Digital Video

Digital Video

Concepts and Applications Across Industries

Edited by

Theodore S. Rzeszewski

Matsushita Television Company

A Selected Reprint Volume
IEEE Consumer Electronics Society, *Sponsor*

The Institute of Electrical and Electronics Engineers, Inc., New York

This book may be purchased at a discount from the publisher when ordered in bulk quantities. For more information contact:

IEEE PRESS Marketing
Attn: Special Sales
P.O. Box 1331
445 Hoes Lane
Piscataway, NJ 08855-1331
Fax: (908) 981-8062

Printed in the United States of America

10 9 8 7 6 5 4 3 2 1

ISBN 0-7803-1099-3

IEEE Order Number: PC4523

Library of Congress Cataloging-in-Publication Data

Digital video : concepts and applications across industries / edited
   by Theodore S. Rzeszewski.
        p.   cm.
    "A Selected reprint volume."
    "IEEE Consumer Electronics Society, sponsor."
    Includes bibliographical references and index.
    ISBN 0–7803–1099–3
    1. Digital television. I. Rzeszewski, Ted. II. IEEE Consumer
Electronics Society.
  TK6678.D537   1995
    621.388′33—dc20
                                              94–33543
                                                  CIP

Contents

CHAPTER 3   DIGITAL VIDEO IN CABLE TELEVISION: TRANSMISSION, APPLICATIONS, AND COMPETITIVE FORCES (W. S. Ciciora)   **293**

Preface

Digital video is an engine driving changes in many industries today. Since we are on the threshold of developing applications of digital video, many of the effects and details of the changes are still unknown. However, it does seem clear that digital video will affect most people's lives significantly over the next decade.

Whether it is the long awaited high definition television (HDTV) standard/market or digital 525-line video, the question is no longer if these services and applications are possible. Rather, it is when will we first see them and how quickly will the markets build? This book is designed to provide the insight needed to understand the areas mentioned above or any digital video application.

The book is organized into five chapters. Each chapter begins with a paper written by a contributing author that puts the material into perspective and provides a bibliography of valuable papers for further reading. The chapters are concerned with:

- Digital Video Concepts
- Digital Video in Consumer Electronics
- Digital Video in Cable Television
- Digital Video in Telecommunications
- Digital Video in Multimedia

The digital video concepts chapter introduces the core material that is needed for a thorough understanding of the subsequent chapters. However, much of the basic theory that is heavily identified with the topic of an individual chapter has been incorporated into subsequent chapters. For example, the second chapter on consumer electronics contains a thorough treatment of the modulation alternatives considered for Grand Alliance HDTV.

The reader will note that chapters two through four are organized along certain industry lines. This is similar to the way that the topic of digital video has been approached in the Annual Electronic Industries Association (EIA)/Institute of Electrical and Electronics Engineers (IEEE) Workshop on Digital Video. It is believed that this arrangement allows the most flexibility in choosing papers at this time.

Chapter two is called Digital Video in Consumer Electronics, and it covers both HDTV and digital video tape recording. Each of the four digital HDTV systems that were proposed to the FCC for a terrestrial service is described in detail. A "Grand Alliance" has been formed to propose a single standard to the FCC. At the time of this writing, there are still some parameters of this grand alliance system that need to be specified. However, it is anticipated that the specification of the grand alliance system will be completed early in 1994, presumably from the best elements of the four systems described in this chapter.

The third chapter is on Digital Video in Cable Television. More than 60% of the viewing public watches their TV from cable in the USA. It is generally believed that cable will be a major force in delivering digital TV into people's homes and businesses. Further, it appears that cable is on the verge of a major thrust into digital TV. The present plans call for the main emphasis to be on 525-line digital TV. The plan calls for extending the upper frequency range utilized by cable; some plans call for extending the upper limit to 1 GHz or beyond. Fiber appears to be an integral part of this effort, and associated network architecture changes seem likely. The fiber backbone architecture was the first of these types of architectural changes. This is an exciting time in the cable industry as these changes are planned, trials are run, and deployment is anticipated shortly. This chapter will introduce the reader to the concepts and hardware involved.

Digital Video in telecommmunications is the topic of the fourth chapter. Elements of the telecommunications industry and the cable industry are coming together by mergers and acquisitions. It is believed that this process is likely to continue for a while as these industries position themselves into the new digital video age. The telecommunications industry comes from a switched services background that is traditionally delivered on a network with a switched star type architecture, and cable comes from a broadcast background with a tree-and-branch type of architecture. However, cable has started to modify its architecture for utilization of fiber. The first example of that was the fiber backbone network introduced several years ago. A major open question in this area is how close to the customer should fiber be deployed. Broadband integrated services digital network (BISDN) looks toward fiber to the access. BISDN is likely to find first application in the business world. This chapter considers many aspects of business-oriented services as well as entertainment services.

The fifth and final chapter of this book is devoted to multimedia. This section goes across several industry lines. The common elements of the present state of the art are compressed digital video initially at a rate around 1.5 Mb/s so that it can be stored on CD-ROM or transmitted on the first level of the digital hierarchy by the telecommunications industry. Multimedia has attracted much attention in such fields as personal computing, games, and teleconferencing.

Theodore S. Rzeszewski
Editor

Digital Video

Chapter 1
Digital Video Concepts:
Theory and Applications

THEODORE S. RZESZEWSKI

Matsushita Television Company
9401 W. Grand Ave.
Franklin Park, IL 60131

Digital video concepts start with the process of obtaining an analog video signal from a capture device such as a camera, and transforming it into a digital video signal. The process involves sampling the analog signal, quantizing the sample value, and coding the samples. But that is just the beginning. The digital video signals are frequently converted from one sampling rate to another, so it is also necessary to understand rate conversion processes.

The first two papers in this book are concerned with sampling and rate conversion, respectively. Sampling video is more involved than the sampling of many other types of signals. Sampling video can be considered as a one-, two-, or three-dimensional process. If we consider it as a one-dimensional process, we find that the repetitiveness of the horizontal and vertical synchronization pulses that interrupt the active video at regular rates typically produce strong components at these frequencies and multiples of these rates. The components that make up the video spectrum appear to be very intricate and complex, obscuring the details of, and inhibiting insight into, some video processing.

Since a still image can be dissected into spatial frequency components, typically horizontal and vertical, we can gain insight and therefore an advantage in looking at the sampling process in two dimensions. However, video implies moving pictures, and that feature injects a temporal element into the equations. Therefore, for certain applications, we can gain additional insight by considering video as a three-dimensional sampling process. Our first paper provides a thorough analysis of 1D, 2D, and 3D sampling.

The second paper is concerned with the rate conversion of video signals. Rate conversion is required whenever we change from a component to a composite format, and usually when the quality level of video service is changed. For example, rate con-version is likely to be part of the processing implemented if we go from an HDTV signal to an IDTV-quality level for economical display.

An extremely important area that will enable many of the video services and applications is video compression. Video compression ratios that were considered impractical just five years ago (1988) are routinely being planned and implemented today. The amazing success of video compression is due, in large part, to two factors. The first factor is the present state of the art in digital integrated circuit design; the second factor is a considerable body of knowledge accumulated over the last 25 years in applying video-compression techniques such as differ-ential pulse code modulation (DPCM), discrete cosine trans-form (DCT), motion compensation techniques (MCT), and entropy coding techniques (ECT) to video compression.

The application of various combinations of these techniques can be thought of as the first generation of high-compression-ratio techniques. We will concentrate on this first generation of high-compression-ratio techniques because they form the basis of the present standards efforts, such as H.261, Joint Photo-graphic Experts Group (JPEG), motion picture experts groups (MPEG), and the Grand Alliance Compression.

The next five papers develop the concepts of video compres-sion. Jain starts from basic concepts and thoroughly develops video compression using basic techniques. The application of a single technique represents the state of the art some years ago before it was considered economically practical to start com-bining several of these techniques to get high compression ra-tios. Upon this base, Musman adds motion compensation techniques and complex combinations of the techniques de-scribed in Jain to achieve a higher compression ratio.

Progress in very large scale integration technology has re-cently allowed the use of transform coding, entropy coding, and motion compensation techniques to be implemented in a sufficiently cost-effective manner that commercial and consumer applications become practical. As explained above, the so-called high-compression-ratio techniques not only use these technologies individually, but they are used in concert to obtain the type of power required for compressing HDTV into a 6-MHz bandwidth (or 4 or more 525-line digital video channels into 6 MHz).

Today, high-compression-ratio techniques usually consists of a predictive coding (DPCM) loop in which the difference signal (so called error signal) is transform-coded with a DCT. The resultant signal produces DCT coefficients with a high-energy concentration in the lower-order coefficients. This, in turn, means that another compression technique called Variable Length Coding (VLC) can be used efficiently. The DCT coefficients are utilized in a zig-zag scan arrangement that bunches these large-valued coefficients together, and the quantization tends to produce large runs of small or zero-valued coefficients, resulting in large runs of zeros that can be efficiently compressed by a combination of VLC and block truncation techniques. An inverse DCT (IDCT) is used to obtain a prediction of the incoming signal (enhanced by the use of motion-compensated prediction) in the DPCM loop. This basic approach to coder/decoder design has been utilized in much of the standards work.

There is more good news in this area. Newer techniques such as fractals and wavelets hold the hope of even greater compression in the future. However, this series of articles concentrates on the first generation of high-compression-ratio techniques for digital video, typically based on using DPCM, DCT, MC and entropy coding in concert.

The paper by Chen describes early work on a scene-adaptive coder, considered to be another important element in the bag of tricks of video coding. It also shows an example of a realization of this type of coder that also utilizes DCT compression techniques. The paper reports on the results of performance testing and describes the realization of such a coder.

MPEG stands for motion picture experts group, an international organization that is developing digital video compression standards. Many of the compression applications are being designed to be MPEG-compliant. The next two papers describe MPEG-1 and some of the concepts that are planned for MPEG-2, respectively.

MPEG-1 presently finds applications in systems that utilize CD-ROMs and/or utilize data rates around the first level of the digital hierarchy (DS-1), that is, approximately 1.5 Mb/s in the US. Therefore, both the telecommunications and multimedia chapters of this book are concerned with applications that could presently utilize MPEG-1.

The seventh paper, by Puri, is primarily concerned with extensions of MPEG to higher data rates, what is commonly called MPEG-2. These rates are particularly appropriate for applications in cable television, terrestrial television broadcast, and telecommunications.

The papers on MPEG have been included because of the broad and general applicability across many applications in many industries. However, there are many other aspects of digital video that have been relegated to the chapters on individual industries, because they are likely to be tailored to the constraints in those industries. For example, the modulation technique, error-correction techniques, and security or conditional access are all very important techniques that have been assigned to the other chapters of the book. Digital-signal processing techniques intended to enhance or improve some aspect of video quality are another important area not included in this chapter.

The final paper in this chapter provides the background needed for a good understanding of advanced television (ATV); consequently, it is included in the concepts chapter. It does not dwell on the specific approaches to ATV; that part is covered for high-definition television (HDTV) in the next chapter on digital video in consumer electronics, where each of the four digital HDTV systems that were originally proposed to the FCC are described in detail. Presumably, the Grand Alliance system will consist of the best elements of these four systems when it is finished.

FURTHER READING

[1] T.S. Rzeszewski, ed., *Television Technology Today,* New York: IEEE Press, 1985.

[2] A. Netravali and B. Prasade, ed., *Visual Communications Systems,* New York: IEEE Press, 1987.

[3] M. Rabbani and P.W. Jones, *Digital Image Compression Techniques,* Bellingham Wash.: SPIE, 1990.

[4] D.E. Dudgeon and R.M. Mersereau, *Multidimensional Digital Signal Processing,* Englewood Cliffs, N.J.: Prentice Hall, 1984.

[5] J.A. Mitchell, "Multirate filters alter sampling rates even after you've captured the data," *EDN,* Aug. pp. 129–40, 1992.

[6] B. Wendland, "Extended definition television with high picture quality," *SMPTE J.,* Oct., pp. 1028–1035, 1983.

[7] E. Fisch, "Scan conversion between 1050 2:1 60 Hz and 525 1:1 30 Hz U and V color components," *IEEE Trans. CE,* Aug., pp. 210–218, 1993.

[8] D.H. Lee, J.S. Park, and Y.G. Kim, "Video format conversion between HDTV systems," *IEEE Trans. CE,* Aug., pp. 219–224, 1993.

[9] J.O. Limb, C.B. Rubinstein, and J.E. Thompson, "Digital coding of color video signals—a review," *IEEE Trans. Comm.,* Nov., pp. 1349–1384, 1977.

[10] T.S. Rzeszewski and R.L. Pawelski, "Efficient transmission of digital component video," *SMPTE J.,* Sept., pp. 889–98, 1986.

[11] R.C. Brainard, A.N. Netravali, and D.E. Pearson, "Predictive coding of composite NTSC color television signals," *SMPTE J.,* March, pp. 245–252, 1982.

[12] T.S. Rzeszewski, "Video coding for EQTV distribution with a rate of approximately 135 Mb/s," *IEEE Trans. CE,* Feb., pp. 147–155, 1988.

[13] S. Kadono and C. Yamamitsu, "A study on high efficiency coding of HDTV at 50 Mbps," *IEEE Trans. CE,* Feb., pp. 49–56, 1993.

[14] H. Gaggioni and D. LeGall, "Digital video transmission and coding for the broadband ISDN," *IEEE Trans. CE,* Feb., pp. 16–34, 1988.

[15] H.C. Huang and J.L. Wu, "Novel real-time software-based video coding algorithms," *IEEE Trans. CE,* Aug., pp. 570–580, 1993.

[16] W.K. Cham, C.S. Choy, and W.K. Lam, "A 2-D integer cosine transform chip set and its application," *IEEE Trans. CE,* May, pp. 43–47, 1992.

[17] Y.S. Jehng, L.G. Chen, and T.D. Chiueh, "A motion estimator for low bit-rate video codec," *IEEE Trans. CE,* May, pp. 61–69, 1992.

[18] T. Liu and W.F. Wedam, "Hardware implementation and cost of decoders for digital HDTV," *IEEE Trans. CE,* Aug., pp. 331–336, 1991.

[19] S.V. Ramaswamy and G.D. Miller, "Multiprocessor DSP architectures that implement the FCT-based JPEG still picture image compression algorithm with arithmetic coding," *IEEE Trans. CE,* Feb., pp. 1–5, 1993.

[20] A. Jalali, V.R. Spelman, J.V. Scattaglia, P.E. Fleischer, and C.D. Novak, "A component codec and line multiplexer," *IEEE Trans. CE,* pp. 156–64.

[21] D. Chin, J. Passe, F. Bernard, H. Taylor, and S. Knight, "The Princeton Engine: a real-time video system simulator," *IEEE Trans. CE,* May, pp. 285–296, 1988.

[22] A. Artieri and O. Colavin, "A Chip Set Core for Image Compression," *IEEE Trans. CE,* Aug., pp. 395–402, 1990.

[23] H. Pemull and D. Draxelmayr, "A digital display processor with integrated 9-bit triple DAC for enhanced TV applications," *IEEE Trans. CE,* Aug., pp. 247–254, 1993.

[24] R. Deubert, "Feature IC's for digivision TV sets," *IEEE Trans. CE,* Aug., pp. 237–241, 1983.

[25] E.J. Berkhoff, U.E. Kraus, and J.G. Raven, "Applications of picture memories in television receivers," *IEEE Trans. CE,* Aug., pp. 251–254, 256–258, 1983.

[26] L.J. Van De Polder, D.W. Parker, and J. Roos, "Evolution of television receivers from analog to digital," *Proc. IEEE.* April, pp. 599–612, 1985.

[27] H.J. Desor, "Single-chip video processing system," *IEEE Trans. CE,* Aug., pp. 182–189, 1991.

[28] H. Altrutz, B. Butera, K. Caesar, F. Lebowshy, S. Rohrer, and G. Stoffel, "A single chip video front end decoder," *IEEE Trans. CE,* Aug., pp. 489–495, 1993.

[29] H. Alrutz, H.J. Desor, P. Flamm, V. Summa, and E. Wagner, "A single chip multistandard video encoder," *IEEE Trans. CE,* Aug., pp. 581–586, 1993.

[30] R.A. Peloso, "Adaptive equalization for advanced television," *IEEE Trans. CE,* Aug., pp. 119–126, 1992.

[31] Y.S. Choi, H. Hwang, and D. I. Song, "Adaptive blind equalization coupled with carrier recovery for HDTV modem," *IEEE Trans. CE,* Aug., pp. 386–391, 1993.

[32] H. Kohne, "2-H adaptive combfilter video processor," *IEEE Trans. CE,* Aug., pp. 303–308, 1991.

[33] H. Rantanen, M. Karlsson, P. Pohjala, and S. Kalli, "Color video signal processing with median filters," *IEEE Trans. CE,* Aug., pp. 157–161, 1992.

[34] T.S. Rzeszewski and P.H. Wyant, "Picture crispening by adaptive digital signal processing," *IEEE Trans. CE,* May, pp. 71–75, 1987.

[35] T. Matsumoto, K. Fujii, F. Koga, H. Ohta, O. Hosoi, S. Suzuki, and K. Yamamoto, "All digital video signal processing system for S-VHS VCR," *IEEE Trans. CE,* Aug., pp. 560–565, 1990.

[36] K. Onishi, T. Itow, H. Nishikawa, K. Sugiyama, H. Yoshida, M. Nagasawa, K. Nakagawa, Y. Ishida, and S. Kunii, "An experimental home-use digital VCR with three-dimensional DCT and superimposed error correction coding," *IEEE Trans. CE,* Aug., pp. 252–259, 1991.

[37] M. Yoneda, J. Kimura, K. Shimoda, M. Tamura, T. Inagaki, K. Ogi, and Y. Uetani, "An experimental digital VCR with new DCT-based bit-rate reduction system," *IEEE Trans. CE,* Aug., pp. 275–282, 1991.

[38] J. Terry, "Alternative technologies and delivery systems for broadband ISDN access," *IEEE Comm.* Aug., pp. 58–64, 1992.

[39] T. DeCouasnon, L. Danilenko, F.J. In der Smitten, and U.E. Kraus, "Results of the first digital terrestrial television broadcasting field-tests in germany," *IEEE Trans. CE,* Aug., pp. 668–675, 1993.

[40] T. Liu, S. Jaffe, D. Downey, C.B. Patel, J. Yang, and S. Roy, "Simulation and implementation of US QAM-based HDTV channel decoder," *IEEE Trans. CE,* Aug., pp. 676–683, 1993.

The Sampling and Reconstruction of Time-Varying Imagery with Application in Video Systems

ERIC DUBOIS, MEMBER, IEEE

Invited Paper

Sampling is a fundamental operation in all image communication systems. A time-varying image, which is a function of three independent variables, must be sampled in at least two dimensions for transmission over a one-dimensional analog communication channel, and in three dimensions for digital processing and transmission. At the receiver, the sampled image must be interpolated to reconstruct a continuous function of space and time. In imagery destined for human viewing, the visual system forms an integral part of the reconstruction process.

This paper presents an overview of the theory of sampling and reconstruction of multidimensional signals. The concept of sampling structures based on lattices is introduced. The important problem of conversion between different sampling structures is also treated. This theory is then applied to the sampling of time-varying imagery, including the role of the camera and display apertures, and the human visual system. Finally, a class of nonlinear interpolation algorithms which adapt to the motion in the scene is presented.

I. INTRODUCTION

Any image transmission system requires an initial sampling and reformatting operation which converts the original signal, in general a function of three independent variables (space and time), into a one-dimensional signal suitable for transmission over a communication channel. At the receiver an interpolation operation is carried out to convert the sampled signal back into a physically displayed image. In conventional analog television, the sampling is carried out in two dimensions only (vertical and temporal), by means of interlaced scanning. In digital processing and transmission systems, a full three-dimensional sampling is required.

A *conceptual* representation of an image sampling and reconstruction system is shown in Fig. 1. A time-varying scene is projected onto an image plane by an optical system, and a component such as luminance or a tristimu-

Manuscript received July 6, 1984; revised October 11, 1984. This work was supported in part by the National Sciences and Engineering Research Council of Canada under Strategic Grant G0845.

The author is with INRS-Télécommunications, Verdun, Que., Canada H3E 1H6.

lus value is extracted to give a continuous function of space and time $u(x_1, x_2, t)$. This signal is filtered by a continuous three-dimensional low-pass filter and then sampled on a discrete set of points in space and time referred to as the sampling structure. The prefilter is required to suitably band-limit the input signal to avoid aliasing introduced by the sampling process. The sampled signal can then be digitally processed, stored, coded, etc. At the receiver, the signal must be interpolated to restore a continuous function of space and time for display and viewing. As will be seen, the operations in Fig. 1 cannot be neatly isolated in most practical systems. The general goal of a sampling system is to give the best possible rendition of the original image for a given spatiotemporal sampling density by appropriate choice of preprocessing, sampling structure, postprocessing, and interpolation. The response of the visual system should be considered when evaluating the performance of a system for the sampling and reconstruction of imagery destined for human viewing. A related problem is the conversion between different sampling structures in systems where more than one structure is used, or in interfacing different systems.

There has recently been intense activity in problems related to the sampling process, in order to provide higher quality pictures for the next generation of television systems. Examples are in high-definition television, extended-definition television, and camera and receiver processing for enhanced-quality television. At the opposite end of the spectrum, subsampling is a key technique in coding systems for very low data rates. These topics are all treated elsewhere in this special issue.

The goal of this paper is to present a general framework for the study of image sampling and interpolation, and to relate it to the specific application areas cited above. In Section II, the mathematical theory of sampling and interpolation of multidimensional signals is presented. The concept of sampling structure is introduced, and the Fourier representation and processing of signals defined on these structures is discussed. The multidimensional sampling the-

Reprinted from *Proc. IEEE*, vol. 73, no. 4, pp. 502–522, April 1985.

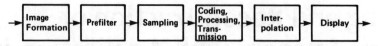

Fig. 1. Conceptual representation of an image sampling and reconstruction system.

orem is then presented, and finally processing for sampling structure conversion is treated. Section III then specializes this theory to the three-dimensional case of time-varying imagery. The role of the camera and display apertures and the human visual system in the sampling and reconstruction process are considered. Then structures suitable for image sampling are presented and evaluated. The sampling of color imagery is also discussed in this section. Techniques for interpolation are presented in Section IV. In particular, a special class of nonlinear interpolation schemes which adapt to the motion in the scene is described. These techniques recognize the special structure present in time-varying imagery due to the motion of objects, and also the differing resolution requirements of the human observer in moving and stationary areas.

II. SAMPLING OF MULTIDIMENSIONAL SIGNALS

The basic operation is any image-sampling system is the specification of the image intensity or color on some regular array of points in space and time. The concept of a lattice, of importance in such areas as the geometry of numbers [1] and solid-state physics [2], is the basic tool in the study of image sampling. The theory of sampling multidimensional signals on a lattice was presented by Petersen and Middleton [3], and was later extended to periodically weighted sampling on a lattice [4]. A special case of periodically weighted sampling is sampling on a superposition of shifted lattices [5], [6]. This section presents the mathematical theory of sampled multidimensional signals, including the necessary results from the theory of lattices, Fourier transform representations, sampling of continuous signals, and conversion between different sampling structures. Image sampling has often been studied by representing it as the multiplication of the continuous signal with a regular array of Dirac delta functions. Although this is quite satisfactory for characterizing the sampling process alone, it makes the subsequent analysis of digital processing of the sampled signal difficult. This approach has thus been virtually abandoned in one-dimensional signal processing. In this paper, we adopt the approach that the sampled signal is truly discrete in space and time, with values only defined at the sample locations [7].

Although we are mainly concerned with the sampling of three-dimensional functions (i.e., time-varying two-dimensional images), the theory is easily developed for arbitrary dimension. Thus the theory in this section will be presented for the arbitrary multidimensional case, and will be equally applicable to still two-dimensional images, still three-dimensional images, and moving three-dimensional images, which are two-, three-, and four-dimensional signals, respectively. Section II-E presents a concise summary of the main results on lattices and sampling of continuous functions in three dimensions which is sufficient background for a first reading of Sections III and IV. Thus the application-oriented reader may wish to proceed directly to Section II-E on first reading.

A. Lattices

Definition [1]: Let $v_1, \cdots, v_D$ be linearly independent real vectors in D-dimensional Euclidean space R^D. A *lattice* Λ in R^D is the set of all linear combinations of $v_1, \cdots, v_D$ with integer coefficients

$$\Lambda = \{ n_1 v_1 + n_2 v_2 + \cdots + n_D v_D | n_i \in Z, i = 1, \cdots, D \}. \tag{1}$$

The set of vectors $v_1, \cdots, v_D$ is called a basis for Λ. A lattice is a discrete additive Abelian group. Fig. 2(a) shows an example of a lattice in two dimensions.

Let V be the matrix whose columns are the representation of the v_i with respect to the standard orthonormal basis for R^D. Then, the lattice is the set of all vectors Vn, with $n \in Z^D$. The basis for a given lattice is not unique. If E is any matrix of integers such that $\det E = \pm 1$, then the matrix $\hat{V} = EV$ provides another basis for Λ [1]. However, $|\det V|$ is unique and independent of the particular choice of basis. This quantity, denoted $d(\Lambda)$, is called the determinant of the lattice Λ and physically represents the reciprocal of the sampling density.

We define a *unit cell* of a lattice Λ as a set $\mathscr{P} \subset R^D$ (not necessarily connected) such that R^D is the disjoint union of copies of $\mathscr{P}$ centered on each lattice point: $(\mathscr{P} + x) \cap (\mathscr{P} + y) = \emptyset$ for $x, y \in \Lambda$, $x \neq y$, and $\bigcup_{x \in \Lambda} (\mathscr{P} + x) = R^D$. The hypervolume of a unit cell of a lattice Λ is $d(\Lambda)$. There are many possible choices for the unit cell of a lattice. One that is very convenient is the *fundamental parallelepiped* given by

$$\mathscr{P} = \left\{ \sum_{i=1}^{D} \alpha_i v_i | 0 \leq \alpha_i < 1 \right\} \tag{2}$$

where $v_1, \cdots, v_D$ is a basis for the lattice Λ. Another unit cell which is often useful is the *Voronoi cell* (also called Dirichlet region, Brillouin zone, Wigner–Seitz cell), the set of all points in R^D closer to 0 than to any other lattice point. Fig. 3 shows these two unit cells for the lattice of Fig. 2(a).

The concepts of sublattices and cosets of a lattice with respect to a sublattice are of importance in the theory of sampling on a superposition of shifted lattices, and conversion between sampling lattices.

Definition: Let Λ and Γ be lattices. Λ is a *sublattice* of Γ if every point of Λ is also a point of Γ. If Λ is a sublattice of Γ, then $d(\Lambda)$ is an integer multiple of $d(\Gamma)$. The quotient $d(\Lambda)/d(\Gamma)$ is called the index of Λ in Γ [1] and is denoted $(\Gamma:\Lambda)$. The set

$$c + \Lambda = \{ c + x | x \in \Lambda \} \tag{3}$$

for any $c \in \Gamma$ is called a *coset* or *class* of Λ in Γ. Two cosets are either identical or disjoint, and $c + \Lambda = d + \Lambda$ if and only if $c - d \in \Lambda$. There are $(\Gamma:\Lambda)$ distinct cosets of Λ in Γ, and the lattice Γ is the disjoint union of these $(\Gamma:\Lambda)$ cosets. A coset is a shifted version of the lattice Λ, and the set of cosets is the set of all shifted versions of Λ which are a subset of Γ.

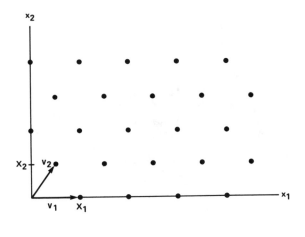

$$V = \begin{bmatrix} X_1 & X_1/2 \\ 0 & X_2 \end{bmatrix}$$

$$d(\Lambda) = X_1 X_2$$

(a)

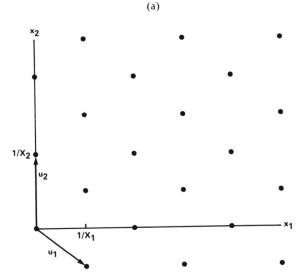

$$U = \begin{bmatrix} 1/X_1 & 0 \\ -1/2X_2 & 1/X_2 \end{bmatrix}$$

$$d(\Lambda^*) = 1/X_1 X_2$$

(b)

Fig. 2. Example of a lattice in two dimensions. (a) Basic lattice Λ. (b) Reciprocal lattice Λ^*.

The intersection $\Lambda_1 \cap \Lambda_2$ of two lattices is also a lattice, although it is possible for the dimension of this lattice to be less than D. A necessary and sufficient condition for $\Lambda_1 \cap \Lambda_2$ to be of dimension D is that $V_1^{-1}V_2$ be a matrix of rational numbers, where V_1 and V_2 are the matrices for the lattices Λ_1 and Λ_2. The sum of two lattices $\Lambda_1 + \Lambda_2$ is defined as $\{x + y | x \in \Lambda_1, y \in \Lambda_2\}$. If $\Lambda_1 \cap \Lambda_2$ is a lattice of dimension D, then so is $\Lambda_1 + \Lambda_2$, and $(\Lambda_1 + \Lambda_2 : \Lambda_1) = (\Lambda_2 : \Lambda_1 \cap \Lambda_2)$. The intersection $\Lambda_1 \cap \Lambda_2$ is the largest lattice which is a sublattice of both Λ_1 and Λ_2, while the sum

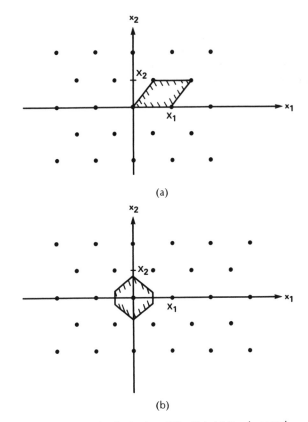

(a)

(b)

Fig. 3. Unit cells for the lattice of Fig. 2(a). (a) Fundamental parallelepiped. (b) Voronoi cell.

$\Lambda_1 + \Lambda_2$ is the smallest lattice which contains both Λ_1 and Λ_2 as sublattices.

A final concept which is very useful in the frequency-domain representation of signals sampled on a lattice is that of the reciprocal lattice.

Definition: Given a lattice Λ, the set of all vectors y such that $y^T x$ is an integer for all $x \in \Lambda$ is called the *reciprocal lattice* Λ^* of the lattice Λ.

The lattice Λ^* is also called the polar lattice in the geometry of numbers. A basis for Λ^* is the set of vectors $u_1, \cdots, u_D$ determined by $u_i^T v_j = \delta_{ij}, i, j = 1, \cdots, D$, or equivalently by $U^T V = I$ where I is a D by D identity matrix. The reciprocal lattice for the lattice of Fig. 2(a) is shown in Fig. 2(b). If Λ is a sublattice of Γ, then it is easily seen that Γ^* is a sublattice of Λ^*. Also, if Λ_1 and Λ_2 are lattices, it can be shown that $\Lambda_1 + \Lambda_2 = (\Lambda_1^* \cap \Lambda_2^*)^*$. Thus an algorithm for determining the intersection of lattices can also be used to determine the sum of lattices.

B. Multidimensional Sampled Signals

A sampling structure Ψ is a discrete set of points in R^D over which the image function is specified. The most general form of sampling structure considered in this paper is the union of selected cosets of a sublattice Λ in a lattice Γ. Thus we have

$$\Psi = \bigcup_{i=1}^{P} (c_i + \Lambda) \tag{4}$$

where $c_1, \cdots, c_P$ is a set of vectors in Γ such that $c_i - c_j \notin \Lambda$ for $i \neq j$. It is assumed that Γ is the smallest lattice containing Ψ and that there is no lattice Υ with $d(\Upsilon) < d(\Lambda)$ such that Ψ is a union of cosets of Υ in Γ. By taking $\Lambda = \Gamma$ and $P = 1$, (4) reduces to a standard lattice. Fig. 4 shows an example of a sampling structure in two dimensions which cannot be represented as a lattice, but can be represented as the union of two shifted lattices. All sampling structures

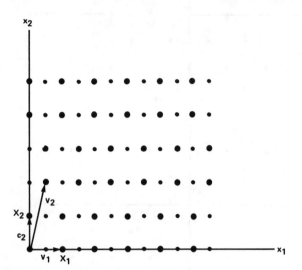

Fig. 4. Sampling structure in two dimensions which is the union of two cosets of the lattice Λ in the lattice Γ: $\Psi = \Lambda \cup (c_2 + \Lambda)$. v_1 and v_2 form a basis for Λ. Ψ is denoted by large dots and Γ by small dots.

known to the author which have been considered for image sampling can be represented in this way. Examples of sampling structures which are not lattices but can be represented using (4) can be found in [5], [6], [8].

The concept of a unit cell can usefully be extended to such a sampling structure. The unit cell is defined as a set $\mathscr{P} \subset \mathbf{R}^D$ such that $\mathscr{P} \cap (\mathscr{P} + x) = \emptyset$ for $x \in \Psi$, $x \neq 0$, and $\bigcup_{x \in \Psi}(\mathscr{P} + x) = \mathbf{R}^D$. For $P = 1$ this reduces to the standard definition.

We now consider the Fourier representation of signals sampled on such a structure. From Fourier analysis, the Fourier transform can be defined for any L^1 function defined on a discrete Abelian group [9]. Since a lattice is an Abelian group, we can define the Fourier transform over a lattice Λ

$$U(f) = \sum_{x \in \Lambda} u(x) \exp\left(-j2\pi f^T x\right)$$
$$= \sum_{n \in \mathbf{Z}^D} u(Vn) \exp\left(-j2\pi f^T Vn\right), \quad f \in \mathbf{R}^D. \quad (5)$$

The Fourier transform is a periodic function over $\mathbf{R}^D$ with periodicity lattice equal to the reciprocal lattice Λ^*, that is

$$U(f) = U(f + r), \quad \forall r \in \Lambda^*. \quad (6)$$

This follows from the fact that $r^T x$ is an integer for $x \in \Lambda$ and $r \in \Lambda^*$, by definition of the reciprocal lattice. Fig. 5 illustrates the periodicity of the Fourier transform for a signal defined on the lattice of Fig. 2. Because of this periodicity, the Fourier transform need only be specified over one unit cell $\mathscr{P}$ of the reciprocal lattice.

The inverse Fourier transform of the sampled signal is given by

$$u(x) = d(\Lambda)\int_{\mathscr{P}} U(f) \exp\left(j2\pi f^T x\right) df, \quad x \in \Lambda. \quad (7)$$

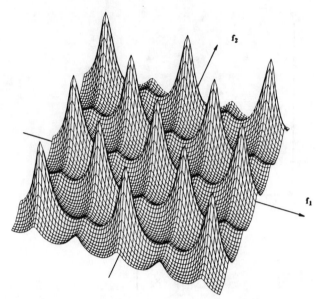

Fig. 5. Periodicity of Fourier transform for a signal defined on the lattice of Fig. 2(a). The periodicity is determined by the reciprocal lattice shown in Fig. 2(b).

For a sampling structure which is not a lattice, the Fourier transform in the usual sense is not defined. However, for the representation of the lattice as the union of certain cosets in a lattice Γ, we can assume that the signal is defined over the lattice Γ, with appropriate sample values set to zero. Then, the usual Fourier transform over Γ becomes

$$U(f) = \sum_{x \in \Psi} u(x) \exp\left(-j2\pi f^T x\right), \quad f \in \mathbf{R}^D \quad (8)$$

and the Fourier transform will have periodicity determined by the reciprocal lattice Γ^*. For a sampling structure as given in (4), the Fourier transform can be written

$$U(f) = \sum_{i=1}^{P} \sum_{x \in \Lambda} u(c_i + x) \exp\left(-j2\pi f^T(c_i + x)\right)$$
$$= \sum_{i=1}^{P} \exp\left(-j2\pi f^T c_i\right) \sum_{x \in \Lambda} u(c_i + x) \exp\left(-j2\pi f^T x\right)$$
$$= \sum_{i=1}^{P} \exp\left(-j2\pi f^T c_i\right) U_i(f) \quad (9)$$

where $U_i(f)$ is the Fourier transform of the function $u_i(x) = u(c_i + x)$ defined on Λ.

In most cases, a sampled time-varying image cannot be considered as a function in $L^1(\Psi)$, but rather may more appropriately be considered as a sample from a discrete random field. For signals defined on a lattice Λ we assume in the usual way that the process is a homogeneous random field with zero mean and autocovariance function

$$R_u(x) = E[u(y)u(y + x)]. \quad (10)$$

The power density spectrum of the random field is given by the Fourier transform of the autocovariance function

$$\Phi_u(f) = \sum_{x \in \Lambda} R_u(x) \exp\left(-j2\pi f^T x\right). \quad (11)$$

A random field defined on the more general sampling structure of (4) cannot be homogeneous since the set of points $\{ x | y + x \in \Psi \}$ varies with y and thus $E[u(y)u(y + x)]$ cannot be independent of y. However, it can be periodic in y, with periodicity given by Λ, yielding a cyclostationary field. Then in the usual fashion [10], an autocovariance averaged over a period can be defined

$$R_u(x) = \frac{1}{(\Gamma : \Lambda)} \sum_{i=1}^{P} E[u(c_i)u(c_i + x)], \qquad x \in \Gamma. \tag{12}$$

The autocovariance function will be nonzero on the set

$$\begin{aligned} \mathscr{D} &= \{ x - y | x, y \in \Psi \} \\ &= \bigcup_{i=1}^{P} \bigcup_{j=1}^{P} (c_i - c_j + \Lambda). \end{aligned} \tag{13}$$

Clearly, not all of the P^2 cosets in this expression are distinct. The power density spectrum is then given by

$$\Phi_u(f) = \sum_{x \in \mathscr{D}} R_u(x) \exp(-j2\pi f^T x). \tag{14}$$

The theory of processing signals defined on a lattice has been presented in [11]. Of main interest to us is the case of linear filtering with finite-impulse response (FIR) filters. FIR filters are generally preferred over infinite-impulse response (IIR) filters for image processing because they allow exact linear phase response, and because stability is assured. For a linear shift-invariant system whose input and output are signals defined on a lattice Λ, the input and output are related by the convolution

$$z(x) = \sum_{y \in \Lambda} u(y)h(x - y), \qquad x \in \Lambda \tag{15}$$

where $h(x)$ is the unit sample response of the system. An FIR filter is characterized by the fact that $h(x)$ is nonzero for only a finite number of points $x \in \Lambda$. The frequency response of the filter is given by the Fourier transform of the unit sample response

$$H(f) = \sum_{x \in \Lambda} h(x) \exp(-j2\pi f^T x). \tag{16}$$

As before, the frequency response is periodic, with periodicity given by the reciprocal lattice Λ^*. If the input to an FIR filter is an L^1 function with Fourier transform $U(f)$, then the output is also an L^1 function with Fourier transform

$$Z(f) = H(f)U(f). \tag{17}$$

On the other hand, if the input to the filter is a homogeneous random field with power density spectrum $\Phi_u(f)$, then the output is also a homogeneous random field with power density spectrum

$$\Phi_z(f) = |H(f)|^2 \Phi_u(f). \tag{18}$$

A number of techniques exist for designing multidimensional FIR filters with frequency response approximating some desired characteristic. An overview of many of these is contained in [7]. The more general problem of linear processing when the input and output are defined on different lattices is considered in detail in Section II-D.

For signals not defined on a lattice, the ideas of shift invariance and frequency response of a linear filter are not straightforward, and this case is not considered here.

C. Sampling and Reconstruction

In general, multidimensional signals defined on a discrete sampling structure are obtained by sampling a continuous function over R^D. If this continuous function is denoted $u_c(x), x \in R^D$, the operation of sampling on a structure Ψ is given by

$$u(x) = u_c(x), \qquad x \in \Psi. \tag{19}$$

Note that while u_c is defined over all of R^D, u is only defined on Ψ. The theory of sampling and reconstruction of both deterministic and random signals on a lattice was presented in [3]. In this section, we review this material, with the extension to structures of the form of (4).

Sampling: Suppose that $u_c \in L^1(R^D)$ has Fourier transform

$$U_c(f) = \int_{R^D} u_c(x) \exp(-j2\pi f^T x) \, dx, \qquad f \in R^D \tag{20}$$

with the inverse Fourier transform relation

$$u_c(x) = \int_{R^D} U_c(f) \exp(j2\pi f^T x) \, df, \qquad x \in R^D. \tag{21}$$

Then, this integral evaluated for $x \in \Lambda$ can be written as a sum of integrals over displaced versions of a unit cell $\mathscr{P}$ of Λ^*

$$\begin{aligned} u(x) &= \int_{R^D} U_c(f) \exp(j2\pi f^T x) \, df \\ &= \sum_{r \in \Lambda^*} \int_{\mathscr{P}} U_c(f + r) \\ &\quad \cdot \exp(j2\pi(f + r)^T x) \, df, \qquad x \in \Lambda. \end{aligned} \tag{22}$$

By the property of the reciprocal lattice, $\exp(j2\pi r^T x) = 1$ so that exchanging the order of summation and integration gives

$$u(x) = \int_{\mathscr{P}} \left[\sum_{r \in \Lambda^*} U_c(f + r) \right] \exp(j2\pi f^T x) \, df. \tag{23}$$

Taking the Fourier transform of this gives

$$U(f) = \frac{1}{d(\Lambda)} \sum_{r \in \Lambda^*} U_c(f + r). \tag{24}$$

Thus the Fourier transform of the sampled signal is the sum of an infinite number of copies of the Fourier transform of the continuous signal, shifted according to the reciprocal lattice. This function has periodicity lattice Λ^* as required. Fig. 6 shows the effect of sampling with the lattice of Fig. 2 on the spectrum of a continuous band-limited signal. Examples where the shifted versions of the analog spectrum overlap and do not overlap are given.

If a homogeneous random field with autocovariance function $R_{uc}(x)$ and power density spectrum $\Phi_{uc}(f)$ is sampled on a lattice Λ, the autocovariance of the sampled signal is $R_u(x) = R_{uc}(x), x \in \Lambda$ so that the above development gives

$$\Phi_u(f) = \frac{1}{d(\Lambda)} \sum_{r \in \Lambda^*} \Phi_{uc}(f + r). \tag{25}$$

The situation for the sampling on a union of shifted lattices can be analyzed by combining the above results

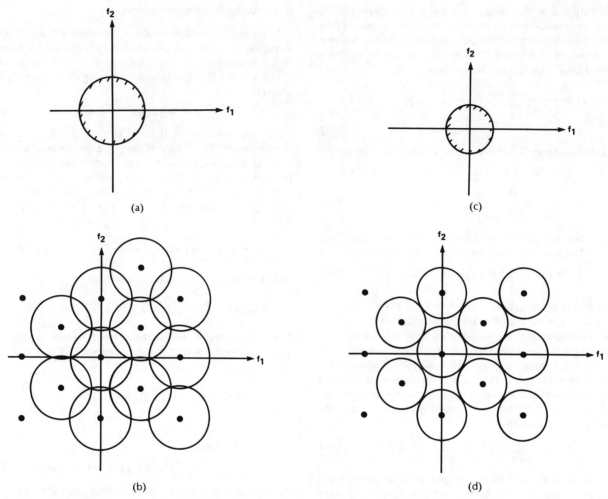

Fig. 6. Sampling of continuous signals. (a) Region of support of spectrum of continuous signal. (b) Spectrum of signal in (a) sampled with lattice of Fig. 2(a), showing overlap in repeated versions of basic spectrum. (c) Spectrum of continuous signal with smaller region of support than (a). (d) Spectrum of signal in (c) sampled with lattice of Fig. 2(a), showing no overlap in repeated versions of basic spectrum.

with (9)

$$U(f) = \frac{1}{d(\Lambda)} \sum_{i=1}^{P} \exp\left(-j2\pi f^T c_i\right) \sum_{r \in \Lambda^*} U_c(f + r)$$

$$\cdot \exp\left(j2\pi (f + r)^T c_i\right)$$

$$= \frac{1}{d(\Lambda)} \sum_{r \in \Lambda^*} \left(\sum_{i=1}^{P} \exp\left(j2\pi r^T c_i\right)\right) U_c(f + r)$$

$$= \frac{1}{d(\Lambda)} \sum_{r \in \Lambda^*} g(r) U_c(f + r). \qquad (26)$$

The function

$$g(r) = \sum_{i=1}^{P} \exp\left(j2\pi r^T c_i\right)$$

is constant over cosets of Γ^* in Λ^*, and may be equal to zero for some of these cosets, so that the corresponding shifted versions of the basic spectrum are not present. It is such a cancellation which would make this pattern of interest, rather than the less dense lattice Λ. Thus we

define Ψ^* to be the union of cosets of Γ^* in Λ^* for which $g(r)$ is nonzero. Fig. 7 shows the reciprocal structure Ψ^* for the structure Ψ of Fig. 4.

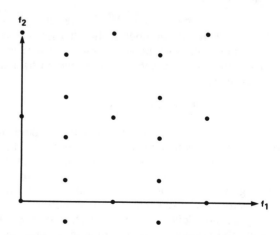

Fig. 7. Reciprocal structure to the sampling structure of Fig. 4.

10

Reconstruction: The final stage in an image communication system involves the reconstruction of the time-varying image as a continuous function of space and time for viewing. This reconstruction is an interpolation process which must fill in the missing values from the existing samples. Exact reconstruction of a continuous function from its samples on a structure Ψ is possible if the image spectrum is confined to a region $\mathscr{W} \in R^D$ such that the regions $\mathscr{W} + r$ for $r \in \Psi^*$ do not overlap with $\mathscr{W}$, i.e., there exists a unit cell $\mathscr{P}$ of Ψ^* such that $\mathscr{W} \subset \mathscr{P}$.[1] This is illustrated in Fig. 6(d). If the above conditions are satisfied, then

$$u_c(x) = \int_{\mathscr{W}} U_c(f) \exp\left(j2\pi f^T x\right) df$$
$$= \frac{d(\Lambda)}{P} \int_{\mathscr{W}} U(f) \exp\left(j2\pi f^T x\right) df. \quad (27)$$

Substituting the definition for $U(f)$ gives

$$u_c(x) = \sum_{s \in \Psi} u(s) t(x - s) \quad (28)$$

where

$$t(s) = \frac{d(\Lambda)}{P} \int_{\mathscr{W}} \exp\left(j2\pi f^T s\right) df. \quad (29)$$

If the smallest region of support of $U_c(f)$ is not a unit cell of the reciprocal structure, then the interpolating formula for $u_c(x)$ is not unique, since $\mathscr{W}$ can be chosen as any subset of a unit cell which contains the region of support. Equation (28) is a hybrid linear filtering, where the input is sampled and the output is continuous. The corresponding frequency response is

$$T(f) = \begin{cases} 1, & f \in \mathscr{W} \\ 0, & f \in \mathscr{W} + r, r \in \Psi^* - \{0\} \\ \text{arbitrary}, & \text{otherwise}. \end{cases} \quad (30)$$

This can in general be interpreted as an ideal low-pass filter. For homogeneous random fields, exact reconstruction (in the sense of vanishing mean-square error) is also obtained using (28) if the power density spectrum is limited to a unit cell of Λ^* [3].

If the signal is not band-limited to a unit cell, then a phenomenon known as aliasing occurs, whereby high frequencies in the original signal are mapped to lower frequencies. The most familiar examples are Moiré patterns, staircase effects on contours, and wagon wheels rotating backwards. A detailed discussion of the different types of aliasing effects which occur for a variety of sampling structures can be found in [6]. Petersen and Middleton [3] showed that if the original signal is not band-limited to a unit cell of the reciprocal lattice of the desired sampling lattice, the mean-square reconstruction error averaged over a cell of the sampling lattice can be minimized by prefiltering with a filter having unit gain over a suitably chosen unit cell, and zero gain elsewhere, again an ideal low-pass filter.

Partial Sampling: To date, all time-varying image recording or transmission systems use sampling in at least one

dimension. Conventional analog television and cinema use only partial sampling, that is sampling in only one or two dimensions. Specifically, in analog television the signal is sampled in only two dimensions (essentially vertical and temporal), while in cinema the signal is sampled in the temporal direction only. We consider here the case of partially sampled signals, i.e., signals defined on a subset of R^D which is the direct sum of a lattice of dimension less than D and its orthogonal complement in R^D.

Let Λ be a C-dimensional lattice in R^D, generated by C linearly independent vectors $v_1, \cdots, v_C$ in R^D, where $C < D$. Let S_1 be the C-dimensional subspace of R^D spanned by $v_1, \cdots, v_C$, and let S_2 be the orthogonal complement of S_1 in R^D. A partially sampled signal defined on the set $\Psi = \Lambda + S_2$ is discrete in the dimensions determined by Λ and continuous in the dimensions determined by S_2. The set $\Lambda + S_2$ is an Abelian group, and the Fourier transform can be defined as

$$U(f_1, f_2) = \sum_{x \in \Lambda} \left(\int_{S_2} u(x, s) \exp\left(-j2\pi f_2^T s\right) ds \right)$$
$$\cdot \exp\left(-j2\pi f_1^T x\right) \quad (31)$$

where $f_1 \in S_1$ and $f_2 \in S_2$. If $u(x)$ is obtained by sampling a continuous signal $u_c(x)$ with Fourier transform $U_c(f)$, then

$$U(f) = \frac{1}{d(\Lambda)} \sum_{r \in \Lambda^*} U_c(f + r). \quad (32)$$

As an example, consider the following approximation to $2:1$ interlaced scanning used in television. The lattice Λ is defined by the vectors $(0, 2X_2, 0)^T$ and $(0, X_2, X_3)^T$ and is simply a hexagonal lattice in the vertical–temporal plane given by $x_1 = 0$. The sampling structure is

$$R + \Lambda = \left\{ (x_1, 2n_2 X_2 + n_3 X_2, n_3 X_3)^T | x_1 \in R, n_1, n_2 \in Z \right\}.$$

D. Sampling Structure Conversion

It is often necessary to interface image communication systems which use different sampling structures. Some examples are conversion between the European and North American scanning standards, or conversion between different sampling structures used in video codecs. Another application of importance is in scan conversion between transmission and display scanning standards [13]. A complete treatment of sampling rate conversion for one-dimensional signals is given in [14], and a brief introduction to the problem of sampling structure conversion for multidimensional signals is found in [11]. This section presents the theory of linear filters with input and output defined on different sampling structures, as illustrated in Fig. 8. We assume that these sampling structures are lattices Λ_1 and Λ_2, and that the input and output signals are in $L^1(\Lambda_1)$ and

[1] If Ψ is not a lattice, exact reconstruction may be possible, even if the translated spectra overlap, by using a different interpolation function for each coset. See [12, p. 194] for a one-dimensional example.

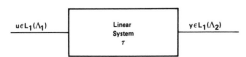

Fig. 8. Linear filter with input and output defined on different sampling lattices.

$L^1(\Lambda_2)$, respectively. The generalization to random fields is straightforward, but the generalization to nonlattice sampling structures is less so.

Let $\mathscr{T}$ be a linear system mapping functions defined on Λ_1 to functions on Λ_2, i.e., $\mathscr{T}:L^1(\Lambda_1) \rightarrow L^1(\Lambda_2)$. By linearity, we mean that $\mathscr{T}[a_1 u_1 + a_2 u_2] = a_1 \mathscr{T}[u_1] + a_2 \mathscr{T}[u_2]$ for any real numbers a_1 and a_2 and for any $u_1, u_2 \in L^1(\Lambda_1)$. Define the unit sample functions on a lattice by

$$\delta_s(x) = \begin{cases} 1, & x = s \\ 0, & x \neq s \end{cases} \tag{33}$$

and the unit sample responses $h_s \in L^1(\Lambda_2)$

$$h_s = \mathscr{T}[\delta_s]. \tag{34}$$

In the usual way, an arbitrary function can be written as a superposition of unit samples

$$u = \sum_{s \in \Lambda_1} u(s)\delta_s \tag{35}$$

and by linearity, the output of the filter is given by

$$\mathscr{T}[u] = \sum_{s \in \Lambda_1} u(s)\mathscr{T}[\delta_s]$$

$$= \sum_{s \in \Lambda_1} u(s)h_s. \tag{36}$$

A general property of interest in digital filters is shift invariance: if the input signal is shifted by p, the output signal is also shifted by p. In our case this is only possible if $p \in \Lambda_1 \cap \Lambda_2$. Thus we assume here that $\Lambda_1 \cap \Lambda_2$ is a D-dimensional lattice, i.e., that $V_1^{-1}V_2$ is a matrix of rational numbers. This is an extension of the condition that the ratio of sampling frequencies be a rational number in one-dimensional multirate systems [14]. Define the shift operator $\mathscr{S}_p$ on $L^1(\Lambda)$ by

$$\mathscr{S}_p u(s) = u(s - p). \tag{37}$$

Then the required shift invariance property is

$$\mathscr{T}[\mathscr{S}_p u] = \mathscr{S}_p \mathscr{T}[u], \qquad p \in \Lambda_1 \cap \Lambda_2 \tag{38}$$

or written out explicitly

$$\sum_{s \in \Lambda_1} u(s - p)h_s = \mathscr{S}_p \sum_{s \in \Lambda_1} u(s)h_s$$

$$= \sum_{s \in \Lambda_1} u(s)\mathscr{S}_p h_s. \tag{39}$$

A simple change of variables on the left side gives

$$\sum_{s \in \Lambda_1} u(s)h_{s+p} = \sum_{s \in \Lambda_1} u(s)\mathscr{S}_p h_s. \tag{40}$$

This equality will hold for arbitrary u if and only if

$$h_{s+p} = \mathscr{S}_p h_s, \qquad \forall p \in \Lambda_1 \cap \Lambda_2. \tag{41}$$

From this equation we see that the unit sample responses over cosets of $\Lambda_1 \cap \Lambda_2$ in Λ_1 are translated versions of each other. Thus the maximum number of such unit sample responses required to completely specify the filter is equal to the index of $\Lambda_1 \cap \Lambda_2$ in Λ_1.

Let the index of $\Lambda_1 \cap \Lambda_2$ in Λ_2 be Q, and let $b_1, \cdots, b_Q$ be representatives for the cosets. If $y = \mathscr{T}[u]$, then the function y restricted to the ith coset can be written

$$y(b_i + p) = \sum_{s \in \Lambda_1} u(s)h_s(b_i + p)$$

$$= \sum_{s \in \Lambda_1} u(p - s)h_{p-s}(b_i + p)$$

$$= \sum_{s \in \Lambda_1} u(p - s)h_{-s}(b_i), \qquad p \in \Lambda_1 \cap \Lambda_2.$$

$$\tag{42}$$

This can be written in the more familiar convolution form

$$y(b_i + p) = \sum_{s \in \Lambda_1} u(p - s)f_i(s) \tag{43}$$

where we define $f_i(s) = h_{-s}(b_i)$ for $i = 1, \cdots, Q$. This can be interpreted for each i as a linear filtering of u by the shift-invariant filter with impulse response f_i followed by a subsampling of the result to $\Lambda_1 \cap \Lambda_2$. The output y is obtained by multiplexing the output of the Q filters.

It is possible to represent this structure by a linear shift-invariant filter operating on a lattice which contains both Λ_1 and Λ_2. This is particularly useful for the application of frequency-domain filter design methods. Recall that $\Lambda_1 + \Lambda_2$ is the smallest lattice containing both Λ_1 and Λ_2. Define the upsampling operator $\mathscr{U}:L^1(\Lambda_1) \rightarrow L^1(\Lambda_1 + \Lambda_2)$ by

$$\mathscr{U}u(x) = \begin{cases} u(x), & x \in \Lambda_1 \\ 0, & x \notin \Lambda_1 \end{cases} \quad x \in \Lambda_1 + \Lambda_2 \tag{44}$$

and the downsampling operator $\mathscr{D}:L^1(\Lambda_1 + \Lambda_2) \rightarrow L^1(\Lambda_2)$ by

$$\mathscr{D}v(x) = v(x), \qquad x \in \Lambda_2. \tag{45}$$

Then the overall filter can be expressed

$$\mathscr{T} = \mathscr{D}\mathscr{T}^+\mathscr{U} \tag{46}$$

where $\mathscr{T}^+:L^1(\Lambda_1 + \Lambda_2) \rightarrow L^1(\Lambda_1 + \Lambda_2)$ is a linear shift-invariant filter. This is illustrated in Fig. 9. The filtering operation is described by

$$v(x) = \sum_{s \in \Lambda_1 + \Lambda_2} w(s)h(x - s) \tag{47}$$

where h is the unit sample response of $\mathscr{T}^+$. However, since

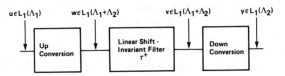

Fig. 9. Decomposition of sampling structure conversion system.

$w(x) = u(x)$ for $x \in \Lambda_1$, and is zero otherwise

$$v(x) = \sum_{s \in \Lambda_1} u(s)h(x - s), \qquad x \in \Lambda_1 + \Lambda_2. \tag{48}$$

Finally, the downsampling operation gives

$$y(x) = \sum_{s \in \Lambda_1} u(s)h(x - s), \qquad x \in \Lambda_2. \tag{49}$$

Comparing this with (36) gives

$$h(x - s) = h_s(x). \tag{50}$$

It can easily be verified that this is a well-defined assignment. The functions f_i are obtained from h by

$$f_i(x) = h_{-x}(b_i) = h(b_i + x). \tag{51}$$

A development very similar to that of Section II-B can be used to obtain the frequency-domain representation of the subsampling operation. Let $r_1, \cdots, r_N$ be coset representatives for the cosets of $(\Lambda_1 + \Lambda_2)^*$ in Λ_2^*, where $N = (\Lambda_1 : \Lambda_1 \cap \Lambda_2)$. Then

$$Y(f) = \frac{1}{N} \sum_{i=1}^{N} V(f + r_i). \tag{52}$$

The overall filter is thus described by

$$Y(f) = \frac{1}{N} \sum_{i=1}^{N} H(f + r_i) U(f + r_i). \tag{53}$$

When the change in sampling structure is such that overlap in the replicated spectra is introduced (as in downsampling), part of the role of the filter $\mathscr{T}^+$ is to eliminate high-frequency signal components which contribute to this overlap. When the sampling density is increased, the filter serves to attenuate repeat spectra in a process of interpolation.

As an example of these ideas, consider a two-dimensional filter whose input and output are defined on the lattices Λ_1 and Λ_2 shown in Fig. 10(a) and (b). These lattices can be represented by the matrices

$$\begin{bmatrix} X_1 & 0 \\ X_2 & 2X_2 \end{bmatrix}$$

and

$$\begin{bmatrix} X_1 & 0 \\ 2X_2 & 4X_2 \end{bmatrix}$$

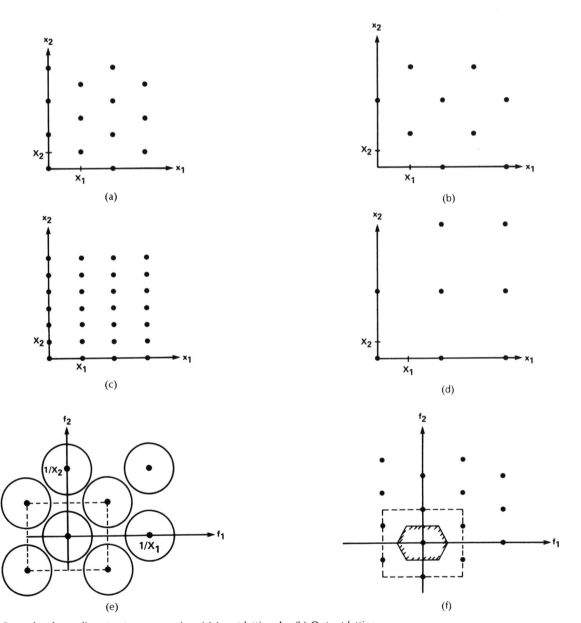

Fig. 10. Example of sampling structure conversion. (a) Input lattice Λ_1. (b) Output lattice Λ_2. (c) $\Lambda_1 + \Lambda_2$. (d) $\Lambda_1 \cap \Lambda_2$. (e) Spectrum of input signal with periodicity Λ_1^*. (f) Passband of filter, equal to Voronoi cell of Λ_2^*. The dashed rectangle shows a basic period of the filter frequency response.

13

with $d(\Lambda_1) = 2X_1X_2$ and $d(\Lambda_2) = 4X_1X_2$. The sum $\Lambda_1 + \Lambda_2$ and intersection $\Lambda_1 \cap \Lambda_2$ of these lattices are shown in Fig. 10(c) and (d), respectively, and can be represented by the matrices

$$\begin{bmatrix} X_1 & 0 \\ 0 & X_2 \end{bmatrix}$$

and

$$\begin{bmatrix} 2X_1 & 0 \\ 0 & 4X_2 \end{bmatrix}.$$

Here, $Q = (\Lambda_1 + \Lambda_2 : \Lambda_1) = (\Lambda_2 : \Lambda_1 \cap \Lambda_2) = 2$. Suppose that the input signal has the spectrum shown in Fig. 10(e), with periodicity given by the reciprocal lattice Λ_1^*, whose matrix is

$$\begin{bmatrix} \dfrac{1}{X_1} & -\dfrac{1}{2X_1} \\ 0 & \dfrac{1}{2X_2} \end{bmatrix}.$$

The filter h defined on $\Lambda_1 + \Lambda_2$ has a frequency response which is periodic with respect to $(\Lambda_1 + \Lambda_2)^*$, and to avoid aliasing, should have a nonzero response only on a unit cell of Λ_2^*, as illustrated in Fig. 10(f). One period of $H(f)$ is indicated by the dashed rectangle in Fig. 10(e) and (f).

E. Summary of Three-Dimensional Sampling

This section highlights the main ideas of Section II, in particular as applied to three-dimensional sampling. A sampling lattice Λ for time-varying imagery is a discrete set of points in $\boldsymbol{R}^3$ given by

$$\Lambda = \{ n_1\boldsymbol{v}_1 + n_2\boldsymbol{v}_2 + n_3\boldsymbol{v}_3 | n_1, n_2, n_3 \in \boldsymbol{Z} \} \qquad (54)$$

where $\boldsymbol{v}_1$, $\boldsymbol{v}_2$, and $\boldsymbol{v}_3$ are linearly independent vectors. The matrix $\boldsymbol{V} = [\boldsymbol{v}_1 | \boldsymbol{v}_2 | \boldsymbol{v}_3]$ is called the sampling matrix, and $d(\Lambda) = |\det \boldsymbol{V}|$ is the reciprocal of the sampling density. The lattice determined by the vectors $\boldsymbol{u}_1$, $\boldsymbol{u}_2$, and $\boldsymbol{u}_3$, where $\boldsymbol{U} = [\boldsymbol{u}_1 | \boldsymbol{u}_2 | \boldsymbol{u}_3] = (\boldsymbol{V}^{-1})^T$ is called the reciprocal lattice Λ^*. Fig. 2 shows an example of a lattice and its reciprocal lattice.

The Fourier transform of a discrete signal defined on a lattice Λ is

$$U(f) = \sum_{\boldsymbol{x} \in \Lambda} u(\boldsymbol{x}) \exp\left(-j2\pi f^T \boldsymbol{x}\right), \qquad f \in \boldsymbol{R}^3.$$

The Fourier transform is periodic with respect to the reciprocal lattice

$$U(f) = U(f + r), \qquad r \in \Lambda^*.$$

One period of $U(f)$ is called a unit cell of the reciprocal lattice; there are many possible ways to define a unit cell (see Fig. 3 for two possible unit cells for a given lattice). If a continuous signal $u_c(\boldsymbol{x})$ with Fourier transform $U_c(f)$ is sampled on a lattice Λ

$$u(\boldsymbol{x}) = u_c(\boldsymbol{x}), \qquad \boldsymbol{x} \in \Lambda$$

the Fourier transform of the sampled signal is

$$U(f) = \frac{1}{d(\Lambda)} \sum_{r \in \Lambda^*} U_c(f + r).$$

The spectrum of the sampled signal is thus the superposition of shifted versions of the original spectrum. Recon-

struction of the continuous signal is in general possible if these do not overlap. The reconstruction filter is an ideal low-pass filter which passes the basic spectrum and eliminates the replicates. If overlap occurs, aliasing is said to take place; see Fig. 6 for an example. The total mean-square error can be minimized by prefiltering the input before sampling, to limit its spectrum to a unit cell of the reciprocal lattice.

III. Sampling and Reconstruction of Time-Varying Imagery

The previous section has presented the mathematical theory of sampling of multidimensional signals. The transmission of a time-varying image over a one-dimensional channel requires the sampling of the image in at least two dimensions. If the original image is band-limited such that the sampling does not cause overlap of the repeated spectra, perfect reconstruction from the samples is possible. However, this is not the case in current television practice. There is aliasing in the sampling process, the reconstruction is far from perfect, and the human visual system is called upon to perform some of the interpolating postfiltering. This section discusses the issues related to sampling and reconstruction of time-varying imagery in television systems, including scanning, sampling structures, and the role of the visual system.

A time-varying image is a function of three independent variables: horizontal and vertical spatial dimensions and time. This will be denoted $u_c(\boldsymbol{x}) = u_c(x_1, x_2, x_3)$ where x_1 and x_2 are the horizontal and vertical coordinates, measured in some convenient unit of length, and x_3 is time in seconds. The ultimate spatial unit of interest in imagery destined for human viewing is distance on the retina (or angle subtended at the eye) of the observer. However, for a given image, this depends on the size of the image display, and the distance of the viewer from the display. Since these quantities cannot in general be controlled, a unit of spatial distance related to the image size is usually used. In this paper the basic unit of spatial distance is the picture height (ph) with the corresponding spatial frequency unit of cycles per picture height (c/ph). If the distance from the viewer to the display in picture heights is known, these can be converted to degrees and cycles per degree subtended at the eye, respectively.

The sampling theory described in the previous section involves the use of ideal point sampling and ideal low-pass prefilters and interpolators. Real image sampling and display involves the use of finite scanning apertures in the camera and display devices. The theory of scanning and display of still pictures with such apertures was first presented by Mertz and Gray [15]. The extension of these ideas to three dimensions, using more convenient mathematical tools, has appeared more recently [16]–[19]. The following two sections develop these ideas within the framework we have established. Structures suitable for sampling time-varying imagery are then discussed. Finally, the sampling of color video signals is treated.

A. Sampling

The process of ideal sampling as discussed in Section II-C requires the measurement of the image intensity at discrete points or lines in space–time. This is not physically possible; a real sampling device measures the integral of the image intensity over a neighborhood of the desired point, weighted by an *aperture function a*, which may in general be space-variant. The sampled signal is thus

$$u(x) = \int_{R^3} u_c(x+s)\, a(x,s)\, ds, \qquad x \in \Psi. \quad (55)$$

Under the assumption that the aperture is space-invariant, (55) becomes

$$u(x) = \int_{R^3} u_c(x+s)\, a(s)\, ds, \qquad x \in \Psi. \quad (56)$$

It is clear from (56) that this is equivalent to the ideal sampling of the function

$$v(x) = \int_{R^3} u_c(x-s)\, h_a(s)\, ds, \qquad x \in R^3 \quad (57)$$

where

$$h_a(s) = a(-s). \quad (58)$$

In other words, this real sampling process is equivalent to the ideal sampling of the original image filtered by a linear continuous three-dimensional filter with frequency response

$$H_a(f) = \int_{R^3} h_a(s) \exp(-j2\pi f^T s)\, ds. \quad (59)$$

The magnitude of $H_a(f)$ for $f_3 = 0$ is referred to as the modulation transfer function (MTF) of the camera.

The aperture function can normally be assumed to be separable in space and time. Although the spatial aperture is generally asymmetric and space-variant, it can be considered to a first approximation to be Gaussian. Fig. 11 shows a contour plot of the MTF for a circularly symmetric Gaussian aperture having a response of 0.5 at 400 TV lines (i.e., 200 c/ph), $H_a(f_1, f_2) = \exp(-(f_1^2 + f_2^2)/(240)^2)$. Miller [20] has given the MTF of several camera tubes, measured using the RCA P-300 test chart; Fig. 11 is typical of the camera tubes described in [20]. The characteristics of the many camera types available are discussed elsewhere in this issue.

To get an idea of the temporal aperture of a camera, consider a tube which exactly integrates the light intensity over a time T and then is completely erased. The temporal aperture in this case is given by

$$h_a(t) = \begin{cases} 1/T, & 0 \leqslant t \leqslant T \\ 0, & \text{elsewhere.} \end{cases} \quad (60)$$

Taking the Fourier transform of this gives the temporal response

$$H_a(f_3) = \exp(-j\pi f_3 T)\frac{\sin(\pi f_3 T)}{\pi f_3 T}. \quad (61)$$

Fig. 12 shows a vertical–temporal slice (at $f_1 = 0$) of the magnitude frequency response of the resulting separable three-dimensional aperture for $T = 1/60$ s.

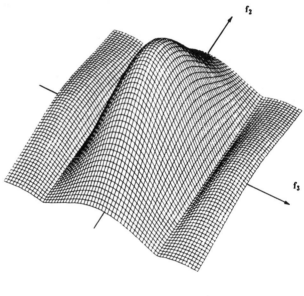

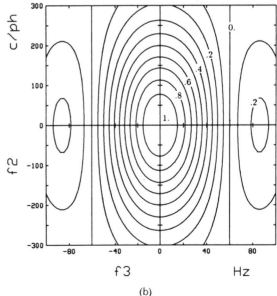

(b)

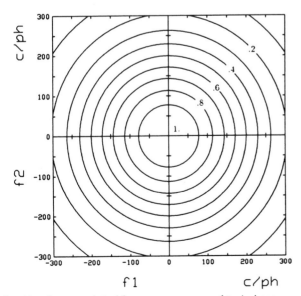

Fig. 11. Contour plot of frequency response of typical spatial Gaussian aperture. The response is 0.5 at 200 c/ph.

Fig. 12. Frequency response of typical vertical–temporal aperture. (a) Perspective view. (b) Contour plot.

The prefiltering provided by the camera aperture does not allow a good approximation to the ideal prefilter described in Section II-C, which passes all frequencies within a unit cell of the reciprocal lattice, and eliminates all frequencies outside the unit cell. There is a delicate balance between leaving high frequencies which will cause aliasing, and excessive attenuation of frequencies within the unit cell, which will compromise system resolution. For example, Schade [21] recommends that the camera MTF be no more than about 0.35 at half the vertical sampling rate to keep aliasing distortion at an acceptable level. However, this still results in significant attenuation of signal components below half the sampling rate, which could in principle be accurately maintained.

Although it is possible that better prefiltering could be obtained by electrooptical means, an alternative approach is to initially scan the image at a high sampling density, such that aliasing is negligible. The signal can then be converted to the desired sampling structure, performing the prefiltering digitally. It is also possible with this filter to compensate for the in-band signal attenuation due to the scanning aperture, a process known as aperture correction. With the use of digital prefilters, an arbitrarily sharp cutoff can be obtained. Although an infinitely sharp cutoff filter gives optimal results in terms of mean-square error, such a filter will cause ringing at sharp transitions, the well-known Gibbs' effect, which can be visually disturbing. A compromise must thus be struck between aliasing, loss of resolution, and ringing, to give optimal picture quality. A good illustration of these tradeoffs can be found in [22].

B. Reconstruction

The sampled image must be converted back to a continuous function of space and time for viewing on some display device such as a cathode-ray tube (CRT). The interpolation process given in (28) and (29) represents an ideal low-pass filtering. For human viewing, it is not necessary to perform perfect reconstruction, even in the ideal case. This is because signal distortions which are below the threshold of visibility can be allowed. In particular, since the visual system has a low-pass characteristic in spatial and temporal frequencies, the reconstruction processing need only reduce the magnitude of the high-order repeat spectra so that they are below threshold. However, since viewing conditions cannot generally be controlled, these thresholds should be based on the worst case viewing distance. Fig. 13 shows a perspective view of the threshold surface of the visual system as a function of spatial and temporal frequency, for particular viewing conditions [23]. Since the visual system is a nonlinear system, this figure can only serve as general indication as to the response to spatiotemporal patterns. A more complete model which accounts for the nonlinearity of the response and masking effects, such as that proposed by Lukas and Budrikis [24], would be required to fully predict the visibility of distortions. Note that the frequencies in Fig. 13 are at the retina, and may not correspond in a simple fashion to the spatiotemporal frequencies present in the imagery, if there is relative motion between the eye and the scene, as when objects are tracked. The relationship when the relative motion is uniform translation is derived in [6].

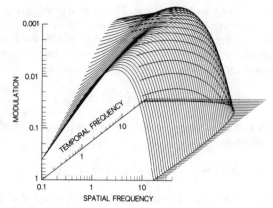

Fig. 13. Perspective view of portion of spatiotemporal threshold surface of human visual system [23]. Spatial frequency in c/deg, temporal frequency in Hz.

As in the camera, it is not easy to manipulate the display aperture to obtain a good approximation to the desired interpolating aperture. The reconstructed signal is given by

$$u_r(x) = \sum_{s \in \Psi} u(s) d(x - s) \qquad (62)$$

where $d(x)$ is the display aperture (impulse response). For a CRT display, the aperture is often assumed to be Gaussian, although more accurate approximations exist [21]. The temporal characteristic (phosphor decay) is usually exponential or logarithmic. The P22 phosphors used in color television decay to less than 10 percent of peak response in 10 μs to 1 ms [25]. Thus virtually no temporal filtering, and very little spatial filtering, is performed, in order to minimize loss of spatiotemporal resolution.

As a result of this imperfect interpolation, the viewer must be placed at a great enough distance for the visual filter to sufficiently attenuate the low-order repeat spectra. This may be at 6 to 8 times the picture height, as compared with a distance of 2 to 4 times which the viewer would naturally choose if no sampling artifacts were present [26]. This effect is illustrated by a rather extreme example of 18:1 subsampling shown in Fig. 14. At a normal reading distance of about 30 cm, the sampling structure obscures the text in Fig. 14(b), making reading difficult. By observing the figure from a greater distance (e.g., 1.5 m), the sampling structure is filtered by the visual system, and the text is more easily read. Fig. 14(c) shows the result of applying a two-dimensional interpolation filter, which attenuates the repeat spectra, making the text readable at 30 cm.

An approach to obtain an improved display aperture, similar to that described in Section III-A for the sampling aperture, can be taken. Digital interpolation to a higher scanning rate is performed, strongly attenuating the lowest order repeat spectra. The remaining repeat spectra are now in bands of lower visibility, and the gentle filtering of the display aperture is adequate to render them below threshold.

With current television practice, the combination of the camera aperture and the display aperture result in a maximum vertical resolution of only about 0.7 of the theoretical limit. This factor is sometimes referred to as the Kell factor, although there is no precise and universally accepted definition. An excellent discussion of the parameters of an

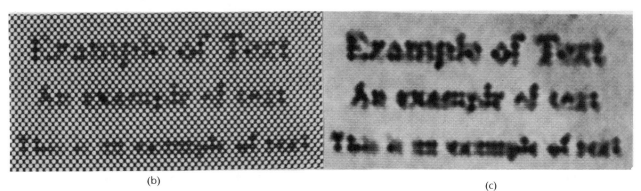

(a)

(b)   (c)

Fig. 14. Example of sampled text. (a) Original image. (b) Subsampled by a factor of 18 with hexagonal lattice and reconstructed with very narrow Gaussian aperture. (c) Reconstructed with two-dimensional interpolation filter.

imaging system which can influence the Kell factor has been given by Tonge [27]. By the approaches described above, significant improvement is possible, and Kell factors much closer to unity may be possible. This topic is discussed in more detail elsewhere in this issue.

C. Sampling Structures

Scanning: Scanning is the two-dimensional sampling process currently used in television, whereby the scene is sampled in the vertical and temporal directions, but is continuous in the horizontal direction. The resulting lines are then abutted to form a one-dimensional signal referred to as the video signal. Two vertical–temporal sampling structures are of interest: the orthogonal and the hexagonal structures shown in Fig. 15(a). These correspond to sequential and 2:1 interlaced scanning, respectively. The reciprocal lattices corresponding to these structures are shown in Fig. 15(b). As shown in Section II-C, the spectrum of the original image is replicated in the vertical–temporal frequency plane according to the reciprocal lattice.

The scanning lines are usually assumed to be perpendicular to the vertical–temporal plane. This is not precisely true; the lines have both a vertical and temporal tilt. For a 525-line sequential image with a 4:3 aspect ratio, this corresponds to rotating the image by about 0.16°. The temporal tilt means that the bottom of the image is scanned X_3 seconds after the top of the image, which could have some minor effect on large rapidly moving objects. However, as argued in [6] and [28], these effects are generally insignificant. We will ignore the tilt of the scanning lines in the remainder of this paper, and assume that they are perpendicular to the vertical–temporal plane. The set of samples taken at a given time t constitute a *field*.

Both scanning patterns shown in Fig. 15 have the same number of lines per picture (counting both fields for the interlaced case) and the same sampling density. Examining the reciprocal lattices, we see that the closest replicated spectra to the origin for sequential scanning are at $(0, 1/X_2, 0)^T$, $(0, 0, 1/2X_3)^T$, and $(0, 1/X_2, 1/2X_3)^T$. For interlaced scanning, the closest replicated spectra to the origin are at $(0, 1/X_2, 0)^T$, $(0, 0, 1/X_3)^T$, and $(0, 1/2X_2, 1/2X_3)^T$. As mentioned previously, these replicated spectra are attenuated very little by the display aperture. The main degradation associated with the replicated spectrum at $(0, 1/X_2, 0)^T$ is visibility of the scanning lines; it is the same with both patterns. The main artifact associated with a component at $(0, 0, F)^T$ is large-area flicker at F hertz. With sequential scanning, large-area flicker is at $1/2X_3$ hertz, while for interlaced scanning, it is at $1/X_3$ hertz. If $X_3 = 1/60$ s (1/50 s), sequential scanning gives 30-Hz (25-Hz) large-area flicker, which is visually unacceptable. Interlaced scanning gives 60-Hz (50-Hz) large-area flicker which is significantly less visible, being almost imperceptible at 60 Hz, but perhaps slightly annoying at 50 Hz. The main distortions associated with the third components at $(0, 1/X_2, 1/X_3)^T$ or $(0, 1/2X_2, 1/X_3)^T$ are interline flicker and line crawl. These distortions are, of course, more visible with interlaced scanning than with sequential scanning, and are generally the most annoying defects in an interlaced display. However, they are still much less visible than the large-area flicker for which they have been traded. In general, 2:1 interlaced scanning display is preferable to sequential scanning for a given scanning density [26], [29].

17

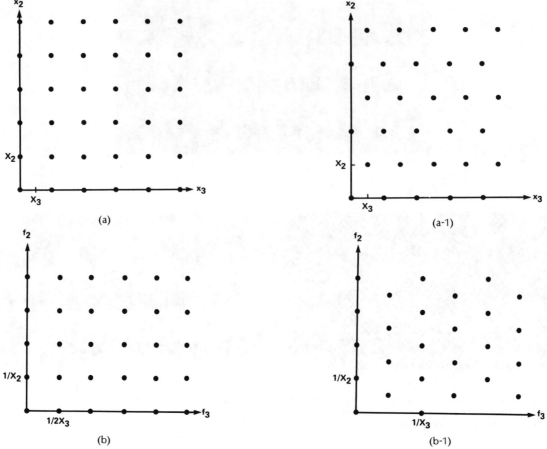

Fig. 15. (a) Two-dimensional sampling patterns for sequential and interlaced scanning of time-varying imagery. (b) Reciprocal lattices.

The spectrum of the one-dimensional video signal obtained by scanning can be related to the three-dimensional spectrum of the time-varying image. It can be shown that the one-dimensional spectrum is basically obtained by scanning the three-dimensional spectrum, giving the familiar comb-type spectrum. A detailed derivation can be found in [18].

Three-Dimensional Sampling Structures: For digital processing, coding, and transmission, the image signal must be sampled in three dimensions. This is usually done by horizontally sampling a signal which has already been scanned in the vertical–temporal dimension. However, with some solid-state sensors, the signal may be inherently sampled in three dimensions. Numerous sampling structures have been proposed for three-dimensional image sampling. A number of these will be presented in this section, and their relative merits discussed.

One of the earliest applications of a sampling lattice to television transmission was described by Gouriet [30] in 1952, in the context of dot-interlaced television. In the mid-1960s, Brainard *et al.* [31] carried out experiments with *replenishment patterns* for low-resolution TV; some were lattices while the rest were the union of two shifted lattices. In this work, no explicit interpolation was carried out, leaving this to the visual system. Further work on sampling structures came with the advent of digital television. Sabatier and Kretz [32] compared several structures for sampling of line-interlaced television signals and later presented an in-depth study of the performance of these sampling struc-

tures [6]. This work also emphasized interpolation by the human visual system. Tonge has described at length the design of three-dimensional digital filters for prefiltering and interpolation in two IBA research reports [28], [33].

Figs. 16–22 show a number of structures which have been proposed for image sampling. Also shown on these figures are the reciprocal structures and the lattice matrices. Sampling structures have often been illustrated by means of perspective drawings, as in [6] and [28]. However, for some of the more complex structures, these figures can be difficult to interpret, so we have chosen to show the spatial and spatial-frequency projections of the structures. All points in the structure occurring at the same time or temporal frequency carry the same number. The spacing in the temporal or temporal-frequency dimension between successive numbers is equal to the $(3,3)$ element of the associated lattice matrix. For convenience, all the matrices are given in upper triangular form, so that the U matrices are not the inverse transposed of the V matrices, although the product UV^T is an integer matrix of determinant one. Fig. 23 shows a perspective view of the lattice and reciprocal lattice of Fig. 18, with the same numbering of the lattice points. Also shown is a Voronoi unit cell of the reciprocal lattice.

The closest lattice points to the origin in the reciprocal lattices indicate which frequencies in the input signal are most likely to cause aliasing problems. Kretz and Sabatier [6] have shown that the most critical structures for the sampling process are periodic structures and contours or

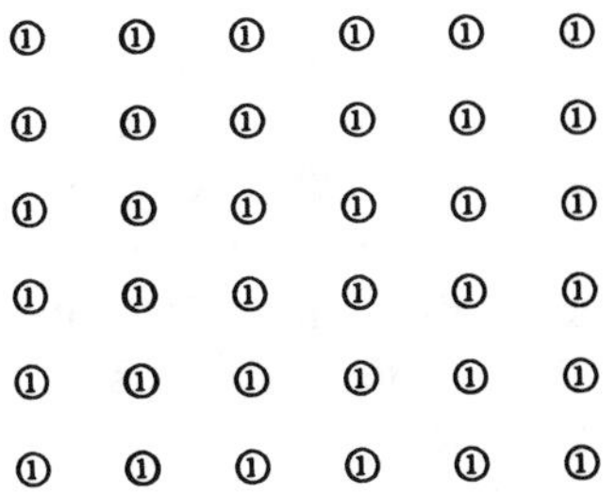

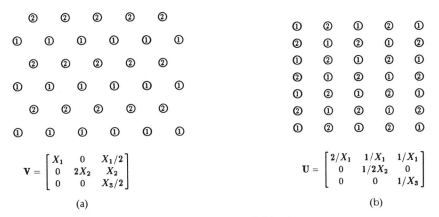

$$\mathbf{V} = \begin{bmatrix} X_1 & 0 & 0 \\ 0 & X_2 & 0 \\ 0 & 0 & X_3 \end{bmatrix}$$

(a)

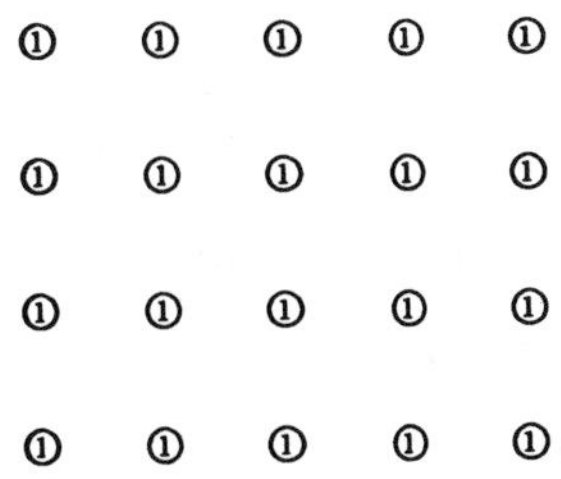

$$\mathbf{U} = \begin{bmatrix} 1/X_1 & 0 & 0 \\ 0 & 1/X_2 & 0 \\ 0 & 0 & 1/X_3 \end{bmatrix}$$

(b)

Fig. 16. (a) Orthorhombic lattice (ORT). (b) Reciprocal lattice.

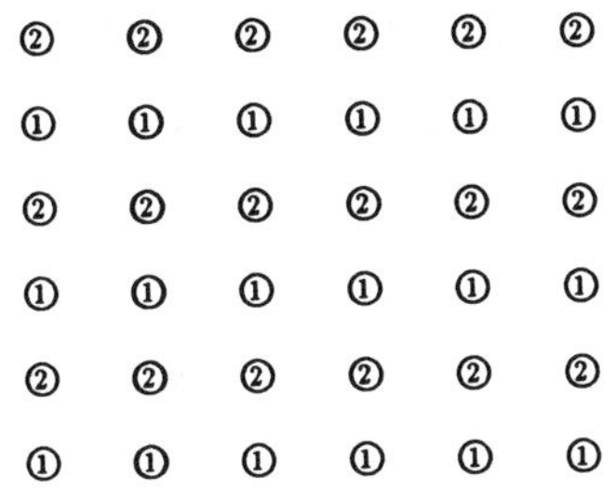

$$\mathbf{V} = \begin{bmatrix} X_1 & 0 & 0 \\ 0 & 2X_2 & X_2 \\ 0 & 0 & X_3/2 \end{bmatrix}$$

(a)

$$\mathbf{U} = \begin{bmatrix} 1/X_1 & 0 & 0 \\ 0 & 1/X_2 & 1/2X_2 \\ 0 & 0 & 1/X_3 \end{bmatrix}$$

(b)

Fig. 17. (a) Lattice obtained by vertically aligned sampling of $2:1$ line-interlaced signal (ALI). (b) Reciprocal lattice.

$$\mathbf{V} = \begin{bmatrix} X_1 & 0 & X_1/2 \\ 0 & 2X_2 & X_2 \\ 0 & 0 & X_3/2 \end{bmatrix}$$

(a)

$$\mathbf{U} = \begin{bmatrix} 2/X_1 & 1/X_1 & 1/X_1 \\ 0 & 1/2X_2 & 0 \\ 0 & 0 & 1/X_3 \end{bmatrix}$$

(b)

Fig. 18. (a) Body-centered orthorhombic lattice (BCO). Also known as field-quincunx (QT). (b) Reciprocal lattice.

edges. The distortion for a periodic structure is worst when any of its significant frequency components are near one of the lattice points of the reciprocal lattice. The distortion appears as a beat frequency at the difference between the structure frequency and the frequency of the closest reciprocal lattice point. When the aliasing is mainly spatial, this phenomenon is referred to as a Moiré pattern. For contours, the distortion appears as a phase perturbation along the length of the contour. This distortion is worst when the Fourier spectrum of the contour is oriented towards one of the points of the reciprocal lattice.

A good indication of the efficiency of a sampling lattice is the ability to pack spheres densely without overlap on the points of the reciprocal lattice. This indicates the sampling density required to sample without aliasing a signal whose spectrum is confined to a spherical region in frequency space. Table 1 gives the minimum sampling density, and the corresponding values of X_1, X_2, and X_3, for each of the sampling structures in Figs. 16–22. The sampling density $C = 8W^3$ of the simple cubic lattice is used as a reference against which the others are compared. The optimum sampling density is $0.707C$, which can be obtained with the lattices BCO, FCO, and HEX3. In all three cases, the reciprocal lattice is equivalent under rotation to the face-centered

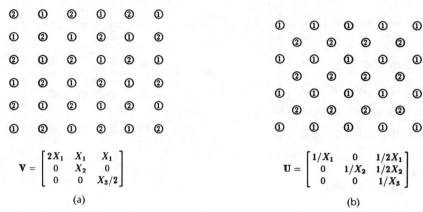

Fig. 19. (a) Face-centered orthorhombic lattice (FCO). (b) Reciprocal lattice.

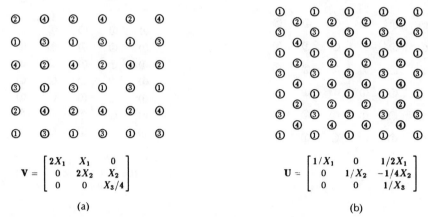

Fig. 20. (a) Hexagonal lattice with four field periodicity (HEX4). Also known as nonstationary line-quincunx (QLNS). (b) Reciprocal lattice.

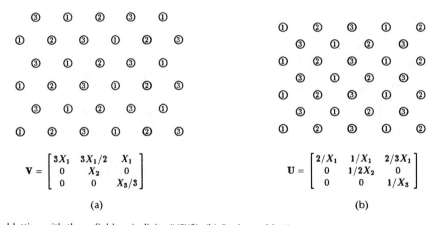

Fig. 21. (a) Hexagonal lattice with three-field periodicity (HEX3). (b) Reciprocal lattice.

Table 1 Minimum Sampling Density for Alias-Free Sampling of Signals Band-Limited to $|f| < W$

Sampling Structure	Minimum Sampling Density $1/X_1 X_2 X_3$	X_1	X_2	X_3
ORT	$8W^3 = C$	$1/2W$	$1/2W$	$1/2W$
ALI	$4\sqrt{3}\,W^3 = 0.866\,C$	$1/2W$	$1/2W$	$1/\sqrt{3}\,W$
BCO	$4\sqrt{2}\,W^3 = 0.707\,C$	$1/\sqrt{2}\,W$	$1/2\sqrt{2}\,W$	$1/\sqrt{2}\,W$
FCO	$4\sqrt{2}\,W^3 = 0.707\,C$	$1/2W$	$1/2W$	$1/\sqrt{2}\,W$
QLNS	$6W^3 = 0.75\,C$	$1/2\sqrt{3}\,W$	$1/2W$	$2/\sqrt{3}\,W$
HEX3	$4\sqrt{2}\,W^3 = 0.707\,C$	$1/\sqrt{3}\,W$	$1/2W$	$\sqrt{3}/2\sqrt{2}\,W$
QL	$3\sqrt{5}\,W^3 = 0.838\,C$	$2/\sqrt{15}\,W$	$1/2W$	$1/\sqrt{3}\,W$

cubic (FCC) lattice, which is known to be the densest possible lattice sphere packing. In order to apply these results to the sampling of time-varying imagery, it is necessary to relate measures of temporal frequency to those of spatial frequency. This may not be strictly possible since these are fundamentally different units. An approach suggested by Tonge [28] is to base this relationship on the spatiotemporal response characteristics of the human visual system, and to assume a worst case viewing distance. If the high-frequency portion of the threshold data, as in Fig. 13, is used for this purpose, an approximate equivalence of 1 Hz and 0.62 cycles per degree (or 8.8 c/ph at a viewing

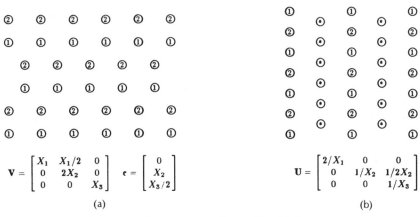

$$\mathbf{V} = \begin{bmatrix} X_1 & X_1/2 & 0 \\ 0 & 2X_2 & 0 \\ 0 & 0 & X_3 \end{bmatrix} \quad \mathbf{c} = \begin{bmatrix} 0 \\ X_2 \\ X_3/2 \end{bmatrix} \qquad \mathbf{U} = \begin{bmatrix} 2/X_1 & 0 & 0 \\ 0 & 1/X_2 & 1/2X_2 \\ 0 & 0 & 1/X_3 \end{bmatrix}$$

(a)   (b)

Fig. 22. (a) Line-quincunx structure (QL). (b) Reciprocal structure. ∗ indicates all multiples of $1/X_3$.

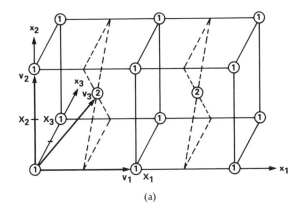

(a)

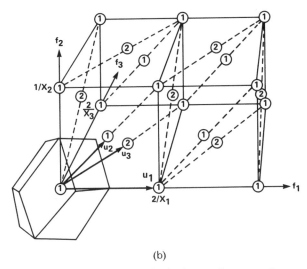

(b)

Fig. 23. (a) Perspective view of BCO lattice. (b) Perspective view of reciprocal lattice (FCO), showing Voronoi region.

distance of four picture heights) is obtained. This ratio would equate a temporal frequency of 60 Hz with a spatial frequency of 528 c/ph, very close to the ratio used in the NTSC system.

An interesting parameter associated with each sampling structure is the ratio of the spatial sampling density per field to the total spatial sampling density, as seen in the spatial projection of the structure. We refer to this as the interlace

order. This was the basic parameter of interest in the original dot-interlace schemes, and is of particular interest in motion-adaptive interpolation, to be discussed in the next section. For a given spatiotemporal sampling density, the potential spatial resolution in stationary areas increases with interlace order. For the sampling structures of Figs. 16–22, the interlace order is equal to the highest sample index on the diagram of part (a) of the corresponding figure. The HEX3 sampling structure has the highest interlace order (three) among the optimal sphere packing lattices we have given. The HEX4 lattice gives an interlace order of four, with only a small decrease in packing efficiency, making it a potentially attractive structure. However, it remains to be verified that the crawling patterns described in [6] can be eliminated by suitable spatiotemporal interpolation filters.

When sampling a signal which has already been scanned (usually with 2:1 line interlace), the samples must lie on the scanning lines. The structures which are compatible with line-interlaced scanning without field subsampling are ALI, BCO, HEX4, and QL. As the sampling density decreases, it may be advantageous to perform field subsampling to maintain similar resolution in the different dimensions. In this case, the ORT, FCO, and HEX3 patterns may also be used. Tonge [28] has proposed preferred sampling structures (choosing between BCO and FCO) compatible with European scanning standards for different sampling densities.

D. Sampling of Color Signals

Sampling Component Color Signals: The sampling theory which has been presented can be applied in a straightforward manner to sampling the three components of color imagery. The main issues which arise are: which three components should be sampled, and what should be the relative sampling densities? The components which appear to be the most advantageous are the luminance and two chrominance components. From a statistical point of view, most signal energy is contained in the luminance component, and the Y, I, and Q components give similar energy compaction to the Karhunen–Loève transformation [34]. From a perceptual point of view, most successful models of color vision incorporate a luminance channel, and two chrominance channels (for example [35] and [36]). It is well known, that for a given total bandwidth, overall picture quality is maximized by allotting more bandwidth to the luminance than to the chrominance components; this forms the basis for existing color television systems. The recent recommendation for a digital component studio standard [37] allows half the luminance sampling density to each chrominance component (R–Y and B–Y). For many coding systems, a much larger ratio of luminance to chrominance sampling density is used. Further work is required to determine more precisely the optimal allocation of relative spatiotemporal sampling density to the luminance and chrominance components.

Sampling Composite Color Signals: The sampling of composite color video signals presents interesting problems, due to the irregular shape of the spectrum. In composite signals, the luminance and chrominance information is frequency-multiplexed in the three-dimensional frequency space. The form of the three-dimensional spectrum of the PAL signal was derived in [38], and that of the NTSC signal in [5]. Fig. 24 shows an idealized view of the three-

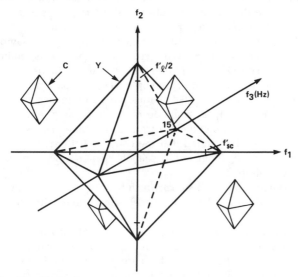

Fig. 24. Three-dimensional spectrum of NTSC signal.

dimensional spectrum of the NTSC signal. The sampling problem is to choose a structure which will optimally pack this spectrum region in three-dimensional frequency space. A number of structures for this purpose, with a horizontal sampling frequency equivalent to $2f_{sc}$, were presented and evaluated in [39]. Although this frequency is "sub-Nyquist" in the one-dimensional sense, appropriate patterns give good separation of the replicated spectra in three dimensions. The preferred sampling pattern was determined to be the body-centered orthorhombic pattern (or field quincunx), and suitable interpolating filters were presented.

IV. FILTERS FOR PREFILTERING AND INTERPOLATION

A. Linear Shift-Invariant Filters

The prefilter and interpolation filters of Fig. 1 are generally hybrid analog/digital filters. The first stage of the prefilter consists of the three-dimensional camera aperture filter, and possibly a one-dimensional analog electrical filter. The output of this stage is sampled on an initial sampling

structure. It may then be digitally filtered, and subsampled to the final sampling structure. At the display, the sampled signal may first be digitally interpolated to a higher sampling density. This is then interpolated to a continuous signal by a one-dimensional analog electrical filter and the display aperture.

There is little flexibility available in shaping the display an camera apertures, whereas there is great flexibility in the design of multidimensional digital filters, and many design techniques are available [7]. Since linear phase is an important requirement in image filtering, finite-impulse response (FIR) filters are most often used, where perfect linear phase can be obtained. Infinite-impulse response (IIR) filters can potentially give equivalent filter performance for a lower order, but introduce problems of phase response and stability. Since the implementation of a filter requires a number of field memories equal to the temporal order of the filter, there may be some advantage to be gained by the use of IIR filters if these problems can be overcome.

There are two basic approaches available for the design of the prefilters and interpolators.

1) *Frequency-domain approach:* for a given filter order, the impulse response coefficients are chosen so that the frequency response approximates in some way the pass-stop characteristics of the ideal prefilter or interpolator, as described in Section II-C.

2) *Spatiotemporal-domain approach:* for a given filter order, the prefilter and interpolator coefficients are chosen so that the interpolated signal approximates as closely as possible the original image.

In video applications, the filters are generally of relatively low order, due to speed and memory constraints. The transition regions of the filters are thus not very sharp, so that in-band components are attenuated, while out-of-band components are not completely eliminated. The filters should be optimized on the basis of subjective criteria, in order to give the best tradeoff between resolution loss, aliasing, and ringing. These do not in general carry equal weight in terms of mean-square error. For example, it has been found on the basis of subjective experiments on still pictures that viewers attach more importance to loss of sharpness than to aliasing distortion [40], [41].

Tonge [28] has presented frequency-domain designs for prefilters and interpolators. For the low filter order usually considered, a simple frequency constraint approach is often successful. This can be accomplished by specifying that the frequency response and its derivatives take on specified values at certain frequencies. For example, the response at the origin can be specified to give the desired dc gain, the response at points of the reciprocal lattice in frequency bands to be attenuated can be set to zero, and the derivatives of the response at these frequencies can be set to zero to give maximally flat response in different directions. Each constraint results in a linear equation. If the number of independent constraints equals the number of degrees of freedom of the filter, a unique solution can be found. Otherwise, the remaining coefficients can be varied in some systematic fashion to obtain the best response. This was the approach used in [28]. The McClellan transformation approach has been proposed for the design of two-dimensional prefilters and interpolators, for use with still images [42].

The spatiotemporal approach has been mainly confined to the use of polynomial-type interpolation. Most prominent among these is the cubic B-spline approach [43], which has been used for spatial interpolation. This technique has the advantage of being able to compute interpolated values anywhere, not just on a rationally related lattice. Another spatiotemporal approach is to choose the interpolation coefficients to minimize the mean-square interpolation error, based on a homogeneous random field model for the image signal. This technique has mainly been used for one-dimensional interpolation [44], [45], but is easily extended to three dimensions.

B. Nonlinear Motion-Dependent Filters

The preceding sections on subsampling and interpolation assume that the signal is reconstructed by means of a linear three-dimensional low-pass filter. The specific nature of time-varying imagery can be exploited to obtain improved reconstruction techniques. Specifically, a time-varying scene generally consists of a fixed background and a number of moving objects. The temporal variation in the imagery is caused by the motion of the objects in the scene. This section presents reconstruction techniques which adapt to the motion. Two main classes of algorithms are considered. In the first, termed *motion-adaptive* processing, a motion *detection* operation is performed, and different filtering algorithms are used in moving and stationary parts of the scene. In the second, *motion-compensated processing*, the displacement of the objects from frame to frame is estimated, and this motion *estimation* is used to determine the filtering which is performed.

Motion-Adaptive Interpolation: Motion-adaptive interpolation can be used when it is desired to interpolate to a higher density sampling structure which has the same spatial projection. The maximum interpolation ratio which can be obtained in this way is equal to the interlace order of the original sampling structure. The idea is to perform temporal interpolation in fixed areas, interpolating a missing sample from samples at the same spatial location in previous and subsequent fields. In moving areas, where this would not give good results, a spatial interpolator is used. The basic concept is shown in Fig. 25. A motion detector generates a motion index M, largely based on the interframe difference in a neighborhood of the sample to be interpolated. To avoid sudden switching between the two

types of interpolators, a weighted sum of the two, with weights determined by the motion index, is used. Thus if $\hat{u}_t(x)$ is a temporal interpolation and $\hat{u}_s(x)$ is a spatial interpolation at point x, the motion-adaptive interpolation is given by

$$\hat{u}(x) = \alpha(M)\hat{u}_s(x) + (1 - \alpha(M))\hat{u}_t(x). \qquad (63)$$

Fig. 26 shows the general form of the function $\alpha(M)$ which relates the weighting factor to the motion index. If the motion index is small, α is close to zero, and the interpola-

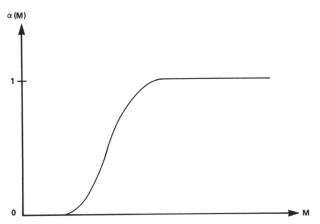

Fig. 26. Nonlinear function of motion index for motion-adaptive interpolation.

tion is mainly temporal. As the motion index increases, α approaches unity, and the interpolation becomes mainly spatial. This type of interpolation can give significantly better results than fixed interpolation, especially in stationary areas where the eye is most critical. The performance of motion-adaptive interpolation is critically dependent on the motion detection algorithm, and most research on this technique centers on this aspect. Motion-adaptive interpolation has been applied in the interpolation from the HEX4 structure to the orthorhombic structure which contains it, in the subsampling subsystem of a low-rate coder for video conferencing [46]. It has also been applied in the interpolation from interlaced scanning to sequential scanning with twice the number of lines per field, for improved display performance [47]–[49]. Motion-adaptive processing, based on the same principles, has also been applied to noise reduction [50] and luminance/chrominance demultiplexing in composite signals [49].

Motion-Compensated Interpolation: Motion compensation is a technique which has received considerable attention recently for application in predictive coding of time-varying imagery (e.g., [51]–[53]), and in noise reduction [54]. This technique can be used to improve the performance of interpolation in moving areas of the picture, especially when pure temporal subsampling has been used, and the spatial interpolation part of the motion-adaptive interpolator is not relevant. The basis of the technique is to estimate the motion of the objects in the scene, and to interpolate a missing field using the corresponding object points in the previous and subsequent transmitted fields. The concept was described by Gabor and Hill [55], using interpolation only along a given scan. The application to general two-dimensional motion was described in a series of papers at

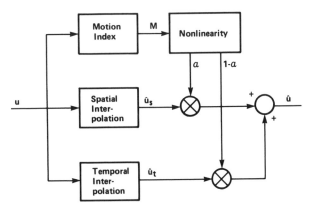

Fig. 25. Motion-adaptive interpolation system.

the 1981 Picture Coding Symposium [56]–[58]. Specific algorithms to perform motion-compensated interpolation are disclosed in [59], and applications in low bit-rate coding are given in [60], [61].

With conventional temporal interpolation, a missing field is reconstructed by forming a weighted combination of pels at the same spatial location in previous and subsequent transmitted fields (using spatial interpolation if necessary). When the subsampling factor is large, this results in both jerkiness (a result of aliasing) and blurring. Motion-compensated interpolation can significantly reduce these effects. The general approach is illustrated in Fig. 27 for the case of 2:1 field subsampling. For each point in the output sampling structure of the nontransmitted field, such as pel A, the spatial location of the corresponding point in the

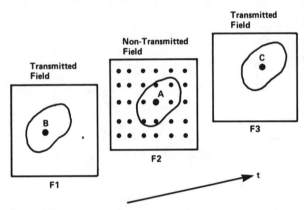

Fig. 27. Principle of motion-compensated interpolation. Point A in field F2 is interpolated using point B in field F1 and point C in field F3, after having estimated the displacement vector.

previous and subsequent transmitted fields must be estimated, B and C in Fig. 27. It is assumed that the points BAC lie on a straight line. A linear combination of the intensities of the points at B and C is used to interpolate the value at A. Many techniques have been developed for displacement estimation, the most important ones being matching [62], [63], the method of spatiotemporal gradients [64], [65], and steepest descent recursive estimation [51]. A review of displacement estimation can be found in [66]. Any of these methods can be applied to motion-compensated interpolation; a matching approach is used in [60], while the steepest descent approach has been used in [59] and [61].

It is important to recognize that there is no correction for errors made in the displacement estimation, as there is in predictive coding and noise reduction applications, and so it is imperative that the displacement field used be as accurate as possible, or else artifacts will appear in the image. Another observation is that where a signal may be considered undersampled and aliased from the point of view of a homogeneous random field, it can be accurately reconstructed on the basis of a more complex model.

V. Conclusion

This paper has presented an overview of techniques for sampling and reconstruction of time-varying imagery. A feature of the presentation is the use of lattices to describe

the sampling process, greatly facilitating the subsequent analysis of digital signal processing algorithms. A good understanding of the principles involved will be required to design systems capable of providing the highest image quality possible for a given transmission format. This is of great importance at this time with the advent of enhanced-quality and high-definition television system proposals, discussed elsewhere in this issue. Further work is required to arrive at three-dimensional linear and nonlinear filters capable of giving the desired image quality with reasonable hardware complexity.

Acknowledgment

The assistance of P. Faubert in the preparation of Fig. 14 is gratefully acknowledged.

References

[1] J. W. S. Cassels, *An Introduction to the Geometry of Numbers*. Berlin, Germany: Springer-Verlag, 1959.

[2] J. M. Ziman, *Principles of the Theory of Solids*. Cambridge, UK: Cambridge Univ. Press, 1972.

[3] D. P. Petersen and D. Middleton, "Sampling and reconstruction of wave-number-limited functions in N-dimensional Euclidean spaces," *Informat. Contr.*, vol. 5, pp. 279–323, 1962.

[4] N. T. Gaarder, "A note on the multidimensional sampling theorem," *Proc. IEEE*, vol. 60, pp. 247–248, Feb. 1972.

[5] E. Dubois, M. S. Sabri, and J.-Y. Ouellet, "Three-dimensional spectrum and processing of digital NTSC color signals," *SMPTE J.*, vol. 91, pp. 372–378, Apr. 1982.

[6] F. Kretz and J. Sabatier, "Echantillonnage des images de télévision: analyse dans le domaine spatio-temporel et dans le domaine de Fourier," *Ann. Télécommunications*, vol. 36, pp. 231–273, Mar.–Apr. 1981.

[7] D. E. Dudgeon and R. M. Mersereau, *Multidimensional Digital Signal Processing*. Englewood Cliffs, NJ: Prentice-Hall, 1984.

[8] J. P. Allebach, "Design of antialiasing patterns for time-sequential sampling of spatiotemporal signals," *IEEE Trans. Acoust., Speech, Signal Process.*, vol. ASSP-32, pp. 137–144, Feb. 1984.

[9] W. Rudin, *Fourier Analysis on Groups*. New York: Interscience, 1962.

[10] L. E. Franks, *Signal Theory*. Englewood Cliffs, NJ: Prentice-Hall, 1969.

[11] R. M. Mersereau and T. C. Speake, "The processing of periodically sampled multidimensional signals," *IEEE Trans. Acoust., Speech, Signal Processing.*, vol. ASSP-31, pp. 188–194, Feb. 1983.

[12] A. Papoulis, *Signal Analysis*. New York: McGraw-Hill, 1977.

[13] B. Wendland, "Extended definition television with high picture quality," *SMPTE J.*, vol. 92, pp. 1028–1035, Oct. 1983.

[14] R. E. Crochiere and L. R. Rabiner, *Multirate Digital Signal Processing*. Englewood Cliffs, NJ: Prentice-Hall, 1983.

[15] P. Mertz and F. Gray, "A theory of scanning and its relation to the characteristics of the transmitted signal in telephotography and television," *Bell Syst. Tech. J.*, vol. 13, pp. 464–515, 1934.

[16] A. Macovski, "Spatial and temporal analysis of scanned systems," *Appl. Opt.*, vol. 9, pp. 1906–1910, Aug. 1970.

[17] A. H. Robinson, "Multidimensional Fourier transforms and image processing with finite scanning apertures," *Appl. Opt.*, vol. 12, pp. 2344–2352, Oct. 1973.

[18] D. E. Pearson, *Transmission and Display of Pictorial Information*. New-York: Wiley, 1975.

[19] Y. Guinet, "Propriétés spectrales et performance du système télévisuel," *Radiodiffusiontélévision*, "1ère partie: Modélisation des systèmes télévisuels scalaires à support continu," no.

56, pp. 9–14, 1979; "2e partie: Propriétés générales des balayages à entrelacement," no. 57, pp. 49–57, 1979; "3e partie: Systèmes scalaires à support continu et à entrelacement de trame d'ordre deux," no. 59, pp. 30–40, 1979; "4ème partie: Modulation du point mobile de balayage par un signal périodique. 1. Le cas du signal sinusoidal," no. 66, pp. 47–55, 1981.

[20] L. D. Miller, "A new method of specifying the resolving power of television camera tubes using the RCA P-300 test chart," *SMPTE J.*, vol. 89, pp. 249–256, Apr. 1980.

[21] O. H. Schade, Sr., "Image reproduction by a line raster process," in *Perception of Displayed Information*, L. M. Biberman, Ed. New York: Plenum, 1973, pp. 233–278.

[22] G. A. Reitmeier, "The effects of analog filtering on the picture quality of component digital television systems," *SMPTE J.*, vol. 90, pp. 949–955, Oct. 1981.

[23] D. H. Kelly, "Motion and vision. II. Stabilized spatio-temporal threshold surface," *J. Opt. Soc. Amer.*, vol. 69, pp. 1340–1349, Oct. 1979.

[24] F. X. J. Lukas and Z. L. Budrikis, "Picture quality prediction based on a visual model," *IEEE Trans. Commun.*, vol. COM-30, pp. 1679–1692, July 1982.

[25] N. A. Diakides, "Phosphor screens," in *Electronics Engineers' Handbook*, D. G. Fink, Ed. New York: McGraw Hill, pp. 11-33–11-39, 1975.

[26] T. Mitsuhashi, "A study of the relationship between scanning specifications and picture quality," NHK, NHK Laboratories Note, no. 256, Oct. 1980.

[27] G. J. Tonge, "The television scanning process," *SMPTE J.*, vol. 93, pp. 657–666, July 1984.

[28] ——, "Three-dimensional filters for television sampling," Independent Broadcasting Authority, Experimental and Development Rep. 117/82, June 1982.

[29] E. F. Brown, "Low-resolution TV: Subjective comparison of interlaced and noninterlaced pictures," *Bell Syst. Tech. J.*, vol. 46, pp. 199–232, Jan. 1967.

[30] G. G. Gouriet, "Dot-interlaced television," *Electron. Eng.*, vol. 24, pp. 166–171, Apr. 1952.

[31] R. C. Brainard, F. W. Mounts, and B. Prasada, "Low-resolution TV: Subjective effects of frame repetition and picture replenishment," *Bell Syst. Tech. J.*, vol. 46, pp. 261–271, Jan. 1967.

[32] J. Sabatier and F. Kretz, "Sampling the components of 625-line colour-television signals," *E. B. U. Rev.—Tech.*, no. 171, pp. 212–225, Oct. 1978.

[33] G. J. Tonge, "The sampling of television images," Independent Broadcasting Authority, Experimental and Development Rep. 112/81, May 1981.

[34] W. K. Pratt, "Spatial transform coding of color images," *IEEE Trans. Commun. Technol.*, vol. COM-19, pp. 980–992, Dec. 1971.

[35] W. Frei and B. Baxter, "Rate-distortion coding simulation for color images," *IEEE Trans. Commun.*, vol. COM-25, pp. 1385–1392, Nov. 1977.

[36] O. D. Faugeras, "Digital color image processing within the framework of a human visual model," *IEEE Trans. Acoust., Speech, Signal Process.*, vol. ASSP-27, pp. 380–393, Aug. 1979.

[37] F. Davidoff, "Digital television coding standards," *Proc. Inst. Elec. Eng.*, pt. A, vol. 129, pp. 403–412, Sept. 1982.

[38] J. O. Drewery, "The filtering of luminance and chrominance signals to avoid cross-colour in a PAL colour system," *BBC Eng.*, pp. 8–39, Sept. 1976.

[39] J.-Y. Ouellet and E. Dubois, "Sampling and reconstruction of NTSC video signals at twice the color subcarrier frequency," *IEEE Trans. Commun.*, vol. COM-29, pp. 1823–1832, Dec. 1981.

[40] J. N. Ratzel, "The discrete representation of spatially continuous images," Massachusetts Institute of Technology, Ph.D. dissertation, Aug. 1980.

[41] R. J. Arguello, H. B. Kessler, and H. R. Sellner, "The effect of sampling, optical transfer function shape, and anisotropy on subjective image quality," *Opt. Eng.*, vol. 21, pp. 23–29, Jan./Feb. 1982.

[42] T. C. Chen and R. J. P. de Figueiredo, "Image decimation and interpolation techniques based on frequency domain analysis," *IEEE Trans. Commun.*, vol. COM-32, pp. 479–484, Apr. 1984.

[43] H. S. Hou and H. C. Andrews, "Cubic splines for image interpolation and digital filtering," *IEEE Trans. Acoust., Speech, Signal Process.*, vol. ASSP-26, pp. 508–517, Dec. 1978.

[44] G. Oetken, T. W. Parks, and H. W. Schüssler, "New results in the design of digital interpolators," *IEEE Trans. Acoust., Speech, Signal Process.*, vol. ASSP-23, pp. 301–309, June 1975.

[45] A. D. Polydoros and E. N. Protonotarios, "Digital interpolation of stochastic signals," *IEEE Trans. Circuits Syst.*, vol. CAS-26, pp. 916–922, Nov. 1979.

[46] K. Takikawa, "Simplified 6.3 Mbit/s codec for video conferencing," *IEEE Trans. Commun.*, vol. COM-29, pp. 1877–1882, Dec. 1981.

[47] C. P. Sandbank and M. E. B. Moffat, "High-definition television and compatibility with existing standards," *SMPTE J.*, vol. 92, pp. 552–561, May 1983.

[48] G. Tonge, "Signal processing for higher-definition television," *IBA Tech. Rev.*, vol. 21, pp. 13–26, Nov. 1983.

[49] M. Achiha, K. Ishikura, and T. Fukinuki, "A motion-adaptive high-definition converter for NTSC color TV signals," *SMPTE J.*, vol. 93, pp. 470–476, May 1984.

[50] J. R. Sanders, "Fully adaptive noise reduction for a television network," *Television: J. Royal Television Soc.*, vol. 18, pp. 29–33, May/June 1980.

[51] A. N. Netravali and J. D. Robbins, "Motion-compensated television coding: Part I," *Bell Syst. Tech. J.*, vol. 58, pp. 631–670, Mar. 1979.

[52] S. Sabri, "Movement compensated interframe prediction for NTSC color TV signals," *IEEE Trans. Commun.*, vol. COM-32, pp. 954–968, Aug. 1984.

[53] T. Koga, A. Hirano, K. Iinuma, Y. Iijima, and T. Ishiguro, "A 1.5 Mb/s interframe codec with motion compensation," in *Rec. Int. Conf. Commun.*, pp. D8.7.1–D8.7.5, June 1983.

[54] E. Dubois and S. Sabri, "Noise reduction in image sequences using motion-compensated temporal filtering," *IEEE Trans. Commun.*, vol. COM-32, pp. 826–831, July 1984.

[55] D. Gabor and P. C. J. Hill, "Television band compression by contour interpolation," Proc. Inst. *Elec. Eng.*, vol. 108, pt. B, pp. 303–315, May 1961.

[56] A. N. Netravali and J. D. Robbins, "Motion adaptive interpolation of television frames," in *Rec. Picture Coding Symp.*, p. 115, June 1981.

[57] H. C. Bergmann, "Motion-adaptive interpolation of eliminated TV fields," in *Rec. Picture Coding Symp.*, pp. 116–117, June 1981.

[58] R. Lippmann, "Air-to-ground TV at low frame rates extended by interpolative frame regeneration," in *Rec. Picture Coding Symp.*, pp. 120–121, June 1981.

[59] A. N. Netravali and J. D. Robbins, "Video signal interpolation using motion estimation," U.S. Patent 4 383 272, May 10, 1983.

[60] A. Furukawa, T. Koga, and K. Iinuma, "Motion-adaptive interpolation for videoconference pictures," in *Proc. Int. Conf. Commun.*, pp. 707–710, May 1984.

[61] S. Sabri, K. Cuffling, and B. Prasada, "Coding of video signals at 50 kb/s using motion compensation techniques," in *Proc. IEEE Military Comm. Conf.*, pp. 809–816, Nov. 1983.

[62] J. R. Jain and A. K. Jain, "Displacement measurement and its application in interframe image coding," *IEEE Trans. Commun.*, vol. COM-29, pp. 1799–1808, Dec. 1981.

[63] Y. Ninomiya and Y. Ohtsuka, "A motion-compensated interframe coding scheme for television pictures," *IEEE Trans. Commun.*, vol. COM-30, pp. 201–211, Jan. 1982.

[64] C. Cafforio and F. Rocca, "Methods for measuring small displacements of television images," *IEEE Trans. Informat. Theory*, vol. IT-22, pp. 573–579, Sept. 1976.

[65] R. Paquin and E. Dubois, "A spatio-temporal gradient method for estimating the displacement field in time-varying imagery," *Comput. Vision, Graph. Image Process.*, vol. 21, pp. 205–221, 1983.

[66] W. B. Thompson and S. T. Barnard, "Lower-level estimation and interpretation of visual motion," *Computer*, vol. 14, pp. 20–28, Aug. 1981.

Sampling-Rate Conversion of Video Signals

By Ajay Luthra and Ganesh Rajan

Encoding analog component video to a composite signal is an established practice. Improvements are constantly being made in encoding techniques, with the result that the quality of the encoded video is closer to that of the component source. Encoding digital components to digital composite signals involves an additional step besides coding: the sampling-rate conversion. The sampling rates of component video signals (CCIR Rec. 601) are 13.5 Msamples/sec and 6.75 Msamples/sec, for the luminance and the color-difference signals, respectively. The sampling rates for NTSC and PAL composite video signals are 14.3181818 Msamples/sec and 17.734475 Msamples/sec, respectively. Clearly, decoding digital composite signals into digital component signals (CCIR 601) will also involve the sampling-rate conversion. This task of sampling-rate conversion further complicates the issues related to the quality of the output video. It introduces a new class of distortions, called linear time varying distortions, in the output signal. This article explores the techniques necessary to convert between digital signals with different sampling rates and presents a qualitative comparison of the two approaches, analog and digital, to the sampling-rate conversion.

Until recent years, video signals have mainly been treated as analog signals. With phenomenal growth in the technology during recent years, digital video signals are becoming more common. The digital form of the signal consists of a sequence of samples having two additional attributes: sampling rate and sample accuracy. In the one-dimensional form, the sampling rate specifies the spacing between two adjacent samples. In two dimensions, it also specifies the spacing between the lines and in three dimensions, the frame rate. In this article, we will limit our discussion to the one-dimensional case.

Unfortunately, there is no single sampling rate that is used to obtain a digital video signal. In one dimension, where the video is treated as a long one-dimensional signal, there are currently two common standards in each of the PAL and NTSC formats. These are the component (CCIR 601) and composite video standards. In the component standard, the luminance and the color-difference video signals, besides being in component form, are sampled at 13.5 Msamples/sec and 6.75 Msamples/sec, respectively. In the composite standard, the NTSC and PAL composite video signals are sampled at 14.3181818 Msamples/sec and 17.734475 Msamples/sec, respec-

tively. Thus, the process of converting component digital signals to composite digital signals, and vice versa, involves not only coding and decoding, but also sampling-rate conversion.

In this article we explore the techniques necessary to convert between digital signals with different sampling rates and present a qualitative comparison of the two approaches, analog and digital, to the sampling-rate conversion. The issue is raised that the sampling-rate conversion introduces a new class of distortions, viz., linear time varying distortions, that the video community is not accustomed to and does not monitor or measure. Typically, one measures linear time invariant distortions, such as chroma-luma gain and phase differences, or nonlinear distortions like differential phase and gain. With the usage of digital sampling-rate conversions systems in the video path, one must now be aware of the relevant distortions that could be introduced into the video signals.

Sampling-Rate Conversion Techniques

There are two broad categories of the techniques used to perform sampling-rate conversion: analog and digital. In analog sampling-rate conversion, the input digital signal is first

converted into analog form, via a digital-to-analog (D/A) converter, and then resampled at the desired output rate. On the other hand, in digital conversion schemes, the signal always stays in the digital form. The values of the signal at the output sampling locations are mathematically calculated from the input samples. As digital hardware becomes faster and more inexpensive, digital approaches are becoming a more economical as well as more accurate means of sampling-rate conversion.

Analog Conversion

The analog conversion method, shown in Fig. 1a, is easy to understand (therefore, not discussed in detail here) but difficult to implement if very high accuracy is desired. Let the magnitude spectrum of the input digital signal be as shown in Fig. 1b, where f_i is the input sampling frequency. The Fourier transform of a discrete time (digital) signal $\{x(n)\}$ is given by

$$X(e^{j2\pi f}) = \sum_{n=-\infty}^{\infty} x(n)e^{-j2\pi nf/f_s}$$

where f_s is the sampling frequency.[1] It is periodic with the period of f_s. Therefore, the spectrum of the input signal consists of the baseband signal and its replicas at the interval of the input sampling frequency f_i. The process of converting digital signals into the analog form involves low-pass filtering of the digital signal so that all the replicas of the baseband are removed completely. It is not possible to realize a perfect, boxcar-shaped, analog low-pass filter, however. The magnitude response of a typical analog low-pass filter is shown in Fig. 1c. The spectrum in the output of the D/A converter contains some energy at frequencies outside the desired baseband (Fig. 1d). When this output is resampled at the desired output sampling rate f_o, these frequencies alias back into the baseband, as shown in Fig. 1e. This aliasing adds to the distortion in the output signal, so to maintain high ac-

Reprinted with permission from *SMPTE J,* pp. 869–879, Nov. 1991. © Society of Motion Pictures and Television Engineers.

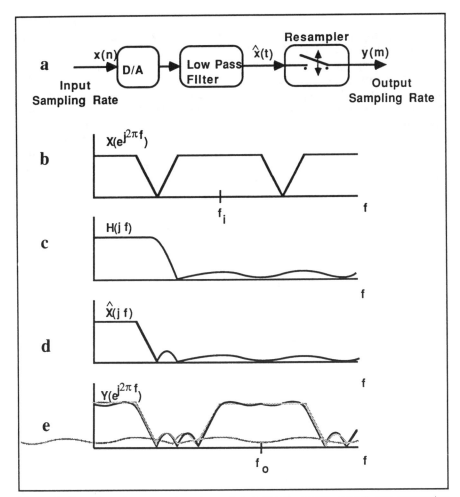

Figure 1. Sampling-rate conversion via analog methods: (a) the overall rate conversion scheme; (b) spectrum of the input signal; (c) spectrum of the analog low-pass filter; (d) spectrum of the filtered analog signal; (e) spectrum of the resampled analog signal (the dotted lines show the original spectrum and its repetitions that give rise to aliasing).

sampled values of the analog signal $x(t)$ at time instants nT_i, where T_i ($=1/f_i$) is the input sampling period. Assuming that the bandwidth of $x(t)$ is less than $f_i/2$, the value of the analog signal at any time instant t can be calculated exactly from $\{x(n)\}$ using the following[1]

$$x(t) = \sum_{n=-\infty}^{\infty} x(n) \frac{\sin[\pi(t-nT_i)/T_i]}{\pi(t-nT_i)/T_i}$$

$$= \sum_{n=-\infty}^{\infty} x(n)\mathrm{sinc}[\pi(t-nT_i)/T_i] \quad (1)$$

This equation essentially represents the low-pass filtering of the input. To perform sampling-rate conversion, one needs to evaluate Eq. 1 at time instants corresponding to the output sample locations, i.e., at $t=mT_o$, $m=-\infty\cdots-2,-1,0,1,2\cdots\infty$, where T_o ($=1/f_o$) is the output sampling period corresponding to desired (output) rate f_o. Therefore, the basic equation to change the sampling-rate can be written as

$$y(m) = x(mT_o) =$$

$$\sum_{-\infty}^{\infty} x(n)\mathrm{sinc}[\pi(mT_o-nT_i)/T_i] \quad (2)$$

Here $y(m)$ is the exact value of the analog signal at the time instant mT_o.

In general, an additional precaution is required. If $f_o<f_i$, we also need to filter out those high-frequency components in the input signal that cannot be sustained by the output sampling rate. This can be easily incorporated in Eq. 2 by narrowing the bandwidth of the sinc function.

Observe that, according to Eq. 2, we require all the input samples to calculate one output sample. It is therefore not possible to evaluate Eq. 2 exactly because the summation index goes from $-\infty$ to ∞. In practice, it is necessary to truncate the sum, which adds to the error in the output signal. (Another source of the error is the finite precision of the calculations, which is not discussed here.) The aim of digital rate conversion schemes is to replace the sinc interpolation function by another function that is of finite duration (we will not worry about infinite impulse response filters here), so that, for a given length of the summation in Eq. 2, the error introduced due to truncation is minimal.

Digital schemes can be classified into three categories: (1) classical in-

curacy throughout, the analog low-pass filter has to have very low sidelobe levels. At the same time, the passband ripple (deviation from unity gain) should be very small, since any distortion in the passband will also be sent on to the output signal. Further, the transition band of the filter is required to be quite sharp. In NTSC, the baseband video extends up to about 4.5 MHz, and in PAL, it goes up to 5.5 MHz. Considering the sampling-rate conversion of a PAL luminance signal from the composite rate to the component rate, the transition bandwidth of the analog low-pass filter is required to be about 2.5 MHz. For the NTSC case, the required transition bandwidth is of the order of 4.5 MHz.

The accuracy of the output signal depends on, besides the accuracy of the D/A and A/D conversion, the passband ripple, the stopband attenuation, and the phase linearity of the low-pass filter, as discussed earlier.

(Although that discussion is for the digital filters, it is also applicable to analog filters.) We show that, in order to match the error performance of an 8-bit quantizer, the deviation of the low-pass filter passband response from unity gain should be less than 0.2%. In addition, the filter's phase response must be linear to within 0.5° over the entire bandwidths of 4.2 MHz and 5.5 MHz for NTSC and PAL signals, respectively. It is very difficult to produce an analog filter to match these specifications. Therefore, although both the D/A and the resampling A/D converters may be accurate to 8 to 10 bits, the output signal may not be that accurate due to imperfections in the analog low-pass filter. The digital methods of rate conversion can relatively easily achieve 10 to 12 bits of accuracy and are also more economical.

Digital Conversion

Let $\{x(n)\}$ denote the sequence of

terpolation based; (2) digital filtering (multirate) based; and (3) hybrid schemes, which are a combination of the methods in (1) and (2).

Classical Interpolation-Based Schemes

The sinc interpolation function in Eq. 2 is replaced by a finite duration classical interpolation function like the splines or the Lagrange interpolation function. Considering Lagrange interpolation, Eq. 2 is now rewritten as

$$\hat{y}(m) = \sum_{k=0}^{N_p-1} x(k+n-\frac{N_p-1}{2})l_k(mT_o)$$

(3)

where $(n-\frac{1}{2})T_i \leq mT_o < (n+\frac{1}{2})T_i$ and N_p is assumed to be odd. The N_p-th order Lagrange polynomial $l_k(t)$ is given by

$$l_k(t) = \frac{(t-t_0)(t-t_1)\cdots(t-t_{k-1})(t-t_{k+1})\cdots(t-t_{N_p-1})}{(t_k-t_0)(t_k-t_1)\cdots(t_k-t_{k-1})(t_k-t_{k+1})\cdots(t_k-t_{N_p-1})}$$

(4)

where $\{t_k\}$ are the time locations of the input samples around the output sample location t. As opposed to the interpolation in Eq. 2, only N_p input samples are considered for the calculation of one output sample. Also observe that the interpolation coefficients $\{l_k(t)\}$ are different, in general, for each output sample. The third-order Lagrange polynomial is an example of a cubic spline.

In general, digital interpolation schemes based on conventional filter design techniques perform much better than the Lagrange interpolator.[2] This is discussed in the following section.

Digital Filtering-Based Schemes

In these schemes, Eqs. 1 and 2 are seen as the convolution of the input digital stream with a filter whose impulse response is the sinc function, i.e., the digital filter is the ideal low-pass (boxcar) filter. This filter is not realizable as it is a noncausal filter. However, there are many techniques for the design of digital filters where the frequency responses come very close to the ideal low-pass filter response. An equiripple Chebyshev design[1,3] is one of the many optimum design techniques that can be used. In

this context, it is also possible to describe sampling-rate conversion using Lagrange polynomials, in the form of a digital filtering-based scheme. We will first explain these schemes and then show how the Lagrange interpolation function can be interpreted as a digital filter.

Digital Filter Synthesis

As the input and the output sampling rates are different, it is difficult to visualize Eq. 2 as a digital filtering equation. It becomes easier to understand, analyze, and design the filters if both the input and output signals of a digital filter have the same sampling rates. This is achieved by artificially creating an intermediate stage consisting of the sampling rate that is the least common multiple of the input and the output rates of the sampling-rate converter. For illustration purposes, let us assume that input and the output sampling rates are related by a ratio of 2:3. If the input sampling rate

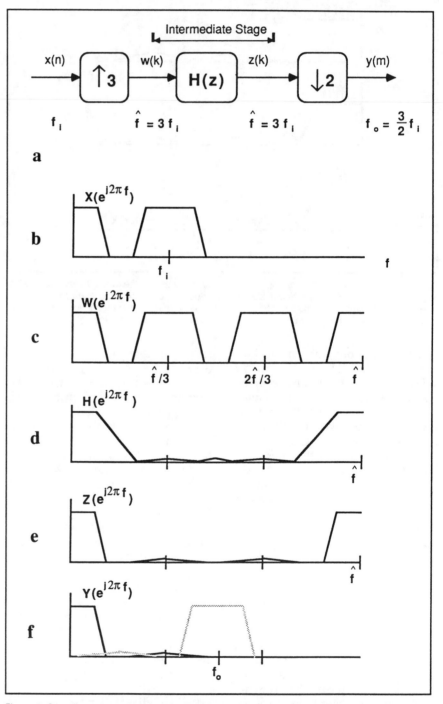

Figure 2. Sampling-rate conversion via digital methods: (a) general 2:3 sampling-rate conversion scheme; (b) through (f) frequency domain description of the block diagram in (a).

were to be increased by a factor of 3, then this intermediate sampling rate is twice the desired output rate and contains sampling locations corresponding to the input as well as the output signal. Now, in order to obtain a sequence at the desired output sampling rate, we discard every alternate sample from the intermediate sequence. This, in general, is the essence of any sampling-rate conversion where the input and the output sampling rates are in a ratio of $M:L$, i.e., $Lf_i = Mf_o$. The emphasis now is on being able to generate the "correct" sequence of samples at the intermediate sampling rate.

The process of going up in the sampling rate is called interpolation (it is unfortunate that this terminology interferes with the classical definition or understanding of interpolation). The process of reducing the sampling rate is referred to as decimation (the reduction does not have to be in the steps of 10, as the name may suggest). Conceptually, it is necessary to first interpolate and then decimate to achieve the desired rate conversion (Fig. 2a-f). We will elaborate on these two steps, as follows.

Let the spectrum of a digital signal $x(n)$ be as shown in Fig. 2b. The spectrum of the interpolator output, assuming a factor of 3 interpolation, is as shown in Fig. 2e (ideally, there will be no energy around $\hat{f}/3$ and $2\hat{f}/3$). Every frequency is now one-third smaller compared to the increased sampling rate. Figure 2c shows the spectrum of the signal obtained by inserting two zeroes after every sample in the original sequence $\{x(n)\}$. Comparing Figs. 2c and 2e, one finds that the only difference in the spectra is that, in Fig. 2c, the low-pass spectrum repeats faster. Therefore, to go from spectrum of Fig. 2c to that in Fig. 2e, we only have to low-pass filter the signal obtained by inserting zeroes. The symbol ↑ 3 indicates that 2 ($=3-1$, i.e., L-1 in general) zeroes are inserted in between every sample of the input data stream. As the input and output of the filter H(z) are at the same rate, the conventional optimum filter design techniques can now be used to design that low-pass filter. To get the final output sampling rate, we discard every other sample (the symbol ↓ 2 indicates that only one out of every two samples is kept in the output ⇒ and the output rate is half that of the intermediate stage). The spectrum of

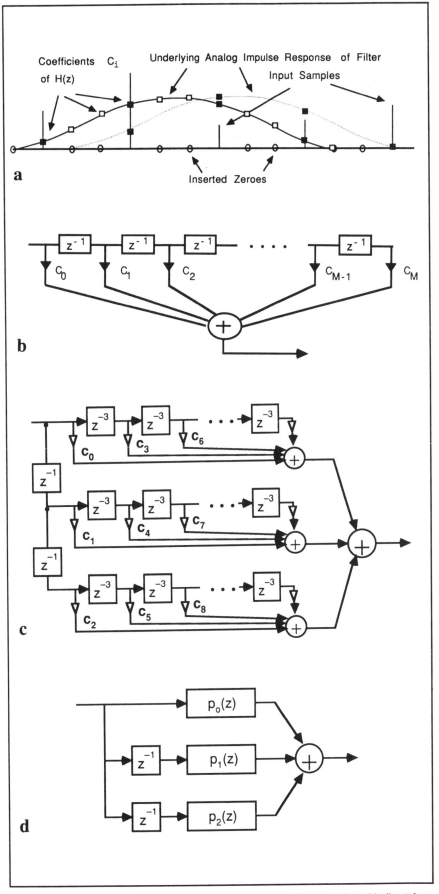

Figure 3. Digital interpolation: (a) a time-domain illustration of interpolation; (b) direct form realization of H(z) in Fig. 2a; (c) a rearrangement of the filter in (b); (d) the polyphase representation of the filter in (b).

29

the signal obtained at the output is shown in Fig. 2f. Thus, for the general case, the concept of a digital scheme to convert the sampling rate by a ratio of L/M is to increase the sampling rate by L and then decimate by M.

Digital Filter Implementation

In practice, to reduce the computational effort, the samples that are discarded by the decimator are not calculated. In addition, the multiplications corresponding to the zeroes inserted in the input sample sequence are also not performed. To implement these two steps, we need to understand the representation (realization) of H(z) in the polyphase form.

Consider the 2:3 sampling rate conversion scheme again. The time-domain representation of the filtering (convolution) is shown in Fig. 3a. The impulse-response envelope of the filter is shown to be centered at some desired output sampling instant. The squares represent the coefficients $\{c_i\}$ used in the realization of

$$H(z) = \sum_{i=0}^{K} c_i z^{-i}$$

the number of coefficients $K + 1$ is also referred as the length of the filter or the number of taps in the filter). The blackened squares represent the filter coefficients that correspond to the actual input samples $\{x(n)\}$ used to calculate an output sample. The dotted curve shows the impulse response envelope of the filter $H(z)$ centered at another output sampling instant. As shown in the figure, the interpolation coefficients that correspond to actual input samples and do not multiply the inserted zeroes are different. Figure 3b shows the direct form structure of the low-pass interpolation filter H(z). Figure 3c indicates a rearrangement of the same structure as

$$H(z) = \sum_{i=0}^{k} c_i z^{-i} = \sum_{i=0}^{R} c_{3i} z^{-3i} + z^{-1}$$

$$\sum_{i=0}^{R} c_{3i+1} z^{-3i} + z^{-2} \sum_{i=0}^{R} c_{3i+2} z^{-3i} \quad (5)$$

with $K = 3R + 2$, without any loss of generality. Here we have grouped every third coefficient of $H(z)$ into one structure. An equivalent block representation is shown in Fig. 3d, where

$$p_k(z) = \sum_{i=0}^{R} c_{3i+k} z^{-3i}, \quad k = 0,1,2 \quad (6)$$

This is the polyphase decomposition of $H(z)^2$. Each subfilter $p_0(z), p_1(z)$ and $p_2(z)$ in this polyphase decomposition is one-third the length of the original filter $H(z)$.

As the input to $H(z)$ has two zeroes inserted in between the actual input samples $\{x(n)\}$, only one subfilter contributes at one time into the final summer. Hence, these subfilters need not be implemented simultaneously. For hardware implementations, we need to provide only one finite impulse response (FIR) filter structure that is only as long as the longest of these subfilters. It can then be multiplexed so that, depending upon the output sample number, it realizes $p_0(z), p_1(z)$ or $p_2(z)$. This is schematically shown in Fig. 4. (In general, by increasing the value of L, only the coefficient storage requirement is increased while the number of actual multipliers required does not significantly change.)

So far, the filter in Fig. 4 is running at three times the original input rate f_i. A tremendous savings is achieved by realizing that, in the case of 2:3 rate conversion, only one out of the two samples is kept. Therefore, only those samples that are kept in the output signal should be calculated. This implies that the subfilters are not implemented according to the sequence of 0, 1, 2, 0, 1, 2 ..... Instead they are realized in the sequence corresponding to the sequence of the samples kept, i.e., 0, 2, 1, ... $2n$ modulo 3, where n is the output sample index. Therefore, the multipliers now need to run at the output rate only.

In short, for hardware realization:
• We only need to realize a short FIR filter, corresponding to the longest subfilter in the polyphase structure, even for large values of L and M.

This length is basically a function of the bandwidth of the signal compared to the sampling rate and does not depend much on the ratio of the ouput and input rates.

• The multipliers need to run at the final output rate only.

Component ⇔ Composite Rate Conversion for NTSC

Let us consider the case of rate conversion for NTSC. In the case of component ⇒ composite rate conversion, the output and input sampling rates for the NTSC luminance component are related by the ratio of 35:33. To achieve the conversion, conceptually we interpolate and increase the input sampling rate by a factor of 35 and then pick every 33rd sample. Therefore, the filter $H(z)$ is now designed in the intermediate domain that is operating at the sampling rate of 472.5 Msamples/sec (= 35 × 13.5 = 33 × 14.3181818). The aim of this filter is to attenuate the replicas of the passband below the desired level, with minimum distortion in the passband itself. No precise formulas exist to calculate the exact length of the desired filter, although one can make use of some empirical formulas to obtain a reasonable estimate of the filter length.[3] From our simulations, we found that a filter of length 350 would suffice to attenuate the passband replicas below −50 dB. This filter can be easily designed using one of the standard FIR filter design packages[4] (this is not so for similar rate conversions in PAL).

We do not, however, have to implement this filter in its entirety. Observe that 34 zero-valued samples are inserted after every input sample in the intermediate data stream. Only 10

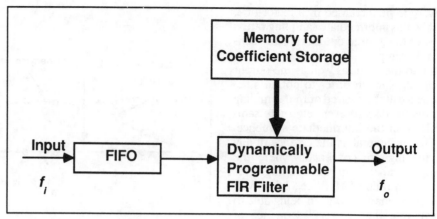

Figure 4. A block diagram of the hardware implementation of the polyphase structure shown in Fig. 3d.

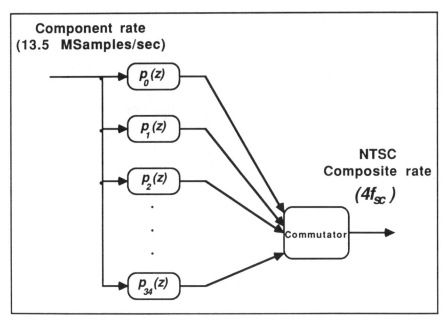

Figure 5. A polyphase implementation of the component (CCIR 601) ⇒ NTSC composite sampling-rate converter.

$$H(z) = \sum_{k=0}^{L-1} z^{-k} q_k(z^L) \qquad (7)$$

where $L = 35$, in this case. The magnitude response of this filter can be compared with that of one obtained via FIR filter synthesis techniques. Figures 6a and 6b compare the magnitude responses of $H(z)$ for N_p equal to 12 and 16 with that obtained from the filter synthesis techniques for $N_p = 12$. Observe that the magnitude responses of $H(z)$ corresponding to the Lagrangian subfilters are very flat at low frequencies, but start to roll off earlier than that for the optimally designed filter. The optimal filter tends to distribute the passband errors evenly over the entire band of interest. Thus, for a given number of multipliers and considering the entire band of interest, the performance of the Lagrange interpolation-based scheme will be poorer than that of digital filtering-based schemes.[2,5]

The results of the simulation work done by us showed that even a 16th-order Lagrange polynomial could barely meet the accuracy of 0.2% (about 8 bits) over the entire frequency range of interest (0 to 4.2 MHz). The error was very small for low-input frequencies but increased as the input frequency increased to 4.2 MHz. Therefore, using this technique, it was necessary to use at least 16 multiplications for each output sample to obtain 0.2% of accuracy over the entire band. The number of required multiplications, in the Lagrangian subfilters, may become prohibitively large if the accuracy of 0.05% (about 10 bits) is desired over the entire band. However, using optimal digital filter design techniques, subfilters of lengths 12 were sufficient (Figs. 6a and 6b) to obtain an accuracy of 0.2% over the desired bandwidth.

(= 350/35) input samples are ever used to calculate one output sample. Therefore, as shown in Fig. 5, the polyphase decomposition of $H(z)$ in this case has 35 subfilters, each of length 10 (i.e., 10 coefficients per subfilter).

In order to generate the desired output samples, the subfilters are implemented in the sequence of indices 0, 33, 31, 29, ..., 33m modulo 35, m being the index of the output sample. The hardware implementation is akin to the structure shown in Fig. 4, with a programmable FIR filter having 10 coefficients (multipliers). Furthermore, the multipliers in the filter structure operate at the rate of 14.3181818 MHz, corresponding to the desired output sampling rate.

A similar structure can be derived for the NTSC composite rate ⇒ CCIR 601 component rate conversion applications.

Component ⇔ Composite Rate Conversion for PAL

Unfortunately, the ratio of $4f_{sc}$ (17.734475 Msamples/sec) and 13.5 Msamples/sec consists of large integers, viz., 709379:540000. In the intermediate stage the sampling rate is very high (about 9.6 Gsamples/sec), so that a signal band of about 6 MHz is very narrow compared to this sampling rate. The low-pass filter required to cancel the many passband replicas has to have a very narrow transition bandwidth, resulting in a very long impulse response sequence

(more than 100 Gsamples). Such a filter cannot be designed using standard equiripple FIR filter design packages. Window-based design techniques[1] or other techniques for the design of very narrowband FIR digital filters have to be considered for this purpose.

The polyphase decomposition of this filter consists of very many subfilters, although these are of fairly short lengths (12-14 coefficients). However, the overall coefficient storage requirement is fairly enormous and this poses a problem. The hybrid scheme of sampling-rate conversion, described in a later section, eases that requirement considerably.[5]

Lagrangian Interpolator as an FIR Filter

Let the length of the Lagrange interpolation polynomial be equal to N_p (see Eqs. 3 and 4). Consider the Lagrange interpolation formula given by Eq. 3 and the component ⇒ composite NTSC rate conversion. To calculate one output sample value we use N_p coefficients. Clearly, in this example, there will be 35 different such sets of such coefficients. For $m = 35$ the sets of coefficients will be the same as those for $m = 0$, and so on. Each set of Lagrange coefficients can be considered to be the coefficients of a polyphase subfilter. If $q_k(z)$ denotes the transfer function of the k-th Lagrange subfilter, the corresponding overall low-pass filter $H(z)$ can be constructed from these polyphase subfilters as

Hybrid Realization

In this approach, the rate conversion consists of two steps. In the first step the digital filtering approach is used to convert the input sampling rate to one that is higher than the final output rate, but is conveniently related (i.e., as a $M:N$ ratio with small values for M and N) to the input sampling rate. This intermediate sampling rate is then converted to the desired ouput sampling rate using polynomial interpolation techniques. Typically, zero to third-order interpolation polynomials are used in this stage. This approach is very useful for PAL component ⇔ composite rate conversion, as the ratio of the two rates contains large integers.

Distortion/Error Analysis

This section will elaborate on the sources of distortions, present qualitative analysis, and raise the issue that the rate conversion introduces another class of distortion, linear time varying, that the video world was missing so far and therefore was neither measuring or monitoring. Typical distortions in video have been classified in two categories: linear time invariant and nonlinear. Linear time invariant distortions include chroma-luma gain and delay differences, as well as nonuniform gain and delay at various frequencies. Nonlinear distortions show up in the form of differential gain and phase, and occur due to the voltage dependencies of the analog amplifiers. Existing vertical interval test signals (VITS) are designed to measure these distortions. However, these may not be satisfactory for measuring the new class of distortions introduced by the sampling-rate converters.

The ideal low-pass filter required in the intermediate stage of the sampling-rate converter (Fig. 2a) cannot be implemented. Practical implementations of low-pass filters show deviations from the ideal frequency response in their passbands and stopbands. Given a low-pass filter $H(z)$, one is therefore interested in a measure of the accuracy that can be obtained at the output of the rate converter. Conversely, in order to obtain a desired accuracy at the output, one is interested in establishing a set of upper bounds on these frequency deviations. Unfortunately, the output accuracy cannot be specified by a single number, yet the simplicity and ease of specifying the accuracy by one number is too tempting to be let go. This leads to the specification of accuracy in terms of "effective bits." The underlying philosophy behind this specification is to compare the power (peak or average) in the error or distortion with that introduced by a b-bit quantizer (sometimes also referred as a digitizer).

We define the instantaneous error $e(m)$ as

$$e(m) = \hat{y}(m) - y(m) \qquad (8)$$

where $\hat{y}(m)$ is the calculated output sample value and $y(m)$ is the corresponding true or "correct" value. Two common error measures are defined as follows. The peak output error e_{max} is given by

$$e_{max} = \max_m |e(m)| = \max_m |\hat{y}(m) - y(m)| \qquad (9)$$

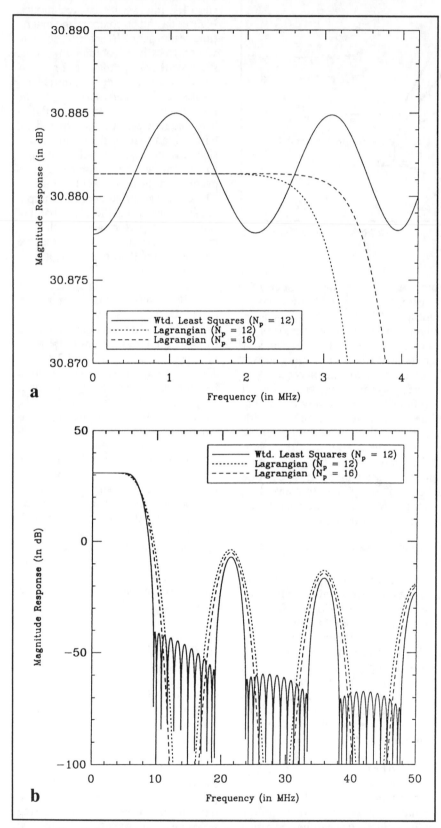

Figure 6. Magnitude responses of the Lagrangian and optimal interpolation filters: (a) magnitude response over 0 to 4.2 MHz; (b) magnitude response over 0 to 50.00 MHz.

The mean square error (MSE) is defined as

$$e_{\text{MSE}} = \frac{1}{2M+1} \sum_{k=-M}^{M} e^2(m+k) \quad (10)$$

calculated over a sufficiently large block of $2M+1$ samples.

In performing tests for accuracy, one generally uses well-known test signals as inputs to the sampling-rate converter. In a practical hardware implementation, however, the true or correct output sample values may not be known due to the errors in the input signal generators themselves. However, accuracy testing can be easily performed via computer simulations with mathematically exact sinusoidal inputs. Since the computer simulation is essentially a software implementation of a digital rate converter, the results should correspond to the actual performance of the hardware system.

If the samples of a sinusoid of frequency f and amplitude A, given by

$$x(t) = A \sin(2\pi f t + \theta)$$

are quantized into b bits, the peak amplitude error e_{max} is given by

$$e_{\text{max}} = \pm \frac{A}{2^b} \quad (11)$$

Assuming that the quantization error is uniformly distributed over the entire frequency band (this assumption is not strictly true but is not too inaccurate, especially for the wideband signals), the mean square error due to a b-bit quantizer is given by

$$e_{\text{MSE}} = \frac{e^2_{\text{max}}}{3} = \frac{A_2}{3} 2^{-2b} \quad (12)$$

It is sometimes more convenient to compare the peak error, and at other times, the average error power. It should be kept in mind that the types of distortion introduced by a quantizer are quite different from those introduced by a sampling-rate converter (especially for narrowband signals like sinusoids). However, comparing the error power in the two cases provides a good quick way of obtaining a preliminary understanding of the performance of the converter.

Errors Due to Nonideal Filtering

In general, every sampling-rate conversion scheme in digital video applications can be considered as a sampling-rate interpolation followed by a sampling-rate decimation. In order to obtain a clearer understanding of the sources of distortion in the overall scheme, it helps to analyze the two stages separately. Consider the interpolation process first, which involves two steps. The first is to increase the sample rate via the insertion of zero-valued samples in between the original samples. The second step is to low-pass filter the upconverted sequence. The nonideal low-pass filtering introduces distortions.

Passband Flatness

The errors due to nonflat passband appear in the output just as they do in conventional filtering because it influences only the baseband frequencies that, unlike the stopband frequencies, do not contribute to aliasing. The deviation in the passband only causes different gain at different frequencies. It does not add random noise (unlike a digitizer) to the output sequence. Peak deviation from the flatness should be less than $\pm (A/2^b)$, to match the peak error of a b bit digitizer. For example, to match the peak error of an 8-bit digitizer with a sinusoidal input, the passband ripple of the filter should be less than 0.2%. The human visual system is generally more tolerant to small variations in the gain at different frequencies, however, so the passband ripple may not be required to be very small (like 0.2%) unless the component $\Leftrightarrow$ composite conversion is to be performed several times on the same signal.

Passband Phase Linearity

The constraints on the phase linearity of the low-pass filter are rather strict. This is not a problem with digital filters because if the filters are made to have symmetric impulse response, they are guaranteed to have perfectly linear phase. However, the phase linearity constraint becomes a problem for analog filters in the analog rate converters.

Consider an input $\{x(n)\}$, given by

$$x(n) = \sin(2\pi f_0 n) + \sin(2\pi f_1 n)$$

to the low-pass filter $H(z)$ in the rate converter. The two frequencies f_0 and f_1 are assumed to be in the passband of the filter. With a linear phase filter, ignoring the filter delay and assuming the passband ripple of the filter to be negligible, the output of the filter is given by

$$y(n) = \sin(2\pi f_0 n) + \sin(2\pi f_1 n)$$

However, if the phase of the filter is nonlinear, so that the frequency f_0 sees a time delay of Δ relative to the frequency f_1, then, after ignoring the common delay, the output of this filter can be written as

$$\hat{y}(n) = \sin(2\pi f_0 n + \Delta\phi) + \sin(2\pi f_1 n)$$

where $\Delta\phi = 2\pi f_0 \Delta$. Using trigonometric identities and assuming $\Delta\phi$ to be small, the output is approximately given by

$$\hat{y}(n) \approx \sin(2\pi f_0 n) + \Delta\phi\cos(2\pi f_0 n) + \sin(2\pi f_1 n)$$

Therefore, the error due to the nonlinearity of the filter phase is given by

$$y(n) - \hat{y}(n) \approx \Delta\phi \cos(2\pi f_0 n)$$

In order that this error be less than e_{max} (see Eq. 11) for all values of n, we obtain

$$\Delta\phi = A/2^b$$

In this example the largest excursion of the signal can be between ± 2, i.e., $A = 2$, and therefore, with $b = 8$, we have

$$\Delta\phi = 0.0078125 \text{ rad.} \approx 0.5^0$$

and with $b = 10$, we have

$$\Delta\phi = 0.0019531 \text{ rad.} \approx 0.11^0$$

These phase constraints are very difficult to achieve using analog filters but are not much of an issue with digital filters. By making FIR filters symmetric, the phase linearity in the passband is guaranteed. However, as is discussed below, finite stopband attenuation will cause small deviations from the linearity in the overall response of the rate converter due to frequency aliasing.

Stopband Ripple

We may not be sensitive to very small errors in the passband magnitude unless the rate conversion is performed many times; however, this may not be so for the errors due to finite stopband attenuation. During the decimation process, the errors caused

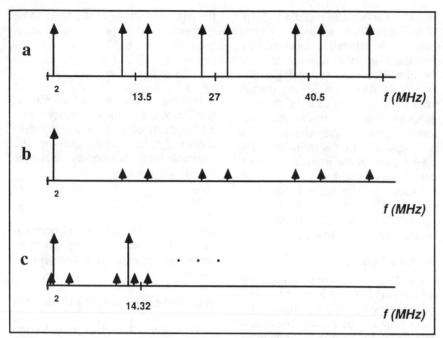

Figure 7. Illustrating the aliasing effects due to the decimation process: (a) line spectrum of a 2-MHz sinusoid sampled at 13.5 MHz; (b) line spectrum of the output of a nonideal low-pass filter at the intermediate stage; (c) line spectrum of the signal in (b) resampled at 14.3181818 MHz, showing the presence of the aliased spectra.

by finite attenuation in the stopband appear in a very interesting and unconventional way. For example, in the component $\Rightarrow$ NTSC composite conversion, the decimation stage implicitly preserves only 1 out of every 33 samples. The replicas of the original low-pass spectrum that were not annihilated completely due to finite stopband attenuation of the nonideal low-pass filter will alias back into the passband at the output of the decimator.

The following example will illustrate this phenomenon. Let the input to the rate converter be a 2-MHz sinusoid sampled at the rate of 13.5 Msamples/sec. The line spectrum of this input is shown in Fig. 7a. Assuming a nonideal low-pass filter in the intermediate stage, the line spectrum of the filter output (before decimation) is shown in Fig. 7b. We observe that the higher-order mirror images of the baseband spectrum have not been annihilated completely. Now, the low-pass filter output is decimated by a factor of 33 to obtain the video signal at the desired output sampling rate of 14.3181818 Msamples/sec. The line spectrum of this output signal is illustrated in Fig. 7c. As shown, the desired output baseband contains the original baseband spectrum as well as some spurious components due to frequency aliasing. The aliasing components are located at frequencies $(2 \pm$

$14.318181 \, m \, \pm \, 13.5 \, n)$ MHz, where m, n are integers. Thus, some aliasing components are located at 1.182 MHz $(=2 + 13.5 - 14.3181818)$, 3.64 MHz

$(=2 - 2 \times 13.5 + 2 \times 14.3181818)$, and so on. These spurious components are not harmonically related to the original signal and their impact on the overall signal depends upon the strengths and the phases of the components present at those frequency locations in the input signal. This leads to the time varying distortions illustrated ahead.

It is difficult to accurately calculate the stopband attenuation required. However, a fairly reasonable estimate can be obtained depending upon the application. Consider, once again, the component $\Rightarrow$ NTSC composite sampling-rate conversion. Let the input to this system be a sinusoid $A \sin 2\pi ft$, $f < 4$ MHz, sampled at the rate of 13.5 Msamples/sec. Due to the nonideal low-pass filter $H(z)$ in the intermediate stage, we will have 34 aliasing components within the band of interest (0 to 6.75 MHz) at the output. We assume that $H(z)$ is optimal with respect to the Chebyshev criterion,[4] so that its stopband is equiripple. In addition, we also assume that the aliasing components add incoherently (randomly or not in phase), so that the total aliasing energy is the sum of the energy in

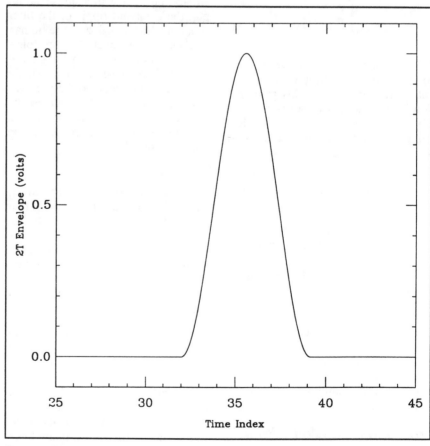

Figure 8. Envelope of 2T pulse.

each aliasing component.

Under these assumptions, the total power in the aliasing components is less than or equal to $34 \times \frac{1}{2}(A \, \delta_s)^2$, where δ_s is the peak sidelobe level of $H(z)$. In order that this power be less than or equal to that of quantization error introduced by a b-bit digitizer, we require that (see Eq. 12)

$$17(A \, \delta_s)^2 \le \frac{A^2}{3} 2^{-2b}$$

or

$$\delta_s \le \frac{2^{-b}}{\sqrt{51}} \qquad (13a)$$

Equivalently,

$$\delta_s \le -(17 + 6b)\text{dB} \qquad (13b)$$

Therefore, to obtain 8 bits of accuracy at the output, on the average, the sidelobe level of $H(z)$ should be less than 0.055% of its nominal passband value. Normalizing the passband gain to 0 dB, this implies that the stopbands of $H(z)$ should be less than -65 dB. Similarly, for a 10-bit output accuracy, the sidelobe level should be below 0.0137% of the nominal passband value (≤ -77 dB).

A more conservative criterion is to ensure that the peak error is always less than the peak quantization error. In this case, one may assume that the spurious components may add coherently (in phase) at some time value for some phase values. Under the circumstances, one would like the stopband level to be such that (see Eq. 11)

$$34 \, A \, \delta_s \le \frac{A}{2^b}$$

or

$$\delta_s \le \frac{2^{-b}}{34} \qquad (14a)$$

In the dB scale, this is equivalent to

$$\delta_s \le -(30 + 6b)\text{dB} \qquad (14b)$$

i.e., the sidelobe attenuation now should be 13 dB greater than before.

Time-Varying Distortion — An Illustration

Consider the example of sampling-rate conversion of NTSC test signals from the component sampling rate to the composite sampling rate. One particular test signal of interest is the 2T pulse (Fig. 8). The pulse has a half-amplitude duration of 250 nsec and consists of a wideband luminance component only. At the sampling rate of 13.50 MHz, the sampled signal is composed of 6 to 7 samples. The scenario for sampling-rate conversion simulation is as follows. The 2T test signals generated according to the component rate (13.5 Msamples/sec)

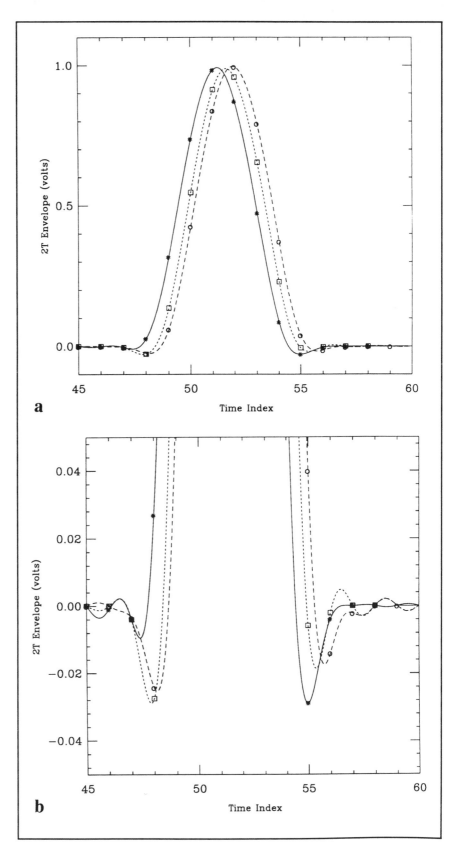

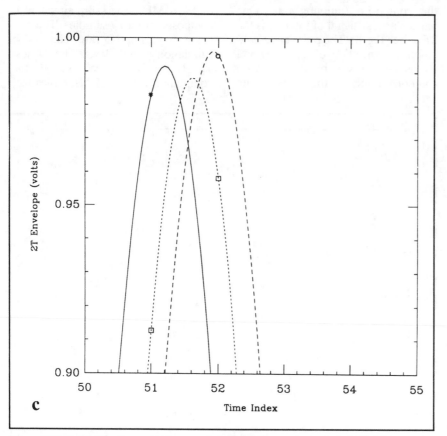

Figure 9. Illustrating the time-varying errors in the sampling-rate conversion of a 2T pulse from the component (CCIR 601) to the NTSC composite sampling rate: (a) reconstruction of the 2T envelopes at the output of the rate converter; (b) magnified view of the base of the reconstructed 2T envelopes; (c) magnified view of the peaks of the reconstructed 2T envelopes.

have to be resampled at the composite rate (14.3181818 Msamples/sec). The input to the sampling-rate converter is a one-dimensional data stream. In the simulation, the samples of the *2T* pulses at the input to the rate converter are the samples of the ideal waveform (i.e., the input signal has no distortions). Any distortion seen at the output is therefore due to the rate-conversion process.

An optimization procedure was used to design the individual polyphase filters. Each polyphase filter has a bandwidth of 4.2 MHz and is of length 4. With 35 such polyphase filters, the overall filter $H(z)$ is of length 140.

The *2T* pulse samples, at the component sampling rate, were passed through the sampling rate converter. Figures 9a to 9c show the reconstructed *2T* pulses at the NTSC composite sampling rate. The squares, circles, and stars represent the reconstructed output samples (composite rate) for different inputs described below. This figure shows the output in the analog form as seen on an analog monitor. An almost ideal sinc interpolation function was used to generate the

analog envelope, so that it does not introduce any noticeable distortion. Whatever distortion that we see is due to the rate converter. Different plots correspond to the same *2T* pulse occurring (centered) at different time locations in the input. This example illustrates the fact that the same *2T* pulse appearing at different time slots in the input will have different degrees of distortions at the output of the rate converter.

Thus, to characterize a rate converter, it is not sufficient to do it for one *2T* pulse located (centered) at one time location. Similarly, for the sinusoidal inputs, it is not sufficient to test the rate converter only for certain set of frequencies. The testing needs to be performed for all frequencies in the bands of interest and for different phases of those sinusoids.

Conclusion

To achieve very high accuracy in digital video signal rate conversion, the requirements are too strict and are difficult to be met with the analog conversion techniques. Digital techniques not only achieve high accuracy relatively easily, but are also econom-

ical. Digital rate conversion can be achieved in hardware by using a relatively small dynamically programmable FIR filter. If an application-specific integrated circuit (ASIC) is developed, the cost of the digital rate converter hardware can easily be far below that of an analog rate converter. Higher scale integration is pushing the digital rate converter from being a small subsystem to a component, consisting of one or two ASICs, of a video system. It also is increasing the accuracy of the finite precision mathematics so that the rate conversion can be easily realized, with accuracy far better than that of input video. This is expected to push the sampling-rate converters, in functionality and usage, as the next level of evolution of A/D and D/A converters. Just as A/D and D/A converters change the form of a video signal between analog and digital forms, the sampling-rate converters change the forms of a digital video signal corresponding to different sampling rates. In a similar manner, they also allow a video signal to have a description inside a video system that is different from that of the input or output signal. Thus the decision of whether to run a particular video system internally at one or another sampling rates will be and should be decided by other limiting factors, related to the internal signal processing algorithms, without worrying too much about the sampling rates of the input and the output signals.

Digital sampling-rate conversion introduces a new class of distortion, viz., linear time varying distortions, where the degree of error is also a function of the time at which the input signal arrives. Existing test patterns and methodologies are not adequate to test, measure, or characterize this type of distortion, which requires a more comprehensive testing procedure.

References

1. A. V. Oppenheim and R. W. Schafer, *Discrete Time Signal Processing*, Prentice-Hall Inc.; Englewood Cliffs, N.J., 1989.
2. R. W. Schafer and L. R. Rabiner, "A Digital Signal Processing Approach to Interpolation," *Proc. IEEE*, 61:692-702, June 1973.
3. L. R. Rabiner and B. Gold, *Theory and Application of Digital Signal Processing*, Prentice-Hall, Inc.; Englewood Cliffs, N.J., 1975.
4. J. H. McClellan, T. W. Parks, and L. R. Rabiner, "A Computer Program for Designing Optimum FIR Linear Phase Digital Filters," *IEEE Trans. Audio Electroacoust.*, *AU-21*:506-526, Dec. 1973.
5. A. Luthra, G. Rajan, and S. Davidson, "OCTOPUS– A 250 MOPS Digital Video Processor for Standard (Sampling Rate) Conversion," presented at 131st SMPTE Technical Conference, Oct. 1989.

Image Data Compression: A Review

ANIL K. JAIN, MEMBER, IEEE

Invited Paper

Abstract—With the continuing growth of modern communications technology, demand for image transmission and storage is increasing rapidly. Advances in computer technology for mass storage and digital processing have paved the way for implementing advanced data compression techniques to improve the efficiency of transmission and storage of images. In this paper a large variety of algorithms for image data compression are considered. Starting with simple techniques of sampling and pulse code modulation (PCM), state of the art algorithms for two-dimensional data transmission are reviewed. Topics covered include differential PCM (DPCM) and predictive coding, transform coding, hybrid coding, interframe coding, adaptive techniques, and applications. Effects of channel errors and other miscellaneous related topics are also considered. While most of the examples and image models have been specialized for visual images, the techniques discussed here could be easily adapted more generally for multidimensional data compression. Our emphasis here is on fundamentals of the various techniques. A comprehensive bibliography with comments is included for a reader interested in further details of the theoretical and experimental results discussed here.

I. Introduction

IMAGE DATA compression is concerned with minimization of the number of information carrying units used to represent an image. Perhaps the simplest and most dramatic form of data compression is the sampling of the band-limited images where an infinite number of image points per unit sampling area is reduced to a single image sample without any loss of information (assuming an ideal low-pass filter is available). Consequently, the number of samples per unit area is infinitely reduced! In digital image processing, each image sample, also called a *pel*, is quantized to a fixed but sufficient number of bits, and then the image is stored (or transmitted) digitally. The usefulness of data compression arises in storage and transmission of images, where the aim is to minimize the memory for storage and bandwidth for transmission. Typically, a compressed image when decoded to reconstruct its original form will be accompanied by some distortion. The efficiency of a compression algorithm is measured by its data compressing ability, the resulting distortion and as well by its implementation complexity. The complexity of data compression algorithms is a particularly important consideration in their hardware implementation.

A. Image Raw Data Rates

Typical television images have spatial resolution of approximately 512×512 pels per frame. At 8-bit/pel intensity resolution and 30 frames/s this translates into a rate of nearly 60×10^6 bit/s. Depending on the application digital image raw data rates typically vary from 10^5 bit/frame to 10^8 bit/frame or 10^6 bit/s to 10^9 bit/s or higher. The large memory and/or channel capacity requirements for digital image transmission and storage make it mandatory to consider data compression techniques.

B. Data Compression versus Bandwidth Compression

The mere process of converting an analog video signal into a digital signal results in increased bandwidth requirements for transmission. For example, a 4-MHz television signal sampled at Nyquist rate with 8 bit/sample would require a bandwidth of 32 MHz when transmitted using a digital modulation scheme, such as phase-shift keying (PSK) which requires 1 Hz per 2 bits. Thus, while digitized information has advantages over its analog form in terms of processing flexibility, easy or random access in storage, higher signal-to-noise ratio (SNR), possibility of errorless transmission, etc., one has to pay the price in terms of this eight-fold increase in bandwidth. Data compression techniques seek to minimize this cost and on occasion use the processing flexibility to reduce the bandwidth of the digital signal below its analog bandwidth requirements.

Applications of data compression are primarily in transmission and storage of information. For transmission, compression techniques are greatly constrained by real time and on-line considerations which tend to limit severely the size and complexity of the hardware. For storage applications, "compressor" requirements are less stringent because much of the preprocessing can be done off line. However, the decoding or decompression (or retrieval) should be quick and efficient to minimize the turn around or response time. Image transmission applications are in broadcast television, remote sensing via satellite, aircraft, radar, sonar, teleconferencing, computer communications, facsimile transmission, etc. Image storage is required most commonly for educational and business documents, medical images used in patient monitoring systems, etc. Because of their wide application, data compression and coding schemes have been of great importance in digital image processing [1]–[10], [209]. Application of data compression is also possible in the development of fast algorithms where the number of operations required to implement an algorithm is reduced by working with the compressed data.

Image data compression methods can be classified in two basically different categories. In the first category are those methods which exploit *redundancy* in the data. Redundancy is a characteristic which is related to *predictability*, *randomness*, *smoothness*, etc., in the data. For example, an image

Manuscript received March 26, 1980; revised October 20, 1980. This work was supported by the Army Research Office, Durham, under Grant DAAG29-78-G-0206.

The author is with the Signal and Image Processing Laboratory, Department of Electrical and Computer Engineering, University of California, Davis, CA 95616.

Reprinted from *Proc. IEEE*, vol. 69, no. 3, pp. 349–389, March 1981.

of constant gray levels is fully predictable once the gray level of the first pel is known. On the other hand, a white-noise random field is totally unpredictable and every pel has to be stored to reproduce the image. Thus many data compression algorithms attempt to represent a given sampled image array $\{u_{i,j}\}$, by another array $\{\epsilon_{i,j}\}$, which has no redundancy, and such that $\{u_{i,j}\}$ can be determined uniquely from $\{\epsilon_{i,j}\}$. The raw data rate of $\{\epsilon_{i,j}\}$ then determines the data rate of $\{u_{i,j}\}$. Often, such a process results in some compression but with an accompanying distortion in the reproduced array $\{u_{i,j}\}$. Efficient compression techniques tend to minimize this distortion. Techniques such as *differential pulse code modulation* (DPCM) and other *predictive coding* methods fall in this category when the field $\{\epsilon_{i,j}\}$ is determined "causally" from $\{u_{i,j}\}$, where causality is imposed by the scanning mechanism of the image.

In the second category, compression is achieved by an energy preserving transformation of the given image into another array such that maximum information is *packed* into a minimum number of samples. Such techniques are labeled "*transform coding*" and are related to noncausal representations [11] of signals. Other image data compression algorithms exist which use a combination of these two methods.

C. Information Rates

Raw image data rates do not necessarily represent information rates. For example, monochrome images, are quantized typically to 8 bits giving the data rate of 8 bit/pel. Whereas, the average information rate is given by the entropy (measured in bits)

$$H(u) = -\sum_{i=1}^{L} p_i \log_2 p_i \tag{1}$$

where p_i is the probability that a quantized sample u takes the value r_i, say, from a set of $L = 2^n$, ($n = 8$ here) values. This is called the zeroth-order entropy since no consideration is given to the fact that a given sample may have statistical dependence on its neighbors. For monochrome images the zeroth-order entropy is generally around 4–6 bits. The first-order entropy is defined as

$$H(u_k|u_{k-1}) = -\sum_{i_1=1}^{L} \sum_{i_2=1}^{L} P_{i_1, i_2} \log_2 (P_{i_1, i_2}/P_{i_2}) \tag{2}$$

where $P_{i_1, i_2} = \text{Prob}[u_k = r_{i_1}, u_{k-1} = r_{i_2}]$; u_{k-1} is a pel "previous" to u_k and P_{i_1}, P_{i_2} are the marginal probabilities of u_k and u_{k-1}, respectively. This is considered as the average information content of u_k if the state of u_{k-1} is known. Second and higher order entropies can be defined similarly. For six-bit raw image data, Schreiber [12] has estimated the zeroth-, first-and second-order entropies to be 4.4, 1.9, and 1.5 bit/pel, respectively.

Since according to Shannon's *noiseless coding theorem* [13]–[16], it is possible to code without distortion, a source of entropy H bit/sample using $H + \epsilon$ bit/sample where ϵ is an arbitrarily small positive quantity, the maximum achievable compression C, defined by

$$C = \frac{\text{Average bit rate of the original raw data}}{\text{Average bit rate of the encoded data}} = \frac{n}{n_a}$$

is $n/(H + \epsilon) \simeq n/H$. Computation of such a compression ratio for images is impractical if not impossible. For example an $N \times M$ digital image with n bit/pel is one of $L = 2^{nNM}$ possible image patterns that could occur. Thus, if p_i, the probability of the ith image pattern were known, one could compute the entropy, i.e., the information rate for n bit/pel $N \times M$ images. Then, one could store all the L possible image patterns and encode the image by its address—using an entropy coding scheme. However, even for relatively small N and M, L is prohibitively large; e.g.,[1] for $n = 8$ and $N = M = 16$, $L = 2^{2048} \simeq 10^{614}$. Although it is physically impractical to measure p_i, it is believed that the entropy of such an ensemble of images is likely to be very low since only a few of the L images are likely to occur often.

D. Fidelity Measures

Techniques commonly employed for image data compression result in some degradation of the reconstructed image. A widely used measure of reconstructed image fidelity for an $N \times M$ size image is the average mean-square error defined as

$$e_{ms}^2 = \frac{1}{NM} \sum_{i=1}^{N} \sum_{j=1}^{M} E(u_{i,j} - u_{i,j}^*)^2 \tag{3a}$$

where $\{u_{i,j}\}$ and $\{u_{i,j}^*\}$ represent the $N \times M$ original and the reproduced images, respectively. Experimentally, the average mean-square error is often estimated by the average sample mean-square error in the given image defined by

$$e_{ms}^2 \simeq \frac{1}{NM} \sum_{i=1}^{N} \sum_{j=1}^{N} (u_{i,j} - u_{i,j}^*)^2. \tag{3b}$$

There are two definitions of SNR that are used corresponding to the above error. These are defined as

$$\text{SNR} =$$

$$10 \log_{10} \frac{(\text{Peak to peak value of the original image data})^2}{e_{ms}^2} \text{ (dB)} \tag{4}$$

$$\text{SNR}' = 10 \log_{10} \frac{\sigma_u^2}{e_{ms}^2} \text{ (dB)} \tag{5}$$

where σ_u^2 is the variance of the original image.

Although SNR′ is more widely used as a measure of SNR in the signal processing literature (since it is related to the signal power and noise power), and is perhaps more meaningful because it gives 0 dB for equal signal and noise power, SNR is used more commonly in the image coding field. Often, the original image raw data is given as discrete samples quantized to a relatively large number of gray levels. Typically, the number of levels is 256 (or 8 bits) so that the peak to peak value is 255. Hence (4) becomes

$$\text{SNR} = 10 \log_{10} \frac{(255)^2}{e_{ms}^2}.$$

The mean-square error criterion of (3a) may not always be desirable especially when one is dealing with images which have to be evaluated visually [17]–[21]. This is because the mean-square error is not an especially accurate measure of visual fidelity. Several visual fidelity measures for images

---

[1] The number of molecules in a gallon of water, by comparison, is only 1.3×10^{26}.

have been recently suggested. In [17], [19], these measures evaluate a weighted mean-square error of contrast (rather than intensity, cf. Section II-E1), e.g.,

$$e = \iiiint |\epsilon(x', y') h(x - x', y - y')|^2 \, dx' \, dy' \, dx \, dy$$

$$\epsilon(x, y) = f(u(x, y) - u^\bullet(x, y)) \tag{6}$$

where $u(x, y)$ is the image intensity field, $f(\cdot)$ is a nonlinear function and $h(x, y)$ is a two-dimensional weighting function. In terms of Fourier domain quantities $\mathcal{E}(\omega_1, \omega_2) = \mathcal{F}\{\epsilon(x, y)\}$ and $H(\omega_1, \omega_2) = \mathcal{F}\{h(x, y)\}$, (6) becomes

$$e = \iint |\mathcal{E}(\omega_1, \omega_2) H(\omega_1, \omega_2)|^2 \, d\omega_1 \, d\omega_2. \tag{7}$$

Mannos and Sakrison [17] have found the following definitions of $f(u)$ and H to be useful (at normal viewing distance)

$$f(u) = u^{1/3}$$

$$H(\omega_1, \omega_2) = H(\omega) = A \left[a + \left(\frac{\omega}{\omega_0} \right)^\alpha \right] \exp - \left\{ \left(\frac{\omega}{\omega_0} \right)^\beta \right\}$$

$$\omega = (\omega_1^2 + \omega_2^2)^{1/2} \quad A = 2.6 \quad a = 0.0192$$

$$\omega_0 = 1/0.114 \quad \alpha = 1 \quad \beta = 1.1. \tag{8}$$

The criterion (7) suggests that for visual evaluation, the image contrast field $(u^{1/3})$ should be passed through a linear spatial filter whose transfer function is $H(\omega)$ defined in (8). Then the output of this filter represents the visual signal whose quality can be measured by the ordinary mean-square criterion. Measurements of $H(\omega)$ show that the human visual response to spatial frequencies in nonuniform and that the mid-spatial frequencies are emphasized more than the low- and high-spatial frequencies [18], [21], [22]. Other measures [20], [209] based on spatial domain characteristics such as "visibility" will be considered in Section III-F.

E. Subsampling, Coarse Quantization Frame Repetition, and Interlacing [23]–[26]

One obvious method of data compression would be to reduce the sampling rate, the number of quantization levels and the refresh rate (number of frames/s for motion images). While this would reduce the amount of data, the associated phenomena of aliasing, contouring, and flickering, respectively, would occur. The compression achieved for acceptable image fidelity by these methods is relatively small compared to more advanced methods available for data compression. For motion images, successive frames have to be refreshed at a rate above the so-called critical fusion frequency (CFF) to avoid a flickering appearance. For most observers this frequency is 50–60 pictures/s. Typically, to capture motion a refresh rate of 25–30 frames/s is generally sufficient. (This, of course, depends on the type of motion e.g., the speed of motion). Thus a compression of 2 to 1 could be achieved by transmitting (or storing) only 30 frames/s, but refreshing at 60 frames/s by repeating each frame [23], [24]. This, however, requires a frame storage and an image breakup [23] or jump effect (not flicker) is often observable. Note that the frame repetition rate is chosen at 60/s rather than, say 55/s, to avoid any interference with the line frequency of 60 Hz (in the U.S.).

Instead of frame repetition, line interlacing is found to give better visual rendition. Each frame is divided into an "odd field" containing the odd line addresses, and an "even field" containing the even line addresses and are transmitted alternately. However, each field is displayed for a duration of $2/n$ s if n is the refresh rate in frames/s. The storage requirement now is $\frac{1}{2}$ frame. Although the jump or image breakup effect is significantly reduced by line interlacing, spatial frequency resolution is somewhat degraded. An appropriate increase in the scan rate (i.e., lines per frame) with line interlacing gives an actual compression of about 37 percent for the same subjective quality as the 60 frames/s refresh rate without repetition [24]. Other interlacing techniques such as vertical line interlace or dot interlace (for higher compression) seem possible [25], [26] but are more objectionable to the viewer.

II. Image Quantization

Since most digital image data compression algorithms require a quantizer, it is helpful to begin with a review of some of the common quantization methods. Let u be a real scalar random variable with a continuous probability density function $p_u(x)$. For example, u could represent the contrast or brightness of an image pel and $p_u(x)$ could be represented by the image histogram. A quantizer maps the continuous variable u into a discrete variable $u^\bullet$ which belongs to a finite set $\{r_1, \cdots, r_L\}$ of real numbers. This mapping is generally a staircase function (Fig. 1) and the quantization rule is as follows.

Define $\{t_j, j = 1, \cdots, L + 1\}$ as a set of increasing *transition* or *decision* levels. If u lies in the interval $(t_j, t_{j+1}]$, then u is mapped to r_j, $j \in [1, L]$. The quantity r_j, called the reconstruction level, is the quantized value of u and also lies in the interval $(t_j, t_{j+1}]$. The quantizer design problem is to determine the optimum transition and reconstruction levels, given the probability density and an optimization criterion. Since the quantizer mapping is irreversible, the quantizer introduces distortion which any reasonable quantizer design must attempt to minimize. There are several quantizer designs available that offer various tradeoffs between simplicity and performance. Some of these are discussed in the sequel. Quantization of image samples for digital transmission is called pulse code modulation (PCM) (Fig. 2).

A. The Optimum Mean Square or Lloyd–Max Quantizer [27]–[28]

Here the criterion is to minimize the mean-square quantization error for a fixed number of quantization levels. This error is defined as

$$E = \int_{u_1}^{u_{L+1}} [x - u^\bullet(x)]^2 \, p_u(x) \, dx = E[(u - u^\bullet)^2]. \tag{9}$$

Minimization of this error gives the transition levels that lie half way between the reconstruction levels and gives reconstruction levels that lie at the center of mass of the density in the transition intervals. Mathematically, they are given by the solutions of the simultaneous nonlinear equations

$$t_k = (r_k + r_{k-1})/2 \tag{10}$$

$$r_k = \int_{t_k}^{t_{k+1}} x p_u(x) \, dx \bigg/ \int_{t_k}^{t_{k+1}} p_u(x) \, dx = E[u | u \in I_k] \tag{11}$$

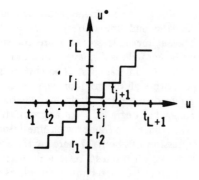

Fig. 1. Typical input–output characteristics of a quantizer.

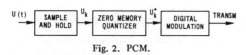

Fig. 2. PCM.

where I_k is the kth transition interval $(t_k, t_{k+1}]$. An estimate for the quantizer distortion is given by

$$E = \frac{1}{12L^2} \left[\int_{t_L}^{t_{L+1}} p^{1/3}(x) \, dx \right]^3. \tag{12}$$

This is a useful expression because it gives an estimate of the quantizer error directly in terms of the probability density and the number of quantization levels.

When u is uniformly distributed, the Lloyd–Max quantizer equations become linear, and yield

$$\left. \begin{array}{l} t_k = t_1 + (k-1)q \\ r_k \triangleq t_k + q/2 \\ q = (t_{L+1} - t_1)/L \end{array} \right\} \tag{13}$$

Thus all the transition as well as reconstruction levels are equally spaced. This quantizer is also called the *"linear quantizer."*

The minimum mean-square quantizer has two interesting properties.

1) The quantizer output is an unbiased estimate of the input, i.e.,

$$Eu^{\bullet} = Eu. \tag{14}$$

2) The quantization error is orthogonal to the quantizer output, i.e.,

$$E(u - u^{\bullet}) u^{\bullet} = 0. \tag{15}$$

This relation[2] gives an interesting model for the quantizer as

$$u = u^{\bullet} + \eta, \quad Eu\eta = E\eta^2 \tag{16}$$

where η denotes *quantizer noise* which is uncorrelated with the *quantizer output*. In Section VII, we will find this model useful in developing data compression techniques for transmission over noisy channels.

---

[2] This result is also of theoretical interest because it *does not* follow from the principle of orthogonality since $u^{\bullet}$ is not constrained to be a linear estimate of u. It does follow, however, from (11) and it implies that regardless of how the transition levels are chosen, the reconstruction level should be the conditional mean of $p_u(x)$ over the corresponding transition interval for the minimization of mean-square error.

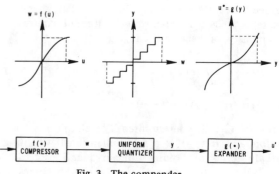

Fig. 3. The compander.

Often a nonuniform random variable is quantized by a uniform quantizer. Then the uniform quantizer which minimizes, with respect to q (the quantization step size), the mean-square error, is called the *optimum uniform quantizer*.

B. A Compander Design [28]–[31]

A compander (compressor–expander) is a uniform quantizer preceded and succeeded by nonlinear transformations as shown in Fig. 3. The random variable u is first passed through a nonlinear memoryless transformation $f(\cdot)$ to yield another random variable w. This random variable is uniformly quantized to give $y \in \{y_i\}$, which is nonlinearly transformed by $g(\cdot)$ to give the output $u^{\bullet}$. The overall transformation from u to $u^{\bullet}$ is a nonuniform quantizer. The functions f and g are determined so that the overall system approximates the Lloyd–Max quantizer. The result is obtained as

$$g(x) = f^{-1}(x)$$

$$f(x) = -a + 2a \left[\int_{t_1}^{x} p_u^{1/3}(z) \, dz \middle/ \int_{t_1}^{t_{L+1}} p_u^{1/3}(z) \, dz \right] \tag{17}$$

for which $[-a, a]$ is the range of w over which the uniform quantizer operates.

As an example, consider the truncated Laplacian density which is used often as a probabilistic model of the prediction error signal in DPCM, i.e.,

$$p_u(x) = c e^{-\alpha|x|}, \quad -a \leqslant x \leqslant a \tag{18}$$

where $c = \alpha/2 [1 - \exp(-\alpha a)]^{-1}$. Use of (17) gives

$$f(x) = \begin{cases} a \dfrac{[1 - \exp(-\alpha x/3)]}{[1 - \exp(-\alpha a/3)]}, & x \geqslant 0 \\[2mm] -f(-x), & x \leqslant 0 \end{cases} \tag{19}$$

$$g(x) = \begin{cases} -\dfrac{3}{\alpha} \ln \left[1 - \dfrac{x}{a} (1 - \exp(-\alpha a/3)) \right], & 0 \leqslant x \leqslant a \\[2mm] -g(-x), & -a \leqslant x < 0. \end{cases} \tag{20}$$

It should be remarked that the transformed random variable $w = f(u)$ is not uniformly distributed in general.[3] Companders for more general criteria have been considered by Algazi [32].

---

[3] Hence, the uniform quantizer in the compander is (by design) not the Lloyd–Max quantizer for w.

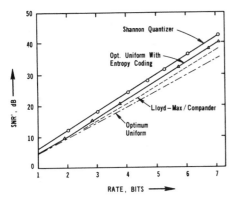

Fig. 4. SNR′ versus rate for Gaussian density quantizers.

C. Comparisons

The Gaussian and the Laplacian densities are two commonly used models for quantization in image data compression algorithms. Comparison among various quantizers could be made in at least two different ways. First, suppose the quantizer output is to be coded by a fixed number of levels. This would be the case for a fixed word length analog to digital conversion. Then one would compare the quantizing error variance as a function of number of quantization bits n. Fig. 4 shows SNR′ curves for the Lloyd–Max, the compander, and the optimum uniform quantizers for the Gaussian case. As expected, the Lloyd–Max quantizer gives the best performance. The performance difference between the Lloyd–Max (optimum nonuniform) and the optimum uniform quantizers is about 2 dB for $n = 6$. In the case of the Laplacian density this difference is about 4.3 dB. The performances of the compander and the Lloyd–Max quantizer are indistinguishable.

From rate distortion theory it is known [35] that block quantization of independent Gaussian samples of variance σ^2, could be achieved at an average bit rate

$$n = \frac{1}{2} \log_2 \frac{\sigma^2}{D} \qquad (21)$$

as the block length approaches infinity (infinite dimensional quantizer), where $D < \sigma^2$, is the average mean-square distortion per sample. This can also be written as

$$D = \sigma^2 2^{-2n}, \qquad n \geqslant 0 \qquad (22)$$

and represents a lower bound on the attainable distortion of any finite length block quantizer for Gaussian random variables. This is also called the Shannon lower bound and the associated (hypothetical) optimal block encoder will be called the *Shannon quantizer*. The various quantizers in Fig. 4 are also compared with this quantizer. Equation (22) also gives an upper bound on attainable distortion by optimal block encoders for non-Gaussian random variables. Zero memory quantizers, also called one-dimensional quantizers (block length is one), for the same rate, generally do not attain distortion levels which are less than given by (22). The optimum one-dimensional quantizer for a uniform random variable of variance σ^2 attains this distortion, however. Thus, for any fixed distortion D, the rate of the Shannon quantizer may be considered to give the minimum achievable by a zero memory quantizer for most probability distributions of interest in coding of images. From Fig. 4 it can be seen that for the Gaussian distributions the zero memory optimum mean-square quan-

tizer performs within about $\frac{1}{2}$ bit of its Shannon quantizer.

The second comparison is based on the entropy of the quantizer output versus its distortion. If the quantized variables are entropy coded by a variable length coding scheme such as Huffman coding, then the average number of bits needed to code them could be less than $\log_2 L$. An optimum quantizer under this criterion would be the one that minimizes the distortion for a specified output entropy [35]–[38]. Entropy coding would undoubtedly increase the complexity of the encoding–decoding algorithm and would require extra buffer storage at the transmitter and receiver to maintain a constant bit rate over the communication channel. From Fig. 4 it is seen that the uniform quantizer with entropy coding has a better performance than the Lloyd–Max quantizer (without entropy coding). It has been found that the uniform quantizer is quite a good approximation of the "optimum quantizer" based on entropy versus mean-square distortion criterion [33], [34], if the quantization step size is optimized with respect to this criterion. In fact, for uniform distributions the one-dimensional optimum mean-square quantizer performs within $\frac{1}{4}$ bit of its Shannon quantizer.

D. Quantization of Complex Gaussian Random Variables [39], [40]

In many situations (e.g., in radar and coherent imaging) one has to quantize complex random variables. Let $z = x + jy$ be a complex random variable, where x and y are independent Gaussian random variables each with zero mean and variance σ^2. One obvious way of quantization of x and y is via their Lloyd–Max quantizers. Now suppose it is desired to quantize the amplitude and phase variables, A and θ defined by

$$z = A \exp(j\theta), \qquad A = \sqrt{x^2 + y^2}, \qquad \theta = \tan^{-1}(y/x). \qquad (23)$$

It is easy to show that when x and y are independent Gaussian random variables, A and θ are also independent where A has a Rayleigh density and θ is uniformly distributed. Let L_1 and L_2 be the number of quantization levels for A and θ, respectively, such that $L_1 L_2 = L = \text{constant}$. Let $\{v_n\}$ and $\{w_n\}$ be, respectively, the decision and reconstruction levels of A, if it were quantized by its own Lloyd–Max quantizer (i.e., without regard to θ or z). Also, let $\{t_n\}$ and $\{r_n\}$ be the corresponding quantities for quantization of A such that the mean-square error of z is minimized (where θ is quantized uniformly). It has been shown [39], [40] that the transition and reconstruction levels of the optimum quantizer of z are related to the Lloyd–Max quantizer of A as follows:

$$\left. \begin{array}{l} t_n = v_n \\[2mm] r_n = w_n \dfrac{\sin \pi/L_2}{\pi/L_2} \end{array} \right\} . \qquad (24)$$

If L_2 is large, then $\sin \pi/L_2 / \pi/L_2 \to 1$ and the phase and amplitude can be quantized independently. For a given number of bits, the optimum allocation of L_1 and L_2 requires that for rates $\geqslant 4.6$ bits, the phase should be allocated 1.37 bits more than the amplitude.

The performance of the amplitude-phase quantizer is found to be only marginally better than the independent quantization of x and y by their Lloyd–Max quantizers. However, the above results could be useful when one is required to quantize

A and θ, e.g., in radar and coherent imaging applications where amplitude and glint (or phase) measurements are made.

E. Visual Quantization [41]–[51]

The foregoing methods can be applied for gray scale quantization of monochrome images. The number of quantization levels or gray levels should be sufficient to suppress any contouring effects. Uniform quantization of typical images, where the pels represent the luminance function, requires about 64 gray levels or 6 bits. Contouring effects start becoming visible at or below 5 bit/pel. Mean-square quantizers matched to the histogram of a given image may need only 5 bit/pel to suppress the contouring effects.

In quantizing images which have to be visually processed (or examined) the eye seems to be quite sensitive to contours and errors which affect the local structure [41]. However, the contours do not contribute very much to the mean-square error. Thus a visual quantization scheme should attempt to hold the quantization contours below the level of visibility over the range of luminances to be displayed. We consider two methods for achieving this (other than allocating the full 6 bit/pel).

1) Contrast Quantization

The human visual system does not perceive equal changes in luminances equally. However, visual sensitivity is nearly uniform with respect to normalized, just noticeable, changes in luminance. That is, if L and $L + \Delta L$ are just noticeably different luminance, then

$$\frac{\Delta L}{L} \simeq \text{constant}. \qquad (25)$$

This is called Weber's law [42]. Define

$$C = \log L \qquad (26)$$

then $\Delta C \simeq \Delta L / L$ is nearly constant. This means visual sensitivity is nearly uniform to changes in C, which is called *contrast*. Several different nonlinear transformations have been suggested in the literature to represent contrast accurately. The common functions are

$$C = \begin{cases} \alpha \log(1 + \beta L), & L \in [0, 1] & (27) \\ \alpha L^\beta & (28) \end{cases}$$

where α and β are constants. For example, in (28) the values $\alpha = 1$, $\beta = \frac{1}{3}$ (see [17]), and in (27) the values $\alpha = \beta/\log(1 + \beta)$ and α lying between 6 and 18 have been suggested (Kretz [43]).

Once the contrast representation $f(\cdot)$ is known, one simply performs the optimum mean-square quantization of the contrast field (see Fig. 5). To display (or reconstruct) the image, the quantized contrast is transformed back to the luminance value by the inverse transformation $f^{-1}(\cdot)$. Experimental studies indicate that with four-bit quantization of contrast, the contouring effects can be greatly minimized [43].

2) Pseudorandom Noise Quantization

Another method for suppressing contouring effects is due to Roberts [44]. First we add a small amount of pseudorandom uniformly distributed noise to the luminance samples before quantization. This pseudorandom noise is also called *dither*. To display the image, the same (or another) pseudorandom sequence is subtracted from the quantizer output. The input noise causes some pels to go above the original

Fig. 5. Visual contrast quantizer.

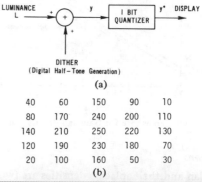

(a)

40	60	150	90	10
80	170	240	200	110
140	210	250	220	130
120	190	230	180	70
20	100	160	50	30

(b)

(c)

Fig. 6. Halftone image quantization. (a) Digital halftone generation. (b) A 5 × 5 halftone dither matrix. Repeat periodically over the image. (c) Clockwise, original 256 × 256 8 bit/pel image; 1 bit/pel quantization; 1 bit/pel halftone with dither; halftone negative 1/bit pel.

decision level and others below the decision level. Thus the average value of the quantized pels is about the same with and without the additive noise. During display, the noise tends to fill-in the regions of contours in such a way that the spatial average is unchanged. The amount of dither added should be kept small enough to maintain the spatial resolution but large enough to allow the luminance values to vary randomly about the quantizer decision levels. Usually, the noise should affect the least significant bit of the quantizer. Reasonable image quality is achievable by a 4- or 5-bit quantizer. For details and examples, see [44]–[49].

3) Halftone Image Quantization

The above method is closely related to the method of generating halftone images from gray level images. Halftone images are binary images which give a gray scale rendition. Examples are the common printed images (e.g., all the images printed in this paper are halftones). To each pel of the given image (often oversampled e.g., a 256 × 256 image may be printed on a 1024 × 1024 grid of black and white dots) is added a random number (dither sample) and the resulting signal is quantized by a one bit quantizer. The output (0 or 1) represents a black or white dot. In practice the dither signal is a finite two-dimensional pseudorandom pattern of thresholds (e.g., a 5 × 5 dither matrix) [50], [51] which is repeated periodically over the image (Figs. 6(a) and 6(b)). The halftone image may exhibit moire patterns if the image and the dither matrix have similar periodicities. Good halftoning algorithms are designed to minimize the Moire effect. Fig. 6(c) shows a 256 × 256 one-bit halftone generated digitally from the original 256 × 256 × 8-bit image. Compared to a one-bit quantized image, the one-bit halftone has a much better visual rendition. The gray level rendition in halftones is due to local spatial averaging performed by the eye.

4) Color Quantization [52]

Perceptual considerations become even more important in quantization of color signals. A pel of a color image could be considered as a three-dimensional vector C, its elements C_1, C_2, C_3 representing the three color primaries. The color gamut (i.e., the set of all perceived colors) is a highly irregular solid in the three-dimensional space. Quantization of a color image requires allocating quantization cells to colors in the color gamut. Moreover, the quantization cells will be unequal in size because equal changes in color coordinates do not, in general, result in equal changes in color perception. In the NTSC (national television systems committee, which has specified U.S. television standards) color coordinate system, the reproducible color gamut is the cube $[0, 1] \times [0, 1] \times [0, 1]$. It has been shown that uniform quantization of each color coordinate in this system provides the best results (based on a color perception measure) as compared to uniform quantization in several other coordinate systems. For more on color image coding see Limb *et al.* [53].

III. PREDICTIVE TECHNIQUES FOR IMAGE DATA COMPRESSION

A. Predictive Quantization

In the previous section we considered zero memory quantization of scalar random variables, i.e., the successive inputs to a quantizer were treated independently. Often, the available data sequence has statistical dependency or redundancy from one sample to the next. Consider a random sequence $\{u_n\}$ and suppose information in the samples up to $n = k - 1$ has been transmitted somehow. Let $u_n^\bullet$ denote the reproduced value of u_n. When u_k is to be transmitted, advantage is taken of the fact that the previously transmitted elements might contain some information about it. Accordingly, a quantity $\overline{u_k^\bullet}$, an estimate of u_k is predicted from the previously transmitted samples and a prediction error sequence defined as

$$e_k \overset{\triangle}{=} u_k - \overline{u_k^\bullet} \qquad (29)$$

is formed. Now it is sufficient to quantize e_k instead of u_k for transmission. If $e_k^\bullet$ is the quantized value of e_k, $u_k^\bullet$ the reproduced value of u_k is given by

$$u_k^\bullet = \overline{u_k^\bullet} + e_k^\bullet. \qquad (30)$$

A common data transmission method utilizing predictive quantization is called DPCM. The overall system concept is shown in Fig. 7. The principal components of a DPCM sys-

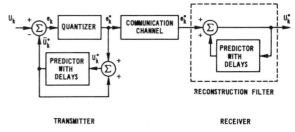

Fig. 7. DPCM.

tem are its predictor and quantizer. From (29) and (30) it is easy to deduce that the error in reproduction of u_k, given by

$$\delta u_k \overset{\triangle}{=} u_k - u_k^\bullet = e_k - e_k^\bullet = q_k \qquad (31)$$

is equal to the error in quantization of e_k. Hence, to minimize $\sigma_e^2(k)$, the variance of the prediction error, $\overline{u_k^\bullet}$ should be the best mean-square estimate of u_k and is given by its conditional mean, i.e.,

$$\overline{u_k^\bullet} = E[u_k | \dot{U}_k^-] \qquad (32)$$

where $\dot{U}_k^-$ is the set of past reproduced values, i.e.,

$$\dot{U}_k^- = \{u_l^\bullet, l < k\}. \qquad (33)$$

From (31), the mean-square distortion of u_k is given by

$$E[\delta u_k^2] = \sigma_q^2(k) \qquad (34)$$

and the minimum achievable rate (using a zero memory quantizer) is[4] (see (21))

$$n_{\text{DPCM}} = \tfrac{1}{2} \log_2 (\sigma_e^2(k)/\sigma_q^2(k)). \qquad (35)$$

If the original sequence were quantized by a zero memory quantizer (PCM), the minimum achievable rate for u_k would be

$$n_{\text{PCM}} = \tfrac{1}{2} \log_2 (\sigma_u^2(k)/\sigma_q^2(k)) \qquad (36)$$

for the same quantizing distortion $\sigma_q^2(k) \leqslant \sigma_e^2(k)$. Since $\sigma_e^2(k) \leqslant \sigma_u^2(k)$, the reduction in achievable rate of predictive quantization over PCM is

$$n_{\text{PCM}} - n_{\text{DPCM}} = \tfrac{1}{2} \log_2 (\sigma_u^2(k)/\sigma_e^2(k)). \qquad (37)$$

From (37), the data compression ability depends on the variance reduction by prediction i.e., the ability to predict u_k and therefore on intersample dependence of the sequence $\{u_n\}$. If all the samples are mutually independent then $\overline{u_k^\bullet} = E[u_k]$ and $\sigma_u^2(k) = \sigma_e^2(k)$, resulting in no advantage over PCM. Hence, the underlying philosophy of predictive quantization is to remove mutual redundancy between successive samples and quantize only the new information, i.e., the residuals. An important aspect of this scheme is emphasized by (32) which says that prediction is based on the output rather than the input samples from the past. This results in the predictor being in the feedback loop around the quantizer (see Fig. 7) so that quantizer noise at a given step is fed back to the quantizer input at the next step. This has a stabilizing effect that prevents accumulation of errors in the reconstructed signal $u_k^\bullet$. At the receiver the feedback loop of the quantizer reconstructs the signal.

[4] Recall from Section II-C our comment that common zero memory quantizers do not achieve a rate lower than the Shannon quantizer for Gaussian distributions.

It is interesting to note that if we consider the error sequence called "innovations"

$$\epsilon_k = u_k - \overline{u}_k \qquad (38)$$

where

$$\overline{u}_k = E[u_k|U_k^-], \quad U_k^- = \{u_l; l < k\} \qquad (39)$$

i.e., the predictor $\overline{u}_k$ is based on the past *input* values, then the variance of this sequence is smaller than that of e_k. Defining[5]

$$E\epsilon_k\epsilon_l \stackrel{\triangle}{=} \beta_k^2 \delta_{k,l} \qquad (40)$$

we must have

$$\beta_k^2 < \sigma_e^2(k). \qquad (41)$$

This is true because $\overline{u}_k^{\:\boldsymbol\cdot}$ is based on the samples $\{u_l^{\:\boldsymbol\cdot}, l < k\}$ which contain quantization noise and could never be quite as good as $\overline{u}_k$. As the number of quantization levels goes to infinity $\sigma_e^2(k)$ will approach β_k^2. Hence, a lower bound on the rate is

$$n_{\min} = \frac{1}{2}\log_2\frac{\beta_k^2}{\sigma_q^2(k)} < n_{\mathrm{DPCM}}. \qquad (42)$$

When the quantization error is small, n_{DPCM} approaches $n_{\min}$. This expression is useful because often it is much easier to evaluate β_k^2 than $\sigma_e^2(k)$ and could be used to estimate the achievable compression. The SNR' corresponding to $\sigma_q^2(k)$ is given by

$$\mathrm{SNR}' = 10\log_{10}\frac{\sigma_u^2(k)}{\sigma_q^2(k)}$$

$$= 10\log_{10}\frac{\sigma_u^2(k)}{\sigma_e^2(k)f(n)} < 10\log_{10}\frac{\sigma_u^2(k)}{\beta_k^2 f(n)} \qquad (43)$$

where $f(n)$ is the quantizer mean-square distortion function for a unit variance input, and n quantization bits. For equal distortion, the gain in SNR of predictive quantization over PCM is

$$\mathrm{SNR}' - (\mathrm{SNR}')_{\mathrm{PCM}} = \Delta\mathrm{SNR}$$

$$= 10\log_{10}\frac{\sigma_u^2(k)}{\sigma_e^2(k)} < 10\log_{10}(\sigma_u^2(k)/\beta_k^2) \qquad (44)$$

which is proportional to the variance reduction ratio.

B. Delta Modulation [57]–[69]

The simplest form of predictive coding is one where the predictor is simply a one-step delay function and a one-bit quantizer is used to achieve a one-bit representation of the signal. Thus we have

$$\overline{u}_k^{\:\boldsymbol\cdot} = u_{k-1}^{\:\boldsymbol\cdot} \qquad e_k = u_k - u_{k-1}^{\:\boldsymbol\cdot}. \qquad (45)$$

This is called "linear modulation" or "delta modulation" (DM) and is shown in Fig. 8(a). An important aspect of this scheme is that it does not require sampling of the input signal. The predictor simply performs integration of the quantizer output signal, which is a sequence of binary pulses. The receiver is also a simple integrator. Fig. 8(b) shows typical input–output signals of a delta modulator. The primary limitations of DM

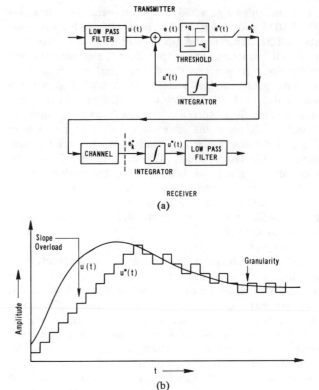

Fig. 8. (a) DM. (b) Input–output signals of DM.

are 1) slope overload 2) granularity noise and 3) instability to channel errors. Slope overload occurs whenever there is a large jump or discontinuity in the signal to which the quantizer can respond only in several delta steps. Granularity noise is the steplike nature of the output when the input signal is almost constant. Both of these errors could be compensated to a certain extent by low-pass filtering the input and output signals. Slope overload can also be reduced by increasing the sampling rate which will reduce the achievable compression. An alternative for reducing granularity, while retaining simplicity, is to go to a *Tristate DM* scheme. Here, the quantizer has three levels and the quantizer output could be coded either by 1) a simple two-bit binary code, or 2) a variable length Huffman code, or 3) a run-length code. The advantage of this method in picture coding is that a large number (65–85 percent) of the pels are found to be in the "level" or "0" state and only the remaining pels are in the "rise" or +1 and "fall" or −1 state. When the output is Huffman coded (which in this case is very simple, e.g., use a code, 0 for 0 states, 10 for +1 states and 11 for −1 states), average rates of around 1.2 bit/pel have been achieved. Alternatively, use of run-length code for 0 states and a two-bit code for the other states have been shown to yield rates around 1 bit/pel for different images [63]. The reconstruction filter of the delta modulator which is a simple integrator is unstable. In the presence of channel errors, the receiver output can accumulate large levels of error. The prediction filter can be stabilized by attenuating the predicted value by a constant $0 < \rho < 1$ (called "leak").

Other variations of DM, such as adaptive DM could further improve its performance (see, e.g., [69]). However, the increase in complexity has to be measured against the more general case of DPCM coding and other techniques for data compression. In application of DM to image coding, the signal is generally presented line by line and no advantage is taken of

---

[5] It is worth noting that while the innovations sequence $\{\epsilon_k\}$ is uncorrelated, the prediction error sequence $\{e_k\}$ is not and therefore still contains some redundancy.

the two-dimensional correlation in the data. The performance of the system will depend largely on how good the previous element prediction rule is. A simple model for many images is to represent each line of the image as a first order Gauss–Markov process

$$u_k = \rho u_{k-1} + \epsilon_k \quad E\epsilon_k^2 = (1 - \rho^2) \sigma_u^2 = \beta^2 \quad Eu^2 \triangleq \sigma_u^2 \quad (46)$$

where ρ, the one-step correlation is approximately 0.95. The mean-square distortion of the delta modulated signal is given approximately by [8]

$$D = E[\delta u^2] = \left[\frac{2(1 - \rho) f(1)}{1 - (2\rho - 1) f(1)} \right] \sigma_u^2. \quad (47)$$

The corresponding SNR' is

$$\text{SNR}' = 10 \log_{10} (\sigma_u^2/D). \quad (48)$$

Assuming the prediction error to be Gaussian and quantized by its Lloyd–Max quantizer, and $\rho = 0.95$, the SNR' is 12.8 dB, which is an 8.4-dB improvement over PCM at 1 bit/pel. This amounts to a compression of 2.5 or a savings of about 1.5 bit/pel. From (47) and (48), the SNR of DM can be improved by increasing ρ which can be done by increasing the sampling rate of the quantizer output. For example, by doubling the sampling rate in this example, ρ will be increased to 0.975 and the SNR' will increase by 3 dB. At the same time the data rate is doubled. Better performance is obtained by increasing the quantizer bits which is done in DPCM. In fact, a large number of ills of DM can be cured by DPCM thereby making it more attractive than DM for data compression.

C. Differential Pulse-Code Modulation of Markov Processes

Many times a signal is modeled by a pth-order Gauss–Markov process

$$u_k - \sum_{j=1}^{p} a_j u_{k-j} = \epsilon_k. \quad (49)$$

For such processes, the best mean-square predictor of u_k given U_k^- is

$$\overline{u}_k = \sum_{j=1}^{p} a_j u_{k-j}. \quad (50)$$

For DPCM of such signals, the predictor $\overline{u}_k^\cdot$ is taken to be the right side of (50) with u_{k-j} replaced by $u_{k-j}^\cdot$ giving

$$\overline{u}_k^\cdot = \sum_{j=1}^{p} a_j u_{k-j}^\cdot. \quad (51)$$

While this is not the optimal estimate of u_k given $\dot{U}_k^-$, it is a good linear approximation if the quantization errors are small. From (40) and (41), assuming u_k is a stationary process (i.e., in steady state), we have

$$\sigma_e^2(k) < \beta^2 = \sigma_u^2 \left(1 - \sum_{j=1}^{p} a_j \rho_j \right) \quad (52)$$

where $\rho_j = E[u_k u_{k+j}]/\sigma_u^2$, is the correlation between u_k and u_{k+j}. For a first-order Markov process, the SNR of the DPCM signal is estimated by

$$\text{SNR}' = -10 \log_{10} ((1 - \rho^2) f(n)/(1 - \rho^2 f(n))). \quad (53)$$

If an image is transmitted line by line then the foregoing Markov model is appropriate. For many images, the probability density of the differential signal e_k, is modeled by the Laplacian density function and roughly 8–10 dB improvement in SNR over PCM is obtained at rates of 1–3 bit/pel.

D. Differential Pulse-Code Modulation of Linear State Variable Systems

Sometimes an image may be modeled by a state variable system [111], [112], e.g., when a scanned image contains additive noise and/or is degraded due to interaction between the sensing elements (e.g., in a charge-coupled device (CCD) camera) or is degraded by other phenomena. It is possible to filter (for restoration and noise smoothing) and compress the digitized scanner output simultaneously. Consider a state variable linear system

$$\left. \begin{aligned} u_{k+1} &= A_k u_k + B_k \epsilon_k \\ y_k &= C_k u_k + n_k \end{aligned} \right\}. \quad (54)$$

The output is y_k but the image pel information is contained in u_k and $C_k u_k$. DPCM of the output can be performed via the associated Kalman filter and the necessary equations are as follows.

Quantizer Input:

$$e_k = y_k - C_k s_k^\cdot$$

where

$$\left. \begin{aligned} s_k^\cdot &= A_{k-1} s_{k-1}^\cdot + G_{k-1} e_{k-1}^\cdot, \\ G_k &= A_k R_k C_k^T Q_k^{-1} \\ Q_k &= N_k + C_k R_k C_k^T \\ R_{k+1} &= A_k R_k A_k^T + B_k K_k B_k^T - G_k Q_k G_k^T, R_0 = P_0 \end{aligned} \right\}. \quad (55)$$

The quantity $s_k^\cdot$ is the one step predictor that arises in Kalman filtering and $e_k^\cdot$ is the quantizer output. The gain G_k is the Kalman filter gain which is computed by solving the Riccati equation for R_k. The matrices K_k, N_k, and P_o represent the covariances of ϵ_k, η_k, and u_0, respectively. At the receiver, the reproduced estimates of u_k and y_k are given by $s_k^\cdot$ and $y_k^\cdot$, respectively, as

$$\begin{aligned} s_{k+1}^\cdot &= A_k s_k + G_k e_k^\cdot \\ y_k^\cdot &= C_k s_k^\cdot + e_k^\cdot. \end{aligned} \quad (56)$$

Note that this method tends to preserve the output y_k as well as $\hat{y}_k = Cs_k$, which is the best linear estimate of Cu_k. In other words, there is no need to first filter the observations and then perform DPCM; the Kalman filter in the prediction loop suffices. Thus filtering as well as DPCM quantization are performed simultaneously. If there is no additive noise, this method is valid if $C_k R_k C_k^T$ is positive definite. The filter gains are obtained by simply setting $N_k = 0$.

E. Two-Dimensional DPCM [73]–[77]

The foregoing DPCM methods are easily extended to two dimensions whenever a reasonable causal predictor for every pel in the two-dimensional image is available. As an example consider the often used causal model for images

$$u_{i,j} = a_1 u_{i-1,j} + a_2 u_{i,j-1} - a_3 u_{i-1,j-1} + \epsilon_{i,j}. \quad (57)$$

If $a_3 = a_1 a_2$ and $\epsilon_{i,j}$ is a white-noise field then this would rep-

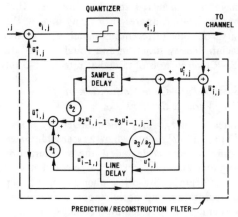

Fig. 9. Two-dimensional DPCM for images represented by the causal model of (57).

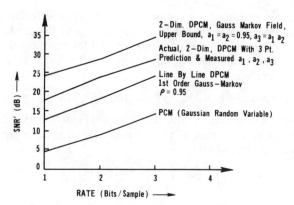

Fig. 10. SNR versus Rate of DPCM of two-dimensional, separable co-variance causal model images and its comparison with line-by-line DPCM and with PCM.

resent a random field whose autocorrelation is

$$r(m, n) = Eu_{i,j}u_{i+m,j+n} = \sigma_u^2 a_1^{|m|} a_2^{|n|}. \tag{58}$$

The quantities a_1, a_2 are the one-step correlations of the random field along the "i" and "j" axes respectively and the prediction error variance is

$$\beta^2 \triangleq E\epsilon_{i,j}^2 = \sigma_u^2 (1 - a_1^2)(1 - a_2^2). \tag{59}$$

The DPCM equations for images represented by (57) would be as follows (Fig. 9)

$$\left. \begin{array}{ll} \textit{Predictor:} & \overline{u}_{i,j}^{\cdot} = a_1 u_{i-1,j}^{\cdot} + a_2 u_{i,j-1}^{\cdot} - a_3 u_{i-1,j-1}^{\cdot} \\[6pt] \textit{Quantizer Input:} & e_{i,j} = u_{i,j} - \overline{u}_{i,j}^{\cdot} \\[6pt] \textit{Reconstructor:} & u_{i,j}^{\cdot} = \overline{u}_{i,j}^{\cdot} + e_{i,j}^{\cdot} \end{array} \right\}. \tag{60}$$

For monochrome images generally $a_1 \simeq a_2 \simeq 0.95$ from which it is deduced that at small distortion levels two-dimensional DPCM should perform better than PCM by about 20 dB or equivalently by about 3.25 bit/pel (see (37) and (44)). In practice two-dimensional DPCM does not achieve quite as much as 20 dB improvement over PCM. This is because the separable covariance model of (58) is "overly optimistic" about the variance of the prediction error. It has also been found [73] that increasing the order of the predictor substantially does not give any appreciable improvement in performance and a three or four point prediction is satisfactory for DPCM coding of images. The predictor coefficients are found by minimizing the mean-square prediction error (of the input data $u_{i,j}$). This leads to a set of linear equations which can be solved from knowledge of the image autocorrelations. Unlike in one dimension, this method of designing a two-dimensional linear predictor could give rise to an unstable causal model [210], [211]. This means while the prediction error will be minimized (ignoring the quantization effects) the reconstruction filter could be unstable causing any transmission error to be amplified greatly at the receiver. Therefore, the predictor rule has to be stabilized (at the cost of either increasing the prediction error variance or increasing the predictor order) before it is used in the DPCM algorithm.

Fig. 10 shows the performance characteristics of various DPCM methods and PCM. Since the entropy of the quantizer output is generally less than the number of quantizing bits, a variable length Huffman code is employed to reduce the average bit rate. Experimental results on images have shown that for a Laplacian density based three-bit Max quantizer, the entropy of the quantized output is roughly 2.3 bits. Thus the compression achieved by two-dimensional DPCM techniques for typical 8 bit/pel raw image data is about 3–3.5.

Overall, DPCM is a simple and easy to implement on-line technique which yields favorable compression results. The major drawbacks are 1) its sensitivity to variations in image statistics, 2) its high sensitivity to channel errors, and 3) its increase in complexity for other types of data such as represented by two dimensional *autoregressive moving average* (ARMA) models (rather than *autoregressive* (AR) models only), and other stochastic models such as semicausal and noncausal models [211]. DPCM techniques can be adapted to local variations in image statistics by adjusting the number of quantization levels according to the local activity (measured by local gradients or variance etc.) in the image and/or modifying the prediction rule whenever a nonstationarity such as slope overload or edge etc., is encountered. Examples of such adaptations are considered in Section VI-C. For ARMA and semicausal fields, vector-DPCM models can yield effective results as we shall see in Section VI. For noncausal random fields DPCM is still possible [8] although other techniques such as transform coding are more suitable (see Section V-C).

F. Differential Pulse-Code Modulation Under a Visual Criterion

Visually, the effect of quantization errors in DPCM is to cause local degradations in areas of large slopes or edges in the picture. Improvement in visual appearance could be made by designing the quantizer which attaches weight to quantization errors according to "visibility" rather than the probability of a given prediction error. Such studies have been made by Candy and Bosworth [78] and Netravali [79].

The visibility of the prediction error e, depends on a combination of factors such as its probability, perceptibility etc. A visibility function is defined as one which relates the subjective visibility of noise added to an image pel to the magnitude of prediction error at the pel. In the case of the previous pel prediction rule, as in DM, e is called the slope of illuminance function. In a more general setting one measures what is called a *masking function* which is a weighted linear combination of the magnitude of the slopes over a window, and the visibility function is related to the value of the masking function.

For prediction errors in a DPCM coder, their visibility function (for a given image) can be measured as follows. For some fixed interval $[x, x + \Delta x]$ (for suitability small Δx), add white noise to all those pels in the original image where the prediction error magnitude $|e|$ (or the masking function) lies in this interval. Let P_m be the power of the noise. Then obtain another image by adding white noise of power P_w to all the pels such that the two images are subjectively equivalent. Then the visibility function $v(x)$ is defined as [20]

$$v(x) = \frac{-dV(x)}{dx} \qquad (61)$$

where $V(x) = P_w/P_m$. The visibility function, therefore, represents the subjective visibility in a scene of unit prediction (or masking) noise. This function varies with the scene. Experimental results have shown that for predictors, such as the one used in (57), the visibility function decays faster than the probability density function of the prediction error. On the other hand, for single element predictors (line-by-line, one-dimensional DPCM), the visibility function of prediction errors decays more slowly than the probability density function.

Given the visibility function of the prediction error, the quantizer in the DPCM loop can be designed to minimize the *mean-square subjective (quantization) error* (MSSE) defined by [8], [79]

$$\text{MSSE} = \sum_{i=1}^{L} \int_{t_i}^{t_{i+1}} v(x) \, (e(x) - r_i(x))^2 \, dx. \qquad (62)$$

With this design, it has been found that a 27-level quantizer ($L = 27$) gives almost no perceptible errors (i.e., all quantization errors are below their visibility threshold). The entropy of the quantizer output is found to be around 3.4 to 3.8 bit/pel (for head and shoulder type images). Equivalent quality is achieved by a 35-level Lloyd–Max quantizer (entropy $\simeq 4.0$). For large but acceptable levels of visual distortions, e.g., corresponding to the output entropy of 2.6 bit/pel of the Lloyd–Max quantizer in DPCM, a quantizer design based on the above criterion could save about 1 bit/pel. Therefore by considering a visual fidelity criterion, DPCM techniques could achieve compressions of about 4 to 5 for acceptable levels of visual distortion (e.g., corresponding to about 30-dB SNR based on peak to peak to rms error ratio) [79].

G. Predictive Coding of Interframe Images

Predictive coding ideas considered above can also be extended to a sequence of motion and other images which have significant frame to frame redundancy. Much of the research on interframe image coding has been done recently and is based on predictive techniques [81]–[97]. This is primarily due to relatively simpler hardware implementation and low storage requirements of these techniques.

Common situations where interframe images occur are broadcast television, teleconferencing, etc. Typically, the pel values from one frame to the next (at a fixed x, y location) differ substantially only in the areas of relative motion. In what follows we will assume that the object being viewed is always within the camera view (i.e., in the image frame), but it may be displaced by translation, rotation, or any other form of motion.

1) Conditional Replenishment

This technique developed by Mounts [81] and subsequently refined by Candy, Haskell, Limb, Pease *et al.* [82]–[85] is based on a simple method of detection and coding of the moving areas which are replenished from frame to frame. If $u_{i,j,k}$ denotes the pel at location (i, j) in frame k, then the interframe difference signal is

$$e_{i,j,k} = u_{i,j,k} - \overset{\bullet}{u}_{i,j,k-1} \qquad (63)$$

where $\overset{\bullet}{u}_{i,j,k-1}$ is the reproduced value of $u_{i,j,k-1}$ at the $(k-1)$th frame. If the magnitude of $e_{i,j,k}$ is greater than a predetermined threshold then it is quantized and coded for transmission. At the receiver, a pel is reconstructed either by repeating the value of that pel location from the previous frame if it came from a stationary area or is replenished by the decoded difference signal if it came from a moving area, i.e.,

$$\overset{\bullet}{u}_{i,j,k} = \begin{cases} \overset{\bullet}{u}_{i,j,k-1} + \overset{\bullet}{e}_{i,j,k}, & \text{if } |e_{i,j,k}| > \eta \\ \overset{\bullet}{u}_{i,j,k-1}, & \text{otherwise.} \end{cases} \qquad (64)$$

For transmission, code words representing the quantized values and their addresses are generated. Evidently the average rate achieved will depend on the extent and duration of moving areas so that a reasonably sized buffer with appropriate buffer control strategy is necessary to achieve a steady bit rate and a small chance of buffer overflow. A common scheme of buffer control is to raise the threshold whenever overflow is imminent.

2) Spatial and Temporal Resolution Exchange by Subsampling

It has been noted by Pease and Limb [82] that the spatial resolution in the moving areas and the temporal resolution in the stationary areas could be reduced without noticeable degradation of the perceived scene. This property of exchange of spatial and temporal resolution could be utilized in obtaining further compression. In the areas of rapid or violent motion, temporal prediction is poor and spatial prediction could be utilized to reduce the prediction error. Experiments based on these ideas have achieved data rates of 0.25 to 1 bit/pel (or 0.25 to 1 Mbit/s) for 1-MHz signal.

3) Conditional Replenishment with Cluster Coding

A typical interframe predictive coding algorithm requires the following sequence of steps:

1) segmentation of moving and stationary areas;
2) prediction of a pel in a given area from pels in the previous frame(s) and from pels in the given frame;
3) spatial and temporal resolution exchange used in bit allocation;
4) temporal filtering to reduce jerkiness of motion in the reconstructed image;
5) buffer control.

Now we consider in some detail an example which utilizes most of the above steps. This method [84]–[86] mainly requires transmitting the addresses and quantized amplitudes of significant interframe differences of consecutive frames. The significant interframe differences tends to occur in clusters along a frame line. Hence their addresses are efficiently coded by transmitting the beginning address of a cluster and a cluster terminator code. Isolated points or very small clusters are ignored to keep the address coding scheme efficient.

Fig. 11 shows a typical buffer control scheme with different control levels. In the beginning the first three lines of the first

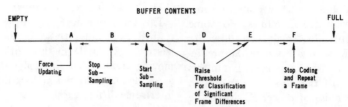

Fig. 11. Buffer control for conditional replenishment interframe coding.

frame are force updated, i.e., transmitted at 8 bit/pel. In subsequent frames the next group of 3 lines is force updated except when the coder is in a buffer overflow state. At this rate, a complete frame is refreshed every 85th frame (for a 256 line image frame) or approximately every 3 s for 30 frame/s. If the contents of the buffer fall below state A, force update is continued. Beyond the state C, the frame differences in a cluster are subsampled by transmitting every other frame difference. At the receiver the missing samples are linearly interpolated. This continues until the buffer contents fall below B. Beyond C, D, and E the threshold is increased to lower the number of significant changes. Beyond the point F, coding is stopped for one frame period and subsampling is continued for the next frame period.

Since the buffer control plays a leading role, the above method is sensitive to available buffer capacity. Often the buffer length is taken to be the average number of bits per frame. Simulation studies [97] have shown that a 1 bit/pel rate could be achieved conveniently with an average SNR of about 33 dB. The SNR in stationary areas is higher (39 dB) and in moving areas it is lower (30 dB). The buffer overflow occurs about 7 percent of the time. Lowering the rate to $\frac{1}{2}$ bit/pel degrades the performance substantially to 59 percent buffer overflow rate and 28-dB SNR. Figs. 12(a) and (b) show encoded images and the encoding error magnitudes[6] for a typical frame at $\frac{1}{2}$ bit/pel and 1 bit/pel rates. A high rate of buffer overflow results in jerky reproduction of motion as evidenced by Fig. 12(a). It should be noted that most distortion is in the temporal direction (because the previous frame is repeated whenever the prediction signal does not replenish) and is evident from the error image. At a 1 bit/pel rate, buffer overflow is significantly reduced leading to a considerable improvement in performance.

H. Adaptive-Predictive Coding and Motion Compensation

Predictive techniques are local in structure and are therefore quite sensitive to changes in the data. Nonstationarities in interframe statistics are introduced by motion in the successive frames. Reasonable adaptations of the predictor and encoder to compensate for the changes due to motion could be made to achieve considerable gains in performance. Several motion compensation schemes [90], [94]–[97] have been proposed to improve the performance of interframe predictive coding methods. We consider one such adaptive scheme which is based on a motion classifier. Fig. 13 shows the overall scheme (for a sequence of frames without interlace). A pel at location (i, j, k) is first classified as belonging to an area of stationary (C_s), moderate/slow (C_M), or rapid (C_R) motion. Classification is based on an activity index $\alpha_{i,j,k}$ which is mea-

sured as a weighted average of the interframe difference signal e.g.,

$$\alpha_{i,j,k} = \sum_{(x, y) \in \mathfrak{N}} w_{x, y} |u^{\bullet}_{i+x,j+y,k} - u^{\bullet}_{i+x,j+y,k-1}| \quad (65)$$

where $w_{x, y} \geq 0$ are some predetermined weights (typically $w_{x, y} = 1$) and $\mathfrak{N}$ is a suitable spatial neighborhood of $(0, 0)$. A large value of $\alpha_{i,j,k}$ indicates a large amount of motion in the neighborhood of the pel. The current pel, $u_{i,j,k}$ is classified by specifying suitable thresholds for the three classes. Its prediction is chosen as

$$\overline{u}^{\bullet}_{i,j,k} = \begin{cases} u^{\bullet}_{i,j,k-1}, & \text{if } u_{i,j,k} \in C_S \\ u^{\bullet}_{i-q,j-r,k-1}, & \text{if } u_{i,j,k} \in C_M \\ \rho^p_r u^{\bullet}_{i,j-p,k} + \rho_h u^{\bullet}_{i-1,j,k} - \rho_h \rho_v u^{\bullet}_{i-1,j-p,k}, \\ & \text{if } u_{i,j,k} \in C_R \end{cases} \quad (66)$$

where $p = 2$ in the 2 to 1 subsampling mode and $p = 1$, otherwise. Also, ρ_h and ρ_v are the one step correlation coefficients along i and j, respectively, and q and r are chosen so that $\overline{u}_{i,j,k}$ is the intensity value at the nearest neighbor of $u_{i,j,k}$. This is done by estimating the average displacement of the neighborhood $\mathfrak{N}$ which gives the minimum activity. Observe that for the case of rapid motion, the two-dimensional causal model in (60) has been used. This is, because due to rapid motion, temporal prediction would be difficult. In the case of moderate motion, we are simply searching the nearest neighbor of $u_{i,j,k}$ in the previous frame. For each class a different quantizer is used, the number of quantization levels of which depends on the variance of the prediction error. Generally, this criterion allocates more bits to areas of high activity and fewer bits to stationary areas. Fig. 12(c) shows the result of this method at 0.5 bit/pel utilizing the same buffer length as in the case of Fig. 12(a). Comparison of error images shows a significant improvement. In terms of the SNR, the improvement is about 7 dB and the buffer overflow rate is 7 percent.

I. Predictive Coding with Motion Compensation and Interpolation

In principle, for compression of interframe motion images, if the motion trajectory of each pel could be measured, then only the initial or reference frame and the trajectory information need to be coded for transmission/storage. To reproduce the images one could simply propagate each pel along its trajectory. In practice, one could only measure the motion trajectory of a group of pels. For example, the interframe motion could be modeled by piecewise linear translations of the moving objects followed by a measurement of the magnitude and direction of this translation. Rocca, Cufforio *et al.* [94]–[96] have considered techniques for segmentation and measurement of displacement of moving objects in a stationary

---

[6] The error magnitudes have been amplified ten times to enhance their display.

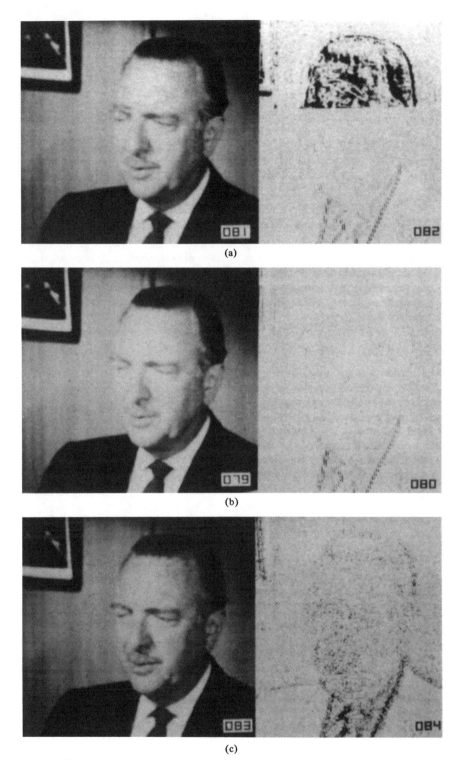

Fig. 12. Encoded images (left) and error images (right) obtained by the interframe conditional replenishment and adaptive predictive coding methods. (a) Encoded images by conditional replenishment, 0.5 bit/pel, SNR = 27.9 dB. (b) Encoded images by conditional replenishment, 1.0 bit/pel, SNR = 33 dB. (c) Adaptive classification prediction coding, 0.5 bit/pel, SNR = 34.8 dB.

background. Another method [97] which does not require coding the moving object boundaries is to divide the image frame into fixed size small rectangular blocks. Each block is assumed to undergo a linear translation and the displacement vector of each block is coded. Image registration techniques such as area correlation, affine transformation and others often employed in geometric correction and interpolation [113]–[114] could be employed. Performance of area correlation techniques has been found to be rather poor for small block sizes, in areas of low spatial activity, and for blocks not under-

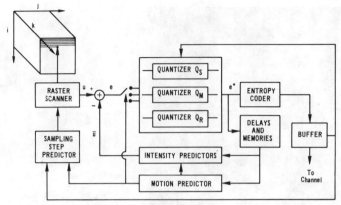

Fig. 13. Adaptive classification predictive coding scheme.

going pure translation. An effective algorithm which searches for the *direction of minimum distortion* (DMD) has been proposed in [97]. The DMD is obtained at a location (i, j) such that the distortion between the current frame and the reference frame block is minimized, i.e.,

$$D(i, j) \triangleq \sum_{m=1}^{M} \sum_{n=1}^{N} \{u(m, n) - u_0(m + i, n + j)\}^2$$

where $\{u(m, n)\}$ and $\{u_0(m, n)\}$ are the current and reference frames respectively, is minimized.

For interframe motion estimation usually the search is limited to a window of 5×5 pels or so. For images with a monotonically nonincreasing correlation function, the search could be speeded up such that the search area is successively reduced to a half or less. For other methods of motion estimation see [212], [213].

Having estimated the motion compression is achieved by skipping the image frames until the next reference frame. For simplicity suppose only the alternate frames are skipped. Frame skipping is a simple and popular method of data compression of interframe images even when no measurements of motion are available. Let U_{2k} be a block of the $2k$th frame which has been skipped for $k = 1, 2, \cdots$. In the absence of motion compensation the reproduced frame could be obtained as follows:

Frame Repetition: $\quad u_{2k}^{\bullet}(m, n) = u_{2k-1}^{\bullet}(m, n)$ (67)

Frame Interpolation: $u_{2k}^{\bullet}(m, n) = \frac{1}{2}[u_{2k-1}^{\bullet}(m, n)$
$$+ u_{2k+1}^{\bullet}(m, n)]. \quad (68)$$

Frame interpolation reduces the jerkiness present in frame repetition methods but requires an additional frame memory. The motion trajectory information can be used in prediction as well as interpolation. Thus with motion compensation one would have

Frame Repetition: $\quad u_{2k}^{\bullet}(m, n) = u_{2k-1}^{\bullet}(m + q, n + l)$ (69)

Frame Interpolation: $u_{2k}^{\bullet}(m, n) = \frac{1}{2}[u_{2k-1}^{\bullet}(m + q, n + l)$
$$+ u_{2k+1}^{\bullet}(m + q', n + l')]$$
(70)

where (q, l) and (q', l') are the displacement vectors of U_{2k} relative to the preceding and following frames, respectively. Fig. 14 shows the effect of motion compensation in interframe

image data compression. Here we show the reproduced images in a skipped frame obtained via (67)–(70) and the corresponding error. The improvement due to motion compensation, roughly 10 dB, is quite significant.

J. Predictive Coding of Facsimile Images [98]–[110]

The principles of predictive coding could be easily applied to binary images. The main difference is that the prediction error is also a binary variable so that no quantizer is needed. If the original data has redundancy, then the prediction error sequence will have large runs of "0"s (or "1"s).

Let $\{u_{i,j}\}$ denote a binary image and $\overline{u}_{i,j}$ denote its predicted value based on the values of pels in its prediction window S^- which contains some of the pels that have already been scanned and encoded. The prediction error e is defined as

$$e_{i,j} = \begin{cases} 0, & \text{if } \overline{u}_{i,j} = u_{i,j} \\ 1, & \text{if } \overline{u}_{i,j} \neq u_{i,j} \end{cases} \quad (71)$$

$$= u_{i,j} \oplus \overline{u}_{i,j} \quad (72)$$

where $\oplus$ denotes the EXCLUSIVE-OR operation. Given the error sequence, the reconstruction is simply

$$u_{i,j} = \overline{u}_{i,j} \oplus e_{i,j}. \quad (73)$$

Since $\overline{u}_{i,j}$ is a causal predictor, it can be determined from $u_{i,j}$ contained in S^-. The binary prediction error sequence can be coded by a run-length or entropy coding scheme [104]–[110] by assuming the variables $e_{i,j}$ to be independent with probability p_i. As an example consider a binary image scanned from top to bottom and left to right. At any (i, j), let the prediction window be

$$S^- = \{(i - 1, j - 1), (i, j - 1), (i + 1, j - 1), (i - 1, j)\}. \quad (74)$$

Then $u_{i,j}$ is decided to be "0" or "1", the state in majority among the pels in S^-. This defines a prediction rule.

1) Choice of Predictors [98]–[103]

A reasonable criterion is to choose a predictor so that the prediction error probability is minimized. If n is the number of pels in the prediction window S^-, then at each pel the elements of S^- can take 2^n different states. Let $k = 1, 2, \cdots, 2^n$ denote the kth state of S^- and define

$$p_k = \text{Probability } S^- \text{ is in state } k$$

$$q_k = \text{Prob } [u_{i,j} = 1 | k]. \quad (75)$$

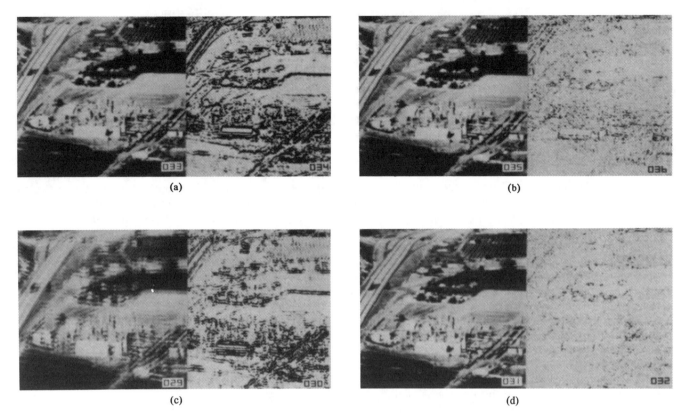

(a)

(b)

(c)

(d)

Fig. 14. Effects of motion compensation on interframe prediction and interpolation. (a) Frame repetition from the preceding frame (i) along temporal axis, SNR = 16.9 dB, equation (67), (ii) along motion trajectory, SNR = 26.69 dB, equation (69). (b) Frame interpolation from the preceding and the following frames (temporal filtering) (i) along temporal axis, SNR = 19.34 dB, equation (68) (ii) along motion trajectory, SNR = 29.56, equation (70).

The optimum prediction rule for minimum probability of prediction error is

$$\overline{u}_{i,j} = \begin{cases} 1, & \text{if } q_k \geqslant 0.5 \\ 0, & \text{if } q_k < 0.5. \end{cases} \quad (76)$$

If the random process $\{u_{i,j}\}$ is assumed to be strict sense stationary, then the various probabilities are the same at every (i, j) and therefore the prediction rule stays the same. In practice a suitable choice of n has to be made to achieve a tradeoff between prediction error probability and the complexity of the predictor due to large values of n. Experimentally 4–7 pel predictors have been found to be adequate. Corresponding to the prediction rule of (76), the minimized prediction error is

$$p_e = \sum_{k=1}^{2^n} p_k \min (q_k, 1 - q_k). \quad (77)$$

2) Adaptive Predictors

Such predictors are useful in practice because the image data is generally nonstationary. In general, any pattern classifier or a discriminant function could be used as a predictor. A simple classifier is a *linear learning machine* or *adaptive threshold logic unit* (TLU) [99], [100] which calculates the threshold q_k as a linear functional of the states of the pels in the prediction window. Another type of pattern classifier is a network of TLU's called layered machines and includes piecewise linear discriminant functions and the so-called "α-perceptron" [99], [100].

A practical adaptive predictor for facsimile images has been proposed by Kobayashi and Bahl [98] where a counter C_k of L bits is associated with each of the $k \in [1, 2^n]$ states. The counter runs from 0 to $2^L - 1$. The adaptive prediction rule is

$$\overline{u}_{i,j} = \begin{cases} 1, & \text{if } C_k \geqslant 2^{L-1} \\ 0, & \text{if } C_k < 2^{L-1}. \end{cases}$$

After prediction of a pel has been performed, the counter is updated as

$$C_k = \begin{cases} \min (C_k + 1, 2^L - 1), & \text{if } u_{i,j} = 1 \\ \max (C_k - 1, 0), & \text{if } u_{i,j} = 0. \end{cases}$$

The value $L = 3$ has been found to yield minimum prediction error for a typical printed page.

3) Performance of Predictive Coders

Experimental results reported in [98] show that a 4-pel adaptive predictor and a 7-pel fixed predictor yield the best tradeoff between the prediction error probability and the predictor complexity. For a typical journal printed page (with no line drawings) the value of p_e is about 0.05, giving the entropy to be 0.286 bit/pel. The maximum achievable compression would be 3.5 if the prediction error sequence was independent. For other printed documents which have line

51

drawings or are less dense, higher compressions have been achieved.

There are other predictive coding algorithms which consider dependency of run lengths by considering one-dimensional Markov models of run lengths (see e.g., Arps [103]) or two-dimensional Markov models of prediction errors (Preuss [101]–[102]). Another technique which makes use of the correlation between scan lines is called the predictive differential quantizing (PDQ) technique. Instead of coding run lengths, the differences between corresponding run lengths of successive scan lines are coded.

IV. ONE-DIMENSIONAL TRANSFORM CODING

An alternative to predictive coding is *transform coding*, which is sometimes also called *block quantization*. Here a long sequence of data samples is divided into blocks of N samples, and each block treated as a vector is quantized independently of other blocks. An optimum block quantizer could be defined as the one that minimizes the average distortion of the quantized elements of the vector for a given number of quantization levels. In optimum predictive coding, the successive inputs to the quantizer are whitened recursively and the optimum predictor is a nonlinear causal filter. In practice, a suboptimal linear predictor is used. In transform coding all the samples are first whitened jointly and then quantized. The optimal whitening filter which minimizes the distortion in the reconstructed signal turns out to be a noncausal, linear filter (as opposed to the causal-predictive filter) known as the Karhunen–Loeve (KL) transform. In practice, the KL transform is substituted by a suboptimal but fast unitary transform.

A. The Karhunen–Loeve Transform and Block Quantization [115]–[118]

Consider a vector u which comes from a (real) Gaussian random process of zero mean and covariance R (see Fig. 15). This vector is linearly transformed by an $N \times N$ (complex) matrix A to produce a (complex) vector v whose components $\{v_k\}$ are mutually uncorrelated. Each component v_k is quantized independently. The output vector $v^{\cdot}$ is linearly transformed by a matrix B to yield a vector $u^{\cdot}$. The problem is to find the optimal decorrelating matrix A, the reconstruction matrix B, and the optimum quantizers such that the overall average mean-square distortion

$$D = \frac{1}{N} E \sum_{k=1}^{N} (u_k - u_k^{\cdot})^2 \qquad (78)$$

is minimized. The solution of this problem is obtained as follows (Segall [116]).

1) The optimal reconstruction matrix B is given by

$$B = A^{-1} \Gamma \qquad (79)$$

where Γ is a diagonal matrix of elements

$$\gamma_k = (E[v_k v_k^{\cdot *}])/(E[v_k^{\cdot} v_k^{\cdot *}]) \qquad (80)$$

where the * indicates the complex conjugate.

2) The optimal decorrelating matrix A is the KL transform of u, i.e., the rows of A are the orthonormalized eigenvectors of the covariance matrix R.

3) For any quantizing scheme, the quantizer minimizing the overall mean-square error is the Lloyd–Max quantizer. Thus the quantizer that minimizes the quantization error between each v_k and $v_k^{\cdot}$ also minimizes the overall mean-square error. With Lloyd–Max quantizers we get $B = A^{*T}$.

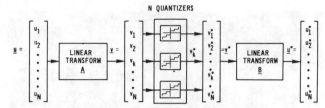

Fig. 15. One-dimensional transform coding.

The KL transform has the property that for any $M \leqslant N$ it packs the maximum average energy into some M samples of v. Although the KL transform is optimal, it is often difficult to compute and has no fast algorithm associated with it. For stationary random sequences there are many fast unitary transforms which approach the energy packing efficiency of the KL transforms. Examples are the cosine, Fourier, and sine transforms. These transforms have been shown to be members of a larger family of sinusoidal transforms [136] all of which have a performance equivalent to the KL transform as the size N of the data vector goes to infinity. For first-order stationary Markov processes [see (46)] the cosine transform matrix defined as [131]

$$C_{i,j} = \begin{cases} \dfrac{1}{\sqrt{N}}, & i = 1, \ 1 \leqslant j \leqslant N \\[2mm] \sqrt{\dfrac{2}{N}} \cos \dfrac{(2j-1)(i-1)\pi}{2N}, & \\[2mm] & 2 \leqslant i \leqslant N, \quad 1 \leqslant j \leqslant N \end{cases} \qquad (81)$$

has been shown to perform very closely to the KL transform when the correlation parameter ρ lies in the interval (0.5, 1), even when N is small [136]. The transformation $y = Cx$ can be computed via the fast Fourier transform (FFT) in $0(N \log N)$ operations. These properties have made the cosine transform a useful substitute for the KL transform in image processing since many images can be modeled by low-order Markov processes with high interpel correlation.

Nonsinusoidal unitary transforms such as the Hadamard, Haar, Slant transforms (which are square-wave transforms) are also used since they are computationally faster than the FFT-based fast sinusoidal transform. Therefore, in transform coding practice, the KL transform is substituted by a suitable fast unitary transform. The Lloyd–Max quantizer may also be substituted by another quantizer.

B. Distortion-Rate Characteristics and Bit Allocation

Regardless of the choice of the unitary transform and the quantizer, the distortion D defined by (78) becomes

$$D = \frac{1}{N} \sum_{k=1}^{N} \sigma_k^2 f(n_k) \qquad (82)$$

where σ_k^2 is the variance of the transform coefficient v_k and $f(n)$, as mentioned before [see (43)], is the distortion function of the quantizer for a unity variance input. To complete the design of the transform coder, one has to determine the bit allocation $\{n_k\}$ among the various samples $\{v_k\}$. Let the average desired bit rate per sample be p. Then

$$\frac{1}{N} \sum_{k=1}^{N} n_k = p. \qquad (83)$$

For a fixed value of p, it is required to find the allocation of $n_k \geqslant 0$ bits to v_k such that the distortion D is minimized. In the case of the Shannon quantizer

$$f(n) = 2^{-2n} \tag{84}$$

the optimum bit allocation is given by

$$n_k = n_k(\theta) = \max \left[0, \frac{1}{2} \log_2 \left(\frac{\sigma_k^2}{\theta} \right) \right] \tag{85}$$

where θ is determined such that

$$\frac{1}{N} \sum_{k=1}^{N} n_k(\theta) = p. \tag{86}$$

The minimized distortion at the rate p is given by

$$D_{\min} = \frac{1}{N} \sum_{k=1}^{N} \min(\theta, \sigma_k^2). \tag{87}$$

Equations (85)–(87) also give the distortion versus rate characteristics of any unitary transform A used in transform coding. We note that the performance of a transform is completely determined by the variances σ_k^2 which are given by

$$\sigma_k^2 = \sigma_k^2(A) = [ARA^{*T}]_{k,k} \tag{88}$$

Since A is unitary, $\sum_{k=1}^{N} \sigma_k^2(A) = N\sigma^2$ is constant for all A's. Hence the distortion versus rate characteristic depends on how the *total energy* $N\sigma^2$ is distributed by A among the various coefficients $\{v_k\}$. The KL transform distributes it in the most efficient way [119]–[129]. The distortion versus rate characteristics when other quantizers are used can also be determined (see e.g., [116], [118]). In practice, the bit allocation requires minimizing (82) subject to (83) and the constraint that the n_k be nonnegative integers. The solution of this problem is found via a theory of marginal analysis due to Fox [117], by the following simple algorithm [118].

Step 1: Start with the allocation $n_k = 0$, $1 \leqslant k \leqslant N$ and set $j = 1$.

Step 2: Let $n_k^j = n_k^{j-1} + \delta_{k,i}$, where $\delta_{k,i}$ is the Kronecker delta function and i is any index for which $\Delta_k = \sigma_k^2 [f(n_k^{j-1}) - f(n_k^{j-1} + 1)]$ is maximum.

Step 3: If $\sum n_k^j > Nr$, stop; otherwise set $j \to j + 1$ and go to step 2. If ties occur for the maximizing index, the procedure is successively initiated with the allocation $n_k^j = n_k^{j-1} + \delta_{i,k}$ for each one. Note that this algorithm simply means that the marginal returns defined by $\Delta_{k,j} = \sigma_k^2 [f(j) - f(j+1)]$; $k = 1, \cdots, N$; $j = 0, 1, \cdots, N$, are arranged in a decreasing order and bits are distributed one by one according to this order. For an average bit rate of p, the total number of marginal returns to be sorted is $N^2 p$ for an $N \times 1$ vector.

C. Fast Karhunen–Loeve Transform Coding

Sometimes it is possible to approach the data compression efficiency of the KL transform by decomposing a random process into two mutually orthogonal processes with fast KL transforms. Consider, for example, the elements u_k, $0 \leqslant k \leqslant N + 1$ of a stationary, first-order Gauss–Markov sequence with zero mean and covariance

$$r_m \triangleq E u_k u_{k+m} = \rho^{|m|}. \tag{89}$$

Let u represent the $N \times 1$ vector of elements $\{u_k, 1 \leqslant k \leqslant N\}$. It has been shown that this vector has a decomposition[7] [137]

$$u = u^0 + u^b \tag{90}$$

where

$$u^b = \alpha Q^{-1} b, \, b = [u_0, \underbrace{0 \cdots\cdots\cdots 0}_{N-2 \text{ zeros}}, u_{N+1}]^T$$

such that u^0 and u^b are zero mean, mutually orthogonal random vectors, i.e., $E[u^0(u^b)^T] = 0$. The matrix Q is a symmetric, tridiagonal, Toeplitz matrix with unity along the main diagonal and $-\alpha$ along the other two diagonals and $\alpha = \rho/(1 + \rho^2)$. The KL transform of the sequence $\{u_k^0\}$ is the fast sine transform defined as

$$\psi_{i,j} = \sqrt{\frac{2}{N+1}} \sin \frac{ij\pi}{N+1}, \quad 1 \leqslant i, j \leqslant N \tag{91}$$

and the KL transform of the 2×1 vector $[u_0, u_{N+1}]^T$ is the 2×2 sine transform

$$\Phi = \frac{1}{\sqrt{2}} \begin{bmatrix} 1 & 1 \\ 1 & -1 \end{bmatrix}. \tag{92}$$

Given the original $(N+2) \times 1$ sequence $\{u_k, 0 \leqslant k \leqslant N+1\}$, the $N \times 1$ sequences $\{u_k^0\}$ and $\{u_k^b\}$ are realized as follows. First the boundary variables (u_0, u_{N+1}) are passed through a time varying finite impulse response (FIR) filter whose impulse response $h_{m,n}$ equals $\alpha [Q^{-1}]_{m,n}$ and its duration is N to give u_k^b and $u_k^0 = u_k - u_k^b$. (See Fig. 16.)

Now instead of transform coding the original $(N+2) \times 1$ sequence by its KL transform we code u^0 and u_b separately by one of the following three methods.

Method I: (see Fig. 17) The boundary variables (u_0, u_{N+1}) and the residual process $\{u_k^0\}$ are transform coded independently by their respective KL transforms and are combined at the receiver according to (90). Fig. 20 shows the performance of this is below the KL transform by only about 0.5 dB at $SNR' = 20$ dB.

Method II: The performance of the above method is improved when the boundary values are quantized before the residual is coded (Fig. 18). Fig. 20 shows the result. Clearly, at small distortion levels ($D \leqslant 3$ percent) the performance is indistinguishable from the KL transform. It is interesting to note that in this method, if the boundary variables are not allocated any bits then $u^0 = u$, the method reduces to sine transform coding of u. Thus the sine transform coder provides a lower bound of the performance of the fast KL transform coder.

Method III: Recursive Block Coding. In all of the foregoing transform coding methods, it is assumed that successive blocks of data are independent. In practice, however, when a long sequence of data is divided into blocks of M samples, the successive blocks are correlated. If the block length is large, the interblock correlation could be ignored. But if the block size is chosen to be small (e.g., when the data statistics are slowly changing or the transform size is kept small to reduce hardware cost) it may be desirable to exploit the interblock redundancy. The noncausal decomposition of (90) could be

[7] This decomposition expresses the finite segment of a stationary process as a two source model. The first source has a fast KL transform and the second source is determined by a few (two in this example) boundary variables.

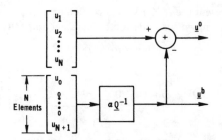

Fig. 16. Realization of fast KL transform decomposition.

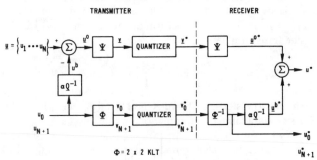

Fig. 17. Fast KL transform coding: Method I.

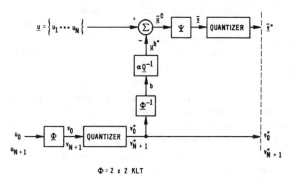

Fig. 18. Fast KL transform coding: Method II.

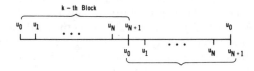

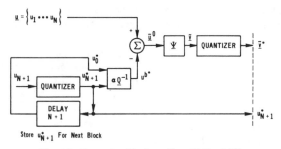

Fig. 19. Recursive block coding: Method III.

exploited to design a *recursive block coding scheme* which does this (Fig. 19). Now in coding of the $(k + 1)$th block of $M = N + 2$ samples, the first sample u_0 comes from the $(N + 1)$th sample of the previous block which has already been coded. Hence for each successive block one only needs to

quantize u_{N+1} and the residual process $\tilde{u}_k^0$. Now, the rate distortion function [214] yields a performance which is better than even the conventional KL transform coding (see Fig. 20). This result can be used in designing small size transform coders which achieve the efficiency of large size coders. For example, it has been shown in [135] that a block recursive coder of size 8 can achieve the efficiency of a KL transform coder of block length 16.

D. Transform Coding versus Differential Pulse-Code Modulation [8], [130]

It is interesting to compare the performances of the KL transform coding and DPCM methods. For first-order stationary Gauss–Markov sequences of N samples, and for a small fixed average mean-square distortion $D < (1 - \rho)/(1 + \rho)$, the rate R_{DPCM} achievable via DPCM could be shown to satisfy the bounds

$$\frac{1}{2N} \log_2 \frac{\sigma_u^2}{D} + \frac{(N - 1)}{2N} \log_2 \left(1 + \frac{\rho^2 D}{(1 - \rho^2)\sigma_u^2}\right) \leqslant R_{\text{DPCM}}$$

$$\leqslant \frac{1}{2N} \log_2 \frac{\sigma_u^2}{D} + \frac{(N - 1)}{2N} \log_2 \left(\rho^2 + \frac{(1 - \rho^2)\sigma_u^2}{D} + \frac{\sigma_u^2}{(N - 1)D}\right).$$

$$(93)$$

The KL transform coding method could achieve a rate

$$R_{\text{KL}} = \frac{1}{2N} \log_2 \frac{\sigma_u^2}{D} + \frac{(N - 1)}{2N} \log_2 \frac{(1 - \rho^2)\sigma_u^2}{D},$$

$$0 < D < (1 - \rho)/(1 + \rho). \quad (94)$$

Comparing (97) and (98), we find $\Delta R = R_{\text{DPCM}} - R_{\text{KL}}$ satisfies

$$\frac{(N - 1)}{2N} \log_2 \left(1 + \frac{\rho^2 D}{(1 - \rho^2)\sigma_u^2}\right) \leqslant \Delta R \leqslant \left(\frac{N - 1}{2N}\right)$$

$$\cdot \log_2 \left(1 + \frac{\rho^2 D}{(1 - \rho^2)\sigma_u^2} + \frac{1}{(N - 1)(1 - \rho^2)}\right). \quad (95)$$

As $N \to \infty$, this gives

$$\Delta R = R_{\text{DPCM}} - R_{\text{KL}} = \frac{1}{2} \log_2 \left(1 + \frac{\rho^2 D}{(1 - \rho^2)\sigma_u^2}\right). \quad (96)$$

For $D = 0.01 \, \sigma^2$, $\text{SNR}' = 20$ dB, and $\rho = 0.95$, one obtains $R_{\text{DPCM}} - R_{\text{KL}} = 0.062$ bit/sample and $R_{\text{KL}} = 1.16$ bit/sample. Thus DPCM performs quite close to KL transform coding at low distortion levels as the block size $N \to \infty$. For $N = 16$ one obtains $0.058 \leqslant \Delta R \leqslant 0.381$ so that the performance of DPCM could get worse if it were reinitialized after short intervals. DPCM is quite sensitive to changes in the data statistics e.g., via (96), it could be shown for small distortions, that

$$\frac{d(\Delta R)}{\Delta R} \simeq \frac{2}{(1 - \rho^2)} \Delta \rho, \quad \text{for } |\rho| \lesssim 1 \quad (97)$$

which shows that a 2.5 percent change in ρ would change the incremental rate of DPCM over KL transform coding by 50 percent at $\rho = 0.95$. This together with the fact that generally the available data is not stationary, leads to a performance of DPCM which is much worse than estimated via (96), especially when the distortion is higher (i.e., for larger compression). At very low distortions, however, $(D \simeq 0.001 \, \sigma_u^2)$ DPCM and KL transform methods are found to perform quite closely on actual images. Finally, we should note that the above analysis

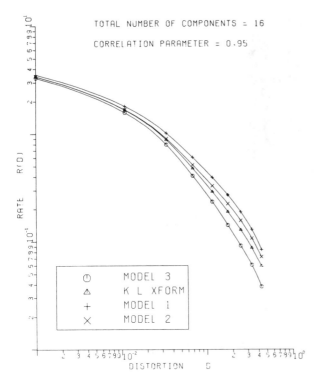

TOTAL NUMBER OF COMPONENTS = 16

CORRELATION PARAMETER = 0.95

○	MODEL 3	
△	K L XFORM	
+	MODEL 1	
×	MODEL 2	

Fig. 20. Distortion versus rate characteristics of fast KL transform coding.

Fig. 21. Two-dimensional transform coding.

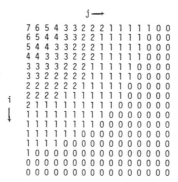

```
j →
7 6 5 4 3 3 2 2 2 1 1 1 1 1 0 0
6 5 4 4 3 3 2 2 1 1 1 1 1 0 0 0
5 4 4 3 3 2 2 2 1 1 1 1 1 0 0 0
4 4 3 3 3 2 2 2 1 1 1 1 1 0 0 0
3 3 3 3 2 2 2 1 1 1 1 1 0 0 0 0
3 3 2 2 2 2 2 1 1 1 1 1 0 0 0 0
2 2 2 2 2 1 1 1 1 1 0 0 0 0 0 0
2 2 2 1 1 1 1 1 1 1 0 0 0 0 0 0
2 1 1 1 1 1 1 1 1 0 0 0 0 0 0 0
1 1 1 1 1 1 1 1 0 0 0 0 0 0 0 0
1 1 1 1 1 1 1 0 0 0 0 0 0 0 0 0
1 1 1 1 1 0 0 0 0 0 0 0 0 0 0 0
1 1 1 1 0 0 0 0 0 0 0 0 0 0 0 0
1 0 0 0 0 0 0 0 0 0 0 0 0 0 0 0
0 0 0 0 0 0 0 0 0 0 0 0 0 0 0 0
0 0 0 0 0 0 0 0 0 0 0 0 0 0 0 0
```

Fig. 22. Typical bit allocation for 16 × 16 block cosine transform coding at approximately 1 bit/pel for images modeled by the exponential covariance function of (103).

is only valid for Markov processes. For general ARMA models, state variable models, or two-dimensional models, ΔR is likely to be more significant.

V. MULTIDIMENSIONAL TRANSFORM CODING

A. Two-Dimensional Transform Coding [145]-[165]

The transform coding results of Section IV-A are easily extended to two-dimensional images by considering an $N \times M$ image $\{u_{i,j}\}$ as a one-dimensional $NM \times 1$ vector u obtained by stacking up the rows of the image. The optimal unitary transform should then be the KL transform of the vector u. Often the image can be characterized such that the KL transform of u is separable, i.e.,

$$\mathcal{A} = A_M \otimes B_N \tag{98}$$

where A_M and B_M are $M \times M$ and $N \times N$, respectively, unitary matrices and $\otimes$ denotes the Kronecker product. Then the transformation

$$\mathcal{V} = \mathcal{A}u \tag{99}$$

can be written in matrix form as

$$V = A_M U B_N^T. \tag{100}$$

Often A and B are the same transforms of appropriate sizes so that

$$V = A_N U A_M^T. \tag{101}$$

If the KL transform is not fast, it is substituted by a fast transform. Fig. 21 shows the overall two-dimensional transform coding algorithm. The bit allocation algorithm for the quantizer design requires the knowledge of the variances (or second moments) of the random variables $\{v_{k,l}\}$. Defining

$$\sigma_{k,l}^2 = E|v_{k,l}|^2 \tag{102}$$

the bit allocation $\{n_{k,l}\}$ can be found as before, by simply mapping $\{\sigma_{k,l}^2\}$ to a one-dimensional sequence of variances and using the algorithms described in Section IV-B. In practice, to make transform coding computationally efficient in terms of storage and speed, a given image is divided into small rectangular blocks, and each block is transform coded independently. For example, if a 256×256 image divided into 16×16 blocks, the storage requirement is reduced by a factor of 256 and the speed is improved by a factor of 2 for a transform which requires $0(N \log_2 N)$ operations to transform an $N \times 1$ vector.

The variances $\sigma_{k,l}^2$ are calculated either directly from transformed blocks of test images or from the knowledge of the power spectral density, or equivalently, the autocorrelation function of the image. The separable covariance function of (58) is often used to estimate the transform domain variances. Another function which generally provides a better fit of covariances is given as

$$r(k,l) = \sigma^2 \exp\{-\sqrt{\alpha_1 k^2 + \alpha_2 l^2}\}. \tag{103}$$

Fig. 22 shows the bit allocation for cosine transform coding of a 16×16 block of an image to achieve an average rate of 1 bit/pel when the image covariance function is modeled by (103). Figs. 23(a) and (b) show the cosine transform coded images (and the error images) at average rates of 0.5 bit/pel and 1 bit/pel, respectively.

B. Zonal Versus Threshold Coding

Examination of the bit allocation pattern of Fig. 22 reveals that a substantial number of transformed samples are allocated zero bits (except at very high average rates). Thus only a small *zone* of transformed image is transmitted. Denoting by I_t, the address set of transmitted samples

$$I_t = \{k, l; n_{k,l} \geq 1\} \tag{104}$$

and letting n_t be the number of transmitted samples, we can define a *zonal mask*

$$m(k,l) = \begin{cases} 1, & k, l \in I_t \\ 0, & \text{otherwise} \end{cases} \tag{105}$$

which takes values of unity in the zone of largest n_t variances

(a)

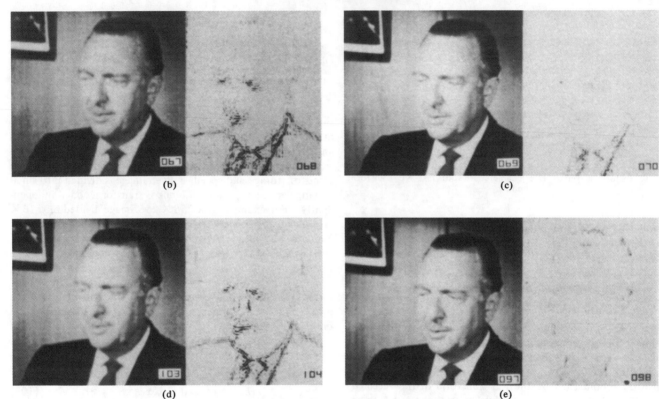

(b)

(c)

(d)

(e)

Fig. 23. Cosine transform coded images and error images. (a) Original. (b) Intraframe 16 X 16 block coded, 0.5 bit/pel, SNR = 34.4 dB. (c) Intraframe 16 X 16 block coded, 1 bit/pel, SNR = 40.3 dB. (d) Interframe transform, 16 X 16 X 16 block coded, 0.5 bit/pel, SNR = 36.8 dB. (e) Adaptive transform coded, 16 X 16 X 16 block coded, SNR = 41.2 dB.

of the transformed samples. Thus in transform coding one applies a zonal mask on the transformed image and quantizes only the nonzero elements for transmission or storage. This method is also called *zonal coding*.

If instead of transmitting/storing the n_t elements of maximum variance, one considers n_t samples of maximum amplitude (for the given image) in the transform domain, we get what is called *threshold coding*. The address set of transmitted samples is now

$$I_t' = \{(k, l): |v_{k,l}| > \eta\} \qquad (106)$$

where η is a suitably chosen threshold which controls the achievable average bit rate. For a given class of images, since the variances of the transform samples are fixed, the zonal mask remains unchanged from one image to the next (or one

block to the next) for a fixed bit rate. However, the *threshold mask m_η* defined as

$$m_\eta(k,l) = \begin{cases} 1, & (k,l) \in I_t' \\ 0, & \text{otherwise} \end{cases} \qquad (107)$$

could change from block to block because the I_t' of largest amplitude samples need not be the same for different blocks. The samples retained after thresholding are typically quantized by a constant word length quantizer followed by a variable word length entropy coder.

Although for the same number of transmitted samples (or the number of quantizing bits) a threshold mask would give a better choice of transmission samples (i.e., lower distortion) it would also result in an increased bit rate because the addresses of the transmitted samples (i.e., the boundary of the threshold mask) have to be coded for every image block. Typically, a sample line by line run-length coding scheme is implemented to code the transition boundaries in the threshold mask. Usually this results in a somewhat more complex scheme than zonal transform coding. However, threshold coding has merits since it is adaptive in nature and is particularly useful when the image statistics might change rapidly so that a fixed zonal mask is inefficient.

C. Transform Coding of Random Fields via Noncausal Models

The fast KL transform decomposition described in Section IV-C arises quite naturally when two-dimensional images or random fields are represented by certain noncausal models [186]. For example, consider a two-dimensional Markov-1 random field image represented by the stochastic difference equation[8]

$$u_{i,j} - \alpha(u_{i-1,j} + u_{i+1,j} + u_{i,j-1} + u_{i,j+1}) = \epsilon_{i,j} \quad (108)$$

where $\alpha < \frac{1}{4}$ and $\epsilon_{i,j}$ is a two-dimensional zero mean random sequence whose covariance function is given by

$$r_\epsilon(k,l) = E\epsilon_{i,j}\epsilon_{i+k,j+l} = \beta^2 \begin{cases} 1, & (k,l) = (0,0) \\ -\alpha_1, & (k,l) = (\pm 1, 0) \text{ or } (0, \pm 1) \\ 0, & \text{otherwise.} \end{cases}$$

$$(109)$$

Let U be an $N \times N$ image block. In matrix form (108) becomes

$$QU + UQ = \epsilon + B_1 + B_2 \quad (110)$$

$$B_1 = \alpha \begin{bmatrix} b_1^T \\ 0 \\ b_3^T \end{bmatrix}, \quad B_2 = \alpha [b_2 \vdots 0 \vdots b_4] \quad (111)$$

where b_1, b_2, b_3 and b_4 are $N \times 1$ vectors which contain the boundary elements of the image (see Fig. 24) and the elements of Q are defined by

$$q_{i,j} = \begin{cases} \frac{1}{2}, & i = j \\ -\alpha, & i - j = 1 \\ 0, & \text{otherwise.} \end{cases} \quad (112)$$

It could be shown that such a random field has a decomposition

$$U = U^0 + U^b$$

where U^b is determined from the boundary values and the KL transform of U^0 is the fast Sine transform. Specifically,

$$\left. \begin{aligned} u^b &= \mathcal{Q}^{-1}(b_1 + b_2), \quad \mathcal{Q} \triangleq (I \otimes Q + Q \otimes I) \\ u^0 &= u - u^b \end{aligned} \right\} \quad (113)$$

where u, u^0, u^b, b_1 and b_2 are $N^2 \times 1$ vectors obtained by lexicographic ordering of the $N \times N$ matrices U, U^0, U^b, B_1, and B_2, respectively. Two-dimensional fast KL transform coding algorithms similar to those discussed in Section IV-C could now be designed. Fig. 25 shows, for example, an appli-

---

[8] It is called a noncausal model because a pel is related directly via this model to neighbors in all the four quadrants.

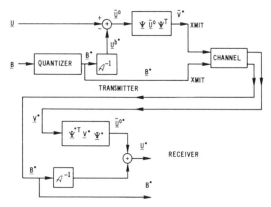

Fig. 24. Boundary variables of the noncausal model.

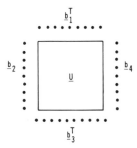

Fig. 25. Fast KL transform coding of images; ψ is the KL transform of U^0.

cation of the method II of Section IV-C. Recursive block coding algorithms which use small image blocks (e.g., for adaptive coding methods) and exploit interblock redundancy could also be designed following Section IV-C.

D. Transform Coding of Two Source Models

It is noteworthy that the foregoing algorithm is based on a two source model of a stationary random field, viz.

$$U = U^0 + U^b \quad (114)$$

where the two source outputs U^0 and U^b are realizable from the given image block U and its boundary variables B. One could extend this idea to represent an image as a nonstationary field

$$U = U_s + U_b \quad (115)$$

where U_s is a stationary component and U_b is a nonstationary component. The two components are coded separately to preserve the different features in the image. Suppose the stationary component has a representation

$$\mathcal{L}[U_s] = \epsilon_s \quad (116)$$

where ϵ_s is a zero mean unity variance white noise field. Applying L on U we get

$$\begin{aligned} \epsilon &\triangleq \mathcal{L}[U] = \mathcal{L}[U_s] + \mathcal{L}[U_b] \\ &\triangleq \epsilon_s + \epsilon_b \end{aligned} \quad (117)$$

The operator $\mathcal{L}$ could be realized in various ways. For example, a common method is to let $\mathcal{L}$ be such that U_s is a low-pass filtered version of U and U_b contains the high spatial frequencies such as edges.

A two source coding scheme similar to the above method

57

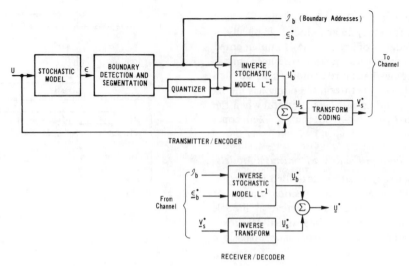

Fig. 26. Two source transform coding.

was first proposed by Schreiber *et al.* [174]–[175]. The given image is segmented into its low and high spatial frequency components. The low-frequency component and the addresses (I_b) of the boundary points are encoded. At the receiver the original image is synthesized by adding to the low-frequency component a quantity proportional to the Laplacian of a step function called *synthetic highs* at the locations of the boundary points. Another two source coding scheme has been studied by Yan and Sakrison [164], where the image decomposition in two sources is performed by subtracting the sharp changes in the local mean of the image from the image. The corner points and the values of changes are coded separately, and the residual image, which is a much better candidate for a stationary random field, is transform coded. Jain and Wang [184] have considered certain stochastic image models to achieve the two source decomposition. For an appropriate $\mathcal{L}$ in (117), $\epsilon_{i,j}$ is a sum of $\epsilon_b(i,j)$ (signal) and $\epsilon_s(i,j)$ (white noise). If the original image data contains only a small amount of additive noise, then ϵ_b and ϵ_s could be segmented by a simple threshold scheme e.g., as follows:

$$\epsilon_b(i,j) = \begin{cases} 0, & |\epsilon_{i,j}| < t \\ t \, \text{sgn} \, \epsilon_{i,j}, & |\epsilon_{i,j}| > t \end{cases} \tag{118}$$
$$\epsilon_s(i,j) = \epsilon_{i,j} - \epsilon_b(i,j)$$

where t is a suitable threshold. A simple connectivity algorithm (e.g., check to see if each feature $\epsilon_b(i,j)$ has at least one neighbor which is also a feature sample) is used to minimize the effects of noise. I_b is the set of addresses where $\epsilon_b(i,j) \neq 0$, and the quantized values $\epsilon_b(i,j)$ are coded for transmission. The residual field

$$U_s = U - \mathcal{L}^{-1}[\epsilon_b] \tag{119}$$

is transform coded. The overall average rate depends on the choice of threshold which has to be found experimentally. For $t = \infty$, this method reduces to the usual transform coding method. Fig. 26 shows the block diagram of this method.

Fig. 27 shows the results of this method for a 256×256 image coded in 64×64 blocks. Figs. 27(a) and (b) show the stochastically segmented components U_s and U_b for the threshold $t = \sigma_\epsilon$ where σ_ϵ is the standard deviation of $\epsilon_{i,j}$. Fig. 27(c) and (d) show the reconstructed components U_s and U_b. Fig. 27(e) shows the final encoded image at 1 bit/pel average rate.

Fig. 27(f) shows the edge map I_b—which is preserved by this coding method.

Compared to ordinary transform coding, for the same mean-square error this method offers several choices in terms of the subjective quality of the receiver image. However, the complexity of the algorithm is increased substantially compared to other adaptive transform coding methods.

E. Transform Coding Under Visual Criteria

In Section I-D it was mentioned that the ordinary mean-square criterion was of limited use for the visual evaluation of images. A weighted mean-square criterion proposed by Mannos and Sakrison [17] has been found to be useful. Fig. 28 shows a transform coding scheme that takes into account the visual criterion. The image luminance field is first converted to a contrast field via a memoryless nonlinear transformation. This image field is then Fourier transformed. The transform domain elements are multiplied by a frequency weighting function $H(\omega_1, \omega_2)$ (see Section I-D) and the resulting samples are quantized using the usual mean-square criterion. Inverse weighting followed by inverse Fourier transformation gives the reconstructed contrast field.

For large image block sizes, the frequency weighting function $H(\omega_1, \omega_2)$ can be applied in the DFT domain. To apply this method for coding images block by block via an arbitrary transform the image constrast field should first be convolved with $h(x, y)$, the Fourier inverse of $H(\omega_1, \omega_2)$. For practical implementation, it would then be desirable to seek discrete finite support approximations of h and h^{-1}. The resulting field $z_{i,j}$ could then be coded by any desired method. At the receiver, the encoded field $z_{i,j}$ must now be convolved with the inverse function $h^{-1}(i,j)$. The reader should note that the transform domain quantizer design and bit allocation now depends on the statistics of the field $\{z_{i,j}\}$.

F. Three-Dimensional Transform Coding

In many applications, (for example, in multispectral imaging interframe video imaging, biomedical cineangiography and computer-aided tomographic (CAT) scanning, etc.), one has to work with three-dimensional (or higher) data. Transform coding schemes are possible for compression of such data. The basic ideas of the foregoing sections are extended in this development.

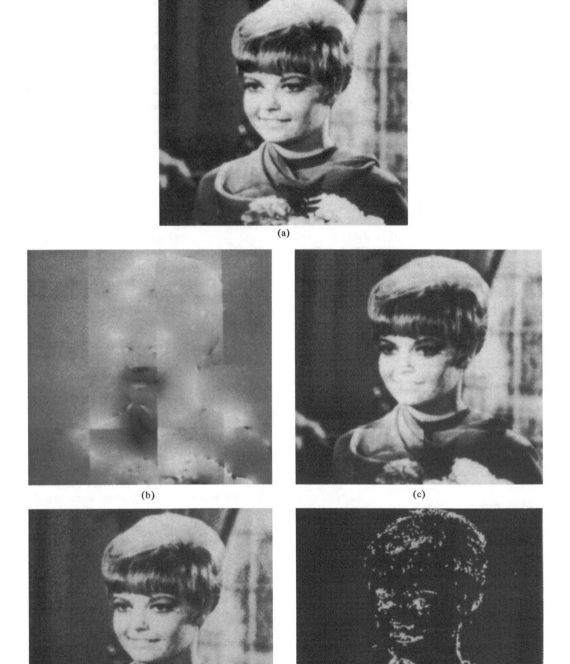

Fig. 27. Images coded by two source transform coding. (a) Original.
(b) U_b, nonstationary component. (c) U_s, stationary component
(d) 1.5 bit/pel coded image. (e) Edges preserved by the coder.

A three-dimensional (separable) transform of an $L \times M \times N$ sequence $\{u_{i,j,k}\}$ is defined as

$$v_{l,m,n} = \sum_{i=1}^{L} \sum_{j=1}^{M} \sum_{k=1}^{N} u_{i,j,k} a_L(l,i) a_M(m,j) a_N(n,k) \qquad (120)$$

where $1 \leqslant l \leqslant L$, $1 \leqslant m \leqslant M$, $1 \leqslant n \leqslant N$ and $\{a_L(i,j)\}$ are the elements of an $L \times L$ unitary matrix A_L. In higher dimensions, one simply takes the A-transform with respect to each index.

59

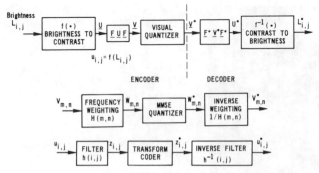

Fig. 28. Transform coding under visual criterion.

For an arbitrary A, the number of operations is $LMN(L + M + N)$. If A is a fast transform, such as the DFT, sine, cosine, etc., then the operation count is generally $LMN(\log_2 LMN)$. The storage requirement for the data is LMN. To reduce the online storage and computation requirements, often one partitions the available data into smaller blocks (e.g., $16 \times 16 \times 16$) and each block is processed independently. The coding algorithm after transformation is the same as before except that one is working with triple indexed variables. Fig. 23(c) shows a frame of a sequence of cosine transform coded images at 0.5 bit/pel. The improvement over intraframe coding is seen by comparing it with Fig. 23(b).

G. Adaptive Transform Coding

Performance of transform coding schemes could be improved substantially by adapting them to changes in image statistics. For three-dimensional data, this could be quite useful because the statistical properties along the temporal dimension could vary quite a lot depending on motion or other temporal changes. There are essentially three types of adaptation that could be made, viz.

1) adaptation of transform
2) adaptation of bit allocation
3) adaptation of quantizer levels.

Theoretically, a change in statistics of the data could require all of these adaptations. Adaptation of the transform basis vectors is the most difficult and expensive, because ideally one should find a new set of KL basis vectors for any change in the statistical parameters. A method of this type was considered by Tasto and Wintz [158]. From a practical standpoint, if one knows the range and type of statistical variations, one may choose a single transform which would be least sensitive to such changes.

A more practical and perhaps more effective method is to adapt the bit assignment to changes in statistics. For example, one could classify an image block into one of several categories and allocate a larger number of bits to blocks that have larger activity and fewer bits to ones having lower activity. This results in a variable average rate from block to block, but gives a better utilization of the total bits over the entire ensemble of image blocks. Adaptations of this type have been considered by Chen [163] for two-dimensional transform coding, by Jain and Wang [118, sec. 6] for hybrid coding and by Jain and Jain [97] for a three-dimensional transform coding. Fig. 23(d) shows a frame of interframe-cosine transform adaptively coded images. The significant improvement over intraframe (Fig. 23(b)) or nonadaptive interframe (Fig. 23(c)) is evident.

Another adaptive scheme is to allocate bits to image blocks so that each block has the same distortion [215]. This results in a uniform degradation of the image and appears less objectionable to the eye. In adaptive quantization schemes, the bit allocation is kept the same but the quantizer levels are adjusted according to changes in the variances of the transform domain samples. Transform domain variances may be estimated by either updating the statistical parameters of the covariance model or may be estimated in real time by local averaging (or prediction) of the squared magnitude of the transform domain samples. One such approach has been considered by Tescher [159].

H. Transform Coding of Tomographic (Computer-Aided Tomographic Scanned) X-Ray Images

In many applications where one has a sequence U_k, of two-dimensional images, where the temporal axis (k) need not be time (as in the case of motion images). Examples are the tomographic X-ray images where a three dimensional object is imaged by illuminating it by an X-ray source on a two-dimensional plane. By rotating the object relatively to the source, several views or projections $\{U_k\}$ of the object are obtained. If $f(x, y, z)$ is the transmissivity of the object, then $U_k(i, j) \triangleq u_{i,j,k}$ is given by

$$u_{i,j,k} = \int_{S_{i,j,k}} f(x, y, z)\, dS \qquad (121)$$

where $S_{i,j,k}$ is the path of the X-ray from the source to the (i, j)th pel on the image in the kth projected view. It is known that if one has several such projection images, one could "reconstruct" a reasonable estimate of $f(x, y, z)$. Once $f(x, y, z)$ or its estimate is known, one could obtain other views (e.g., cross sections) which may otherwise be impractical to obtain. The number of projection views and the associated data rates with such images often achieves unmanageable proportions [169]. Hence compression of projection images for storage of this data for subsequent reconstruction and analysis becomes very desirable.

Fig. 29(a) shows an 8 bit/pel projection image (128×128) of a dog's thorax. Figs. 29(b) and (c) show results of three-dimensional transform coded projections at 0.5 bit/pel and 0.04 bit/pel giving compressions of 16 and 200, respectively. The size of each image block for three-dimensional transform coding was chosen to be $32 \times 16 \times 8$. Note that high SNR values are achieved even at large values of compression. The high values of compression are achieved because imaging a projection is equivalent to low-pass filtering so that the data has large interpel correlation. Also, there is substantial redundancy from one projection to the next.

From a clinical standpoint, one is more interested in the reconstructed images than the projection images. Fig. 30(a) shows a cross section of the object reconstructed from the original (uncompressed) and the transform coded projections. Hence the fidelity criterion is to minimize the error in the reconstructed object for a given bit rate of the projection data. Fig. 30(b) shows the error images of the reconstructed cross section. These results show compression ratios of 16 and above may be achieved for projection images while preserving medically useful information. Higher compression is achievable for X-ray cineangiographic images where the third dimension represents time [97], [169].

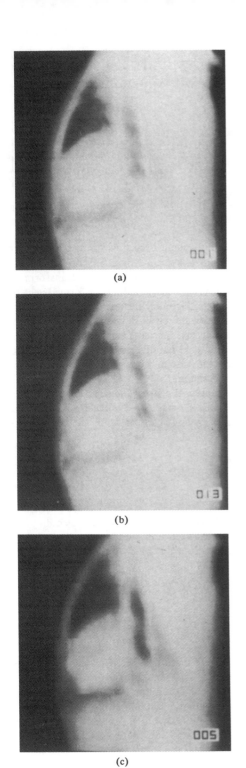

(a)

(b)

(c)

Fig. 29. Transform coding of CAT scanned images, CR = compression ratio. (a) original 8 bit/pel. (b) 0.5 bit/pel, CR = 16, SNR = 49.3 dB. (c) 0.04 bit/pel, CR = 200, SNR = 40.7 dB.

I. Summary of Transform Coding

In summary, transform coding achieves relatively larger compression compared to predictive methods. Generally, any distortion due to quantization and channel errors gets distributed, over the entire image, during the inverse transformation. Visually, this is less objectionable than the errors in predictive coding where it is distributed locally at the source. Although for one-dimensional autoregressive processes, transform and

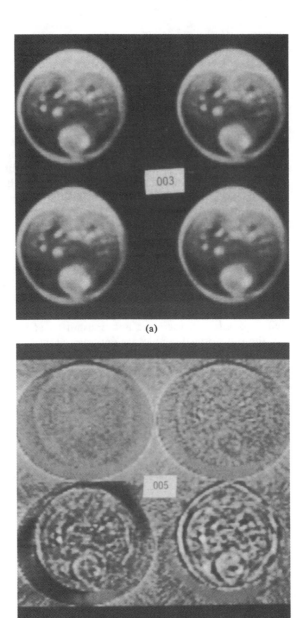

(a)

(b)

Fig. 30. Reconstructed cross section from compressed projection images. (a) Reconstructed images clockwise from top left, original, CR = 4, CR = 16, CR = 8. (b) Error in reconstructed images due to data compression, clockwise from top left, CR = 4, CR = 16, CR = 200, CR = 64.

predictive coding schemes are theoretically close in performance, their differences on real world data are substantial. This is because of two reasons. First, often the real world data is not stationary. Predictive coding compared to transform coding, is quite sensitive to changes in the statistics of the data. Hence, in practice, only adaptive predictive coding algorithms achieve the efficiency of (nonadaptive) transform coding methods. Second, in two dimensions finite order causal predictors may never achieve a compression ability close to transform coding because a finite order autoregressive representation of a two-dimensional random field may not exist [211]. From an implementation point of view, predictive coding has much lower complexity both in terms of memory requirements and number of operations to be performed. However, with rapidly decreasing cost of digital hardware and computer memory, the hardware complexity of transform coders may not remain a disadvantage for very long.

VI. Hybrid Image Coding and Vector Differential Pulse-Code Modulation

A. Hybrid Coding

The term refers to techniques which combine transform and predictive coding techniques. Typically, first a two-dimensional image is unitarily transformed in one of its dimensions to obtain a sequence of one dimensional, independent, sequences. Each of these sequences is then coded independently by a one dimensional predictive technique such as DPCM. This technique combines the advantages of hardware simplicity of DPCM and the robust performance of transform coding. Fig. 31 shows the overall scheme. The hardware complexity of this method is that of a one-dimensional transform coder and at most N DPCM channels, where N is the size of the transform basis vectors. The number of DPCM channels is significantly less than N because many elements of the transformed vector are allocated zero bits and therefore not transmitted at all. In practice, the transformed samples are multiplexed into a single DPCM channel which adjusts its quantizer and predictor according to the statistics of the input samples. Consider an $N \times M$ image and let u_j denote its jth column, i.e.,

$$u_j = [u_{1,j} u_{2,j} \cdots u_{N,j}]^T. \tag{122}$$

A unitary transformation

$$v_j = \Psi u_j, \quad 1 \leqslant j \leqslant M. \tag{123}$$

is performed on each vector u_j such that the elements of v_j are mutually uncorrelated. Further, for each i, the sequence $\{v_j(i)\}$, is modeled by a suitable autoregressive process. It has been shown [118], [184] that several random field models for images lead to a first-order Markov model

$$v_j(i) = \rho_i v_{j-1}(i) + e_j(i), \quad 1 \leqslant i \leqslant N \tag{124}$$

for the transformed vector v_j. For example, consider a random field represented by the semicausal stochastic finite difference equation

$$\left. \begin{array}{l} u_{i,j} = \alpha(u_{i-1,j} + u_{i+1,j}) + \gamma u_{i,j-1} + \epsilon_{i,j} \\ E\epsilon_{i,j} = 0, E\epsilon_{i,j}\epsilon_{k,l} = \beta^2 \delta_{i,k} \delta_{j,l} \quad \alpha < \tfrac{1}{2}, |2\alpha + \gamma| < 1 \end{array} \right\}. \tag{125}$$

This is called a semicausal model (because a pel at (i, j) is related to pels that occur both before and after it in the "i" direction and to pels that occur only before it in the "j" direction). If we assume that at the boundaries of the image $u_{i,j} \simeq u_{i-1,j}$ (highly correlated) then the cosine transform plays the role of Ψ and (125) reduces to (124) with

$$\rho_i = \gamma \lambda_c(i), E[e_j^2(i)] = \beta^2/\lambda_c^2(i)$$

$$\lambda_c(i) = 1 - 2\alpha \cos \frac{(i-1)\pi}{N}, \quad 1 \leqslant i \leqslant N. \tag{126}$$

The DPCM equations for the ith channel now follow from Section III-C as

Predictor: $\bar{v}_j(i) = \rho_i v_{j-1}(i)$ (127a)
Quantizer Input: $\tilde{e}_j(i) = v_j(i) - \bar{v}_j(i)$ (127b)
Reconstruction Filter: $v_j(i) = \bar{v}_j(i) + \tilde{e}_j(i)$.   (127c)

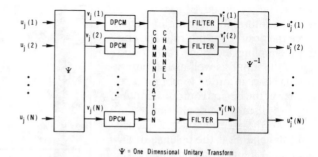

Ψ = One Dimensional Unitary Transform

Fig. 31. Hybrid coding of two-dimensional images.

The encoding scheme requires, first, taking the transform of each column vector u_j. This is followed by the DPCM channels for predictive coding of successive transform vectors. The receiver simply reconstructs the transformed vectors according to (127a) and (127c) and performs the inverse transformation Ψ^{-1}. It has been shown [118] that in practice a fast sinusoidal transform such as the sine or cosine (depending how the boundary values are handled) is useful for monochrome images. To complete the design we now need to specify the quantizer in each DPCM channel.

Letting p denote the average desired bit rate in bit/pel, n_i the number of bits allocated to the ith DPCM channel and $\sigma_e^2(i)$ the quantizer mean-square error in the ith channel we could write

$$p = \frac{1}{N} \sum_{i=1}^{N} n_i, \quad n_i \geqslant 0. \tag{128}$$

Assuming that all the DPCM channels are in their steady state, the average (mean-square) distortion in coding of any vector (for noiseless channels) can be shown to be simply the average distortions in various DPCM channels, viz.

$$D = \frac{1}{N} \sum_{i=1}^{N} g_i(n_i) \sigma_e^2(i) \tag{129}$$

$$g_i(x) = \frac{f(x)}{1 - \rho_i^2 f(x)}$$

where $f(x)$ is the distortion-rate function of the quantizer and $g_i(x)$ represents the mean square distortion of the ith DPCM channel if the corresponding Markov process prediction error variance were unity. The bit allocation problem for hybrid coding is to minimize (129), subject to the constraints of (128). This is now in the framework of the problem defined in Section IV-B and the solution could be obtained as indicated there. In a typical hybrid coding scheme with $N = 16$ (block size) the bit allocations are (3, 3, 3, 2, 2, 1, 1, 1, 0, 0, 0, 0, 0, 0, 0, 0) for an average rate of 1 bit/pel. Fig. 32 shows a 256 $\times$ 256 image hybrid coded in blocks of 16 $\times$ 256 using the cosine transform and the semicausal model of (125).

B. Hybrid Coding of Noisy Images

In many situations the observed image may be noisy (and/or blurred). Then, it is desirable to design a coder which does not waste bits in coding the noise. As explained in Section III-D, a Kalman filter could be employed for prediction, in each DPCM channel of the hybrid coder. This is particularly useful when the image data is represented by a suitable semi-

Fig. 32. Hybrid encoded images via semicausal model of (125) at 1 bit/ pel. (a) Nonadaptive, SNR = 31 dB. (b) Adaptive variance estimation, SNR = 31.5 dB. (c) Adaptive classification, SNR = 33 dB.

Fig. 33. Hybrid coding of noisy images via semicausal model. (a) Noisy image. (b) Restored image 8 bit/pel. (c) Encoded image 1 bit/pel.

causal model [184], since the Kalman predictor equations for the noisy image would correspond to the simple one-dimensional state variable model

$$v_j(i) = \rho_i v_{j-1}(i) + e_j(i) \qquad (130)$$

$$z_j(i) = v_j(i) + \eta_j(i). \qquad (131)$$

Fig. 33 shows the result of hybrid coding of a noisy image. The following observations have been made.

1) Because of presence of noise, the encoded data could have higher fidelity than the observed data due to filtering

63

combined with encoding. Fig. 33 shows this. Except at low rates and small noise (e.g., at rate = 0.5 bit/pel and $\sigma_n = 0.2\,\sigma_u$), the encoded data has a better SNR then the observed data.

2) The overall coder performance depends on additive noise in observed image versus quantizer noise (or bit rate). At large noise levels ($\sigma_n > 0.5\,\sigma_u$), the additive noise dominates so that quantization noise due to compression results in only a marginal degradation in performance. At small noise levels ($\sigma_n \gtrsim 0.2\,\sigma_u$), quantization effects are more visible (as in the noise free case) since this effect starts to dominate.

C. Extensions of Hybrid Coding

The coding scheme of the previous section could be adapted to images whose spatial statistics vary slowly by updating the parameters of the model. It is important to consider adaptive schemes which offer reasonable tradeoffs between performance and complexity of the coder.

For a fixed predictor in the feedback loop of a DPCM channel, the variance of the prediction error will fluctuate with changes in the image statistics. A simple method is to update the variance of the prediction error at each step j, and use it to adjust the spacing of the quantizer levels in each DPCM channel. For a mean-square error criterion, this adaptation is achieved by simply normalizing the prediction error using its updated standard deviation. Then the quantizer levels are designed for a unit variance input random variable.

Let $\tilde{\sigma}_j^2(i)$ be the variance of $\tilde{e}_j(i)$, the prediction error at step j of the ith DPCM loop, and let $\dot{\sigma}_j^2(i)$ denote the variance of the quantized values. Since the quantized variables $\tilde{e}_j(i)$ are available both at the receiver and the transmitter, it is easy to estimate $\dot{\sigma}_j^2(i)$. A simple estimate of $\dot{\sigma}_j^2(i)$, called an exponential average variance estimator, is of the form [189]

$$\dot{\sigma}_{j+1}^2(i) = (1-\gamma)e_j^{\cdot 2}(i) + \gamma\dot{\sigma}_j^2(i), \quad j = 1, 2, \cdots . \quad (132)$$

For small quantization errors one may use $\dot{\sigma}_j$ as an estimate of $\tilde{\sigma}_j$. For the Lloyd–Max quantizers (or approximations thereof) a more accurate estimate of $\tilde{\sigma}_j$ is possible. Since the variance of a Lloyd–Max quantizer input equals the sum of the variances of the quantizer output and the quantization error (Section II-C), one could obtain the recursion [118]

$$\tilde{\sigma}_{j+1}^2(i) = \frac{1-\gamma}{1-f(n_i)}e_j^{\cdot 2}(i) + \gamma\tilde{\sigma}_j^2(i), n_i > 1, \quad 0 < \gamma < 1.$$

$$(133)$$

The above estimates become poor for DPCM channels which are assigned a small number of bits ($n_i \simeq 1$). For these channels $\tilde{\sigma}_j(i)$ could be estimated by an extrapolation procedure [118].

Another adaptation is based on the classification method discussed earlier in Section V-G. Here each image column is classified as belonging to one of K predetermined classes that are fixed according to the activity in that image column, which is measured by its variance. Quantization bits are allocated according to their dynamic activity. The classification information is communicated by sending an extra $\log_2 K$ bits per column. Fig. 32 shows results of adaptive hybrid coding and compares them with the nonadaptive algorithm. Experimentally, it is found that the compression increases by a factor of 2 for the adaptive techniques [118].

Hybrid coding is particularly useful in interframe image data

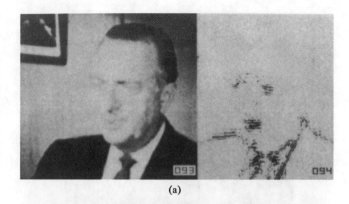

(a)

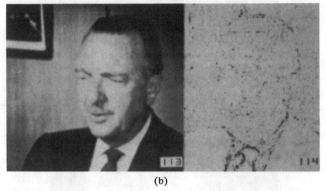

(b)

Fig. 34. Interframe adaptive hybrid coding. (a) Nonadaptive without motion compensation, 0.5 bit/pel, SNR = 34 dB. (b) Adaptive with motion compensation, 0.125 bit/pel, SNR = 36.7 dB.

compression of motion images. A two-dimensional $M \times N$ block of the kth frame, denoted U_k, is first transformed to give V_k. For each (m, n) the sequence $\{v_k(m,n), k = 1, 2, \cdots\}$ is considered a one-dimensional random process, and is coded independently by a suitably designed DPCM method. The receiver simply performs the two-dimensional inverse transform of the sequence $\{v_k(m, n)\}$. Since motion is characterized by deterministic variations along the temporal axis, the various motion compensation schemes discussed in Section III-I on predictive coding can be applied. Fig. 34 shows an interframe, 0.125 bit/pel via an adaptive hybrid coding method with motion compensation based on trajectory estimation and frame skipping. Such adaptations are not feasible in three-dimensional transform coding. Thus with motion compensation the adaptive hybrid coding method performs better than adaptive predictive coding as well as adaptive three-dimensional transform coding [97].

D. Hybrid Coding–Conclusions

In practice, hybrid coders combine the advantages of simple hardware complexity of DPCM coders and the high performance of transform coders, particularly at moderate bit rates (e.g., 1 bit/pel for two-dimensional images). In general, hybrid coding performance lies between transform coding and DPCM. It is easily adaptable to coding and filtering of noisy images and to changes in data statistics. It is less sensitive to channel errors than DPCM, but is not as robust as transform coding. Hybrid coders have been implemented for real-time data compression of images acquired by remotely piloted vehicles (RPV) [188].

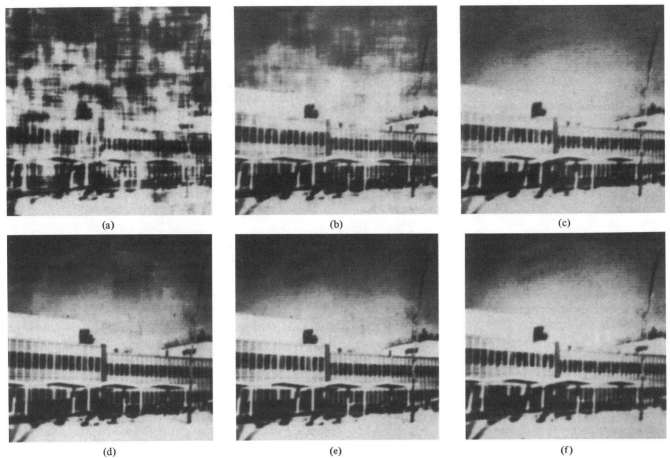

Fig. 35. Effect of channel errors in DPCM coding of images at 3 bit/pel; n = bit/pel assigned to the quantizer, k = length constraint on the channel code word, R = code rate for the convolutional codes used, SNR_i = signal to noise ratio at the channel input. From Modestino and Daut [216].

VII. IMAGE CODING IN THE PRESENCE OF CHANNEL ERRORS

In the data compression designs considered in the foregoing sections we ignored the channel effects by assuming noiseless channels (for transmission or storage). In practice, error correcting bits are appended to quantized samples before encoding to compensate for channel errors. Often, the error correcting codes used are designed to reduce the probability of bit errors, and for simplicity, equal protection is provided to all the samples. To account for channel errors, one has to add redundancy to the input. On the other hand, the data compression techniques tend to remove the redundancy in the source data. Thus a proper tradeoff between source coding (redundancy removal) and channel coding (redundancy injection) has to be achieved in the design of data compression systems.

In predictive coding, it is essential that the reconstruction filter be stable. Otherwise the channel errors could accumulate to arbitrarily large values. For example, as mentioned in Section III-B, the predictor of the delta modulator has to be stabilized by providing a "leak" factor. For multidimensional predictive coding, special care has to be taken to ensure the stability of the predictor model. Even when the predictor models are stable, the channel error is usually amplified by the reconstruction filter. For example, in DPCM coding of a first-order Markov process with intersample correlation ρ, the distortion that appears in the output signal in steady state due to channel noise (assumed white) is amplified by a factor of $(1 - \rho^2)^{-1}$. For $\rho = 0.95$, this amplification factor is 10. At the same time the achievable compression is also proportional to this factor. Therefore, while high compression is achievable for large value of ρ, the channel distortion is also large. Visually, channel noise in DPCM tends to create streaks that originate at the time the first channel error occurs and terminate when the coder is reinitialized. When isolated erroneous scan lines appear, post processing such as its replacement by the previous line or an average of the neighbors can be done [218]. A median filter operating orthogonally to the scanning direction could also be effective. Other techniques involve using error correcting codes at the source or modifying the reconstruction filter. These and related considerations have been studied in [76], [216]–[220].

Modestino and Daut have considered a combined source-channel coding approach for DPCM transmission of images. Error control protection is provided to bits which contribute most significantly to the reconstruction error. Fig. 35 shows that a proper bit allocation between the quantizer and the channel coder for error protection can improve the performance of DPCM schemes designed for unaided channels.

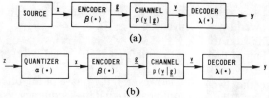

(a)

(b)

Fig. 36. (a) Channel encoding system. (b) PCM transmission with channel encoding.

In this section we consider source channel encoding methods based on optimal allocation of bits between the various error sources as well as the use of "optimal channel coder-decoder" which minimize the overall mean-square error. Crimmins, Horwitz et al. [190], [191], Wolf and Redinbo [192] and others [194], [195] have considered this criterion for the design of channel encoding–decoding methods. Jain and Jain [97], [193] have used this criterion for optimization of PCM and transform image coding algorithms to compensate for channel errors. The key result is that the overall optimal transform coder is a cascade of the optimal transform (KL), the optimal mean-square quantizer (Lloyd–Max) and the optimal channel coder–decoder.

A. Definitions

Consider Fig. 36(a). Let S be the set of $K = 2^k$ data symbols representing k bit source output words x_i. Let V be an n-dimensional binary vector space and let C be a k-dimensional subspace of V, $k \leqslant n$. If v_1 and v_2 are elements of V, then

$$v = v_1 \oplus v_2 \tag{134}$$

is also an element of V. Here "$\oplus$" sign implies the EXCLUSIVE-OR operation. C contains n-bit binary words of order K such that if $g_1, g_2 \in C$, then $g = g_1 \oplus g_2 \in C$. Since C is a k-dimensional subspace of V, it could be described by a set of k basis vectors, each being an n-tuple. Moreover, every k-dimensional binary vector can be mapped onto C.

Let the channel be a memoryless, binary symmetric channel with bit-error probability p_e. We will assume the channel error does not depend on the channel input. Let $\beta(\cdot)$ denote the mapping which maps the k-bit source output $x_i \in S$ into the n-bit code words $g_i \in C$ by a one-to-one encoding rule. The channel maps the elements of C into the elements of V. At the receiver, $\lambda(\cdot)$ denotes the mapping of elements of V into elements on the real line R, i.e.,

$$\lambda : V \xrightarrow{\text{into}} R. \tag{135}$$

B. The Optimum Mean-Square Decoder [192]

The mean-square error between the decoder output and the encoder input is given by

$$\sigma_c^2 = \sigma_c^2 (\beta, \lambda) \triangleq E(y - x)^2 \tag{136}$$

and depends on the mappings β and λ. It has been shown that for a fixed encoding rule β, the decoder that minimizes this error is given by the conditional mean of x, i.e.,

$$y = \lambda(v) = \sum_{x \in S} x p(x|v) = E(x|v) \tag{137}$$

where $p(x|v)$ is the conditional probability of x given the channel output v [192].

The function $\lambda(v)$ does not, in general, map the channel output into the set S even if $n = k$. Sometimes it may be desired to map the decoder output into a predefined set of levels $y^{\cdot}$ which contain 2^n or less levels. Then it could be shown [192] that the best decoding rule is to find $\lambda(v)$ according to (137) and then round off each value to $[y]$; the nearest $y^{\cdot} \in y^{\cdot}$, i.e., the optimum mapping $\lambda^{\cdot}$ is now given by

$$\lambda^{\cdot}(v) = [\lambda(v)]^{\cdot}. \tag{138}$$

If β is the natural encoding of the integers into binary k-tuples $(n = k)$, and the source outputs are equiprobable, then the optimum decoding rule is given by

$$\lambda(v) = (2^k - 1)p_e + \sum_{i=1}^{k} v_i (1 - 2p_e) 2^{k-i} \tag{139}$$

where $v_i = 0, 1$ are the elements of the channel output vector v. For $p_e \ll 1$, this yields $\lambda = \beta^{-1}$, i.e.,

$$\lambda(v) \simeq \sum_{i=1}^{k} v_i 2^{k-i} \tag{140}$$

which says for small bit-error probability that the inverse of the natural encoding rule is the optimum decoding rule. (See Yamaguchi and Huang [195].)

C. The Optimum Encoding Rule

In the foregoing we considered the optimum decoding rule for any given encoding rule β. It is desirable to find as well the encoding rule (i.e., the pair β, λ) which minimizes the mean-square error. This requires finding the optimum subspace C as well as the encoding rule β. For uniformly distributed source output, Wolf and Redinbo [192] have given a procedure for obtaining the optimal mapping β. In general, an exhaustive minimization procedure which searches over all subspaces of V is required. In practice suboptimal solutions are found by restricting the search to a particular set of subspaces. Table I shows a set of suboptimal basis vectors calculated by Jain and Jain [97] for various combinations of pairs (n, k), from which β is obtained as follows. Let $b = [b(1), b(2), \cdots, b(k)]$, be the binary representation of an element of S, then

$$g = \beta(b) = \sum_{j=1}^{k} \oplus b(j) \cdot \phi_j \tag{141}$$

where $\Sigma \oplus$ denotes EXCLUSIVE-OR summation, "·" denotes the binary product and $\{\phi_j\}$ are the basis vectors of C as listed in Table I. The codes generated by this method are called (n, k) Group Codes. These codes for other combinations of n and k have been tabulated in [97].

Example: Let $n = 4$, $k = 2$. Then $\phi_1 = [1\ 0\ 1\ 1]$. $\phi_2 = [0\ 1\ 0\ 1]$ and β is given as follows:

x	b	$g = \beta(b)$	
0	0 0	0 0 0 0	$= 0 \cdot \phi_1 \oplus 0 \cdot \phi_2$
1	0 1	0 1 0 1	$= 0 \cdot \phi_1 \oplus 1 \cdot \phi_2$
2	1 0	1 0 1 1	$= 1 \cdot \phi_1 \oplus 0 \cdot \phi_2$
3	1 1	1 1 1 0	$= \phi_1 \oplus \phi_2.$

In general the basis vectors ϕ_i depend on the bit error probability p_e. In the special cases of Table I and those tabulated in [97], these vectors have been found to be almost independent of p_e [97], [192]. For most image coding applications, the

TABLE I
Basis Vectors $\{\phi_i, i = 1, \cdots, k\}$ of Group G for (n, k) Group Codes

i	k \ $n-k$	0	1	2	3	4
1	4	1000	10001	100011	1000110	10001110
2		0100	01000	010001	0100101	01001010
3		0010	00100	001000	0010011	00100101
4		0001	00010	000100	0001111	00010011
1	3	100	1001	10011	100110	1001110
2		010	0100	01001	010101	0101010
3		001	0010	00100	001011	0010101
1	2	10	101	1011	10110	010111
2		01	010	0101	01101	101110
1	1	1	11	111	1111	11111

group codes given in [97] are sufficient. Although these codes are for equiprobable source outputs, we shall use these codes for other distributions as well. This will degrade the performance of the channel encoder somewhat, but it is a second-order effect compared to the overall improvement in performance.

D. Optimization of PCM Transmission

In PCM the source is a memoryless quantizer whose outputs are independently coded for transmission. Let k be the number of quantizer bits for each sample, $\{x_i\}$ the output levels arranged in the ascending order of their values, and $\{p(x_i)\}$ their probabilities. If b_i is the binary vector representation of the index i, we use (141) to define the mapping β for any given pair (n, k). The decoder equation (137) gives the reproduced values. Consider the PCM scheme in Fig. 36(b) where a continuous random variable z is quantized for transmission. The mean square distortion between the quantizer input z and the decoder output is given by

$$\sigma_t^2 = E(z - y)^2. \tag{142}$$

It has been shown [97] that for a fixed n-bit channel encoder $\beta(\cdot)$, the k-bit quantizer $\alpha(\cdot)$ and the channel decoder $\lambda(\cdot)$ that minimize the mean-square error σ_t^2 are given by

$$\lambda(v) = E(x | v) \tag{143}$$

$$x = \alpha(z) = E(z | z \in I_j) \tag{144}$$

where $I_j, j = 1, \cdots, 2^k$ denotes the jth quantization interval of the quantizer.

This means that the optimum decoder is independent of the optimum quantizer, which is the Lloyd–Max quantizer. Thus the optimal design can be accomplished by designing the quantizer and the decoder individually.

Let $f(k)$ and $c(n, k)$ denote the mean-square distortions due to the k-bit Lloyd–Max quantizer and the channel respectively when the quantizer input is a unit variance random variable. Then we could write the total mean-square error for the input z of variance σ_z^2,

$$\left.\begin{array}{l} \sigma_t^2 = \sigma_z^2 \hat{\sigma}_t^2 \\ \hat{\sigma}_t^2 \triangleq [f(k) + c(n, k)] \\ \sigma_q^2 \triangleq \sigma_z^2 f(k), \sigma_e^2 \triangleq \sigma_z^2 c(n, k). \end{array}\right\} \tag{145}$$

where σ_q^2 and σ_e^2 represent the quantizer and channel distortions, respectively. The channel distortion depends on the

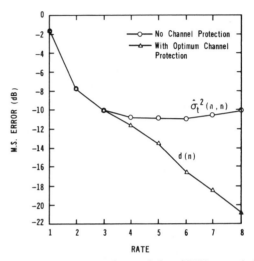

Fig. 37. Distortion versus rate characteristics of PCM transmission over a binary symmetric channel.

(n, k) group code as well as the bit error probability p_e. For a fixed n and $k \leqslant n$, $f(k)$ is a monotonically decreasing function of k, whereas $c(n, k)$ is a monotonically increasing function of k. Hence for every n there is an optimum value of $k = k(n)$ for which $\hat{\sigma}_t^2$ is minimized. Let $d(n)$ denote the minimum value of $\hat{\sigma}_t^2$ with respect of k. Fig. 37 shows the plot of the distortions $\hat{\sigma}_t^2(n, n)$ and $d(n)$ versus the rate for n-bit PCM transmission of a Gaussian random variable when $p_e = 0.01$. It shows, for example, the optimum combination of error protection and quantization could improve the system performance by about 11 dB for an 8-bit transmission. The quantity $\hat{\sigma}_t^2(n, n)$ represents the distortion of the PCM system if no channel error protection is provided and all the bits are used for quantization. With k optimized, we write

$$k = k(n)$$

$$d(n) = \min_k \{\hat{\sigma}_t^2(n, k)\} = \hat{\sigma}_t^2(n, k(n)). \tag{146}$$

Thus $d(n)$ represents the optimized distortion function.

E. Optimization of Transform Coding

The results above could be exploited in designing transform coders which are protected against channel errors. A transform coder contains several PCM channels, each operating on one transformed sample. If we represent z_j as the jth trans-

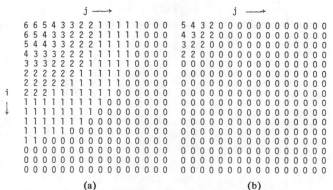

j ⟶   j ⟶

```
6 6 5 4 3 3 2 2 1 1 1 1 1 0 0 0    5 4 3 2 0 0 0 0 0 0 0 0 0 0 0 0
6 5 4 3 3 2 2 2 1 1 1 1 1 0 0 0    4 3 2 2 0 0 0 0 0 0 0 0 0 0 0 0
5 4 4 3 3 2 2 2 1 1 1 1 0 0 0 0    3 2 2 0 0 0 0 0 0 0 0 0 0 0 0 0
4 3 3 3 2 2 2 1 1 1 1 1 0 0 0 0    2 2 0 0 0 0 0 0 0 0 0 0 0 0 0 0
3 3 3 2 2 2 2 1 1 1 1 0 0 0 0 0    0 0 0 0 0 0 0 0 0 0 0 0 0 0 0 0
2 2 2 2 2 2 1 1 1 1 0 0 0 0 0 0    0 0 0 0 0 0 0 0 0 0 0 0 0 0 0 0
2 2 2 2 2 1 1 1 1 1 0 0 0 0 0 0    0 0 0 0 0 0 0 0 0 0 0 0 0 0 0 0
2 2 2 1 1 1 1 1 1 0 0 0 0 0 0 0    0 0 0 0 0 0 0 0 0 0 0 0 0 0 0 0
1 1 1 1 1 1 1 1 0 0 0 0 0 0 0 0    0 0 0 0 0 0 0 0 0 0 0 0 0 0 0 0
1 1 1 1 1 1 1 0 0 0 0 0 0 0 0 0    0 0 0 0 0 0 0 0 0 0 0 0 0 0 0 0
1 1 1 1 1 1 1 0 0 0 0 0 0 0 0 0    0 0 0 0 0 0 0 0 0 0 0 0 0 0 0 0
1 1 1 1 1 0 0 0 0 0 0 0 0 0 0 0    0 0 0 0 0 0 0 0 0 0 0 0 0 0 0 0
1 1 0 0 0 0 0 0 0 0 0 0 0 0 0 0    0 0 0 0 0 0 0 0 0 0 0 0 0 0 0 0
0 0 0 0 0 0 0 0 0 0 0 0 0 0 0 0    0 0 0 0 0 0 0 0 0 0 0 0 0 0 0 0
0 0 0 0 0 0 0 0 0 0 0 0 0 0 0 0    0 0 0 0 0 0 0 0 0 0 0 0 0 0 0 0
0 0 0 0 0 0 0 0 0 0 0 0 0 0 0 0    0 0 0 0 0 0 0 0 0 0 0 0 0 0 0 0
```

i ↓

(a)   (b)

Fig. 38. Bit allocations for quantization and error protection in 16×16 block cosine transform coding of images. Images modeled by the exponential covariance function of (103). Average bit rate is 1 bit/pel and channel error rate is 1 percent. (a) $k_{i,j}$, bits allocated to quantizers (b) $n_{i,j} - k_{i,j}$, channel protection bits allocated to quantizer outputs.

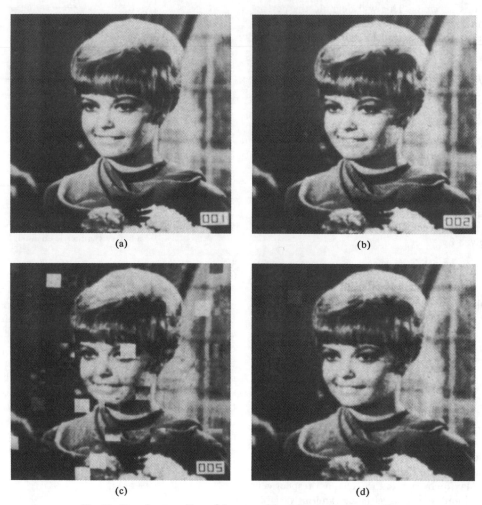

Fig. 39. Transform coding of images with channel error protection.
(a) original (b) 1 bit/pel with no channel errors (c) 1 bit/pel, $p_e = 0.01$, without channel error protection (d) 1 bit/pel, $p_e = 0.01$ with error protection.

form domain sample and let $\sigma_j^2 = \text{var}(z_j)$, then the average mean-square distortion of a transform coding scheme in the presence of channel errors becomes

$$D = \sum_j \sigma_j^2 \, d(n_j) \qquad (147)$$

where n_j is the total number of bits allocated to the jth PCM channel.

The index j takes values over the set of integers $\{1, 2, \cdots, J\}$, where J is the number of PCM channels. Since we could evaluate the function $d(n)$ via (146), any transform coding scheme could be designed by finding the bit allocation n_j for

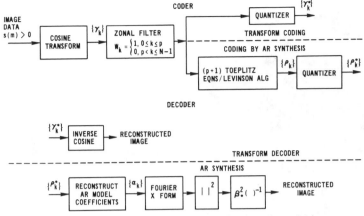

Fig. 40. Transform coding versus coding by AR synthesis.

a desired average rate by following the integer bit allocation algorithm of Section IV-C. Knowing n_j, we can find $k_j = k(n_j)$, the optimum number of quantizer bits corresponding to n_j.

Fig. 38 shows the bit allocation (k_j) pattern for the quantizers and the allocation of channel protection bits $(n_j - k_j)$ at an overall average bit rate of 1 bit/pel for 16×16 block coding of an isotropic random field. Clearly, more protection is provided to samples which have larger variances (and hence are more important for transmission). The overhead due to channel protection, even for the high value of $p_e = 0.01$, is only 15 percent. For $p_e = 0.001$, the overhead is about 4 percent.

Fig. 39 shows the results of applying the foregoing techniques to transform coding of an image in the presence of channel errors. The improvement in SNR is 10 dB at $p = 0.01$ and is also significant visually. This scheme is quite robust with respect to fluctuations in the channel error rates (p_e).

VIII. OTHER METHODS

Several specialized methods not described so far include variable velocity scanning, pseudorandom scanning, image coding by splines, interpolative coding, countour coding, cluster and feature coding, singular value decomposition (SVD) coding, autoregressive coding, etc. We briefly discuss them now.

In variable velocity scanning [203], the image is sampled at a rate proportional to the slope of the scanned intensity. This provides a higher number of samples in areas of edges and large activity and fewer samples in smooth areas. Pseudo random scanning proposed by Huang and Tretiak [205] for binary facsimile images, is a multiplexing scheme where pseudorandom scans of 1's and 0's from several images are passed sequentially through a logical OR gate. At the receiver the transmitter pseudorandom scanning sequence is repeated by each channel. A "1" will be displayed correctly in some of the channels but will appear as random noise in others. Up to four channels have been found to be easily multiplexed giving a 4 to 1 compression.

Since image activity is not regularly spaced in common images, non-uniform sampling could be performed via the use of variable knot splines [208]. Basically the image is sampled at locations (called knots) where its Laplacian (for cubic splines) exceeds a threshold. Cubic splines in two dimensions are then fitted through the knots. This method becomes quite similar to the stochastic decomposition method of Section V-D, if we identify $\mathcal{L}$ to be the Laplacian operator and al-

locate all the quantization bits to the deterministic part ϵ_b. The reconstructed image is obtained by finding a least squares smoothing solution of the problem $\mathcal{L}[u] = \epsilon_b$. A somewhat different approach to this problem is via splines [208]. For other interpolative coding schemes, see [206], [207].

Contour coding is useful for boundaries and curves and has applications in transmission of weather maps as well as in two source coding discussed in Section V-C. These algorithms have been studied by Wintz, Wilkins et al., Freeman, Graham, Schreiber, and others [171]–[181]. An important class of algorithms useful for multispectral images is called cluster or feature coding. In multispectral images, at each (x, y) location a vector of multispectral intensities is represented. Each vector is mapped into a feature vector. Areas of the images which have similar features "cluster" together in the feature space. First, a set of cluster centroids is determined. Then, for each pel, its membership to this set is found. Only the information pertaining to its membership and the set of feature vectors are coded. Hilbert, Wintz, and others [222], [223] have developed algorithms for cluster coding. Usually, the fidelity criterion for these algorithms is the classification (rather than mean square) accuracy of the encoded data.

Since an image is most easily represented by a matrix, its SVD can be used for data compression. Consider an $N \times M$ image U of rank r. Its SVD could be written as

$$U = \sum_{i=1}^{r} \lambda_i \boldsymbol{\phi}_i \boldsymbol{\psi}_i^T \tag{148}$$

where $\boldsymbol{\phi}_i$ and $\boldsymbol{\psi}_i$ are, respectively, $N \times 1$ and $M \times 1$ vectors, and $\lambda_1 \geqslant \lambda_2 \geqslant \lambda_3 \cdots \geqslant \lambda_r > 0$ are called the singular value of U. The first term $\lambda_1 \boldsymbol{\phi}_1 \boldsymbol{\psi}_1^T$ represents the best least squares, rank one matrix approximation of U. To achieve data compression, define

$$U_1 = U - \lambda_1^{\bullet} \boldsymbol{\phi}_1^{\bullet} (\boldsymbol{\psi}_1^{\bullet})^T$$
$$U_{k+1} = U_k - \lambda_{1,k}^{\bullet} \boldsymbol{\phi}_{1,k}^{\bullet} (\boldsymbol{\psi}_{1,k}^{\bullet})^T, \quad k = 1, 2, \cdots, k_m \tag{149}$$

where $\lambda_{1,k} \boldsymbol{\phi}_{1,k} \boldsymbol{\psi}_{1,k}^T$ is the best least squares rank one approximation of U_k and $\lambda_{1,k}^{\bullet}, \boldsymbol{\phi}_{1,k}^{\bullet}, \boldsymbol{\psi}_{1,k}^{\bullet}$ are the quantized values of $\lambda_{1,k}, \boldsymbol{\phi}_{1,k}$ and $\boldsymbol{\psi}_{1,k}$, respectively. Generally, one chooses $k_m \ll r$. At the receiver, the reproduced image is given by

$$U^{\bullet} = \sum_{k=1}^{k_m} \lambda_{1,k}^{\bullet} \boldsymbol{\phi}_{1,k}^{\bullet} (\boldsymbol{\psi}_{1,k}^{\bullet})^T. \tag{150}$$

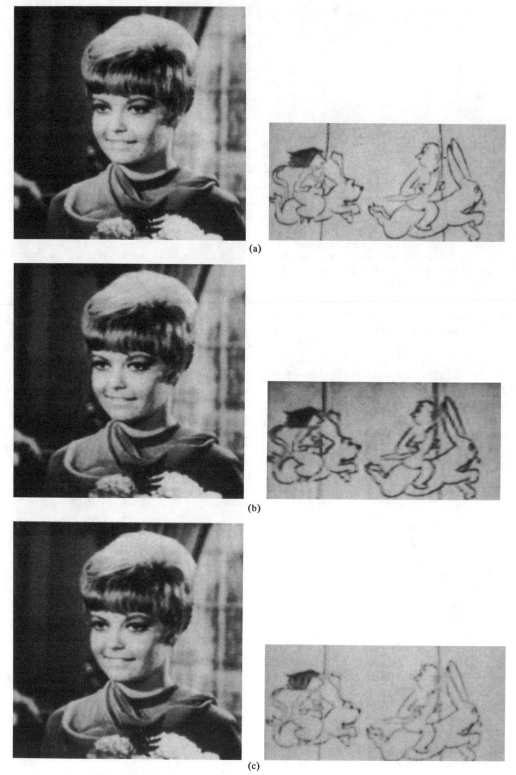

Fig. 41. Line-by-line compression of images by AR synthesis with 4 to
1 sample reduction. (a) Original. (b) Cosine transform coded.
(c) Coding by AR synthesis.

For small quantization errors, one would have $\lambda_{1,k}^{\cdot} \simeq \lambda_k$, calculated as
$\boldsymbol{\phi}_{1,k}^{\cdot} \simeq \boldsymbol{\phi}_{1,k}$ and $\boldsymbol{\psi}_{1,k}^{\cdot} \simeq \boldsymbol{\psi}_k$. Andrews and Patterson [173]
have used the expansion of (148) although differently for cod-
ing of images. All the quantities $\lambda_k, \boldsymbol{\phi}_k$ and $\boldsymbol{\psi}_k$ are calculated
first, then quantized and coded. The received image is simply

$$U^{\cdot} = \sum_{k=1}^{k_m} \lambda_k^{\cdot} \boldsymbol{\phi}_k^{\cdot} (\boldsymbol{\psi}_k^{\cdot})^T. \qquad (151)$$

70

TABLE II
SUMMARY OF IMAGE DATA COMPRESSION METHODS

Method	Typical Average Rates Bits/Pixel	Comments
Zero Memory Methods		Simple to implement
PCM	6–8	
Contrast Quantization	4–5	
Pseudorandom Noise – Quantization	4–5	
Line Interlace	4	
Dot Interlace	2–4	
Predictive Coding		
Delta Modulation	1	Performance poorer than DPCM over sample data for improvement.
Intraframe DPCM	2–3	Predictive methods are generally
Intraframe Adaptive DPCM	1–2	simple to implement, are sensitive
Interframe Conditional – Replenishment	1–2	to data statistics. Adaptive techniques improve performance
Interframe DPCM	1–1.5	substantially. Channel error
Interframe Adaptive DPCM	0.5–1	effects are commulative and severely degrade image quality.
Transform Coding		
Intraframe	1–1.5	Achieve high performance, small
Intraframe Adaptive	0.5–1	sensitivity to fluctuation in data
Interframe	0.5–1	statistics, channel and quantization
Interframe Adaptive	0.1–0.5	errors distributed over the image block. Easy to provide channel protection. Hardware complexity is high.
Hybrid Coding		
Intraframe	1–2	Achieve performance close to trans-
Intraframe Adaptive	0.5–1.5	form coding at moderate rates
Interframe	0.5–1	(.5 to 1 bit/pixel). Complexity
Interframe Adaptive	0.25–0.5	lies midway between transform coding and DPCM.

Bit rates of 2 bit/pel have been achieved at acceptable distortion levels. The method according to (149) and (150) should perform better, since the quantization error at any step is fed to the next step for correction. Compared to usual transform coding, SVD coding is not very attractive because the vectors ϕ_i, ψ_i have to be computed for each image.

In recent years AR models have been found to have extensive applications [198]. Their success has been notable in high resolution spectral estimation and in the theory of linear prediction. Recently, it has been shown [197] that the AR models can be useful in image data compression also.

From the theory of image formation, since the intensity distribution of an image is nonnegative, it can be considered as a power spectrum. Therefore its Fourier transform is an autocorrelation function. In AR modeling an underlying AR random process is realized such that the Fourier transform of the image is the autocorrelation of that random process. For simplicity we consider the one-dimensional case. It has been shown [197] that the discrete cosine transform of a positive sequence $\{u_m\}$

$$\gamma_k = \gamma_{-k} = \frac{1}{N} \sum_{m=0}^{N-1} u_m \cos \frac{\pi k}{N} \left(m + \frac{1}{2} \right), \quad 0 \leq k \leq N - 1 \tag{152}$$

is an autocorrelation sequence. Hence, there exists a p th-order

AR model, viz.

$$a(k) = \sum_{m=1}^{p} \alpha_m a(k - m) + \epsilon(k) \tag{153}$$

where $\epsilon(k)$ is a stationary zero-mean white noise process, such that its first $(p + 1)$ autocorrelations are the same as $\{\gamma_k, 0 \leq k \leq p\}$. The corresponding power spectrum of the sequence $\{a(k)\}$ is given by

$$s(x) = \beta^2 / |1 - \sum_{m=1}^{p} \alpha_m \exp \{-j2\pi mx\}|^2, \quad -\frac{1}{2} \leq x \leq \frac{1}{2} \tag{154}$$

$$\beta^2 \triangleq E[\epsilon^2(k)] = \gamma_0 - \sum_{m=1}^{p} \alpha_m \gamma(m). \tag{155}$$

The information in the image line $\{u_m\}$ is thus coded into the $(p + 1)$ coefficients α_m and β^2. The quantity $s(x)$ gives an interpolated estimate of the samples image sequence $\{u_m\}$. The α_m and β^2 may be obtained by solving a system of linear Toeplitz equations whose solution can be obtained via Levinson's algorithm [197]–[200], which gives the quantities ρ_m, known as reflection coefficients. These are less than 1 in magnitude and have been shown in speech synthesis [201], [202] to be more desirable for quantization. Fig. 40 shows

71

the AR coding algorithm and compares it with transform coding.

For highly correlated gray-level images, this method has only a marginal advantage over the cosine transform coding. However for binary and high contrast images (with few gray levels) this method performs much better than transform coding (Fig. 41). Hence it could be considered as a universal transform coding algorithm which could be used for transform coding of composite images. Further development is required to extend this method to two-dimensional block coding (rather than line by line).

IX. SUMMARY AND CONCLUSIONS

We have discussed the fundamentals as well as details of several basic and state of the art techniques in image data compression. Many of these techniques, e.g., predictive, transform and hybrid coding have been hardware implemented for image transmission/storage applications (see [9], [188]). Table II provides a summary of performance of the three classes of algorithms considered in detail here. Excluded from our specific discussion here is color image coding. The principles outlined here are valid for color images. However, the details differ substantially because of perceptual considerations in color. A recent survey article [53] addresses these issues.

Much of our discussion in this paper has been devoted to pel by pel reproduction of an image. In many applications such as image understanding systems, one desires to code only the description of the image. For example, if the various objects of the scene could be recognized by a machine, then it may suffice to synthesize a similar scene at the receiver from the description of the objects. Such a technique is called coding by synthesis. One method of coding by synthesis is to code the unrecognized objects pel by pel and synthesize the image background or other areas which may contain some easily identifiable texture such as grass, ivy, brick, or a nearly uniform background. Such an approach requires a marriage of image analysis and segmentation techniques with the pel by pel coding techniques discussed here. Future image coding advances seem to point in this direction.

BIBLIOGRAPHY AND COMMENTS

Section 1

Data compression has been a topic of immense interest in digital image processing. Several special issues and review papers have been devoted to this. For details, see

[1] Special Issue on Redundancy Reduction, *Proc. IEEE*, vol. 55, Mar. 1967.
[2] Special Issue of Digital Communications, *IEEE Commun. Tech.*, vol. COM-19, part I, Dec. 1971.
[3] T. S. Huang and O. J. Tretiak, Eds., *Picture Bandwidth Compression*. New York: Gordon and Breach, 1972.
[4] Special Issue of Image Bandwidth Compression, *IEEE Trans. Commun.*, vol. COM-25, Nov. 1977.
[5] L. D. Davisson and R. M. Gray, Eds., *Data Compression* (Benchmark Papers in Electrical Engineering and Computer Science). Stroudsberg, PA: Dowden Hutchinson & Ross, 1976.
[6] T. S. Huang, "PCM picture transmission," *IEEE Spectrum*, vol. 12, pp. 57–60, Dec. 1965.
[7] W. K. Pratt, *Digital Image Processing*. New York: Wiley, 1978, pp. 591–710.
[8] A. K. Jain, *Multidimensional Techniques in Digital Image Processing*. To be published.
[9] P. Camana, "Video bandwidth compression: A study in trade-offs," *IEEE Spectrum*, pp. 24–29, June 1979.
[10] W. K. Pratt, Ed., *Image Transmission Techniques*. New York: Academic Press, 1979.

[11] A. K. Jain, "Some new techniques in Image Processing," in *Image Science Mathematics*, C. O. Wilde and E. Barrett, Eds. North Hollywood, CA: West Periodical Co., 1977, pp. 201–223.

For entropy and probability measures of image data, see [10] and

[12] W. F. Schreiber, "The measurement of third order probability distributions of television signals," *IRE Trans. Inform. Theory*, vol. IT-2, pp. 94–105, Sept. 1956.

For Shannon's original work, see

[13] C. E. Shannon, "The mathematical theory of communication," Parts I and II, *Bell Syst. Tech. J.*, vol. 27, pp. 379 and 623, 1948. Also see, C. F. Shannon and W. Weaver, *The Mathematical Theory of Communication*. Urbana, IL: The University of Illinois Press, 1949.

Shannon's theory and the fundamentals of source coding and different encoding schemes can be found in textbooks on Information theory, e.g.,

[14] F. M. Reza, *An Introduction to Information Theory*. New York: McGraw-Hill, 1961.
[15] N. Abramson, *Information Theory and Coding*. New York: McGraw-Hill, 1963.
[16] R. G. Gallagher, *Information Theory and Reliable Communication*. New York: Wiley, 1968.

For visual fidelity criteria based on spatial frequency response, see Sakrison in [4, p. 1251] and

[17] J. L. Mannos and D. J. Sakrison, "The effects of a visual fidelity criterion on the encoding of images," *IEEE Trans. Inform. Theory*, vol. IT-20, pp. 525–236, July 1974.

For other related results on visual fidelity criterion and visual perception,

[18] D. H. Kelly, "Effects of sharp edges on the visibility of sinusoidal gratings," *J. Opt. Soc. Amer.*, vol. 60, pp. 98–103, Jan. 1970.
[19] V. R. Algazi, "The psycho-physics of vision and their relation to picture quality and coding limitations," *Acta Electron.*, vol. 19, no. 3, pp. 225–232, 1976.
[20] A. Netravali and B. Prasada, "Adaptive quantization of picture signals using spatial masking," *Proc. IEEE*, vol. 65, pp. 536–548, April 1977.
[21] Z. L. Budrikis, "Visual fidelity criterion and modeling," *Proc. IEEE*, vol. 60, pp. 771–779, July 1972.
[22] T. N. Cornsweet, *Visual Perception*. New York: Academic Press, 1970.

For effects of frame rate reduction, interlacing and related methods of compression, see

[23] M. W. Baldwin, "Demonstration of some visual effects of using frame storage in television transmission," in *IRE Conv. Rec.*, p. 107, 1958.
[24] R. C. Brainard, F. W. Mounts, and B. Prasada, "Low resolution TV: Subjective effects of frame repetition and picture replenishment," *Bell Syst. Tech. J.*, vol. 56, no. 1, pp. 261–271, Jan. 1967.
[25] S. Deutsch, "Pseudo-random dot scan television systems," *IEEE Trans. Broadcasting*, vol. BC-11, pp. 11–21, July 1965.
[26] G. G. Gouriet, "Dot Interlaced Television," *Electron. Eng.*, vol. 24, no. 290, pp. 166–171, Apr. 1952.

Section II

[27] S. P. Lloyd, "Least squares quantization in PCM," unpublished memorandum, Bell Laboratories, 1957 (Copy available by writing the author).
[28] J. Max, "Quantizing for minimum distortion," *IRE Trans. Inform. Theory*, vol. IT-6, pp. 7–12, 1960.
[29] P. F. Panter and W. Dite, "Quantizing distortion in pulse-code modulation with nonuniform spacing levels," *Proc. IRE*, vol. 39, pp. 44–48, 1951.

[30] B. Smith, "Instantaneous companding of quantizing signals," *Bell Syst. Tech. J.*, vol. 27, pp. 446–472, 1948.

[31] G. M. Roe, "Quantizing for minimum distortion," *IEEE Trans. Inform. Theory*, vol. IT-10, pp. 384–385, 1964.

[32] V. R. Algazi, "Useful approximations to optimum quantization," *IEEE Trans. Commun.*, vol. COM-14, pp. 297–301, 1966.

[33] T. J. Goblick and J. L. Holsinger, "Analog source digitization: A comparison of theory and practice," *IEEE Trans. Inform. Theory*, vol. IT-13, pp. 323–326, Apr. 1967.

[34] H. Gish and J. N. Pierce, "Asymptotically efficient quantization," *IEEE Trans. Inform. Theory*, vol. IT-14, pp. 676–681, 1968.

[35] T. Berger, *Rate Distortion Theory*. Englewood Cliffs, NJ: Prentice-Hall, 1971.

[36] ——, "Optimum quantizers and permutation codes," *IEEE Trans. Inform. Theory*, vol. IT-16, pp. 759–765, Nov. 1972.

[37] A. N. Netravali and R. Saigal, "An algorithm for the design of optimum quantizers," *Bell Syst. Tech. J.*, vol. 55, pp. 1423–1435, Nov. 1976.

[38] D. K. Sharma, "Design of absolutely optimal quantizers for a wide class of distortion measures," *IEEE Trans. Inform Theory*, vol. IT-24, pp. 693–702, Nov. 1978.

[39] N. C. Gallagher, Jr., "Quantizing schemes for the discrete fourier transform of a random time-series," *IEEE Trans. Inform. Theory*, vol. IT-24, pp. 156–163, Mar. 1978.

[40] W. A. Pearlman, "Quantizing error bounds for computer generated holograms," Stanford University Information Systems Laboratory, Stanford, CA, Tech. Rep. 6 503-1, Aug. 1974. Also see Pearlman and Gray, *IEEE Trans. Inform. Theory*, vol. IT-24, pp. 683–692, Nov. 1978.

[41] F. W. Scoville and T. S. Huang, "The subjective effect of spatial and brightness quantization in PCM picture transmission," *NEREM Rec.*, pp. 234–235, 1965.

[42] S. Hecht, "The visual discrimination of intensity and the Weber–Fechner law," *J. Gen. Physiol.*, vol. 7, p. 241, 1924.

[43] F. Kretz, "Subjectively optimal quantization of pictures," *IEEE Trans. Commun.*, vol. COM-23, pp. 1288–1292, Nov. 1975.

[44] L. G. Roberts, "Picture coding using pseudo-random noise," *IRE Trans. Inf. Theory*, vol. IT-8, pp. 145–154, Feb. 1962.

[45] J. E. Thompson and J. J. Sparkes, "A pseudo-random quantizer for television signals," *Proc. IEEE*, vol. 55, pp. 353–355, Mar. 1967.

[46] J. O. Limb, "Design of dither waveforms for quantized visual signals," *Bell Syst. Tech J.*, vol. 48, pp. 2555–2583, Sept. 1969.

[47] B. Lippel, M. Kurland, and A. H. March, "Ordered dither patterns for coarse quantization of pictures," *Proc. IEEE*, vol. 59, pp. 429–431, Mar. 1971.

[48] B. Lippel and M. Kurland, "The effects of dither on luminance quantization of pictures," *IEEE Trans. Commun. Tech.*, vol. COM-19, pp. 879–889, Dec. 1971.

[49] J. E. Thompson, "A 36-MBIT/S television coder employing pseudorandom quantization," *IEEE Trans. Commun. Tech.*, vol. COM-19, pp. 872–879, Dec. 1971.

[50] C. N. Judice, "Digital video: A buffer-controlled dither processor for animated images," *IEEE Trans. Commun.*, vol. COM-25, pp. 1433–1440, Nov. 1977.

[51] P. G. Roetling, "Halftone method with edge enhancement and moiré suppression," *J. Opt. Soc. Amer.*, vol. 66, pp. 985–989, 1976.

[52] A. K. Jain and W. K. Pratt, "Color image quantization," in *Nat. Telecommunication Conf. 1972 Rec.* (Houston, TX), Dec. 1972 (IEEE Publication No. 72CH0601-S-NTC).

[53] J. O. Limb, C. B. Rubinstein, and J. E. Thompson, "Digital coding of color video signals," *IEEE Trans. Commun.*, vol. COM-25, pp. 1329–1385, Nov. 1977.

Section III

For some initial work on predictive coding, see

[54] B. N. Oliver, "Efficient coding," *Bell Syst. Tech. J.*, vol. 31, pp. 724–750, July 1952.

[55] C. W. Harrison, "Experiments with linear prediction in television," *Bell Syst. Tech. J.*, pp. 764–768, July 1952.

[56] P. Elias, "Predictive Coding—Part I and Part II," *IRE Trans. Inform. Theory*, vol. IT-1, pp. 16–33, Mar. 1955.

For delta modulation analysis of Markov and Wiener processes, see

[57] D. Slepian, "On delta modulation," *Bell Syst. Tech. J.*, vol. 51, pp. 2101–2137, Dec. 1972.

[58] T. L. Fine, "The response of a particular nonlinear system with feedback to each of two random processes," *IEEE Trans. Inform. Theory*, vol. 14, pp. 255–264, Mar. 1968.

For applications of delta modulation in transmission of signals and video images, see

[59] R. Steele, *Delta Modulation Systems*. New York: Wiley, 1975.

[60] J. B. O'Neal, Jr., "Delta modulation quantizing noise—Analytic and computer simulation results for gaussian and television inputs signals," *Bell Syst. Tech. J.*, vol. 45, pp. 117–141, Jan. 1966.

[61] R. S. Bosworth and J. C. Candy, "A companded one-bit coder for PICTUREPHONE transmission," *Bell Syst. Tech. J.*, vol. 58, no. 5, pp. 1459–1479, May 1969.

[62] H. R. Schindler, "Delta modulation, " *IEEE Spectrum*, vol. 7, pp. 69–78, Oct. 1970.

[63] I. M. Paz, G. C. Collins, and B. H. Batson, "A tri-state delta modulator for run-length encoding of video," *Proc. Nat. Telecomm. Conf.* (Dallas, TX), vol. I, pp. 6.3-1–6.3-6, Nov. 1976.

For adaptive delta modulation algorithms and applications to image transmission, see

[64] J. E. Abate, "Linear and adaptive delta modulation," *Proc. IEEE*, vol. 55, pp. 298–308, Mar. 1967.

[65] C. L. Song, J. Garodnick, and D. L. Schilling, "A variable step-size robust delta modulator," *IEEE Trans. Commun.*, vol. COM-19, pp. 1033–1044, Dec. 1971.

[66] N. S. Jayant, "Adaptive delta modulation with one bit memory," *Bell Syst. Tech. J.*, vol. 49, pp. 321–342, Mar. 1970.

[67] D. Mitra, "Mathematical analysis of an adaptive quantizer," *Bell Syst. Tech. J.*, vol. 53, no. 5, pp. 867–896, May 1974.

[68] C. C. Cutler, "Delayed encoding: Stabilizer for adaptive coders," *IEEE Trans. Commun.*, vol. COM-19, pp. 898–906, Dec. 1971.

[69] T. R. Lei, N. Scheinberg, and D. L. Schilling, "Adaptive delta modulation systems for video encoding," *IEEE Trans. Commun.*, vol. COM-25, Nov. 1977.

The original design of DPCM systems was developed in

[70] C. C. Culter, "Differential quantization of communication systems," U. S. Patent 2 605 361, July 29, 1952.

For other early work in DPCM and its applications in image data compression see [54], [55] and

[71] R. E. Graham, "Predictive quantization of television signals," in *IRE Wescon Conv. Rec.*, Part 4, pp. 147–156, Aug. 1958.

[72] J. B. O'Neal, Jr., "Predictive quantizing systems (differential pulse code modulation) for the transmission of television signals," *Bell Syst. Tech. J.*, vol. 45, pp. 689–721, May–June 1966.

For more recent work on DPCM of two-dimensional images, see

[73] A. Habibi, "Comparison of the nth-order DPCM encoder with linear transformations and block quantization techniques," *IEEE Trans. Commun. Tech.*, vol. COM-19, pp. 948–956, Dec. 1971.

[74] S. K. Goyal and J. B. O'Neal, Jr., "Entropy coded differential pulse code modulation for television," *IEEE Trans. Commun.*, vol. COM-23, pp. 660–666, June 1975.

[75] J. B. O'Neal, Jr., "Differential pulse-code modulation (DPCM) with entropy coding," *IEEE Trans. Inform. Theory*, vol. IT-21, pp. 169–174, Mar. 1976.

[76] R. Lippmann, "Influence of channel errors on DPCM picture coding," *Acta Electron.*, vol. 19, no. 4, pp. 289–294, 1976.

[77] J. B. O'Neal, Jr., and T. R. Natarajan, "Coding isotropic images," *IEEE Trans. Inform. Theory*, vol. IT-23, pp. 697–707, Nov. 1977.

For DPCM techniques based on visual fidelity, see [20] and

[78] J. C. Candy and R. H. Bosworth, "Methods for designing differential quantizers based on subjective evaluations of edge busyness," *Bell Syst. Tech. J.*, vol. 51, no. 7, pp. 1495–1516, 1972.

[79] A. N. Netravali, "On quantizers for DPCM coding of picture signals," *IEEE Trans. Inform. Theory*, vol. IT-23, pp. 360–370, May 1977.

[80] D. K. Sharma and A. N. Netravali, "Design of quantizers for DPCM coding of picture signals," *IEEE Trans. Commun.*, vol. COM-25, pp. 1267–1274, Nov. 1977.

Predictive coding techniques have been studied extensively for interframe image data compression. Greater details of the techniques described in the text may be found in

[81] F. W. Mounts, "A video encoding system with conditional picture-element replenishment," *Bell Syst. Tech. J.*, vol. 48, pp. 2545–2554, Sept. 1969.
[82] R.F.W. Pease and J. O. Limb, "Exchange of spatial and temporal resolution in television coding," *Bell Syst. Tech. J.*, vol. 50, pp. 191–200, Jan. 1971.
[83] J. O. Limb and R.F.W. Pease, "A simple interframe coder for video telephony," *Bell Syst. Tech. J.*, vol. 50, pp. 1877–1888, Aug. 1971.
[84] J. C. Candy *et al.*, "Transmitting television as clusters of frame-to-frame differences," *Bell Syst. Tech. J.*, vol. 50, pp. 1889–1917, Aug. 1971.
[85] B. G. Haskell *et al.*, "Interframe coding of video-telephone pictures," *Proc. IEEE*, vol. 60, pp. 792–800, July 1972.
[86] J. O. Limb *et al.*, "Combining intraframe and frame-to-frame coding for television," *Bell Syst. Tech. J.*, vol. 53, pp. 1137–1173, Aug. 1974.
[87] D. J. Connor and J. O. Limb, "Properties of frame-difference signals generated by moving images," *IEEE Trans. Commun.*, vol. COM-22, p. 1564, Oct. 1974.
[88] B. G. Haskell, "Entropy measurements for nonadaptive and adaptive frame-to-frame, linear predictive coding of videotelephone signals," *Bell Syst. Tech. J.*, vol. 54, pp. 1155–1175, Aug. 1975.
[89] B. G. Haskell and R. L. Schmidt, "A low bit-rate interframe coder for video-telephone," *Bell Syst. Tech. J.*, vol. 54, pp. 1475–1495, Oct. 1975.
[90] B. G. Haskell *et al.*, "Interframe coding of 525-line, monochrome television at 1.5 Mbits/s," *IEEE Trans. Commun.*, vol. COM-25, pp. 1339–1348, Nov. 1977.

For other designs and considerations of interframe DPCM, see

[91] H. Yasuda *et al.*, "Transmitting 4-MHz TV signals by combinational difference coding," *IEEE Trans. Commun.*, vol. COM-25, pp. 508–516, May 1977.
[92] T. Ishiguro *et al.*, "Composite interframe coding of NTSC color television signals," *Nat. Telecommunications Conf.* (Dallas, TX), pp. 6.4-1–6.4-5, 1976.
[93] J. O. Limb *et al.*, "Digital coding of color video signals—A review," *IEEE Trans. Commun.*, vol. COM-25, pp. 1349-1385, Nov. 1977.

For adaptive interframe predictive coding methods, see [84], [86] and

[94] F. Rocca and S. Zanoletti, "Bandwidth reduction via movement compensation on a model of the random video process," *IEEE Trans. Commun.*, vol. COM-20, pp. 960–965, Oct. 1972.
[95] C. Cafforio and F. Rocca, "Methods for measuring small displacements of television images," *IEEE Trans. Inform. Theory*, vol. IT-22, pp. 573–579, Sept. 1976.
[96] S. Brofferio and F. Rocca, "Interframe redundancy reduction of video signals generated by translating objects," *IEEE Trans. Commun.*, pp. 448–455, Apr. 1977.
[97] J. R. Jain and A. K. Jain, "Interframe adaptive data compression techniques for images," Sig. & Image Proc. Lab., Dep. Elec. and Comput. Eng., Univ. CA, Davis, Aug. 1979.
Also see, J. R. Jain, Ph.D. dissertation, Dep. Elec. Eng., SUNY, Buffalo, Sept. 1979.

For predictive coding of facsimile images, different prediction rules and data compression results, see

[98] H. Kobayashi and L. R. Bahl, "Image data compression by predictive coding I: Prediction algorithms" and "II: Encoding algorithms," *IBM J. Res. Dev.*, vol. 18, no. 2, pp. 164–179, Mar. 1974.
[99] N. J. Nilsson, *Learning Machines*. New York: McGraw-Hill, 1965.
[100] K. S. Fu, "Learning control systems—Review and outlook," *IEEE Trans. Automat. Contr.*, vol. AC-15, p. 210, 1970.

[101] T. S. Huang, "Coding of two tone images," *IEEE Trans. Commun.*, vol. COM-25, pp. 1406–1424, Nov. 1977.
[102] D. Preuss, "Two-dimensional facsimile source coding based on Markov Model," *Nachrichtentech. Z.*, vol. 28, pp. 358–363, Oct. 1975.
Also see, H. G. Musmann and D. Preuss, "Comparison of redundancy rendering codes for facsimile transmission of documents," *IEEE Trans. Commun.*, vol. COM-25, no. 11, pp. 1425–1433, Nov. 1977.
[103] R. B. Arps, "Entropy of printed matter at the threshold of legibility for efficient coding in digital image processing," Stanford Electronics Lab., Stanford, CA, Rep. No. 31, 1969.

For other encoding schemes with applications to facsimile image data, see Huang [3, p. 221] and

[104] J. Capon, "A probabilistic model for run-length coding of pictures," *IRE Trans. Inform. Theory*, vol. IT-5, pp. 157–163, Dec. 1959.
[105] S. W. Golomb, "Run length encodings," *IEEE Trans. Inform. Theory*, vol. IT-12, pp. 399–401, July, 1966.
[106] J. O. Limb, "Efficiency of variable length binary encoding," in *Proc. UMR Mervin J. Kelly Communications Conf.* (Rolla MO), pp. 13.3-1–13.3-9, Oct. 1970.
[107] T. S. Huang, "An upper bound on entropy of runlength coding," *IEEE Trans. Inform. Theory*, vol. IT-21, pp. 00–00, Sept. 1975.
[108] H. Meyr, H. G. Rosdolski and T. S. Huang, "Optimum runlength codes," *IEEE Trans. Commun.*, vol. COM-22, pp. 00–00, June 1974.
[109] D. A. Huffman, "A method for the construction of minimum redundancy codes," *Proc. IRE*, vol. 40, pp. 1098–1101, Sept. 1952.
[110] A. E. Laemmel, "Coding processes for bandwidth reduction in picture transmission," Microwave Res. Inst., Poly. Inst. Brooklyn, NY, Rep. R-246-51, PIB-187, Aug. 30, 1951.

Other references for Section III

[111] N. E. Nahi and T. Asseffi, "Bayesian recursive estimation," *IEEE Trans. Comput.*, vol. C-21, pp. 734–738, July 1972.
[112] S. R. Powell and L. M. Silverman, "Modelling of two-dimensional random fields with application to image restoration," *IEEE Trans. Automat. Contr.*, vol. AC-19, pp. 8–13, Feb. 1974.
[113] R. Bernstein, Ed., *Digital Image Processing for Remote Sensing*. New York: IEEE Press, 1978.
[114] G. L. Turin, "An introduction to matched filters," *IRE Trans. Inform. Theory*, vol. IT-6; pp. 311–329, June 1960.

Section IV

For the optimality of the KL transform in one-dimensional transform coding, bit allocations, and related results see

[115] J.J.Y. Huang and P. M. Schultheiss, "Block quantization of correlated Gaussian random variables," *IEEE Trans. Commun. Syst.*, pp. 280–296, Sept. 1963.
[116] A. Segall, "Bit allocation and encoding for vector sources," *IEEE Trans. Inform. Theory*, vol. IT-22, pp. 162–169, Mar. 1976.
[117] B. Fox, "Discrete optimization via marginal analysis," *Management Sci.*, vol. 13, pp. 201–216, Nov. 1966.
[118] A. K. Jain and S. H. Wang, "Stochastic image models and hybrid coding," Dep. Elec. Eng., SUNY, Buffalo, Final Rep., NOSC Contract N00953-77-C-003MJE, Oct. 1977.

The KL transform is often also called the method of *Principal Components* or the *Hotelling Transform* due to original work of Hotelling reported in

[119] H. Hotelling, "Analysis of a complex of statistical variables into principal components," *J. Educ. Psychology*, vol. 24, pp. 417–441, and 498–520, 1933.

For theory of KL transform and its further historic development see

[120] H. Karhunen, "Ueber Lineare Methoden in der Wahrscheinlichkeitsrechnung," *Ann. Acad. Science Fenn*, Ser. A.I. 37,

Helsinki, 1947. (see translation by I. Selin, The Rand Corp., Doc. T-131, Aug. 11, 1960.)

[121] M. Loeve, "Fonctions aleatoires de seconde ordre," in P. Levy, *Processus Stochastiques et Mouvement Brownien.* Paris, France: Hermann, 1948.
Also see, M. Loeve, *Probability Theory.* New York: Van Nostrand, pp. 478–479, 1960.

[122] A. Koschman, "On the filtering of nonstationary time series," in *Proc. Nat. Electron Conf.*, p. 126, 1954.

[123] J. L. Brown, Jr., "Mean square truncation error in series expansion of random functions," *J. SIAM*, vol. 8, pp. 18–32, Mar. 1960.

[124] I. Selin, *Detection Theory.* Princeton, NJ: Princeton University Press, 1965.

[125] R. E. Totty and J. C. Hancock, "On optimum-finite dimensional signal representation," in *Proc. 1st Annu. Allerton Conf. on Circuits and System Theory*, 1963.

[126] S. Wantanabe, "Karhunen-Loeve expansion and factor analysis, theoretical remarks and applications," *Prague Conf. Inform. Theory, Statistics, Decision Functions, and Random Processes* (Prague, Czechoslovakia), pp. 635–660, 1965.

[127] W. D. Ray and R. M. Driver, "Further decomposition of the Karhunen Loeve series representation of a stationary random process," *IEEE Trans. Inform. Theory*, vol. IT-11, pp. 663–668, Nov. 1970.

For results on energy compaction properties see Wantanabe [126] and

[128] H. P. Kramer and M. V. Mathews, "A linear coding for transmitting a set of correlated signals," *IRE Trans. Inform. Theory*, vol. IT-2, pp. 41–46, Sept. 1956.

[129] V. R. Algazi and D. J. Sakrison, "On the Optimality of Karhunen-Loeve Expansion," *IEEE Trans. Inform. Theory*, pp. 319–321, Mar. 1969.

For rate distortion aspects of KL transform coding see [35] and

[130] L. D. Davisson, "Rate distortion theory and application," *Proc. IEEE*, vol. 60, pp. 800–808, July 1972.

For Cosine, Sine, and other sinusoidal transforms, their relationship to the KL transforms and asymptotic properties see

[131] N. Ahmed, T. Natarajan, and K. R. Rao, "Discrete cosine transform," *IEEE Trans. Comput.*, vol. C-23, pp. 90–93, Jan. 1974.

[132] Y. Yemini and J. Pearl, "Asymptotic properties of discrete unitary transforms," School Eng. Appl. Sci., UCLA, Los Angeles, UCLA-ENG-REPORT-7566, Nov. 1975.

[133] M. Hamidi and J. Pearl, "Comparison of the cosine and Fourier transforms of Markov-1 signals," *IEEE Trans. Acoust., Speech, Signal Processing*, vol. ASSP-24, pp. 428–429, Oct. 1976.

[134] R. M. Gray, "Toeplitz and circulant matrices: A review," Stanford Univ. Stanford, CA, Tech. Rep. SV-SEL-71-032, June 1971.
Also see, "On the asymptotic eigenvalue distribution of Toeplitz matrices," *IEEE Trans. Inform. Theory*, vol. IT-18, pp. 725–730, Nov. 1972.

[135] A. K. Jain, "Some new techniques in image processing," in *Proc. Symp. on Current Mathematical Problems in Image Science* (Naval Post Graduate School, Monterey, CA) Nov. 1976.

[136] A. K. Jain, "A sinusoidal family of unitary transforms," *IEEE Trans. Pattern Anal. Machine Intell.*, vol. PAMI-1, pp. 356–365, Oct. 1979.

For details of the Fast KL transform and related results see [135] and

[137] A. K. Jain, "A fast Karhunen-Loeve transform for a class of stochastic processes," *IEEE Trans. Commun.*, vol. COM-24, pp. 1023–1029, Sept. 1976.

[138] A. K. Jain, S. H. Wang, and Y. Z. Liao, "Fast KL transform data compression studies," *National Telecomm. Conf.*, Dallas, Texas, Nov-Dec. 1976.

[139] A. Z. Meiri, "The pinned Karhunen-Loeve transform of a two-dimensional Gauss-Markov field," in *Proc. 1976 SPIE Advances in Image Transmission Techniques* (San Diego, CA), vol. 87, pp. 155–164, Aug. 1976.

For fast transforms and the general theory of transforms see

[140] N. Ahmed and K. R. Rao, *Orthogonal Transforms for Digital Signal Processing.* New York: Springer Verlag, 1975.

[141] E. O. Brigham, *The Fast Fourier Transform.* Englewood Cliffs, NJ: Prentice-Hall, 1974.

[142] H. F. Harmuth, *Transmission of Information by Orthogonal Signals.* New York: Springer Verlag, 1970.

[143] B. S. Nagy, *Introduction to Real Functions and Orthogonal Expansions.* New York: Oxford Univ. Press, 1965.

[144] *Proc. Symp. Applications of Walsh Functions* (University of Maryland, IEEE-EMC), 1970-1973, and Catholic Univ. America, 1974.

Section V

Transform coding of two-dimensional images was introduced by Andrews and Pratt. The original work is reported in

[145] H. C. Andrews and W. K. Pratt, "Fourier transform coding of images," in *Proc. Hawaii Int. Conf. System Science*, pp. 677-679, Jan. 1968.

[146] H. C. Andrews, J. Kane, and W. K. Pratt, "Hadamard transform image coding," *Proc. IEEE*, vol. 57, pp. 58-68, Jan. 1969.

[147] W. K. Pratt and H. C. Andrews, "Application of Fourier-Hadamard transformation to bandwidth compression," in *Picture Bandwidth Compression*, T. S. Huang and O. J. Tretiak, Eds. New York: Gordon and Breach, 1972, pp. 515-554.

[148] H. C. Andrews and W. K. Pratt, "Transform image coding," in *Proceedings Computer Processing Communications.* New York: Polytechnic Press, 1969. pp. 63-84.

[149] H. C. Andrews, *Computer Techniques in Image Processing.* New York: Academic Press, 1970.

For subsequent developments and refinements, see

[150] A. Habibi and P. A. Wintz, "Image coding by linear transformation and block quantization," *IEEE Trans. Commun. Tech.*, vol. COM-19, pp. 50–63, Feb. 1971.

[151] H. Enomoto and K. Shibata, "Orthogonal transform coding system for television signals," *IEEE Trans. Electromagn. Compat.*, Special Issue on Walsh Functions, vol. EMC-13, pp. 11–17, Aug. 1971.

[152] J. W. Woods and T. S. Huang, "Picture bandwidth compression by linear transformation and block quantization," in *Picture Bandwidth Compression*, T. S. Huang and O. J. Tretiak, Eds. New York: Gordon and Breach, 1972, pp. 555–573.

[153] P. A. Wintz, "Transform picture coding," *Proc. IEEE*, vol. 60, pp. 809–823, July 1972.

[154] G. B. Anderson and T. S. Huang, "Piecewise Fourier transformation for picture bandwidth compression," *IEEE Trans. Commun.*, vol. COM-20, pp. 388–491, June 1972.

[155] W. K. Pratt, W. H. Chen, and L. R. Welch, "Slant transform image coding," *IEEE Trans. Commun.*, vol. COM-22, pp. 1075–1093, Aug. 1974.

[156] A. K. Jain, "A fast Karhunen-Loeve transform for finite discrete images," in *Proc. Nat. Electronics Conf.* (Chicago, IL), pp. 322–328, Oct. 1974.

[157] K. R. Rao, M. A. Narasimhan, and Revuluri, "Image Data Processing by Hadamard-Haar Transform," *IEEE Trans. Comput.*, vol. C-23, pp. 888–896, Sept. 1975.

[158] M. Tasto and P. A. Wintz, "Image coding by adaptive block quantization," *IEEE Trans. Commun. Tech.*, vol. COM-19, pp. 956–972, Dec. 1971.

[159] H. C. Andrews and A. G. Tescher, "The role of adaptive phase coding in two and three dimensional Fourier and Walsh image compression," in *Proc. Walsh Function Symp.* (Washington, DC), Mar. 1974.
Also see, A. G. Tescher, "The role of phase in adaptive image coding," Ph.D. dissertation, Univ. Southern California, Los Angeles, Jan. 1974.

[160] J. I. Gimlett, "Use of activity classes in adaptive transform image coding," *IEEE Trans. Commun.*, vol. COM-23, pp. 785–786, July 1975.

[161] R. V. Cox and A. G. Tescher, "Channel rate equalization techniques for adaptive transform coder," *Proc. SPIE Conf. Advances in Image Transmission Techniques* (San Diego, CA), Aug. 1976.

[162] C. Reader, "Intraframe and interframe adaptive transform coding," *Proc. SPIE*, vol. 66, pp. 108–118, Aug. 1975.

[163] W. H. Chen and C. H. Smith, "Adaptive coding of monochrome and color images," *IEEE Trans. Commun.*, vol. COM-25, pp. 1285–1292, Nov. 1977.

[164] J. K. Yan and D. J. Sakrison, "Encoding of images based on a two component source model," *IEEE Trans. Commun.*, vol. COM-25, pp. 1315–1322, Nov. 1977.

[165] A. Habibi, "Survey of adaptive image coding techniques," *IEEE Trans. Commun.*, vol. COM-25, pp. 1275–1284, Nov. 1977.

For three-dimensional transform coding with applications in data compression of color images, medical X-ray images, etc., see

[166] W. K. Pratt, "Spatial transform coding of color images," *IEEE Trans. Commun. Tech.*, vol. COM-19, pp. 980–982, Dec. 1971.

[167] J. A. Rose and W. K. Pratt, "Theoretical performance models for interframe transform and hybrid transform/DPCM coders," in *Proc. SPIE Conf. Advances in Image Transmission Techniques* (San Diego, CA), Aug. 1976.

[168] J. A. Roese, W. K. Pratt, and G. S. Robinson, "Interframe cosine transform image coding," *IEEE Trans. Commun.*, vol. COM-25, pp. 1329–1338, Nov. 1977.

[169] J. R. Jain, A. K. Jain, and R. A. Robb, "Data compression of multidimensional X-ray Images," to be published.

[170] T. R. Natrajan and N. Ahmed, "On interframe transform coding," *IEEE Trans. Commun.*, vol. COM-25, pp. 1323–1329, Nov. 1977.

For other topics related to transform image coding, see

[171] W. K. Pratt, "Transform image coding spectrum extrapolation," in *Proc. Hawaii Systems Science Conf.*, Jan. 1974.

[172] M. N. Huhns, "Optimum restoration of quantized correlated signals," University of Southern California, Los Angeles, Image Processing Institute, USCIPI 600, Aug. 1975.

[173] H. C. Andrews and C. L. Patterson, "Singular value decomposition (SVD) image coding," *IEEE Trans. Commun.*, vol. COM-24, pp. 425–432, Apr. 1976.

For contour and boundary coding algorithms, see

[174] W. F. Schreiber and C. F. Knapp, "TV bandwidth reduction by digital coding," *IRE Nat. Conv. Rec.*, vol. 6, part 4, pp. 88–89, 1958.

[175] W. F. Schreiber, C. F. Knapp, and N. D. Kay, "Synthetic highs: An experimental TV bandwidth reduction system," *J. Soc. Motion Pict. Telev. Eng.*, vol. 68, pp. 525–537, Aug. 1959.

[176] H. Freeman, "On the encoding of arbitrary geometric configurations," *IRE Trans. Electron. Comput.*, vol. EC-10, pp. 260–268, June 1961.

[177] D. N. Graham, "Image transmission by two-dimensional contour coding," *Proc. IEEE*, vol. 55, pp. 336–346, Mar. 1967.

[178] H. Freeman, "Boundary encoding and processing," in *Picture Processing and Psychopictorics*, B. S. Lipkin and A. Rosenfeld, Eds. New York: Academic Press, pp. 241–266.

[179] P. A. Wintz and L. C. Wilkins, "Studies on data compression, Part I: Picture coding by contours, Part II: Error analysis of run-length codes," Purdue University, Lafayette, IN, School of Engineering, Rep. TR-EE-70-17, Sept. 1970.

[180] L. C. Wilkins and P. A. Wintz, "Image coding by coding contours," *Proc. Int. Conf. Communications* (San Francisco, CA), vol. 1, 1970.

[181] W. F. Schreiber, T. S. Huang, and O. J. Tretiak, "Contour coding of images," in *Picture Bandwidth Compression*, T. S. Huang and O. J. Tretiak, Eds. New York: Gordon and Breach, pp. 443–448, 1972.

Section VI

[182] A. Habibi, "Hybrid coding of pictorial data," *IEEE Trans. Commun.*, vol. COM-22, pp. 614–624, May 1974.

[183] R. A. Jones, "Adaptive hybrid picture coding," *Proc. SPIE*, vol. 87, pp. 247–255, Aug. 1976.

For detailed analysis of hybrid coding via stochastic models and simulation results, see Jain and Wang [118] and

[184] S. H. Wang, "Applications of stochastic models for image data compression," Ph.D. dissertation, Dep. Elec. Eng., State Univ. New York, Buffalo, Sept. 1979.

For interframe hybrid coding and its applications, see Roese *et al.* [168], Jain *et al.* [97]. For other hybrid processing

applications, see

[185] A. K. Jain, "A semicausal model for recursive filtering of two-dimensional images," *IEEE Trans. Comput.*, vol. C-26, pp. 343–350, Apr. 1977.

[186] A. K. Jain, "Partial differential equations and finite difference methods in image processing, Part I: Image representation," *J. Optimiz. Theory Appl.*, vol. 23, pp. 65–91, Sept. 1977.

[187] A. K. Jain and J. R. Jain, "Partial differential equations and finite difference methods in image processing, Part II: Image restoration," *IEEE Trans. Automat. Contr.*, vol. AC-23, pp. 817–834, Oct. 1978.

[188] R. W. Means, E. H. Wrench, and H. J. Whitehouse, "Image transmission via spread spectrum techniques," Naval Ocean Systems Center, San Diego, CA, ARPA Quarterly Tech. Rep. ARPA-QR6, Jan.–Dec. 1975.
Also see, ARPA-QR8, Annu. Rep., Jan–Dec. 1975.

For variance estimation in DPCM, see

[189] P. Castellino, G. Madena, L. Nebbia, and C. Sengliala, "Bit rate reduction by automatic adaptation of quantizer step-size in DPCM systems," in *Proc. 1974 Int. Zurich Sem. Digital Communications*, pp. B6(1)–B6(6), 1974.

Section VII

Use of Fourier transform theory on finite Abelian groups, to find the optimal mean-square encoding rule β for nonredundant codes ($n = k$) is reported in

[190] T. R. Crimmins, H. M. Horwitz, C. J. Palermo, and R. V. Palermo, "Minimization of mean square error for data transmitted via group codes," *IEEE Trans. Inform. Theory*, vol. IT-15, pp. 72–78, Jan. 1969.

[191] T. R. Crimmins and H. M. Horwitz, "Mean square error optimum coset leaders for group codes," *IEEE Trans. Inform. Theory*, vol. IT-16, pp. 429–432, July 1970.

Extension to include redundant codes ($n \geqslant k$) and the optimal mean-square decoding rule was proposed in

[192] G. A. Wolf, "The optimum mean square estimate for decoding binary block codes," Ph.D. dissertation, Dep. Elec. Eng., Univ. Wisconsin, Madison, 1973.
Also see, G. A. Wolf and R. Redinbo, *IEEE Trans. Inform. Theory*, vol. IT-20, pp. 344–351, May 1974.

Extension of these results to optimize PCM and image transform coding methods are discussed in [97] and

[193] J. R. Jain and A. K. Jain, "Optimization of image data compression algorithms for transmission over noisy channels," Presented at Int. Picture Coding Symp., Ipswich, U.K., July 1979. (To be published.)

Other designs of mean-square quantizers cascaded to noisy channels (with a fixed encoding rule) have been considered for PCM transmission, e.g., see

[194] A. J. Kurtenbach and P. A. Wintz, "Quantizing for noisy channels," *IEEE Trans. Commun. Tech.*, vol. COM-17, pp. 291–302, Apr. 1969.

For other related results, see

[195] Y. Yamaguchi and T. S. Huang, "Optimum binary fixed length block codes," Research Lab of Electronics, Massachusetts Institute of Technology, Cambridge, MA, Quarterly Report, vol. 78, July 1965.

[196] W. Rudin, *Fourier Analysis on Groups*. New York: Interscience, 1967.

Section VIII

[197] A. K. Jain and S. Ranganath, "Image coding by autoregressive synthesis," in *Proc. IEEE ICASSP* (Denver, CO), Apr. 1980.

[198] J. Makhoul, "Linear prediction: A tutorial review," *Proc. IEEE*, vol. 63, pp. 561–580, Apr. 1975.

[199] J. P. Burg, "Maximum entropy spectral analysis," Ph.D. disserta-

tion, Stanford University, Stanford, CA, 1975.

[200] T. J. Ulrych and T. N. Bishop, "Maximum entropy spectral analysis and autoregressive decomposition," *Rev. Geophysics Space Phys.*, vol. 13, pp. 183–200, Feb. 1975.

[201] J. D. Markel and A. H. Gray, "On autocorrelation equations as applied to speech analysis," *IEEE Trans. Audio and Electro-acoustics*, vol. AU-21, #2, pp. 69–77, April 1973.

[202] R. Viswanathan and J. Makhoul, "Quantization properties of transmission parameters in linear prediction systems," *IEEE Trans. Acoust., Speech, Signal Processing*, vol. ASSP-23, pp. 309–321, June 1975.

Section IX

For variable velocity scanning, pseudorandom scanning, interpolative coding, variable knot splines, SVD, and other methods, see

[203] E. E. Wright, "Velocity modulation in television," *Proc. Phys. Soc. (London)* vol. 46, p. 512–514, July 1934.

[204] M. P. Beddoes, "Experiments with slope feedback coder for TV compression," *IRE Trans. Broadcasting*, vol. BC-7, pp. 12–28, Mar. 1961.

[205] T. S. Huang and O. J. Tretiak, "A pseudorandom multiplex system for facsimile transmission," *IEEE Trans. Commun. Tech.*, vol. COM-16, pp. 436–438, June 1968.

[206] C. M. Kortman, "Redundancy reduction: A practical method of data compression," *Proc. IEEE*, vol. 55, pp. 253–263, Mar. 1967. (See this issue for other data compression schemes also.)

[207] L. D. Davisson, "Data compression using straight line interpolation," *IEEE Trans. Inform. Theory*, vol. IT-14, pp. 390–394, May 1968.

[208] D. McCaughey, "The degrees of freedom of sampled images," Ph.D. dissertation, USCIPI Rep. No. 730, University of Southern California, Los Angeles, June 1977.

ADDITIONAL BIBLIOGRAPHY

[209] A. N. Netravali and J. O. Limb, "Picture coding: a review," *Proc. IEEE*, vol. 68, pp. 366–406, Mar. 1980.

[210] J. Woods, "Stability of DPCM coders for television," *IEEE Trans. Commun.*, vol. COM-23, pp. 845–846, Aug. 1975.

[211] A. K. Jain, "Advances in mathematical models for image processing," *Proc. IEEE*, to be published.

[212] A. N. Netravali and J. D. Robbins, "Motion compensated television coding—Part I," *Bell Syst. Tech. J.*, pp. 631–670, Mar. 1979.

[213] J. A. Stuller and A. N. Netravali, "Transform domain motion estimation," *Bell Syst. Tech J.*, pp. 1673–1702, Sept. 1979. (Also see pp. 1703–1718 of the same issue for application to coding.)

[214] A. K. Jain, "The rate vs distortion characteristics of some fast Karhuenen Loeve transform coding algorithms," Tech. Rep. Signal and Image Processing Lab., Dep. Elec. and Comput. Eng., Univ. California, Davis, Sept. 1980.

[215] V. R. Algazi and D. J. Sakrison "Computer processing in communications," pp. 85–100, Polytechnic Institute of Brooklyn, Brooklyn, NY, 1969.

[216] J. W. Modestino and D. G. Daut, "Combined source channel coding of images," *IEEE Trans. Commun.*, vol. COM-27, pp. 1644–1659, Nov. 1979.

[217] H. G. Musmann, "Predictive image coding," in *Image Transmission Techniques.* New York: Academic Press, 1979.

[218] E. G. Bowen and J. O. Limb, "Subjective effects of substituting lines in a video telephone signal," *IEEE Trans. Commun.*, pp. 1208–1211, Oct. 1976.

[219] N. F. Maxemchuk and J. A. Stuller, "Reduction of transmission error in adaptively predicted DPCM encoded picture," *Bell Syst. Tech. J.*, vol. 58, pp. 1413–1425, July–Aug. 1979.

[220] W. Zschunek, "DPCM picture coding with adaptive prediction," *IEEE Trans. Commun.*, vol. COM-25, pp. 1295–1302, Nov. 1977.

[221] I. Dukhovich and J. B. O'Neal, "A three dimensional spatial nonlinear predictor for television," *IEEE Trans. Commun.*, vol. COM-26, pp. 578–583, May 1978.

[222] F. E. Hilbert, "Cluster compression algorithm, a joint clustering/data compression concept," Jet Propulsion Laboratory, Pasadena, CA, JPL Publication 77-43, Dec. 1, 1977.

[223] J. N. Gupta and P. A. Wintz, "A boundary finding algorithm and its applications," *IEEE Trans. Circuits Syst.*, vol. CAS-22, pp. 351–362, Apr. 1975.

Advances in Picture Coding

HANS GEORG MUSMANN, PETER PIRSCH, MEMBER, IEEE, AND HANS-JOACHIM GRALLERT

Invited Paper

This paper presents a review of the advances in digital coding of video signals during the last four years. Displacement estimation algorithms for coding applications are compared first and the relationship between the algorithms is pointed out. The developments in predictive and transform coding are described and discussed with view to broadcast television and video-conferencing applications. One chapter summarizes the first promising results of motion adaptive frame interpolation. Some problems to be solved in the future are pointed out in the conclusions.

I. INTRODUCTION

In this paper advances in image coding are reported starting from the state of image coding as presented in [1]–[3]. In the book edited by Pratt [1], a comprehensive overview is given of the state of image coding in 1979, while [2] and [3] are two reviews on picture coding by Netravali and Limb in 1981 and Jain in 1982. The focus in this paper is oriented to advances in digital coding of television and video-conference signals. Facsimile coding is not included, no hardware systems or codec realizations are described. The emphasis is on new coding algorithms.

One of the main recent developments in image coding is the application of mathematical models describing the motion of objects. Motion considerations have become more and more important, specially for low bit-rate coding. It allows one to improve predictive, transform, and interpolative coding. Because of computation complexity and the required real-time processing mainly motion models describing only the translational component of a motion have been investigated for coding so far. A translational movement generates a frame-to-frame displacement of the moving object. Several methods have been developed to estimate the displacement vector of a moving object from two successive frames. Knowing the displacement vector, we can use it to realize motion-compensated predictive coding, motion-compensated transform coding, and motion-adaptive frame interpolation.

In view of the central role of the displacement estimation techniques for the various coding concepts the whole Section II is devoted to the problems of displacement estimation. Essentially, two groups of estimation algorithms are explained, which are known as recursive algorithms and block-matching algorithms. These displacement estimation techniques are compared with respect to estimation accuracy, convergence rate, and computation complexity.

In Section III advances in predictive coding are discussed. First, the design of differential pulse-code modulation (DPCM) techniques for digital coding of broadcast color television signals is considered, where no visible coding distortions are allowed. Such design methods are based on masking functions which represent visibility thresholds for the quantization error. The design takes care that the DCPM system does not exceed the visibility thresholds. By refinements of this technique improved predictors, as well as fixed and adaptive quantizers have been found. Also new algorithms to adapt the predictor to the nonstationary statistics of an image signal have been developed. This applies to contour prediction as well as to adaptive intra-inter-frame prediction. A considerable research activity can be observed in the field of motion-compensated prediction. Predictors with forward motion estimation generally apply block-matching techniques to estimate the displacement of objects and transmit the displacement vector in addition to the prediction error, whereas predictors with backward motion estimation use recursive estimation techniques and need not transmit the displacement vector.

Advances in transform coding are presented in Section IV. To optimize the quantization of the spectral coefficients the mean-square quantization error has been used as an optimization criterion in the past. New approaches try to control the quantization by the local picture content and to adapt the quantization to the characteristics of the human visual perception. Another attempt to exploit the properties of the human observer for transform coding is the M-transform. This transform uses basis functions of a noise-like structure and generates quantizing error patterns which are

Manuscript received August 27, 1984; revised December 3, 1984.

H. G. Musmann is with the Universität Hannover, Institut für Theoretische Nachrichtentechnik und Informationsverarbeitung, 3000 Hannover, West Germany.

P. Pirsch is with the Standard Elektrik Lorenz Forschungszentrum, 7000 Stuttgart 40, West Germany.

H -J. Grallert is with Siemens AG, Unternehmensbereich Nachrichten-und Sicherungstechnik Zentrallaboratorium, 8000 München 70, West Germany.

Reprinted from *Proc. IEEE*, vol. 73, no. 4, pp. 523–548, April 1985.

less visible than those of known transforms. In connection with hybrid coding also motion-adaptive techniques have been investigated.

At present, there are only a few publications on motion-adaptive frame interpolation techniques which are described in Section V. A considerable reduction of the data rate can be obtained when frames are skipped at the transmitter and then interpolated at the receiver. However, these techniques run into difficulties if there is motion in the scene. Moving objects become blurred by normal linear interpolation. First promising results show that the blur can be reduced by motion-adaptive frame interpolation. The investigations have also revealed many problems to be solved in the future.

II. DISPLACEMENT ESTIMATION FOR IMAGE SEQUENCE CODING

In a sequence of television pictures a moving object generates frame-to-frame luminance changes. These luminance changes can be used to estimate the parameters of a mathematical model that describes the movement of the object. Huang [4] has investigated a motion model that describes translation and rotation of a three-dimensional rigid object. Several methods [5]–[8] have been proposed for estimating the parameters of such motion models from a sequence of television pictures for applications in dynamic scene analysis.

Motion models can also be used to improve the efficiency of predictive and interpolative television coding techniques. Because of the real-time computing requirements, only relatively simple models considering the translational component of motion have been investigated for television coding so far. A translational movement generates a displacement of the moving object from frame to frame. Displacement estimation algorithms for television coding have been proposed for the first time by Limb and Murphy [9] in 1975 and by Cafforio and Rocca [10] in 1976.

The algorithm of Limb and Murphy can be explained by considering a simple moving edge as shown in Fig. 1. The displacement D is estimated by

$$\hat{D} = \hat{dx} = \sum_M |FD| \Big/ \sum_M |ED| \qquad (1)$$

where $|FD|$ denotes the magnitude of the frame difference signal and $|ED|$ that of the element difference signal. The summation is carried out over the area M which is defined by frame differences greater than a given threshold. The numerator

$$\sum_M |FD|$$

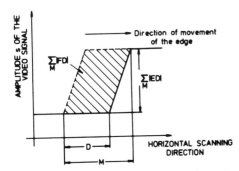

Fig. 1. Illustration of the displacement estimation scheme proposed by Limb and Murphy [9]. The dashed line indicates the position of the edge in the previous frame.

corresponds to the hatched area and the denominator

$$\sum_M |ED|$$

to the height of the parallelogram. Equation (1) does not indicate the direction of the displacement. Cafforio and Rocca start with a different approach and show that their algorithm for displacement estimation includes that of Limb and Murphy as a special simplified solution, whereby the latter one is easier to implement.

Let $s_k(x, y)$ be the luminance value at point x, y of a moving object in frame k. The moving object is assumed not to change its luminances from frame to frame. Then, in case of a pure translational movement that generates a displacement vector D with components dx, dy, the frame differences FD are

$$FD(x, y) = s_k(x, y) - s_{k-1}(x, y)$$
$$= s_k(x, y) - s_k(x + dx, y + dy)$$
$$= -\frac{\delta s_k(x, y)}{\delta x} \cdot dx - \frac{\delta s_k(x, y)}{\delta y} \cdot dy - n(x, y)$$
$$= -D^T \nabla s_k(x, y) - n(x, y) \qquad (2)$$

where $n(x, y)$ represents the higher order terms of the Taylor series expansion which will be neglected. The gradient ∇s is a vector whose components are element differences ED and line differences LD.

To explain (2), a one-dimensional displacement in the x-direction is considered in Fig. 2. In this special case, the

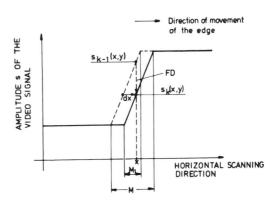

Fig. 2. Illustration of the displacement estimation algorithm proposed by Cafforio and Rocca [10]. The dashed line indicates the position of the edge in the previous frame.

estimate of the displacement vector D reduces to

$$\hat{D} = \hat{dx} = -\frac{FD(x, y)}{\partial s(x, y)/\partial x}. \qquad (3)$$

If the boundary of the moving object is known, (2) can be evaluated for all picture elements of the moving object. Then, using linear regression and neglecting the x, y cross terms, the displacement vector D is approximated by

$$\hat{dx} = -\frac{E[FD(x, y) \cdot \partial s(x, y)/\partial x]}{E[(\partial s(x, y)/\partial x)^2]} = -\frac{\Sigma(FD \cdot ED)}{\Sigma(ED)^2}$$

$$\hat{dy} = -\frac{E[FD(x, y) \cdot \partial s(x, y)/\partial y]}{E[(\partial s(x, y)/\partial y)^2]} = -\frac{\Sigma(FD \cdot LD)}{\Sigma(LD)^2}$$
$$\qquad (4)$$

where the statistical averages are calculated by summing over the entire area M of the moving object.

The described displacement estimation algorithm of Cafforio and Rocca assumes a linear luminance function at point x, y. For the example in Fig. 2 this assumption is only valid within the area M_1. This area decreases with increasing displacement. Therefore, this estimation algorithm can only be used for measuring small displacements D.

To overcome this problem new estimation algorithms have been developed recently. The algorithms can roughly be classified into two groups, which are denoted as recursive algorithms [11]–[17] and block-matching algorithms [18]–[23]. However, this terminology has not been uniform till now.

A. Recursive Displacement Estimation Algorithms

In 1978, Netravali and Robbins [11] published a first recursive estimation algorithm to improve the estimation accuracy and to increase the measuring range of D. In recursive estimation algorithms it is assumed that an initial estimate $\hat{D}_i$ is used to produce a new improved estimate $\hat{D}_{i+1}$ according to

$$\hat{D}_{i+1} = \hat{D}_i + U_i \tag{5}$$

where U_i is the so-called update term of iteration i. The iterations can be executed either for a single picture element at consecutive picture elements along a scanning line, from line to line, or from frame to frame. Correspondingly, these techniques may be denoted as pel-recursive estimation algorithms with horizontal, vertical, or temporal recursion. Knowing $\hat{D}_i$, a function of the displaced frame difference DFD

$$\text{DFD}\left(x, y, \hat{D}_i\right) = s_k(x, y) - s_{k-1}\left(x - \hat{d}x_i, y - \hat{d}y_i\right) \tag{6}$$

can be used as a criterion for calculating the estimate $\hat{D}_{i+1}$. Netravali and Robbins propose an estimation algorithm that attempts to minimize the squared value of the displaced frame difference recursively with i using the gradient method

$$\hat{D}_{i+1} = \hat{D}_i - \frac{1}{2}\epsilon \nabla_{\hat{D}_i}\left[\text{DFD}(x, y, \hat{D}_i)\right]^2 \tag{7}$$

where $\nabla_{\hat{D}_i}$ is the gradient operator with respect to $\hat{D}_i$ and ϵ is a positive constant. Fig. 3 illustrates how this algorithm approaches the actual displacement D after several iterations. The choice of ϵ requires a compromise. A high value

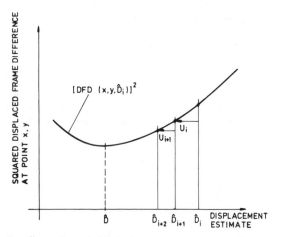

Fig. 3. Illustration of the displacement estimation scheme proposed by Netravali and Robbins [11]. The update term U_i at each iteration is proportional to the gradient $\nabla_{\hat{D}_i}[\text{DFD}(x, y, \hat{D}_i)]^2$ and to the constant ϵ according to (7).

of ϵ yields a quick convergence but a noisy estimate, whereas a small ϵ leads to more accurate displacement estimates. In [11] the ϵ is chosen to be $1/1024$ for motion-compensated predictive coding. Evaluating (7) gives

$$\hat{D}_{i+1} = \hat{D}_i - \epsilon \text{DFD}\left(x, y, \hat{D}_i\right) \cdot \nabla_{\hat{D}_i}\left[\text{DFD}\left(x, y, \hat{D}_i\right]\right] \tag{8}$$

and with the definition (6)

$$\hat{D}_{i+1} = \hat{D}_i - \epsilon \text{DFD}\left(x, y, \hat{D}_i\right) \cdot \nabla s_{k-1}\left(x - \hat{d}x_i, y - \hat{d}y_i\right) \tag{9}$$

where ∇ is a gradient operator with respect to the horizontal and vertical coordinates x, y.

$$\nabla s_{k-1}\left(x - \hat{d}x_i, y - \hat{d}y_i\right) = \begin{bmatrix} \dfrac{\partial}{\partial x} \\ \dfrac{\partial}{\partial y} \end{bmatrix} \cdot s_{k-1}\left(x - \hat{d}x_i, y - \hat{d}y_i\right). \tag{10}$$

The algorithm (7) can be extended by calculating the update term from several picture elements, e.g., of an area M, in order to smooth out the effect of quantization noise [11]. Then the update term is given by

$$U_i = -\frac{1}{2}\epsilon \nabla_{\hat{D}_i} \sum_{j \in M} W_j\left[\text{DFD}\left(x, y, \hat{D}_i\right)\right]^2 \tag{11}$$

where $W_j \geq 0$ and

$$\sum_{j \in M} W_j = 1.$$

The evaluation of DFD and ∇s_{k-1} in (9) requires an interpolation of the luminance $s_{k-1}(x - \hat{d}x_i, y - \hat{d}y_i)$ for nonintegral displacements $\hat{d}x_i, \hat{d}y_i$. Four neighboring picture elements s_A, s_B, s_C, s_D are considered for this interpolation as demonstrated in Fig. 4. First, the integral parts of $\hat{d}x_i$ and

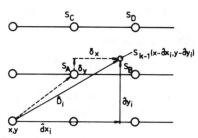

Fig. 4. Position of picture elements in frame s_{k-1} used for interpolation of $s_{k-1}(x - \hat{d}x_i, y - \hat{d}y_i)$.

$\hat{d}y_i$ determine the position of s_A. Then, the fractional parts $\delta x, \delta y$ of $\hat{d}x_i, \hat{d}y_i$ are used for linear two-dimensional interpolation according to

$$s_{k-1}\left(x - \hat{d}x_i, y - \hat{d}y_i\right) = (1 - \delta y)\left[(1 - \delta x)s_A + \delta x s_B\right] + \delta y\left[(1 - \delta x)s_C + \delta x s_D\right]. \tag{12}$$

In order to reduce the implementation complexity Netravali and Robbins also propose simplified versions for the interpolation (12) and displacement estimation algorithm (9) in [11] and [12].

Stimulated by the work of Netravali and Robbins, several new recursive displacement estimation algorithms have been developed. Compared to the algorithm (7) the constant ϵ is substituted by variables in the following displacement estimation techniques to achieve a better adaptation to the local image statistics. The main aim is to improve the rate of convergence and thus also the accuracy of the displacement algorithms if the number of iterations is limited. To simplify the description of these algorithms only the dx-component of the displacement vector is considered.

Applying the Newton–Raphson algorithm [13] to search for the minimum of DFD^2 results in an update term as

$$U_i = -\frac{\sum_M \frac{\partial}{\partial dx}[DFD(x,y,\hat{D}_i)]^2}{\sum_M \frac{\partial^2}{\partial dx^2}[DFD(x,y,\hat{D}_i)]^2}. \tag{13}$$

Instead of ϵ, a denominator term corresponding to the second-order derivative of DFD^2 is introduced.

In 1982 Cafforio and Rocca [14] published an extended recursive version of their former algorithm (4) which is considered here in a somewhat simplified form

$$U_i = -\frac{\frac{1}{2}\sum_M \frac{\partial}{\partial dx}[DFD(x,y,\hat{D}_i)]^2}{\sum_M \left[\frac{\partial}{\partial x}s_{k-1}(x-\hat{d}x_i, y-\hat{d}y_i)\right]^2 + \eta^2} \tag{14}$$

with $\eta^2 = 100$.

In (14), a correction term η^2 is introduced to avoid problems which would occur in areas of nearly constant luminance where $\partial s_{k-1}/\partial x$ is small.

Bergmann [15] starts from a proposal of Burkhard and Moll [16] and develops a displacement estimation algorithm where the average of two second-order derivatives are used as a denominator

placement estimation algorithms (11), (13), (14), and (15) we use

$$E[DFD^2] = E\left[\{s_k(x,y) - s_{k-1}(x-dx, y-dy)\}^2\right]$$
$$= E[s_k^2(x,y)] - 2E[s_k(x,y)$$
$$\cdot s_{k-1}(x-dx, y-dy)]$$
$$+ E[s_{k-1}^2(x-dx, y-dy)]. \tag{16}$$

In the case of

$$E[s_k^2(x,y)] = E[s_{k-1}^2(x-dx, y-dy)] = \text{constant} \tag{17}$$

(16) proves that minimizing $E[DFD^2]$ corresponds to maximizing the cross correlation

$$R_{s_k s_{k-1}}(x,y,D) = E[s_k(x,y) \cdot s_{k-1}(x-dx, y-dy)]. \tag{18}$$

Using (16), (18), and approximating the expectations E by summations over an area M, the described estimation algorithms can be simplified to the expressions in Table 1.

A comparison of the displacement estimation algorithms in Table 1 shows that these algorithms only differ in the denominator of the update term. Fig. 5 illustrates the updating for the Newton–Raphson and Bergmann algorithms. The slope of line ⓐ corresponds to the denominator term of the Newton–Raphson algorithm, while Bergmann's algorithm takes the average of the slopes of line ⓐ and line ⓑ. From Fig. 5 it becomes evident that in this example the Bergmann algorithm converges quicker to the actual dis-

$$U_i = -\frac{\frac{1}{2}\sum_M \frac{\partial}{\partial dx}[DFD(x,y,\hat{D}_i)]^2}{\frac{1}{2}\sum_M \left[\frac{\partial}{\partial x}s_{k-1}(x-dx_i, y-dy_i) + \frac{\partial}{\partial x}s_k(x,y)\right]\frac{\partial}{\partial x}s_k(x,y)}. \tag{15}$$

The summations in (11), (13), (14), and (15) are taken over the picture elements of an area M. Of course, M can be reduced to contain only one picture element.

To demonstrate the close relationship between the dis-

placement dx than the Newton–Raphson algorithm. Since the exact slope of line ⓑ is unknown, the second-order derivative of the cross-correlation function at the actual displacement is approximated by the second-order deriva-

Table 1 Pel-Recursive Displacement Estimation Algorithms, Simplified for Comparison by Assuming (17)

Algorithm	x-Component of the Displacement Estimate $\hat{D}_{i+1}$
Netravali and Robbins [11]	$\hat{d}x_{i+1} = \hat{d}x_i + \epsilon\frac{\partial}{\partial x}R_{s_k s_{k-1}}(x,y,\hat{D}_i), \qquad \epsilon = 1/1024$
Newton–Raphson [13]	$\hat{d}x_{i+1} = \hat{d}x_i - \dfrac{\frac{\partial}{\partial x}R_{s_k s_{k-1}}(x,y,\hat{D}_i)}{\frac{\partial^2}{\partial x^2}R_{s_k s_{k-1}}(x,y,\hat{D}_i)}$
Cafferio and Rocca [14]	$\hat{d}x_{i+1} = \hat{d}x_i + \dfrac{\frac{\partial}{\partial x}R_{s_k s_{k-1}}(x,y,\hat{D}_i)}{\left|\frac{\partial^2}{\partial x^2}R_{s_{k-1}s_{k-1}}(x,y,0)\right| + \eta^2}, \qquad \eta^2 = 100$
Bergmann [15]	$\hat{d}x_{i+1} = \hat{d}x_i - \dfrac{\frac{\partial}{\partial x}R_{s_k s_{k-1}}(x,y,\hat{D}_i)}{\frac{1}{2}\left[\frac{\partial^2}{\partial x^2}R_{s_k s_{k-1}}(x,y,\hat{D}_i) + \frac{\partial^2}{\partial x^2}R_{s_k s_k}(x,y,0)\right]}$

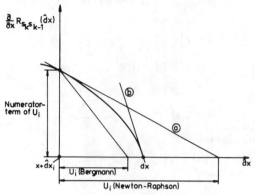

Fig. 5. Illustration of the Newton–Raphson algorithm and a displacement estimation scheme proposed by Bergmann according to Table 1. U_i are the update terms at one iteration. The actual displacement is dx corresponding to maximum cross correlation or minimum of the squared displaced frame differences.

tive of the autocorrelation function at point x, y to calculate the estimate.

Bergmann [15] has investigated the convergence rate of the algorithms in Table 1 in computer simulations using a test sequence showing vertical black bars that move horizontally. The test sequence has been recorded with a camera, sampled with 10 MHz, quantized, and coded with 8 bits per sample. Fig. 6 shows the displacement estimates at consecutive steps of iterations for the different algorithms.

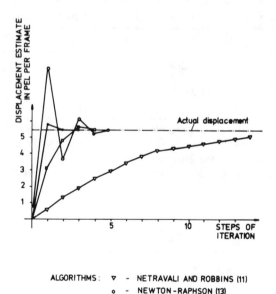

ALGORITHMS: ▽ – NETRAVALI AND ROBBINS (11)
○ – NEWTON-RAPHSON (13)
□ – CAFFORIO AND ROCCA (14)
● – BERGMANN (15)
AREA M: 11 × 11 PEL

Fig. 6. Displacement estimates at consecutive steps of iterations for various recursive estimation algorithms.

A quicker updating of Netravali and Robbins algorithm can be achieved by increasing the constant ϵ. However, this also implies a decrease of the achievable estimation accuracy which is limited to ϵ. Comparing the Newton–Raphson algorithm with that of Cafforio and Rocca, the results indicate that the correction term η^2 prevents the overshoots. In the case of this special test sequence Bergmann's algorithm

proves most favorable. He found that for a good initial estimate the extent of the area M should be chosen about twice as large as the maximum displacement, i.e., $M = 11 \times 11$ pels if $D = dm$ is 5.5 pels. However, it must be pointed out here that the convergence behavior of the recursive estimation algorithms depends also very strongly on the local image details. To illustrate the convergence behavior in the case of a natural test sequence, in Fig. 7 the displaced frame differences of two successive frames are shown after

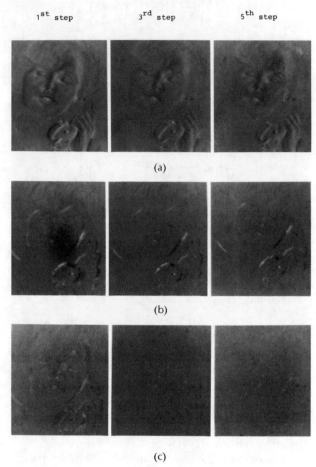

Fig. 7. Illustration of the displaced frame differences of two successive frames at the 1st, 3rd, and 5th step of iteration for various recursive estimation algorithms. $M = 7 \times 5$ pels. (a) Algorithm of Netravali and Robbins [11]. (b) Algorithm of Cafforio and Rocca [14]. (c) Algorithm of Bergmann [15].

consecutive steps of iterations. Positive and negative differences are represented by white and black picture elements, while a zero difference is gray. Also this test confirms the favorable behavior of Bergmann's algorithm. It also indicates some places with residual large differences where the estimation algorithm cannot compensate the displacement.

A second important feature of an estimation algorithm is its range of stability in which the algorithm converges to the correct correlation peak or actual displacement. The stability constraint is given by

$$|D - \hat{D}_{i+1}| < |D - \hat{D}_i|. \tag{19}$$

It requires that the update vector is always directed towards and not opposite to the actual displacement. From this requirement, bounds for the stability ranges of the discussed estimation algorithms can easily be found by considering only the sign of the update terms. In Fig. 8, these bounds are shown for a typical example of a cross-correla-

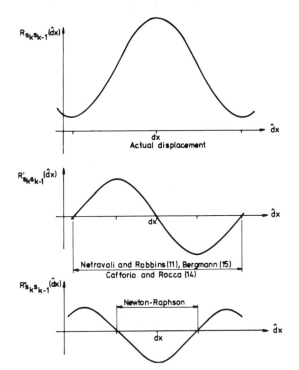

Fig. 8. Stability ranges for various recursive estimation algorithms.

tion function. The Newton–Raphson algorithm has a smaller stability range compared to that of algorithms (11), (14), and (15). It diverges at the point where the second-order derivative of the cross-correlation function changes its sign.

When displacement estimation algorithms are applied to improve predictive or interpolative coding, the behavior of an estimation algorithm can be affected by quantizing noise superimposed to the image signal. The influence of noise on the accuracy of recursive displacement estimation techniques has been investigated by Sabri [17].

B. Displacement Estimation by Block Matching

Instead of estimating a displacement recursively, a normalized two-dimensional cross-correlation function NCCF

$$NCCF(D) = \frac{R_{s_k s_{k-1}}(D)}{\sqrt{R_{s_k s_k}(0) \cdot R_{s_{k-1} s_{k-1}}(0)}} \qquad (20)$$

can be measured and a displacement estimate be obtained

from the position of the correlation peak. To find the displacement for a point x, y, a block of $M \times N$ picture elements centered at point x, y is taken from frame k and correlated with the picture elements in a search area SR of frame $k - 1$ to find the best match. Assuming a maximum horizontal or vertical displacement of dm picture elements the search area SR is given by

$$SR = (M + 2dm) \times (N + 2dm) \qquad (21)$$

as shown in Fig. 9. In case of a block size 7×7 and a maximum displacement $dm = 10$ the search area is $SR = 27 \times 27$.

The search for the correlation peak requires an evaluation of NCCF at

$$Q = (2dm + 1)^2 \qquad (22)$$

different horizontal and vertical shifts resulting in an excessive number of computations.

On the other hand, investigations by Beyer [24] have shown that a special correlation technique which takes into account the nonstationary behavior of the second moments can reach a very high accuracy of the displacement estimate which is close to the theoretical bounds as given in Fig. 10. These results indicate that an estimation accuracy of 1/10 pel can be obtained with correlation techniques using a practical block size of 7×7 pels.

A first and simple way to reduce the computation complexity is to segment an image into a fixed number of rectangular blocks and to assume that all picture elements of one block have the same displacement. Thus only one displacement vector has to be calculated per block. This technique is called block matching.

A second possibility to reduce the computation complexity is to simplify the matching criterion $D(i, j)$. Instead of evaluating the normalized cross-correlation function NCCF as a matching criterion according to

$$NCCF(i, j) = \frac{\displaystyle\sum_{m=1}^{M} \sum_{n=1}^{N} s_k(m, n) \cdot s_{k-1}(m + i, n + j)}{\left[\displaystyle\sum_{m=1}^{M} \sum_{n=1}^{N} s_k^2(m, n)\right]^{1/2} \left[\displaystyle\sum_{m=1}^{M} \sum_{n=1}^{N} s_{k-1}^2(m + i, n + j)\right]^{1/2}} \qquad (23)$$

where $-dm \leqslant i, j \leqslant dm$, J. R. Jain and A. K. Jain [18] apply the mean-square error MSE

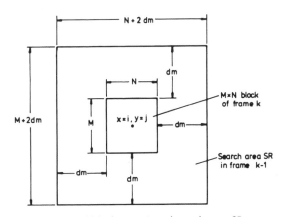

Fig. 9. Geometry of block $M \times N$ and search area SR.

83

$$MSE(i,j) = \frac{1}{MN} \sum_{m=1}^{M} \sum_{n=1}^{M} \left[s_k(m,n) - s_{k-1}(m+i,n+j) \right]^2 \qquad (24)$$

and Koga *et al.* [19] propose to use the mean of the absolute frame difference MAD

$$MAD(i,j) = \frac{1}{MN} \sum_{m=1}^{M} \sum_{n=1}^{N} |s_k(m,n) - s_{k-1}(m+i,n+j)|$$

$$(25)$$

with $-dm \leqslant i,j \leqslant +dm$. The MAD criterion has the advantage that no multiplications and no divisions are required.

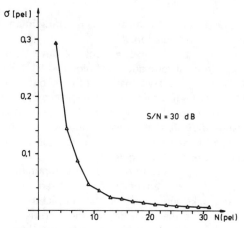

Fig. 10. Lower bound for the standard derivation σ of the displacement estimation error versus block size $N \times N$ according to [24].

In addition to the matching criterion, J. R. Jain and A. K. Jain in 1981 also suggested a method to reduce the number Q of required shifts to find the best match. The importance of such search procedures can be recognized by considering the extreme situation when an object moves across the television scene of 512×512 picture elements within 1 s. This corresponds to a frame-to-frame displacement of about $dm = 20$ and $Q = 1681$ required shifts. For each shift, the criterion (23), (24), or (25) has to be evaluated. To overcome this difficulty, several methods for simplifying the search procedure have been recently investigated [19]–[23]. Three of these techniques, the 2D-logarithmic search [18], the three-step search [19], and the modified conjugate direction search [21] are discussed briefly in the following.

The 2D-logarithmic search procedure, published by J. R. Jain and A. K. Jain, is based on the assumption that the matching criterion $D(i,j) = MSE(i,j)$ increases monotonically as the search moves away from the direction of minimum distortion. The direction of minimum distortion is defined by (i,j), such that $D(i,j)$ is minimum. The 2D-logarithmic search procedure tracks the direction of minimum distortion. In each step, five search points are checked, as shown in Fig. 11. The distance between the search points is reduced if the minimum is in the center of the search locations or at the boundary of the search area. In this example, five steps are required to find the displacement vector at point $(i+2, j+6)$.

At almost the same time, Koga *et al.* [19] have published

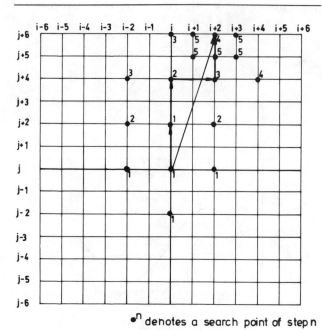

Fig. 11. 2D-logarithmic search procedure [18]. The search points in the search area of frame $k-1$ are shown with respect to a picture element ($x=i, y=j$) in frame k. In this example, the approximated displacement vectors $(i,j+2)$, $(i,j+4)$, $(i+2,j+4)$, $(i+2,j+6)$, $(i+2,j+6)$ are found in step 1, 2, 3, 4, and 5.

a three-step search procedure which is closely related to the 2D-logarithmic search. Excepting the starting point (i,j), eight search points are tested in the first step. These points are relatively coarsely spaced around the center $x=i, y=j$ as demonstrated in Fig. 12. In this example, point ($i+3$,

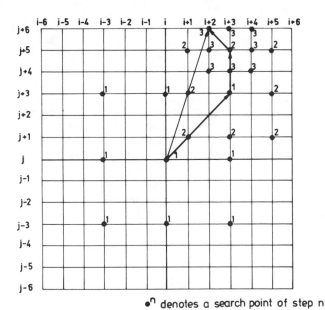

Fig. 12. Three-step search procedure [19]. In this example the points $(i+3, j+3)$, $(i+3, j+5)$, and $(i+2, j+6)$ are the approximated displacement vectors found in step 1, 2, and 3.

84

$j + 3$) is found as a first approximation of the displacement vector using the MAD criterion (25). In a second step, eight search points are spaced less coarsely around the first approximation and point $(i + 3, j + 5)$ is found. The second step is repeated until the required accuracy is achieved. In the case of a search area with $dm \leqslant 6$ the third step gives the final displacement vector which is at point $(i + 2, j + 6)$ in this example.

Recently, Srinivasan and Rao [21] presented an efficient new search procedure, called conjugate direction search. A simplified version of this procedure will be described using the example in Fig. 13. The algorithm searches for the

Table 2 Required Number of Search Points and Sequential Steps for Various Search Procedures and a Search Area Corresponding to a Maximum Displacement of $dm = 6$ Pels per Frame. Total Number of Search Points is $Q = 169$

Search Procedure	Required Number of Search Points		Required Number of Sequential Steps	
	a	b	a	b
2D-logarithmic	18	21	5	7
Three step	25	25	3	3
Conjugate direction (simplified)	12	15	9	12

a) For a special displacement vector $(i + 2, j + 6)$.
b) For a worst case situation.

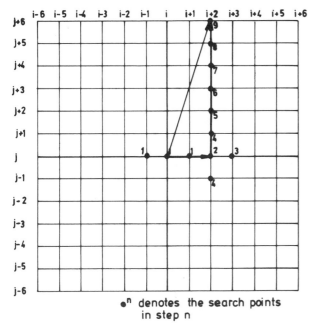

●^{n} denotes the search points in step n

Fig. 13. Conjugate direction search in simplified version [21]. In this example, point $(i + 2, j + 6)$ is the displacement vector found in step 9.

direction of minimum distortion $D(i, j)$ which is defined by the MAD (i, j) criterion (25). In a first search, the minimum in the i-direction is determined by computing $D(i - 1, j)$, $D(i, j)$, $D(i + 1, j)$. If $D(i + 1, j)$ proves to be the smallest, $D(i + 2, j)$ also is computed and the smallest value of $D(i, j)$, $D(i + 1, j)$, $D(i + 2, j)$ is found. Proceeding in this fashion, the minimum in the i-direction is detected when the smallest value is situated between two higher values. In a second search, the minimum in the j-direction is determined by the same procedure starting at the minimum of the first search. In case of the example shown in Fig. 13, the first search results in the point $(i + 2, j)$ and the second search in $(i + 2, j + 6)$.

The computing complexity of a search procedure can be measured by the number of required points. In the above examples, a maximum displacement of $dm = 6$ is assumed. For this case the brute force method requires $Q = 169$ search points. Table 2 presents a comparison of the number of search points and sequential steps required by the explained search procedures. For a real-time hardware realization, the number of the required sequential steps can be a more important feature than the number of search points,

since some of these can be evaluated by parallel computations. If displacement estimates are available from preceding measurements also a tracking method [23] can be used to reduce the search area.

In experiments it has been found that the matching criterion $D(i, j)$ has no significant influence on the search [21]. Therefore, the MAD criterion (25) is recommended since it is relatively simple to implement.

Comparing block matching and recursive estimation algorithms we recognize that the estimation accuracy of the described block-matching algorithms is limited to $+0.5$ picture element. Recursive algorithms allow a more accurate estimate for the cost of more complex computations. However, it should be mentioned that the accuracy of the block-matching techniques could also be improved by additional interpolation.

C. Feature-Based Displacement Estimation Algorithms

These techniques originate from research in the field of dynamic scene analysis where special features of an object are extracted to track and describe its movement. Especially features with high luminance gradients allow a good displacement estimate. The feature-based displacement estimation algorithms which are going to be developed for predictive image coding extract edges in a first step and then use one of the described basic algorithms to estimate the displacement of the edge [25]–[27]. These techniques are still in an early stage requiring very complex computations.

III. Predictive Coding

One of the promising methods for transmission bit-rate reduction of digital video signals is predictive coding. Differential pulse-code modulation (DPCM) is a predictive coding scheme which has been studied extensively since its invention. A block diagram of the basic DPCM system is shown in Fig. 14. In such a system, a prediction $\hat{s}$ of the present sample s is made based upon previously transmitted and decoded information. The difference between the predicted and the present value of the sample is then quantized, coded, and transmitted. After decoding of the transmitted code words, the receiver reconstructs the sample by adding the prediction value to the quantized prediction error. To have the same prediction value at both the transmitter and the receiver, also at the transmitter side the prediction is based on reconstructed samples.

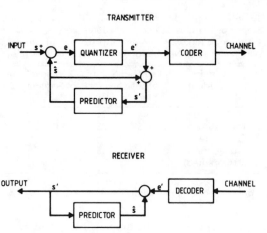

Fig. 14. Block diagram of basic DPCM system.

Methods for designing predictors, quantizers, and coders have been investigated to achieve the smallest transmission rate for a desired picture quality. Several extensions of the basic DPCM system have been made and used for both intraframe and interframe coding of video signals. Besides various adaptive DPCM systems, combinations of different source coding schemes, e.g., DPCM and transform coding, have also been proposed.

The complexity of coding schemes applied to video transmission depends on the kind of service and the tradeoff between hardware expense and transmission costs. Essential for broadcast television is high picture quality. Furthermore, digital cable TV calls for simple hardware realization, because the additional expense for the terminal equipment should be kept small. For video-conference and video-phone services, reduction of transmission rate is important. For this reason, more sophisticated coding techniques can be applied. This discussion shows that for an economical coding scheme with reasonable hardware size and cost, there is no general solution. Various factors have impact on the economical solution for a given application. Even if the recent progress in VLSI and digital technology have made complicated signal processing feasible, in addition to new sophisticated predictive coding schemes also improvements in simple DPCM systems are of interest.

A. Subjectively Optimized Quantizers

The transmission bit-rate reduction of DPCM is achieved, to a large extent, by the quantization of the prediction error. An optimum quantizer design for a DPCM system with fixed-length code words should yield a minimum number of quantization levels, and impairments which should be as close as possible to the visibility threshold. Because of the difficulty of incorporating the observer's perception in the quantizer design, simple error measures like "minimum mean-squared error" (MMSE) have frequently been used. Using this distortion measure

$$D_{MMSE} = \sum_{i=0}^{k-1} \int_{d_i}^{d_{i+1}} (e - r_i)^2 p(e) \, de \qquad (26)$$

has to be minimized, where $d_0 < d_1 < \cdots < d_K$ and $r_0 < r_1 < \cdots < r_{K-1}$ are decision and representative levels, respectively, and $p(e)$ is the probability density function of

the prediction error e. For a given number of levels K, Max [28] has developed a set of equations for optimum decision and reconstruction levels. Subjective tests have shown that the statistically optimized quantizers have too many levels for small prediction errors and *vice versa* too few for large prediction errors. For a small number of levels, these quantizers generate visible edge business and slope overload effects. For this reason several modifications of the MMSE distortion measure have been proposed. A better match to the visibility of distortions is given by a distortion measure with a power of 4 or 6 [29]. Another method of psychovisual quantizer design replaces the probability density function $p(e)$ by a visual weighting function. Limb [30] used the product $p(e)w(e)$, where $w(e)$ is a measure of the local signal change

$$D_{WMSE} = \sum_{i=0}^{k-1} \int_{d_i}^{d_{i+1}} (e - r_i)^2 w(e) p(e) \, de. \qquad (27)$$

Candy and Bosworth [31] and Netravali [32] considered the visual masking effect by introducing a visibility function. A visibility function of a particular picture is measured by determination of the visual sensitivity of the eye to distortions added to points where the horizontal signal slope of a video signal exceeds a threshold. A quantizer design procedure according to Max [28] can be applied if the probability density function $p(e)$ is replaced by the visibility density function $v(e)$.

$$D_{SV} = \sum_{i=0}^{k-1} \int_{d_i}^{d_{i+1}} (e - r_i)^2 v(e) \, de. \qquad (28)$$

The optimum choice of visual weighting functions for quantizer design is not known. In all cases, physiological as well as statistical effects are considered. A disadvantage of the design methods described above is that the quantization error feedback of the DPCM is not taken into account since the visual weighting functions are determined by added noise [33] instead of real quantization error pattern of DPCM. In addition, an optimal quantizer design, particularly for broadcast television should consider visibility thresholds and should provide the smallest number of levels with no visible impairments.

The first attempt in this direction was made by Kretz [34] who investigated visibility thresholds of specific patterns which imitate the quantization errors of one-dimensional DPCM systems. Real quantization error patterns of various test pictures were generated by non-real-time DPCM simulations on a computer and have been used for threshold measurements by Erdmann [35] and Pirsch [36]. The visibility thresholds were determined by subjective comparison tests of a PCM-encoded picture with a picture which is impaired by DPCM. By selecting specific quantization characteristics and test pictures, thresholds were measured in subjective tests for the various types of impairments such as granular noise, edge busyness, and slope overload [36].

With respect to the masking effect, the measured visibility threshold function is called a masking function. In most investigations on masking, the visibility thresholds were determined for several edge slopes and signal differences on either side of the edge. For signal patterns other than simple one-dimensional edges, a measure for signal change had to be defined, which was denoted as activity function.

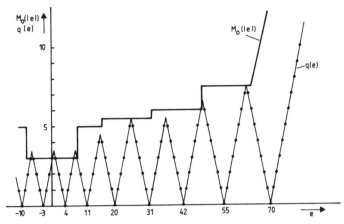

Fig. 15. Masking function and quantization error characteristic versus prediction error of luminance signals sampled at 10 MHz from [38].

In the case of fixed quantizers the maximum quantization error q is dependent on the prediction error e. Hence, the prediction error can be considered as an activity function.

A measured masking function is shown in Fig. 15. The staircase structure of the masking function in Fig. 15 results from the test method and has no subjective evidence. For a given masking function, it is relatively easy to determine a quantizer with a minimum number of levels which always produce quantization errors below threshold [37]. The masking function depends on the predictor used for the subjective tests. Linear predictors with only positive coefficients are advantageous for quantizers with a minimum number of levels [38]. For two-dimensional prediction the algorithm

$$\hat{s}_0 = \frac{1}{2}s_1' + \frac{1}{8}s_2' + \frac{1}{4}s_3' + \frac{1}{8}s_4' \qquad (29)$$

is recommended [38]. The subscripting of the pels is shown in Fig. 16.

There are several publications on nonadaptive quantizer design based on subjectively measured thresholds. The results can be summarized as follows. For the luminance component sampled at 10 MHz, 13 levels are required for natural test pictures and 21 levels for resolution charts [38].

It has been recognized that the chrominance component B−Y can be quantized more coarsely than R−Y [39], [40]. The number of quantization levels for natural test pictures sampled at 4.4 MHz is 9 for R−Y and 5 for B−Y [40].

The measured threshold functions are picture dependent, but the variation for a class of pictures is not significant. Viewing distance and sampling frequency strongly influence the threshold values. The results reported so far are valid for fixed intraframe prediction. Recent investigations of masking functions for interframe prediction support the known effect that interframe predictors are better than intraframe predictors only for scenes of very slowly moving objects (velocity smaller than 1 pel per frame) [41]. Hence, intraframe predictors are to be prefered for nonadaptive DPCM systems. In the case of interframe prediction, critical test material generates new distortion effects which are described as "temporal overload" and "busy areas" [41]. Measurements of masking functions adapted to these distortions are required for interframe coding.

Subjectively measured masking functions can also be used for the design of adaptive quantizers. By means of more complex activity functions, a picture can be divided into several segments which are quantized differently. There are some proposals for activity functions used for quantizer control in the literature [42], [43], [33], [36]. A typical example of an activity function A is

$$A_{MD} = \max_{i,j \in DN} |d_{i,j}| \qquad (30)$$

where

$$d_{i,j} = s_i' - s_j' \qquad (31)$$

is the difference between neighboring pels and DN describes the index set of pels used for calculation of A_{MD}. To avoid the transmission of additional control information, a causal neighborhood as $DN = \{1,2,3,4\}$ is used in most cases. A heuristic approach leads to a combined masking function which is the maximum of two parts.

$$M = \max \left\{ M_0(e_0), M_n(A_{MD}) \right\}. \qquad (32)$$

Here M_0 describes the masking by the present prediction error and M_n describes the masking by surrounding pels. If we assume no interactions between M_0 and M_n than they can be measured independently by subjective threshold tests [36]. An adaptive quantizer can be realized by a set of

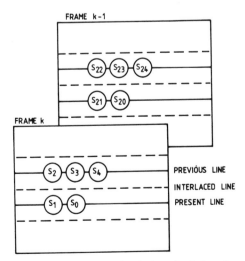

Fig. 16. Sampling raster and subscripting of pels for schemes other than contour predictions.

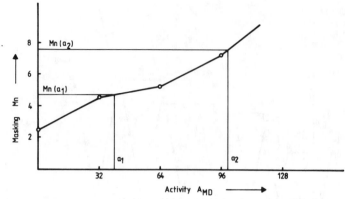

Fig. 17. Masking function $M_n(A_{MD})$ of luminance signals sampled at 10 MHz [36]. The a_1 indicate activity values used for quantizer control.

L separate quantizers which are switched on by the activity value A_{MD} according to

$$Q(e) = \begin{cases} Q_1(e) & A_{MD} < a_2 \\ Q_2(e) & a_2 \leqslant & A_{MD} < a_3 \\ \vdots & \vdots & \vdots \\ Q_L(e) & a_L \leqslant & A_{MD} \end{cases} \quad (33)$$

To each of the specific activity values a_1, a masking value $M_n(a_1)$ can be assigned (Fig. 17). Corresponding to (32), each quantization characteristic Q_1 has a uniform quantization with $M_n(a_1)$ as maximum quantization error as long as $M_0(e_0) < M_n(a_1)$. For $M_0(e_0) > M_n(a_1)$, a nonuniform quantization characteristic similar to that of Fig. 15 can be designed. Because of the masking characteristic, the number of levels becomes smaller as the activity becomes greater. Investigations on the statistics of switched quantizers have shown that for smaller activity values, large prediction errors are very rare, particularly for natural pictures. For this reason, a constant word length coding is possible, if for small activity values, the representative levels for large prediction errors are omitted in such a way that for all L characteristics, the same number of levels is used. In this case the largest threshold $M_n(a_L)$ fixes the number of levels.

The described technique has shown some limitations for very detailed pictures [36]. Recent investigations [44] improve adaptive quantizers by extension of the activity function. The term $M_n(A_{MD})$ is replaced by $M_n(A_{MWD})$ where

$$A_{MWD} = \max \{A_{MD}, A_{WD}\} \quad (34)$$

and the activity

$$A_{WD} = \max_{i \in DN} \left\{ |\delta_i| + \frac{1}{4}(\delta_i + |\delta_i|)(1 - \text{sign}(e_0)) \right\} \quad (35)$$

is based on weighted differences $\delta_i = s'_i - s_0$. The sign function is defined as

$$\text{sign}(x) = \begin{cases} 1, & x > T \\ 0, & |x| \leqslant T \\ -1, & x < -T \end{cases}$$

$$T = 1. \quad (36)$$

The function A_{WD} considers that transitions to bright values are more strongly masked than transitions to dark values. Application of the extended activity function (34) results in a switched quantizer with four different characteristics each having 11 levels corresponding to 3.5 bits per pel [44]. The representative levels of the four characteristics are listed in Table 3.

Table 3 Positive Representative Levels of Adaptive Quantization with Four Symmetrical Characteristics Each Having 11 Levels [44]

Positive Representative Levels	Activity Range	Masking Value
0, 3, 8, 15, 24, 35	$A_{MWD} < 15$	
0, 7, 14, 23, 34, 47	$15 \leqslant A_{MWD} < 35$	$M_n(15) = 3$
0, 11, 22, 35, 48, 65	$35 \leqslant A_{MWD} < 100$	$M_n(35) = 5$
0, 15, 30, 45, 64, 85	$100 \leqslant A_{MWD}$	$M_n(100) = 7$

Even with very sophisticated control techniques, adaptive quantizers allow only a relatively small reduction of the bit rate in case of constant word length coding. Significantly lower bit rates can be achieved by combining adaptive quantization with variable word length coding. In addition to quantizer control, the activity function is used to assign different codes of variable length to the quantized prediction error. The activity function divides a picture in segments of different statistics. Statistic measurements shows that by variable length coding of the prediction errors, the mean transmission rate could be further reduced by about 0.5 to 1 bit per pel.

Entropy coding with mean transmission rates of less than 2.5 bits per pel for the luminance signal can be reached only if adaptive quantization is combined with subsampling of picture segments at the transmitter side and interpolation of skipped samples at the receiver side [45]. Another well-known approach for low bit-rate coding is conditional replenishment where only pels with significant change from frame to frame are coded and transmitted. Up to now, quantizers for sophisticated, low bit-rate systems have been designed by trial and error and not by psychovisual criteria. The problem of visibility tests for such coding systems starts by selection of scenes with adequate spatial as well as temporal variations.

B. Adaptive Prediction

The picture signal is highly nonstationary and therefore the prediction error can be reduced by adapting the prediction to the local properties of the picture signal. Adaptive prediction reduces the range of possible prediction errors. Hence, picture quality will be improved for a given quantizer.

Contour Prediction: Let the picture be segmented into different areas where to each segment a predictor function h_i is assigned. Differences between proposed adaptive predictors are given by the chosen features of the segments and the control strategy. In case of adaptive intraframe prediction, four different kinds of segments as given below could be used

$$\hat{s}_0 = \begin{cases} h_1 & \text{flat area} \\ h_2 & \text{horizontal contour} \\ h_3 & \text{straight-line contour other than horizontal} \\ h_4 & \text{texture.} \end{cases} \tag{37}$$

Selection of predictor functions is controlled by the state of the neighboring pels. To avoid the transmission of additional information, most predictor selection schemes are based on previously transmitted pels. Frequently signal differences $d_{i,j}$ (31) are used to select the predictor at the present position.

Examples of this approach are adaptive predictors by Graham [46] and Zschunke [47]. Graham used horizontal and vertical prediction only.

$$\hat{s}_0 = \begin{cases} s'_7, & |d_{1,6}| < |d_{6,7}| \\ s'_1, & \text{otherwise.} \end{cases} \tag{38}$$

Because contour prediction requires a larger surrounding of pels for predictor control, a special subscripting according to Fig. 18 is used. Zschunke improved Graham's scheme by

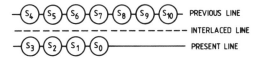

Fig. 18. Subscripting of pels for contour prediction.

separating contour pels from non-contour pels and considering the orientation of straight-line contours.

$$\hat{s}_0 = \begin{cases} s'_k, & \text{straight-line contour} \\ & k \in \{6,7,8\} \\ s'_1, & \text{otherwise.} \end{cases} \tag{39}$$

Contour points from the previous line are determined with reference to the previous pel s_1 by searching for the minimum of $\{|d_{1,5}|,|d_{1,6}|,|d_{1,7}|\}$. In addition, at a detected contour, the sign of the signal change (rising or falling) must be the same at both the previous line and the present line.

Selection control of most adaptive predictors is such that relations of signal differences with reference to the previous pel are used to predict corresponding relations of signal differences at the present pel. This sometimes results in bad prediction for high-detailed picture areas. To reduce the effects of wrong predictor selection, improved selection schemes and predictor functions, with coefficients smaller than one, are proposed. Recent investigations by Zhang [48] recommend the following predictor functions:

$$h_1 = \frac{5}{8}s'_1 + \frac{1}{8}\left(s'_6 + s'_7 + s'_8\right)$$

$$h_2 = \frac{3}{4}s'_1 + \frac{1}{4}s'_7$$

$$h_3 = \frac{1}{4}s'_{k-1} + \frac{1}{2}s'_k + \frac{1}{4}s'_{k+1}, \qquad k \in \{6,7,8,9\}$$

$$h_4 = \frac{1}{5}\left(s'_5 + s'_6 + s'_7 + s'_8 + s'_9\right). \tag{40}$$

The main steps of Zhang's selection scheme can be summarized as follows:
Predictor h_1 for flat areas is used if

$$\min\{|d_{1,2}|,|d_{1,5}|,|d_{1,6}|,|d_{1,7}|\} < 20 \text{ out of } 256.$$

A horizontal edge is assumed for

$$\max\{|d_{1,2}|,|d_{2,3}|\} < \min\{|d_{1,5}|,|d_{1,6}|,|d_{1,7}|,|d_{1,8}|\}.$$

The direction of a contour other than horizontal is identified by

$$\min\{|d_{1,k-1}|\}, \qquad k = 6,7,8,9$$

as long as the minimum is smaller than 51 out of 256. In addition, the sign of the signal change at a detected contour has to be identical for neighboring lines. This is checked by

$$\text{sign}(d_{1,2}) \times \text{sign}(d_{k-1,k-2}) = 1.$$

In order to avoid the influence of noise in the contour estimate, the result of the sign function is set to zero for arguments smaller than 7.

Texture is identified by rapid signal changes which will be recognized by

$$\text{sign}(d_{1,2}) \times \text{sign}(d_{k,k-1}) = -1, \qquad k = 6,7$$

and

$$\text{sign}(d_{k-1,k-2}) \neq \text{sign}(d_{k,k-1}) = \text{sign}(d_{k+1,k}).$$

Another approach to contour prediction by an edge orientation extrapolation process has been presented by Kretz [26]. An advantage of this recent proposal is the reduced sensitivity to transmission errors.

Adaptive Intra/Interframe Prediction: Contour prediction improves picture quality of scenes with high activity and many high contrast edges. However, for a large class of natural scenes, transmission bit rate reduction is more successful with adaptive intra/interframe predictors. A frame of a scene can be segmented into unchanged and changed areas. The unchanged areas consist of a stationary background with very small frame-to-frame differences whereas changed areas are caused by moving objects. It is obvious, that the best predictor function for unchanged areas is the previous frame predictor. Intraframe predictor is very efficient for changed areas. Hence, several adaptive predictors are proposed. Here either a previous frame or an intraframe predictor is selected, depending on surrounding signal changes. Variations of the coding schemes are basically given by the switching control.

Two approaches will be discussed here. According to the subscripting in Fig. 16 let

$$h_1 = \frac{1}{2}s'_1 + \frac{1}{8}s'_2 + \frac{1}{4}s'_3 + \frac{1}{8}s'_4 \tag{41}$$

be the intraframe predictor and let

$$h_2 = s'_{20} \tag{42}$$

be the previous frame predictor. In the first method [49], switching between both predictors is controlled by a special activity function A_{Sj} which is the sum of the magnitudes of the prediction errors for each pel in a small window of neighboring pels. The predictor function, which gives the smallest activity value, is chosen for prediction. The basic selection rule is as follows:

$$\hat{s}_0 = \begin{cases} h_1, & \text{if } A_{s1} < A_{s2} \\ h_2, & \text{otherwise} \end{cases} \tag{43}$$

where

$$A_{sj} = \sum_{i \in DN} |s'_i - h_j(s'_i)|. \tag{44}$$

The notation $h_j(s'_i)$ means the value of predictor function h_j calculated at pel position s_i relative to the present pel s_0.

It has been recognized that the selection schemes described above are sensitive to quantization noise because of recursive control. Better performance for the case of coarse quantization can be provided by activity functions similar to (30) [50]. Here

$$A_{MD1} = \max_{i,j,\, \in DN} |d_{i,j}| \tag{45}$$

is used as a measure of intraframe activity, and

$$A_{MD2} = \max_{i \in DN} |d_{i,i+20}| \tag{46}$$

as a measure of activity between successive frames. The switching control has been further improved by introducing a weighting factor b and a transitional state. In the transitional state, a three-dimensional predictor

$$h_3 = \frac{1}{4}s'_1 + \frac{1}{8}s'_3 + \frac{5}{8}s'_{20} \tag{47}$$

is used. The adaptation process of this scheme can be described by a state diagram as shown in Fig. 19. A further improvement of picture quality for highly detailed moving areas is possible if the intraframe predictor is combined with contour prediction. An adaptive predictor similar to

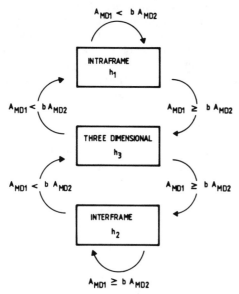

Fig. 19. State diagram of an adaptive intra/interframe predictor [50].

the one described above has been also proposed by Grallert and Starck [51]. Subjective investigations have shown that an eight-level quantizer is sufficient for most television scenes [50].

The application of variable-length coding does not require the restriction to a very small number of quantization levels and allows much lower bit rates than constant word length coding. Using a quantization level zero, optimized prediction provides this level very frequently. Very efficient for such a case is the application of a run-length code for the zero–nonzero pattern of quantization levels within a frame [49], [52].

Other coding schemes cluster a picture in predictable (prediction error level zero) and unpredictable pels and code clusters of predictable pels by run-length [53]. It has been recognized that in case of adaptive prediction, segmentation control by the prediction error is more efficient than a forward segmentor based on frame-to-frame differences as in standard conditional replenishment.

Inter and intraframe prediction are the best for scenes with small and very large motion, respectively. For scenes with moderate motion, interfield predictors are better. This is due to the fact that spatial and interframe correlation is effected differently by motion. For this reason, adaptive inter/intrafield has been proposed [51], [54].

Most of the adaptive schemes are controlled by signal changes of previously transmitted pels to avoid the transmission of overhead information. It has been also shown that systems with overhead information can be as efficient as those without [54]. To keep the transmission costs for overhead information small, switching is performed by clusters of pels.

Motion-Compensated Prediction: Adaptive prediction can be further significantly improved by taking into account the frame-to-frame displacement of moving objects. The success of these schemes obviously depends on the ability to estimate the displacement of moving objects. Methods for displacement estimation are described in Section II of this paper.

In Fig. 20, the transmission bit rate of moving objects is shown as a function of the velocity for the three kinds of predictors. The transmission bit rates have been calculated by assuming a simple signal model [55]. For objects or segments of a scene with small velocity, interframe prediction is obviously the best. For segments with higher velocity, above 1 pel per frame, intraframe prediction does better than interframe prediction. Hence, the transmission rate of adaptive intra/interframe predictors depends on the percentage of pels with slow motion. By application of motion-compensated prediction, transmission rate of moving areas with a velocity above 0.5 pel per frame can be further reduced. It should be recognized, that even with an ideal displacement estimation, there still remains a significant transmission bit rate for highly detailed moving objects in case of noninteger displacements. For this kind of displacement, prediction by the nearest neighbor performs poorer than an interpolation of the four neighboring pels [11].

The methods of motion-compensated prediction can be roughly split into two groups. One set of techniques uses a forward motion estimation on a block-by-block basis (Fig. 21(a)). Block matching is performed by searching for the maximum of the correlation between a block in the present frame and a displaced block in the previous frame [18]–[20].

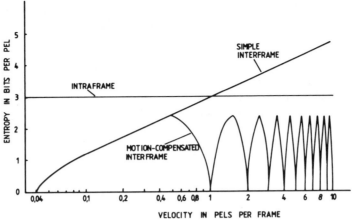

Fig. 20. Transmission rate of moving areas versus velocity for three basic predictors [55].

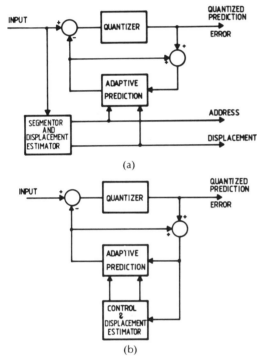

Fig. 21. Block diagram of motion-compensated DPCM codecs. (a) Forward segmentor and motion estimator. (b) Recursive control and motion estimator.

Block size for these correlation techniques is on the order of 7 × 7. To reduce realization expense, the searching of displacement is restricted to a total certain number of possible positions (25) [20]. One of the problems of block-based motion estimation is the segmentation method for moving objects. It is obvious that boundary lines of moving objects within a block influence the estimate.

Instead of block matching, significant spatial luminance gradients within a block can be used for displacement measurement [26]. The results of a two-stage system based on gradients are very promising [56]. Such a system allows separation of objects with different motion within one block.

A disadvantage of the block-wise forward displacement estimator is that the displacement vector needs to be transmitted. To restrict the amount of overhead information, most of the coding schemes with forward estimators use only integer displacements. Overhead information is not necessary with pel recursive displacement estimation based on transmitted pels (Fig. 22(b)). The pel recursive algorithm of Netravali and Robbins [11], [12] has been applied to component and composite color video signals [57], [58]. For stability reasons, the update of the displacement from pel to pel in recursive systems is restricted. Hence, it is advantageous to do predictor selection between motion-compensated prediction and other frame-to-frame and intraframe predictors [53]. Computer simulations on several test sequences have shown the efficiency of motion-compensated prediction with pel recursive displacement estimate. This

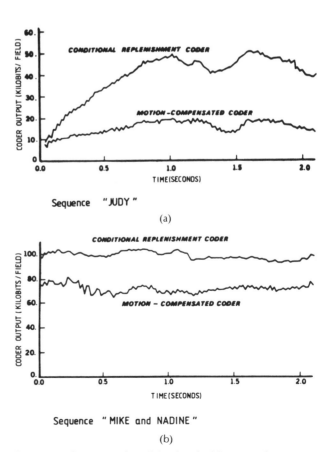

Sequence "JUDY"

(a)

Sequence "MIKE and NADINE"

(b)

Fig. 22. Performance of conditional replenishment and motion-compensated prediction for two scenes with different activity [12].

kind of prediction reduces the coder bit rate by 30 to 70 percent compared to conditional replenishment (Fig. 22). Using a 35-level quantizer, the maximum bit rates of the scenes are on the order of 0.5 to 2.8 bits per pel depending on the kind of scene [12].

In most cases, motion-compensated prediction based on a forward estimator provides more accurate displacements of large moving objects than recursive systems. But a comparison of prediction techniques with forward and backward estimation using the same bit rate has not yet been reported. Here it has to be considered that the amount of overhead information for a prediction with a forward estimator can be used in addition for prediction error coding in case of recursive estimators. Although the optimal compromise between coding efficiency and hardware costs is not yet known, for low bit-rate systems such as video conferencing with 1.5 Mbits/s and below, a motion compensated predictor performs much better in terms of picture quality than conventional interframe coders. Recent investigations are directed to computationally simpler as well as more robust and effective methods to reduce hardware size and implementation costs [23], [59]. Supported by the progress of VLSI, complex systems such as motion compensation are going from theoretical investigations to actual implementation [60].

IV. TRANSFORM CODING

Transform coding denotes a procedure in which the PCM-coded video signal s_n is subjected prior to transmission to an invertible transform with subsequent quantizing and coding. The aim of the transform algorithm is to convert statistically dependent picture elements into independent coefficients. Probably the best known method is the discrete Fourier transform. Fig. 23 shows a block diagram for transform coding of video signals. The input signal s_n representing the picture elements of a sequence of successive television frames is first segmented into blocks (subpictures) of size $M \times N \times K$ (Fig. 24). Typical block sizes are $4 \times 4 \times 4$, $8 \times 8 \times 1$, and $16 \times 16 \times 1$. The coordinates within a block are indicated by i, j, k. Owing to line-by-line and frame-by-frame sampling of television signals, block

segmentation calls for M line stores for two-dimensional and K-field or frame stores for three-dimensional transforms. Block-segmentation networks precede the transform circuit at the transmitter and follow it on the receiver side.

A one-dimensional transform

$$S = \bar{T} \cdot s \qquad (48)$$

converts the vector s of the sampling values of a block $(1, N, 1)$ into the vector S of the transform coefficients, which, in order to achieve data compression, are quantized and then subjected to redundancy and irrelevancy reduction. Irrelevancy reduction introduces an irreversible distortion to the video signal whereas elimination of redundancy is a reversible coding operation. At the receiver, the inverse transform

$$s = \bar{T}^{-1} \cdot S = \bar{T}^{-1} \cdot \bar{T} \cdot S = s \qquad (49)$$

restores the picture signal which is affected by the errors produced by irrelevancy reduction. The tolerable distortion is determined by the human observer exclusively. In this paper we distinguish between broadcast picture quality and video telephone quality. The lines of the transform matrix $\bar{T}$ correspond to the samples of the basis functions, e.g., Walsh functions, cosine functions, which determine the characteristics of a transform. For natural pictures, Discrete Cosine Transform (DCT), Karhunen–Loève transform (KLT), Walsh transform (WT), and Slant transform (SLT) lead to an energy concentration in only a few coefficients containing the main part of the picture information. The M transform uses orthogonal pn-sequences as basis functions allowing particularly effective irrelevancy reduction. Various basis function systems are presented in [2], [3]. Fig. 25 shows the basis functions of a one-dimensional M transform for $1 \times 15 \times 1$ blocks [89].

In the past three years investigations have concentrated on the following problems:

- adaptive coding, i.e., quantizing and coding of spectral coefficients controlled by the picture content;
- hybrid coding, i.e., combination of transform coding and DPCM;
- investigation of new basis function systems.

In addition to these investigations, which will be explained in detail, also techniques for reducing the visibility of the block boundaries have been developed.

Transform coding takes advantage of the statistical dependencies of picture elements for redundancy reduction. Because of block segmentation, statistical dependencies beyond block boundaries are not considered. Furthermore, due to irrelevancy reduction at data rates below 1 bit per pel these boundaries may become visible. Schlichte [61], [62], Pearson [63], and Chen [64] are attempting to overcome this deficiency by transform coding with overlapping blocks. This increases the number of blocks per frame or the block size. It is still unknown whether this technique will result in greater reduction factors. This method, however, does make the block boundaries less visible. As the locations of the block boundaries are known, also digital low-pass filtering can be applied to reduce the visibility of the block edges. Reeve and Lim [65] propose two-dimensional filtering for this use. They report that filtering or block overlap coding give almost the same results.

Investigations covered both component and composite

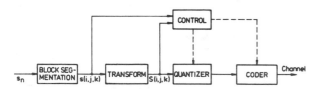

Fig. 23. Block diagram of a transform coder with adaptive control.

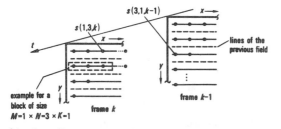

Fig. 24. Sampling structure. The indices x, y, k denote the positions of picture elements in a sequence of frames.

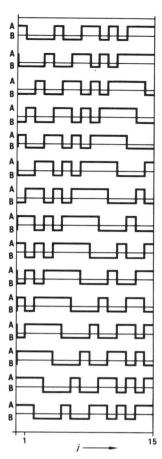

Fig. 25. A one-dimensional *m* function system with *N* = 15.

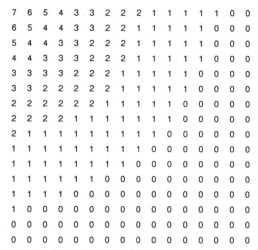

7	6	5	4	3	3	2	2	2	1	1	1	1	1	0	0
6	5	4	4	3	3	2	2	1	1	1	1	1	0	0	0
5	4	4	3	3	2	2	2	1	1	1	1	1	0	0	0
4	4	3	3	3	2	2	2	1	1	1	1	1	0	0	0
3	3	3	3	2	2	2	1	1	1	1	1	0	0	0	0
3	3	2	2	2	2	2	1	1	1	1	1	0	0	0	0
2	2	2	2	2	2	1	1	1	1	1	0	0	0	0	0
2	2	2	2	1	1	1	1	1	1	1	0	0	0	0	0
2	1	1	1	1	1	1	1	1	1	0	0	0	0	0	0
1	1	1	1	1	1	1	1	1	0	0	0	0	0	0	0
1	1	1	1	1	1	1	1	0	0	0	0	0	0	0	0
1	1	1	1	1	1	0	0	0	0	0	0	0	0	0	0
1	1	1	1	0	0	0	0	0	0	0	0	0	0	0	0
1	0	0	0	0	0	0	0	0	0	0	0	0	0	0	0
0	0	0	0	0	0	0	0	0	0	0	0	0	0	0	0
0	0	0	0	0	0	0	0	0	0	0	0	0	0	0	0

Fig. 26. Typical bit allocation table for 16 × 16 × 1 block cosine transform coding at approximately 1 bit per pel according to Jain [3].

coding of PAL and NTSC signals. The following statements refer to component coding. Composite coding will be described briefly in Section IV-D.

A. Adaptive Coding

The aim of adaptive transform coding is to control the quantizing and coding of the individual coefficients as a function of the picture content or its spectral energy distribution within a block in such a way that the distortions as a result of irrelevancy reduction are kept below a visibility threshold, which is fixed by the human observer. The problems that have to be overcome here are the unique classification of the picture content and the design of suitable quantizers and coders.

From the knowledge of the variances of the spectral coefficients determined from an evaluation of many transform blocks, the so-called bit-allocation or bit-assignment tables can be drawn up which contain the necessary number of quantizing steps for each coefficient. The results of comprehensive investigations on the design of quantizers have been carried out by Mauersberger [66]. Jain [3] gives a typical example in Fig. 26. S (1,1,1) is coded with 7 bits. With increasing indices (i, j) the coefficients S $(i, j, 1)$ are quantized more and more coarsely according to the frequency weighting function of the human eye until eventually high-order coefficients are completely suppressed. Once established, the bit-allocation table applies to all the blocks. With such methods it is possible to achieve a

reduction to approximately 1 bit per pel for video telephone pictures. This does not, however, apply to highly structured picture contents as it leads to mismatching of the quantizer. Therefore, adaptive coding has to be used for broadcast TV signals or reduction factors greater than 8.

In der Smitten and Hildebrandt [67] have investigated adaptive coding of the Slant coefficients for the transmission of broadcast color TV signals on 34-Mbit/s channels. Classification is based on an analysis of the magnitude spectrum of two-dimensional blocks. If there are predominantly horizontal (H), vertical (V), diagonal (D), or no (0) structures in the picture the investigated block of size 4 × 4 × 1 is assigned to one of the four activity categories H, V, D, or 0. For each category there is a special bit-allocation table. Activity category 0 applies if none of the coefficients achieves 8 percent of its maximum amplitude. Decision for activity category H, V, or D is taken by the activity functions h, v, and d, which are the weighted sums of the absolute values of the coefficients. The following matrix shows the arrangement of the two-dimensional Slant coefficients of one block:

$$
\begin{array}{cccc}
S(1,1) & S(1,2) & S(1,3) & S(1,4) \\
S(2,1) & S(2,2) & S(2,3) & S(2,4) \\
S(3,1) & S(3,2) & S(3,3) & S(3,4) \\
S(4,1) & S(4,2) & S(4,3) & S(4,4).
\end{array}
$$

Activity functions h, v, and d are calculated by

$$
\begin{aligned}
h = {} & 2 \cdot |S(2,1)| + 2 \cdot |S(3,1)| + 2 \cdot |S(4,1)| \\
& + |S(3,2)| + |S(4,2)| \\
v = {} & 2 \cdot |S(1,2)| + 2 \cdot |S(1,3)| + \quad |S(1,4)| \\
& + |S(2,3)| + |S(2,4)| \\
d = {} & 4 \cdot |S(2,2)| + 8 \cdot |S(3,3)| \\
& + 2 \cdot |S(3,4)| + 2 \cdot |S(4,3)|. \quad (50)
\end{aligned}
$$

If the relevant information is concentrated in one of the categories 0, H, or V, quantizing is controlled by a corresponding bit-allocation table. In case of activity category D the coefficients are subjected to structure coding. The basic

93

idea behind this form of coding is to combine groups of coefficients into a pattern. The actual pattern is compared with a set of basic patterns and the basic pattern that bears the greatest similarity is selected. All the possible basic patterns are stored at the receiver, so that only the storage address needs to be transmitted. Using this coding method and a set of 752 basic patterns, In der Smitten and Hildebrandt have achieved a picture quality that shows no discernible difference between the original and the coded picture under CCIR viewing conditions: [98]. In Fig. 27 the original and the coded luminance signals are represented.

Original

34 Mbit/s

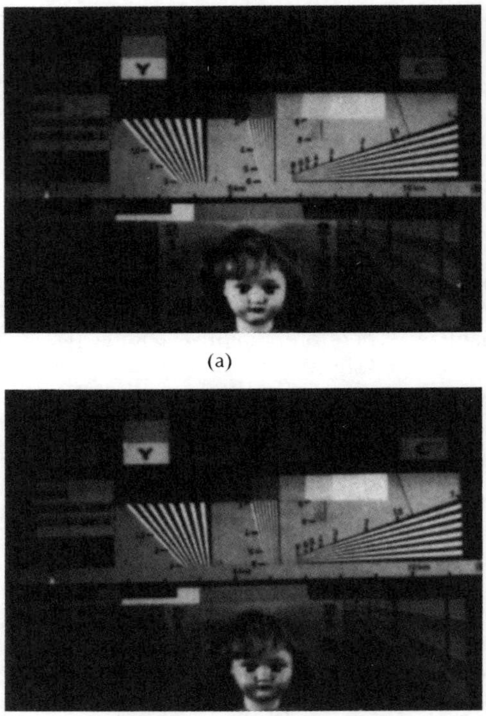

(a)

(b)

Fig. 27. Luminance component of the test picture. (a) PCM, sampling rates: 10 MHz for luminance, 2.5 MHz for chrominance, line-alternating transmission. (b) Adaptive Slant transform, bit rate 34 Mbits/s, according to [67].

Ngan [68] has conducted a comparative study of five different bit-allocation algorithms using WT and DCT at bit rates between 0.5 and 2 bits per pel. The author comes to the conclusion that bit allocation and type of basis function system are not independent of each other. In general, DCT is clearly superior to WT in terms of data compression achieving a lower bit rate for the same picture quality for all schemes.

Wong and Steele [69], [70] have achieved a data rate of 0.55 bit per pel for monochrome video telephone signals using bit allocation and adaptive selection of the DCT coefficients. For a block size of 16 × 16 × 1, bit allocation takes place in accordance with the following formula:

$$b(i,j) = \text{INTEGER}\left[1/2 \log_2\left(\frac{E[S^2(i,j)]}{E_{\text{mean}}} \cdot C\right)\right] \quad (51)$$

where $b(i,j)$ corresponds to the number of bits made available for coding $S(i,j,1)$. E_{mean} is defined as $E[s^2(x,y)]$

for all x, y of the whole field. C is a weighting factor for the individual spectral coefficients. $E[S^2(i,j)]$ as well as E_{mean} must be known to the receiver, which requires the transmission of overhead information. This transform coding scheme reduces the bit rate to approximately 1 bit per pel. In a second step, the squares of the current coefficients $S^2(i,j)$ in a block are estimated from coefficients already coded according to

$$\hat{S}^2(i,j) = 1/3\left[S^2(i,j-1) + S^2(i-1,j) + S^2(i-1,j-1)\right]. \quad (52)$$

If $\hat{S}^2(i,j_0)$ falls below a specified threshold none of the residual coefficients in the same line $S(i,j = j_0,\cdots,16)$ is transmitted. Since $S^2(i,j)$ generally decreases at higher orders i,j this method seems justifiable.

Götze and Ocylok [71] describe a system with adaptive coding of the three-dimensional DCT coefficients for 8 × 8 × 4 blocks. Coding is controlled by the activity vector $\Delta = (\Delta h, \Delta v, \Delta t)$. The variables Δh and Δv denote the maximum absolute difference between adjacent pels s in the horizontal and vertical direction. Δt denotes the maximum absolute difference in the temporal direction within a block

$$\Delta t = \max\left\{(\max s(i,j,k+1) - \min s(i,j,k))k = 1,\cdots,3, \right.$$
$$\left. i,j = 1,\cdots,8\right\}. \quad (53)$$

If Δt is less than a certain threshold, the block does not contain any visible change in the temporal direction. In this case only coefficients $S(i,j,1)$ $(i,j = 1,\cdots,8)$ are encoded and transmitted. If the classifier detects changes in the temporal direction, the coefficients are divided into 14 activity categories as a function of Δh and Δv. A bit-allocation table is available for each activity category. The authors have achieved a signal-to-noise ratio of about 24 dB for video telephone signals at 0.4 bit per pel.

Attention is drawn to further work on adaptive transform coding, some of it in conjunction with a study of channel coding [72]–[78]; there is no room within this paper for discussing this work in detail.

Lohscheller [79], [80] studies the transmission of still pictures on digital telephone channels. His intention is to overcome the long transmission time by making a coarse structure of the image visible at the receiver after only a few seconds. After two-dimensional DCT with block size 8 × 8 × 1 and quantization according to Mauersberger [66] the coefficients are transmitted in an order according to the size of their spectral variance. After transmission of the first three coefficients of a block, a coarse picture is already visible.

A similiar method allows the inclusion of high-quality photographic images within Videotex data [81]–[83]. Further investigations of the progressive transmission of still pictures in conjunction with transform coding are published by Takikawa [84] and Ngan [85].

B. Hybrid Coding

Hybrid coding denotes the combination of transform coding and DPCM. Owing to the line structure of the television signal, M line stores are used for two-dimensional block segmentation and K frame stores for three-dimensional block segmentation. In order to save memory, it may be suitable to combine a one-dimensional transform in the line direction with DPCM in the column direction or a two-dimensional transform with DPCM in the temporal direction. The block diagram of a hybrid coder based on one-dimensional transform is shown in Fig. 28.

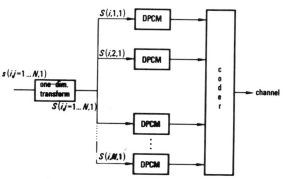

Fig. 28. Block diagram of a hybrid encoder using a one-dimensional transform and DPCM encoders in the second dimension. The block consists of N pels s $(i, j = 1, \ldots, N, 1)$ along a line.

Habibi [86] proposes a system with one-dimensional DCT of block size $1 \times 16 \times 1$. The DPCM is simplified to a previous coefficient predictor that encodes the differences between successive spectral coefficients in the column direction. Then the differences are arranged in blocks of size 64×16. A cutout of such a block is given in Fig. 29.

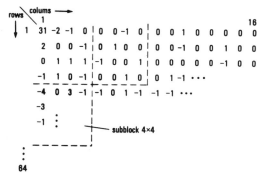

Fig. 29. Typical values of the differences between successive coefficients in column direction [86].

Investigations have shown that a great many of these differences within a block are equal to zero. Habibi divides a block of 64×16 into subblocks of 4×4 differences and applies a special code with variable word length. If a block consists only of zeros, one short code word (01) is transmitted. Otherwise, individual samples of the subblock are encoded corresponding to Table 4.

A buffer is provided to smooth the variable data rate. In order to avoid buffer overflow the resolution of the A/D converter at the system input is controlled by the level to which the buffer is filled. A coarser quantization of the samples results in an increase of the number of zeros in the subblocks. With this adaptive coding scheme, Habibi achieves a signal-to-noise ratio of approximately 36 dB at 1.2 bits per pel with aerial photographs. The quality of these test pictures can be compared with video telephone pictures.

Table 4 Coding with Variable Word Length of Individual Samples of One Subblock According to Habibi [86]

Difference	Code Word
0	1
1	001
−1	0001
2	00001
−2	000001
other	0000001 + PCM

Kamangar and Rao [87] as well as Pearlman and Jakatdar [88] have focused their attention on a two-dimensional transform combined with DPCM in the temporal direction. Pearlman has carried out a full-frame DFT. The differences between temporally successive spectral values are quantized by separate Max quantizers for the real and the imaginary components. Proof that this procedure can be used for videotelephony was furnished with the aid of the test sequence "Walter Cronkite." The signal-to-noise ratio is given as 30 dB for 1 bit per pel per frame and 21.6 dB for 0.2 bit per pel per frame.

By means of two-dimensional DCT, Kamangar and Rao [87] transform blocks of $8 \times 8 \times 1$ picture elements in the field with subsequent one-dimensional DPCM in the temporal direction. Since DPCM fails if there is fast motion in the picture it makes sense to control the coding adaptively. Each block representing the prediction error of DCT coefficients is divided into four subblocks according to Fig. 30.

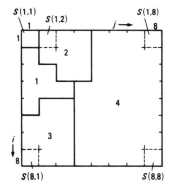

Fig. 30. Structure of subblocks in an 8×8 block of prediction errors in the two-dimensional DCT domain according to Kamangar and Rao [87].

The spatial activity of each subblock is determined by the variance of the coefficients. If the activity exceeds a threshold, more bits are assigned to the prediction errors in that subblock. This method results in a variable output bit rate which requires a buffer to smooth the data stream. The magnitude of the prediction error of the dc coefficient $S(1, 1)$ indicates temporal activity. If a block is recognized as temporally active no extra bits will be assigned to subblocks 3 and 4. Coding is thereby adapted to the reduced capacity of the eye to resolve detail in rapid movement. The system supplies a variable data flow. The authors have achieved a signal-to-noise ratio of about 30 dB at 1 bit per pel with the test sequence "Wheel of Fortune." Compared to the test sequence "Walter Cronkite" this sequence shows finer structured details.

95

Jain and Jain [18] as well as Hein [96] improve the prediction in temporal direction by motion-compensation methods which are carried out in the spatial domain and not in the spectral domain. Jain and Jain calculate the displacement vector for one block of size $16 \times 16 \times 1$ by using the samples $s(i,j,1)$. Then they shift the corresponding block of DCT coefficients $S(i,j,1)$ according to that displacement vector and improve a DPCM in temporal direction in the spectral domain. With 0.253 bit per pel they obtain a signal-to-noise ratio of 38.74 dB in the test sequence "Walter Cronkite."

C. M Transform

M transform is derived from the basis function system of m functions which is presented in [89], [90]. An m-function system arises from the cyclic shifting of one m sequence of binary symbols and subsequent orthonormalization. An m sequence is the maximum-length sequence generated by a feedback shift register [97]. Fig. 25 shows a system of one-dimensional m functions with $N = 15$. The condition for the orthonormalization of this function system reads

$$\frac{1}{15} \sum_{j=1}^{15} m_u(j) \cdot m_v(j) = \begin{cases} 1, & u = v, \\ 0, & u \neq v, \end{cases} \quad u, v = 1, \cdots, 15$$
(54)

with

$$\frac{8}{15} A^2 + \frac{7}{15} B^2 = 1, \quad \text{for } u = v$$

and

$$\frac{4}{15} A^2 + \frac{3}{15} B^2 + \frac{8}{15} AB = 0, \quad \text{for } u \neq v \quad (55)$$

the amplitudes A and B can be calculated.

The M transform does not lead to an energy concentration to only a few coefficients and does not reduce redundancy due to statistical dependencies of the picture elements, but allows particularly effective reduction of irrelevancy in the M spectrum. The basis functions have a noise-like structure as shown in Fig. 25. Therefore, the quantizing errors are superimposed on the video signal after the inverse transform as noise-like patterns. The human eye is less sensitive to these patterns than to structures as produced by WT, for example. Measurements have shown that the visibility threshold for the patterns of the m functions are higher than those of Walsh functions.

Using the m functions presented in [89] as a basis, Keesen developed a two-dimensional basis function system, which is shown in Fig. 31. The spectrum produced by this modified M transform is free of dc components [91], [92]. In addition, the mean value of the input function has no effect on the form of the spectrum. Measurements have shown that the variances of all spectral values are nearly the same. Therefore, the same quantizer can be used for all the coefficients.

Fig. 32 shows the block diagram of a coder which has been optimized for the transmission of broadcast color TV signals in 34-Mbit/s channels. The sampling values $s(i,j,1)$ are segmented into blocks of $3 \times 3 \times 1$ prior to transformation. Coding is carried out in three parallel channels. First, the coefficients (S), the activity (a), and the mean value $E(s)$ of a block are computed. Activity is defined as the

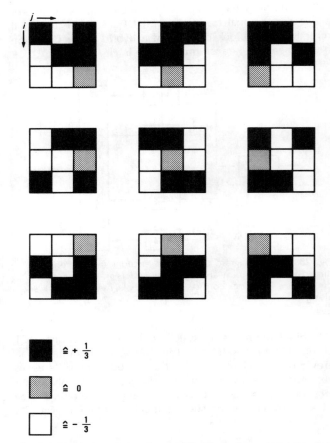

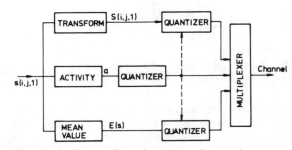

Fig. 31. Basis functions of a modified two-dimensional M transform with block size $3 \times 3 \times 1$.

difference between the maximum and the minimum sample value in a block. The activity controls bit allocation for the quantizing of the mean value and the coefficients. In a block with low activity the mean value is quantized very

Fig. 32. Block diagram of an adaptive transform coder using modified m functions.

finely and up to 8 bits are spent for its transmission. For high activities about 6 bits are sufficient. Investigations with a realized coder for the luminance signal have shown that for natural pictures there are no visible differences compared with a PCM picture, when 32 bits are used on the average for encoding the information of one block.

D. Composite Coding of NTSC and PAL Signals

In principle, similar procedures to those used for the adaptive coding of component signals are applied to the adaptive coding of NTSC and PAL signals. The difficulty lies in finding block boundaries in which there is maximum correlation between sampling values.

Playsongsang and Rao [95] describe two different hybrid DCT/DPCM coding schemes for NTSC composite video signals. The first scheme is based on one-dimensional DCT with block size $1 \times 32 \times 1$ with subsequent DPCM in the vertical direction. The authors report, that at 3.5 bits per pel the overall quality for video telephone pictures was good, but there appeared isolated color streaks in areas of sharp changes in color and luminance. The second scheme involves a special form of DCT with block size of $4 \times 4 \times 1$ followed by DPCM between the blocks. The NTSC signal is sampled at three times color subcarrier frequency $3 f_{sc}$ and quantized with 8 bits per sample. The samples are arranged in a block consisting of 4 lines of a field and 12 pels per line as shown in Fig. 33. Each block is divided into three sub-blocks of 4×4 samples having the same subcarrier phase as that in Fig. 34. The data in the subblocks are then

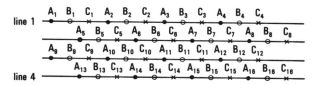

Fig. 33. Samples of one block $4 \times 12 \times 1$. Picture elements indicated with the same symbols have the same subcarrier phase according to Playsongsang and Rao [95].

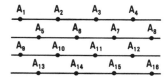

Fig. 34. One subblock with size $4 \times 4 \times 1$ of the block in Fig. 11.

rearranged to be one-dimensional and the DCT of those samples is performed. The first coefficient of each subblock corresponding to the mean value is compared with those of already transmitted adjacent subblocks of the subcarrier phase, as indicated in Fig. 35. The neighboring subblock

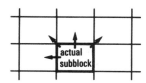

Fig. 35. Intersubblock DPCM according to Playsongsang and Rao [95].

whose mean value is closest to that of the actual block is assumed to have maximum correlation. DPCM is applied between the coefficients of these two subblocks. Two additional bits per subblock indicate the nearest neighbor that has been chosen for DPCM. The signal-to-noise ratio obtained with this method is about 37 dB at a bit rate of 3.5 bits per pel.

Ekambaram and Kwatra [93], [94] describe another adaptive method using two-dimensional DCT with which they

achieve a data rate of approximately 2 bits per pel at a "good" picture quality. Unfortunately, the authors do not describe their test sequences.

V. MOTION-ADAPTIVE FRAME INTERPOLATION

Skipping frames at the transmitter and interpolating the skipped frames at the receiver appears as a very attractive method of television coding since it can be combined with known coding techniques to further reduce the bit rate. However, it has been proven that simple frame reconstruction techniques as, e.g., frame repetition, generates jerkily moving objects in the displayed picture [99] or linear interpolation by temporal filtering exhibits blurring in moving areas [100]. The visibility of these degradations is in proportion to the speed of movement. Therefore, linear frame interpolation techniques can only be applied for television sequences with slow movement.

A certain improvement can be achieved if field interpolation is applied instead of frame interpolation [101], since there is less displacement of a moving object between fields than between frames. However, transmitting every second field also reduces the vertical resolution in stationary areas of the displayed picture.

A first step into the direction of motion-adaptive frame interpolation is an adaptive interpolator which is controlled by a movement detector [102]. This technique attempts to improve the picture quality by switching between two different interpolation algorithms in stationary and moving areas. If one of the picture elements F or Z in a present field according to Fig. 36 belongs to a moving area then the picture element in the field to be interpolated is replaced

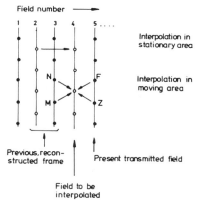

Fig. 36. Position of lines in subsequent fields. The arrows indicate which picture elements are used for interpolation in stationary and moving areas.

by an average of four picture elements Z, F, M, and N. Otherwise it is substituted by the corresponding picture element from the previous reconstructed frame. Compared to linear field interpolation, this nonlinear technique preserves the vertical resolution when combined with coding techniques where no permanent field skipping is applied as, e.g., in conditional replenishment coding.

To avoid blurring in the case of both moderate and rapid movement, the interpolation algorithm must "compensate" the motion of objects. Fig. 37 illustrates that a linear inter-

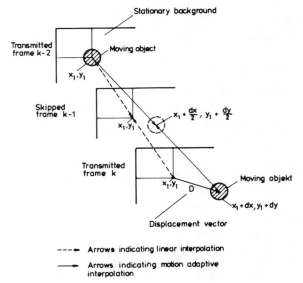

Fig. 37. Illustration of linear and motion-adaptive frame interpolation.

polator reconstructs a picture element with coordinates x_1, y_1 in a skipped frame $k - 1$ from corresponding picture elements x_1, y_1 of the transmitted frames k and $k - 2$. Blurring will be introduced, since picture element amplitudes from a moving object and static background are mixed in the interpolation. For a correct reconstruction of the moving object, its displacement vector $D(dx, dy)$ has to be considered. Thus a picture element at position $x_1 + (dx/2)$, $y_1 + (dy/2)$ in the skipped frame $k - 1$ has to be interpolated from picture elements x_1, y_1 in frame $k - 2$ and $x_1 + dx, y_1 + dy$ in frame k as indicated by arrows. Of course, if there are several moving objects with different displacements in a television scene, the interpolation has to be locally adapted to the individual displacements of the objects.

For this reason, the investigations on motion-adaptive frame interpolation have started with special television scenes which show only one uniformly moving object. Lippmann [103], [104] proposed in 1980 a motion-adaptive frame interpolation scheme for reducing the bit rate of an airborn television camera which scans the ground as demonstrated in Fig. 38. Let A_0, B_0 be two locations on the

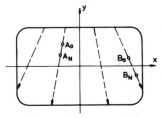

Fig. 38. Geometric imaging configurations of an oblique air-to-ground view. The dashed lines represent the motion paths of fixed ground locations in the television image sequence due to a moving camera.

ground in frame k_0 and A_N, B_N be the corresponding measured, displaced locations in frame k_N. Then all locations C_n in the skipped frames $k_1, \cdots, k_{N-1}$ of Fig. 39 can be calculated from the two measured displacement vectors by use of a simple linear motion model which approximates

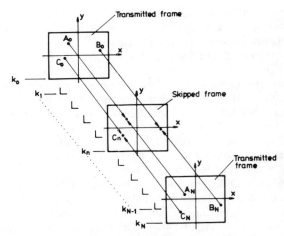

Fig. 39. Interpolation of skipped frames $k_1, \ldots, k_{N-1}$ for a television scene with uniformly moving background according to Lippmann [104].

the motion paths in the image plane by linear trajectories according to

$$y_{C0} = h_1 y_{Cn} + h_2$$
$$x_{C0} = g_1 x_{Cn} + g_2$$

and

$$y_{CN} = h_3 y_{Cn} + h_4$$
$$x_{CN} = g_3 x_{Cn} + g_4 \tag{56}$$

where the coefficients $g_1, \cdots, g_4$ and $h_1, \cdots, h_4$ are defined by the measured locations A_0, A_N and B_0, B_N. Once the locations C_0 and C_N with amplitudes S_{C0} and S_{CN} have been determined, an amplitude S_{Cn} at location C_n in frame n is interpolated as

$$S_{Cn} = \frac{1}{N}[(N - n)S_{C0} + nS_{CN}]. \tag{57}$$

This interpolation scheme requires that two point correspondences are measured in two transmitted frames k_0 and k_N. For a more accurate interpolation, the motion has to be described by a model that also considers the rotational components of motion. Assuming that the ground is flat, then five point correspondences have to be measured [4].

Using the explained interpolation scheme for these special aerial television scenes, Lippmann [104] reduces the frame rate at the coder from 25 frames per second to 1 frame per second achieving a bit rate reduction factor of 25.

First research results about motion-adaptive frame interpolation of television signals considering several randomly moving objects have been presented at the 1981 Picture Coding Symposium by Netravali and Robbins [105] and Bergmann [106]. Bergmann points out three major problems which are associated with motion-adaptive frame interpolation and which have to be solved.

i) Moving objects, areas decovered in the present frame and areas going to be covered in the next frame have to be detected and segmented.

ii) Displacement estimation algorithms must be improved to give more accurate estimates for single picture elements. Otherwise, the interpolation will introduce errors, e.g., at the boundaries of moving objects.

iii) An appropriate interpolation filter and algorithm for adapting the coefficients has to be developed.

In 1982 Lenz and Gerhard [107] presented some proposals

for solving the segmentation problem. Sabri, Cuffing, and Prasada reported experiments with 4:1 motion-adaptive field interpolation in noise-free conditions and in low bit-rate coding environment [108], [111]. The first more detailed description of a complete motion-adaptive frame interpolator was published by Bergmann [109] in 1984.

Fig. 40 shows a block diagram of the motion-adaptive frame interpolator. Bergmann uses a displacement estimator

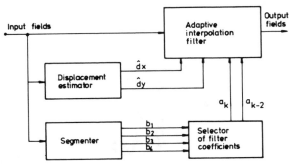

Fig. 40. Block diagram of a motion-adaptive frame or field interpolator.

based on the algorithm (15) as described in Section II. The segmenter according to Fig. 41 indicates for the transmitted field k:

b_1: moving areas
b_2: areas decovered in the present field
b_3: areas going to be covered in the next field
b_4: stationary background.

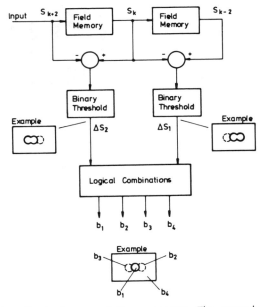

Fig. 41. Block diagram of the segmenter. The examples show the segmentation of a ball moving from right to left.

The segmentation is required for a correct reconstruction of skipped fields. Fig. 42 illustrates how the individual segments have to be reconstructed using image information from field k and $k - 2$, respectively. It also explains that the segments b_2, b_3 cannot be interpolated but must be

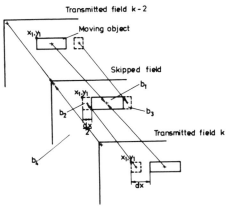

Fig. 42. Ideal segmentation and interpolation of a skipped field. The moving object is assumed to have a horizontal displacement of dx between the transmitted fields k and $k - 2$. Arrows indicate the image information used to reconstruct the skipped field.

extrapolated, since the required image information is available only in the subsequent field for b_2 and in the preceding field for b_3. The stationary background b_4 can be interpolated linearly. To interpolate the moving object b_1, a uniform displacement between field $k - 2$ and field k is assumed.

Unfortunately, the described segmenter only gives a segmentation for transmitted fields. Therefore, Bergmann [109] extrapolates from a segmentation in field k to that in the skipped field. For simplification he assumes that at a picture element position x, y in a skipped field $k - 1$ the same displacement vector is true, as measured for the picture element x, y in field k. Only the size of the displacement vector is divided by a factor of two.

Depending on the segmenter information $b_1, \cdots, b_4$, for a FIR interpolation filter, coefficients a_k, a_{k-2} are selected according to Table 5. Table 5 also shows the resulting interpolation algorithms for the amplitude $s_{k-1}(x, y)$ of the picture element at position x, y. These algorithms correspond to the arrows in Fig. 42.

In case of nonintegral displacements the amplitudes $s_k[x + (dx/2), y + (dy/2)]$ and $s_{k-2}[x - (dx/2), y - (dy/2)]$ have to be evaluated by bilinear interpolation using the four adjacent picture elements according to (12) in Section II. Therefore, the block diagram of the motion-adaptive interpolation filter includes two bilinear spatial interpolators as shown in Fig. 43.

If only every Nth field is transmitted, where $N = 2, 3, 4, \cdots$, then for interpolating the nth field, where $n = 1, 2, 3, \cdots, N - 1$, the filter coefficients have to be chosen according to

$$a_{k-2} = \frac{N - n}{N} \qquad a_k = \frac{n}{N} \qquad (58)$$

for areas b_1 and b_4.

In order to investigate the performance of the proposed motion-adaptive interpolation technique, simulation with the television test sequence "Ellen" has been carried out. The maximum displacement in this sequence is 16.5 pels per frame. No degradations have been observed in the case that every second field has been skipped ($N = 2$). When skipping two fields ($N = 3$) interpolation errors become visible due to erroneous displacement estimates.

Table 5 Selection of Filter Coefficients and Interpolation Output in Case that Every Second Field is Interpolated ($N = 2$)

Information from Segmenter	Coefficients	Interpolator Output $s_{k-1}(x, y)$
b_1	$a_k = a_{k-2} = \dfrac{1}{2}$	$\dfrac{1}{2} \cdot s_{k-2}\left(x - \dfrac{dx}{2}, y - \dfrac{dy}{2}\right) + \dfrac{1}{2} \cdot s_k\left(x + \dfrac{dx}{2}, y + \dfrac{dy}{2}\right)$
b_2	$a_k = 1 \quad a_{k-2} = 0$	$1 \cdot s_k(x, y)$
b_3	$a_k = 0 \quad a_{k-2} = 1$	$1 \cdot s_{k-2}(x, y)$
b_4	$a_k = a_{k-2} = \dfrac{1}{2}$	$\dfrac{1}{2} \cdot s_{k-2}(x, y) + \dfrac{1}{2} \cdot s_k(x, y)$

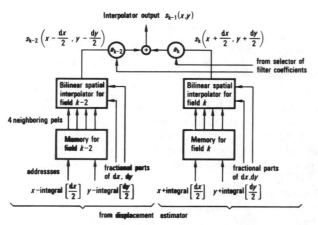

Fig. 43. Block diagram of the motion-adaptive interpolation filter.

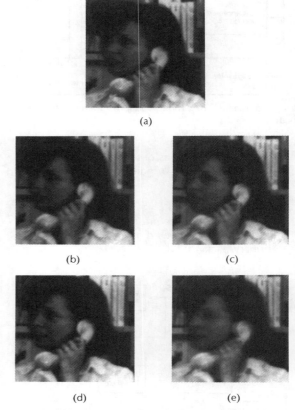

(a)

(b)   (c)

(d)   (e)

Fig. 44. Interpolated sequence of fields from the test sequence "Ellen." Every third field is transmitted ($N = 3$). (a) Transmitted field k_0. (b), (c) Motion adaptively interpolated fields k_1 and k_2. (d) Transmitted field $k_{N=3}$. (e) Field, reconstructed by linear interpolation.

The photos in Fig. 44 demonstrate the picture quality of the transmitted and motion adaptively interpolated fields in comparison to a field which is reconstructed by pure linear interpolation.

In a recent publication by Furukawa, Koga, and Iinuma [110] the problem of erroneous displacement estimates in motion-adaptive interpolation is discussed. The authors propose a preprocessing of the measured vectors based on a rigid moving object assumption to provide more reliable displacement vectors for the interpolation.

VI. Discussion and Conclusion

The main advances in digital coding of video signals during the last five years are outlined including the areas of predictive coding, transform coding, and motion-adaptive frame interpolation.

In a special section on displacement estimation, the fundamentals and the relationship of two important classes of displacement estimation, known as recursive and block-matching algorithms, are elaborated. It is shown that both classes are iterative estimation techniques which only differ in the search procedure. In the first class, the search procedure is based on measured derivatives of the optimization criterion, in the second the search procedure is based on matching results which are nothing else but checks of the local optimization criterion. Also, it is shown that the algorithms within the first class are closely related although there are essential differences in the performance. In the beginning, only displacements of up to 2 pels per frame

could be estimated with an acceptable accuracy in one or two steps of iteration. Now, block-matching techniques allow to measure displacements of up to 6 pels per frame within three steps of iteration while those techniques which are based on derivatives require one to two steps of iteration to reach an accuracy of about ±0.5 pel per frame.

In the future, especially for application in motion-adaptive frame interpolation, we will need displacement estimation techniques with a measuring range of up to 20 pels per frame. Furthermore, methods will have to be developed which will assure a correct convergence of the estimation algorithms.

Predictive coding is discussed with a view to two areas of application. For coding of broadcast television signals there is the demand that digital encoding should not degrade the picture quality. For such a quality requirement, quantizer design methods based on subjectively measured visibility thresholds are described. Definition and application of activity and masking functions are the main part of this section. More work is needed in order for the activity functions to be better matched to the visual system and for the quantizer control to consider the dynamic feedback of DPCM systems.

Better coder performance in terms of picture quality as a function of bit rate can be reached by adaptive prediction. For high detailed picture areas the use of contour prediction is proposed. Up to now there is a big distinction between adaptive prediction for intraframe and interframe coding because of the hardware expense for the frame store.

Due to the stringent requirements of bit rate reduction for video conferencing, sophisticated adaptive intra/interframe prediction schemes can be applied. Furthermore, in video conferencing, we are allowed to restrict the variety of television scenes to be considered for coding to scenes with slow and moderate movement. Certain distortions may be introduced in coding of rapid movement. A few examples of adaptive prediction schemes are outlined within the paper. Also, two basic approaches of motion-compensated prediction are explained. Better models for describing a scene by an extended set of motion parameters and the development of more robust and accurate motion adaptive prediction schemes are required to improve coder performance.

Transform coding denotes a procedure in which the PCM-coded video signal is subjected prior to transmission to an invertible transform with subsequent quantizing and coding. So far the aim of the transform algorithm has been to convert statistically dependent picture elements into independent coefficients.

In recent years, investigations have focussed on an improvement of adaptive transform coding. Several techniques are discussed where quantizing and coding is controlled by the local picture content and adapted to the perception of the human eye. In addition, a new transform is introduced which does not reduce the statistical redundancy but exploits masking effects of the eye. Three bit per picture element seems to be a lower bound which is attainable in coding of broadcast television signals. In video conferencing the data rate can be reduced to about 0.5 bit per picture element because of the special picture content, e.g., head and shoulder scenes.

It is expected that the combination of transform coding with other pre- and postprocessing methods as motion-compensated three-dimensional transformation or motion-adaptive interpolation will decrease the data rate furthermore in the future. Compared to motion-compensated prediction, motion-adaptive frame interpolation is still in a very early stage. The presented interpolation techniques indicate that at least for video-conferencing scenes a reduction of the field rate by a factor of 2 can be achieved without introducing image degradation. Skipping more than every second field leads to an increase of the displacements and requires more reliable displacement estimation algorithms as well as a development of refined techniques for segmenting the frame to be interpolated. In spite of these problems to be solved, motion-adaptive frame interpolation appears very promising.

REFERENCES

[1] W. K. Pratt, *Image Transmission Techniques*. New York: Academic Press, 1979.
[2] A. N. Netravali and J. O. Limb, "Picture coding: A review," *Proc. IEEE*, vol. 68, pp. 366–406, Mar. 1980.
[3] A. K. Jain, "Image data compression: A review," *Proc. IEEE*, vol. 69, pp. 349–384, Mar. 1981.
[4] T. S. Huang and R. Y. Tsai, "Image sequence analysis: Motion Estimation," in *Image Sequence Analysis*. Berlin, Germany: Springer-Verlag, 1981, pp. 1–18.
[5] J. W. Roach and J. K. Aggarwal, "Determining the movement of objects from a sequence of images," *IEEE Trans. Pattern Anal. Machine Intell.*, vol. PAMI-2, no. 6, pp. 554–562, 1980.
[6] R. Y. Tsai and T. S. Huang, "Estimating three-dimensional motion parameters of a rigid planar patch," *IEEE Trans. Acoust., Speech, Signal Process.*, vol. ASSP-29, no. 6, pp. 1147–1152, Dec. 1981.
[7] R. J. Schalkoff and E. S McVey, "A model and tracking algorithm for a class of video targets," *IEEE Trans. Pattern Anal. Machine Intell.*, vol. PAMI-4, no. 1, pp. 2–10, Jan. 1982.
[8] H. H. Nagel, "Overview on image sequence analysis," in *Image Sequence Processing and Dynamic Scene Analysis*, T. S. Huang, Ed., Berlin, Germany: Springer-Verlag, 1983, pp. 2–39.
[9] J. O. Limb and J. A. Murphy, "Measuring the speed of moving objects from television signals," *IEEE Trans. Commun.*, vol. COM-23, no. 4, pp. 474–478, Apr. 1975.
[10] C. Cafforio and F. Rocca, "Methods for measuring small displacements of television images," *IEEE Trans. Inform. Theory*, vol. IT-22, no. 5, pp. 573–579, Sept. 1976.
[11] A. N. Netravali and J. D. Robbins, "Motion compensated television coding—Part I," *Bell Syst. Tech. J.*, vol. 58, pp. 631–670, Mar. 1979.
[12] J. D. Robbins and A. N. Netravali, "Recursive motion compensation: A review," in *Image Sequence Processing and Dynamic Scene Analysis*, T. S. Huang, Ed. Berlin, Germany: Springer-Verlag, 1983, pp. 76–103.
[13] H. C. Bergmann, "Displacement estimation based on the correlation of image segments," in *IEEE Proc. Int. Conf. on Electronic Image Processing* (York; England), pp. 215–219, July 1982.
[14] C. Cafforio and F. Rocca, "The differential method for image motion estimation," in *Image Sequence Processing and Dynamic Scene Analysis*, T. S. Huang, Ed. Berlin, Germany: Springer-Verlag, 1983, pp. 104–124.
[15] H. C. Bergmann, "Ein schnell konvergierendes Displacement-Schätzverfahren für die Interpolation von Fernsehbildsequenzen," Ph.D. dissertation, Tech. Univ. of Hannover, Hannover, Germany, Feb. 1984.
[16] H. Burkhard and H. Moll, "A modified Newton-Raphson search for the model-adaptive identification of delays," in *Identification and System Parameter Identification*, R. Isermann, Ed. Oxford, England, and New York: Pergamon Press, 1979, pp. 1279–1286.
[17] S. Sabri, "Movement-compensated interframe prediction for NTSC colour TV signals," in *Image Sequence Processing and Dynamic Scene Analysis*, T. S. Huang, Ed. Berlin, Germany: Springer-Verlag, 1983, pp. 156–199.
[18] J. R. Jain and A. K. Jain, "Displacement measurement and its application in interframe image coding," *IEEE Trans. Commun.*, vol. COM-29, pp. 1799–1806, Dec. 1981.
[19] T. Koga, K. Iinuma, A. Hirano, Y. Iijima, and T. Ishiguro, "Motion-compensated interframe coding for video conferencing," in *NTC 81, Proc.*, pp. G5.3.1–G5.3.5 (New Orleans, LA, Dec. 1981).
[20] Y. Ninomiya and Y. Ohtsuka, "A motion-compensated interframe coding scheme for television pictures," *IEEE Trans. Commun.*, vol. COM-30, pp. 201–211, Jan. 1982.
[21] R. Srinivasan and K. R. Rao, "Predictive coding based on efficient motion estimation," in *ICC 1984, Proc.*, pp. 521–526, May 1984.
[22] C. M. Lin and S. C. Kwatra, "Motion compensated interframe color image coding," in *ICC 1984, Proc.*, pp. 516–520, May 1984.
[23] K. Matsuda, T. Tsuda, T. Ito, and S. Make, "A new motion compensation coding scheme for video conference," in *ICC*

1984, Proc., pp. 234–237, May 1984.

[24] S. Beyer, "Displacementschätzverfahren für Fernsehbild-signale mit minimaler Schätzfehlervarianz," pending dissertation at the Tech. Univ. of Hannover, Hannover, Germany.

[25] F. May and W. Wolf, "Picture coding with motion analysis for low bit rate transmission," in *ICC 82, Proc.*, pp. 2G.7.1–2G.7.5, June 1982.

[26] F. Kretz, "Edges in visual scenes and sequences: Applications to filtering, sampling and adaptive DPCM coding," in *Image Sequence Processing and Dynamic Scene Analysis*, T. S. Huang, Ed., Berlin, Germany: Springer-Verlag, 1983, pp. 125–155.

[27] C. Labit and A. Benveniste, "Motion estimation in a sequence of television pictures," in *Image Sequence Processing and Dynamic Scene Analysis*, T. S. Huang, Ed. Berlin, Germany: Springer-Verlag, 1983, pp. 292–306.

[28] J. Max, "Quantizing for minimum distortion," *IEEE Trans. Inform. Theory*, vol. IT-6, pp. 7–12, Mar. 1960.

[29] P. Pirsch and L. Stenger, "Statistical analysis and coding of color video signals," *Acta Electronica*, vol. 19, no. 4, pp. 277–287, 1976.

[30] J. O. Limb, "Source-receiver encoding of television signals," *Proc. IEEE*, vol. 55, pp. 364–379, Mar. 1967.

[31] J. C. Candy and R. H. Bosworth, "Methods for designing differential quantizers based on subjective evaluations of edge busyness," *Bell Syst. Tech. J.*, vol. 51, pp. 1495–1516, Sept. 1972.

[32] A. N. Netravali, "On quantizers for DPCM coding of picture signals," *IEEE Trans. Inform. Theory*, vol. IT-23, no. 3, pp. 360–370, May 1977.

[33] J. O. Limb and C. B. Rubinstein, "On the design of quantizers for DPCM coders: A functional relationship between visibility, probability, and masking," *IEEE Trans. Commun.*, vol. COM-26, pp. 573–578, May 1978.

[34] F. Kretz et al., "Optimization of DPCM video coding scheme using subjective quality criterions," presented at the Conf. on Digital Processing of Signals in Communications, Loughborough, (also in *Proc. IERE Conf.*, no. 37), Sept. 1977.

[35] W. D. Erdmann, "Ein an die Wahrnehmbarkeitseigenschaften des menschlichen Auges angepaßter, gesteuerter Quantisierer für Bildsignale," Ph.D. dissertation, Tech. Univ. of Hannover, Hannover, Germany, 1978.

[36] P. Pirsch, "Design of DPCM quantizers for video signals using subjective tests," *IEEE Trans. Commun.*, vol. COM-29, no. 7, pp. 990–1000, July 1981.

[37] D. K. Sharma, "Design of absolutely optimal quantizers for a wide class of distortion measures," *IEEE Trans. Inform. Theory*, vol. IT-24, pp. 693–702, Nov. 1978.

[38] P. Pirsch, "A new predictor design for DPCM coding of TV signals," in *ICC Conf. Rec.*, pp. 31.2.1–31.2.5, (Seattle, WA), 1980.

[39] F. Lukas and F. Kretz, "DPCM quantization of color television signals," *IEEE Trans. Commun.*, vol. COM-31, no. 7, pp. 927–932, July 1983.

[40] R. Schäfer, "DPCM coding of the chrominance signals for the transmission of color TV signals at 24 Mbit/s," to appear in *Signal Processing*.

[41] D. Westerkamp, "The influence of motion on the masking of quantization errors in 3-dimensional DPCM coding," *Signal Processing*, vol. 7, no. 3, pp. 283–292, Dec. 1984.

[42] A. N. Netravali and B. Prasada, "Adaptive quantization of picture signals using spatial masking," *Proc. IEEE*, vol. 65, pp. 536–548, Apr. 1977.

[43] H. G. Musmann, "Predictive image coding," in *Image Transmission Techniques*, W. K. Pratt, Ed. New York: Academic Press, 1979.

[44] R. Schäfer, "Design of adaptive and nonadaptive quantizers using subjective criteria," *Signal Processing*, vol. 5, no. 4, pp. 333–345, July 1983.

[45] D. Anastassiou et al., "Series/1 based video conferencing system," *IBM Syst. J.*, vol. 22, nos. 1, 2, pp. 97–110, 1983.

[46] R. E. Graham, "Predictive quantizing of television signals," in *IRE WESCON Conv. Rec.*, vol. 2, pt. 4, pp. 147–157, 1958.

[47] W. Zschunke, "DPCM picture coding with adaptive prediction," *IEEE Trans. Commun.*, vol COM-25, no. 11, pp. 1295–1302, Nov. 1977.

[48] C. Zhang, "Ein neuer adaptiver Prädiktor für die DPCM-Codierung von Fernsehsignalen," *Frequenz*, vol. 36, pp. 161–184, June 1982.

[49] P. Pirsch, "Adaptive intra-interframe DPCM coder," *Bell Syst. Tech. J.*, vol. 61, no. 5, pp. 747–764, May 1982.

[50] D. Westerkamp, "Adaptive intra-interframe DPCM coding for transmission of TV signals with 34 Mbit/s," in *Conf. Rec. Int. Zurich Seminar on Digital Communications*, Mar. 1984.

[51] H. J. Grallert and A. Starck, "Component encoding of color television signals for transmission in 34, 70 and 140 Mbit/s channels," in *Conf. Rec. Int. Zurich Seminar on Digital Communications*, Mar. 1984.

[52] T. Koga et al., "A 1.5 Mb/s interframe codec with motion compensation," in *ICC Conf. Rec.*, pp. 1161–1165, June 1983.

[53] J. A. Stuller et al., "Interframe television coding using gain and displacement compensation," *Bell Syst. Tech. J.*, vol. 59, no. 7, pp. 1227–1240, Sept. 1980.

[54] H. Yamamoto, Y. Hatori, and H. Murakami, "30 Mbit/s codec for NTSC color TV signal using an interfield-intrafield adaptive prediction," *IEEE Trans. Commun.*, vol. COM-29, no. 12, pp. 1859–1867, Dec. 1981.

[55] T. Ishiguro and K. Iinuma, "Television bandwidth compression transmission by motion compensated interframe coding," *IEEE Commun. Mag.*, pp. 24–30, Nov. 1982.

[56] F. May, "Codierung von Bildfolgen mit objektbezogener Bewegungskompensation und Signifikanzklassifikation," Ph.D. dissertation, University of Karlsruhe, Karlsruhe, Germany, Feb. 1984.

[57] K. A. Prabhu and A. N. Netravali, "Motion compensated component color coding," *IEEE Trans. Commun.*, vol. COM-30, no. 12, pp. 2519–2527, Dec. 1982.

[58] K. A. Prabhu and A. N. Netravali, "Motion compensated composite color coding," *IEEE Trans. Commun.*, vol. COM-31, no. 2, pp. 216–223, Feb. 1983.

[59] R. Srinivasan and K. R. Rao, "Predictive coding based on efficient motion estimation," in *ICC'84 Conf. Rec.*, pp. 521–526, May 1984.

[60] K. Iinuma et al., "A 1.5 Mb/s full motion videoconference system," in *Conf. Rec. 6th Int. Conf. on Digital Satellite Communications* (Phoenix, AZ, Sept. 1983).

[61] M. Schlichte, "Block-overlap transform coding of image signals," *Siemens Forsch.-u. Entwickl.-Ber.*, vol. 13, no. 3, 1984.

[62] E. Marschall, M. Schlichte, W. Tengler, and E. Hundt, "Blockübergreifende Transformationscodierung: Theorie und numerische Simulation an Hand von Bildsignalen," in *NTG-Fachberichte 84*, ISBN 3-8007-1302-0, pp. 249–257.

[63] D. E. Pearson and M. W. Whybray, "Transformcoding with interleaving blocks," in *Proc. Conf. on Transform Techniques in Image Processing* (London, England), pp. 511–513, May 1983.

[64] T. C. Chen and J. P. de Figueiredo, "An image coding scheme based on spatial domain considerations," *IEEE Trans. Pattern Anal. Machine Intell.*, vol. PAMI-5, pp. 332–337, May 1983.

[65] H. C. Reeve and J. S. Lim, "Reduction of blocking effect in image coding," in *Proc. ICASSP 83* (Boston, MA), pp. 1212–1215.

[66] W. Mauersberger, "Adaptive Transformationskodierung von digitalisierten Bildvorlagen," Ph.D. dissertation, Tech. Univ. of Aachen, Aachen, Germany, 1980.

[67] H. G. Hildebrandt, "Untersuchungen zur Optimierung einer adaptiven Transformationscodierung von Farbfernsehsignalen in Echtzeit bei einer Bitflußrate von 34 Mbit/s," Ph.D. dissertation, Univ. of Wuppertal, Wuppertal, Germany, 1983.

[68] K. N. Ngan, "Adaptive transform coding of video signals," *Proc. Inst. Elec. Eng.*, vol. 129, pp. 28–40, Feb. 1982.

[69] W. C. Wong and R. Steele, "Adaptive discrete cosine transformation of pictures using an energy distribution logarithmic model," *Radio and Electron. Eng.* (GB), vol. 51, pp. 571–578, Nov.–Dec. 1981.

[70] ———, "Adaptive coding of discrete cosine transform video telephone pictures," presented at PCS Ipswich, England, 1979, paper 12.3.

[71] M. Götze and G. Ocylok, "An adaptive interframe transform coding system for images, in *Proc. IEEE ICASSP 82*, pp. 448–451.

[72] L. Stenger, Th. Kremes, and R. Govaerts, "Optimization of coding algorithms by computer simulation," in *Proc. IEEE Globecom 82* (Miami, FL), pp. 305–309, Dec. 1982.

[73] M. Guglielmo, R. Marion, and A. Sciarappa, "Subjective

quality evaluation of different intraframe adaptive transform coding schemes," *CSELT Rapporti Tecnici*, vol. X, pp. 177–181, June 1982.

[74] A. G.. Tescher, "Adaptive transform coding of color images at low rate," in *Proc. IEEE NTC 80* (Houston, TX), pp. 36.3/1–4, Dec. 1980.

[75] M. Götze, "Kombinierte Quellen- und Kanalcodierung in adaptiven Transformationscodierungen," in *NTG-Fachberichte 84*, ISBN 3-8007-1302-0, pp. 259–275.

[76] J. W. Modestino, D. G. Daut, and A. L. Vickers, "Combined source-channel coding of images using the block cosine transform," *IEEE Trans. Commun.*, vol. COM-29, pp. 1261–1274, Sept. 1981.

[77] R. Zelinski, "An adaptive transform coding system based on cepstral control and entropy coding," *Frequenz*, vol. 36, pp. 193–198, 1982.

[78] M. Götze, "Combined source channel-coding in adaptive transform coding systems for images," in *Proc. ICC 1984* (Amsterdam, The Netherlands).

[79] H. Lohscheller, "Video-Einzelbildübertragung über Schmalbandkanäle mit zeitlich zunehmender Auflösung," *NTG-Fachberichte*, vol. 74, pp. 335–342, 1980.

[80] _____, "Adaptive transform coding for still picture communication," in *Proc. IEEE Zurich Sem. on Digital Communication, 1984*, pp. 25–31, Mar. 1984.

[81] J. A. Robinson and F. P. Coakley, "Picture coding for photovideotex," *Comput. Commun.*, vol. 6, pp. 3–13, Feb. 1983.

[82] F. Coakley and E. Bisheruwa, "Transform coding techniques for photovideotex," in *Proc. Colloquium on Transform Techniques in Image Processing*, pp. 9/1–9/7 (London, England, May 1983).

[83] "Picture prestel," *Funkschau*, vol. 26, p. 28, 1982.

[84] K. Takikawa, "Fast progressive reconstruction of a transformed image," *IEEE Trans. Informat. Theory*, vol. IT-30, no. 1, pp. 111–117, 1984.

[85] K. N. Ngan, "Image display techniques using cosine transform, *IEEE Trans. Acoust. Speech, Signal Process.*, vol. ASSP-32, no. 1, pp. 173–177, 1984.

[86] A. Habibi, "An adaptive strategy for hybrid image coding," *IEEE Trans. Commun.*, vol COM-29, pp. 1736–1740, Dec. 1981.

[87] F. A. Kamangar and K. R. Rao, "Interfield hybrid coding of component color television signals," *IEEE Trans. Commun.*, vol. COM-29, pp. 1740–1753, Dec. 1981.

[88] W. A. Pearlman and P. Jakatdar, "Hybrid DFT/DPCM interframe image," in *Proc. ICASSP'81* (Atlanta, GA), pp. 1121–1124, Mar. 1981.

[89] H.-J. Grallert, "Application of orthonormalized m-sequences for data reduced and error protected transmission of pictures," in *Proc. IEEE Int. Symp. on Electromagnetic Compatibility, 1980* (Baltimore, MD), pp. 282–287.

[90] _____, "Source encoding and error protected transmission of pictures with help of orthonormalized m-sequences," in *Proc. 12th Int. Television Symp.* (Montreux, Switzerland, 1981), pp. 441–454.

[91] W. G. Keesen, U. Reimann, and H.-J. Grallert, "Codierung von Farbfernsehsignalen mittels modifizierter M-Transformation für die Übertragung über 34-Mbit/s-Kanäle," *Frequenz*, vol. 38, no. 10, pp. 238–243, Oct. 1984.

[92] W. Keesen, U. Reimann, and H.-J. Grallert, "Component encoding using a modified M-transform for transmission over 34-Mbit/s-channels," presented at PCS 84, Rennes, France, July 1984.

[93] C. Ekambaram and S. C. Kwatra, "A new architecture for adaptive transform compression of NTSC composite video signals," in *Proc. IEEE NTC 81* (New Orleans, LA), pp. C9.6/1–5, Dec. 1981.

[94] S. C. Kwatra and H. Fatmi, "NTSC composite video at 1.6 bits/pel," in *Proc. IEEE ICC 83* (Boston, MA), pp. 458–462, June 1983.

[95] A. Playsongsang and K. R. Rao, "DCT/DPCM processing of NTSC composite video signal," *IEEE Trans. Commun.*, vol. COM-30, pp. 541–549, Mar. 1982.

[96] D. N. Hein, "Video data compression using motion compensation," in *MIDCON 82 Conf. Rec.*, pp. 3/4,1–9 (Dallas, TX, Nov. 1982).

[97] S. W. Golomb, *Digital Communications*. Englewood Cliffs, NJ: Prentice-Hall, 1974.

[98] CCIR, Rep. 405-4, in *Recommendations and Reports of the CCIR*. Geneva, Switzerland: CCIR, 1982.

[99] B. G. Haskell and R. L. Schmidt, "A low bit-rate interframe coder for videotelephone," *Bell Syst. Techn. J.*, vol. 54, no. 8, pp. 1475–1495, Oct. 1975.

[100] J. Klie, "Codierung von Fernsehsignalen für niedrige Übertragungsbitraten," Ph.D. dissertation, Tech. Univ. of Hannover, Hannover, Germany, 1978.

[101] H. C. Bergmann, "Übertragung von Bewegtbildern mit niedrigen Übertragungsbitraten," *NTG-Fachberichte*, vol. 74, pp. 370–378, 1980.

[102] B. G. Haskell, P. L. Gordon, R. L. Schmidt, and J. V. Scattaglia, "Interframe coding of 525-line monochrome television at 1.5 Mbit/s," *IEEE Trans. Commun.*, vol. COM-25, no. 11, pp. 1339–1348, Nov. 1977.

[103] R. Lippmann, "Video transmission of aerial scenes at reduced frame rates using motion compensation," presented at the ICC, Seattle, WA, June 1980.

[104] _____, "Continuous movement regeneration in low-frame-rate aerial images," in *Proc. IEEE Int. Conf. on Electronic Image Processing*, Conf. Publ. No. 214, pp. 194–198, July 1982.

[105] A. N. Netravali and J. D. Robbins, "Motion-adaptive interpolation of television frames," presented at the Picture Coding Symp., Montreal, Canada, 1981.

[106] H. C. Bergmann, "Motion-adaptive interpolation of eliminated TV-fields," presented at the Picture Coding Symp., Montreal, Canada, 1981.

[107] R. Lenz and A. Gerhard, "Image sequence coding using scene analysis and spatio-temporal interpolation," in *Image Sequence Processing and Dynamic Scene Analysis*, T. S. Huang, Ed. Berlin, Germany: Springer-Verlag, 1983, pp. 264–274.

[108] S. Sabri, K. Cuffing, and B. Prasada, "Coding of video signals at 50 kbit/s using motion compensation techniques," in *Proc. IEEE Military Communications Conf.*, pp. 809–816, Nov. 1983.

[109] H. C. Bergmann, "Motion adaptive frame interpolation," in *Proc. Int. Zurich Seminar on Digital Communications*, pp. D2.1–D2.5, Mar. 1984.

[110] A. Furukawa, T. Koga, and K. Iinuma, "Motion-adaptive interpolation for videoconference pictures," in *Proc. ICC 1984*, vol. 2, pp. 707–710, May 1984.

[111] B. Prasada, E. Gulko, and S. Sabri, "Evaluation of spatio-temporal interpolation techniques," presented at the Picture Coding Symp., Rennes, France, 1984.

Scene Adaptive Coder

WEN-HSIUNG CHEN, MEMBER, IEEE, AND WILLIAM K. PRATT, SENIOR MEMBER, IEEE

Abstract—An efficient single-pass adaptive bandwidth compression technique using the discrete cosine transform is described. The coding process involves a simple thresholding and normalization operation on the transform coefficients. Adaptivity is achieved by using a rate buffer for channel rate equalization. The buffer status and input rate are monitored to generate a feedback normalization factor. Excellent results are demonstrated for coding of color images at 0.4 bits/pixel corresponding to real-time color television transmission over a 1.5 Mbit/s channel.

I. INTRODUCTION

TRANSFORM image coding, developed about 15 years ago, has been proven to be an efficient means of image coding [1]–[6]. In the basic transform image coding concept, an image is divided into small blocks of pixels, and each block undergoes a two-dimensional transformation to produce an equal-sized array of transform coefficients. Among various transforms investigated for image coding applications, the cosine transform has emerged as the best candidate from the standpoint of compression factor and ease of implementation [7]–[11]. With the basic system, the array of transform coefficients is quantized and coded using a zonal coding strategy [3]; the lowest spatial frequency coefficients, which generally possess the greatest energy, are quantized most finely, and the highest spatial frequency coefficients are quantized coarsely. Binary codes are assigned to the quantization levels, and the code words are assembled in a buffer for transmission. At the receiver, inverse processes occur to decode the received bit stream, and to inverse transform the quantized transform coefficients to reconstruct a block of pixels.

The basic transform image coding concept, previously described, performs well on most natural scenes. A pixel coding rate of about 1.5 bits/pixel is achievable, with no apparent visual degradation. To achieve lower coding rates, without increasing coding error, it is necessary to adaptively quantize transform coefficients so that those blocks of coefficients containing large amounts of energy are allocated more quantization levels and code bits than low energy blocks. In almost all adaptive transform coding designs to date, transforms are computed, and transform energy is measured or estimated on a first pass through the image. This information is then utilized to determine the quantization levels and code words for a second pass [9]. With this scheme, compression factors can be reduced by a factor of two or more as compared to nonadaptive coding. The practical difficulties are the memory required for the second pass and the complexity of the quantization algorithm. Both these problems are eliminated in the scene adaptive coder described in this paper.

The scene adaptive coder is a single-pass adaptive coder of relative simplicity. The following sections describe the coding scheme and present subjective and quantitative performance evaluations.

Paper approved by the Editor for Communication Theory of the IEEE Communications Society for publication after presentation at the International Conference on Communications, Philadelphia, PA, June 1981. Manuscript received September 2, 1982; revised July 8, 1983.

W. Chen is with Compression Labs, Inc., San Jose, CA 95131.

W. K. Pratt is with VICOM Systems, Inc., San Jose, CA 95131.

II. COSINE TRANSFORM REPRESENTATION

The two-dimensional discrete cosine transform of a sequence $f(j, k)$ for $j, k = 0, 1, \cdots, N - 1$, can be defined as [6]

$$F(u,v) = \frac{4C(u)C(v)}{N^2} \sum_{j=0}^{N-1} \sum_{k=0}^{N-1} f(j, k)$$
$$\cdot \cos\left[\frac{(2j + 1)u\pi}{2N}\right] \cos\left[\frac{(2k + 1)v\pi}{2N}\right] \tag{1}$$

for $u, v = 0, 1, \cdots, N - 1$, where

$$C(w) = \begin{cases} \dfrac{1}{\sqrt{2}} & \text{for } w = \phi \\ 1 & \text{for } w = 1, 2, \cdots, N - 1. \end{cases}$$

The inverse transform is given by

$$f(j, k) = \sum_{u=0}^{N-1} \sum_{v=0}^{N-1} C(u)C(v)F(u, v)$$
$$\cdot \cos\left[\frac{(2j + 1)u\pi}{2N}\right] \cos\left[\frac{(2k + 1)v\pi}{2N}\right] \tag{2}$$

for $j, k = 0, 1, \cdots, N - 1$. Among the class of transform possessing fast computational algorithms, the cosine transform has a superior energy compaction property [6]–[9]. The following sections present some other properties of the cosine transform, which are useful to the subsequent discussion.

A. Statistical Description of DCT Coefficients

Let the pixel array $f(j, k)$ represent a sample of a random process with zero mean represented in two's complement format over an integer range $-M \leq f(j, k) \leq (M - 1)$. The probability density of the cosine transform coefficients $F(u, v)$ has been modeled by a number of functions [3], [12]. Among them, the Laplacian density has been shown to provide the best fit [12]. This function can be written as

$$p(x; u, v) = \frac{1}{\sqrt{2}\,\sigma(u, v)} \exp\left\{\frac{\sqrt{2}\,|x|}{\sigma(u, v)}\right\} \tag{3}$$

where $\sigma(u, v)$ denotes the standard deviation of a coefficient.

B. Coefficient Bound

The maximum coefficient value for the cosine transform can be derived from (1) as

$$F_{\max}(0, 0) = 2f_{\max} \tag{4a}$$

and

$$\frac{16}{\pi^2} f_{\max} \leq F_{\max}(u, v) \leq 2f_{\max} \tag{4b}$$

Reprinted from *IEEE Trans. Commun.* vol. COM-32, no. 3, pp. 225–232, March 1984.

where $f_{\max}$ is the maximum value of the discrete array $f(j, k)$ and $F_{\max}$ is the maximum value for the coefficient $F(u, v)$. If the transform is performed in a vector length of $N = 16$, then

$$F_{\max}(0, 0) = 2f_{\max} \tag{5a}$$

$$F_{\max}(u, v) = 1.628 f_{\max}. \tag{5b}$$

C. Mean Square Error Representation

The mean square quantization error between an original image $f(j, k)$ and its reconstructed image $\hat{f}(j, k)$ can be written as

$$\text{MSE} = \frac{1}{N^2} \sum_{j=0}^{N-1} \sum_{k=0}^{N-1} E\{[f(j, k) - \hat{f}(j, k)]^2\}. \tag{6}$$

The unitary property of the cosine transform allows one to express the MSE in the transform domain as

$$\text{MSE} = \frac{1}{4} \sum_{u=0}^{N-1} \sum_{v=0}^{N-1} E\{[F(u, v) - \hat{F}(u, v)]^2\} \tag{7}$$

which reduces to

$$\text{MSE} = \frac{1}{4} \sum_{u=0}^{N-1} \sum_{v=0}^{N-1} \sum_{n=-\infty}^{\infty} \int_{D_{n-1}}^{D_n} (x - x_n)^2$$
$$\cdot p(x; u, v) \, dx \tag{8}$$

where $p(x; u, v)$ is the probability density function, D_n is a set of decision levels, and x_n is a set of reconstruction levels. With Laplacian modeling of the probability density function, as represented in (3), the MSE becomes

$$\text{MSE} = \frac{1}{4} \sum_{u=0}^{N-1} \sum_{v=0}^{N-1} \left\{ \sigma^2(u, v) - \sum_{k=1}^{\infty} \left[(2x_n D_{n-1} \right. \right.$$
$$+ \sqrt{2}\sigma(u, v)x_n - x_n{}^2) \exp\left(\frac{-\sqrt{2}D_{n-1}}{\sigma(u, v)}\right)$$
$$- (2x_n D_n + \sqrt{2}\sigma(u, v)x_n - x_n{}^2)$$
$$\left. \left. \cdot \exp\left(\frac{-\sqrt{2}D_n}{\sigma(u, v)}\right) \right] \right\}. \tag{9}$$

This result has been verified by computer simulation.

III. Scene Adaptive Coder

Fig. 1 contains a block diagram of the scene adaptive coder. In operation, the input image undergoes a cosine transform in 16×16 pixel blocks. An initial threshold is established, and those transform coefficients whose magnitudes are greater than the threshold are scaled according to a feedback parameter from the output rate buffer. The scaled coefficients are quantized, Huffman coded, and fed into the rate buffer. The rate buffer operates with a variable rate input, dependent upon the instantaneous image energy, and a constant channel output rate. The buffer status (fullness) and input rate are monitored to generate the coefficient scaling factor. At the receiver, the received fixed rate data are fed to a rate buffer that generates Huffman code words at a variable rate to the decoder. The decoded transform coefficients are then inverse normalized by the feedback parameter, added to the threshold, and inverse

transformed to reconstruct the output pixel block. The following sections describe the coding algorithm in greater detail.

A. Cosine Transform

Referring to the block diagram in Fig. 1, the original image is first partitioned into 16×16 pixel blocks. Each block of data is then cosine transformed as defined by (1). The resultant transform coefficients $F(u, v)$ are stored in a register according to the zigzag scan of Fig. 2. Scanning the data in this fashion minimizes the usage of runlength codes during the subsequent coding process.

B. Thresholding

The transform coefficients in the register undergo a threshold process in which all the coefficients, except $F(0, 0)$, that are below the threshold are set to zero, and those coefficients above the threshold are subtracted by the threshold. This results in

$$F_T(u, v) = \begin{cases} F(u, v) - T & \text{if } F(u, v) > T \\ 0 & \text{if } F(u, v) \leqslant T \end{cases} \tag{10}$$

where T is the threshold. Fig. 3 shows a plot of the percentage of coefficients below a threshold versus the threshold for the original images exhibited in Figs. 8(a) and 9(a). As demonstrated, more than 90 percent of the coefficients have absolute magnitude of less than a value of 3, even though the maximum coefficient value could be as large as $1.628 f_{\max}$ [see 5(b)]. Therefore, the thresholding process indicated in (10) will set a major portion of coefficients to zero, and thereby limit the number of coefficients to be quantized. The value of the threshold varies with respect to the globally desired bit rate. However, it can be adjusted locally on a block-to-block basis if desired.

C. Normalization and Quantization

The threshold subtracted transform coefficients $F_T(u, v)$ are scaled by a feedback normalization factor D from the output rate buffer according to the relation

$$F_{TN}(u, v) = \frac{F_T(u, v)}{D}. \tag{11}$$

The scaling process adjusts the range of the coefficients such that a desired number of code bits can be used during the coding process.

The quantization process is simply a floating point to integer roundoff conversion. No decision and reconstruction tables are required. Therefore, there is a significant simplification and saving for a hardware implementation. Because many of the threshold subtracted coefficients are of fractional value, the roundoff process will set some of the coefficients to zero and leave only a limited number of significant coefficients to be amplitude coded. The quantized coefficients can now be represented as

$$\hat{F}_{TN}(u, v) = \text{integer part of } [F_{TN}(u, v) + 0.5]. \tag{12}$$

It should be noted that a lower bound has to be set for the normalization factor in order to introduce meaningful transform coefficients to the coder. This lower bound is dependent upon how accurately the cosine transform is computed. Generally speaking, setting the minimum value of D to unity is sufficient for most of the compression applications. In this case, the worst-case quantization error can be obtained from (9) by letting $D_{n-1} = n - 0.5$, $D_n = n + 0.5$, and $x_n = n$.

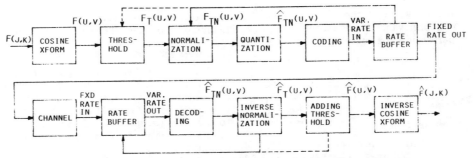

Fig. 1. Block diagram of scene adaptive coding/decoding system.

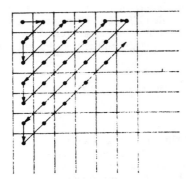

Fig. 2. Zigzag scan of cosine transform coefficients.

Thus

$$\text{MSE} = \frac{1}{4} \sum_{u=0}^{N-1} \sum_{v=0}^{N-1} e(u, v) \qquad (13)$$

where

$$e(u, v) = \sigma^2(u, v) - (1/2) \sum_{n=1}^{\infty} \left\{ [n^2 + (\sqrt{2}\sigma(u, v) - 1)n] \right.$$

$$\cdot \exp\left[\frac{-\sqrt{2}(n - 0.5)}{\sigma(u, v)}\right] - [n^2 + (\sqrt{2}\sigma(u, v)$$

$$\left. + 1)n] \exp\left[\frac{-\sqrt{2}(n + 0.5)}{\sigma(u, v)}\right] \right\}.$$

Fig. 4 shows the functional relationship between $e(u, v)$ and $\sigma(u, v)$. As can be seen, $e(u, v)$ is always less than 1/12. (Note: 1/12 is the quantization error for a uniform density.) Therefore, the MSE represented by (13) is always less than $N^2/48$. For $N = 16$, this MSE is less than 16/3, which corresponds to a normalized error of 0.0082 percent. This MSE also corresponds to a peak-to-peak signal-to-quantization-noise ratio of more than 40.9 dB, which is relatively insignificant.

D. Coding

The coefficient $F(0, 0)$ in the upper left-hand corner of each luminance transform block is proportional to the average luminance of that block. Because block-to-block luminance variations resulting from quantization of $F(0, 0)$ are easily discerned visually, $F(0, 0)$ is linearly quantized and coded with a 9 bit code. As for the other nonzero coefficients, their magnitudes are coded by an amplitude lookup table, and the addresses of the coefficients are coded using a runlength lookup table. The amplitude and runlength lookup tables are simply Huffman codes derived from the histograms of typical

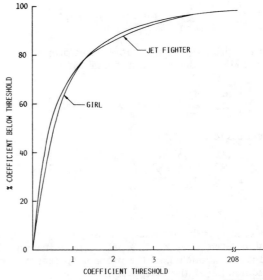

Fig. 3. Distribution of cosine transform coefficients.

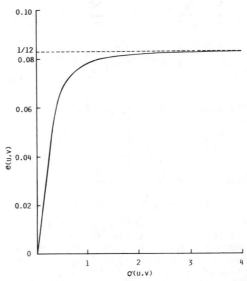

Fig. 4. Quantization error $e(u, v)$ versus coefficient standard deviation $\sigma(u, v)$ at normalization factor of unity and coding threshold of zero. (Probability density function of the coefficient is assumed to be Laplacian.)

transform coefficients. As demonstrated by the histograms of Fig. 5, the domination of low amplitudes and short runs of zero-valued coefficients indicates that both Huffman tables are relatively insensitive to the type of input images and the de-

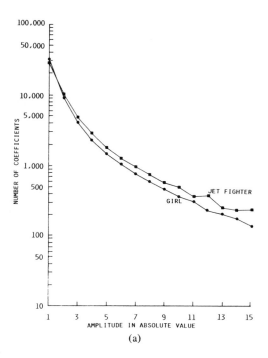

(a)

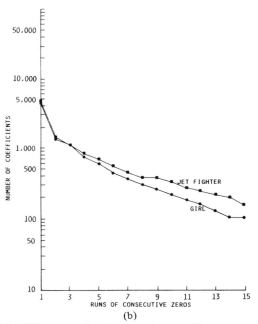

(b)

Fig. 5. (a) Histogram of cosine transform coefficients obtained with threshold of zero and normalization factor of one. (b) Histogram of runs of consecutive zero counts obtained with threshold of zero and normalization factor of one.

sired bit rate. This suggests that only two predetermined tables are needed for the coding process.

The length of the Huffman table for the amplitude codes is a function of the normalization factor and the transform bound represented by (5b). For a two-dimensional cosine transform of 16×16 pixels, the maximum length is

$$L_A = \frac{1.628 |f_{max}|}{D_{min}} \qquad (14)$$

where D_{min} is the minimum allowable normalization factor. For $|f_{max}|$ and D_{min} equal to 128 and 1, respectively, the length will be 208. As for the runlength of zero counts, the

TABLE I
HUFFMAN CODE TABLE FOR COEFFICIENT AMPLITUDE IN ABSOLUTE VALUE

AMPLITUDE	NUMBER OF CODE BITS	HUFFMAN CODES
1	1	1
2	3,	001
3	4	0111
4	5	00001
5	5	01101
6	6	011001
7	7	0000001
8	7	0110001
9	8	00000000
10	8	01100000
11	8	00000001
12	8	01100001
13	6+8	000001+8 BITS
EOB	4	0001
RL PREFIX	3	010

length of the table can be represented by

$$L_R = (N^2 - 1) \qquad (15)$$

where N is the transform block size. The subtraction of unity is because the dc coefficient in individual blocks is separately encoded. For a transform block size of 16×16 pixels, the length is 255. In practice, the length of both tables can be shortened to less than 30 entries by assigning Huffman codes to only the low amplitude coefficients and short runlengths (using a fixed length code elsewhere). Again, due to the domination of the low amplitude coefficients and short runlengths, the loss of coding efficiency is insignificant.

Tables I and II show typical truncated Huffman code tables for the amplitude and runlength, respectively. It should be noted that the amplitude codes in Table I include an "end of block (EOB)" code and a "runlength prefix" code. The EOB code is used to terminate coding of the block as soon as the last significant coefficient of the block is coded. The runlength prefix code is required in order to distinguish the runlength code from the amplitude code.

It should be noted that there are many ways to improve the coding efficiency of the coder. One way is to cut down the number of runs in the runlength coder. This can be accomplished by skipping single isolated coefficients with absolute magnitude of one, or by introducing an amplitude code for the isolated coefficients with zero amplitude. The coding improvement is generally quite significant; this is especially true if the average coding rate is low.

E. Rate Buffer

The rate buffer in the SAC performs channel rate equalization. The buffer has a variable rate data input and a constant data output. The differentials are monitored from block to block, and the status is converted into a scaling factor that is fed back to the normalizer. The buffer always forces the coder to adjust to the local coding variations, while ensuring global performance at a desired level. The general operation of a rate buffer is well documented [13], [14]. The specific method used in this paper is described as follows.

Let $B(m)$ represent the number of bits into the rate buffer for the mth block and let $S(m)$ represent the normalized buffer status at the end of the mth block ($-0.5 < S(m) < 0.5$). Then, $B(m)$ and $S(m)$ can be written as

$$B(m) = \sum_{\substack{u=0 \\ (u,v) \neq (0,0)}}^{15} \sum_{v=0}^{15} H\{[\hat{F}_{TN}(u,v)]_m\} + 9 \qquad (16)$$

TABLE II
HUFFMAN CODE TABLE FOR THE NUMBER OF CONSECUTIVE ZERO-VALUED COEFFICIENTS

RUN-LENGTH	NUMBER OF CODE BITS	HUFFMAN CODE
1	2	11
2	3	101
3	3	011
4	4	0101
5	4	0011
6	5	01000
7	5	10010
8	5	01001
9	5	10001
10	5	10011
11	6	001000
12	6	100000
13	6	001010
14	6	001001
15	6	100001
16	6	000011
17	6	001011
18	7	0000000
19	7	0000100
20	7	0000010
21	7	0001110
22	7	0000001
23	7	0000101
24	7	0000011
25	7	0001111
26	8	00011000
27	8	00011010
28	8	00011001
29	8	00011011
30	5+8	00010+8 BITS

$$S(m) = S(m-1) + \frac{[B(m) - 256R]}{L} \qquad (17)$$

where

$[\hat{F}_{TN}(u, v)]_m$ quantized coefficients of the mth block, as defined in (12)

$H\{\cdot\}$ Huffman coding function

R average coding rate

L rate buffer size.

The buffer status $S(m)$ is used to select an instantaneous normalization factor $\hat{D}(m)$ according to an empirically determined "normalization factor versus status" curve. This relationship is described by

$$\hat{D}(m) = \Phi\{S(m)\}. \qquad (18)$$

In order to smooth out this instantaneous normalization factor such that the desired normalization factor does not fluctuate too much, a recursive filtering process is applied to generate

$$D(m) = cD(m-1) + (1-c)\hat{D}(m) \qquad (19)$$

where c is a constant with value less than unity.

The desired operating conditions for the rate buffer algorithm are: a) the feedback normalization factor is as stable as possible; b) the buffer status is able to converge rapidly and stay as close to the half full position ($S(m) = 0$) as possible. Both these conditions may be satisfied using the above set of equations. Fig. 6 shows typical values of the normalization factor and buffer status as a function of block indexes for the images shown in Figs. 8(a) and 9(a).

The rate buffer can be guaranteed not to overflow. This is because the normalization factor can get very large within a few blocks of operation, and effectively limit the data going into the buffer. However, there is no guarantee that the buffer will not underflow if a minimum allowable normalization factor is set to a fixed value. Therefore, the buffer status has to be constantly monitored and, if the status is closer to -0.5, fill bits must be introduced into the channel.

IV. SCENE ADAPTIVE CODING OF COLOR IMAGES

Fig. 7 contains a block diagram of a color image coding system based on the scene adaptive coder. In this system, a color image, represented by tristimulus signals $R(j, k)$, $G(j, k)$, $B(j, k)$, is first converted to a new three-dimensional space defined by

$$\begin{bmatrix} Y(j, k) \\ I(j, k) \\ Q(j, k) \end{bmatrix} = \begin{bmatrix} 0.299 & 0.589 & 0.114 \\ 0.596 & -0.274 & -0.322 \\ 0.211 & -0.253 & 0.312 \end{bmatrix} \begin{bmatrix} R(j, k) \\ G(j, k) \\ B(j, k) \end{bmatrix} \qquad (20)$$

where $Y(j, k)$ is the luminance signal and $I(j, k)$ and $Q(j, k)$ are chrominance signals. This conversion compacts most of the signal energy into the Y plane such that more efficient coding can be accomplished [15]. The I and Q chrominance planes are spatially averaged and subsampled by a factor of 4 to 1 in both the horizontal and vertical directions. The luminance and subsampled chrominance images are then partitioned into 16×16 pixel blocks and coded by the SAC in the order of 32 Y, two I, and two Q sequences. At the receiver, the received code bits are decoded. Inverse cosine transform and inverse coordinate conversions are then performed to reconstruct the source tristimulus signals. The inverse coordinate conversion is described by

$$\begin{bmatrix} R(j, k) \\ G(j, k) \\ B(j, k) \end{bmatrix} = \begin{bmatrix} 1.000 & 0.956 & 0.621 \\ 1.000 & -0.272 & -0.647 \\ 1.000 & -1.106 & 1.703 \end{bmatrix} \begin{bmatrix} Y(j, k) \\ I(j, k) \\ Q(j, k) \end{bmatrix}. \qquad (21)$$

V. SIMULATION RESULTS

Computer simulations have been conducted to evaluate the performance of the scene adaptive coder. The original test images shown in Figs. 8(a) and 9(a) are of size 512×512 pixels with each red, green, and blue tristimulus value uniformly quantized to 8 bits/pixel. Figs. 8(b) and 9(b) show the reconstructed images at a combined average bit rate of 0.4 bits/pixel. This rate corresponds to a channel bandwidth of 1.5 Mbits for a 15 frame/s intraframe coding system. The excellent reconstruction of the images is clearly demonstrated. Table III tabulates the average mean square error between the original and the reconstructed images. Also included in the table is the peak signal-to-noise ratio for the reconstructed image.

VI. SUMMARY

The scene adaptive coder described herein encodes cosine transform coefficients in a simple manner. The coding process involves only thresholding, normalization, roundoff, and rate buffer equalization. The performance of the coder is quite good in terms of mean square error and subjective evaluation. Because the coding process is dependent upon the instantaneous coefficient content inside the block and the accumulated rate buffer content, it is well suited for intraframe coding of moving images. At Compression Labs, Inc., the coder has been implemented with real-time hardware to code NTSC color video at a channel rate of 1.5 Mbits/s.

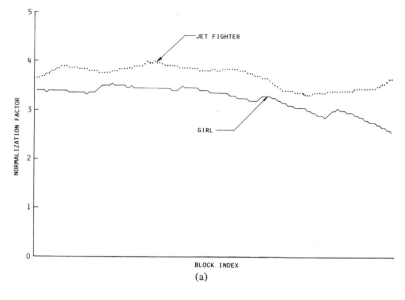

(a)

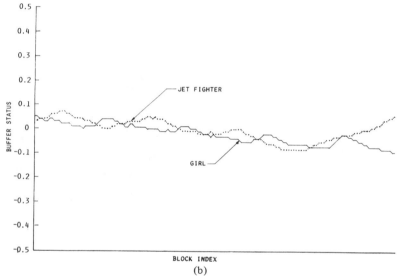

(b)

Fig. 6.   Buffer status for the last 114 blocks of images shown in Figs. 8(a) and 9(a).

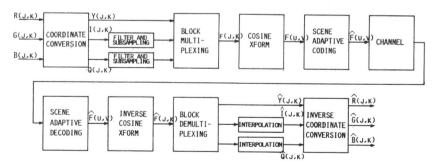

Fig. 7.   Cosine transform color image coding/decoding system.

(a)

(a)

(b)

Fig. 8. Cosine transform scene adaptive coding. (a) Original. (b) Reconstructed image at 0.4 bits/pixel.

(b)

Fig. 9. Cosine transform scene adaptive coding. (a) Original. (b) Reconstructed image at 0.4 bits/pixel.

TABLE III
MEAN SQUARE ERROR BETWEEN ORIGINAL AND
RECONSTRUCTED IMAGES AT 0.4 BITS/PIXEL;
MEAN SQUARE ERROR IS COMPUTED AT
THE INPUT OF CODER AND THE OUTPUT
OF DECODER WITH $f_{\max}(j, k)$
NORMALIZED TO 1

IMAGES	MEAN SQUARE ERROR	SNR
GIRL	0.0359%	34.45 DB
JET	0.0521%	32.84 DB

110

ACKNOWLEDGMENT

The authors wish to express their sincere gratitude to Dr. A. Tescher for his valuable discussions and suggestions in the area of rate buffer stabilizations.

REFERENCES

[1] H. C. Andrews and W. K. Pratt, "Fourier transform coding of images," in *Proc. Hawaii Int. Conf. Syst. Sci.*, Jan. 1968, pp. 677–678.

[2] W. K. Pratt, J. Kane, and H. C. Andrews, "Hadamard transform image coding," *Proc. IEEE*, vol. 57, pp. 58–68, Jan. 1969.

[3] W. K. Pratt, W. H. Chen, and R. Welch, "Slant transform image coding," *IEEE Trans. Commun.*, vol. COM-22, pp. 1075–1093, Aug. 1974.

[4] A. Habibi and P. A. Wintz, "Image coding by linear transformation and block quantization," *IEEE Trans. Commun. Technol.*, vol. COM-19, pp. 50–62, Feb. 1971.

[5] W. K. Pratt, *Digital Image Processing*. New York: Wiley-Interscience, 1978.

[6] N. Ahmed, T. Natarjan, and K. R. Rao, "Discrete cosine transform," *IEEE Trans. Comput.*, vol. C-23, pp. 90–93, Jan. 1974.

[7] M. Hamidi and J. Pearl, "Comparison of the cosine and Fourier transforms of Markov-1 signals," *IEEE Trans. Acoust., Speech, Signal Processing*, vol. ASSP-24, pp. 428–429, Oct. 1976.

[8] A. K. Jain, "A sinusoidal family of unitary transforms," *IEEE Trans. Pattern Anal. Mach. Intell.*, vol. PAMI-1, Oct. 1979.

[9] W. H. Chen and C. H. Smith, "Adaptive coding of monochrome and color images," *IEEE Trans. Commun.*, vol. COM-25, pp. 1285–1292, Nov. 1977.

[10] W. H. Chen, C. H. Smith, and S. Fralick, "A fast computational algorithm for the discrete cosine transform," *IEEE Trans. Commun.*, vol. COM-25, pp. 1004–1009, Sept. 1977.

[11] R. M. Haralick, "A storage efficient way to implement the discrete cosine transform," *IEEE Trans. Comput.*, vol. C-25, pp. 764–765, July 1976.

[12] R. C. Reininger and J. D. Gibson, "Distributions of the two-dimensional DCT coefficients for images," *IEEE Trans. Commun.*, vol. COM-31, pp. 835–839, June 1983.

[13] A. Tescher, "Rate adaptive communication," in *Proc. Nat. Telecommun. Conf.*, 1978.

[14] ——, "A dual transform coding algorithm," in *Proc. Nat. Telecommun. Conf.*, 1980.

[15] W. K. Pratt, "Spatial transform coding of color images," *IEEE Trans. Commun. Technol.*, vol. COM-19, pp. 980–992, Dec. 1971.

8.4: *Invited Address*: Video Coding Using the MPEG-1 Compression Standard

A. Puri

AT&T Bell Laboratories, Holmdel, NJ

ABSTRACT

The first phase of the Motion Picture Experts Group (MPEG-1) activity has resulted in a standard for compression of digital video. The standard, however, only specifies a syntax for the bit-stream and the decoding process; encoders can be designed to allow the best tradeoff of performance versus complexity depending on the application. We discuss such tradeoffs as well as various potential improvements in encoding that are key to obtaining good picture quality with this standard.

1. INTRODUCTION

The first phase of MPEG activity has resulted in a standard [3] for the compression of digital audio and video. The MPEG-1 video compression standard, although primarily aimed at coding of video for digital storage media (DSM), at rates of 1 to 1.5 Mbit/s is well suited for a wide range of applications at a variety of bit-rates. The standard mandates real-time decoding and supports features to facilitate interactivity with stored bit-stream. It only specifies a syntax for the bit-stream and the decoding process; sufficient flexibility is allowed regarding the encoding complexity. Encoders can, therefore, be designed to allow optimal trade-off of performance versus complexity as suited for a specific application. A simple view of a few application profiles, for which this standard may be suitable, is shown in Table 1.

The MPEG-1 video syntax supports group-of-pictures structure to facilitate interactivity in the form of fast forward, fast reverse and random access on bit-streams stored on compact disk (CD) or other DSM, as well as channel switching or late-tune-in for cable/satellite TV or broadcast TV applications. The video coding syntax allows temporal redundancy to be exploited via motion-compensation while it permits spatial and perceptual redundancy reduction by Discrete Cosine Transform (DCT) coding and visually-weighted adaptive quantization. The exact bit-stream and decoding syntax can be found in [3], its explanation and detailed overview is described in [1,2], here we focus on various encoding choices and their impact on complexity.

Table 1: A Few Application Profiles

Compressed Rate	Coding Resolution and Format	Applications
0.3 – 1 Mbit/s	360 × 240, 30Hz non-interlaced	Video Conferencing
1 – 2 Mbit/s	360 × 240, 30Hz non-interlaced	Video on Compact Disks, Network Video Services
2 – 4 Mbit/s	360 × 480, 30Hz interlaced	Cable/Satellite TV, Video on LANs
4 – 9 Mbit/s	720 × 480, 30Hz interlaced	Cable/Satellite TV, Broadcast TV Future Digital Storage Media
7 – 15 Mbit/s	960 × 480, 30Hz interlaced 960 × 480, 30/60Hz progressive	Extended Definition TV
15 – 30 Mbit/s	1440 × 960, 30Hz interlaced 1280 × 720, 60Hz progressive	High Definition TV

2. GROUP-OF-PICTURES

An input video sequence is divided into units of group-of-pictures (GOP's), consisting of an Intra (I-) picture, coded without reference to other pictures, and an arrangement of Predictive (P-) pictures, coded with reference to previous (I- or P-) pictures and Bidirectional (B-) pictures coded with reference to an immediate previous (I- or P-) picture, as well as an immediate future (P- or I-) picture. A GOP serves as a basic access unit, with an I- picture as a natural entry point to facilitate random seek or channel switching. A GOP is defined by its length, N, the distance between I- pictures, and M, the distance between P- pictures. An example of a GOP with N=15 and M=3, consisting of one I- picture, 4 P- pictures and 10 B- pictures is shown in Fig. 1. With a GOP of N= 15, the worst case random seek or channel switching delay is 0.5 secs, if a shorter delay is necessary, a smaller value of N should be used. For interpersonal communications, such as videophone or video-conferencing, total (encoding, transmission and decoding) delay becomes extremely important and may require GOP's with large N and shortest possible M(=1) to reduce the coding delay.

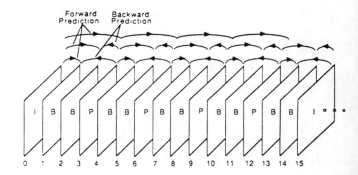

Fig. 1   Group-of-Picture structure with M=3 and N=15

Each picture within GOP is composed of one or more slices, the basic unit at which resynchronization information is associated. The number of slices per picture is directly related to the amount of resynchronization information that can be afforded and may be different for each picture type. Since loss of synchronization in I- or P- pictures can have a propagative effect throughout the GOP, it is common to have several slices in these pictures but only one slice in B-pictures, in order to minimize resynchronization overhead. Typically in I- or p- pictures a slice consists of a row of macroblocks. A macroblock, in turn, consists of a 16 × 16 block (or alternately 4, 8 × 8 blocks) of luminance along with each of 8 × 8 blocks of Cb- and Cr- chrominance blocks.

In the compression sense, I- pictures are the least efficient as they exploit only spatial redundancies, P- pictures are more efficient as they exploit causal-temporal, as well as, spatial redundancies and B- pictures are the most efficient as they also exploit non-causal-temporal redundancies in addition to those that P- pictures exploit. Even though it appears that increasing the value of M (and therefore the frequency of B- pictures) would increase overall coding efficiency, in reality, the amount of improvement depends on the characteristics of video scene and saturates quickly. It is often regarded [2,4] that a GOP with M=3, already exploits significant benefits that accrue from use of B- pictures. Moreover, increasing the value of M also increases the complexity of temporal redundancy reduction schemes. In MPEG-based-coding, temporal redundancies are reduced by estimation and compensation of movement of objects on a block-wise basis and is one of the primary contributors not only to encoding efficiency but also to encoding complexity; we now discuss such tradeoffs.

Reprinted with permission from *SID 92 Digest*, pp. 123–126, May 1992. © Society for Information Display.

3. MOTION ESTIMATION AND COMPENSATION

A motion-vector is computed by the well known technique of block-matching using luminance blocks of 16×16 pixels. A simple distortion measure, Mean Absolute Difference, between pixels of a current block in *reference* picture and candidate displaced blocks in *target* picture is computed, the motion-vector corresponding to minimum value of distortion yields the best match. The syntax permits forward motion-compensation by one motion-vector for each macroblock of P- pictures but allows up to two independent motion vectors for forward and/or backward motion-compensation for each macroblock belonging to B-pictures.

In integer pixel search, distortion criterion is evaluated at all positions within the search range. The search range employed between consecutive pictures depends on the picture resolution being coded. Typically, when coding 360×240 resolution, a motion range often found suitable is given by $(7 + 8 \times (d-1))$, and for coding 720×480 resolution a suitable range is given by $(15 + 16 \times (d-1))$, where $d(\geq 1)$ is the distance between pictures. For other picture resolutions in Table 1, or if motion estimation for severe motion can be afforded, the ranges can be modified using given examples as a guide.

The syntax supports motion-vectors with half-pixel resolution to allow precise motion compensation. If half pixel motion estimates are computed by full search, it requires too many computations. A reduced half-pixel search that performs reasonably well, starts from the best integer pixel estimate obtained by the full search and further evaluates the distortion measure at surrounding 8 additional half pixel locations obtained by spatial interpolation of pixels in target picture.

3.1 Full vs Telescopic Search

If k is the search range between consecutive pictures, the full search for a block between these pictures requires $(2 \times d \times k + 1)^2$ distortion evaluations, whereas with *telescopic* search [2] it, at most requires $d \times (2 \times k + 1)^2$ evaluations to find the best match. In reality, for a GOP with M=3, the number of computations needed for a macroblock in B- pictures by telescopic method is only $2 \times (2 \times k + 1)^2$, about one third, as compared to, $(2 \times k + 1)^2 + (4 \times k + 1)^2$ required for full search. For the same M, a macroblock in P- pictures with *telescopic* search, requires only $(2 \times k + 1)^2$ evaluations, about 9 times, as many as compared to $(6 \times k + 1)^2$ required for full search.

3.2 Symmetric Search for B- pictures

In many cases, forward and backward motion of a block in B- pictures is highly correlated, this often happens for blocks with smooth translatory motion. The symmetric (or fitted) search method [4] allows explicit joint minimization of distortion measure for forward and backward estimates, rather than separate minimization of the two. This results in maintaining spatio-temporally smooth motion and has significant advantage at low bit-rates when enough bits to code prediction error may not be available. This method, however can be significantly computation intensive.

4. DCT AND PERCEPTUAL QUANTIZATION

In order to exploit spatial redundancies present in either Intra- (original) blocks or NonIntra- (prediction error) blocks, the DCT is applied which transforms blocks of pixels to blocks of transform coefficients. The DCT is an orthogonal transform that preserves energy in a block, except that energy in pixel-domain that may have been spread throughout the block, is in most case, localized in a few low frequency coefficients. Thus, an input block of 8×8 pixels is converted into an 8×8 block of DCT coefficients, on which further redundancy reduction schemes can be applied. Towards this end, the accuracy of DCT coefficients is reduced via quantization. In order not to cause undue visible impairments in reconstructed video, the degree of quantization of a specific coefficient is decided based on frequency sensitivity of that coefficient to visible noise. We now discuss this frequency sensitivity of DCT coefficients which is given as a weighting matrix.

4.1 Visual Weighting Matrices

The MPEG syntax allows use of separate visually weighted quantization matrices for Intra- and NonIntra-blocks. This allows differences in frequency characteristics of each block type to be exploited to suit their requirements. Since, in most cases, the high frequency coefficients of a DCT block can be quantized more coarsely than the low frequency coefficients, higher quantization weights are associated with these terms when compared to middle or low frequency terms. Moreover, the shape of weighting matrix depends on whether a block is coded Intra or NonIntra. In general, the shape of the weighting matrix may also depend on the bit-rate and complexity of a scene. If scenes are relatively easy to encode (low or medium complexity at relatively high bit-rate), matrices may have a slow variation with ratio of highest frequency term to non-dc lowest frequency terms in the range of 1 to 3. For somewhat harder to code scenes (medium complexity scenes at low to mid bit-rates), the ratio of weights may be between 3 to 5, and for even more challenging scenes (high complexity scenes at low to mid bit-rates), the ratio may be between 4 to 7. An example of Intra matrix W_I, [2], and NonIntra matrix W_{NI} that are well suited for a wide range of scenes is shown in Fig. 2. The syntax allows these matrices along with other video parameters called the "context" information to be specified before encoding a sequence.

$W_I[i,j]$

```
 8 16 19 22 26 27 29 34
16 16 22 24 27 29 34 37
19 22 26 27 29 34 34 38
22 22 26 27 29 34 37 40
22 26 27 29 32 35 40 48
26 27 29 32 35 40 48 58
26 27 29 34 38 46 56 69
27 29 35 38 46 56 69 83
```

$W_{NI}[i,j]$

```
16 17 18 19 21 23 25 27
17 18 19 21 23 25 27 29
18 19 20 22 24 26 28 31
19 20 22 24 26 28 30 33
20 22 24 26 28 30 32 35
21 23 25 27 29 32 35 38
23 25 27 29 31 34 38 42
25 27 29 31 34 38 42 47
```

Fig. 2 Visual Weighting Matrices

4.2 Quantization Operation

The operation of quantization, i.e., application of quantization (step-size) parameter on weighted DCT coefficients is discussed in this section. This operation is applied somewhat differently on Intra- and NonIntra- blocks to take into account noise visibility characteristics of these blocks. In particular [1,2], Intra blocks are coded without a dead-zone, while NonIntra- blocks are coded with a deadzone. In either case, the process of "forward" quantization is a two step process comprising of, first, computing visually weighted coefficient called *actmp*, and then, applying *quant* parameter to weighted coefficient *actmp* to compute quantization level, $Qac[i,j]$. The quantization operation, being inherently lossy in nature, is another major contributor to overall compression. The operation loosely referred to as "inverse" quantization, merely performs reverse mapping of a given $Qac[i,j]$ back to the quantized coefficient.

It is worth noting that MPEG-1, being a decoder standard, mandates use of specified inverse quantization operation [3], whereas forward quantization operations of [2] can be modified for better performance [5]. As an example, we suggest a possible improvement in encoding of Intra- blocks by carefully selecting rounding parameter p in the following generalized equations.

$$actmp = \frac{16 \times ac[i,j] + \dfrac{W_I[i,j]}{2}}{W_I[i,j]}$$

$$Qac[i,j] = \frac{actmp + sign(actmp) \times p \times quant}{2 \times quant}$$

The resulting $Qac[i,j]$'s are clipped to be in range ± 255.

Our experiments indicate that p of 5/6 (or 3/4) results in a negligible increase in visual distortion when compared to that with p of 1, while it saves bits. It is also essential to note that the standard does not specify how to choose *quant* parameter, which is simply transmitted as part of the bitstream, in the form of either *squant* at the slice layer, or as often as can be afforded, as *mquant* at the macroblock layer. Whether *mquant* provides a significant improvement in picture quality over *squant* depends on whether *squant* itself is derived based on feedback of buffer fullness as a mechanism of rate control, or some other means. Typically, *mquant* is derived based on local contents of the macroblock, and is even more intimately related to rate control and warrants a joint discussion.

5. QUANTIZER ADAPTATION

There have been several proposals [6]-[8] for adapting the quantizer to the local characteristics of a scene, such that visual quality of reconstructed video can be optimized. These schemes, though they appear somewhat different, basically all adapt *mquant* parameter to local contents of the macroblock, such that, an overall target bit-rate can be maintained. Unlike *squant*, which is typically based on feedback rate-control, *mquant* adaptation can exploit feedback or feedforward rate-control. It should be pointed out that *mquant* adaptation, though it can significantly improve picture quality, also adds to increase in complexity and processing delay at the encoder. Although schemes [6]-[8] differ somewhat in complexity and performance, they are suitable for real-time encoding as they are one-pass and incur short delay. We now discuss various steps in quantizer determination with particular emphasis on scheme of [8].

5.1 Target Allocation

Initially, target bits are allocated to each of the different picture types, I-, P-, and B- used in a GOP, such that, these targets result in meeting the quota for that GOP and thus the desired bit-rate for coding the scene. Typically, I- pictures are assigned 2 to 3 times as many bits as P- pictures, which, in turn, is assigned 4 to 6 times the bits assigned to B- pictures. This initial assignment of bits is updated for each picture type as the coding progresses and better estimation of complexity of scene is obtained. At the end of a GOP, any bits left over are used to increment the quota of allocated bits to the next GOP, if too many bits are used for coding of current GOP, the excess bits are differenced from the quota for the next GOP.

5.2 Rate Control

Local variations in three separate virtual buffers for I-, P- and B- pictures are tracked to allow instantaneous control on rate of generation of bits. Before a macroblock is coded, the contents of virtual buffers are updated by removing (virtual) bits from these buffers, assuming a linear rate of depletion. Based on the fullness of virtual buffers, a quantizer value is derived and used as reference in actual *mquant* calculations. One undesirable property of this rate-control mechanism is that different areas of picture with similar spatial contents may get quantized fairly differently, making distortion more visible. In practice, as long as local variations in virtual buffer of that picture type is tracked

once every macroblock, the rate of generation of bits can be kept close to linear rate of depletion thus avoiding the need to make drastic changes in quantizer and minimizing the sacrifice of picture quality.

5.3 Mquant Assignment

A measure of spatial activity of a macroblock is computed as the minimum of the variances of its 4 luminance blocks, using original pixel values. A normalized activity measure is computed as the average activity of entire previous picture of the same type. Next, the value of *mquant* parameter is computed as a product of this normalized activity and the quantizer value obtained from the rate control. The *mquant* value is restricted to be in range of 1 to 31, and is sent in bitstream whenever its value is different from the value being used at that time. At relatively lower bit-rates, if every macroblock is quantized with *mquant*, the overhead necessary for *mquant* may be excessive and actually result in lowering of overall performance. Many experiments suggest that at these bit-rates, there is little to be gained by using *mquant* for B- pictures. When *mquant* is used effectively, it saves bits in busy areas of picture, as more distortion can be hidden there, but costs bits in low detailed and edge regions, as these areas are more sensitive to distortion and need to be quantized relatively better.

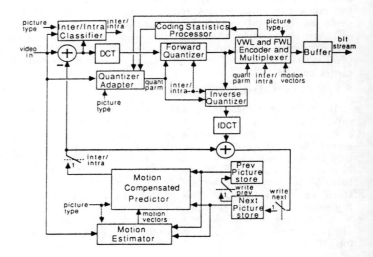

Fig. 3 MPEG-1 Encoder

6. OTHER CODING ISSUES

Fig. 3 shows a block diagram of a MPEG-1 encoder. The functionality of many of the individual blocks has already been discussed. An input macroblock is differenced with its motion-compensated prediction, resulting in prediction error which is compared with original (intra) block to determine which would be most efficient to encode. The chosen macroblock is transformed by the *DCT* and quantized by the *forwardquantizer* using quantization parameter provided by the *quantizeradapter*. Since during the quantization process, many of the resulting $Qac[i,j]$'s get truncated to zero; for every coefficient with a non-zero level, a pair consisting of run along the zig-zag scan path [1], and level is variable word length (VWL) coded. At the macroblock layer, data items such as inter/intra decision, quantizer parameter and motion vectors are transmitted, while at slice and picture layer, synchronization codes are multiplexed into the MPEG bit-stream. The decoder of Fig. 4 does the inverse processing consisting of demultiplexing, followed by inverse

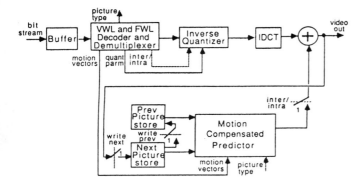

Fig. 4 MPEG-1 Decoder

quantization and DCT and addition of motion-compensated prediction to reconstruct each macroblock.

It is worth noting that MPEG-1 video coding syntax was developed for low resolution (360×240) non-interlaced video. Even though it performs relatively well over a range of bitrates and coding resolutions and formats, it can easily be improved on for coding high resolution (720×480 and above) video. The video coding activity for the second phase (MPEG-2) standard is already in progress and is aimed both at optimizing the syntax for coding of high resolution video, as well as supporting additional functionalities of backward compatibility with MPEG-1 standard and multi-resolution scalable video.

7. SUMMARY

The MPEG-1 standard, being generic in nature, is well suited for a wide range of applications at variety of bitrates. The standard, while it specifies a syntax for the bitstream and the decoding process, offers considerable flexibility in optimizing the encoding process. We have discussed various choices in encoding parameters and schemes, as well as, suggested potential improvements and their impact on picture quality and encoder complexity.

The next phase of this standard is in progress and is addressing the problems of optimized coding of high resolution video of various formats and at the same time supporting additional features such as compatibility and scalability.

REFERENCES

[1] D. Le. Gall, "MPEG: A Video Compression Standard for Multimedia Applications," *Communications of the ACM,* vol.34, pp. 47-58, April 1991.

[2] Source: MPEG Simulation Model Editing Committee, "MPEG Video Simulation Model 3 (SM3)," July 1990.

[3] Source: ISO MPEG, "ISO CD 11172-2: Coding of Moving Pictures and Associated Audio for Digital Storage Media at up to about 1.5 Mbit/s," Nov. 1991.

[4] A. Puri and R. Aravind, "On Comparing Motion-Interpolation Structures for Video Coding," *Proc. SPIE Visual Commun. and Image Processing,* pp.1560-1571, Lausanne, Switzerland, Oct. 1990.

[5] Source: Norweign Telecom, "Improvements in Hybrid DCT Coding," *MPEG Document 91/78,* Paris, France, May 1991.

[6] A. Puri and R. Aravind, "Motion Compensated Video Coding with Adaptive Perceptual Quantization," *IEEE Trans. on Circuits and Systems for Video Technology,* vol.1, no.4, pp. 351-361, Dec. 1991.

[7] C. Gonzales and E. Viscito, "Motion Video Adaptive Quantization in the Transform Domain," *IEEE Trans. on Circuits and Systems for Video Technology,* vol.1, no.4, pp.374-378, Dec. 1991.

[8] Source: MPEG Preliminary Working Draft Editing Committee, "MPEG Video Preliminary Working Draft of Test Model 0," Feb. 1992.

Adaptive frame/field motion compensated video coding

Atul Puri, R. Aravind and Barry Haskell

AT&T Bell Laboratories, Crawfords Corner Road, Holmdel, NJ 07733, USA

Abstract. The second phase of the Motion Pictures Experts Group (MPEG-2) activity is in progress and is primarily aimed at coding of high resolution video with high quality at bit-rates of 4 to 9 Mbit/s. In addition, this phase is also required to address many issues including forward and backward compatibility with the first phase (MPEG-1) standard. For MPEG-2, an adaptive frame/field motion-compensated video coding scheme is proposed. This scheme builds on the proven framework of DCT and motion-compensation based techniques already optimized in MPEG-1 for coding of lower resolution video at low bit-rates. Various adaptations include techniques to improve efficiency of coding for interlaced video source as well as improving quality by better exploitation of characteristics of the video scenes. Statistics and subjective tests confirm that these adaptations provide significant improvement as compared to purely MPEG-1 based coding. We then discuss issues of compatibility with the MPEG-1 standard and of implementation complexity of the proposed scheme.

Keywords. Adaptive video coding; motion-compensated DCT coding; interlaced video coding; MPEG 2.

1. Introduction

The second phase activity of the Motion Pictures Experts Group (MPEG-2) standard is currently in progress and is primarily aimed at coding of high resolution video with high quality. The first phase (MPEG-1) standard [4] is nearly complete, the video coding syntax for this phase is primarily optimized for coding video of low resolution (luminance of 360×240) and non-interlaced format at bit-rates of 1 to 1.5 Mbit/s. The MPEG-2 standard is focussed on coding CCIR 601 resolution (luminance of 720×480) and interlaced format at bit-rate ranging from 4 to 9 Mbit/s.

The MPEG-2 video coding scheme is not only required to provide good picture quality and to satisfy all the features of MPEG-1, but also to support additional features [6] such as compatibility with MPEG-1, ability to derive multiresolution scales, robustness to cell loss for transmission on ATM networks, and low-delay modes for visualconferencing. It is also desirable that the coding scheme satisfy as many requirements as it can while maintaining relatively low implementation complexity.

We propose an adaptive frame/field motion-compensated video coding scheme [10] that primarily addresses the issue of attaining good picture quality at desired bit-rates. This scheme builds on the proven framework of discrete cosine transform (DCT) and motion-compensation based coding techniques already optimized for MPEG-1. As in MPEG-1 based coding [1–3, 5], temporal redundancies are exploited via estimation and compensation of block-wise motion of objects, whereas spatial and perceptual redundancies are exploited via DCT and perceptual (visually weighted) quantization. In addition, various adaptations improve efficiency by adapting to the characteristics of the video source and improve quality by better exploitation of the locally varying contents of the video scene. Finally, we also discuss issues of compatibility with MPEG-1 [7, 8] and that of implementation complexity [11].

2. Organization basics

We now discuss basics of pre- and post-processing of input video source as well as its organization into access, synchronization and processing units for coding.

2.1. Pre- and post-processing

The input video resolution is CCIR-601, 4:2:2, and corresponds to luminance resolution of 720×480 and two chrominance components of 360×480 each. The luminance signal is retained as full resolution and is neither pre- nor post-processed. The chrominance signal is pre-processed by vertical filtering and decimation to half of its original resolution. The resulting luminance and chrominance signal referred to as 4:2:0, is input to the video encoder. The output of the video decoder has the same 4:2:0 format and is postprocessed to 4:2:2 for display. The filters employed for pre- and post-processing are those used in [5].

2.2. Group-of-pictures

An input video sequence is divided into units of group-of-pictures (GOP's), consisting of an Intra (I-)picture coded without reference to other pictures, and an arrangement of Predictive (P-)pictures coded with reference to previous (I- or P-)pictures, and Bidirectional (B-)pictures coded with reference to an immediate previous (I- or P-)picture as well as an immediate future (P- or I-)picture. The GOP arrangement is very much like that for MPEG-1 [4, 5], and here, also, a GOP serves as a basic access unit, with an I-picture as a natural entry point. The length of the GOP, N, is chosen to be 12, the distance between I-pictures; whereas M, the distance between P-pictures is chosen as 3. Such a GOP is shown in

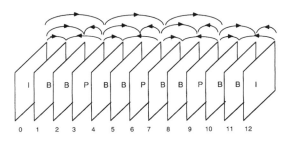

Fig. 1. Group-of-picture structure with $M = 3$ and $N = 12$.

Fig. 1. Each picture corresponds to a frame which, in turn, is composed of a pair of fields. The chosen GOP length ensures that a complete I-picture occurs every 0.4 seconds, consistent with the maximum random access delay requirements for MPEG-2 [6].

2.3. Slices and macroblocks

As in MPEG-1 [5], each picture is composed of a number of slices, where a slice is the basic unit at which resynchronization information is associated. There are 30 slices per picture and each slice contains a row of macroblocks that start from the left edge of a picture and end at the right edge of the picture. In our coding scheme we have assumed a 4:2:0 source, which means that a macroblock consists of a 16×16 block (or alternately 4, 8×8 blocks) of luminance along with each of the 8×8 Cb- and Cr-chrominance blocks. The macroblock structure employed can also support 4:2:2 format, the only difference being that now a macroblock would have 2 Cb- and 2 Cr-chrominance blocks in addition to the same number of luminance blocks. Since the video source is interlaced, each macroblock contains lines both from odd- and even-fields, and may require this distinction to be made for specific operations. In any case, an entire macroblock is always processed together and is the basic unit at which motion-estimation and compensation as well as quantizer selection is performed.

3. Motion estimation and compensation

The well-known block-based techniques are employed for motion estimation and compensation. In order to exploit the presence in a macroblock of lines from two temporally separated fields, two fundamental modes of motion compensation are defined: the *frame-MC* and the *field-MC* modes. The frame-MC mode does not discriminate between the two fields inside a macroblock; it compensates a macroblock with another macroblock containing lines from both fields. In the field-MC

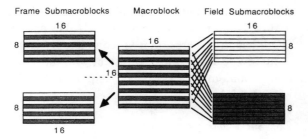

Frame Submacroblocks   Macroblock   Field Submacroblocks

Fig. 2. Macroblock organization into submacroblocks for motion compensation.

mode, the lines from each field in a macroblock are compensated with a block containing only lines from the field of the same parity.

For the frame-MC mode two block sizes are allowed, with horizontal × vertical dimensions of 16×16 and 16×8, respectively. In the latter case, a macroblock is divided into two horizontal halves (a top half and a bottom half), which are called frame submacroblocks. In the field-MC mode a macroblock is separated into two field submacroblocks each containing lines from only one field. Since a macroblock contains 16 lines, each field submacroblock contains 8 lines and is of size 16×8. Figure 2 illustrates how a macroblock is divided into frame- and field-submacroblocks. Motion compensation is performed with half-pixel precision. Precise details on motion compensation modes are given in Section 3.2; we now consider motion-estimation schemes for the frame- and field-MC modes.

3.1. Frame/field motion estimation

As in the MPEG-1 simulation models, motion estimation is performed in two steps: a search for the integer motion vector, followed by a local search for the half-pixel refinement. In general, exhaustive (full) search is employed for the integer motion vector, with a range of $(15 + 16 \times (d-1))$ for a distance d between the target and reference pictures.

Considering first the frame-MC mode, we note that it is very similar to MPEG-1 motion compensation and therefore needs no significant modifi-

cations to the motion estimation methods used for MPEG-1 [2]. Here, motion vectors are required for the 16×16 macroblock and the 16×8 frame submacroblocks, all of which are computed by full search followed by a half-pixel update. Half-pixel positions in the frame-MC mode are defined as in MPEG-1, midway between the lines and pixels of the whole picture. Bilinear spatial interpolation is employed for the half-pixel update (Section 3.3) in both the frame- and field-MC modes.

For the field-MC mode, the search is performed by matching the field submacroblock of a certain parity only with 16×8 blocks from the reference field of the same parity. The vertical range for the integer motion-vector search is halved, since one field-line shift is equivalent to a two-line shift in the picture. The half-pixel positions for the field-MC mode are obtained as follows. A first intra-field spatial interpolation operation places the interpolated pixels where the lines of the other field lie. Since these positions correspond to integer-line locations of the picture, a second intra-field interpolation step is performed that places the interpolated pixels at half-line positions of the picture, which is equivalent to quarter-line positions inside the field. Motion vectors for the field-MC mode are defined with respect to these quarter-line field positions. The 'half-pixel' search thus consists of updating the field integer motion vector in two successive steps. The effect is that the frame-mode and field-mode motion vectors have the same resolution relative to the picture.

In P-pictures, motion vectors are computed for the 16×16 macroblock, the 16×8 frame submacroblocks and the 16×8 field submacroblocks. In B-pictures, which have two references, the motion estimation process is performed independently for each reference picture. We note however that the search range in B-pictures is smaller than that in P-pictures on account of the smaller distances to the reference picture.

3.2. Frame/field motion compensation

We now discuss the specifics of the motion compensation modes in P- and B-pictures, which are related to either the frame-MC or the field-MC modes.

3.2.1. P-picture modes

1. 16×16 frame-MC mode: In this mode, the 16×16 luminance block is compensated by another 16×16 block from the reference picture that is fetched using one (forward) motion vector. The prediction block also contains pixels of both fields of the reference picture. This MC mode is identical to that in MPEG-1 for P-pictures, and is retained to provide syntactical compatibility with MPEG-1.

2. 16×8 frame-MC mode: Each 16×8 frame sub-macroblock is independently compensated using a (forward) motion vector. Two motion vectors are transmitted per macroblock.

3. 16×8 field-MC mode: Each field submacroblock is compensated independently using a (forward) motion vector with a 16×8 block derived only from the field of the same parity in the reference picture. Two motion vectors are transmitted per macroblock.

3.2.2. B-picture modes

1. 16×16 bidirectional frame-MC mode: This mode is identical to the bidirectional prediction mode in MPEG-1. A forward motion vector is used to obtain a 16×16 block from the past reference picture, and a backward motion vector, a 16×16 block from the future reference picture. These blocks are averaged to yield the final prediction block.

2. 16×16 forward unidirectional frame-MC mode: This mode is identical to the forward unidirectional prediction mode in MPEG-1. Only one forward motion vector is used for a macroblock.

3. 16×16 backward unidirectional frame-MC mode: This mode is identical to the backward unidirectional prediction mode in MPEG-1. Only one backward motion vector is used for a macroblock.

4. 16×8 frame-MC mode; top-forward with bottom-backward: The top frame-submacroblock is compensated using a forward motion vector, and the bottom frame-submacroblock is compensated using a backward motion vector. Two motion vectors are transmitted per macroblock in this mode.

5. 16×8 frame-MC mode; top-backward with bottom-forward: This mode is very similar to the above, with the top half compensated using a backward motion vector and the bottom half using a forward motion vector.

6. 16×8 field-MC mode; odd-forward with even-backward: The odd-field submacroblock is compensated using a forward motion vector with another 16×8 block derived only from the odd field of the past reference picture. Similarly, the even-field submacroblock is compensated using a backward motion vector with a 16×8 block derived only from even field of the future reference picture. Two motion vectors are transmitted per macroblock in this mode.

7. 16×8 field-MC mode; odd-backward with even-forward: This mode is very similar to the one above, with the odd-field submacroblock is compensated using a backward motion vector and the even-field submacroblock compensated using a forward motion vector. Two motion vectors are again required per macroblock in this mode.

As can be seen from the above discussion, at most two motion vectors are transmitted for a 16×16 macroblock. For a given macroblock, the mode giving the error signal with the smallest energy is selected at the encoder. After motion compensation is finished, the difference pixels are replaced in the original interlaced order to form a frame-difference macroblock.

Each motion vector component is encoded differently, with respect to a previously transmitted component.

3.3. Filtering for half-pixel prediction

For half-pixel prediction, we employ a 4 tap symmetrical filter with coefficients $(-1, 9, 9, -1)$. This filter, among others, has been investigated in

[9]. We apply this filter identically in horizontal and vertical directions while the center pixel is computed using the circumference pixels, as shown in Fig. 3. For fairly detailed scenes with fine textures and edges undergoing slow-to-medium pan, this filter provides an improvement in visual quality as compared to a simple linear averaging filter [4, 5]. The visual improvement is due to enhancement of fine edges and texture; this filter yields the best tradeoff between enhancing image details versus coding artifacts. The improvement in picture quality comes at the expense of increase in complexity, as extra pixels outside the boundary of every block need to be accessed.

4. DCT and quantization

On a macroblock basis, to adapt to local spatial contents of a scene, either frame or field coding can be selected. The splitting of the 16×16 luminance block of a macroblock into frame- or field-8×8 blocks for DCT coding is shown in Fig. 4. The

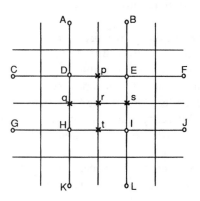

$$p = (9 \times (D+E) - (C+F)) / 16$$
$$q = (9 \times (D+H) - (A+K)) / 16$$
$$s = (9 \times (E+I) - (B+L)) / 16$$
$$t = (9 \times (H+I) - (G+J)) / 16$$
$$r = (18 \times (D+E+H+I) - (A+B+C+F+G+J+K+L)) / 64$$

Fig. 3. Filtering for computing prediction at half-pixel positions.

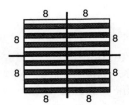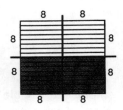

Fig. 4. Macroblock organization into frame/field blocks for DCT coding.

chrominance 8×8 blocks are retained without splitting.

4.1. Frame/field coding selection

The decision to select frame- or field-coding for a macroblock is made independent of the mode chosen for motion-compensation. Often, block matching provides the best prediction for a macroblock but may not always estimate the exact motion and the resulting prediction error signal can still have considerable correlation among frame or field lines. Motion estimates may also result in significantly correlated frame- or field-prediction errors due to inadequate motion vector range, background and foreground regions within the same blocks, as well as blocks with partially occluded objects undergoing complex movement.

One-step correlation coefficients are calculated for the frame and field lines of an either 16×16 original or motion-compensated difference luminance block. If one-step correlation coefficient of frame lines, ρ_F, is greater than or equal to one-step correlation coefficient of field lines, ρ_f, frame-coding is selected, otherwise field-coding is chosen. The fundamental reason for the choice is that the DCT is more efficient on signals with higher correlation.

4.2. Frame/field quantization matrices

In general, quantization matrices should depend on the bit-rate and complexity of scenes. If either the bit-rate is high or the scenes are relatively easy to encode, these matrices should have a small variation in weights for low and high frequency terms.

For lower bit-rates and medium complexity scenes or for relatively higher bit-rates and difficult scenes, an appropriate ratio of weights of high and low frequency terms may be between 4 and 7. Conversely, for either higher bit-rates and medium complexity scenes or relatively lower bit-rates and easier scenes, this ratio could be between 3 and 5.

Since the field lines are twice apart as compared to the frame lines, the correlation chartacteristics of the two are quite different. If there is significant movement in a scene, the DCT of intra macroblocks processed in frame or field modes show major differences in the location of significant coefficients. Even for scenes where such movement can be compensated, there may still be important differences. For example, the DCT of frame blocks undergoing motion shows significant coefficients in the bottom left-hand corner. This effect occurs due to false edges created by the interlace, and appears as interline flicker if these coefficients are quantized too coarsely. Frame quantization matrices keep this under the visibility threshold by giving preferential treatment to these coefficients during quantization. Field quantization matrices, on the other hand, treat vertical spatial frequencies more carefully as compared to horizontal spatial frequencies to account for the difference in spacing between adjacent samples in horizontal and vertical directions.

Quantization matrices for field- and frame-coding of intra- and non-intra-macroblocks for 3 to 5 Mbit/s coding of medum to high complexity scenes are shown in Fig. 5.

4.3. The quantization operation

For Intra-macroblocks, we shift quantizer decision levels by employing rounding similar to that in [2, 9]. This results in savings of bits, while increase in distortion is hardly visible. A careful selection of decision level shift ensures no recursive loss within a GOP.

First, weighted DCT coefficient is computed as before [5]:

$$\text{actmp} = (16 \times \text{ac}[i, j]) // W_I[i, j].$$

Intra frame matrix

```
 8  16  19  22  26  27  29  34
16  16  22  24  27  29  34  37
19  22  26  27  29  34  34  38
22  22  26  27  29  34  37  40
22  26  27  29  32  35  40  48
26  27  27  32  35  40  48  58
26  27  27  32  35  40  56  69
26  26  27  29  32  40  56  83
```

Intra field matrix

```
 8  16  19  22  26  27  29  34
16  16  22  24  27  29  34  37
19  22  26  27  29  34  34  38
22  22  26  27  29  34  37  40
22  26  27  29  32  35  40  48
26  27  29  32  35  40  48  58
26  27  29  34  38  46  56  69
27  29  35  38  46  56  69  83
```

Non-intra frame matrix

```
16  17  19  21  23  25  28  31
17  18  20  22  24  27  30  33
18  19  21  24  26  29  32  35
19  21  23  26  28  31  34  39
20  22  25  26  31  34  36  43
22  24  25  28  33  38  42  48
22  24  25  28  33  38  48  54
22  22  25  26  31  38  48  63
```

Non-intra field matrix

```
16  17  19  21  23  25  28  31
17  18  20  22  24  27  30  33
18  19  21  24  26  29  32  35
19  21  23  26  28  31  34  39
20  22  24  28  31  34  36  43
22  24  26  30  33  38  42  48
24  25  28  32  35  40  48  54
25  27  31  35  40  47  54  63
```

Fig. 5. An example of quantization matrices for frame/field coding at 4 Mbit/s.

Next, coefficient quantization-level is calculated using the weighted DCT coefficient by the following generalized equation:

$$Q_{\text{ac}}[i, j] = \frac{\text{actmp} + \text{sign}(\text{actmp}) \times (p \times \text{mquant} // q)}{2 \times \text{mquant}}.$$

Here p and q control the offset of quantizer decision levels. In our experiments we have used $p = 5$ and $q = 6$, although $p = 3$ and $q = 4$ result in higher bits savings at the expense of slight increase in blurriness. Since the changes discussed here only affect the encoding, no change in inverse quantization equations [4, 5] is necessary.

Also, the NonIntra-macroblocks are coded with a dead-zone as in [5]; the forward and inverse quantization operations remain unchanged.

5. Quantizer adaptations and rate control

Here, we discuss the issue of adapting the quantizer to the characteristics of a scene such that visual quality of the reconstructed scene can be optimized, given a certain target data-rate. More specifically, the mquant parameter is varied based on the local contents of a macroblock. Unlike the slice quantizer, squant, which is typically based on feedback rate-control, our mquant adaptation exploits both feedback and feedforward rate-control. In performing mquant adaptation we also impose an additional constraint that the scheme should be one-pass causal in nature to limit the implementation complexity of the encoder. Since there is often a considerable interaction between mquant selection based on contents of a macroblock versus what can actually be afforded based on rate-control, both these issues are discussed jointly. Since the scheme for mquant adaptation in I- and P-pictures is very similar to that in [3], we include only a brief description. For B-pictures we employ mscale, which is derived from the mquant parameter.

5.1. Target allocation

Initially, target bits are allocated to each of the different picture types, I-. P- and B-, used in a GOP such that these targets result in meeting the quota of bits assigned to that GOP and thus, the desired bit-rate for coding that scene. Typically, each I-pictures is assigned 2 to 3 times the bits assigned to a P-picture, which, in turn, is assigned 3 to 5 time the bits assigned to a B-picture. This initial assignment of bits is updated for each picture type as the coding progresses and better estimate of complexity of the scene is obtained. At the end of a GOP, any left over bits are used to increment the quota of allocated bits to the next GOP. If too many bits are used in the current GOP, excess bits are differenced from the quota of the next GOP.

5.2. Rate control

A target picture quality is chosen based on bit-allocations targeted and the complexity of each of the I-, P- and B-picture types. An accumulated histogram of occurrence of classes in the previous picture of the same type and an experimentally derived bits-model are used to predict the number of bits required to code the current picture. If the bits estimate exceeds the target bits, a search for a new target quality is conducted that may provide bits estimate closer to the target bits. For further regulation of coding rate, a Q_p string corresponding to target quality is updated based on the fullness of the buffer. This selectively influences the picture quality of busier blocks, depending on the contents of the buffer.

5.3. Mquant assignment

A macroblock is first classified to be either homogeneous or non-homogeneous depending on whether the variances of its four luminance blocks are 'close' to one another. If it is homogeneous, it is further classified into one of the sixteen possible classes depending on the average variance of its four luminance blocks. Typically, such a macroblock contains a low-detail area of fairly regular texture. The mquant assigned to this macroblock is determined from the average mquant assigned to that variance class in the previous picture of the same type. This potentially permits the same mquant to be assigned to all macroblocks in the picture that have the same variance class irrespective of their location in the picture. If a macroblock is non-homogeneous each of the luminance blocks within the macroblock is individually assigned to a variance based on an edge based category. They are then merged forming union of 8×8 block regions, which may be homogeneous or may have edges passing through them. The mquant assigned to such a macroblock is dependent on the lowest variance of the blocks within the macroblock.

5.4. Mscale computation

While picture quality of B-pictures can be selectively improved by adapting the quantizer depending on the spatial contents, the overall quality of the scene may actually decrease due to relatively high overhead of this adaptation especially at lower data-rates. As a solution to this problem, we introduce mscale, a scaling parameter, that helps minimize overhead by using the concept of relative quantization. First, mquant is calculated for a macroblock following method in previous section. It is then multiplied by a global scale factor depending on the scene, and a ratio is computed with respect to the slice quantizer, squant. For B-pictures, the value of squant is the average of mquant values used for coded macroblocks in the same slice of the immediately previous P-picture. The ratio is compared to four ratios called mscales, loaded at the start of coding of sequence along with other parameters. The closest representative ratio is the chosen mscale, a 2-bit code identifying one of the 4 candidate values is sent to the decoder. It can be invoked just like mquant; when sent, it resets the previous mscale to the current value, until a new value is needed. At the decoder, the absolute quantizer for a macroblock is obtained by multiplying mscale to the slice quantizer, squant.

6. VWL coding of DCT coefficients

The non-zero quantized coefficients are Variable Word Length (VWL) coded as two-dimensional events of run-length and amplitude, as in MPEG-1.

6.1. DC prediction for intra-blocks

The efficiency of DC prediction for Intra-macro-blocks [4, 5] is increased by adapting it to frame/field-coded macroblocks. Two DC predictors, one for the top row of 8×8 luminance blocks and, second, for the bottom row of 8×8 blocks in a slice are employed. For frame-coded macroblocks, using two predictors instead of one simply means better prediction, whereas for field-coded macro-blocks, the top row carries prediction for blocks of odd and the bottom row for the blocks of even fields. All DC predictions are reset at the beginning of a slice or whenever a NonIntra macroblock is encountered.

Since macroblocks coded in frame-mode may be preceded by those that are coded in field-mode or vice-versa, i.e., whenever there is change in mode, an average of DC values of the top-right and bottom-right 8×8 blocks of the previous macroblock is used to predict the DC value of top-left 8×8 block of the next macroblock; further, this block's DC value is used as a prediction for the bottom-left 8×8 block of the same macroblock. Figure 6 shows an example of the DC prediction in a row of all Intra-macro-blocks coded with frame/field mode transitions. The DC prediction employed for chrominance Cb- and Cr-blocks is fairly straightforward [4].

6.2. Frame/field coefficient scans

In our scheme, the adaptation of coefficient scans does not require additional overhead as we utilize the coding mode information sent for each macroblock. This adaptation is designed to exploit major differences in structure of coefficients produced by the DCT applied to blocks of frame- or field-coded macroblocks. Typically, DCT coefficients resulting from frame-coded blocks exhibit significant values not only in low frequency

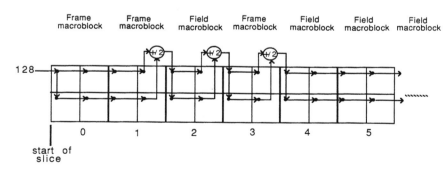

Fig. 6. An example of DC prediction of luminance for intra-frame/field macroblocks.

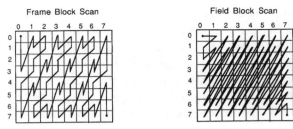

Fig. 7. Scanning of DCT coefficients for frame and field coded blocks.

terms around the upper left-hand corner of coefficient block, but also in the lower left-hand corner term. The DCT coefficients for the field coded blocks, on the other hand, due to larger vertical spacing between field lines exhibit significant values in higher vertical but lower horizontal frequency terms. Two scans, one suitable for frame-coded blocks and the other field-coded blocks, are shown in Fig. 7, and allow significant non-zero coefficients to be quickly scanned with short zero-runs for efficient VWL coding of pairs of runs and levels.

6.3. Adaptive VWL coding

In MPEG-1 [4, 5], pairs of runs of zero quantized coefficients and level of non-zero quantized coefficients are coded with a 2-dimensional VWL code table. The end-of-block (EOB), a unique codeword, is sent after the last significant coefficient in each coded block. The 2-dimensional table is derived by observing the relatively high frequency of occurrence of events with short run-lengths and small levels, as well as events with large run-lengths and small levels, which are coded efficiently. At relatively low data-rates, the frequency of occurrence of EOB code becomes significantly high and it is desirable to code it efficiently. For efficient VWL encoding, it is crucial to assign optimum code lengths to first few most significantly occurring events including the EOB. In using a fixed VWL table, the potential for mismatch of code lengths assigned to freqently occurring events can be significant due to variation in characteristics of the scene. Moreover, within a scene I- and P-macroblocks themselves differ in statistical distribution of coefficient run/level combinations, a single table represents a compromise between the two.

When multiple VWL tables are used to improve the coding efficiency, not only the number and size of tables but also the mechanism for adaptation between the tables is important as it affects the overall coding complexity. We propose two base-tables (each of the same size as MPEG-1), where each base-table is further optimized in most frequent events by choosing one of the 4 templates consisting of a subtable of 32 events each. On a macroblock basis, one of the 4 templates containing subtable (which maps into one of the two appropriate base-tables) is adaptively selected for each of the I- and P-pictures. This represents an affordable overhead of only 2-bits per coded macroblock. These subtables differ in code lengths assigned to most frequently occurring events including the EOB. In order to select the best sub-table, all the 4 subtables are tried at the encoder and the one that produces the least number of bits for all blocks within a coded macroblock is selected. For B-pictures, a fixed table consisting of the first subtable (and corresponding base table) of P-pictures is employed. Experiments have indicated relatively little gain by adaptively selecting VWL code tables for B-pictures. An example of the shape of the templates, and subtables corresponding to lengths of VWL codes for each template for I- and P-pictures is shown in Figs. 8a and 8b. We note that in Fig. 8a three out of 4 subtables have similar template shapes but differ in codeword length assigned to EOB and other frequently occurring events, while the other template is different in shape but not the EOB length. Similarly, Fig. 8b contains 3 subtables of identical template shapes and one of different shape, as before.

7. Details of encoder and decoder

The encoder is shown in Fig. 9. Video input is assumed to be already reordered appropriately for MPEG-1 style I-, P- and B-picture coding. Thus,

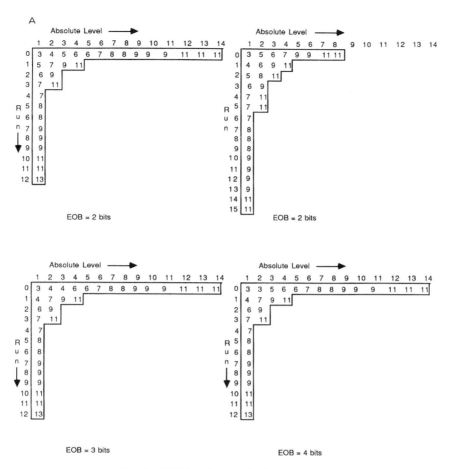

Fig. 8a. VLC length tables for intra-pictures.

macroblocks comprised of six blocks go to Subtractor, Inter/Intra-analyer, DCT, Quantizer and Motion Estimator. On the other input to the Subtractor is pixel-estimate signal, which is either produced by the Motion-Compensated Predictor or is set to zero for Intra coded macroblocks. The output of the subtractor is the well known error signal which passes to the Inter/Intra-analyzer, which decides if macroblock should be coded Intra. The Frame/Field-Analyzer determines if the error signal macroblock should be coded in 'Frame' or 'Field' mode; this decision is output as 'coding type' signal, which goes to several modules as shown in Fig. 9. The block formatter reformats the macroblock for the field mode into a form where pixels from one field are rearranged at the top and pixels from the other field go at the bottom; the (possibly reformatted) block then goes to DCT for transformation. Motion Compensation modules determine the 'motion-compensation type' for each macroblock, and this signal is sent to Motion Compensated Predictor, Motion Vector Predictor and Macroblock Classifier. The Macroblock Classifier has as input the 'picture type', 'coding type', 'motion-compensation type' and 'inter/intra type'. From these it generates macroblock classification that is sent to VWL Encoder and used to control the choice of VWL tables.

For Intra-macroblocks, DC coefficient of DCT block is coded separately and is fed to the DC

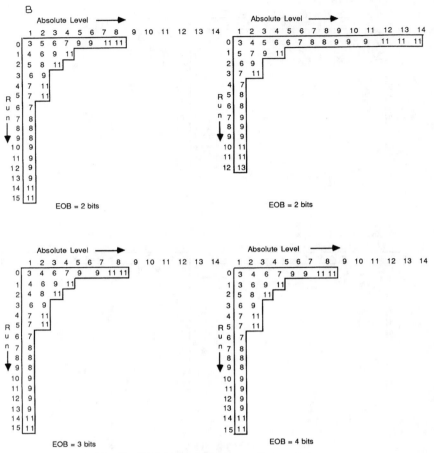

Fig. 8b. VLC length tables for prediction pictures.

predictor. The resulting differential DC coefficients are VWL coded. The non-DC coefficients of Intra macroblock and all coefficients of NonIntra macroblock are quantized by the Quantizer. One of the four quantization matrices is chosen for each macroblock depending on its type. Scan selector applies a scan depending on 'coding type' and reorders the coefficients on which 2-dimensional VWL encoding is carried out. The VWL encoder selects appropriate base-tables and sub-tables depending on the 'picture type' and the 'macroblock type'. VWL encoder also codes and multiplexes the macroblock class, intra-differential DC coefficients, differential motion-vectors and the quantization step size parameter, Qp. Coded bits are then sent to buffer and await transmission. Inverse Scan Selector restores the original order to the (now) quantized DCT coefficients. IDCT produces the quantized error signal, Block Unformatter restores the original pixel order for field mode and adder produces the decoded pixels in the usual manner. The operation of Inverse Scan Selector and Block Unformatter convert coefficient and pixel-domain data back to original order. For non-B-pictures, decoded pixels pass to the Next Picture Store and from here to the Previous Picture Store. These pictures are then used in the usual way for P-picture prediction or B-picture interpolation.

The decoder is shown in Fig. 10. It is almost the inverse of the encoder; most modules in the

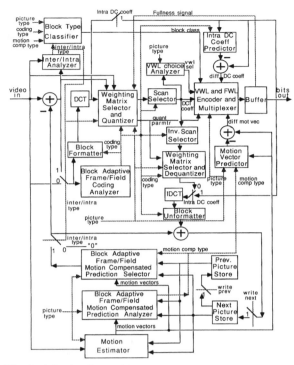

Fig. 9. Adaptive frame/field motion compensated predictive encoder.

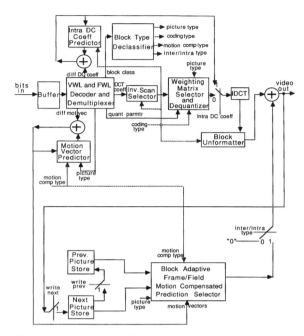

Fig. 10. Adaptive frame/field motion compensated predictive decoder.

decoder also appear at the encoder and their operation is fairly straightforward.

8. Macroblock types and coding syntax

Earlier, in Section 3, we have discussed details of macroblock motion-compensation modes allowed in P- and B-pictures. In Section 4, details of macroblock coding modes were also discussed. Here, we first discuss all macroblock types resulting from combination of motion-compensation and coding modes in each of I-, P- and B-pictures, followed by a discussion of the coding syntax when using these macroblock types.

8.1. Macroblock types

An explanation of nomenclature used in Tables 1a–1c that contain details of macroblock_types

seems necessary. The terms macro_mc_f and macro_mc_b refer to macroblock motion-compensation modes that use a single motion-vector in forward and backward directions, respectively, and these columns in tables take binary values (of 0 or 1). In the next three columns, macro_sub_frmfldmc_fb, macro_sub_frmfldmc_bf and macro_sub_frmfldmc_ff all refer to submacroblock motion-compensation with two motion-vectors, the postfix fb means that the first motion-vector refers to the forward direction and the second motion-vector to the backward direction, whereas bf means the inverse of fb, and ff means that both vectors refer to the forward direction. The term macro_sub_frmfldmc is common to all three, and simply refers to use of frame- or field-submacroblocks for motion-compensation. The three corresponding columns in tables take one of the three values, with entry of '0' when that mode does not exist, a '1' when frame submacroblocks are used, and a '2' when field submacroblocks are used. The next column, macro_frmfld_cod takes a value of

127

Table 1a

VLC table for macroblock_types in I-pictures

VLC code	Macro_ mc_f	Macro_ mc_b	Macro_sub_ frmfldmc_fb	Macro_sub_ frmfldmc_bf	Macro_sub_ frmfldmc_ff	Macro_ frmfldcod	Macro_ Intra
1	0	0	0	0	0	1	1
01	0	0	0	0	0	2	1

Table 1b

VLC table for macroblock_types in P-pictures

VLC code	Macro_ mc_f	Macro_ mc_b	Macro_sub_ frmfldmc_fb	Macro_sub_ frmfldmc_bf	Macro_sub_ frmfldmc_ff	Macro_ frmfldcod	Macro_ Intra
10	0	0	0	0	1	1	0
11	0	0	0	0	2	1	0
01	1	0	0	0	0	1	0
0010	0	0	0	0	1	2	0
0011	0	0	0	0	2	2	0
0001	1	0	0	0	0	2	0
00001	1	0	0	0	0	2	1
000001	0	0	0	0	0	1	1

Table 1c

VLC table for macroblock_types in B-pictures

VLC code	Macro_ mc_f	Macro_ mc_b	Macro_sub_ frmfldmc_fb	Macro_sub_ frmfldmc_bf	Macro_sub_ frmfldmc_ff	Macro_ frmfldcod	Macro_ Intra
10	1	1	0	0	0	2	0
11	1	1	0	0	0	1	0
010	0	1	0	0	0	1	0
011	0	1	0	0	0	2	0
0010	1	0	0	0	0	2	0
0011	1	0	0	0	0	1	0
00010	0	0	0	1	0	1	0
00011	0	0	2	0	0	1	0
000010	0	0	1	0	0	1	0
000011	0	0	0	2	0	1	0
0000010	0	0	2	0	0	2	0
0000011	0	0	0	1	0	2	0
00000010	0	0	0	2	0	2	0
00000011	0	0	1	0	0	2	0
000000010	0	0	0	0	0	1	1
000000011	0	0	0	0	0	2	1

'1' when frame-coding is chosen and a value of '2' when field coding is selected. The last column simply indicates whether the macroblock is coded as Intra or not. Overall, for I-pictures 2 macroblock_types, for P-pictures 8 macroblock_types, and for B-pictures 16 macroblock_types result. The first column in these tables shows VLC codes assigned to the event explained by appropriate entries in that row for each of the 7 columns, depending on the frequency of occurrence.

8.2. The coding syntax

We now discuss the exact coding syntax necessary for using the macroblock types listed. This syntax can be best explained with the help of syntax

Sequence Layer:

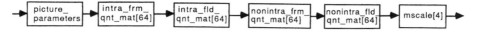

Macroblock Layer in Intra Macroblocks:

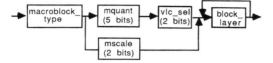

Macroblock Layer in Predictive Macroblocks:

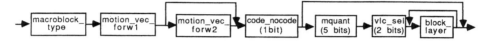

Macroblock Layer in Bidirectional Macroblocks:

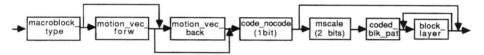

Block Layer in Intra Macroblocks:

Block Layer in NonIntra (Predictive and Bidirectional) Macroblocks:

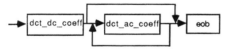

Fig. 11. Syntax diagrams for sequence, macroblock and block layers.

diagrams shown in Fig. 11. These syntax diagrams not only specify the parameters, control information and data necessary to decode specific modes, but also help in visualizing organization of syntax hierarchies. At the sequence layer, picture and bit-rate parameters are followed by Intra and NonIntra-quantizer matrices for frame and field coding, and mscale parameters (discussed in Section 5.4). The syntax of macroblock layer for Intra macro-

blocks in I- and P-pictures requires macro-block_type, mquant and vlc_select, whereas for Intra macroblocks in B-pictures only macro-block_type and mscale are required and are followed by the block_layer data. The syntax diagram for macroblock layer in Predictive macroblocks shows macroblock_type, motion_vec_forw1 and an optional motion_vect_forw2 followed by and depending on code_nocode decision, mquant, vlc_-

select and coded block_layer data. The macroblock layer in bidirectional macroblocks requires macro-block_type, and either motion_vec_forw or motion_vec_back or both followed by and depending on code_nocode decision, mscale, coded_block_pattern and block_layer data. We have found that use of coded_block_patterns is useful for saving bits in B-pictures, while its use does not benefit coding of P-pictures; also, it provides bigger gain at 4 Mbit/s rather than at 9 Mbit/s. In some sense, this is to be expected as coded_block_pattern is most efficient when not many blocks within a picture (and in each macroblock) are coded. For B-pictures and 4 Mbit/s this condition is satisfied resulting in significant advantage. The last two syntax diagrams show black_layer for Intra and Non-Intra (Predictive and Bidirectional) macroblocks; the difference in these diagrams is that the DC prediction is employed for Intra-macroblocks.

9. Performance of coding scheme

Before we discuss performance of our coding scheme, it is important to understand the framework and its implications on results. Earlier, in Fig. 5, we have shown examples of quantizer matrices employed at 4 Mbit/s; we employ less steep matrices at 9 Mbit/s as at this bit-rate it is necessary to code even high frequency coefficients relatively well to meet expectation of overall high picture quality. It is also necessary to point out that signal-to-noise-ratio (SNR) comparison of schemes that use less sophisticated quantization [5] and fairly adaptive quantization based on [3] used here, can be misleading. This is so because schemes that adapt quantizers tend to coarsely quantize highly detailed texture regions where quantization errors can be hidden; the bits saved are used in low-detail and edge regions. However, these high detail texture regions typically are major contributors to high SNRs. It is quite reasonable to compare SNR values to judge relative improvements in going from 4 to 9 Mbit/s bit-rates, given a similar quantization strategy. Also, if Intra- and

NonIntra-quantization matrices are very different, similar SNR values in I-, P- and B-picture types could still mean non-uniformity in coding quality within a scene.

9.1. Statistical and subjective results

Some statistical results of performance of our coding scheme on MPEG-2 standard test scenes at 4 and 9 Mbit/s are presented in Tables 2a–2g. At 4 Mbit/s the ratio of bits taken by I-picture to that taken by P-picture varies from around 2 to 3 and is the highest for the 'Mobil calendar' scene. Due to spatial details in this scene, I-pictures need a significant amount of bits to code them well and in turn provide good prediction for compensation of linear pan, thus requiring relatively fewer bits for P-pictures. The 'Flower garden' scene, though also fairly detailed, due to angular pan, requires more bits for coding of P-pictures and requires I-pictures to be coded with at most twice as many bits required for coding a P-picture. The 'Table tennis' scene on the other hand contains zoom on detailed texture, a linear pan, and scene changes; in terms of ratio of I- to P-picture bits it behaves between the two extremes. Next, at 4 Mbit/s observing the ratio of P-picture to B-picture bits, we find that this ratio varies between 4.75 to 6, and is the lowest for the 'Table tennis' scene; this is so because in case of zoom, B-pictures cannot be very well predicted from P-pictures and require relatively higher bits. For the 'Flower garden' scene this ratio is the highest, implying that details in B-pictures can be coded coarsely, whereas it is lower for the 'Mobil calendar' scene, where a uniform picture quality is expected and B-pictures cannot be coded as coarsely as in the 'Flower garden' scene.

At 9 Mbit/s, for the same three scenes, the bits-ratio between I- and P-pictures varies from around 1.5 to 2.5 and follows the same trend as in 4 Mbit/s case, i.e., it is the highest for 'Mobil calendar' and the lowest for 'Flower garden' scene. The ratio of bits between P- and B-pictures varies between 3.75 to 6, and follows trend similar to 4 Mbit/s case, i.e., it is the highest for the 'Flower garden' and

Table 2a

'Flower garden' at 4 Mbit/s

Statistic	I-picture	P-picture	B-picture	Overall
Average bits	499 813	241 563	41 544	131 802
Average step-size	13.82	10.81	23.48	19.46
Average SNR (Y), dB	31.26	30.48	29.68	30.02
Average SNR (Cb), dB	34.56	34.16	34.34	34.32
Average SNR (Cr), dB	34.86	34.59	34.74	34.72

Table 2b

'Table tennis' at 4 Mbit/s

Statistic	I-picture	P-picture	B-picture	Overall
Average bits	368 941	169 086	35 306	98 057
Average step-size	11.95	9.31	19.21	16.10
Average SNR (Y), dB	31.35	31.06	30.52	30.73
Average SNR (Cb), dB	39.16	39.14	39.05	39.08
Average SNR (Cr), dB	39.30	39.30	38.94	39.02

Table 2c

'Mobil calendar' at 4 Mbit/s

Statistic	I-picture	P-picture	B-picture	Overall
Average bits	566 373	186 787	36 791	120 807
Average step-size	13.98	10.82	24.22	19.97
Average SNR (Y), dB	29.15	28.48	27.77	28.07
Average SNR (Cb), dB	33.50	33.18	33.31	33.29
Average SNR (Cr), dB	33.89	33.43	33.49	33.51

Table 2d

'Flower garden' at 9 Mbit/s

Statistic	I-picture	P-picture	B-picture	Overall
Average bits	949 489	565 742	93 515	286 758
Average step-size	13.82	10.81	23.48	19.46
Average SNR (Y), dB	37.37	36.54	33.50	34.60
Average SNR (Cb), dB	39.53	38.58	38.01	38.29
Average SNR (Cr), dB	39.15	38.14	37.93	38.09

Table 2e

'Table tennis' at 9 Mbit/s

Statistic	I-picture	P-picture	B-picture	Overall
Average bits	686 249	394 449	103 254	227 261
Average step-size	7.17	5.08	8.87	7.77
Average SNR (Y), dB	35.52	35.34	33.66	34.24
Average SNR (Cb), dB	40.91	41.65	40.91	40.95
Average SNR (Cr), dB	41.38	41.54	41.28	41.35

Table 2f

'Mobil calendar' at 9 Mbit/s

Statistic	I-picture	P-picture	B-picture	Overall
Average bits	1 080 333	437 418	87 325	262 072
Average step-size	7.61	6.07	13.21	10.93
Average SNR (Y), dB	34.27	33.49	31.10	31.97
Average SNR (Cb), dB	37.32	36.74	36.42	36.58
Average SNR (Cr), dB	37.80	37.12	36.66	36.87

Table 2g

'Popple' at 9 Mbit/s

Statistic	I-picture	P-picture	B-picture	Overall
Average bits	589 530	434 061	198 726	281 869
Average step-size	6.35	5.17	10.25	8.88
Average SNR (Y), dB	36.46	35.31	33.59	34.11
Average SNR (Cb), dB	40.88	39.75	38.30	38.74
Average SNR (Cr), dB	41.30	40.02	38.82	39.21

the lowest for the 'Table tennis' scene. In addition, for 'Popple', a scene containing fast zoom, we observe that the ratio of bits between I- and P-pictures is the lowest of all 4 scenes, as is the ratio of bits between P- and B-pictures. This is so because block matching motion-compensation has trouble compensating zoom and thus both P- and B-pictures require a relatively large number of bits to encode, which are taken from I-pictures.

In comparing luminance SNRs between 4 and 9 Mbit/s coding, we observe the difference to be between 3.5 to 4.5 dB, with the 'Flower garden' scene, the highest, and the 'Table tennis' scene the lowest. The significant increase in SNR for 'Flower garden' is attributed to a large amount of textural detail that can be coded well at 9 Mbit/s, whereas the contributing factor for 'Mobil calendar' is the increased coding quality of edges and details that are spatially distributed in the scene. In comparing ratio of bits at 9 and 4 Mbit/s for P-pictures, we find the ratio to be nearly the same for all scenes, whereas the ratio is slightly smaller for the 'Table tennis' scene; this also accounts for slightly higher bits-ratio for B-pictures, in this scene. The results of MPEG-2 subjective tests confirm that the picture quality offered by our coding scheme is impressive, both at 4 and 9 Mbit/s, and ranked among the top performing coding schemes.

10. Compatibility

One of the requirements [6] for MPEG-2 is that forward and backward compatibility with MPEG-1 be maintained. While forward compatibility can be achieved by requiring MPEG-2 standard decoders to be able to decode MPEG-1 bit-streams, backward compatibility, on the other hand, requires that MPEG-1 decoders be able to decode pictures from full or partial bit-streams produced by MPEG-2 encoders. The demand of backward compatibility can be met if MPEG-2 bit-streams contain in them an embedded MPEG-1 bit-stream that can be played on MPEG-1 decoders. A strict backward compatibility with MPEG-1 means that embedded MPEG-1 bit-stream satisfy the constrained parameter specifications of a bit-rate less than 1.856 Mbit/s and a pixel rate of at most 396×25 macroblocks/s. A less strict form of compatibility that may be even more useful could require bit-rates of less than 3 Mbit/s and pixel rates of up to $2 \times 396 \times 25$ macroblocks/s, such that the embedded bit-stream would still be MPEG-1 but designed for bit-rates and resolutions lower than that addressed by MPEG-2, allowing more flexibility in optimizing picture quality. It is worth noting that the forward and backward compatibilities discussed here also imply upward and downward compatibilities with respect to MPEG-1 [6], where the upward compatibility requires that the higher resolution (MPEG-2) decoder be able to decode signal from lower resolution (MPEG-1) encoder, and the downward compatibility, where low resolution (MPEG-1) decoder be able to decode part of the signal from higher resolution (MPEG-2) encoder.

10.1. Compatible coding scheme

We assume that the issue of forward compatibility can be resolved by a flexible MPEG-2 decoder that can decode MPEG-1 bit-streams, as discussed earlier. To resolve the issue of backward compatibility, we propose a spatial layered coding scheme; a high level functional view of such a scheme is shown in the example of Fig. 12. In this example it is further assumed that functionally there is an embedded MPEG-1 encoder that operates at lower pixel rates within an MPEG-2 encoder, and produces an MPEG-1 bit-stream embedded within MPEG-2 bit-stream. Locally decoded pictures from MPEG-1 bit-stream are spatially interpolated and used for compatible prediction, one of the many modes that can be adaptively selected on a macroblock basis. This mode is selected only if the mean square value of

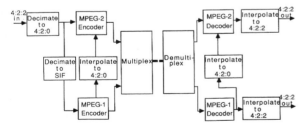

Fig. 12. A functional diagram of a compatible 2-spatial layered codec.

spatial-interpolation difference is smaller than that of either the motion-compensated difference or the mean removed original signal. Various coding modes in each of the I-, P- and B-pictures and relevant syntax extensions necessary to support these modes can be derived by extending Tables 1a–1c, following examples given in [7, 8]. The decoding operation simply consists of unsampling MPEG-1 reconstructed pictures and adding this signal to the decoded spatial-interpolation difference signal for macroblocks where compatible prediction is selected at the encoder. Even though the proposed scheme seems straightforward, it is important to note that the interpolation of SIF (luminance of 360×240), non-interlaced format to CCIR 601, interlaced format poses unique problems. One possible solution could be to use a scheme with three spatial layers, where two layers operate on SIF resolution odd- and even-fields. In all cases, it is assumed that systems multiplex/demultiplex can identify (perhaps, on a picture basis), different bit-streams that correspond to each of the spatial layers.

11. Implementation complexity

We encode 525-line CCIR 601 (deinterlaced) pictures with chrominance subsampled vertically by 2:1. Thus, each picture store requires $480 \times 720 \times 1.5 = 518\,400$ bytes.

11.1. Picture and buffer stores

If there are $M-1$ bidirectionally interpolated pictures, the encoder must have a minimum of $M+1$ picture stores. Our test pictures were generated with $M = 3$.

If the video input is progressively scanned, $M+1$ picture stores are easily sufficient. If the input is interlaced and the encoder can code two fields in one field period, $M+1$ picture stores are sufficient. If the input is interlaced and the encoder takes two field periods to code two fields, $M+1$ picture stores are sufficient if some line-ping-pong complexity can

133

be added to the memory controller. Otherwise, an extra half field store for a total of $M + 1.25$ picture stores are required by the encoder.

Buffer stores for compressed data are sized to give about one-half second delay, i.e., approximately 250 000 bytes for 4 Mbit/s and 562 500 bytes for 9 Mbit/s.

11.2. Memory size and bandwidth

The width of off-chip memory is chosen by trading off the pin count, memory size and speed. Assuming $M = 3$, our encoder needs $4 \times 518\,400$ bytes of external picture store, i.e., four 4 Mb DRAMs. Our decoder needs 2.5×518400 bytes of external picture store, i.e., three 4 Mb DRAMs. The major piece of on-chip memory occurs in the encoder motion estimation module, and depends strongly on which motion estimation algorithm is employed, we assume 12 kbytes of memory, which could be DRAM since it is refreshed at a high rate.

The major memory bandwidth constraint is for P-frame motion estimation in the encoder. For each 16×16 macroblock (384 pels) to be encoded a new batch of 16×106 pels must be read in plus 2 color blocks. That is a total of $(384 + (16 \times 106) + 128) \times (720 \times 480 \times 30/256) = 89.4$ Megabytes/sec being read. Coded macroblocks must also be written at a rate of $(6 \times 64) \times (720 \times 480 \times 30/256) = 15.5$ Megabytes/sec.

At the decoder, motion compensated macroblocks are read for B-frames at a peak rate of $2 \times (6 \times 64) \times (720 \times 480 \times 30/256) = 31.0$ Megabytes/sec, and coded macroblocks are written at a rate of $(6 \times 64) \times (720 \times 480 \times 30/256) = 15.5$ Megabytes/sec.

11.3. Table sizes and lookups

The major stored tables in the system are the quantization matrices, perceptual quantization tables and variable word-length (VWL) tables. Each of the six quantization matrices contains 64 8-bit numbers. The total size is $6 \times 64 = 384$ bytes.

Each of the six perceptual quantization tables contains 16 classes, 10 qualities and 5-bit Qp values. The total size is $6 \times 16 \times 10 \times 5/8 = 600$ bytes. For a fixed bit-rate, this could be ROM. If a wide range of bit-rates is contemplated, ROM could still be used if the number of qualities were increased. Otherwise, downloadable RAM could be used.

VLC tables are very similar to MPEG-1, except there are several of them, corresponding to the various modes of system operation. The largest of these are the two-dimensional DCT coefficient run-length/value tables. We use eight (8) tables. However, a large part of the tables corresponding to the longer code words can be reused. Only the shorter code words change from table to table. The total size is less than a few hundred bytes. VLC tables are ROM.

All tables are accessed basically at the pixel rate of $720 \times 480 \times 30 \times 1.5 = 15.6$ Megabytes/sec.

12. Summary

The MPEG-2 video coding standard is primarily aimed at coding of CCIR-601 or higher resolution video with fairly high quality at challenging bit-rates of 4 to 9 Mbit/s. Moreover, being even more generic in nature, it imposes several new requirements that were not considered for MPEG-1.

The MPEG-1 video coding scheme, even though it performs reasonably well [1, 2, 5], was optimized at lower bit-rates and resolutions leaving substantial room for impovement of coding efficiency for higher resolution video. Various adaptations including techniques to improve efficiency of coding for interlaced video source as well as improving quality by better exploitation of characteristics of a video scene have been investigated. Statistics and subjective tests confirm that these adaptations provide significant improvement as compared to purely MPEG-1 based coding. Issues related to compatibility with MPEG-1 and implementation complexity have also been discussed.

References

[1] D. Le Gall, "MPEG: A video compression standard for multimedia applications", *Comm. ACM*, Vol. 34, April 1991, pp. 47–58.

[2] A. Puri, "Video coding using the MPEG-1 compression standard", *International Symposium of Society for Information Display 92*, Boston, MA, May 1992, invited paper.

[3] A. Puri and R. Aravind, "Motion compensated video coding with adaptive perceptual quantization", *IEEE Trans. Circuits Systems for Video Technology*, Vol. 1, No. 4, December 1991, pp. 351–361.

[4] ISO CD 11172-2: Coding of Moving Pictures and Associated Audio for Digital Storage Media at up to about 1.5 Mbit/s, November 1991.

[5] MPEG Video Simulation Model 3 (SM3), MPEG Simulation Model Editing Committee, July 1990.

[6] Source: Chair of Requirements Subgroup, "Proposal package description for MPEG phase 2", *MPEG Document 91/100 Rev.*, August 1991.

[7] Source: AT&T, "Syntax extension for scalability and compatibility", *MPEG Document 92/59*, Singapore, January 1992.

[8] Source: British Telecom, "Compatibility proposal for TM", *MPEG Document 92/76*, Singapore, January 1992.

[9] Source: Norwegian Telecom, "Improvements in hybrid DCT coding", *MPEG Document 91/78*, Paris, France, May 1991.

[10] Source: AT&T, "MPEG-2 video coding proposal", *MPEG Document 91/201*, Kurihama, Japan, November 1991.

[11] Source: AT&T, "MPEG-2 coding proposal implementation document", *MPEG Document 91/233*, Kurihama, Japan, November 1991.

A Technical Assessment of Advanced Television

THEODORE S. RZESZEWSKI, SENIOR MEMBER, IEEE

Invited Paper

This paper contains a traditional description of the video spectrum, and a three-dimensional representation of video that is useful in understanding Advanced Television (ATV). Next, component video systems are described. Virtually all ATV systems strive to provide the desirable characteristics of component systems, such as no crosstalk between the components that make up the color signal. The three categories of ATV: High-Definition Television (HDTV), Enhanced Definition or Extended Quality Television (EDTV/EQTV), and Improved Definition Television (IDTV) are explained. The next topic is the basic approaches to ATV, and the influence that the FCC has had on shaping the typical systems in these categories. The original NHK system and the SMPTE (Society of Motion Picture and Television Engineers) 240M production standard are described, as well as the MUSE (MUltiple sub-Nyquist Sampling and Encoding) family of transmission systems. An evaluation of the standards arena is given. Also, it is concluded that the two delivery systems with long range potential for highest quality ATV are fiber based networks, and pre-recorded material for home players. The likely time windows for the success of different forms of ATV are predicted, along with speculation about the effect of competition between the three areas of ATV for market share. Next, the general ATV market potential is considered. Video processing is addressed with a specific example of a picture crispening technique for digital video that may be extended to line doubling applications. The importance of display technology for ATV, and the need for a CRT replacement are discussed. It is asserted that some form of ATV will be coming soon, and that there is a synergy between ATV and fiber networks. Finally, consideration is given to a new fiber network that capitalizes on the strengths of both traditional telecommunications networks and CATV networks.

I. INTRODUCTION

Advanced Television (ATV), and more specifically that which is currently referred to as High Definition Television (HDTV), is generally believed to have been started by NHK (Japan Broadcasting Corporation) almost two decades ago. They developed a provisional standard in 1980, and they demonstrated the system in the USA in 1981.

In view of this time frame, a logical question might be: why are we not enjoying HDTV in our homes today? The answer is rather complicated, and involves political as well as technical aspects. To get a feeling for some of the technical requirements, human factors decisions, and what are

Manuscript received November 2, 1989; revised February 20, 1990.
The author is with AT&T Bell Laboratories, 200 Park Plaza, Naperville, IL 60566, USA.
IEEE Log Number 9035641.

the important parameters in the selection of an ATV system, it is helpful to understand some of the history and limitations of the present USA television standard, NTSC (National Television System Committee) television.

A. NTSC—Color Television in the USA

The original NTSC made recommendations for a monochrome television standard that was adopted in the USA in 1941 [1]. Product introduction had to wait until after World War II; however, market development was very rapid. The need for color TV was seen immediately, and the FCC adopted a non-compatible field sequential color TV standard in 1950, and broadcasts began in 1951 [2].

A second NTSC was convened to work on a compatible color standard in 1950, and it became obvious that a compatible standard was possible. The field sequential broadcasts stopped in 1951, and the FCC reversed itself in December of 1953 and adopted the NTSC color system. Broadcasts were authorized after January 22, 1954 [3], [4]. However, it took a number of years before color television achieved a significant percentage of the TV market. Color TV sales began to take-off in the early to mid-1960s.

NTSC TV utilizes 525 lines total; however, only 483 of these lines are typically active. That means that 483 lines are used to transmit video information. The remaining lines are used for synchronization and retrace blanking. It would be logical to assume that the vertical resolution is approximately 483 lines; however, the scanning process is a sampling process with substantially no vertical pre-filtering. Consequently, there will be aliasing if a pattern with a high vertical spatial-frequency is displayed. Equation 1 expresses the actual vertical resolution displayed in the TV picture by the addition of a Kell factor (k) that takes this extra loss into account.

$$R_v = (N_t - 2N_v)k \qquad (1)$$

- R_v is the vertical resolution;
- N_t is the total number of scan lines in a frame (525 for NTSC);
- N_v is the number of lines in each of the two vertical intervals of a TV frame (nominally 21 for NTSC); and
- k is the Kell factor.

Reprinted from *Proc. IEEE*, vol. 78, no. 5, pp. 789–804, May 1990.

The typical vertical resolution for NTSC TV normally ranges between 290 and 338 lines. Therefore, the Kell factor is typically between 0.6 and 0.7 for NTSC TV systems.

The measure of resolution is usually expressed as TV-lines of resolution, which is the number of lines that will fit into the picture height [5], [6]. This way a single measure of resolution (horizontal or vertical) is utilized. Equation 2 can be used to determine the horizontal resolution of a television system per unit of video bandwidth (R'_h).

$$R'_h = 2T_a/AR \qquad (2)$$

- T_a is the total active time for a horizontal line;
- AR is the aspect ratio.

T_a and AR are 53.5 μsec and 4/3 respectively for the NTSC system.

The 4 to 3 AR used for NTSC TV means that the picture is four units wide and three units high. Therefore, the same horizontal resolution, as vertical, will result in 4/3 more resolution elements displayed across the TV screen horizontally (vertical lines) than vertically.

Occasionally, the horizontal resolution will be expressed in lines per picture width, then the adjustment for the aspect ratio should be made when comparing it to the vertical resolution in order to get a proper comparison of resolving power of the system in the two directions.

A convenient rule-of-thumb for NTSC TV is that the horizontal resolution per unit bandwidth (R'_h) equals 80 lines/MHz of bandwidth [7]. The horizontal resolution capability (R_h) in TV-lines, is directly proportional to the system bandwidth. It is simply the product of R'_h and the system bandwidth. The 4.2 MHz of luminance bandwidth for NTSC TV results in a maximum of 336 lines of horizontal resolution. The bandwidth limitations on the components of the composite NTSC signal are illustrated in Fig. 1.

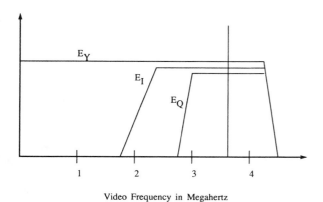

Y is the Luminance Signal
I is the Inphase Component of Chrominance
Q is the Quadrature Component of Chrominance

Fig. 1. NTSC luminance and chrominance bandwidth allocation.

B. Defects and Limitations of NTSC

A tenet of the NTSC was compatibility. They followed an approach that added color to the existing monochrome signal. The signal specifications are based on the complete system. That includes the taking characteristics (camera), the transmission channel, the receiving characteristics, and the human visual system [3].

A color signal needs three components [4]. The camera utilizes Red, Green, and Blue (RGB) primaries that result in RGB signals. However, in the interest of compatibility and bandwidth conservation, these three signals are transformed into Luminance, Inphase color, and Quadrature color (YIQ) components. The Luminance (Y) signal carries the brightness component which is the original NTSC monochrome signal. The two color components are Quadrature Modulated as Double Sideband Suppressed Carrier Signals (QAM-SC). This color signal is added to the monochrome (luminance) signal along with the appropriate color synchronizing signal to form a composite color signal. Equation 3 represents the composite NTSC signal (E_{NTSC}).

$$E_{NTSC} = E'_Y + [E'_Q \sin(\omega t + \theta) + E'_I \cos(\omega t + \theta)] \qquad (3)$$

- E'_Y is the gamma-corrected luminance signal;
- E'_Q is the gamma-corrected quadrature color component;
- E'_I is the gamma-corrected inphase color component; and
- θ is an angle equal to 33 degrees.

The relationship of I, Q, R–Y, B–Y, and the color burst are illustrated in Fig. 2.

The color signal contains two quadrature modulated signals that are phase shifted 33° compared to a reference burst and added to the luminance or monochrome signal in such a way as to interleave with the luminance signal so that both the high-frequency luminance and the color signal can band-share the same frequency region. This is possible because the luminance signal tends to have energy at multiples of the horizontal line frequency and the modulated color signal tends to have energy at odd multiples of half the horizontal line frequency. Therefore, the two signals tend to interleave and can be separated by a comb filter.

Some TV sets do utilize a comb filter to get the full 336 lines of horizontal resolution talked about in the previous section. Lower cost TV sets utilize Y selectivity that simply filters out the high-frequency luminance region, which also contains chrominance. These sets may have a horizontal resolution as low as 240 lines, but 260 or 270 lines are more typical.

It is generally agreed that HDTV should have horizontal and vertical resolution capabilities of approximately twice that of NTSC TV, and other forms of ATV (such as EDTV) will usually add some additional resolution capability beyond that of NTSC TV as well [8].

Another category of deficiencies in NTSC TV is the crosstalk that occurs between the luminance and the color signals [6]. Luminance (Y) to Color (C) crosstalk is called cross color. It shows up as spurious unwanted color when there is a detailed luminance pattern in the horizontal direction (a tweed suit, a picket fence, or a referee's shirt). The second form of crosstalk is C into Y, and it is called cross-luminance. It shows up as a series of dots usually moving up the edges of color regions of a picture. These two defects of NTSC TV should be eliminated or greatly reduced in ATV.

Another defect of NTSC TV that needs to be corrected for ATV is the bandwidth limitation of the chrominance signals [4], [6]. It is known that the bandwidth of the chrominance signals does not need to equal the luminance bandwidth for entertainment video. However, the Q component of the NTSC signal is only 0.5 MHz in bandwidth, less than 1/8 the

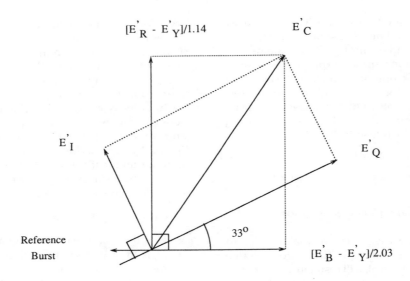

E_C is the Chrominance Signal

E_I is the Inphase Chrominance Component

E_Q is the Quadrature Chrominance Component

E_R is the Red Signal

E_B is the Blue Signal

The Primes Indicate Gamma Correction

Fig. 2. Vector diagram of the chrominance signal.

Y bandwidth. This ratio is too extreme. A ratio of 1/3 to 1/2 gives essentially the same entertainment quality as full bandwidth RGB.

II. Traditional Representation of a Video Spectrum

It is well known that the energy in a video signal tends to cluster at multiples of the horizontal frequency [2], [4], [7].

$$V(f) = \sum_{i=0}^{\infty} V_i(f - if_H) \qquad (4)$$

- $V(f)$ is the video spectrum;
- V_i is the weighting factor for the ith cluster of energy;
- f is frequency; and
- f_H is the horizontal line scanning frequency.

This characteristic of video was used by the NTSC Committee in the early 1950s to add color information to the existing monochrome signal (luminance) in a compatible fashion. They placed a subcarrier signal (the color information) at an odd multiple of half the horizontal frequency,

$$f_{sc} = 455 \left(\frac{f_H}{2} \right) \qquad (5)$$

which is midway between two of these peaks of energy in the monochrome signal. This modulated signal has a spectral density with peaks spaced at multiples of f_H from the subcarrier frequency. Consequently, the high frequency monochrome and the chrominance information interleave when the modulated color subcarrier is added to the monochrome to produce the composite NTSC color signal. It is because of these properties that the chrominance and the luminance information in the composite NTSC signal can be separated into Y and C signals by comb filters.

It should be remembered that the above properties are tendencies. If there are diagonal patterns, or motion in the picture, the energy at the peaks tends to spread into the regions away from the multiples of the horizontal line frequency.

Further, if one examines the video spectrum closer, one finds that the clusters of energy at multiples of f_H are themselves divided into energy that is spaced at multiples of the field and frame frequencies from each f_H frequency [9], [10], [4]. The interleaving of the spectral components is illustrated in Fig. 3. The interleaving of the field and frame frequency components makes the use of field or frame combs possible. The comb filters that have been discussed so far can be called line combs, because the delay increment needed to implement them is a horizontal line of delay. Field or frame combs introduce a temporal element into the analysis of television systems. To properly analyze television systems with processing that affects not only the two spatial directions (horizontal and vertical), but in the temporal domain as well, a three-dimensional representation which represents spatiotemporal frequencies is used.

III. Three-Dimensional Representation of Video

There has been a number of recent papers that use a three-dimensional representation of video to analyze and perhaps improve NTSC video [11]–[14]. Any moving image of dimension A by B over a time interval C can be represented by a Fourier series. This representation has the form of equation 6 [12].

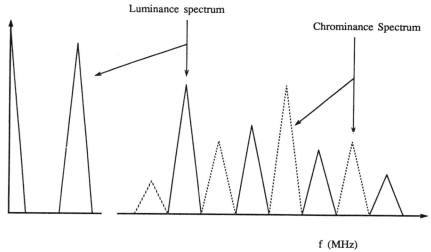

Fig. 3. Luminance/chrominance interleaving.

$$U(x, y, z) = \sum_{n=-\infty}^{n=\infty} \sum_{m=-\infty}^{m=\infty} \sum_{l=-\infty}^{l=\infty} U\left(\frac{n}{A}, \frac{m}{B}, \frac{l}{C}\right)$$
$$\cdot \exp\left[j2\pi\left(\frac{nx}{A} + \frac{my}{B} + \frac{lz}{C}\right)\right] \quad (6)$$

The coefficients $U(n/A, m/B, l/C)$ define the spatiotemporal spectrum of the image, and give the relative weight of the different frequency component of the image. They are complex numbers that specify the magnitude and phase of the components. Since the time interval C can be arbitrarily long, the temporal frequency components can be spaced arbitrarily closely, and are usually considered to be continuous. However, the horizontal and vertical frequency components are constrained to be multiples of one cycle per picture width and one cycle per picture height, respectively.

Temporal frequencies are expressed in Hz. The coefficients of the Fourier series can be obtained from the image by the Fourier transform operation given by equation 7.

$$U\left(\frac{n}{A}, \frac{m}{B}, \frac{l}{C}\right) = \frac{1}{ABC} \int_0^C \int_0^B \int_0^A u(x, y, z)$$
$$\cdot \exp\left[-j2\pi\left(\frac{nx}{A} + \frac{my}{B} + \frac{lz}{C}\right)\right] dx \, dy \, dz$$
$$(7)$$

If a fixed spatial pattern denoted as $u(x, y, z)$ has a frequency domain representation $U(f_x, f_y, f_z)$, and the transfer function of a three-dimensional filter is denoted by $H(f_x, f_y, f_z)$, the spectral shaping of the filter can be expressed by equation 8, where $Z(f_x, f_y, f_z)$ is the output signal after filtering.

$$Z(f_x, f_y, f_z) = H(f_x, f_y, f_z) U(f_x, f_y, f_z) \quad (8)$$

The use of the three-dimensional frequency spectrum can provide extra insight into the analysis and synthesis of television systems. The discrete three-dimensional spatiotemporal frequency is illustrated by a region in Fig. 4, where f_x is the horizontal spatial frequency, f_y is the vertical spatial frequency component, and f_z is the temporal frequency component. Fig. 5 illustrates the spectrum of a conventionally encoded NTSC signal [11]. Note the overlap of the

Y, I, and Q signals. Next, Fig. 6 illustrates the spectrum of a NTSC signal encoded by using 3-dimensional pre-filtering.

It is believed that the human visual system cannot see high-frequency detail in moving objects [15]. Therefore, many of the HDTV systems that are being proposed restrict the amount of detail in moving scenes. It is convenient to use the type of three-dimensional frequency representation of the spectrum that was shown above to illustrate the processing and compare the parameters of the various systems.

IV. Component Video

RGB is the ultimate component system, because that is the way that the signals come from the camera. Each signal is full bandwidth. However, it is well known that humans do not visualize color with the same resolution as Y. Therefore, the color bandwidths are usually reduced in the range of 1/3 to 1/2 of Y in the interest of bandwidth compression. Figure 7 illustrates the component system arrangement where each of the components is maintained as a separate signal.

CCIR Recommendation 601 is a digital international production (or studio) standard for 4:2:2 components that is approximately equivalent to RGB quality for entertainment. Further, it is used as the basis for ATV in Broadband Integrated Services Digital Network (B-ISDN). While B-ISDN standards are not yet established, the currently preferred method within the CCITT of providing the digital component coding service quality is to use Recommendation 601 as the basis for a digital component system that represents an intermediate level of quality between HDTV and a digital composite signal. This intermediate level of quality is usually called Extended Quality Television (EQTV) [8].

Recommendation 601 uses an 8-bit PCM signal for all three components, with 13.5 MHz sampling for the luminance and a 6.75 MHz sampling rate for the two color components. This results in a 216 Mb/s data rate; however, extra capacity is normally required for error correction and sound. The EQTV distribution signal will be a compressed version of 601. The transmission rate will be between 30 Mb/s and 135 Mb/s.

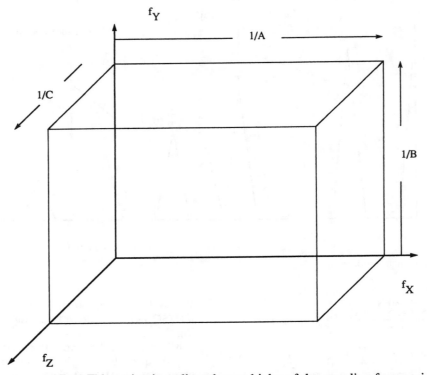

Note: This region is replicated at multiples of the sampling frequencies
1/A, 1/B, and 1/C, and the spectrum has even symmetry with the axis

Fig. 4. Discrete three-dimensional spectral region.

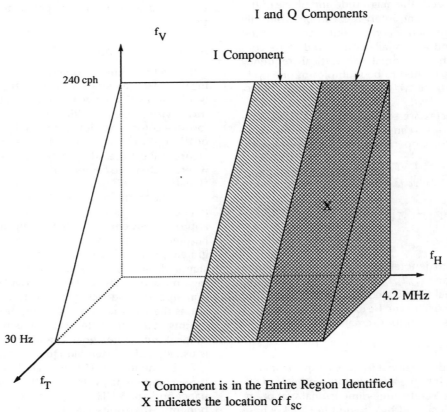

Y Component is in the Entire Region Identified
X indicates the location of f_{sc}

Note: This spectrum has even symmetry with respect to the axis, and
replicates at multiples of the sampling frequencies in the f_V and f_T directions

Fig. 5. Discrete spatiotemporal spectral region for NTSC.

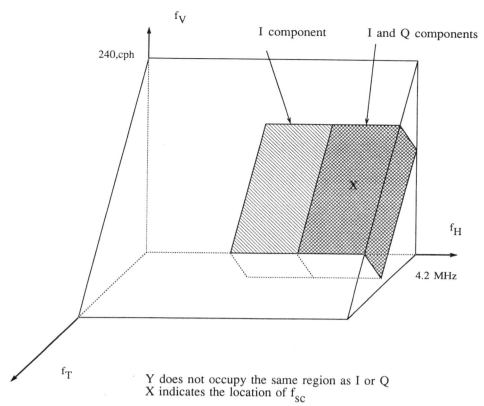

Fig. 6. NTSC Spectrum encoded by using three-dimensional pre-filtering.

In the figure: f_V axis labeled 240,cph; I component; I and Q components; f_H axis; 4.2 MHz; f_T axis; X; Y does not occupy the same region as I or Q; X indicates the location of f_sc

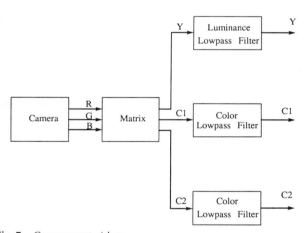

Fig. 7. Component video.

Part of the appeal of 601 is that the same monitor can be used to display a 601 signal or an NTSC signal. Both of these signals incorporate 525 lines for scanning in the USA. The appropriate type of TV sets, with baseband inputs, and monitors are already on the market. Therefore, the start-up time of this type of system can be fast. Further, 601 components provide a significant improvement over present NTSC TV, the subjective effect (which is approximately equivalent to RGB) appears to be midway between HDTV (35-mm movie film quality) and the present NTSC TV [16]. Further, the improvement can be made even larger by allowing a slight modification of the CCIR Recommendation 601 [7].

CCIR 601 may also be used as the basis for HDTV in B-ISDN. One plan is to scale recommendation 601 up to provide twice the horizontal and vertical resolution capability, while changing the aspect ratio to 16 to 9 or 5 to 3, compared to the present 4 to 3 aspect ratio. This leads to an approach called Common Data Rate (CDR). With this approach, different countries can have different image formats, but they use the same recording or transmission format, as they do with CCIR 601. CDR is based on a common sampling frequency and number of bits per sample for all images regardless of structure and frame rate, this provides the common data rate.

Another approach is called Common Image Format (CIF); this approach forces the same image parameters. A CIF system is based upon a standard active-image structure having the same number of active lines per frame and active pels per line regardless of the frame rate. In current discussions before the CCIR, CIF would also imply common colorimetry and transfer characteristics, common image aspect ratio, and common digital level representation.

Equation 6 calculates the new data rate (D_n) of a system that has been scaled-up from a reference system.

$$D_n = \frac{R_{vn} R_{hn} AR_n}{R_{vo} R_{ho} AR_o} D_o \qquad (9)$$

- D_o stands for old data rate
- R stands for resolution, subscript v for vertical, h for horizontal, n for new, and o for old; and
- AR stands for aspect ratio, subscript n for new, and o for old.

This implies an uncompressed data rate of at least 5 times that of CCIR 601, or almost 1.2 Gb/s for the 16 to 9 aspect

141

ratio HDTV. The present plan in the CCITT is to compress this signal down to fit into the H_4 channel, which is approximately 135 Mb/s, for distribution.

However, that represents a compression ratio of almost 10 to 1. In order to maintain quality and a low cost for the local loop, it may be necessary to utilize a higher rate.

V. THREE CATEGORIES OF ATV

The topic of ATV can be divided into the following three categories [8]:

1. High Definition Television (HDTV),
2. Enhanced Television, also called Enhanced Definition Television (EDTV), or Extended Quality Television (EQTV), and
3. Improved Definition Television (IDTV), also called Improved NTSC in the USA.

The three levels of video quality listed above are being worked by both analog and digital video coding experts. The previous section contained a description of the digital effort that comes from B-ISDN. A great deal of attention is centered on analog transmission today, and the analog area usually designates the three quality levels of ATV as HDTV, EDTV, and IDTV.

The boundaries between these three levels is not very clear in the analog area, because different proponents stress different aspects of picture quality. Therefore, the relative level of quality of one system compared to another may be somewhat controversial. For that reason there is a tendency to refer to these levels as simply ATV for analog transmission systems.

A. HDTV

HDTV is used to represent the highest level of quality in both the analog and digital areas. It is generally agreed that HDTV means about twice the horizontal and twice the vertical resolution along with a wider aspect ratio than 4 to 3 (this means five times the number of pels as NTSC TV for a 5 to 3 aspect ratio). HDTV should have a quality and aspect ratio approximately equivalent to 35-mm motion pictures as projected in the average theater. There are two different standards in both the analog and digital areas; the first is called production, in the analog area, or contribution in B-ISDN. This is a rugged signal suitable for many generations of processing such as chroma key and special effects that are part of the making of the program. Secondly, there is transmission, in the analog area, or distribution in B-ISDN. This is a compressed signal that is suitable for transmission. Further, this last area of distribution/transmission may have two different signals, one for long distance transmission and one for distribution in the local loop.

Analog HDTV transmission systems normally can be classified as compatible augmentation channel systems or as non-compatible simulcast systems.

B. EDTV/EQTV

The usual level of image quality that EDTV or EQTV systems provide is approximately midway between HDTV and present TV; further, they may or may not provide an increase in the aspect ratio from the present value of 4 to 3. However, some people consider an increased aspect ratio alone to be a sufficient attribute for a system to be considered in this category. EDTV systems may be based on a component or a composite format. However, EQTV is normally considered to be a component system; therefore, the three component signals that are needed to reproduce the color image are transmitted as separate signals so that no crosstalk will occur between the components. Systems proposed for the EDTV/EQTV area display a larger variation in image quality than in the other two categories. For example, some system proposals may use essentially the same resolution values as the present NTSC system, while others may utilize resolution values that are near the values generally associated with HDTV. Some proposals use a 4 to 3 aspect ratio, others use a 16 to 9 aspect ratio, and still others use a value between these two.

EDTV usually means either a 525 or 1050 line format for display, in the USA. It could have a significant market share early (1993 or 4). However, there needs to be a significant enough improvement in quality over IDTV, and/or the same or lower cost. New ICs are needed for tuning and detection as well as for processing similar to those mentioned in the next section on IDTV.

However, EDTV could also take a different approach than IDTV that is less IC intense, and uses a less costly display. It could incorporate a TV with NTSC scanning and an intermediate level of resolution capability (500 to 600 lines) in the display. These types of TV receivers are on the market, so some people may already have this capability in their home without realizing it. The baseband signal would have extra horizontal resolution capability, compared to NTSC. Extra vertical resolution capability could also be added if desired. Super VHS (S-VHS) type tape systems can be thought of as the start of this type of an approach. S-VHS provides an increase in picture quality; however, there are possible improvements on S-VHS that could increase its quality further. However, the main obstacle that the S-VHS delivery system has in the USA is to get on the shelves of the video rental stores along with VHS and Beta (a non-technical challenge) quickly.

The nice part about the S-VHS type of an approach is that there is a number people who already have the appropriate TV sets or monitors for displaying the signal, and that number is likely to grow as time goes by, independent of whether this type of EDTV transmission system drives it or not. Therefore, this type of a transmission system can fit into the market very easily, and complement the pre-recorded tape type of delivery systems that are already getting started.

C. IDTV

IDTV is sometimes referred to as Improved NTSC (I-NTSC), and there is a caution needed when talking about this area. Different people may have a different set of improvements in mind when they are referring to this area. A case could be made that IDTV or I-NTSC started when the first improvements to the first NTSC decoder were realized. Some others believe that IDTV started when the first major change in the NTSC decoder capability for increased resolution took place, with the use of comb filters. However, it is generally agreed today that IDTV means a change in the display scanning parameters to either a 1050 line display or a 525 line progressive display even though the NTSC transmission format is still 525 lines interlaced.

IDTV generally incorporates some combination of progressive scanning or line doubling, improved horizontal and vertical resolution, better Y/C separation, ghost cancellation, and noise reduction [17], [18]. These types of TV sets have been demonstrated at a number of technical conferences and trade shows.

These TV sets will use an extensive amount of digital signal processing. The main feature is the line doubling or progressive scan, which involves the display of extra lines that are not transmitted, usually by interpolation of the extra lines from the values of picture elements (pels) of the transmitted lines. The ICs should include A/Ds and D/As, Finite Impulse Response (FIR) filters (horizontal as well as vertical), and field or frame memory in some cases.

One approach uses multiple field memories and line memories. The digital image (internal to the TV set) is represented by a matrix of pels that define the image to be a size represented by the number of lines (525) by the number of pels on a line. This matrix is subdivided into cells that are a small number of lines by that same number of pels. Activity within a cell is used for detection of significant motion in that area, and the amount of motion determines which interpolation method will be used for that cell.

Another approach implements line interpolation through the use of median filters. This filter generates extra lines by selecting, on a pel by pel basis, the median value of a pel on each of three lines. Two of these lines are spatially just above and below the interpolated line from the current field, with the pel that is either directly above or below the current pel. The third line and pel are from the previous field which spatially corresponds to the interpolated line and pel, respectively. The median filter essentially results in field insertion in still areas and line repeat in motion areas. However, no motion detection is required, and only one line memory and one field memory are required.

Other approaches to interpolation of the extra lines are possible; one will be described in the section called Signal Processing.

It is possible that some TV set manufacturers may also use IDTV as an opportunity to introduce Gallium Arsenide (GaAs) into the tuning systems of their TVs [19]. It has been known for some time that GaAs will improve the performance of a TV tuner by providing better noise performance and interference immunity. However, the TV set manufacturers have been reluctant to incorporate it into sets because of the added cost. Since these new IDTV sets will add a significant amount of extra processing (and cost) with the objective of an improved picture, it is logical to increase the RF performance as well. However, cost is a real concern for IDTV.

VI. Basic Approaches to ATV

Much of the direction in analog ATV in the USA is being set by the Federal Communications Commission (FCC) for over-the-air transmission (terrestrial broadcasting) of HDTV, even though there are other delivery systems for ATV. In fact, terrestrial broadcasting may not be the most important delivery system for HDTV. The reason is that it has many limitations for HDTV. There will be a severe problem getting the image quality expected in many locations because of multipath and interference. Even in those locations that may sometimes provide sufficient quality, there is the ques-

tion of consistency; variability due to weather conditions alone is a factor. There also is a shortage of spectrum space needed for extra HDTV capability that results in a higher cost set and/or a compromise in quality.

For now, it is sufficient to say that the FCC's decisions on terrestrial broadcasting seem to be driving the analog HDTV standardization effort in the USA. The FCC has decided that HDTV must be transmitted in a compatible fashion, or an NTSC signal must be simulcast with a HDTV broadcast that occupies no more than 6 MHz. It has also decided that no extra spectrum will be made available for HDTV, so it must live within the present TV channel allocations.

A. Compatible Systems Approaches

Most compatible systems approaches to HDTV seem to use an NTSC channel and an augmentation channel [20]. The augmentation channel carries all the improvements that are added to the NTSC signal to provide HDTV. This second channel can occupy anywhere from 2.1 to 6 MHz in bandwidth depending upon the system. Sometimes this channel is analog and in some systems it is digital.

The thing that these systems have in common is that at least a portion of the spectrum contains an NTSC TV signal at a current NTSC frequency allocation so that present NTSC TV receivers can tune to it and display a picture that is substantially the same as they presently display.

However, systems that do not have that capability still find it advantageous to maintain some aspect of compatibility. For example, they may be compatible with the NTSC scanning format, or just provide a simple conversion to or from NTSC scanning parameters. Another aspect of the NTSC system that is important to systems that do not provide compatibility in the way described above is the 6 MHz frequency allocations of the NTSC signal. Therefore, a non-compatible systems approach can be spectrum compatible.

B. Non-Compatible System Approaches

From the FCC direction mentioned above, non-compatible systems also must be simulcast systems. In other words they require a 6 MHz NTSC signal be broadcast along with the non-compatible HDTV signal. Even though these systems are non-compatible in the sense that the HDTV signal cannot cause an NTSC receiver, without a converter, to display substantially the same picture as an NTSC signal, these systems realize an advantage if they keep a simple relationship to the NTSC scanning format so that conversion is both simple and economical.

The proposed production standard for these types of systems usually contains 1.5 or 2 times the number of scanning lines of NTSC in the USA.

A system that either uses the present 525 lines, or allows for a simple conversion method (by providing a simple mathematical relationship between the number of scanning lines that it uses compared to NTSC) is sometimes called compatible with the scanning format. The belief is that this type of system not only provides economies for the conversion to NTSC, but that the presentation of NTSC on the displays of this new system can be made more economical than a system that does not have compatibility with the scanning format of NTSC.

However, there are non-compatible systems with no simple relationship to NTSC scanning parameters. The original NHK proposal is an example of this type of system.

VII. NHK HDTV AND SMPTE 240M

The original NHK HDTV system has historical significance in that it is usually credited with starting the present movement toward HDTV and the general effort in ATV as well. Also, the NHK family of systems illustrate many of the categories of ATV that were just considered, such as HDTV, EDTV, as well as augmentation and simulcast systems.

The NHK system is also the basis for the evolution into the (MUltiple sub-Nyquist Sampling and Encoding) MUSE family of transmission systems which are presently backed by the Japanese as a transmission standard for both Japan and the USA.

Many of the parameters that are commonly used to identify HDTV have come from the NHK effort, such as the use of approximately double the horizontal and vertical resolution of present TV, an aspect ratio of approximately 5 to 3, and a viewing distance of approximately three times the picture height.

Further, it is the foundation upon which the SMPTE (Society of Motion Picture and Television Engineers) 240M production standard is based. The NHK system utilizes 1125 lines, originally with a 5 to 3 aspect ratio; however, 240M uses a 16 to 9 aspect ratio. The SMPTE changed many other parameters of the NHK system in 240M. Some of the other parameters of 240M are [21]:

- There are 1035 active lines per frame;
- The field rate is 60 fields per second (not 59.94 fields per second);
- A 2 to 1 interlace scanning format is used;
- The line repetition rate is 33.75 kHz;
- There are 2200 Y samples per line total;
- Of those, 1920 are active Y samples per line;
- It uses 960 active color-difference samples per line;
- There are 280 blanking samples per line.

The Y (or RGB) sampling frequency is 74.25 MHz, and a sampling rate of 37.125 MHz is used for the color difference signals. Direct 8-bit PCM encoding of this component signal gives a data rate of about 1.2 Gb/s.

The three components of the 240M signal are specified by the following equations.

$$E'_Y = 0.701E_G + 0.087E_B + 0.212E_R \qquad (10)$$

$$E'_{PB} = \frac{E'_B - E'_Y}{1.826} \qquad (11)$$

$$= -0.384E_G + 0.500E'_B - 0.116E'_R$$

$$E'_{PR} = \frac{E'_R - E'_Y}{1.576} \qquad (12)$$

$$= -0.445E_G + 0.055E'_B + 0.500E'_R$$

- E'_Y is the gamma corrected luminance signal;
- E_G is the gamma corrected green signal;
- E'_B is the gamma corrected blue signal;
- E'_R is the gamma corrected red signal;
- E'_{PB} is the gamma corrected and amplitude scaled blue color difference signal;
- E'_{PR} is the gamma corrected and amplitude scaled red color difference signal.

If we assume the same range on the value for the Kell factor as for NTSC TV (between 0.6 and 0.7), the vertical resolution is somewhere between 621 and 725 TV lines of resolution, from equation 1.

A 30-MHz Y bandwidth is specified by 240M, although the original NHK system only used 20 MHz of Y bandwidth. The 30 MHz bandwidth can be accommodated conveniently, given the sampling frequency of 74.25 MHz, with conventional analog filtering. Equation 2 predicts a horizontal resolution (R_h) of approximately 870 TV lines, given the 30 MHz bandwidth and an active horizontal line time of 25.86 μsec.

The SMPTE 240M standard was also adopted as an Advanced Television Systems Committee (ATSC) standard; it once represented the USA position for a single world-wide production standard in the CCIR. More recently, the USA has decided not to advocate the adoption of a single world-wide production standard during the current study period of the CCIR, recognizing that agreement on a single field rate will not be adopted in the near future. Further, the use of 1080 active lines per frame is being considered in some organizations to achieve square pels.

It should be remembered that this is a production standard, and it is unlikely that the full resolution capabilities of 240M will be delivered to the home by any delivery system other than fiber or pre-recorded material. Further, it is unlikely that even they will be delivering a 240M signal to the home in the near future. Delivery to the home is the role of the transmission standard.

Some of the transmission standard possibilities that are being proposed by NHK are considered further in the next few paragraphs. However, the original MUSE proposal allows only a maximum of 20 MHz of bandwidth for an R_h of approximately 580 TV lines on the static scenes. This number goes down to approximately 360 lines in the moving portions of the picture. The horizontal resolution for color in moving areas is 90 lines. Newer versions of MUSE provide less resolution capability, in the interest of accommodating the initial FCC requirements that were described previously.

NHK has recently developed experimental equipment for three systems that they call Advanced Definition Television (ADTV) that put emphasis on compatibility with the current channel allocation and the NTSC system. They are NTSC-Compatible MUSE-6, NTSC-Compatible MUSE-9, and Narrow-MUSE.

MUSE-6 has the following features:

- NTSC and 6 MHz compatibility,
- Improved resolution over NTSC for the static portion of the picture,
- Upward compatibility with MUSE-9, and
- 2-channel digital audio.

It is reported as capable of 420 TV-lines (750 lines/picture width) of horizontal resolution of luminance on static portions of the picture, and 230 TV-lines for moving portions. The static vertical resolution is 690 lines for low horizontal detail scenes, and 345 lines for high detail scenes.

The moving (dynamic) vertical resolution for low and high horizontal resolution is 345 and 173 lines respectively.

The static chrominance spatial resolution for the I signal is 345 and 158 lines for the vertical and horizontal directions, respectively. The dynamic resolution is 173 and 79 lines, respectively. The numbers for the Q channel are 345 and 107 for static, and 173 and 28 for the dynamic resolution.

The features of the MUSE-9 system are:

- Compatible with NTSC and MUSE-6,
- Improved static and dynamic resolution over NTSC TV,
- Improved resolution for the moving portion of the picture over MUSE-6, and
- 4-channel digital audio.

MUSE-9 uses two RF channels, a main channel that is the same as MUSE-6, and an augmentation channel. The augmentation channel base bandwidth is about 2.1 MHz, and it transmits information for improving the dynamic resolution and digital audio.

Narrow-MUSE is intended for ATV simulcast. It has the following features:

- 6-MHz RF channel compatibility,
- Highest picture quality among the three NHK ADTV systems, and
- 4-channel digital audio.

The horizontal static resolution is improved to 568 lines, and the dynamic value is 377 TV lines.

VIII. ZENITH SC-HDTV

The Zenith Spectrum Compatible (SC) HDTV system uses a 37 MHz RGB source signal which is first video processed into a 6 MHz signal. It is subsequently encoded into an NTSC-like signal for transmission by suppressed-carrier, double-sideband, amplitude modulation of two carriers in quadrature.

The source and display utilize a 787.5 line progressive scan format that has a frame rate of 59.94 Hz. The horizontal line rate is exactly three times the NTSC horizontal line rate (47.702 kHz), and the aspect ratio is 16 to 9 or 4 to 3. The progressive scan source signal is encoded into spatial-temporal frequency subbands which are adaptively selected for transmission. This process reduces the number of subbands for transmission (in analog form) to one in eight on the average. Low-frequency video is transmitted digitally during the vertical blanking interval.

The major benefits claimed by the SC-HDTV system are efficient utilization of the VHF/UHF spectrum, since new SC-HDTV channels can be added to existing NTSC channels. SC-HDTV realizes significant power reduction for the same coverage area as NTSC. The NTSC-like RF format allows precision cochannel carrier offset which effectively reduces mutual NTSC–SC-HDTV interference. The system provides high definition resolution capabilities within a 6-MHz channel. It also easily converts to a frequency modulated format for satellite service and VCR use. The VCR is no more complex than a current S-VHS unit. SC-HDTV allows delivery of premium services with optional encrypted security, because of the digital encoding of the low-frequency video signals.

IX. SARNOFF ACTV-I EDTV

ACTV-I is a channel-compatible and receiver-compatible system that delivers an aspect ratio of 16 to 9 and approximately a 30% improvement in horizontal resolution over NTSC to ACTV-I receivers. The ACTV-I signal, when viewed on an NTSC receiver, is reported to display NTSC-quality images without letterbox, the blanking of active picture lines on the top and bottom of the picture.

To transmit the increased information required by the wider aspect ratio and the extra resolution, ACTV-I exploits three "subchannels" in the NTSC spectrum:

- the horizontal overscan portion of active video that is hidden behind the bezel on consumer NTSC receivers,
- a Fukinuki subcarrier at 3.58 MHz (generated by inverting the phase of an interlaced carrier on alternate fields) that is quadrature-modulated, and
- quadrature modulation of the RF picture carrier.

The spectrum of the Fukinuki subcarrier signal can be analyzed by the three-dimensional processing described previously.

The ACTV-I signals are assigned to these "subchannels" as follows. The horizontal overscan on each side of the picture contains the time-compressed luminance low frequencies of the side panel. The time-expanded side panel luminance high frequencies and the Q portion of the side panel chrominance are modulated onto one phase of the quadrature-modulated Fukinuki subcarrier. The other phase contains the I portion of the side panel chrominance. Extra horizontal luminance high frequencies are quadrature-modulated onto the picture carrier.

X. FAROUDJA IDTV

This system is called Super NTSC. A 525-line progressively scanned source is used together with a series of innovative processing techniques at the transmission end. The appropriate receiver processing to go with the transmission processing is applied together with line doubling.

The resulting image is reported to have the following characteristics:

- 1050 lines, 2 to 1 interlace, 60 Hz,
- Apparent horizontal bandwidth increase,
- Aspect ratio of 4 to 3,
- No visible cross color,
- No visible cross luminance,
- No visible vertical aliasing,
- No apparent chroma bandwidth loss.

XI. ATTC

The Advanced Television Test Center (ATTC) is scheduled to test the following group of systems for the FCC.

- Faroudja
- Production Services Inc
- Sarnoff (ACTV I)
- NHK (Narrow MUSE)
- NHK (MUSE 6)
- Zenith
- Sarnoff (ACTV II)
- Philips
- MIT

There may be some changes in this list, because of the fluid nature of this field. A description of all these systems is beyond the scope of this paper. Further, most of the above systems, and many other systems that are not being tested by the ATTC, have been described in the literature [8], [20].

XII. Standards

A. FCC

It was mentioned earlier, in the section called Basic Approaches to ATV, that the FCC decisions on terrestrial broadcasting seem to be driving the analog HDTV standardization effort in the USA. On September 1, 1988, the FCC issued MM Docket No. 87-268. It is called: Tentative Decision and Further Notice of Injury. In that document, the FCC announced fundamental policies and defined boundaries for development of advanced television. The FCC issued several preliminary findings and conclusions narrowing the policy issues and requesting comments on four spectrum authorization plans.

The Commission announced three major tentative conclusions. First, it found that providing for terrestrial broadcasting use of ATV techniques would benefit the public by continuing the existing systems of privately-owned and operated stations. It tentatively concluded that the benefits of this technology can be realized by the public most quickly if existing broadcasters are permitted to implement ATV.

Second, it concluded that it will require the initial ATV signals to either be compatible with existing TV (NTSC standard) receivers or that ATV broadcasters duplicate them on another channel by simulcasting. Thus, consumers will continue receiving TV signals using existing equipment.

Third, based on the work of the Advisory Committee on Advanced Television Service and the Office of Engineering and Technology, the Commission said that if additional spectrum is needed for ATV, it can be found within the existing VHF and UHF TV bands. It said that consideration of additional spectrum outside the existing allocations would delay the implementation of ATV service because suitable spectrum not already being used for other purposes has not been identified; differences in propagation characteristics between the existing allocations and other spectrum bands limit their attractiveness for ATV broadcast purposes; and proceedings involving reallocation likely would be lengthy and result in further delay of ATV broadcasting service to the public.

B. ATSC

The Advanced Television Systems Committee (ATSC) was established in 1983. It contains a broad base of membership of organizations that are interested in ATV. The original structure of the ATSC contained three technology groups (areas of interest) plus an executive committee. The three groups were: HDTV, EDTV, and I-NTSC. Each technology group consisted of four specialists groups on Production, Transmission and Distribution, Reception and Display, and Measurements and Test Procedures. Separate production and transmission standards were considered likely.

More recently, the ATSC reorganized itself into two groups called production and distribution technology groups. This is consistent with the present trend that considers all systems as ATV and only makes a distinction between production/contribution and distribution/transmission.

Much of the early standards work on ATV was done by the ATSC, and by the ATSC together with the SMPTE. Also, it has been one of the advisory organizations that supports the FCC with technical expertise.

C. International Organizations

The International Telegraph and Telephone Consultative Committee (CCITT) is a sister organization to the International Radio Consultative Committee (CCIR) that is concerned with telecommunications issues. These are two organs of the four permanent organs of the International Telecommunications Union (ITU). The ITU is the specialized agency of the United Nations for telecommunications.

The CCITT began looking into B-ISDN in 1986. B-ISDN is a fiber based network that is intended to deliver many services in digital form to the home and office. Since one of the important issues in B-ISDN is how to handle video, the CCIR and CCITT jointly arranged for a group in the Mixed Telephone and Television Committee (CMTT) that is intended to answer the video needs of the CCITT.

The direction of ATV in B-ISDN has already been described in the section called Component Video. The currently preferred plan is for the contribution standard to use CCIR 601 directly for the intermediate level called EQTV, and to scale it up by a factor of two-to-one for HDTV.

D. SMPTE

A significant effort of the SMPTE has been directed into 240M, a production standard for HDTV. The 240M standard was described in the section called NHK HDTV and SMPTE 240M. Also, a significant amount of the early work on HDTV in the USA was done by the SMPTE.

E. Standards Outside the USA

The standards situation in other countries seems to be advancing rapidly. This is particularly true of Japan. However, there is division within Japan. The independent broadcaster association is advocating compatible EDTV type systems. In spite of this, much of the Japanese effort is set by NHK, and that effort was described in the section called NHK and SMPTE 240M.

Europe is focused on one common Multiplexed Analog Component (MAC) approach with DBS as the delivery system. This approach has started with a Direct Satellite Broadcast (DBS) service of PAL in the England. Next, there should be a DBS version of MAC, and the process should culminate with HD-MAC. HD-MAC doubles the number of lines of the present 625 line, 50 Hz European systems to make a 1250 line, 50 Hz system. Of course, the PTTs are looking toward a B-ISDN digital fiber solution as the ultimate delivery system in the future.

XIII. Delivery Systems

The likely candidates for the important delivery systems for ATV are listed below.

- Terrestrial
- Coaxial Cable CATV
- Fiber
  —Fiber CATV
  —Switched Video Services like B-ISDN
  —B-ISHN
- Pre-Recorded
  —Video Tape
  —Video Disc
- DBS

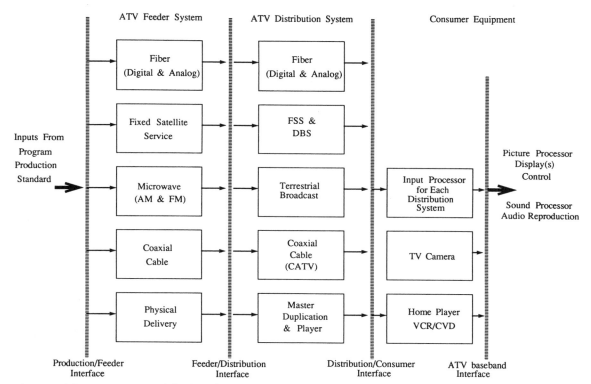

Fig. 8. Production, delivery systems, and display of ATV.

Figure 8 illustrates the entire ATV system from production through display, with an emphasis on the delivery systems. The two types of delivery systems that are likely to be the most important, long term, are fiber based solutions and pre-recorded solutions. Further, it is likely that these two categories will complement each other. The relationship may be similar to the present relationship that terrestrial/CATV has with pre-recorded VCRs. In this case, fiber based solutions will not only provide transmission capability, but will eventually provide full networking capabilities.

Fiber networks with switched video capability and signaling are likely to be the most practical delivery systems for video-on-demand services. Further, fiber networks with switched video capability are ideal for pay-per-view services as well, the reason being the clean customer interfacing provided by a network that provides efficient signaling and billing.

An alternative approach to B-ISDN is a hybrid analog and digital solution that is called B-ISHN for Broadband Integrated Services Hybrid Network [22]. This type of network has the same type of appeal as B-ISDN in that it can produce an integrated solution that provides all services with a single network. However, residential B-ISDN may be some years away. The need for a fiber based solution to entertainment video is here now. If a switched fiber CATV system is installed in the early-1990s, the other services to make it B-ISHN could be added later if the network topology is a switched star.

A switched fiber system that starts with either video-on-demand or pay-per-view video services may be the way to get started. However, the basic CATV services do have a great deal of appeal. Alternatively, a distribution system for CATV with a star topology could be a way to get started, with the idea of adding switched services later. Fortunately, the

two-layer approach that has been called B-ISHN can provide the vehicle to provisioning both services, but not necessarily starting both at the same time.

ATV will likely be more demanding of the delivery system than NTSC TV, because of the higher level of image quality that it is intended to display. Pre-recorded video will provide a high level of ATV quality and be available from the local video store. The consumer also requires a better quality receiver to realize the full benefit of ATV; however, the appropriate receivers for S-VHS has been on the market for several years, and many people already have the appropriate capability in their TVs without realizing it.

Consequently, CATV will need to go fiber (probably a hybrid fiber and coaxial solution first) soon to improve performance and system reliability. If the CATV industry does not, they may face shrinking markets because of competition with pre-recorded video from the corner video store with ATV quality video.

The CATV industry is aware of this movement in the pre-recorded programming area and may come up with a fiber CATV architecture for deployment soon. It is likely that the short term solution will be an analog fiber CATV system without switching capability, because it is generally believed that that type of system will likely result in the lowest cost solution of providing ATV on fiber to the home. If this is the case, this will leave a market opportunity for switched video services, before a second generation fiber CATV system with switched video service capability is introduced.

A synergistic effect will occur between ATV and fiber networks. Any network planned for the 1990s that is intended to provide entertainment video must be able to handle some form of ATV in order to be competitive with other delivery systems of that time. A new fiber network needs the product distinction that ATV can offer. Also, in order to fully appreciate ATV, a good delivery system (transmission system) is needed so that the quality of the received signal is not lowered by channel impairments. Fiber provides the highest quality channel because of its wide bandwidth together with immunity from interference and noise. Therefore, both fiber video networks and ATV benefit by the presence of the other.

Earlier it was stated that over-the-air terrestrial broadcasting may not be the most important delivery system for HDTV, because of the problem of maintaining quality. Unfortunately, coaxial CATV also has a problem. The CATV companies have been in a horsepower type race with each other on the number-of-channels capability of their systems. ATV will require wider bandwidth and result in fewer channels carried than with the present systems. Further, it will be very difficult to provide the level of video quality that would be needed for ATV. Some CATV installations presently provide second-rate quality to subscribers that are some distance from the headend, because transmission through many repeaters noticeably degrades the video quality of the present NTSC TV reception. ATV will be more demanding of the delivery system than NTSC TV, because of the higher quality that it is intended to display.

A big question that needs to be resolved on fiber networks that carry video is analog versus digital transmission. Another big question is switched versus non-switched networks.

There is no doubt that analog transmission of video is more economical than digital at this time. However, some CATV publications are starting to acknowledge that digital may be competitive for certain CATV applications in just a few years. Some believe that digital will cost the same as analog FM video in just 2 years, and therefore, replace FM [23].

One of the reasons is that digital has a much further reach; consequently, it may require no, or fewer, repeaters in some CATV environments. This has a large impact on reliability and maintenance. Further, digital transport offers a higher grade of service than analog.

Digital and switched services also seem to go together. While switched services can be provided in an analog network, it is generally believed that digital is the way to go, because of the extra performance of digital and the belief that cost differentials between analog and digital should be smaller in switched than non-switched networks.

XIV. HDTV versus EDTV/IDTV

Some of the questions that need to be answered before one can select one system approach over another are listed below.

- Relative Costs
- Ease of Acceptance
- Quality Differences
- How Much Improvement (over NTSC) is enough

Even though this section is named HDTV versus EDTV/IDTV, it should be recognized that all areas are in competition with each other, with some type of a criterion for a cost/performance trade-off that is not clearly understood at this time.

The relative costs of the competing systems are obviously important; however, ease of acceptance is also important. Systems that allow TV sets or monitors that can display either the NTSC signal or the new ATV signal are definitely preferred over systems that require two different displays in the same room to get the full range of programming.

The quality improvement of ATV must be sufficiently better than NTSC to even be considered; however, after that there will be some sort of a cost performance trade-off in the buyer's mind. Also, the acceptance of one level of video quality, like IDTV, will make it more difficult for another level, like EDTV, to get started.

HDTV could have a significant market share in the late 1990s. However, if other forms of ATV are a success sooner, a HDTV volume market may not come until after the year 2000. The reasons for this are that HDTV has the highest cost display and processing of all three levels of ATV. The extra resolution translates directly into higher cost displays and more processing. Another consideration is that HDTV volume will probably wait for standards which are not likely until the very end of 1992, or 1993. IDTV and some of the EDTV/EQTV approaches may not require any wait for standards. Further, some EDTV/EQTV could use today's high quality NTSC displays and less processing than HDTV. A form of EDTV is already getting started with video tape, like S-VHS. The main problem that it has is to get into the video stores with movies along with VHS. A second problem is with the relatively narrow chrominance bandwidth; however, that could be cured with a chrominance bandwidth expansion circuit.

Chroma Bandwidth Expansion is a technique that creates a replica of the high-frequency chrominance that was filtered out of the signal at the encoder. Since too high a ratio of luminance to chrominance bandwidths is one of the defects of the NTSC system, this technique is mostly applicable to IDTV/EDTV. However, it could be used to require less capacity from a HDTV by transmitting less chrominance bandwidth in the two color components. Also, it could be used to improve S-VHS to give better performance.

It is likely that there will be a time window for IDTV that is approximately between 1990 and 1994. If it does not receive a significant amount of success in that time frame, it is not likely to be accepted at all.

The EDTV/EQTV level of quality will likely have a time window between 1990 and 1997. The time window for HDTV starts in the 1992/5 time frame, and HDTV will succeed. The only question is when?

XV. ATV Market Potential

According to the Nathan Marketing Report for the Electronic Industries Association (EIA), the total market for TV receivers in the USA in the year 2000 will be 35.6 million TV sets. However, this number is relatively insensitive to the success of ATV.

In other words, ATV will have little impact on the total number of TV sets sold in the year 2000. It will just get a certain percentage of that total number. Lower priced NTSC receivers will be replaced by high-priced ATV receivers, with little volume change due to ATV.

This supports the idea that success in one level or facet of ATV will impede the acceptance of the other levels or areas of ATV. The time window for HDTV starts in 1992/5, and the exact time of start is influenced by the standards situation in HDTV. Therefore, the other levels have an opportunity to get started before it, and delay the acceptance of HDTV.

Another factor that could delay HDTV is the likely high initial cost of HDTV receivers. The firm of Booze, Allen & Hamilton has made some predictions of both the ATV receiver costs and consumer adoption scenarios [24]. The market scenarios vary widely; however, they all indicate that significant market penetration will be more than 7 years after introduction. How much more seems to vary widely with the scenario.

A nominal ATV receiver retail cost in 1991 is projected to be $4,342 for a 35-inch CRT display with medium resolution (500 to 600 lines) capability, and $5,483 for high resolution (1,000 lines) capability. The $4,342 number drops to $3,620 for a 1992 introduction, and $3,095 for a 1993 introduction.

The point is that there is a price to be paid for the high resolution display, especially during the early product introduction. Another point from the previous figures is that there is a price to be paid for early ATV product.

XVI. Signal Processing

Signal processing is a general term that can refer to a large number of techniques. Video processing is a category that has some familiar examples such as Analog-to-Digital (A/D) and D/A conversions, spectral shaping, and video coding. However, there are some less familiar techniques that may be used in ATV. An example of one of these less familiar techniques is mentioned next.

Picture Crispening is a technique for shortening the risetime of edges in a digital video signal. Traditionally, video engineers perform this type of function utilizing a technique that is called peaking or aperture correction. Unfortunately, these techniques tend to produce associated ringing and other undesirable effects. The following algorithms were developed for an adaptive technique of picture crispening of digital video that eliminates the undesirable side effects. It inserts extra pels between the transmitted pels, locally at the receiver, to achieve this improvement. Two somewhat different algorithms can be used to achieve the desired result; the first is shown as Equation 13 below [25].

If

$$|A - B| < K \; XOR \; |B - C| < K \qquad (13)$$

then

$$X = B$$

else

$$X = \frac{A + B}{2}$$

- A is the previous pel;
- B is the present pel;
- C is the next pel;
- K is a small constant; and
- X is the new pel that is added between A and B.

Figure 9 shows the nine basic patterns that are used to insert the extra pels into the waveform. The improvement makes the displayed picture appear more crisp, so that it appears to have more resolution than was transmitted. The reason

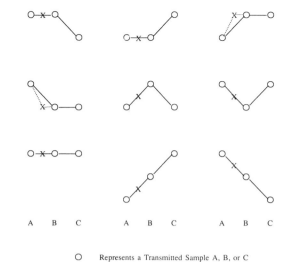

| O | Represents a Transmitted Sample A, B, or C |
| X | Represents an Added Sample |

Fig. 9. Nine basic patterns used to insert extra pels.

Fig. 10. The crispening effect of the first algorithm.

for this is the shorter risetimes. Figure 10 illustrates the crispening effect of the first algorithm.

Alternatively, a second, slightly more complicated algorithm, may have some advantages in some cases. This algorithm inserts two pels at a time in some cases.

If

$$|A - B| < K \; XOR \; |B - C| < K \qquad (14)$$

then

$$X_{AB} = B$$

$$X_{BC} = B \; and \; skip \; a \; pel$$

else

$$X_{AB} = \frac{A + B}{2}$$

- X_{AB} is the pel added between pels A and B;
- and X_{BC} is the pel added between pels B and C.

Fig. 11 illustrates the nine basic patterns of the second algorithm. The crispening effects of the second algorithm are illustrated in Fig. 12.

This same technique can be carried over to two-dimensions so that the improvement can also be obtained in the vertical direction. This fits right in with a need in the IDTV/ EDTV area to increase the number of lines in the display. TV set manufactures appear to be planning to simply repeat the transmitted lines twice, interpolate between two lines to get the values for the extra line, or some more complicated technique that usually involves a combination of these two techniques. Two of these more complicated techniques were described in the section on IDTV. However,

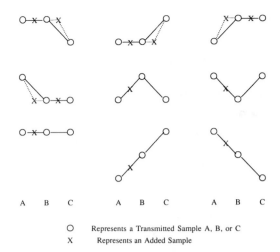

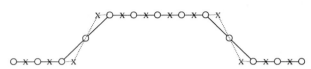

O   Represents a Transmitted Sample A, B, or C
X   Represents an Added Sample

Fig. 11. Alternative nine basic patterns for pel insertion.

Fig. 12. Picture crispening effects of the second algorithm.

this new technique will allow them to select the values for this new line that will provide crispening in the vertical direction, and therefore provide even more improved performance than other techniques.

A RF processing opportunity exists in the GaAs area; GaAs varactor diodes and/or tuner ICs will provide improved performance over Si varactor diodes and circuits. While this opportunity has not been exploited in NTSC, TV, ATV requires improved performance in order to consistently display its better images. Also, especially initially, manufacturers will be willing to experiment with higher-cost solutions in the interest of seeking the right competitive (cost/performance) advantages for their product. Therefore, there is an opportunity for these types of higher cost, but also higher performance, devices to enter the market.

The two examples above are just one video and one RF processing example, respectively. Many more are possible.

XVII. Displays

It is generally believed that HDTV will only be fully appreciated when viewed on large display devices. The intent is to have the viewer sit approximately three picture heights away from the display. This will fill up the field of vision and give a better sense of realism. However, this is not as desirable with NTSC TV, because of the poor resolution and artifacts that would be annoying at that distance.

Therefore, the display technology is believed to be an important ingredient for HDTV success. The display device is the largest contributor to the cost of an HDTV set. Consequently, it is important that the display not only be of high quality, it must also be at an affordable cost, and provide sufficient brightness. The CRT does not seem to be the long term solution, because of cost and other problems. Some of the other problems with direct view CRTs appear to be fundamental. For example, even if a very large, six-to-eight-foot size, direct view CRT display could be made econom-

ically, it is unlikely that it could pass through typical doorways, and the weight would likely be prohibitive for normal homes. Therefore, if a CRT based technology is used for displays of this size, they are likely to be projection TVs.

It is likely that the initial ATV sets will utilize mainly CRT based displays for both projection and smaller size direct-view. However, there is a definite need for a CRT replacement, and the most likely candidates are plasma panels and liquid crystal based technology.

XVIII. Conclusion

Some form, or forms, of ATV will be introduced to the consumer soon. In other words, the question is no longer if ATV will come, but rather, when and how many versions will be introduced, and be successful.

One of the important points identified in this paper is the synergy between ATV and fiber networks as a delivery system. The only other delivery system that is likely to provide comparable quality is pre-recorded material, tape and disc.

There is a way of capitalizing on the strengths of both the traditional telecommunications networks and the CATV networks in a single fiber network that has more capability and customer appeal than a CATV distribution approach [22]. This type of a network can provide switched video services such as video-on-demand. Also, it provides the flexibility of getting started with either a switched video network or a distribution (likely a subcarrier approach) system initially and growing the network into integrated services later.

Some predict that it will take until the year 2000 for fiber Plain Old Telephone Service (POTS) to be less costly than copper [26]. Others predict that an integrated services approach should be economical long before that, perhaps in the mid-1990s. Further, a mostly fiber network approach to CATV called fiber-to-the-curb has been estimated to break-even with copper costs before 1993 [27].

REFERENCES

[1] D. G. Fink, *Television Standards and Practice—NTSC.* New York, NY: McGraw-Hill, 1943.
[2] K. McIlwain and C. E. Dean, *Principles of Color Television.* New York, NY: Wiley, 1956.
[3] D. G. Fink, *Color Television Standards—NTSC.* New York, NY: McGraw-Hill, 1955.
[4] T. S. Rzeszewski, *Color Television.* New York, NY: IEEE Press, 1983.
[5] K. B. Benson, *Television Engineering Handbook.* New York, NY: McGraw-Hill, 1986.
[6] T. S. Rzeszewski, "A compatible high-definition television system," *BSTJ,* pp. 2091–111, Sept. 1983.
[7] T. S. Rzeszewski, "Video coding for EQTV distribution with a rate of approximately 135 Mb/s," *IEEE Trans. Consumer Electronics,* pp. 147–155, Feb. 1988.
[8] T. S. Rzeszewski, Special Issue on Advanced Television Systems, *IEEE Trans. Consumer Electronics,* Feb. 1988.
[9] P. Mertz and W. Gray, "Theory of scanning and its relation to the transmitted signal in telephotography and television," *BSTJ,* pp. 464–515, July 1934.
[10] P. Mertz, "Television—the scanning process," *Proc. IRE,* pp. 529– , Oct. 1941.
[11] M. A. Isnardi, "Multidimensional interpretation of NTSC encoding and decoding," *IEEE Trans. Consumer Electronics,* pp. 179–183, Feb. 1988.
[12] E. Dubois and W. F. Schreiber, "Improvements to NTSC by multidimensional filtering," *SMPTE J.,* pp. 446–463, June 1988.
[13] E. Dubois *et al.,* "Three-dimensional spectrum and processing of digital NTSC color signals," *SMPTE J.,* pp. 372–378, April 1982.

[14] M. A. Isnardi, "Exploring and exploiting subchannels in the NTSC spectrum," *SMPTE J.*, pp. 526–532, July 1988.

[15] W. E. Glenn and K. G. Glenn, "HDTV compatible transmission system," *SMPTE J.*, pp. 242–246, March 1987.

[16] B. L. Jones and L. E. Marks, "Picture quality assessment: A comparison of ratio and ordinal scales," *SMPTE J.*, pp. 1244–1248, Dec. 1985.

[17] T. Kurita *et al.*, "A practical IDTV system improving picture quality for nonstandard TV signals," *IEEE Trans. Consumer Electronics*, pp. 387–396, Aug. 1988.

[18] S. Naimpally *et al.*, "Integrated digital IDTV receiver with features," *IEEE Trans. Consumer Electronics*, pp. 410–419, Aug. 1988.

[19] H. Mizukami *et al.*, "A high quality GaAs IC tuner for TV/VCR receivers," *IEEE Trans. Consumer Electronics*, pp. 649–659, Aug. 1988.

[20] K. R. Donow, *HDTV Planning for Action.* Washington, D.C.: National Association of Broadcasting, 1988.

[21] "Signal Parameters—1125/60 High-Definition Production System," Proposed American National Standard, 240M, *SMPTE Journal*, November, 1987, pp. 1150–1152.

[22] T. S. Rzeszewski, "A two layer fiber network for broadband integrated services," *IEEE Trans. Consumer Electronics*, pp. 81–85, May 1989.

[23] J. W. Linebarger, "Introducing fiber in a coaxial world," *Communication Technology*, pp. 120–126, June 1989.

[24] M. J. Mackell, "Likely costs of consumer advanced television (ATV) technology," *IEEE Trans. Consumer Electronics*, pp. 63–71, May 1989.

[25] T. S. Rzeszewski, "Picture crispening by adaptive digital signal processing," *IEEE Trans. Consumer Electronics*, pp. 71–75, 1987.

[26] C. A. Willcock, "Service implications of fiber networking," *IEEE Trans. Consumer Electronics*, pp. 92–96, May 1989.

[27] G. Kotelly, "Fiber-to-the-curb cuts delivery costs," *Lightwave*, pp. 8–9, June 1989.

Chapter 2
Digital Video in Consumer Electronics: High Definition Television and Digital Video Recording

SAIPRASAD NAIMPALLY

PANASONIC ADVANCED TV-VIDEO LABORATORIES, INC.
95 E. CONNECTICUT DR.
BURLINGTON, NJ 08016

Recent advances in digital video compression and transmission technologies promise to revolutionize the television viewing experience. They will enable the compression of pictures with very high resolution and color fidelity and multi-channel compact disc quality sound into 6 megahertz television channels. Consumers will be able to enjoy a movie theater-like audio-visual experience in their own homes when they watch High Definition Television programs, which might be delivered by several different media, for example, by terrestrial transmission or by cable, satellite, or telecommunications channels. Also, advances in digital recording technologies will soon make it possible for consumers to record and play back high-quality video and audio programs with the same clear, noise-free performance as the original signals back in the studio. The new digital VCRs will feature a very small cassette, much smaller in size than the VHS cassettes currently used by consumers. This section will provide the reader with an overview of digital video compression and transmission techniques used in HDTV systems tested by the Advanced Television Test Center in Alexandria, Virginia under the auspices of the Federal Communication Commission's (FCC) Advisory Committee on Advanced Television Service (ACATS). This section also provides a brief overview of some prototype digital VCR systems and the issues related to trick-play features with compressed video recording.

In 1987 the FCC issued a Notice of Inquiry on Advanced Television. Initially there were several proposals that attempted to transmit enhanced-definition and high-definition television pictures through one 6-megahertz channel, using analog transmission schemes. In March 1990, the FCC expressed a preference for simulcast HDTV systems in which an HDTV signal could be sent in a 6-megahertz channel in a manner incompatible with current NTSC receivers; that is, NTSC receivers would not be able to receive the HDTV signal and decode it to provide pictures and sound. An NTSC version of the HDTV signal would be simulcast on a separate channel. Thus, additional 6-megahertz channels would be needed to transmit HDTV. Of course, it would be a requirement that these HDTV signals not interfere with NTSC signals being transmitted from adjacent channels within the same local area, or from co-channels from nearby areas. It would also be a requirement that NTSC signals not interfere with clean reception of the HDTV signals. In June 1990, General Instrument Corp. submitted to the FCC's ACATS a system description of an all-digital HDTV system for terrestrial broadcast in a 6-megahertz channel. Within six months, three other all-digital HDTV systems were also submitted. Papers 1–11 provide an overview of these systems. All of the HDTV systems use a motion-compensated discrete cosine transform (DCT) compression system for compressing the HDTV video signal by a roughly 50 to 1 ratio. Three of the four systems use a quadrature amplitude modulation (QAM) scheme for digital transmission; the fourth uses a closely-related scheme called vestigial sideband modulation (VSB).

Paper 1 gives an overview of the General Instrument Digicipher HDTV System and provides brief descriptions and performance specifications for the key parameters of each subsystem. It also provides a tutorial type of treatment of basic video compression concepts such as motion estimation, motion compensation, Huffman coding, DCT, rate buffer control, etc. Paper 2 describes the video compression technology used in the Digicipher HDTV System, which is designed for interlaced video signals and the closely related Channel Compatible Digicipher (CCDC) HDTV System, which is designed for progressively-scanned video signals. The CCDC system uses a somewhat more sophisticated video encoding system since it has a lower bits per pixel (bpp) ratio than the Digicipher system (i.e., it has a higher compression ratio). For instance, CCDC uses sub-pixel accuracy and variable block size motion estimation, whereas Digicipher uses pixel accuracy and fixed 32×16 block size motion estimation. CCDC uses a method called vector coding for sending the non-zero DCT coefficients, whereas Digicipher uses two-dimensional Huffman coding. In common with virtually all HDTV compression systems, 24-frames-per-second film material is transmitted at its original, lower temporal rate since the resulting compression ratio is lower and results in higher quality compressed video with fewer compression artifacts.

The Digicipher and CCDC system both use 32-QAM or 16-QAM digital transmission schemes. The 32-QAM mode is the preferred mode since it allows a higher data rate to be transmitted within the same bandwidth as compared to 16-QAM mode, albeit at the expense of coverage area. The reason is that, given the same symbol rate in symbols per second, 32 QAM maps five data bits into one of 32 symbols, whereas 16 QAM maps four data bits into one of 16 symbols. Paper 3 describes the 32-QAM transmission system used in Digicipher. Paper 4 explains how the concatenated coding schemes previously developed for QPSK modulation could be adapted for QAM modulation.

Paper 5 describes the video compression subsystem used in the Zenith/AT&T Digital Spectrum Compatible (DSC) HDTV System. This video codec compresses progressively-scanned video with a compression ratio of 50 to 1. It uses a sophisticated model of the Human Vision System (HVS) to quantize the DCT coefficients in a manner that leads to a minimum loss of perceptual image quality. It employs sub-pixel and variable-block-size motion estimation, vector quantization of quantizer selection patterns, and a forward analyzer to analyze the video information in the frame being coded, to improve the buffer control operation. Also, in order to overcome the abrupt loss of picture resulting from a slight decrease in S/N near the limits of the service area (the so-called "cliff effect"), the DSC HDTV System is capable of switching between a 2-bits-per-symbol transmission mode and a more robust 1-bit-per-symbol mode. This switching results in a bi-rate coding of the video, and the ratio of 1-bit-per-symbol to 2-bits-per-symbol transmission is selected adaptively in the encoder as part of the buffer control system.

Paper 6 gives an overview of the DSC HDTV transmission system. It uses a vestigial sideband modulation system called 4VSB, whose performance is very similar to that of 16 QAM. A pilot carrier is used at the band edge on the slope of the channel VSB characteristic. It is claimed that this pilot carrier aids in carrier acquisition even under poor S/N conditions. Paper 7 provides details of a unique method for NTSC interference rejection that uses a precoder at the transmitter and a comb filter at the receiver. It is claimed that this method makes it possible to ensure satisfactory HDTV reception at a D/U ratio of 0 dB.

Paper 8 explains how it is possible to include the Zenith-type comb filtering approach in an HDTV system based on a QAM-type digital transmission.

Paper 9 describes the video used in the Advanced Digital HDTV (AD-HDTV) System. The AD-HDTV codec uses a modified form of the MPEG-1 video coding standard [1] called MPEG++. MPEG-1 and its successor MPEG-2 [2], which has special techniques to deal with interlaced material, are video coding standards that have found acceptance among a wide range of applications, such as cable television, direct broadcast satellite television, interactive storage media, video conferencing, video telephony, and HDTV. AD-HDTV, following MPEG, has three coded frame types: I, P and B. I frames are used periodically within a sequence for refresh purposes, and are coded without reference to any other frame. P frames are coded with reference to a previous I or P frame. I and P frames are called anchor frames. B frames are bidirectionally predictive-coded with reference to a past and future anchor frame. AD-HDTV attempts to combat the "cliff effect" by a combination of a spectrally-shaped QAM (SS-QAM) transmission scheme and prioritization of coded video data into high-priority (HP) and standard-priority (SP) data. The more important HP data is modulated onto a narrow-band QAM carrier located in the vestigial sideband portion of an NTSC co-channel. It has 5 dB more power than the other (SP) QAM carrier onto which is modulated the less important SP data. This digital transmission scheme is explained in Paper 10.

Multiplexing of compressed video, audio, and data, and the transmission of synchronizing information, is accomplished in a packed-oriented transport layer within MPEG++, as described in Paper 11. The transport layer contains several sublayers. The datalink/network sublayer provides generic transport services, such as priority support, asynchronous cell multiplexing, and error control. The adaptation header sublayer provides for logical resynchronization and error concealment support, and contains MPEG-specific error recovery information, including an "entry pointer" that locates the start of the first decodable video unit in a cell. The video service sublayer contains highly service-specific information and provides the higher-level resynchronization mechanism needed for error recovery.

In February 1993, a special panel of the FCC's Advisory Committee met to choose a "winner" among the tested HDTV systems. However, the test results of the four digital systems were judged to be very close in performance. The special panel was therefore unable to choose a "winning" system and recommended that the systems be retested. In May 1993, the companies that had proposed the four original HDTV systems formed a "Grand Alliance" to work together to develop a single Grand Alliance HDTV System. The key system characteristics of the Grand Alliance HDTV System are as follows [3]:

SCANNING FORMATS

The video encoder will accept either of two scanning formats:

- 1920(h) $\times$ 1080(v)/ 2:1 (interlaced)/ field rate of 60 or 59.94 Hz

- 1280(h) $\times$ 720(v)/ 1:1 (progressive)/ frame rate of 60 or 59.94 Hz

Internally the encoder will detect film-derived program material (detection of 3:2 pulldown in the case of 24-Hz original film material) and convert it to its original frame rate. The lower frame rate video is then compressed and transmitted. Other (non-film) video is compressed as received, except that in the case of interlaced video, horizontal prefiltering could reduce the pixel number per active line to 1440.

The transmitted (compressed) formats could therefore be any of the following:

- 1920(1440) $\times$ 1080/ 2:1/ 60,59.94 Hz
- 1280 $\times$ 720/ 1:1/ 60,59.94,30,29.97,24,23.976 Hz
- 1920 $\times$ 1080/ 1:1/ 30,29.97,24,23.976

VIDEO COMPRESSION

A subset of the MPEG-2 Main Profile @ High Level as constrained by the Grand Alliance [4] will be used as the video compression system. [2] describes the coded representation of video coded in accordance with MPEG-2 and the video decoding process required to produce pictures for display.

TRANSMISSION SYSTEM

The digital transmission system for terrestrial broadcast will be VSB; for cable it will be 16 VSB. The data rate for 16 VSB is double that for 8 VSB, thus making it possible to transmit two HDTV programs in a 6-MHz cable channel.

The key system parameters for the 8-VSB and 16-VSB transmission systems are listed in the table below:

TABLE 1 VSB PARAMETERS

Parameter	Terrestrial Mode (8 VSB)	High Data Rate Cable Mode (16 VSB)
Channel Bandwidth	6 MHz	6 MHz
Excess Bandwidth	11.5%	11.5%
Symbol Rate	10.76 MSPS	10.76 MSPS
Bits per Symbol	3	4
Trellis FEC	2/3 rate	None
Reed-Solomon FEC	T = 10 (208,188)	T = 10 (208,188)
Segment Length	836 Symbols	836 Symbols
Segment Sync	4 symbols per segment	4 symbols per segment
Frame Sync	1 per 313 segments	1 per 313 segments
Payload Data Rate	19.3 Mb/s	38.6 Mb/s
NTSC Co-Channel Rejection	NTSC Rejection Filter in Receiver	N/A
Pilot Power Contribution	0.3 dB	0.3 dB
C/N Threshold	14.9 dB	28.3 dB

TRANSPORT LAYER

The transport layer will follow the MPEG-2 Systems (transport streams only) specification with constraints as defined by the Grand Alliance. The transport layer protocol and syntax are described in [5] and [6].

AUDIO

Audio will be encoded at 384 kbps using the Dolby AC-3 system [7], [8].

In the design of an HDTV video decoder, a function that poses a real challenge is the variable-length decoder or entropy decoder. Paper 12 explains the difficult design issues involved and some hardware solutions. The VLD has very high throughput requirements and its operation is inherently recursive and difficult to pipeline, since one needs to know the length of a given variable-length codeword to establish the starting point of the next codeword in the bitstream. Therefore, one cannot start the decoding of the next codeword before one decodes at least the length of the first codeword.

Paper 13 reports on the VLSI implementation of a Reed Solomon codec. Reed Solomon coding is a block-coding method for forward error correction in which parity bytes are appended to fixed-length blocks of "information bytes." Errors that may occur during transmission are detected and wherever possible corrected by the Reed Solomon decoder. Decoding is a computation-intensive operation. The mathematical background, operation, and VLSI architecture of the decoder are explained in this paper.

Research in the area of Digital VCRs for consumer use started in the 1980s and matured in the 1990s. Paper 14 reports on the development of a prototype digital VCR that records CCIR 601 component video at 19 Mbps using a DCT-based coding scheme. The input bit rate of the uncompressed video is 162 Mbps. This moderate level of compression was considered necessary in order to provide sophisticated editing functions similar to those used in professional VTRs and to maintain high picture quality during trick plays such as fast search. Paper 15 examines the requirements imposed on the video coding scheme and the formation of compression blocks and sync blocks by the need to provide good picture quality during trick plays.

MPEG-type compression schemes inherently assign a variable number of bits to the frames within a video sequence, to the slices within a frame, to the macroblocks within a slice, and to the blocks within a macroblock. Stationary images without much detail are assigned very few bits, whereas highly detailed images with rapid motion are assigned a large number of bits. An MPEG-type compression scheme is optimized for continuous transmission, recording, and playback. Even the simplest trick-play operation, such as fast forward, at any speed poses a significant challenge, since the recovered bits would produce no recognizable video output. Paper 16 examines this problem and proposes some clever solutions that provide acceptable pictures at even fairly high speed search.

REFERENCES

[1] ISO/IEC 11172-2, MPEG-1 Video, "Coding of moving pictures and associated audio for digital storage media at up to about 1.5 Mbits/s," ISO/IEC, 1993, Switzerland.

[2] ISO/IEC 13818-2, MPEG-2 Video Committee Draft, "Information technology—generic coding of moving pictures and associated audio," Seoul, Korea, Nov. 1993, ISO/IEC.

[3] Grand Alliance, "Grand Alliance HDTV system specification—draft document," submission to the FCC ACATS Technical Subgroup, Feb. 24, 1994.

[4] Grand Alliance, "Grand Alliance video compression report," submission to FCC ACATS Technical Subgroup, Oct. 21, 1993.

[5] ISO/IEC 13818-1, MPEG-2 Systems Committee Draft, "Information technology—generic coding of moving pictures and associated audio," Seoul, Korea, Nov. 1993, ISO/IEC.

[6] Grand Alliance, "Transport layer functional description for the Grand Alliance ATV system," submission to FCC ACATS Technical Subgroup, Oct. 21, 1993.

[7] Dolby Laboratories, "Dolby AC-3 multichannel audio coding," submission to the Grand Alliance Audio Specialist Group, Aug. 17, 1993.

[8] Steve Forshay and Dolby Laboratories, "Dolby AC-3 multi-channel digital audio compression system algorithm description," MPEG Document 93/972, Seoul, Korea, Nov. 1993.

FURTHER READING

[1] Advance Television Research Consortium, "Advanced digital television," submission to FCC ACATS, Jan. 20, 1992.

[2] AT&T, "DSC HDTV encoder implementation," submission to FCC ACATS Systems Subcommittee, Working Party 3, June 11, 1992.

[3] G.C. Clark, Jr. and J.B. Cain, *Error-Correction Coding for Digital Communications*. New York: Plenum Press, 1988.

[4] General Instrument Corp., "Digicipher HDTV encoder information," submission to FCC ACATS Systems Subcommittee, Working Party 3, June 10, 1992.

[5] General Instrument Corp., "Digicipher HDTV system description," submission to FCC ACATS, Aug. 22, 1991.

[6] J.H. Lee, J.T. Seo, Y. C. Park, D.H. Youn, and T.S. Oh, "A study on new DCT-based bit rate reduction algorithm and variable speed playback for a home-use digital VCR," *IEEE Trans. Consumer Electronics*, vol. 38, no. 3, pp. 236–242, 1992.

[7] D. A. Luthi, P. Tong, and P.A. Ruetz, "A video-rate JPEG chip set," *IEEE Custom Integrated Circuits Conf.*, pp. 26.2.1–26.2.4, 1992.

[8] Massachusetts Institute of Technology, "Channel compatible digicipher HDTV system—encoder description and implementation," submission to FCC ACATS Systems Subcommittee, Working Party 3, June 12, 1992.

[9] Massachusetts Institute of Technology, "Channel compatible digicipher HDTV system," submission to FCC ACATS, May 14, 1992.

[10] T. Miyazaki, T. Nishitani, M. Edahiro, I. Ono, and K. Mitsuhashi, "DCT/IDCT processor for HDTV developed with DSP silicon compiler," *J. VLSI Signal Process.*, vol. 5, pp. 151–158, 1993.

[11] J. G. Proakis, *Digital Communications*. New York: McGraw-Hill, 1989.

[12] A. Puri and R. Aravind, "Motion-compensated video coding with adaptive perceptual quantization," *IEEE Trans. Circuits and Syst. Video Tech.*, vol. 1, no. 4., pp. 351–361, 1991.

[13] B. Sklar, *Digital Communications—Fundamentals and Applications*. Englewood Cliffs, N.J.: Prentice-Hall, 1988.

[14] SMPTE 240M, *1125/60 Production Systems Signal Parameters*. White Plains, N.Y.: SMPTE, 1988.

[15] SMPTE 260M, *1125/60 HDTV Production Systems Digital Representation and Bit Serial Interface*. White Plains, N.Y.: SMPTE, 1992.

[16] K. Yang and S. Singhal, "Design of a multi-function video decoder based on a motion-compensated predictive-interpolative coder," *SPIE Visual Communications and Image Processing*, vol. 1360, pp. 1530–1539, 1990.

[17] Zenith and AT&T, "Digital spectrum compatible HDTV system," submission to FCC ACATS, Sept. 23, 1991.

[18] Zenith Electronics Corp., "VSB transmission system technical details," submission to FCC ACATS Technical Subgroup, Dec. 17, 1993.

DIGICIPHER™- ALL DIGITAL, CHANNEL COMPATIBLE, HDTV BROADCAST SYSTEM

Woo Paik
General Instrument Corporation
6262 Lusk Boulevard
San Diego, California 92121

ABSTRACT

General Instrument's DigiCipher™ System is an all digital HDTV system that can be transmitted over a single 6 MHz VHF or UHF channel. It provides full HDTV performance with virtually no visible transmission impairments due to noise, multipath, and interference. It offers high picture quality, while the complexity of the decoder is low. Furthermore, low transmitting power can be used, making it ideal for simulcast HDTV transmission using unused or taboo channels. The DigiCipher™ HDTV System can also be used for cable and satellite transmission of HDTV. There is absolutely no satellite receive dish size penalty (compared to FM-NTSC) in the satellite delivery of DigiCipher™ HDTV. This is important not only for DBS, but for broadcast and cable since broadcast network and cable programming is typically delivered to affiliates via satellite. To achieve the full HDTV performance in a single 6 MHz bandwidth, a highly efficient unique compression algorithm based on DCT transform coding is used. Through the extensive use of the computer simulation, the compression algorithm has been refined and optimized. Computer simulation results show excellent video quality for a variety of HDTV material. For error free transmission of the digital data, powerful error correction coding combined with adaptive equalization is used. At a carrier-to-noise ratio of above 19 dB, essentially error free reception can be achieved.

INTRODUCTION

The DigiCipher™ HDTV System is an integrated system that can provide high definition digital video, CD-quality digital audio, data and text services over a single VHF or UHF channel. Bandwidth for conditional access capability that allows the encryption of video, audio, and data services is also provided.

Figure 1 shows the overall system block diagram. At the HDTV station, the encoder accepts one high definition video and four audio signals and transmits one 16-QAM modulated data stream. The control computer can supply program related information such as program name, remaining times, and program rating. At consumer's home, the DigiCipher™ HDTV receiver receives the 16-QAM data stream and provides video, audio, data, and text to the subscriber. On screen display can be used to display the program related information.

Figure 2 shows the block diagram of the encoder. The digital video encoder accepts YUV inputs with 16:9 aspect ratio and 1050-line interlaced (1050/2:1) at 59.94 field rate. The YUV signals are obtained from analog RGB inputs by RGB-to-YUV matrix, low pass filtering, and A/D conversion. The sampling frequency is 51.80 MHz for Y,U, and V. The digital video encoder implements the compression algorithm and generates video data stream. The digital audio encoder accepts four audio inputs and generates audio data stream. The data/text processor accepts four data channels at 9600 baud and generates a data stream. The control channel processor interfaces with the control computer and generates control data stream.

The multiplexer combines the various data streams into one data stream at 15.8 Mbps. The FEC encoder adds error correction overhead bits and provide 19.42 Mbps of data to the 16-QAM modulator. The symbol rate of the 16-QAM signal is 4.86 MHz.

Figure 3 shows the block diagram of the decoder. The 16-QAM demodulator receives IF signal from the VHF/UHF tuner and provides the demodulated data at 19.42 Mbps. The demodulator has an adaptive equalizer to effectively combat multipath distortions common in VHF or UHF terrestrial transmission. The FEC decoder corrects virtually all random or burst errors and provides the error-free data to the Sync/Data selector. The Sync/Data Selector maintains overall synchronization and provides video, audio, data/text, and control data streams to appropriate processing blocks.

The control channel processor decodes the program related information. The user microprocessor receives commands from the remote control unit (RCU) and controls various functions of the decoder including the channel selection.

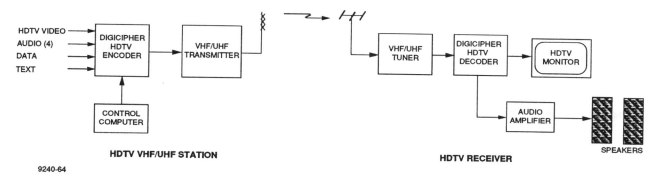

Figure 1. System Block Diagram

Reprinted from *IEEE Trans. Broadcasting,* vol. 36, no. 4, pp. 245–254, Dec. 1990.

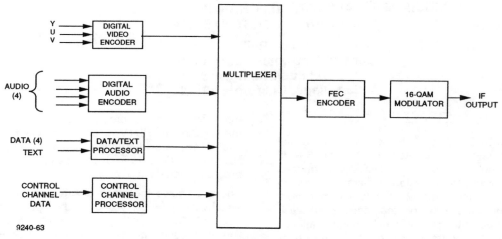

Figure 2. Encoder Block Diagram

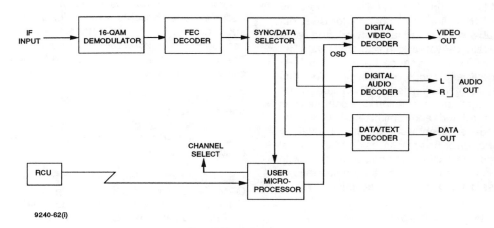

Figure 3. Decoder Block Diagram

DIGITAL VIDEO PROCESSING

The compression process can be broken down into five different subprocesses:

1. Chrominance Preprocessor
2. Discrete Cosine Transform (DCT)
3. Coefficient Quantization (Normalization)
4. Huffman (Variable Length) Coding
5. Motion Estimation and Compensation

Basic block diagrams for the encoder and the decoder video processing are shown in Figures 4 and 5 respectively. The subsequent discussions refer to certain basic picture processing elements:

- **Pixel:** An 8 bit active video sample (luminance or chrominance). Unless mentioned, the term "pixel" refers to luminance pixels. Representing an image by digitized samples is generally referred to as PCM coding.

- **Block:** An image area 8 pixels horizontally by 8 pixels vertically.

- **Superblock:** An image area 4 luminance blocks horizontally by 2 luminance blocks vertically; associated with 1 chrominance block each for U and V derived from that image area.

- **Macroblock:** An image area 8 superblocks horizontally.

These elements are described further in the appropriate sections.

Chrominance Preprocessor

The resolution of chrominance information can be further reduced relative to luminance resolution with only a slight effect on the perceived image quality. Therefore, to take advantage of this phenomenon, the input signal must first be separated into luminance and chrominance components if it does not already exist in this form. The Y,U,V color space (See CCIR 601) representation has been chosen for this purpose. The U and V chrominance components are decimated horizontally by a factor of 4 and vertically by a factor of 2.

The decimation requires the application of a prefilter prior to subsampling. In this case, simple boxcar filters are used. That is, pixels are averaged in groups of four horizontally, and groups of two vertically. Since the vertical averaging is performed across two different fields, some degradation in motion rendition occurs. In practice, however, this degradation is very difficult to detect. We are not only less sensitive to reductions in chrominance spatial resolution, but in temporal resolution as well.

The luminance signal (Y) bypasses the chrominance preprocessor, and therefore full resolution is maintained. The chrominance components are then multiplexed with the luminance component, one block at a time, and all components are then subjected to the same processing. At the decoder, the components are again separated and the chrominance signals are interpolated back to full resolution.

Discrete Cosine Transform

The Discrete Cosine Transform (DCT) transforms a block of pixels into a new block of transform coefficients. A block size of 8 x 8 has been chosen because the efficiency of the transform coding doesn't improve much while the complexity grow substantially beyond the 8 x 8 block size [1-3]. The transform is applied in turn to each such block until the entire image has been transformed. At the decoder, the inverse transformation is applied to recover the original image.

If $f(i,j)$ represents pixel intensity as a function of horizontal position j and vertical position i, and $F(u,v)$ represents the value of each coefficient after transformation, then the equations for the forward and inverse transformations are

$$F(u,v) = \frac{4C(u)C(v)}{N^2} \sum_{i=0}^{N-1} \sum_{j=0}^{N-1} f(i,j) \cos\frac{(2i+1)u\pi}{2N} \cos\frac{(2j+1)v\pi}{2N} \quad - \quad (1)$$

$$f(i,j) = \sum_{u=0}^{N-1} \sum_{v=0}^{N-1} C(u)C(v) F(u,v) \cos\frac{(2i+1)u\pi}{2N} \cos\frac{(2j+1)v\pi}{2N} \quad - \quad (2)$$

where $C(w) = \begin{cases} 1/\sqrt{2} & \text{for } w=0 \\ 1 & \text{for } w=1,2,\cdots,N-1 \end{cases}$

where N is the horizontal and vertical dimension of the block.

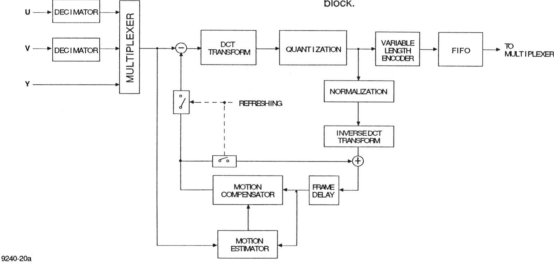

9240-20a

Figure 4. Digital Video Encoder Block Diagram

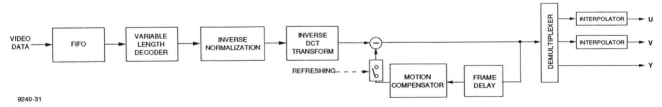

9240-31

Figure 5. Digital Video Decoder Block Diagram

159

The DCT merely transforms an image area from a fixed number of pixels to an equal number of transform coefficients. In order to compress the image, it is necessary to take advantage of an important property of the DCT. For typical images, a very large proportion of the signal energy is compacted into a small number of transform coefficients [4-6].

Coefficient Quantization (Normalization)

Coefficient quantization, or normalization, is a process that introduces small changes into the image in order to improve coding efficiency. This is done by truncating the DCT coefficients to a fixed number of bits. The truncation is performed by shifting a coefficient from left to right, spilling the least significant bits off the end of its register. In this way, the amplitude of the coefficient is also reduced. The number of bits remaining are preassigned individually for each of the 8 x 8 coefficients. However, the number of bits can be further reduced or increased as necessary to maintain a constant bit rate.

In the best case, the encoder will allocate 9 bits (not including sign bit) for each of the transform coefficients. At such times, the system is operating at maximum level on a performance scale ranging from 0 to 9 (the "quantization level"). If the targeted bit rate is exceeded, however, the quantization level is decremented to 8 before encoding the next block. At this level, the low frequency coefficients continue to be represented with 9 bits; however, some of the higher frequency coefficients are now truncated to 8 bits. If the quantization level is then decremented to 7, then those coefficients that were previously truncated to 8 bits will then be truncated to only 7 bits. In addition, a few of the coefficients that were previously 9 bits will now be truncated using 8 bits.

Table 1 is used to determined the number of bits assigned to each coefficient of an 8 x 8 block as a function of the quantization level. If the number in Table 1 corresponding to a specific coefficient is n, then the number of bits will remain at 9 until the quantization level becomes less than n, after which the number of bits will begin decrementing. In other words, the number of bits is always the minimum of 9 and $9-n+qlevel$.

Table 1. Table for Determining the Number of Bits to Allocate for Each of 8 x 8 DCT Coefficients

```
2 3 4 5 6 7 8 9
3 4 5 6 7 8 9 9
4 5 6 7 8 9 9 9
5 6 7 8 9 9 9 9
6 7 8 9 9 9 9 9
7 8 9 9 9 9 9 9
8 9 9 9 9 9 9 9
9 9 9 9 9 9 9 9
```

Huffman Coding

Normalization improves the compressibility of an image by reducing the amplitude of the transform coefficients. In order to take advantage of the result, an algorithm for assigning a variable number of bits to these coefficients is required. At this stage, a statistical coding technique is used, which unlike the normalization process, is information preserving, and therefore, does not degrade the image.

Huffman coding is an optimum statistical coding procedure capable of approaching the theoretical entropy limit, given a priori knowledge of the probability of all possible events. The encoder can generate such probability distributions and send them to the decoder prior to the transmission of a given frame. This table is then used to derive Huffman code words where relatively short code words are assigned to events with the highest probability of occurrence. The decoder maintains an identical code book and is able to match each code word with the actual event.

In order to apply Huffman coding for this application, the 8 x 8 DCT coefficients are serialized into a sequence of 64, and "amplitude/runlength" coded. Scanning the sequence of 64, an event is defined to occur each time a coefficient is encountered with an amplitude not equal to zero. A code word is then assigned indicating the amplitude of the coefficient and the number of zeros preceding it (runlength). Table 2 shows the length of each code word in bits. It does not include the sign bit which must be also included with each code word. When the coefficient amplitude is greater than 16 or the number of preceding zeros is more than 15, a special code word is used to tell the decoder not to use the code book to interpret the bits that follow. Instead, the runlength is sent uncoded. The coefficient amplitude is also sent uncoded with the number of bits determined by the normalization process described previously. In addition, it is sometimes more efficient to directly code the amplitude and runlength even if it can be coded through the use of the two-dimensional table. The encoder detects these occasions and will switch to direct coding if necessary to shorten the length of the code word. A special code word is also reserved to indicate the end of a block. It is always inserted after the last non-zero coefficient.

The efficiency of this coding process is heavily dependent on the order in which the coefficients are scanned. By scanning from high amplitude to low amplitude, it is possible to reduce the number of runs of zero coefficients

Table 2. Number of Bits Used for Each code word of Two-Dimensional Huffman code book

RUNLENGTH	AMPLITUDE															
	1	2	3	4	5	6	7	8	9	10	11	12	13	14	15	16
0	2	3	5	5	6	7	8	8	9	9	9	10	10	11	11	11
1	4	5	7	8	9	10	10	11	12	12	13	14	14	15	15	16
2	4	7	8	10	11	12	13	14	15	16	16	16	18	18	19	19
3	5	8	10	11	13	14	15	16	17	18	18	19	19	19	21	21
4	6	9	12	14	15	17	18	18	20	21	20	22	28	29	29	29
5	7	10	13	16	18	19	22	21	21	29	29	29	29	29	29	29
6	7	11	14	17	18	19	19	17	20	21	28	28	28	28	28	28
7	8	12	16	18	19	22	20	28	28	28	28	28	28	28	28	28
8	9	14	17	21	28	28	28	28	28	28	28	28	28	28	28	28
9	9	15	19	28	28	28	28	28	28	28	28	28	28	28	28	28
10	10	16	20	28	28	28	28	28	28	28	28	28	28	28	28	28
11	11	18	28	22	28	28	28	28	28	28	28	28	28	28	28	28
12	11	17	28	22	28	28	28	28	28	28	28	28	28	28	28	28
13	11	17	28	22	28	28	28	28	28	28	28	28	28	28	28	28
14	12	20	28	22	28	28	28	28	28	28	28	28	28	28	28	28
15	13	20	28	22	28	28	28	28	28	28	28	28	28	28	28	28

typically to a single long run at the end of the block. As defined above, any long run at the end of the block would be represented efficiently by the "end of block" code word.

Motion Compensation

There is a limit to the amount of compression possible by spatial processing alone. An interframe coder, however, can benefit from temporal correlation as well as spatial correlation. A very high degree of temporal correlation exists whenever there is little movement from one frame to the next. Even if there is movement, high temporal correlation may still exist depending on the spatial characteristics of the image. If there is little spatial detail, then frame-to-frame correlation remains high even at high velocities. If the image is highly detailed, however, and contains high spatial frequencies, then even slight displacements of one pixel or less can significantly reduce the amount of correlation that exists.

In the DigiCipher™ system, we compress the signal by first predicting how the next frame will appear and then sending the difference between the prediction and the actual image.

A reasonable predictor is simply the previous frame. This sort of temporal differential encoding (DPCM) will perform very well if little movement occurs or if there is little spatial detail. At other times, it will be less effective and occasionally worse than if the next frame had simply been encoded without prediction (PCM).

Motion compensation is a means of improving the performance of any temporal compression scheme when movement occurs. In order to apply motion compensation, it is first necessary to determine what has moved since the previous frame and where it has moved to. If this information is known at the decoder site, then the previous frame can be shifted or displaced in order to obtain a more accurate prediction of the next frame that has yet to be transmitted. The encoder would reproduce the same prediction as the decoder and then determine the difference between the prediction and the actual image. If the movements match the model used to estimate motion and if the motion estimates are accurate and the signal is free of noise, then this error signal would, in fact, be zero.

Displacement of the previous frame can be performed on a frame, partial frame, or pixel basis. That is, a unique displacement (motion vector) could be generated for every frame, part of a frame, or pixel respectively. The usefulness of generating a single motion vector per frame, however, is limited since it can only model simple panning of the entire image. Ideally, a unique motion vector would be generated for each pixel. However, since motion estimation is a complex process and requires knowledge of the next frame, it can only be performed at the encoder, and the overhead involved in making this per-pixel motion information available to the decoder would be excessive. Therefore, the motion estimation is performed on a partial frame basis with the area of the portion chosen to equal a superblock. The superblock has a horizontal dimension equal to 4 DCT blocks and a vertical dimension equal to 2 DCT blocks. This sizing is compatible with the 4 times horizontal subsampling and 2 times vertical subsampling of the chrominance components, thus allowing the same

motion vector to be used to displace a single chrominance DCT block.

The process of displacing portions of the previous frame in order to better predict the next frame is illustrated in Figure 6.

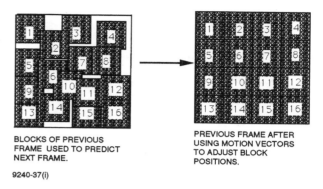

BLOCKS OF PREVIOUS
FRAME USED TO PREDICT
NEXT FRAME.

PREVIOUS FRAME AFTER
USING MOTION VECTORS
TO ADJUST BLOCK
POSITIONS.

9240-37(i)

Figure 6. Using Motion Compensation to Predict Next Frame

Motion Estimation

Before describing the integration of motion compensation with the overall compression process, an explanation of how motion vectors are derived is necessary.

Motion estimation algorithms can be divided into two classes - those which focus primarily on extracting three dimensional motion parameters from a sequence of two dimensional images or projections, and those which estimate velocities on a point-by-point or region-by-region basis without any consideration of how the object(s) is (are) moving as a whole. In the first case, a common formulation of the problem is to assume rigid three-dimensional bodies with movement patterns that can be described by a translation component, a rotation component, a zooming component, and a center about which the rotation or zooming is occurring. It is clear, however, that typical television imagery is far too complex to be satisfactorily characterized by this simple motion description. Therefore, we restrict ourselves to the second class of algorithms. Unlike the first class, these algorithms are unintelligent; they have no understanding of the higher level motion events that are occurring. These algorithms are usually based on translational models. However, if the region over which each estimation is performed is small, then more complex (large area) movements can be modeled satisfactorily. The selected method determines a good match between superblock regions in the current and the previous frames. The overhead required to send a single motion vector to the decoder is 9 bits per superblock (approximately 0.018 bits/pixel).

Motion Picture Processing

Almost all movies developed for the cinema and a significant amount of program material developed for television are initially shot on film. Except for a few special cases, the display rate used for film is 24 frames/second, and therefore the motion rendition is degraded in comparison to normal television video. Eventually, when this program material is converted to the NTSC or HDTV television standard, a process called three-two pulldown is used. As shown in Figure 7, it involves alternating between three repetitions and two repetitions of each frame of the film. Since the three-two pulldown process increases the

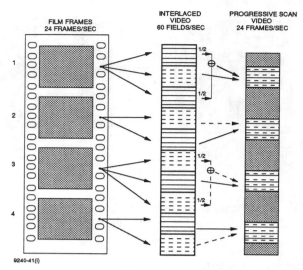

Figure 7. Conversion of Film to Interlaced Video and Restoration of Progressive Scan

number of video frames from 24 to 30 without increasing the amount of information in the signal, the first step in the source coding process is to restore the signal to its original state. Since one of every five fields is redundant, it can either be discarded, or averaged with the other identical field as shown in Figure 7. In the latter case, a 3 dB noise reduction results; however, its significance is questionable, since it will benefit only one of every four fields.

After the 24 frame/second signal is reconstructed at the decoder, it must be converted back to 60 fields/second before it can be displayed. This is easily accomplished by applying the three-two pulldown process once again.

The DigiCipher™ System processes material shot on film in this manner to further improve the performance. Other video source material is, of course, handled without going through this process.

Rate Buffer Control

Each single channel video processing section in the encoder requires a rate buffer in order to match the variable rate of the Huffman-coded data to the fixed output rate necessary for channel transmission. This rate buffer is implemented as a one frame FIFO located after the Huffman encoder. The total storage size is large enough to handle variations of plus and minus one field.

In order to prevent the video output buffer FIFO from overflowing or underflowing, the FIFO input rate must be continuously adjusted. This is the purpose of the multi-quantization level coding structure. As the quantization level is decremented, quantization is increased, blocks are shortened, and an increase in the FIFO input block rate results. As the quantization level is incremented to a maximum level of 9, finer quantization results in longer

blocks, and a reduced FIFO input block rate. This adjustment has the required effect of keeping the bit rate into the FIFO relatively constant. The status of the buffer is continuously monitored, and as long as the number of stored blocks remains within a predetermined window, the quantization level will remain unchanged. If the buffer level drops below the lower threshold or rises above the higher threshold, then the quantization level will decrement or increment respectively. Fill bits are inserted into the channel in order to prevent underflows during the transmission of very simple images.

DIGITAL AUDIO PROCESSING

Digital Audio Encoding

Figure 8 shows the digital audio processing at the encoder. The system uses the emphasis characteristics specified by the EIAJ standard for PCM VTR Adapters ($T_1 = 50$ μsec; $T_2 = 15$ μsec.) Digital audio sample pairs are processed into compressed floating point notation, as used in the VideoCipher™ II Plus system. A 15 to 10 bit instantaneous μ-law compression technique was selected, which produces 1 sign bit, 3 exponent bits, and 6 mantissa bits per audio sample. The sampling rate is 44.056 kHz, which is also common to the VideoCipher™ II Plus system.

Error correction for all DigiCipher™ transmitted bits is performed in a separate decoder block, and is *not* integrated with the audio processing. Detected errors can be used to mute the audio. Furthermore, error concealment is not used since the bit error rate performance curve is very steep.

Overall, audio compression produces a 10 bit coded representation of each audio sample. Given the 44.056 kHz sampling rate, 56 audio bits must be transmitted per line time to support 4 audio channels.

Digital Audio Decoding

Figure 8 shows the digital audio processing at the decoder. Received audio bits are decrypted along with the received video bits. After buffering and μ-law expansion, precision audio reconstruction at the decoder is accomplished with a switched capacitor filter followed by analog deemphasis and a 18 kHz lowpass filter.

DIGITAL DATA TRANSMISSION

Data Channel Processing

The DigiCipher™ transmission format has 4 bits per line time assigned to data channel capacity. This allocation of 125.87 kbps is sufficient capacity for 13 9600 baud data streams. The initial DigiCipher™ design will support 4 such data streams, with the remaining capacity reserved.

Control Channel Processing

The DigiCipher™ transmission format has 4 bits per line time, which amounts to 125.87 kbps. There is great flexibility allowed in message mixing within the control channel on a bit stream.

Data Multiplex Format

This section defines the data multiplex for video, audio,

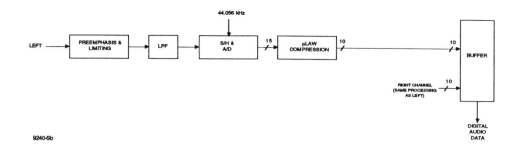

9240-5b

Figure 9. Digital Audio Encoder

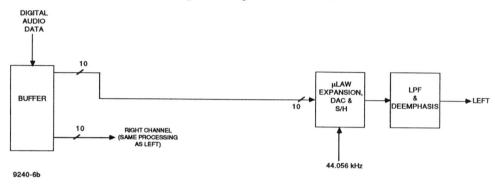

9240-6b

Figure 10. Digital Audio Decoder

data, text, and control channel.

Prior to forward error coding at the encoder, each video line time includes 504 information bits. Figure 10 shows the data transmission format. Each line has a fixed allocation of 4 control channel bits followed by 4 allocated data channel bit positions. The next 56 bits represent audio data. The remainder of the 504 bits are dedicated to video for lines 2 through 1050. Line 1 differs in that the 48 bit positions 457 through 504 represent 3 specific fields, as listed below.

- 457 through 480: The 24-bit **sync pattern** provides frame synchronization for the decoder. All the decoder timing signals are derived from this per-frame sync.

- 481 through 488: The **system control** field contains LSBits of the nominal frame count number as well as other system control information.

- 489 through 504: The **Next Macroblock Position** (NMP) field indicates the number of video multiplex data bits from the end of the NMP field to the beginning of the next macro block. This 15 bit parameter is necessary to support the acquisition process. Additionally, if errors cause a loss of sync within the decoder, the unit can always recover through a reacquisition. Note that there is a 16th bit in the field, reserved for future use.

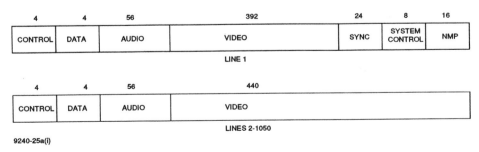

9240-25a(i)

Figure 11. Data Multiplex Format

163

Digital Transmission

Modulation and channel coding are key elements of the DigiCipher™ system. The modulation technique must be efficient in order to send the required number of information bits through a single VHF or UHF channel. The channel coding technique must be powerful in order to maintain a very low error rate; the more compression (source coding), the more serious the effect of a single error.

Figure 11 shows the basic communication system blocks, including coding, modulation, pulse shaping (transmit filtering), receive filtering, demodulation, tracking, and decoding. The modulation selected for digital transmission over the VHF or UHF channel is 16-QAM at 4.86 Msps. The 16-QAM provides two times the data rate with moderate penalty (approximately 5 dB) in power compared to QPSK. Figure 12 shows the BER performance of uncoded 16-QAM. The implementation of the modulator and the demodulator for the 16-QAM is similar to the QPSK design, except that the I channel and the Q channel have 4-level signals present, rather than two-level signals.

Adaptive equalization is employed to handle the reflections (multipath) found typical VHF or UHF reception. Forward error correction using Reed Solomon coding of rate 130/154 (t=12) is used to correct transmission errors caused by noise and/or interference. The system threshold is 19 dB C/N including 2.5 dB of implementation margin. At 19 dB C/N there will be one undetected error event per day. The threshold C/N is much lower than C/N required for satisfactory reception of analog VHF/UHF signals. Proper signal filtering (a 15% roll-off raised cosine, for example) will be provided to prevent adjacent channel interference (See Figure 13).

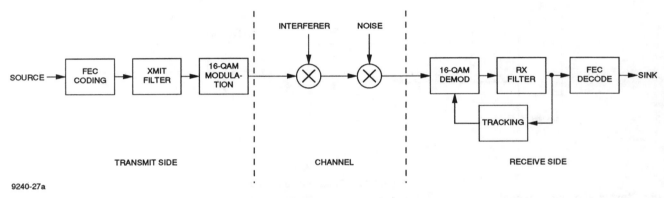

9240-27a

Figure 12. Communication System Blocks

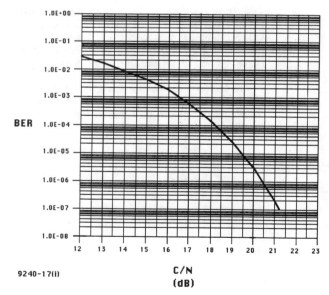

9240-17(I)

Figure 13. BER Performance of 16-QAM

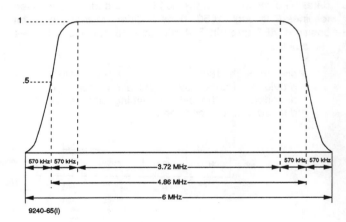

9240-65(I)

Figure 14. IF Output Spectrum

164

SYNCHRONIZATION

Frame Synchronization

Once clock synchronization is achieved, frame synchronization is achieved by using the twenty-four bit sync sequence transmitted every frame (33.4 msec). The sync detection algorithm is similar to the one used in VideoCipher II Plus for detecting its twenty-four bit frame sync sequence. The overall acquisition time of the decoder through to the start of the video decompression process should be less than 100 msec after a channel change.

Digital Video Acquisition and Recovery

When a decoder tunes to a channel, its video data FIFO must be flushed. Once 24 bit frame sync is established, the decoder must monitor the macroblock stream for the FIRST macroblock. Once identified, data can be stored in the FIFO, and subsequent sections of the decoder can be notified as to the early or late status. All decoder processing from the Huffman decoder output side through to the filtered decompressed output video has a static timing alignment to the 24 bit pattern location. This alignment is computed based on nominal FIFO operation (half full), plus all the processing delays and buffering from decoder input to output. Likely alignment values are between 0.7 and 0.9 frames, as measured from the 24 bit pattern received *before* a late FIRST macroblock, or from the 24 bit pattern received *after* an early FIRST macroblock. Although processing can commence based on this static alignment, the video output will remain blanked for a full second more, while the decoder builds up the PCM blocks received during the one second long interval.

Uncorrected error events, although rare, must be recoverable. That is, the decoder may lose the picture momentarily, but not indefinitely. Currently, a decoder can detect an error in two ways. First, the Reed-Solomon decoder outputs a flag that is a robust, but not a guaranteed, error detector. Secondly, the Huffman decoder counts pixel flow, and expects an end-of-block code word for pixel 64 of every block. If this code word is not detected, or is detected early, an error has occurred.

SUMMARY OF DIGICIPHER™ SYSTEM PARAMETERS

Key parameters of the DigiCipher™ HDTV System are listed in Table 3. The sampling frequency has been chosen to optimize the video performance as well as to reduce the hardware complexity of the decoder. The video data includes both luminance and chrominance data as well as various overhead information.

ALTERNATE MEDIA DISTRIBUTION

Cable Transmission

One of the main features of the DigiCipher™ HDTV System is its potential to provide digital transmission starting at the satellite uplink all the way to the cable subscriber. This cable pass-through approach offers the following advantages:

- Subscribers can enjoy HDTV services free from signal degradations caused by the cable.

Table 3. DigiCipher™ System Parameters

Parameters	Value
VIDEO	
Aspect Ratio	16:9
Raster Format	1050/2:1 Interlaced
Frame Rate	29.97 Hz
Bandwidth	
Luminance	22 MHz
Chrominance	5.5 MHz
Horizontal Resolution	
Static	660 Lines per Picture Height
Dynamic	660 Lines per Picture Height
Horizontal Line Time	
Active	26.446 µsec
Blanking	5.332 µsec
Sampling Frequency	51.8 MHz
Active Pixels	
Luminance	960(V) x 1408(H)
Chrominance	480(V) x 352(H)
AUDIO	
Bandwidth	15 kHz
Sampling Frequency	44.05 kHz
Dynamic Range	85 dB
DATA	
Video Data	14.38 Mbps
Audio Data	1.76 Mbps
Async Data and Text	126 Kbps
Control Data	126 Kbps
Total Data Rate	16.40 Mbps
TRANSMISSION	
FEC Rate	130/154
Data Transmission Rate	19.43 Mbps
16-QAM Symbol Rate	4.86 MHz

- Addressing and authorization for cable subscribers can be inserted centrally although local (cable headed) control would still be provided.

- Subscribers can enjoy the quality of digital audio.

Since the DigiCipher™ HDTV System requires substantially lower C/N, it helps reduce intermodulation problems and the power loading of the cable system. Also, extra channels can be placed above usable channels where VSB-AM signals cannot be placed due to low C/N or FCC emission requirements.

Satellite Transmission

The DigiCipher™ HDTV System can be transmitted over C-band or Ku-band satellite channels using QPSK modulation.

The system can support both FSS and BSS satellite transponders. A satellite channel can carry two HDTV signals. The threshold C/N is 8 dB measured over a 24 MHz bandwidth, therefore the DigiCipher™ HDTV System allows the use of smaller dish size compared to other analog or hybrid HDTV systems.

Other Terrestrial Distribution

Since the DigiCipher™ HDTV System is an all-digital system, it can be readily applied to other transmission media such as microwave distribution service (MDS), multi-channel MDS (MMDS) and fiberoptic cables (FO).

An inherent characteristic of the all-digital system is that the HDTV service is free from transmission artifacts caused by various transmission media. Also, the complexity of the interface equipment between various transmission media is substantially lower.

VCR and Video Disc Recorders

All-digital recording and playback of HDTV signals using the signal format of the DigiCipher™ HDTV System is within the reach of current technology for consumer use since the total data rate is less than 20 Mbps. The cost and performance benefits of digital recording will be significant compared to analog recording.

CONCLUSION

The DigiCipher™ HDTV System offers many advantages over analog or hybrid HDTV systems. It can deliver full HDTV performance to consumer's home through terrestrial, cable, or satellite channels. Lower transmitting power requirement of the DigiCipher™ system makes it ideal for simulcast HDTV transmission. All digital transmission enables seamless interface between various transmission

media. Furthermore, all digital VCR or VDP can be easily developed using existing consumer grade mechanism.

References

[1] W. K. Pratt, Digital Image Processing, John Wiley and Sons, Inc., New York, NY, 1978.

[2] D. E. Dudgeon and R. M. Merserau, Multidimensional Digital Signal Processing, Prentice-Hall, Inc., 1984.

[3] S. Ericsson, "Fixed and Adaptive Predictors for Hybrid Predictive/Transform Coding," IEEE Trans., on Comm., Vol. CQM-33, No. 12, December 1985.

[4] W. Chen and W. K. Pratt, "Scene Adaptive Coder," IEEE Trans. on Comm., Vol. Com-32, No. 3, March 1984.

[5] D. Hatfield, "Report on the Potential for Extreme Bandwidth Compression of Digitalized HDTV Signals," Hatfield Associates, Inc., March 20, 1989.

[6] R. C. Reininger and J. D. Gibson, "Distribution of Two-Dimensional DCT Coefficients for Images, "IEEE Trans. on Comm. Vol. iCOM-31, No. 6, June 1983.

[7] A. Fernandez, R. Ansari, D. J. Gall and C. T. Chen, "HDTV Subband/DCT Coding: Analysis of System Complexity," IEEE Globecom Proceedings, 343.1.1 - 343.1.4, 1990.
[8] M. Barbero, R. Del Pero, M. Muratori and M. Stroppiana," Bit-Rate Reduction Techniques Based on DCT for HDTV Transmission," IEEE Globecom Proceedings, 343.2.2 - 343.3.5, 1990.

[9] G. K. Wallace, "Overview of the JPEG (ISO/CCITT) Still Image Compression Standard, "Visual Communications and Image Proceeding '89, SPIE, Philadelphia, November 1989.

DigiCipher™ Video Compression Technology for All Digital, Channel Compatible, HDTV Broadcast System

Woo H. Paik, Edward Krause, and Jerrold Heller

General Instrument Corporation--VideoCipher Division, 6262 Lusk Boulevard, San Diego, CA 92121

Abstract

This paper describes the video compression technology used for the DigiCipher™ HDTV and the Channel-Compatible DigiCipher (CCDC) HDTV Systems. To achieve full HDTV performance in a single 6 MHz bandwidth, a highly efficient, unique compression algorithm based on DCT transform coding is used. The compression algorithm used in the DigiCipher™ system has been optimized for 1050-line interlaced scanning and the compression algorithm used in the CCDC system has been optimized for 787.5-line progressive scanning. The CCDC system has additional refinements in the compression algorithm to compensate for the lower coding rate (0.34 bits/pixel) due to the higher video sampling rate (75.5 MHz).

1. INTRODUCTION

The DigiCipher™ HDTV system is an all digital HDTV system that has been designed to deliver full HDTV performance with virtually no visible transmission impairments in a 6 MHz bandwidth. Due to the bandwidth and interference constraints, the maximum data rate that can be transmitted reliably over a terrestrial channel is limited to 20 Mbps while uncompressed HDTV signals require a data rate exceeding 1 Gbps. The DigiCipher compression algorithm requires minimal hardware complexity and achieves more than a 50:1 compression ratio without introducing any visible degradation. The key features of the DigiCipher compression algorithm are:

- Adaptive Field/Frame Decision (DigiCipher™ system only)
- Full Search Motion Estimation
- Sub-Pixel Accuracy and Variable Block Size Motion Estimation (CCDC system only)
- Adaptive PCM/DPCM Decision
- Progressive Refreshing
- Four-Panel Processability
- Low Processing Delay
- Two-Dimensional Huffman Coding (DigiCipher™ system only)
- Vector Coding of non-zero DCT Coefficients (CCDC system only)
- 24-Frame Film Processing

Key parameters of the DigiCipher™ and CCDC HDTV video compression systems are shown in Table 1.

Table 1. DigiCipher™ and CCDC HDTV System Parameters

Parameters	DigiCipher™	CCDC
Raster Format	1050/2:1 Interlaced	787.5/1:1 Progressive
Aspect Ratio	16:9	16.9
Frame Rate	29.97 Hz	59.94 Hz
Bandwidth		
Luminance	21.5 MHz	34.0 MHz
Chrominance	5.4 MHz	17.0 MHz
Active Pixels		
Luminance	960(V) x 1408(H)	720(V) x 1280(H)
Chrominance	480(V) x 352(H)	360(V) x 640(H)
Sampling Frequency	53.65 MHz	75.5 MHz
Compressed Video Data Rate		
32-QAM	17.47 Mbps	18.88 Mbps
16-QAM	12.59 Mbps	13.60 Mbps
Compression Rate		
32-QAM	0.43 bits/pixel	0.34 bits/pixel
16-QAM	0.31 bits/pixel	0.25 bits/pixel

2. IMPLEMENTATION

A block diagram of the DigiCipher video encoder is shown in Figure 1 and a block diagram of the video decoder is shown in Figure 2. These are described in the following sections.

2.1 Adaptive Field/Frame Processing

The DigiCipher™ system uses a novel method to maintain high compression efficiency when processing interlaced video. It adaptively selects between frame processing and field processing on a block by block basis. Field processing generally works better than frame processing in detailed moving areas. This is because the interleaving of the even and odd fields introduces spurious high vertical frequencies when frame processing mode is selected. This reduces the correlation between lines and therefore the effectiveness of the compression algorithm.

Frame processing works better than field processing when there is little or no motion. Since there are twice as many lines per picture height when frame processing mode is selected, there will be more correlation between samples and hence compressibility will be improved. Therefore, to achieve the same accuracy, field processing will require a higher data rate, or alternatively, for equal data rates, frame processing will achieve greater accuracy.

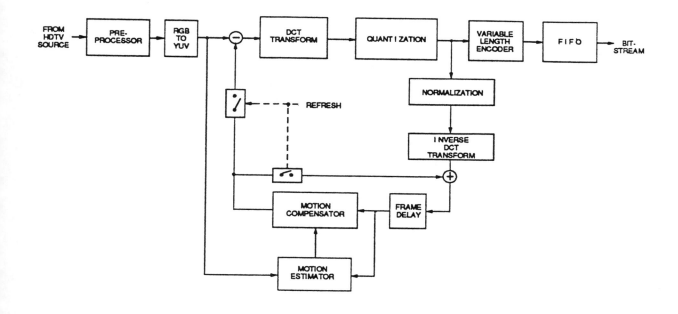

Figure 1. Digital Video Encoder Block Diagram

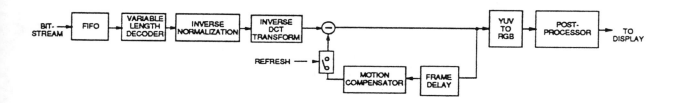

Figure 2. Digital Video Decoder Block Diagram

The selection between frame processing and field processing modes is made by comparing the errors in the quantized DCT coefficients. A total of eight DCT's are required to transform each block of 16x32 pixels, which consists of eight lines from field one and eight lines from field two. The transform is applied in both frame mode and field mode and the absolute quantization errors occurring after coefficient weighting are summed over all eight blocks. The mode which results in the least total error is selected. This technique has been found to be very efficient in its allocation of bandwidth for both high vertical resolution and good motion rendition.

2.2 Motion Estimation and Compensation

To exploit the temporal redundancy in the video signal, the DigiCipher™ and CCDC systems use interframe (DPCM) coding. Motion vectors are determined and used to identify the regions of maximum correlation in the previous frame. A block matching method is used where the selected motion vector (d_x, d_y) is the one which minimizes

$$\sum_{i=1}^{N} \sum_{j=1}^{M} |x(i,j) - y(i+d_y, j+d_x)|$$

where $x(i,j)$ and $y(i,j)$ represent pixel intensities in the current and previous frames respectively, at some location determined by i and j and the displacement vector d_x and d_y. A full search is performed and therefore all possible displacements are evaluated. The summation limits N and M specify the size of the rectangular regions that are being compared. $N = 16$ and $M = 32$ in the interlaced DigiCipher™ system.

In the CCDC system, two different block sizes are compared: 16x16 and 8x8. The smaller block size allows better adaptation for complex, non-translational motion but with increased overhead due to the additional motion vectors that must be transmitted. The CCDC system selects the block size which results in the least number of bits when the block is compressed and the motion vector overhead is included. This bit-counting decision criterion is the most effective method of comparing the trade-off between improved compression efficiency and the overhead required to achieve it. The CCDC system also uses sub-pixel accuracy to further improve the interframe coding efficiency. All horizontal and vertical half-pixel displacements are evaluated using the full search method.

As shown in the encoder and decoder block diagrams in Figures 1 and 2 respectively, motion compensation is easily integrated into the overall system design. Instead of transform coding the image directly, an estimate of the image is first generated using motion compensation. The difference between this estimate and the actual image is then transformed using the DCT and the transform coefficients are quantized and statistically coded. The second of the two frames from which the motion estimates are derived is always the previous frame as it appears after reconstruction by the decoder. The encoder thus must include a model of the decoder processing.

Scene changes or complex motion can reduce the efficiency of interframe coding. Occasionally, intraframe coding (PCM) will provide better efficiency and therefore an adaptive scheme is used to select between the two modes. In order to obtain the lowest possible bit rate, the encoder determines the number of bits required for each of the two methods and then selects the method requiring the fewest bits, on an 8x8 block basis. For most scenes, the motion compensation rate averages between 85% to 100%. During scene changes, however, the motion compensation rate can drop to less than 10%.

2.3 Acquisition and Refreshing

Differential processing in general causes a basic problem for the decoder. When a decoder is tuned to a new channel, it has no "previous frame" information. Acquisition would be delayed until at least 1 PCM version of every block was received, which would result in an unbounded acquisition time.

DigiCipher™ uses a distributed refreshing technique for low processing delay and simplified buffer control. With this method, the mode is periodically switched from adaptive DPCM/PCM to PCM. The image frame is divided into four strips or panels as shown in

Figure 3A. The first vertical strip of each panel is always processed in PCM mode. The width of this vertical strip is 32 pixels in the DigiCipher™ system and 16 pixels in the CCDC system. This corresponds to the width of one superblock.

After processing the entire frame, the four panels are shifted to the left by one superblock (32 pixels for DigiCipher™; 16 pixels for CCDC). Therefore, after several frames, the partition would be as shown in Figure 3B. Upon completion of one refresh cycle, the partition would be as shown in Figure 3C. The refresh cycle completes after 11 frames (11/30 seconds) in the interlaced DigiCipher™ system and 20 frames (20/60 seconds) in the progressive CCDC system.

One reason for partitioning the image frame in this way is that it easily permits the use of independent processors without any loss in compression efficiency. This is important since the high pixel sampling rates will continue to dictate the use of parallel processors in the near future. This four-panel processability contributed to extremely compact prototype systems, despite complex, state of the art compression technology.

The four independent processors used in the DigiCipher™ prototypes each have their own current frame and previous frame memories and each is responsible for updating or refreshing a particular region of the image. The distributed use of PCM coding must be applied carefully, so that subsequent motion compensation by the acquiring decoder relies only on the now guaranteed PCM blocks. This is accomplished by restricting the direction of the motion vectors corresponding to each superblock in the second column of each panel. The previous frame data in this column is assumed to be reliable since its data was recently refreshed by PCM coding during the previous frame. Similarly, the data in the third column can be assumed to be reasonably reliable since its contents was refreshed two frames earlier. The least reliable data, on the other hand, is that contained in the first column of each panel. Although this column will be completely refreshed upon completion of the current frame, the data is not yet available to the motion compensator. The solution, therefore is to limit the horizontal direction of the motion vectors in the second column in order to avoid referencing data in the first column.

In order to maintain complete independence among the different panel processors, it is necessary to insure that the motion estimation process never requires a memory access that exceeds the bounds of the previous frame memory associated with a particular processor. Otherwise, this would greatly complicate the design by requiring a certain amount of memory overlap in each processor or alternatively, a shared memory system with multiple random-access capability.

One method of insuring that the bounds of the previous frame memory are not exceeded is to impose additional restrictions on the motion estimator. However, this would impair coding efficiency and further complicate the design of the encoder. In this case, since each panel shifts to the left after each frame, we find that no additional restrictions are required. For example, consider the first column of superblocks at the left edge of each of the four panels. As shown in Figure 3, this column is always the one that is due to be refreshed. Since refreshing is performed by PCM coding, access to the previous frame memory is not required. Next consider the second column of superblocks in each of the four panels. Since

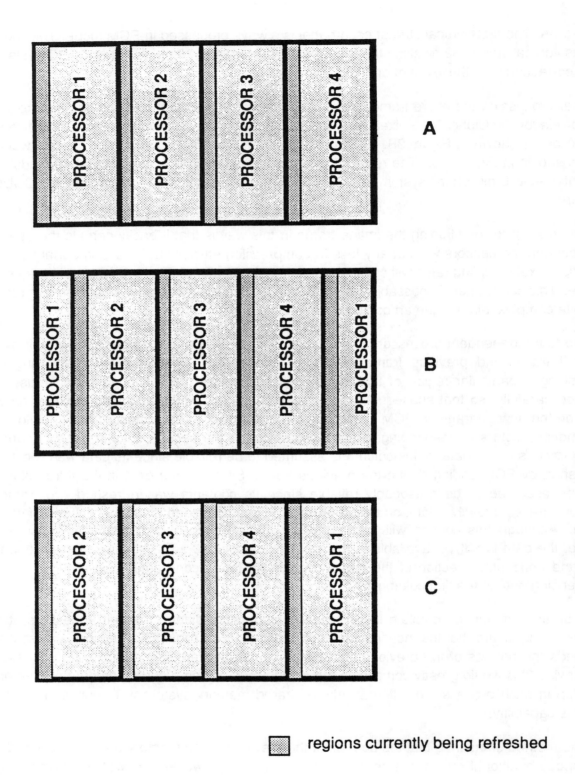

regions currently being refreshed

Figure 3. Partition of Image Frame into Four Panels

the current frame is misaligned one block left of the previous frame, there is insufficient data in the previous frame memory if the movement is from left to right. Fortunately, such motion vectors are avoided as a result of the image refreshing process described previously. If such displacements were permitted, then the column of superblocks refreshed in the previous frame could be quickly corrupted by previous frame data that has not yet been refreshed. Therefore, this restriction is necessary to insure a rapid refresh rate.

Finally, consider the right-most column of superblocks in each of the four panels in Figure 3. A problem might be anticipated when movement is from right to left since this would suggest a match in the portion of previous frame memory that exists only in the adjacent processor. However, since the current frame has been shifted to the left relative to the previous frame, displacements to the left are permitted.

One important advantage of distributed refreshing is that it permits the use of a small channel buffer and simplifies the feedback mechanism for controlling the quantizer precision as a function of buffer fullness. By inserting the forced PCM refresh blocks into the bit stream one at a time and at frequent intervals, large fluctuations in the channel buffer level are avoided. Therefore, since the buffer responds only to variations in video complexity, quantizer adjustments can be made more rapidly and with greater precision.

2.4 Quantization Level Control

Each single channel video processing section in the encoder uses a rate buffer to match the variable rate of the Huffman-coded data to the fixed output rate necessary for transmission. This rate buffer is implemented as a one frame FIFO located after the Huffman encoder. The total storage size is large enough to handle variations of plus and minus one field.

In order to prevent the channel buffer from overflowing or underflowing, the FIFO input rate must be continuously adjusted. This is the purpose of the multi-quantization level coding structure. As the quantization level is increased to a maximum level of 31, quantization is increased, blocks are shortened, and an increase in the block rate out of the encoder's FIFO results. As the quantization level is decremented to a minimum level of 0, finer quantization results in longer blocks, and a reduced FIFO output block rate. This adjustment has the required effect of keeping the bit rate into the FIFO relatively constant.

The quantization level is checked and, if necessary, adjusted after sending one row of superblocks from each video channel. Since all processors are synchronized and since compressed data blocks are removed from the individual buffers and multiplexed for transmission one at a time, it follows that each channel buffer will contain the same number of compressed data blocks. Since the quantization level responds to the number of blocks in the channel buffers and since the same quantization level is broadcast to all four processors, the dynamic allocation of channel bandwidth among the four processing units, occurs automatically and in an optimal manner.

In some cases, the quantization level will be varied locally and independently within each processor. This adjustment to the established quantization level is made on the basis of local scene complexity. Local scene complexity is measured by pre-analyzing each superblock of the image to determine the amount of data that will result if the block is compressed using the established quantization level. The result is compared with a set of three pre-determined thresholds to obtain a complexity measure ranging from 0 to 3. Most image blocks are classified into level 0, meaning that no adjustment is required. Otherwise one of three pre-determined adjustment factors associated with levels 1 to 3, is applied to the current quantization level. The block is again compressed, this time with the new quantization level, and the resulting data is used for transmission. The quantization level change is temporary and does not affect the next region to be processed.

The idea behind weighting based on scene complexity is that the human eye is less sensitive to artifacts in detailed, randomly organized regions of most images. This phenomenon is often referred to as spatial masking.

In order to uniformly distribute visible errors, the quantizer precision is also varied as a function of inter/intra decisions. The CCDC system can also use different quantizers for luminance and chrominance data.

2.5 Statistical Coding

The DigiCipher™ system uses optimized two-dimensional Huffman coding for lossless compression of the quantized DCT coefficients. The coefficients are first serialized using a zig-zag scan. A single Huffman codeword specifies not only the amplitude of the next non-zero coefficient in the scan, but also the number of preceding coefficients which are zero.

The CCDC system uses lossless vector coding to specify the location of non-zero coefficients. This is done by first partitioning the block of coefficients into four sections as shown in Figure 4. A single huffman codeword is used to represent the coefficient selection pattern within each of the block sections. A maximum of four codewords are transmitted in sequence, beginning with the codeword corresponding to the section with the lowest frequency coefficients, and ending with the codeword corresponding to the section with the highest frequency coefficients. A codeword is not transmitted if all of the coefficients in the current and following sections are zero.

Huffman codewords are also sent to convey the amplitude of each non-zero coefficient identified by the vector coding process. Codewords depend not only on the amplitude, but also on the coefficient frequency, the inter/intra decision, and whether the data is luminance or chrominance.

2.6 Motion Picture Processing

Almost all movies developed for the cinema and a significant amount of program material developed for television are initially acquired on film. Except for a few special cases, the display rate used for film is 24 frames/second, and therefore the motion rendition is significantly degraded in comparison to normal television video. Eventually, when this program material is converted to the NTSC or HDTV television standard, a process called

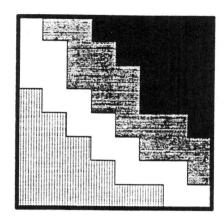

Figure 4. Block Partitions for Vector Coding

three-two pulldown is used. Since the three-two pulldown process increases the number of video frames from 24 to 30 without increasing the amount of information in the signal, the first step in the source coding process is to restore the signal to its original state. Since one of every five fields is redundant, it can either be discarded, or averaged with the other identical field. After the 24 frame/second signal is reconstructed at the decoder, it must be converted back to 60 fields/second before it can be displayed. This is easily accomplished by applying the three-two pulldown process once again.

The DigiCipher™ and CCDC Systems process film material in this manner in order to further improve performance. Other video source material is, of course, handled without going through this process.

3. CONCLUSION

Prototypes of the DigiCipher™ and CCDC HDTV video compression systems have been built and successfully tested by the ATTC. Both systems provide excellent picture quality and proved to be acceptable as the new U.S. HDTV standard.

4. REFERENCES

1. J. S. Lim, Two-Dimensional Signal and Image Processing, Prentice Hall, Englewood Cliffs, NJ, 1990.

2. S. Ericson, "Fixed and Adaptive Predictors for Hybrid Predictive/Transform Coding," IEEE Trans., on Comm., Vol. Com-33, No. 12, December 1985.

3. W. Chen and W. K. Pratt, "Scene Adaptive Coder," IEEE Trans. on Comm., Vol. Com-32, No. 3, March 1984.

4. W. Paik, "DigiCipher™ - All Digital, Channel Compatible, HDTV Broadcast System," IEEE Trans. on Broadcasting, Vol. 36, No. 4, December 1990.

A High Performance, Robust HDTV Transmission System--DigiCipher[TM]

Woo H. Paik, Scott A. Lery, and John M. Fox[a]

[a]General Instrument Corporation--VideoCipher Division, 6262 Lusk Boulevard, San Diego, CA 92121

Abstract

The DigiCipher[TM] HDTV transmission system is an all-digital system developed by the General Instrument Corporation--San Diego, CA, employing the latest in state of the art technology. The system is well suited for broadcast television, as well as cable and satellite transmission, providing full HDTV performance within a 6 MHz bandwidth with virtually no visible transmission impairments due to noise, multipath, and interference. Furthermore, high picture quality is achieved at low transmitter power and system complexity.

Spectrum efficiency and a low noise threshold are achieved by using a concatenated coding scheme, consisting of a Reed-Solomon code and trellis coded QAM modulation. A powerful adaptive equalizer combats multipath interference and other channel distortions. Robustness against burst noise and interference is made possible with multilayer interleaving. Fast and reliable acquisition and synchronization occur in the presence of noise and interference.

1 Introduction

The DigiCipher[TM] HDTV transmission is designed to deliver a high rate digital stream with high reliability, even under severe channel conditions. This result is achieved by using the most modern modulation and coding techniques available, two layers of interleaving, and fast adaptive equalization.

Reprinted with permission from *Proc. International Workshop on HDTV '92,*
pp. 25.1–25.8, Nov. 1992. © Elsevier Science Publishers.

The basic HDTV transmission system requirements are:

- Data Rate: 20 Mbps.

- Bandwidth Occupancy: 6 MHz NTSC channel.

- Data Reliability: one error event per minute.

- Channel Conditions: thermal noise, multipath, burst interference, NTSC interference, and other channel distortions.

- Receiver Complexity: low cost in volume production.

The data rate requirement arises from the need to provide a high quality compressed television picture. The bandwidth constraint is a consequence of the U. S. FCC requirement that HDTV signals occupy existing television channels; they must coexist with the current broadcast NTSC signals. This combination of data rate and bandwidth occupancy requires a modulation system that has high bandwidth efficiency, which is why QAM was chosen.

The need for very high data reliability follows from the fact that highly compressed source material (i.e., the compressed video) is intolerant of channel errors; the natural redundancy of the signal has been removed in order to obtain a concise description of the intrinsic value of the data. Low error rate requirements are met in practice via the use of a concatenated coding approach (divide and conquer approach). The standard concatenated coding approach is to use a convolutional or trellis code [9], [10], [11] for the inner code with some form of the Viterbi algorithm [2] for the trellis decoder, and a block code for the outer code [1], [5]. The optimization of the trellis modulation code for concatenated and non-concatenated coding systems can lead to different solutions. It is our contention that simple extensions of modulation codes developed for QPSK to QAM modulation provide the correct solution to the concatenated coding problem. This leads directly to an implementable structure that is both efficient in bandwidth and data reliability.

Since in a broadcast environment the channel conditions are unknown to the receiver, an adaptive equalizer is required. The DigiCipher[TM] system employs an equalizer structure that is both fast and effective at handling single/multiple reflections, time varying multipath (e.g., airplane flutter), as well as other channel distortions such as non-ideal frequency response and group delay.

The carrier recovery scheme is decoupled from the equalization scheme such that both initial equalization and carrier recovery occur together, thus decreasing initial acquisition time. In addition, the symbol timing recovery is independent of the equalization/carrier recovery, and is robust in the face of channel impairments.

To combat the effects of burst noise/interference, two layers of interleaving are provided. The first level is used to protect against short impulsive noise, while the second level protects against burst errors generated by the trellis decoder. Pseudo random scrambling is employed to assure random signal transmission to eliminate troublesome data patterns. Fast synchronization of the decoders, deinterleavers, and descrambler is achieved by utilizing the trellis (Viterbi) decoder and unique synchronization words.

2 Implementation

The DigiCipher™ transmission system has been efficiently implemented, without sacrificing performance. The transmitter, shown in Figure 1, takes compressed video and audio data and scrambles it. The scrambling randomizes the data to remove undesirable patterns. Then the data is Reed Solomon (RS) encoded, block interleaved, and trellis encoded, producing 32-QAM symbols. These symbols are interleaved again, using a "channel interleaver" implemented as a random convolutional interleaver. The interleaved symbols are filtered with a square-root-raised-cosine FIR filter, converted to analog and quadrature modulated to an IF of 44 MHz. Finally, the tuner translates the IF signal to VHF/UHF.

The receiver, shown in Figure 2, takes the VHF/UHF signal and translates it to IF, where it is quadrature demodulated and sampled at four times the baud rate (4.88 MHz). The samples are filtered by a square-root-raised-cosine FIR filter and presented to the adaptive equalizer, which produces equalized symbols at the baud rate. These symbols are deinterleaved by the random convolutional deinterleaver ("channel deinterleaver") and presented to the trellis decoder. The trellis decoded symbols are formatted into RS code words, block deinterleaved, and RS decoded. Finally, the data from the RS decoder is descrambled, resulting in compressed video and audio data.

Further details of the transmitter and receiver are presented in the following sections.

2.1 Equalization

The adaptive equalizer is designed for rapid convergence under various channel conditions such as multipath and NTSC interference. The equalizer is a complex transversal filter, with coefficients spaced at one half the baud period. A quantized version of the LMS algorithm is used to update the coefficients. As shown in Figure 3, 2 bits of data and 2 bits of error are used to update the 10-bit coefficients. A blind equalization scheme called the Constant Modulus Algorithm (CMA) [3] is first used to initialize the coefficients; once initialized, a Decision Directed (DD) approach is used to complete the equalizer convergence. Since the CMA is insensitive to carrier phase, initial coefficient adjustment can occur in the absence of carrier recovery. By utilizing parallel processing elements, the equalizer not only converges faster, but

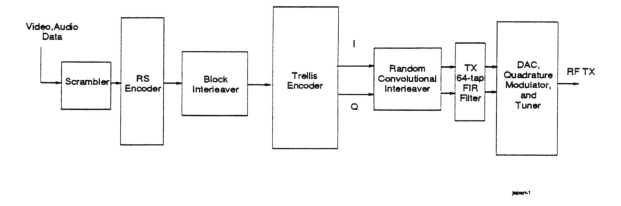

Figure 1. DigiCipher^{TM} Transmitter

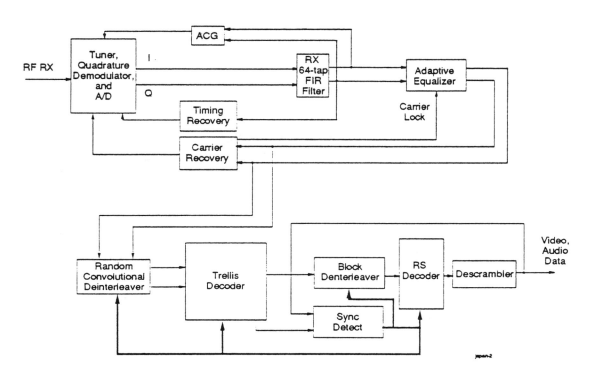

Figure 2. DigiCipher^{TM} Receiver

also its structure lends itself to a VLSI implementation. Also, spacing the equalizer taps at half the baud period speeds up convergence, while making the equalizer less sensitive to timing offsets.

179

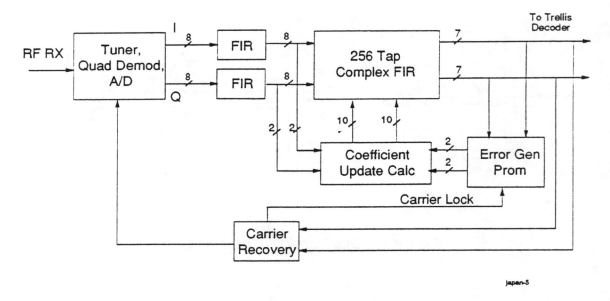

Figure 3. Adaptive Equalizer

2.2 Modulation/Demodulation and Coding/Decoding

To support the data rate and reliability requirements, a concatenated code was developed consisting of a RS outer code and a novel 32-QAM trellis coded modulation (TCM). This TCM outperforms conventional TCM codes found by Ungerboeck [11] at "low" signal-to-noise ratios (SNR), thus making them ideally suited for use as inner codes in concatenated coding schemes. (The inner code just needs to be good enough to bring the symbol error rate down to where the outer code is most effective; i.e., beyond the knee of the error rate vs SNR curve.) The TCM uses the industry defacto standard rate 1/2, 64-state convolutional code, with octal generators G1=171 and G2=133 [6].

The trellis encoder is shown in Figure 4. Eight bit data bytes are split into 4 bit nibbles. The least significant bit of the nibble is convolutionally encoded and the resulting 2 encoded bits, called the "coded bits", select 1 of 4 constellation (32-QAM) subsets; the remaining 3 bits of the nibble, called the "uncoded bits", select 1 of 8 constellation points with the subset. The 32-QAM mapping has the property that the uncoded bits are 90 degrees rotationally invariant. The coded bits are 180 degrees complimentary, and they are made 180 degrees rotationally invariant using differential coding and a transparent convolutional code [7].

The trellis decoder is depicted in Figure 5. The pruner PROM outputs two types of data: four branch Metrics for the Viterbi decoder and four 3-bit conditional hard decisions on the "uncoded" bits. The four Metrics correspond to the Euclidean distances (quantized to 4 bits) from the received signal point to the closet point in each of the four subsets, and the four 3-bit hard decisions are the bits associated with each aforementioned point. A decision on the "uncoded" bits is delayed until the

Viterbi Decoder in conjunction with a "re-encoder" (consisting of a differential encoder and another convolution encoder) makes a decision as to which subset (2 "coded" bits) was transmitted. The resulting 4-bit decisions are formatted into 8-bit bytes for processing by the block deinterleaver and RS decoder.

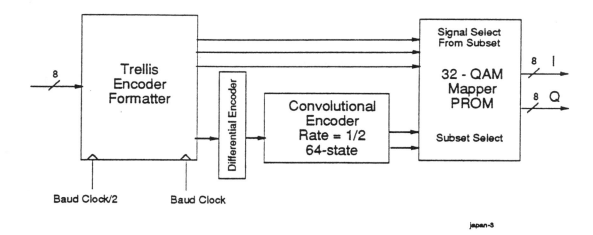

Figure 4. Trellis Encoder

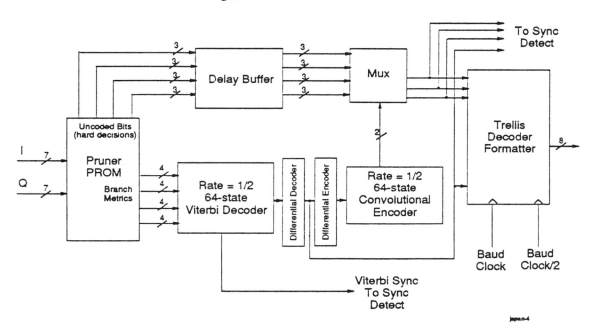

Figure 5. Trellis Decoder

2.3 Interleaving/Deinterleaving

Two interleavers are used. The first one, used to time-spread short impulsive interference, is randomly addressed to prevent periodic interference from defeating the interleaver. It interleaves/randomizes the QAM symbols over the channel, thus, it is referred to as the channel interleaver. The second interleaver spreads the errors

181

caused by the trellis decoder over several Reed-Solomon code words, thus, in effect, increasing the burst error correcting capability of the code [8].

2.4 Synchronization

2.4.1 Carrier Recovery

A novel approach is used to recover the carrier. Usually, carrier recovery is performed after adaptive equalization, which requires not only a phase rotator after

the adaptive equalizer, but also a phase de-rotator to rotate the error signal at the input to the equalizer's coefficient update section. In the DigiCipher^{TM} system, the adaptive equalizer is located inside the carrier recovery loop, as show in Figure 3, which eliminates the two rotators (digital) and only requires one quadrature (analog) mixer. In addition, the second order carrier recovery loop contains a simple, yet very effective phase detector, which does not exhibit the false lock associated with other types of phase detectors [4].

Initial carrier recovery works in conjunction with equalizer convergence. During initial equalizer convergence (CMA), the carrier recovery loop pulls in the carrier phase. When the carrier phase is within a certain region, indicating the signal eye is open, a lock indicator is asserted, which signals the equalizer to switch from CMA to DD mode. This turns out to be a very simple and reliable way of switching the adaptive equalizer's coefficient update procedure.

2.4.2 Symbol Timing

A simple transition detector, operating on the in-phase part of the signal, is used in a second order phase locked loop to control the sampling of the QAM waveform.

2.4.3 Decoders, Deinterleavers, and Descrambler

Fast synchronization of the decoders and deinterleavers is made possible by utilizing the Viterbi decoder's (VD) path metric renormalization rate. Synchronization is basically a three step process. First the VD is used to synchronize the channel deinterleaver. Next a unique word is used to synchronize the other deinterleaver. Finally, another unique word is used to synchronize the RS decoder and descrambler.

3 Laboratory and Field Testing

The DigiCipher^{TM} system was the first all-digital HDTV system to be successfully tested at the Advanced Television Test Center (ATTC). As recently released test results indicate, the system performed very well in all areas. Recently, General Instrument has undertaken field testing of the system in the Los Angeles area. The purpose of the testing was to verify the performance of the system in a real world environment, and to help anticipate how the system would perform in the FCC field testing in Charlotte, North Carolina. The results indicate that reliable reception can be achieved at distances as far as 42 miles from the transmitter, with only 137 watts of average power in the presence of strong cochannel and adjacent channel interference.

References

1. George C. Clark and J. Bibb Cain. *Error-Correction Coding for Digital Communications.* Plenum Press, 1981.

2. G. D. Forney, Jr. "The Viterbi Algorithm". *Proceedings of the IEEE 61* (March 1973).

3. Godard D. "Self-Recovering Equalization and Carrier Tracking in Two-Dimensional Data Communication Systems". *IEEE Transactions on Communications COM-28*, 11 (November 1980), 1867-1875.

4. Leclert A., Vandamme P. "Universal Carrier Recovery Loop for QASK and PSK Signal Sets". *IEEE Transactions on Communications COM-31*, 1 (January 1983), 130-136.

5. Shu Lin and Daniel J. Costello. *Error Control Coding: Fundamentals and Applications.* Prentice-Hall, 1983.

6. J. P. Odenwalder. *Optimal Decoding of Convolutinal Codes.* Ph.D. Th., Dept. of Elec. Eng., Univ. of Calif. at Los Angles, January 1970.

7. Odenwalder, Joseph P. Error Control Coding Handbook. Linkabit Corporation, July, 1976.

8. Sklar, Bernard. *Digital Communications Fundamentals and Applications.* Prentice Hall, 1988.

9. G. Ungerboeck. "Channel Coding with Multilevel/Phase Signals". *IEEE Transactions on Information Theory IT-28* (January 1982), 55-67.

10. G. Ungerboeck. "Trellis-Coded Modulation with Redundant Signal Sets--Part I: Introduction". *IEEE Transactions on Communications Magzine 25* (February 1987), 5-11.

11. G. Ungerboeck. "Trellis-Coded Modulation with Redundant Signal Sets--Part II: State of the Art". *IEEE Transactions on Communications Magzine 25* (February 1987), 12-21.

Practical Coding for QAM Transmission of HDTV

Chris Heegard, *Member, IEEE,* Scott A. Lery, *Member, IEEE,* and Woo H. Paik, *Member, IEEE*

Abstract—This paper describes a practical approach to digital transmission of compressed HDTV. We demonstrate how modulation schemes based on QPSK modulation can be directly incorporated into QAM-based modulation systems. We shall argue that this leads directly to an easily implementable structure that is both efficient in bandwidth and data reliability.

The use of a concatenated code is known to provide an effective and practical approach to achieving low BER, high data rate, and modest implementation complexity. It is our contention that the correct solution to the concatenated coding problem for HDTV transmission is to simply extend the modulation codes developed for QPSK - to - QAM modulation.

In nonconcatenated situations, a trellis code based on a binary code at rate 2/3 is usually best; this fact follows from the study of the asymptotic coding gain of a trellis code. However, this is not the case for higher error rates at the output of the trellis decoder (e.g., when a symbol error correcting decoder follows as in a concatenated code). The reason for this follows from an analysis of the effect of the number of "nearest neighbors" on the error rate.

A four-way partition of QAM is a natural extension of QPSK modulation; it is a simple matter to incorporate any good QPSK code into a trellis coding scheme for QAM modulation. We propose a concatenated coding scheme based on QPSK trellis codes and symbol error correcting coding. A specific example is presented which shows the advantages of this approach.

I. INTRODUCTION

THIS paper describes a practical approach to the digital transmission of compressed high definition television (HDTV). The transmission system for this application has the following requirements.

- Data rate: 15–30 Mb/s
- Bandwidth occupancy: 6 MHz
- Data reliability: one error event per minute
- Receiver complexity: low cost in volume production

The data rate requirement arises from the need to provide a high-quality compressed television picture. The bandwidth constraint is a consequence of the U.S. Federal Communications Commission (FCC) requirement that HDTV signals occupy existing television channels; they must coexist with the current broadcast National Television System Committee (NTSC) signals. This combination of data rate and bandwidth occupancy requires a modulation system that has high bandwidth efficiency; the number of transmitted bits per second per unit of bandwidth (i.e., the ratio of data rate to bandwidth) must be on the order of 3 to 5. This means that modulation systems such as quadrature phase shift keying (QPSK), a

common scheme for satellite transmission systems (which are usually "power limited"), is unsuitable because its bandwidth efficiency without coding is 2. A more bandwidth-efficient modulation (for "bandlimited" transmission-like terrestrial and cable video systems), most notably quadrature amplitude modulation (QAM), is required.

On the other hand, since QPSK systems are so well established, coded modulation schemes for such systems are well understood and routinely implemented. Typically, a binary convolutional code at rate 1/2 (or the same code "punctured" to some higher rate [11], [12]) is incorporated as the modulation code. As a consequence, integrated circuits that realize trellis-coded QPSK modulation are readily available and easily obtained. In this paper, we demonstrate how modulation schemes based on QPSK modulation can be directly incorporated in QAM-based modulation systems. We shall argue that this leads directly to an implementable structure that is both efficient in bandwidth and data reliability.

The need for very high data reliability follows from the fact that highly compressed source material (i.e., compressed video) is intolerant of channel errors; the natural redundancy of the signal has been removed in order to obtain a concise description of the intrinsic value of the source data.

Low error rate requirements are met in practice via the use of a concatenated coding approach (divide and conquer), as depicted in Fig. 1. In such a coding framework, two codes are employed: an "inner" modulation code and an "outer" symbol error-correcting code. The inner code is usually a "coded modulation" that can be effectively decoded using "soft decisions" (i.e., finely quantized channel data). The inner code "cleans up" the channel and exploits the soft decision nature of the received signal. The output of the inner code delivers a small (but unacceptably high) symbol error rate to the outer decoder. This second decoder then removes the vast majority of symbol errors that have eluded the inner decoder in such a way that the final output error rate is extremely small.

The standard concatenated coding approach is to use a convolutional or trellis code [1], [2], [4], [7]–[9] as the inner code with some form of the Viterbi algorithm [3] as the trellis decoder. The outer code is most often a "t error correcting" Reed–Solomon code [2], [4] over a finite field with 2^q symbols (q is usually on the order of 5–10). Such Reed–Solomon coding systems, that operate in the required data rate range, are widely available and have been implemented in the integrated circuits of several vendors.

The optimization of the modulation code for concatenated and nonconcatenated coding systems can lead to different solutions. In a concatenated coding system, one needs to consider the required error rate of the modulation (inner)

Manuscript received June 1992; revised August 1992.

C. Heegard is with the School of Electrical Engineering, Cornell University, Ithaca, NY.

S. Lery and W. H. Paik are with the VideoCipher Division, General Instrument Corporation, San Diego, CA 92121.

IEEE Log Number 9204409.

Reprinted from *IEEE J. Selected Areas Commun.,* vol. 11, no. 1, pp. 111–118, Jan. 1993.

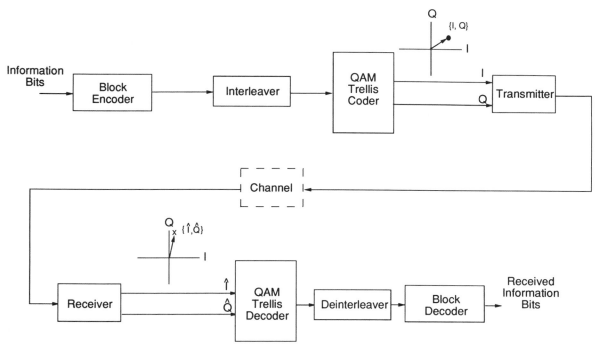

Fig. 1. QAM transmission system using concatenated coding.

code to achieve a specified bit or block (codeword) error rate from the outer code. In a nonconcatenated coding system, the required error rate of the modulation code is usually much lower than in a concatenated coding system. For example, modulation code A may perform better at "low" signal-to-noise ratio (SNR) where the error rate is "large" than modulation code B, which performs better at "high" SNR where the error rate is "small." Code A may be the better choice for a concatenated coding system, and code B may be the better choice for a nonconcatenated coding system.

In light of this, it is our contention that simple extensions of modulation codes developed for QPSK-to-QAM modulation provide the correct solution to the concatenated coding problem. This is true even though these extensions are known to be weaker than other known modulation codes used in nonconcatenated systems (i.e., when used in the domain where the output error rate of the modulation code is "small").

The organization of this paper is as follows. In Section II, a brief description of trellis/modulation coding is given. In Section III, the optimization of coding gain for trellis codes used in concatenated and nonconcatenated systems is discussed. In Section IV, QPSK-based trellis codes are described in detail, along with a trellis decoder implementation. In Section V, performance comparisons between QPSK-based trellis codes and Ungerboeck codes are shown with and without outer coding. A short summary in Section VI concludes the paper.

II. TRELLIS/ MODULATION CODING

In uncoded QAM transmission, n bits per symbol are transmitted by mapping n data bits onto the 2^N points of a QAM constellation. Thus, in the uncoded case, the number of data bits is equal to the number of input bits of the QAM modulator $N = n$. In a trellis code [1], [7]–[9], the constellation is expanded by one bit (i.e., the constellation size is doubled), and the number of data bits per symbol is one less than the number of input bits of the QAM modulator $N = n + 1$. This expansion of the signal constellation is what allows for a coding gain to be achieved (i.e., it allows for redundancy to be introduced in the transmitted signal).[1]

A two-dimensional trellis code for the transmission of n bits per QAM symbol is obtained by the combination of an n-bit input, an $n + 1$ bit output, a 2^ν-state finite state machine (FSM) (i.e., encoder), and an $N = n + 1$ bit QAM mapper (i.e., a 2^N point QAM mapper/modulator), as depicted in Fig. 2. As discovered by Ungerboeck [7], the most economical approach to this problem involves two components. The signal constellation is partitioned into 2^{N-m} subsets, each of size 2^m, in such a way that the distance between points within each subset is maximized.[2] The n input bits are split into k "coded" bits and $m = n - k$ "uncoded" bits. The k-bit coded data is then encoded by a FSM with $k + 1$ output bits (i.e., redundancy in time is introduced) and used to select the subset, while the m-bit uncoded data is used to select the point within the subset selected by the FSM. One way of labeling the QAM constellation points, corresponding to a mapping of the $n + 1$ bits to a QAM constellation point, is described in [7]–[9].

[1] In the "pragmatic" approach described in [10], QAM modulation is obtained from the one-dimensional PAM model. This approach leads to a quadrupling of the QAM signal constellation $N = n + 2$. In many applications, this extra expansion is undesirable.

[2] Caulderbank and Sloane [1] have shown that Ungerboeck's method of set partitioning is best described in terms of lattices and their cosets.

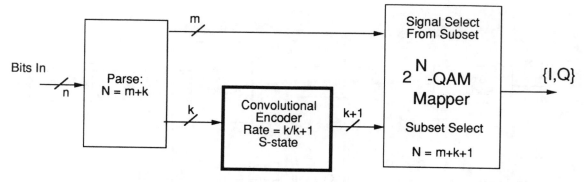

Fig. 2. Trellis encoder.

III. CODING GAIN

A. Asymptotic Coding Gain

In nonconcatenated situations, a trellis code based on a binary code at rate 2/3 (not a punctured rate 1/2 code) is usually the best solution.[3] This fact follows from the study of the asymptotic coding gain (ACG) of a trellis code.

The ACG, γ, of a QAM-based trellis code is given by [8]

$$\gamma = \frac{d_{\text{free}}^2(\text{coded})/Ec(\text{coded})}{\Delta_o^2/Ec(\text{uncoded})} \tag{1}$$

where $Ec(\text{coded})$ and $Ec(\text{uncoded})$ denote the average constellation energies of the coded and uncoded schemes, respectively, and Δ_o is the minimum spacing of the QAM constellation points. The free Euclidean distance of the trellis code is given by [8]

$$d_{\text{free}}^2(\text{coded}) = \Delta_o^2 \min\left\{d_{\text{free}}^2[\text{FSM}(k,\nu)], 2^{k+1}\right\} \tag{2}$$

where the Euclidean distance of the FSM (i.e., the convolutional encoder) is $d_{\text{free}}^2[\text{FSM}(k,\nu)]$. The free distance of the FSM depends on the structure of the encoder.

For a given number of encoder states parameterized by ν and the number of inputs given by k, the encoders that maximize the FSM free distance have been tabulated for small values of ν [1], [8]. The results show why $k = 2$ (i.e., an encoder FSM at rate 2/3) is the most practical for maximizing the ACG. For a given value of k and small ν, the ACG is determined by the FSM

$$\gamma = \frac{Ec(\text{uncoded})}{Ec(\text{coded})} d_{\text{free}}^2[\text{FSM}(k,\nu)]. \tag{3}$$

However, because the ACG involves a minimum as the complexity of the encoder (as measured by ν) is allowed to grow, it becomes

$$\gamma = \frac{Ec(\text{uncoded})}{Ec(\text{coded})} 2^{k+1}. \tag{4}$$

Thus, for a given value of k, there is a natural value of trellis complexity $\nu^*(k)$ such that the ACG is not improved by making $\nu > \nu^*(k)$. We note that $\nu^*(k)$ is monotonically increasing in k, since the rate of the encoder $k/(k + 1)$

<hr>

[3] This assumes a two-dimensional trellis code [8].

increases with increasing k. Now from [9] it is seen that, for QAM trellis coding, $\nu^*(1) = 2$ and $\nu^*(2) = 7$. Thus, for a four-way partition ($k = 1$, rate 1/2 encoding), the maximum ACG (equal to 3.01 dB) is achieved with four states while, for an eight-way partition ($k = 2$, rate 2/3 encoding), the maximum ACG (equal to 6.02 dB) is achieved with 128 states. Note that since the complexity of the decoder (with Viterbi decoding [2], [4], [7]) depends on the number of states of the encoder, a 16-way partition ($k = 3$, rate 3/4 encoding) may not be practical since the number of states required to achieve a large ACG might be prohibitive.

B. Optimization of Coding Gain

The conclusion from the above discussion is that if the ACG is to be maximized, then the obvious practical choice for trellis coding is an eight-way partition of the QAM constellation with a rate 2/3 encoder. Furthermore, in nonconcatenated systems, where the output error rate of the trellis code is to be small, maximizing the ACG is the appropriate thing to do. However, this is not the case for higher error rates at the output of the trellis decoder (e.g., when a symbol error correcting decoder follows). The reason for this follows from an analysis of the effect on the error rate of the number of "nearest neighbors."

The probability of error, P_{sym}, at the output of the trellis decoder can be predicted by the behavior of the formula [6], [8]

$$P_{\text{sym}} \approx M_{nn}Q\left[\frac{d_{\text{free}}(\text{coded})}{\sqrt{2N_o}}\right] \tag{5}$$

or, using (1) and (2),

$$P_{\text{sym}} \approx M_{nn}Q\left[\Delta_o \frac{\sqrt{\gamma\rho}}{\sqrt{2Ec(\text{uncoded})}}\right] \tag{6}$$

where the Q-function is

$$Q(x) = \frac{1}{\sqrt{2\pi}} \int_x^\infty \exp\left(-y^2/2\right) dy.$$

M_{nn} is the average number of nearest neighbors, N_o is the one-sided spectral density of the additive Gaussian noise, and ρ is the signal-to-noise ratio (i.e., the energy per transmitted symbol divided N_o).

For "high" signal-to-noise ratio ρ, the error probability is more seriously effected by the ACG, γ, than the number of nearest neighbors M_{nn}. However, in the domain of "low" ρ, this is simply not the case; the number of the nearest neighbors has a significant effect. Thus, a code with a smaller ACG and smaller M_{nn} may be more reliable than a code optimized for the ACG.

For example, for the rate 2/3 32-QAM Ungerboeck code with 16 states, the ACG is 4.77 dB [9]. However, the number of nearest neighbors is estimated to be 56 [9]. On the other hand, if a strong QPSK-based code modulation code is used with a four-way partition of 32-QAM, the ACG is only 3.01 dB yet the number of nearest neighbors is 2.5. (The free distance of this code is determined by the "uncoded" bits. A four-way partition of 32-QAM yields four subsets, each with eight points. Among these eight points, five have two nearest neighbors, two have three nearest neighbors, and one has four nearest neighbors. So the average number of nearest neighbors is 2.5.) For low signal-to-noise ratios, the latter code has a smaller probability of error.

It is this simple realization that leads to the conclusion that, in fact, a four-way partition with $\nu \gg \nu^*(1) = 2$ is a very efficient method of trellis coding in a concatenated coding system. Furthermore, a four-way partition of QAM is a natural extension of QPSK modulation. It is a simple matter to incorporate any good QPSK code into a trellis coding scheme for QAM modulation.

IV. PRACTICAL QPSK-BASED TRELLIS CODE

Two issues showing how a QPSK code is incorporated into a QAM modulation system are detailed. The first addresses transmission (encoding): how the "codewords" of the QPSK code and the "uncoded" bits are assigned to the QAM constellation. The method described has the following desirable features: 1) it addresses the 90° phase ambiguity of QAM; and 2) the most significant digits control the constellation size. The second issue involves the decoder: how the received signal is prepared for decoding by the soft-decision QPSK decoder, and how the "uncoded" bits are decided.

A. Labeling of QAM Points

For purposes of QAM transmission, the codewords of the QPSK code and the uncoded bits must be assigned to the QAM constellation. This is accomplished by labeling the QAM constellation points by a modulation function $\text{MOD}(\boldsymbol{m}) \in R^2$,

$$(\text{mod} :)\{0, 1\}^N \to R^2.$$

The method described has the following desirable features: 1) the consequences of the 90° phase ambiguity of QAM is imposed on the QPSK codewords, while the uncoded bits are invariant to the ambiguity (i.e., the 90° phase ambiguity can be dealt with in the same manner as the QPSK system); and 2) the most significant digits control the constellation size (i.e., a nested scheme for 16/32/64-QAM).

Consider the labeling (modulation function $\text{MOD}(\boldsymbol{m})$) given in Fig. 3, and depicted in Fig. 4. The outputs of the QPSK encoder form the least significant bits (LSB's), m_1, m_0, of the constellation label; the LSB's select the column of the matrix. The most significant bits (MSB's) determine the

constellation size. With no uncoded bits, QPSK is generated; with two uncoded bits, 16-QAM is generated; with three uncoded bits, 32-QAM is generated; and with four uncoded bits, 64-QAM is generated. Furthermore, the effect of rotating the QAM constellation by 90° is to rotate the columns of the matrix

$$00 \to 01 \to 11 \to 10 \to 00$$

which leaves the rows invariant. Thus, the label of the uncoded bits is unaffected by 90° rotations. The handling of the 90° phase ambiguity at the receiver (decoder) is left solely to the QPSK encoder. The same method used to resolve the ambiguity with a QPSK receiver can be incorporated into the QAM system using this labeling. For example, differential encoding could be used if the QPSK code is itself rotationally invariant.

As a final note, the assignment of the two coded bits, m_1, m_0, to the four constellation subsets is such that the intersubset Hamming distance is proportional to the intersubset Euclidean distance squared (the proportionality factor is Δ_o^2, the square of the minimum spacing of the constellation) as is normally done in coded QPSK systems. (See Fig. 4 for the coded bit assignment.)

B. Pruning and Decoding

Consider the process of signal detection when a soft decision QPSK decoder is incorporated into a system employing the previously described QAM modulator. First, in hard decision detection of QPSK or QAM signals, the received signal $y_k = x_k + w_k$ is quantized, where the signal x_k belongs to the QPSK or QAM constellation (i.e., in the range of $\text{MOD}[\boldsymbol{m}]$), and w_k is the noise. The quantization function provides an estimate of both the signal x'_k and the data $\boldsymbol{m}'$ according to the relation $x'_k = \text{MOD}(\boldsymbol{m}')$. For maximum likelihood (ML) detection, the log-likelihood function $-\log(p(y_k|\text{MOD}(\boldsymbol{m})))$ is minimized over the possible messages $\boldsymbol{m} \in \{0, 1\}^N$, where $p(y_k|x_k)$ is the conditional probability of receiving y_k given that x_k was transmitted. For random messages, ML detection minimizes the probability of error. The most common method of quantization is nearest (Euclidean) neighbor detection, which satisfies

$$\|y_k - x'_k\|^2 = \min \|y_k - \text{MOD}(\boldsymbol{m})\|^2$$

where the minimum is taken over $\boldsymbol{m} \in \{0, 1\}^N$, and $\| \bullet \|^2$ is the Euclidean distance squared (i.e., the sum of squares). In the case of additive Gaussian noise, nearest neighbor detection is ML.

In coded QPSK and QAM systems, soft decision information should be provided to the decoder for more effective decoding of the codeword. This soft decision information is often described as a symbol metric, which indicates the quality of deciding a particular symbol was sent when y_k is received. For nearest neighbor decoding, the metric of choice is

$$\text{metric}(y_k; \boldsymbol{m}) = \|y_k - \text{MOD}(\boldsymbol{m})\|^2.$$

(In practice, the metric itself is quantized for purposes of implementation.) In QPSK, for example, for each possible

For QPSK with m5=m4=m3=m2=0, and 16-QAM:

m1m0

	00	01	11	10
0000	+1,+1	-1,+1	-1,-1	+1,-1
0001	+1,-3	+3,+1	-1,+3	-3,-1
0011	-3,-3	+3,-3	+3,+3	-3,+3
0010	-3,+1	-1,-3	+3,-1	+1,+3

(rows labeled m5 m4 m3 m2)

For 32-QAM add:

m1m0

	00	01	11	10
0100	+5,-3	+3,+5	-5,+3	-3,-5
0101	+1,+5	-5,+1	-1,-5	+5,-1
0111	+5,+1	-1,+5	-5,-1	+1,-5
0110	-3,+5	-5,-3	+3,-5	+5,+3

(rows labeled m5 m4 m3 m2)

For 64-QAM add:

m1m0

	00	01	11	10
1100	+5,+5	-5,+5	-5,-5	+5,-5
1101	+5,-7	+7,+5	-5,+7	-7,-5
1111	-7,-7	+7,-7	+7,+7	-7,+7
1110	-7,+5	-5,-7	+7,-5	+5,+7
1000	-3,-7	+7,-3	+3,+7	-7,+3
1001	-7,+1	-1,-7	+7,-1	+1,+7
1011	+1,-7	+7,+1	-1,+7	-7,-1
1010	-7,-3	+3,-7	+7,+3	-3,+7

(rows labeled m5 m4 m3 m2)

Fig. 3.   Modulation function for 16/32/64-QAM.

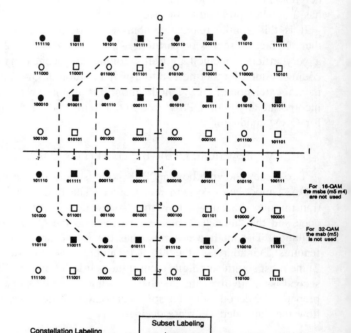

Fig. 4.   16/32/64-QAM mapping.

message $m_1, m_0 \in \{0,1\}^2$, the nearest neighbor metric $\|y_k - \mathrm{MOD}(m_1, m_0\|^2)$ is the ML metric for additive Gaussian noise.

In coded QAM modulation based on a soft-decision decodable QPSK code, four symbol metrics must be supplied to the decoder as well as four conditional hard decisions ("uncoded" bits). For nearest neighbor detection, for each choice of $m_1, m_0 \in \{0,1\}^2$

$$\mathrm{metric}\,(y_k; m_1, m_0)$$
$$= \min \|y_k - \mathrm{MOD}(m_{N-1}, \cdots, m_2, m_1, m_0)\|^2$$

where the minimum is taken over $m_{N-1}, \cdots, m_2 \in \{0,1\}^{N-2}$. The conditional hard decisions correspond to

the choice of $m_{N-1}, \cdots, m_2$ that obtain the minimum. The process of determining the symbol metrics and conditional hard decisions is known as pruning. In trellis-coded QAM, the uncoded bits appear as "parallel" branches of the trellis; the computation of the symbol metrics and conditional hard decisions act to prune all but the single best branch from the set of parallel branches.

Once the pruning operation has been completed, the soft decision information is presented to the decoder of the QPSK code. During this time, the conditional hard decisions are stored (delayed) until QPSK decisions become available. The

188

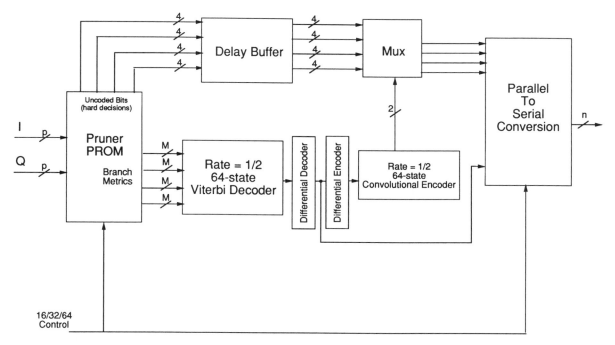

Fig. 5.   Trellis decoder for 16/32/64-QAM.

QPSK decoder, using the soft decision information, decodes the QPSK information (i.e., m_1, m_0). The remaining information (i.e., $m_{N-1}, \cdots, m_2$) is then decided using the decoded QPSK information and the previously stored conditional hard decisions.

Note that if the QPSK decoder is ML (for QPSK modulation), then the pruning/QPSK decoding method is also ML. For example, if the QPSK code is a binary convolutional code with nearest neighbor (Viterbi) decoding, then the aforementioned QAM decoding algorithm is also nearest neighbor (i.e., finds the closest codeword to the received sequence). [7]–[9].

Fig. 5 shows a decoder implementation for 16/32/64-QAM. Notice that QPSK-based trellis codes allow a very practical trellis decoder design. The Viterbi decoder can be the "standard" off-the-shelf variety instead of a custom part (as would be the case if, say, a rate 2/3 convolutional code were used).

V. PERFORMANCE RESULTS

Using (1), (2), and (6) with $\Delta_o = 2$ (i.e., constellations based on the odd integer lattice), the performance of QAM-based trellis coded modulation (TCM) using two different convolutional codes is plotted in Fig. 6. The rate 1/2 code is the "standard" 64-state code with octal generator vector [171 133] found by Odenwalder [5]. The rate 2/3 code is a 16-state code with octal generator matrix rows [5 1 2] and [2 7 0] found by Ungerboeck [9]. In this paper, the rate 1/2 code is referred to as the "practical" code, and the rate 2/3 code is referred to as the "Ungerboeck" code. The Ungerboeck code was chosen because it requires a Viterbi decoder whose complexity is about the same as the decoder for the practical code.

For the concatenated system, the error rate of interest is the Reed–Solomon (RS) code block error rate. The reason the block error rate was chosen as the error rate of interest, as opposed to bit error rate, is because it is natural to block code

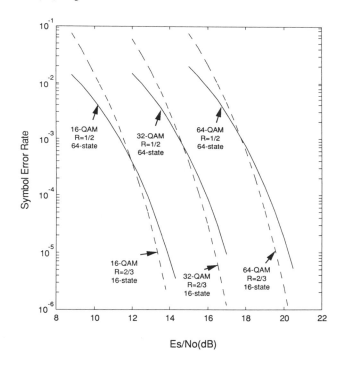

Fig. 6.   Theoretical TCM performance using two different convolutional codes.

HDTV lines of data, and when an uncorrectable RS symbol error occurs in the line, some action is taken regardless of the number of bit errors that occurred. The block error rate can be approximated by

$$P_{\text{block}} \approx \sum_{i=t+1}^{L} \binom{L}{i} P_{\text{RSsym}}^{i} (1 - P_{\text{RSsym}})^{L-i} \quad (7)$$

where L is the RS block length (number of m-bit symbols per block), and t is the number of RS symbol errors that can be

189

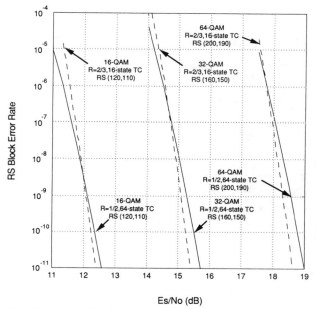

Fig. 7. Theoretical RS+ TCM performance using two different convolutional codes.

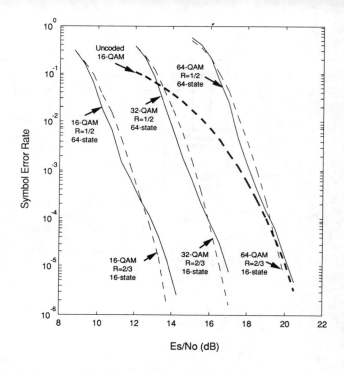

Fig. 8. Simulated TCM performance using two different convolutional codes.

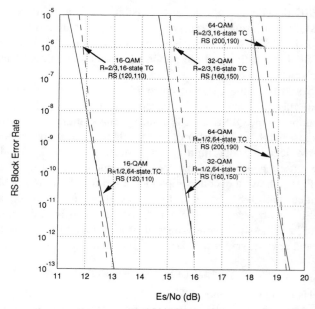

Fig. 9. Simulated TCM+ calculated RS performance using two different convolutional codes.

corrected per block. P_{RSsym} is the probability of an m-bit RS symbol being in error, and is approximated by

$$P_{RSsym} \approx 1 - (1 - P_n)^{m/n} \qquad (8)$$

where P_n is the n-bit symbol error rate out of the trellis decoder. (Note that the above approximations assume that the channel is memoryless.)

Based on our experience with video compression systems, a block error rate of 10^{-6} defines an acceptable viewing threshold. If blocks are transmitted at the NTSC TV horizontal line rate of 15.734 kHz, a 10^{-6} block error rate corresponds to about one block error per minute. If in addition the baud rate is restricted to 5 MHz (sufficient for transmission over a 6 MHz NTSC channel), then it is required that each of the three TCM's corresponding to three, four, and five RS coded bits per symbol (16, 32, and 64-QAM, respectively) be concatenated with RS codes with block lengths of 120, 160, and 200 RS symbols, respectively. Commercial RS chips that can correct five, eight-bit symbol errors are readily available. Therefore, the RS codes (over GF[256]) chosen for concatenation with the 16, 32, and 64-QAM TCM's are RS(120, 110), RS(160, 150), and RS(200, 190), respectively.

Fig. 7 shows the theoretical performance of concatenating the aforementioned RS codes with practical and Ungerboeck trellis codes. Notice that all practical codes are better at a block error rate of 10^{-6} or more. However, simulations reveal even better results for practical codes.

Fig. 8 compares the simulated performance of the practical and Ungerboeck codes. Notice here that the curves cross at 10^{-4} compared to the theoretical curves in Fig. 6, which cross near 10^{-3}. This result is reflected in the concatenated case, shown in Fig. 9, where the practical codes are shown to be better than the Ungerboeck codes at a block error rate of 10^{-10} or more. This clearly shows the performance advantage of the practical codes.

VI. SUMMARY

In this paper, it was argued that for concatenated coding systems employing QAM-based trellis coded modulation, optimization of coding gain is achieved by analysis of the number of nearest neighbors, where as for nonconcatenated systems the ACG is the parameter of interest. A practical concatenated coding scheme based on a QPSK trellis code employing a "standard" rate 1/2 64-state code was shown to perform better than a rate 2/3 16-state code. Furthermore, the practical scheme has a distinct implementation advantage over other trellis coding schemes due to the fact that a standard off-the-shelf Viterbi decoder can be used in the trellis decoder rather than a custom part.

REFERENCES

[1] A. R. Caulderbank and N. J. A. Sloane, "New trellis codes based on lattices and cosets," *IEEE Trans. Inform. Theory*, vol. IT-33, pp. 177–195, Mar. 1987.

[2] G. C. Clark and J. B. Cain, *Error-Correction Coding for Digital Communications.* New York: Plenum, 1981.

[3] G. D. Forney, Jr., "The Viterbi algorithm," *Proc. IEEE*, vol. 61, Mar. 1973.

[4] S. Lin and D. J. Costello, *Error Control Coding: Fundamentals and Applications.* Englewood Cliffs, NJ: Prentice-Hall, 1983.

[5] J. P. Odenwalder, "Optimal decoding of convolutional codes," Ph.D. thesis, Dept. of Elec. Eng., Univ. of Calif. at Los Angeles, Jan. 1970.

[6] E. Biglieri, D. Divsalar, P. McLane, and M. Simon, *Introduction of Trellis-Coded Modulation With Applications.* New York: Macmillan, 1991.

[7] G. Ungerboeck, "Channel coding with multilevel/phase signals," *IEEE Trans. Inform. Theory*, vol. IT-28, pp. 55–67, Jan. 1982.

[8] G. Ungerboeck, "Trellis-coded modulation with redundant signal sets—Part I: Introduction," *IEEE Commun.*, vol. 25, pp. 5–11, Feb. 1987.

[9] G. Ungerboeck, "Trellis-coded modulation with redundant signal sets—Part II: State of the Art," *IEEE Commun.*, vol. 25, pp. 12–21, Feb. 1987.

[10] A. Viterbi, J. K. Wolf, E. Zehavi, and R. Padovani, "A pragmatic approach to trellis-coded modulation," *IEEE Commun. Mag.*, vol. 27, pp. 11–19, July 1989.

[11] Y. Yasuda, Y. Hirata, K. Nakamura, and S. Otani, "High rate punctured convolutional codes for soft decision Viterbi decoding," *IEEE Trans. Commun.*, vol. COM-32, pp. 315–319, Mar. 1984.

[12] Y. Yasuda, Y. Hirata, K. Nakamura, and S. Otani, "Development of a variable-rate Viterbi decoder and its performance characteristics," in *Proc. 6th Ann. Conf. Satel. Commun.*, Phoenix, AZ, Sept. 1983.

A CODEC FOR HDTV

Arun Netravali, Eric Petajan, Scott Knauer,
Alireza F. Faryar, George Kustka, Kim Matthews, Robert J. Safranek
AT&T Bell Laboratories
600 Mountain Avenue
Murray Hill, New Jersey 07974

Abstract

A high quality digital video codec has been developed for the Zenith/AT&T HDTV system which adaptively selects between two transmission modes with differing rates and robustness. The codec works on an image progressively scanned with 1575 scan lines every 1/30th of a second and achieves a compression ratio of approximately 50 to 1. The high compression ratio facilitates robust transmission of the compressed HDTV signal within an NTSC taboo channel. Transparent image quality is achieved using motion compensated transform coding coupled with a perceptual criterion to determine the quantization accuracy required for each transform coefficient. The codec has been designed to minimize complexity and memory in the receiver.

1.0 Introduction

The Zenith/AT&T Digital Spectrum Compatible (DSC)-HDTV system uses a video compression algorithm which is optimized for the terrestrial broadcast environment. A very high compression ratio is achieved which enables robust transmission without sacrificing the image quality. The algorithm is designed for practical implementation and results in a decoder which is realizable in a small number of VLSI chips.

Three basic types of redundancy are exploited in the video compression process. Motion compensation removes temporal redundancy, spatial frequency transformation removes spatial redundancy, and perceptual weighting re-moves amplitude redundancy by putting quantization noise in less visible areas.

Temporal processing occurs in two stages. The motion of objects from frame to frame is estimated using hierarchical block matching. Using the motion vectors, a displaced frame difference (DFD) is computed which generally contains a small fraction of the information in the original frame. The DFD is transformed using a two dimensional discrete cosine transform (DCT) to remove the spatial redundancy. Each new frame of DFD is analyzed prior to coding to determine its rate versus perceptual distortion characteristics and the dynamic range of each coefficient. Quantization of the DCT coefficients is performed based on the perceptual importance of each coefficient, the precomputed dynamic range of the coefficients, and the rate versus distortion characteristics. The perceptual criterion uses a model of the human visual system to determine a human observer's sensitivity to color, brightness, spatial frequency and spatial-temporal masking. This information is used to minimize the perception of coding artifacts throughout the picture. Parameters of the coder are optimized to handle the scene changes that occur frequently in entertainment/sports events, and channel changes made by the viewer. The motion vectors, compressed DCT coefficients and other coding overhead bits are packed into a format which is highly immune to transmission errors. In case of transmission errors, the decoder uses a recovery technique which masks the errors. If loss of signal is detected or the channel is changed, the decoder switches to a

Reprinted from *IEEE Trans. Consumer Electron.*, vol. 38, no. 3, pp. 325–340, Aug. 1992.

special mode which quickly builds the picture to full quality.

The video coder takes full advantage of the transmission systems ability to switch between 1 bit/symbol and 2 bit/symbol modes. Depending on scene complexity, an improvement in error performance is achieved by adapting the ratio of 1 to 2 bit symbols in the Encoder. The encoder will automatically select optimum error performance for each scene.

In choosing the video compression algorithm the need for a modular architecture and low cost was considered. Particular attention has been given to minimizing the Decoder circuits that will be part of every DSC-HDTV receiver. Some elements of the encoding algorithms that affect picture quality can be altered without requiring modifications to the Decoder. This feature provides an opportunity for future improvement without affecting the installed base of equipment. Some coding applications may also require an inexpensive Encoder. The DSC-HDTV system has a modular architecture which allows a subset of the encoder to be used at a much lower cost without requiring a different transmission format.

2.0 Encoder

The Encoder is shown in **Figure 1**. Motion from frame to frame is estimated using a hierarchical block-matching Motion Estimator. The Motion Estimator produces motion vectors, which are compressed and sent to the output buffer for transmission. Each frame is analyzed before being processed in the encoder loop. The motion vectors and control parameters resulting from the forward analysis are input to the encoder loop which outputs the compressed prediction error to the channel buffer. The encoder loop control parameters are weighted by the buffer state which is fed back from the channel buffer.

In the predictive encoding loop, the generally sparse differences between the new image data and the motion-compensated predicted image data are encoded using adaptive transform coding. The parameters of the encoding are controlled in part by forward analysis. The data output from the encoder consists of some global parameters of the video frame computed by the Forward Analyzer and transform coefficients that have been selected and quantized according to a perceptual criterion.

Each frame is composed of a luminance frame and two chrominance difference frames which are half the resolution of the luminance frame horizontally and vertically. The compression algorithm produces a chrominance bit-rate which is generally a small fraction of the total bit-rate, without perceptible chrominance distortion.

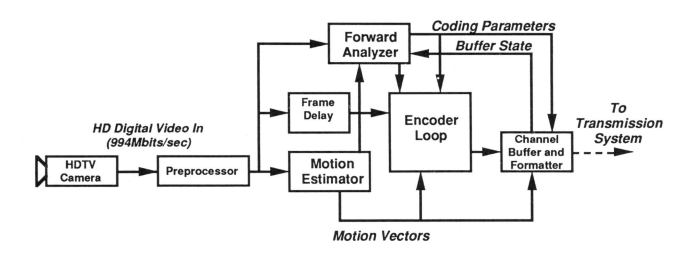

Figure 1. Encoder

The output buffer has an output rate varying between 9 and 17 Mbits/sec and has a varying input rate that depends on the image content. The buffer history is used to control the parameters of the coding algorithm so that the average input rate equals the average output rate. The feedback mechanism involves adjustment of the allowable distortion level, since increasing the distortion level (for a given image or image sequence) causes the Encoder to produce a lower output bit-rate.

The encoded video is packed into a special format before transmission which maximizes immunity to transmission errors by masking the loss of data in the Decoder. The duration and extent of picture degradation due to any one error or group of errors is limited.

2.1   Motion Estimation

Motion is estimated in stages on a block by block basis using the luminance frames only. At each stage the best block match is defined to be that which has the least absolute difference between blocks. The results from one stage are used as a starting point for the next stage to minimize the number of block matches per image. The motion estimator is capable of handling large frame-to-frame displacements typical of entertainment and sport scenes. Finally, the resolution of motion estimation is adapted spatially to those places in the picture which could have the most benefit within the limit of the compressed motion vector bit-rate.

The Motion Estimator compares a block of pels in the current frame with a block in the previous frame by forming the sum of the absolute differences between the pels, known as the prediction error. Each block in the current image is compared to displaced blocks at different locations in the previous image and the displacement vector that gives the minimum prediction error is chosen as being the best representation of the motion of that block. This is the motion vector for that block. The end result of motion estimation is to associate a motion vector with every block of pels in the image.

The Motion Estimator is shown in **Figure 2**. To reduce the complexity of the search, hierarchi-cal motion estimation is used in which a first stage of coarse estimation is refined by a second, finer estimation. The first stage matching is performed on the images after they have been decimated by a factor of two both vertically and horizontally. This reduces both the block size and the search area by factors of four. A block size of 16H X 8V pels in the decimated image is used with 1 pel accuracy. This is equivalent to 32H X 16V Pel blocks and 2 pel accuracy in the original image. The motion vectors that are generated are passed to the second stage which performs a subpixel accuracy search centered around this coarse estimate.

The second Motion Estimator stage generates the prediction errors of the 8x8 pel blocks for each location within the search window. The prediction errors of the coarse blocks are derived from the sums of the appropriate small block prediction errors and the coarse motion vectors are refined to subpel accuracy.

The final stage of the Motion Estimator uses the prediction errors to generate the motion vectors by finding the minimum prediction error for all blocks in every location. The resulting 8x8 motion vectors are then passed on to the vector selector stage with the associated prediction errors. In addition, 32H X 16V pel block motion vectors and associated prediction errors are sent to the Motion Vector Selector.

Half pixel motion is deduced by extrapolation of the prediction errors around the region of minimum error. A simple scheme used is to derive the half pixel motion independently horizontally and vertically. A parabola is fit to the three points around the minimum, and the resulting equation is solved to find the position of the minimum of the curve. This process simplifies to solving the following:

$$x' = x - 1/2; \quad (3p_{x+1} - 2p_x - p_{x-1}) < 0$$
$$x' = x + 1/2; \quad (3p_{x-1} - 2p_x - p_{x+1}) < 0$$
$$x' = x; \qquad \text{otherwise}$$

where p_x is the prediction error at x, and x' is the deduced half pixel motion vector. The use of this approximation results in a great reduction in the size of the Motion Estimator implementation.

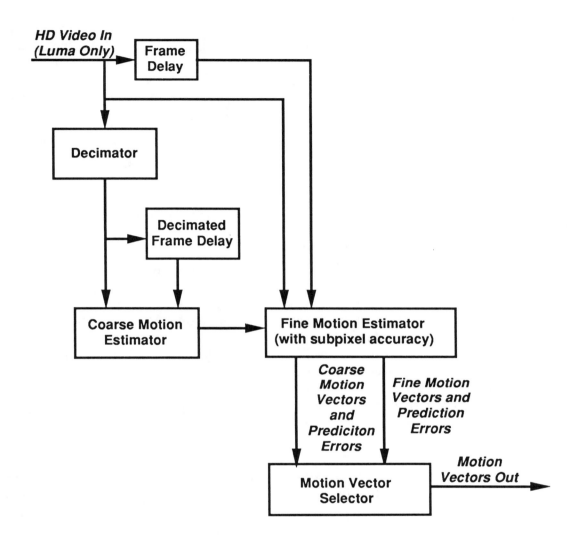

Figure 2. Motion Estimator

2.1.1 Motion Vector Encoding

Given the motion vectors from the motion estimator, the motion vector encoder must select the set of motion vectors that will give the best prediction of the next frame while limiting the bit-rate of the compressed motion vector data to less than a user defined limit.

This is achieved by sending two resolutions of motion vectors, the first set representing the motion vectors of the 32Hx16V blocks which is unconditionally transmitted, and the second set which represents the 8x8 motion vectors. However, not all of the 8x8 motion vectors are transmitted, but only those which can be sent within the bandwidth remaining after the 32Hx16V motion vectors have been sent.

2.1.2 32Hx16V Block Motion Vector Encoding

The coarse block size of 32Hx16V has been chosen to ensure that, even in the worse case, these 1800 motion vectors can be transmitted within a reasonable budget. This block size is also useful because an integer multiple of them are contained in the slice size of 64Hx48V defined for the data transmission format. Hence for each slice, six motion vectors are sent. In order to improve coding efficiency, five of the six motion vectors are sent as the difference between itself and the sixth motion vector. If the six motion vectors constituting the slice are numbered as shown in **Figure 3**, then the motion vectors which are sent represent the values of the motion vectors A, B-A, C-B, D-C, E-D, and F-E.

2.1.3 8x8 Motion Vector Encoding

The next stage in the coding scheme is the refinement of some of these larger 32Hx16V block motion vectors by sending the differences between the motion vector of the larger block and those of eight 8x8 block motion vectors. As long as this process improves the prediction of the next frame, it is repeated until the bit budget remaining has been consumed.

The criterion for deciding which blocks should be subdivided is the improvement in prediction error of the smaller blocks compared with that of the single large block, that is to say the improvement is defined as the difference between

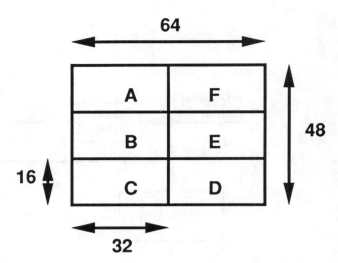

Figure 3. Motion Vectors in a Slice

the prediction error of the 32Hx16V block and the sum of the eight prediction errors of the 8x8 blocks. The improvement values are sorted to give a list which is ordered by the relative importance of subdividing a motion vector block. Concurrently with the calculation of the improvement, the number of extra bits associated with the subdivision of this 32Hx16V block must be calculated. This consists of the bits required for the eight new 8x8 motion vectors. The motion vectors are encoded using a variable length coding. Once the ordered list of improvements and the bit information has been generated, it is a simple task to select the motion vectors which give the greatest improvement in prediction error until the motion vector bit budget is exhausted.

In addition to the six motion vectors representing the 32Hx16V motion vectors of the slice, information is transmitted indicating which of the 32Hx16V motion vectors have been subdivided into eight 8x8 motion vectors. In its simplest form, this would require an extra six bits per slice to represent this information. However, because of the spatial correlation of the regions that require improvement, this information can be compressed by providing one extra bit which indicates whether any of the motion vectors are subdivided, and the other six bits are sent only if this first bit is set.

2.2 Encoder Loop

The Encoder Loop is shown in **Figure 4**. The Encoder Loop generates a transformed and quantized displaced frame difference (DFD) using the motion vectors, perceptual thresholds and loop control parameters. The Motion Compensated Predictor applies the motion vectors to the predicted frame which is stored in a buffer. A variable portion of the resulting displaced frame (DF) is subtracted from the input frame to generate the DFD. The DFD is then spatially transformed using DCT and adaptively quantized by the Quantizer Vector Selector. The quantized DCT coefficients and coded selection vectors are passed to the Channel Buffer and Formatter. The DFD coefficient quantization and spatial transform are inverted resulting in prediction of the DFD as received by the Decoder. This predicted DFD is added to the DF resulting in the next reconstructed or predicted frame which replaces the current reconstructed frame in the buffer.

The mean of each frame is calculated in the Forward Analyzer and subtracted from each frame before differencing with the zero-mean DF. This results in a zero-mean DFD for greater DCT efficiency. The mean is added back to the reconstructed frame in order to accurately estimate the quantization effects of mean addition prior to display in the receiver.

2.2.1 Adaptive Postprocessing

Under certain circumstances, coarse quantization of the transformed DFD coefficients can produce random noise from frame to frame resulting in increased visibility. To avoid this potential flickering of quantized information, postprocessing is applied at the receiver. At each pixel a weighted average of temporally successive pixels is stored in the reconstructed frame buffer if it differs from the current pixel by an amount less than some threshold. If the pixel differs by an amount larger than the threshold, the new pixel is used without averaging.

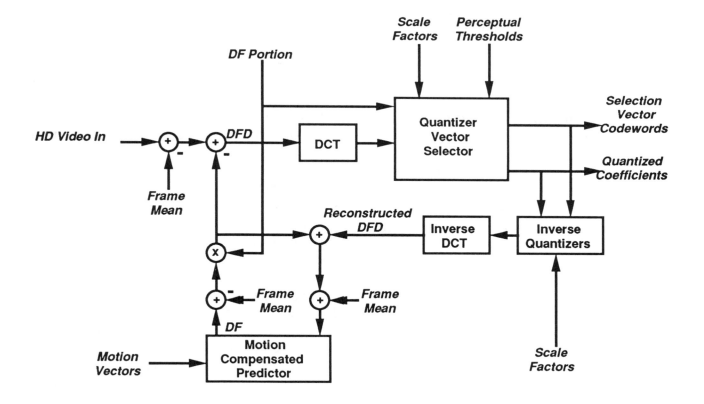

Figure 4. Encoder Loop

2.2.2 Spatial Transform

8x8 blocks of pixels containing the DFD are transformed using an 8x8 two dimensional DCT. The DCT implementation is based on an algorithm that minimizes the number of multiplications required and results in an economic implementation. [4]

2.2.3 Adaptive Quantization of DCT Coefficients

A principal means of reducing the number of bits needed to represent an image is to control the number of bits used to represent the individual DCT coefficients. The algorithm described here recognizes that DCT coefficients vary in importance based on the limitations of human vision. By adjusting the coarseness of quantization of individual coefficients in local regions of the image, the algorithm can minimize the amount of transmitted information, while retaining the flexibility to apply better coefficient precision where needed.

A set of non-uniform quantizers is used to quantize the coefficients. Each quantizer has a zero level and is adaptively scalable to maximize its efficiency given the amplitudes of coefficients. A coefficient may also be dropped or forced to zero. The quantized coefficients are variable length encoded using a codebook matched to each quantizer.

2.2.4 Vector Quantization of Selection Patterns

A variety of quantizers are available for each coefficient. However, constraints on the selection of quantizers is needed to accommodate the quantizer selection overhead. Within the bit budget, Vector Quantization is used to represent the possible combinations or patterns of quantizers which can be applied to a given 8x8 block of coefficients (i.e. a set of coefficients from a block of 8x8 pixels). Coding efficiency is achieved by variable length coding and transmitting the index associated with a given quantizer selection pattern instead of the pattern itself.

The Quantizer Vector Selector is shown in **Figure 5**. Unquantized DCT coefficients are input to the Quantizer Selector and buffered to accommodate Quantizer Selector Delay. Each entry in the Quantizer Selection Vector Codebook is retrieved in sequence and applied to a given block of coefficients. Each of the 64 elements of a selection vector contains a quantizer code which selects one of three quantizers (or drop) which are applied to a set of coefficients. A given set of luminance coefficients is composed of the four coefficients from a 16x16 super block (2x2 DCT blocks) which have the same coefficients number (0,0 ... 7,7 where 0,0 is the DC coefficient). A given set of chrominance coefficients is composed of 6 coefficients from a 16Hx48V super block (2Hx3V DCT blocks) which have the same coefficient number. In other words a 16x16 pixel or coefficient sample super block is the domain of a given selection vector for luminance images and a 16Hx48V super block is the domain of a given selection vector for chrominance images. The luminance and two chrominance frames are quantized using separate codebooks and quantizers. The luminance codebook contains less than two thousand vectors and each chrominance codebook contains less than five hundred vectors. The codebooks are organized differentially such that only differences between successive vectors are computed. This results in a great reduction in the number of computations and the size of the implementation. In the Quantizer Vector Selector each coefficient set is either quantized or dropped and variable length encoded in order to compute the number of bits per coded coefficient set. The quantization error is compared to a perceptual error threshold and the result is summed to produce the selection error for the vector. The optimal vector is selected by considering both selection error and the bit-rate.

The selected vector is now applied to the buffered unquantized coefficients via the quantizers as shown in **Figure 5**. Scale factors are computed in the Forward Analyzer and applied to the quantizers to increase quantization efficiency. The vector selects which quantizer to apply to each coefficient. The quantized coefficients are sent to the inverse quantizers and inverse transform in the encoding loop, and to the Channel Buffer and Formatter for transmission after variable length encoding.

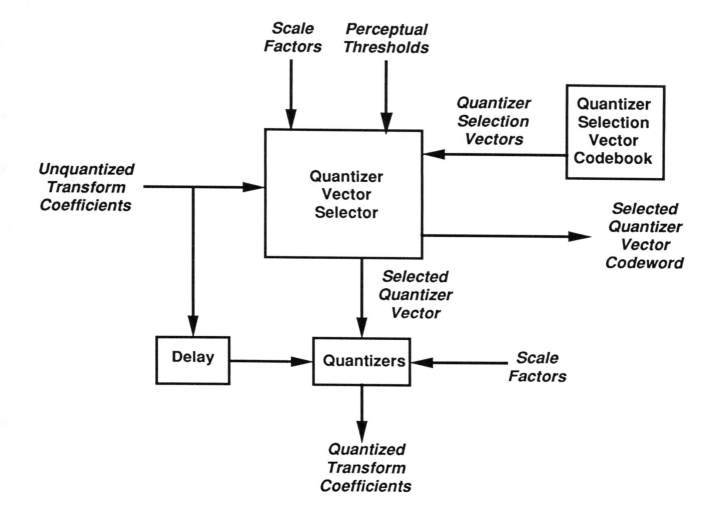

Figure 5. Quantizer Vector Selector

2.3 Forward Analyzer

The Forward Analyzer is show in **Figure 6**. The original frame is transformed and analyzed by the Perceptual Weight Calculator which passes weights to the Buffer Controller. The perceptual thresholds are computed by the Buffer Controller using the weights and the buffer state.

The Forward Analyzer also approximates the operation of the encoding loop in order to optimize encoding loop control parameters. These parameters depend on the results of analysis of the entire original frame and DFD and would be available one frame too late if computed in the loop. Examples of control parameters are the image mean and the quantizer scaling which increase the efficiency of the quantizers.

2.3.1 Perceptual Criterion

The concept of perception-based coding depends on matching the coding algorithm to the characteristics of the human visual system (HVS). If one considers the coding artifacts and the ways in which a coding algorithm can affect their distribution, it is apparent that if artifacts are concentrated in localized regions of the image,

the coded image distortion will be more visible. Conversely, the visibility of coding artifacts will be minimized if the coding distortions are uniformly distributed across the image. The use of perceptual thresholds results in an allocation of coding distortions so that the visibility of distortions is uniformly distributed.

The Perceptual Weight Calculator is show in **Figure 7**. The unpredicted picture information represented by the DFD is coded into DCT coefficients that will be transmitted with varying precision. The precision needed for a particular coefficient will be determined by a local perceptual threshold. For every coefficient the perceptual threshold generator produces a threshold value. The coarseness of quantization (number of bits used for sending the coefficient value to the decoder) depends on the local perceptual thresholds and on a global target distortion related to the time history of the channel buffer fullness. A lower perceptual threshold value implies that a low quantization error is allowed and more bits will be allocated for the corresponding DCT coefficient.

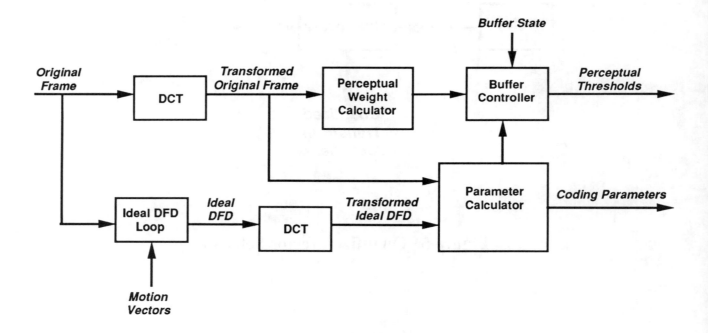

Figure 6. Forward Analyzer

Separate luminance and chrominance (both U and V) perceptual thresholds are generated for every coefficient in each frame. The perceptual thresholds are not transmitted, but are used to ensure that the information transmitted is allocated in an optimum manner, minimizing perceptible artifacts and maximizing picture quality.

The set of perceptual thresholds, one for each coefficient sample, provides an estimate of the relative visibility of the coding distortion. Note that these thresholds depend on the content of the original image and, therefore, the bit allocation algorithm can adapt to variations in the input. The module implements a model of the human visual system (HVS) that has been optimized to work with this coder's architecture.

Frequency sensitivity in the HVS model exploits the fact that the visual system modulation transfer function (MTF) is not flat. The MTF indicates that more quantization error can be tolerated at high frequencies than at low frequen-cies. Therefore, the perceptual thresholds for higher frequency coefficients are larger than those for low frequency coefficients.

For a flat field stimulus, the HVS has varying sensitivity to distortion which is related to the brightness of the flat field. This is called Contrast Sensitivity. By examining the local brightness, the perceptual thresholds can be locally adjusted to account for this property.

Up to this point, we have modeled the HVS response to flat field inputs of varying brightness levels. Since most images of interest are not flat fields, we have incorporated a model of spatial masking which further adjusts the perceptual thresholds based on the amount of local texture present at each location in the input. Our definition of texture is the amount by which the input deviates from a flat field. This results in Spatial Masking being proportional to the AC energy at each location.

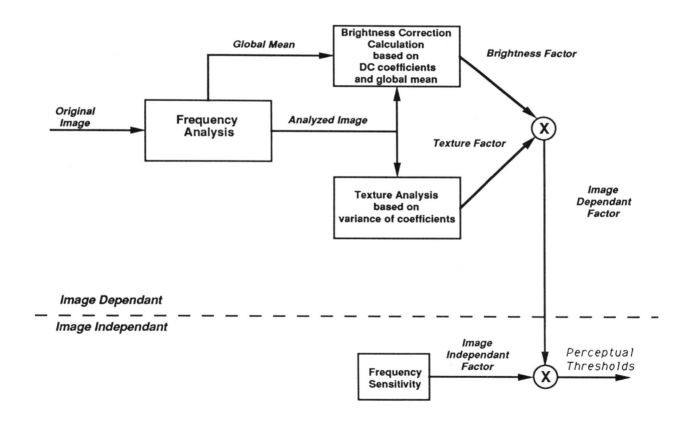

Figure 7. Perceptual Weight Calculator

2.3.2 Channel Buffer Control

In general, the buffer controls the coding algorithm by feeding back the history of the buffer state to the forward analyzer. The effect of the buffer state signal is to slow the information rate out of the encoder when the buffer fullness is high, and to allow an increase in information rate from the encoder when the buffer is less full. The buffer state is controlled by the global target distortion level. If the target distortion level is increased (to decrease the buffer fullness), more distortion is allowed.

The history of the buffer state and target distortion is stored and is also used in the current target distortion calculation. The forward analyzer maintains a certain average buffer fullness without increasing the target distortion beyond perceptible limits. At a scene change, the buffer fullness and the target distortion are allowed to increase for a few frames.

The buffer state is transmitted to the receiver for each frame. The size of the decoder channel buffer and latency in the Decoder are minimized by resetting the buffer state upon receiver startup caused by channel changes or severe loss of transmitted data.

2.4 Channel Buffer and Formatter

As shown in **Figure 8**, the Channel Buffer and Formatter receives an assortment of partially encoded video data from the rest of the Encoder and packs it into the compressed frame buffer. Since an error at a given point in a variable length coded data stream causes data after that point to be lost, the variable length codes are packed into slices which correspond to fixed 64Hx48V pixel regions in the original image. To avoid channel error propagation beyond a slice, the slice boundaries are periodically marked in the data stream to allow a restart of variable length decoding. The encoded video data stream is divided into fixed length data segments for transmission. Since the variable length slices do not correspond to the fixed length segments, each segment contains

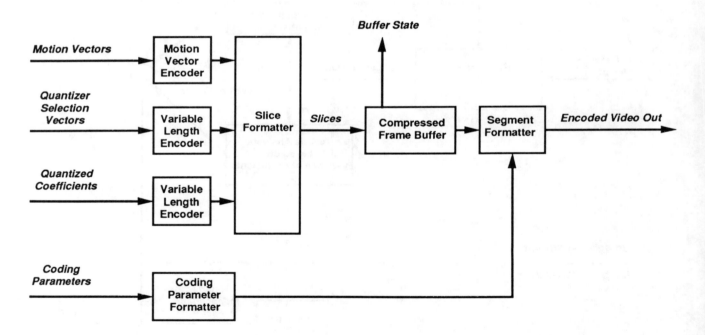

Figure 8. Channel Buffer and Formatter

header information which marks the first slice boundary in the segment.

The motion vectors, quantizer selection vectors, and quantized coefficients are variable length encoded. Various other coding parameters are fixed length encoded and put into special global segments by the segment formatter. The following coding parameters are contained in the global segments:

- Scale factors
- Luminance and chrominance mean values
- DF-factor
- Buffer fullness
- Frame number
- Frame number of frame following this global segment (for synchronization)

The state of the compressed frame buffer is calculated periodically and relayed back to the Forward Analyzer. The Forward Analyzer alters the perceptual thresholds to prevent overflow or underflow of the buffer which is being emptied into the channel via the transmission system. In case underflow is unavoidable, special underflow segments are transmitted which contain pseudo-random data.

2.4.1 Variable Length Coding

The data representing information like motion vectors, quantizer selection patterns, and transform coefficients, are seldom statistically uniform. Usually, the data are statistically clustered, and the probability distributions can be estimated from analysis of real scenes. The use of variable length codes takes advantage of this statistical non-uniformity by assigning short code words to the most frequent values, and assigning longer words to less frequent values.

2.4.2 Bi-Rate Coding

The main criticism of digital transmission systems is that the error rate as a function of S/N increases sharply at the noise threshold resulting in the complete loss of transmitted data. HDTV viewers near the limits of the service area would suffer from abrupt loss of picture resulting from a small decrease in S/N. This situation is considered to be unacceptable.

The DSC-HDTV transmission system is capable of time division multiplexing between 1 bit per symbol (binary) and 2 bits per symbol transmission resulting in more robust transmission (or higher noise threshold) for the binary portion of the video data. The ratio of 1 vs. 2 bit/symbol transmission is adaptively selected in the encoder as part of the buffer control system. The majority of HD video source material can be compressed and transmitted using a high percentage of binary transmission without any loss of picture quality. The most challenging source material may result in a slight reduction in picture quality to achieve more robust transmission. However, protection of the highest priority video segments results in a significant improvement in error masking capability.

Although the Encoder automatically optimizes between picture quality and robustness, interactive control of this balance will be possible at the point of encoding, such as at the network source.

Each segment within a given channel field is assigned a priority. The buffer control determines the number of segments (N) which will be transmitted using the 1 bit/symbol (binary) channel coding mode. The N highest priority segments are selected for binary transmission for each channel field. The binary segment selection information (or binary selection mask) is packed into the global segment with the coding parameters for each HD frame. The global segment heads each channel field, is always binary, and is repeated to ensure correct transmission. The receiver uses the binary selection mask for channel decoding the mixture of binary and 4-level video data segments.

3.0 Decoder

The Decoder is shown in **Figure 9**. The compressed video data enters the buffer which is complementary to the compressed video buffer at the Encoder. The Decoding Loop uses the motion vectors, DCT coefficient data, and other side information to reconstruct the HDTV images. The Postprocessor converts the luminance and chrominance frames into RGB for display. Channel changes and severe transmission errors are

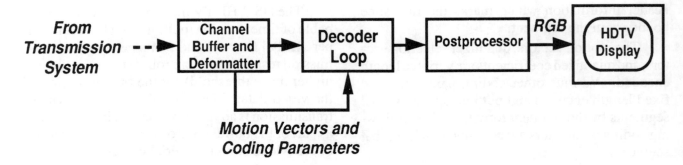

Figure 9. Decoder

detected in the Decoder causing a fast picture recovery process to be initiated. Less severe transmission errors are handled gracefully by several algorithms depending on the type of error.

Processing and memory in the Decoder are minimized. Processing consists of one inverse DCT and a variable length decoder which are realizable in a few VLSI IC's. Memory in the Decoder consists of one full frame and a few compressed frames.

3.1 Channel Buffer and Deformatter

After Reed-Solomon error detection and correction the encoded video data stream enters the segment deformatter as shown in **Figure 10**.

The receiver system indicates the presence of detected and corrected errors in the header of each segment. The error detection and concealment controller causes erroneous data to be replaced by estimated values during variable length decoding. Entire slices are replaced if a slice marker is lost or an insufficient portion of a particular slice is recovered. If one of the global data segments is lost, the duplicate global segment is used

After the beginning of each slice is determined in the slice deformatter the motion vectors, quantizer selection vectors and quantized coefficients are variable length decoded. The coding parameters are extracted from the global segments for use in the decoder loop.

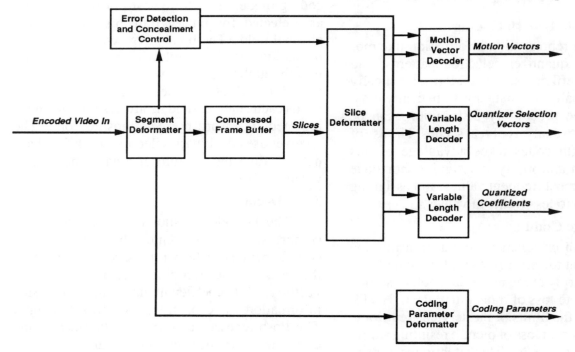

Figure 10. Buffer and Deformatter

3.2 Decoder Loop

The decoder loop is show in **Figure 11**. Quantized coefficients, quantizer selection vector codewords, motion vectors and loop control parameters are received from the Channel Buffer and Deformatter. Each quantizer selection vector codeword is used to lookup a quantizer selection vector which is an array of quantizer selection codes. One of the inverse quantizers is applied to each quantized coefficient as selected by the corresponding selection code in the vector. The quantized coefficients are received in a fixed order which corresponds to the selection code order in the vectors.

The fully decoded coefficients are inverse transformed producing the DFD. The DFD is added to the DF resulting in the frame which is displayed. The frame mean is added prior to display and storage in the frame buffer. After some portion of the frame is written into the buffer

the motion vectors are applied to generate the next DF.

4.0 Scalability, Extensibility and Inter-operability

The rapid proliferation of video coding and transmission applications is creating a demand for an HDTV standard which is scalable and can be easily adapted to meet the requirements of alternate media. In the future, improvements in camera and display resolution will result in a need for extensions to the DSC-HDTV system. The DSC-HDTV system was designed with the need for scalability, extensibility and inter-operability in mind.

The use of progressive scanning and square pixels facilitates resampling to other scanning formats and computer workstation image manipulation. Computer graphics workstations can display the 787.5 format directly with no need for pixel resampling. Extra space on the workstation

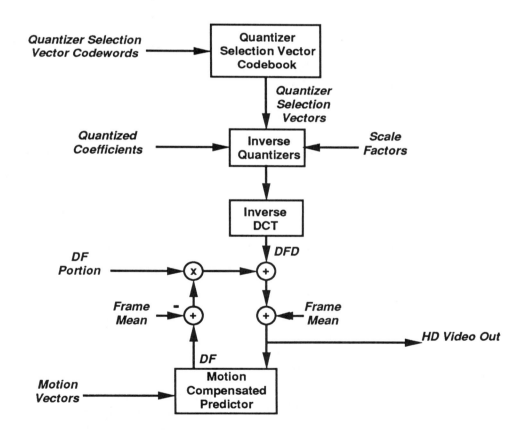

Figure 11. Decoder Loop

display is conveniently available for text or control windows. Where up/down conversion is required, filtering and resampling are greatly eased by progressive scan and square pels. For applications which require frame rate conversions or still frame capture, progressive scan is again ideal. And, of course, progressive scan provides flicker-free display of computer generated text and graphics.

The video encoder and decoder architectures are inherently modular and the compressed video data format is designed to accommodate virtually any ratio of intra-frame to inter-frame data. As a result of this high degree of flexibility, the video coder can be easily scaled or extended for:

- Higher quality pictures given higher bit-rate transmission media
- Lower cost encoder given higher bit-rate media and/or less complex source material
- Compressed video transmission over packet networks

Business video and camcorder applications would require less picture quality and a simple encoder, and could provide somewhat higher transmission and storage bit-rates. Again, the DSC-HDTV coder can be easily scaled to provide the right combination of encoder simplicity and picture quality.

Another simple extension of the DSC-HDTV video coder would meet the growing need for high quality video transmission over packet networks. The packet-like format used in the DSC-HDTV system is easily converted to standard packet formats by a simple redefinition of the ample header space used for terrestrial broadcasting and cablecasting. The existing error concealment algorithm in the DSC-HDTV system would be used for packet-loss concealment.

Eventually, the demand for ever higher picture quality will produce a need for additional video compression standards which, ideally, would be upwardly compatible with the HDTV standard. A higher resolution extension of the DSC-HDTV system could be conveniently implemented by splitting the new higher resolution frames into HD frames and high frequency residual frames by straightforward filtering techniques. The standard HDTV system would code and transmit the HD frames and an augmentation encoder would code and transmit the augmentation signal on an additional channel. The splitting, merging and filtering would be greatly simplified due to progressive scans and square pixels in the DSC-HDTV system.

5.0 Summary

The video compression algorithm includes a unique set of features that maximizes picture quality within the available channel bandwidth.

The principal features are:

- Hierarchical, subpixel motion estimation within a motion vector budget
- Handling of scene changes with no perceptible distortion
- Quick buildup of picture after channel change by the viewer
- Adaptive post-processing of reconstructed images to improve picture quality
- Perceptual quantization and dropping of transform coefficients
- Vector quantization of quantizer selection patterns
- Smooth control of quantization based on buffer fullness history
- Forward analyzer to determine coding parameters of each new frame
- Randomizing and limiting effects of transmission errors
- Adaptive channel coding for maximum coverage area
- Simple receiver

Transparent image quality is achieved using motion compensated transform coding coupled with a perceptual criterion to determine the quantization accuracy required for each transform coefficient. The combination of a sophisticated encoded video format and advanced bit error protection techniques and adaptive channel coding results in a highly robust reception and decoding of the compressed video signal.

The DSC-HDTV Video Coder algorithm is optimized to simplify the Decoder. The motion estimator, Forward Analyzer, Vector Quantizer, and buffer state control are all functions which exist only in theEncoder. An additional attribute of the DSC-HDTV Video Coder algorithm is the ability to improve the Encoder in the future without modifying the Decoder. The Decoder is realizable in a small number of VLSI chips. Frame memory and processing in the receiver are minimized while maintaining transparent image quality.

References

[1]   Netravali, Haskell: Digital Pictures, Plenum Press, 1988.

[2]   Netravali, Stuller: "Motion-Compensated Transform Coding", Bell System Technical Journal, Vol. 58, No. 7, September 1979, pp. 1703-1718.

[3]   Netravali, Robbins: "Motion-Compensated Television Coding, Part I", Bell System Technical Journal, Vol. 58, No. 3, March 1979, pp. 631-670.

[4]   Netravali, Prasada: "Adaptive Quantization of Picture Signals Using Spatial Masking", IEEE Proceedings, Vol. 65, No. 4, April 1977, pp. 536-548.

THE DIGITAL SPECTRUM-COMPATIBLE HDTV TRANSMISSION SYSTEM

R. Citta, P. Fockens, R. Lee, and J. Rypkema
Zenith Electronics Corporation
Glenview, IL 60025

Abstract

The Digital Spectrum-Compatible HDTV (DSC-HDTV) System allows noise-free and imperfection-free display of a received signal throughout a television broadcast station's service area. Compared to an NTSC station with the same service area, the DSC-HDTV station radiates less power for two reasons. The DSC-HDTV transmission signal is more efficient and, secondly, a digital receiver operates with a lower carrier-to-noise ratio. As a result, the DSC-HDTV transmitter can operate closer to a cochannel NTSC station than another NTSC station without increasing the interference into receivers tuned to the cochannel NTSC station and yet achieve a HDTV service area comparable to NTSC.

The decreased cochannel spacing does not cause unacceptable NTSC interference into DSC-HDTV receivers for three reasons. First, there is a newly devised interference rejection system; secondly, the receiver operates with a lower acceptable carrier-to-interference ratio compared to an NTSC receiver; and, thirdly, a directional antenna is assumed for the new service.

Introduction

The DSC-HDTV system [1] is an all-digital simulcast system designed to operate on a 6 MHz channel in the existing TV bands. The previous Spectrum-Compatible (SC-HDTV) HDTV system [2] was part digital; conversion to an all-digital system was made possible by the efficient video compression (source coding) described in a companion paper [3].

The video source signal is the same as for the previous system: it has 787.5 lines per frame, 59.94 frames per second, is progressively scanned at 47,203 Hz (three times NTSC rate) and is of 34 MHz bandwidth. The aspect ratio is 16:9 and there are 1280 x 720 active pixels in a frame; the pixels are square. Note that there are 1575 lines displayed in 1/29.97 second.

The source signal's simple ratios to NTSC horizontal and vertical rates result in easy up and down conversion between formats. Addition of high-definition facilities to an NTSC broadcast station initially requires a transmitter and an antenna. This enables HDTV network program feed-through. Local signals can be inserted with an Upconverter. Note that the Upconverter makes all NTSC equipment usable for HDTV; purchase of additional HDTV equipment can be deferred. Upconverted signals are not of HDTV quality but are of NTSC studio quality when upconverted from component source signals. Such signals do include all the advantages of digital transmission as noise-free display (without NTSC artifacts) and CD quality sound.

Using linear RGB source signals for DSC-HDTV, the color matrix produces chroma and true constant luminance signals.

If all active pixels of an RGB video source were encoded at 9 bits, the total bit rate would be 1.49 Gigabit/second. The source coding reduces this to 17.2 Mbit/second. The total data rate is 21.52 Mbit/second due to the addition of digital audio (four independent channels), captioning, text, forward error correction, box address, cryptography and other ancillary data.

The following sections will detail station coverage aspects and give a general systems description.

DSC-HDTV Station Coverage

According to the FCC [4] all current TV broadcast stations can be assigned a second channel if the minimum station distance is reduced to 100 miles. At 112 miles only 0.17% of current stations cannot be assigned an additional channel. It is generally agreed that the problem of cochan-

Reprinted from *IEEE Trans. Consumer Electron.,* vol. SMC37, no. 3, pp. 469–474, Aug. 1991.

nel interference will be the most difficult to solve in the resulting channel assignments. The following paragraphs give an outline of the calculations and lab tests that are the basis of predictions for the new service in the same bands with existing NTSC service. The consideration of adjacent channel interference may slightly modify the conclusions but is not included.

First, a worst-case UHF NTSC-into-NTSC situation is analyzed (Figure 1). Both stations are assumed to have maximum power (37 dBK) and average antenna height (1250 ft) and are at the minimum distance of 155 miles. The Grade B contour of these stations is at 57 miles. The acceptable limit of cochannel interference for nominal carrier frequency offset operation is a D/U (Desirable-to-Undesirable) Ratio of 28 dB. (This includes F(50,50) field-strength[*] for D and F(50,10) for U.) It turns out that this ratio is not yet reached on the Grade B contour of the D station (on the right) at the point closest to the U station. Moving 15 miles closer to the D station reaches the point

Next, a lab test was performed to compare the interference of NTSC into NTSC at D/U = 28 dB to DSC-HDTV interference into NTSC.

The DSC-HDTV RF level was adjusted until it was equally objectionable as the NTSC interference. The D/U ratio that resulted from this test was 28 dB as well. (DSC-HDTV power is defined as the power at the highest digital state.) Subjective evaluation was used in the comparison since both interferences differ in character.

Based on the information obtained from the described subjective test, it is now possible to determine the power of a DSC-HDTV transmitter at 100 miles distance from a NTSC transmitter while providing the NTSC transmitter with a cochannel protection equal to the present value. This results in 12 dB reduction to a maximum power level of 25 dBK (UHF). This situation is illustrated in Figure 2.

Note that at 112 miles distance (accommodating 99.83% of all current stations) the NTSC stations will

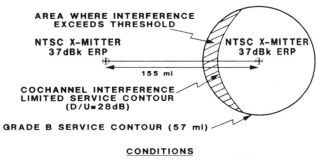

CONDITIONS	
BAND	UHF
TRANSMITTER SPACING	155 ml
TRANSMITTER HAAT	1250 ft
FRONT TO BACK RATIO	6 dB
D/U THRESHOLD	28 dB
GRADE B SERVICE CONTOUR	57 ml
% GRADE B AREA LOST	14 %

FIG. 1   NTSC INTO NTSC COCHANNEL INTERFERENCE

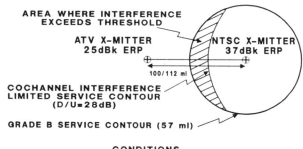

CONDITIONS	
BAND	UHF
TRANSMITTER SPACING	100/112 ml
TRANSMITTER HAAT	1250 ft
FRONT TO BACK RATIO	6 dB
D/U THRESHOLD	28 dB
GRADE B SERVICE CONTOUR	57 ml
% GRADE B AREA LOST (100ml)	18.4 %
% GRADE B AREA LOST (112ml)	14.2 %

FIG. 2   DSC-HDTV INTO NTSC COCHANNEL INTERFERENCE

where D/U = 28 dB. The area within the Grade B contour of the D station where the D/U ratio is less than 28 dB is approximately 14% of the total area within the Grade B contour of D. This includes the assumption of a receiving antenna front-to-back (F/B) ratio of 6 dB.

experience the same protection from ATV as currently from each other as expressed by the 14.2% (versus 14%) loss in Grade B service area.

Given the 12 dB power reduction, the noise limited DSC-HDTV service area can be determined. The following assumptions are made for the receiver: 10 dB noise figure and 8 dB net antenna gain (antenna gain minus down-lead loss). A carrier-to-noise ratio of 18 dB is sufficient for error-free data reception of DSC-HDTV, especially since the F(50,90) instead of the F(50,50) fieldstrength is

[*] F(A,B) refers to fieldstrength on a contour. The field-strength is reached or exceeded at A % of the points on the contour and is reached or exceeded B % of the time.

assumed. By coincidence, the DSC-HDTV noise-limited service area so defined is equal to that of an NTSC transmitter (57 miles) of 37 dBK power. Both antenna heights are assumed to be 1,250 feet.

The analysis is completed by determining how much the noise-limited DSC-HDTV service area is decreased by an NTSC cochannel at 100 miles distance. This depends, of course, on the tolerable D/U ratio. It is evident, that with 12 dB less power and an interfering station at 100 miles rather than at 155 miles, operation with a D/U ratio much less than 28 dB is required.

It is reasonable to assume under certain extreme conditions that the new service may require a new receiving antenna. For a receiver in-line between the two stations, a 16 dB F/B ratio is assumed. This is a realistic value, especially at UHF. The F/B ratio is assumed to gradually reduce to 0 dB as the angle between the two incoming signals reduces from 180 degrees to zero.

The calculations have shown that at D/U = 3 dB the area within the noise-limited service area where D/U is less than 3 dB, is approximately 14% of the noise limited service area. DSC-HDTV is able to satisfactorily operate under that condition due to the Interference Filter, the lower carrier-to-interference ratio for a digital receiver and the directional antenna. Figure 3 illustrates the conditions and shows an ATV protection that corresponds to 14% loss of service area at 100 mile distance. The loss would be somewhat smaller at 112 mile distance. (DSC-HDTV is identified by the generic term "ATV"; "DES" stands for "Desired".)

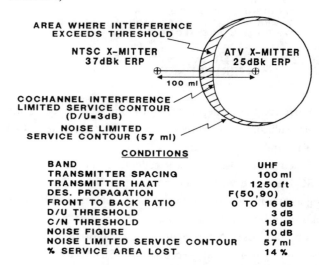

CONDITIONS	
BAND	UHF
TRANSMITTER SPACING	100 ml
TRANSMITTER HAAT	1250 ft
DES. PROPAGATION	F(50,90)
FRONT TO BACK RATIO	0 TO 16 dB
D/U THRESHOLD	3 dB
C/N THRESHOLD	18 dB
NOISE FIGURE	10 dB
NOISE LIMITED SERVICE CONTOUR	57 ml
% SERVICE AREA LOST	14 %

FIG. 3   NTSC INTO DSC-HDTV COCHANNEL INTERFERENCE

The service area in Figures 1 and 2 is based on F(50,50) for the desired signal and on F(50,10) for the undesired signal. This is the conventional treatment for the case where NTSC is the desired signal. In Figure 3, however-

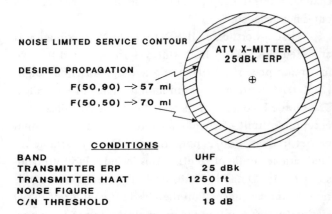

CONDITIONS	
BAND	UHF
TRANSMITTER ERP	25 dBk
TRANSMITTER HAAT	1250 ft
NOISE FIGURE	10 dB
C/N THRESHOLD	18 dB

FIG. 4   DIGITAL ATV SERVICE CONTOUR

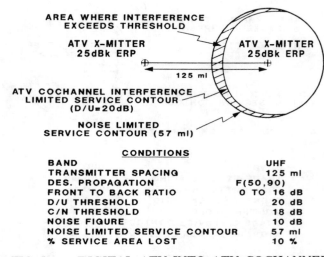

CONDITIONS	
BAND	UHF
TRANSMITTER SPACING	125 ml
DES. PROPAGATION	F(50,90)
FRONT TO BACK RATIO	0 TO 16 dB
D/U THRESHOLD	20 dB
C/N THRESHOLD	18 dB
NOISE FIGURE	10 dB
NOISE LIMITED SERVICE CONTOUR	57 ml
% SERVICE AREA LOST	10 %

FIG. 5   DIGITAL ATV INTO ATV COCHANNEL INTERFERENCE

er, DSC-HDTV is the desired signal and the noise-limited service area is here based on F(50,90). Both the NTSC Grade B service contour based on F(50,50) and the DSC-HDTV noise-limited service contours based on F(50,90) are at 57 miles distance.

Figure 4 shows the considerable difference in service area depending on whether the time factor is 50% or 90%.

A study has shown that two cochannel ATV stations will need a minimum distance of 125 miles. This worst-case situation is illustrated in Figure 5 and shows a loss in service area of 10%.

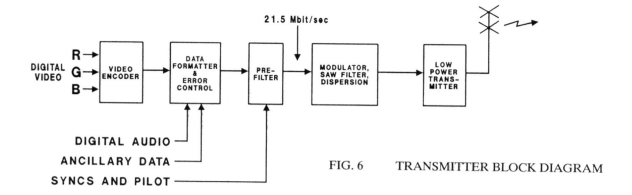

FIG. 6   TRANSMITTER BLOCK DIAGRAM

Transmitter

The Transmitter Block Diagram is shown in Figure 6. After the Video Encoder [3] follows the Data Formatter and the Error Control Block. The Pre-Filter fulfills a preliminary function for the Interference Filter in the receiver where NTSC cochannel interference is rejected. Next follow the Modulator, the Bandpass Filter which is further explained below, and the actual Transmitter.

As mentioned, the DSC-HDTV signal consists of a digital signal with a bit rate of 21.52 Mbit/second which corresponds to 718.2 Kbit/frame or 89.775 Kbytes/frame. The time arrangement of those bytes is illustrated in Figure 7, one so-called Data Frame. The NTSC-like transmission format of the partly analog SC-HDTV system is retained: one Data Frame corresponds in time to one NTSC frame. There are also Data Fields and Data Segments corresponding to NTSC fields and NTSC horizontal lines, respectively. (The new terms are used to avoid confusion with "frame", "field" and "line" which are the terms used for HDTV video source and display.)

One Data Segment contains 171 bytes, four of which are sync bytes. The first byte of these four is intended to synchronize the Receiver Video Data Clock. Each Data Field is preceded by a Data Field Sync Signal of one Data Segment duration consisting of pseudo-random data sequences. This signal is used for field synchronization but also as a training signal for a Ghost-Canceler/Channel-Equalizer in the receiver. The rest of the Data Field is occupied by interleaved program and service data to which are added Reed-Solomon bytes for forward-error correction. Syncs are not so protected since, in the receiver, syncs are detected before error correction; they have their own protective redundancy, however.

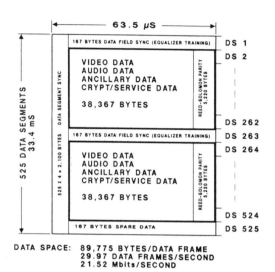

FIG. 7   ONE DATA FRAME

In order to aid carrier recovery in a receiver under strong cochannel interference conditions, a CW pilot signal is transmitted. CW signals are potential sources of interference. Near the low end of an NTSC channel, however, there is a region where CW interference has no effect due to the selectivity of an NTSC receiver's IF Nyquist slope. For this reason, the DSC-HDTV carrier frequency is chosen near the low end of the 6 MHz band. The pilot signal is also at that frequency; the modulation thus becomes vestigial sideband. By choosing 4 level symbols, the symbol rate becomes 21.52/2 = 10.76 Msymbol/second. A 6 MHz channel can accommodate this data rate; the modulation has been designated "4-VSB".

The nominal DSC-HDTV and NTSC transmitted spectra are shown in Figure 8. The horizontal scales correspond but the spectra are not drawn to vertical scale.

211

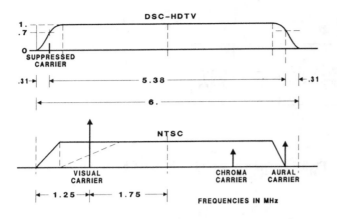

FIG. 8   DSC-HDTV/NTSC RF COCHANNELS

take place under extremely strong cochannel interference conditions. The pilot signal aids in channel acquisition. This is further helped by the choice of a frequency-and-phase-locked loop (FPLL) [5] for carrier regeneration. The FPLL's wide pull-in range, narrow hold-in range and stable operating points at 90 and 270 degrees contribute to reliable acquisition and hold-in.

The receiver SAW Filter has a group delay characteristic that provides dispersion which is complementary to that in the transmitter.

Data Segment sync is detected in a Correlator Circuit that uses the sync's repetitive and periodic character. Data Field Sync detection correlates the input with a Look-Up

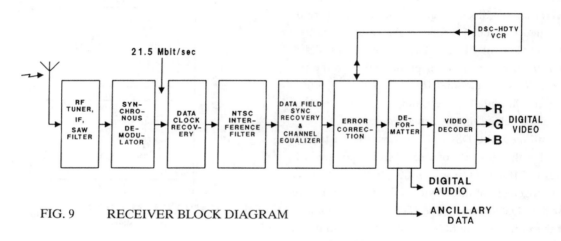

FIG. 9   RECEIVER BLOCK DIAGRAM

The only transmitted data that occur so regularly that they would cause a noticeable, non-random interference pattern on an NTSC set, are the data segment syncs. To avoid this effect, even though minor, a data dispersion operation is introduced by the non-constant group delay of the transmitter Bandpass (SAW) filter (Figure 6 and Figure 8, top). As a result, the random level of the data adjacent to the sync spreads into the sync data. This effectively removes the visibility of the described interference.

DSC-HDTV Reception

A receiver block diagram is shown in Figure 9. The functions are those of the transmitter in reverse order with a few additions. The additions include sync and clock recovery, Ghost-Cancellation/Channel-Equalization and error correction.

The receiver front-end is basically a conventional analog device except that channel acquisition may have to

Table that contains the transmitted pseudo-random sequence information.

The NTSC Interference Filter acts in conjunction with the transmitter's Pre-Filter to effectively reject NTSC cochannel interference.

The Ghost-Canceler/Channel-Equalizer uses the Data Field sync signal as a training signal. Multiple ghosts can be handled. The amount of cancellation required for data signals is much less than for analog signals due to the much higher threshold for imperfections which can be tolerated for data signals.

Summary

The paper describes the Digital Spectrum-Compatible HDTV System, including a new modulation system, a new NTSC Interference Filter and reduced radiated power compared to NTSC. The system is designed to operate in the existing TV bands at 100 miles minimum cochannel distance. The NTSC interference-limited service area is unchanged. A UHF example shows that the DSC-HDTV noise-limited and interference limited service areas are equal to those of NTSC.

Acknowledgement

The many contributions of the technical staff of AT&T Bell Laboratories and AT&T Microelectronics are recognized as are those of the staff of Zenith's Electronic Systems Research and Development department.

References

[1] Digital Spectrum Compatible HDTV, "Technical Description", Monograph published by Zenith Electronics Corporation and AT&T Bell Laboratories, Glenview, IL, February 22, 1991.

[2] "Spectrum-Compatible HDTV System", Monograph published by Zenith Electronics Corporation, Glenview, IL, September 1, 1988.

[3] "A High Performance Digital HDTV Codec" by A. Netravali, E. Petajan, S. Knauer, K. Matthews, B. Safranek, P. Westerink, this issue.

[4] Interim Report: "Further Studies on the Availability of Spectrum for Advanced Television", by R. Eckert, A. Stillwell, and B. Franca. Technical Memorandum FCC/OET TM89-1, December 1989.

[5] "Frequency and Phase Lock Loop", by R. Citta, IEEE Transactions on Consumer Electronics, Vol. CE 23, No. 3, August 1977, pp. 358-365.

THE DSC-HDTV INTERFERENCE REJECTION SYSTEM

Carl Eilers, Pieter Fockens
Zenith Electronics Corporation
Glenview, Illinois

Abstract

The Digital Spectrum-Compatible HDTV receiver, operating in a terrestrial simulcast situation, needs exceptional immunity against NTSC cochannel interference. This is provided by a receiver comb filter with nulls near all three NTSC carriers. The correlative action caused by the comb filter is complemented by digital precoding.

CoChannel Interference.

The FCC intention to introduce HDTV terrestrial broadcasting by simulcasting in the existing TV bands is only possible by making use of currently taboo channels and by reducing the minimum distance between cochannels and adjacent channels. The current UHF minimum cochannel distance of 155 miles will have to be reduced to as little as 100 miles for NTSC-HDTV cochannel operation.

DSC-HDTV can achieve a noise-limited service area comparable to NTSC Grade-B service area with 12-15 dB less power. This is due to the efficient use of the 6 MHz channel spectrum.

In general terms, reducing minimum distance will increase interference while reducing an interfering station's power will reduce interference. A detailed analysis [1] has shown that the interference into NTSC from a DSC-HDTV cochannel at the reduced distance and power is comparable to that from another NTSC station at the current minimum distance. The minimum ratio commonly receiver's RF terminals, to define service, is D/U = 28 dB.

The reverse situation is quite different. Reduced channel spacing and an NTSC signal 12-15 dB stronger than the DSC-HDTV signal cause more serious interfer-ence into a DSC-HDTV receiver by an NTSC cochannel. To obtain an interference limited area that is again comparable to that of an NTSC/NTSC situation, requires satisfactory operation of the DSC-HDTV receiver with a D/U ratio near 0 dB. The Interference Rejection System makes this possible.

NTSC Interference Rejection

The three parts of the NTSC Interference Rejection System are shown in the block diagram of Figure 1. The circuit that performs the actual rejection is the Receiver Comb Filter. This filter has response nulls at or very close to the frequencies where the NTSC spectrum peaks: the NTSC visual, chroma and aural carriers.

Figure 1   Block Diagram

The Comb Filter causes intersymbol interference (ISI) to the desired data signal. Due to an added feature of the Comb Filter: a delay equal to an integer number of symbol intervals, the ISI is reduced to the manageable kind known as "correlative", or partial response. The Pre-Coder is a digital circuit that pre-compensates before transmission for the correlation at the receiver.

The Comb Filter output requires "modulo-interpre-tation" before the originally transmitted data are repro-duced.

Digital precoding and modulo-interpretation are explained in the next section.

The cochannel situation is shown in Figure 2. The suppressed DSC-HDTV carrier is at the frequency loca-

Reprinted from *IEEE Trans. Consumer Electron.*, vol. 38, no. 3, pp. 101–106, Aug. 1992.

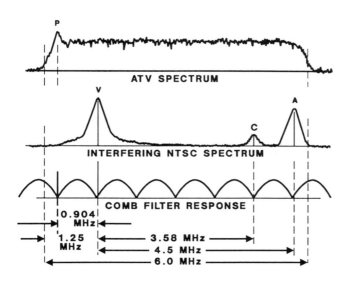

Figure 2　NTSC Cochannel Interference Rejection
Spectral Relationships

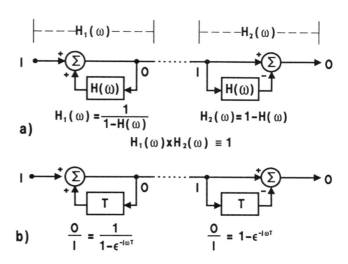

Figure 3　Transparent Networks

tion of pilot P. The spectral distance between P and the NTSC carriers V, C and A is in the approximate ratio of 1:5:6, respectively, leading to a comb filter response as shown. The NTSC carriers fall at or near the comb filter nulls with significant attenuation at their sidebands.

One of the original design criteria of the DSC-HDTV transmission signal is its noise-like and flat spectrum which is optimum from a cochannel interference point-of-view. The Pre-Coder is placed before transmission but it retains the desired transmitted signal characteristics.

Pre-Coding and Modulo Reduction

The function and operation of the Pre-Coder and of Modulo-Reduction are explained in this section. It is also shown how these two combine with the comb filter to a transparent system e.g., a system with identical output and input.

The networks of Figure 3a and 3b are each transparent. Note that transmitter and receiver are complementary, one uses feedback and a summer, the other feedforward and a subtracter. Replacing the transfer function $H( )$ by a constant time delay T in $H_2( )$ generates a receiver comb filter. Its nulls are determined by the delay time T. The complementary transmitter network $H_1( )$ is a feedback comb filter. At this time no input signal assumptions are made; the input can be analog or quantized or multi-level periodic.

The feedback comb filter is undesirable for two reasons. One, it is unstable. It could be stabilized by some attenuation in the feedback path but transparency then requires the same attenuation in the receiver comb filter delay path. This is undesirable because it reduces the nulls to a finite attenuation compromising its interference rejection function. Secondly, the summer in the feedback comb increases the number of possible levels in case of discrete (quantized) inputs and the dynamic range in case of analog (continuous) inputs.

As an example of discrete level inputs, assuming that the system is somehow stabilized, suppose that the transmitter summer has a direct input of a level 3 and a feedback input at the same instant of a level 2. The output would be a transmitted level 5. The receiver subtracter would have a direct input of 5 and a delayed input of 2 (just as in the transmitter - same delay) yielding an output of 5 - 2 = 3, the original input. If the possible input levels are 0, 1, 2 and 3, the possible transmitted levels are 0, 1, 2, 3, 4, 5 and 6: 4 possible levels have expanded to 7 possible transmitter levels. With a power-limited transmitter, distinguishing between 7 different levels instead of 4 reduces the noise margin in the receiver.

The system of Figure 3b works equally well for continuous signals (assuming stability). A direct input of 3.6 and a simultaneous feedback of 2.1 results in 5.7 transmitted level. After the receiver comb the 5.7 reduces by 2.1 to 3.6, the input.

215

Operating the circuit of Figure 3b only with discrete signals opens the possibility of a transformation that stabilizes the circuit, that does not increase the number of levels and that does not change the general spectrum shape of the transmitted signal. All this is done with the Modulo Reduction process the principle of which is explained in reference to Figure 4. Applications to analog as well as digital systems are found in References [2], [3].

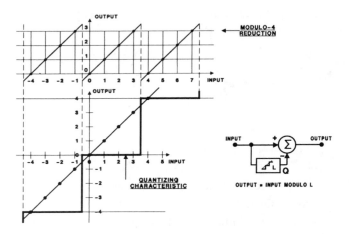

Figure 4   Modulo Reduction Process

Figure 4 shows a summer with a direct input and a quantized, negative input Q. The quantizing characteristic L, as shown, pertains to a modulo-4 reduction process for multi-level data signal inputs but is equally applicable to a continuous signal input. Its operation is best explained by examples.

Multi-level data symbol inputs of 0, 1, 2 or 3 generate the same outputs of 0, 1, 2, or 3 since the quantizing characteristic shows zero output. Inputs outside the range of 0, 1, 2, 3 are reduced or augmented by integer times the number of 4 to again generate outputs in the range of 0, 1, 2, 3 shown in Figure 4, top. For example, an input of 5 results in an output of 1 and an input of -1 causes an output of -1 - (-4) = +3.

Next consider Figure 5a. The transmitter summer output of 5 in the above discrete example is now reduced to a transmitted level of +1. The subtracter in the receiver comb filter has the +1 as the direct input and at the same instant the delayed input of 2. The subtracter yields 1 - 2 = -1. The Modulo Reducer (Modulo Interpreter) translates the -1 to +3, the original input thus showing the transparency.

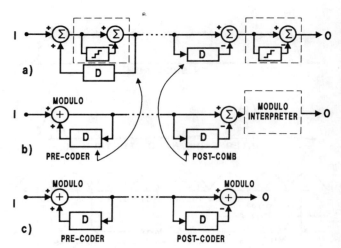

Figure 5   Transparent Pre and Post Processing

The Modulo Reduction process works equally well for continuous signals as mentioned. In the continuous example above the transmitter summer output of 3.6 + 2.1 = 5.7 Modulo-4 reduces to 1.7. The receiver summer output is 1.7 - 2.1 or -0.4 which modulo-4 increases to +3.6, as before.

In the case of 4 different discrete levels, the two summers of Figure 5a can be combined to one digital modulo-4 adder as the Pre-Coder in Figure 5b. This circuit no longer works for continuous signals but it is considerably simplified. The delay need no longer be a wideband delay line but can be realized digitally. The circuit is stable and it has only 4 different output levels instead of 7. Its output spectrum will be considered later. The receiver retains the comb filter "Post-Comb", followed by a Modulo Interpreter that reduces the 7 possible output levels to the original 4. The Post-Comb has the spectral nulls needed for interference rejection.

The discretization of Figure 5a can be continued another step by transforming the Post-Comb with the subsequent Modulo-Interpreter into the Post-Coder of Figure 5c with the Modulo Subtracter and digital delay. Neither the Pre-Coder nor the Post-Coder of Figure 5c do any spectral shaping as will be explained below. Thus, the nulls of the Post-comb are no longer present so that this version cannot perform interference rejection but there is no signal-to-noise ratio loss.

The issue of the transmitted spectrum shape is addressed next.

The transparency of the two networks of Figure 3b

with nulls in the feedforward version is complemented by "poles" in the feedback version. The poles are at the same frequencies as the nulls. The poles signify instability of the feedback version: there is uncontrolled output.

The output can be controlled by a modulo-reduction circuit as shown in Figure 5a. When this circuit is driven by an analog signal there is still a tendency to peak at the pole frequencies output but the peaks are limited by the modulo reduction circuit. Driven by discrete multi-level signals, Figure 5a and 5b are identical. The Pre-Coder of Figure 5b when considered in the time domain with binary input can be recognized as the well-known exclusive-or circuit which is stable.

It can be shown [4] that if randomly-distributed discrete-level symbols enter the Pre-Coder of Figure 5b, the output also consists of randomly-distributed discrete-level symbols and that their spectrums have the same general shape. In the case of DSC-HDTV the individual 4-level transmission symbols have a spectrum shape that is flat from DC to 5.38 MHz and a controlled cosine rolloff

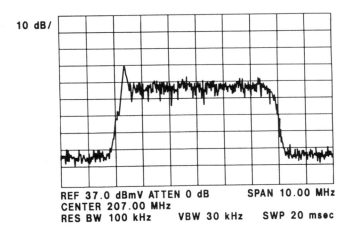

REF 37.0 dBmV ATTEN 0 dB   SPAN 10.00 MHz
CENTER 207.00 MHz
RES BW 100 kHz   VBW 30 kHz   SWP 20 msec

Figure 6   DSC-HDTV Radiated Spectrum

shape from 5.38 to 6 MHz. The pre-coded transmitted spectrum of a random sequence of such symbols is thus of the same generally flat shape. This has been confirmed by computer simulation and by hardware implementation. A measured radiated spectrum plot is shown in Figure 6 which also includes a pilot component.

All explanations involving modulo-4 operations hold equally for modulo-2 operations. For this reason the circuits in Figures 5b and 5c carry identification "Modulo" only.

The DSC-HDTV Interference Rejection Processor

The DSC-HDTV circuit is shown in Figure 7. The Post Comb delay and the Pre-Coder delay have to be equal to 12 symbol intervals in order to provide the nulls shown in Figure 2. The Pre-Coder is placed in the digital processor of the Transmitter (Reference [1], Figure 6, "Pre-Filter") and the Post-Comb in a corresponding location in the receiver (Reference [1], Figure 9, "NTSC Interference Filter").

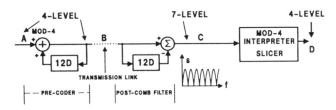

Figure 7   DSC-HDTV Processing

The Post-Comb causes a loss in S/N ratio which can be explained as follows. The Post-Comb has two parallel paths to the output. The thermal noise voltages from the transmission path arriving simultaneously at the subtracter are uncorrelated so that their powers add. The noise power sum is thus 3 dB stronger than on the transmission path. The difference between two adjacent nominal signal levels at a sampling instant determines the margin of detection safety, i.e. the noise margin. Since this difference is equal before and after the subtracter (although 4 nominal levels have increased to 7), the Post-Comb causes 3 dB loss in S/N ratio.

The Post-Coder of Figure 5c when placed subsequent to a symbol detector (4-level Data Slicer) does not cause any decrease in S/N ratio and is thus preferable in regions where cochannel interference is no problem.

A receiver arrangement that allows the use of either circuit is shown in Figure 8. The Data Field sync (vertical sync) consists of a pseudo-random sequence of one segment (line) duration each field. The sequence is kept in memory and is compared to the detected sequence by calculating the bit-error rate (BER) at each circuit's output. If the Post-Coder shows the smaller BER it is activated, otherwise the Post-Comb is selected. If both BERS are zero or equal the Post-Coder is selected [5]. When, eventually, NTSC ceases to be a cochannel prob-

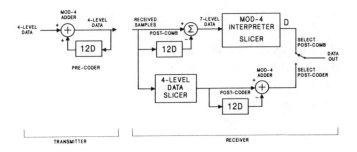

Figure 8   Post-Comb/Post-Coder Modes

lem, receivers no longer need the Post-Comb and the selection circuit. Only the Post-Coder is then needed.

Figure 9 and 10 show coding examples of 4-level symbols and 2-level symbols, respectively. Column B shows the precoded data stream. Column C shows the post-coded data; note the 7 different levels in Figure 9 and 3 in Figure 10. Column D (Figure 9) illustrates the modulo-interpretation of Figure 4.

Ⓐ	Ⓑ	Ⓒ	Ⓓ
0	0	0	
1	1	1	
2	2	2	
3	3	3	
1	1	1	12
3	3	3	SYMBOLS
0	0	0	IGNORED
3	3	3	
3	3	3	
2	2	2	
0	0	0	
1	1	1	
3	3	3	3
3	0	-1	3
1	3	1	1
3	2	-1	3
3	0	-1	3
0	3	0	0
3	3	3	3
1	0	-3	1
2	1	-2	2
3	1	-1	3
0	0	0	0
2	3	2	2
1	0	-3	1
1	1	1	1
2	1	-2	2
2	0	-2	2
1	1	1	1
1	0	-3	1
3	2	-1	3
3	3	3	3
2	3	2	2
3	0	-1	3
3	3	3	3
0	3	0	0

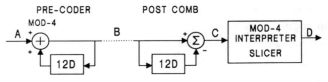

Figure 9   4-Level Data Coding Example

Ⓐ	Ⓑ	Ⓒ	Ⓓ
0	0	0	
2	2	2	
2	2	2	
0	0	0	
0	0	0	
0	0	0	12
2	2	2	SYMBOLS
0	0	0	IGNORED
0	0	0	
2	2	2	
2	2	2	
2	2	2	
2	0	-2	2
0	2	0	0
2	2	2	0
0	0	0	0
0	0	0	0
0	2	2	0
2	2	2	2
0	2	0	0
2	0	-2	2
2	0	-2	2
0	2	0	0
0	0	0	0
0	2	0	0
2	2	2	2
2	2	2	2
0	2	0	0
2	0	-2	2
2	0	0	0
0	0	-2	2
0	0	0	0
2	2	2	2

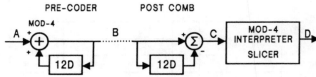

Figure 10   2-Level Data Coding Example

<u>Comparisons With Duo-Binary Signal Processing</u>

The NTSC Interference Rejection system shows both similarities and differences when compared to duo-binary signaling techniques [6], [7]. Here follow some comparisons.

Two versions of Duo-Binary signaling are shown in Figure 11. Spectral shaping in these circuits is performed at the transmitter by a comb filter identified here as "Correlative Level Filter" (A. Lender: "Conversion Filter"). This filter provides a spectral null at the Nyquist frequency (= 1/(2x symbol rate)). This enables maximum signaling speed (at the Nyquist rate) for a given bandwidth. Without the spectral null, signaling at the Nyquist rate is impractical. The price to pay for gaining signaling speed is a loss in S/N ratio due to the transmission of 3 instead of 2 levels for constant transmitter power. Error propagation can be avoided by digital precoding so that each bit on the transmission path is independent of other bits.

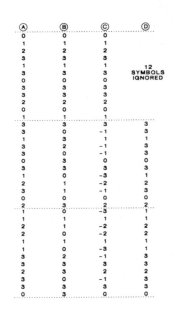

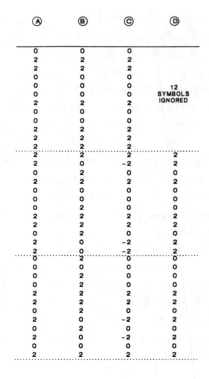

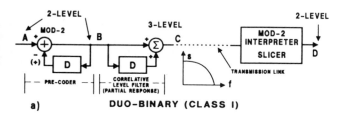

a) **DUO-BINARY (CLASS I)**

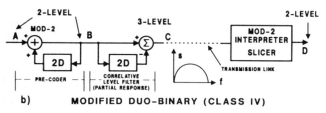

b) **MODIFIED DUO-BINARY (CLASS IV)**

Figure 11   Duo-Binary Processing

A significant difference between duo-binary signaling and interference rejection is the location of the comb filter. It is needed at the receiver for interference rejection. In duo-binary signaling it is needed at the transmitter for bandwidth reduction (which is equivalent to signaling speed increase).

Note that addition at the summer (Figure 11a) causes non-zero DC of the transmitted spectrum while subtraction at the summer (Figure 11b) causes a null at DC. The latter arrangement is also used in DSC-HDTV Post-Comb processing as shown in Figure 7 at point C.

Conclusion

An efficient system for rejection of NTSC interference in DSC-HDTV receivers is described and explained. A receiver comb filter with nulls at the NTSC spectrum peaks is complemented by a transmitter Pre-Coder that causes essentially no change in the transmitted spectrum. The comb filter is followed by a modulo-interpreter. The comb filter causes 3 dB S/N ratio loss which loss can be regained by using a Post-Coder instead of the Post-Comb when cochannel interference is no problem.

References

[1]   Citta, Fockens, Lee, Rypkema: "The Digital Spectrum-Compatible HDTV Transmission System", IEEE Transactions on Consumer Electronics, Vol. 37, No. 3, August 1991, pp. 469-475. (The section "DSC-HDTV Station Coverage").

[2]   Tomlinson: "New Automatic Equalizer Employing Modulo Arithmetic", Electronic Letters, Vol. 7, No's. 5/6, March 25, 1971, pp. 138-139.

[3]   Harashima, Miyakawa: "Matched-Transmission Technique for Channels With Intersymbol Interference", IEEE Transactions on Communications, Vol. COM-20, No. 4, August 1972, pp. 774-780.

[4]   Kabal, Pasupathy: "Partial Response Signaling" IEEE Transactions on Communications, Vol. COM-23, No. 9, September 1975, page 926.

[5]   "Digital Spectrum Compatible" Monograph with Technical Details of the DSC-HDTV System, published by Zenith Electronics Corporation and AT&T, September 23, 1991.

[6]   A. Lender: "Correlative (Partial Response) Techniques and Applications to Digital Radio Systems", Chapter 7 in "Digital Communications, Microwave Applications" editor K. Feher, Prentice Hall, Inc., 1981.

[7]   Kretzmer: "Generalization of a Technique for binary Data Communication", IEEE Transactions on Communication Technology, (Concise Paper), Vol. COM-14, February 1966, pp. 67-68.

Precoding Technique for Partial-Response Channels with Applications to HDTV Transmission

Lee-Fang Wei, *Fellow, IEEE*

Abstract—An equivalent partial-response (PR) channel $1 - Z^{-k}$ arises in the envisioned terrestrial over-the-air broadcasting of digital high definition television (HDTV) signals when a comb filter is used by an HDTV receiver to reduce the NTSC cochannel interference. In this paper, we consider the design of signal constellations and their associated precoders for this PR channel. Besides PAM and square QAM, we show that generalized square and hexagonal constellations can also be used here. Coded modulation and graceful degradation in the received signal quality are discussed. The results are extended to a more general PR channel $1 - \Sigma_{i=1}^{J} c_i Z^{-i}$ with integer coefficients c_i.

I. INTRODUCTION

IN the envisioned terrestrial over-the-air broadcasting of digital high-definition television (HDTV) signals using taboo channels, one of the major transmission issues is the cochannel interference between an HDTV signal and an existing National Television System Committee (NTSC) signal [1], [2]. To avoid the interference from an HDTV signal to an NTSC signal, the transmitted power of the HDTV signal can be set at a value at least 10 dB below that of the NTSC signal. Reducing the transmitted power of the HDTV signal, however, makes it more susceptible to interference from the much stronger NTSC signal. To solve this problem, it is proposed in the Zenith/AT&T Digital Spectrum Compatible HDTV system that a comb filter be used in the HDTV receiver, as briefly explained below [3], [4].

The energy of an NTSC signal is concentrated in the three narrowbands centered at the luminance, chrominance, and sound carriers, which are located at 1.25, 4.83, and 5.75 MHz, respectively, from the lower band edge of a TV channel. The present Zenith/AT&T HDTV transmission system is based on a vestigial-sideband pulse amplitude modulation (VSB/PAM). By carefully choosing the carrier frequency f_c to be 0.35 MHz higher than the lower band edge of the channel and the symbol rate $1/T$ to be 10.76 Mbaud, a comb filter of the form $1 - Z^{-12}$ can be used at the output of the VSB demodulator to remove most of the NTSC cochannel interference. In this paper, the impulse response of a digital filter is represented by its Z-transform, where Z^{-k} stands for a delay element of kT seconds.

Not surprisingly, the same comb filter approach for reducing cochannel interference can be used in an HDTV system based on a double-sideband quadrature amplitude modulation (DSB/QAM) [4]. In this case, the symbol rate $1/T$ may be

chosen to be 5.38 Mbaud, half of that of the earlier VSB/PAM system in order for the transmitted signal to be accommodated in the same 6 MHz channel. The carrier frequency f_c may be chosen to be 3.04 ($= 0.35 + 1/(2T)$) MHz higher than the lower band edge of the channel. Conceptually, the front end of the receiver may operate as follows (in reality, the signal $r_+(t)$ below is formed at a more convenient intermediate frequency). It first forms a complex-valued signal $r_+(t) = r(t) + j\hat{r}(t)$ from the received signal $r(t)$ and its Hilbert transform $\hat{r}(t)$ [5]. $r_+(t)$, which has frequency content for only positive frequencies, is then down shifted in the frequency domain by an amount $(f_c - 2.69)$ MHz. A comb filter $1 - Z^{-6}$, whose frequency response is identical to that in the VSB/PAM system (Z^{-6} rather than Z^{-12} is used here because the symbol interval T is twice as long as earlier), is next used to remove the NTSC cochannel interference. Another down shifting by 2.69 MHz brings the filtered signal to the baseband for further processing.

For both VSB/PAM and DSB/QAM systems, an equivalent discrete-time baseband HDTV transceiver is shown in Fig. 1. Note that the comb filter $1 - Z^{-k}$ for some integer k shown in this figure is the equivalent baseband comb filter. For the VSB/PAM system, the original comb filter is already in the baseband. With the frequency for the second down shifting in the DSB/QAM system being *properly* chosen to be 2.69 ($= 1/(2T)$) MHz, the equivalent baseband comb filter happens to be identical to the original passband comb filter. The reader is cautioned that an undesirable, more complicated equivalent baseband comb filter with coefficients other than ± 1 may result if an improper frequency is chosen for the second down shifting in the DSB/QAM system.

In Fig. 1, l and r denote the average number of information bits input to and the average number of redundant bits introduced by, respectively, the channel encoder in each symbol interval. Each of the numbers l, r and their sum $l + r$ could be either an integer or a fractional number. In the case where $l + r$ is a fractional number, a fractional bit encoder is used to convert that number into an integer $m > l + r$ [6]–[8]; otherwise, $m = l + r$. P_n is a symbol selected from a signal constellation C (PAM or QAM) and broadcasted in the nth symbol interval. The equivalent discrete-time baseband TV channel is modeled as an intersymbol interference channel with an impulse response $1 + \Sigma_{i=1}^{L} h_i Z^{-i}$ and an additive noise N_n, the latter including both the NTSC cochannel interference and background noise.

The adaptive equalizer in the receiver is meant to compensate for only the intersymbol interference $\Sigma_{i=1}^{L} h_i Z^{-i}$ from

Manuscript received June 1992; revised August 1992.
The author is with AT&T Bell Laboratories, Holmdel, NJ 07733.
IEEE Log Number 9204419.

Reprinted from *IEEE J. Selected Areas Commun.*, vol. 11, no. 1, pp. 127–135, Jan. 1993.

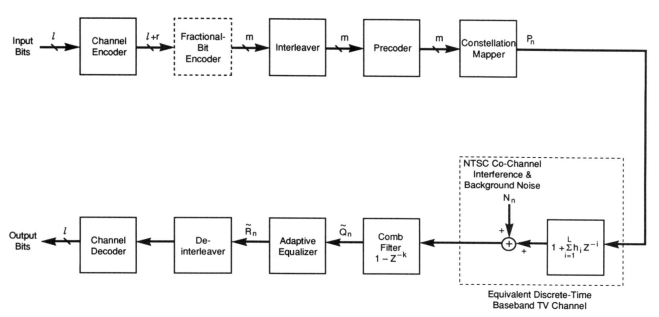

Fig. 1. Equivalent discrete-time baseband HDTV transceiver with comb filter for reduction of NTSC cochannel interference.

the TV channel. Let R_n be $(P_n - P_{n-k})$ and denote C' as the set formed by all possible R_n. The output $\tilde{Q}_n$ of the comb filter can then be expressed as

$$\tilde{Q}_n = R_n + \sum_{i=1}^{L} h_i R_{n-i} + (N_n - N_{n-k}). \tag{1}$$

From this equation, it is clear that in order to cope with the intersymbol interference from the TV channel, the equalizer should use C' instead of C as the reference constellation in its processing (that is, the equalizer should treat C' as if it were the constellation used in the transmitter). As a notation, C and C' will be hereinafter referred to as the transmitter and receiver constellations, respectively.

The equalizer for the HDTV transmission is most likely implemented as a decision feedback equalizer (DFE) [3], [4], [9], [10]. It is not the intention of this paper to address the performance of DFE for the TV channel. Instead, the purpose of the discussion here is to show the role played by the receiver constellation C' in the equalizer and to bring out a requirement on the design of an HDTV transceiver based on a comb filter. A commonly known problem of DFE is the propagation of past decision errors. In order to reduce this error propagation, it is desirable that the receiver constellation C' have a small size, which is, in turn, determined by both the transmitter constellation C and the equivalent baseband comb filter. The transmitter constellation, therefore, should also be kept as small as possible, and the equivalent baseband comb filter should be as simple as possible. The comb filter of Fig. 1, which has only two taps with both coefficients being ± 1, is already in its simplest form.

To simplify the presentation, assume that the equalizer has done a perfect job in eliminating the intersymbol interference from the TV channel. The portion of the baseband transceiver

from P_n to $\tilde{R}_n$ in Fig. 1 can then be modeled as an equivalent partial-response (PR) channel $1 - Z^{-k}$ as shown in Fig. 2 [11]. To further eliminate the "forced" intersymbol interference $-Z^{-k}$ from the PR channel (or the comb filter), a well-known precoding technique can be used, as shown by the precoder in Fig. 1 (see, for example, [11]–[13]). The essence of this technique is twofold: First, precoding does not alter the transmitter constellation C; second, the bits input to the precoder in the nth symbol interval can be recovered from the received symbol $\tilde{R}_n$ alone.

The main purpose of this paper is to consider the design of signal constellations and their associated precoders for such a PR channel. Besides PAM and square (SQ) QAM constellations, we show in Section II that the precoding technique can also be used with the so-called generalized square (GSQ) and generalized hexagonal (GHX) constellations [14]. The GSQ and GHX constellations typically have smaller peak-to-average power ratios (PAR) than those for PAM and SQ constellations of comparable bandwidth efficiencies. The PAR of a constellation is defined here as the ratio of the peak power over the average power of its symbols. The results for PR channel $1 - Z^{-k}$ are also extended in this section to a more general PR channel, namely $1 - \Sigma_{i=1}^{J} c_i Z^{-i}$ with integer coefficients c_i.

Any of the following three categories of error correction codes may be used in the channel encoder of Fig. 1: conventional codes such as Reed–Solomon codes, coded modulation, and their concatenations. Coded modulation is discussed in Section III. The interleaver/deinterleaver of Fig. 1 is meant to enhance the decoder performance in the presence of bursty noise which may come from the TV channel, comb filter, or adaptive equalizer. Another major issue in HDTV transmission is the so-called graceful degradation, which is the ability to gradually reduce the received signal quality as the distance from the transmitter increases [2]. This issue is also addressed in Section III.

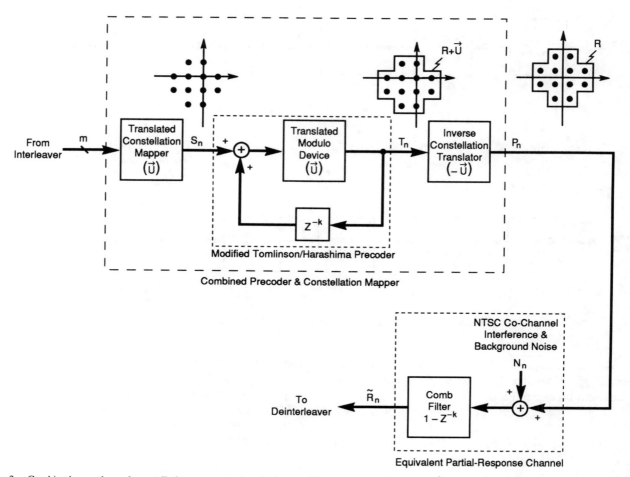

Fig. 2. Combined precoder and constellation mapper and equivalent partial-response channel $1 - Z^{-k}$ for baseband HDTV transceiver of Fig. 1.

II. PRECODING TECHNIQUE FOR PARTIAL-RESPONSE CHANNELS

A generalization of the precoding technique for a PR channel is the so-called Tomlinson/Harashima (TH) precoding technique for an intersymbol interference channel with arbitrary impulse response [11],[14]–[17]. In this paper, we differentiate between an intersymbol interference channel and a PR channel. An intersymbol interference channel $1 - \Sigma_{i=1}^{J} c_i Z^{-i}$ is also referred to as a PR channel only if its coefficients c_i are integers. For notational convenience, the precoding technique for a PR channel is referred to as a PR precoding technique. In Section II-A, we shall first compare the PR and TH precoding techniques. A general structure for a combined precoder and constellation mapper for PR channel $1 - Z^{-k}$ is then described in Section II-B. This general structure can be applied to all four classes of transmitter constellations defined below.

The first class consists of M-PAM for any integer $M > 1$. The second class consists of SQ constellations which can be further divided into two groups, the first group consisting of M^2-SQ with $90°$ phase symmetries for any integer $M > 1$ and the second group consisting of $(1/2) \cdot M^2$-SQ with $180°$ phase symmetry for any even integer $M > 2$. Each constellation $(1/2) \cdot M^2$-SQ in the second group is derived from its corre-

sponding M^2-SQ in the first group in a chessboard fashion. The third class consists of GSQ(M) constellations for any integer $M > 1$, which can also be divided into two groups. The first group contains $90°$ phase symmetries and $2M(M+1) \cdot J_1^2$ symbols for any positive integer J_1, and the second group contains $180°$ phase symmetry and $M(M+1) \cdot J_2^2$ symbols for any positive even integer J_2. Each constellation in the second group is again derived from a corresponding constellation in the first group in a chessboard fashion. The fourth class consists of GHX constellations, each corresponding to a GSQ constellation in the third class and typically having only $180°$ phase symmetry. Readers may refer to [14] for more details about the GSQ and GHX constellations. Examples for the first three classes of transmitter constellations are shown on the left side of Fig. 3. The constellations shown on the right side of this figure are the corresponding receiver constellations C' associated with the PR channel $1 - Z^{-k}$, as defined in Section I.

Section II-C proves a uniform signaling property of the precoded transmitter constellation for PR channel $1 - Z^{-k}$. The advantages of the GSQ and GHX constellations are discussed in Section II-D. The results in Sections II-A–D for PR channel $1 - Z^{-k}$ are then extended in Section II-E to a more general PR channel $1 - \Sigma_{i=1}^{J} c_i Z^{-i}$ with integer coefficients.

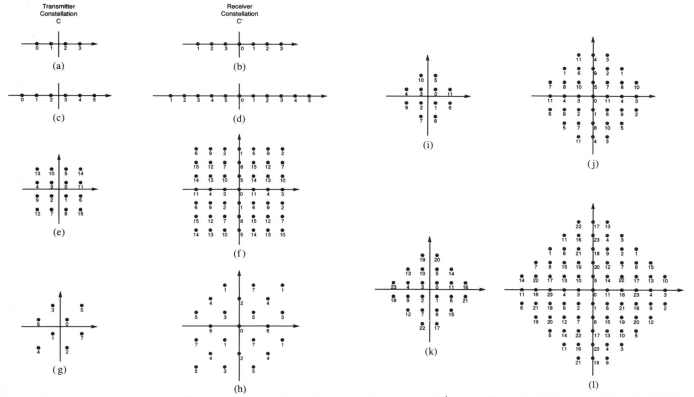

Fig. 3. Transmitter and receiver constellations associated with partial-response channel $1 - Z^{-k}$. (a) 4-PAM. (b) 7-PAM. (c) 6-PAM. (d) 11-PAM. (e) 16-SQ. (f) 49-SQ. (g) 8-SQ. (h) 23-QAM. (i) 12-GSQ(2).(j) 37-QAM. (k) 24-GSQ(3). (l) 81-QAM.

A. Comparisons to the Tomlinson/Harashima Precoding Technique

Both the PR and TH precoding techniques compensate for the intersymbol interference of a channel by preprocessing the signal at the transmitter. A major difference between the two techniques is in the transmitter constellations C formed by all possible symbols transmitted to the channel. On one hand, the transmitter constellation is not altered by the PR precoder. On the other hand, the constellation with a TH precoder is, generally speaking, quite different from and much larger (measured by the number of symbols) than that without the precoder. There is usually some penalty in the transmitted signal power that comes with the larger constellation associated with a TH precoder. As a result, for an intersymbol interference channel such as a PR channel where both the PR and TH precoding techniques are applicable, the PR precoding technique is preferred.

Nevertheless, the TH precoding technique, especially with its recent developments for the GSQ and GHX constellations [14], can be used to advance the PR precoding technique, as shown in the next subsection.

B. Combined Precoder and Constellation Mapper

Fig. 2 shows the general structure for a combined precoder and constellation mapper for PR channel $1 - Z^{-k}$. The structure can be converted to the separate precoder and constellation mapper of Fig. 1, if so desired, and can be applied to all four classes of constellations defined earlier (PAM, SQ, GSQ,

and GHX). For notational convenience, however, we shall not mention PAM in the following discussion unless otherwise specified. Also, for ease of discussion, assume that all of these constellations are taken from half-integer lattices. That is, the coordinate of each symbol in a constellation is always in a form of $i + 0.5$ for some integer i.

Let D be $C + \vec{U}$, which is a constellation obtained by translating the transmitter constellation C by an amount $\vec{U}$, where $\vec{U}$ is chosen such that one of the symbols of D is at the origin. Referring to Fig. 2, the m bits from the interleaver first select a symbol S_n from the translated constellation D. S_n is then processed by a modified TH precoder. Recall from [14] that each SQ, GSQ, or GHX constellation is associated with a template R centered at the origin and a pair of vectors $\vec{V}_1$ and $\vec{V}_2$. The only modification in the TH precoder of Fig. 2, as compared to that in [14], is that the output symbol T_n of the precoder is in a region defined by a translated template $R + \vec{U}$ rather than the original template R, where $\vec{U}$ is the same vector used for translating the constellation C into D. The input and output of the modified TH precoder, therefore, bear the following relationship:

$$T_n = S_n + T_{n-k} + k_1 \cdot \vec{V}_1 + k_2 \cdot \vec{V}_2 \qquad (2)$$

for some integers k_1 and k_2 such that T_n is in the region $R + \vec{U}$.

The reason for using a translated constellation mapper and a modified TH precoder in Fig. 2 is to ensure that the transmitter constellation C is not altered by the precoding, as explained below for two different cases. The first case is for SQ and GSQ constellations with $90°$ phase symmetries, and the second is for 180° phase symmetry. The explanation for each GSQ constellation can also be applied to its corresponding GHX constellation. In the first case, the translated constellation D is taken from the integer lattice, i.e., each symbol of D has integer coordinates. From [14], each of the two vectors, $\vec{V}_1$ and $\vec{V}_2$, also has integer coordinates. As a result, the output T_n of the modified TH precoder has integer coordinates and the constellation E formed by all possible T_n is the same as D. An inverse translation by an amount $-\vec{U}$ can then be used to bring the constellation E back to the original transmitter constellation C as shown in Fig. 2.

In the second case, the two coordinates of each symbol of the translated constellation D are either both even or both odd integers. From [14], both coordinates of $\vec{V}_i$, for $i = 1$ and 2, are even integers. As a result, the two coordinates of the output T_n of the modified TH precoder are also either both even or both odd integers. The constellation E formed by all possible T_n, therefore, is the same as D. Inverse translation by an amount $-\vec{U}$ again brings E back to the original transmitter constellation C.

It is straightforward to show that the output $\tilde{R}_n$ of the PR channel in Fig. 2 is

$$\tilde{R}_n = S_n + k_1 \cdot \vec{V}_1 + k_2 \cdot \vec{V}_2 + (N_n - N_{n-k}). \tag{3}$$

Let an inverse constellation mapping for the receiver constellation C' (formed by all possible $R_n = P_n - P_{n-k}$ as defined in Section I) be as follows: a symbol R_n of C' and a symbol S_n of D are assigned the same m-bit pattern if the two symbols can be obtained from each other through a translation by an amount $j_1 \cdot \vec{V}_1 + j_2 \cdot \vec{V}_2$ for some integers j_1 and j_2. With this arrangement, it is obvious from (3) that the m bits at the input of the combined precoder and constellation mapper of Fig. 2 can be recovered from the received symbol R_n alone in the absence of additive noise $\{N_n\}$.

Equation (3) also says that the minimum squared Euclidean distance (MSED) between symbols of the receiver constellation C' is the same as that for the transmitter constellation C. In other words, although the PR channel expands the constellation from C into C', it does not alter the MSED of the constellation. This property can be easily verified using the characteristics of the coordinates of the two vectors $\vec{V}_i$ mentioned earlier.

As an example, Fig. 2 also shows the constellations D, E, and C, together with their templates R and $R + \vec{U}$, used at various stages of the transmitter for the case where C is the 12-GSQ(2) of Fig. 3(i). In this example, $\vec{U} = (-0.5, -0.5), \vec{V}_1 = (2, 3)$, and $\vec{V}_2 = (2, -3)$. The 12-GSQ(2) can be used to carry, on the average, $l + r = 3.5$ bits per symbol. A fractional bit encoder is used in Fig. 1 in this case to convert the 3.5 into $m = 4$ bits, which can assume values from 0 to 11 (in this paper, a bit pattern is represented by its decimal equivalent). Not all of these twelve bit patterns appear equally likely. Fig. 3(i) shows a bit mapping for the 12-GSQ(2) which, after a translation by an amount $\vec{U}$, can be used by the translated constellation mapper of Fig. 2. Fig. 3(j) shows the corresponding inverse bit mapping for the receiver constellation 37-QAM.

Fig. 3 also shows the bit mappings for the other transmitter and receiver constellations associated with PR channel $1 - Z^{-k}$. In these examples, the $\vec{U}$ associated with an SQ or GSQ transmitter constellation is always chosen to be $(-0.5, -0.5)$. The $\vec{U}$'s for the 4-PAM and 6-PAM are scalars, which are chosen to be 1.5 and 2.5, respectively. In the case of 4-PAM, the precoding arrangements are equivalent to what would be found in a textbook [12].

C. Uniform Signaling Property

For PR channel $1 - Z^{-k}$, an interesting property of the combined precoder and constellation mapper of Fig. 2 is that each symbol of the transmitter constellation C is used with equal probability, whether the size of the constellation is a power of 2 or not. This property is called uniform signaling. As a result of this property, in the case where patterns for the m input bits of Fig. 2 do not appear equally likely, any bit mapping can be used for the translated constellation D because they all result in the same amount of transmitted signal power. Note that this is in contrast to the case where a precoding technique is not used. In that case, to save the transmitted signal power, an input bit pattern which appears more often is assigned to a symbol which requires less energy [6]–[8]. In the remainder of this subsection, we shall prove this uniform signaling property. Readers may skip this proof without loss of continuity.

To prove the uniform signaling property, it is equivalent to prove the following: For each *given* pattern of the m input bits, each symbol of C is equally likely to be selected as P_n for transmission. The selection for P_n in this case depends solely on that for P_{n-k}. Assume tentatively that each symbol of C is equally likely to be selected as P_{n-k}. If we can show that different selections for P_{n-k} always lead to different selections for P_n for the same given input bit pattern, then each symbol of C is also equally likely to be selected as P_n and our proof is completed.

Denote A_{n-k} and B_{n-k} as two different selections from C for P_{n-k}. For a given pattern of the m input bits, if the two corresponding selections for P_n are the same, then it can be shown that A_{n-k} and B_{n-k} must have the following relationship:

$$A_{n-k} = B_{n-k} + j_1 \cdot \vec{V}_1 + j_2 \cdot \vec{V}_2 \tag{4}$$

for some integers j_i, where $\vec{V}_i$ are the vectors associated with the constellation C mentioned earlier. On one hand, either j_1 or j_2 must not be zero because A_{n-k} and B_{n-k} are different. On the other hand, both j_1 and j_2 must be zero because, otherwise, either A_{n-k} or B_{n-k} does not belong to C by the definition for $\vec{V}_i$. Because of this contradiction, the two corresponding selections for P_n cannot be the same, which completes the proof.

D. Advantages of Generalized Square and Hexagonal Constellations

Table I lists some PAM, SQ, GSQ, and GHX constellations together with their bandwidth efficiencies and PAR's. The bandwidth efficiency of a constellation is expressed as the

Constellation	Bandwidth Efficiency (bits per dimension)	Peak-to-Average Power Ratio	Coded Modulation
2-PAM	1	1	X
3-PAM	1.5	1.5	
4-PAM	2	1.8	X
5-PAM	2.25	2	
6-PAM	2.5	2.14	X
8-PAM	3	2.33	X
10-PAM	3.25	2.45	X
12-PAM	3.5	2.54	X
4-SQ	1	1	X
8-SQ	1.5	1.8	X
12-GSQ (2)	1.75	1.36	
16-SQ	2	1.8	X
24-GSQ(3)	2.25	1.70	
32-SQ	2.5	2.33	X
48-GSQ(2)	2.75	1.85	X
48-GHX(2)	2.75	1.89	X
64-SQ	3	2.33	X
96-GSQ(3)	3.25	2.05	X
96-GHX(3)	3.25	2.09	X
128-SQ	3.5	2.65	X

number of bits carried by each dimension of the constellation, which is the $l + r$ in Fig. 1 normalized by the number of dimensions of the constellation. (In the case where the size of a constellation is not a power of 2, it is possible for the constellation to have a bandwidth efficiency slightly higher than what is shown in the table, the latter being determined on an assumption that a simple fractional bit encoder is used [8].) The average power used for determining the PAR of a constellation is calculated on the uniform signaling property of the precoded constellation.

Only four GSQ and two GHX constellations are shown in Table I. They are the 12-GSQ(2) of Fig. 3(i), the 24-GSQ(3) of Fig. 3(k), and the 48-GSQ(2), 96-GSQ(3), 48-GHX(2), and 96-GHX(3) in [14, Figs. 6 and 7]. Readers may refer to [14] for more GSQ and GHX constellations. Note in Table I that the PAR's of these GSQ and GHX constellations are consistently smaller than those for PAM and SQ constellations of comparable bandwidth efficiencies. For example, 12-GSQ(2) has an impressive PAR of only 1.36, which is much smaller than the 1.8 for 4-PAM, 8-SQ, and 16-SQ, and also smaller than the 1.5 for 3-PAM. The bandwidth efficiency of 1.75 (bits per dimension) for 12-GSQ(2) is slightly lower than the 2 for both 4-PAM and 16-SQ, but slightly higher than the 1.5 for both 3-PAM and 8-SQ. As another example, the PAR of 1.7 for 24-GSQ(3) is smaller than the 2 for 5-PAM, both having the same bandwidth efficiency of 2.25. The GHX constellation generally has the same peak power but a slightly smaller average power than that for its corresponding GSQ constellation with the same size, which results in a slightly larger PAR for the former.

For the HDTV transceiver of Fig. 1, the GSQ and GHX transmitter constellations have another advantage: they provide more choices for the corresponding receiver constellation C'. These added choices for C' are useful because C' affects the equalizer performance, as discussed in Section I. Generally speaking, the receiver constellations C' associated with GSQ and GHX constellations are good constellations by themselves, in the sense that they have a more circular shape. Such examples are the 37-QAM and 81-QAM of Fig. 3(j) and (l).

E. Generalization to Partial-Response Channels $1 - \Sigma_{i=1}^{J} c_i Z^{-i}$ with Integer Coefficients c_i

The combined precoder and constellation mapper for a specific PR channel $1 - Z^{-k}$ can be easily generalized to any PR channel $1 - \Sigma_{i=1}^{J} c_i Z^{-i}$ with integer coefficients c_i. This is done by replacing the PR channel $1 - Z^{-k}$ in Fig. 2 with $1 - \Sigma_{i=1}^{J} c_i Z^{-i}$ and the feedback portion Z^{-k} in the modified TH precoder with $\Sigma_{i=1}^{J} c_i Z^{-i}$.

In this generalized case, the transmitter constellation C, whether it is a PAM, SQ, GSQ, or GHX constellation with $90°$ or $180°$ phase symmetries, is again not altered by the precoding. The receiver constellation C' is now defined as the set formed by all possible $R_n = P_n - \Sigma_{i=1}^{J} c_i P_{n-i}$. The output $\tilde{R}_n$ of the generalized PR channel is given by

$$\tilde{R}_n = S_n - \left(1 - \sum_{i=1}^{J} c_i\right) \cdot \vec{U} + k_1 \cdot \vec{V}_1 + k_2 \cdot \vec{V}_2$$
$$+ \left(N_n - \sum_{i=1}^{J} c_i N_{n-i}\right) \qquad (5)$$

for some integers k_i, where the vectors $\vec{U}$ and $\vec{V}_i$ have the same meaning as before. Note the constant term of $-(1 - \Sigma_{i=1}^{J} c_i) \cdot \vec{U}$ in this equation, which does not appear in (3) for the specific

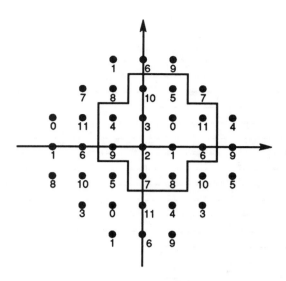

Fig. 4. Inverse bit mapping for receiver constellation 37-QAM associated with partial-response channel $1 + Z^{-k}$.

PR channel $1 - Z^{-k}$. Accordingly, inverse bit mapping for the receiver constellation C' associated with the general PR channel is modified as follows. A symbol R_n of C' is assigned the same bit pattern as that of a symbol S_n of D in the transmitter if R_n can be obtained from S_n through a translation by an amount $-(1 - \Sigma_{i=1}^{J} c_i) \cdot \vec{U} + j_1 \cdot \vec{V}_1 + j_2 \cdot \vec{V}_2$ for some integers j_i. In addition, (5) says that although the general PR channel expands the constellation from C into C', it does not alter the MSED of the constellation, just as in the case for the specific PR channel $1 - Z^{-k}$.

As an example, for a transmitter constellation 12-GSQ(2), the corresponding receiver constellation C' associated with PR channel $1 + Z^{-k}$ is the 37-QAM of Fig. 3(j), the same as that for PR channel $1 - Z^{-k}$. With the same bit mapping for the translated 12-GSQ(2) obtained by translating the 12-GSQ(2) of Fig. 3(i) by an amount $(-0.5, -0.5)$, the inverse constellation mappings for PR channels $1 - Z^{-k}$ and $1 + Z^{-k}$ are, however, different, as shown in Figs. 3(j) and 4, respectively. Note that, apart from a translation, the bit mapping for the 12 symbols circumscribed by solid lines in Fig. 4 is identical to that in Fig. 3(i), as dictated by (5).

The uniform signaling property of the precoded constellation for PR channel $1 - Z^{-k}$ is not preserved for the general PR channel. However, we expect that this property is valid for a large subclass of PR channels, which remains to be determined. Furthermore, when the patterns for the m input bits of the combined precoder and constellation mapper appear equally likely and the number of these patterns is equal to the constellation size, it is straightforward to show that the uniform signaling property is valid for the general PR channel.

III. CODED MODULATION

Coded modulation is a forward error correction technique that has already found wide commercial applications for channels with additive white Gaussian noise (AWGN) [6], [7],[18]. More recently, the technique has been adapted for intersymbol interference channels with TH precoders (see,

for example, [14],[17] and the references therein). Since the combined precoder and constellation mapper of Section II is based on a modified TH precoder, it is easy to show the following: If a coded modulation scheme originally designed for an AWGN channel can be *perfectly* used for an intersymbol interference channel with a TH precoder, then it can also be *perfectly* used for a general PR channel with a precoder. In the present paper, the word "perfectly" means that in addition to the transmitter constellation C not being altered by the precoder, the MSED between different sequences of symbols $\{\tilde{R}_n\}$ received from the PR channel in the absence of additive noise $\{N_n\}$ is equal to the MSED between different sequences of symbols $\{S_n\}$ at the output of the translated constellation mapper. The latter is also the MSED of the coded modulation scheme when applied to an AWGN channel.

Section III of [14] describes a simple method for determining whether a coded modulation scheme can be perfectly used for an intersymbol interference channel with a TH precoder. The same method can be used here for a general PR channel with a precoder. The method examines only the constellation and its partition. Table I also shows whether each constellation there can be used to construct at least one such perfect coded modulation scheme. A mark "X" in an entry means "yes."

Table II lists the characteristics of some simple trellis-coded modulation schemes that can be perfectly used in the HDTV transceiver of Fig. 1. These schemes are either taken directly from [6], [7], [18] or can be easily constructed using the rules described in those references. The 1D, 2D, or 4D in the table denote the number of dimensions of the constellation used by a scheme. A 4D 4-PAM means that the constellation is formed by concatenating four constituent 4-PAM constellations in the time domain, and likewise for the other constellations. The bandwidth efficiency of a coded modulation scheme is expressed as the number of *information* bits carried by each dimension of the constellation, which is the l in Fig. 1 normalized by the one or two dimensions of the constituent PAM or QAM constellation. The nominal coding gain of a coded PAM (or QAM) scheme, relative to uncoded 4-PAM (or 16-SQ) at the same symbol rate, is determined based on the gain in the MSED between sequences of symbols $\{S_n\}$ at the output of the translated constellation mapper in Fig. 2 normalized by the average transmitted signal power $E\{|P_n|^2\}$, where $E\{|P_n|^2\}$ is calculated using the uniform signaling property of the precoded constellation. Note that the uncoded 4-PAM or 16-SQ here means that it is not encoded with an error correction code, but it *is* encoded with a precoder. With proper interleaving, the real coding gain in the transmitted signal power of a scheme in Table II is expected to be at most 1 dB less than its nominal coding gain. The difference is caused by the larger error coefficient associated with the coded scheme.

For graceful degradation in HDTV transmission, the different coded modulation schemes of Table II may be applied to different classes of bits from an HDTV video/audio source encoder [19]. The resulting signals are then multiplexed together in the time domain before they are further processed by the precoder in Fig. 1 (or the combined precoder and constellation mapper in Fig. 2). As an example, in the present Zenith/AT&T

TABLE II
CHARACTERISTICS OF TRELLIS-CODED MODULATION SCHEMES FOR PARTIAL-RESPONSE CHANNEL $1 - Z^{-k}$ WITH PRECODER

Scheme	Constellation	Number of Trellis States	Rate of Trellis Code	Bandwidth Efficiency (information bits per dimension)	Nominal Coding Gain* (dB)
1	1D 4-PAM	8	1/2	1	10.00
2	4D 4-PAM	8	2/3	1.75	6.02
3	4D 6-PAM	8	2/3	2.25	2.34
4	2D 8-SQ	8	2/3	1	10.00
5	4D 16-SQ	8	2/3	1.75	6.02
6	2D 32-SQ	8	2/3	2	3.77
7	4D 32-SQ	8	2/3	2.25	2.80
8	4D 48-GSQ(2)	8	2/3	2.5	1.06

Relative to uncoded 4-PAM or 16-SQ at the same symbol rate.

HDTV transmission system based on VSB/PAM, one may use Scheme 1 of Table II for a more important class of bits and Scheme 2 for a less important class. The transmitter constellation C in this case is always a 4-PAM. Alternatively, in an HDTV system based on DSB/QAM, Schemes 4 and 5 may be used for the more and less important classes of bits, respectively. With proper multiplexing, the transmitter constellation C in this latter case alternates between an 8-SQ and a 16-SQ. If the 8-SQ is chosen to be a subset of the 16-SQ, as it should be, then the transmitter constellation C is at most a 16-SQ, no matter how the multiplexing is done.

It is unfortunate that coded modulation schemes based on the two nice and small GSQ constellations, 12-GSQ(2) and 24-GSQ(3), cannot be perfectly used in the HDTV transceiver of Fig. 1. If these constellations are chosen because of their nice bandwidth efficiencies and small PAR's, then some conventional error correction codes, such as Reed–Solomon, should be used in the channel encoder. For graceful degradation in this case, one can again multiplex together symbols from different constellations, say the 4-SQ, 8-SQ, 12-GSQ(2), 16-SQ, and/or 24-GSQ(3), in the time domain before they are further processed by the precoder. The bits carried by different constellations are separately encoded in the channel encoder. Again, with proper multiplexing, the transmitter constellation C alternates between the above constellations.

IV. CONCLUSIONS

Motivated by the comb filter used in the present Zenith/AT&T HDTV transmission system, we have considered the precoding technique for a general partial-response channel. Using a variation of the Tomlinson/Harashima precoder, we have greatly expanded the list of constellations for such applications. The significance of this expansion is twofold. First, one can have a better match between the bit rate of an HDTV signal and the size of the constellation and, hence, a better error rate performance. Second, these constellations

can be used jointly to provide graceful degradation in the received signal quality. As an alternative for conventional error correction codes, coded modulation may also be nicely used in such HDTV systems.

ACKNOWLEDGMENT

The author wishes to thank V. B. Lawrence for inviting him to a meeting with Zenith engineers, which brought the author's attention to the use of comb filters in HDTV transmission.

REFERENCES

[1] R. K. Jurgen, "Consumer electronics: Digital HDTV," *IEEE Spectrum,* vol. 28, pp. 65–68, Jan. 1991.
[2] R. K. Jurgen and W. F. Schreiber, "All-digital TV's promise/problems," *IEEE Spectrum,* vol. 28, pp. 28–30, and 71–73, Apr. 1991.
[3] Zenith and AT&T, "Digital spectrum compatible HDTV," submitted to the FCC/ACATS, Feb. 1991.
[4] J.-D. Wang, "Transmission system design for all-digital HDTV terrestrial broadcasting using VSB or QAM modulation," AT&T internal memo., Apr. 1991.
[5] D. J. Sakrison, *Communication Theory: Transmission of Waveforms and Digital Information.* New York: Wiley, 1968, pp. 132–134.
[6] G. D. Forney, Jr. *et al.,* "Efficient modulation for band-limited channels," *IEEE J. Select. Areas Commun.,* vol. SAC-2, pp. 632–647, Sept. 1984.
[7] L.-F. Wei, "Trellis-coded modulation with multidimensional constellations," *IEEE Trans. Inform. Theory,* vol. IT-33, pp. 483–501, July 1987.
[8] G. D. Forney, Jr. and L.-F. Wei, "Multidimensional constellations-Part I: Introduction, figures of merit, and generalized cross constellations," *IEEE J. Select. Areas Commun.,* vol. SAC-7, pp. 877–892, Aug. 1989.
[9] C.A. Belfiore and J.H. Park, Jr., "Decision feedback equalization," *Proc. IEEE,* vol. 67, pp. 1143–1156, Aug. 1979.
[10] S.U.H. Qureshi, "Adaptive equalization," *Proc. IEEE,* vol. 73, pp. 1349–1387, Sept. 1985.
[11] P. Kabal and S. Pasupathy, "Partial-response signaling," *IEEE Trans. Commun.,* vol. COM-23, pp. 921–934, Sept. 1975.
[12] J. G. Proakis, *Digital Communications.* New York: McGraw-Hill, 1983, pp. 342–346.
[13] J.W. Ketchum, "Performance of trellis codes for M-ary partial response," in *Proc. GLOBECOM'87,* Tokyo, Japan, Nov. 1987, pp. 1720–1724.
[14] L.-F. Wei, "Generalized square and hexagonal constellations for intersymbol-interference channels with generalized Tomlinson/Harashima precoders," to appear in *IEEE Trans. Commun.,* Jan. 1992.

[15] M. Tomlinson, "New automatic equaliser employing modulo arithmetic," *Electron. Lett.*, vol. 7, pp. 138–139, Mar. 1971.

[16] H. Harashima and H. Miyakawa, "Matched-transmission technique for channels with intersymbol interference," *IEEE Trans. Commun.*, vol. COM-20, pp. 774–780, Aug. 1972.

[17] M.V. Eyuboglu and G.D. Forney, Jr., "Trellis precoding: Combined coding, precoding and shaping for intersymbol interference channels," *IEEE Trans. Inform. Theory*, vol. IT-38, pp. 301–314, Mar. 1992.

[18] G. Ungerboeck, "Trellis-coded modulation with redundant signal sets, Part I: Introduction & Part II: State of the art," *IEEE Commun. Mag.*, vol. 25, pp. 5–21, Feb. 1987.

[19] L.-F. Wei, "Coded modulation with unequal error protection," to appear in *IEEE Trans. Commun.*

THE DIGITAL SIMULCAST AD-HDTV CODING SYSTEM

Regis Saint Girons*, Yo-Sung Ho, Tristan Savatier*
Joel Zdepski** and Kiran Challapali

*Thomson Consumer Electronics Inc.
Philips Laboratories, North American Philips Corporation
**David Sarnoff Research Center

Abstract

Advanced Digital High Definition Television (AD-HDTV) is an all-digital simulcast system that is designed to deliver high-quality HDTV services to a large coverage area through a single 6 MHz terrestrial broadcast channel. This paper describes the AD-HDTV coding system with emphasis on the unique features added to the emerging International Standards Organization (ISO) Moving Picture Experts Group (MPEG) coding standard.

1. Introduction

AD-HDTV [1] is an all-digital simulcast system developed by the Advanced Television Research Consortium (ATRC) for terrestrial broadcasting of HDTV in the United States. The AD-HDTV system is designed to offer high-quality HDTV services to a large coverage area in an NTSC co-channel environment with excellent noise and interference limited performance needed for a successful HDTV simulcast system. Figure 1 shows a high-level system block diagram of the AD-HDTV system.

The AD-HDTV system attempts to achieve the performance requirements for terrestrial simulcast by customizing international video and audio coding standards. Specifically, the AD-HDTV coding system is based on the emerging ISO MPEG-1 coding standard [2]. By building upon a widely-accepted coding standard, AD-HDTV ensures a low-cost implementation taking the potential benefits of leveraging ongoing technological advances and VLSI developments. It also facilitates inter-operability with other potential consumer electronics applications involving digital HDTV.

This paper provides a detailed description of the AD-HDTV coding system with its important features that enables the transmission of high-quality HDTV pictures and stereo audio signals in a single 6 MHz terrestrial simulcast channel.

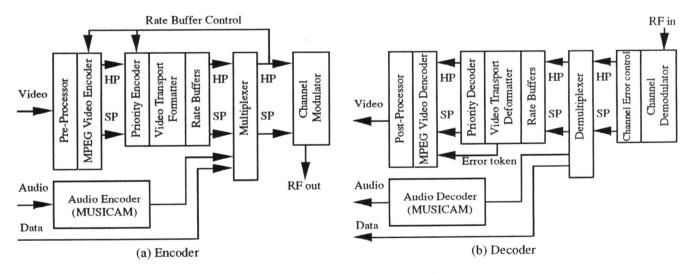

Figure 1: HD-ADTV System Block Diagram.

2. Video Encoder

The AD-HDTV video codec, also known as "MPEG++", is based on the highly-refined and widely-accepted MPEG-1 video compression standard, and has been extensively optimized by the ATRC to achieve high-quality HDTV performance. The MPEG++ encoder produces a coded bit-stream in the range of 15-20 Mb/s that conforms to the MPEG-1 video coding standard. Excellent subjective picture quality has been observed by the ATRC through significant improvements in quantization and bit-rate control techniques.

Reprinted from *IEEE Trans. Consumer Electron.*, vol. 38, no. 4, pp. 778–783, Nov. 1992

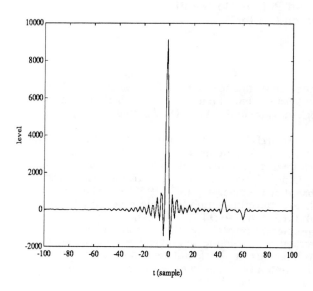

(a) Correlator Output

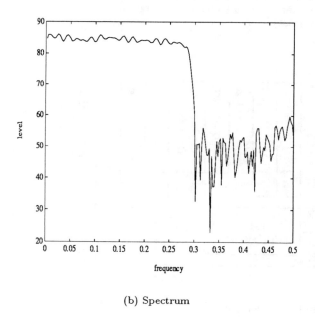

(b) Spectrum

Figure 7: Two Ghosts: 1st Cancellation

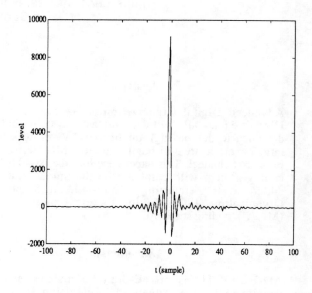

(a) Correlator Output

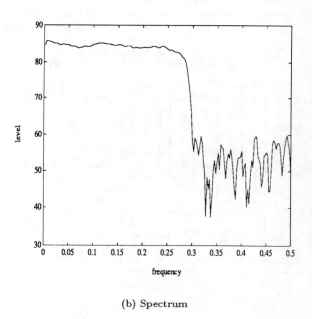

(b) Spectrum

Figure 8: Two Ghosts: 9th Cancellation

As in the MPEG coding standard, picture frames are categorized into three different types: Intra-coded frames (I-frames), Predictively-coded frames (P-frames), and Bidirectionally-coded frames (B-frames). I-frames use purely spatial compression, and are processed independently of other frames. P-frames are coded by a motion- compensated predictive coder using the previous I-frames or P-frames. B-frames are coded by a bidirectional motion-compensated predictive coder using the two adjacent I-frames or P-frames. Figure 2 represents different types of picture frames.

The AD-HDTV video encoder includes preprocessing, motion-compensated prediction, coding mode decision, discrete cosine transform (DCT), adaptive quantization with perceptual weighting, sophisticated bit allocation and rate buffer control, and flexible prioritization of coded data. Figure 3 shows the functional block diagram of the AD-HDTV video encoder.

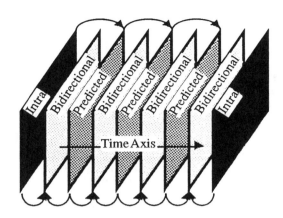

Figure 2: Different Picture Types.

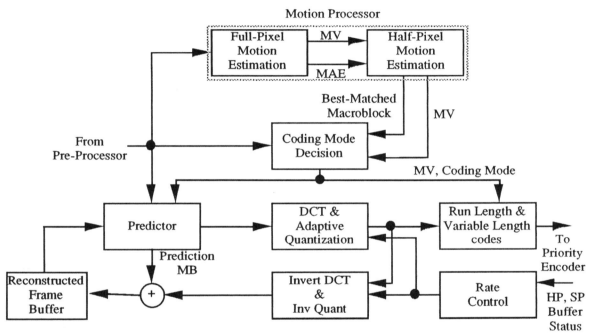

Figure 3: Functional Block Diagram of Video Encoder.

2.1 Preprocessing

In the MPEG++ encoder, video processing is performed on picture frames that are formed by appropriately filtering two successive interlaced fields. RGB color components are converted into one luminance (Y) and two chrominance components (U and V) using a suitable mapping matrix. The two color difference signals in U and V are each filtered and decimated, both horizontally and vertically, by a factor of two, resulting in signals that are each one fourth the sampling density of the luminance signal. Each luminance and chrominance frame is then divided into non-overlapping blocks of 8 x 8 pixels for the DCT coding operation. For motion compensation and adaptive quantization, a macroblock is defined as 16 x

16 luminance pixels and their corresponding two chrominance blocks, as shown in Figure 4.

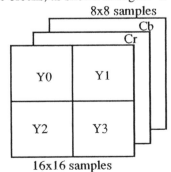

Figure 4: Block and Macroblock Structures.

2.2 Motion Estimation and Motion Compensation

In order to exploit the temporal redundancy in a sequence of video frames, motion estimation of half-pixel accuracy is performed on a unit of 16 x 16 luminance pixels. A displacement vector for each macroblock is obtained using a two-step block matching algorithm with the mean absolute error criterion.

In the first step of the algorithm, an exhaustive search of full pixel accuracy is performed over a predetermined search region. During the second step, the eight neighboring locations of half-pixel distance surrounding the integer displacement estimate from the first step are checked for a better match. Interpolation between sampled pixels is used to produce the missing sample values at the half-pixel locations. Figure 5 shows an illustrative example.

The inferred displacement vector for the chrominance blocks is derived by truncating the component values of the corresponding macroblock motion vector into integer values toward zero and then halving those component values.

Once the motion vector for each macroblock is estimated, pixel values for the target macroblock can be predicted from the previously reconstructed picture. The displacement is then compensated by subtracting the predicted values from the target macroblock. The result from the subtraction process is another macroblock called the prediction residual, or simply the residual macroblock. Note that for bidirectional motion compensation, the prediction macroblock is a weighted average between two macroblocks from the two anchor frames.

Full-pixel Best-matched Block
MV=(+3,-2)

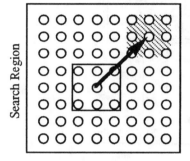

Full-pixel Motion Estimation (first step)

Half-pixel Best-matched\Block
MV=(+2.5,-1.5)

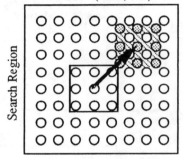

Half-pixel Motion Estimation (second step)

Figure 5: Example of Two-Step Motion Estimation.

2.3 Coding Mode Decision

In addition to the motion estimation process, the motion processor also selects the coding mode for each macroblock. Within a given picture, each macroblock is further analyzed and coded in one of several different coding modes. A macroblock in a P- frame or a B-frame can be coded directly without using motion-compensated prediction if such a coding would result in a lower variance of the macroblock to be encoded. Coding modes for both the P-frame and the B-frame macroblocks are determined based on the luminance component of each macroblock. Table 1 lists all possible coding modes for the three types of frames.

Frame Type	Coding Modes			
	Intraframe Mode	Interframe Modes		
		Forward Motion	Backward Motion	Bidirectional Motion
I	✔			
P	✔	✔		
B	✔	✔	✔	✔

Table 1: Macroblock Coding Modes

2.4 DCT and Adaptive Quantization

The picture information resulting from the motion compensation with a selected coding mode is then transformed by an 8 x 8 DCT operation to exploit the remaining spatial redundancy in the image. Since the human visual system is less sensitive to quantization noise at higher frequencies, the DCT coefficients are first weighted according to their perceptual importance. Different quantization weighting matrices are used for the quantization of intra-frame and inter-frame coded macroblocks. The same weighting matrix is used for both the luminance and chrominance blocks. Figure 6 shows an example of two typical weighting matrices for the intra-frame and the inter- frame coded macroblocks.

8	16	19	22	26	27	29	34
16	16	22	24	27	29	34	37
19	22	26	27	29	34	34	38
22	22	26	27	29	34	37	40
22	26	27	29	32	35	40	48
26	27	29	32	35	40	48	58
26	27	39	34	38	46	56	69
27	29	35	38	46	56	69	83

Intraframe-Coded Quant Matrix.

16	17	18	19	20	21	22	23
17	18	19	20	21	22	23	24
18	19	20	21	22	23	24	25
19	20	21	22	23	24	25	27
20	21	22	23	24	25	27	28
21	22	23	24	25	27	28	30
22	23	24	25	27	28	30	31
23	24	25	27	28	30	31	33

Interframe-Coded Quant Matrix.

Figure 6: Quantization Weighting Matrices.

The MPEG++ encoder uses a forward analyzer that allows better bit allocation to be performed within each frame, thus significantly reducing coding artifacts. The perceptually-weighted DCT coefficients are adaptively quantized according to the local activity measure and the transmission buffer occupancy. The quantized coefficients are scanned in a zig-zag pattern. Because the high-frequency coefficients are most likely to be zero, this ordering results in the longest runs of zeros, which is favorable for the following run-length coding.

The quantized DCT coefficients and other information such as the motion vectors are losslessly encoded by differential coding, runlength coding (RLC), and variable length coding (VLC). Differential coding is applied to the luminance d.c. coefficients within an intraframe-coded macroblock, and to motion vectors within a slice. The a.c. coefficients and the differentially coded d.c. coefficients are coded with a two- dimensional modified Huffman code [2]: the zero runs and following non-zero values are then coded with a single variable-length code. For the less likely combinations of zero runs and non-zero values, fixed-length coding is used instead of VLC. In addition, an end-of-block (EOB) code is used to indicate when all the remaining coefficients in a block are zero.

2.5 Rate Buffer Control

Buffers are needed at the encoder and at the decoder to allow fixed rate transmission of variable rate data. In order to control the fluctuation of the coded bit stream and ensure a constant transmission rate for a band-limited channel, a sophisticated buffer control scheme is incorporated in the MPEG++ encoder. The buffer control is designed to provide excellent subjective quality without external assistance or intervention, i.e., the buffer control is performed automatically.

The Rate Control shown in Figure 3, in conjunction with the rate buffers, smoothes out the time variations in the number of coded bits which must be transmitted. The three different types of frames (I, P, and B) need different number of bits to be coded. I- frames require the maximum number of bits as they do not use any temporal prediction. Conversely, B-frames use the minimum number of bits as they can be very efficiently coded by the bi-directional motion compensated predictive coding.

2.6 Data Priority Processing

The MPEG++ encoder incorporates a robust approach that is essential to permit the bit- stream to survive transmission errors that will inevitably occur during terrestrial simulcast broadcasting. In general, compressed video data is highly vulnerable to bit errors that result from noise in the transmission channel.

To overcome these potentially serious error effects, the AD-HDTV codec separately transmits two classes of data: high-priority (HP) data that is essential for viewable pictures, and standard-priority (SP) data that is additionally required for high-quality HDTV pictures. The prioritization encoder analyzes the MPEG codewords and assigns each codeword to either the HP or SP channel. This assignment is made adaptively to maximize the subjective quality of the decoded video in the presence of channel errors.

The HP data is transmitted at a higher power level to provide additional reliability and robustness, thus ensuring the reception of viewable pictures under virtually all conditions, even at the fringe areas of coverage.

3. Video Decoder

Figure 7 shows the functional block diagram of the AD-HDTV video decoder.

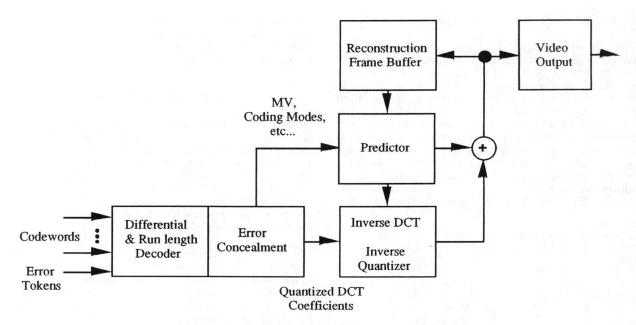

Figure 7: Functional Block Diagram of Video Decoder

3.1 Differential and Run Length Decoding

The MPEG++ decoder receives corresponding fixed length internal MPEG codes from the priority decoder subsystem. These codes are processed to interpret parameters specifying the coding mode used by the encoder, and then video decoding is performed.

The differential and runlength decoder reconstructs motion vectors, the quantized DCT coefficients, and the quantization scale factor. These values are subsequently used by the inverse quantizer and inverse DCT units to reconstruct the individual macroblocks of video pixels or residuals.

Prediction macroblocks are generated from the reconstruction frame stores based on coding modes and the received motion vectors for a particular macroblock. The reconstruction process of I-frames or P-frames also involves updating the content of the frame memory. For intraframe-coded macroblocks, the output macroblocks from the inverse DCT replaces the macroblocks in the appropriate frame store. For interframe-coded macroblocks, the output macroblocks from the inverse DCT are added to appropriate prediction macroblocks. The resultant macroblocks then replace the corresponding macroblocks in the frame stores. Finally, as the reconstructed frames exit the video compression decoder, they are put back into the correct field sequence for proper display.

3.2 Error Concealment

The MPEG++ decoder provides for error concealment functionality. When there are errors in the transmitted bit stream, the video decoder receives an appropriate "error token" from the priority subsystem, indicating the type of error event along with the internal MPEG code. Based on these error tokens, the decoder implements a set of error concealment procedures.

The error concealment unit in Figure 7 estimates and replaces video information lost due to uncorrectable channel errors. When no errors are present, data passes through the error concealment block unaltered. When there are uncorrectable transmission errors in the bit-stream, the received erroneous video data are discarded. The decoder then performs error concealment operations aimed at mitigating the effects of this lost data. Within the video decoder, each missing macroblock is replaced with either co-located macroblocks from the previous reconstructed frame, or spatial concealment in which corrupted a.c. coefficients of the DCT block are replaced by zero values.

These concealment procedures enable the AD-HDTV decoder to deliver a useful picture, and thus provides an important feature of "graceful degradation", even in the presence of significant channel errors.

3.3 Postprocessing

The postprocessor at the receiver reconstructs analog RGB color signals from the decoded YUV signals. The postprocessor receives YUV 4:2:0 component signals in a 1050/29.97/1:1 internal format from the video compression decoder. Horizontal and vertical interpolation filtering is applied to the color difference signals to recreate a full raster, and the component signals are converted from the internal compression format (1050/29.97/1:1) to interlaced fields

(1050/59.94/2:1). Finally, the signals are converted to analog form and matrixed to RGB signals.

4. Audio Coding

The AD-HDTV system is designed to carry two stereo pairs of audio signals. A stereo pair of audio signals uses 16-bit digital audio at a 48 kHz sampling rate. The audio program is coded using the MPEG Layer-2 audio compression algorithm [2]. Its core technique is based on the Masking-pattern-adaptive Universal Subband Integrated Coding And Multiplexing (MUSICAM) system [3], which achieves high aural quality by varying the quantization of frequency subbands in a manner that the resulting quantization distortion is psycho-acoustically masked. Listening tests have shown that this coding provides performance virtually indistinguishable from CD quality.

5. Conclusion

AD-HDTV is designed to provide high-quality HDTV pictures and stereo audio signals in a single 6 MHz simulcast channel. AD-HDTV has flexible operating characteristics that allow it to provide a broad scope of services, as well as the inter- operability and extensibility needed to form the basis for new and innovative applications of HDTV in many industries. By building upon widely-accepted coding standards, AD-HDTV ensures cost-effective solutions to new products in the variety of markets.

Acknowledgment

The AD-HDTV system has been developed as a joint effort among many engineers from Philips Laboratories at Briarcliff, David Sarnoff Research Center, Thomson Consumer Electronics Inc., and LEP in Paris. The authors wish to express their sincere gratitude to many individuals from these research laboratories who contributed to the system development.

References

[1] System Description of Advanced Digital Television, Submitted to the FCC by the Advanced Television Research Consortium, Jan. 1992.
[2] Coding of Moving Pictures and Associated Audio for Digital Storage Media at up to about 1.5 Mb/s, MPEG Committee Draft ISO11172, ISO/MPEG, Nov. 1991.
[3] G. Theile, G. Stoll and M. Link, "Low Bit-Rate Coding of High-Quality Audio Signals: An Introduction to the MUSICAM System," EBU Review - Technical, No. 230, pp. 158-181, Aug. 1988.

Advanced Digital HDTV Transmission System for Terrestrial Video Simulcasting

Samir N. Hulyalkar, Yo-Sung Ho, Kiran S. Challapali, David A. Bryan, *Member, IEEE*, Carlo Basile, Hugh White, Newman D. Wilson, and Bhavesh Bhatt

Abstract—Transmission aspects of the Advanced Digital High Definition Television (AD-HDTV) system, proposed by the Advanced Television Research Consortium (ATRC) for terrestrial simulcast delivery of HDTV, are described. The terrestrial simulcast HDTV channel can be viewed as an interference-limited channel due to the presence of a cochannel NTSC signal, which limits the total transmitted power of an HDTV signal. In AD-HDTV, two quadrature-amplitude modulated (QAM) carriers, with different power spectral densities, are employed in a frequency division multiplex (FDM) mode within the standard 6 MHz channel. The resulting spectral shaping allows a larger power to be transmitted, compared to that for a single QAM carrier, for the same level of perceptual interference into cochannel NTSC. In addition, the coded video data is split into high-priority (HP) data and standard-priority (SP) data and the vital information is sent on the appropriate QAM carrier. This prioritization results in a robust audio and video transmission system. Besides, the availability is higher in scenarios where the received signal level is such that the carrier-to-noise ratio (CNR) is above the threshold for HP reception but below the threshold for SP reception. This is important in fringe areas where an abrupt drop in reception quality, typical of a digital transmission, is to be avoided. The NTSC planning factors, suitably modified for HDTV delivery, are used to estimate the coverage area for AD-HDTV. The calculated AD-HDTV coverage area of 54.5 miles is comparable to that for NTSC transmission.

I. INTRODUCTION

BY the middle of the last decade, television broadcasting had been in existence in the United States for nearly fifty years and had grown into a successful and mature industry. As a result, the implementation of high-definition television (HDTV) broadcasting in the terrestrial environment has become of interest to the industry as well as the regulatory bodies. Faced with the complex problem of a limited electromagnetic spectrum and the desire to occupy this scarce spectrum with a variety of new services, the Federal Communications Commission (FCC) decided that the spectrum presently allocated to terrestrial television broadcasting must suffice for HDTV broadcasting as well.

The implication here is that a new television service will be broadcast in severely constrained 6 MHz channels [1], presently called *taboo* channels. In addition, the worst-case taboo channels carry a full-power NTSC transmission originating in a geographically adjacent service area resulting in a strong cochannel interfering signal. The requirement of coexistence with NTSC transmissions also limits the power available for HDTV broadcasting; however, the viability of terrestrial broadcasting relies on coverage areas of approximately 50 miles. Given the state-of-the-art in digital image compression, it is clear that what the broadcasters require of HDTV images can be supported by approximately 20 Mb/s and that the capacity of the terrestrial broadcast channel matches this fairly well. Considering these issues, the challenge undertaken by several research and development institutions, with the encouragement of the FCC, is to design a joint source/channel coding scheme for this environment.

Coexistence with NTSC vestigial sideband (VSB) transmissions, containing a high amplitude picture carrier at 1.25 MHz from the lower band edge, suggests that the new transmission must be designed to mitigate the effect of this strong interferer. Furthermore, due to the characteristics of the human visual system, analog NTSC transmissions are most sensitive to interference which occurs near the picture carrier itself, thus requiring a solution which minimizes disturbance to the NTSC signal in this region of the spectrum. A solution proposed by the Advanced Television Research Consortium (ATRC) consists of two separate quadrature-amplitude modulated (QAM) signals inside the 6 MHz channel referred to as spectrally-shaped QAM (SS-QAM). Using this technique, a narrowband QAM signal is placed below the interfering NTSC picture carrier and a wideband QAM signal is placed above the picture carrier. The narrowband and wideband spectra are entirely contained on either side of the picture carrier and, therefore, are protected from cochannel NTSC transmissions while providing substantial protection to the cochannel transmission.

VSB transmissions require that the transmitted signal be processed through a Nyquist slope filter, and in the case of NTSC transmissions this filter is located at the receiver rather than the transmitter. The narrowband QAM signal has been placed so that it coincides with the slope of the Nyquist filter. Therefore, the affected NTSC receiver enjoys protection when subjected to this interferer, derived from the attenuation of the input filter. These facts suggest an opportunity for further optimization of the AD-HDTV signal by increasing the power level of the narrowband QAM signal while maintaining the interference-limited coverage due to the wideband signal.

Having optimized the transmission as described, the resulting composite AD-HDTV broadcast contains two data streams with widely different bit error probability versus carrier-to-

Manuscript received June 1992; revised August 1992.

S. N. Hulyalkar, Y.-S. Ho, K. S. Challapali, D. A. Bryan, and C. Basile are with Philips Laboratories, North American Philips Corporation, Briarcliff Manor, NY 10510.

H. White, N. Wilson, and B. Bhatt are with the David Sarnoff Research Center, Princeton, NJ 08543.

IEEE Log Number 9204411.

Reprinted from *IEEE J. Selected Areas Commun.*, vol. 11, no. 1, pp. 119–125, Jan. 1983.

noise ratio (CNR) performances. Narrowband transmission will have a lower error rate than the wideband transmission at any given receive location by virtue of its higher power density. This assumes that most of the interfering cochannel NTSC power is concentrated around the picture, color, and sound carriers, thus resulting in a robust narrowband transmission. Coupling these transmission characteristics with the payload of broadcast television (i.e., compressed video high-quality audio), it is desirable to "prioritize" the data at the source and place high-priority (HP) data in the more secure narrowband channel while routing the standard-priority (SP) data through the wideband channel. Due to the variability in the received signal level in the terrestrial channel, this type of broadcasting scheme allows for the information which is essential to transmission such as picture synchronization, motion vectors, and compressed audio to be received with a greater reliability. Error concealment algorithms in the receiver can then utilize the essential information received to reconstruct at least a *recognizable* picture and sound. Clearly, the time availability of recognizable pictures and sound should be close to 100%, with good quality pictures available at least 90% of the time. Both of these requirements must be satisfied at the fringe areas. This criterion can be used to evaluate the *coverage area* of a transmitted HDTV signal.

This paper describes the effective embodiment of the above ideas in the advanced digital HDTV (AD-HDTV) system. In Section II, an overview of the AD-HDTV system is presented. Then, the prioritization algorithm, which selects more important data for transmission over the HP channel, is described in Section III. The channel coding and modulation strategies, along with performance calculations which specify the effective coverage area, are described in Section IV. Section V draws some conclusions.

II. AD-HDTV SYSTEM OVERVIEW

AD-HDTV [2] is an all-digital simulcast HDTV system developed by the Advanced Television Research Consortium (ATRC). It is designed to offer high-quality HDTV service to a large coverage area through a single 6 MHz channel subject to cochannel NTSC interference. It combines practical approaches to video and audio data compression, prioritized data transport, and digital modulation to provide both the robustness and reliability required for digital simulcasting. It holds promise for low-cost implementation by building upon the emerging International Standards Organization (ISO) Moving Picture Experts Group (MPEG) coding standard [3]. It also provides the flexibility that will form the basis for new and innovative services through the use of a packetized data transport system. The AD-HDTV system is shown in Fig. 1.

The video coding scheme, also known as "MPEG++," is based on the well-refined and widely accepted MPEG video compression standard, which has been further optimized by the ATRC to achieve high-quality HDTV performance. Excellent subjective picture quality has been achieved through significant improvements in various aspects of the video processing. The MPEG++ encoder includes preprocessing, motion-compensated predictive coding, frequency transforma-

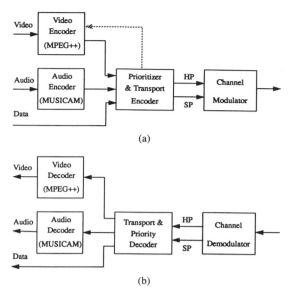

Fig. 1. System overview. (a) AD-HDTV encoder. (b) AD-HDTV decoder.

tion by discrete cosine transform (DCT), adaptive quantization with perceptual weighting, and sophisticated bit allocation and rate control.

The digital video encoder operates on YUV 4 : 2 : 0 video inputs that are converted from RGB color components using a suitable mapping matrix. The video signals have a 2 : 1 interlaced scanning format at 59.94 fields/second with 960 active lines per frame and 1440 active pixels per line. The video encoder produces a coded bit stream at about 20 Mb/s that conforms to the ISO MPEG-1 draft standard.

The AD-HDTV system is designed to carry two pairs of stereo audio signals. The audio programs are coded using the MPEG Layer-2 audio compression algorithm [3], whose core technique is based on the MUSICAM (masking-pattern-adaptive universal subband integrated coding and multiplexing) system [4]. Data reduction is accomplished by varying the quantization of data from frequency subbands in such a way that the resulting quantization noise is psychoacoustically masked.

The AD-HDTV encoder incorporates a robust delivery strategy that is essential to permit the bit stream to survive transmission errors that will inevitably occur during terrestrial simulcast broadcasting. In general, compressed data are highly vulnerable to bit errors that result from noise in the transmission channel. To overcome these potentially serious error effects, the AD-HDTV codec separately transmits two classes of data: HP data that are essential for viewable pictures, and SP data that are additionally required for high-quality HDTV pictures. The HP data in the two-tier delivery system are transmitted at a higher power level to provide additional robustness and reliability, thus ensuring the reception of viewable pictures under virtually all conditions, even at the fringe areas of coverage.

The data transport processor is responsible for service-independent data multiplexing, cell formatting, error detection, and error correction as well as service-specific logical error recovery. The prioritized data transport format used in the AD-HDTV system provides for reliable transport and synchronization of the MPEG++ bit-stream over a two-tier transmission system. It uses a powerful Reed–Solomon (RS) error correction code to correct the bit errors that can occur under channel noise and interference.

The channel modulator performs the tasks of modulation, channel equalization, and frequency translation. The HP and SP MPEG++ bit streams are sent over the simulcast channel with appropriate transmission priority using a two-tier modulation technique which delivers approximately 20% of the data with greater reliability. In addition to providing two-tier transmission matched to the data prioritization process, AD-HDTV's two-carrier SS-QAM approach mitigates the effect of NTSC cochannel interference, thus permitting the low-power operation necessary for terrestrial simulcast. Finally, reliable demodulation of the low-power AD-HDTV signal is achieved without sacrificing bandwidth efficiency through the use of a high-rate set partition code.

The AD-HDTV video decoder receives a sequence of MPEG codewords from the priority decoder. These codewords are processed to interpret parameters specifying the mode coded by the encoder, and then video decompression is performed. When there are uncorrectable transmission errors in the bit stream, the received erroneous video data are discarded. The decoder then performs error concealment operations aimed at mitigating the effects of the transmission errors. These concealment procedures, combined with priority data encoding, enable the AD-HDTV decoder to deliver useful pictures even in the presence of significant channel errors.

The key technical features of the AD-HDTV system are provided in [2]. Detailed descriptions of video coding, data prioritization, and channel coding and modulation follow.

III. VIDEO CODING FOR PRIORITIZED TRANSMISSION

A. Introduction

An elegant way to minimize the effect of channel errors would be to encode and transmit a low-resolution image (for example, of standard-definition quality) at higher power than the associated enhancement information. In that way, the first part of the coded video to be affected by transmission errors is the enhancement information, which is the least important visually. However, the current transmission conditions in North America (namely, a 6 MHz channel capable of carrying about 20 Mb/s) require a highly optimized coding scheme in order to deliver true HDTV quality images. This situation will be exacerbated with improvements in HD camera technology, producing images with greater spatial and temporal resolution. Schemes that impose constraints, such as the simple hierarchical scheme described above, compromise the visual quality of the HD signal and were therefore deemed unacceptable in the design of the AD-HDTV system.

The ATRC has proposed a scheme whereby the HD signal is coded without constraint (with the intention of fully utilizing the 20 Mb/s). A part of the coded video is tagged as "high priority" and is transmitted with higher power. The decision as to which data are tagged as HP depends upon the importance of the data in reconstructing a presentable picture and the availability of bandwidth on the HP channel. After a priority is assigned to it, each data element is multiplexed to one of the two output channels according to the assigned priority.

The HP data are transmitted with much higher power than the SP so that the fringe areas receive the HP data reliably even though the SP signal may be lost. The error concealment in the receiver then utilizes the HP data in reconstructing a presentable picture. Error concealment is defined as any-and-everything done in the receiver to mitigate the effects of channel errors. Some of the error concealment algorithms investigated by the ATRC have been reported in [5].

The priority processor can be designed so that it can either be included in the source coder or as a separate unit located between the source and channel coders. The latter scheme is employed in the AD-HDTV system. An advantage of such a scheme is that the priority processor could be designed independently of the video codec, without sacrificing coding efficiency.

In summary, the function of the MPEG++ encoder is to generate high-quality coded HD video with two priority levels in such a manner as to give acceptable image quality under severely impaired reception conditions, while delivering superb quality under typical transmission impairments.

B. The Prioritization Algorithm

The HP transmission capacity is only one-fifth of the total capacity available for compressed video. Hence, it is important to utilize the HP capacity wisely. As a first step, the priority encoder determines the number of bits that can be sent as HP on a frame basis (defined as HP_{frac}). Experiments have shown that splitting encoded video data into HP/SP uniformly for all frames does not produce the best image. The distribution of information between HP and SP depends upon the degree of importance of the information in reconstructing a good quality image. The MPEG I-frames [3] are protected the most, since they are the "refresh" frames and MPEG B- and P-frames [3] are predicted from I-frames. The B-frames are protected the least because degradation that affects them persists for only one frame. Other important information, such as timing data, audio, and key MPEG headers, are given high priority. HP_{frac} is set so that as much important information as possible goes into HP while ensuring that the buffers associated with HP and SP do not overflow or underflow.

Having computed HP_{frac} on a frame-by-frame basis, we proceed to decide where to set the priority breakpoint (PBP) so that the HP/SP split given by HP_{frac} is achieved. A PBP is that point in an ordered sequence of encoded codewords which defines the HP/SP split. Codewords before the PBP go into HP, while codewords after the PBP go into SP. The inherent ordering of data types in MPEG according to importance [3] is utilized, and a simple PBP is defined accordingly. The interested reader is referred to [2] for more details. The following section describes the channel coding/modulation strategy.

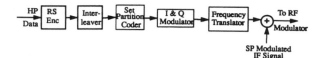

Fig. 2. AD-HDTV transmission system.

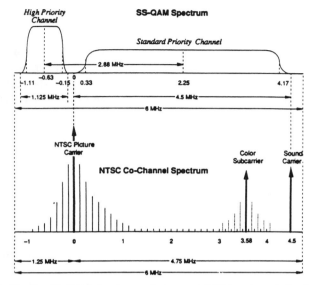

Fig. 3. SS-QAM signal spectral shape and NTSC cochannel signal.

IV. CHANNEL CODING/MODULATION

A. Introduction

Fig. 2 shows the overall block diagram of the AD-HDTV transmitter, where only the HP signal path is shown. An essentially identical description applies to the SP signal path. As explained earlier, two QAM transmitters are used in a frequency division multiplex (FDM) mode with the QAM carrier corresponding to the HP data sent with higher (5 dB more) power to ensure better reliability, where the two QAM carriers are placed such that the cochannel interference into the NTSC receiver is minimized, as shown in Fig. 3.

The symbol rate corresponding to the HP signal is 0.96 MHz; the symbol rate for the SP signal is four times higher. With 32 QAM used to modulate both carriers, the total encoded bit rate that can be transmitted is 24 Mb/s. The channel coding strategy for both carriers is identical and consists of using a (147,127) RS code followed by an interleaver. A sync byte is placed before each packet, resulting in a total FEC frame size of 148 bytes. Then, a 0.9 rate set-partition code (described in more detail later) is applied. Hence, the actual payload that can be transmitted with two 32 QAM modulated streams is 18.5 Mb/s.

The modulator, shown in Fig. 2, uses square-root raised-cosine pulse shaping with 17% excess bandwidth. The design of the pulse-shaping filters takes into account the higher power of the HP signal such that no interference of the HP signal into the SP signal is observed. The HP and SP signals are then added together at IF (with appropriate frequency translations and gain adjustments). This IF signal is then passed to the

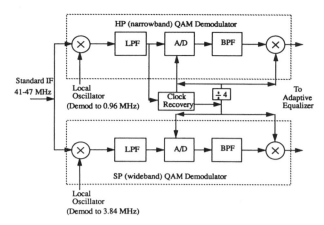

Fig. 4. SS-QAM filtering, sampling, and demodulation.

RF modulator for simulcast transmission over the terrestrial channel.

In addition to the introduction of noise in actual transmission channels, echoes or multipath may be introduced [6]. UHF channels exhibit time-varying multipath, but these variations are slow compared to the rate of symbol transmission. In most cases, the number of echoes are less than 8 and these echoes do not exceed 35 microseconds in delay. Thus, the multipath effects can be modeled as a slowly varying channel filter which can be corrected by use of an adaptive equalizer at the receiver. Interleaving (following RS encoding) is used to combat impulse noise and SS-QAM is employed to mitigate cochannel interference from NTSC.

At the receiver front end, a double-conversion tuner [2] is used to bring the signal down to an IF of 41–47 MHz. This process of translating the received spectrum to the first IF, centered at 611 MHz, and then translating it again to the final IF avoids problems related to image frequencies and thus obviates some of the "UHF taboos" present in current UHF TV broadcasting. The use of UHF taboos can free significant portions of television spectrum for broadcast use.

The SS-QAM IF signal is then passed through two different demodulators (i.e., one for the HP and the other for the SP signal), as shown in Fig. 4. As can be seen, the two QAM carriers are demodulated separately. The incoming IF signals are frequency translated close to baseband, lowpass filtered, and then sampled at four times the (HP or SP) symbol rate using a clock generated from the HP signal. The precise relationship between the symbol rates of the HP and the SP signals allows the clock generated from the HP carrier to be used, after multiplication by four, for sampling the SP signal. Hence, the resulting synchronization can be made quite robust. The current AD-HDTV hardware uses a square-law timing recovery circuit [7], which is found to be sufficient for operation over the range of carrier-to-noise ratios required for reliable transmission of 32 QAM signals.

The outputs of the demodulators are then sent to the equalizers and decision-directed carrier recovery circuits [7] corresponding to the HP and SP signals, respectively, as shown in Fig. 5. A blind equalizer using the constant modulus algorithm [8] is used to provide initial convergence. This is then followed by a decision-directed least mean square (LMS)

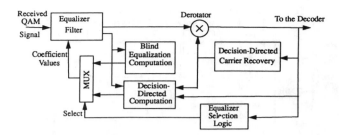

Fig. 5. Equalization and carrier recovery.

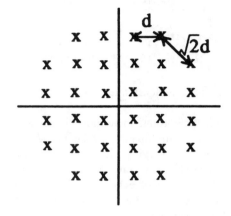

Fig. 6. 32-QAM constellation used for set-partition coding.

adaptation of the equalizer coefficients such that the equalizer is implemented in a passband mode, i.e., the error signal, obtained using a slicer, is rotated appropriately by the carrier recovery circuit. The carrier recovery is also operated in a decision-directed mode using the phase error thus computed as input to a digital phase-locked loop that tracks and minimizes the frequency and the phase offset between the carriers of the transmitter and the receiver. During acquisition, both the blind equalizer and the carrier recovery circuit are operated in parallel since the blind equalization algorithm is independent of phase.

The soft-decision output of the derotator shown in Fig. 5 is then sent to the set-partition decoder, deinterleaver, and RS decoder for both the HP and SP signals, respectively, providing the inverse processing to that shown in Fig. 2. Fig. 6 shows the 32-QAM constellation used in AD-HDTV. The set-partition coder operates on this constellation and is a 0.9 rate code as described in [9]. A set-partition coding gain of 3 dB can then be obtained by use of a convolutional or block encoder as shown in [9]. Almost all of this coding gain is realized by performing soft-decision decoding at the receiver.

B. Performance Analysis

The RS block error rate performance of the HP and SP signals is shown in Fig. 7 as a function of CNR, where the carrier power is measured for both the HP and SP signals and the noise power is measured over a 6 MHz bandwidth [2]. Here, the performance of the set-partition encoder/decoder is also included. Error concealment experiments have shown that a viewer will typically begin to notice picture artifacts for RS

block error rates of 10^{-3} in the SP signal. This then determines the CNR threshold for reliable operation.

The following set of thresholds have been calculated using simulations and/or measured subjective testing [2]. These can be used to determine the coverage area of the AD-HDTV SS-QAM signal as limited by random noise and cochannel interference.

- CNR threshold for the SP signal is 16.1 dB.
- CNR threshold for the HP signal is 11.1 dB.
- Desired-to-undesired signal power ratio (DUR) required to receive full-quality AD-HDTV reception (full quality is defined to be the CNR threshold for SP reception), when AD-HDTV is subjected to interference from an NTSC cochannel station, is −2 dB [2].
- DUR required to receive full-quality AD-HDTV (SP reception), when subjected to interference from another AD-HDTV cochannel station, is 16.1 dB.
- Noise equivalent (NEQ) advantage factor, which is defined as the ratio of power of AD-HDTV interference to the power of 6 MHz random noise interference that causes the same subjective degradation to the picture quality of the NTSC signal subject to the interference, is 1.4 dB. This has been determined by a combination of actual viewer simulations and analysis [2].

There are two advantages that accrue from the shaping of the SS-QAM spectrum with respect to performance under interference from cochannel NTSC. First, for the same interference into NTSC, a larger amount of total power can be transferred to the HDTV receiver. This is represented by the NEQ factor. The second advantage relies on the fact that the effective CNR available at a receiver is statistical in nature. To overcome this variability, the FCC has calculated field strengths $F(x, y)$ at different distances for different antenna heights, where $F(x, y)$ is defined as the field strength in dB μV/m relative to 1 kW available at $x\%$ of the stations with a $y\%$ availability. The presence of the high-power HP signal increases the availability of recognizable pictures and sound and thus provides a larger coverage area. This will be stated more precisely in the following.

The effective coverage area in NTSC transmission is defined by specifying the grade B contour corresponding to the distance associated with the $F(50, 90)$ contour for "marginal" or better pictures. Based on Television Allocation Study Organization (TASO) test results, 85% of the viewers regard an NTSC peak-of-sync power to average noise power ratio of 26.7 dB as "marginal" or better, which, for typical antenna heights and antenna radiated power, can result in a coverage area of approximately 55 miles. A loss in power of 3.5 dB results in a decrease in the percentage of viewers who rate the picture as "marginal" or better to 65%. Hence, NTSC exhibits graceful degradation. Nonetheless, for the grade B contour, the picture never disappears totally since the audio and synchronization are available even with a CNR of 15 dB. Thus, the time availability of the NTSC signal is almost 100% at the NTSC grade B contour.

If the CNR falls below a certain threshold for a digitally transmitted signal, then the entire picture can be lost. From preceding remarks regarding NTSC, it is clear that important

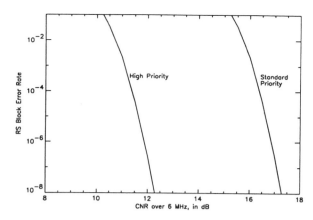

Fig. 7. RS block error rates for 32 SS-QAM with a 5 dB power difference in HP and SP power densities.

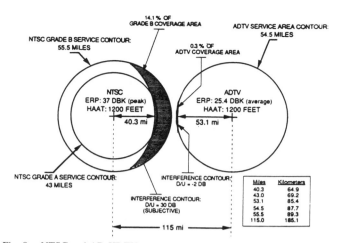

Fig. 8. NTSC and AD-HDTV cochannel stations with 115 miles separation.

data (for example, the audio data) must be available at the receiver with a higher percentage availability as compared to the rest of the data. This important consideration allows a digital HDTV system's noise-limited coverage area to be defined by the following.

- 90% time availability for perfect or slightly degraded pictures. For AD-HDTV, this would correspond to a CNR threshold for SP reception equal to 16.1 dB.

- A much higher availability, for example 97%, for audio and recognizable pictures to protect against loss of service for all but a small fraction of the time. For AD-HDTV, this corresponds to the availability provided with a CNR threshold for HP reception equal to 11.1 dB.

Both of these requirements must be satisfied for the coverage area of interest. In [2], many examples are provided using typical antenna heights and antenna radiated powers. Fig. 8 shows the results of these calculations. As much as 54.5 miles of HDTV signal coverage can be provided using the AD-HDTV approach. In Fig. 8, the AD-HDTV and NTSC transmitters are assumed to be operating at a distance of 115 miles. The NTSC transmitter is assumed to operate with an effective radiated power (ERP) of 37 dBK. To set the AD-HDTV signal power, it is assumed that the AD-HDTV signal is allowed to interfere with 14.1% of the NTSC coverage area, which is the same as the amount that an NTSC signal would interfere if it is placed at the minimum allowed distance of 155 miles. This signal penetration of AD-HDTV into NTSC is reached at 40.3 miles from the NTSC transmitter. To specify the DUR for the NTSC signal with an AD-HDTV signal acting as interference, we first note that if the AD-HDTV signal is equivalent to the subjective effect of noise then the DUR is 30 dB. However, due to the strategically placed carriers, an NEQ advantage factor was determined in [2], as described earlier, to be given by 1.4 dB, i.e., the effective DUR for the NTSC signal is 28.6 dB. In [2], it is shown that for the signal penetration of 40.3 miles with a DUR of 28.6 dB, the AD-HDTV *average* ERP is 25.4 dBK. The noise-limited contour distance of AD-HDTV for this ERP is at a distance of 54.5 miles [2]. For this region, the area in which the DUR for the AD-HDTV signal that is less than or equal to −2 dB is 0.3%, which is the coverage area interfered by NTSC into

AD-HDTV. These results are obtained assuming the height of antenna above average terrain (HAAT) to be 1200 feet. Other examples with different heights, different NTSC ERP, and different spacing between the NTSC and the AD-HDTV transmitters result in similar numbers for the noise-limited coverage area. The interested reader is referred to [2] for more details.

V. CONCLUSIONS

The FCC has set a goal of achieving HDTV simulcasting within the existing 6 MHz wide taboo channels, which are subject to strong cochannel interference from existing NTSC broadcast stations. Fairly recently, it became clear from viewing of decompressed images that this would require a transmission rate of approximately 20 Mb/s.

Minimization of interference from cochannel NTSC into AD-HDTV and vice versa led to the specifications of two QAM carriers—one below and one above the NTSC picture carrier. Due to the well-known Nyquist slope of the NTSC receiver filter, it became possible to transmit the lower-frequency QAM carrier with much higher power. Having this high-power signal available led to the prioritization of information such that the most essential information for delivering a viewable picture with sound, even at the fringe areas of coverage, can be transmitted with great reliability or availability. The manner in which the output of the MPEG++ encoder is prioritized has been described, as have the channel coding and receiver processing strategies that allow reliable reception in the face of noise and multipath. A coverage of as much as 54.5 miles is possible using the AD-HDTV transmission system as shown above using typical antenna parameters.

Thus, we conclude that the AD-HDTV system has achieved the goal of providing a robust HDTV transmission system through the use of a SS-QAM modulation system, prioritized video encoding and transport, powerful forward error correction, and adaptive equalization at the receiver. Furthermore, the system holds the promise for low-cost implementation by building on the MPEG coding standard, and provides the flexibility for new and innovative services through the use of a packetized data transport system.

Acknowledgment

The described AD-HDTV system design was a joint effort among many engineers at Philips Laboratories in Briarcliff Manor, NY, David Sarnoff Research Labs in Princeton, NJ, and Thomson Consumer Electronics in Indianapolis, IN. The authors wish to thank the many individuals from these research laboratories who contributed to the system and these results.

References

[1] K. Blair Benson, *Television Engineering Handbook.* New York: McGraw Hill, 1986.
[2] "AD-HDTV system description," prepared by ATRC for ACATS Cert., Feb. 1992.
[3] "Coding of moving pictures and associated audio for digital storage media at up to about 1.5 Mbits/s," MPEG Comm. Draft ISO11172, ISO/MPEG, Nov. 1991.
[4] G. Theile, G. Stoll, and M. Link, "Low bit-rate coding of high-quality audio signals: An introduction to the MUSICAM system," *EBU Rev.—Tech.,* no. 230, pp. 158–181, Aug. 1988.
[5] H. Sun, K. Challapali, and J. Zdepski, "Error concealment in digital simulcast ADTV decoder," presented at ICCE '92, Rosemont, IL, June 1992.
[6] "Field tests of ghost canceling systems for NTSC television broadcasting," Nat. Assoc. of Broadcasters and Assoc. of Maximum Service Television Rep., Jan. 31, 1992.
[7] E. A. Lee and J. G. Messerschmitt, *Digital Communication.* Boston, MA: Kluwer Academic, 1988.
[8] D. N. Godard, "Self-recovering equalization and carrier tracking in two-dimensional data communication systems," *IEEE Trans. Commun.,* vol. COM-28, no. 11, pp. 1867–1875, Nov. 1980.
[9] G. D. Forney, R. G. Gallager, G. R. Lang, F. M. Longstaff, and S. U. Qureshi, "Efficient modulation for band-limited channels," *IEEE J. Select. Areas Commun.,* vol. SAC-2, no. 5, pp. 632–646, Sept. 1984.

Flexible and Robust Packet Transport for Digital HDTV

Robert J. Siracusa, *Member, IEEE,* Kuriacose Joseph, *Member, IEEE,*
Joel Zdepski, and Dipankar Raychaudhuri, *Senior Member, IEEE*

Abstract— This paper describes a packet-oriented transport approach used in the recently proposed Advanced Digital Television (ADTV) system for terrestrial HDTV broadcast. ADTV achieves the primary design goal of providing robust HDTV delivery on terrestrial simulcast channels via MPEG video compression, prioritization of MPEG data, and "cell-relay" type packet transport in conjunction with a two-tier physical transmission scheme. General design issues relevant to the development of the proposed transport protocol are discussed. To provide context for the two-tier transport approach described, ADTV's prioritization algorithm for partitioning MPEG-encoded video into high-priority (HP) and standard-priority (SP) bit streams is first outlined. The data transport format which supports these prioritized compressed video bit streams over the terrestrial channel and other applicable media (e.g., cable, satellite, ATM) is then described. The three principal sublayers of the ADTV transport protocol include a generic data link/network level for addressing, priority support and error control, an adaptation layer for service-specific error recovery, and a video service level for higher-level resynchronization of the video decoder. Each of these layers is discussed in terms of specific functions, impact on system performance, and hardware implementation factors. A "proof-of-concept" simulation model which incorporates transport encoding and decoding functionality is outlined, and performance evaluation results are given for illustrative transmission scenarios.

I. INTRODUCTION

THIS paper describes a packet-oriented transport approach used in the recently proposed Advanced Digital Television (ADTV) system [1], [2] for terrestrial broadcast of high-definition television. ADTV achieves the primary design goal of reliably delivering HDTV over terrestrial simulcast channels through the use of MPEG video compression, prioritization of MPEG data, and "cell-relay" type packet transport in conjunction with a two-tier physical transmission scheme. The ADTV system incorporating this protocol is currently being developed by the Advanced Television Research Consortium (ATRC), and is scheduled for FCC testing in the second quarter of 1992. This proposal for digital HDTV is distinguished from other candidate systems [3], [4] by the use of a layered "cell-relay" type data transport protocol similar to that being considered for the CCITT broadband ISDN/ATM standard [5], [6]. While ADTV's transport represents the first application of a layered cell-relay protocol to HDTV broadcasting, similar approaches have been proposed by others for video over B-

Manuscript received June 1992; revised August 1992.

The authors are with the David Sarnoff Research Center, Princeton, NJ 08543–5300.

IEEE Log Number 9204420.

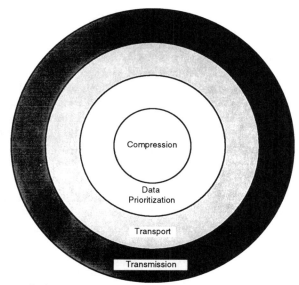

Compression Layer
- Input/Output Pre-/post-processing.
- Data Compression/Decompression

Prioritization Layer
- Separation (merging) of data to (from) standard and high priority.

Transport Layer
- Service multiplexing/demultiplexing.
- Error control.
- Video-specific adaptation control.

Transmission Layer
- Physical level modulation.
- Adaptive equalization.
- Frequency translation to/from r.f.

Fig. 1.   Conceptual view of an ADTV system architecture.

ISDN/ATM, most notably in a recent pioneering prototyping effort by Bellcore [7].

Before proceeding to a detailed discussion of ADTV's transport approach, the overall system architecture is briefly reviewed. Fig. 1 shows that the ADTV system has been defined in terms of four major layers, each with a clearly defined function and interface. These are the compression, prioritization, transport, and physical transmission layers. Such a layered digital system design approach offers many benefits including simplicity, hardware modularity, relative ease with which functionality may be upgraded, the availability of simple interfaces for testing, processing, transmission or storage, etc. The compression, prioritization, and transport layers of ADTV taken together are also referred to as the "MPEG++" bit stream, which is discussed in a more general paper [8]. This work focuses on the design, specification, and validation of the MPEG++ data transport layer intended to support flexible and robust delivery of video over relatively unreliable media. The closely related prioritization layer will also be described here at a level sufficient to provide context for the transport

Reprinted from *IEEE J. Selected Areas Commun.,* vol. 11, no. 1, pp. 88–98, Jan. 1993.

discussions to follow. Note that although the transport protocol is described here in the context of HDTV, MPEG++ is a scalable video compression and transport approach with broad applicability to various one-way and two-way video transmission scenarios.

At the compression layer, the ADTV video encoder produces a bit stream conforming to the MPEG-1 standard video representation [9], [10]; on the receive side is an MPEG-1 decoder augmented to incorporate appropriate error concealment procedures. The prioritization layer (optional for channels other than terrestrial broadcast) performs the media-specific function of separating/remerging the MPEG-encoded video into (from) subjectively important high-priority (HP) and less important standard-priority (SP) bit streams. The data transport layer to be described in this paper is responsible for reliable delivery of these HP and SP video streams over applicable media, as well as for generic functions such as service multiplexing. The ADTV physical layer is based on two frequency multiplexed trellis-coded QAM carriers at 4.8 and 19.2 Mb/s (for a total bit rate of 24 Mb/s) positioned to avoid the NTSC picture carrier region for immunity from cochannel interference. In addition, the modem exploits the vestigital sideband rolloff in a TV receiver to transmit the 4.8 Mb/s carrier at a power level 5–6 dB higher than that of the 19.2 Mb/s carrier, thus providing two-tier transmission matched to the prioritized HP/SP video representation. Taken together, these four layers of ADTV provide the robust "graceful degradation" property necessary for channels with occasional channel impairments, while retaining an efficient standards-based media-independent video compression approach.

The transport layer considered here may be viewed as the essential platform for robust HDTV delivery over difficult media, since its packet structure provides the basis for error detection, logical resynchronization, and error concealment at the receiver. The ADTV transport format consists of three distinct sublayers: a "data link/network" sublayer, an "adaptation" sublayer, and a "video service layer." The data link/network layer provides generic transport services such as priority support, asynchronous cell multiplexing, and error control. The video adaptation header has been designed for efficient packing of variable-length MPEG data into fixed-length cells, while providing for rapid logical resynchronization and error concealment support at the video decoder after uncorrectable error events. This adaptation header contains MPEG-specific error recovery information including an "entry pointer" which locates the start of the first decodable video unit (i.e., slice or macroblock) in a cell, along with positional information that helps to locate the received video unit in the decoded picture. An additional "video service" sublayer contains highly service-specific information (e.g., key MPEG parameters, priority breakpoint), providing a higher-level resynchronization mechanism needed for decoder recovery after certain error events.

The sections that follow provide a more detailed view of the MPEG++ transport format outlined above. First, in Section II, we provide a discussion of general design considerations that led to the selection of particular approaches at each sublayer. This is followed, in Section III, by a brief review of the video

TABLE I
MPEG++ PROTOCOL SUBLAYERS AND FUNCTIONS

Sublayer	Scope	Functions
Data Link/Network	Generic and channel specific transport functions	Service multiplexing, HP/SP priority support, error detection (CRC), cell sequence indicator
Video Adaptation	Service-specific interface to data link/network sublayer	Segmentation and reassembly of video data, alignment of HP/SP streams, logical video resynchronization after cell loss, error concealment support
Video Service	Higher level service specific	Video decoder parameter and priority decoder reset

data prioritization process used to achieve robustness, mainly to set the stage for a detailed description of the transport protocol. Each of the sublayers of the transport format are described in Section IV, along with applicable design issues where appropriate. This is followed by Section V, which contains an outline of a detailed software model that has been developed as a "proof of concept" for MPEG++ transport. Simulation results illustrating the protocol's performance (in terms of key measures such as percentage overhead, end-to-end HDTV quality versus bit-error rate, etc.) are given in, for example, two-tier terrestrial transmission scenarios. Finally, Sections VI and VII contain concluding remarks and references, respectively.

II. DESIGN CONSIDERATIONS

A number of requirements must be addressed in the design of a new data format for digital HDTV. In this section, a brief overview of some of the major design considerations is given.

1) Protocol Layering: One of the most important issues in protocol design is that of providing well-defined layers, each with a carefully defined interface and functionality. This type of design provides various advantages including design simplicity, testability, flexibility for various applications and media, etc. However, for connection-oriented HDTV delivery, the use of many ISO-type layers is not recommended in view of the high data rates involved. As in most fast packet switching approaches, we recommend the use of a simplified protocol stack that collapses the necessary ISO-layer functions into just a few layers. Also, it is noted that HDTV services will generally require fewer services than conventional data communications, so that many simplifications are appropriate. In our view, services needed by HDTV can be effectively segregated into the three MPEG++ protocol sublayers with functions described in Table I.

2) Service Multiplexing: At the lowest layers (i.e., ISO data link/network layers), new digital HDTV services will require service multiplexing capabilities for flexible support of a mix of video audio and data services. While conventional constant bit-rate circuit multiplexing approaches often considered for video distribution can serve initial needs, there is a basic problem in that the specific service mix (i.e., number of audio, video, and data channels) and their individual bit rates must be known in advance. In view of the fact that HDTV service standards are at an early stage, it would be inappropriate to design a system with fixed bit-rate partitions that cannot accommodate future evolution of HDTV, TV, and digital audio rates. These requirements motivate an ATM-type asynchronous mutiplexing approach in which channel capacity can be dynamically assigned to services by marking each cell (i.e., packet) on the channel with an appropriate "service type." Such a data format can support both constant bit rate (CBR) and variable bit rate (VBR) transmission modes [note that the VBR mode is unlikely to be used in initial systems, but may be potentially useful in future wideband cable and satellite scenarios].

In addition to flexibility, it is noted that in the HDTV broadcast context, asynchronous packet multiplexing provides useful "backward compatibility" with respect to equipment designed to receive particular services. New services can be added at any time without any impact on the existing sets since the service address will simply be ignored.

3) Applicability to Different Delivery Media: The design of a new HDTV data transport format should take into account (to the extent possible) the needs and limitations of various delivery media alternatives. This means that the lower protocol layers (e.g., data link/network levels) should have features and parameters ranges intended for efficient support on various protocol-free media alternatives, including terrestrial broadcast, satellite, and cable. Such a design requirement can be approached in a practical manner by determining typical modulation and forward error correction (FEC) parameters associated with modems for these media, and then accounting for the range of values in the design. For example, block-size parameters associated with typical Reed-Solomon error correction VLSI used in terrestrial and satellite applications range between 128 and 256 bytes, thus motivating a cell size in this range. Also, considering the bit error rate regimes experienced on each of the above media, a cyclic redundancy check (CRC) code for reliable error detection is considered appropriate (however, they may not be required in implementations in which the FEC used is both correcting and detecting). Considerations such as efficiency (i.e., percentage overhead), minimum detectable errored data block size, and cell header processing speeds must also be factored into the selection of cell size. Taking into account all these factors, an ADTV cell size in the region of 128 bytes was considered appropriate. Note that this is larger than the ATM cell size of 53 bytes, which was chosen mainly for error-free fiber media on which a relatively fine-grain selection of bit rate is required. It is observed here that when ADTV is supported on protocol-assisted media such as ATM, the signal can either be transported transparently as ATM payload or by replacement of the ADTV data link/network level with ATM's lower layer protocol.

4) Robust Video Transport: At the more service-specific video adaptation layer, the primary design goal is to provide robustness with respect to channel errors or cell loss. Although a limited class of dedicated fiber-optic media may be reliable

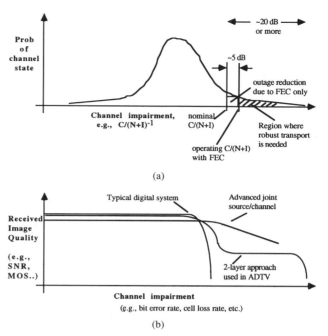

Fig. 2. (a) Illustration of signal variations relative to FEC in terrestrial broadcasting. (b) Conventional versus graceful degradation characteristics of HDTVdelivery systems.

enough for unprotected transport of compressed video, most practical media (including terrestrial simulcast, coaxial cable, digital satellite, and ATM/B-ISDN) are characterized by unavoidable bit error and/or cell loss events. The primary terrestrial simulcast scenario (which is based on low-power VHF/UHF transmission in the presence of cochannel NTSC interference) is especially error-prone, even after all reasonable error protection measures have been taken. It is noted that in addition to time-varying cochannel interference, the simulcast HDTV signal is subject to temporal and spatial signal strength variations of as much as $\pm$ 10–20 dB at the edge of coverage. This means that error correcting codes, which are limited to no more than about 3–6 dB of "coding gain," cannot adequately compensate for all potential signal variations, as illustrated in Fig. 2(a). These considerations motivate the development of a "graceful degradation" characteristic for video, in which the characteristic digital "brickwall effect" is ameliorated by joint source/channel approaches, as outlined in Fig. 2(b).

From Fig. 2(b), it is observed that an advanced joint source/channel coding approach, e.g. [11], has the potential for achieving an analog-type graceful degradation characteristic. However, such an approach was considered impractical in view of the importance of maintaining a clean layering of functions between the modulation, transport, and compression subsystems. Accordingly, a compromise "two-tier" approach was adopted for ADTV. This two-tier method avoids a strong coupling between modulation, transport, and compression by reducing the problem to one of segregating the video into a high-priority (HP) and standard-priority (SP) bit stream for subsequent prioritized transport. This general approach has earlier been suggested for robust video transmission over ATM [12], [13], where the ATM transport system provides two different quality of service (QOS) levels during network congestion. In ADTV, the priority mechanism is at the physical level, and is achieved by transmitting two QAM signals on the 6 MHz simulcast channel for HP and SP, respectively. The HP signal (which is situated in the VSB rolloff region of NTSC) is operated at a substantially higher power density level than the SP carrier.

With appropriate prioritization of video data, error detection at the link/network level, error recovery support at the video adaptation level, and error concealment within the video decoder, such an arrangement can provide useful images at relatively high SP channel error rates. The basic idea is to convert all channel errors to cell loss/erasure events by adding a reliable error detection code, thus essentially avoiding the handling of erroneous data within the video decoder, and redundantly add vital video decoding information at a video-specific adaptation layer in order to facilitate rapid decoder recovery after detecting the loss of one or more cells on the channel. Using the redundant transport information, the decoder identifies regions of the image affected by errors, and applies appropriate concealment algorithms such as temporal replacement and spatial interpolation [14]. Thus, the adaptation layer proposed here is central to achieving the robust video delivery over terrestrial simulcast and other error-prone media.

It is noted that the MPEG++ signal need not be transmitted with priorities if the medium is considered to be relatively reliable. For example, when transmitted via infrastructural satellite links, it may be appropriate to use a single priority while ignoring cell priority information carried at the transport level. A reasonable amount of graceful degradation can still be achieved with one-tier prioritization by utilizing cell error detection and video adaptation level features to support error concealment.

5) Other Requirements: In addition to the major design considerations discussed previously, a number of other criteria were taken into account. An important issue is that of high-speed hardware implementation: generally, this motivates a cell-relay approach with fixed-length packets rather than conventional variable-length packets (which are otherwise better suited to the natural characteristic of compressed video). In addition, the cell relay approach has the advantage of being associated with rugged channel synchronization, and is compatible at the physical level with practical block coding approaches (such as Reed-Solomon). Other factors considered include the need to minimize hardware complexity in order to meet an aggressive schedule for FCC prototype evaluation. In this prototype design, the following constraints were met to simplify hardware:

- equal cell sizes for high-priority (HP) and standard-priority (SP) channels
- one-byte service header
- four-byte adaptation header for both the HP and SP cells
- cell payload is a multiple of four bytes.

III. PRIORITIZATION FOR TWO-TIER TRANSPORT

The basic goals of MPEG++ priority processing are to split the encoded video bit stream into two priority levels for subsequent transmission over a terrestrial channel, and to provide adequate image quality under impaired channel conditions. Since the high-priority (HP) signal is transmitted at a significantly higher signal power than the standard-priority (SP) signal, degradation to the signal quality is dominated by the transmission losses on the standard-priority channel at the fringes of the coverage areas. Hence, the strategy is to determine the "importance" of different data types in the MPEG bit stream and to route the more important data, to the extent possible, to the HP channel.

It is observed that MPEG produces a bit stream consisting of variable-length codewords conveying information about different picture attributes such as headers (initialization values, adaptation parameters, etc.), motion vectors, DCT coefficient values, run lengths, etc. The subjective impact of losing each of these codeword types in the presence of channel errors can vary considerably. For example, loss of motion vector information may cause serious errors in decoding, whereas a few DCT coefficients may be missed with relatively minor impact on the picture. Accordingly, dynamic separation of MPEG data into high-priority (HP) and standard-priority (SP) streams may be carried out using an adaptive prioritization algorithm which takes into account the codeword type, the MPEG frame type (i.e., I, B, or P), and the relative occupancies of HP and SP rate buffers at the output of the MPEG encoding system.

For the MPEG bit stream, I-frame information tends to be the most important for transmission on the HP channel for two reasons. First, the effect of losses on this frame last the longest, i.e., until the next I frame. Perhaps more important is the fact that since there is no temporal prediction for this frame, loss of DCT coefficient information results in loss of all information in this frame. This is different from what happens in P and B frames, where availability of partial motion vector information may be sufficient to produce reasonable lower-resolution images, even in the event of absence of DCT coefficient information due to channel losses. Hence, the general objective is to transmit a large fraction of the I frame data on the HP channel to the extent allowed by the HP buffer occupancies. For the P frames, the fraction of the channel data transmitted HP allows for all motion vector data to go HP if possible, and more DCT coefficient data to be transmitted HP only if additional capacity is available. It is important to transmit motion information for these frames HP since the effect of losses will tend to propagate until the next I frame. The B frame is considered the least important, primarily since the effect of errors in these frames does not propagate. The fraction of data for B frames transmitted on the HP channel is minimal.

The computed threshold of what data is placed on HP and SP remains constant over a MPEG slice and is called the priority breakpoint. The priority breakpoint can fall anywhere within the MPEG data stream, beginning at the headers and ending at the high-frequency coefficients, depending on the precomputed HP target for the total frame. Certain breakpoint computation overrides are also enforced depending on frame type, with the assurance that none of these overrides cause rate buffers to overflow or underflow. An example of an 8x8 DCT block with the ac coefficient corresponding to the priority

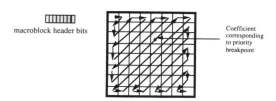

macroblock header bits

Coefficient corresponding to priority breakpoint

Fig. 3. Example of HP/SP prioritazation within a DCT coefficient scan.

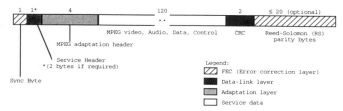

MPEG video, Audio, Data, Control

CRC

Reed-Solomon (RS) parity bytes

MPEG adaptation header

Service Header
*(2 bytes if required)

Sync Byte

Legend:
FEC (Error correction layer)
Data-link layer
Adaptation layer
Service data

Fig. 4. Logical structure of a transport cell.

TABLE II
VIDEO TRANSPORT FORMAT SPECIFICATION

Tiers	2 (HP and SP)
Cell Size (bytes)	127 HP /127 SP
Entry Points	HP: Slice SP: Macroblock
Entries/Cell (goal)	1 (avg)
Mblks/Frame	4680
Slices/Frame *	60 Vertically 6 Horizontally (360 total)
MBlks/Slice	13
Transport Overhead/Cell	6 %

* The FCC prototype divides the raster into three vertical stripes, each of which contains two slices.

breakpoint is shown in Fig. 3. In this case, some coefficient information goes high priority and the rest low priority for each block in a macroblock.

Information about the priority breakpoint must also be included in the transmitted bit stream, so that there is knowledge at the receiver to decode MPEG bits from the correct HP or SP channel even under channel loss conditions. This mechanism for transporting the priority breakpoint will be described further in the next section.

IV. ADTV TRANSPORT PROTOCOL

This section provides specific details about the transport protocol implemented in the ADTV prototype. It is remarked here that the data format given should be considered as preliminary since the ADTV system is still evolving. Nevertheless, the general principles discussed here are expected to carry over into subsequent generations of MPEG++. The MPEG++ transport protocol formats the HP/SP prioritized compressed video bit streams into sequences of fixed-length 148-byte cells, each containing a one-byte synchronization header, a one-byte link layer header, a four-byte adaptation layer header, a 120-byte transport block, a two-byte frame check sequence trailer, and a 20-byte forward error correction code. This fixed-length cell structure, shown in Fig. 4 and further specified in Table II, is similar to the "cell relay" asynchronous time division multiplexing (ATM) concept, but with cell header and payload sizes more appropriate for the terrestrial broadcast medium. The data-link layer header contains generic transport information such as priority indicator, service I.D., and sequence number. The adaptation layer has been designed to support segmentation and reassembly and to permit rapid decoder resynchronization after cell losses. The highest-layer "video service" contains highly video-specific information needed to reestablish the MPEG decoding environment after a data loss.

1) Data Format Definition: The ADTV transport protocol refers to three communication protocol layers: data link/network layer, adaptation layer, and service layer. With the exception of the link layer, the adaptation and service layers are specific with regards to video, audio, and auxiliary data services.

Data Link/Network Layer: The data link/network header consists of a service-type (ST) byte containing generic transport information such as cell priority, service identity to support multiplexing, and a cell continuity counter for detecting cell loss. Fig. 5 shows the logical structure of a transport cell in which the ST field has been broken down to its components. The ST byte carries a priority-level indicator to allow immediate identification of a transport cell to be either HP or SP. The service I.D. field allows up to eight services to be uniquely identified. The video timing service is a timing signal used to establish a frame rate, as well as to synchronize the arrival of codewords to the video decoder. This timing service uses just-in-time delivery and hence is given highest priority when all services are multiplexed on the channel. In this implementation, the reserved service channel identity (0,0,0) can be used to extend the address space of the primary services by indicating the presence of a one-byte service header extension following the ST byte. This optional extension would provide 256 additional service addresses per channel. The four-bit continuity counter (CC) in the ST byte increments by 1 for each cell transmitted. It is service- and priority-dependent, i.e., separate continuity counters are maintained for each service identity and for each transmission-priority tier. The value of the CC sequences from 0 through 15. The CC allows receivers to detect cell discontinuity (due to cell errors) for a particular transport service. Table III shows the receiver responses when decoding the ST byte.

There are two situations in which an errored cell can migrate into a service application:

1) An undetected error is located in any byte after the ST byte.
2) There are modulo 16 losses between two nonerrored cells for the same service i.d. and priority.

The last two bytes of each transport cell include a 16-bit frame check sequence (FCS) to provide CRC error detection over the ST byte and the 124-byte transport block. This is used to detect errors not corrected by the forward error correction system.

Video Adaptation Layer: An MPEG-specific adaptation sublayer has been designed to efficiently pack variable-length

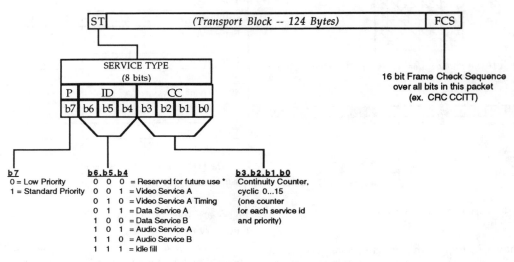

Fig. 5. Transport packet format at data link/network layer.

TABLE III
RECEIVER RESPONSES WHEN DECODING ST BYTE

Cell Error	Service I.D.	Continuity	Data link/network layer response
No Error	valid	continuous	declare good continuity, deliver cell to service
	valid	discontinuous	declare bad continuity, deliver cell to service
	invalid	–	drop cell
Error	–	–	drop cell

TABLE IV
ADAPTATION HEADER ENTRY POINT COMPONENTS

Tier	Entry Point Identity
HP	entry position pointer, frame type, frame number, slice number, MPEG "f codes"
SP	entry position pointer, frame type, frame number, Mblk number

video into fixed-length cells and to support rapid decoder resynchronization after error events that result in the loss of one or more cells. Adaptation headers contain information fields which aid error recovery at the video decoder; for MPEG-encoded video, these fields include frame-type indicators, slice/macroblock I.D.'s, and reentry pointers needed to support segmentation and error control in variable-length coded video. Table IV indicates the entry-point components found in the two-tier adaptation header (AH).

The frame type, slice number, macroblock number, and "f codes" are supplied by the video processor, while the position pointer and frame number are supplied by the transport processor. The *entry position pointer* addresses the first bit of the entry point in the MPEG data portion of the cell. If the pointer value equals 0 x 3 *ff*, the transport cell has no entry point. AH *frame type* indicates whether the data refers to an I, P, or B frame or the first cell of a GOP. The *frame number* is used as a transport frame continuity counter, incrementing once per frame. The *slice number macroblock numbers* are unique over the frame. Fig. 6 shows the logical structure of a transport cell in which the AH field has been broken down to its components.

The adaptation layer protocol allows the decoder to synchronize to variable-length codes within the service. The first usable entry point in each cell is identified and stored in the adaptation header (AH). While having one entry point per cell is a design goal, there is a wide range of data per slice dependent upon the priority channel and frame type. Entry points allow data blocks to segment across cell boundaries. Illustrating this concept in Fig. 7, four variable-length input data blocks (*B*1, *B*2, *B*3, and *B*4) are formatted into three transport cells. As shown in this figure, transport cells 1 and 3 have AH entry pointers to the beginning of data blocks *B*1 and *B*3, respectively. Transport cell 2 has no entry point. Using this method, the entry pointer always points to the beginning of a decodable block of variable-length codes. In the event of cell loss, say cell 2 in this example, decoding of block *B*2 is terminated at the end of cell 1, and decoding resumes at the start of block *B*3. The entry point information is used in the decoder only if there is a break in cell continuity.

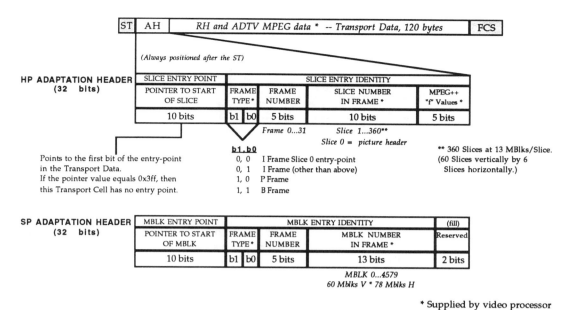

HP ADAPTATION HEADER (32 bits)	SLICE ENTRY POINT	SLICE ENTRY IDENTITY		
	POINTER TO START OF SLICE	FRAME TYPE * (b1 b0)	FRAME NUMBER	SLICE NUMBER IN FRAME *	MPEG++ "f" Values *
	10 bits	b1 b0	5 bits	10 bits	5 bits

Frame 0...31   Slice 1...360**
Slice 0 = picture header

Points to the first bit of the entry-point in the Transport Data. If the pointer value equals 0x3ff, then this Transport Cell has no entry point.

b1,b0
0, 0   I Frame Slice 0 entry-point
0, 1   I Frame (other than above)
1, 0   P Frame
1, 1   B Frame

** 360 Slices at 13 MBlks/Slice. (60 Slices vertically by 6 Slices horizontally.)

SP ADAPTATION HEADER (32 bits)	MBLK ENTRY POINT	MBLK ENTRY IDENTITY		(fill)
	POINTER TO START OF MBLK	FRAME TYPE *	FRAME NUMBER	MBLK NUMBER IN FRAME *	Reserved
	10 bits	b1 b0	5 bits	13 bits	2 bits

MBLK 0...4579
60 Mblks V * 78 Mblks H

* Supplied by video processor

Fig. 6.   Transport packet format at video adaptation level.

INPUT VLC DATA BLOCKS:

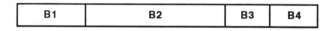

OUTPUT TRANSPORT CELLS:

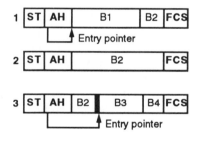

Fig. 7.   Example to illustrate the concept of entry point.

This particular adaptation format implementation is based on slice numbers for high-priority data, since MPEG macroblocks by themselves are not generally useful to the decoder. On the other hand, macroblock (MB) numbers are used to recover from standard-priority data loss since header data for those MB's will be received over the more reliable HP bit stream. It is observed that the HP slice pointer serves as the resynchronization function of the MPEG slice start code, which for ADTV is removed from the bit stream to improve transmission efficiency. In this prototype implementation, a mechanism is added to carry the MPEG picture layer motion vector f-codes for the HP slice entry point. This data should be added to the video service layer discussed later but, to simplify hardware, a reduced set of ADTV prototype f-codes were placed in the HP adaptation header. In the presence of errors, the motion vector f-codes allow decoders to process data at the entry point without waiting for a MPEG picture header.

Video Service Layer: All information contained in the video service layer is supplied by the video encoder and the priority processor. The record header (RH) appears in the HP channel only, and at the beginning of each slice. Any number of record headers may appear in a cell, but only the first is used as an entry point in the AH. (On the SP channel, any number of macroblocks may begin in one cell, but only the first is used as an entry point in the AH.) Slice 0, designated as the picture header, does not have a record header and has no corresponding data in the SP channel. Fig. 8 shows the logical structure of a transport cell in which the RH field has been broken down to its components. The RH contains the following information: priority breakpoint, vertical position, quantizer scale, and RH extensions (as defined within MPEG).

The priority breakpoint splits the one-tier encoded video data stream into a two-tier data transport format (as discussed earlier). The breakpoint, along with the MPEG encoded data, is input to the transport encoder. All MPEG codewords arriving at the input of the transport encoder are tagged with length and type. If the codeword type is less than or equal to the priority breakpoint, the codeword is placed on the HP channel; otherwise, it is placed on the SP channel. Similarly, the transport decoder can use the breakpoint value to determine the data source (HP or SP) of each codeword. The priority breakpoint remains constant over a slice. The remaining fields of the record header are unmodified from the MPEG slice header, except for the slice vertical position, which has been reduced from eight to six bits, as there are 60 slices vertically in the ADTV prototype.

(2) Transport Decoder Issues: The transport decoder receives cells from two separate paths for the high-priority (HP) and standard-priority (SP) data, respectively. A 124-byte transport cell is received from the data link/network layer containing the four-byte adaptation header (AH) and the 120-byte transport data block. The data link/network layer uses the continuity counter in the transport cell service type byte to

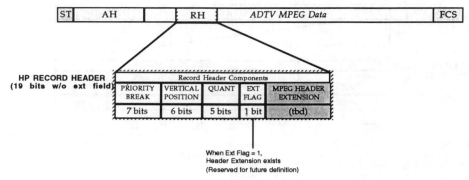

Fig. 8. Transport cell format at video service level.

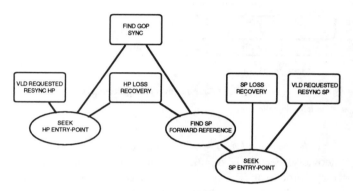

Fig. 9. Transport decoder resynchronization tasks.

inform the transport decoder of lost (or discontinuous) data. Only error-free transport blocks are delivered to the transport decoder. The transport decoder provides a constant stream of data to services identified in the ST byte. For the video service, the data stream is supplied to the inverse priority processor/variable-length decoder (IPP/VLD). The transport decoder also strips off the adaptation header (AH) from the transport cell, decodes this header, and presents it to the IPP/VLD in a suitable format.

If there is cell discontinuity, the video transport decoder initiates a sequence of resynchronizing tasks. These tasks are summarized in Fig. 9. If synchronization to the start of a Group of Pictures (GOP) is required (e.g., at initialization), the decoder will continue reading HP transport blocks from the data link/network layer until an entry point is found with frame type 0,0 (start of GOP). The decoder will then examine the SP stream until an entry point is found with the same or future frame number. The GOP start will be coincident with the start of a new cell on both HP and SP channels, and only the first cell in the GOP (for both channels) will have frame type 0,0.

If a loss is indicated on the SP stream, the decoder will set an error flag on the last SP data word delivered to the IPP/VLD and seek the next entry point on the SP stream. Entry point seek is accomplished by continuously reading the SP stream until the AH indicates an entry point is present. The decoder then positions the entry point within the next word available to the IPP/VLD. No changes are made to the HP stream. The IPP/VLD can also request this resynchronization.

If a loss is indicated on the HP stream, the decoder will set an error flag on the last SP data word delivered to the IPP/VLD and seek the next entry point on the HP stream. Entry point seek is accomplished by continuously reading the HP stream until the AH indicates an entry point is present. The decoder then positions the HP entry point within the next word available to the IPP/VLD. Once the IPP/VLD reads this newly acquired HP entry point, the SP stream is resynchronized by finding the next available SP entry point and positioning this entry within the next SP word available to the IPP. The IPP/VLD can also request this resynchronization.

Other more hardware-intensive options are available for the transport decoder design. Given the information available in the transport protocol alone, a transport decoder can merge cells together forming a single bit stream for the VLD. In such a design, the decoder continuously reads cells from each tier until it finds an entry point in a nonerrored cell. The AH at this entry point is fully decoded, and data beginning at this entry point is extracted from the transport cell and stored in a holding buffer. Data from subsequent cells are appended to this holding buffer until either the next entry point is encountered or a cell is found in error. Once bit streams are captured for both HP and SP, they are held until a VLD request matches the entry point identity being held by the transport decoder. When the VLD request and bit stream identity are aligned, the VLD gets the HP or SP bit stream containing the requested codeword. The selection of HP or SP is determined by the codeword type being requested by the VLD and the current priority breakpoint read from the active record header. The VLD extracts bits from this stream until a codeword is built, and returns a count of the number of bits used. The TP decoder maintains pointers into each bit stream until all available data has been extracted. At that point, the transport decoder acquires the next "bit stream" from the rate buffer.

(3) Transport Protocol — Future Evolution: The design of the ADTV transport format for FCC prototyping is a subset of the transport protocol needed to support a wide extent of transmission systems and to fully support all MPEG requirements. Several aspects of the ADTV prototype protocol were influenced by the aggressive hardware build schedule to meet FCC testing. Some simplicities and inefficiencies in the current design will be revisited before standardization takes place. In the ATDV prototype design, there are no provisions to retransmit the MPEG Sequence Header layer, no provisions to handle scramble codes for data encryption, and no support for one-tier transmission systems such as DBS. In addition to these

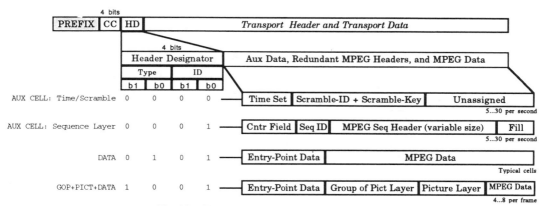

Fig. 10. Future ADTV transport design concepts.

TABLE V
ENTRY POINT DATA AND OVERHEAD STATISTICS

Item	I-Frame	P-Frame	B-Frame	Weighted Means
Number of Frames Processed	2	4	14	
Avg HP Cells/Frame	1012.0	66.5	7.4	119.7
Avg SP Cells/Frame	560.5	968.5	385.6	520.0
Avg HP+SP Cells/Frame	1572.5	1035.0	392.2	639.7
% HP Cells/Frame	64.5%	6.4%	1.9%	9.1%
% SP Cells/Frame	35.5%	93.6%	98.1%	90.9%
HP Rate/Frame (Mb/s)	30.8	2.0	0.2	3.6
SP Rate/Frame (Mb/s)	17.1	29.5	11.8	15.8
Total Rate/Frame (Mb/s)	47.9	31.5	12.0	19.5
Avg HP Slices/Cell*	0.36	5.4	49.3	3.0
Avg SP MBlks/Cell*	8.5	4.8	12.5	9.2
127 Byte Cell Components				
Link (ST+FCS)+Adaptation (AH)	5.5%	5.5%	5.5%	5.5%
Video Data (RH + data)	94.5%	94.5%	94.5%	94.5%

* 13 MBlks/Slice, 360 slices/frame

omissions, future protocol designs will include mechanisms to support synchronizing timestamps and application-defined data fields requiring redundant transmissions. Fig. 10 illustrates design concepts under consideration which incorporate some of these features for advanced ADTV-like systems.

V. SOFTWARE MODEL AND PERFORMANCE RESULTS

The ADTV prototype system has been simulated using detailed software models running on multiple Sun/Unix workstations. The software was written in a modular fashion to facilitate design changes and improvement. The simulation model for ADTV has been used extensively in system performance evaluation work as well as in assisting parameter finetuning for hardware implementation. Fig. 11 shows the primary functional modules of the ADTV system software. Functions for the entire ADTV simulation are written for single frame (frame-at-a-time) processing. After processing a frame, the program state is saved in a file associated with each module. Before processing the next frame, these files are read to restore the program state. Statistical data for all frames processed are accumulated over a selectable set of frames. Fully formed transport cells are stored in two binary files (HP and SP). This allows encoding to be simulated once for multiple runs of the decoder (e.g., for varying the characteristics of the channel model). Each of the software modules mimic principal interface requirements of the prototype hardware, thus providing a secondary benefit as a source of test-vector generators for hardware testing. Additionally, output data from some hardware modules can be captured and inserted directly into appropriate software functional equivalents. Table V is a sample of the transport encoding statistics which indicate cell packing characteristics and overhead for three different frame types. These metrics are from data collected using 28 frames of "typical" source material. Data for the first eight frames were dropped for start-up transients.

A series of experiments to investigate the effect of channel errors were performed in order to assess robustness. In this case, the channel model assumed a 19.2 Mb/s video bit rate (corresponding approximately to a typical 32 QAM mode at the transmission level) with a nominal standard to high-

251

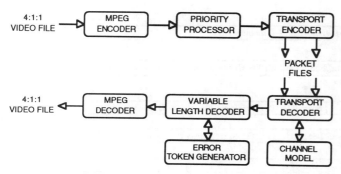

Fig. 11. Functional modules for ADTV system software.

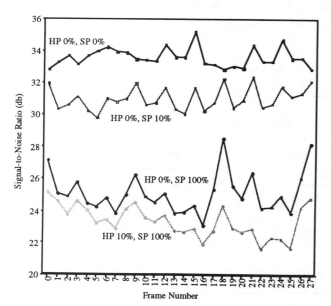

Fig. 12. Simulation results showing video under various cell loss scenarios.

TABLE VI
SUBJECTIVE QUALITY OF MPEG++ UNDER DIFFERENT CHANNEL SCENARIO

Percentage of Lost Cells		Subjective Quality
HP (%)	SP (%)	
0	1	Nearly transparent
0	10	Good image quality
0	50	Annoying, but viewable image
0	100	Degraded, but viewable image
10	100	Very degraded image quality
50	100	Severely degraded image

scenario when an appropriate transmission scheme with two-tier reliability is used. This robustness property should also be useful on other delivery media (such as ATM fiber) capable of prioritized transport.

VI. CONCLUDING REMARKS

This paper has described an HDTV transport protocol designed for efficient and robust delivery of HDTV over the error-prone terrestrial simulcast channel. The protocol provides flexible service multiplexing and other ATM-like service features, along with video-specific adaptation features designed to mitigate the impact of channel errors. Simulation results have validated the proposed MPEG++ compression and transport approach, demonstrating graceful degradation of image quality down to relatively high cell loss (bit error) rates. The proposed protocol has been implemented in the ADTV prototype system that was tested by the FCC during the second quarter of 1992. We believe that the general principles embodied in the ADTV transport protocol are applicable to a wide range of HDTV and TV delivery applications involving unreliable transmission media.

priority data rate ratio of 1:4. Several scenarios corresponding to various levels of channel impairments were simulated. In all cases, the HP data is transmitted with better reliability than the SP data; the percentage of transmitted data that is lost is used as a measure of the channel reliability. Fig. 12 is a plot of the frame-to-frame SNR variation of the system under different channel impairment levels for a particular error concealment approach. The four curves correspond to increasing levels of HP and SP channel losses: i) no channel losses on HP and SP data; ii) no loss on HP data, 10% loss of SP data; iii) no loss of HP data, 100% loss of SP data; and iv) 10% loss of HP data, 100% loss of SP data. It is observed that the signal-to-noise ratio of the decoded video is not severely degraded by moderate loss of standard-priority information. Also, even when 100% standard-priority loss is experienced, a useful SNR level is maintained from the high-priority bit stream alone. A subjective image quality assessment with channel errors present is shown in Table VI.

Image quality is strongly dependent upon error concealment algorithms; this particular experiment used simple temporal replacement. Preliminary results from these experiments indicate that the proposed two-layer MPEG++ approach provides a significant level of robustness for the terrestrial broadcast

REFERENCES

[1] Advanced Television Research Consortium, "ADTV system description," FCC Pre-Cert. Doc., Feb. 1991.
[2] Advanced Television Research Consortium, "ADTV system description," FCC Final Cert. Doc., Jan. 1992.
[3] General Instruments Corp., "Digicipher HDTV system description," FCC Final Cert. Doc., July 1991.
[4] AT&T and Zenith Corp., "Digital spectrum compatible," FCC Final Cert. Doc., Sept. 1991.
[5] CCITT, Recom. Drafted by Working Party XVIII/8 (General B-ISDN Aspects) approved in 1990, Study Group XVIII-Rep. R 34, June 1990.
[6] S. Minzer, "Broadband ISDN and asynchronous transfer mode (ATM)," IEEE Commun. Mag., pp. 17–24, Sept. 1989.
[7] Bellcore, "Advanced television for broadband ISDN," Seminar Proc., Iselin, NJ, Mar. 19–20, 1990.
[8] K. Joseph, S. Ng, D. Raychaudhuri, R. Saint Girons, T. Savatier, R. Siracusa, and J. Zdepski, "MPEG++: A robust compression and transport system for digital HDTV," to appear in Image Commun.
[9] D. LeGall, "MPEG: A video compression standard for multimedia applications," Commun. ACM, vol. 34, no. 4, Apr. 1, 1991.
[10] "MPEG video committee draft," MPEG Video CD Edit. Com., ISO-IEC JTC1/SC2/WG11 MPEG 90, Dec. 18, 1990.
[11] K. Sayood and J. Borkenhagen, "Use of residual redundancy in the design of joint source/channel coders," IEEE Trans. Commun., pp. 838–846, June 1991.
[12] G. Karlsson and M. Vetterli, "Packet video and its integration into the network architecture," IEEE J. Select. Areas Commun., pp. 739–751, June 1989.

[13] F. Kishino, K. Manabe, Y. Hayashi, and H. Yasuda, "Variable bit-rate coding of video signals for ATM networks," *IEEE J. Select. Areas Commun.*, vol. 7, no. 5, pp. 801–806, June 1989.

[14] R. Saint Girons, J. Zdepski, and D. Raychaudhuri, "Transport and error concealment for MPEG-2," ISO-IEC JTC1/SC2/WG11 MPEG 91, Kurihama, Nov. 1991.

[15] H. Sun, K. Challapali, and J. Zdepski, "Error concealment in simulcast ADTV decoder," presented at *ICCE '92*, Chicago, IL, June 2–4, 1992.

An Entropy Coding System for Digital HDTV Applications

Shaw-Min Lei, *Member, IEEE,* and Ming-Ting Sun, *Senior Member, IEEE*

Abstract—Run-length coding (RLC) and variable-length coding (VLC) are widely used techniques for lossless data compression. A high-speed entropy coding system using these two techniques is considered for digital high definition television (HDTV) applications. Traditionally, VLC decoding is implemented through a tree-searching algorithm as the input bits are received serially. For HDTV applications, it is very difficult to implement a real-time VLC decoder of this kind due to the very high data rate required. In this paper, we introduce a parallel structured VLC decoder which decodes each codeword in one clock cycle regardless of its length. The required clock rate of the decoder is thus lower and parallel processing architectures become easy to adopt in the entropy coding system. The parallel entropy coder and decoder will be implemented in two experimental prototype chips which are designed to encode and decode more than 52 million samples/s. Some related system issues, such as the synchronization of variable-length codewords and error concealment, are also discussed in this paper.

I. INTRODUCTION

RUN-LENGTH coding (RLC) [1] and variable-length coding (VLC) [2] are two widely adopted techniques for lossless data compression. They have become part of the international digital facsimile coding standard [3], and will be included in the low-bit rate video coding standard [4] as well. In image or video coding applications, these two statistical coding techniques are often used in conjunction with various lossy coding techniques, such as DCT, subband, or DPCM [5]–[7], to reduce the data rate further without adding any degradation to the data. The RLC represents consecutive zeros[1] by their run lengths thus reducing the number of samples. The VLC assigns shorter codewords to more frequent source symbols, and vice versa, so that the average bit rate is reduced. Usually, the output distribution of a lossy coder is very uneven for different quantization levels and there are many zeros clustering together. Thus, RLC and VLC can compress the data effectively.

In the digital advanced television (ATV) project of Bellcore, these two techniques are used along with subband/DPCM source coding algorithms [6], [7] as data compression algorithms for the high definition television on broadband integrated services digital network (HDTV-on-BISDN) experimental research prototype system [25]. Although there are other lossless data compression techniques, the combination of RLC and VLC was chosen because it achieves very good compression efficiency, feasible hardware implementation, and reasonable means of recovering from errors. The overall compression performance was reported in [6] and [7]. A discussion of the overall proposed

HDTV system can be found in [7] and [25]. In this paper, we focus on the entropy coding part of the whole system.

Some of the important parameters of our prototype system are as follows. The sampling rate of the HDTV system is about 52 MHz[2]. The sampling ratio between luminance (Y) and chrominance (U and V) components is $4:2:2$. Thus, the total sample rate is about 104 MHz. The video data will be compressed to roughly 130 Mbps, and then carried in SONET STS-3c [8] at a gross rate of 155.52 Mbps. The data rates involved in this HDTV application are much higher than those in the digital facsimile or low-bit rate video applications. The design of a real-time implementation of an entropy coding (RLC/VLC) system with such a high throughput is an important and challenging problem.

Other issues also need to be considered in the design of the high-throughput entropy coding system. Since there is no explicit word-boundary in the variable-length coded data stream, a transmission error will cause the succeeding codewords to be decoded erroneously. Means must be provided to recover from such error propagation and minimize its effect on the quality of the reconstructed picture.

The organization of this paper is as follows. A parallel architecture for the entropy coding system that can achieve high throughput with lower speed requirement is discussed in Section II. The implementation of a parallel entropy coder and decoder which can achieve the required throughput for HDTV applications is described in Section III. The codeword synchronization and error concealment are discussed in Section IV. Finally, a summary is given in the last section.

II. THE SYSTEM ARCHITECTURE

In this section, we will discuss a parallel architecture for the entropy coding system which achieves high throughput with lower speed requirement. First, we will discuss the structures for the VLC coder and decoder that are suitable for parallel signal processing. Second, the overall entropy coding system is described.

A. The Structures of the VLC Coder and Decoder: Parallel Versus Serial

VLC encoding is a table look-up operation corresponding to a mapping between source symbols and variable-length codewords. The concatenation of these variable-length codewords is usually done by shifting out each codeword bit serially. On the other side, the VLC decoding is usually carried out by tracing along a coding tree at the input serial bit rate until a leaf (i.e.,

Manuscript received July 3, 1990; revised October 20, 1990. This paper was presented in part at the IEEE International Symposium on Circuits and Systems, New Orleans, LA, May 1990 and the 3rd International Workshop on HDTV, Italy, August 1989.

The authors are with Bellcore, 331 Newman Springs Road, Red Bank, NJ 07701.

IEEE Log Number 9041881.

[1]Although RLC on the other symbols is also possible, only zero run-length coding is really effective in our applications.

[2]Although some of the existing HDTV systems have sampling rates higher than 70 MHz, 51.84 MHz (1/3 of SONET STS-3c rate) has been chosen for this experimental prototype HDTV system. As the VLSI technology advances, higher sampling rates will be achieved automatically with the same architecture.

Reprinted from *IEEE Trans. Circuit Syst.,* vol. 1, no. 1, pp. 147–154, March 1991.

254

decoded data) is reached [9]. The operations of these encoding and decoding methods are bit-serial. For the real-time HDTV system, the lowest bit-serial rate is the coded compressed data rate which is about 130 Mbps. Such high clock rate processing is not easy to achieve with today's low-cost CMOS VLSI technology. Can parallel processing reduce this rate? Unfortunately, the partition of the source data into multiple paths cannot guarantee that the coded data rate is equally distributed for each path. Thus, the possible peak rate for each path may still be close to 130 Mbps. The other possibility is to operate these serial coder and decoder at the rate derived from the source sample rate such that parallel processing can effectively reduce the clock rate. If the maximal code length of VLC is 16, the maximum bit-serial rate is 104M × 16 = 1664 Mbps. In order to reduce the clock rate to lower than 100 MHz, which is more comfortable for today's CMOS VLSI technology, more than sixteen paths are needed. This implies too many hardware duplications.

In Section III, we will introduce VLC coder and decoder structures based on a parallel approach [12]–[14]. The parallel coder (or decoder) encodes (or decodes) each codeword in one clock-cycle regardless of its code length and thus can operate at the video sample rate, instead of a high bit-serial rate. Since they operate at the video sample rate, the parallel VLC coder and decoder also permit a system design based on parallel paths to further reduce the speed requirement. For example, if two paths are used in the entropy coding system, each VLC coder or decoder need to operate only at a peak rate of 52 MHz.

Other parallel decoding methods can be found in [10] and [11]. In [10], Peake used a barrel shifter and two programmable logic arrays (PLA's) to achieve decoding of each codeword in one clock cycle. However, the decoder's interface and control circuitry for the barrel shifter were not discussed. In [11], a read only memory (ROM) and an N-shift register were used, and the VLC was modified to allow fewer code lengths for a high-speed implementation. Such constraints on the VLC usually introduce some degradation on compression efficiency.

B. A System Overview

A general block diagram of an ATV codec is shown in Fig. 1. The video codec consists of an A/D and D/A, a video source coder/decoder, an entropy coder/decoder, and channel interfaces. The input of the entropy coder comes from the source coder. In order to achieve the required data compression, the source coder may transform its input video signals into multi-subband signals (such as in the DCT or subband coding [25], [7]) so that each subband can be quantized more efficiently. The source coder outputs can then be further compressed by the entropy coder. After the entropy coder, the instantaneous data rate may vary over a wide range. Thus, a large buffer is needed to smooth out the data rate so that the average rate is near the channel rate.

It is very inefficient to use one entropy coder/decoder for each subband since a lot of hardware would have to be duplicated. It has been suggested[3] that the multi-subband signals generated by the source coder be multiplexed into the least number of paths such that the speed requirement of the entropy coder/decoder is still feasible for implementation. A data shuffler is added after the multiplexer to shuffle the data on a line-by-line basis (i.e., one line of data from one subband followed by one line of data from another subband) so that the zero-runs of each subband are preserved [25], [7].

[3]The idea was suggested by Dr. J. A. Bellisio.

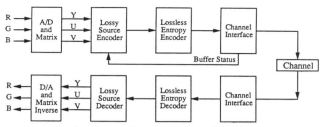

Fig. 1. System diagram of generic HDTV codec.

It is possible to multiplex all the luminance and chrominance subbands into a serial data stream with a total sample rate of 104 MHz[4] so that only one entropy coder/decoder is needed. However, assuming a maximum codeword length of 16, the VLC coder/decoder would need to achieve a worst-case throughput of 1.664 Gbps. Also, the required interface bandwidth of the VLC decoder and the buffer would have to be 1.664 Gbps. It is very difficult and expensive to implement circuits to achieve this rate. Moreover, the 104 MHz clock is more difficult to obtain in a system where the video sampling clock is 52 MHz.

A block diagram of a two-path entropy coder is shown in Fig. 2. This architecture is more general and can be easily extended to systems having more paths. In Fig. 2, the subbands are separated into two paths, one for luminance and the other for chrominance, such that the peak-rate in each path is only 52 MHz. Since the output of the VLC coder is bursty, a small line first-in-first-out buffer (FIFO) is added after each VLC coder. This FIFO can accommodate the maximal amount of data that buffer can absorb within one line period so that the data can be multiplexed into the buffer on a line-by-line basis. Also, this FIFO smooths out the data rate over one line period and the resulting average rate is much lower than the peak rate. Thus, the interface bandwidth to the buffer can be reduced from 1.664 Gbps to a moderate amount (e.g., 416 Mbps in our system) so that this interface is easier to implement while still having enough bandwidth to accommodate most lines. Since the entropy coder only compresses data statistically, in some very rare but possible cases, the actual output rate of the entropy coder within a line may be higher than the reduced interface bandwidth. Some data have to be discarded by the multiplexer in these cases. The degradation caused by this loss of data is minimized by coding the important subbands first. Thus, if some data need to be discarded, only the less important subbands are affected. A special codeword may be needed to mark this forced-end-of-line case. The entropy decoder is an inverse of the entropy coder except some error-handling functions are included.

III. The Implementation of the Entropy Coder and Decoder

In this section, the structures of the entropy coder and decoder based on a parallel approach are described first. Then full-custom VLSI implementations of these two experimental prototype chips are introduced.

A. The Entropy Coder

The entropy coder consists two major parts: RLC and VLC coders. The input data is run length coded first, and then variable length coded. In the RLC coder, input data that is not part of a zero run is passed through, otherwise the length of the zero run is determined and properly encoded. For both cases,

[4]Many source coders preserve the sample rate.

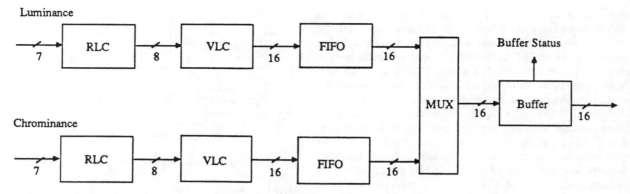

Fig. 2.   Block diagram of two-path entropy coder.

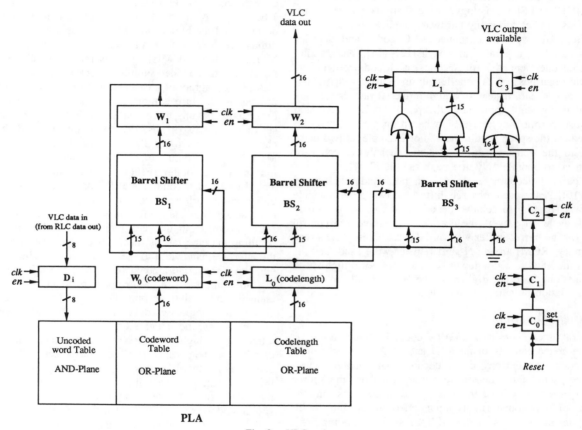

Fig. 3.   VLC coder.

one extra bit is added to indicate whether the symbol represents a zero run or a single sample. The RLC coder can be easily implemented by a counter, some registers and logic gates. When a zero run is present, the RLC coder generates no output until the last zero or maximum run length is reached. Therefore, the output of the RLC coder is not continuous, and the operation of the downstream VLC coder is gapped.

The VLC coder maps the input data into variable-length codewords, concatenates them together, and segments them into 16-bit words for output. The parallel VLC coder shown in Fig. 3 encodes each codeword in one clock cycle regardless of its length. The functions of some major circuit components in Fig. 3 are as follows. The PLA does the table look-up of the codewords. The barrel shifter BS_1 concatenates these codewords together and the barrel shifter BS_2 segments them into 16-bit words for output. The function of a 4-bit accumulator of code

lengths is mimicked by the barrel shifter BS_3 and the register L_1. The carry-out of the accumulator forms the output-available signal of the VLC coder. The signal *en* in Fig. 3 is an enable signal which is derived from the data-available of the RLC coder. When there is a zero run in the source data, operation of the VLC coder is suspended until the RLC coder obtains its run length. During this time period, *en* is low and the registers in the VLC coder will retain their old data.

The codeword look-up table can be implemented by a read only memory (ROM), programmable logic array (PLA), or random access memory (RAM). Using RAM, a user programmable VLC can be implemented. However, the size will be larger, the speed will be slower than the other two approaches, and extra circuitry is needed for preloading the codebooks. A ROM is more suitable when the number of codebook entries is 2^n, where n is an integer, otherwise some address locations are wasted. For these reasons, a PLA is used in our current implementation. Although there is only one PLA shown in Fig. 3, multiple paged PLA's will be implemented to allow different tables for different subband signals to achieve higher compression efficiency.

Registers W_0 and L_0 store the results of the PLA table look-up, i.e., codeword and code length respectively. The maximal code length is 16 bits in our implementation[5]. The codeword from the PLA and in W_0 is left-adjusted and stuffed with 1's, if necessary, on the right. The first bit is on the left. The code length is represented by 16 bits in a decoded form, i.e., the position of the only 1 indicates the length. W_1 stores the concatenated previous codeword which have not yet been output. We will call these codeword bits the residual bits. W_2 is the output latch. L_1 records the number of the residual bits in W_1. C_3 indicates whether there is an output available in the output latch W_2.

The parallel concatenation of codewords is done by barrel shifters BS_1 and BS_2. Functionally, the output of a barrel shifter is a sliding window on its input data. BS_1 and BS_2 both provide 16-bit wide windows on their 31 input bits. BS_3 has a 32-bit wide window on its 47 input bits. They all have 16 different shift positions. BS_1 is controlled by the current code length stored in L_0 and shifts the codeword from W_0 into W_1 so that the rightmost bit of W_1 is the last bit of the codeword. Consequently, the data stored in register W_1 is ready to concatenate with the next codewords. The barrel shifter BS_2 is controlled by the number of residual bits as recorded by L_1. The residual bits in W_1 are left-adjusted by BS_2. If the sum of the residual bits and the current codeword is more than 16, the output of BS_2 contains the first 16 bits which have not yet been output but are ready for output.

The combination of the barrel shifter BS_3 and the latch L_1 functions as a 4-bit accumulator of code lengths. If the residual bit length is greater than 16, the right 16 bits of BS_3's output are all 0's and $C3$ is set to 1 to indicate output-available. The 16-bit pattern from the latch L_1 is partially duplicated into a 31-bit input to BS_3 so that the barrel shifter functions as a rotator. The other 16 input bits of BS_3 are connected to "0" for detecting the carry-out condition. If the right 16 bits of BS_3's output are all 0's, there is a carry-out. The left 16 bits of BS_3's output update the new number of residual bits in W_1. The number of residual bits is usually between 1 and 16 except at the beginning of the operation when it is zero. Since L_1 is 16 bits long, it can only represent 1 to 16 in the decoded form. Thus, at the beginning of the operation, L_1 needs to be set to 16, which is modulo-16 equivalent to zero, and C_2 is set to 1 to indicate this is a zero, not 16. The example in Fig. 4 illustrates how this VLC coder works.

There are several reasons for using the barrel shifter BS_3 instead of a 4-bit accumulator: 1) a barrel shifter is faster than an accumulator; 2) since the output is already a 16-bit decoded pattern, a 4-to-16 decoder is not required for BS_2; and 3) the decoded representation of a code length reduces the capacitive loading on the bit-line in the PLA code length OR-plane. Consequently, using the barrel shifter results in faster circuitry and also saves design time since the design of the barrel shifter is available anyway.

[5] The 16-bit maximal code length limitation has been found to incur very little penalty (less than 1%) on the coding rates of all the test sequences we used. The circuits discussed here can also be modified easily to accommodate longer code length.

Time	W_0 (codeword)	L_0 (code leng.)	W_1 (residual register)	W_2 (output register)	L_1 (res. leng.)	C_3	C_2
0	0000 0000 0001 0001	16	X	X	16	X	1
1	0101 0••• •••• ••••	5	0000 0000 0001 0001	X	16	0	0
2	0100 01•• •••• ••••	6	•••• •••• •••0 1010	0000 0000 0001 0001	5	1	0
3	0110 0101 1•• ••••	9	•••• ••10 1001 0001	0101 0010 001• ••••	11	0	0
4	0000 0000 0001 001•	15	•••• •••0 1100 1011	0101 0010 0010 1100	4	1	0
5	1111 1111 1111 0000	16	1000 0000 0000 1001	1011 0000 0000 0001	3	1	0
6	1010 0101 10•• ••••	10	1111 1111 1111 0000	0011 1111 1111 1110	16	1	0
7	0010 0100 •••• ••••	8	•••• ••10 1001 0110	1111 1111 1111 0000	10	1	0
8	1111 1111 1111 0000	16	1001 0110 0010 0100	1010 0101 1000 1001	2	1	0
9	0101 0•• •••• ••••	5	1111 1111 1111 0000	0011 1111 1111 1100	16	1	0
10	0100 01•• •••• ••••	6	•••• •••• •••0 1010	1111 1111 1111 0000	5	1	0

Fig. 4. Example of VLC coder operations.

B. The Entropy Decoder

The entropy decoder contains a VLC decoder followed by a RLC decoder. It performs an inverse function of the entropy coder. The RLC decoder passes the VLC-decoded codewords through if they are not run-length codes, otherwise it outputs the specified number of zeros. During a zero run, while zeros are being output, the operation of the VLC decoder must be suspended. Thus, the output of the RLC decoder is continuous, but the operation of the VLC decoder needs to be intermittent in analogy to the VLC coder. Similar to the RLC coder, the RLC decoder can also be easily implemented by a counter, some register, and logic gates.

The VLC decoder is more difficult to implement than the VLC coder. The input to the VLC decoder is a bit stream without explicit word-boundaries. The VLC decoder has to decode a codeword, determine its length, and shift the input data stream by the number of bits corresponding to the decoded code length, before decoding the next codeword. These are recursive operations that cannot be pipelined.

A block diagram of a parallel VLC decoder is shown in Fig. 5. The functions of its major components are described as follows. The PLA is the codebook table. It matches a codeword and outputs the corresponding symbol and code length. The code length is accumulated by barrel shifter BS_1 and register D_2. The barrel shifter BS_0 then shifts its opening window to the next codeword according to this accumulated code length. An example of this VLC decoder operations is shown in Fig. 6.

In principle, a decoding table could be implemented by a ROM, however, it would require a 2^{16}-word ROM which would be very wasteful. It is much more efficient to use a content addressable memory (CAM) [12] or a PLA [10] whose sizes are determined only by the number of code-book entries. A user programmable VLC decoder can be implemented by using a CAM [12], however, it would result in a circuit much larger and slower than a circuit using a PLA. In the following discussion, use of a PLA is assumed. The operation of the circuitry is as follows.

The input data are stored in registers D_0 and D_1. The 16-bit pattern in D_2 represents the number of decoded bits (i.e., accumulated codelength) in D_1. The number can lie between 0 and 15. This pattern controls the barrel shifter BS_0 so that the undecoded bits appear at the output of the barrel shifter.

The AND-plane of the PLA essentially performs a parallel pattern matching on the data stream. When a codeword is matched, the corresponding word-line in the PLA AND-plane is activated which enables the corresponding word transistors in the OR-planes to output the decoded codewords and the code length.

The decoded code length is used to control the second barrel shifter BS_1 whose function is a 4-bit accumulator, analogous to

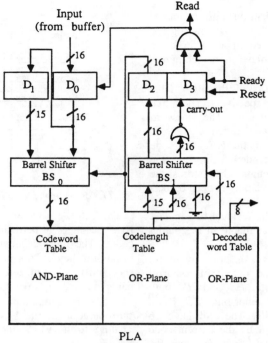

PLA

Fig. 5. VLC decoder.

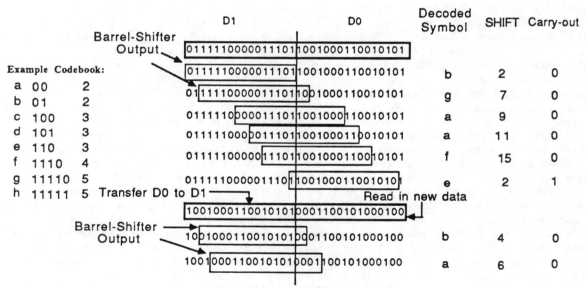

Fig. 6. Example of VLC decoder operations.

the BS_3 in the VLC coder. BS_1 shifts the pattern of D_2's output according to the newly decoded code length. The resultant new pattern corresponds to the accumulated code length. This new pattern controls BS_0 so as to output the correct window of 16 bits for the next decoding cycle.

When the accumulated code length exceeds 15, a carry-out bit becomes 1. It indicates that all the bits in D_1 have been used and that D_0 may not contain the whole next codeword. In this case, when the gapped ready clock generated by the RLC decoder latches the decoded output, a read signal is generated. The contents of D_0 is loaded into D_1, a new 16-bit word is loaded into D_0, and the barrel shifter shifts to the new position, all at the same time, to prepare for the next decoding cycle.

If the accumulated code length does not exceed 15, the

carry-out signal is 0. Since the maximum code length is 16 and at least 16 bits of data in D_0 and D_1 are not used yet, there are always enough bits for the next decoding cycle. D_0 and D_1 are left unchanged. The new accumulated code length pattern simply controls the BS_0 to shift to the correct position for the next decoding cycle. Thus, VLC decoding is achieved in one clock cycle regardless of the code length.

C. A Full-custom IC Implementation

Since the circuit components of the entropy coder are similar to those of the entropy decoder and the speed requirement of the entropy decoder is more difficult to achieve, we will focus on the entropy decoder here. The mask-size and the simulated speed of some critical parts, barrel shifters and the PLA, are shown in

Fig. 7.   Chip layout of entropy decoder.

TABLE I
THE LAYOUT SIZE AND SIMULATION SPEED OF THE CRITICAL PARTS

Technology	1.2 μm double-metal CMOS
Barrel shifter BS_0	Mask-size 304 μm $\times$ 271 μm Delay-time ~ 1.5 ns from input and shift to output
Barrel shifter BS_1	Mask-size 598 μm $\times$ 282 μm Delay-time ~ 1.5 ns from input and shift to output
PLA (with 160 entries)	Mask-size 557 μm $\times$ 2937 μm Evaluation-time ~ 4.2 ns to wordlength OR-Plane output, including an output buffer. (assuming the maximum number of entries with same length is 60)

Table I. A mask layout of the decoder chip is shown in Fig. 7. Six codebooks are included in the chip. The core of the chip contains about 37K transistors in an area about 3.8 mm × 4.0 mm. Operating speed higher than the required 52 MHz is anticipated. For our usage, the maximum number of entries in a codebook is 160. However, extension to more codebook entries is easy.

The PLA's are implemented using Domino CMOS circuits [15] which achieve high speed operations with low power consumption [16]. The AND-plane and OR-plane of the PLA are precharged in the first half clock cycle and evaluated in the second. During the precharge time of VLC decoder, the signals are propagating through D_0, D_1, BS_0, and the PLA address buffers. Thus, the time during the precharge is not wasted.

The critical path of the VLC decoder includes the PLA AND-plane evaluation time, the code length OR-plane evaluation time, and the BS_1 delay time. The PLA AND-plane evaluation is speeded up by employing larger-than-minimum size transistors. The OR-plane evaluation time is very dependent on the capacitive loading on the bit-lines. Since the code length is fully decoded, the transistors in the code length OR-plane are

very sparsely populated. This greatly reduces the capacitive loading and increases the evaluation speed. To further speed up the operation in the OR-plane, each bit is implemented by multiple transistors sharing drain diffusions. This improves the ratio of transistor strength to load capacitance. Also, the word-lines from the PLA address decoder are buffered between the code length OR-plane and the decoded-word OR-plane. This minimizes the capacitive loading on the word-lines which address the code length OR-plane.

To minimize the capacitive loading on the bit-line of the codeword OR-plane, the transistors on the OR-plane are populated in such a way that no bit-line ever has more than 50% occupancy of transistor drains on it. If a bit-line has more "1" entries, the polarity of that bit-line is inverted and the output polarity is corrected by an inverting sense amplifier [17].

The PLA layouts are generated by a PLA generator written in the C Language. This PLA generator makes the chips mask-programmable for other systems using different codebooks.

IV. CODEWORD SYNCHRONIZATION AND ERROR CONCEALMENT

One major concern on using variable-length code is its error propagation property. An erroneous bit from transmission or storage of the encoded bit stream will cause the codeword to be misinterpreted and as the codeword's length is not fixed, this may result in a loss of synchronization of the bit stream. Decoding errors may propagate to the subsequent source symbols. Although resynchronization may naturally occur after a while [18], [19] or it can be guaranteed by careful designs of the code [20]–[22], the number of the decoded symbols may not be correct. In video or image coding applications, this would result in a shift on part of the reconstructed picture which is very objectionable. A technique for resynchronizing both the code-word and the sample position is the use of synchronizing words at suitable intervals. These synchronizing words have to be recognizable whether the decoding is synchronized or not. A codeword with this property is called a clear codeword. Basically, a clear codeword is a codeword which cannot be generated by any concatenations of other codewords. The end-of-line (EOL) codeword used in the international digital facsimile coding standard [3] is an example of the clear codeword.

The identification of these clear codewords is not dependent on the correct decoding of their proceeding symbols; they can be identified by their special codeword patterns. Thus, if there is any bit error in the coded data stream, the error propagation is confined at most until the next clear codeword. Furthermore, since the number of codewords between each pair of clear codewords is known, most of the errors can be detected by counting the decoded samples between the clear codewords. Such error detection not only can prevent a possible position shift of the decoded samples following the erroneous segment, but also can activate error concealment mechanisms for the erroneous segment. For example, if a bad line is detected, we may repeat the previous line. If the erroneous segment is a high-frequency subband, we can retain other correct subbands and only replace the erroneous subband by zeros. According to the study in [23], these two error concealment techniques are very effective.

If multiple variable-length coded bit streams have to be multiplexed together, usually they cannot be multiplexed directly in a word-interleaving fashion due to a different number of words for each bit stream. By using clear codewords as segment delimiters, they can be multiplexed segment by segment. These clear

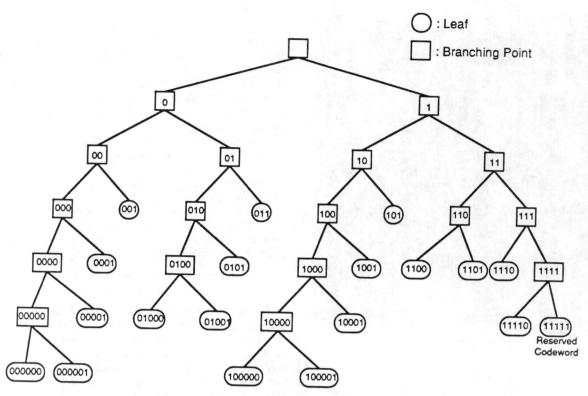

Fig. 8. Example of construction of code tree with shorter clear codeword.

codewords are recognizable to the demultiplexer and the segments can be demultiplexed without the requirement of variable-length decoding first.

Although the clear codeword, EOL, is used in the international digital FAX coding standard [3], the design of an optimal Huffman codebook which also includes clear codewords has not been shown. A clear codeword cannot be obtained automatically from the Huffman algorithm. Usually, the codewords generated by the Huffman algorithm are not clear, i.e., they can be generated by a concatenation of other codewords. In order to make a clear codeword, a reserved codeword has to be extended by several bits. Naturally, it is desired to make these extension bits as few as possible. With the codelengths given by the Huffman algorithm, there are many different codes. For different codes or different reserved codeword patterns, the number of the needed extension bits may be different.

A method of finding an efficient code with a clear codeword will be introduced here. As shown heuristically in [24], a good bit pattern for the reserved codeword is all 1's (or all 0's). (Since they are equivalent, we will only discuss the former case without loss of any generality.) The all-one reserved codeword tends to require shorter extension bits than others in order to make it clear. To convert the reserved all-ones codeword into a clear codeword, a suffix of a few more 1's followed by a 0 is needed. The suffice 0 after the all 1's pattern in the clear codeword is needed to mark the end of the clear codeword. Otherwise, an all 1's clear codeword cannot be clearly located when it succeeds a codeword with suffix 1's or when it precedes a codeword with prefix 1's.

If the reserved codeword and the clear codeword should have the patterns we described above, it is simple to observe that we should arrange the code tree such that a concatenation of codewords other than the reserved codeword will not form a long segment of consecutive 1's in order to obtain a shorter clear codeword. For any code tree, all codewords (except the reserved

all-ones codeword) must contain at least one 0, otherwise the prefix property[6] is contradicted. Thus, we only have to consider the consecutive 1's formed by the concatenation of two codewords. The longest possible run of 1's in the concatenation of codewords, other than the reserved codeword, is formed by the codeword with longest suffix of 1's followed by the codeword with longest prefix of 1's. If the reserved codeword is n 1's, there must be at least one codeword having a prefix of $n - 1$ 1's and one 0. Also, no codeword except the reserved codeword has a prefix of 1's longer than $n - 1$ as this would contradict the prefix property. Thus, for the codewords other than the reserved one, the maximal number of the prefix 1's is always $n - 1$. Therefore, in order to obtain the shortest clear codeword, we only need to minimize the maximal number of consecutive 1's in the suffixes of the codewords. The resulting clear codeword is the reserved all 1's appended by this number of longest suffix 1's and a 0. Thus, knowing the code length for each codeword from the Huffman algorithm, we can rearrange the *shape* of the code tree such that the longest suffix 1's of the codewords (excluding the reserved codeword) is minimized.

In the tree representation of a variable-length code, the number of the leaves on level k is the number of codewords with length k, while the root is viewed as level 0. The key idea for minimizing the suffix 1's of codewords is the assignment of nodes with the longest suffix 1's (except the all-one reserved pattern) as leaves on each level. Thus, the nodes with longer suffix 1's are terminated into leaves, thereby thwarting the suffix 1's growth to the next level. The assignment will result in a code tree with shortest suffix 1's of its codewords. This code tree is thus the *optimal* code tree in the sense that its reserved all-one codeword needs least extension bits to make it clear.

An example of this *optimal* code tree is shown in Fig. 8. In this example, the variable-length code contains three 3-bit code-

[6]No codeword is a prefix of any other codeword.

260

words, six 4-bit codewords, six 5-bit codewords, and four 6-bit codewords. Totally, there are 19 codewords, including the reserved codeword with codelength of 5 bits. The first and second level have no leaves since no codeword is one or two bits long. On the third level, there are 8 nodes and three of them must be assigned as leaves, since three 3-bit codewords are required. The nodes with longer suffix 1's (except the all-one node) are assigned to be leaves first. For example, node 011 has the longest suffix 1's (except the all-one pattern), so it is the first node we want to assign as a leaf. Besides this, nodes 001 and 101, which have the second longest suffix 1's, are also assigned as leaves. The leave assignment for other levels is similar except, on level 5, the node 11111 is first chosen as a leaf since it is the required 5-bit reserved codeword. In this example, the longest suffix 1's is 2 bits. To make the reserved 11111 clear, it has to be extended three more bits as 11111110.

V. Summary

In this paper, a complete entropy coding system for HDTV applications is described. Parallel structures of the entropy coder and decoder are introduced. This parallel entropy coder (or decoder) encodes (or decodes) each codeword in one clock cycle regardless of its code length. Thus, the required clock rate is lower and a parallel processing system is also easy to design. These parallel entropy coder and decoder are implemented in two experimental prototype chips which are capable to encode and decode 52 million samples/s. Clear codewords are introduced for variable-length codeword synchronization and multiplexing. A systematic method of designing an efficient code with clear codewords is described.

Acknowledgment

We would like to thank J. A. Bellisio, P. E. Fleischer, and M. E. Lukacs for stimulating discussions and valuable comments. We also like to thank S. Palaniraj for helping us on doing layouts and writing the PLA generator.

References

[1] W. K. Pratt, *Digital Image Processing*. New York: Wiley, pp. 632, 1978.
[2] D. A. Huffman, "A method for the construction of minimum redundancy codes," *Proc. IRE*, vol. 40, pp. 1098–1101, Sept. 1952.
[3] R. Hunter and A. H. Robinson, "International digital facsimile coding standards," *Proc. IEEE*, vol. 68, no. 7, pp. 854–867, July 1980.
[4] CCITT SGXV, "Draft Revised Recommendation H.261—Video code for audiovisual services at p × 64 kbit/s," *OM XV-R 17-E, CCITT Study Group XV—Report R 17*, Specialist Group on Coding for Visual Telephony, Jan. 1990.
[5] W. H. Chen and W. K. Pratt, "Scene Adaptive Coder," *IEEE Trans. Commun.*, vol. COM-32, no. 3, pp. 225–232, Mar. 1984.
[6] T.-C. Chen, P. E. Fleischer, and S.-M. Lei, "A subband scheme for advanced TV coding in BISDN applications," presented at *3rd Int. Workshop on HDTV*, Italy, Aug. 1989.
[7] P. E. Fleischer, T.-C. Chen, and S.-M. Lei, "Coding of advanced TV for BISDN using multiple subbands," *Proc. of Int. Symp. on Circuits and Systems*, New Orleans, LA, pp. 1314–1318, May 1990.
[8] R. Ballart and Y.-C Ching, "SONET: Now it's the standard optical network," *IEEE Communications Magazine*, Mar. 1989.
[9] J. L. Sicre and A. Leger, "Silicon complexity of VLC decoder vs Q-coder," JPEG N258, ISO/JTC1/SC2/WG8, CCITT SGVII, Feb. 1989.
[10] J. W. Peake, "Decompaction," *IBM Technical Disclosure Bulletin*, vol. 26, no. 9, pp. 4794–4797, Feb. 1984.
[11] M. E. Lukacs, "Variable word length coding for a high data rate DPCM video coder," in *Proc. Picture Coding Symp.*, pp. 54–56, 1986.
[12] M.-T. Sun, K.-M. Yang, and K.-H. Tzou, "A high-speed programmable VLSI for decoding variable-length codes," *Applications of Digital Image Processing XII*, A. G. Tescher, ed., Proc. SPIE 1153, Aug. 1989.
[13] M.-T. Sun and S.-M. Lei, "A parallel variable-length-code decoder for advanced television applications, presented at *3rd Int'nl Workshop on HDTV*, Italy, Aug. 1989.
[14] S.-M. Lei, M.-T. Sun, K. Ramachandran, and S. Palaniraj, "VLSI implementation of an entropy coder and decoder for advanced TV applications," in *Proc. of Int. Symp. on Circuits and Systems*, New Orleans, LA, pp. 3030–3033, May 1990.
[15] R. H. Krambeck, C. M. Lee, and H. S. Law, "High speed compact circuits with CMOS," *IEEE J. Solid-State Circuits*, vol. SC-17, pp. 614–619, June 1982.
[16] J. A. Pretorius, A. S. Shubat, and A. T. Salama, "Charge redistribution and noise margins in domino CMOS logic," *IEEE Trans. Circuits Syst.*, vol. CAS-33, no. 8, pp. 786–793, Aug. 1986.
[17] P. C. Rossbach, R. W. Linderman, and D. M. Gallagher, "An optimizing XROM silicon compiler," *Proc. IEEE Custom Integrated Circuits Conf.*, Portland, OR, pp. 13–16, May 4–7, 1987.
[18] J. C. Maxted and J. P. Robinson, "Error recovery for variable length codes," *IEEE Trans. Inform. Theory*, vol. IT-31, no. 6, pp. 794–801, Nov. 1985.
[19] B. Rudner, "Construction of minimum-redundancy codes with an optimum synchronizing property," *IEEE Trans. Inform. Theory*, vol. IT-17, pp. 478–487, July 1971.
[20] T. J. Ferguson and J. H. Rabinowitz, "Self-synchronizing Huffman codes," *IEEE Trans. Inform. Theory*, vol. IT-30, no. 4, pp. 687–693, July 1984.
[21] P. G. Neumann, "Self-Synchronizing Sequential Coding with Low Redundancy," *Bell Sys. Tech. Journal*, vol. 50, no. 3, pp. 951–981, Mar. 1971.
[22] P. G. Neumann, "Efficient Error-Limiting Variable-Length Codes," *IRE Trans. Inform. Theory*, vol. IT-8, pp. 292–304, July 1962.
[23] D. S. Lee and K. H. Tzou, "Hierarchical DCT coding of HDTV for ATM networks," *Proc. ICASSP*, vol. 4, pp. 2249–2252, Apr. 1990.
[24] S.-M. Lei, "The construction of efficient variable-length codes with clear synchronizing codewords for digital video applications," *Packet Video '91*, Kyoto, Japan, Mar. 18–19, 1991.
[25] T.-C. Chen, P. E. Fleischer, and K.-H. Tzou, "Multiple Block-size Transform Coding for Video Using a Subband Structure," *IEEE Trans. Circuits Syst. Video Technol.*, vol. 1, no. 1, Mar. 1991.

Reed Solomon VLSI Codec For Advanced Television

Sterling R. Whitaker, *Member, IEEE*, John A. Canaris, *Student Member, IEEE* and Kelly B. Cameron

Abstract—A VLSI implementation of a Reed Solomon codec circuit is reported. The 1.6-μm double metal CMOS chip is 8.2 mm by 8.4 mm, contains 200 000 transistors, operates at a sustained data rate of 80 Mbits/s and executes up to 1000 MOPS while consuming less than 500 mW of power. The 10-MHz sustained byte rate for the data is independent of the error pattern. The circuit has complete decoder and encoder functions and uses a single data/system clock. Block lengths of 255 bytes as well as shortened codes are supported with no external buffering. Erasure corrections as well as random error corrections are supported with selectable correction of up to ten symbol errors. Corrected data is output at a fixed latency. These features make this Reed Solomon processor suitable for use in advanced television systems.

I. INTRODUCTION

ADVANCED television systems require the transmission of image and audio data over noisy channels. Due to limited bandwidth in the available channels this data must be compressed in a variety of ways. Since even single bit errors can significantly degrade compressed images, it is necessary to use error correction codes to protect the transmitted data. The large frame buffers in advanced television receivers may also require error correction between the memory and the rest of the system. The combination of high data rates and the need for powerful error correcting codes places a significant real time computational burden on advanced television systems. A VLSI Reed Solomon (RS) processor chip, originally designed for the Hubble Space Telescope (HST) [1], is described in this paper. The computation rate and powerful error correcting features of this processor make it suitable for use in advanced television applications [2]–[6].

Images transmitted from the Hubble Space Telescope are encoded with a (255 239) RS code. Reed Solomon codes are efficient and powerful but real time decoding of the received message requires operation rates that far exceed the present capabilities of stored program computers. For each message block, the HST code requires the evaluation of 16 equations of order 254, the recursive evaluation of an algorithm utilizing polynomials of degree 16 and 15 255 evaluations for each of two polynomials of degree 8255 evaluations of a polynomial of degree 7, plus 255 divisions, multiplications and additions of field elements. The total number of calculations per message in the HST (255 239) code is 19 386. Operating

Manuscript received January 1, 1991; revised April 22, 1991. This research was sponsored in part by NASA under the NASA Space Engineering Research Center Grant NAGW-1406.

The authors are with NASA Space Engineering Research Center for VLSI System Design, University of Idaho, Moscow, ID 83843.

IEEE Log Number 9101087.

at 80 Mbits/s, the number of operations per second is 750 million. Real time decoding of information sent from the HST is accomplished in the ground communications link by the single full custom CMOS chip described in this paper. The full capability of the chip, a (255 235) RS code, requires 1000 MOPS.

A pipelined architecture was designed to achieve these real time processing rates. This required a reformulation of the basic RS mathematics. The architecture was also conceived with VLSI layout considerations in mind. This led to an implementation which was highly structured and which can be easily scaled for different error correction capabilities. The flexibility and error correcting ability of this processor can provide significant advantages in advanced television systems. Error correction codes can either be used to extend the coverage area for a broadcast television signal or to reduce the transmitter power required for a given coverage area. With a (167 147) shortened RS code, transmitter power can be reduced by at least 6 dB without a loss in coverage [6]. Reed Solomon codes are also extremely efficient. A (167 147) RS code proposed for digital HDTV introduces only an 11% overhead to achieve a 10-byte error correction capability. This overhead is small when compared with other conventional error correction schemes. Terrestrial digital HDTV also requires about a 20 MBits/s data rate. The features of the HST chip allow all of these code and speed requirements to be met by the VLSI codec presented here, with no modifications. Other RS decoders which have been reported in the literature include a single chip 40 MHz decoder which corrects 8 byte errors [7], a single chip 10 Mbits/s decoder which corrects 16 byte errors [8] and implements the standard for concatenated coding for spacecraft-to-ground telemetry (CCSDS) [9] and a multi-chip 80 Mbits/s CCSDS decoder [10].

This paper presents the capabilities and VLSI architecture for the special purpose processor introduced here. In Section II, a mathematical background is presented for Reed Solomon codes. Basic equations are presented for each of the decoding steps. Section III presents some of the operational features of the IC. The VLSI architecture is presented in Section IV. Section V describes implementation issues related to logic design and layout. Conclusions and acknowledgements are given in Section VI.

II. MATHEMATICAL BACKGROUND

The following is a brief summary of basic definitions found in [11]. For Binary Reed Solomon codes, each symbol

Reprinted from *IEEE Trans. Circuits Syst.*, vol. 1, no. 2, pp. 230–236, June 1991.

is represented by a binary word consisting of m bits. Given the number of bits representing a symbol, there are $2^m - 1$ unique, nonzero, symbols possible. An RS code is defined over the finite field $GF(2^m)$. The elements of the field are specified by an irreducible, primitive polynomial $p(x)$. A code block consists of $N \leq 2^m - 1$ symbols. Each code block includes both information symbols and parity symbols. In order to correct t symbol errors, $2t$ parity symbols are calculated and appended to a group of information symbols during an encoding process. The decoding process uses this parity information to identify the magnitude and location of up to t errors or to mark the code block as uncorrectable if more than t errors have been introduced during transmission through the channel. Since each code block contains $N \leq 2^m - 1$ symbols and $2t$ parity symbols are required for decoding, a code block contains $k = N - 2t$ information symbols. An RS code is classified as a (N, k) code. $N = 2^m - 1$ for a full length code. If $N < 2^m - 1$, the code is said to be shortened. For this processor, $m = 8$, $t \in \{1, 1.5, 2, 2.5, \cdots, 10\}$, and the primitive polynomial is $p(x) = x^8 + x^7 + x^2 + x^1 + x^0$. The code block may be as long as $N = 255$ or as short as $N = 23 + 10t$. The chip can therefore decode a family of RS codes.

The RS code block can be defined as a polynomial $c(x)$, of order $N - 1$, formed from an order $k - 1$ information polynomial, $m(x)$, and an order $N - k$ generator polynomial, $g(x)$, as in (1). A shift in time, due to the addition of the parity symbols, is represented by x^{2t}:

$$c(x) = x^{2t}m(x) + x^{2t}m(x) \bmod g(x). \qquad (1)$$

Consequently, every valid code block is a multiple of the generator polynomial

$$g(x) = \prod_{i=s+1}^{s+2t} (x - \beta^i) = \sum_{j=0}^{2t} g_j x^j \qquad (2)$$

where $\beta = \alpha^h$ is a primitive element of the field, s is an offset term and t is the error correcting ability of the code. For the HST, $s = 119$, $\beta = \alpha^1$ and $t = 8$. The architecture of the chip is flexible. The same chip can decode Reed Solomon codes having the values of s and β given above and any value of t less than or equal to 10. Error correction ability is pin selectable. The offset term and primitive element are single mask programmable. The primitive polynomial, $p(x)$ can also be altered by the same mask change.

A transmitted code block, $c(x)$, may be modified by the introduction of errors in a noisy channel. The received polynomial, $R(x)$, can be represented by the sum of the transmitted $c(x)$ and an error polynomial, $E(x)$, as follows:

$$R(x) = c(x) + E(x) \qquad (3)$$
$$= R_{N-1}x^{n-1} + \cdots + R_1 x + R_0 \qquad (4)$$

where each R_i is a received symbol, viewed as a field element and symbols R_i, $i < 2t$ are the parity symbols.

The first step in the decoding algorithm is to calculate the syndrome polynomial $S(x)$ which contains information to correct correctable errors or detect uncorrectable errors.

Each coefficient, S_j, of the syndrome polynomial is defined as

$$S_j = \sum_{i=0}^{N-1} R_i \alpha^{i(j+s+1)}, \qquad 0 \leq j \leq 2t - 1. \qquad (5)$$

The syndrome polynomial can be expressed as

$$S(x) = \sum_{j=0}^{2t-1} S_j x^j. \qquad (6)$$

In order to correct an error, it is necessary to determine both the location and the magnitude of the error. The solution for a minimum degree error location polynomial, $\lambda(x)$, which satisfies the following key equation, (7), is the next step in decoding Reed Solomon codes. Furthermore, if time domain decoding [11] is used, an error magnitude polynomial, $\Omega(x)$, must also be calculated. These polynomials have the following relationship with the syndrome polynomial

$$S(x)\lambda(x) \equiv \Omega(x) \bmod x^{2t}. \qquad (7)$$

Berlekamp was the first to develop a computationally efficient method of solving this key equation [12]. Since then, several different methods have been developed. Sugiyama [13] showed that Euclid's algorithm for finding the greatest common divisor could also be adapted to this purpose. Reed developed a closely related method based on continued fractions [14], [15]. All of these methods have roughly the same computational complexity. The method based on Euclid's procedure was selected because its implementation is highly regular and the data flow requirements of the machine are such that it can easily be implemented in VLSI. Time domain decoding was selected, as opposed to a frequency domain transformation method [16], because it can be implemented as a small array of identical cells.

The error location and error magnitude polynomials can be obtained by using a recursive operation, Euclid's greatest common divisor algorithm [11]. Once the two polynomials are known, the location and magnitude of a given error are found as follows:

Let α^i be a zero of $\lambda(x)$ (i.e., $\lambda(\alpha^i) = 0$), then the corresponding error is located at R_{254-i}. The error magnitude is

$$-\frac{\Omega(\alpha^i)}{\lambda'(\alpha^i)} \alpha^{si} \qquad (8)$$

where $\lambda'(x)$ is the first derivative of $\lambda(x)$ with respect to x and α^{si} is an offset term.

If errors are detected in other parts of the system, the probable location of an error may actually be available before decoding. The correction capability of a code can be extended by marking symbols for erasure correction, relieving the decoder of the burden of determining the error location. For each R_i, of $R(x)$ to be erased, the $\lambda(x)$ and $S(x)$ polynomials are premultiplied:

$$\Lambda(x) = \lambda(x) \prod (1 - \alpha^i x) \qquad (9)$$
$$S(x) \equiv S(x) \prod (1 - \alpha^i x) \bmod x^{2t} \qquad (10)$$

where $\Lambda(x)$ and $S(x)$ are the modified locator and syndrome polynomials, respectively [17]. The RS processor described in this paper supports erasure corrections.

III. OPERATION

This section provides a description of the RS processor operations. The coder circuit has one data input port and one data output port. Data is input at a constant rate, and output with a fixed latency. The coder can operate as either an encoder or a decoder. Encoder operation is accomplished by marking all $2t$ parity locations for erasure correction as a block of data is passed through the decoder. All buffering required is internal to the chip. The block length of the code is variable, as large as 255 bytes and as small as $23 + 10t$ bytes. The correction/detection ability of the code is quite flexible, with limits given by

$$t = E/2 + e + d/2 \qquad (11)$$

where $2t$ is the number of parity symbols, E is the number of erasures, e is the number of random errors, $e + E/2$ is the correction ability of the code and d is the additional detection ability of the code, as specified by the user.

An erasure is any symbol that is identified to be in error prior to the actual decoding process. Any byte flagged as an erasure will count against the correcting ability of the code whether that byte is in error or not. The detection ability of the code is the ability to detect errors beyond the correction ability of the code.

Let P be the number of parity symbols that will be used for correction. During operation, the parameters P and $2t$ are fixed. Full correction ability of the coder is achieved when $P = 2t$. Making P smaller does not change how the data path will perform correction, but it does change how the coder reports the integrity of the output data.

During initialization, the parameter P is read from input pins. After initialization, the coder is ready to receive data. DataEn is an input timing signal which must be high when the message symbols are input and low when the parity symbols are input. The coder takes in code blocks consecutively, performs the appropriate coding operation and outputs the data with a fixed latency of $2N + 10t + 34$ clock pulses. The number of parity symbols, $2t$, is set by the number of clock pulses that DataEn is low during the first block. In subsequent blocks, if DataEn is low for more than $2t$ clocks, data will be passed through the decoder with no correction applied. Those bytes passed through will be treated as data inserted between code blocks and not as an element of a code block.

The coder will allow two different block lengths to be intermixed. The latency is a function of the longest block length, N_l. If the shorter block of length N_s is processed first, the latency will be $2N_s + 10t + 34$ until the first large block is ready to be output, at which time the latency will become $2N_l + 10t + 34$.

DataRdy is the timing signal for outputting data. It is high while the message bytes are output and low for the parity symbols. If the Correct line is high, the message was correctable and corrected, if it is low, the message was determined to be uncorrectable and is passed to the output unchanged. If StatEn was low during initialization, the chip will output the corrected message followed by parity. If StatEn was high during initialization, the chip will output the data followed by the status words. The status words will report the number of erasures, the total number of errors, and whether or not the message was correctable.

IV. VLSI ARCHITECTURE

Full custom VLSI was used to achieve both circuit density and speed. The VLSI architectures implemented here are similar to previous full custom designs presented in the literature [10], [18], [19]. The HST chip requires only 200 000 transistors including the 384×18 FIFO which buffers incoming data and the 256×8 ROM's used in calculating field inverses. The low transistor count was achieved through the use of nonclassical CMOS structures. Full custom design controls the amount of interconnect, increasing speed which is a function of capacitive load. Interconnect was minimized in this design thereby increasing speed and circuit density.

Message data, DI, enters the chip and is stored in the FIFO and input to the syndrome module as shown in the block diagram of Fig. 1. Messages are processed in a pipeline fashion through each of the modules. The syndrome module accepts data from the input port and produces the syndrome values according to (5). Circuitry exists to calculate $2t$ syndromes in parallel; since $t_{max} = 10$, there are 20 parallel syndrome computational cells.

The Euclid multiply and divide modules implement (7) and operate on the syndrome polynomial to determine the error magnitude $\Omega(x)$ and error location $\lambda(x)$ polynomials. The Euclid modules use an internal ROM to calculate the field inverse. The error magnitude and error location polynomials are then passed to the polynomial solver.

Erasure positions are generated by a counter which counts in powers of α. Each time the erasure flag, Erase, is activated, the current count is stored in a 20×8 LIFO. Since the length of a given code block is not known prior to the initial block of data passing through the chip, these values only represent *relative* erasure positions. Each of these values are subsequently divided by the counter value associated with the last (lowest order) coefficient of the code block to obtain the actual erasure locations, expressed as powers of α. An erasure in the jth coefficient is represented by α^j. These erasure locations are used to create the initial conditions for Euclid's algorithm:

$$\lambda_0(x) = \Pi(1 - \alpha^j x) \qquad (12)$$

and

$$\Omega_0(x) = S(x)\Pi(1 - \alpha^j x) \bmod x^{2t}. \qquad (13)$$

These operations are performed in the divide and multiply sections of the chip just prior to the commencement of Euclid's algorithm.

The polynomial solver modules evaluate all three polynomials $\lambda(x)$, $\Omega(x)$ and $\lambda'(x)$ in parallel. The error location polynomial solver produces a single bit answer that denotes a

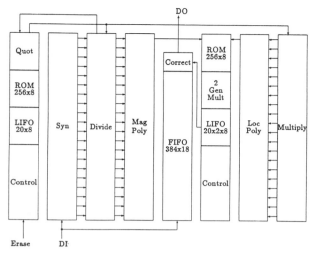

Fig. 1. Architectural block diagram.

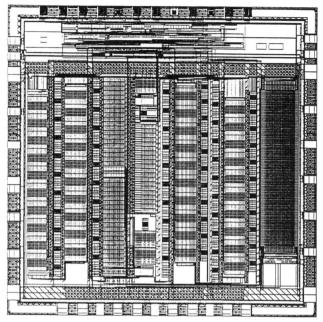

Fig. 2. VLSI chip plot.

zero found or not found. The other two polynomial calculators produce 8 bit answers that correspond to the evaluation of the polynomial at a given field element. This evaluation identifies the location of an error and produces the values to calculate the error magnitude according to (8).

The correction module performs the field division and multiplication as specified by (8) to determine the error magnitude. The error magnitude is divided by the derivative of the error location polynomial and is multiplied by a constant to determine the magnitude of the error for a given field element. If a zero was found by the polynomial solver, then the magnitude is output, otherwise zero is output. This output is exclusive or-ed with the raw data which has been stored in the FIFO and thus corrects the errors as the processed data leaves the chip through the output port, DO.

V. VLSI LAYOUT

The success of the project required a synergy between engineering and layout to attain the density and speed required. The layout of the chip is depicted in Fig. 2 which is a plot of the metal layers and cell outlines. Each module was configured to minimize interconnect. This was accomplished through mental Roubik's cube like manipulations to carefully place the data path elements such that interconnect related modules were adjacent and through careful planning of the base level cells to connect by abutment.

As an example, Fig. 3 shows the functional diagram for a single syndrome computational cell. The basic function is a multiply accumulate with a parallel in, serial out shift register (D2) added to allow the resulting syndromes from one code block to be transferred to the Euclid divide module while the syndromes from the next code block are being calculated. Fig. 4 shows the layout of the syndrome computational cell. The constant multiplier consists of an 8×8 array of XOR/ZERO cells. The XOR cell is a 4 transistor cell performing an Exclusive OR operation and the ZERO cell is a 4 transistor cell performing a connection operation. Precharge and evaluate logic is also required. Each column of the constant multiplier is a single bit of the 8 bit symbol. The U/D cell contains the precharge logic for one column

and the evaluate logic for the adjacent column. Every other XOR column is flipped alternating the bits between the top and bottom of the cell. The ADD function, shown in Fig. 3, has been folded into the evaluate logic. The pitch was set by the XOR/ZERO cell and all cells were constructed to connect by abutment, eliminating interconnect.

Occasionally the basic mathematical algorithms were manipulated away from the forms derived for minimum operations as described in the literature to forms that minimized the VLSI layout and maximized the performance. For example, there is actually only one field GF(2^m). There are, however, many different representations of this field determined by the primitive polynomial, $p(x)$. The chip actually works in a basis defined by a working primitive polynomial $p_w(x)$ rather than the $p(x)$ specified by the HST code. The working $p_w(x)$ was chosen to minimize the number of feedback terms and the carry paths in the general GF multipliers. This reduces the layout and increases the performance of the circuit although the computational burden is actually increased since data must be transformed into and out of this working basis by forward and reverse transform cells.

At times, specific logic configurations were modified to enhance characteristics desirable for better layouts. Logic diagrams were drawn to include geometric data, such as placement of interconnects, and reflected the physical size of the cells. A bit slice approach was taken at the very base levels, with geometric manipulations overlaid to minimize routing channels. The overall area dedicated to routing is much less than 5% of the total die area and extremely dense active areas were achieved. Fig. 5 shows the functional diagram for the chien search computational cell from which the polynomial solver sections were constructed. The basic operation is a multiply accumulate followed by a compare. A serial in, parallel out shift register, D is also included to receive data for the next code block while continuing to

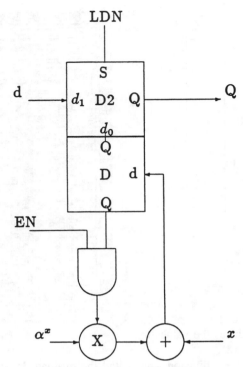

Fig. 3. Syndrome computational cell.

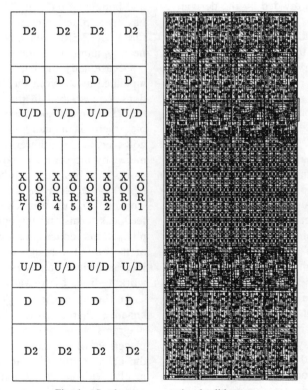

Fig. 4. Syndrome computational cell layout.

process the current code block data. Fig. 6 is a plot of the two metal layers for this cell illustrating the density achieved.

The primitive and generator polynomials can be altered on the current design with a single mask level change. Each of the constant multipliers in the syndrome, chien search, transform and erasure computational cells can be altered with a single mask. That is, the XOR and ZERO cells are actually the same cell which is programmed by a single, metal mask change. Since a working basis is used, the GF multipliers and field inverse ROM's are unaffected by changes in $p(x)$ and $g(x)$. Layout and architectural planning of this full custom design also considered the desire to produce additional chips

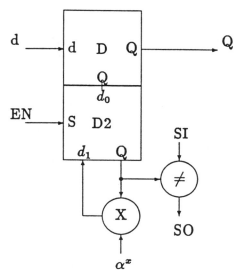

Fig. 5. Chien search computational cell.

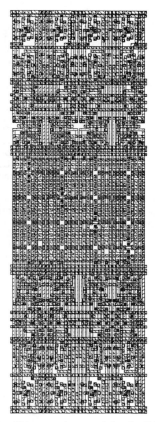

Fig. 6. Chien search computational cell layout.

with different maximum error correction capabilities. Integrated circuits for other applications have been designed and fabricated using the basic cells and organization described here. Two configurations requiring a maximum error correction ability of $t = 5$ and a $t = 3$ codec have been fabricated. These designs required different primitive and generator polynomials. Each of these developments required a small fraction of the effort and cost of the original design.

VI. CONCLUSION

A VLSI coder, that can function either as an encoder or decoder for Reed Solomon codes, was presented. Originally designed for the Hubble Space Telescope, the error correction/detection capability of the coder can be selected by the user. The maximum error correction is 10 symbol errors and the maximum data rate is 10 Mbytes/s (under worst case conditions). The correction time is independent of the number of errors in the incoming message. The computation rate and powerful error correcting features of this processor make it suitable for use in advanced television applications.

The chip was designed in a 1.6 μm CMOS process and fabricated at Hewlett Packard's Circuit Technology Group. The circuit was tested on a Fairchild Sentry 50 tester with sets of test vectors which were developed from a combination of functional and structural tests. The pipelined data path architecture allows easy access to internal nodes for testing purposes. Blocks were studied individually using methods ranging from path sensitization and fault folding tables to computer generation by extensive search and replacement algorithms to develop the test vector sets. The fault set addressed include stuck at 1 and stuck at 0 with as many of the transistor shorts and transistor opens addressed as feasible. Additional logic was introduced where needed to ease testing. Standard checker board, walking 1's and walking 0's tests were applied to the FIFO by patterns passed as data to the decoder. Patterns were developed using a high level input language written for a 21 state logic simulator. The simulator output was converted to Sentry 50 test vectors by software. This chip was delivered to Goddard Space Flight Center in April, 1989, and has been installed in the ground communication link for service in the Space Telescope system.

ACKNOWLEDGMENT

The authors wish to acknowledge the support from Warner Miller at Goddard Space Flight Center, G. Maki at the NASA Space Engineering Research Center for VLSI Systems Design, P. Owsley at Advanced Hardware Architectures and R. Hauge at Zenith Electronics Corporation.

REFERENCES

[1] S. Whitaker, K. Cameron, G. Maki, J. Canaris, and P. Owsley, "VLSI Reed Solomon processor for the Hubble space telescope," *VLSI Signal Processing IV*, IEEE Press, 1991, Chap. 35.

[2] G. W. Meeker, "High definition and high frame rate compatible N.T.S.C. broadcast television system," *IEEE Trans. Broadcast.*, vol. 34, no. 3, pp. 313–322, Sept.1988.

[3] T. Fujio, "A study of high-definition TV system in the future," *IEEE Trans. Broadcast.*, vol. BC-24, no. 4, pp. 92–100, Dec. 1978.

[4] B. C. Mortimer, M. J. Moore, and M. Sablatash, "Performance of a powerful error-correcting and detecting coding scheme for the North American basic teletext system (NABTS) for random independent errors: Methods, equations, calculations and results," *IEEE Trans. Broadcast.*, vol. 36, no. 2, pp. 113–131, June 1990.

[5] K. Niwa, T. Araseki, and T. Nishitani, "Digital signal processing for video," *IEEE Circuits and Devices Magazine*, vol. 6, no. 1, pp. 27–33, Jan. 1990.

[6] *Digital Spectrum Compatible*, Tech. Description, Zenith Electronic Corporation and AT&T, Feb. 22, 1991.

[7] P. Tong, "A 40-MHz encoder-decoder chip generated by a Reed-Solomon code compiler," in *IEEE 1990 Custom Integrated Circuits Conf. Rec.*, May 1990, pp. 13.5.1–13.5.4.

[8] N. Demassieux, F. Jutand, and M. Muller, "A 10 MHz (255,223) Reed-Solomon decoder," in *IEEE 1988 Custom Integrated Circuits Conf. Rec.*, May 1988, pp. 17.6.1–17.6.4.

[9] H. F. Reefs and A. R. Best, "Concatenated coding on a spacecraft-to-ground telemetry channel performance," *Proc. ICC-81*, 1981.

[10] G. Maki, P. Owsley, K. Cameron, and J. Venbrux, "VLSI Reed Solomon decoder design," *IEEE Military Communications Conf. Rec.*, Oct. 1986, pp. 46.5.1–46.5.6.

[11] G. C. Clark and J. B. Cain, *Error Correcting Coding For Digital Communications*, New York: Plenum, 1981.

[12] E. Berlekamp, *Algebraic Coding Theory*. New York: McGraw Hill, 1968.

[13] Y. Sugiyama, M. Kasahara, S. Hirasawa, and T. Namekawa, "A method for solving key equation for decoding Goppa codes," *IEEE Trans. Contr.*, vol. 27, pp. 87–99, 1975.

[14] S. Reed, R. Scholtz, T. Truong, and L. Welch, "The fast decoding of Reed Solomon codes using Fermat theoretical transforms and continued fractions," *IEEE Trans. Inform. Theory*, vol. IT-24, Jan. 1978.

[15] L. Welch and R. Scholtz, "Continued Fractions and Berlekamp's algorithm," *IEEE Trans. Inform. Theory*, vol. IT-25, pp. 19–27, Jan. 1979.

[16] D. Carhoun, B. Johnson, and S. Meehan, "Transform decoding of Reed Solomon codes, vol. I: Algorithm and signal processing structure," ESD TR-82-403, vol. I, Nov. 1982.

[17] G. Forney, "On decoding BCH codes," *IEEE Transactions on Inform. Theory*, vol. IT-11, pp. 549–557, 1965.

[18] G. Maki and P. Owsley, "Parallel Berlekamp vs. conventional VLSI architectures," in *Government Microcircuit Applications Conf. Rec.*, Nov. 1986, pp. 5–9.

[19] G. Maki, P. Owsley, K. Cameron, and J. Shovic, "A VLSI Reed Solomon encoder: An engineering approach," in *IEEE Custom Integrated Circuit Conf. Rec.*, May 1986, pp. 177–181.

AN EXPERIMENTAL STUDY FOR A HOME-USE DIGITAL VTR

C. Yamamitsu,* A. Ide,* A. Iketani,* T. Juri,*
S. Kadono,* C. Matsumi,* K. Matsushita,** H. Mizuki**
*Central Research Laboratories
Matsushita Electric Industrial Co., Ltd., Osaka, Japan
**Development Center
Matsushita-Kotobuki Electronics Industries Ltd., Tokushima, Japan

1. INTRODUCTION

Higher quality of picture and audio is requested for a home-use VTR, in addition to that, it becomes more important to keep the high quality through dubbings because of the generalizing video movies. On the other hand, digital audio equipments such as a compact disc and a digital audio tape recorder are already available on the market. Also in the video field, there are some equipments with digital technologies, e.g. a digital TV for home-use and a digital VTR for professional-use. Especially, a digital VTR has a valuable feature of keeping the picture quality high even if the picture was taken by dubbings.

Some serious technological problems, however, must be solved to bring about a home-use digital VTR. The most serious one is how to record a digital video signal for long hours. The digital video data, which has a large amount of information of 100-200 Mbps that is 100 times as much as audio data, needs much more tape to be recorded. So, long-hour recording of the video data into a compact cassette tape needs the following two technologies, the first one is a bit rate reduction which reduces the data quantity to be recorded down by extracting a small amount of essential information from the video data, and the second is a high density recording which makes a stable playback possible under high packing density.

A bit rate reduction technology consisting of a sub-Nyquist sampling, an Hadamard transformation and a vector quantization for an NTSC composite signal is already reported[1]. This technology has a feature of small error propagation range which is desirable for a digital VTR. Under the condition of high recording density, so many errors, ie., random errors and burst errors with various length, disturb the playback data very often. In the circumstances any bit rate reduction technology of which decoding process propagates an undetected error is not appropriate for a digital VTR at all. Furthermore, it is also necessary to develop a technology of bit rate reduction which reproduces a picture only with incomplete data got at intervals as in a trick play mode. From this point of view, smallness of error propagation range is a important factor for a bit rate reduction technology for a digital VTR.

By the way, considerations on a picture quality and a compatibility between the 525/60 TV system and the 625/50 TV system gave an answer that signal processes in a component form could result in a better bit rate reduction technology. In comparison with an amount of data, a composite signal has less data quantity than component signals, and it is necessary to reduce more data in the component way. A new technology of bit rate reduction with a discrete cosine transform(DCT) was developed for the target. DCT is a well-known technology for bit rate reduction superior to others and is popular in the field of TV conference systems. The DCT, however, needs so many multipliers and so fast operations in a digital VTR that the scale of circuit can not be compact. This is a fatal problem for a home-use digital VTR, and a new fast DCT algorithm which needs less than half as many multipliers as the conventional DCT is developed for this system and is described

Reprinted from *IEEE Trans. Consumer Electron.*, vol. 35, no. 3, pp. 450–457, Aug. 1989.

hereinafter.

Variable length coding also used in the TV conference systems makes the efficiency of the data transmission higher, but causes wide error propagations. The conventional variable length coding has a serious problem that errors occurring during the transmission often disturb the word synchronization. A new variable length coding developed this time has the minimum range of error propagation while keeping the picture quality acceptable.

In addition to the bit rate reduction, a new technology of high density recording was also developed. The target of recording density was 270 Mbpi² of area packing density and was cleared by a narrow track recording. Furthermore, an error correction suitable for the bit rate reduction was also developed for this system.

2. STRUCTURE OF AN EXPERIMENTAL DIGITAL VTR

A block diagram of the experimental digital VTR is shown in Fig.1. We use component TV signal considering common use between 525/60 TV system and 625/50 TV system. In a component TV signal, chrominance signals are not superimposed on a luminance signal, so it is easier to develop a bit rate reduction and variable speed play than the case of a composite TV signal.

We adopted sampling frequencies 13.5MHz for luminance signal and 3.375MHz for both of color difference signals (4:1:1) for realizing more than 500 horizontal resolution as for a next generation VTR, and to interface between D1 digital VTR easily. Computer simulations show very little visible difference between (4:1:1) and (4:2:2). So we got high quality of picture for a home-use VTR, though the sampling frequency of color difference signals is half of D1 format. The input data rate including H & V blanking is 162Mbps.

An unit of the bit rate reduction is constructed from both luminance and color difference signals using the formatting memory. We call this unit a compression block. And input video signal is compressed to 19Mbps. These compressed data are error-correcting-encoded and formed into a so-called sync-block with ID-information and synchronization-pattern. And it is recorded on the tape at 27Mbps with audio signals. Specifications of this experimental VTR are listed in Table 1.

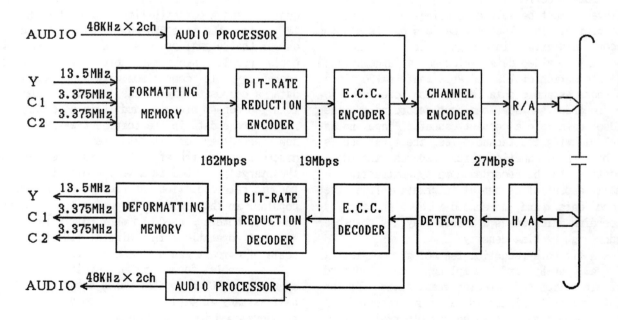

Fig.1 STRUCTURE OF THE DIGITAL VTR

270

Table 1 SPECIFICATIONS OF THE DIGITAL VTR

Input video signals	Y : 13.5MHz
	R-Y,B-Y : 3.375MHz
Input video rate	162Mbps
Bit rate reduction	DCT & V.L.C.
Compressed video rate	19Mbps
Audio signals	48kHz×16bit×2ch
Error correction	Reed-Solomon code
Recording rate	27Mbps
Channel code	Interleaved NRZI
Detection	Partial response
Track pitch	6.8μm
Area packing density	270Mbpi²
Head	Amorphous
Tape	ME
Recording time	3 hours

3. BIT RATE REDUCTION

In order to compress the video data rate from 162Mbps to 19Mbps (about 1/8 compression), a new bit rate reduction technology using DCT has been developed. It adopts a 2-dimensional DCT for a block which is constructed by horizontal 8 samples × vertical 8 samples. And the structure of the bit rate reduction is shown in Fig.2. It is mainly composed of the blocks of
(1) Modified DCT.
(2) Data compression (adaptive quantizer, variable length encoder).
(3) Data quantity estimator.

3.1 Modified DCT

A DCT is known as one of the most efficient method for bit rate reduction. But it needs many multipliers or huge ROMs. So, many fast DCT algorithms have been invented, and a conventional fast DCT algorithm for N points DCT, it needs about N×log₂(N) multiplyings [2][3].

By the way, in the case of using DCT for the bit rate reduction, some weighting functions can be multiplied to the DCT components. Human eye is less sensitive for high frequency components than low frequency. And block degradation caused by the distortion of low frequency components is very uncomfortable. So it is important to encode lower frequency components in high fidelity than higher frequency. By encoding high frequency coarsely with the weighting, the compression performance can be improved. This weighting needs one multiplication for each DCT coefficient. But by getting weighting and DCT operation together, the number of multiplyings can be decreased. And if some specific values of weighting are adopted, it needs less multipliers than the conventional fast DCT. We call this algorithm modified DCT.

It is difficult to find the most efficient weighting function. But by the computer simulations, there are little visible differences among several weighting functions. So it is possible to select a weighting function for decreasing multiplyings of DCT. One example of the weighting functions for the 8-th order modified DCT is listed in Table 2.

In comparison with about 12 multiplyings for the conventional fast DCT algorithm, the modified DCT needs only 6 multiplyings and 9 bit-shiftings (multiplification with 2's power). The signal flow chart of the modified DCT is shown in Fig.3. In Fig.3, arrows mean addition point and a dot line means a subtraction.

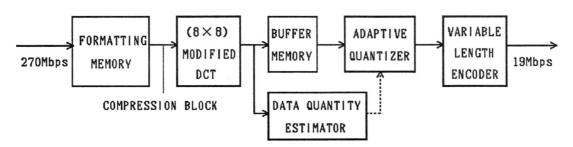

Fig.2 STRUCTURE OF THE BIT RATE REDUCTION

Table 2 WEIGHTING FUNCTION OF A MODIFIED DCT

i	Wi
0	1
1	$\sin(\pi/4)/\sin(\pi/16)/4$
2	$\sin(\pi/4)/\sin(2\pi/16)/2$
3	$3\sin(\pi/4)/\sin(3\pi/16)/4$
4	$\sin(\pi/4)/\sin(4\pi/16)$
5	$\sin(\pi/4)/\sin(5\pi/16)$
6	$\sin(\pi/4)/\sin(6\pi/16)$
7	$\sin(\pi/4)/\sin(7\pi/16)$

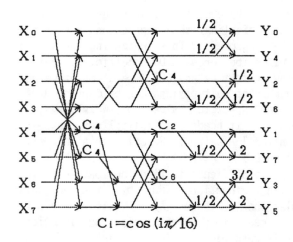

$C_i = \cos(i\pi/16)$

Fig. 3 ALGORITHM OF MODIFIED DCT

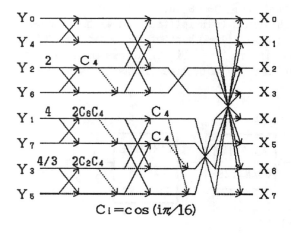

$C_i = \cos(i\pi/16)$

Fig. 4 ALGORITHM OF MODIFIED IDCT

Furthermore, numerics and characters on the arrows mean multiplying constants. As multiplying constants are classified into only 4 classes C_2, C_4, C_6 and 3/2, its hardware is realized simply by 4 constant multipliers or ROMs. Fig. 4 shows the signal flow chart of the modified inverse DCT (modified IDCT) for the modified DCT in Fig. 3. The modified IDCT needs 6 multiplyings and 2 bit-shiftings. The multiplying constants are C_4, $2C_2C_4$, $2C_6C_4$ and 4/3. As described above, it is able to decrease not only the number of multiplyings but also the number of constants for multiplyings. One sample of weighting functions for modified DCT is listed in Table 2, and we already found other weighting functions of the modified DCT.

3.2 Data compression

In this section, how the DCT coefficients are compressed is explained. At first we prepare some quantizers, and one of them is selected to quantize the DCT coefficients by a result of the data quantity estimator (explained in next section). An example of quantized (8×8) DCT coefficients are shown in Fig. 5. In this figure, right upper part indicates horizontal higher frequency, left lower part indicates vertical frequency and left upper corner indicates the quantized value of the lowest frequency coefficient (DC component). As ordinary pictures have much energy in low frequencies and the DCT coefficients are weighted at the modified DCT, most of the quantized values of higher coefficients come to zero. Then in this system, only the quantized values in a area that is enclosed by the minimum rectangle which includes all non-zero quantized values and one of the corner of which is DC component are transmitted (this rectangle is indicated the thick line in Fig. 5). And this rectangle is decided by a corner that is an opposite corner of the DC component (it is a point of that (H, V) = (5, 4) in Fig. 5). So by transmitting only this point, many of zero quantized values are compressed easily. And this point can be encoded into 6 bits for this system.

Then transmitting quantized values are encoded by variable length encoder, and outputted.

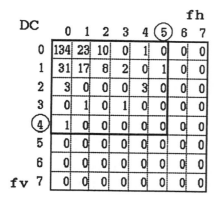

DC   fh

	0	1	2	3	4	⑤	6	7
0	134	23	10	0	1	0	0	0
1	31	17	8	2	0	1	0	0
2	3	0	0	0	3	0	0	0
3	0	1	0	1	0	0	0	0
④	1	0	0	0	0	0	0	0
5	0	0	0	0	0	0	0	0
6	0	0	0	0	0	0	0	0
fv 7	0	0	0	0	0	0	0	0

Fig.5 EXAMPLE OF QUANTIZED VALUES OF DCT

3.3 Data quantity estimator

For using variable length coding, errors occurred during transmission make enormous degradation by out of synchronization of code words. As many data can be dropped out in play back, variable length code must be resetted within a specific area. Especially, considering high speed playing, it is desirable that the variable length code is completing within each sync-block. So we developed the new variable length coding method that a compressed data quantity from a compression block (mentioned above) is limited in the sync-block (Fig.6).

For realizing this method, data quantity of variable length codeword from each quantizer is estimated previously, and the best quantizer to compress the compression block into the same length of the sync-block is selected. As the encoded data quantity is estimated previously, this system has following merits.

(1) The best quantizer can be selected at adaptive quantizer.

(2) The variable length coding can be completed within a small specific area such as a sync-block.

Generally, estimating a quantity of variable length encoded data needs large scale of hardware. Then a variable length code encoding zero component to a codeword of 1bit is adopted. So a encoded data quantity of (8 × 8) DCT block (D) is calculated by the following equation.

$$D = \sum_{i=0}^{63}(L_i - 1) + N$$

The L_i means a length of the i-th codeword, and the N means the number of transmitting quantized values. Because the N is equal to the area of the rectangle mentioned above, it can be calculated easily (ex. N = 6×5 = 30 in Fig.5). By these ways, it is possible to estimate the data quantity in a simple hardware.

4. ERROR CORRECTION

In case of the digital VTR using bit rate reduction, error correcting method is very important because of the possibility that only one bit error causes wide area propagation. The structure of error correcting code is shown in Fig.7. First, compressed data in each sync-block

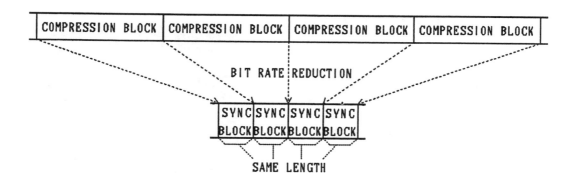

Fig.6 DATA COMPRESSION

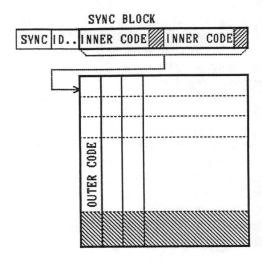

SYNC BLOCK

Fig. 7 STRUCTURE OF THE ERROR CORRECTING CODE

is coded into two Reed-Solomon codewords (each codeword is of the inner code) like Fig. 7. Second, several inner codewords are coded into Reed-Solomon codewords orthogonal to them (that makes outer code). In such a way, the sync-block size is fixed and is equal to the variable length code size of the bit rate reduction.

At play back, error correction and detection method is as follows.

(1) Error correction by inner code.
(2) Error correction and erasure correction by outer code using flags from the inner correction.
(3) Error detection by the inner code, on every sync-block.

By using correcting performance of the inner and the outer codes, and moreover using the third detection, miscorrection is enough suppressed. Three times decoding makes correction and detection performance very high. And that, errors are detected in every sync-block, which is equal to a variable length code size. Even if there occurs an error which cannot be corrected, the error propagation is restricted in a narrow area. And in case of high speed play, where data cannot be got totally but got sync-blocks at intervals, it is possible to decode a compression code and construct a picture by decoding the inner code.

An error-detected sync-block is replaced with the sync-block of a previous field for error concealment. In our VTR, variable speed play is enabled by appropriating the memory for concealment.

5. HIGH DENSITY RECORDING

3-hour recording, the target of this experimentation, needs extremely high area packing density of 270Mbpi², and a narrow track recording can not be helped adopting to bring about the target. The following two problems, however, are taken place in the narrow track recording.

(1) Lower playback signal level.
(2) Mutual interference between pilot tones and playback data.

5.1 Signal processes for playback wave

Metal amorphous heads and ME(Metal Evaporated) tape which reproduces higher playback signal level are used in the DVTR to solve the first problem. In addition to that, an optimization of the playback signal processes, ie., development of a low noise head amplifier and an equalizer efficiently compensating the high frequency component of the playback wave, makes noise level lower at the detection point. As the results, about 48 dB of the C/N ratio is obtained, herein C is a peak level read out of a recorded alternatively changing binary sequence at 27MHz, and N is an effective noise level. Under the condition the average bit error rate including burst errors is kept 1-5×10-5. An eye pattern at the point of the detection is shown in Fig. 8.

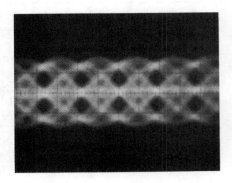

Fig. 8 EYE PATTERN

By the way, a channel code used in this DVTR is Interleaved NRZI code and a signal detection system is Partial response detection[4]. Both of the code and detection system are the same in the previous DVTR[1]. Although the minimum wave length is set to the relatively longer in this DVTR, the high frequency components of the play back signal are attenuated so that intersymbol interferences causing errors have occurred. Therefore, an equalization compensating the attenuated high frequency components are needed to eliminate the intersymbol interference. Furthermore, it is necessary to make the increase of the noise caused by the equalization as small as possible and to reduce the influence of the high frequency noise emphasized by the equalization. From the points of view, an equalization which emphasizes the high frequency component efficiently has been developed and is suitable for the channel code and the signal detection.

5.2 Tracking control

Pilot tones lower than 1MHz for the tracking is added to the recording data and then those signals are recorded. On the other hand, the recorded data has a large amount of energy in the low frequency components which interfere the pilot tones and the pilot tones also interfere the playback data. This mutual interference causes error rate worse. From this point of view, it can be said that Partial response detection is suitable for the high density recording on a narrow track, because the detection depends little on the low frequency components of the playback data. In addition, a better extraction of the pilot tones from the playback signals has made a stable playback possible under the narrow track recording.

6. AUDIO RECORDING

Audio data is also recorded on the same track on which video data is recorded, but audio and video data are separated completely. Two channels of audio data are sampled at 48kHz each, quantized into 16bits/sample/channel and then synchronized to video data. In order to make after-recording possible, audio data of one channel is separated from that of other channel completely, and then processed and recorded independently. In addition, shuffling pattern of audio data makes it possible to reproduce audible sounds with the playbacked audio data even in double speed play mode. The technologies of shuffling and interpolation developed this time is to give us an acceptable sound without 2/3 of the complete audio data.

7. CONCLUSIONS

The results of this experimentation are summarized as follows.
(1) The Modified DCT developed for this system which needs only one half multipliers of a conventional DCT has made the hardware scale smaller.
(2) THe data quantity estimator controls the variable length coding to complete within a sync-block keeping the picture quality high. This control limits the propagation of errors at most in a sync-block even in the trick play modes.
(3) Three stages of error correction, repeating the inner correction and the outer correction, corrects more errors and makes the probability of miscorrection lower.
(4) High area packing density of 270Mbpi^2 is brought about by a low noise head amplifier, an optimization of the playback signal processing, high performance magnetic heads and tapes, and a stable tracking to narrow tracks.

8. ACKNOWLEDGMENTS

The authors hereby express their sincere gratitudes to Mr. Ken Takahashi, Mr. Yoshiaki Doyama colleagues in our laboratories and AV Laboratories for their useful suggestions, cooperation and encouragements.

REFERENCES

[1] C. Yamamitsu, A. Ide, A. Iketani and T. Juri : "An Experimental Study on Bit Rate Reduction and High Density Recording for a Home-Use Digital VTR", IEEE Trans. on CE, CE-34, No. 3, pp. 588-596 (Aug. 1988)

[2] Chen, W., Smith, C. H. and Dralick, S: "A Fast Computational Algorithm for the Discrete Cosine Transform", IEEE Trans, Commun., COM-25, 9, pp. 1004-1009 (Sept. 1977)

[3] Y. MORIKAWA, H. HAMADA, N. YAMANE: "A Fast Algorithm for the Cosine Transform Based on Successive Order Reduction of the Tchebycheff Polynomial", IECE Vol. J68-A No. 2, pp. 173-180 (Feb. 1985)

[4] H. Kobayashi and D. T. Tang: "Application of Partial-Responce Channel Coding to Magnetic Recording Systems", IBM Jour. Res. Develop, pp. 368-375 (July 1970)

A STUDY ON TRICK PLAYS FOR DIGITAL VCR

C. Yamamitsu, A. Ide, M. Nishino, T. Juri, and H. Ohtaka
Matsushita Electric Industrial Co., Ltd.

Introduction

In recent years, video equipment for home use give us high picture quality and many function. Digital VCR is expected to be a next generation VCR with a feature that very little degradation is caused by dubbing and is already produced for broadcasting or professional use. Considering a home use digital VCR, however, it is not possible to obtain enough playing time because of a high recording rate when a conventional TV signal is recorded. In order to achieve a long playing time in a small cassette, a bit rate reduction technology without a visible degradation in picture quality and high density recording technology must be developed. A bit rate reduction technology for a home use digital VCR which compress a conventional component signal to 1/6.4 was reported [1]. (8 samples $\times$ 8 lines) Discrete cosine transform (DCT) and Variable Length Coding (VLC) are adopted for the bit rate reduction. We confirmed that picture quality was enough for a home use in normal play. Specifications of an experimental digital VCR is shown in Table 1. On the other hand, there are trick plays for the functions of VCR and it is

Table 1 Specifications of an experimental Digital VCR

Input video signals	Y : 13.5MHz
	R-Y,B-Y : 3.375MHz
Input video rate	162 Mbps
Bit rate reduction	DCT & VLC
Compression video rate	19 Mbps
Recording rate	27 Mbps
Error correction	Reed-solomon code
Area packing density	270 Mbpi ^{2}
Recording time	3 hours

one of important items to realize an acceptable picture quality in high speed play even in case of using DCT and VLC.

In these points of view, we investigated the approaches to improve the picture quality in high speed play with keeping enough picture quality in normal play.

In this paper, the problems in high speed play are listed at first, and secondly the approaches to high speed play and the results of computer simulation are described.

High speed play in digital VCR

Fig.1 shows the head trace on the tape in normal play and high speed play. In normal play, a head traces over a complete track as shown in Fig.1(a) and the data on each track are continuously reproduced. Accordingly, picture is constructed by the data on the same track. On the contrary, the head traces the plural number of tracks in high speed play as shown in Fig.1(b). In the part that the head crosses over the two tracks, a level of reproduced signal is small and data cannot be correctly detected. Therefore, the problems in high speed play are listed below.

(a) Data is not reproduced continuously.
    Data reproduced from a track are continuous, but data from different tracks are not continuous.
(b) The picture is constructed by the data in different fields.
    It is one case that the head crosses the plural number of fields. Furthermore, data which is not detected are replaced by a corresponding data in a previous field.
(c) Error rate is higher than that of normal play.

Reprinted from *IEEE Trans. Consumer Electron.*, vol. 37, no. 3, pp. 261–265, Aug. 1991.

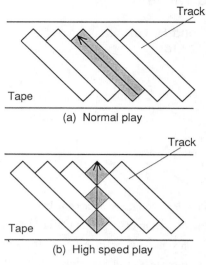

(a) Normal play

(b) High speed play

Fig. 1   Head trace on the tape

Approaches to high speed play

1.   Data quantity control

In our bit rate reduction technology, VLC is adopted to get enough picture quality in high compression rate. The length of code-word is variable depending on data in a VLC. If error occurs, data is not correctly decoded because of out of synchronization of code-word. In case of using DCT, one error spreads over the whole DCT block and it is difficult to interpolate the errornous pixels by surrounding pixels. If the length of VLC is controlled to be fixed in a long range, error propagation over a large area of screen occurs, which causes a visible degradation.

The minimum recording unit on the tape is called a sync block and a valid data is detected by the unit of the sync block. Therefore, VLC is controlled to be completed within a sync block to keep the data quantity a constant. Fig.2 shows the control method of data quantity. At first, the plural number of DCT blocks in both luminance and chrominance signals are gathered to form a compression block. And then the control of data quantity can be accomplished by calculating the data quantity in advance by utilizing an adaptive quantizer and VLC characteristics. One sync block is constructed by encoded data of one compression block.

In these method, even if a sync block or data cannot be

detected, the range of error propagation of VLC is limited within a compression block. Furthermore, there is an advantage that error concealment with other compressed data can be easily realized. A sync block with a detected error is replaced with the corresponding sync block in a previous field.

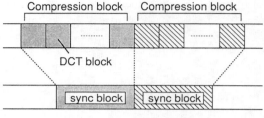

Fig. 2   Data quantity control

2.   Compression block forming method

As described above, the compression block consists of the plural number of DCT blocks. One method of forming the compression block is shown in Fig.3(a). DCT blocks are gathered sequentially on the screen. However it happens that the information amount among the compression block is unbalanced. Some compression block have much information and the others have less information. Since the data quantity in each compression block is controlled to be a constant, the deviation of information amount causes degradation in picture quality. Such degradation is caused in the compression block which contains much information. Considering picture quality in normal play, we cannot accept the picture quality by this sequential forming method.

We adopted an another forming method that each compression block is formed by DCT blocks which are separated each other on the screen. Fig.3(b) is a view showing the method of forming the compression block. First, the screen is divided into segment both for luminance and chrominance signal and a DCT block in each segment is taken out to form the compression block. By constituting above, the position of DCT blocks within a compression block is shuffled and separated each other on the screen. Accordingly, with respect to each compression block, the information amount is less apt to become unbalanced and the efficiency of VLC can be improved. From these reasons, the method as shown in Fig.3(b) is effective for normal play, but has a disadvantage in high speed

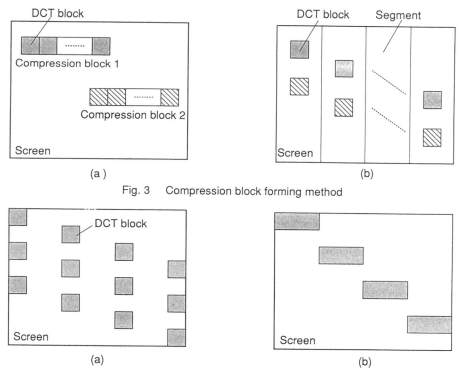

Fig. 3   Compression block forming method

Fig. 4   Reproduced DCT blocks in high speed play

play. Reproduced picture in high speed play is constructed by using the DCT blocks which were detected and decoded correctly. So the picture is constructed by using the DCT blocks which have time interval. In these situation, there is little problem in a still picture, but no continuity among the DCT blocks is visible in a motion picture. And reproduced DCT blocks are scattered over the screen because the DCT blocks in a compression block are separated each other on the screen, which is shown in Fig.4(a).

According to our evaluation of computer simulation, it is visibly desirable for the picture quality in high speed play that the adjacent DCT blocks are reproduced in the same time as much as possible, which is shown in Fig.4(b). There is a high possibility that the sync blocks which are recorded on the adjacent position on the tape are reproduced in the same time. Therefore, it is performed that the corresponding DCT blocks contained in the sync block adjacent on the tape are in the adjacent position on the screen.

Fig.5 shows a relationship between the DCT blocks and the corresponding sync blocks. Sync block n, n+1, n+2 are recorded in the adjacent position on the tape and the corresponding DCT blocks n, n+1, n+2 are in the adjacent

position on the screen. By using these arrangement, when sync block n, n+1, n+2 are simultaneously detected in high speed play, the corresponding DCT blocks n, n+1, n+2 are reproduced continuously. The number of DCT blocks which are reproduced continuously is decided by the tape speed.   So a large area on the screen is continuously reproduced in lower speed. But only small area is reproduced continuously and there is little improvement of picture quality in higher speed.

3. Data format in a sync block

Faster the tape speed is, the less the number of detected sync blocks is. Furthermore, it is often occurred that a part of data in a sync block is only detected. In order to improve picture quality in higher speed, we investigated data format in a sync block.

Concerning error correction, encoded data is divided into two part, a first part (s1) and the second part (s2) and error correction check words are added to each s1 and s2.

Fig.6 is one of the data format about a sync block. Data is located sequentially by the unit of DCT block. In this case, if error occurs in s2, s2 must be concealed and s1 is also

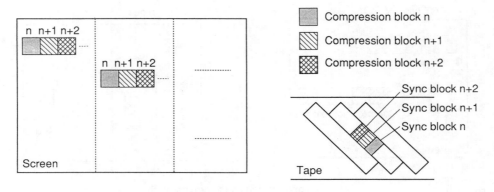

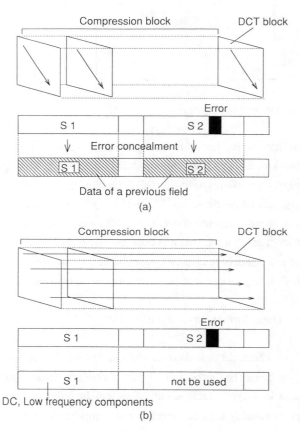

Fig. 5   The DCT blocks and the corresponding sync blocks

Compression block   DCT block

Error

| S 1 | | S 2 | ■ | |

↓   Error concealment   ↓

| S 1 | | S 2 | |

Data of a previous field

(a)

Compression block   DCT block

Error

| S 1 | | S 2 | ■ | |

| S 1 | | not be used | |

DC, Low frequency components

(b)

Fig. 6   Data format in a sync block

concealed because the error concealment is performed by the unit of sync block. In higher speed play, picture quality is improved by reproducing the DCT blocks as much as possible. So the format shown in Fig.6(a) is not effective.

In these reasons, we adopted the format shown in Fig.6(b). Since the original picture data is transformed to frequency, the sync block is filled with the data in lower frequency components in order. Consequently, lower frequency components with DC components are located in s1 and high frequency components are located in s2. This filling procedure makes `it possible that even if error exists in s2 and s1 is only detected, all DCT blocks in the corresponding compression block can be decoded by lower frequency components including DC components and additional information for decoding. The loss of s2 which mainly consists of high frequency components is not vital for picture reconstruction in high speed play.

Results of simulation

It is difficult to evaluate the picture quality in high speed play in quantity. Therefore, a computer simulation was done for a evaluation of visible picture quality. It was done in the condition that valid data were got in the case that a half width of a track was traced by a head of which azimuth angle was equal to the track's.

Results of evaluation which were got by changing the playing speed and the method of compression block forming which are listed below.

(1) The compression block is constructed by DCT blocks which are adjacent on the screen.

(2) The compression block is constructed by the DCT blocks which are separated each other on the screen. The corresponding DCT blocks contained in sync block adjacent on the tape are separated each other on the screen.

(3) The compression block is constructed by DCT blocks which are separated each other on the screen. The corresponding DCT blocks contained in the sync block adjacent on the tape are adjacent each other on the screen.

Table 2 Evaluation of picture quality

	2 times	4 times	8 times
(1)	A	B	B
(2)	B	C	D
(3)	A	B	B

A : good   B : acceptable
C : unacceptable D : terrible

In case of (1), the borders between DCT blocks are not visible and reproduced picture has a good quality. In case of (2), the borders are easy to be minded and reproduced picture in 2 times speed is acceptable. However the picture in higher speed is not acceptable because of a degradation like a mosaic. On the other hand, in case of (3), which is proposed in this time, although the borders between areas which consists of DCT blocks are visible slightly in about 4 times play, picture quality is acceptable. At last in over 8 times speed, the borders are remarkable especially in the fast moving area because of time difference.

Conclusions

Summarization of approaches to improve picture quality in high speed play and results are listed below.

(1) VLC is controlled to be completed within a sync block.

(2) Each compression block is constructed by DCT blocks which are separated each other on the screen. The DCT blocks which are in the adjacent sync block on the tape are in the adjacent position on the screen.

(3) Lower frequency components are located at the first half in a sync block.

Computer simulation about an evaluation of reproduced picture quality in high speed play gave us a result that the best method of coding for high speed play is to form a compression block with DCT blocks adjacent on the screen. However there is a problem in picture quality in normal play because of the efficiency of VLC. From these points of view, our new format satisfying the need for picture quality in both normal play and high speed play is optimum to a home use digital VCR.

Acknowledgements

The authors would like to express their sincere appreciation to A.Iketani and C.Matsumi of our laboratory for their support, valuable advises, and cooperation to their project.

Reference

[1] C.Yamamitsu, A.Ide, A.Iketani, T.Juri, S.Kadono, C.Matsumi, K.Matsushita and H.Mizuki "An Experimental Study on a Home -Use Digital VTR", ICCE, 89 June 1989.

Scalable Speed Search Technique for Digital VCRs

Masaaki KOBAYASHI, Akihiro TAKEUCHI, Yasuo HAMAMOTO,
Chojuro YAMAMITSU, Ichiro ARIMURA
MATSUSHITA ELECTIRIC INDUSTRIAL CO. ,LTD.
OSAKA JAPAN ,540

ABSTRACT

The requirement to develop a VCR, which is capable of performing search play at variable speeds (picture in shuttle) in both forward and reverse directions of interframe coded signals presents a difficult task.

This paper describes a new trick play technique for interframe coded (MPEG like) HD-VCR data. The technique is based on analysis made on required picture quality and it involves special positioning of the data for the "trick" play mode. The basic criteria is that picture quality which is inversely proportional to tape speed (lower quality at higher speed) is acceptable to the viewers.

1 INTRODUCTION

In developing the digital broadcasting system, for example ATV, the inter-frame relationship between the signal frames is generally utilized in order to increase the compression ratio of video signals. In this method, higher compression ratio can be obtained by transmitting only the differences between the continuous frames utilizing the correlationship between the video signal frames.

However, when thus compressed video signals are recorded on VCR are searched at a high-speed, though the video data can be partly retrieved, several partial images separated by several frame distances would be inevitably included in a reproduced picture since the picture which is easy to see can not be reproduced from difference signals only.

This paper is to report that the present authors have determined the subjective picture qualities from the relationship between the picture quality and the search speed, and accordingly, the video data are hiearchically classified.

Based on these facts, the hiearchical data area on video tape on which acquired data are distributed according to the search speed is determined, and the hiearchical video data are disposed thereon accordingly. Thus, easily recognizable search pictures at plural search speed became available without adding extra data for the search operation.

2 THE RELASIONSHIP BETWEEN SEARCH SPEED AND NECESSARY PICTURE QUALITY

The high-speed search is an often-used VCR function for searching desired pictures or to skip unwanted picture regions. In these cases, however, the picture quality must not necessarily be the one reproducible at standard speed.

Since the pictures reproduced at high-speed would change at a very fast rate, the loss of high-frequency components would not be very serious problem considering the visual characteristics to moving objects. Moreover, considering the purposes of search also, the recognition of rough outline, if obtained, would be satisfactory for practical purpose.

Thus, the relationship between the search speed and the allowances for resolution loss is subjectively determined. In this study, various evaluation images with different picture qualities are prepared after selecting conventional HDTV images with high image movements.

Assuming a DCT compression (8×8), the images shown in Fig.1 prepared for evaluation are grouped into four groups from No. 1 to No. 4 in an order of lower resolution first. No. 1 group contains DC components only, and after No. 2 group, the widths of both the horizontal and the vertical frequency bands thereof are succeedingly doubled, and in addition to these groups, a No. 5 group containing all of the components is prepared.

The relationships between the search speed and the picture quality of the evolution images have been determined by using a picture simulator when the search speed is increased at a step of 2, 4, 8, and 16-times speeds the subjective evaluation time at 1 second. Fig.2 shows a result of this, proving that a higher loss of high-frequency components is permissible at higher search speed.

3   CONCEPT OF HIERARCHICAL DATA DISPOSITION

As shown in the above, since it is found that the amount of data constituting a reproduced picture is less at higher search speed, a reliable method to acquire these data is studied based on this fact.

The head traces on the magnetic tape made at various search speeds are shown in Fig.3 wherein the solid lines show the traces left at 16-times search speed, fine lines at 4-times search speed, and the broken lines the respective traces in reverse directions of these. As shown in Fig.3, these respective traces cross at several points on the recording tracks.

For an example, the point Y identified by o marks shows the point crossed at a 4-times speed, while the point X identified by ● marks shows the point crossed at a speed of 16 times, and a part of points X and Y is shared each other, and these are in a hierarchical rationship.

By disposing the image data for searching at these points concentratively, the data can be commonly used at both searching and reproducing speeds so that high-speed search can be accomplished without any aditional data. The relationships between these points can be conceptually expressed in a hierarchical structure shown in Fig.4.

For example, the recording video data are expressed by a hierarchical structure as shown in Fig.5. Fig.6 shows data dispositions when intraframe (I-frame) period GOP is expressed by N and the number of tracks per frame for VCR is expressed by M. The recording data which are classified as shown in Fig.5 are allocated by a relationship as shown in Fig.4.

4   EXPERIMENT

4.1   Data Disposition

A disposition of picture data according to the below shown specification is considered here.
Compression :

Intraframe period(GOP): 16 frames
Intraframe data volume : 2 Mbit
Data-rate   :18 Mbps

VCR :

> Track construction : 300 tracks/sec
> Data-rate : 30 Mbps (l00kb/track)

As shown in Fig.7, the heads are disposed at one side of the rotating cylinder, and supplemental reproducing head of same construction is disposed additionally on its opposite side in order to secure the data acquisition rate. Fig.8 shows concrete data dispositions corresponding to various search modes made at 16-, 8-, and 4-times speed.

A: Data for 16-times search speed are disposed at every 8 pair-tracks in common with the data for 8-and 4-times search speeds and normal speed reproduction.

B: Data for 8-times search speed are disposed at an area enlarged to upper and lower direction including the center area of track where A data are disposed in common with the data for 4- times search speed and normal speed reproduction.

C: Data for 4-times search-speed are disposed at an area enlarged to upper and lower directions including the center area of the A and B tracks in common with the data for normal speed reproduction .

In order to meet with these arrangements, three kinds of search data, i. e., A, B, and C, are disposed at an area around the center of track.

A paired head at 16-times search-speed should pass through the tracks at an interval of every 16 pair-tracks, and this means that the head and the supplemental head pass through the track at an interval of every 8 pair-tracks. Like a case of search speed of 8-times, the head passes through the track at every 4 pair-tracks, and in a case of 4-times speed, the head passes at every 2 pair-tracks.

The length on the data track when a head having a width which is l.5 times of the track width allowing a head output decrease of -6 dB is determined as shown in Fig. 9. The burst data acquired at one scanning pass is shown in the solid black region therein. One intraframe data are disposed over the length of 1GOP(80 pair-tracks). When a 16-times speed is used for 80 pair-tracks, the reproducing head scans the five regions times so that, counting the scanning duties of the supplemental reproducing head, the scanning head acquires 20 bursts at every 10 scanning operations.

4.2 Hiearchical Allocations of Intra-Data

Assuming, both the numbers of horizontal and vertical pixels are set at orders of 1400 x 1000, and one frame is compressed into about 2 Mb/frame by using DCT (8 x 8) system, 2 Mb data are hiearchically separated into the data shown in Table2. So that about one-tenth of single complete frame data 200kbit is acquired at the 16-times search speed. Fig.10 shows a block diagram of VCR system.

An I-frame components separated from the inputted data are hiearchically isolated according to the rule shown in Table2, and are distributed on the intermittent regions provided on the tape. The components other than the I-frame are recorded on the tape region other than the above specified. At reproduction at a standard speed, all of these data are acquired through the head.

4.3 Simulated Results

By constructing a recorded tape in a computer simulation study, the hiearchical data are disposed thereon. Furthermore, pictures are reproduced by scanning the tape by using a simulated heads.

Changes of resolution in one frame according to the search speed are observed by this.

Though the observed moving speed becomes faster when the search speed is increased, the reproduced pictures are only to observe the resultantly produced visual effects. Fig.11 to Fig.13 show the reproduced pictures together with the original pictures at two reproducing speeds.

5 CONCLUSION

A new high-speed searching method for VCR in which highly compressed TV signals are recorded utilizing the inter-frame relationship has been studied and developed.

As the result of these processes, a search system having the below-shown characteristics have been obtained:

1. Since the resolution is higher when the search speed is lower, natural reproduced images can be produced.
2. Both the positive and negative plural search speeds including 16-, 8-, and 4-times speeds are possible.
3. Since no additional data for high-speed search is required, the tape utilization factor is high.

The presently developed high-speed reproduction technique is hereby named as Scalable Speed Search (SSS) Technique utilizing the hiearchical data disposition.

References

[1] A. Takeuchi, Y. Hamamoto, M. Kobayashi, C. Yamamitsu, I. Arimura: "A Study of High Speed Search Technique for Digital VCR with High Bit Rate Reduction System", TECHNICAL REPORT OF IEICE. MR93-28,pp.21-26 (1993).

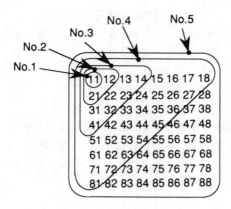

Fig. 1 DCT components for evaluation images

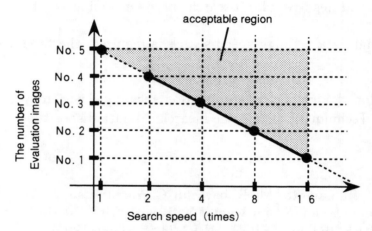

Fig.2 Acceptable picture quality at each search speed

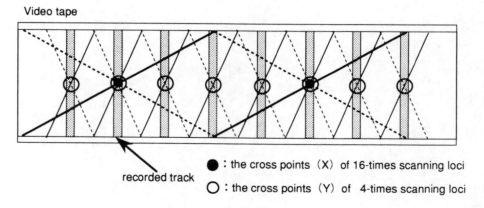

● : the cross points （X） of 16-times scanning loci

○ : the cross points （Y） of 4-times scanning loci

Fig.3 Recorded tracks and scanning loci

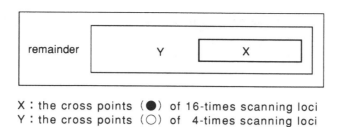

X : the cross points (●) of 16-times scanning loci
Y : the cross points (○) of 4-times scanning loci

Fig. 4   The relationship of the cross points

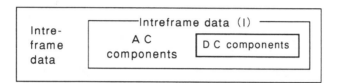

Fig. 5   Example of recording data structure

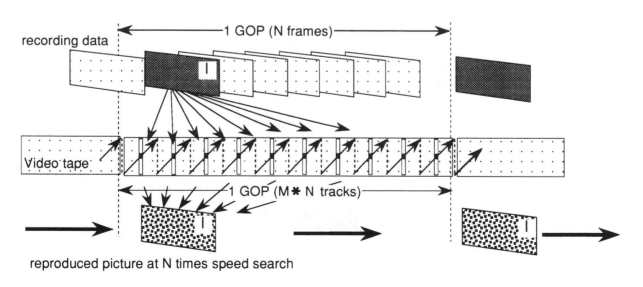

reproduced picture at N times speed search

Fig. 6   Dispositions of Intraframe data (I)

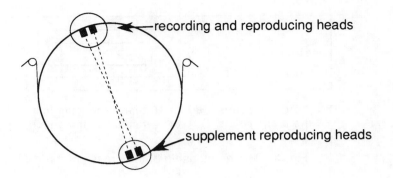

Fig. 7   heads construction

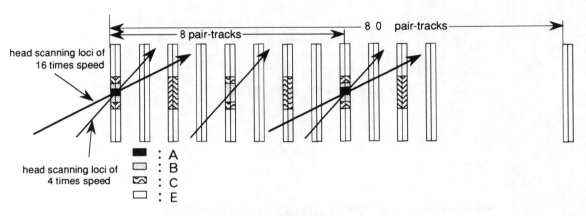

head scanning loci of
16 times speed

head scanning loci of
4 times speed

■ : A
▨ : B
▧ : C
▢ : E

8 pair-tracks

8 0   pair-tracks

Fig. 8   Data dispositions on a video tape

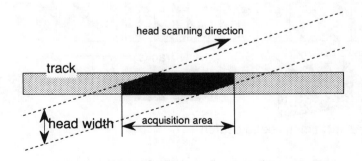

head scanning direction

track

head width

acquisition area

Fig. 9   acquisition area

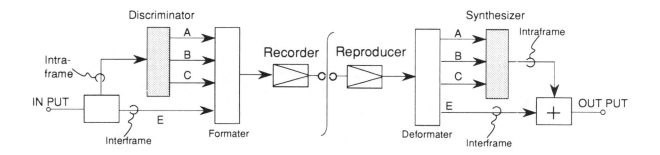

Fig. 10   Block diagram of VCR

TCR 01:03:44:14

Fig. 11   Original picture

Fig. 12   Computer simulated reproduced picture
(8-times speed)

Fig. 13   Computer simulated reproduced picture
(16-times speed)

Table 1 Acquired Burst Lengths

Search Speed (times)	Length (%)	Number of Bursts	Data Volume (k bit)
1 6	1 0	2 0	2 0 0
8	2 0	4 0	8 0 0
4	5 0	8 0	4 0 0 0

recorded track length is defined at 100%

Table 2 Allocations of I-frame Data

	Data area	A (200kbit)	B (230kbit)	C (1.57Mbit)		
	DCT components	·DC Upper(e) ·ACL Upper	·DC Upper(O)	·DC Lower ·ACH		
Search	1 6	○			200kbit	Reproduced data amount
Speed	8	○	○		430kbit	
(times)	4	○	○	○	2Mbit	

DC Upper(e) ： Subsumpled (even) significant five bits of DC components
DC Upper(o) ： Subsumpled (odd) significant five bits of DC components
DC Lower   ： Unsignificant bits of DC components
ACL Upper   ： Significant bits of low frequency DCT components
ACH   ： High frequency DCT components and unsignificant bits of low frequency DCT components

Chapter 3
Digital Video in Cable Television: Transmission, Applications, and Competitive Forces

WALTER S. CICIORA, Ph.D.
45 HULLS FARM RD
SOUTHPORT, CT 06490-1027

INTRODUCTION

Digital television techniques found first applications in the defense and space exploration areas where priorities other than cost dominated. These early applications financed and stimulated the technology at a time when no other area could afford the costs. Next, digital television was applied in situations that generated short segments of creative video to be used repeatedly for commercials, logos, and channel identification segments. Here the costs could be amortized over many viewers and multiple showings. Then followed the digital studio, where multiple processing of signals and tape storage required a method that did not show degradation in successive generations.

A major step in the expansion of digital resulted from the need to squeeze high-definition television into six megahertz. The video generated by an HDTV camera totaled near 100 megahertz. The compression demanded by HDTV could best be implemented in digital form. A natural question arose regarding the possibility of using these same techniques to put multiple NTSC-like signals into the same spectrum required for one analog NTSC signal. The advantages of that strategy include rapid deployment, since consumers could continue to use their existing TV receivers and VCRs. Only the external converter was needed to transform the digital signal into something the existing consumer products could use. Those converters could be supplied by vendors of services and financed as part of a monthly subscription.

CABLE TELEVISION AND ITS COMPETITORS

Major opportunities for compressed digital video are in cable television and in areas that compete with cable. Cable's main advantage has always been choice. Tens of channels expanding to 150 analog channels occupying a gigahertz of bandwidth in the cable system serving Queens, New York, have made cable compelling. Direct Broadcast Satellite (DBS) and microwave distributed multi-channel multi-point distribution service (MMDS) had little chance to compete with cable as long as they were limited to ten or twenty channels. The hope for over a hundred channels gives these media an opportunity to become viable competitors.

The telephone "twisted pair" had no chance of delivering entertainment quality video until compressed digital video became practical. Broadcasters would like to participate as well. From a technical perspective, the broadcast environment has reflections and interference that limit what might be achieved. Public policy issues, perhaps more restrictive than the technical problems, limit what is allowed.

Cable television with its gigahertz spectrum can apply compressed digital video in ways that competitors have difficulty matching. Add to this the local nature of cable television, and its two-way transmission capability, to understand the potential for expanded and new services. "Information Age" services and "multi-media" applications become possible. The combination of hybrid fiber/coaxial plant and compressed digital video make the national information infrastructure (NII) a practical initiative.

MAKING IT AFFORDABLE

What was unthinkable just a decade or two ago is now practical. Integrated-circuit technology advances have made this possible. When the first IBM computer was introduced in the early 1980s it was based on an Intel microcomputer containing only 30,000 transistors. The 80486, which forms the core of most of the personal computers sold today has 1.2 million transistors. The latest version, the Pentium, has in excess of three million transistors. External to these core devices are memory systems containing tens of millions of transistors. All this is at affordable consumer prices. Application-specific integrated circuits (ASIC's) containing 50,000 to 100,000 logic gates are not unusual. ASICs with ten or twenty thousand gates are considered unremarkable. We can only speculate on what the next five to ten years will bring.

It is this tremendous digital power at very low cost that makes it possible to extend digital technology to consumer and cable applications. Simply put, digital video compression is practical now because we can afford to put several million transistors in a consumer product.

APPLICATION SCENARIOS

Before delving into the details of digital technology as applied to cable, it is important to motivate that study by considering how the technology might be used. If the consumer does not find the technology useful and compelling, it remains an academic curiosity. That is not the focus of the IEEE Consumer Electronics Society! Large-scale applications that interest and benefit the consumer are what drive the industry, which supplies the membership of this Society.

CABLE TRANSMISSION

Cable television's hybrid fiber/coaxial infrastructure gives it unique advantages, which promise higher capacity than other media. Cable's coaxial spectrum is sealed in an aluminum shell to minimize interference from other users of the free-space spectrum. The same immunity applies to the portions of the cable plant utilizing fiber.

A well designed cable system keeps noise under control. Error detection and correction techniques further relax transmission constraints, making multi-level signaling possible, yielding as many as eight bits per Hertz of spectrum. Reflections from impedance discontinuties are also kept to low enough levels so that affordable time-domain equalizers can cope with the effects of these transmission impairments. It appears likely that cable systems will be able to routinely carry at least double the data capacity of broadcast, over-the-air six-megahertz channels. In excess of forty Megabits per second is expected in six megahertz. Since there are 150 of these six-megahertz channels in a gigahertz cable system, the data-carrying capacity is truly awesome.

CABLE CHANNEL CHARACTERIZATION

A number of measurements of practical cable systems have been reported that support theoretical studies. There is reason to expect that the projected data capacities will be realizable. Interestingly, the limitations appear to be most severe in the home where the subscriber modifies the wiring and adds opportunities for signal ingress and reflections. The hybrid fiber/coaxial plant, when well maintained, is benign to digital signals.

CONCLUSION

While digital techniques were first applied to video in a variety of other fields, cable television will rapidly expand its impact on the average citizen's life. Just one manufacturer has orders for over two-and-a-half million decompression units for use on cable. Some time in 1994, the number of transistors applied to digital video (since video was first digitized) will double. In the next few years, digital video will become a part of the lives of most cable subscribers.

REFERENCES

There are very few papers published in this new and exciting field. There are, however, two places to look. First, there is the National Cable Television Association's (NCTA, Washington, DC) Convention Technical Record and, second, there are the Conference proceedings published by the Society of Cable Television Engineers (SCTE, Exton, Penn.). The SCTE has two yearly functions, one called Cable-Tech Expo, and the other the "Conference on Emerging Technologies." In addition, two trade magazines carry technical articles with a more popular orientation. They are the *Communications Engineering & Design* (CED), and *Communications Technology* (CT). The following papers are from the 1994 SCTE Emerging Technologies Proceedings:

[1] K. Metz et al., "MPEG-2 video decoder implementation considerations," pg. 15.
[2] C.E. Holoborow, "MPEG2 systems: a standard packet multiplex format for cable digital services," pg. 25.
[3] G.S. Roman, "Compressed digital program delivery: system issues," pg. 35.
[4] A. Paff, "Evolution of the sonet regional interconnect in the cable television environment," pg. 87
[5] H.J. Kafka, "Video servers—moving trials to the interactive mainstream," pg. 167.
[6] W.L. Hoarty, "Multimedia on cable television systems," pg. 181.
[7] E.L. Langenberg, "Integrated switched voice with video services," pg. 199.
[8] R. Citta et al., "Practical 43 MBIT/Sec digital CATV modem using 16-VSB modulation," pg. 219.

Scenarios for Compression On Cable

Walter S. Ciciora, Ph.D.
Vice President, Technology
Time Warner Cable
Stamford, CT 06902-6732
U.S.A.

Introduction

Digital Video Compression, DVC, is the hottest technical subject in television. It has left HDTV behind in the dust. This is because it offers more, sooner.

When most Americans are given the choice between "more" and "better", they almost always choose "more". An interesting example of this is the $2.00 blank video cassette. Most Americans will put their VCR into the six hour mode even though the two hour mode will give them noticeably better video and dramatically better audio. When the VCR was introduced, the Beta machine had better quality, the VHS machine had six hour mode. Soon after, another difference arose. There were many more movies available on VHS than on Beta. Better image quality was forsaken in favor of more choice and longer playing times. The same is likely to be the case in the contest between HDTV and DVC.

What is DVC?

Compression is motivated by the desire to get more information through limited channels and to be more efficient about it. Another motivation is to require less storage space. Some of the earliest motivations were from the desire to put limited pictures through twisted pairs. PicturePhone was a technology to put images through somewhat extended audio links. To accomplish this, the images had to be compressed. A modern day version of this is Teleconferencing. Military and space communications also deal with images through challenging channels. The most recent motivation for compression is HDTV. An analog HDTV television camera puts out 30 + MHz each of red, blue, and green signals. Along with the other signals involved in producing the picture, there is a raw bandwidth of around 100 MHz. However, the Federal Communications Commission allows only 6 MHz. To squeeze all of that information into 6 MHz requires the elimination of most of the redundancies. A practical question arises. If it is possible to force 100 MHz of HDTV into 6 MHz, wouldn't it be possible to put many NTSC signals into the same 6 MHz. The answer is in the affirmative.

DVC is based on the principal of removing redundancies from images. There are three kinds of redundancies:

1) Redundancies in each picture

2) Redundancies between pictures

3) Information we don't see

A picture can be considered to be made up of a tremendous number of points of light called picture elements, or pixels. When compared with each other, many of the adjacent pixels are found to be identical. In ordinary television, these pixels are transmitted one at a time without any regard for their redundancies. This wastes a huge amount of spectrum, but makes possible simple, inexpensive hardware. DVC minimizes pixel redundancy and saves transmission capacity at the expense of increased hardware complexity.

Reprinted with permission from W. S. Ciciora, from
1993 International Television Symposium, vol. 242, pp. 435–443, 1993.

Motion pictures are made up of a succession of still pictures. Movies have 24 pictures per second and video has 30. There are large redundancies from picture to picture because objects cannot not move very quickly. DVC attempts to remove most of this redundancy.

The final form of redundancy is the information which the human visual system does not use. The human visual system has evolved over time to be very sensitive to horizontal motion and horizontal detail. It is much less sensitive to motion and detail in the vertical direction and even less sensitive in the diagonal direction. This is probably because prey and predators most often move horizontally, rarely vertically, and even less rarely diagonally. Those of our predecessors who had high sensitivity to horizontal motion probably ate well. Those who did not have this sensitivity probably were eaten. As descendents of the survivors, we have this high sensitivity to horizontal motion and detail.

Photographic and television cameras don't differentiate between these directions. They respond essentially equally in all directions. As a result, there is a lot of information in electronic and photographic images which we don't appreciate. It would not be missed if it was deleted.

Yet one more technique can sometimes be used to advantage. It is called "statistical multiplexing" or "stat mux". In this scheme, the compression of all of the programs to be placed in a 6 MHz slot is done in one location at the same time under the control of a processor. The processor analyzes the video in each program to be compressed to determine the level of difficulty involved. Data capacity is reallocated from programs which are relatively unchallenging to those which are challenging. Better results can be expected. If enough programs are involved, it may be possible to add another program on average. There are some circumstances where stat mux can break down and cause trouble. Stat mux must be used carefully.

There are several methods of DVC under investigation:

Discrete Cosine Transform, DCT

Vector Quantization, VQ

Fractals

Wavelets

Magic

In the case of the last category, calls are received at least every other month insisting that there has been some great advance. Computer simulations, loaded with defects are proudly shown. All the defects are explained away. Dramatic claims are made. Usually there is a request for several millions of dollars to bring the promise to fruition. In at least one case, outright fraud was involved. Usually, it's just simple-minded over-optimism.

The DCT is a technique that divides the image into blocks eight lines high and eight pixels wide. The information inside the block is converted into a spectrum. Once in the spectrum format, it can be processed more easily. For example, removing detail involves low pass filtering. This is computationally much more convenient in the frequency domain. Approximations are made. Blocks from succeeding pictures are compared and redundancies minimized. Models of the human visual response are applied to minimize information we do not respond to.

The VQ approach also breaks the image up into eight by eight blocks. It compares the block to a look up table with approximate representations of what the block looks like. It chooses the closest match and transmits the location in the look-up table of that representation. In the receiver, an identical look-up table exists. When the location of the approximating image is received, the image is moved to memory to approximate the picture. The original promise of VQ was greater simplification and lower cost. Originally, the compression was to be done only on a picture by picture basis. It was found that when this was done, the compression amount was not adequate. Too much redundancy was left in because of the similarities picture to picture. When redundancies between pictures were removed, the complexity approached DCT but the video quality did not. A persistent shimmering remained which was very annoying.

Wavelets and fractals have not yet received the same degree of attention as DCT and VQ and are therefore in an earlier stage of development. Their advocates make high claims for these approaches. Time will tell if the promises are fulfilled.

DVC has the promise of significantly better pictures. Transmission noise, ghosts, micro-reflections, beats be-

tween carriers, all are not evident in the picture. Either they are below a threshold which has no impact on the final result or they destroy the signal entirely. There is a sharp cliff between near perfect reception and total disaster. It is possible to avoid the NTSC artifacts of dot crawl and cross color. By using the same S-connector intended for Super VHS, color artifact free images can be presented. For the older TV or VCR, the usual channel 3 signal will be provided.

This does not mean that there are no problems. DVC brings a new set of artifacts which are minimal when DVC is properly done. If implemented poorly or too aggressively in the pursuit of high levels of compression, DVC can cause some very bothersome artifacts. When the processing between the eight by eight blocks is not coordinated, the boundaries can become evident. Naturally, this is called "blocking". Some images appear to be as if seen through a dirty window. In some implementations, there are ripples around sharp edges. In particular, letters in the credits of movies appear to be placed in puddles of water with ripples surrounding them. Foliage tends to have serrated edges as if little crystals of salt have grown there. In one version of DCT, slow pans yield the appearance of a picture painted on a sheet of rubber. Some parts of the image move before others and then they catch up. A mountain scene appears to be having an earth quake. All of these artifacts occur when the implementation is poor or overly aggressive in the pursuit of high compression rates. These artifacts are very unpleasant because they do not look natural. In contrast, analog picture artifacts appear much more like what we might see in nature.

Since video has 30 pictures per second and movies have 24, there is a 25% capacity penalty for transmission of video when compared to movies in the same resolution.

What Can It Do? When?

DVC is being used to put four channels in one transponder to improve the efficiency of use of the transponder. HBO is utilizing the General Instruments DigiCipher I system to deliver its multiplex service to cable headends. At the headend, the digital signals are converted to analog form for delivery down the cable system. In some cases the signal is scrambled before being put on the system. Multiplexing is a marketing approach introduced by HBO to offer the same set of movies on three different channels arranged so that different genre appear on the channels. In that way subscribers are most likely to find something of interest nearly all of the time. Generally, the multiplexed service is offered at no extra charge. Therefore cost containment is important. The incremental costs for multiplexing is primarily the transponder costs. DVC saves most of that by using advanced hardware to better utilize the satellite.

There are a number of others promising to use DVC soon. SkyPix was the original announced user of DVC. It demonstrated an early version using DCT. Because it was a pioneering effort, it did not benefit from subsequent experience. The pictures origin-

ally were quite impaired with artifacts. More recently, Direct TV has announced plans to use a Hughes high powered satellite to be launched at the end of 1993. Thomson Electronics will provide hardware. Initially fifty channels will be offered. Service is expected to begin in 1994.

TCI has announced that it will provide compressed signals via satellite to cable headends. At the headend, the signal will be remodulated onto carriers which are more appropriate for cable. The decompression will occur in the home. Addressing and servicing of the subscription will take place from a central site. Some have called this a "headend in the sky".

Time Warner Cable is building an advanced system in Orlando Florida. Extensive fiber links will connect servers and digital switches via Asynchronous Transfer Mode, ATM, signals to nodes in the neighborhood. The nodes will serve about five hundred homes. The servers will utilize terra bytes of semiconductor memory to store movies. The silicon memory will be supplemented with high capacity hard drives. Subscribers will be able to order movies in true Video On Demand, VOD, format. All normal VCR features will be available including pause, fast forward, and rewind. Other communications services will be provided as well. These include telecommunication services such as wireless Personal Communications Services, PCS, multimedia, video games, information age services, shopping services, etc. Accordingly, this is called the Full Service Network.

Others have also announced the use

of DVC. Several phone companies are promising video dial tone using Asymmetrical Digital Subscriber Loop, ADSL, technology.

Standards

There have been calls for standardization of DVC. It is much too early to create standards for DVC. When NTSC was created some fifty years ago, having a dozen vacuum tubes in a receiver was a major accomplishment. Very slowly over time, the number of "active devices" (originally tubes, then transistors) increased. Transistors greatly reduced the constraints on active devices. It became possible to have dozens of active devices in a TV. The analog integrated circuity made possible a few hundreds of transistors in a TV set. When digital techniques were introduced, the number increased to a few thousand. The road from a dozen to a few thousand active devices took around fifty years. In just the last five years or so, the number of digital devices that can be employed in consumer products has exploded to a few million. We are on the steep part of the technical progress curve.

The principal reason we can implement DVC now is because we can afford a million or two transistors in a cable provided decompression unit. The nature of digital electronics is that the number of transistors available at a given price approximately doubles every eighteen to twenty four months. This has been going on for several decades and appears to have at least one more decade to go. About ten years ago, the Intel 8086 microcomputer had 30,000 transistors on one piece of silicon. The Intel 80486 intro-

duced a couple of years ago has 1,200,000 transistors. The recently introduced 80586, also called the "Pentium", has 3.1 million transistors. In roughly ten years, the doubling every eighteen to twenty four months has held true. From this we can project dramatic future growth in computing power affordable in cable provided decompression boxes. If the experience of the last few decades extends one more decade, there will be about six and a half doublings of transistors. Today's million transistors will become around a hundred million in a decade. Any more conservative estimate still promises five to ten million transistors in five to six years. We can surely do better compressed digital NTSC with five to ten million transistors than we can do with just one million.

The DVC "standards" process by the international Motion Pictures Experts Group, MPEG, has already created one standard, MPEG I. Before it experienced significant implementation, an MPEG II standards setting process was launched. It is likely that there will be an MPEG III, MPEG IV, and who knows how far it will go. The rich availability of millions of transistors at very affordable prices will make this progress possible.

The Four Scenarios

It appears that there are four possible scenarios for the application of DVC to cable:

1) DVC for only Impulse Pay Per View, IPPV

2) DVC for IPPV and Pays

3) DVC for IPPV, Pays, and Tiers

4) DVC for everything

In the first scenario, DVC is only used for movies. This allows for the maximum compression for two reasons. First, movies have only 24 pictures per second. Secondly, movies can be compressed "off line" using human intervention to obtain optimum results. The movies can be provided in the Near Video On Demand, NVOD, format pioneered in the Time Warner Queens New York Quantum system. In that application, advanced fiber techniques were used to provide 1 GHz bandwidths delivering 150 analog channels to subscribers' homes. Some 57 channels are allocated to IPPV. The top five or so movies are stagger started every half hour, occupying four channels. The next most popular movies start every hour, occupying two channels each. The remainder just repeat on one channel. At any one time, fifteen movies are available at differing repeat rates. If DVC were applied to Quantum, the top 75 channels would be compressed. If ten to one compression were available, 750 simultaneous movies would be possible. That would create a very attractive movie service indeed, a Mega Quantum!

An important characteristic of this scenario is that decompressors are only provided in homes that generate new revenue. Thus the cost of the relatively expensive new hardware can be covered in a reasonable period of time. Since movies will be purchased, it is likely that only one decompressor is needed per home. Because of the high rate of repetition, there is no need for a separate decompressor for the VCR. Time shifting is unnecessary. The decompressor will be located in the principal viewing area, where the largest and newest TV is located. This scenario is the one most likely to pay for itself in a reasonable period of time.

The second scenario clears out a few low penetration pay channels. For example if a 33 channel cable system has three low penetration pays, they can be deleted. If ten to one compression is possible, thirty new slots are created. Three are required for the pays which were deleted. This yields 27 new "synthetic" channels. This is an especially useful scenario for responding to a competitive move. It does have some drawbacks. The pay subscribers must be given the relatively expensive decompression box. Some of them will not take any or much of the new IPPV services generating little or no new income. The need for more than one decompressor in some homes will be felt. These subscribers may be accustomed to viewing pay programming in more than one room in the house. This is especially true if the Pay services were originally trapped. Subscribers who take more than one pay may also wish to tape from time to time. It is important to get all of the Pay service providers to utilize the same DVC technology so that only one box is needed in the home. These pay providers will have to continue to deliver satellite signals in analog form for some time to come for the cable operators who have not yet adopted compression to the home. In addition, Pay services are not all movies. There are live sporting events and concerts which must be done in video. Further more, the live events will require live compression in "real time". The benefits of human intervention in the compression process are lost because there is no second chance. What goes through the compressor, goes out over the satellite. This scenario is less likely to pay for itself quickly.

Scenario # 3 adds Tiered programming to the IPPV and Pays to clear out still more channels. This adds further complications. This is now likely to include subscribers who will not take the new revenue producing IPPV services. There is very much greater likelihood of a need of multiple decompressors per home for additional outlets and VCR's. A major new headache arises. Many of these tier channels are advertiser supported. Some of these are local ads. These ads must all be of the same technology as the programming so that the in-home box can decompress all of these signals. This is not what is being considered for ad compression now. Still another problem is that American subscribers have become accustomed to holding the channel-up or channel-down button on their remote controls to scan through channels quickly to determine what to watch. This has been called "channel surfing". Channel surfing is all but impossible with DVC. Since redundancy has been removed from the signal, it takes from one to thirty seconds to build up a picture, depending on the system. Channel surfing is not important with IPPV since a decision is made and the program is watched until it is over. It is not too important when there is just one or two pay services. However, when a tier of channels is compressed, channel surf-

ing can become very important. This scenario is even less likely to pay for itself quickly than scenario # 2.

The last scenario compresses everything. This approach requires a decompressor for each and every TV and VCR in each and every subscribers' home. This is the most expensive approach and the one least likely to pay for itself in a reasonable period of time. Any local origination programming will also have to be compressed. Some of it may have to be compressed in "real time". Channel surfing will be mandatory. Changing channels and waiting seconds for a picture will be a problem. Since a decompressor yields only one output program at a time, this approach has the consumer electronics friendliness of 100% scrambling. Depending on how the regulations eventually turn out, this option may even be precluded.

Feeding The Monster

The creation of systems which use extensive DVC gives rise to a problem called "feeding the monster". Multiple hundred channel systems or systems with true VOD have a monstrous appetite for compressed programming.

There is a school of thought that holds that the best results will be obtained if human intervention is allowed in the compression process. A movie would be first compressed by a best estimate of the compression parameters for each scene. Then, an experienced and talented operator would go back to the difficult scenes and adjust the parameters. This is all the more important as lower data rates are used. This approach appears to preclude the use of stat mux because the central processor which controls the process for the 6 MHz slot will be dealing with pre-compressed material. There is an opinion that human intervention in the compression process may produce better results than stat mux. But that is just an opinion. There is no experience to back this up.

To implement human intervention, a compression suite must be designed and built and experience gained. A compression suite is a console with appropriate controls, time code equipment, monitors, tape machines, etc. to allow a skilled operator to efficiently and effectively compress the product. Such suites are available for film to tape transfer. Similar set ups will be required for compression.

It would be desirable to compress a movie once for many purposes. This is not likely to be the case, at least initially. Movies to be stored in servers which include semiconductor memory and large hard drives would best be compressed with a variable data rate. Frames which need a lot of bits for compression would get them. Frames which did not need many would get fewer. That way excessive bits won't be needed in storage. Pre-recorded devices on the other hand seem to need a constant data rate. Rotational playback devices either have constant linear velocity or constant angular velocity. Using variable data rates would require a buffering memory along with some constraints on cumulative difference in rate.

It appears that most of the systems that have announced that they will use G.I. DigiCipher I will migrate to DigiCipher II in the near future. Movies compressed for DigiCipher I will have to be recompressed if they are to be used with DigiCipher II. The same is likely to be true of Direct TV. And if neither Direct TV nor DigiCipher II end up being compatible with MPEG II, there may be a need for yet another compression of the same movie. This makes the Beta vs VHS vs 8 mm issue seem simple.

Unfortunately, in all the excitement about compression, inadequate attention has been paid to feeding the monster. No compression suites are designed or available, no compression technicians are being practiced, no inventory of movies is being built up at present. Much must be done before the first monster is let out of the cage.

Conclusion

Digital Video Compression is upon us. There are many exciting new services which depend on it. There are a number of important challenges to the implementation. It appears that there will be at least another decade of rapid development and change. Life will not be soon dull for the television technologist. That's the good news. The bad news is that the technologist might as well forget about vacations and weekends. They will be consumed with the digital challenge.

The Author

Walter S. Ciciora, Ph.D. is Vice President of Technology at Time Warner Cable. Walt joined American Television and Communications, the predecessor to Time Warner Cable, in December of 1982 as Vice President of Research and Development. Prior to that he was with Zenith Electronics Corporation since 1965. He was Director of Sales and Marketing, Cable Products, from 1981 to 1982. Earlier at Zenith he was Manager, Electronic System Research and Development specializing in Teletext, Videotext and Video Signal Processing with emphasis on digital television technology and ghost canceling for television systems.

He has nine patents issued. He has presented over one hundred papers and published about fifty, two of which have received awards from the Institute of Electrical and Electronic Engineers. Walt wrote monthly columns for Communications Engineering and Design magazine and for Communications Technology magazine for three years each.

He currently serves on the Executive Committee of the Montreux Television Symposium, and is a member of the board of directors of the Society of Cable Television Engineers, SCTE. He was chairman of the National Cable Television Association, NCTA, Engineering Committee for four years and chairman of the Technical Advisory committee and also a member of the board of directors of CableLabs for four years, and was president of the Institute of Electrical And Electronic Engineers, IEEE, Consumer Electronics Society for two years. He is a past chairman of the IEEE International Conference on Consumer Electronics .

Walt is a Fellow of the IEEE, a Fellow of the Society of Motion Picture and Television Engineers, SMPTE, and a Senior Member of the SCTE. He chaired the Joint Engineering Committee of the NCTA and the Electronic Industry Association for eight years and co-chairs the Cable Consumer Electronics Advisory Group for the FCC, CCEAG .

Other memberships include Tau Beta Pi, Eta Kappa Nu, and Beta Gamma Sigma. He has served on several industry standard-setting committees. Current interests center on competitive technology, the consumer electronics interface with cable, Digital Video Compression, and High Definition Television.

Walt received the 1987 NCTA Vanguard Award for Science and Technology and was named "1990 Man of the Year" by Communications Engineering and Design magazine.

Walt has a Ph.D. in Electrical Engineering from Illinois Institute of Technology dated 1969. The BSEE and MSEE are also from IIT. He received an MBA from the University of Chicago in 1979. He has taught Electrical Engineering in the evening division of IIT for seven years.

Hobbies include helping his wife with her horses, reading, wood working, photography, skiing, and a hope to someday become more active in amateur radio (WB9FPW).

PERFORMANCE OF DIGITAL TRANSMISSION TECHNIQUES FOR CABLE TELEVISION SYSTEMS

Richard S. Prodan, Ph.D.
Cable Television Laboratories, Inc.

Abstract

An evaluation of complex modulation techniques for the transmission of digital information for advanced television applications is currently underway at CableLabs. The performance of various digital modulation techniques in the cable television transmission medium co-existent with standard NTSC analog video channels has been investigated. Both laboratory and field evaluations on existing cable systems are presented.

Introduction

The performance measure customarily utilized in characterizing digital modulation is the bit error rate. The bit error rate (BER) is dependent upon the carrier to noise ratio, or more precisely the bit energy to noise spectral density ratio. Either of these metrics provide the probability of error in terms of the distance between signals in energy space divided by the noise power for the additive white Gaussian noise environment.

The optimum receiver receives a waveform which is comprised of a transmitted signal corrupted by adding white Gaussian noise. The signal can be replaced by an equivalent vector form, and the noise process by a relevant noise process that can also be represented in vector form. This is done by defining a set of orthonormal time waveforms which can be used in linear combinations to represent both the signal and noise vector components (e.g., two quadature modulated carrier phases).

The vector components are derived at the receiver through a correlator or matched filter to the orthonormal time waveforms. The decision as to which signal was sent is made by comparing the distance of the received vector to all possible signal vectors. The receiver decides that a particular signal was sent if the received signal vector is closest to it. An error occurs if the received vector is closer to a signal vector that is different from the originally transmitted one.

For PAM modulated signals with non binary symbols, a rectangular constellation and decision regions result. The constellation diagram represents the signal vectors in a two dimensional space. The rectangular nature of the signals and their resulting decision boundaries are shown for 16 QAM and 4 VSB in Figures 1 and 2 respectively.

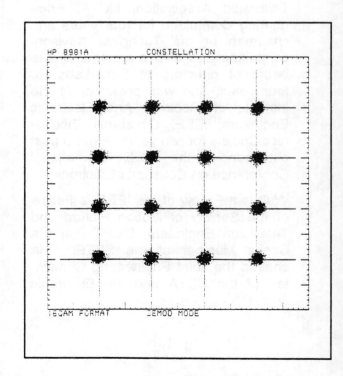

Figure 1 - 16 QAM Constellation

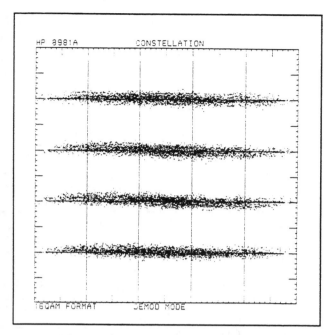

Figure 2 - 4 VSB Constellation

This Euclidean distance concept in signal energy in the presence of such noise can be reduced in the presence of additional impairments such as channel nonlinearities, intermodulation, and intersymbol interference due to channel bandwidth restrictions or reflections from impedance mismatches. These impairments reduce the "effective" carrier to noise ratio of an equivalent noisy but unimpaired channel. The bit error rate is calculated as the probability of the equivalent noisy signal erroneously crossing a decision boundary associated with the transmitted symbol (or group of bits) into another region associatedwith a different symbol. The effective carrier to noise with reduced implementation noise margins degraded by channel impairments has been studied to estimate the expected bit error rate of modern terminal equipment with practical performance limitations.

Transmission Testing Method

Two modulation formats were studied. The first format is 16 QAM double sideband pulse amplitude modulation format with quadrature carrier multiplexing and 4 levels (representing 2 bits) per carrier phase with the carrier placed symmetrically in the center of the band. The second format is 4 VSB, which is a (nearly) single sideband pulse amplitude modulation format with a small (5 percent) vestige about the carrier at the band edge. The modulated average signal power was set approximately 10 dB below NTSC carrier level.

The approach suggested for the performance evaluation of digital modulation on the cable distribution plant is vector modulation or constellation analysis. The digital data carrier is discretely modulated in phase and amplitude to convey groups of binary digits (words) as vectors in carrier phase space. The instantaneous switching between carrier phase states requires infinite channel bandwidth. Restrictions on the modulating data signal bandwidth result in intersymbol interference in practical systems.

Evaluation of ISI is possible by examination of the baseband data modulating channel response given by an eye pattern or diagram, where overlapping data symbol periods are superimposed to determine the reduction of noise margin due to ISI. The closure of the eye results in increased bit error rate, since noise in the channel is much more likely to force the signal to cross a decision boundary. The spread in the signal constellation clusters as well as shifts in position due to other channel impairments can be characterized by the constellation diagram. The constellation is a set of sampled points in carrier phase space with the carrier sampling times optimally chosen to coincide with the maximum eye openings in time of the inphase (I) and (for QAM only) the quadrature (Q) channels.

The performance of generalized digital modulation signal sets can be generated and analyzed with vector modulation equipment. Although bit error rate cannot be directly measured, it can be inferred from the constellation and eye pattern parameter measurements. These measurements can be made without constructing modems that require carrier recovery, symbol synchronization, clock recovery, data detection, differential decoding, etc.

Laboratory Tests

Vector modulation equipment available from Hewlett Packard along with prototype digital Nyquist pulse shaping filters and frequency conversion equipment was employed for the digital transmission evaluations. A pseudorandom bit sequence (PRBS) generator provided the data for the digital carrier modulation. The random data modulates I and Q IF carriers in both formats. Channel filters must be designed and inserted to shape the modulation spectrum and limit the modulated carrier bandwidth. A 6 MHz channel is utilized within the 41 to 47 MHz range with an appropriate Nyquist response rolloff characteristic.

A source bit rate of 18 Mbps from the PRBS generator divided between I and Q carrier phases (for 16 QAM) or carried in the I phase only (for 4 VSB) with 10 percent rolloff (excess bandwidth) occupied a 6 MHz channel. The coherent reference from the vector generator was normally used (except for phase noise testing) to demodulate the modulated data IF carrier at the vector modulation analyzer. Constellation and eye pattern measurements were made without the need for carrier recovery.

The modulated IF signal was supplied to a Scientific Atlanta RF modulator IF input with a crystal oscillator selected for the television channel desired for data transmission. A complementary RF demodulator recovers the modulated data carrier at IF, after being degraded by added impairments.

The recovered I and Q data bitstreams can be examined for mean square eye closure, phase offsets, and dispersion in the recovered constella-

tion samples from the vector modulation analyzer. Several hundred thousand points were downloaded via a GPIB interface to a computer for further analysis and estimation of effective carrier to noise ratio and expected error rate.

Some mean square eye closure results from the lab tests done on the CableLabs test bed in the Advanced Television Test Center in Alexandria, VA are given in Table 1 for various cable

LAB DATA - FROM CableLabs TEST BED			
TTS	DESCRIPTION	QAM %	VSB %
1	Unimpaired	13.0	14.5
2	Echo @ 300ns -15.7dBc	35.0	33.4
2A	Echo @ 300ns -20.7dBc	21.5	20.5
2B	Echo @ 300ns - 25.7dBc	15.3	15.6
3	CW Ingress at -23dBc	30	32
4	CTB at -32.5dBc (cw carriers)	16.6	18.8
5	Phase Noise -91.6dBc (1Hz) at + 20kHz from carrier	23.5	25.0
6	Composite Second Order at -32dBc (cw carriers)	15.0	16.5
7	Hum Mod, 120Hz, 4.6%	16.5	17.5

Table 1 - Lab results from the CableLabs test bed in Alexandria, VA.

impairments. The "unimpaired" eye closure of 14% is due to implementation loss, analog filtering, and the modulation and frequency translation equipment. Data for a short duration reflection characteristic of cable systems is shown for -15, -20, and -25 dB. The composite triple beat level for comparable eye closure is higher than would be present for satisfactory NTSC reception. The same situation applies for composite second order interference. Phase jitter from oscillator phase noise and power supply induced residual FM show a significant degredation at levels that would be unnoticeable on NTSC.

Field Tests

The laboratory tests may be repeated in the field on the TCI cable system in Boulder, CO. An additional complication arises due to the need

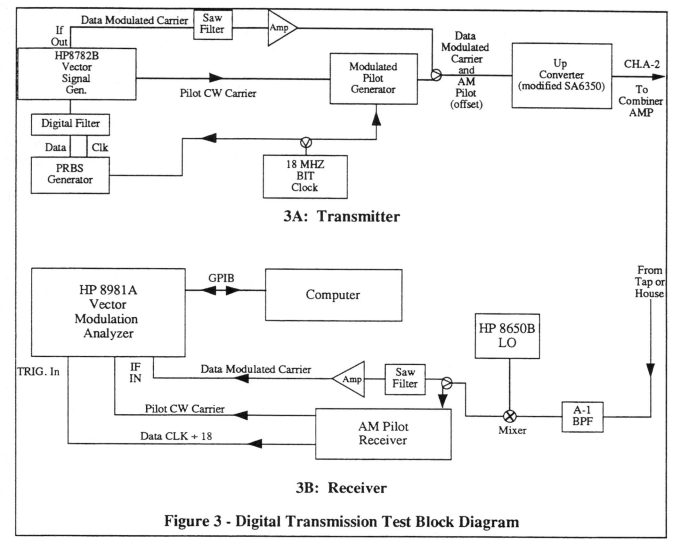

3A: Transmitter

3B: Receiver

Figure 3 - Digital Transmission Test Block Diagram

for a recovered carrier reference and symbol timing for vector demodulation and sampling of the I and Q modulated carrier phases. This unmodulated carrier reference should be phase locked precisely to the data modulated carrier IF frequency.

During the field tests, both 4 VSB and 16 QAM signals were generated to study the effect of cable impairments. The complete test setup for the field (and the lab without the carrier and symbol timing reference recovery portions) is shown in Figure 3. The generation of the I and Q baseband data streams were done in the headend in the same way as in the test bed facility using a pseudo-random binary sequence generator

(PRBS) and a digital filter. The digital filter generated the necessary Nyquist shaped, bandlimited data signals which drove the external inputs of an HP8782B Vector Signal Generator. The HP Vector Signal Generator generated both a coherent pilot CW carrier at the output frequency, and a data modulated carrier with the I and Q data.

At the receive site (which was kilometers away in the field test, but less than one meter in the lab test), a coherent pilot CW carrier reference was needed by the HP8981A Vector Modulation Analyzer to demodulate its received data carrier into baseband I and Q data streams. Additionally, the Vector Modulation Analyzer needed an external input data clock to accurately determine symbol timing. This presented a design problem to the recovery of the data over the cable TV plant because the coherent pilot reference occupies the same spectral space as the data modulated carrier.

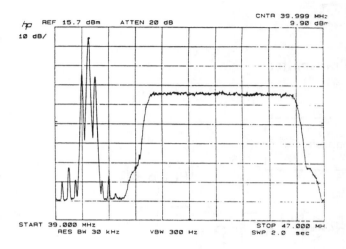

Figure 4 - Spectrum of Modulated Data Carrier and AM Pilot Tone

The solution implemented was not to build a modem, but to use an offset AM carrier pilot to achieve both carrier and data timing references. The AM pilot carrier was offset out of band from the modulated data carrier, and a 200 kHz AM modulation tone was put on the offset pilot. The AM pilot carrier was now 1 MHz below the 41-47 MHz IF band used by the modulated data carrier. Figure 4 shows the spectrum of the data modulated carrier and the offset AM modulated pilot tone.

The 200 kHz tone was used in the AM Pilot Receiver to both regenerate the carrier off-set, and provide a data clock to trigger the external trigger on the vector analyzer.

At RF the spectrum is inverted from IF. The Modulated Pilot Generator at the headend used the 18 MHz Bit Clock and the pilot CW carrier to generate the offset AM pilot, and it was summed with the data modulated carrier for an input to an upconverter. A Scientific Atlanta 6350 modulator with a frequency agile output converter (FAOC) was used for upconversion of the pilot plus modulated carrier. Normally, the phase noise of the agile upconverter would have been troublesome, but the offset carrier recovery scheme provided immunity to phase noise, as both the out of band AM pilot and modulated carrier undergo identical phase jitter in the conversion process.

It can be shown that any frequency offset in the RF local oscillator will be present in both the modulated IF data carrier and the recovered carrier reference. Hence carrier recovery without phase error is achieved at the remote measurement site, and all the measurements previously described for the laboratory testing may be done in the field.

At the receive site, the signal was amplified and put through a bandpass filter (BPF). Channel A-1 was used in the TCI Boulder, CO system. An HP8656B Signal Generator was used as a downconverter local oscillator (LO), and a double balanced mixer brought the data modulated carrier and the offset AM pilot to the IF frequency band. At IF, the signals were split and the data modulated carrier was bandpassed through a saw filter and presented to the input of the demodulator in the HP8981A Vector Modulation Analyzer. Off of the other split, the AM modulated carrier was put into the AM Pilot Receiver. The AM pilot receiver performed two tasks. The first was to recover an unmodulated carrier reference for demodulation, and the second was to provide a data clock that the Vector Modulation Analyzer could use for triggering, which provided the correct sampling times for the symbols.

The Transmitter and Receiver carrier and data clock reference circuitry was used for both

16 QAM and 4 VSB. With both transmission methods, the AM modulated pilot carrier remained at an IF frequency of 40 MHz. With 4 VSB, the regenerated carrier at 42 MHz was offset by 2 MHz from the 40 MHz AM carrier. In the 16 QAM case, the regenerated carrier at 44 MHz was offset by 4 MHz from the 40 MHz AM carrier. The same 41 to 47 MHz IF band was used for both VSB and QAM modulated data carriers.

Some mean square eye closure results from the field tests done on the TCI system in Boulder, CO are given in Table 2 for various tap and subscriber home locations. The signal received both at the tap and inside the house at the TV receiver input were measured. The mean square eye closure for several locations including

FIELD DATA		
FIELD LOCATION	QAM EYE CLOSURE %	VSB EYE CLOSURE %
TCI Headend	13.2	14
CableLabs Lab	14.2	15.7
House 1	32	34
Tap 1	16	17.9
House 2	16	(Note 1)
Tap 2	14.7	16.2
House 3	14.7	15.9
Tap 3	14.4	17.1
House 4	19.9	23.3
Tap 4	17.2	19
House 5	22.1	22.5
Tap 5	20.9	24.4
House 6	16	15.5
Tap 6	14.8	15.2
Field Fiber HUB	19.9	21.6
Lab Fiber + 12AMPS	16.1	16.2

Note 1: Equipment out of service

Table 2 - Field Results from the TCI System in Boulder, CO.

a fiber hub are shown. The large variability on the resulting impairment between location in the system and between the tap and the premises wiring in this small sample is significant. The variability of performance for digital modulation within the cable plant at the subscriber drop merit additional investigation.

Conclusion

It can be noted that rather small reflections causing intersymbol interference results in significant eye closure. This source of interference is most readily caused by cable reflections due to mismatches inside the house. This suggests that adaptive equalization may be required in many receive locations for a uniform level of reliable reception (suitably low error rate) at the lower signal levels that are nominally suggested (and used in this evaluation) for digital cable transmission.

The results obtained in both laboratory and field trials can be used to infer required modem performance in terms of the relative level of importance of the residual impairments at the receiver. A test of actual bit error rate requires the modem, as the carrier recovery, data, clock recovery, and symbol timing and synchronization information (and resulting equipment implementation losses) are needed to recover and evaluate the continuous baseband data stream at the destination. However it is possible to estimate the error rate obtained using the raw data acquired in the present study. This is the subject of a future companion paper.

PRACTICAL IMPLEMENTATION OF A 43 MBIT/SEC. (8 BIT/HZ) DIGITAL MODEM FOR CABLE TELEVISION

Rich Citta, Ron Lee

Zenith Electronics Corporation

Glenview, IL. 60025

1. INTRODUCTION

The paper describes the main features of 16-VSB, a new digital modulation system for cable TV. One 6 MHz channel can carry 23 movie channels (each compressed to 1.5 Mbit/sec.) or 9 live video channels (compressed to 4 Mbit/sec.) or 2 Digital Spectrum-Compatible high definition channels. The results of a field test have shown ample signal-to-noise ratio for error-free operation of the digital signal an existing analog environment. The 16-VSB picture and audio are free of the effects of NTSC-caused composite triple beat (CTB) and 16-VSB does not contribute to CTB.

2. 16-VSB MODULATION METHOD

The modulation method for 16-VSB is based on the digital modulation used in the Digital Spectrum Compatible High Definition Television (DSC-HDTV) system which is 4-VSB [1], [2]. In 16-VSB, symbols of 16 discrete levels are suppressed-carrier vestigial-sideband amplitude modulated (SC-VSB-AM) in a 6 MHz channel. The suppressed carrier is located approximately 310 kHz above the lower channel edge. The 16-VSB channel occupancy in comparison to NTSC is shown in Figure 1.

An explanation of the system's bit capacity is as follows. The theoretical Nyquist rate for a 6 MHz channel is 12 gasymbols/second. This is an unobtainable maximum; 10.7 Megasymbols/second is possible in practice. To trans-

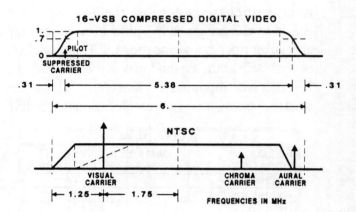

16-VSB AND NTSC CHANNEL OCCUPANCY

FIGURE 1

mit 43 Mbit/sec., each symbol must carry 43/10.7 = 4 bits. To carry 4 bits each symbol must have 16 different levels (2^4 = 16). In comparison, 4 level DSC-HDTV carries 21.5 Mbit/sec. at 2 bits/symbol. Expressed in bits/Hz, 16-VSB in a 6 MHz channel carries 43/6 = 7.17 bits/Hz while 4-VSB carries 3.58 bits/Hz. Using the customary maximum channel capacity, 16-VSB has 8 bits/Hz and 4-VSB has 4 bits/Hz.

The symbol shape is chosen to have a flat frequency spectrum in order to uniformly load the channel. This produces a minimum of composite triple beat. Any residual CTB is noise-like, rather than consisting of discrete components.

The 16-VSB signal includes a pilot carrier at the location of the suppressed carrier. The pilot is a significant aid in 16-VSB signal detection. Its contribution to CTB is negligible because of its low level. This is discussed in Section 5.3.

3. CARRIER-TO-NOISE (C/N) RATIOS AND SIGNAL-TO-NOISE (S/N RATIOS

3.1 NTSC

The analog NTSC RF signal power is defined at peak of sync. Even though the power of a given video signal varies all the time, the peak of NTSC sync power is constant.

The nominal cable TV channel bandwidth is 6 MHz; nevertheless, the cable TV C/N Ratio is defined for an RF bandwidth equal to the video bandwidth (= 4.2 MHz).

NTSC video power is defined for (constant) 100 IRE units of video.

It can be shown that the video S/N ratio of an ideal NTSC receiver is 6.8 dB less than the cable TV C/N ratio. (Factors contributing to this number are the level reduction of the carrier by a factor of two on the IF Nyquist slope and the reduction from peak of sync to video; these two combine to a 7.1 dB reduction in signal power. Single sideband AM detection of a portion of the RF noise reduces the noise by 0.3 dB. Overall, the S/N ratio is thus reduced by 7.1 - .3 = 6.8 dB, compared to the C/N ratio). In a non-ideal receiver the reduction can be greater than 6.8 dB.

3.2 16-VSB

The digital 16-VSB RF signal has no easily identifiable peak and the peak levels vary all the time. Therefore, the RF power is defined as the average power which is essentially constant when averaged over several frames.

Instantaneous RF signal peaks can constitute significantly greater power than average. A convenient way to provide a measure of the power at the peaks is by a distribution curve as in Figure 2. For example, Figure 2 shows that the average power is exceeded by not more than 6 dB for 0.6% of the time.

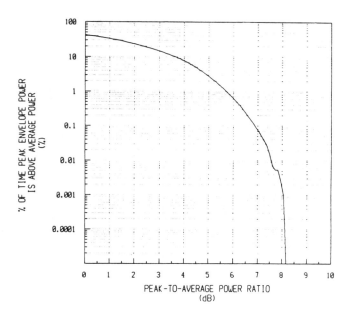

16-VSB PEAK-TO-AVERAGE POWER RATIO DISTRIBUTION

FIGURE 2

The pilot portion of the 16-VSB signal adds 0.4 dB to the data power.

RF noise power is defined for a 6 MHz bandwidth.

The 16-VSB detection process is considerably more efficient than NTSC detection, due to the suppressed carrier. RF signal power is only reduced by the 0.4 dB pilot power.

The noise bandwidth of the IF is 5.4 MHz. This reduces the noise power by .47 dB from 6 MHz RF to baseband.

Combining the above numbers shows that the digital 16-VSB baseband S/N ratio is .07 dB higher than the RF C/N ratio. Thus 16-VSB C/N ratio and S/N ratio are essentially equal.

In practice, with a non-ideal receiver, the S/N will be less than the C/N ratio; specifically tuner local oscillator phase noise may cause such a reduction.

3.3 Noise Impairment of Digital TV

The effect of noise on a digitally transmitted picture is quite different than on a picture that results from analog transmission.

A cable system that delivers an analog NTSC television signal with a C/N ratio of 40 dB (resulting in a video S/N ratio of not more than 40 - 6.8 = 33.2 dB) will provide an average picture. A higher C/N ratio will give less snow, a smaller C/N ratio results in more.

In contrast, a digitally delivered picture is snow-free (except for possible source noise) over a wide range of RF levels. If the RF level gets too low, the data detector produces uncorrected errors which result in "artifacts" in the picture, but it remains snow-free. At even lower RF levels, the picture is frozen and displayed as a previous error-free frame, still snow-free.

The 16-VSB system has built-in error protection so that incorrectly detected symbols not necessarily result in errors in the display or in the sound.

The previous reasoning shows that the S/N ratio is not a sufficient measure of the quality of the displays. The S/N ratio measure must be interpreted in terms of the probability of error or the error rate.

Probability of error as a function of baseband digital S/N ratio is shown in Figure 3. The two right-hand curves are for 16-VSB, the steep one for the error protected case; the curve that rolls off more gradually is for the unprotected case.

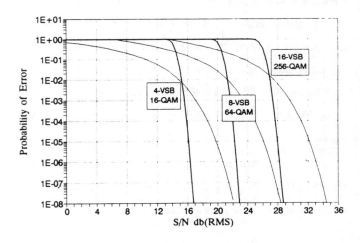

ERROR PRORABILITIES
OF VSB AND QUAM SYSTEMS

FIGURE 3

When the probability of error equals 10^{-6} or lower, visible artifacts occur so rarely that they go unnoticed. This requires a protected S/N ratio of 28 dB. The non-ideal receiver used in the field test, described in Section 4.2, required approximately 30 dB C/N ratio for visually artifact-free operation.

3.4 QAM Systems

Another modulation method proposed for data symbol transmission is QAM (Quadrature Amplitude Modulation) Compared to VSB systems, QAM systems have two separate symbol streams at half the VSB rate, each stream modulating one of two carriers in quadrature. Quadrature modulation only works with double sideband modulation (SC-DSB-AM). For a given number of levels per symbol and for a given channel bandwidth, VSB and QAM have the same data capacity: QAM has two channels in quadrature versus only a single channel for VSB but each QAM channel has only half the modulation bandwidth of VSB.

Figure 3 shows the equivalence of some representative systems (x-VSB and x^2-QAM).

3.4.1 64-QAM

This modulation scheme has 6 bits/Hz data capacity. Thus, it can only accommodate 6/8 x 43 = 32 Mbit/sec., assuming proportional overhead for error protection. Compared to 16-VSB, a trade-off is at work: 16-VSB has 33% greater data capacity while 64-QAM needs 6 dB less S/N ratio for the same error probability. This trade-off is evaluated at the end of Section 3.5.

3.4.2 256-QAM

This modulation scheme has a data capacity identical to 16-VSB and it needs the same S/N ratio as shown in Figure 3. However, when considering the practical implementation of the systems, 16-VSB has a significant advantage.

the carrier for channel tuning instead of a pilot carrier. This means that during noise bursts or ghosting when data detection fails, carrier and data synchronization signals also fail. These circuits have to re-acquire when the noise burst or ghost ends and this typically takes time. As will be shown in some detail in Section 4.2, the pilot carrier of a VSB system makes it possible to retain carrier synchronization and sync operation even during noise bursts and ghosts.

Frequent noise bursts are not typical for cable TV operation but are very important for terrestrial broadcasts. (It may be assumed that at some time in the future the receiver will be used for both cable and terrestrial reception.)

As will be described in Section 4.2.1 below, an essential part of a digital TV receiver is the Channel Equalizer, the principal function of which is ghost cancellation. QAM channel equalization not only requires equalizer sections in the I channel and the Q channel but also cross-coupled sections between I and Q, four equalizers in total. 16-VSB channel equalization requires just one equalizer.

3.5   16-VSB RF Signal Levels on Cable

In a cable system that carries both NTSC and 16-VSB channels it is important to have a basis of comparison of signal power. NTSC systems are characterized by a minimum C/N ratio of 40 dB (after 6/1/93). If it is assumed for a moment that the signal level is 0 dBm, then the noise level is -40 dBm which is in 4.2 MHz. The noise level over the wider bandwidth of 6 MHz is then -38.5 dBm. If 16-VSB requires 30 dB C/N ratio, the RF signal level must be at least -38.5 + 30 = -8.5 dBm which is 8.5 dB lower than the NTSC signal level.

If the average 16-VSB level equals -8.5 dBm, the peaks do not reach 0 dBm (the NTSC level) as can be derived from Figure 2. Increasing the 16-VSB level to - 6dBm, the NTSC level is exceeded still only 0.6% of the time, a negligeable percentage. The 16-VSB C/N ratio is now 32.5 dB.

A cable system with 45 dB NTSC C/N ratio increases the

Comparing 16-VSB operation under these conditions with 64-QAM shows that the extra 6 dB S/N ratio available when operating 64-QAM is not needed. The loss in data capacity is thus not warranted.

4. 16-VSB EXPERIMENTAL EQUIPMENT

4.1   Transmitter

The 16-VSB transmitter bit capacity is 43 Mbit/sec., twice the 4-VSB capacity, as mentioned. A 16-VSB Multiplexer/Formatter/Modulator unit is fed by two 21.5 Mbit/sec., compressed DSC-HDTV sources on D3 tape via Interface Equipment. The Modulator IF output feeds a Cable Channel Converter. The set-up is shown in Figure 4.

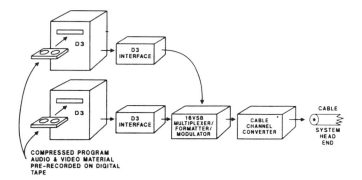

16-VSB CABLE FIELD TEST HEAD-END

FIGURE 4

4.2   Receiver

The receiver front-end is fed by the cable. The tuner is of the dual-conversion type; the first conversion stage is an upconverter. [1, Section 6.3] The local carrier is generated in a Frequency/Phase Locked Loop (FPLL) circuit [3], controlled by the pilot carrier. The phase-locked loop part of the FPLL has a bandwidth under 10 kHz. As a result, channel tuning can be accomplished with even a negative C/N ratio. A simplified block diagram of the receiver is shown in Figure 5.

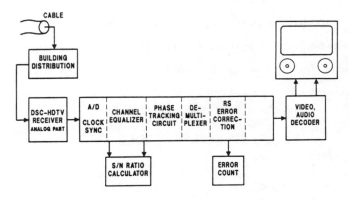

16-VSB CABLE FIELD TEST RECEIVER

FIGURE 5

After channel tuning, data segment sync detection takes place. This can also be accomplished with low C/N ratio when proper data detection is not yet possible. AGC (Automatic Gain Control) is not required for sync detection due to the repetitive nature of the sync.

Next, the data clock is synchronized and proper AGC is set. The data slicers can now function properly and field sync can be detected.

The field sync signal consists of a constant pseudo-random symbol sequence of 63 microseconds duration. Synchronization is established by comparing the received sequence to the nominal reference sequence stored in receiver memory. The receiver sequence is also used to adjust the Channel Equalizer, described in the next Section 4.2.1. The principal function of the Channel Equalizer is ghost elimination.

The receiver is now able to properly detect data but an extra margin is provided by a phase-tracking circuit, described in Section 4.2.2. This circuit counteracts the phase noise which originates in the tuner's first local oscillator.

The detected data stream is separated into the two original data sets; this takes place in the Demultiplexer. Either of the two sets can be selected for further processing. This includes error correction and deformatting. The Reed-Solomon (RS) error-correcting code used in the system is RS (167,147) t = 10. The receiver chip for the code allows the read-out of byte-error count. Deformatting achieves separa-

tion of the error corrected data stream into video, audio and ancillary signals.

The Video Decoder restores the original analog signal for display and the Audio Decoder restores the audio.

4.2.1 Channel Equalization

As described in the previous Section 4.2, channel equalization takes place following field sync detection and synchronization. The difference between the detected field sync and the reference field sync is used to adjust the taps of the automatic channel equalizer circuit.

The equalizer corrects primarily ghosts and micro-reflections but also distortions in the transmitter at the head-end and in the receiver front-end.

Included in the equalizer is a computer circuit that uses the difference between detected and reference sequence to calculate signal-to-noise (S/N) ratio. This can be done before and after equalization. The equipment thus allows evaluation of both S/N ratio and byte-error count prior to and therefore independent of video decoding and display.

4.2.2 Phase Noise Tracking

The data capacity of the 16-VSB system, 43 Mbit/sec., is close to the Nyquist rate of 48 Mbit/sec. for an 8 bit/Hz, 6 MHz channel. A consequence of the high data efficiency is narrow "eyes". ("Eye" height and eye width are a measure of detection margin.) Phase noise in the data signal acts as timing jitter which narrows the eye. A limit to this disturbance is achieved by a phase tracking circuit. This circuit significantly reduces the narrowing of the eye.

Phase disturbances in the data signal are principally due to phase noise of the first l.o. in the tuner and to hum frequency modulation and microphonics of the l.o. These disturbances are conveniently measured through substitution of the l.o. by an external oscillator that has inherent phase noise of at least an order of magnitude less than the level to be measured. The external oscillator is FM modulated by an

314

external noise source or by 120 Hz. The modulated l.o. spectrum is recorded. Two cases are compared; in the first case the modulation is applied with phase tracking and in the second case without phase tracking. In each case the modulation level is adjusted until the error counter registers just a few errors/second.

First the external l.o. is FM modulated by noise. As expected, much more noise modulation can be tolerated with phase tracking than without it. This is shown by comparing Figure 6 (with) and Figure 7 (without). The phase noise level in 1 Hz bandwidth at a distance of 20 kHz from the carrier is recorded in the top right-hand corner of Figures 6 and 7. With phase tracking, almost 20 dB more noise can be tolerated than without (-51.70 dB versus -71.20 dB).

To measure spurious hum and microphonics, the external l.o. is modulated by 120 Hz. Without phase tracking, the carrier can only be deviated by less than 500 Hz for 0 to 1 error/second. With phase tracking, the deviation can be increased to approximately 3 kHz, an improvement of more than 16 dB. The l.o. spectrum with phase tracking is shown in Figure 8.

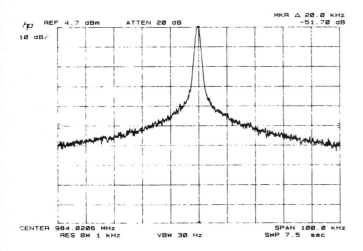

16-VSB TUNER L.O. SPECTRUM
WHITE NOISE FM, 0-2 ERRORS/SEC.
WITH PHASE TRACKING

FIGURE 6

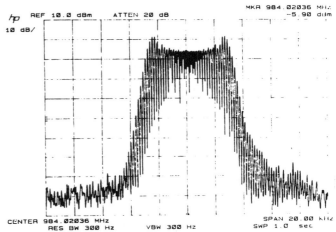

16-VSB TUNER L.O. SPECTRUM
120 HZ FM, 0-1 ERROR/SEC.
WITH PHASE TRACKING

FIGURE 8

4.3 Composite Triple Beat

The 16-VSB signal does not contribute to CTB but CTB due to the NTSC channels can act as interference during 16-VSB detection. The digital system reacts to CTB in the same way as it reacts to thermal noise. CTB is either totally absent from the picture (and audio) or it causes artifacts and may eventually cause a freeze. As a result the signal-to-CTB ratio can approach the S/N ratio (within approximately 3 dB) and still be totally ignored.

Under normal operating conditions in the cable system, CTB can be assumed to be at a lower level than thermal

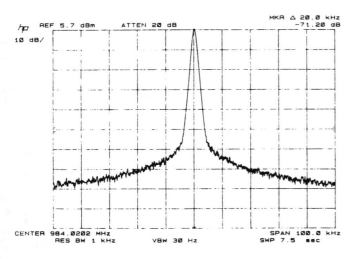

16-VSB TUNER L.O. SPECTRUM
WHITE NOISE FM, 0-2 ERRORS/SEC.
WITHOUT PHASE TRACKING

FIGURE 7

noise. This remains the case if the reference is shifted from the NTSC RF signal level to the 16-VSB RF signal level. Thus, CTB is generally not a problem.

5. 16-VSB FIELD TEST

5.1 Conditions

The 16-VSB experimental equipment was tested on the Washington, D.C. cable system "District CableVision" during the first week of February 1993. Transmitter equipment was placed at the system's head-end; receiver equipment at a location fed by a cable system section that had 11 trunk amplifiers and a building distribution system in cascade.

The cable system has a full complement of TV channels. The FM band is occupied by digital audio channels. The channel assigned for the 16-VSB test was channel A-2 (108-114 MHz). Channel A-1, upper adjacent to A-2, was in operation as well as all higher channels. Immediately below A-2 was the FM band with the digital audio channels. The low VHF channels completed the full channel system.

The 16-VSB head-end equipment is shown schematically in Figure 4. The Cable Channel Converter was set for Channel A-2.

The equipment at the receiver site is shown schematically in the simplified block diagram of Figure 5. The cable fed an existing distribution system in the building in which the receiver was located. The 16-VSB DSC-HDTV experimental receiver was connected to one of the outlets on the tenth floor.

During the demonstrations of early February 1993, the two available digital HDTV programs (video and audio) were sequentially error-free displayed and enjoyed by hundreds of guests.

5.2 Initial Problems

After setting up the equipment, the levels were adjusted and verified but no satisfactory operation could be obtained: the error rate was too high.

First, it was discovered that the receiver was fed from an unmatched tap. Feeding from a matched tap changed the received spectrum to its normal flat shape from one with a significant broad dip, apparently caused by the unmatched tap. The error rate, however, remained far too high.

Investigating with the spectrum analyzer showed strong CTB. Finally, an overloaded amplifier was found at the head of the building distribution. Padding its input cured the CTB and restored proper functioning of the 16-VSB. The nominal 16-VSB level was set at -12 dB with respect to NTSC sync level.

5.3 Nominal Measurements

The received A-2 channel spectrum is shown in the center of Figure 9 with the upper adjacent picture carrier and the lower adjacent digital sound channel off on the sides.

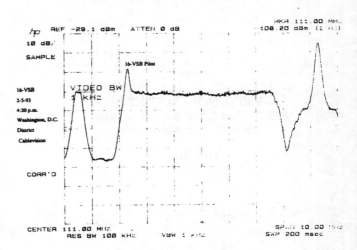

16-VSB RECEIVED SPECTRUM (10 MHZ SPAN)

FIGURE 9

The pilot at the left side of the 16-VSB channel appears to be much stronger than the data but this is misleading. The spectrum analyzer was adjusted for 100 kHz RF bandwidth, displaying the pilot at full strength but strongly attenuating the noise-like data signal. In 6 MHz bandwidth, the data symbols are on the average 10 dB higher than the pilot as is the case in the time domain.

Figure 10 shows more surrounding channels on a 50

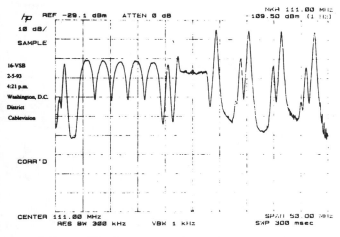

16-VSB RECEIVED SPECTRUM (50 MHZ SPAN)

FIGURE 10

MHz span; the 16-VSB channel is in the middle of the plot.

Figure 11 shows data S/N ratios for a 12 hour period as measured and subsequently computed from errors before and after the channel equalizer. Note the 31-32 dB before equalization and the improvement to approximately 35 dB after equalization.

The resulting sampled error count after correction is shown in Figure 12. The two high counts towards the end of a 12 hour period correlate with the S/N ratio loss in Figure 11. Their origin is unknown but they appear to be transient.

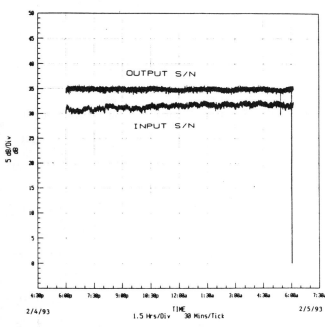

MEASURED S/N RATIO

FIGURE 11

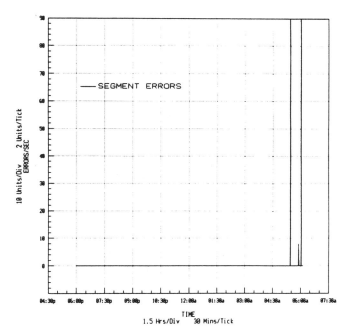

ERROR COUNT AFTER EQUALIZATION

FIGURE 12

5.4 Microreflections and Ghosts

It was of particular interest to test the channel equalizer's capability to cancel reflections and ghosts.

Figure 13 shows the received 16-VSB RF spectrum when a 25 percent (-12 dB) ghost, 1.3 microsecond delayed, was locally added in-phase to the primary signal. (It obviously could not be added to the whole cable system.) Note that the ripples in the spectrum are approximately 6 dB peak-to-peak as expected from paired-echo theory. Note also that 25 percent constitutes four of the 16 RF signal levels and that noise or interference exceeding even one of these levels, if uncorrected, is sufficient to cause errors in detection. This is illustrated in Figure 14 where the lower line represents the S/N ratio at the input of the equalizer which reads between 12 and 13 dB, far below the minimum required 30 dB. At the output of the equalizer the S/N ratio consistently reads 33 dB.

The sampled error count after correction for the ghosted situation is shown in Figure 15. The few errors measured in a six hour period correlate with the slight S/N ratio loss shown in Figure 14. The errors are transient and now so

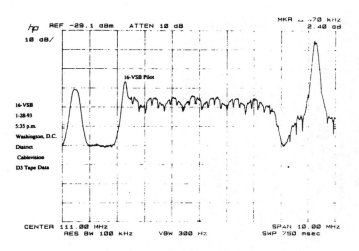

16-VSB RECEIVED SPECTRUM
INCLUDING -12 DB IN-PHASE GHOST

FIGURE 13

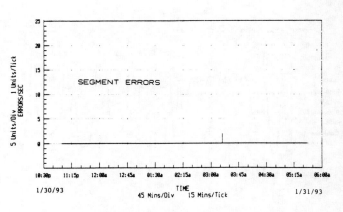

GHOSTED ERROR COUNT
AFTER EQUALIZATION

FIGURE 15

minor that they hardly would have been noticed in the dis-played picture nor in the reproduced sound.

6. SUMMARY

A new high data capacity digital modulation method for Cable TV is described. The signal-to-noise ratio in the system is ample for error-free 16-VSB operation, and existing composite triple beat interference is not a problem. The 16-VSB RF signal is injected on the cable system at significantly lower levels than NTSC signals which makes it possible to add digital channels at the high frequency end of the system. 16-VSB does not contribute to composite triple beat inter-ference.

7. REFERENCES

[1]   "Digital Spectrum-Compatible High Definition Tele-vision: Technical Details", Monograph published by Zenith Electronics Corporation and AT&T, September 23, 1991.

[2]   "The Digital Spectrum-Compatible HDTV Transmis-sion System" by R. Citta, P. Fockens, R. Lee, J. Rypkema, IEEE Transactions on Consumer Electron-ics, Volume 37, No. 3, August 1991, pp. 469-475.

[3]   "Frequency and Phase Lock Loop" by R. Citta, IEEE Transactions on Consumer Electronics, Volume CE 23, No. 3, August 1977, pp. 358-365.

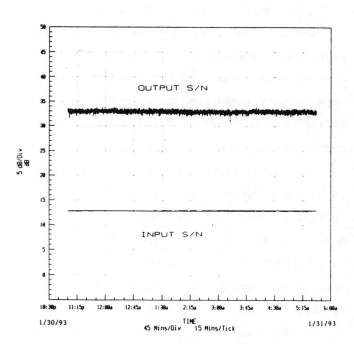

MEASURED S/N RATIO
INCLUDING -12 DB IN-PHASE GHOST

FIGURE 14

A DIGITAL COMPRESSED VIDEO TRANSMISSION SYSTEM
- WITH SIMULATION RESULTS OF ECHOES IN 64-QAM TRANSMISSION

Jeff Hamilton, Zheng Huang, and Dan Sutorius
Jerrold Communications

Abstract

Digital compressed transmission is developing as an attractive method of video delivery to both headends and subscribers. This paper will review compression and transmission, and then focus on some key performance parameters for digital transmission. Finally we present the results of computer simulations of the effect of echoes on 64-QAM digital transmission.

Introduction

The US space program, through a multitude of outstanding examples, made the creation of spin-off technologies famous. Digital compression for Cable was born as just such a spin off, not from NASA, but from the desire to deliver high definition TV to consumers. The need to squeeze a high bandwidth HDTV signal into existing 6 MHz TV channel bands created the means to deliver several standard NTSC programs in the spectrum currently occupied by just one.

Various methods of transmitting HDTV signals have been proposed to the FCC. Of the six advanced TV systems under review four propose digital transmission. Each of these digital HDTV proponents has also proposed a multichannel NTSC delivery system in response to the CableLabs compression request for proposal.

Compression

Since the landmark announcement of the DigiCipher system in 1990, several other digital video compression systems have been proposed. Most of these, including all of the digital HDTV proponent systems and the work of the International Standards Organization's MPEG[1] committee, have been similar in function, based on the discrete cosine transform (DCT) and motion compensated inter-frame processing. This has proved to be an efficient technique for removing the many redundancies and, as needed, lower value components, from the video signal, with a minimum perceived effect on the reconstructed picture.

The use of digital compression offers operators and subscribers much more than just an increased number of programs. Digital transmission means every subscriber will get the same very high quality picture. It will be free of the noise and distortion common in analog systems. Most digital compression systems use component, not composite, color. With these systems there will be, for the first time a means of delivering a true component signal to the S-Video jack on high end consumer TV's and VCR's. Sound quality will also be uniformly excellent, indistinguishable from compact disc. True digital encryption will provide a level of security never before possible for video on Cable. Programming these new digital channels will become easier and more reliable with the introduction of digital switchers and digital compressed storage at the headend.

With satellite delivered digital compressed programs passing through to digital transmission on the Cable plant, the operator will no longer need to worry about picture quality anywhere in his operation. Headend processing to realize this, ranges from changing only the modulation, which offers very limited local features, to full video decompression and recompression, which allows all the control and programming options the operator now has with analog video.

The advantages of digital media have been realized by the telephone industry. They are arriving in TV network studios now, and they will soon offer major benefits to Cable operators system-wide.

Transmission

For analog video transmission, different forms of modulation are required on satellite and Cable. The satellite channel has a bandwidth of at least 24 MHz, but a reliable carrier to noise ratio (C/N) of only about 8dB. The Cable channel has only a 6 MHz bandwidth but typically 40 dB or more C/N. To make effective use of these very different transmission paths, we use a unique form of modulation in each. Frequency modulation (FM), a wide band noise insensitive technique, is carried on satellite. Amplitude modulation (AM), a noise sensitive but bandwidth efficient approach is appropriate for Cable.

For digital transmission of video the same logic applies. Satellite systems use quadrature phase shift keying (QPSK) which is an FM-like modulation for digital carriers. QPSK requires a wide bandwidth channel but offers high immunity to noise. For Cable, two AM techniques are proposed for digital carriers: double side band quadrature amplitude modulation (QAM), and the vestigial sideband multi-amplitude technique often called 4-VSB. These two approaches to amplitude modulation are very similar in performance. Both trade off noise immunity for spectral efficiency relative to QPSK. The following work addresses QAM with 6 bits per symbol.

To compare the data capacity of the disparate satellite and Cable channels we turn to Claude Shannon's pioneering work in information theory[2]. He developed a formula for calculating the maximum theoretical capacity of a channel based on bandwidth and S/N alone. For a signal of power S transmitted over a channel with noise power N and bandwidth W, the channel capacity C in bits per second is:

$$C = W \log_2\left(1 + S/N\right).$$

A satellite channel with 24 MHz bandwidth and 8 dB optimum signalling S/N would have a Shannon limit of 69 million bits per second (Mbps). Of course, this is for an ideal modem, operating in a channel free of secondary impairments. Commercial satellite modems commonly approach about one half this theoretical maximum rate.

A Cable channel with 6 MHz bandwidth and 35 dB optimum signalling S/N has almost the same Shannon limit as the above satellite channel: 70 Mbps. The Cable channel may have more secondary impairments and certainly the tolerable modem cost is much lower, but it is clear the Cable channel has a data transmission capacity similar to that of satellite.

Transmission Analysis

In designing a new digital communications system many factors must be considered. Among these are a wide variety of channel impairments, many of which will occur simultaneously in a working system. It is the combined effects of these impairments that define the transmission system operating parameters.

For the traditional Cable environment there are three principle impairments to the transmission of digital QAM carriers: channel noise, echoes, and modem implementation loss. Although there are many other impairments they are expected to be either avoidable, like not running high-level sweeps through active digital spectrum, or of lesser significance to digital transmission, like CTB and CSO.

Many prior papers have defined the effect of the primarily white channel noise on QAM. The following analysis will briefly discuss the specification of digital C/N in the Cable plant. We will then detail the results of our simulations

of echoes on QAM transmission in the presence of white noise. Modem implementation loss, the third major factor, will be significant due to the severe cost constraints on the subscriber terminal for Cable applications. It includes such factors as filter imprecision, phase noise, receiver noise figure, clock jitter, and computation error. These factors are hardware specific and beyond the scope of this paper.

The block diagram for the following simulations is shown in Figure 1. It consists of a random data source, 64-QAM modulator, 5 MHz Nyquist bandwidth (BW) transmit filter, white noise and recursive echo sources, a matched receive filter, 64-QAM demod, and an error counter. All blocks are ideal floating point simulation models. Figures 2 and 3 show the eye-diagram and constellation with the noise and echo sources set to zero amplitude.

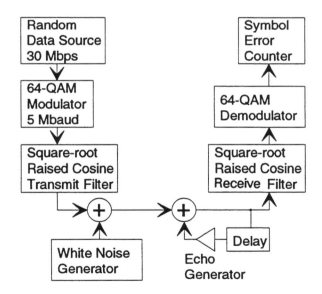

Figure 1: Simulation Block Diagram

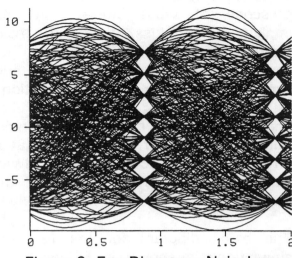

Figure 2: Eye Diagram - Noiseless

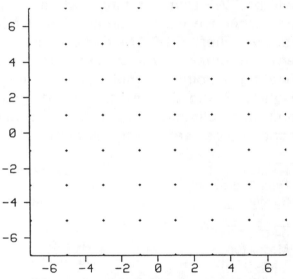

Figure 3: 64-QAM Constellation

Noise
Channel noise is the familiar broadband white noise floor we now measure as C/N on the Cable distribution plant. Easily seen with a spectrum analyzer, it comes primarily from the active devices in the distribution plant: trunk amps, line extenders, AML, and fiber links. Digital carrier to noise as referred to in the literature and this paper, is average modulated digital carrier power divided by rms noise power in the modulation bandwidth. Digital carrier modulation bandwidth will be about 5 MHz. This contrasts with our standard analog C/N spec. We measure analog carrier power during sync tip peak level and divide by noise power in the 4 MHz video bandwidth.

To relate these different C/N measures, consider that average modulated analog carrier power depends on picture content. Indeed, this is why it's impractical to measure average power on a modulated analog carrier. The peak to average ratio ranges from 7 dB to 2 dB for 0 to 100 IRE pictures respectively. A long time average of all possible picture contents will eventually yield a peak to average ratio near that for a 50 IRE flat field: 5dB. From this we can say that a digital carrier with the same average power as an analog carrier will have a 6 dB lower measured C/N. Five dB for the peak vs. average power measurement method and 1 dB for the 4 vs 5 MHz noise bandwidth.

Figure 4 shows symbol error rate as a function of (average modulated) digital carrier to noise. Simulation results are shown to be close to calculated theoretical values. Symbol error rate (SER) is very close to bit error rate (BER) when error rates are low ($< 10^{-2}$). Figures 5 and 6 show the effects of -24 dB white noise on the eye-diagram and constellation.

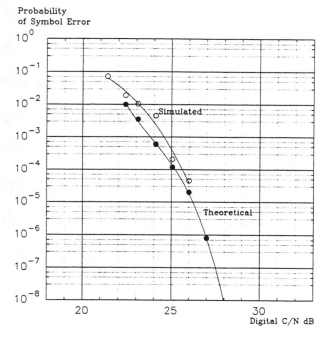

Fig.4: Error Performance
of 64 QAM with White Noise

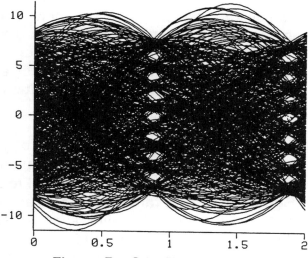

Figure 5: 24 dB Digital C/N

Echoes

There are many sources of echoes in the traditional Cable plant. Most of these are the result of imperfect impedance matching at the myriad connection points along the RF distribution path. At each of these points a

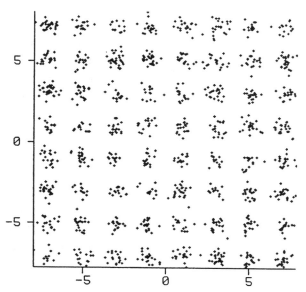

Figure 6: 24 dB digital C/N

small amount of the downstream RF power reflects back to its source. The example in figure 7 shows the reflection through the 8 dB return loss of a digital receiver input. Reflected power returns to the next upstream device, delayed and attenuated by its double pass through the connecting coax. A fraction of this returning power then reflects again through a second return loss. The twice reflected signal is now a downstream echo with a delay and power relative to the primary signal.

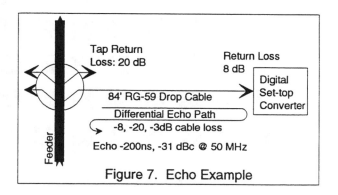

Figure 7. Echo Example

The simulation model for echo generation is a recursive structure as shown in

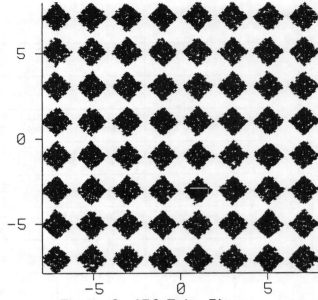

Figure 9: 45° Echo Phase

Figure 1. This is appropriate as the echo is by nature a repeating effect. A -20 dB 200ns delayed impulse will be followed by impulses at -40 dB 400ns, -60 dB 600ns, ..., as the twice reflected signal continues to be reflected four, six, ..., times with diminishing amplitude.

Echoes will have a specific phase relative to the primary signal carrier, determined by their exact delay in carrier cycles. A 200ns echo on a 50 MHz carrier will have a 0 degree phase because the delay is exactly 10 cycles of carrier. The constellation of a signal with this echo is shown in Figure 8. A 205ns echo on a 50 MHz carrier will have a 45 degree phase as shown in Figure 9. In this example, the difference would be an 86 versus 88 foot run of coax between the reflecting devices.

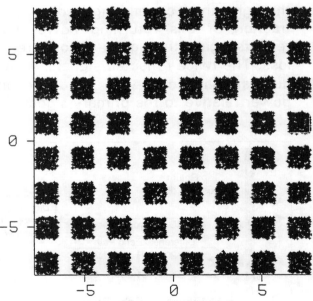

Figure 8: 0° Echo Phase

The effect of phase on QAM transmission in the presence of other impairments is shown in figure 10. We used white noise at -30dBc to model the combined effect of all non-echo impairments for this example. The phase of echo has a 1 to 2 dB effect on sensitivity, with the maximum effect at 45 degrees. All following simulations assume a 45 degree echo phase.

Figure 11 shows the effects of a range of echo powers on QAM with three different levels of white noise. From Figure 4, the SER for -25 dB noise alone is 10^{-4}. At this noise level even a -37 dB echo increases the SER substantially, to 10^{-3}. With white noise in the range of -27 dB echoes of -30 dB are still significant. As used here 'white noise' includes all of the non-echo transmission impairments including: channel noise, implementation loss, and secondary transmission impairments. For the sum of these in the range of -25 to -30 dB, even very low level echoes will be significant.

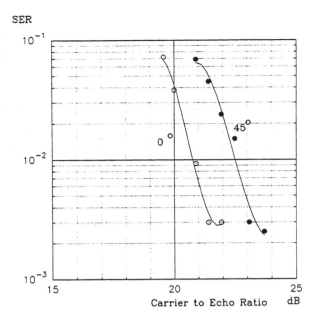

Fig. 10: Effect of Echo Phase

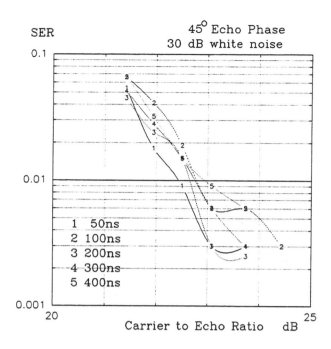

Fig. 12: Effect of Delay on Echo Sensitivety

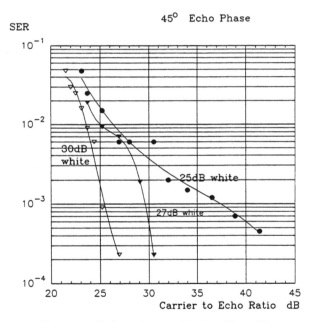

Fig.11: Echo Sensativity For Three Level of Added White Noise

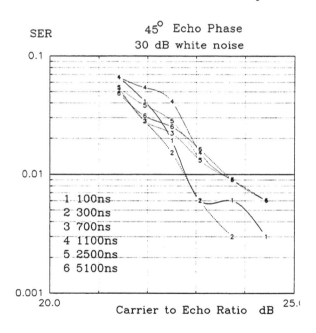

Fig.13: Effect of Delay on Echo Sensitivity

Figures **12** and **13** show the results of simulations over a range of echo powers for several different delays. All include white noise of -30 dB. The echo

power is far more significant to SER than the delay. The effect on SER is almost unchanged over the range of delays. Even the short delays of 50ns and 100ns, one quarter and one half the 200ns symbol period, have the same general level of impairment as the longer echoes.

Conclusion

Digital compressed transmission will offer substantial benefits to the Cable operator and subscriber. Data rates similar to those of satellite systems are feasible using unique modulation, and demodulation, optimized for the Cable environment. These new digital carriers will require a new C/N measurement specification.

Digital transmission of 64-QAM will be sensitive to echoes at very low power. For a sum of other impairments equivalent to white noise of -30dBc or above, even echoes below -30dBc, will be significant.

---

[1] Motion Picture Expert Group (MPEG)
[2] Shannon, Claude E., a series of papers including "A Mathmatical Theory of Communications," Bell System Technical Journal, volume 27, pages 379-423, July 1948.

MODULATION AND CODING TECHNIQUES FOR HIGH CAPACITY COAXIAL CABLE AND SCM FIBER DIGITAL TV-HDTV DISTRIBUTION

DR. KAMILO FEHER

Director, Consulting Group, DIGCOM, Inc.
Professor, Department of Electrical and Computer Engineering
University of California, Davis, CA 95616
Tel. 916-752-8127, 916-753-1788; Fax 916-752-8424

ABSTRACT

New emerging digital modulation-demodulation (modem) and coding techniques suitable for spectrally and power efficient digital TV and HDTV distribution systems over coaxial cable and subcarrier multiplexed (SCM) fiber optics systems are described. Efficient and robust modulators/demodulators (modems) combined with low redundancy forward error correction (FEC) - integrated circuits attain a spectral efficiency in the 2 b/s/Hz to 7 b/s/Hz range and a bit error rate (BER) in the 10^{-7} to 10^{-10} range. Recently developed VLSI-ASIC chips, having a universal QPSK-QAM-QPRS modem architecture combined with FEC-chips, operating up to 100 Mb/s, with a 3% to 10% redundancy will enable the transmission of 30 Mb/s rate (or even higher bit rate) digitized TV signals in one conventional analog TV band.

Requirements for FDM shared analog and digitized TV distribution systems are highlighted. The performance of a new class of QPRS filtered modems invented by the author is compared to conventional QPRS and QAM-8-PSK cable systems. The performance advantages of our new class of "above Nyquist rate" modems and of an operational SQPRS (staggered) QPRS system developed by Digital Radio Laboratories are highlighted.

1. MODEM AND CODED MODEM ARCHITECTURES FOR DIGITAL CABLE TELEVISION AND SCM FIBER OPTICS DISTRIBUTION

Numerous modulation/demodulation (modem) architectures have been implemented and considered for digital cable TV and subcarrier multiplexed (SCM) fiber optics digital TV distribution systems. From simple QPSK, 8-PSK to more advanced coded 64-QAM and even 1024-QAM cable systems have been designed and studied.

In general, the purpose of increasing the number of modulation states is to increase the spectral efficiency expressed in terms of b/s/Hz. For example, a theoretical QPSK system could transmit 12 Mb/s while a 16-QAM system 24 Mb/s in a 6 MHz wide video channel. The theoretical spectral efficiency and BER = f(C/N) performance of ideal coherent a = 0 filtered (raised-cosine-Nyquist filtered with a roll-off parameter of a = 0) uncoded modems is illustrated in Figure 3 and 4. The practical spectral efficiency is typically 5% to 50% below the theoretical values of QAM systems and is 4% to 30% above the "theoretical ISI-free" values for QPRS systems [1; 6; 11; 12; 13]. Steep filters, having an a = 0.1 to a = 0.2 and 60 dB out-of-band rejection have been used in several modem designs [1; 2] in order to approach the theoretical spectral efficiency limit of QAM, within 5%.

For example, in the **DigiCipher** radio broadcast system [J.A. Kraus, 18] trellis coded and Reed-Solomon FEC coded 16-QAM and 32-QAM a 19.51 Mb/s and a 24.39 Mb/s rate modulated signal is transmitted in bandwidth of 6 MHz. This corresponds to a 19.51 Mb/s: 6 MHz = 3.25 b/s/Hz (as compared to a theoretical uncoded of 4 b/s/Hz for a = 0, 16-QAM system.

For the DSC-HDTV (Digital Spectrum-Compatible High-Definition Television) system of **Zenith** [Luplow & Fockens, 8], the transmission of 11.1 Mb/s and of 21.0 Mb/s data (representing the digitized video, audio, ancillary data and error protection bits) 2-level VSB and 4-level VSB pilot aided methods are described [8]. The symbol rate is 10.76 M Symbols/second.

For the **ATVA-Progressive System**, a 19.43 Mb/s rate, 16-QAM system is described for the 6 MHz wide video channel [10].

For relatively lower data rate cable systems (1.544 Mb/s to 2.048 Mb/s) and hybrid FDM, analog video and digital data cable systems, more spectrally efficient modems have been implemented by our design teams including 256-

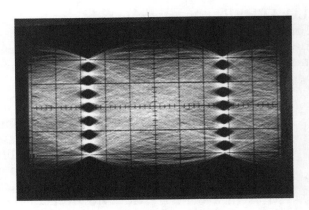

Fig. 1 Experimental 45M b/s coherently demodulated I-channel of a 64-QAM system with a = 0.1 filtering [1 and 2].

Fig. 2 Measured constellation of a 1024-QAM subsystem [1 and 2].

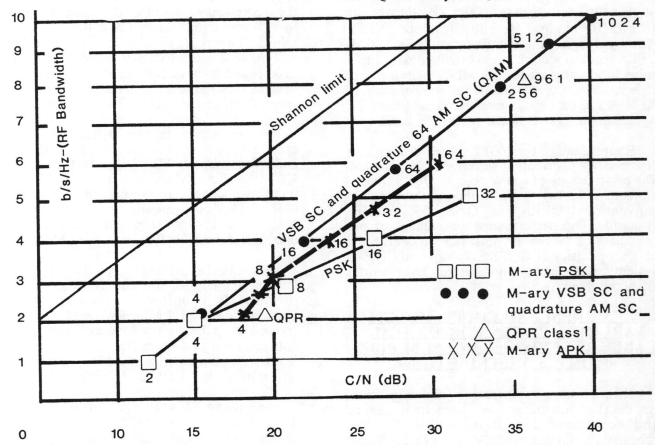

Fig. 3 Theoretical bit rate efficiency of uncoded-modulated coherent systems as a function of the available C/N at P(e) = 10^{-8}. The average C/N is specified in the double-sided Nyquist bandwidth which equals the symbol rate. Ideal a = 0 filtering has been assumed. Shannon limit is for coded-modulated systems [1 - 5].

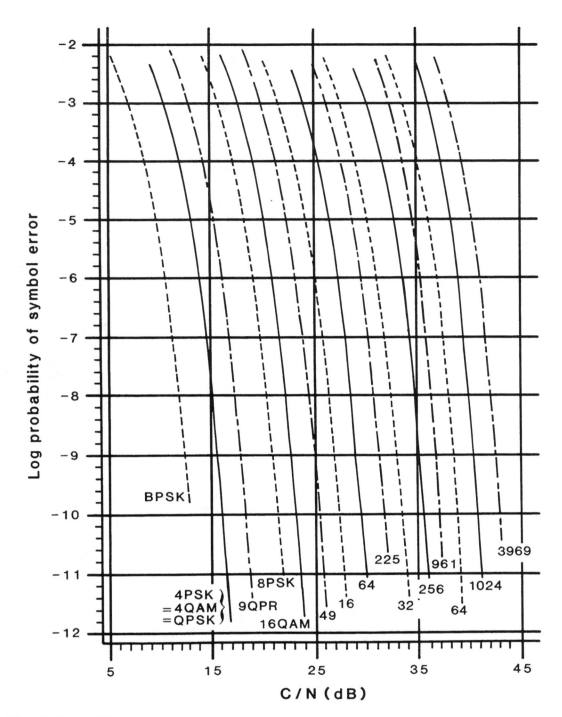

Fig. 4 Probability of error-theoretical performance curves of M-ary PSK, M-ary QAM and M-ary QPR modulation systems vs. the carrier-to-thermal noise ratio in dB. White Gaussian noise channel only - no phase noise. Double-sided Nyquist RF bandwidth equals the symbol rate bandwidth [1 - 5].

QAM modems which achieve a practical spectral efficiency of 6.66 b/s/Hz specified at the 60 dB out-of-band attenuation point [1; 2; 14]. A practical block and implementation diagram of an FEC-coded 256-QAM modem (could be extended to 1024-QAM) modem is illustrated in Figure 5. Even though our modem designs incorporate advanced baseband adaptive time equalizers (BATE) (fully digital), we found that the residual group delay, i.e., group delay and/or echo not equalized by the BATE and IF adaptive equalizer could significantly degrade the performance, as illustrated in Figure 6. We also found that by "staggering" or "offsetting" the 256-QAM or 1024-QAM systems, for short S-QAM we could reduce the sensitivity of the cable system to residual imperfections, see Figures 5 and 6. Experimental field data of one of our (2196, 2136)-BCH-FEC coded (2.7% redundancy) 256-QAM cable systems is illustrated in Figure 7 - Figure 9. For a BER = 10^{-6} our 256-QAM required a C/N = 32 dB and had a spectral efficiency of 6.66 b/s/Hz [2]. Extensive field experiments over LOS hybrid microwave and coaxial cable systems indicated that 99.875 percent or better EFS (error free second) performance could be obtained with these modems over regenerative spans exceeding 1000 km and excellent performance was also obtained on the cable system between Vancouver, Canada and Hawaii.

Probably one of the most spectrally efficient digital modulation cable systems studied so far has been the 1024-QAM system described by Feher in [2]. See the experimental constellation/hardware photograph of Figure 2. Evidently such an efficient system having the theoretical potential of **10 b/s/Hz** and practical potential of more than **9 b/s/Hz** requires an increased C/N requirement and very advanced complex equalization and interference (including echo) cancellation subsystems. For a 6 MHz video channel, a future 1024-QAM system could have the potential of 54 Mb/s. However, it could take some time prior to design completion and implementation of these types of systems.

Simpler, more robust modem architectures have also been considered for digital TV and digital audio cable distribution systems and for **SCM fiber optics** system applications [15-17]. A spectral efficiency in the 2 b/s/Hz to 3

b/s/Hz range has been found to be a good compromise for low C/N requirements, robust performance and low cost ASIC implementations.

Among the simplest and most robust digital modems are the BPSK, G-MSK and QPSK [1]. For a raw BER = 10^{-6} a low C/N in the range of 8 dB to 14 dB is sufficient. The spectral efficiency of these modems is less than 2 b/s/Hz, that is, these modem architectures are not suitable for spectrally efficient digital cable TV and digital audio cable distribution applications. Among the robust, i.e., low C/N operation, modems 8-PSK and staggered 9-state QPRS or S-QPRS are of significant interest. For coaxial cable and for SCM fiber optics systems [15], 8-PSK modems have been considered by several corporations. A brief comparative study of these techniques is highlighted in the next section.

2. COMPARISON OF 9-QPRS AND 8-PSK SYSTEMS: MULTIPLEXED DIGITAL AUDIO CABLE, TV AND SCM FIBER SYSTEMS

QPRS and S-QPRS systems offer several advantages over 8-PSK systems, including a 3 dB lower C/N requirement, simpler architecture, less sensitive to filter imperfections including group delay or cable roll-off, and more robust performance in a phase noise dominated channel. The 3 dB lower C/N could be potentially even further reduced, i.e., to a lower C/N with non-redundant QPRS error correction and/or Viterbi decoding.

The 8-PSK system has 3 b/s/Hz theoretical spectral efficiency, while the Nyquist rate for 9-QPRS is 2 b/s/Hz. However, as highlighted in our publications and patent [1; 12-14], we note that the practical spectral efficiency of 8-PSK systems is in the 2.5 b/s/Hz range with more complex filters - leading to significant system sensitivities. The practical spectral efficiency of the 9-QPRS system is in the 2.2 b/s/Hz to 2.6 b/s/Hz range. It has been proven by numerous organizations (since Dr. Lender's discovery around 1960) that it is feasible to transmit with simple/robust hardware significantly above the Nyquist binary rate with 3-level partial response (PR) signals - which are the baseband part of 9-QPRS modems. See Lender's chapter in [4].

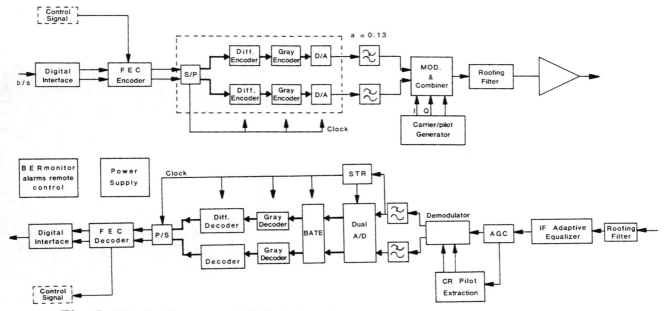

Fig. 5 Block diagram of FEC-Coded QAM and QPRS systems including baseband adaptive time equalizers (BATE).

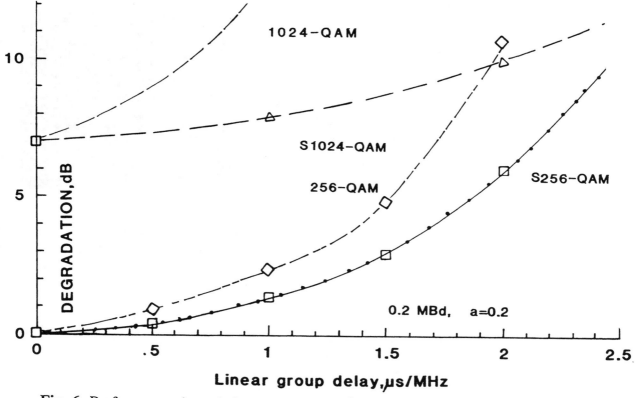

Fig. 6 Performance degradation at BER = 10^{-6} of conventional QAM and of staggered QAM, i.e., SQAM due to residual (unequalized) linear group delay distortions of a cable TV system. These normalized curves are for a scaled-down 0.2 M Baud system [1 and 2].

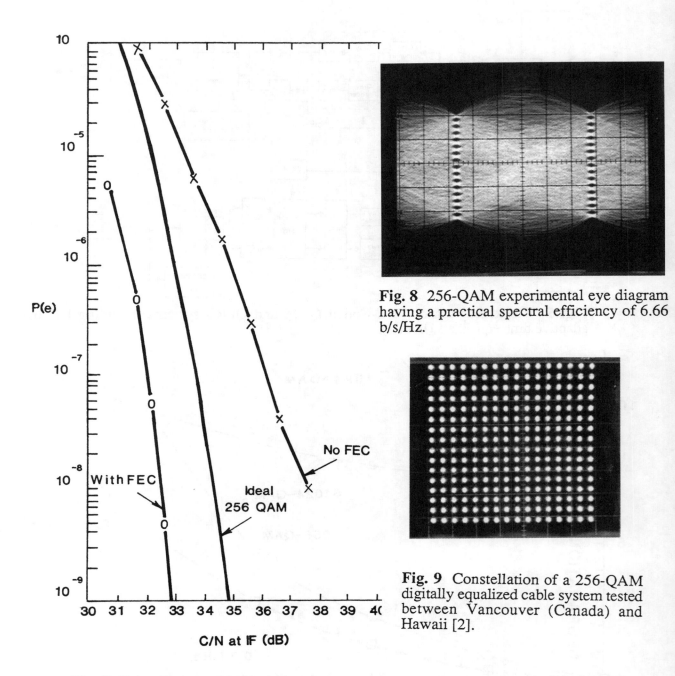

Fig. 8 256-QAM experimental eye diagram having a practical spectral efficiency of 6.66 b/s/Hz.

Fig. 9 Constellation of a 256-QAM digitally equalized cable system tested between Vancouver (Canada) and Hawaii [2].

Fig. 7 Experimental 256-QAM-FEC coded performance in cable systems and LOS microwave systems, measured by the author [1 and 2].

The theoretical BER = P(e) = f(C/N) advantage of 9-QPRS systems as compared to 8-PSK is illustrated in Figure 4 and Table 1.

Table 1 <u>Reduced C/N requirement of 9-QPR as compared to 8-PSK in AWGN systems. The 9-QPR system is about 3 dB more robust than the 8-PSK system.</u>

	9-QPR	8-PSK
10^{-4}	13.5 dB	16.5dB
10^{-6}	16 dB	19 dB
10^{-8}	17.5 dB	20.5 dB

The practical efficiency of 8-PSK is in the 2.5 b/s/Hz to 3 b/s/Hz range if an out-of-band rejection of 20 dB to 30 dB is sufficient. For cable TV applications, we assume that an integrated our-of-band spectral rejection of about 60 dB is required, thus the practical efficiency of 8-PSK is assumed to be less than 2.5 b/s/Hz.

An additional advantage of 9-QPRS systems (as compared to 8-PSK) is that they are approximately 3 dB more robust to **phase noise** [1; 14]. For example, at BER = 10^{-6} the integrated phase noise requirement is (C/N_p) = 23 dB for a 2 dB degradation in case of 8-PSK, while it is only 20 dB in case of 9-QPRS. thus the 9-QPRS has an additional 3 dB phase noise advantage.

Increased capacity-improved performance QPRS systems, i.e., $3 \times 3 = 9$ state; $7 \times 7 = 49$-QPRS and even $15 \times 15 = 225$-QPRS systems can be designed by using a new invention (see [13], patent by Feher et al.). The advantage of the patented QPRS are illustrated in Figs. 14 and 15. A capacity increase of 8% without increasing the number of states and thus the C/N requirement is attained in the experimental results of Fig. 15.

3. DRL'S NEW SQPRS MULTIPLEXED DIGITAL AUDIO CABLE BROADCAST SYSTEM

Staggered 9-QPRS or S-QPRS systems have additional advantages as compared to conventional QPRS. In references [1; 11; 12], it is demonstrated that staggering reduces the peak-factor and the potential intermodulation problems and leads to simpler, better performance coherent demodulator design. In Figure 10, the constellation diagram of a 9-state SQPR digital cable system is presented, courtesy of Digital Radio Laboratories (DRL), Carson, CA. The DRL modem, 9-SQPR is the **'industry first'** operational staggered QPRS cable system implemented in ASIC, see Figure 11. The 9-QPR modem is currently in operation, see Figure 12. The DRL digital audio system carries 18.56 Mb/s data, i.e., two 9.28 Mb/s in two 4 MHz SAW filtered channels. Exceptionally high fidelity MUX (multiplexed) digital audio channels and commercial free music and audio is distributed to cable broadcast systems and directly into homes.

REFERENCES

[1] K. Feher, Ed.: "<u>Advanced Digital Communications: Systems and Signal Processing Techniques,</u>" Prentice-Hall, Inc., Englewood Cliffs, New Jersey 07632 (1987-710 pages).

[2] K. Feher: "1024-QAM and 256-QAM Coded Modems for Microwave and Cable System Applications," <u>IEEE Journal on Selected Areas in Communications,</u>Vol. SAC-5, No. 3, April 1987.

[3] K. Feher: "<u>Digital Communications: Satellite/Earth Station Engineering,</u>" Prentice-Hall, Inc., Englewood Cliffs, New Jersey 07632 (1983-480 pages).

[4] K. Feher: "<u>Digital Communications: Microwave Applications,</u>" Prentice Hall, Inc., Englewood Cliffs, NJ 07632 (1981).

[5] K. Feher and Engineers of Hewlett-Packard: "<u>Telecommunications Measurements, Analysis and Instrumentation,</u>" Prentice-Hall, Inc., Englewood Cliffs, NJ (1987).

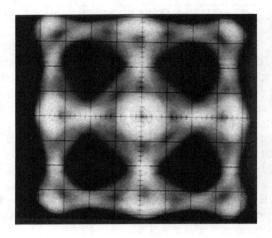

Fig. 10 Constellation and eye diagram of a SQPR digital cable system operated at an 9.28 Mb/s rate. Courtesy of Digital Radio Laboratories, Carson, CA [6].

Fig. 11 Cable TV - digital audio receivers for Digital Planet and other highest quality audio receivers. ASIC implementations by Digital Radio Laboratories of Carson, CA led to a compact size, versatility and low-cost original-proprietary SQPR systems design [6].

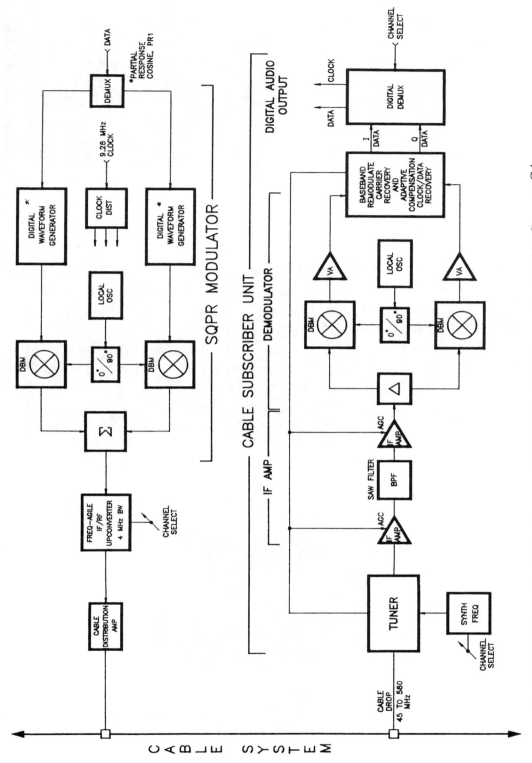

Fig. 12 Digital Audio Cable System of Digital Radio Laboratories (DRL), Carson, CA. This original ASIC implemented staggered SQPRS already operational cable system outperforms conventional 8-PSK systems, see Table I and [6].

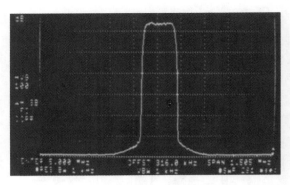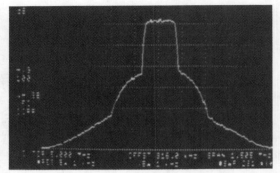

Fig. 13 Spectrum of a 64-QAM linearly and nonlinearly amplified (NLA) system. Spectral regrowth and interference into adjacent TV channels [7 and 11].

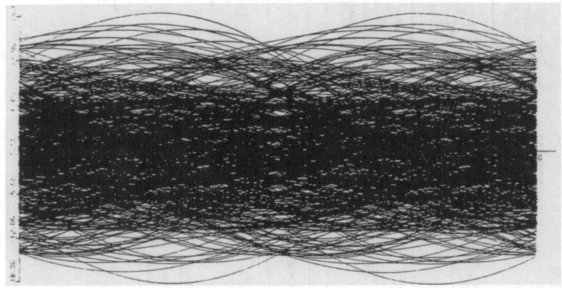

Fig. 14 Conventional 225-QPRS (15 × 15 baseband) operated at 4% above the Nyquist rate with 6.24 b/s/Hz-computer simulation [1; 12; 13] leads to closed eye diagrams.

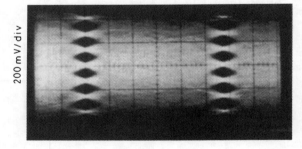

Fig. 15 New 49-QPR and other QPR filter methods, see Feher et al. Patent [13], enable transmission above the Nyquist rate. In this hardware experiment, instead of 4 b/s/Hz we had 4.32 b/s/Hz (an 8% increase and "open eye diagrams" [1; 4; 11; 12; 13].

[6]   D. Talley and T. Schnerk: "D.R. L. Digital Audio System - Cable Transmission with SQPR Modems-ASIC Implementation'" Digital Radio Laboratories Inc., 22010 Wilmington Ave, Ste 208, Carson, CA 90745, <u>Technical Information Package</u> No. 7/20/91, July 1991.

[7]   Z. Chen, J. Wang, K. Feher: "Effect of HPA Non-Linearities on Crosstalk and Performance of Digital Radio Systems," <u>IEEE Transactions on Broadcasting</u> Vol. 34, No. 3, September 1988 (pp. 336-343)

[8]   W.C. Luplow and P. Fockens: "Source Coding, Channel Coding and Modulation Techniques Used in Digital Spectrum-Compatible HDTV System," <u>IEEE Transactions on Broadcasting</u>, Vol. 37, No. 4, December 1991.

[9]   G.A. Reitmeier, C. Basile and S.A. Keneman: "Source Coding, Channel Coding and Modulation Techniques Used in the ADTV System," <u>IEEE Transactions on Broadcasting</u>, Vol. 37, No. 4, December 1991.

[10] J.A. Kraus "Source Coding, Channel Coding and Modulation Techniques Used in the ATVA-Progressive System.

[11] K. Sreenath, I. Sasase, K. Feher: "QAM and QPRS Digital Broadband Cable Systems," <u>International Journal of Digital and Analog Cabled Systems</u>, a John Wiley & Sons Ltd. Journal, Vol. 2, 1989 (pp. 139-148).

[12] K. T. Wu, I. Sasase, K. Feher: "Class IV PRS above the Nyquist Rate," <u>I E E</u>

[13] K. Feher, K. T. Wu, J. C. Y. Huang, D. E. MacNally: "<u>Improved Efficiency Data Transmission Technique</u>," U.S. Patent No. 4-720-839, Washington, DC. Issued January 19, 1988.

[14] A. Kucar, K. Feher: "Practical Performance Prediction Techniques for Spectrally Efficient Digital Systems," <u>RF Design</u>, (Cardiff Publishing Company) Vol. 14, No. 2, February 1991, (pp. 58-66, p. 5).

[15] W.I. Way: "Fiber-Optic Transmissions of Microwave 8-Phase-PSK and 16-ary Quadrature-Amplitude-Modulated Signals at the 1.3-μm Wavelength Region," <u>IEEE Journal of Lightwave Technology</u>, February 1988.

[16] W.I. Way: "Subcarrier Multiplexed Lightwave System Design Considerations for Subscriber Loop Applications," <u>IEEE Journal of Lightwave Technology</u>, November 1989.

[17] S.S. Wagner, R.C. Menendex: "Evolutionary Architectures and Techniques for Video distribution on Fiber," <u>IEEE Communications Magazine</u>, December 1989.

[18] J.A. Kraus: "Source Coding, Channel Coding and Modulation Techniques used in the DigiCipher system," <u>IEEE Transactions on Broadcasting</u>, December 1991.

Proceedings, Vol. 135, Pt. F, No. 2, April 1988 (pp. 183-191).

DIGITAL TELEVISION AND CABLE TV

Geoffrey S. Roman and Joseph B. Waltrich
General Instrument Communications, USA

ABSTRACT:

There is great interest in obtaining the benefits of digital television: picture quality in difficult transmission environments, security and compatibility with multimedia computing. However, transmission of uncompressed digital television signals requires much more bandwidth than is required for their analog counterparts. Compression techniques are now available which allow the transmission of as many as 10 or more television signals in the bandwidth traditionally occupied by a single analog channel, yielding not only the benefits of digital picture quality but also dramatically increasing the variety of programming that can be provided over a given transmission medium.

Compressed digital video is already being transmitted over satellite and subsequent transmission over cable is not far away. Digital signals will soon begin to share the cable spectrum with analog channels and mixed analog/digital systems are likely to become commonplace in the near future. Since the effect of transmission media on analog and digital signals is quite different, it is important to understand how channel characteristics affect the behavior of a mixed analog/digital system.

BACKGROUND:

Transmission of digital video in uncompressed form is impractical because of bandwidth requirements. It has been shown [1] that, for transmission of uncompressed component video, sampled at CCIR-601 rates, the bit rate exceeds 200 Mb/s. Depending on the spectral efficiency of the modulation technique, transmission at this data rate would require a bandwidth in the range 60 - 120 MHz.

Fortunately, video compression is capable of effecting a significant reduction in bit rate without sacrificing picture quality. All compression engines accomplish their intended purpose in the following manner:

- Those portions of the video signal which are not perceptible to the human eye are not transmitted.

- Frame to frame redundancies in the video signal are not transmitted.

- The remaining information is coded in an efficient manner for transmission.

DIGITAL TRANSMISSION TECHNIQUES:

Transmission of digital data can be accomplished using a variety of modulation techniques. The choice of modulation format is based on the best compromise between channel bandwidth, data rate and signal robustness.

The required bandwidth for digital transmission is a function of the total data rate and the spectral efficiency of the modulation technique. The transmission bandwidth may be calculated as follows:

$$W = R_d / E_s \qquad (1)$$

where W = bandwidth (Hz)
R_d = total data rate (b/s)
E_s = spectral efficiency (b/s/Hz)

Spectral efficiencies for modulation schemes currently proposed for digital video transmission range from 2 - 6 b/s/Hz. Additional information regarding modulation formats for digital transmission may be found in Feher [2].

For a power limited system such as a satellite link, Quadrature Phase Shift Keying (QPSK) is a good choice of modulation. QPSK is extremely robust and is less affected by noise than most other modulation formats. The bandwidth penalty exacted by QPSK (in the neighborhood of 24 MHz) is not a problem for satellite transmission.

In a relatively benign but bandwidth limited environment such as cable, other modulation formats, which offer greater spectral efficiency, are a better choice. Several different techniques have been proposed for digital video transmission over cable. These include Quadrature Amplitude Modulation (QAM), 4 Level Vestigial Sideband Modulation (4-VSB), and Orthogonal Frequency Division Multiplexing (OFDM). A review of some of these modulation techniques may be found in [2] and [3].

The use of 16QAM has proved to be very rugged for cable transmission. Using 16QAM, it is possible to transmit a total data rate of slightly less than 20 Mb/s in a 6 MHz bandwidth. At the DigiCipher information rate of 13.46 Mb/s, 16QAM permits the addition of a significant amount of overhead for error correction and transmission of ancillary data. If a QPSK satellite transmission is transcoded to 16QAM at the downlink, then it is possible to transmit the contents of one phase of the satellite transponder in a single cable channel. For the DigiCipher signal, this allows transmission of up to 5 NTSC signals in 6 MHz.

It is possible that the choice of 16QAM for cable transmission may be overly conservative. If a more efficient modulation scheme such as 64QAM is used in conjunction with error correction more suited to the medium, then it should be possible to double the information rate, thereby enabling transmission of up to 10 NTSC signals in 6 MHz.

A comparison of 16QAM vs. 64QAM is shown in Table 1. The data presented in the table is based on the DigiCipher information rate of

13.46 Mb/s per satellite transponder phase. The error correction used for satellite transmission can be replaced with a different error correction scheme which, although it results in a lower data overhead, is nevertheless sufficient for cable transmission. This permits transmission of an information rate of 26.92 Mb/s, thereby allowing up to 10 NTSC signals to be compressed into 6 MHz.

Table 1 Comparison of 16QAM with 64QAM		
	16QAM	64QAM
Information Rate (Mb/s)	13.46	26.92
Error Correction Data (Mb/s)	6.05	2.34
Total Data Rate (Mb/s)	19.51	29.26
NTSC Signals in 6 MHz	5	10

A simplified block diagram of the proposed transcoding scheme is shown in Fig. 1. The received signal from the satellite is demodulated and decoded into its in-phase and quadrature (I and Q) data streams. Following error correction of the satellite transmission, the parity bits which were inserted at the satellite uplink are removed and the data streams are re-encoded using both convolutional (trellis) and Reed-Solomon coding. The data streams are then modulated in 64QAM format and up-converted for cable transmission.

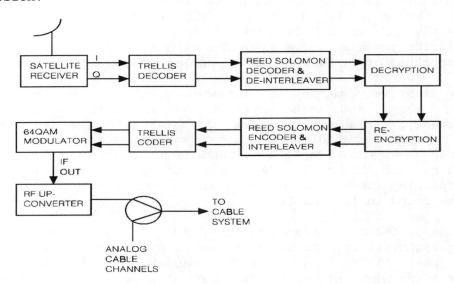

FIG. 1 DIGITAL TRANSCODER BLOCK DIAGRAM

EFFECTS OF CHANNEL IMPAIRMENTS:

Analog cable systems are designed to minimize noise and distortions. Other impairments such as group delay and micro-reflections are generally considered to be less significant since they have a lesser effect on analog signals. The effect of typical cable impairments on digital signals is, however, quite different.

In general, noise is not a problem for digital transmission over cable. This is true even when the digital signals are operated at reduced power levels. Furthermore, techniques such as trellis coding and Reed-Solomon error correction are very effective in overcoming errors caused by poor Carrier/Noise ratios.

The noise performance of digital transmission is illustrated in Fig. 2 which shows a plot of bit error rate vs. C/N for 64QAM transmission. If one assumes an analog C/N of 40 dB (FCC minimum requirements for U.S. cable systems in 1995), then the digital signal could be operated at -10 dB relative to the peak analog carrier power and still yield a bit error rate of less than 10^{-9}. Error correction will improve the C/N performance by 5-7 dB. However, implementation loss in the modem will probably reduce this improvement by 1-2 dB.

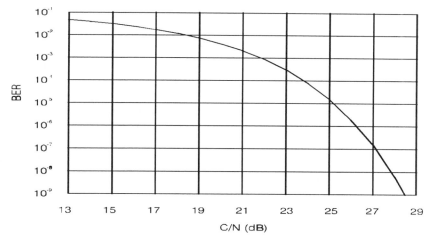

FIG. 2 64QAM BIT ERROR RATE VS. CARRIER/NOISE RATIO

Digital signals are also much less sensitive to CTB. Carrier/Interference ratios for digital signals can be 10 to 20 dB worse than those for analog signals before uncorrectable errors are observed in the digital picture. However, multiple contiguous digital channels can generate their own form of distortion. This appears as random noise in parts of the analog spectrum as shown in Fig. 3. Second order distortion produces a triangular spectrum, centered around DC, which may affect low end or return path channels. Third order distortion generates a bell-shaped spectrum which spreads into the adjacent analog channels. As is the case with analog signals, second and third order digital distortions increase by 2 dB and 3 dB, respectively, for each dB increase in digital power. However, third order distortion also increases by 6 dB for each octave increase in digital bandwidth. As digital signals proliferate in the cable spectrum, this may be a limiting factor on the digital signal power, although it is not likely to be a problem in the near future.

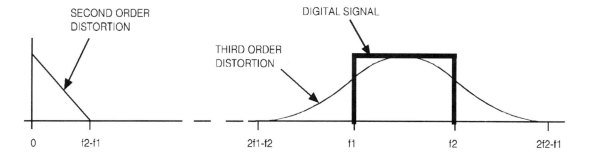

FIG. 3 SPECTRA PRODUCED BY DIGITAL DISTORTION

341

Microreflections can have a severe effect on digital transmission. In particular, short ghosts of relatively high amplitude, most of which are found in the subscriber's home, can cause significant bit error rates unless corrected by adaptive equalization. Group delay can also cause severe errors, particularly near the edge of the cable spectrum which is where many operators plan on putting their digital channels.

TEST RESULTS:

Considerable testing has been done at Jerrold using 16QAM. Uncorrected bit error rates of 10^{-6} to 10^{-7} were measured in field tests on cable trunks containing more than 20 amplifiers. Digital C/N ratios at the receiving sites were on the order of 30 dB or less. Field tests also showed that reflections can produce significant bit error rates. In tests on two different systems, unterminated drop and splitter connections produced bit error rates of about 10^{-3}. Correcting the misterminations resulted in a BER decrease of 2-3 orders of magnitude. Test results also showed that group delays in excess of 200 nS can produce BER's of up to 10^{-3}.

16QAM testing was also conducted on AML, fiber, MMDS and twisted pair systems. Test results on these systems were not significantly different from those for cable.

Since the results obtained with 16QAM were encouraging [4], it was decided to conduct a series of channel characterization studies to determine the feasibility of using 64QAM.
A block diagram of the 64QAM test system is shown in Fig. 4. A pseudorandom data generator, internal to the digital modulator,

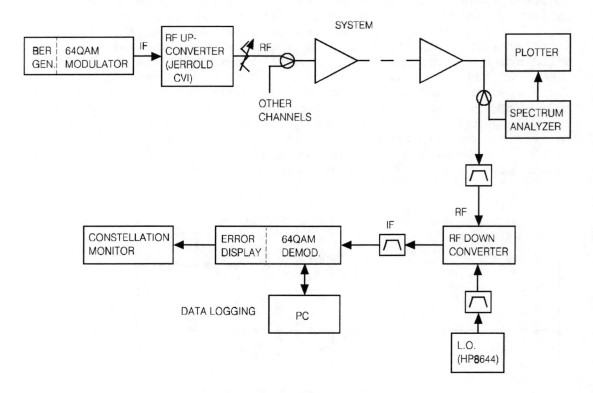

FIG. 4 64QAM CHANNEL CHARACTERIZATION - BLOCK DIAGRAM

serves as the data source. The 64QAM modem incorporates both convolutional and Reed Solomon error correction, either or both of which may be disabled in order to determine the optimum error correction technique for use in cable transmission.

The IF output of the digital modulator is a double sideband suppressed carrier AM signal centered at 44 MHz with a 3 dB bandwidth of 4.88 MHz. The output is up-converted to the appropriate cable channel using the RF section of a Jerrold Commander VI modulator. The digital RF signal is combined with the analog cable channels at the headend and transmitted over the cable system in the normal manner.

At the receiving site, the RF signal is converted to IF using a frequency agile down converter. In order to insure low phase noise, the down converter's local oscillator input was supplied by a HP8644 frequency synthesizer. Spectral purity of the L.O. was maintained by a tunable bandpass filter at the HP8644's output.
The digital demodulator incorporates display capability for readout of errors/second. The displays show both raw errors and errors which escape correction (coded errors). This data is also output to an RS-232 port in order to permit data collection via a personal computer. The demodulator also incorporates a 64 tap adaptive equalizer for correction of multipath and group delay effects. The values of the adaptive equalizer coefficients are also output to the serial port in order to provide information on the nature and extent of echoes resident on the system under test. The PC software permits storage of the error data and adaptive equalizer coefficients in separate ASCII files for off-line printout and analysis.

64QAM transmission tests were conducted over several cable systems. System configurations included trunk cascades of 23 - 41 amplifiers plus distribution systems consisting of 1 -2 line extenders and up to 26 taps. Uncorrected bit error rates were on the order of 10^{-4}. These bit error rates were somewhat higher than those measured in tests with 16QAM and were due in part to group delay in the IF filter used in the down converter. Group delay in this filter was on the order of 6-700 nS and was adequately, although not totally compensated for by the adaptive equalizer. Subsequent tests, conducted using a SAW filter in place of the original analog filter, yielded uncorrected BER's on the order of 10^{-5} to 10^{-6}.

Tests ranged from 2 to 51 hours in length, with the average test duration being on the order of 16 hours. Error correction was quite effective, resulting in a corrected BER of zero over an average of 99.85% of the total test time. Test results over fiber optics links were not significantly different than those over cable.

Test results over AML were somewhat less effective in terms of error free operation. This was due to phase noise in the AML transmitter/receiver combination which ranged from -70 dBc/Hz to -103 dBc/Hz, measured at 10 KHz from an unmodulated carrier, over a 12 hour period. Previous tests with 16QAM have shown that phase noise on the order of -80 dBc/Hz was a threshold level for production of significant errors. It is reasonable to expect that this threshold would be lower for 64QAM. Additional laboratory and field tests are required to determine more precisely the effects of phase noise on 64QAM transmission.

As previously mentioned, a good part of the adaptive equalizer's effort was spent in compensating for the effects of group delay in the down converter's IF filter. However, this did not consume much of the available equalization budget. Significant change in equalizer coefficient values from one test to the next was observed on about 8-14 taps of the equalizer. This implies that system echoes which were corrected by the equalizer were relatively short - a finding which is not inconsistent with the results of previous analyses and testing [5], [6].

EVOLUTION TO HDTV:

There is essentially no difference in transmission of digital HDTV vs. digital NTSC. Although the digital bitstream is different for HDTV (one or two HDTV signals as compared to 5 - 10 NTSC signals), as long as the information rates are comparable, the same modulation technique and the same transmission hardware can be used. Hardware differences would, of course, exist in the compression and decompression circuitry, but, once the data is encoded into a serial bitstream, the transmission technique is the same.

This also applies to transmission of PAL video in digital form with some minor changes. Since both the information rate and the available bandwidth for PAL are higher than for NTSC, minor modifications to the transmission system filters would have to be made in order to accommodate these differences. However, the net result is that, if NTSC can be transmitted over cable using 64QAM, then PAL can also be transmitted.

CONCLUSIONS:

Judging from the results obtained to date, 64QAM appears to be feasible for cable transmission. The problems encountered in transmission over AML are indicative of the need for careful design of phase locked loops in both the AML equipment and the digital transmission hardware. Adaptive equalization appears to be capable of handling echoes in both the cable system and the transmission equipment. Additional laboratory and field tests are required in order to determine more conclusively the effects of system impairments.

REFERENCES:

[1]   A. Netravali, B. Haskell, "Digital Pictures: Representation and Compression", Plenum Press, 1989.

[2]   K. Feher, "Telecommunications Measurement, Analysis and Instrumentation", Prentice-Hall, 1987.

[3]   R. Monnier, J. Rault, T. deCousanon, "Digital Television Broadcasting with High Spectral Efficiency", IBC Technical Papers, 1992.

[4]   J. Waltrich, J. Glaab, "Digital Transmission in 16QAM Format Over Cable and Alternate Media", IBC Technical Papers, 1992.

[5]   R. Prodan, "Performance of Digital Transmission Techniques for Cable Systems", NCTA Technical Papers, 1992.

[6]   J. Glaab, M. Muller, M. Ryba, J. Waltrich, "The Impact of Microreflections on Digital Transmission Over Cable and Alternate Media", NCTA Technical Papers, 1992.

APPLICATION OF ERROR CONTROL TECHNIQUES TO DIGITAL TRANSMISSION VIA CATV NETWORKS

JOHN T. GRIFFIN

JERROLD COMMUNICATIONS
APPLIED MEDIA LAB

ABSTRACT

Digital carriage of data via CATV networks is becoming more prevalent with each passing year. Digital radio services are presently being offered by numerous cable operators. Digital compression of video is just over the horizon, and other data services will likely follow. Although these digital delivery systems do not exhibit the impairments of their analog counterparts, bit errors may cause catastrophic distortions. Forward error correction is one aspect of a solution to this problem.

This paper introduces the CATV system engineer to the concepts of forward error correction, and discusses its benefits, complexity, and limitations. It also touches on the interdependence of forward error correction with channel equalization and efficient modulation. Several important concepts, such as coding gain, are discussed in detail.

INTRODUCTION

A CATV system meets the definition of a communication system because it connects multiple information sources to users of this information. A general communication system is illustrated in Figure 1. For purposes of this paper, the source is any source of television programming; the **source encoder** might be some form of video and audio compression. The **forward error encoder** and decoder in Figure 1 are the subject of this paper.

Error control techniques can be very effective against random noise impairments, but are not a panacea for microreflections on digital transmission in a CATV network. Error control can be teamed with channel equalization, as shown in Figure 1, to develop a very robust and cost effective communication channel. Both the rate at which the errors occur and their distribution must be known before the optimum error correction scheme may be designed. This may be accomplished by a combination of simulation, laboratory tests, and field tests.

Error control applied to future CATV networks using video and audio compression (the source encoder and source decoder in Figure 1) is essential because compression eliminates the redundancy from the original analog signals. Errors occurring during transmission may cause severe impairments to the reconstituted analog signals. In general, errors will propagate through the decompression process.

HISTORY

The history of error control began in 1948 with Claude Shannon's famous paper on channel capacity[1]. His channel capacity theorem says the following:

$$C = W \log_2(1 + S/N) \text{ bits/sec} \quad (1)$$

where:

C = capacity in bits/sec
W = bandwidth in Hz
S = signal power
N = noise power

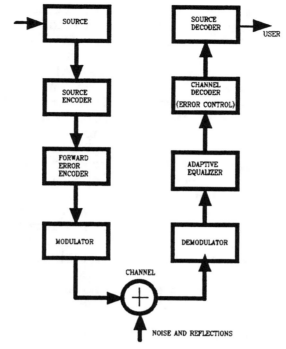

DIGITAL COMMUNICATIONS SYSTEM

FIGURE 1

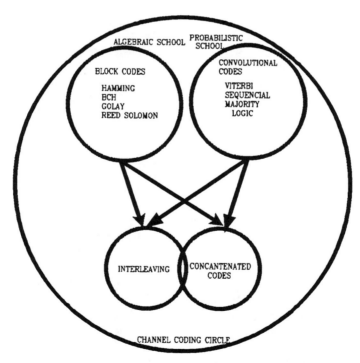

CODING FOR ERROR CONTROL
FIGURE 2

What Shannon said was that the noise limits the rate at which we can send information, but not the accuracy. Today designers are moving ever closer to this limit with a combination of error control and efficient modulation. Shannon's work also tells us it is more cost effective to employ error coding than to try to build an error-free channel.

During the 1950's and 1960's the search for good codes continued. It was during this period that two mathematical bases developed to solve the error coding problem. This concept is illustrated in Figure 2. The two bases are the **algebraic** and **probabilistic** approaches. The algebraic codes are most commonly known as "block codes". The first of these were introduced in 1950 by Hamming; his are a class of single error correcting codes. Another major milestone occurred in 1960 when Bose, Ray-Chaudhuri, and Hocquenghem found a class of multiple-error-correcting codes now known as BCH codes . Reed and Solomon also developed their codes in 1960; these codes are related to the BCH, but for non-binary channels.[2,3]

The second mathematical approach to coding, the probabilistic approach, led to the development of "convolutional" or "tree" codes. In the late 1950's, studies led to the notion of sequential decoding and to the introduction of non-block codes of indefinite length. However, the most well known algorithm, the Viterbi algorithm, did not appear until 1967. Such techniques have allowed reception of digital data from deep space probes. The steady improvement in the performance of telephone modems has also resulted from advances in error coding and sophisticated modulation techniques.

ERROR CONTROL AND EQUALIZATION

Error control is very effective at mitigating the impairments caused by additive noise. A CATV channel presents other phenomena that limit channel performance. Chief among these are microreflections due to impedance mismatches at the television receiver or unterminated taps. This results in **intersymbol interference** (ISI), which is the tendency of received symbols to flow into one another.[2] This can not be overcome by increasing signal power; there is an ISI noise floor that increases with signal power. ISI may be overcome by **adaptive equalization**, which is outside the scope of this paper. Error control and adaptive equalization may be combined to result in a very robust communication system (refer to Figure 1).

DEFINITIONS

Certain terms appear throughout the literature of coding theory. These are defined here for the convenience of the reader:[2,3]

Symbol A symbol is a group of bits within an error control block. It is also defined as a signal representing a group of "k" bits in some analog manner, such as amplitude or phase. Thus, there are error control symbols and modulation symbols.

Weight The weight of a symbol, codeword, or "vector" is the number of non-zero elements.

Hamming distance The Hamming distance between two vectors having the same number of elements is defined as the number of positions in which the elements differ. This is a key concept in error control and will be discussed in more detail later in this paper.

Minimum distance The minimum distance "d" of a linear block code is the smallest distance between pairs of different codewords in the code.

Codeword A codeword or "code block" is a group of bits or symbols made up of information elements and parity (error control) elements.

Code rate Assume that a block encoder accepts information in successive "k"-bit blocks and for each k bits generates a block of "n" bits, where n > k. The code rate R = k/n is a dimensionless ratio that indicates the portion of an encoded block that carries information.

Overhead This is the percentage of parity bits that must be appended to the information bits in constructing a code.

Hard decision A hard decision demodulator makes an absolute 1/0 choice on each received bit (or symbol). The symbol is quantized to two levels.

Soft decision In making a soft decision, the demodulator makes a bit-quality measurement on each bit or symbol. The symbol is quantized to more than two levels.

Erasure This is the process of flagging a bit or symbol as unreliable. It is the result of a soft decision. This flag is passed along to the error control circuitry.

Coding gain This term describes the amount of improvement that is achieved when a particular coding scheme is used. Figure 3 illustrates coding gain on a logarithmic plot of bit error rate vs E_b/N_0 (energy/bit divided by spectral noise density). At low signal to noise ratios, the gain will become negative.

Vector This term is based in linear algebra and is familiar to us from physics. In coding theory vector space is one of the most important algebraic concepts. The vector provides a convenient representation of field elements that may be implemented with simple digital functions. The term is also used in matrix notation, where the vector consists of the coefficients of a polynomial. Refer to section 3.3 of reference 2.

The syndrome The syndrome is defined in the dictionary as "a number of symptoms occurring together and characterizing a specific disease".[6] In coding theory, a syndrome is a sequence of discrepancies which occur when received parity bits are compared with calculated parity bits. The syndrome may take on the form of a "vector" in a matrix. Calculations of syndromes are used in many decoding algorithms to locate errors in received data.

Constraint length In a convolutional code, the constraint length is the number of data frames used in the generation of the encoded data. Each input frame may consist of one or more bits. The process occurs on a continuous basis. In terms of the actual circuit elements, the constraint length is the length of the input data shift register in the encoder.

Galois field A field having a finite number of elements is called a finite or Galois (pronounced gall-wa) field. It is denoted by GF(q), where q is the number of elements in the field. These fields are named after Evariste Galois (1811-1832), a French mathematical prodigy who established group theory mathematics by age 17.[2] Chapter 4 in reference 3 treats this theory in detail.

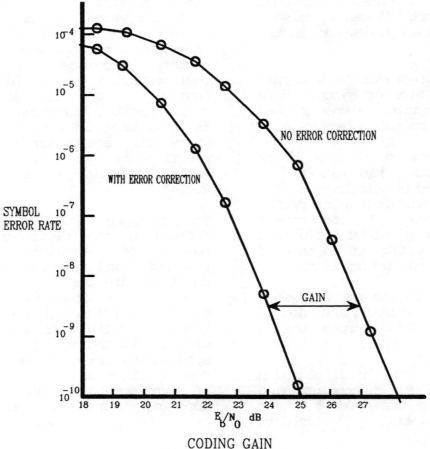

SYMBOL ERROR RATE

NO ERROR CORRECTION

WITH ERROR CORRECTION

GAIN

E_b/N_0 dB

CODING GAIN
FIGURE 3

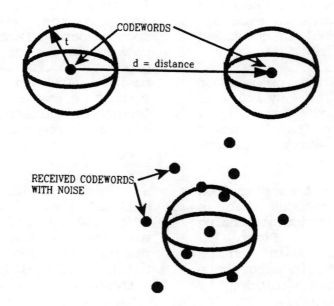

CODEWORDS

t

d = distance

RECEIVED CODEWORDS
WITH NOISE

DECODING SPHERES
FIGURE 4

THE DISTANCE CONCEPT

This concept is crucial in visualizing the operation of error control circuitry. Figure 4 illustrates "decoding spheres" in a geometric fashion. Recall the definition of minimum distance d_m. We will define t as the number of errors that a particular code can correct. If more than t errors occur in transmission, the decoder may incorrectly decode the data or it may indicate with a flag that it can not decode the message. [3]

In Figure 4, the code is designed so that the minimum distance between codewords is defined as:

$$d \geq 2t + 1 \qquad (2)$$

where t is the number of errors that can be corrected. A codeword received error free will land at the center of a sphere. If t errors occur, the codeword will be on the surface of the sphere, and the decoder will correct the error(s). Received codewords with more than t errors may fall between spheres or within another sphere; those falling in another sphere will be incorrectly decoded. Those falling between spheres may or may not be correctly decoded, but would be erased in a soft decision decoder. One can see that the minimum distance is a critical property of a code.

BLOCK CODES

In a block (algebraic) code the encoder accepts k information bits and appends r parity-check bits to form a block of n bits, such that:

$$n = k + r \qquad (3)$$

where n = block length
r = number of parity bits

The code is referred to as an (n,k) code. The code rate R is k divided by n. Each block is independent of all others; the check bits are completely determined by the information bits within the same codeword. Also, there are 2^k codewords in the code set. The code is designed to make the codewords very different from each other to resist channel errors.

Arithmetic operations in the Galois field GF(2) are simple because no overflow or round-off error is permitted. The operations of addition and multiplication are mod-2. This is illustrated in the following tables:

+	0	1		*	0	1
0	0	1		0	0	0
1	1	0		1	0	1

ADDITION   MULTIPLICATION

Addition bit-by-bit is accomplished with an "X-OR" gate. Multiplication is done with an "AND" gate.

Polynomial arithmetic in a Galois field (in this case GF(2)) can be used in the description of block codes. Fortunately, digital logic circuits may be constructed to mimic this special polynomial arithmetic. These circuits take the form of digital filters, and are constructed of shift register elements, X-OR gates, AND gates, and multiplexers (Figure 5). The form of the encoders and decoders are similar.

We choose for this paper "binary cyclic block codes" to illustrate the relationship of the GF(2) polynomial arithmetic to the actual circuits. We do so because these codes have proven useful and efficient in practice. Binary cyclic block codes are a subset of

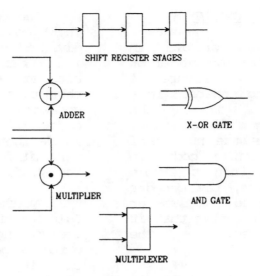

CIRCUIT ELEMENTS

FIGURE 5

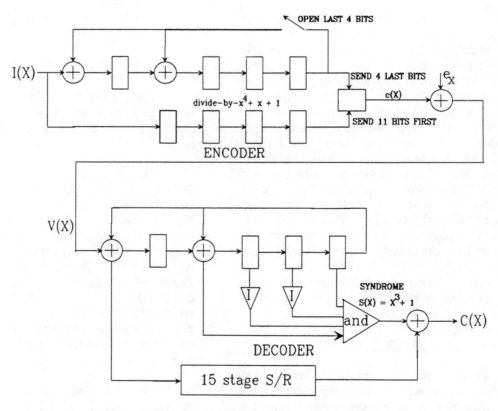

CYCLIC BLOCK ENCODER/DECODER

FIGURE 6

linear block codes, and fall in the "algebraic school" circle of Figure 2. A binary code must meet two criteria to be cyclic:

a. The code is linear; bit-by-bit addition of two codewords in GF(2) is again a codeword.

b. Any cyclic (end around) shift of a codeword is also a codeword. [2]

Chapters 4, 5 and 6 of reference 3 give the reader a clear understanding of the mathematical basis and implementation of cyclic block codes. The polynomial description of a codeword is also found in chapter 4 of reference 2 as follows (in general form):

let $c(x) = c_0 + c_1x + c_2x^2 + \ldots + c_{n-1}x^{n-1}$ (4)

where n = block length, and the polynomial is of degree n-1. Now we will develop an example, as shown in Figure 6. If the information polynomial is:

$i(x) = i_0 + i_1x + i_2x^2 + \ldots + i_{k-1}x^{k-1}$ (5)

and the generator polynomial is:

$g(x) = x^4 + x + 1$ (6)

(derivation of generator polynomials is given in references 2 and 3)

then the codeword takes the form:

$c(x) = x^{n-k}i(x) + t(x)$ (7)

where t(x) is the remainder, and is equal to:

$t(x) = -R_{g(x)}[x^{n-k}i(x)]$ (8)

this reads "t(x) is the remainder after dividing by g(x)".

and thus

$$R_{g(x)}[c(x)] = 0 \qquad (9)$$

The encoder in Figure 6 is a systematic encoder that implements a divide-by-g(x) using shift registers and X-OR gates; it produces a (15,11) Hamming code. Assume that the register stages are first cleared to zero. Eleven information bits are shifted into the circuit; division begins after four clock shifts. The circuit produces eleven information bits followed by four parity bits, to produce a fifteen bit codeword. The four parity bits are the result of the division.

Refer again to Figure 6. As the codeword passes through the channel, noise may cause bit errors. This noise is represented as the error polynomial e(x), which has degree n-1. The sum of the codeword c(x) and noise e(x) is v(x), the received codeword:

$$v(x) = c(x) + e(x) \qquad (10)$$

The decoder in the figure implements a divide by g(x), where g(x) is the same generator polynomial used in the encoder. If no error has occurred, the remainder is zero. If the remainder is non-zero, it is calculated as:

$$s(x) = x^3 + 1 \qquad (11)$$

s(x) is the **syndrome** defined earlier! The decoder circuit in the figure calculates s(x) by dividing by g(x); if s(x) is non-zero, the appropriate information bit is inverted, yielding the original information codeword c(x). The encoder and decoder of Figure 6 constitute a single-error-correcting system. Note the simplicity of the circuit, but remember it is limited to correcting single errors.

The example just presented is of a **binary** block code; the coefficients of all the polynomials are either binary 0 or 1. As you may recall from our brief history lesson, Reed and Solomon developed multiple error correcting codes in a 1960 paper. These codes (and there are many) are are very effective in the presence of burst errors. The **overhead** of these codes is typically 10% or less, making them very efficient. However the decoding hardware is far more complex than described above for the binary code. Algorithms for decoding of R/S codes must calculate two syndromes, one for error location, and one for error magnitude. This is because the mathematics is over a Galois field $GF(2^m)$, where m is a small integer on the order of 7 or 8. In hardware, a parallel bus m bits wide is required. The data bits are arranged into "symbols" of m bits, and the arithmetic calculations are done on these symbols. A number of sophisticated decoding algorithms have been developed for the many Reed Solomon codes. They have found many practical applications, such as compact discs.

CONVOLUTIONAL CODES

These codes are based on a probabilistic approach to the problem of error control. They were originally called **recurrent** codes, and are also referred to as **tree** codes, from the use of a tree or trellis diagram used to visualize the sequence of events. A convolutional code does not have a simple block structure, with each codeword independent from all others. Rather, the codewords are generated using a **sliding window** over the information symbols. A continuous stream of encoded symbols is produced, where successive codeword frame are coupled together by the encoder.

Figure 7 illustrates a generic convolutional encoder, and will be used to define terms common in the literature. The input information is broken into **information** frames of k_0 symbols; **m** is the number of these frames stored in the encoder shift register. The length of the shift register is $m \times k_0$, which is the **constraint length**, denoted by **v**. The output **codeword frame** is made up of n_0 symbols. The code is referred to as an (n_0, k_0) **code**. K is the **wordlength** of the code and is equal to $(m + 1)k_0$. **Blocklength N** is equal to $(m + 1)n_0$, and is the length of the output code that may be influenced by an input frame k_0. The rate **R** of the code is k_0/n_0. The input to the encoder is data at a rate of k_0 symbols per second, and the output is data at a rate of n_0 symbols per second.[3]

Next we will consider the mathematical basis for these codes. We used a **generator polynomial** in constructing a block code. Convolutional codes require a set of multiple polynomials to describe them; these are best described by a mathematical **matrix**. Matrix notation provides a means of writing a number of simultaneous equations (polynomials) in compact form. Appendix A of reference 2 presents a summary of matrix definitions and manipulations.

A matrix is made up of row and column **vectors**, whose elements are the coefficients of the polynomials.

The generator-polynomial matrix is given by:

$$G(x) = [g_{ij}(x)] \qquad (12)$$

This is a k_0 by n_0 matrix of polynomials. Further, if d(x) is a

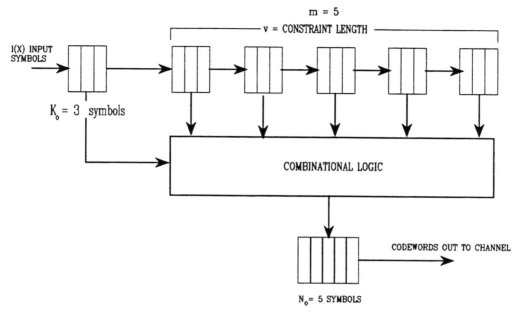

GENERIC CONVOLUTIONAL ENCODER

FIGURE 7

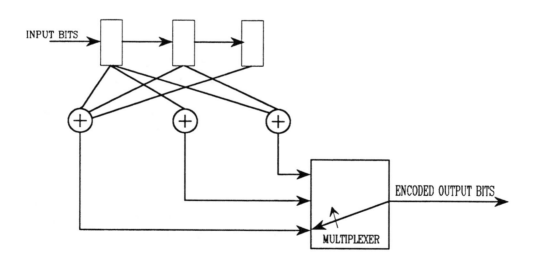

(3,1) CONVOLUTIONAL ENCODER

FIGURE 8

set of k_0 information polynomials and c(x) is a matrix of n_0 codeword ploynomials, then:

$$c(x) = d(x)g(x) \qquad (13)$$

Also, there is a parity check matrix H(x) that satisfies

$$G(x)H(x)^T = 0 \qquad (14)$$

and there is a **syndrome-polynomial vector** given as

$$s(x) = v(x)H(x)^T \qquad (15)$$

where v(x) represents the received codewords.

We will now go on to describe the **tree** and **trellis** structures, as these are very useful in visualizing the generation of the convolutional code. We will use an example taken from a paper by Batson. [4] Figure 8 shows a simple encoder made up of a three stage shift register, three XOR gates, and a multiplexer. This is a (3,1) tree encoder. The coefficients of the generator polynomials specify which stages of the shift register are connected to each modulo 2 adder. In Figure 9, we see the tree that describes the operation of the encoder. Assume the shift register contains all zero's to start the sequence. In the tree, an input of zero causes the circuit to follow the upper branch, a logic one the lower branch. The labels on the branches indicate the resulting output code. An input sequence of 1011 results in an output sequence of 111 101 011 010. It can be seen that this tree would grow very large after a relatively short input stream, and would be unwieldy.

An alternate structure which is much more compact is the **trellis diagram**. This may be seen in Figure 9. The **state** of the encoder is the most recent contents of the k_0-1

stages of the encoder shift register. Time is from left to right. The circuit steps from state to state at clock times. The path is up for a logic zero, and down for a logic 1. The encoded output bits are shown on the branches. The repetitive structure of the trellis is immediately apparent.

The trellis structure is useful is understanding decoding algorithms for convolutional codes, such as the Viterbi algorithm[4], which has found wide application. It basically attempts to find a valid path through the trellis that is as close as possible to the received sequence. This method is very effective, but it should be noted that the hardware requirements for the Viterbi decoder grow exponentially with constraint length.

The coding gain of the Viterbi algorithm may be improved by the use of a **soft decision** demodulator. Such a demodulator takes into account the distance of a received symbol from the center of it's decoding sphere. This is accomplished with an analog-to-digital converter (A/D) to quantize the received signal.

We made brief mention of the **syndrome vector** earlier. Next, we will illustrate its use in a syndrome feedback decoder of a convolutional code. Figure 10 illustrates both the encoder and decoder for such a code. The encoder and decoder both calculate the same parity bits if the data is received error-free. However, if a data bit is received in error, the locally calculated parity will differ from the received parity. When this difference occurs, a logic 1 will appear in the syndrome register. It is the function of the decoder decision table to find the **most likely** bit error location. [2]

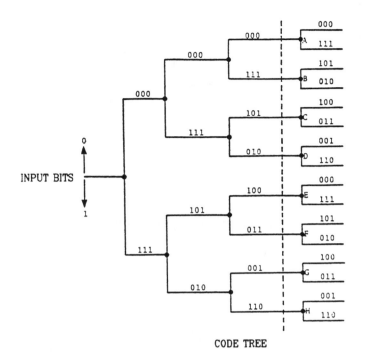

CODE TREE

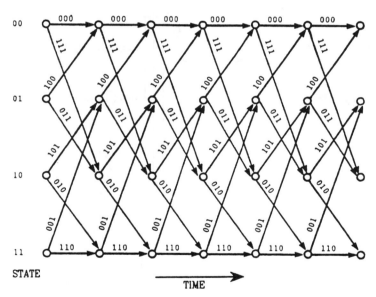

TRELLIS DIAGRAM

FIGURE 9

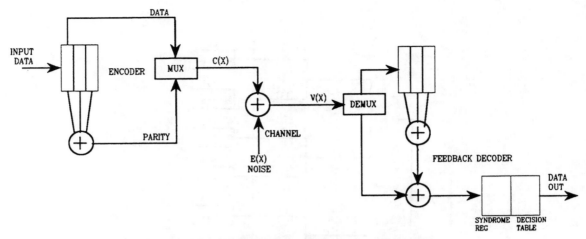

CONVOLUTIONAL SYNDROME FEEDBACK DECODER

FIGURE 10

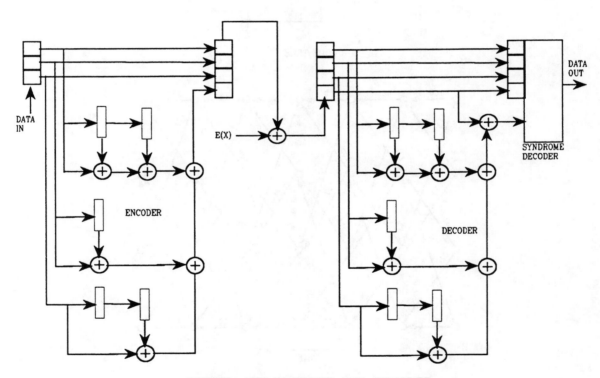

WYNER–ASH ENCODER AND DECODER

FIGURE 11

More than one error pattern can result in the same syndrome; the decoder will choose the pattern with the least errors and compensate for that pattern.

One more example of a convolutional encoder/decoder combination is illustrated in Figure 11; the Wyner-Ash code is used here.[3,5] The decoder uses the syndrome concept. The Viterbi decoder described earlier is a better method of improving coding gain.

INTERLEAVING AND CONCANTENATED CODES

Figure 2 illustrates how these two techniques relate to block codes and convolutional codes. Figure 12 depicts a hardware block diagram of a system employing these techniques.

Interleaving is used to transform a bursty channel into an independent error channel by scrambling the encoded symbols before transmission. An interleaver structure is built from semiconductor memory in a rectangular array. Encoded data is written into the array by rows and out by columns before transmission. After reception and decoding by the decoder, the process is reversed. This techniques has proven effective in satellite links that are subject to long bursts of errors.

Concantenated codes are used to increase coding gain. A Reed-Solomon code is used with the Viterbi decoder in Figure 12 due to the bursty nature of uncorrected errors out of the Viterbi decoder.[2,3]

CONCLUSIONS

This paper is intended as an introduction to error control theory for the CATV system engineer. In order to determine the optimum strategy to develop a practical digital delivery system for CATV, a number of factors should be considered:

1. The worst-case allowable symbol-error-rate. This determines the required coding gain.

2. The environment in which the system will operate, to include channel C/N, expected reflections, and other impairments.

3. The type of digital modulation selected (eg, 16QAM, 64QAM, etc). The digital channel bandwidth, the allowable signal power relative to AM channels, and any effect on those AM channels must be considered.

4. The required parity overhead, which increases the symbol rate.

5. The distribution of errors in the channel. A CATV channel is subject to random errors, not burst errors.

6. The behavior of the required adaptive equalizer under various conditions.

7. The circuit complexity and cost of the hardware, especially in the subscriber terminal.

Figure 13 illustrates the likely functional blocks in a CATV subscriber terminal employing digital data delivery. The demodulator, adaptive equalizer, error decoder, and decompression hardware must be designed to operate in concert. A properly designed system promises to deliver consistent high quality video and audio to all subscribers.

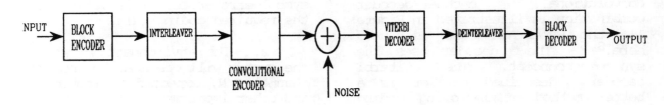

INTERLEAVING AND CONCANTENATED CODES

FIGURE 12

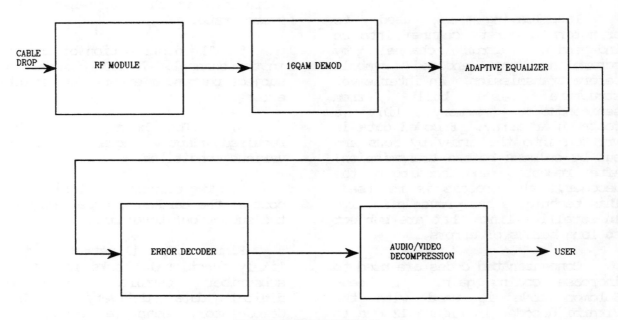

SUBSCRIBER TERMINAL

FIGURE 13

REFERENCES

1. Shannon, C.E., A Mathematical Theory of Communication, Bell Syst. Tech. J., Vol XXVII (1948)

2. Michelson, A, and Levesque, A., Error-Control Techniques For Digital Communication, John Wiley & Sons, New York, 1985

3. Blahut, R., Theory and Practice of Error Control Codes, Addison-Wesley Publishing Co., Reading Mass., 1983

4. Batson, B., A Description of The Viterbi Decoding Algorithm, NASA Report EE70-8008(U), May 1970

5. Wyner, A., and Ash, R., Analysis of Recurrent Codes, IEEE Trans. Inf. Theory, IT-9 (1963): 143-156

6. Webster's New World Dictionary, The World Publishing Company, Cleveland, 1964

CATV Channel Characterization for Digital Data Transmission Applications

Steve Dehart[+], Richard Serafin[+], Samir Hulyalkar[#], David Bryan[#], and Larry Bennett[*]

[+]Philips Broadband Networks Inc., 100 Fairgrounds Drive, Manlius, NY 13104.
[#]Philips Laboratories, 345 Scarborough Road, Briarcliff Manor, NY 10510.
[*]Hewlett Packard, 8600 Soper Hill Road, Everett, Washington 98205.

ABSTRACT

To transmit digitally compressed video with co-existing analog video over cable television (CATV) systems, the entire CATV bandwidth is frequency-division-multiplexed (FDM) into 6 MHz wide channels. For reliable data transmission, it is necessary to design an adaptive digital equalizer to compensate for the linear distortion effects, for example, the microreflections, introduced in such a 6 MHz CATV channel. This paper describes the characterization of the linear distortion effects as viewed by a digital adaptive equalizer in a 6 MHz CATV channel by developing measurement techniques using existing equipment. In contrast to other proposed techniques, this method has the added advantage of *non-intrusive* characterization of the channel, i.e., it is not necessary to interrupt existing cable service to characterize the channel. The advent of a new type of spectrum analyzer has greatly facilitated our work. Laboratory tests are performed to validate the measurement techniques. Finally, channel measurements are obtained for an in-house cable system.

INTRODUCTION

A typical cable system has a tree-type network structure, originating from the headend, then going through the trunk cable, distribution (or feeder) cable and the drop cable to the in-house wiring, and finally terminating at some consumer electronics equipment [1]. Numerous amplifiers are required to maintain the signal at specified levels. These amplifiers are generally operated in the linear region. The nonlinear effects, for example, the composite-triple-beats (CTB) and the composite-second-order (CSO) products are at least 53 dB below the main signal which is small compared to the NTSC peak carrier-to-noise ratio (CNR) of 43-46 dB. Hence, for testing the performance of digitally modulated signals, it is sufficient to assume that the CATV channel is a time-invariant linear channel with noise, which could be impulsive in nature.

The received signal at a specific consumer site can be represented simply by a sum of variously attenuated multiple reflections of the same signal caused because of improper termination of the numerous taps in the system. Since the channel is assumed to be linear, the effect of these 'microreflections' can be characterized completely by the frequency-response of the CATV channel. In older analog systems, precise channel characterization was not necessary. Crude methods were sufficient to "measure" amplitude response and group delay, such as observing the envelope of a frequency sweep or the base-line of a two-tone burst on an oscilloscope display. These methods are clearly inadequate as digitally modulated signals are added to these older systems.

A conventional network analyzer is capable of measuring the characteristics of a communication channel if both ends are in the same location. However, in a typical cable television (CATV) system, the receiving location may be twenty miles or more from the cable head-end. With the exception of only a few systems, this spatial restriction limits the use of a network analyzer to laboratory simulations.

In formulating the channel characterization technique described in this paper we made certain assumptions about the channel data required to characterize performance of digital modulation techniques over CATV channels. By the time-frequency duality, a channel characterization of X MHz should be able to resolve all microreflections of $1/X$ μsec or greater. This implies that the general problem of characterizing *all* the linear-distortion effects of the CATV channel is extremely complex, since this implies that the entire channel frequency-response be known. However, for a digitally modulated signal with a specific center frequency, only a 6 MHz section need be known to evaluate the performance of the digital modulation strategy. This channel characterization technique then concentrates only on the characterization of 6 MHz wide channels and, in this respect, is different from other approaches as described in [2], [3].

The other constraint that is assumed is the fact that such 6 MHz channels in most cable channels are already occupied with analog NTSC. It is possible to remove channels from service temporarily, but that may not always be commercially acceptable. Simulated cable plants at any lab fail to generate 'typical'

channel characteristics and tests on actual user-sites are required. The technique presented in this paper can be used for *both* the cases when analog NTSC is present or when empty channel space is available, using the same equipment for either case and thus is different from the technique proposed in [3]. One way to characterize a channel even when an analog NTSC channel is being used, is to make use of the recently adopted Ghost Cancellation Reference (GCR) signal used for echo cancellation. This reference signal is sent during the vertical blanking interval (VBI) of analog NTSC. The received signal is then a convolution of the transmitted GCR reference and the channel impulse response. Thus, the channel characteristics are obtained quite simply by dividing the received frequency response by the frequency response of the known reference. It should be emphasized that both the magnitude and the phase-response of the channel is of interest for determining the performance of the adaptive equalizer.

The above 'one-shot' technique of determining the channel frequency response usually has some noise added to it. Using averaging techniques, implemented efficiently using the new HP 89440A vector signal analyzer, it is possible to eliminate this noise, by assuming that the channel frequency response is time-invariant, at least during the total time required for averaging. One problem associated with averaging is the possibility of having a random initial phase-offset for each measurement because of sampling time jitter. This uncertainty causes the amplitude-response to be attenuated at high frequencies. Using the NTSC sync pulse, a stable reference can be generated which has provided sufficiently accurate channel measurements and is limited only by the timing-jitter present in the sync-regenerator circuits of an NTSC receiver. A similar sync pulse can be provided for the case when empty channel space is available.

An inherent problem associated with channel measurements obtained using the existing analog NTSC channels is that the bandwidth of channel measurement is limited to at most 4 MHz because the picture carrier is placed 1.25 MHz away from the band-edge and also because of the presence of the sound-carrier at 5.75 MHz. In fact, the GCR signal, introduced in the VBI of analog NTSC, has a 3 dB bandwidth equal to 4.15 MHz. To determine the frequency response over a 6 MHz bandwidth, an interpolation technique can be used, which is not included here and will be described in [4]. Thus, the output of the channel measurement scheme will be a frequency-response measurement of at least 6 MHz bandwidth obtained either by using empty-channel locations or using the GCR signal in existing analog NTSC channels.

In the next section, the measurement philosophy and setup are described in more detail. Following that, validation experiments performed in a laboratory are described using a simple single-echo channel simulator. Finally, measurements are provided for an in-house cable system.

MEASUREMENT SETUP

As discussed in the previous section, the GCR signal is used as a reference signal to characterize the linear CATV channel. Fig. 1 describes the measurement setup used for laboratory validation tests. For the purposes of the validation tests, the GCR pulse along with the synchronization pedestal was sent repetitively. An HP 89410 spectrum analyzer was used extensively, a description of which follows.

The HP 89410A (dc-10 MHz) vector signal analyzer (VSA) represents a new class of measurement instrument. These analyzers calculate both frequency and modulation domain characteristics from a time-record. The time-record of the desired frequency span is produced by accurately digitizing the input waveform, mixing with a digital quadrature local oscillator and band-limiting with digital filters. Selectable trigger delay and time-record length control the portion of the time-domain waveform that is captured. In addition, time-gating allows a subset of the time-record to be selected for subsequent calculations. The HP 89410A also has an arbitrary source generator.

For the laboratory setup shown in Fig. 1, the HP 89410A arbitrary source generator is configured to send the test signal repetitively. Fig. 2 shows the signal sent by the HP89410A source which consists of a GCR signal on an NTSC sync waveform. This signal is then modulated by the HP 8780A vector modulator, thus resulting in a double-sideband (DSB) modulated signal with the synchronization pulse providing a carrier similar to the visual carrier in analog NTSC. Note that the DSB signal will have a much larger bandwidth than 6 MHz, and is used only for this setup: typically another filter will remove one of the sidebands as used, for example, in an NTSC modulator. For the demodulation, a Tektronix VSB demodulator with sufficiently wide bandwidth filters is used to obtain the signal at baseband. A separate frame synchronization waveform can also be generated by using the HP 1133A. The receiving HP 89410A is then set to trigger on this sync and a time-record is generated which is sufficient to capture the entire transmitted signal, as shown in Fig. 2. This captured time record is then converted to a vector spectrum in the frequency domain. The spectrum contains both amplitude and phase information for every frequency component of the test signal. Fig. 2 also shows the amplitude spectrum of the time-record, which has a small attenuation over the 4 MHz bandwidth.

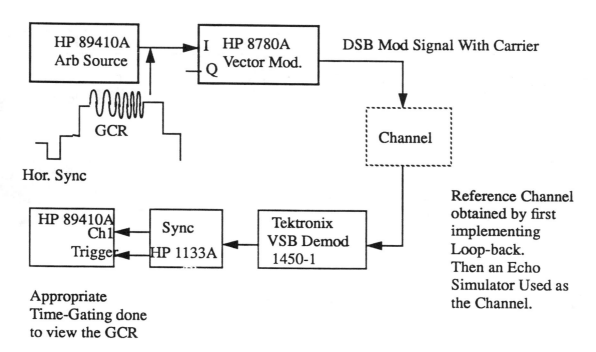

Fig. 1: Laboratory Setup Used for Channel Measurement.

For the purposes of calibration, the reference measurement is made by using a loop-back technique, i.e., the DSB modulated signal is fed directly into the Tektronix demodulator. This ensures that the frequency responses of the different instruments have also been taken into account. Fig. 3 shows the amplitude and phase variations across the entire frequency band. After creating this reference, the spectrum of the channel is measured. Dividing this spectrum by the previously measured reference yields the transfer function of the channel with an arbitrary delay term (phase ramp). The actual propagation delay cannot be measured with this technique: however, in most applications, the delay is irrelevant and only the deviation from linear phase is of interest. If necessary, improved signal-to-noise ratio is achieved by time averaging several measurements. Because the noise is not correlated with the repetitive test signal, the noise averages to zero over time. Due to the use of the HP

1133A sync generator, timing jitter is kept small which allows for such averaging to be done without any degradation to the measurement.

For measurement over a CATV network, when empty channel-space is available, a different arbitrary source generator must be used since the instruments are at different locations. For the case when analog NTSC is present, the trigger for HP 89410A is the frame sync passed through a divide-by-8 counter. This is because the GCR signal is sent with different phases over an eight field sequence to compensate for the dc offset and the color burst [5]. This will be described in more detail in the following sections.

VALIDATION TESTS

To validate the channel measurement technique, a single-echo simulator was used as shown in Fig. 4. The HP 8753 network

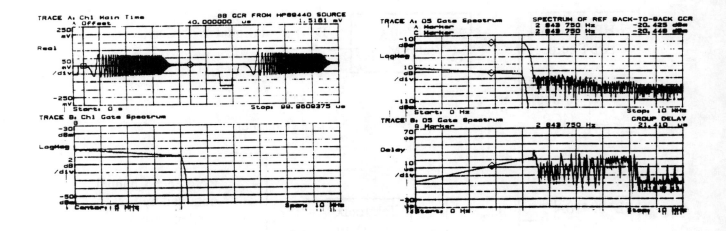

Fig. 2: GCR With the Timing Pulse.

Fig. 3: Reference Amplitude and Group-Delay Response.

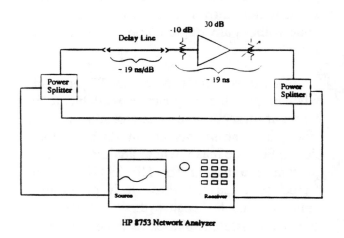

Fig. 4: Single-Echo Generator.

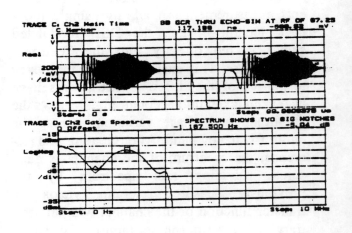

Fig. 5: GCR With a 10 dB Echo at 420 nsec.

analyzer was used to obtain the amplitude and group delay variations across a frequency band of 12 MHz, which is compared with our results.

Fig. 5 shows the GCR pulse received at the HP 89440A when a 10 dB attenuated echo was added to the main signal at a delay of 420 nsec, along with the amplitude spectrum of the appropriately gated time-record. In Fig. 6, amplitude and group delay measurements are shown for a section of 12 MHz bandwidth between 60-72 MHz using the network analyzer. This can be compared with two 4 MHz measurements shown in Fig.'s 7 and 8, between 61.25-65.25 MHz and between 67.25-71.25 MHz. Note that there is a small ripple in the group-delay measurement. This is because the dc offset in the signal was removed by subtracting the signal by a constant and then performing an FFT as can be seen by the expression shown in Fig.'s 7 and 8. Unfortunately, the AGC control in the VSB demodulator was not very accurate and this level jitter caused a ripple in both the amplitude and the group delay response. A simple method of removing this jitter will be described in the next section.

Fig. 9 shows the amplitude and the group delay measurements obtained using the network analyzer when the echo amplitude is 25 dB below the main signal. Note that the peak-to-peak variation in both the amplitude and the group delay is smaller than the 10 dB case. The corresponding measurements using our setup are shown in Fig.'s 10 and 11 which are close to the measurement made by the network analyzer.

CHANNEL MEASUREMENTS

The channel used is as shown in Fig. 12. The sixteen amplifier cascade is part of an in-house cable system with a bandwidth of 50-600 MHz. The output of this cascade was then passed through a 21 dB 8-way splitter, seven of which were unterminated. To simulate possible home-wiring the output of this splitter was passed though another splitter, the attenuation of which was varied between 0 and 3 dB for two different experiments. The other end of the 3 dB splitter was left open-ended.

Fig.'s 13-16 show the amplitude and group delay measurements performed at different bandwidths for the 16 amplifier cascade only. Note the flat spectrum in Fig.'s 14 and 15 for mid-range frequencies of 295.25-299.25 MHz and of 567.25-571.25 MHz. Also note the expected attenuation and increasing ripple for both the low frequncy of 67.25-71.25 MHz and 627.25-631.25 MHz.

Fig. 17 shows the case when the bottom path is selected for the channel shown in Fig. 12, i.e., a 3 dB splitter is used. As can be seen the amplitude ripple for 567.25-571.25 MHz is only 0.5 dB. Finally, in Fig. 18, the amplitude and group delay response for a 0 dB splitter is shown, where an open-ended cable of RG-59 of length 56 inches is used at the other end. This causes a deep null to occur near the 572 MHz frequency, as is seen by as much as 3 dB attenuation in the amplitude response as in Fig. 18.

In most of the figures on channel measurement, the effect of incorrect dc offset is observed clearly at the low frequencies. As explained earlier, this dc offset is because of the AGC present in the VSB demodulator. This dc offset can be removed quite easily by using the HP 89440A delayed trigger mode. The arbitrary source generator is used to send the GCR signal of opposite phases at successive intervals. At the receiver, a synchronization trigger to the HP 89440A is created by passing the frame sync from the HP 1133A through a divide-by-2 counter. The received baseband signal is fed in to both the Ch1 and the Ch2 inputs of the HP 89440A. The gated window for Ch2 is set to be a time-offset win-

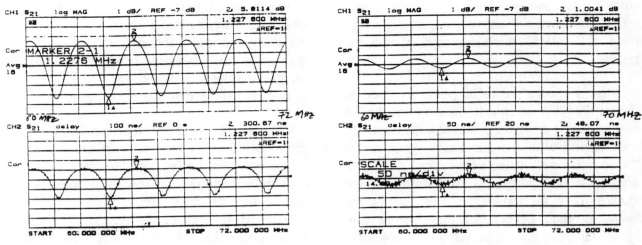

Fig. 6: Amplitude and Group Delay Measurements Using a Network Analyzer for 10 dB Echo.

Fig. 9: Amplitude and Group Delay Meas. Using a Network Analyzer for 25 dB Echo.

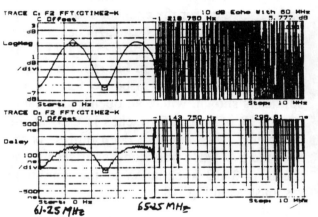

Fig. 7: Amplitude and Group Delay Meas. From 61.25-65.25 MHz for 10 dB Echo

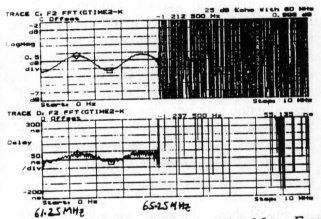

Fig. 10: Amplitude and Group Delay Meas. From 61.25-65.25 MHz for 25 dB Echo.

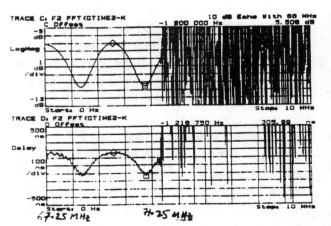

Fig. 8: Amplitude and Group Delay Meas. From 67.25-71.25 MHz for 10 dB Echo.

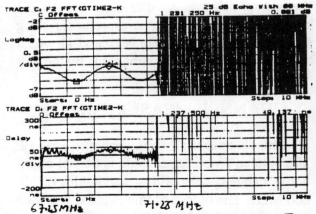

Fig. 11: Amplitude and Group Delay Meas. From 67.25-71.25 MHz for 25 dB Echo.

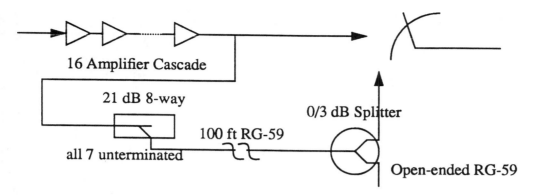

Fig. 12: Channel Setup for CATV Measurement

dow of Ch1 so that now a difference between the gated window of Ch1 and Ch2 removes the dc offset but does not cancel out the GCR. This technique can also be used with the analog NTSC GCR 8-field signal sequence, where the opposite phase is present every fourth field, and, now, a divide-by-8 counter is used. Another technique to remove this dc offset is by observing the trailing edge of the time-gated signal and using the mean value of the samples of this trailing edge to calculate the required dc offset. This trailing edge can be obtained as a time-gated signal on Ch2. A software program which performs such an averaging can be easily written using the BASIC programming options available with the HP 89440A. This investigation will form part of our future work.

CONCLUSIONS

Using the GCR signal, proposed for echo-cancellation, a channel characterization technique is described. Assuming that digital modulation techniques could be used over channels currently used for NTSC, it then becomes necessary to characterize these channel with 6 MHz bandwidth. The channel characterization technique described above allows for non-intrusive channel characteriza-

tion. The measurement technique was validated in the laboratory by using a single-echo ghost simulator. Some channel measurements are shown with an in-house cable system.

REFERENCES

[1]   W. Ciciora, "An Overview of Cable Television in the United States," Cable-Labs Report.

[2]   R. Voyer, "HDTV Cable Tests: Method of Measurement," NCTA, Nov. 1989.

[3]   R. Prodan, M. Chelehmal, T. Williams and C. Chamberlain, "Digital Transmission Characterization of Cable Television Systems," proposed project in CableLabs, Jan. 1993.

[4]   S. Hulyalkar, "Methods of Interpolation of Channel Frequency-Response in a CATV Channel," to be published, 1993.

[5]   C. Greenberg, "Effects on Ghost Cancellation of VBI Lines Before and After GCR," to be presented at ICCE 1993.

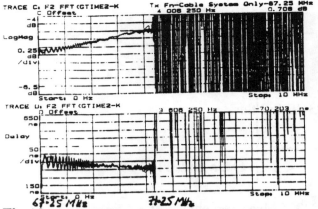

Fig.13: Amplitude and Group Delay Meas. For Just the Cable System- 67.25-71.25 MHz.

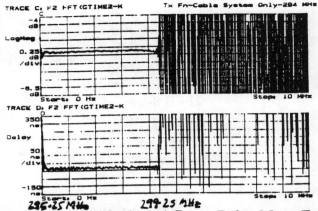

Fig. 14: Amplitude and Group Delay Meas. For Just the Cable System - 295.25-299.25 MHz.

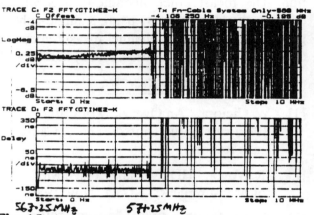

Fig. 15: Amplitude and Group Delay Meas. For Just the Cable System - 567.25-571.25 MHz.

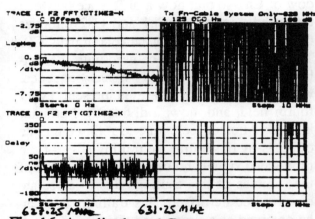

Fig. 16: Amplitude and Group Delay Meas. For Just the Cable System - 627.25-631.25 MHz.

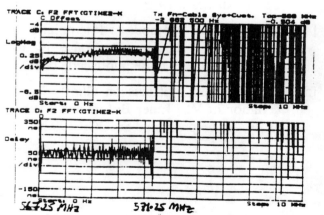

Fig. 17: Amplitude and Group Delay Meas. For Cable System+3dB Splitter-567.25-571.25. MHz.

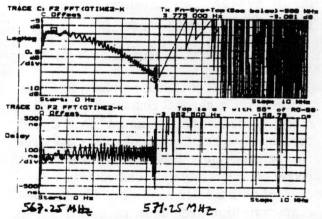

Fig. 18: Amplitude and Group Delay Meas. For Cable System+0dB Splitter-567.25-571.25 MHz.

THE IMPACT OF MICROREFLECTIONS ON DIGITAL TRANSMISSION OVER CABLE AND ASSOCIATED MEDIA

Joseph B. Waltrich
Joseph B. Glaab
Marc Ryba
Mathias A. Muller

Jerrold Communications
Applied Media Lab

ABSTRACT

Microreflections on cable systems are usually not severe enough to cause a problem with analog video transmission. However, this is not necessarily the case with digital transmission. Reflections which produce negligible degradation in an analog picture can cause significant bit errors in a digital signal. This paper discusses the overall effect of reflections and analyzes the relative contributions of the trunk and distribution systems as well as the system configuration in the subscriber's home. Analyses are correlated with test results in the laboratory and in the field.

INTRODUCTION

Generally, the effects of microreflections on cable transmission of analog video are relatively innocuous. At the most, a slight edge degradation or very low level ghosts are observed. This is not the case with digital transmission. Reflections which are barely observable in an analog video signal can cause bit error rates of up to 10^{-3} or more in the digital bit stream.

The effect of reflections on a quadrature amplitude modulated signal may be expressed mathematically by a few simple equations. The equation of a QAM signal without reflections is:

$$x(t) = I(t)\mathrm{Cos}w_c t + Q(t)\mathrm{Sin}w_c t \quad (1)$$

where: $x(t)$ = received signal
$I(t)$ = in-phase component of the baseband signal
$Q(t)$ = quadrature component of the baseband signal
w_c = modulating carrier frequency in rad/sec.

$I(t)$ and $Q(t)$ are multi-level analog signals corresponding to digital data. The number of levels assumed by $I(t)$ and $Q(t)$ depends on the type of modulation. For a 16QAM signal, $I(t)$ and $Q(t)$ each have four values.

If we now assume that the signal is impaired by $n=1...N$ multiple reflections, each having an amplitude α_n and a delay τ_n relative to the main signal $x(t)$, then the received signal $r(t)$ can be written:

$$r(t) = x(t) +$$

$$\sum_{n=1}^{N} \alpha_n I(t-\tau_n)\mathrm{Cos}(w_c(t-\tau_n)) \quad +$$

$$\sum_{n=1}^{N} \alpha_n Q(t-\tau_n)\mathrm{Sin}(w_c(t-\tau_n)) \quad (2)$$

When $r(t)$ is demodulated by $\cos w_c t$ and $\sin w_c t$ and the double frequency terms are removed, the in-phase and quadrature components of the recovered baseband signal are:

$$r_I(t) = I(t) +$$

$$\sum_{n=1}^{N} \alpha_n (I(t-\tau_n)\cos w_c \tau_n - Q(t-\tau_n)\sin w_c \tau_n)$$

$$(3)$$

$$r_Q(t) = Q(t) +$$

$$\sum_{n=1}^{N} \alpha_n (Q(t-\tau_n)\cos w_c \tau_n + I(t-\tau_n)\sin w_c \tau_n)$$

$$(4)$$

The effect of reflections is best observed by examining the signal constellation - that is, by looking at all possible combinations of in-phase and quadrature data plotted in I-Q space. If the above equations are plotted for a single reflection, the result is a miniature replica of the entire constellation about each point in the original constellation. The size of the replicated constellation is equal to α times the size of the original constellation and the replicated constellation is rotated by an angle $w_c \tau$ relative to the original constellation. This effect is shown in Fig. 1. Multiple reflections occurring at various amplitudes and delays will result in a number of superimposed replicas of the original constellation, producing a smearing of the constellation points. However, if one echo is dominant, the pattern will still have a square or diamond shaped configuration.

SOURCES OF REFLECTIONS

For purposes of analysis, the reflections generated on a cable system may be separated into those produced by the trunk, the distribution system and by the subscriber environment. If each of these sources of reflections is analyzed separately, the results may be combined to determine a complete pattern of reflections as seen at the consumer terminal.

Trunk Echoes:

Reflections generated along the trunk are produced when signals are reflected from amplifier inputs and outputs as a result of amplifier return loss. The reflected signal paths are shown in Fig. 2. The transmitted signal from a given trunk amplifier is reflected due to the return loss of the next amplifier in the cascade and reflected again due to the transmitting amplifier's output mismatch. The power of the echo relative to the transmitted signal is:

$$P = -2(R_A + \mu_0 L) \qquad (5)$$

where: R_A = amplifier return loss (dB)
μ_0 = cable attenuation (dB/ft)
L = amplifier spacing (ft.)

Equation (5) assumes equal input and output return loss for the amplifiers. The echo is delayed by two path lengths. The delay time is:

$$t = 2\tau L \qquad (6)$$

where τ = cable delay (nS/ft)

For N amplifiers in cascade, the worst case reflection is produced by the sum of the echoes at the end of the cascade. If all the amplifiers are equally spaced, all primary echoes will have the same delay. The total reflected power at the Nth stage of the cascade is:

$$P_T = 10 \text{Log}(N*10^{P/10}) \qquad (7)$$

For a 20 amplifier cascade with 22 dB spacing at 300 MHz (2472 ft. using the cable data from Table 1), the total reflected power vs frequency is:

f(MHz)	P_T(dB)
55	-37
300	-63
450	-74
550	-83

The echoes are delayed by about 5.7 μS. Although the trunk generates rather long delays, the amplitude of the echoes is quite low and, therefore, not a major contributor to signal degradation.

Distribution System:

A worst case situation for reflections on a distribution system would occur in a section consisting of N equally spaced taps, located between two line extenders, with equal length drops from each tap. A simple example of such a system, containing 4 taps, is shown in Figs. 3-5 to illustrate reflection paths. However, the echo analysis, as shown in this paper, has been extended to an N tap system. The following notation will be used for purposes of analysis:

k = 0....N+1 = Tap no.

For simplification of the analysis, the first line extender (LE1) is considered to be tap 0 and the second line extender (LE2) is considered to be tap N+1.

j = 1,2....k = No. of taps behind the kth tap. (i.e. - the receiving site of interest).

n = 1,2...N+1 = No. of taps ahead of the kth tap.

Referring to Figs. 3-5. reflections on the system can be categorized into the following types:

(1) Backward reflections from the kth tap to the (k-j)th tap and then returning to the kth tap. (Fig. 3).

(2) Forward reflections from the (k+n)th tap, returning to the kth tap. (Fig. 4).

(3) Bi-directional reflections. These are a special case of backward reflections in which the reflected signal from n taps ahead passes through the kth tap and is reflected from j taps behind (Fig. 5).

(4) From unterminated drops within the same tap. (Fig. 6).

Note that the above paths include the reflections from LE1 (tap 0) and LE2 (tap N+1).

In the 4 tap example of Fig. 3, there are 5 reflections from adjacent taps, 4 reflections from two taps back, 3 reflections from 3 taps back, etc. As these echoes are propagated through the system, they add, producing the maximum reflected power at the input of the second line extender (i.e. - for k = N+1). Extending the analysis to an N tap system and computing the echoes at each tap, one obtains:

$$t1(k-j) = 2j\tau L \tag{8}$$

The reflected power associated with each echo is:

$$P1(k-j) = -(R_k + R_{(k-j)} + 2j\mu_1 L$$

$$+ 2\sum_{i=k-j+1}^{k-1}\epsilon_i) \tag{9}$$

where: $P1(k-j)$ = reflected power from the $(k-j)$th tap
$t1(k-j)$ = delay of reflection from $(k-j)$th tap
$R_{(k-j)}$ = I/O return loss of $(k-j)$th tap
R_k = kth tap I/O return loss
μ_1 = feeder cable loss (dB/ft.)
ϵ_i = insertion loss of taps between the $(k-j)$th and kth taps

For a given delay, the echo power at the input of the second line extender is :

$$P1_T(j) = 10Log[10 \cdot \frac{1}{k}\sum P1(j,k)] \tag{10}$$

In Fig. 4 there are 4 reflections from adjacent taps, 3 reflections from two taps ahead, etc. These echoes do not propagate through the system and are attenuated by the tap to output isolation. Therefore they may be considered negligible. For an N tap system, the delay and reflected power at the kth tap are:

$$t2(k+n) = 2n\tau L \tag{11}$$

$$P2(k+1) = -(R_{(k+1)} + \mu_1 L + \delta_k) \tag{12}$$

$$(k=1,2..N; n=1)$$

$$P2(k+n) = -(R_{(k+n)} + n\mu_1 L + \delta_k$$

$$+ \sum_{i=k+1}^{k+n-1}\epsilon_i) \tag{13}$$

$$(k=1,2..N; n=2,3..N+1-k)$$

where: $P2(k+n)$ = reflected power from the $(k+n)$th tap
δ_k = tap to output isolation

If the 4 tap example of Fig. 5 is extended to N taps, the equations for delay time and echo power are:

$$t3(k,n,j) = (n+2j)\tau L \tag{14}$$

$$P3(k,n,j) = -(R_{(k+n)} + R_{(k-j)}$$

$$+ \mu_1(n+2j)L + 2\sum_{i=k-1}^{k-j+1}\epsilon_i$$

$$+ \sum_{i=k+1}^{k+n-1}\epsilon_i + \epsilon_k) \tag{15}$$

For reflections from unterminated drops on the same tap (Fig. 6), the equations are:

$$t4(k) = 2\tau D \tag{16}$$

$$P4(k) = 10Log(m_k-1)$$

$$- (\beta_k + 2\mu_2 D) \tag{17}$$

where: m_k = no. of outputs on the kth tap
β_k = tap to tap isolation

An example of part of a typical urban distribution system is shown in Fig. 7. In order to obtain worst case conditions, the assumption is made that all taps are equally spaced and all drops are the same length.

Using the data from Table 1 and Fig. 7 in equations (8)-(17), it is seen that the worst case echoes of type 1 are backward reflections from adjacent taps (j=1). The total echo power at the input of LE2 due to these reflections is as follows:

f(MHz)	$P1_T(1)$ (dB)
55	-28
300	-29
450	-29
550	-29

The delay associated with this reflection is 115 nS. Other type 1 reflections are delayed up to about 1.5 μS in increments of 115 nS, but, since their levels are lower, their effect on digital transmission is relatively small.

Other dominant echoes are those from unterminated drops on the same tap. For the example of Fig. 7, these reflections are delayed about 300 nS and have the following power levels relative to the transmitted signal:

f(MHz)	P4(dB)
55	-24
300	-30
450	-32
550	-33

Different drop lengths will not have a significant effect on the power levels shown in the above table. However, for drop lengths in the range 75-175 ft. and cable velocity factors of 82-87%, the delay of the echoes will vary from about 170 nS to 440 nS. For an 8-port tap, the levels shown in the above table will be 3 dB worse.

Subscriber Environment:

It is not possible to predict the nature of reflections in every subscriber's home since such installations vary considerably, depending on the number of TV receivers, VCR's and converters which are connected to the cable drop. Also, customers may add their own variations to the installation, in the form of splitters, cable, connectors and switches purchased from retail stores. Therefore, investigation of echoes in the home environment was limited to the following:

o   Performance analysis of a variety of splitters purchased from local retail outlets.

o   Computational analysis of an installation consisting of a single 4-way splitter feeding various devices.

o   Verification of the computed data by laboratory measurements.

The splitters were tested using a HP8753B Network Analyzer to measure return loss and isolation. Performance varied considerably among devices. However, worst case results yielded return losses of about -8 dB and tap to tap isolation of about -15 dB.

Analysis and testing were performed on what might be considered a typical home installation. The test setup is shown in Fig. 8. The test configuration consisted of a 4 way splitter with one output correctly terminated and the remaining three outputs connected to reflective devices (a cable ready TV receiver, a VCR and a converter). Return loss of each of these devices was measured. Although there was some variation with frequency, worst case return loss was very near zero for all of the active devices.

From an analysis of the test system configuration, it is seen that there are three significant reflections from each of the three mis-terminated ports into the fourth port. The first echo path consists of a reflection from each of the devices, through the splitter's interport connections, to the fourth port. The reflected signal power and delay, relative to the main signal are:

$$P_{s1} = 10Log[\sum_{i=1}^{3}10^{-.1(\mu(D_i+D_4)+Rd_i+\beta_{i4})}]$$

$$(18)$$

$$t_{s1} = \tau(D_i + D_4) \qquad (19)$$

where: P_{s1} = total reflected power
μ = cable loss (dB/ft.)
D_i = connection length from ith port to device
D_4 = connection length from 4th port to termination
Rd_i = return loss of device on ith port
β_{i4} = isolation between ith port and port 4

The second reflection occurs due to the return loss of the splitter output port. The signal is reflected back from the splitter to the device and then from the device, through the splitter, to the termination. The delay and reflected power are:

$$P_{s2} = 10Log[\sum_{i=1}^{3}10^{-.1(\mu(3D_i+D_4)}$$

$$+2Rd_i+R_i+\beta_{i4})] \qquad (20)$$

$$t_{s2} = \tau(3D_i + D_4) \qquad (21)$$

where: P_{s2} = total reflected power for second echo
R_i = return loss of ith port on splitter

A third echo is caused by a double reflection between the splitter and the device which then travels through the splitter to the termination. The equations for this reflection are:

$$P_{s3} = 10Log[\sum_{i=1}^{3}10^{-.1(\mu(5D_i+D_4)}$$

$$+3Rd_i+2R_i+\beta_{i4})] \qquad (22)$$

$$t_{s3} = \tau(5D_i+D_4) \qquad (23)$$

Using the cable data from Table 1 and worst case values for splitter and device return loss (R_i = 15 dB and Rd_i = 0), it is possible to compute expected echo amplitudes and delays as a function of both frequency and interconnection length. Results of these computations are shown in Table 2. It is seen that first echoes can have amplitudes on the order of −10 dB at delays in the range 20 − 120 nS. The level of second echoes is about −20 dB and the delay range is 40 − 250 nS. Third echoes range from 26 − 45 dB at delays up to about 350 nS.

LABORATORY TESTS

The calculations of equations (18) − (23) were verified using the test setup of Fig. 8. The signal input to the system was an RF burst, produced by modulating a carrier with the output of a Tektronix PG507 generator. The pulse generator output was filtered to generate a Gaussian RF burst with a half amplitude duration of about 25 nS. The pulse repetition rate was set to 2.44 μS and the modulator output level was adjusted to produce about 7 dBmV at the splitter input port.

Reflections were measured using a Tektronix DAS602 Digital Scope with an 11A52 input amplifier. The bandwidth of the scope, as configured for the test, was 600 MHz. The scope vertical display was set to display the log of the absolute value, thereby permitting direct readout of reflected signal amplitudes in dB relative to the main signal. The displayed signals were averaged over 512 readings in order to minimize the effect of transients.

Fig. 9 presents a printout of a scope trace obtained using the test setup. All three echoes are clearly visible.

A comparison between calculated and measured values is shown in Table 3. The calculations of Table 3 differ from the worst case situation of Table 2 in that cable loss and velocity factors were taken from specifications for the RG6 cable used in the test. Also, return loss and interport isolation are those measured for the specific splitter used in the test. From Table 3, it is seen that the agreement between calculated and measured values is quite good, differing by only 1 or 2 dB in most cases.

The effect of test configuration echoes on bit error rates was evaluated using 16QAM transmission of pseudorandom data through the test system. Fig. 10 shows the test configuration. Results are presented in Table 4. Depending on which devices are turned on, bit error rates range from 5×10^{-3} to 8.5×10^{-5}.

FIELD TESTS

Bit error rate tests were conducted on two cable systems using the following configurations within the systems:

o   A three amplifier cascade plus a minimal distribution system.

o   A 21 amplifier cascade and a more extensive distribution system.

o   An 11 amplifier cascade in conjunction with a 13 mile AML link.

Tests were first run over a cascade of three trunk amplifiers, plus a bridger, a line extender and a 7 dB tap. Bit error rates were about 10^{-7}. This test was conducted on Channel 57 (91 MHz).

Following the initial test, a second bit error rate test (also using Channel 57) was conducted over a link consisting of 21 trunk amplifiers, a bridger, two line extenders and three taps. The received signal was taken from the third tap and fed through an A/B switch into a 4-way splitter. Initial bit error rates were on the order of 5×10^{-3}. The received signal constellation clearly indicated the presence of reflections (Fig. 11). These were traced to 3 unterminated outputs of the 4-way splitter. When these outputs were terminated, the BER dropped to between 10^{-5} and 10^{-6}.

A third test was conducted on an 11 amplifier cascade, followed by a 13 mile AML link. The output from the AML receiver was fed through a bridger and one tap to the test system. The BER measured for this test was about 3×10^{-6}.

CONCLUSIONS

Judging from the results of theoretical analyses, corroborated by laboratory and field tests, it would seem that the principal source of reflections in a cable system is the home installation. Since this is the part of the system over which the operator has the least control, it is necessary to compensate for the effects of reflections in the converter design. This can be done using an adaptive equalizer. Considerable literature has been devoted to adaptive equalizer design [1] – [3]. Since most of the echo power is concentrated in a rather small delay range, the use of relatively short equalizers is possible.

REFERENCES

[1] E. Lee, D. Messerschmitt, "Digital Communication", Kluwer Academic Publishers, 1988.

[2] J. Treichler, C. Johnson, M. Larimore, "Theory and Design of Adaptive Filters", Wiley, 1987.

[3] J. Proakis, "Digital Communications", McGraw-Hill, 1989.

Table 1

Cable Data

Attenuation (dB/100 ft)

Frequency (MHz)	Trunk (.750)	Feeder (.625)	Drop RG-6	Subscriber RG-59
55	.36	.46	1.55	1.9
300	.89	1.10	3.75	4.57
450	1.12	1.35	4.63	5.64
550	1.29	1.51	5.15	6.25

Velocity Factor for all cables = 87%   (τ = 1.15 nS/ft)

Table 2

Worst Case Echoes Computed for Installation of Fig.8

f(MHz)	D(ft)	P1	t1	P2	t2	P3	t3
55	10	-11	23	-19	46	-27	69
300	10	-11	23	-20	46	-29	69
450	10	-11	23	-20	46	-30	69
550	10	-11	23	-21	46	-30	69
55	20	-11	46	-20	92	-29	138
300	20	-12	46	-22	92	-32	138
450	20	-12	46	-23	92	-33	138
550	20	-13	46	-23	92	-34	138
55	50	-12	115	-22	230	-32	345
300	50	-15	115	-27	230	-39	345
450	50	-16	115	-30	230	-43	345
550	50	-16	115	-31	230	-45	345

All power levels in dB.
All times in nS.

R_i = 8dB Rd_i = 0 β_{i4} = 15dB

τ = 1.15 nS/ft   (87% velocity factor)

For 82% velocity factor, delays range from 25 -375 nS.

Table 3

Test Results vs. Calculations

f(MHz)	P1	t1	P2	t2	P3	t3	
75	-17	124	-26	248	-36	372	Calculated
	-15	126	-26	250	-36	376	Measured
100	-17	124	-27	248	-37	372	Calculated
	-17	121	-30	249	-38	374	Measured
200	-18	124	-28	248	-39	372	Calculated
	-19	125	-28	252	-38	371	Measured
250	-18	124	-29	248	-40	372	Calculated
	-20	124	-32	249	-36	371	Measured

$R_i = 8$ dB $Rd_i = 0$ $D_i, D_4 = 50$ ft.

$\beta_{i4} = 15$ dB $\beta_{24}, \beta_{34} = 30$ dB

$\tau = 1.24$ nS/ft. (82% velocity factor)

$\mu = .018$ dB/ft.   (75 MHz)
   .022   "   (100 MHz)
   .028   "   (200 MHz)
   .033   "   (250 MHz)

Table 4

Bit Error Rate Test Results

VCR	TV Receiver	Converter	BER
OFF	OFF	OFF	5×10^{-3}
ON	OFF	OFF	1.8×10^{-3}
OFF	OFF	ON	6.4×10^{-4}
OFF	ON	OFF	5×10^{-4}
ON	ON	OFF	2.3×10^{-4}
ON	ON	ON	1.4×10^{-4}
ON	OFF	ON	1×10^{-4}
OFF	ON	ON	8.5×10^{-5}

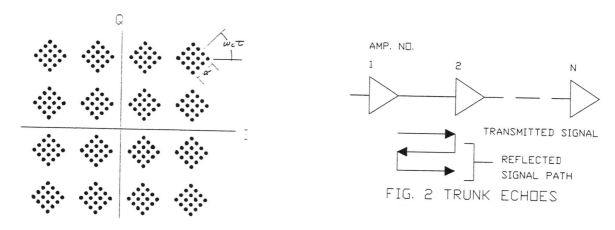

FIG. 1 16QAM CONSTELLATION
WITH SINGLE REFLECTION

AMP. NO.

FIG. 2 TRUNK ECHOES

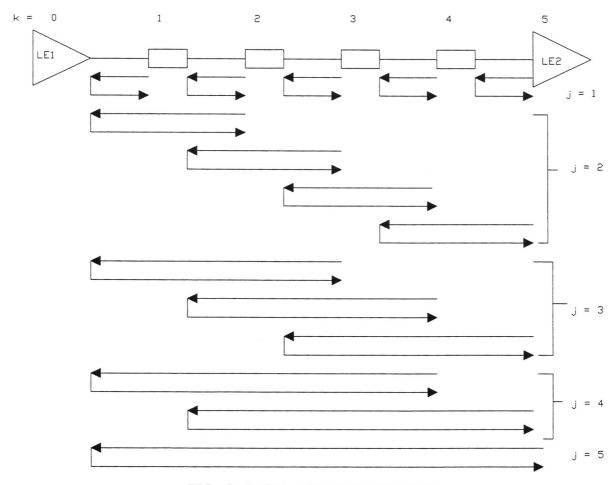

FIG. 3 BACKWARD REFLECTIONS

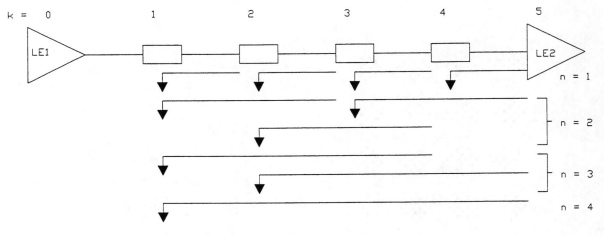

FIG. 4 FORWARD REFLECTIONS

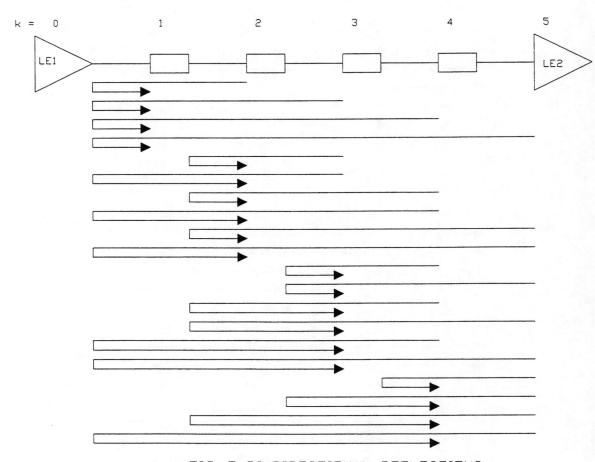

FIG. 5 BI-DIRECTIONAL REFLECTIONS

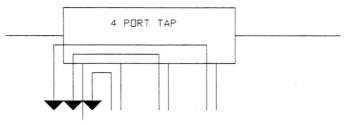

FIG. 6 REFLECTIONS FROM UNTERMINATED DROPS

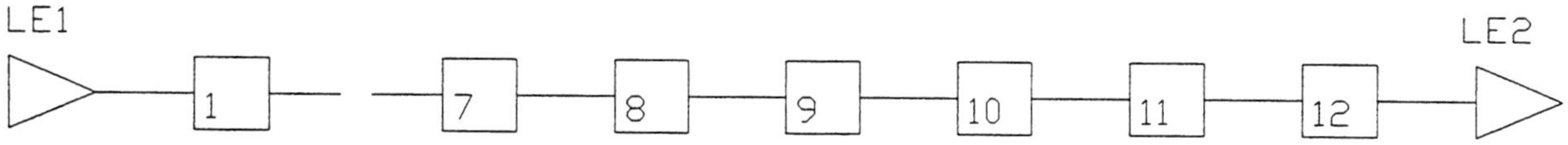

LE1   LE2

| 1 | 7 | 8 | 9 | 10 | 11 | 12 |

Tap Value (dB)	26	26	23	20	17	17	15.5

Tap Insertion Loss (dB)

55 MHz	.3	.3	.5	.6	.7	.7	1.1
300 MHz	.4	.4	.5	.7	.8	.8	1.3
450 MHz	.5	.5	.6	.7	.9	.9	1.5
550 MHz	.6	.6	.8	.9	1.1	1.1	1.9

Tap to Output Isolation (dB)

55 MHz	45	45	40	35	30	30	30
300 MHz	45	45	40	35	30	30	30
450 MHz	45	45	40	35	30	30	30
550 MHz	45	45	40	35	30	30	25

Tap to Tap Isolation: 25 dB (all taps)

Tap I/O Return Loss (all taps): 20 dB (30-450 MHz), 18 dB (450-600 MHz)

Tap Spacing: 50 ft.

Drops/Tap: 4 (all taps)

Drop Length: 125 ft. (all drops)

Line Extender Return Loss: 16dB

FIG. 7 DISTRIBUTION SYSTEM

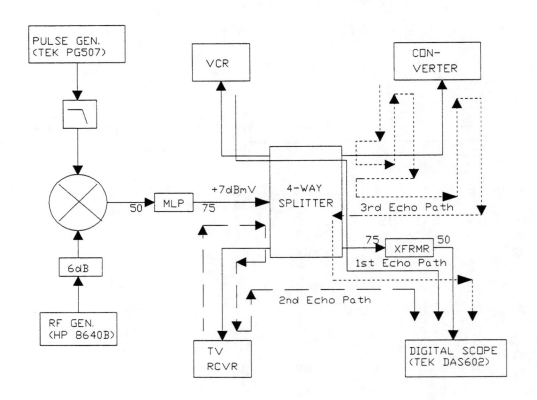

All splitter output cables are 50 ft.
All cables are RG-6 (CommScope F660BV)

FIG. 8 HOME INSTALLATION - TEST SETUP

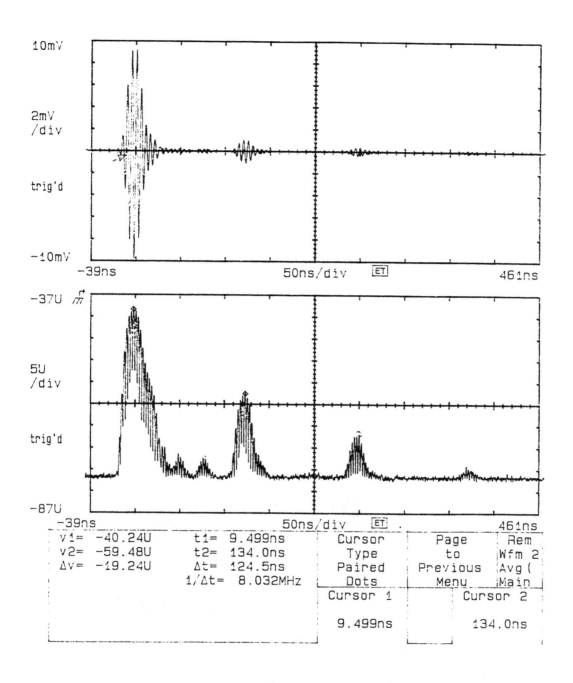

Fig. 9 Scope Trace Showing Transmitted Signal With Echoes

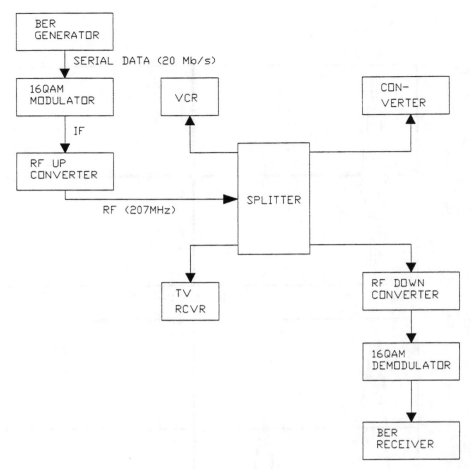

FIG. 10 BER TEST SETUP

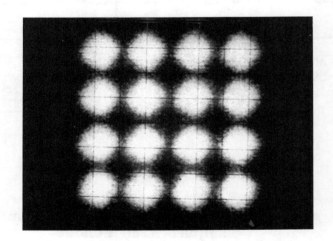

**FIG. 11 Received Signal
Constellation With
Reflections**

THE EFFECT OF DIGITAL CARRIERS ON ANALOG CATV DISTRIBUTION SYSTEMS

Jeff Hamilton and Dean Stoneback[1]

Jerrold **GI** General Instrument

Abstract

The introduction of digital carriers into existing CATV distribution plants will bring significant benefits to cable operators but will also introduce a new set of impairments to the analog video carriers. In general, the digital carriers have a noise-like spectral energy distribution. This signal will be superimposed on the analog video carriers by second and third order distortion effects similar to CSO and CTB. Digital transmission will not create the familiar beats and patterns created by the distortion products of analog carriers. The picture impairment of digital carrier distortion will be reduced video signal to noise on analog channels. This paper will describe the level of this impairment in quantitative terms. Theoretical calculations and test results will provide some insight into what levels to carry the digital signals to allow for their robust transmission while minimizing the impairment of the analog carriers.

INTRODUCTION

The technology of distributing analog video carriers through a CATV plant has been developed over many years. Specifications, test methods, and performance criteria are all well established. Much of this technology is based on practical experience and the logic is not always obvious.

Distortion performance, for example, is specified as Composite Second Order (CSO) and Composite Triple Beat (CTB) and is measured with unmodulated "CW" carriers. In an operating system, however, the carriers are modulated. This drops the distortion beat power substantially below the specified levels. If only one carrier was modulated with video while performing the distortion test, a system meeting the -53 dB specifications would create a terrible picture on that one modulated channel. Only when you modulate the rest of the carriers will the visible picture beats and patterns disappear. Proper cable system operation depends on the effect of lower beats when the carriers are modulated. The specifications were set based on operating the plant with modulated carriers while testing with CW carriers.[2]

The way CATV distribution plant is specified and designed will require some new thinking as we introduce digital carriers into the mix. In particular, the basic physics of how digital carriers behave with amplifier distortion offers new opportunities and risks to distribution plant design.

As plant bandwidth is extended with analog video carriers, the number of distortion products or beats increases exponentially. Distribution amplifier power output levels are reduced to keep the composite of all of these beats, CSO and CTB, below an acceptable threshold. This means closer amplifier spacing, more amplifiers, better coaxial cable, and a higher cost plant.

Adding digital carriers to a distribution system does not add new CSO or CTB beats. Instead, distortion beats of digital carriers generate the new impairment, *Intermodulation Noise*. As the analog carriers are switched over to digital modulation the distortion beats rapidly become Intermodulation Noise. In a 750 MHz system with 77 analog and 33 digital carriers, only 30 % of the carriers are digital but 67% of the third order beats on the last analog channel are Intermodulation Noise.

This paper will describe our work to quantify the level of this new impairment to analog transmission and how to minimize its impact.

DIGITAL TRANSMISSION SPECTRUM

Using an advanced 64-QAM modulation and error correction technology built upon the art developed for HDTV broadcast testing, a 27 Mbps information rate can be provided in each 6 MHz cable channel. This high density modulation in 6 MHz channels makes optimum use of cable spectrum while offering maximum compatibility with existing CATV equipment, practices, and procedures.

In the frequency domain these Quadrature Amplitude Modulation (QAM) digital carriers will look like 5 MHz bands of white noise. The modulation is balanced double sideband suppressed carrier. Transmit filtering is square-root raised cosine with an excess bandwidth under 0.2 and a symbol frequency of just over 5 MHz. The compressed video multiplex is bit scrambled to insure the data stream is sufficiently random to maintain this noise like appearance by equally exciting each of the 64 modulation states. One advantage of this balanced modulation is the absence of residual carrier. The distribution amplifiers are not loaded by unnecessary carrier power as they are with analog video modulation and other forms of digital modulation. All of the transmitted power is in the modulation sidebands which carry the information. This avoids generating additional discrete CTB and CSO beats, increases amplifier headroom, and reduces analog carrier distortion levels by operating

further from the knee in the curve of amplifier non-linearity (crash point).

DISTORTION BEAT THEORY

Individual (Single) Beats

When CW carriers mix with each other through amplifier non-linearity, they produce second and third order beats. Some of these beats contribute to CSO and CTB in the transmission band. These *ISO's* (*Individual Second Order*) and *ITB's* (*Individual Triple Beats*) are the result of multiplication of the carriers in the time domain which is convolution in the frequency domain. Since the CW carrier spectra are all impulses, the beats also appear as impulses in the frequency domain.

Due to the DC bias used in AM video modulation, most of the analog video carrier power remains at the frequency of the CW carrier. Analog modulated video carriers have lower average power but the same peak power and approximately the same impulsive spectral shape as CW carriers. The spectrum of ISO and ITB from analog modulated carriers look like impulses. See Figure 1.

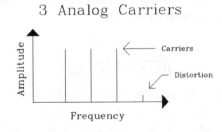

3 Analog Carriers

Figure 1

This is not true for digitally modulated carriers. The 64-QAM modulated carrier looks like a 5 MHz band of white noise (a pulse in the frequency domain). See Figure 2. When this "pulse" is convolved with two analog carriers, the result will be a "pulse" of noise. This is called Intermodulation Noise. If the digital carrier is at the same average power as the CW carrier, the Intermodulation Noise beat will have the same total average power as the ISO or ITB of the CW carriers.

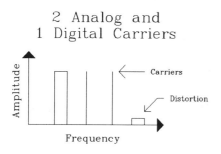

Figure 2

If the distortion beat involves two digital channels and one analog channel, the resulting distortion energy will appear as a triangle of noise in the frequency domain. See Figure 3. The triangle will have twice the width of the "pulse" shaped distortion and will have the same amplitude. The spectral broadening is from each spectral component of the digital carrier beating with each component of the second digital carrier.

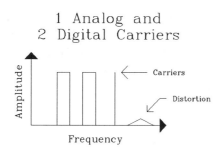

Figure 3

Finally, if the distortion is a result of three digital channels beating against each other, the distortion will appear as a band limited gaussian shape. See Figure 4. The width will be three times the digital carrier width (15 MHz). The height will be ¾ as high as the "pulse" shaped distortion and the total average power will be the same as a CW carrier beat.

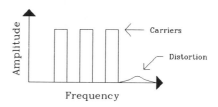

Figure 4

All the results above assume that all channels are transmitted at the same total power.

Multiple Beats

Just as many discrete beats of CW carriers add to produce CTB in an all analog system, the various intermodulation noise beats will add to produce *Composite Intermodulation Noise* (*CIN*). The level of this noise will depend on the location of both the analog and digital channels, and on their level. *CIN3* is the composite of all of the third order beats involving at least one digital carrier and so giving the beat one of the above described spectral shapes. The second order digital beat composite is *CIN2*. Since the principle significance of either type of CIN is as an impairment to analog video transmission we normalize levels to a 4 MHz noise bandwidth.

CALCULATED CIN PERFORMANCE

A computer program was written to calculate all the beats produced by carriers. These carriers can be any combination of CW or digital and may have any amplitude assigned to them. The output of the program contains both the total number of each type of beat and the total amplitude of the beats at every frequency. If digital carriers are involved, the computer also produces the total CIN2 and CIN3 at each channel. This program was used to predict the performance of 550 and 750 MHz channel loadings for a hypothetical device which has a flat distortion vs frequency characteristic.

The simulations were done with tilted output spectrums. In order to establish a baseline for a mixed analog/digital system, all output levels are referenced to the level at 547.25 MHz. For ease of measurement, this reference is called 0 dB. See Figure 5.

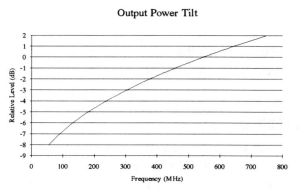

Figure 5

This tilt was used in the computer program to produce the levels of the beats for both 77 and 110 channel CW loading. When these beats are compared to the carrier level at that channel, the results are given in dB below carrier (dBc). The results shown in Figure 6 have been evenly scaled across the spectrum to produce a worst case CTB of -60 dBc for 77 CW carriers. As expected, significant CTB performance degradation occurs as more CW carriers are added.

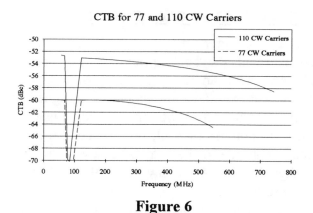

Figure 6

If instead of adding more CW channels, digital carriers are used above 550 MHz, the discrete beat levels will be the same as they were for 77 CW carriers. This is because no new discrete beats are produced as digital carriers are added. However, Intermodulation Noise will be produced. The levels of CTB and CIN3 are shown in Figure 7 for a channel loading of 77 CW carriers from 50 to 550 MHz and 33 digital carriers from 550 to 750 MHz.

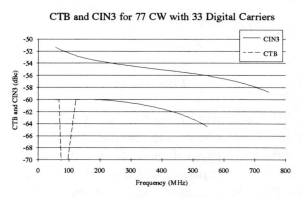

Figure 7

It is unlikely that the digital channels will be operated at the same power as the analog channels. Figure 7 showed that the CIN3 is very bad under these conditions. Since digital transmission requires less carrier to noise to maintain picture quality, the digital carriers can be lowered by several dB. Figure 8 shows the output levels of a system with digital carriers above 550 MHz. The digital carriers are 8 dB lower than the equivalent analog level.

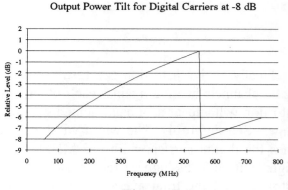

Figure 8

The CTB and CIN3 for the reduced digital levels is shown in Figure 9. Note that the CIN3 performance has improved significantly from Figure 7.

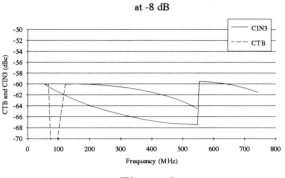

Figure 9

REAL AMPLIFIERS

Frequency Dependence of Distortion

Figures 5 through 9 have been for a hypothetical device with a flat distortion vs frequency curve. In order to account for the performance of real amplifiers, several 750 MHz power doubling amplifiers were characterized for distortion with CW carriers. These results were tabulated so that the behavior of the amplifiers could be determined. Since different numbers of beats contribute to the CTB at different frequencies, the CTB results of the amplifier tests were converted to their equivalent Individual Triple Beat (ITB) performance. The number of beats at each channel was determined by the computer program described previously. To simplify computation, we hypothesized that the amplitude of the distortion at a particular frequency depends only on the frequency of each ITB, its type (A±B±C, 2A±B, 3A), and the number of beats adding at that frequency and not on the frequency of the original carriers that mixed to create the ITB. Furthermore, since intermodulation beats (2A±B) are 6 dB smaller and occur much less often than triple beats (A±B±C), they are insignificant. Based on

these assumptions, the ITB performance at a given frequency can be estimated as:

$$ITB = CTB - 10\log(\# \text{ of beats}) + 3$$

The +3 term corrects for a response error in the spectrum analyzer. When the analyzer is subjected to large numbers of carriers (or beats) in close proximity to each other, the detector and video filter create an error. The correction factor of 3 dB was determined by experimentation. The test results are shown in Figure 10. Data was taken for both 77 channel (550 MHz) and 110 channel (750 MHz) CW loading. All amplifier output levels were +44 dBmV flat. The measured CTB and calculated ITB are shown for both tests.

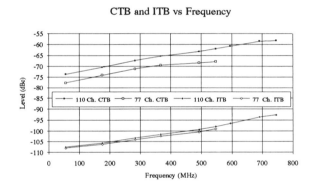

Figure 10

The ITB curves closely match. This supports the hypothesis that the beat size is not strongly influenced by the frequencies of the carriers which caused the beats. Notice that the ITB is <u>not</u> flat across the frequency band. Instead, it has a strong frequency dependence, increasing with increasing frequency. This effect should be factored into CIN3 projections.

Test Method

In order to conduct testing of mixed analog/digital systems, the device under test was driven with a combined spectrum designed to model analog carriers from 50 to 550 MHz and digital carriers from 600 to 750 MHz. Twenty-five digital carriers were simulated by bandpass filtering the output of a broadband noise source. In order to accurately make measurements at the highest likely analog carrier, 547.25 MHz, the noise was band limited to between 600 MHz and 750 MHz. See Figure 11.

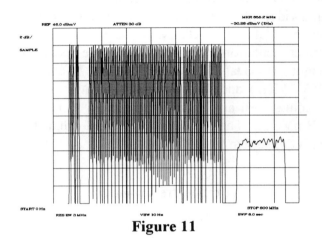

Figure 11

The digital carriers shown in Figure 11 are 6 dB below the CW carriers. Note that they appear lower than this in the figure. The power in a digital carrier is distributed over the channel so its apparent power on a spectrum analyzer display is highly dependent on the resolution bandwidth setting. This is the same effect as exhibited with broadband noise. Digital carrier power is measured with the noise power measurement facility of the analyzer and normalized to its 3 dB bandwidth of 5 MHz.

Projected and Measured Performance

The next step in determining actual system performance is to combine the calculated beat levels with the ITB frequency dependence. A similar procedure is followed for the second order beats. In order to produce the best possible prediction of Composite Intermodulation Noise, the third order and second order beat performance curves were

scaled to provide an exact match to the CTB and CSO performance of the amplifier under test. The measured thermal carrier to noise of the amplifier was also used in the prediction of total carrier to noise.

The predicted performance of a single amplifier is shown in Table 1. The output level is +47 dBmV with a 10 dB tilt from 50 to 750 MHz. The total carrier to noise is the sum of CIN2, CIN3, and thermal noise on a 10*log basis. The total carrier to noise of the amplifier was then measured. The predicted and measured results for 55.25 MHz are shown in Figure 12. The results for 547.25 MHz are shown in Figure 13.

Single Amplifier Carrier to Noise Performance Prediction

Digital level below Analog level	55.25 MHz				547.25 MHz			
	CIN2 (dBc)	CIN3 (dBc)	Thermal C/N	C/N Total	CIN2 (dBc)	CIN3 (dBc)	Thermal C/N	C/N Total
0	64.8	60.0	65.2	57.9	65.2	56.3	68.9	55.6
2	68.7	62.2	65.2	59.8	67.2	59.3	68.9	58.3
4	72.4	64.3	65.2	61.4	69.2	62.1	68.9	60.6
6	76.0	66.4	65.2	62.5	71.2	64.6	68.9	62.6
8	79.4	68.4	65.2	63.4	73.2	66.9	68.9	64.2
10	82.6	70.5	65.2	64.0	75.2	69.1	68.9	65.5

Table 1

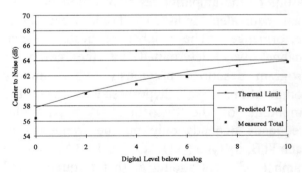

Figure 12

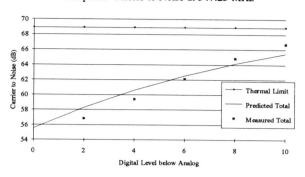

Figure 13

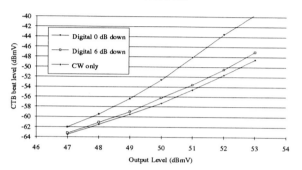

Output Level	CTB		
	Analog Only (550 MHz)	Analog with Digital 6 dB Lower (750 MHz)	Analog and Digital at Equal Levels (750 MHz)
47	-63.5	-63.2	-62.0
48	-61.5	-61.1	-59.5
49	-59.5	-59.0	-56.4
50	-57.3	-56.2	-52.6
51	-54.6	-53.6	-48.1
52	-51.6	-50.5	-43.5
53	-48.5	-47.0	-39.6

Table 2

Figure 14

The figures show a very good correlation between the calculated and measured results.

Crash Point

Under normal behavior, CTB is expected to get 2 dB worse for every dB increase in output level. As the amplifier is driven into compression, the performance will deviate from this expectation. With 77 CW carriers the amplifiers are operating with a certain total load and driving a range of peak-to-peak output voltage levels. When the digital carriers are added, they increase the total amplifier load and require larger peak-to-peak output voltages. This increases CTB on the 77 CW carriers as the amplifier is driven further beyond its "well behaved" range. The crash point of an amplifier is defined as the point at which CTB deviates by 1 dB from the expected 2:1 behavior.

A line extender was tested with 77 channel loading with a 10 dB cable equivalent tilt between 50 and 750 MHz. The CTB distortion was measured at 547.25 MHz. The test was then repeated with noise added between 600 and 750 MHz. The noise was adjusted so that the noise power in any 6 MHz bandwidth was equal to the power of one of the analog carriers. The test was then repeated with the digital channels (noise) 6 dB lower. The test results are shown in Table 2 and Figure 14.

The crash point is seen to be +51 for the analog only system, +50 for the digital carriers at -6, and between +48 and +49 for the digital carriers equal to the analog carriers. All of these crash points are well above normal operating conditions.

AMPLIFIER CASCADES

Theory

In 100% analog CATV cascades, impairment addition is well understood. Third order distortion beats tend to add on a voltage basis. Therefore, when designers are cascading CTB, they add the contributions together on a 20*log basis. Second order distortion beats tend to add somewhere between a power and a voltage. This is because the phase of the second order beats produced by one amplifier is not likely to be the same as the phase of the same beat when produced by a different amplifier. As a result, CSO tends to add on a 10*log to 15*log basis. Thermal noise adds on a 10*log basis since the noise produced by one amplifier is totally uncorrelated with the noise produced by another amplifier.

The addition of amplifier noise is not quite as obvious in systems with mixed analog and digital carriers. The noise of each amplifier consists of CIN2, CIN3, and thermal noise. As these units are cascaded, the CIN2 is expected to add like CSO, the CIN3 is expected to add like CTB, and the thermal noise is expected to add like noise. This means that the total carrier to noise of one amplifier can no longer be added to the total carrier to noise of a second amplifier to get the result. Each of the individual components must be added according to their own addition factors.

Distortion Performance

To test the theory, a cascade of one Mini-Bridger™ and three JLX™ line extenders was built. The distortion performance of the four amplifier cascade was measured for 77 CW channels and for 77 CW with 25 digital channels at both 0 and 8 dB below the CW channels. All tests had a 10 dB output power tilt (cable equivalent) from 50 to 750 MHz. The output level was selected to produce a worst case cascade CTB of roughly -53 dBc. The corresponding operating level was +47 dBmV at the highest CW channel. The CTB results are shown in Figure 15.

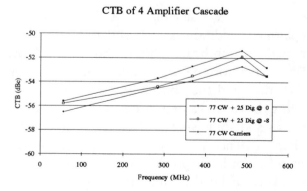

Figure 15

The graph indicates that the CTB is slightly dependent on the presence of the digital channels. This correlates to the results for a single device shown in Table 2.

The CSO measurements show no significant impact from the addition of the digital carrier power. The performance of the four amplifier cascade is shown in Figure 16.

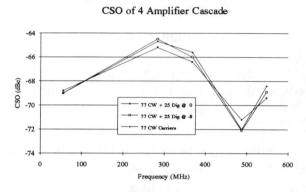

Figure 16

When 110 CW carriers were tested, the output level had to be lowered to 43.5 dBmV at 750 MHz to meet the required CTB distortion of -53. This equates to +41.5 dBmV at 550 MHz.

Carrier to Noise Performance

Once again, in order to produce the best possible prediction of Composite Intermodulation Noise, the third order and second order beat performance curves were scaled to provide an exact match to the CTB and CSO performance of the cascade. In this case, the CSO of the cascade was actually better than the CSO of a single unit. This was probably due to cancellation effects. The CTB added on a 19*log basis. The measured thermal carrier to noise was used in the calculation of total carrier to noise. The predicted results are shown in Table 3.

Cascade Carrier to Noise Performance Prediction

Digital level below Analog level	55.25 MHz				547.25 MHz			
	CIN2 (dBc)	CIN3 (dBc)	Thermal C/N	C/N Total	CIN2 (dBc)	CIN3 (dBc)	Thermal C/N	C/N Total
0	64.3	48.3	57.4	47.7	64.7	44.6	61.9	44.4
2	68.2	50.5	57.4	49.6	66.7	47.6	61.9	47.4
4	71.9	52.6	57.4	51.3	68.7	50.4	61.9	50.0
6	75.5	54.7	57.4	52.8	70.7	52.9	61.9	52.3
8	78.9	56.7	57.4	54.0	72.7	55.2	61.9	54.3
10	82.1	58.8	57.4	55.0	74.7	57.4	61.9	56.0

Table 3

The total carrier to noise of the amplifier was then measured. The predicted and measured results for 55.25 MHz are shown in Figure 17. The results for 547.25 MHz are shown in Figure 18.

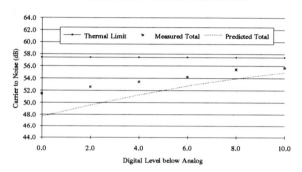

Figure 17

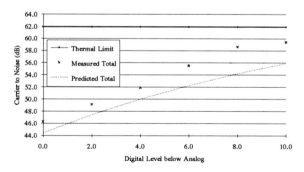

Figure 18

The figures show that the measured performance was much better than the prediction. Several experiments are being conducted in an attempt to explain this phenomena. Perhaps the CIN did not add like distortion because of the various group delays and amplitude ripples in the system. Since noise was used to simulate the digital carriers, the performance improvement might not be representative of the behavior with real digital carriers. In any case, we will show that CATV systems will work even if the real digital carriers cause the performance to degrade to the predicted values.

PREDICTED PERFORMANCE IN A MIXED ANALOG / DIGITAL SYSTEM

To predict what would happen in a real system with both analog and digital carriers, the calculated Intermodulation Noise spectrum was combined with extrapolated amplifier ITB performance.

A system was simulated consisting of:
- a STARFIRE™ 750 optical link driving two Mini-Bridger™ amplifiers and three JLX™ line extenders
- 77 CW carriers from 55.25 to 547.25 MHz
- 33 digital carriers from 555 to 747 MHz
- CW carrier levels set for -53 dB CTB on the analog channels alone
- analog channel C/N of 49 dB before introduction of the digital carriers
- amplifier spacing set for 750 MHz
- 10 dB of tilt on the RF device outputs

Figure 19 shows how C/N is affected in the analog channels of this system as digital carrier power is reduced relative to the CW carriers. For 33 digital carriers at nine dB below the CW level, worst case effect is 0.8 dB degradation of C/N. This simulation assumes CIN3 adds through a cascade on a 20 log basis. If initial cascade tests prove out, CIN and the degradation will actually be lower than shown here.

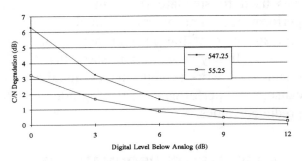

Analog Channel C/N Degradation by CIN with
77 CW and 33 Digital Carriers

Figure 19

Although CTB is measured with CW carriers and the above curve is 'correct', cable systems are not run with CW carriers in the field. In an operating plant the 77 carriers from 50 to 550 MHz will be modulated with analog video. This does not change their nominal level since video carriers are measured during sync tip peak, but average power is reduced when modulated with video. Across all 77 analog carriers, average power will drop three to five dB with modulation. The exact figure for each carrier depends on video picture content but the average across all 77 channels will be in this narrow range. A three dB drop in average carrier power reduces the operating level of the second order beats six dB and third order beats by nine dB.

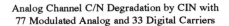

Analog Channel C/N Degradation by CIN with
77 Modulated Analog and 33 Digital Carriers

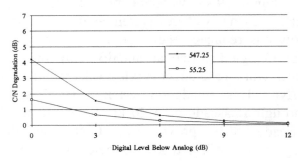

Figure 20

Figure 20 shows the C/N degradation of analog carriers due to CIN with modulated analog carriers. The conservative number of

three dB lower average power is used. For digital carriers nine dB down, worst case degradation drops to 0.3 dB.

DESIGN LEVEL FOR 64-QAM DIGITAL CARRIERS

To minimize the effects of CIN on analog video it is desirable to carry digital carriers at a level several dB below analog. How low 64-QAM carriers can be run and still provide reliable robust transmission will depend on many parameters.

In the satellite transmission environment, channel noise (C/N) is the only significant impairment. The CATV transmission environment is quite different. It has an array of simultaneous impairments which occur at a wide range of levels across cable systems and even from site to site within a system.

To design a digital transmission system for this environment, an estimate must be made of the level of each impairment, how it will interact with the other impairments, and the performance of the digital receiver including error correction. Through extensive simulations each impairment can be described in terms of equivalent noise power. A loss budget can then be assigned based on expected channel impairment levels and achievable transmitter and receiver performance.

With high performance error correction, the sum of all impairments can be below -25 dBc while maintaining the required very low error rates. A reasonable budget for the sum of tuner thermal noise and channel noise in this total might be -30 dBc. It is assumed that CTB, CSO, and CIN in the digital channels will all be well below this level.

For a tuner noise figure of 10 dB the relationship of required digital carrier level to channel C/N is shown in Figure 21.

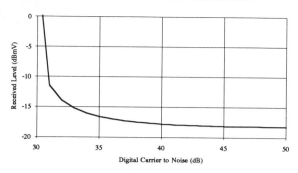

-30 dB Sum of Tuner and Channel Noise

Figure 21

Any combination of received level and digital C/N above the plotted line meets the total noise budget of -30 dBc. Other impairments will further constrain the operating point to no more than 10 dB below analog levels.

The -30 dBc budget leaves substantial room for reducing the level of digital carriers on CATV plant to minimize the impact of CIN. For a plant with 49 dB analog carrier C/N and a guaranteed minimum 0 dBmV analog carrier level at the digital video consumer terminal, the digital carriers could be carried 10 dB below the analog carriers with several dB of margin. This margin may be required to accommodate secondary effects like consumer splitters, poor in-home wiring, drop effects, and variation of tap levels with time and temperature.

Cable plants with lower analog C/N will run the digital carriers closer to analog carrier level to provide the same margin. This will increase CIN, but since there is more noise in the plant to start with it is less sensitive to degradation by CIN.

IMPACT ON SYSTEM DESIGN

Typical line extender drive levels for 550 MHz, 77 channel, all analog plant design are +47 dBmV. For a 110 channel plant drive level is backed off about 5.5 dB to +41.5 dBmV at

550 MHz to meet the -53 dB CTB specification.

Effectively, the distribution amplifiers in a mixed analog and digital system can use the output drive levels of the 550 MHz plant. A half dB back off to make up for the compression effect shown in Figure 15 may be appropriate.

This has significant impact on the active count and therefore system cost. There is still some premium over 550 MHz plant cost due to the requirement to design the distribution system for unity gain at 750 MHz instead of 550 MHz.

Preliminary work indicates a plant cost premium of 60% for 110 channel analog over a 77 channel system. Designing for digital carriers from 550 to 750 MHz reduces this premium to 30% with current component prices. Both of these premiums are expected to come down as 750 MHz components reach volume production.

CONCLUSIONS

1) Distortion products involving digital carriers will look like noise, not discrete frequency tones.

2) Composite Intermodulation Noise (CIN) of a device can be calculated based on beat counts and device performance characterized with CTB and CSO.

3) Digital video carriers can be run eight to ten dB down in new system designs with reasonable margin.

4) Designing systems for mixed mode transmission provides bandwidth for future digital services at very modest premiums.

[1] Acknowledgments: The authors wish to thank David Grubb, Zheng Huang, and Joseph Waltrich for their substantial contributions to the technical basis of this paper.

[2] CTB and CSO are measured with a matrix of CW carriers because it provides an available, stable, and repeatable measurement. The many required independently modulated video carriers are often not available. When they are, the measured level of CTB and CSO would depend on the video modulation, and so would not provide a stable and repeatable measurement.

A NEW TECHNIQUE FOR MEASURING BROADBAND DISTORTION IN SYSTEMS WITH MIXED ANALOG AND DIGITAL VIDEO

Lamar West
Scientific-Atlanta

I. ABSTRACT

Several proposals have been made to augment the channel capacity of existing or proposed CATV systems by adding compressed digital video signals to conventional analog VSB signals. Such a proposal brings with it the difficulties of quantifying the degradation of broadband distortion performance (CTB, XMOD, DSO and CSO) associated with the additional loading caused by the new digital signals. Conventional techniques that measure device and system distortion performance by modeling the digital signals with CW carriers at the picture carrier frequencies of conventional analog VSB channels will give extremely disappointing results.

A new technique is described that models the digital signals in a manner that accurately represents the digital channel energy spectral density. Measurements using this technique are given that accurately predict distortion performance that is far better than that predicted by conventional CW carrier techniques.

A simple means of generating this signal is described. Test results are given that compare the performance of test devices when loaded with only conventional analog VSB signals to the performance of the test devices when loaded with mixed analog and digital signals.

II. CONVENTIONAL DISTORTION TECHNIQUES

It is a primary goal in the electronic processing of CATV signals to minimize any corruption of these signals. This design goal, as it interplays with economic considerations, has set the practical limits for performance of the system components (whether they be program supplier studio electronics, satellite delivery systems, headend electronics, distribution plant or subscriber electronics). In the case of broadband electronics, the principle technical trade-offs have been between broadband distortion and noise limitations.

Well established techniques have been used throughout the industry for several years in order to characterize the broadband distortion performance of conventional CATV electronics. Composite triple beat, discrete second order, composite second order and crossmodulation have historically been used as figures of merit for system performance. These techniques are closely linked with the types of signals used in conventional CATV applications.

In the United States, Canada, Mexico, Japan and several other countries, NTSC-M is the standard for color television transmission. As we are all aware, this system utilizes vestigial sideband modulation with a 6 MHz channel bandwidth. The picture carrier contains the most significant amount of channel energy, from a distortion standpoint, and is located 1.25 MHz from the lower channel edge. Another significant characteristic is the horizontal line frequency of 15734.264 Hz. The distortion techniques mentioned above utilize this characteristic in order to quantify system performance.

Knowing that the majority of the energy in an NTSC-M television signal is located at or very near the picture carrier leads to the understanding that the majority of the distortion in a CATV system results from that energy. In many laboratory or test applications the modulated video signal is replaced with a CW carrier at the picture carrier frequency. In a CATV system with a standard frequency line-up (not HRC or IRC) the frequency characteristics of these carriers have the useful property that third order distortion products fall at or very near to the picture carrier frequencies of affected channels. A simple examination of the possible linear combinations of an odd number of picture carrier frequencies will demonstrate this fact (for example: Channel 7 + Channel 8 - Channel 37 = 175.25 MHz + 181.25 MHz - 301.25 MHz = 55.25 MHz = Channel 2). This is the driving factor in the definition of CTB (composite triple beat). Note that the name CTB is somewhat of a misnomer as this distortion product is composed of not only third order beats, but also many higher odd-order distortion products.

Reprinted with permission from NCTA, from the *1992 NCTA Technical Papers,* pp. 273–279, 1992.
© National Cable Television Association.

A similar examination of the linear combination of the frequencies of any two picture carriers will result in a frequency that falls at 1.25 MHz above or below the picture carrier frequency of an affected channel in a standard system. The result is of course discrete second order distortion. A simple extension of this phenomena to any combination of an even number of carrier frequencies results in an explanation of composite second order, a phenomena that grows significantly as the broadband system bandwidth exceeds 450 MHz.

Crossmodulation is closely linked to the frequency components contained within the modulating signal of the RF spectrum. In the case of NTSC-M, there is a significant spectral content at 15.734 kHz. In a test environment, the modulating waveform is simplified to a 15.734 kHz square wave. Under these test conditions, it is relatively easy to quantify the parasitic modulation impressed upon an unmodulated carrier when included in a broadband spectrum where all other carriers are modulated and then passed through a device that can create nonlinear distortion. The ratio of the amplitude of that parasitic modulation to the modulation generated by 100% modulating that carrier with a 15.734 kHz square wave is defined as the crossmodulation.

In all of the cases mentioned above, the distortion measurements, by definition, are linked closely to the baseband video format and RF modulation techniques. An easy extension of these concepts may be used to quantify broadband distortion in the case of HRC or IRC frequency line-ups. It is also possible to extend these concepts to apply to other video formats, such as PAL and SECAM as well as their various RF spectrum formats, such as I, B, G, N, etc.

III. INITIAL STUDIES OF LOADING OF CATV DEVICES FOR DIGITAL VIDEO

A popular scenario for expanding the capabilities of a CATV plant is based on the inclusion of digital video in the upper part of the CATV broadband spectrum. Digital video promises to greatly increase the capability of this spectrum by permitting digital compression of the analog video signal. This compression will allow the carriage of up several times the number of channels in a given block of spectrum as would be possible using conventional VSB techniques. For example, one scenario might be to include conventional analog signals in the spectrum

from 54 MHz to 550 MHz in order to serve the existing base of CATV subscribers. Additional digital video services could be included from 550 MHZ to 750 MHz. However, it is not clear how the inclusion of this potentially large number of video signals would affect the overall system distortion performance.

Initial testing of typical equipment was performed by Scientific-Atlanta in order to quantify the performance of 550 MHz CATV electronics when loaded with video carriers from a Matrix signal generator from 54 MHz to 750 MHz. This is the natural extension of the existing art of distortion measurements. Under these test conditions it was shown that distortion deteriorates significantly when conventional video carriers between 550 MHz and 750 MHz are included in the spectrum. These results were initially somewhat discouraging.

IV. AN EXAMINATION OF DIGITAL VIDEO SIGNAL CHARACTERISTICS

As one might expect, the RF characteristics of the compressed digital video spectrum are substantially different from those of the conventional VSB analog signal. For the purposes of this discussion, we will examine the characteristics of the 4-level VSB modulation technique employed by Scientific-Atlanta. However, the significant characteristics as described herein may be applied to most other compressed digital video RF modulation systems. Most of the conclusions drawn are easily extended to all systems.

Upon examining the RF spectrum of the digital video, the most striking characteristic is the uniform distribution of the energy as a function of frequency. There are no discrete high level carriers that result in the concentration of the RF energy at particular frequencies. The distribution of the energy is further homogenized by various multiplex techniques that allow the inclusion of several video programs within one 6 MHz slice of spectrum. A final smoothing of the energy is accomplished by the various encryption techniques that allow conditional program access. In the case of the S-A 4-level VSB technique, there is a suppressed pilot carrier at the very low end of the spectrum, but its impact upon the overall energy distribution is negligible.

Another significant difference in the signal characteristics is level. The average level of the signal is reduced with respect to the level of a conventional analog signal. The average level of the power in the channel is 10 dB below the peak envelope power (sync tip power) of a conventional analog channel. There are instantaneous peak powers that are higher than the average power but because of the multiplex and encryption techniques mentioned above, it is virtually impossible to relate the frequency components of these peaks to any characteristics of the original video waveforms.

Finally, a performance advantage is obtained with the compressed digital video that allows it to be more robust with respect to undesirable interference. Excellent bit error rates (BER) may be obtained with average channel power to interference ratios of only 20 dB. This results in a required channel dynamic range of 30 dB (resulting from operation at a level of -10 dB with respect to the peak carrier power of the analog video and the the requirement for a 20 dB signal to interference ratio), as compared with the dynamic range required by conventional analog video of 57 dB.

These characteristics result in a channel energy distribution that very closely resembles Gaussian noise at an average channel power that is -10 dB with respect to a peak power of a conventional analog signal.

V. DISTORTION TESTING TECHNIQUES

A new distortion measurement technique was developed that allowed the simulation of a mixed system containing both conventional analog channels and compressed digital channels. For the purposes of this test it was proposed that the device under test (DUT) would be loaded with conventional analog carriers from 54 MHz to 550 MHz and loaded with simulated digital channels from 550 MHz to 750 MHz. The device chosen to be tested in this experiment was the Scientific-Atlanta Model number 9504 four-port interdiction unit.

The test set-up for this experiment is shown in figure 1. The conventional analog carriers were supplied from a matrix generator. A conventional distribution equalizer was cascaded with the matrix generator in order simulate the typical tilt encountered in a conventional feeder leg of a distribution plant. The optional video generator, optional modulator, and optional directional coupler will be discussed in detail

later. The conventional analog signals are combined with the output of the digital video signal simulator.

For the purposes of this test, the digital video is simulated with band limited gaussian noise. The noise was generated by amplifying thermal noise in a cascade of two high gain indoor distribution amplifiers. The noise must be band limited to the 550 MHz to 750 MHz band in order to match the desired test conditions. It was determined that a very complex and high order band-pass filter would be required to meet the shape factor requirements of limiting the noise to this band.

A simpler approach was identified that utilized a series of low-pass filters that produce a noise spectrum occupying the band from approximately 3 MHz to 100 MHz. This spectrum is then mixed with a 650 MHz LO to produce band limited noise spectrum from 550 MHz to 750 MHz. The SBL-1X type mixer used gave adequate LO rejection at the output to ensure that the LO content would not significantly affect the distortion measurements. Finally a 550 MHz high-pass filter is included to ensure that any inadequacies in the mixer isolation would not degrade the distortion measurements by masking distortion products in "leaked" noise. An added benefit of this technique is the ability to "turn-off" the digital channels by simply removing the LO from the mixer. Comparisons could therefore be easily made between performance with and without the additional loading of the digital video signals.

The resulting total RF spectrum is shown in figure 2. Note that in the simulated digital portion of this spectrum, the average level is -12.5 dB with respect to the peak analog carrier level. This apparent discrepancy with respect to the normal operating conditions described above is due to the resolution bandwidth of the spectrum analyzer. The widest available resolution bandwidth was 3 MHz. Correcting this for 6 MHz and compensating for the equivalent noise bandwidth of the analyzer filter, the resulting observed average power level is -10 dB with respect to the analog carriers, as described above.

Also note the relatively low level of the mixer LO leakage and the narrow gap of noise introduced around 650 MHz by the inability of the indoor distribution amplifiers to amplify the noise all the way to DC. It was decided that these characteristics would cause negligible effects on the measured

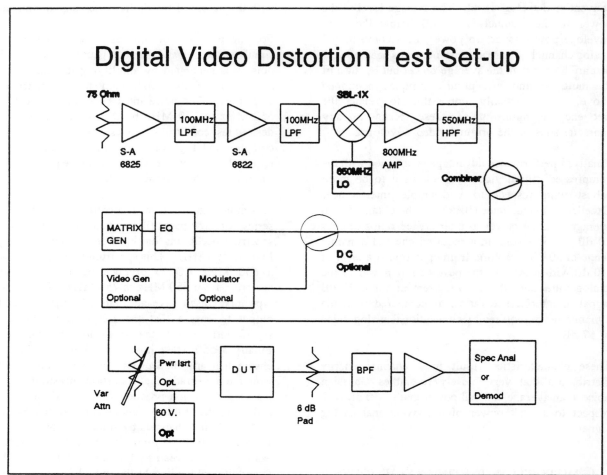

Digital Video Distortion Test Set-up

Figure 1

VI. MEASURED DISTORTION RESULTS

Conventional distortion techniques were utilized to quantify the distortion performance on the analog channels with and without the loading of the digital video. The distortion results were initially measured on a total of 4 different subscriber ports. Distortion was measured at five different frequencies spaced throughout the 54 MHz to 550 MHz band. CTB, CSO, and XMOD were measured. The data from this initial experiment is given in figure 3.

In general, the additional noise loading of the simulated digital video signals causes a deterioration of the distortion performance of only a few tenths of a dB. In no instance does the addition of the noise degrade the signal by more than 1 dB (note that in a few cases the signal appears to actually get better with the addition of the noise, but these measurements are limited by the measurement system noise floor).

To further confirm the results, an additional 20 ports were measured for CTB at elevated output levels to ensure that system noise would not mask the results. A summary of this data is shown in figure 4. Note again, that the performance, though clearly deteriorated by the higher levels and now clearly above the system noise floor, shows distortion performance impacts of only tenths of a dB when the

distortion performance.

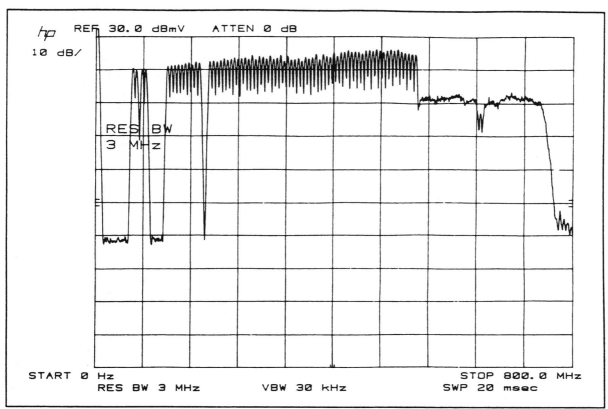

Figure 2

additional noise loading of digital video is added. This encouraging result implies that the additional loading of compressed digital video at frequencies above the conventional analog channels will have a minimal impact on system performance.

VII. EXPLANATION OF RESULTS

As described above, the energy in a conventional NTSC-M VSB channel is primarily concentrated around the frequencies of discrete RF carriers. Therefore the loading of a DUT with these types of signals results in discrete distortion products or beats that fall at easily predicted discrete frequencies (CTB, DSO, CSO, XMOD). In the case of compressed digital video signals, however, the energy is at a much lower average level and evenly distributed across the entire 6 MHz channel.

The distortion products from such a signal do not lie on discrete frequencies, but rather spread themselves

across the entire 6 MHz of an affected channel. Fortunately, as the energy is spread, its impact on perceived picture quality is minimized. It was theorized that the result would appear as a slight degradation of the video signal to noise on the affected channel.

VIII. VIDEO S/N EFFECTS

The S/N effects were quantified using the optional video generator, optional modulator and optional directional coupler mentioned above. To use these devices, a single carrier of the matrix generator was turned off. The modulator was then used to replace that carrier with modulated video. An S-A agile modulator was used to allow the modulated carrier to be moved throughout the 54 MHz to 550 MHz band, and specifically to the frequencies where the distortion had been measured earlier.

Distortion Data		55.25 MHz		199.25 MHz		295.25 MHz		379.25 MHz		499.25 MHz	
		w/o dig	w/ dig	w/o dig	w/ dig	w/o dig	w/ dig	w/o dig	w/ dig	w/o dig	w/ dig
CTB (dB)	Port 1	73.6	73.6	72.7	72.8	74.3	74.1	72.7	72.5	75.5	75.2
	Port 2	74.4	74.0	72.9	72.6	74.5	74.5	72.5	72.4	75.5	75.3
	Port 3	73.5	73.4	72.3	72.6	73.7	73.8	70.6	70.3	74.2	74.4
	Port 4	73.4	73.4	72.3	72.3	72.5	72.7	70.7	70.6	75.3	75.2
CSO- (dB)	Port 1	64.8	65.0	64.0	64.0	62.9	63.3	63.5	63.5	77.1	77.3
	Port 2	64.0	64.0	63.0	62.8	62.8	62.8	62.8	62.9	77.5	77.6
	Port 3	64.5	64.6	64.2	64.0	63.8	63.8	63.5	63.4	75.7	75.5
	Port 4	64.0	64.6	64.0	63.8	63.6	63.2	63.2	63.1	76.5	76.4
CSO+ (dB)	Port 1	74.8	75.0	76.8	76.6	71.7	71.5	66.7	66.6	64.2	65.0
	Port 2	75.5	75.6	76.7	76.9	71.5	71.3	66.2	66.3	64.3	64.2
	Port 3	74.6	74.8	74.7	74.6	71.1	70.9	66.8	66.8	66.7	66.6
	Port 4	74.6	74.7	74.7	74.7	71.1	71.1	66.1	65.9	64.0	63.8
XMOD (dB)	Port 1	65.1	65.1	66.1	66.4	66.8	66.4	65.3	65.6	66.2	68.9
	Port 2	67.1	66.4	64.9	65.5	66.6	67.5	65.7	65.8	67.0	67.0
	Port 3	69.8	69.3	65.1	67.6	67.1	67.6	65.0	65.2	66.7	66.2
	Port 4	68.5	68.6	66.6	66.5	66.8	66.0	64.2	64.0	65.5	67.4

Figure 3

COMPOSITE TRIPLE BEAT (dB)
Measured at elevated operating levels

Analog Video Only					
	55.25 MHz	199.25 MHz	295.25 MHz	379.25 MHz	499.25 MHz
Minimum	53.5	55.0	51.1	49.8	48.0
Mean	54.5	55.2	51.7	50.8	49.0
Maximum	55.5	55.4	52.0	51.8	49.8
Analog And Digital Video					
	55.25 MHz	199.25 MHz	295.25 MHz	379.25 MHz	499.25 MHz
Minimum	53.3	54.4	50.4	49.4	47.4
Mean	54.3	54.6	51.1	50.2	48.7
Maximum	55.3	54.8	51.4	51.1	49.6

Figure 4

Reduction of Unweighted Video S/N
With the Addition Of Digital Video Signals
In the 550 MHz to 750 MHz Band

Frequency	55.25 MHz	199.25 MHz	295.25 MHz	379.25 MHz	499.25 MHz
Average Change of S/N	0.3 dB	0.4 dB	0.5 dB	0.5 dB	0.3 dB

Figure 5

During this test, the spectrum analyzer was replaced with a video demod and a Tektronix VM-700 video analyzer. The VM-700 was then used to measure the video S/N on that channel. Care was taken to ensure that adequate pre-selection filtering was placed in front of the demod so that additional distortion was not generated by that demod. The results of these measurements are summarized in figure 5.

The Video S/N degradation resulting from the loading of the simulated compressed digital video was typically less than 0.5 dB.

IX. CONCLUSIONS

It has been analytically shown that band-limited Gaussian noise is a good simulation for compressed digital video. Testing with noise of this type may be used for quantification of distortion performance of broadband devices. This method easily allows the simulation of mixed systems with partial analog video and partial compressed digital video.

Additional study of this subject is required. However, based on the preliminary data presented, the distortion performance impact of system or device loading with compressed digital video should be substantially less than the effect of loading the same amount of spectrum with conventional analog signals. In particular, the Scientific-Atlanta model 9504 4-port interdiction device shows very little distortion deterioration (less than 1 dB) with the additional loading of simulated digital video from 550 MHz to 750 MHz. The deterioration of the video signal to noise ratio resulting from this loading is typically less than 0.5 dB.

ACKNOWLEDGEMENTS

The author wishes to gratefully acknowledge the invaluable assistance of the following people: Charles Bramhall, John Canning, Scott Cheek, Dean Fredriksen and Steve Webb. This paper would not have been possible without their help.

THE IMPACT OF COMPRESSION TECHNOLOGY ON SATELLITE TRANSMISSIONS TO CABLE HEADEND EARTH STATIONS

Marvin Freeling - GE American Communications, Inc.
Allan Guida - David Sarnoff Research Center

Abstract

Developing technology in digital video compression will have a profound technical impact on satellite transmissions to cable headend earth stations. Implementation of this new technology will enable the transmission of as many as 10 digital video channels through a single 36 MHz bandwidth C-Band satellite transponder. Conventional modulation methods that are employed at present limit the capacity of a saturated satellite transponder to 1 analog video channel.

This paper examines the leading digital video systems that are presently under development. It describes a hierarchy of picture quality as a function of data rate, ranging from HDTV to VCR quality.

The capacity of a typical C-Band satellite transponder broadcasting to a typical cable headend is derived in this paper for each level of picture quality.

In addition to increasing transponder capacity, use of digital as opposed to analog video transmission techniques will increase the margins available to compensate for rain and pointing error losses. Examples are given in the paper.

1.0 Introduction

Much work is presently underway in the United States and in the rest of the world directed toward the development of compressed digital video systems. Implementation of these systems will have a profound technical impact on satellite transmissions to cable headend earth stations.

This paper describes a number of typical compressed digital video systems that are now under development. It describes a hierarchy of picture quality as a function of data rate, ranging from High Definition (HDTV) to Video Cassette Recorder (VCR) movie quality. It is shown that, depending upon desired picture quality, anywhere from 2 to 10 digital video channels could be transmitted through a single C-Band satellite transponder. Conventional analog modulation methods that are employed at present limit the capacity of a standard C-Band satellite transponder to 1 analog video channel into a typical headend. A capacity of two analog video channels can be achieved only through significant reduction in the power available to each video channel. Transmission of two analog video channels through one C-Band satellite transponder is not achievable for the typical cable television systems considered.

It is also shown that in addition to increasing transponder capacity, use of compressed digital, as opposed to analog video, transmission techniques will increase the system margins available to compensate for rain and pointing error losses.

This paper describes the two transmission modes employed in the compressed digital video systems under development: time division multiplex (TDM) and single channel per carrier (SCPC), and discusses the advantages and disadvantages to the cable operator of each mode.

2.0 Conventional Analog Television Transmission By Satellite To Cable Headend Earth Stations

The transponders of present generation C-Band satellites are equipped with amplifiers with output powers typically in the 5.5 watt to 10 watt range. Such amplifier powers generally result in an Equivalent Isotropic Radiated Power (EIRP) level of approximately 34 dBW at the edge of CONUS coverage. The bandwidth of C-Band satellite transponders is almost universally 36 MHz. At a cable headend earth station equipped with a 3.7 meter diameter receive antenna (G/T = 23.7 dB/K), located on the 34 dBW EIRP contour and receiving television transmissions in a 36 MHz wide channel, filtered to a receiver bandwidth of 30 MHz, the system carrier-to-noise ratio, $(C/N)_{system}$, will be about 13 dB in clear weather. LNB noise temperature in this example and for the rest of this article, was assumed to be 40K, yielding a receive system noise temperature of about 75K, which results in the earth station G/T of 23.7 dB/K used in the calculation. This calculation of $(C/N)_{system}$ takes into account thermal noise as well as interference from adjacent satellites (for which it was assumed that the sidelobe performance of the earth station antennas involved conformed to the FCC's 2° spacing guidelines), and interference from cross-polarized transponders on the same satellite.

Some cable headend earth stations are equipped with antennas smaller than 3.7 meters in diameter. At a 3.0 meter diameter antenna earth station located on the 34 dBW EIRP contour $(C/N)_{system}$ would be about 11 dB, lower of course than for the 3.7 meter diameter antenna.

For an earth station with a 3.0 meter diameter antenna located in the interior of the coverage pattern, on the 37 dBW EIRP contour, $(C/N)_{system}$ would be equal to that achieved at the larger antenna earth station located at the edge of coverage.

The figure of merit for quality of received television is $(S/N)_{video}$, the ratio of peak-to-peak signal to rms weighted noise including pre- and de- emphasis improvement. For cable headend earth stations the minimum desired value of $(S/N)_{video}$ is generally in the 49 dB to 50 dB range. This value is consistent with the FCC's guideline that system carrier-to-noise ratio be about 3 dB above threshold. $(S/N)_{video}$ is related to $(C/N)_{system}$ by the transmission parameters of the television signal. For a peak deviation of the video carrier of 10.75 MHz, $(S/N)_{video}$ = 51.3 dB in clear weather for $(C/N)_{system}$ = 13 dB.

This is the video signal-to-noise ratio achieved at the 3.7 meter earth station on the 34 dBW EIRP contour and the 3.0 meter earth station on the 37 dBW EIRP contour.

Many satellite operators currently plan to increase the amplifier power output on the next generation of C-Band satellites to the 16 watt to 20 watt range, resulting in a 3 dB increase in EIRP level at the edge of CONUS coverage from 34 dBW to 37 dBW. At the cable headend earth stations cited in the example above (3.7 meter diameter antenna earth station located now on the 37 dBW EIRP contour and 3.0 meter diameter antenna earth station now located on the 40 dBW EIRP contour), $(C/N)_{system}$ and $(S/N)_{video}$ would increase to 15 dB and 53.3 dB respectively in clear weather.

In a number of areas in the United States, particularly in the eastern and southeastern regions, attenuation due to rainfall has a great impact on satellite system performance. Figure 1 shows the regions of different rainfall rate into which the United States may be divided. These regions differ in the severity of rainfall. For example, in region B, a rain rate of 5.6 mm/hr. is exceeded 0.1% of the time or 8.8 hours in a year. On the other hand, in the worst case rainy southeastern area, rain zone E, a rain rate of 35.4 mm/hr. is exceeded for the same time interval.

In addition to increasing the uplink and downlink losses, rainfall raises the noise temperature of the system, as the rain is at 290K, substantially higher than the background temperature of space.

The parameter Y is designated as the sum total of the rain loss and noise temperature increase effects:
$$Y = L_{rain} + \Delta (G/T)$$

The decrease in G/T of the receive earth station corresponding to the increase in noise temperature caused by rain is given by:

$$\Delta (G/T) = 10 \log \left\{ \frac{Ts + To ([Lrain -1] /Lrain)}{Ts} \right\}$$

where L_{rain} = attenuation due to rain
T_s = system noise temperature
T_o = ambient (rain) temperature = 290K

Table 1 shows Y values at a number of cities located throughout the United States.

TABLE 1

Y Factors [$Y = L_{rain} + \Delta (G/T)$]
For Selected Cities In The United States

City	Rain Zone	Y Factor For 99.99% Availability (dB)
Atlanta	D3	2.8
Boise	B1	0.7
Boston	D2	3.6
Brownsville, TX	D1	1.3
Chicago	D2	2.4
Denver	B2	0.8
Duluth, MN	D1	1.9
Eastport, ME	D1	3.5
Houston	E	2.3
Las Vegas	F	0.8
Los Angeles	F	0.7
Miami	E	3.9

TABLE 1 (Continued)

City	Rain Zone	Y Factor For 99.99% Availability (dB)
Mobile	E	3.6
New Orleans	E	3.5
New York	D2	3.2
San Diego	F	0.7
San Francisco	C	0.9
Seattle	C	1.1
Tampa	E	3.9
Virginia Beach, VA	D3	3.5

NOTES: Satellite Location = 131° West Longitude
System Temperature = 75K

Each rain zone is represented in the table. The Y values shown are for a satellite located at 131° West Longitude, a system noise temperature of 75K and for an availability of 99.99%; that is for rainfall of such intensity that it (and the corresponding downlink loss) is exceeded only 0.01% of the time or 53 minutes in a year. Table 2 summarizes the performance described above for present generation and next generation satellites. The values of clear weather $(S/N)_{video}$ shown in the table (51.3 dB and 53.3 dB) were calculated taking into account uplink carrier-to-noise ratio, $(C/N)_{up,}$ and carrier-to-total interference ratio, $(C/I)_T$ in addition to downlink carrier-to-noise ratio, $(C/N)_{down}$. Overall space segment availability, however, is determined basically by loss on the downlink due to the fact that sufficient reserve uplink power is usually available to compensate for rain at the transmit location. Table 2 shows the maximum downlink loss permissible to allow achievement of a faded video signal-to-noise ratio of 49 dB. For this signal-to-noise ratio, and for the future 16 watt to 20 watt transponders, a minimum availability greater than 99.999% would

be achieved throughout the United States, compared to 99.972% for the present generation of satellites. Table 2 also shows availability to the impulse noise threshold level [$(C/N)_{system}$ is approximately 9.5 dB, corresponding to a $(S/N)_{video}$ ratio of approximately 48 dB]. For future transponders availability to this level would be greater than 99.999%. The corresponding availability for present generation satellites is 99.995%.

It will be shown below in Sections 3.1 and 3.2 that implementation of a digitally compressed television transmission system by satellite will enable the achievement of greater margins than are currently available using analog transmission techniques. These additional margins would be available to compensate for rain losses or to enable the headend system to reduce any newly installed or replacement antennas to smaller sizes if current margins are maintained. It will also be shown below that use of digital video compression techniques will allow the transmission of as many as 10 digital video channels through a single 36 MHz bandwidth C-Band satellite transponder.

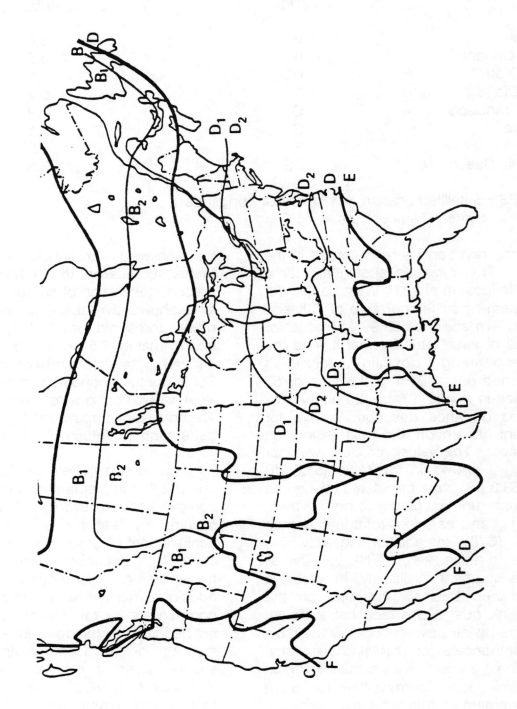

FIGURE 1 - RAIN RATE REGIONS

TABLE 2

Performance of Present Generation and Next Generation Satellites - Clear Weather and Rain Fade

Satellite	Clear Weather (S/N) Video (dB)	Downlink Margin Available In Clear Weather or Maximum Permissible Downlink Loss [For Faded (S/N)$_{video}$ = 49 dB] (dB)	[To Impulse Noise Threshold] (dB)
Present Generation	51.3	3.1	4.5
Next Generation	53.3	6.1	7.5

3.0 Compressed Digital Television Transmission By Satellite To Cable Headend Earth Stations

Digitization, or the conversion of an analog television signal into a stream of 0's and 1's, can result in a picture that is free of noise and distortions. This is similar to the situation in the audio domain in which digital compact disks reproduce music without hisses and pops. Use of the digital format also has the advantage that it allows the bits which represent the video images to be stored, moved and manipulated more easily than conventional analog signals. Program encryption and multiple digital audio channels would also be facilitated by use of digital compressed transmissions.

Conversion to digital format requires that approximately 10 million pixels per second be sampled. Representation of each sample by 8 binary digits or bits results in a data rate of 80 MBps. However, about 25% of the samples would be for synch periods and would convey no video information. Therefore, digital representation of a television signal requires transmission at a rate of 60 MBps. Since the capacity of a C-Band satellite for digital transmissions is also about 60 MBps, it can be seen that C-Band satellite capacity is 1 uncompressed digital video channel per transponder; basically no increase over analog capacity. It is the use of compression that results in increased capacity.

In compressed digital video systems fewer bits are transmitted than would be required for complete reproduction of the original picture. Among the techniques employed in this bit reduction are:

● Intraframe Compression - Each frame is processed to contain fewer visual details and fewer bits.

● Interframe Compression - Elements that are repeated in successive frames are not transmitted. Only changes are transmitted.

Universally accepted compressed digital video standards are still under development and have not yet been firmly established. The rate at which data must be transmitted will depend upon the desired picture quality and the desired fidelity of the reproduction of motion, either of the live action programming or of the recorded program source. Some developers of compressed digital video systems have suggested the following hierarchy of picture quality as a function of data rate:

Channel Data Rate (MBps)	Picture Quality
15 - 30	Network/HDTV Quality
10 - 15	Sports Events
6.5 -7.0	VCR - SP Quality
3.3 -4.0	Old Movies/VCR - EP Quality

This suggested ranking of television services is neither definitive nor constraining. In the final analysis, the customer will determine the data rate for each television service.

3.1 Time Division Multiplexed (TDM) Transmission

Digital compressed television systems are still under final development, and no standard format has yet been established. A typical time division multiplexed (TDM) digital compressed television system that is being developed is described in this section. The parameters of this typical TDM system presently under development are:

Digital Information Rate	30 MBps
Error Correction Code Rate	3/4
Transmitted Data Rate	40 MBps
Modulation	QPSK
Channel Bandwidth	24 MHz
Carrier-To-Noise Ratio Required	8.0 dB

(For a Bit Error Rate of 1×10^{-12})

In this traffic mode a number of digitized and compressed television channels will be time division multiplexed to form a single 30 MBps (before forward error correction, 40 MBps after forward error correction) data channel. As stated previously the capacity of the transmitted data channel will depend on the desired picture quality and the desired fidelity of the reproduction of motion, either of the live action programming or of the recorded program source. For example, the transmitted data stream could consist of:

2 channels at a rate of 15 MBps
or 4 channels at a rate of 7.5 MBps
or 6 channels at a rate of 5 MBps
or 8 channels at a rate of 3.75 MBps
or 10 channels at a rate of 3 MBps

Table 3 shows the downlink margins available at a typical cable headend earth station located at the edge of CONUS coverage and receiving the 40 MBps data transmissions described above. This earth station is assumed to be equipped with a receive antenna 3.7 meters in diameter and 40K LNB. The margins shown in Table 3 are with respect to the carrier-to-noise ratio required for a Bit Error Rate of 1×10^{-12} [$(C/N)_{system} = 8.0$ dB], the nominal operating point.

$= 8.0$ dB] would be achieved in the presence of rainfall so intense that it is experienced for less than about 5.3 minutes in a year.

TABLE 3

Digital Compressed Television
Time Division Multiplexed (TDM) Transmission Mode
Downlink Margin Available in Clear Weather

Satellite	Downlink Margin Available in Clear Weather or Maximum Permissible Downlink Loss [For Faded Bit Error Rate = 1×10^{-12}] (dB)
Present Generation (Transponder Power = 5.5 to 10 Watts)	7.9
Next Generation (Transponder Power = 16 to 20 Watts)	10.9

The downlink margins shown in Table 3 would compensate for losses due to rain and due to pointing errors of the satellite and earth station antennas. For a satellite located at 131° West Longitude and a system noise temperature of 75K, the maximum Y factor anywhere in the contiguous United States for a space segment availability of 99.999% would be 6.0 dB. The permissible downlink losses shown in Table 3 are greater than this value and the resulting availabilities will be greater. That is, at the cable headend earth station under consideration the required system carrier-to-noise ratio [$(C/N)_{system}$

The above example illustrates the great technical impact that digital compression technology will have on satellite transmissions to cable headend earth stations. Present analog modulation techniques limit the capacity of a saturated satellite transponder to 1 television channel with downlink margin in the 3.1 dB to 6.1 dB range (see Table 2). The introduction and use of Time Division Multiplex techniques will increase saturated transponder capacity to as many as 10 television channels, depending on picture quality, and at the same time increase margin to the 7.9 dB to 10.9 dB range.

3.2 Single Channel Per Carrier (SCPC) Transmission

An obvious disadvantage of the multiplexed mode of transmission is that all of the uplink signals must originate at the same location. To allow the flexibility of multiple site origination of the desired channels, the single channel per carrier(SCPC) transmission mode is necessary. The major operating parameters of a leading SCPC compressed digital video system are listed below.

satellites (EIRP = 37 dBW at edge of CONUS coverage), five 6.6 MBps compressed digital video channels could be transmitted through a single transponder. Since the bandwidth of each channel is only 3.3 MHz and the transponder bandwidth is 36 MHz, it might at first appear that more than 4 or 5 channels could be transmitted through a single channel. However, in this system transponder capacity is determined by power rather than by bandwidth considerations. For example, if it were attempted to transmit five 6.6 MBps digital video channels in a single

Digital Information Rate	=	5.0 MBps
Modulation	=	QPSK
Forward Error Correction	=	Rate 3/4
Transmitted Data Rate	=	6.6 MBps
Channel Bandwidth	=	3.3 MHz
Carrier-To-Noise Ratio Required For Satisfactory Operation (Bit Error Rate of 1×10^{-7})	=	8.8 dB

A transponder of a C-Band satellite operating in this system would be capable of receiving compressed digital video channels uplinked from earth stations located anywhere in the United States and retransmitting these channels to receive earth stations similarly dispersed throughout the United States. For the parameters listed above, four 6.6 MBps compressed digital video channels could be transmitted through a single present generation C-Band satellite transponder. For next generation

transponder to a typical headend earth station located on the 34 dBW EIRP contour, system carrier-to-noise ratio, $C/N_{system,}$ would be less than the required 8.8 dB. Table 4 shows the typical margins that would be experienced at a cable headend earth station located at the edge of CONUS coverage, equipped with an antenna 3.7 meters in diameter (G/T = 23.7 dB/K), and receiving either 4 or 5 digital video channels in a single satellite transponder.

TABLE 4

Single Channel Per Carrier (SCPC) Transmission
4 or 5 Compressed Digital Television Channels Per Transponder
Downlink Margin For Each Channel

Satellite	Maximum Permissible Downlink Loss (For Bit Error Rate = 1×10^{-7}) (dB)
Present Generation (Transponder Power = 5.5 to 10 Watts) (4 Channels)	3.9
Next Generation (Transponder Power = 16 to 20 Watts) (5 Channels)	2.3

The margins shown in Table 4 could be used to compensate for losses due to rain and for antenna pointing error losses.

Since the bit rate is fixed as a part of the system design, the flexibility in adjusting the bit rate to the program content is not available in an SCPC architecture.

4.0 High Definition Television (HDTV)

Much work is now being done directed toward the development of a television system that will provide a picture of higher definition and quality than is currently available in conventional NTSC transmissions. A number of High Definition Television (HDTV) systems are under development. The specific parameters vary from system to system: not every new system incorporates every proposed feature. Among the suggested new characteristics are: increase in the number of lines per frame from the present 525 up to 1125, increase in aspect ratio from the current 4:3 up to 16:9, and use of a progressive scan format instead of the existing 2:1 interlace.

While, as in the case of digital compressed television, HDTV standards are still under final development, a typical digital HDTV system will be considered here. This system, which is currently under development, may be considered both as exemplar of all the proposed systems and at the same time as the most difficult to implement via satellite because the transmitted data rate per HDTV channel is the highest of all the candidate systems. The conclusions reached concerning performance of this system at cable headend earth stations will be representative of all the systems now under development. Some of the outstanding baseband television characteristics are:

Lines Per Frame	1050
Aspect Ratio	16:9
Scan	2:1 Interlaced

In the satellite transmission scheme that is currently being planned, two HDTV channels will be time division multiplexed into one data channel.

The operational parameters for satellite transmission are:

System carrier-to-noise, $(C/N)_{system}$, and the corresponding margin above the value required for satisfactory operation will, of course, be lowest where the satellite EIRP value is lowest: at the edge of CONUS. Table 5 shows the downlink margins available at a typical cable headend earth station located at the edge of CONUS coverage and equipped with a receive antenna 3.7 meters in diameter. Table 5 also shows the space segment availability that would be achieved in the transmission of the two time division multiplexed HDTV channels.

Digital Information Rate Per HDTV Channel	24 MBps
Total Digital Information Rate	48 MBps
Error Correction Code Rate (Using concatenated codes)	0.82
Total Transmitted Data Rate	58.5 MBps
Modulation	QPSK
Channel Bandwidth	29.3 MHz
Carrier-To-Noise Ratio Required (For a Bit Error Rate of 1×10^{-12})	8.9 dB

TABLE 5

Digital High Definition Television (HDTV)
Two Time Division Multiplexed Channels per Transponder
Downlink Margin Available in Clear Weather and Space Segment Availability

Satellite	Downlink Margin Available in Clear Weather or Maximum Permissible Downlink Loss [For $(C/N)_{system}$ = 8.9 dB]	Space Segment Availability %	Minutes/Year Below [$(C/N)_{system}$ = 8.9 dB]
Present Generation (Transponder Power = 5.5 to 10 Watts)	5.3	99.9986	7.4
Next Generation (Transponder Power = 16 to 20 Watts)	8.3	>99.9990	<5.3

The above example again illustrates the great technical impact that digital compression technology will have on satellite transmissions to cable headend earth stations. For analog or partially digitized HDTV systems, the capacity of a C-Band satellite would be one channel per transponder. Use of digital compression techniques would double this capacity and at the same time increase space segment availability.

5.0 Conclusion

It has been seen in this paper that technology now developing in digital video compression will have a profound technical impact on satellite transmissions to cable headend earth stations. Transmission of digital compressed video signals through a satellite will result, compared to conventional analog transmissions, in:

- Multiple television channels per transponder

- Greater margins with respect to system requirements.

The following table summarizes the increases in transponder capacity and in system operating margins that have been described in this paper.

SUMMARY TABLE

Impact Of Digital Compression Technology
On Satellite Television Transmissions

Transmission Mode	Satellite Capacity (Channels/Transponder)	Downlink Margin Available In Clear Weather (dB)	
		Present Generation Satellite	Next Generation Satellite
● Analog	1	3.1	6.1
● Compressed Digital-TDM	(See Note 1)	7.9	10.9
● Compressed Digital-SCPC (Bit Rate = 6.6 MBps)	4	3.9	6.9
● Compressed Digital-SCPC (Bit Rate = 6.6 MBps)	5	-	2.3
● Compressed Digital High Definition Television (HDTV)-TDM	2	5.3	8.3

NOTES:
1. Depending upon desired picture quality, ranging from HDTV to VCR, the number of channels per digital channel, and therefore per transponder, would range from 2 to 10.

Chapter 4
Digital Video in Telecommunications: Interoperability in Multi-Format Digital Video Networks

ROBERT E. KEELER
AT & T BELL LABORATORIES

Abstract—Numerous applications and services will take advantage of digital video technologies, which will include unique characteristics not encountered in analog television. In order to realize the full potential of digital video applications, provision must be made for affordable, effective interoperability. Interoperability will enable unplanned cross-connections among industries, among consumer stakeholders, including producers, distributors, and consumers, who will need to adjust to the diversity and complexity that are associated with these opportunities in order to derive the maximum possible benefit from digital video services.

INTRODUCTION

The interoperability discussed in this paper serves as a thematic backdrop to the other papers in this telecommunications-oriented chapter. The chapter's papers include tutorial material on telecommunications standards for the digital telecommunications hierarchy for a broad range of transmission rates, and a review of image and video coding standards that will be applicable for network-based digital video. Several papers introduce diverse digital video applications that will take advantage of the emerging digital telecommunications connectivity.

A major initiative, called the National Information Infrastructure (NII), is now being planned jointly by the federal government and private industry. [1] This initiative will add to the telecommunications options for the public in a national information "superhighway." This effort to improve the nation's information infrastructure will lead, among other things, to an extension to the wider public of functions currently performed by the Internet, now used so much by industrial, academic, and government interests. This extension will combine increased functionality with vastly greater access and performance of the network.

The purpose of this paper is to explore the need and potential for interoperability within the rapidly growing and evolving field of digital video, particularly as it relates to telecommunications. The telecommunications industries will provide an ever-widening range of delivery means for digital services, and it will be feasible to address niche markets for video services that previously have not been economically supportable or feasible. Consequently, digital video services and applications, in many forms, will become a ubiquitous accompaniment to our daily lives, for both business and pleasure.

There is a common base of technology for digital video, and it includes advances in the miniaturization, speed, power, and cost effectiveness of semiconductors; advances in compression algorithms; and advances in digital communications. These technologies are making possible the realization of advanced image systems for a very wide range of applications including video telephony and teleconferencing, multi-media interactions and presentations, broadcast and entertainment television, educational television, medical imaging, and many others.

CONVERGENCES AND DIVERGENCES

In the author's opinion, the evolution and revolution taking place in video communications involve both converging and diverging forces. While the underlying technology for digital video converges in the fields of algorithms, integrated semiconductor circuits, communications techniques, and display devices, the applications are diverging, that is, becoming more diverse. Examples of convergence include joint use of communications networks and the adherence to common compression algorithms for many applications. Examples of diversity abound, and some typical applications will be listed later. They include differences in resolution and frame rate, as well as compression algorithms tailored for specific applications.

Matching Formats to Applications

Rapid advances in digital video technology are creating opportunities for numerous video applications in traditional as well as non-traditional fields. Different formats and standards will emerge for different market segments, and the use of digital technology will remove or reduce impediments to interconnections among formats and across industries and applications, so that market forces can determine how the applications, including cross-industry applications, evolve.

The concept of a single "one-size-fits-all" format for television and video applications no longer makes sense, now that we can customize image systems to particular applications without the risk of being stranded when connections across applications boundaries are needed. The author therefore believes it is a mistake to think that a proliferation of formats and systems is undesirable, or that it is an indication that we are in an interim state while waiting to define some single ultimate standard for all image communications. The very diversity of image uses means that no single system will be optimum for all applications.

Interoperability Essential for Multi-Format Environment

The reason interoperability is so important, and cross-connections among disparate applications so necessary, is the fundamental need for options and choice in modern information systems. Consumers indicate clearly that they desire choice in television programming, as evidenced by the success of multiple-channel cable systems. End-users in business applications want and need access to arbitrary information, including video information, without regard to source, location, or format. With disparate systems optimized for specific purposes (no longer one-size-fits-all), effective cross-connections are imperative.

Interoperability will therefore be essential for the full realization of video opportunities. The importance of digital video in this context is that digital representation and processing of video information will foster effective, affordable, and necessary interoperability among these diverse video applications and services.

Varying Degrees of Interoperability

The interoperability idea does not mean that effortless, zero-cost, zero-degradation connection is guaranteed among all kinds of applications, media, and so forth. The ideal of a "plug-and-play" cross-connection can be realized, if plug-and-play refers to the end-users' perception and involvement, that is, if the effort needed to accomplish the appearance of effortless, transparent connections is concealed from the user. The idea of

"submerged complexity" in this context will be discussed in a later section. If a useful connection can be made, it can be considered interoperable. Interoperability is thus a matter of degree: the easier, more affordable, and more useful the connection, then the more the different video regimes are interoperable.

There are several dimensions to the issue of interoperability, and they include scalability and extensibility. Scalability refers to the ability to use different subsets of digital video data for different applications; extensibility refers to the ability to incorporate new technology while retaining backward compatibility. These dimensions will be discussed in a later section.

Changing Market Forces for Video

As communications options proliferate, users of video information will be confronted with choices not previously encountered (when most roads led to NTSC). For example, the user may be faced with a choice between a video service that has performance limitations (perhaps delay is excessive for interactive conferencing), and a better grade of service that may cost several times as much (using much more channel capacity to guarantee good quality with low delay). Users of video services will need to be equipped with knowledge or tools that will provide appropriate tradeoffs among features, performance, and cost, so the users can make informed decisions among many choices. Not all complexity will be submerged.

II. SOME UNIQUE CHARACTERISTICS OF DIGITAL VIDEO

(Implications and Characteristics Specific to Digital Video)

A. Digital Processing Is Fundamentally Non-Real-Time, Effectively Off-Line

Unlike the traditional analog television processing steps, which have been locked to analog sync signals, the use of digital compression forces a non-real-time mode of operation in which processing is intrinsically off-line, even if the results occur fast enough to appear to be happening in real time.

The compression algorithms involve disassembling sequences of images both temporally and in the image plane (i.e., spatially) as the images are processed. The processed elements cease to be recognizably related to the images and are only reassembled at the receiver after decoding and reformatting.

This disassembling should be viewed as a step forward, rather than as an undesirable complication. The result is a virtual decoupling of the capture and production phase of the television chain from the storage and transmission phase, and again a decoupling of the transmission from the eventual display or displays. By moving the difficult process-intensive steps in image compression out of the real-time mode (rigidly controlled by end-to-end synchronization) to an off-line mode, we can bring to bear as much processing power as is needed (or as can be afforded). In particular, this decoupling and the off-line processing facilitate the kinds of interoperability that will be important for future digital video services.

B. Indirect Synchronization

In digital video systems, because synchronization cannot be counted on as a byproduct of the regular occurrence of periodic features in analog signals, digital video will need to rely on a reconstructed synchronization or clock. For example, in a packetized transport environment there will be no stable reference points in the data stream on which to base a video clock, and indirect means will be used to recreate a stable reference from information imbedded in the payloads of the packetized data stream. In general, the modern digital video communications systems will devote a far smaller part of channel capacity to synchronization than does an analog system like NTSC. While this feature increases efficiency, it will require careful engineering to minimize jitter in the reconstructed clock signals, and to assure rapid acquisition and robust locking of the sync signals. The tolerance to synchronization perturbations in the receiver will need to be matched to realistic timing variations of all the communications networks that may be used to deliver the signal.

C. Changing Evaluation of Video Quality

There has been a shift in the way video quality is evaluated, by consumers and by professionals, especially in video quality after compression. In general, this shift is a result of increased sophistication in our recognition of diversity among applications, and increased practicality in tolerating insignificant picture artifacts.

For example, simplistic measures like mean-square error were used in early studies to quantify picture degradations. Those measures are now recognized as being of less utility for compressed digital images than they were for analog television or digitally represented (sampled) analog television. By using models of the human visual system, there have been attempts to measure the *perception* of the degradations rather than the degradations themselves. [2] This approach has led to designs for compression algorithms that attempt to minimize the perceived amount of degradation, irrespective of the degradation itself, which may be substantial but irrelevant if not noticeable.

A more recent and more sophisticated approach, at least in the entertainment industry, is to acknowledge that the expectation of artifact-free (or perceptually artifact-free) compression and transmission is unrealistic, and that for practical reasons some perceptible artifacts will be accepted. This view can be justified on the grounds that the *average* picture quality can be dramatically improved, while occasional very active and/or detailed images will include some built-in artifacts after decompression.

For a constant bit rate channel, the economics favor such an approach. For example, if 20 Mb/sec will suffice in a high-definition television system for all but the extremely rare cases just described, but 40 Mb/sec would be needed to eliminate the perceptible artifacts almost completely, it might be difficult to justify the expense of the extra channel bandwidth needed for near perfection, for a limited-bandwidth broadcast television channel. In the recent past, the professional mind-set was to exclude or try to eliminate any perceptible *or measurable* image defects in the signal before transmission. (Consider, for example, some of the analog television test signals such as the 2T pulse and differential phase-and-gain measurements.)

D. Video Impairments Not Directly Related to Transmission Impairments

The digital nature of signals in digital video means that transmission impairments all map into the same effect in the decoded signal; that is, a transmission error if bad enough, or no error if not a bad enough impairment. [3] Some applications are more sensitive to errors than others, and error management will need to be considered when multiple uses are contemplated for digital video.

The error effects in the decoded signal (either errored symbols or error-free symbols) then map into "artifacts" that depend on the data affected, and not directly upon the impairment that caused the error. In other words, we will no longer have a single-stage process in which, for example, poor S/N ratio causes snow in a picture, multipath causes repeated horizontally-displaced image edges, impulse noise causes sparkles on the screen, differential phase causes color shifts, or co-channel interference (from sporadic-E) causes unrelated ghost images to roll through an image. We will have a first stage where those effects, if severe enough, will all lead to digital (i.e., symbol) errors. In a second stage, statistically uncorrelated with the first, errors that cannot be corrected will lead to a variety of effects. The type, visibility, and severity of the effect will not be predictable from the type of impairment that caused the error (except that more severe transmission impairments will likely cause more noticeable picture impairments). The visibility of the effects will depend entirely on the specific digital information that was affected, which cannot be predicted based on either the cause of the error or the picture content. (This view makes the reasonable assumption that naturally occurring transmission impairments are statistically independent of features in the transport protocol and of the details of the images being transmitted.)

E. Nonlinearity of Digital Video Compression

The non-linear relationship between video quality and compressed bit rate has been alluded to earlier. By resorting to various kinds of predictions, algorithms, and tricks, and employing a certain low cunning, engineers have been able to extract most of what is important for an image's perception by a human observer, and to represent that extracted information with relatively very few bits. The result is that, for a given algorithm, a sharp knee occurs in the quality vs. bit-rate curve. This knee is sharpest for the best algorithms, and less sharp for algorithms that use fewer tricks, or employ less cunning. The

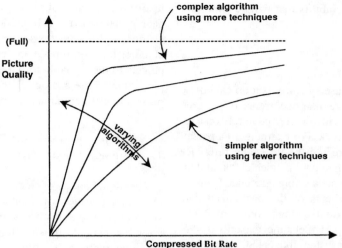

Figure 1. Nonlinear relationship between compressed video bit rate and picture quality

curves in Figure 1 illustrate the point, without referring to any particular algorithm.

This observation is relevant to the discussion of interoperability because of the hope in many quarters for the desirable feature called "scalability." In a scalable system for compression, there would be many different levels of performance that correspond to many different bit rates after compression.

III. DIGITAL VIDEO ENVIRONMENT

Evolving digital video systems are bringing substantial changes in the telecommunications environment, in digital video processing capabilities, and in related end-user information appliances. If handled properly, the resulting combinations of digital video and digital communications will add enormous value to our information wealth. The seeming chaos of diverse image systems and communications systems will represent opportunities rather than an unstable collection of incoherent capabilities. [4]

A. EMERGING DIGITAL TELECOMMUNICATIONS ENVIRONMENT

Digital Telecommunications Media

The telecommunications infrastructure in the U.S. is changing at an accelerated rate, with more media, more choice of transmission rates, more transport protocols, more communications standards, more means of access, and more variety of information for the end-user. The media over which digital video services will deliver images to users will include:

- telephone wire pairs,
- coaxial cable,
- fiber transmission (analog and digital),

- terrestrial broadcast (over-the-air radio),
- DBS (direct broadcast satellite),
- microwave radio ("wireless cable"),
- cellular radio (and PCN),
- stored media (tapes, laser discs, CD-ROM).

Networks to Support Digital Video Services

Among the telecommunications disciplines, protocols, and networks for delivering digital video services will be:

- ISDN (integrated services digital network),
- frame relay packet services,
- MPEG-2 transport stream packetized video services,
- ATM (asynchronous transfer mode) packet services,
- digital modems for telephone lines,
- ADSL (asymmetric digital subscriber line) and HDSL (high bit-rate digital subscriber line).

The above lists are not exhaustive, but indicate the increasing range of options compared to a recent past that involved mostly over-the-air terrestrial broadcast of entertainment television. The trend in these communications developments is toward more flexibility, leading to more choices and a wider range of possible features. For the packetized services, like ATM, and the transport layers of some compression algorithms, like MPEG-2, there is almost complete flexibility in dynamic allocation and multiplexing of channel capacity. This flexibility adds complexity, but opens the possibility of non-constant-rate services. For example, a viewer might choose to receive a different language or an additional language in the sound channels, or surround-sound, or additional camera angles, in each case perhaps for only part of a program, such as a sports event.

National Information Infrastructure (NII)

While capable of supporting the highest bandwidth communications requirements, the goal of the NII will be to support all types of information users, including those with modest information needs as well as the most demanding. The NII is envisioned to become a "seamless web of communications networks, computers, databases, and consumer electronics that will put vast amounts of information at users' fingertips." [5] The plan includes the concept of "universal service" to ensure that all Americans have access to the information available through the NII at affordable prices. Individuals connected to the NII will be able to access, generate, store, process, transmit, and receive all kinds of information: text, audio, images, video, and multimedia services. They will be able to get them anywhere, at any time. Barriers of distance, location, time, and even language can eventually be overcome even if not eliminated.

Such an ambitious plan for a publicly accessible network directly supports the notion of multiple image formats matched to the needs of particular applications but interconnecting via the "seamless web" of networks. While all the details of the NII have not yet been worked out, such a powerful network infrastructure promises to provide access for the public at large to an arbitrary range of diverse information sources. The success of this activity will require that video and image information accessible through the NII be widely available to end users with a variety of interactive information appliances. Use of communications protocols that share common elements will make it relatively simple for networks to serve the needs of customers with differing performance requirements, and differing monitoring equipment.

B. Evolving Digital Video
Compression Standards

Video compression techniques have developed rapidly over the last two decades, and are still the subject of very active and productive research. Standards chosen now must allow for the likely substantial advances in compression technology that are yet to come, and that cannot be predicted.

Common Algorithmic Techniques for
Digital Video Compression

The current dominant digital video compression algorithms have several important processing and transmission techniques in common. These common techniques include:

- motion-compensated predictive coding,
- block-oriented spatial transforms (specifically, discrete cosine transforms, or DCTs),
- adaptive quantization of transform coefficients,
- entropy coding of data to be transmitted,
- transmission buffers with feedback to adaptively control the compression.

Many other approaches are under investigation, including use of fractals, wavelets, sub-band coding, and model-based representation. The architecture of new digital video networks needs to allow for incorporating advances in compression technology. By providing the hooks for different levels of interoperability, we can treat these advances as additions to our video capability, instead of replacements for existing capabilities.

The emerging digital standards include those for standard-definition and high-definition television, video telephony, and multi-media business video. These different applications reflect different customer needs, and represent different market segments previously addressed, if at all, by a relatively ubiquitous NTSC television standard. Some of the most prominent video compression standards are discussed in the following sections.

1. P*64 Algorithms

The P*64 compression algorithms, designated as Recommendation H.261 by the CCITT, [6] are the subject of international agreement under the CCITT, and they focus on video telephony, with a requirement for minimum processing delay. This standard was motivated by the needs of interactive video telephony and video teleconferencing. The requirements of this market application include a symmetry between coder and decoder in terms of cost and complexity, and a need for minimum processing delay (less than 150 microseconds each way). Picture quality is important, but the applications do not generally involve the range of motion and scene changes expected for broadcast and entertainment television. In the decoder, where improved picture quality might result from processing over many picture frames, the delay criterion requires an algorithm that minimizes multiple-frame processing.

The P*64 standard is relatively open and extensible, being intended for multiples of 64 kb/sec transmission up to about 2 Mb/sec, although the algorithms could be used at higher speeds as well. Parameters within the P*64 standard can be chosen to optimize performance for specific applications. The algorithms with different parameters will produce different compressed bit-streams. (That is, a lower rate H.261 bit-stream will not generally be a subset of a higher rate H.261 bit-stream produced with different parameters.) This means that the standard does not provide a perfect subset kind of scalability.

2. MPEG-1

The MPEG-1 standard (MPEG stands for Moving Pictures Experts Group) has been established with international agreement under the auspices of the ISO (International Organization for Standardization). [7] The goal, different from the P*64 standard, was to address the requirements for multi-media applications and interactivity with digital storage media in particular, such as CD-ROM. Among the requirements were the inclusion of easily implemented VCR features like fast forward and reverse searching, full-quality stop motion, and slow motion. An asymmetry between coder and decoder costs is desirable because of a need for low decoder costs and "reasonable" encoder costs. The decoder must be inexpensive for consumer decoding of mass-distributed video on pre-recorded storage media like CD-ROM. The video formats considered were those associated with CCIR Recommendation 601, which supports digital moving images (525-line and 625-line) that can be stored in compressed form on affordable storage media.

Like the P*64 standard, the MPEG-1 standard includes many parameters that can be changed to fit particular applications. Also like the P*64 standard, the bit-streams resulting from different parameter choices within the MPEG-1 syntax will be different, and not interchangeable.

3. MPEG-2

The MPEG-2 standard is intended to extend the performance of multi-media applications above the 4-Mb/sec range, with corresponding improvements in picture quality. MPEG-2 will allow "profiles" to be defined for various applications and formats, such as different quality levels for broadcast CCIR 601, and HDTV.

MPEG-2 includes a detailed specification for packetized transport using either fixed-length or variable-length packets. [8] MPEG-2 also makes provisions for an optional "layering" of compression algorithms that can potentially make the system "scalable."

4. High-Definition Television—HDTV

High-definition television is intended to be a replacement for the current NTSC television system in the U.S., in which the resolution will be roughly doubled, colorimetry will be improved (better contrast and more accurate colors), and multi-channel CD-quality sound will be incorporated. The implications of the increased resolution are that viewing distances will be approximately halved, so that the TV screen will subtend a bigger solid angle than with current television. (A good working assumption for optimal NTSC viewing distances is about five to six times the height of the picture. For HDTV, the optimum viewing distances will typically be about two-and-a-half to three times the picture height.) Also, the aspect ratio will change from the current 4:3 (width to height) to 16:9 (5 1/3 to 3), giving an aspect ratio wider than current television, more like a movie screen. Since people will tend to continue watching television at the same viewing distances (because of room sizes and furniture placement), the market will tend toward larger screen sizes. Homes with HDTV will have dazzling pictures, without snow or ghosts, in a home theater setting, including surround-sound.

The attributes of the HDTV system proposed [9] for the U.S. include:

- all-digital signal representation, transmission, and processing;
- roughly double the horizontal and vertical resolution compared to current TV;

- packetized transport conforming to MPEG-2 transport specifications, easily carried over networks using ATM;
- self-identifying data streams for various elementary data such as multiple audio, multiple video, and auxiliary data streams;
- multiple formats, including 24-Hz, 30-Hz, and 60-Hz update rates, with progressive and interlaced scanning included among the 720-line (i.e., 720 active lines) and 1080-line formats (all progressive-scan except for the 1080-line 60 Hz mode, which is interlaced 2:1);
- HDTV receivers to support the multiple formats, agile in the sense they will identify formats and convert a variety of received formats to the receiver's common display format (alternatively, a receiver could have an agile "multi-sync" display);
- compression algorithms conforming to international digital video standards (MPEG-2);
- signal for HDTV contained in standard 6-MHz TV channel (with modulation producing about 25 Mb/sec); signal can also be carried directly by any U.S. cable system (the cable medium has the capability of carrying more than one HDTV signal in a 6-MHz channel, because it has less interference than terrestrial broadcasting).

The implications are that agile HDTV receivers will pave the way for interoperability among visual services, including those envisioned for the national information infrastructure (NII). Either as stand-alone HDTV receivers, or in combination with set-top boxes, HDTV will constitute a high-performance constellation of image capabilities in the spectrum of digital video services accessible to the U.S. public, providing a digital pipe into U.S. homes for many digital services in addition to HDTV. While applications will doubtless evolve with specific parameters and capabilities different from HDTV, the digital HDTV system can serve as a paradigm for future digital, self-identifying, interoperable video applications.

5. Digital 525-Line TV for Cable and Other Broadcast Applications

The cable industry in the U.S. is preparing to implement digital television compression systems for standard-definition television. Included will probably be compression algorithms with various performance characteristics in the (roughly) 1.5-Mb/sec to 10-Mb/sec range for 525-line broadcast/entertainment television. Several proprietary compression algorithms have been proposed, as well as versions of MPEG-1 and MPEG-2 compression, for this "standard-definition TV" or SDTV market segment. There is an opportunity for compatibility on several levels with a digital HDTV system (for example, for format harmonization, compression algorithms, and transport protocols).

6. Other Digital Video Standards

Proprietary standards for video teleconferencing and video telephony have also been introduced, in addition to open standards. As niche markets emerge, such nonstandard systems will always be a part of the information environment. These systems have evolved in such a way that direct interconnection among disparate systems often is not possible. In such cases, a telecommunications network can provide access to a conversion service when needed to achieve some level of interoperability.

C. NEW INFORMATION APPLIANCES

New kinds of information appliances will doubtless evolve to satisfy the needs of future users of digital video services. An assumption for this paper is that there will be multiple different formats and types of video applications for different purposes. It will be most practical for information appliances to be relatively agile, flexible, and capable of linking consumers/users with various kinds of information.

Diversity of New Video Applications

Coincident with the search for practical uses for increasingly large bandwidths that can be supported by the evolving local (and national and international) information infrastructure, there is a growing realization that consumers want a broader choice of viewing options and more diverse programming, tailored to the needs of the individual consumer. When one considers the variety of relevant market segments, it is clear that consumers will need to manage a wide range of video services that provide different levels of image (and sound) performance. Some will be niche applications, and some will be mass-market offerings.

Caution Concerning Convergence

While the underlying technologies supporting digital video services are converging, it would be a mistake to assume that mean the applications themselves will automatically converge. In other words, personal computers and television sets will use nearly identical technology, including communications protocols, processing elements, memory, and perhaps displays. That similarity does not mean that the viewing habits of television couch potatoes will shift in the direction of computer applications. It also does not mean that users of personal computers will prefer to watch dramatic productions like movies in a window on a PC display. Just because a technical feasibility exists, one should not assume that a genuine market for a product exists. The value of interoperability in this regard is important, since an emerging market for a particular combination of features can be observed as users deploy their resources and focus on certain most useful cross-connections.

Regarding specifically the often-mentioned convergence between computers and television applications, there will continue to be a distinction between applications that are viewed from a short distance, with low brightness, and applications that are viewed from a longer distance (three or more picture heights), with brighter screens. The short-distance applications will be more individual and personal, requiring more intense concentration, and the long-distance viewing will be more casual and informal. Computer displays will generally require more accurate presentation geometry, while entertainment displays can tolerate less accurate geometry but need more accurate color and smoother motion rendition.

Typical Digital Video Information Appliance

Figure 2 shows the elements of a future canonical digital video information appliance. It includes:

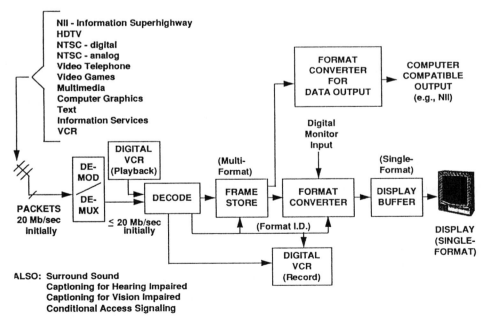

Figure 2. Canonical Digital Information Appliance

- several communications interfaces (tuners, modems);
- direct digital input ports;
- demultiplexers that sort out several input streams, and direct sub-streams appropriately;
- decompression processing for audio, video, other;
- frame stores for storing bit-mapped images before display;
- display formatters that convert arbitrary input images to the format of the local display device;
- display;
- output ports (analogous to TV baseband monitor outputs).

Such an appliance can provide the television household with far more than advanced television, and can be the home's window into numerous digital services.

IV. PLANNING FOR INTEROPERABILITY

In pre-digital times, different image applications evolved separately, and interconnections were awkward at best. One approach, when interconnections have been needed, has been to use NTSC television standards for all images, but undesirable compromises were necessary.

A much better solution, made possible with digital technologies that foster affordable interconnections, is to allow different applications, such as medical imaging, entertainment television, video telephony, and others, to use formats and features appropriate to each application, but with the formats and features chosen to be harmoniously related. [10] In this way, the possibility of easy conversions and interconnections among applications will be assured.

A. NECESSITY FOR INTEROPERABILITY AMONG VIDEO APPLICATIONS

The strong trend among consumers is toward more choice. The historical trend in consumer choice is from a common viewing experience for the vast majority of an earlier viewing population, to a multiple-channel cable option today, to a future in which viewing will be increasingly individualistic. For the planned interactive services, programming will be primarily for an individual information appliance controlled by a single end-user.

As digital communication becomes accessible to a continually broader segment of the public, there will be increasing needs and opportunities to interconnect applications and services that have been separate. Therefore, a diversity of digital video systems and formats tailored to specific digital video applications will only be a completely positive development if it is easy to move among different formats, applications, industries, and media. [11] The utility of video images will be magnified through unanticipated cross-connections that cannot all be planned for. This unpredictability is related to the market need for choice and options in image communication important for business as well as residential users.

For example, connecting entertainment television production facilities with medical imaging in a distance-learning application is a likely use for interoperable digital video, and yet the native images for medical imaging may have very different formats and performance criteria from traditional television. It will be important to retain the advantages of the native modes for (say) medical imaging even when a different-quality image is used for the learning environment and the diagnostic environment.

B. DEFINITIONS FOR INTEROPERABILITY

The usefulness of the term "interoperability" for digital video relates to the idea of achieving a kind of universality of images, in which consumers can obtain image information of any kind, in a form chosen by the consumer to match the consumer's needs, instantly available (or at least in a timely fashion), at an affordable cost. One definition that has some acceptance in the television and computer industries is:

Interoperability: The capability of providing useful and cost-effective interchange of electronic image, audio, and associated data among different signal formats, among different transmission media, among different applications, among different industries, among different performance levels. [12]

Examples include film to HDTV to NTSC to ultra-high definition images, for different formats. Terrestrial broadcast, satellite, fiber optic networks and coaxial cable represent different media that will need to interconnect. Education to medical imaging to entertainment television is an example of different industries that can usefully exchange image information. CAD-CAM, image databases, computer art, and entertainment TV are different applications of image technology with a potential need to interoperate. Education, history, and entertainment can benefit from interoperation among different epochs, using archived as well as current images. Transfer of image data among the U.S., Africa, Antarctica, Australia, Asia, Europe, South America, and the rest of the world represents a geopolitical dimension to openness and interoperability.

Measures of interoperability could include ease of processing for conversions, delay associated with such processing, and picture impairments introduced by such processing.

Extensibility

The concept of extensibility relates to the ability of systems to evolve over time in a way that retains some measure of interoperability. The underlying digital video technology relies on a common base of semiconductors, processing elements, and modern digital communications techniques; rapid progress in those fields is continuing. New standards need to allow for future advances which cannot be predicted, but must allow for important extensions to performance without rendering the new standards obsolete.

Extensibility: A property of a system, format or standards that allows future improvements in performance or format within a common framework, while retaining partial or

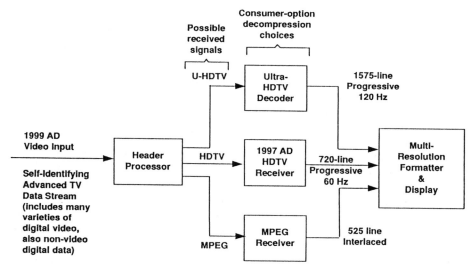

Figure 3(a). Example of Extensibility

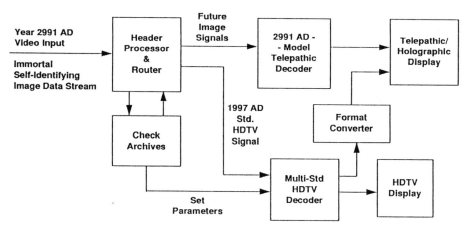

Figure 3(b). Additional Example of Extensibility

complete compatibility among systems that belong to the common framework. [12]

Extensibility reduces the risk of choosing a standard while the underlying technology is in a state of flux. Extensibility means that interoperability with the future is assured. An example might be a future 3-D (stereoscopic) television that is compatible with the initial version of HDTV.

An important element of systems that provides some measure of extensibility is the incorporation of headers and descriptors that makes blocks of image data self-identifying. The headers in packetized transport allow data types to be self-identifying, thus re-definable, thus extensible.

The needed general principle seems to be to allow both compatible and noncompatible signals, but to require that all information appliances respond intelligently to all signals. That is, an older TV receiver may be partially compatible with a new multimedia signal, and usefully decode and display the information contained in packets or data it understands, while ignoring packets and data that for the older receiver are undefined. Figure 3 shows two examples of extensibility.

Scalability

Scalability means that the image data representation allows for functionally different performance levels. The idea is that a common data stream can serve the needs of various end-users whose requirements may differ.

Scalability: The degree to which video and image formats can be combined in systematic proportions for distribution over communications channels for varying capacities. In particular, this means that different subsets of compressed video data can be decoded and used for different applications and for different performance levels. [12]

Several advantages are claimed for systems that have the scalable property. These include:

a. Only a needed portion of the entire data stream has to be transmitted, saving transmission costs. Consider a frugal customer with modest resources to spend on access charges, whose application does not need the full quality of HDTV or highest resolution of stored video images.

b. Only a needed portion of the entire received stream must be decoded, thereby saving processing cost (power, speed, time) at the decoder. Think of a wrist TV that may be hard-pressed to decode an entire HDTV data stream, but would like to decode a 100-line subset of the HDTV picture.

c. Related to the previous item, consider a windowing application in which, for some window sizes, much of the detail information for a full NTSC-quality image might be unnecessary and discarded for the windowed display, saving processing power in the local computer for simultaneous other applications.

The scalability idea is motivated by the thought that one could usefully deal with (transmit, receive, manipulate, process) a fraction of the complete image data and thereby save the cost of dealing with the entire data stream. For example, if 90 percent of the data gives a 90 percent quality image, and 30 percent of the data gives an image with 30 percent of the entire data's quality, one can imagine a scheme with several performance levels corresponding to different data rates, all subsets of the total data stream. This scheme might be practical if the performance curve were linear as indicated by the straight line in Figure 4. In that case, different performance levels could be spread out rationally, and there could be an economic incentive for supporting performance levels different enough to satisfy different needs.

However, the curve of performance vs. bit rate for video compression is highly nonlinear, as mentioned previously, and it has been found that there is a penalty in terms of performance to structure the compression algorithms so that they can be subdivided in a completely scalable way. Some estimates suggest

about a 15 percent penalty in bit rate to achieve a given picture quality with the scalable property. In the case of broadcast television, for example, the strict limitation on channel bandwidth puts a hard constraint on bit rates, and a loss of performance due to compression inefficiency cannot be made up by transmitting more bits.

A Possible Approach to Scalability

The digital systems that use spatial transforms can achieve some degree of scalability by selecting a subset of transform coefficients (like lower frequency DCT coefficients) for decoding at the receiver. Also, a layered or pyramidal coding architecture [13] can be employed to extend any of the digital compression techniques to higher-quality compression. (See Figures 5a and 5b.)

A conceptual approach to scalability, one that addresses the need for efficiency in dominant applications as well as the advantages of scalable systems, is to design the compression algorithms without scalability for an operating point that approximates the dominant usage for the system.

For performance better than the initial dominant applications, a layered approach can be taken, in which the main data stream is augmented with additional data that provides the needed extra information. [14] Lesser performance subsets will not be directly available in the original data stream, and the original data stream will not be readily scalable. However, for additional performance, a scalable approach that uses layered coding can be used. (Thus, scaling up from the initial operating point is defined, but not scaling down.)

If there is a need for the lesser-quality images, it may be economical and attractive to send a separate encoding of images for the lesser-performance applications, with little loss, because of the steeper slope of quality vs. bit rate for a lesser-resolution image. This overhead may be smaller than the cost in compression efficiency for the scalable version of an algo-

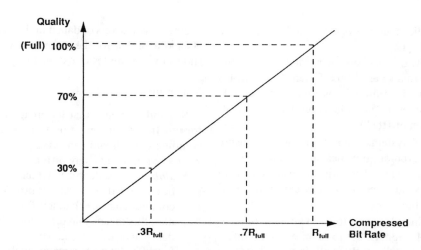

Figure 4. Hypothetical linear relationship allows significant differences in compressed bit rate to result in corresponding significant picture quality differences

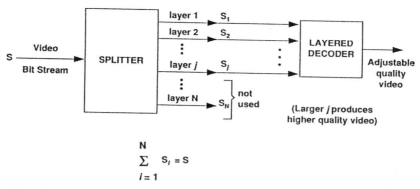

Figure 5(a). Layered Coding of Video

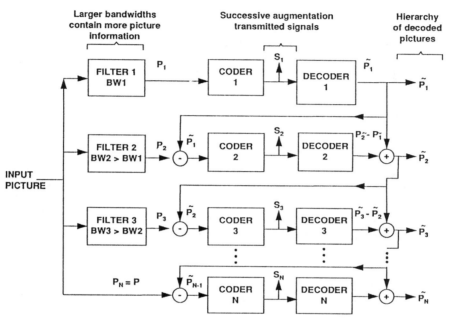

Figure 5(b). Hierarchical Layered Coder Example

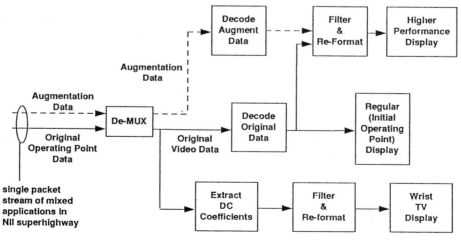

Figure 6. Example with limited scalability achieved using layered coding

rithm. Then if there is a genuine market need for a lower-bit-rate, lower-cost digital video service, one could simply add a completely separate data stream (using less than 15 percent of the channel capacity for the higher performance system) to the data that is routinely transmitted. A low-bit-rate digital video compression algorithm for a movie might require 1 Mb/sec, while the higher performance HDTV version of the same movie would require about 20 Mb/sec. Always sending both of those signals (20 Mb/sec + 1 Mb/sec = 21 Mb/sec) would be less costly in terms of channel capacity than sending a single scalable data stream that would include the 1 Mb/sec equivalent as a subset and would retain the HDTV quality (20 Mb/sec + 15 percent or 23 Mb/sec).

Decoding only the DC terms of transform blocks would provide a scalable subset for lower-resolution uses like a wrist television. This signal might not be scalable in the sense of a simple subset, but the DC coefficients might be readily extracted with minimum processing. Figure 6 shows several ways in which a scalable signal could be decoded and used.

C. Attributes Required for Interoperability in Digital Video

The most important attributes for a digital video system to achieve interoperability include:

1. *All-digital signal representation, transmission and processing:* Digital representation of signals is the key element in achieving interoperability for images and video. The digital nature of the signal means that all systems that process the signal will have identical material to process (barring errors, which can be controlled effectively). Digital representation also allows the utilization of advances in speed and processing power of digital semiconductors, as well as advances in digital signal processing theory;

2. *Packetized transport:* The use of packets for delivering video data provides great flexibility in handling multiple video and audio data streams. Data of different types can be easily partitioned and labeled, and channel capacity can be dynamically allocated;

3. *Self-identifying data streams:* In a multi-format, multi service, multi-media environment, self-identifying data will allow information systems to identify and adapt to received data with a minimum of external coordination;

4. *Support for multiple image formats;*

5. *Agile receivers to support the multiple formats and multiple services;*

6. *Compression algorithms that conform to widely accepted digital video standards.*

V. OPPORTUNITIES AND NEED FOR NEW FUNCTIONALITY

Submerged Complexity

To be effective, the complexity associated with modern telecommunications networks and digital video must not obscure for the user the system features with which the user must interact. In other words, inevitably there will be so much (useful) complexity that we will need to shield users from all except those elements the user needs to know about. Much more effort than in the past will need to be devoted to "submerging" unneeded detail from end-users, who will need all the help they can get to control and make decisions about the information available to them. Examples of choices to be made by consumers/users are:

- network access, network codes;
- grades of service for telecommunications;
- network-mediated processing, like conversions, translations;
- identification of desired data and form of data;
- identification of other participants in conferences, sessions, calls.

Behind the scenes, the network may turn somersaults to locate information, route calls, integrate information from disparate databases, edit image files, and so on. The interface with the customer should involve only control and status information, plus the actual desired content.

The idea of submerged complexity is to siphon off a tiny fraction of the enormous processing power necessarily present in realistic information appliances, and use that power to make routine, predictable decisions and default connections, to guide the user and, in effect, to do all the tedious detail work that the user will not have time for.

An example might be a future VCR that, on recognizing that its clock display is flashing "12:00," inconspicuously connects itself to a telephone line or a time stamp on a TV channel and resets itself. A trickier VCR could, on being plugged in for the first time, identify itself to all the other video appliances and connect itself to a default virtual input port on one of the TV sets, and to the main television source signal in the residence.

Flexible Compositing

The processing of images for compression necessarily involves their disassembly for processing, and in effect non-real-time processing. Thus, the limits previously imposed on compositing, editing and other processing will diminish.

Current practice for television production centers on a single format, and additional formats, such as 24-Hz or 30-Hz film, or 50-Hz European formats, constitute costly complications in editing and mixing television signals. In the future, we can expect to have editing equipment in which each output frame will be created using various image inputs and various processing steps that now are specialty functions applied to isolated image frames. The inputs to such editing equipment need not be synchronized to one another, nor adhere to a single format.

NETWORK MEDIATED POST PROCESSING

Just as more flexible processing will exist in the origination of images, the information for the end-user can be modified in the network or at the destination.

In some cases, the network can deliver differently subsets of the information adaptively depending on an end-user's profile or feedback from an interactive connection. Different camera angles, different languages, and other variations were mentioned previously. Processing steps that are specialized and expensive will be accessible to end-users through the information networks. At the destination information appliance, totally arbitrary processing will be possible, with cost being the major constraint.

VI. CONCLUSIONS

Digital video services are becoming an increasingly important part of the fabric of our lives, from entertainment television and video games to learning and business applications of all types. Rather than a single format for video services, many formats will flourish, although some will be numerically more important because they address mass markets.

In the author's opinion, the risk of users being stranded on an island of video formats that cannot interconnect will be minimized by incorporating features that facilitate interoperability in the transport and compression standards for digital video. In order to support the kind of interoperability needed, digital video systems should incorporate.

- digital representation, processing, and transmission;
- packetized transport;
- formats that are harmoniously related.

These developments are made possible by use of new levels of speed, complexity, and processing power that previously have not been feasible. Much of the complexity will be shielded from the end-user, in a process of "submerged complexity," but the complexity will exist in a beneficial sense, and it will be an essential part of the new communications and information infrastructure. The beneficiary of these developments will be the information consumer, who will have image information of any kind instantly available, in a form chosen by the consumer, at an affordable cost.

REFERENCES

[1] U.S. Commerce Dept., "An NII task force—the national information infrastructure: agenda for action," September 1993.
[2] W. E. Glenn, "Digital image compression based on visual perception and scene properties," SMPTE J. vol. 102, no. 5, May, pp. 392–397, 1993.
[3] "Report of Analysis Task Force on system-specific tests for digital systems," FCC Advisory Committee on Advanced Television Services, November 26, 1991.
[4] R. F. Cohen, "Estimating the economic value of interoperability," draft report for planning subcommittee of FCC Advisory Committee on Advanced Television Service, Working Party 4, February 24, 1992.
[5] R. Brown, Commerce Dept. Secretary, "An NII Advisory Council," Remarks by Secretary Brown at Museum of Television and Radio, January 1994.
[6] CCITT, "Recommendation H.261—video codec for audiovisual services at px64 kbits/s," Geneva, August 1990.
[7] ISO, "Coding of moving pictures and associated audio for digital storage media up to about 1.5 Mb/s." Committee Draft 11172, information technology, 1993.
[8] ISO, "Draft Systems Standard for MPEG-2," 1993.
[9] Grand Alliance (for HDTV), "HDTV systems specification," submitted to FCC Advisory Committee on February 24, 1994.
[10] G. Reitmeier, C. Carlson, E. Geiger, and D. Westerkamp, "The digital hierarchy—a blueprint for television in the 21st century," SMPTE J., vol. 101, no. 7, July, pp. 466–470, 1992.
[11] R. E. Keeler, "Interoperability considerations for digital HDTV," IEEE Transactions Broadcasting, vol. 37, no. 4, December, pp. 128–130, 1991.
[12] Planning Subcommittee Working Party 4 of FCC Advisory Committee on Advanced Television Service, "Final Report on Interoperability," 1993.
[13] B. G. Haskell, "Layered coding of video for broadband ISDN (ATM)," Talk given at EIA 3rd Annual Workshop on Digital Video, October 11, 1991.
[14] J. S. Lim, "A migration path to a better digital television system," SMPTE J., vol. 103, no. 1, January, pp. 2–6, 1994.

FURTHER READING

TELECOMMUNICATIONS BACKGROUND

[1] G. Clapp and M. Zeug, "Components of OSI: Asynchronous transfer mode (ATM) and ATM adaptation layers," ConneXions, April, pp. 22–31, 1992.
[2] G. Falk, "LAN interconnection over X.25," ConneXions, Feb., pp. 2–14, 1993.
[3] H. Rubin and N. Natarajan, "A distributed software architecture for telecommunications networks," IEEE Network, Jan./Feb., pp. 8–17, 1994.
[4] W. Stallings, "Components of OSI: Broadbank ISDN," ConneXions, April, pp. 2–12, 1992.
[5] W. Stallings, "Components of OSI: Synchronous optical network," ConneXions, April, pp. 13–21, 1992.
[6] W. Stallings, "Components of OSI: International standardized profiles," ConneXions, Jan., pp. 2–15, 1993.
[7] SMPTE Engineering Committee, "SMPTE Header/Descriptor task force: Final report," SMPTE J., June, pp. 411–429, 1992.
[8] G.-H. Im and J. J. Werner, "Bandwidth efficient digital transmission up to 155 Mb/s over unshielded twisted pair wiring," ICC '93 Geneva, pp. 1–7, 1993.
[9] D. L. Waring, D. S. Wilson, and T. R. Hsing, "Fiber upgrade strategies using high-bit-rate copper technologies for video delivery," IEEE J. Lightwave Technology, Nov., pp. 1743–1750, 1992.

DIGITAL VIDEO TRENDS

[1] H. Aldermeshian, W. H. Ninke, and R. J. Pile, "The video communications decade," AT&T Tech. J., Jan./Feb., pp. 2–6, 1993.
[2] H. Aiko and K. Aoyama, "Technical trends in visual communications systems."
[3] R. Brown, Commerce Dept. Secretary, "All NII advisory council," Remarks by Secretary Brown at Museum of Television and Radio, Jan. 1994.

[4] U.S. Commerce Dept., "An NII task force—the national information infrastructure: agenda for action," September, 1993.

[5] R. F. Cohen, "Estimating the economic value of interoperability," Draft report for planning subcommittee of FCC Advisory Committee on Advanced Television Service, Working Party 4, Feb. 24, 1992.

[6] R. E. Keeler, "Interoperability considerations for digital HDTV," *IEEE Trans. Broadcasting,* Dec., pp. 128–130, 1991.

[7] G. Reitmeier, C. Carlson, E. Geiger, and D. Westerkamp, "The digital hierarchy—A blueprint for television in the 21st century," *SMPTE J.,* July, pp. 466–470, 1992.

[8] "Report of analysis task force on system-specific tests for digital systems," *FCC Advisory Committee on Advanced Television Services,* Nov. 26, 1991.

DIGITAL VIDEO APPLICATIONS IN CURRENT TELECOMMUNICATIONS NETWORK

[1] B. D. Ackland, et al, "A video-codec chip set for multimedia applications," AT&T Tech. J., Jan./Feb., pp. 50–66, 1993.

[2] D. T. Chai, et al, "Networked compact disc interactive," *SMPTE J.* Sept., p. 773, 1993.

[3] M. Ghanbari and C. J. Hughes, "Packing coded video signals into ATM cells," IEEE/ACM *Trans. Networking,* Oct., pp. 505–509, 1993.

[4] J. T. Powers, Jr, et al, "Video on demand: Architecture, systems and applications," *SMPTE J.,* Sept., p. 791, 1993.

[5] T. R. Hsing, C.-T. Chen, and J. Bellisio, "Video communications and services in the copper loop," *IEEE Comm.,* Jan., pp. 62–68, 1993.

[6] S. Ichinose, H. Sakai, Y. Nakamura, and K. Takita, "Visual telephone," *NTT Review,* March, pp. 59–66, 1993.

[7] S. Early, A. Kuzma, and E. Dorsey, "The VideoPhone 2500—Video telephony on the public switched telephone network," AT&T Tech. J., Jan/Feb., pp. 22–32, 1993.

[8] P. E. Crouch, J. A. Hicks and J. J. Jetzt, "ISDN personal video," *AT&T Tech. J.,* Jan./Feb., pp. 33–40, 1993.

[9] B. G. Haskell, "Layered coding of video for broadband ISDN (ATM)," Talk given at EIA 3rd Annual Workshop on Digital Video, Arlington, Va., Oct. 11, 1991.

[10] D. N. Horn, T. G. Lyons, J. C. Mitchell, and D. L. Skran, "A standards-based multimedia conferencing bridge," *AT&T Tech. J.,* Jan./Feb., pp. 41–49, 1993.

[11] Planning Subcommittee Working Party 4, "Final Report on Interoperability," FCC Advisory Committee on Advanced Television Service, 1993.

[12] S. Shiwa, Nakazawa, T. Komatsu, and S. Ichinose, "Eye contact display technologies for visual telecommunications," *NTT Review,* March, pp. 67–73, 1993.

[13] G. Suzuki, S. Sugawara, K. Watanabe, and Y. Nagashima, "Virtual collaborative workspace," *NTT Review,* March, pp. 74–81, 1993.

[14] Y. Tonomura, K. Otsuji, A. Akutsu, and Y. Ohba, "Stored video handling techniques," *NTT Review,* March, pp. 82–90, 1993.

BROADBAND DIGITAL VIDEO IN THE TELECOMMUNICATIONS NETWORK

[1] Karlsson, M. Vetterli, "Packet video and its integration into the network architecture," *IEEE J. Selected Areas in Comm.,* June, pp. 739–751, 1989.

[2] A. R. Riebman and B. Haskell, "Constraints on variable bit-rate video for ATM networks," *IEEE Trans. Circuits and Systems for Video Tech.,* Dec., pp. 361–372, 1992.

[3] P. Skelly, M. Schwartz, and S. Dixit, "A histogram-based model for video traffic behavior in an ATM multiplexer," *IEEE/ACM Tans. Networking,* Aug., pp. 446–459, 1993.

[4] W. Verhiest and L. Pinnoo, "A variable bit rate video codec for asynchronous transfer mode networks," *IEEE J. Selected Areas in Comm.,* June, pp. 761–770, 1989.

VIDEO CODING AND CODING STANDARDS

[1] R. Aravind, et al, "Image and video coding standards," *AT&T Tech. J.,* Jan./Feb., pp. 67–89, 1993.

[2] CCITT, Recommendation H.261, "Video codec for audiovisual services at px64 kbits/s," Geneva, August 1990.

[3] W. E. Glenn, "Digital image compression based on visual perception and scene properties," *SMPTE J.,* May, pp. 392–397, 1993.

[4] Grand Alliance (for HDTV), "HDTV systems specification," submitted to FCC Advisory Committee, February 24, 1994.

[5] ISO Committee Draft 11172, information Technology, "Coding of moving pictures and associated audio for digital storage media up to about 1.5.

[6] ISO Draft Systems Standard for MPEG-2, 1993.

[7] A. G. MacInnis, "The MPEG systems specification: Multiplex, coding, and constraints," *SID 92 Digest,* pp. 127–129, 1992.

[8] A. Puri, "Invited address: Video coding using the MPEG-1 compression standard," *SID 92 Digest,* pp. 123–126, 1992.

[9] A. Puri and R. Aravind, "Motion- compensated video coding with adaptive perceptual quantization," *IEEE Trans. Circuits and Systems for Video Tech.,* Dec., pp. 351–361, 1991.

[10] T. Hanamura, W. Kameyama, and H. Tominaga, "Hierarchical coding scheme of video signal with scalability and compatibility," *Signal Processing: Image Comm.,* Feb., pp. 159–184, 1993.

[11] A. Puri, R. Aravind, and B. Haskell, "Adaptive frame/field motion compensated video coding," *Signal Processing: Image Comm.,* pp. 39–58, 1993.

[12] C.-T. Chen and T. R. Hsing, "Digital coding techniques for visual communications," *J. Visual Comm. and Image Representation,* March, pp. 1–16, 1991.

[13] A. Puri, R. Aravind, B. G. Haskell, and R. Leonardi, "Video coding with motion-compensated interpolation for CD-ROM applications," *Signal Processing: Image Comm.,* pp. 127–144, 1990.

[14] H. Jozawa and H. Watanabe, "Video coding using lapped orthogonal transform," *NTT Review,* March, pp. 91–96, 1993.

[15] H. Buley and L. Stenger, "Inter/intraframe coding of color TV signals for transmission at the third level of the digital hierarchy," *Proc. IEEE,* April, pp. 765–772, 1985.

[16] W. Y. Zou, "Digital HDTV compression techniques for terrestrial broadcasting," *SMPTE J.,* Feb., p. 127, 1993.

Components of OSI:
Broadband ISDN

by William Stallings, Comp-Comm Consulting

Introduction

The planning for ISDN began as far back as 1976 and is only now moving from the planning stage to prototypes and actual implementations. It will be a number of years before the full spectrum of ISDN services is widely available, and there will continue to be refinements and improvements to ISDN services and network facilities. Nevertheless, with the publication of the 1988 "Blue Book" set of Recommendations from CCITT, the bulk of the work on ISDN is complete. To be sure, future versions of the CCITT standards will provide refinements and enhancements to ISDN. But, since 1988, much of the planning and design effort became directed toward a network concept that will be far more revolutionary than ISDN itself. This new concept has been referred to as *Broadband ISDN* (B-ISDN).

CCITT modestly defines B-ISDN as "a service requiring transmission channels capable of supporting rates greater than the primary rate." Behind this innocuous statement lie plans for a network and a set of services that will have far more impact on business and residential customers than ISDN. With B-ISDN, services, especially video services, requiring data rates orders of magnitudes beyond those that can be delivered by ISDN will become available. These include support for image processing, video, and high-capacity workstations and local area networks (LANs). To contrast this new network and these new services to the original concept of ISDN, that original concept is now being referred to as *Narrowband ISDN*.

In 1988, as part of its I-series of recommendations on ISDN, CCITT issued the first two recommendations relating to B-ISDN: I.113, "Vocabulary of Terms for Broadband Aspects of ISDN," and I.121, "Broadband Aspects of ISDN." [1, 2] These documents represent the level of consensus reached among the participants concerning the future B-ISDN, as of late 1988. They provide a preliminary description and a basis for future standardization and development work.

With both demand (user interest) and supply (the technology for high-speed networking) evolving rapidly, the usual four-year cycle would be fatal to hopes of developing a standardized high-speed network utility. To head off the possibility of a fragmentation of effort and a proliferation of non-standard products and services, CCITT issued an interim set of 1990 Draft Recommendations on B-ISDN. The set of thirteen documents (Table 1) provide, for the first time, a detailed and specific master plan for the broadband revolution. Although much work remains to be done, the 1990 standards are sufficient to allow field trails to follow within a few years of the issue date.

B-ISDN services

The driving force behind B-ISDN is *services.* The services that B-ISDN will support form the set of requirements that the network must satisfy. CCITT classifies the services that could be provided by a B-ISDN into "interactive services" and "distribution services." Interactive services are those in which there is a two-way exchange of information (other than control signaling information) between two subscribers or between a subscriber and a service provider. Distribution services are those in which the information transfer is primarily one way, from service provider to B-ISDN subscriber.

Reprinted with permission from W. Stallings, from *ConneXions*, pp. 2–12, Jan. 1993.

Interactive services

Interactive services are further classified as *conversational, messaging,* and *retrieval.* Conversational services provided for real-time dialogue between a user and an application or a user and a server. This category encompasses a wide range of applications and data types, including the transmission of video, data, and document. An example of a conversational service that would require higher capacity than can be provided by narrowband ISDN is a remote image application, such as CAD/CAM or the review and manipulation of medical images from a hospital image data base server. Another example is video teleconferencing. Conversational services will place the greatest demand on the network, requiring high throughput and short response time.

Number	Title	Description
I.113	Vocabulary of Terms for Broadband Aspects of ISDN	Defines terms considered essential to the understanding and application of the principles of B-ISDN.
I.121	Broadband Aspects of ISDN	States the basic principles of B-ISDN and indicates the evolution of ISDN required to support advanced services and applications.
I.150	B-ISDN ATM Functional Characteristics	Summarizes the functions of the ATM layer.
I.211	B-ISDN Service Aspects	Serves as a guideline for evolving Recommendations on B-ISDN services. Includes a classification of B-ISDN services an a consideration of necessary network aspects
I.311	B-ISDN General Network Aspects	Describes networking techniques, signaling principles, traffic control, and resources management for B-ISDN. Introduces concepts of transmission path, virtual path, and virtual channel.
I.321	B-ISDN Protocol Reference Model and Its Application	Describes additions to the ISDN protocol reference model needed to accommodate B-ISDN services and functions.
I.327	B-ISDN Functional Architecture	Describes additions to the ISDN functional architecture needed to accommodate B-ISDN services and functions.
I.361	B-ISDN ATM Layer Specification	Describes the ATM layer, including cell structure, cell coding, and ATM protocol.
I.362	B-ISDN ATM Adaptation Layer (AAL) Functional Description	Provides a service classification for AAL and indicates the relationship between AAL services and AAL protocols.
I.363	B-ISDN ATM Adaptation Layer (AAL) Specification	Describes the interactions between the AAL and the next higher layer; the AAL and the ATM layer; and AAL peer-to-peer operations.
I.413	B-ISDN User-Network Interface	Gives the reference configuration for the B-ISDN user-network interface and examples of physical realizations.
I.432	B-ISDN User-Network Interface Physical Layer Specification	Defines physical layer interface for B-ISDN. Includes physical medium specification, timing and framing aspects, and header error control.
I.610	OAM Principles of B-ISDN Access	Describes the minimum functions required to maintain the physical layer and the ATM layer of the customer access.

Table 1: 1990 CCITT Interim Recommendations on Broadband ISDN

Messaging services offer user-to-user communication between individual users via storage units with store-and-forward, mailbox and/or message handling (e.g., information editing, processing and conversion) functions. In contrast to conversational services, messaging services are not in real time. Hence, they place lesser demands on the network and do not require that both users be available at the same time. Analogous narrowband services are X.400 and Teletex. One new form of messaging service that could be supported by ISDN is *video mail,* analogous to today's e-mail (text/graphic) and voice mail.

Retrieval services enable users to retrieve information stored in information centers, data bases, or libraries of television and film. With this service, a user could order full-length films or videos from a film/video library facility. Of greater interest to business, educational, and medical organizations, the envisioned broadband retrieval service would also allow the retrieval of high-resolution images such as X-ray or computerized axial tomography (CAT) scans, mixed-media documents, and large data files. This service could also be used for remote education and training.

The B-ISDN distribution services are classified into those without and those with user presentation control.

Broadcast services

Distribution services *without* user presentation control are also referred to as *broadcast services.* They provide a continuous flow of information which is distributed from a central source to an unlimited number of authorized receivers connected to the network. Each user can access this flow of information but has no control over it. In particular, the user cannot control the starting time or order of the presentation of the broadcasted information. All users simply tap into the flow of information.

The most common example of this service is broadcast television. Currently, broadcast television is available via radio waves and through cable television distribution systems. With the capacities planned for B-ISDN, this service could be integrated with the other telecommunications services. In addition, higher resolutions can now be achieved and it is anticipated that these higher-quality services will also be available via B-ISDN.

Distribution services *with* user presentation control also distribute information from a central source to a large number of users. However, the information is provided as a sequence of information entities (e.g., *frames*) with cyclical repetition. So, the user has the ability of individual access to the cyclical distributed information and can control start and order of presentation. Due to the cyclical repetition, the information entities, selected by the user, will always be presented from the beginning.

B-ISDN architecture

B-ISDN will differ from a narrowband ISDN in a number of ways. To meet the requirement for high-resolution video, an upper channel rate of on the order of 150Mbps is needed. To simultaneously support one or more interactive services and distributive services, a total subscriber line rate of about 600Mbps is needed. In terms of today's installed telephone plant, this is a stupendous data rate to sustain. The only appropriate technology for widespread support of such data rates is *optical fiber.* Hence, the introduction of B-ISDN depends on the pace of introduction of fiber subscriber loops.

Internal to the network, there is the issue of the switching technique to be used. The switching facility has to be capable of handling a wide range of different bit rates and traffic parameters (e.g., burstiness). Despite the increasing power of digital circuit-switching hardware and the increasing use of optical fiber trunking, it is difficult to handle the large and diverse requirements of B-ISDN with circuit-switching technology. For this reason, there is increasing interest in some type of fast packet switching as the basic switching technique for B-ISDN. This form of switching readily supports a new user—network interface protocol known as *Asynchronous Transfer Mode* (ATM).

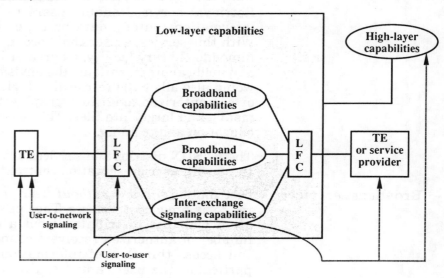

LFC - Local Function Capabilities
TE - Terminal Equipment

Figure 1: B-ISDN Architecture

Functional architecture

Figure 1 depicts the functional architecture of B-ISDN. As with narrowband ISDN, control of B-ISDN is based on common-channel signaling. Within the network, *Signaling System 7* (SS7), enhanced to support the expanded capabilities of a higher-speed network, will be used. Similarly, the user—network control signaling protocol will be an enhanced version of I.451/Q.931.

B-ISDN must of course support all of the 64Kbps transmission services, both circuit-switching and packet-switching, that are supported by narrowband ISDN. This protects the user's investment and facilitates migration from narrowband to broadband ISDN. In addition, broadband capabilities are provided for higher data rate transmission services. At the user—network interface, these capabilities will be provided with the connection-oriented ATM facility.

Transmission structure

In terms of data rates available to B-ISDN subscribers, three new transmission services are defined. The first of these consists of a full-duplex 155.52Mbps service. The second service defined is asymmetrical, providing transmission from the subscriber to the network at 155.52Mbps, and in the other direction at 622.08Mbps. The highest-capacity service yet defined is a full-duplex 622.08Mbps service.

A data rate of 155.52Mbps can certainly support all of the narrowband ISDN services. That is, it readily supports one or more basic or primary rate interfaces. In addition, it can support most of the B-ISDN services. At that rate, one or several video channels can be supported, depending on the video resolution and the coding technique used. Thus, the full-duplex 155.52Mbps service will probably be the most common B-ISDN service.

The higher data rate of 622.08Mbps is needed to handle multiple video distribution, such as might be required when a business conducts multiple simultaneous videoconferences. This data rate makes sense in the network-to-subscriber direction. The typical subscriber will not initiate distribution services and thus would still be able to use the lower, 155.52Mbps, service. The full-duplex 622.08Mbps service would be appropriate for a video distribution provider.

The 1988 document (I.121) discussed the need for a 150Mbps and 600Mbps data rate service. The specific rates chosen for the 1990 documents were designed to be compatible with defined digital transmission services. The 1988 document also included a list of specific channel data rates to be supported within these services. The 1990 documents drop all reference to channel rates. This allows the user and the network to negotiate any channel capacity that can fit in the available capacity provided by the network. Thus, B-ISDN becomes considerably more flexible and can be tailored precisely to a wide variety of applications.

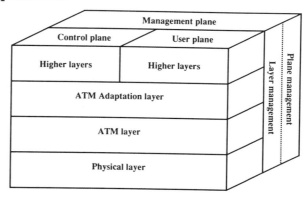

Figure 2: B-ISDN Protocol Reference Model

B-ISDN Protocol Reference Model

The protocol architecture for B-ISDN introduces some new elements not found in the ISDN architecture, as depicted in Figure 2. For B-ISDN, it is assumed that the transfer of information across the user–network interface will use Asynchronous Transfer Mode. ATM is, in essence, a form of packet transmission across the user–network interface in the same way that X.25 [3] is a form of packet transmission across the user–network interface. One difference between X.25 and ATM is that X.25 includes control signalling on the same channel as data transfer, whereas ATM makes use of common-channel signaling. Another difference is that X.25 packets may be of varying length, whereas ATM packets are of fixed size, referred to as "cells."

The decision to use ATM for B-ISDN is a remarkable one. This implies that B-ISDN will be a packet-based network, certainly at the interface and almost certainly in terms of its internal switching. Although the recommendation also states that B-ISDN will support circuit-mode applications, this will be done over a packet-based transport mechanism. Thus, ISDN, which began as an evolution from the circuit-switching telephone network, will transform itself into a packet-switching network as it takes on broadband services.

Adaptation Layer

Two layers of the B-ISDN protocol architecture relate to ATM functions. There is an ATM layer common to all services that provides packet transfer capabilities, and an *ATM Adaptation Layer* (AAL) that is service dependent. The AAL maps higher-layer information into ATM cells to be transported over B-ISDN, then collects information from ATM cells for delivery to higher layers. The use of ATM creates the need for an adaptation layer to support information transfer protocols not based on ATM. Two examples listed in I.121 are PCM voice and LAP-D. PCM voice is an application that produces a stream of bits. To employ this application over ATM, it is necessary to assemble PCM bits into packets (called *cells* in the recommendation) for transmission and to read them out on reception in such a way as to produce a smooth, constant flow of bits to the receiver.

For LAP-D, it is necessary to map LAP-D frames into ATM packets; this will probably mean segmenting one LAP-D frame into a number of packets on transmission, and reassembling the frame from packets on reception. By allowing the use of LAP-D over ATM, all of the existing ISDN applications and control signaling protocols can be used on B-ISDN.

The protocol reference model makes reference to 3 separate planes:

- *User Plane:* Provides for user information transfer, along with associated controls (e.g., flow control and error control).

- *Control Plane:* Performs call control and connection control functions.

- *Management Plane:* Includes *plane management,* which performs management functions related to a system as a whole and provides coordination between all the planes, and *layer management,* which performs management functions relating to resources and parameters residing in its protocol entities.

The 1988 I.121 Recommendation contains the protocol reference model depicted in Figure 2, but provides virtually no detail on the functions to be performed at each layer. The 1990 documents include a more detailed description of functions to be performed, as illustrated in Table 2. Let us examine each of these briefly.

The physical layer consists of two sublayers: the *physical medium sublayer* and the *transmission convergence sublayer.*

CS   = Convergence sublayer
SAR = Segmentation and reassembly sublayer
AAL = ATM adaptation layer
ATM = Asynchronous transfer mode
TC   = Transmission control sublayer
PM = Physical medium sublayer

	Higher Layer Functions	Higher Layers	
Layer Management	Convergence	CS	AAL
	Segmentation and reassembly	SAR	
	Generic flow control Cell header generation/extraction Cell VPI/VCI translation Cell multiplex and demultiplex	ATM	
	Cell rate decoupling HEC header sequence generation/verification Cell delineation Transmission frame adaptation Transmission frame generation/recovery	TC	Physical layer
	Bit timing Physical medium	PM	

Table 2: Functions of the B-ISDN Layers

Physical Medium Sublayer

The *Physical Medium Sublayer* includes only physical medium dependent functions. Its specification will therefore depend on the medium used. One function common to all medium types is bit timing. This sublayer is responsible for transmitting/receiving a continuous flow of bits with associated timing information to synchronize transmission and reception.

The 1988 document (I.121) does not address the issue of the physical medium on the subscriber's premises. In contrast, the 1990 documents provide preliminary specifications of the medium for the interface between the user and B-ISDN.

438

For the full-duplex 155.52Mbps service, either coaxial cable or optical fiber may be used. The coaxial cable is to support connections up to a maximum distance of 100 to 200 meters, using one cable for transmission in each direction. The parameters defined in the 1988 Recommendation G.703 are to be used.

Optical fiber is to support connections up to a maximum distance of 800 to 2000 meters. The details of the optical media (e.g., single mode versus multimode, single full-duplex fiber versus dual fiber) have been postponed for further study.

For a service that includes the 622.08Mbps rate in one or both directions, optical fiber is to be used. Again, the details of the fiber parameters are left for further study.

Transmission Convergence Sublayer

The *Transmission Convergence Sublayer* is responsible for the following functions:

- *Transmission frame generation and recovery:* Transmission at the physical layer consists of frames, such as we saw in the basic and primary rate interfaces. This function is concerned with generating and maintaining the frame structure appropriate for a given data rate.

- *Transmission frame adaptation:* Information exchange at the ATM layer is a flow of ATM cells. This sublayer is responsible for packaging these cells into a frame. One option is to have no frame structure but to simply transmit and receive a flow of cells.

- *Cell Delineation:* For transmission purposes, the bit flow may be scrambled. This sublayer is responsible for maintaining the cell boundaries so that cells may be recovered after descrambling at the destination.

- *HEC Sequence Generation and Cell Header Verification:* Each cell header is protected by a header error control (HEC) code. This sublayer is responsible for generating and checking this code.

- *Cell Rate Decoupling:* This includes insertion and suppression of idle cells in order to adapt the rate of valid ATM cells to the payload capacity of the transmission system.

A key issue at this sublayer is the transmission structure to be used to multiplex cells from various virtual channels. The 1988 document discussed this issue in general terms and proposed three alternatives. For the 155.52Mbps data rate, the 1990 documents reduce the number of options to two and provide more detail. For the 622.08Mbps data rate, the multiplex structure is left for further study.

HEC

The first of the two options for the 155.52Mbps data rate is the use of a continuous stream of cells, with no multiplex frame structure imposed at the interface. Synchronization is on a cell-by-cell basis. That is, the receiver is responsible for assuring that it properly delineates cells on the 53-octet cell boundaries. This task is accomplished by using the *header error control* (HEC) field. As long as the HEC calculation is indicating no errors, it is assumed that cell alignment is being properly maintained. An occasional error does not change this assumption. However, a string of error detections would indicate that the receiver is out of alignment, at which point it performs a hunting procedure to recover alignment.

SDH

The second option is to place the cells in a synchronous time-division multiplex envelope. In this case, the bit stream at the interface has an

439

external frame based on the *Synchronous Digital Hierarchy* (SDH) defined in Recommendation G.709. In the U.S., this frame structure is referred to as SONET(*Synchronous Optical Network*). The SDH frame may be used exclusively for ATM cells or may also carry other bit streams not yet defined in B-ISDN.

The SDH standard defines a hierarchy of data rates, all of which are multiples of 51.84Mbps, and including 155.52Mbps and 622.08Mbps. Therefore, the SDH scheme could also be used to support the higher B-ISDN data rate. However, the 1990 specification does not address this possibility.

As noted, B-ISDN will use ATM, making it a packet-based network at the user interface and almost certainly also in terms of its internal switching. Although the basic nature of B-ISDN is packet-switching, the recommendation also states that it will support circuit-mode applications. Thus, ISDN, which began as an evolution from the circuit-switching telephone networks, will transform itself into a packet-switching network as it takes on broadband services.

ATM Layer ATM is similar in concept to Frame Relay[4], a packet interface technique planned to be used in narrowband ISDN and available today in some products that transmit over dedicated T-1 circuits. Both ATM and Frame Relay use a streamlined set of functions to provide maximum throughput, taking advantage of the reliability and fidelity of modern digital networks to provide high-speed packet-switching by avoiding repeated error checking and other protocol functions. ATM takes this streamlining process much further than Frame Relay to be able to exploit transmission channels in the tens and hundreds of megabits per second. In contrast to the variable-length frames used in Frame Relay, ATM uses fixed-length cells and is often referred to as *cell relay*.

In ATM, transmission capacity is assigned to a connection based on subscriber requirements and available capacity. Data transfer is connection oriented, using the concepts similar to the *virtual circuit* in X.25.

ATM uses two connection concepts: *virtual path* and *virtual channel*. A virtual channel, much like an X.25 virtual circuit, provides a logical packet connection between two users. A virtual path defines a route from source to destination through a network. Multiple virtual channels may be bundled together to use the same virtual path.

The use of two connection concepts has certain advantages. For one thing, much of the work of setting up connections is done when a virtual path is first established. The addition of a new virtual channel to an existing virtual path requires little overhead. In addition, a number of data transport functions, such as flow control, can be done at the virtual-path level, simplifying the network architecture.

The ATM cell Each ATM cell consists of a 5-octet header and a 48-octet information field. The format for the header at the user–network interface is shown in Figure 3 on the previous page. The header includes the following fields:

- *Generic flow control:* This field is to be used for end-to-end flow control between ATM users. Its specific use is not defined but is left for further study.

- *Virtual path identifier:* Identifies the path or route between source and destination.

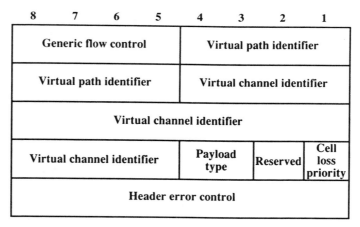

8	7	6	5	4	3	2	1
Generic flow control				Virtual path identifier			
Virtual path identifier				Virtual channel identifier			
Virtual channel identifier							
Virtual channel identifier				Payload type		Reserved	Cell loss priority
Header error control							

Figure 3: ATM cell format at User–Network interface

- *Virtual channel identifier:* Defines a logical connection between two ATM users.

- *Payload type:* Type 00 is for user information; that is, for information from the next higher layer. Other values are not defined but are left for further study. Presumably, network management and maintenance values will be assigned.

- *Cell loss priority:* A value of 1 means that this cell is subject to being discarded, whereas a value of 0 indicates a higher-priority application for which discarding is inappropriate. Discarding might occur in the case of high network congestion.

- *Header error control:* This is an 8-bit error code that can be used to correct single-bit errors in the header and to detect double-bit errors.

All of the details just described are new to the 1990 draft Recommendations. In the 1988 document, the header fields and header size were undefined, and it had not yet been decided to use fixed-size cells.

ATM Adaptation Layer (AAL) The use of ATM creates the need for an adaptation layer to support information transfer protocols not based on ATM. Two examples listed in the 1988 Recommendation are PCM (Pulse Code Modulation) voice, and the standard data link control protocol for ISDN, *Link Access Protocol-D* (LAP-D).

PCM voice is an application that produces a stream of bits from a voice signal. To use this application over ATM, it is necessary to assemble PCM bits into cells for transmission and to read them out on reception in such a way as to produce a smooth, constant flow of bits to the receiver.

To carry LAP-D signaling across the network, it is necessary to map LAP-D frames into ATM cells. This procedure will probably involve segmenting one LAP-D frame into a number of cells on transmission, and reassembling the frame from cells on reception. By allowing the use of LAP-D over ATM, all of the existing ISDN applications and control signaling protocols can be used on B-ISDN.

Four service classes The 1988 Recommendation briefly mentions AAL and points out its functions of mapping information into cells and performing segmentation and reassembly. The 1990 documents provide greater detail of the functions and services of this layer. In the area of services, four classes of service are defined (Table 3). The classification is based on whether a timing relationship must be maintained between source and destination, whether the application requires a constant bit rate, and whether the transfer is connection-oriented or connectionless.

	Class A	Class B	Class C	Class D
Timing relation between source and destination	Required		Not Required	
Bit rate	Constant	Variable		
Connection mode	Connection-oriented			Connectionless

Table 3: Service Classification for ATM Adaption Layer (I.362)

An example of a class A service is circuit emulation. In this case a constant bit rate, which requires the maintenance of a timing relation, is used, and the transfer is connection-oriented.

An example of a class B service is variable-bit-rate video, such as might be used in a teleconference. Here, the application is connection-oriented and timing is important, but the bit rate varies depending on the amount of activity in the scene.

Classes C and D correspond to data transfer applications. In both cases, the bit rate may vary and no particular timing relationship is required; differences in data rate are handled by the end systems using buffers. The data transfer may be either connection-oriented (class C) or connectionless (class D).

To support these various classes of service, a set of protocols at the AAL level are defined. In the 1990 version, a preliminary definition is provided, which is primarily functional. However, the document does include some detail concerning header formats and procedures. The details of the AAL protocols remain to be worked out.

The future direction of ISDN

Since the publication of the 1988 Blue Book, the central focus of CCITT has been the development of specifications for B-ISDN. B-ISDN is based on a fast packet-switching technology namely ATM. ATM specifies the manner in which data is to be structured for transmission over virtual channels. To accommodate a variety of applications, the ATM adaptation layer (AAL) provides a mapping from various application transfer techniques to ATM. The physical medium to be used on the subscriber's premises can be either coaxial cable or optical fiber, depending on data rate and distance requirements.

Although many issues remain to be resolved, the network architecture and supported services for broadband ISDN are beginning to solidify with the publication of the 1990 draft Recommendations for B-ISDN. Sufficient detail now exists for both providers and users to begin to plan for the arrival of this exciting new network facility.

[This article is based on material in Bill Stallings' *ISDN and Broadband ISDN,* Second Edition, ISBN 0-02-415475-X, Copyright © 1992 by Macmillan Publishing Company. Used with permission. —*Ed.*]

References

[1] CCITT Blue Book: "I.113 Vocabulary of Terms for Broadband Aspects of ISDN," 1988.

[2]   CCITT Blue Book: "I.121 Broadband Aspects of ISDN," 1988.

[3]   Vair, D., "Components of OSI: X.25—the Network, Data Link, and Physical Layers of the OSI Reference Model," *ConneXions*, Volume 4, No. 12, December 1990.

[4]   Kozel, E., "The Cisco/DEC/NTI/StrataCom Frame Relay Specification," *ConneXions*, Volume 5, No. 3, March 1991.

[5]   Blackshaw, R., "Components of OSI: Integrated Services Digital Networks (ISDN)," *ConneXions*, Volume 3, No. 4, April 1989.

[6]   Leifer, D., "ISDN: Why use it?," *ConneXions*, Volume 4, No. 10, October 1990.

Image and Video Coding Standards

Rangarajan Aravind
Glenn L. Cash
Donald L. Duttweiler
Hsueh-Ming Hang
Barry G. Haskell
Atul Puri

Most image or video applications involving transmission or storage require some form of data compression to reduce the otherwise inordinate demand on bandwidth and storage. Compatibility among different applications and manufacturers is very desirable, and often essential. This paper describes several standard compression algorithms developed in recent years.

Introduction

The International Organization for Standardization (ISO) Joint Bilevel Image Group (JBIG) has perfected a progressive coding algorithm for bilevel (two-tone, black/white, or facsimile) images that transmits these images in stages of successively higher resolution. (See Panel 1 for definitions of abbreviations, acronyms, and terms.) This enables users to browse through remotely located image databases. It also allows output displays with differing resolutions to access documents that reside in the same database. New coding techniques make it possible to provide this progressive capability, while at the same time achieving significantly better compression than that attained by previous facsimile coding standards.

The ISO Joint Photographic Experts Group (JPEG) has developed an algorithm for coding single-frame color images. It is based on the discrete cosine transform (DCT), but it also has extensions for progressive coding. Starting from an original red, green, blue (RGB) picture of 24 bits per picture element (pel or pixel), the JPEG algorithms give good image quality at compression factors of 10 to 20, i.e., bit rates between 1 and 2 bits per pixel.

The International Telegraph and Telephone Consultative Committee (CCITT) Study Group 15 (SG15) and its experts group on video telephony has finalized a set of coding standards, known informally as the P×64 standard, for sending videotelephone or videoconference pictures on integrated services digital network (ISDN) facilities. The standard is applicable over a bandwidth range from 56 kilobits per second (kb/s) to 2 megabits per second (Mb/s). It relies not only on the DCT, but also on motion-compensated prediction to compress data generated by the moving imagery.

The ISO Motion Picture Experts Group (MPEG) has developed both audio and video compression algorithms that can compress entertainment or educational video for storage or transmission on various digital media, including compact disk, remote video databases, movies on demand,[1] cable television (CATV), fiber to the home, etc. Requirements are for implementation of normal play, fast forward/reverse, random access, normal reverse, and simple very-large-scale integration (VLSI). The MPEG algorithm utilizes all the P×64 methodology, as well as some new techniques, most notably conditional motion-compensated interpolation.

JBIG Progressive Bilevel Image Coding

This section presents the JBIG bilevel image coding standard and how it relates to other standards. It also describes progressive coding and compares the compression performance of various algorithms.

Standards Framework. JBIG was chartered in 1988 to establish a standard for the progressive coding of bilevel images. The "joint" in its name reflects the fact that it reports to both ISO (specifically, ISO–IEC/JTC1/SC29/WG9) and CCITT (specifically, CCITT/SGVIII/Q16). The JBIG standard[2,3] is nearly finalized.

On average, since 1988 the chair of the working group has scheduled three JBIG meetings a year, each with about 15 attendees from large, well-known companies in the fields of telecommunications, photography, and computer science.

Reprinted with permission from *AT&T Technical Journal*, vol. 72, no. 1, pp. 67–88, Jan./Feb. 1993.

Relationship to Existing Standards. For bilevel image coding, the G3 and G4 algorithms[4] of CCITT Recommendations T.4[5] and T.6[6] are well established. JBIG coding, like the coding of the G3/G4 algorithms, is lossless (bit-preserving), with decoded images digitally identical to input images. Hence, image quality is not an issue using any of the available algorithms. However, compared to G3/G4 coding, JBIG coding offers better compression and, if desired, progressiveness. Numerical data relating JBIG and G3/G4 compression are discussed later in this paper. Progressive coding will be defined and discussed as well, along with identifying applications in which it is valuable.

Another standard that has applicability overlapping that of JBIG is the JPEG standard,[7] described later in this paper. Although JBIG was chartered for work on bilevel compression, the JBIG algorithm can also be used effectively for the lossless coding of grey scale images (monochrome with shades of grey) and color images. The simple expedient of letting each bit plane of such images define an independent image for bilevel coding works quite well as long as the bit planes are defined using something like a folded-binary (Gray) representation[8] of intensity. This minimizes the total number of transitions in the images of the various bit planes. When intensity resolution is highly precise and there are eight or more bits per pixel, JBIG coding and lossless JPEG coding are about equal in compression efficiency. When the intensity resolution is coarser, JBIG coding is more efficient. Of course, if lossless coding is not required, JPEG coding in any of its normal (lossy) modes will provide the greatest compression.

The JBIG approach to lossless grey scale and color image coding offers coding unification. One underlying algorithm efficiently codes bilevel images, grey scale photographic images, color photographic images, and computer-generated images with bit-plane overlays.

Progressive Coding. Progressive codings are multiresolution encodings. An image is captured as a compression of a low-resolution rendition plus a sequence of "delta" files that each allow one doubling of resolution. When an image that has been progressively encoded is decoded, the low-resolution rendition of the original becomes available first, with subsequent doublings of resolution following as more data are decoded.

The number, D, of doublings that are to be available is a free parameter for the JBIG algorithm. When progressiveness is desired, it is typically chosen as 4, 5, or 6. It can, however, be chosen as 0, in which case progressiveness is disabled, but the JBIG compression advantage remains.

Progressive coding offers advantages for:
- Storing images in databases intended to serve displays of differing resolution capability
- Browsing through images
- Transmitting images over a packet network.

By storing progressive encodings of images, a database can efficiently serve output devices that have differing resolution capability. The database sends the coding of the low-resolution rendition and only as many delta files as needed. If a user first views an image on a comparatively low-resolution display, such as a cathode-ray tube (CRT), and later requests a hard copy on a higher-resolution display, such as a laser printer, only a few additional delta files need be sent.

In contrast, an image database storing images nonprogressively can use one of two methods to serve output terminals with different resolutions. Most simply, it can store multiple compressions at various resolutions. Alternatively, it can store only a compression at the highest resolution and require output devices to decode to this high resolution and map down to the lower resolution of the display available. The first alternative wastes storage and is inefficient when an update to higher

resolution is requested. The second alternative wastes both transmission capacity and processing power. The output device must receive and decode the highest resolution rendition, even though it only can show a lower resolution rendition.

Progressive codings can be advantageous for document browsing. A low-resolution rendition can be rapidly transmitted and displayed, and then followed by as much resolution enhancement as desired. Progressive coding makes it easy for a user to recognize the image being displayed quickly and to interrupt the transmission of an unwanted image.

This advantage for progressive coding only occurs on medium-rate links, roughly those with speeds between 9.6 and 64 kb/s when bilevel images are being retrieved. Were the communication link slower, no viewer would have the patience to browse through images, no matter what the form of presentation. On high-speed links, the image is delivered so rapidly relative to human reaction times that the way it develops is immaterial.

The third application for progressive coding is in packet networks,[9] where packets can or must be classified as droppable (i.e., those that the network is free to discard during times of congestion) or nondroppable (i.e., those that the network must always deliver). The packets carrying the information for the final resolution doubling would be sent at low priority; if they had to be dropped, no image regions would be lost or destroyed. The only penalty would be an image that is slightly less sharp in some regions.

One potential disadvantage of progressive coding is its need for a frame buffer large enough to hold the image at the second-to-highest resolution. When the display is a CRT, this buffer always exists and this need is inconsequential. It is of greater concern in hard-copy devices. The JBIG algorithm has a feature called "compatible-sequential" mode, which can obviate the need for the frame buffer whenever a database is storing images progressively (to support a range of display resolutions efficiently), but can also serve hard-copy devices. For a hard-copy device, the intermediate resolution images are of no interest. In serving such a device in the compatible-sequential mode, the same information is transmitted as would be transmitted for normal progressive decoding. However, it is rearranged to eliminate the need for a full-image buffer. Reference 2 describes how this is accomplished.

Table I. Compressed File Sizes in Bytes for Various Coding Algorithms

Image	Bytes					
	Raw	**G3D1**	**G3D2**	**G4**	**Nonprogressive JBIG**	**Progressive JBIG**
CCITT #1	513216	37423	25967	18103	14715	16771
CCITT #2	513216	34367	19656	10803	8545	8933
CCITT #3	513216	65034	40797	28706	21988	23710
CCITT #4	513216	108075	81815	69275	54356	58656
CCITT #5	513216	68317	44157	32222	25877	28086
CCITT #6	513216	51171	28245	16651	12589	13455
CCITT #7	513216	106420	81465	69282	56253	60770
CCITT #8	513216	62806	33025	19114	14278	15227
Halftone	834048	483265	572259	591628	131479	103267

Compression Comparison. Table I shows compression performance on the eight standard CCITT test images and one additional image. The additional image is a binary image, rendering grey scale using halftoning. It is image number 20 of the so-called "JBIG testing" image set and is a picture of a Japanese woman holding flowers. The eight CCITT images are all sampled at 200 dots per inch (dpi) and contain 1728×2376 pixels. The halftone image contains 2304×2896 pixels. Compressed-file byte counts are provided for coding with one-dimensional G3 (G3D1), two-dimensional G3 (with a k factor of 4) (G3D2), G4, nonprogressive JBIG, and progressive JBIG with four delta layers.

Over the eight CCITT images, nonprogressive JBIG coding has about a 22-percent coding advantage over G4, the most efficient of the G3/G4 algorithms. The progressive JBIG algorithm provides progressivity and still shows an average 15-percent coding gain over G4.

The G3/G4 algorithms are not suitable for coding bilevel images rendering grey scale using halftoning, as is evident in the last row of Table I, where the JBIG compression advantage is about a factor of five.

Overview of JBIG Algorithm. This section describes some of the main functional blocks of an encoder. Decoders, similar to encoders, and somewhat simpler because resolution reduction is not needed, will not be described.

Conceptually, a JBIG encoder can be decomposed (see Figure 1) into a chain of D identical differential layer encoders, followed by a bottom-layer encoder. In Figure 1a, I_D denotes the image at layer D and C_D denotes its encoding. Generally, implementations will time-share one physical differential layer encoder, but for heuristic purposes, the decomposition of Figure 1a is helpful.

The heart of both the differential-layer encoder (Figure 1b) and bottom-layer encoder (Figure 1c) is an adaptive arithmetic encoder. Arithmetic coders are distinguished from other entropy coders such as Huffman coders and Ziv-Lempel coders in that, conceptually at least, they map a string of symbols to be coded into a real number on the unit interval [0.0,1.0). What is transmitted instead of the symbols is a binary representation of this number. The process to derive the representative real number is known as interval subdivision. Abramson[10] credits Elias with having conceived it soon after Shannon's seminal work on information theory was published. However, practical application of arithmetic coding had to wait almost thirty years for the discovery of ways to realize arithmetic coders with finite-precision arithmetic, as well as ways to make pipelining possible. Pipelining enables an encoder to start outputting the bits of the binary representation before it has seen the entire input stream to be coded, and for a decoder to start outputting the reconstructed symbol stream before it has seen the entire binary expansion of the representative real number. The JBIG and JPEG arithmetic coders are identical.

An algorithmic subfunction of differential-layer encoders, but not bottom-layer encoders, is resolution reduction, which is the mapping of a given resolution

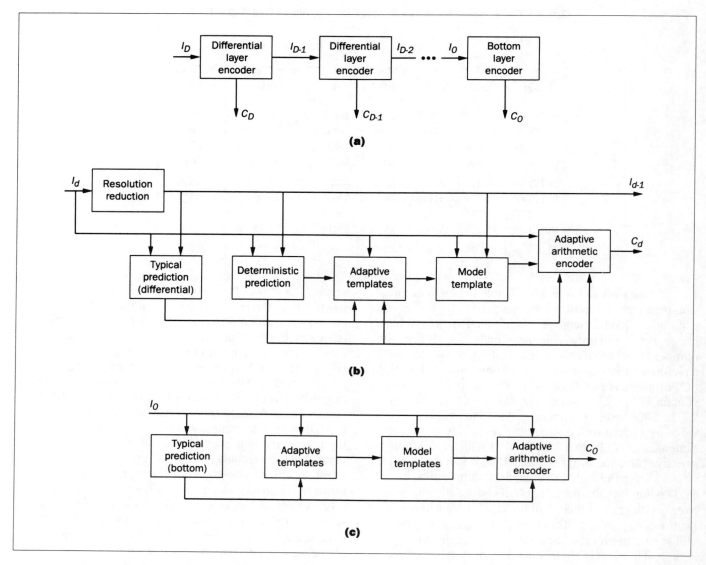

(a)

(b)

(c)

image to a half-resolution image. One way to do this would be simply to discard every other row and column, but such subsampling leads to images that are poorer in subjective quality than need be. The table-based JBIG resolution-reduction algorithm creates excellent quality, low-resolution renditions for text, line art, dithered grey scale, halftoned grey scale, and error-diffused grey scale. The low-resolution image is created pixel by pixel in the usual raster scan order, that is, from top to bottom and left to right. The color of any given low-resolution pixel is uniquely determined by the colors of nine particular

Figure 1. (a) A JBIG encoder can be decomposed into a chain of (b) *D* differential layer encoders, followed by a (c) bottom-layer encoder.

high-resolution neighbors that are in fixed spatial relationship to it and three particular low-resolution neighbors that are in causal and fixed spatial relationship to it. Decoders have no counterpart to this block.

Other algorithmic subfunctions of interest are adaptive templates, deterministic prediction (differential-layer encoder only), and typical prediction. The adaptive

448

templates algorithm searches for periodicities typical of halftone images and, when they are found, can exploit them to greatly enhance compression. Deterministic prediction exploits idiosyncrasies of the resolution reduction algorithm to gain about a 5-percent coding advantage. Typical prediction looks for large regions of continuous color and, when they are present, can substantially speed both software and hardware implementations. Reference 2 provides further details.

JPEG Still-Color-Image Coding

The need for an international standard for continuous-tone still image compression resulted, in 1986, in the formation of JPEG. This group was chartered by ISO and the CCITT to develop a general-purpose standard suitable for as many applications as possible. After thorough evaluation and subjective testing of a number of proposed image-compression algorithms, the group agreed, in 1988, on a DCT-based technique. From 1988 to 1990, the JPEG committee refined several methods incorporating the DCT for lossy compression. A lossless method was also defined. The committee's work has been published in two parts: "Part 1: Requirements and guidelines"[7] describes the JPEG compression and decompression method. "Part 2: Compliance Testing"[11] describes tests to verify whether a coder-decoder (codec) has implemented the JPEG algorithms correctly.

To appreciate the need for image compression, consider the storage/transmission requirements of an uncompressed image. A typical digital color image has 512×480 pixels. At three bytes per pixel (one each for the red, green and blue components), such an image requires 737,280 bytes of storage space. To transmit the uncompressed image over a 64-kb/s channel takes about 1.5 minutes. The JPEG algorithms offer "excellent" quality for most images compressed to about 1.0 bit/pixel. This 24:1 compression ratio reduces the required storage of the 512×480 color image to 30,720 bytes, and its transmission time to about 3.8 seconds. Applications for image compression may be found in desktop publishing, education, real estate, and security, to name a few.

In the next section, we give an overview of the JPEG algorithms. In subsequent sections, we present some operating parameters and definitions, and describe each of the JPEG operating modes in more detail.

Overview of the JPEG Algorithms. The JPEG committee could not satisfy the requirements of every still-image compression application with one algorithm. As a result, the committee proposed four different modes of operation:

- *Sequential DCT-based* — Figure 2 presents a simplified diagram of a sequential DCT codec. In this mode, 8×8 blocks of the input image are formatted for compression by scanning the image left to right and top to bottom. A block consists of 64 samples of one component that make up the image. Each block of samples is transformed to a block of coefficients by the forward discrete cosine transform (FDCT). The coefficients are then quantized and entropy-coded.

- *Progressive DCT-based* — This mode offers a means of producing a quick "rough" decoded image when the medium separating the coder and decoder has a low bandwidth. The method is similar to the sequential DCT-based algorithm, but the quantized coefficients are partially encoded in multiple scans.

- *Lossless* — In this mode, the decoder renders an exact reproduction of the digital input image. The differences between input samples and predicted values, where the predicted values are combinations of one to three neighboring samples, are entropy-coded.

- *Hierarchical* — This mode is used to code an input image as a sequence of increasingly higher-resolution frames. The first frame is a reduced resolution version of the original. Subsequent frames are coded higher-resolution differential frames.

The color space conversion process in Figure 2 is not a part of the standard. In fact, JPEG is color-space-independent. As a first step in the compression process, many image-compression schemes take advantage of the human visual system's low sensitivity to high-frequency chrominance information[12] by reducing the chrominance resolution. Many images (usually RGB) are typically converted to a luminance-chrominance representation before this processing takes place.

Either Huffman or arithmetic techniques can be used for entropy coding in any of the JPEG modes of operation (except in the *baseline* system, where Huffman coding is mandatory). A Huffman coder compresses a series of input symbols by assigning short code words to frequently occurring symbols and long code words to improbable symbols.[13,14] The output of an arithmetic coder is a single real number. After initialization to a range of 0 to 1, the probability of each input symbol is used to restrict the range of the output number further. Unlike a Huffman coder, an arithmetic coder does not

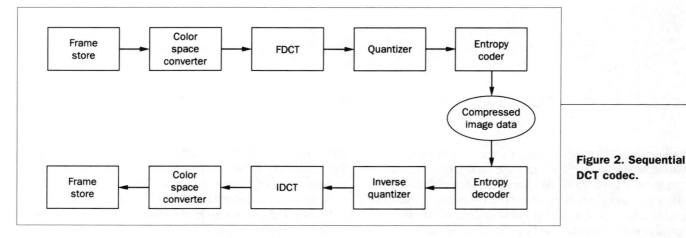

Figure 2. Sequential DCT codec.

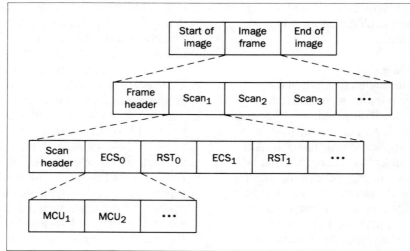

Figure 3. Structure of compressed-image data.

require an integral number of bits to represent an input symbol. As a result, arithmetic coders are usually more efficient than Huffman coders.[15,16] For the JPEG test images, Huffman coding (using fixed tables) resulted in compressed data requiring, on average, 13.2 percent more storage than arithmetic coding.

JPEG Operating Parameters and Definitions. A number of parameters related to the source image and the coding process may be customized to meet the user's needs. In this section, we discuss some of the important variable parameters and their allowable ranges. Also, as an aid to the algorithm descriptions in the following sections, we define some JPEG terms and present the hierarchical structure of the compressed data.

Parameters. An image to be coded using any JPEG mode may have from 1 to 65,535 lines and from 1 to 65,535 pixels per line. Each pixel may have from 1 to 255 components (only 1 to 4 components are allowed for progressive mode). The operating mode determines the allowable precision of the component. For the DCT modes, either 8 or 12 bits of precision are supported (only 8-bit precision is allowed for *baseline*). Lossless mode precision may range from 2 to 16 bits. If a DCT operating mode has been selected, the quantizer precision must be defined.

For 8-bit component precision, the quantizer precision is fixed at 8 bits. Twelve-bit components require either 8- or 16-bit quantizer precision.

Data interleaving. To reduce the processing delay and/or buffer requirements, up to four components can be interleaved in a single scan (for progressive mode, only the DC scan may have interleaved components). A data structure called the *minimum-coded unit* (MCU) has been defined to support this interleaving. An MCU consists of one or more data units, where a data unit is a component sample for the lossless mode, and an 8×8 block of component samples for the DCT modes. If a scan contains only one component, then its MCU is equal to one data unit. For multiple component scans, the MCU for the scan consists of interleaved data units. The maximum number of data units per MCU is 10. As an interleaving example, consider an International Radio Consultative Committee (CCIR) 601 digital image in which the chrominance components are subsampled 2:1 horizontally. For a DCT coder, a CCIR-601 MCU could consist of two Y blocks, followed by a C_R block and a C_B block, where Y is the luminance of the image and C_R and C_B are proportional to the two color differences $(R - Y)$ and $(B - Y)$, respectively.

Marker codes. JPEG has defined a number of two-byte marker codes to delineate the various sections of a compressed data stream. All marker codes begin with a byte-aligned hexadecimal "FF" byte, making it easy to scan and extract parts of the compressed data without actually decoding it. Because it is possible to create a byte-aligned hexadecimal "FF" byte within the entropy-coded data, the coder must detect this situation and follow the "FF" byte with a zero byte. When the decoder encounters the hexadecimal "FF00" combination, the zero byte must be removed.

Compressed-image data structure. At the top level of the compressed data hierarchy is the *image* (see Figure 3). A nonhierarchical mode image consists of a *frame* surrounded by "start of image" (SOI) and "end of image" (EOI) marker codes. There will be multiple *frames* in a hierarchical mode image. Within a frame, a start of frame (SOF) marker identifies the coding mode to be used. The SOF marker is followed by a number of parameters (see Reference 7), and then by one or more *scans*. Each scan begins with a header identifying the components to be contained within the scan, and more parameters. The scan header is followed by an entropy-coded segment (ECS). An option exists to break the ECS into chunks of MCUs called *restart intervals* (RST$_0$, RST$_1$, etc.). The restart interval structure is useful for identifying select portions of a scan, and for recovery from limited corruption of the entropy-coded data. Quantization and entropy-coding tables may either be included with the compressed image data or communicated separately.

Sequential DCT. The sequential DCT mode offers excellent compression ratios, while maintaining image quality. A subset of the sequential DCT capabilities has been identified by JPEG for a "*baseline system.*" All DCT-based JPEG implementations are required to include baseline capability. This requirement should help to ensure interoperability between codecs from different vendors. Restrictions on the baseline system related to sample and quantizer precision were pointed out in the "Parameters" subsection. One further restriction should be noted: Although a full sequential DCT coder may employ either Huffman or arithmetic entropy coding, a baseline coder can only use Huffman coding. In addition, only two AC and two DC tables may be used per scan (up to four sets of tables are allowed for full sequential mode).

The following subsections describe the processing steps for a baseline coder. A decoder is formed by reversing the coder steps.

DCT and quantization. All JPEG DCT-based coders begin the coding process by partitioning the input image into non-overlapping 8×8 blocks of component samples. After level-shifting the 8-bit samples so that they range from −128 to +127, the blocks are transformed to the frequency domain using the FDCT.[17,18] The equations for the forward and inverse discrete cosine transforms are given by:

$$FDCT\colon F(u,v) = \frac{1}{4} C(u) C(v) \sum_{x=0}^{7} \sum_{y=0}^{7} f(x,y)$$

$$\cos \frac{\pi u (2x+1)}{16} \cos \frac{\pi v (2y+1)}{16} \quad (1)$$

$$IDCT\colon f(x,y) = \frac{1}{4} \sum_{u=0}^{7} \sum_{v=0}^{7} C(u) C(v) F(u,v)$$

$$\cos \frac{\pi u (2x+1)}{16} \cos \frac{\pi v (2y+1)}{16} \quad (2)$$

where

$$C(u), C(v) = \frac{1}{\sqrt{2}} \text{ for } u,v = 0; \ C(u) C(v) = 1 \ otherwise.$$

The DCT concentrates most of the energy of the component samples' block into a few coefficients, usually in the top-left corner of the DCT block. The coefficient in the immediate top-left corner is called the DC coefficient because it is proportional to the average intensity of the block of spatial domain samples. The AC coefficients corresponding to increasingly higher frequencies of the sample block progress away from the DC coefficient.

The next step in the process, quantization, is the key to most of the JPEG compression. A 64-element quantization matrix, where each element corresponds to a coefficient in the DCT block, is used to reduce the amplitude of the coefficients, and to increase the number of zero-value coefficients. The quantization and dequantization is performed according to equations (3) and (4), respectively.

$$Fq(u,v) = round \left\lfloor \frac{F(u,v)}{Q(u,v)} \right\rfloor \quad (3)$$

$$R(u,v) = Fq(u,v) Q(u,v) \quad (4)$$

A carefully designed quantization matrix will produce

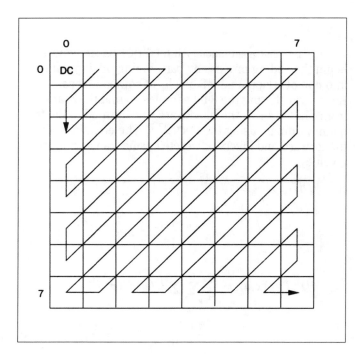

Figure 4. Zig-zag scan.

Table II. Lossless Mode Predictors

Selection value	Prediction
0	No prediction
1	a
2	b
3	c
4	a + b - c
5	a + ((b - c)/2)
6	b + ((a - c)/2)
7	(a + b)/2

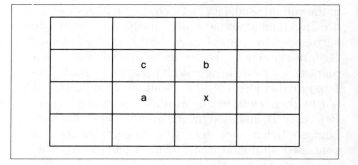

Figure 5. Prediction neighborhood.

high compression ratios while introducing negligible "visible" distortion.[19] Up to four quantization matrices are allowed by JPEG. The standard does not mandate quantization matrices, but includes a set that gives good results for CCIR-601 type images. Many JPEG implementations control the compression ratio (and output image quality) by using a *q-factor*, which is usually just a scale factor applied to the quantization matrices.

    DC coefficient entropy coding. Greater compression efficiency can be obtained if a simple predictive method is used to entropy-code the DC coefficient separately from the AC coefficients. Recall that the DC coefficient corresponds to the average intensity of the component block. Adjacent blocks will probably have similar average intensities. It is, therefore, advantageous to code the *differences* between the DC coefficients of adjacent blocks rather than their values. Each differential DC value is coded using a variable-length code (VLC) and a variable-length integer (VLI). The VLC corresponds to the size, in bits, of the VLI, while the VLI gives the amplitude of the differential DC value.

    Zig-zag scan and AC coefficient entropy coding. After they have been quantized, the coefficient blocks usually contain many zero-value AC coefficients. If the coeffi-

cients are reordered, using the zig-zag scan illustrated in Figure 4, there will be a tendency to have long runs of zeroes. Only the nonzero AC coefficients are entropy-coded. As in the DC coefficient coding, a VLC-VLI pair results from the coding of an AC coefficient. However, the AC VLC corresponds to two pieces of information: the number of zeroes (run) since the last nonzero coefficient, and the size of the VLI following the VLC.

    Progressive DCT. A progressive DCT mode has been defined by JPEG to satisfy the need for a fast decoded picture when a low-bandwidth medium separates a coder and decoder. By partially encoding the quantized DCT coefficients in multiple scans, the decoded image quality builds progressively from a coarse level to the quality attainable with the quantization matrices. Either spectral selection, successive approximation, or a combination of the two is used to code the quantized coefficients.

    Spectral selection. In this method, the quantized DCT coefficients of a block are first partitioned into non-overlapping bands along the zig-zag block scan. The

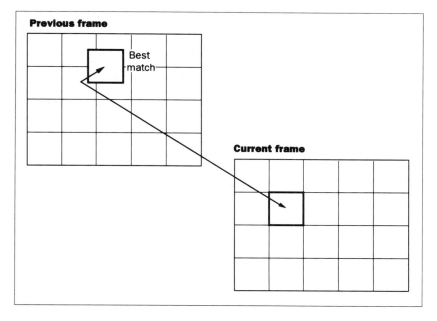

Figure 6. Block motion compensation.

bands are then coded in separate component scans. Before an AC coefficient band of a component may be coded, its DC coefficient must be coded. DC coefficients from as many as four components may be interleaved in a single scan. Interleaving is not permitted for AC bands because of the introduction of an efficient means for coding contiguous blocks of zero-valued coefficients. From 1 to 32,767 blocks can be coded with a single VLC–VLI combination called an end-of-band code.

Successive approximation. With this method, the precision of the coefficients is successively increased during multiple scans. Following a scan for a specified number of most significant bits of the quantized coefficients, subsequent scans increase the precision in increments of one bit until the least significant bits have been coded.

Lossless Mode. The lossless mode was defined for applications in which output pixels from a decoder must be identical to the input pixels to the coder. The compression ratios achievable with the lossless mode, typically around 2:1, are much smaller than those afforded by the lossy modes. This method is similar to the one used to code the DC coefficients in the DCT-based modes, but the predictor is selectable from one of seven choices, as shown in Table II. Samples a, b, and c in the table correspond to neighbors of the sample x to

be predicted. Figure 5 illustrates the prediction neighborhood. Entries 1 to 3 in Table II are used for one-dimensional predictive coding, and 4 through 7 form two-dimensional predictors. Entry 0 identifies differential coding for the hierarchical mode. As in the DC coefficient entropy coding described earlier, differences between the actual and predicted values are entropy-coded.

Hierarchical Mode. In the hierarchical mode, an image is coded as a succession of increasingly higher-resolution frames. This "pyramidal" approach offers an alternative to the previously described methods for achieving progression. It also allows decoders with different resolution capabilities to use the same compressed data stream.

The first coded frame is created by reducing the resolution of the input image by a power of two in one or both dimensions, and then processing the lower resolution image using one of the lossy or lossless techniques of the other operating modes. Subsequent frames are formed by upsampling the decoded image by a factor of two in the dimension(s) having reduced resolution, subtracting the upsampled image from the input image at the same resolution, and coding the difference. "Missing" pixels in the upsampled image are filled in using linear (or bilinear) interpolation. This process continues until the decoded image has the same resolution as the

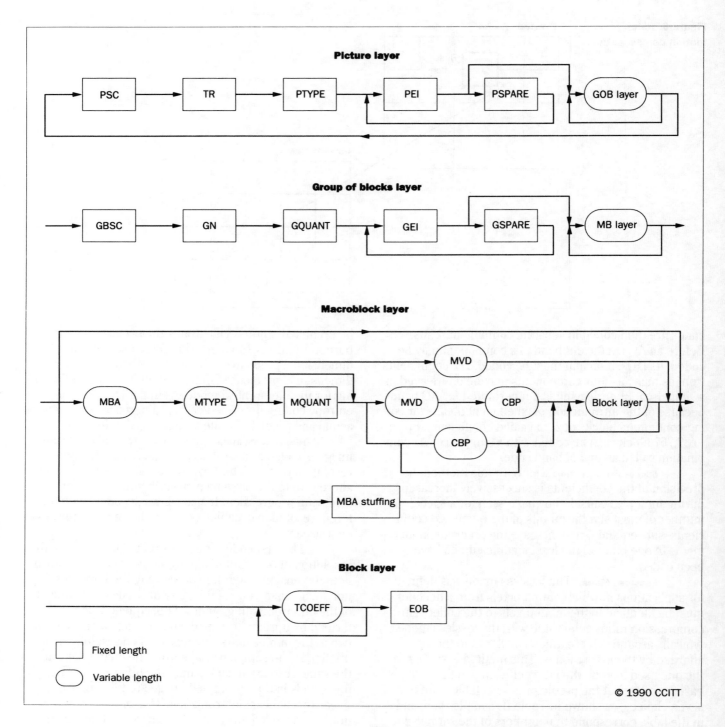

© 1990 CCITT

Figure 7. Syntax diagram of the video multiplex coder.[20]

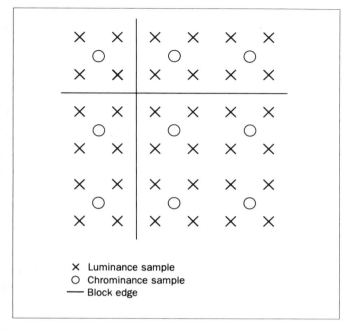

× Luminance sample
○ Chrominance sample
— Block edge

Figure 8. Relative positioning of the luminance and chrominance samples.

full-resolution input image. After that, one or more full-resolution difference images may be coded. A hierarchical decoder may abort the decoding process after it has decoded a frame that provides the desired resolution.

Any coding methods described in the other three modes of operation may be used to code the hierarchical mode frames, with the following restrictions:
- If a lossy method is chosen, all but the last frame must be coded using that method. A lossless method may be used optionally to code the last frame.
- If a lossless method is chosen, all frames must be coded with that method.
- The same entropy-coding technique (Huffman or arithmetic) must be used for all frames.

The hierarchical coding/decoding process is not symmetrical. Indeed, a hierarchical coder must also include the greater part of a decoder. However, a hierarchical decoder is only more complex than a nonhierarchical decoder in that it must provide a way to upsample and add. This increased complexity may be justified, given the flexibility afforded in matching the decoder to the application. This type of codec is well suited for "one-to-many" applications, as in a number of decoders (possibly having different resolution capabilities) accessing a database of images precoded by a hierarchical coder.

Videoconferencing Coding Standards H.261

From an algorithmic point of view, the extension from JPEG, intraframe DCT coding, to H.261, motion-compensated DCT video coding, is a rather natural one. Historically, H.261 was developed long before JPEG. In December 1984, CCITT Study Group XV (Transmission Systems and Equipment) established a "Specialists' Group on Coding for Visual Telephony." The development of this video transmission standard for low-bit-rate ISDN services has gone through several stages. At the beginning, the goal was to design a coding scheme for a transmission rate of $m \times 384$ kb/s, where m was between 1 and 5. Later, $n \times 64$ kb/s transmission rates (n from 1 to 5) were considered. However, by late 1989, the final CCITT recommendation H.261[20] was made for a $p \times 64$ kb/s video codec, where p is between 1 and 30.

In fact, the H series of audiovisual teleservices is a group of standards (or recommendations) consisting of H.221 — frame structure; H.230 — frame synchronous control; H.242 — communication between audiovisual terminals; H.320 — systems and terminal equipment; and H.261 — video codec. Audio codecs at several bit rates have also been specified by other CCITT recommendations, such as G.725. In this paper, we concentrate on the H.261 video codec system.

Both JPEG baseline and H.261 codecs use DCT and VLC techniques. The major difference between the JPEG compression scheme and H.261 is that JPEG codes each frame individually, whereas H.261 performs interframe coding. In H.261, block-based motion compensation is performed to compute interframe differences, which are then DCT coded. Here, the picture data in the previous frame can be used to predict the image blocks in the current frame, as shown in Figure 6. As a result, only differences, typically of small magnitude, between the displaced previous block and the current block have to be transmitted.

There are several interesting characteristics or design considerations in H.261.
- First, it defines essentially only the *decoder*. However, the *encoder*, which is not completely and explicitly specified by the standard, is expected to be compatible with the decoder.

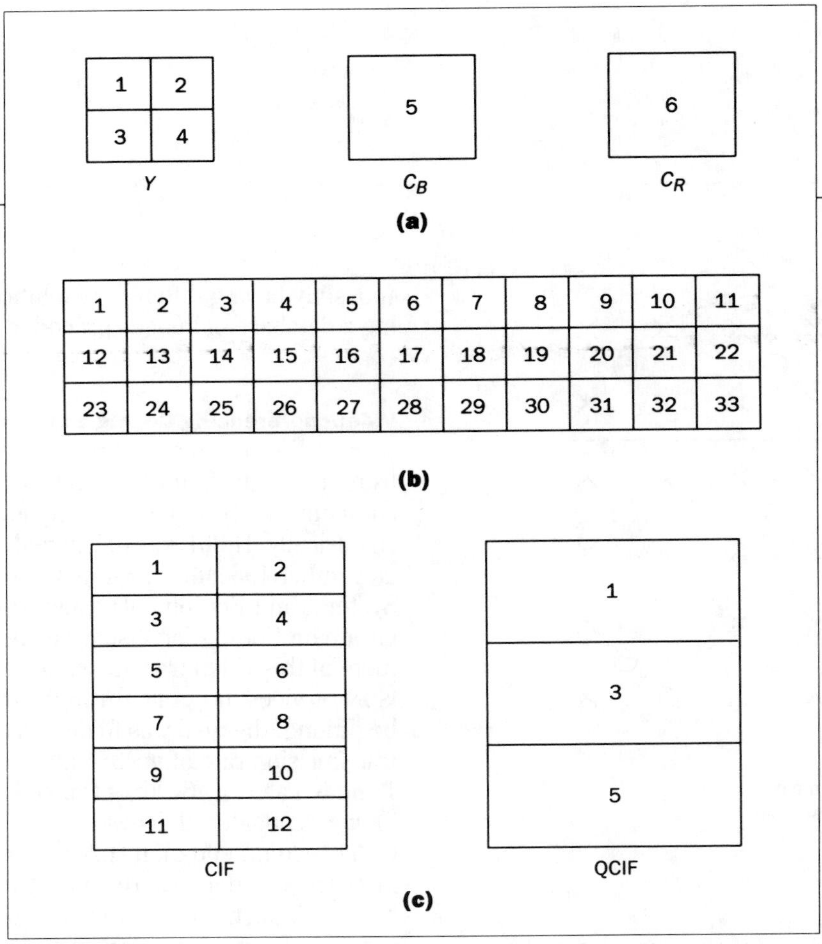

Figure 9. Successive arrangement of (a) blocks in a macroblock, (b) macroblocks in a GOB, and (c) GOBs in a picture.

- Second, because H.261 is designed for real-time communications, it uses only the closest previous frame as prediction to reduce the encoding delay.
- Third, it tries to balance the hardware complexities of the encoder and the decoder, since they are both necessary for a real-time videophone application. Other coding schemes, such as vector quantization (VQ), may have a rather simple decoder, but a very complex encoder.
- Fourth, H.261 is a compromise between coding performance, real-time requirement, implementation complexity, and system robustness. Motion-compensated DCT coding is a mature algorithm, and after years of study, quite general and robust in that it can handle various types of pictures.
- Fifth, the final coding structures and parameters are tuned more toward low-bit-rate applications. This choice is logical, because selection of the coding structure and coding parameters is more critical to codec performance at very low bit rates. At higher bit rates, the less-than-optimal parameter values do not affect codec performance very much.

Decoder Structures and Components. H.261 specifies a set of protocols that every compressed bit stream has to follow, and a set of operations that every standard compatible decoder must be able to perform. The actual hardware codec implementation and the encoder structure can vary drastically from one design to another. In a few places, user-defined bit streams may be inserted into the standard bit stream. We will first explain briefly the data structure in an H.261 bit stream and then the functional elements in an H.261 decoder.

The compressed H.261 bit stream[20] contains several layers (see Figure 7). They are *picture* layer, group of blocks (GOB) layer, macroblock (MB) layer, and *block* layer. The higher layer consists of its own header and a number of the lower layer data.

Only two picture formats — common intermediate format (CIF) and quarter-CIF (QCIF) — are allowed. CIF pictures are made of three components: luminance Y and color differences C_B and C_R, as defined in CCIR Recommendation 601. The CIF picture size for Y is 352 pixels per line by 288 lines per frame. The two-color difference signals are subsampled to 176 pixels per line and 144 lines per frame. Figure 8 shows the sampling pattern of Y, C_B, and C_R. The picture aspect ratio is 4 (horizontal):3 (vertical), and the picture rate is 29.97 non-interlaced frames per second. All standard codecs must be able to operate with QCIF; CIF is optional.

A picture frame is partitioned into 8 lines by 8

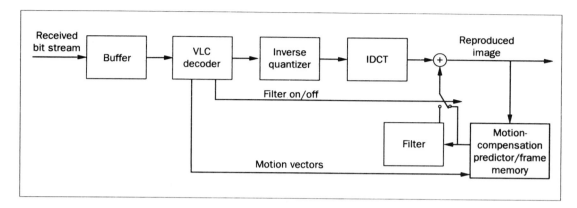

Figure 10. A typical H.261 decoder.

pixel image blocks. The so-called MB is made of 4 Y blocks, one C_B block, and one C_R block at the same location, as shown in Figure 9a. Figure 9b contains 33 MBs grouped into a GOB. Therefore, one CIF frame contains 12 GOBs and one QCIF frame contains 3 GOBs, as shown in Figure 9c.

In a compressed bit stream, we start with the picture layer. Its header contains:

- Picture start code (PSC) — a 20-bit pattern
- Temporal reference (TR) — a 5-bit input frame number
- Type information (PTYPE) — such as CIF/QCIF selection
- User-inserted bits.

Then, a number of GOB layer data follow.

At the GOB layer, a GOB header contains:

- Group of blocks start code (GBSC) — a 16-bit pattern
- Group number (GN) — a 4-bit GOB address
- Quantizer information (GQUANT) — quantizer step size normalized to lie in the range 1 to 31
- User-inserted bits.

Next come a number of MB layer data. An 11-bit stuffing pattern can be inserted repetitively right after a GOB header or after a transmitted macroblock.

At the MB layer, the header contains:

- Macroblock address (MBA) — VLC location relative to the previously coded MB
- Type information (MTYPE) — 10 types in total
- Quantizer (MQUANT) — normalized quantizer step size
- Motion vector data (MVD) — the differential displacement
- Coded block pattern (CBP) — the coded block location indicator.

The lowest layer is block layer, consisting of quantized

transform coefficients (TCOEFF), followed by the end of block (EOB) symbol.

Not all header information need be present. For example, at the MB layer, if an MB is not motion-compensated (as indicated by MTYPE), MVD does not exist.

Figure 10 is a functional diagram of a typical H.261 decoder. The received bit stream is first kept in the receiver buffer. The VLC decoder decodes the compressed bits and distributes the decoded information to the elements that need that information. The VLC tables are given by the standard.

There are essentially four types of MBs:

- Intra — original pixels are transform-coded
- Inter — the difference pixels (with zero-motion vectors) are coded
- Inter with motion compensation (MC) — the displaced (nonzero-motion vectors) differences are coded
- Inter MC with filter — the displaced blocks are filtered by a predefined filter, which may help reduce visible coding artifacts at very low bit rates.

Certain MB types in this list allow the optional transmission of MQUANT and TCOEFF information. The received MTYPE information controls various switches at the decoder to produce the right combination.

A single-motion vector (horizontal and vertical displacement) is transmitted for one inter-MC macroblock, that is, the four Y blocks, one C_B, and one C_R block all share the same motion vector. The range of motion vectors is ±15 pixels with integer values. Using both MVD and MTYPE information, the predictor can choose the right pixels for prediction.

The transform coefficients of either the original or the differential pixels are ordered according to the zig-zag scanning pattern in Figure 11. These transform

1	2	6	7	15	16	28	29
3	5	8	14	17	27	30	43
4	9	13	18	26	31	42	44
10	12	19	25	32	41	45	54
11	20	24	33	40	46	53	55
21	23	34	39	47	52	56	61
22	35	38	48	51	57	60	62
36	37	49	50	58	59	63	64

Increasing cycles-per-picture width →

Increasing cycles-per-picture height ↓

Figure 11. Transmission order for transform coefficients.

coefficients are selected and quantized at the encoder, and then variable-length-coded. Just as with JPEG, successive zeros between two nonzero coefficients are counted and called a *RUN*. The magnitude of a transmitted nonzero quantized coefficient is called a *LEVEL*. The most likely occurring combinations of (RUN, LEVEL) are encoded with the standard supplied VLC tables. The other combinations are coded with a 20-bit word consisting of a 6-bit ESCAPE code, 6 bits RUN, and 8 bits LEVEL. EOB is appended to the last nonzero coefficient, indicating the end of a block.

The inverse quantizer or the reconstruction process for all the coefficients other than the intra DC is defined by the following formula:

If *QUANT* is odd,

$$REC = QUANT \times (2 \times LEVEL + 1), \text{ for } LEVEL > 0,$$

$$REC = QUANT \times (2 \times LEVEL - 1), \text{ for } LEVEL < 0;$$

if *QUANT* is even,

$$REC = QUANT \times (2 \times LEVEL + 1) - 1, \text{ for } LEVEL > 0,$$

$$REC = QUANT \times (2 \times LEVEL - 1) + 1, \text{ for } LEVEL < 0,$$

where REC is the reconstructed value of a quantized coefficient. Almost all the reconstruction levels are odd numbers to reduce problems of mismatch between

encoders and decoders from different manufacturers. The intra-DC coefficient is uniformly quantized with a fixed step size of 8, and coded with 8 bits.

The standard requires a compatible inverse DCT (IDCT) to be close to the ideal 64-bit floating point IDCT. H.261 specifies a measuring process for checking a valid IDCT. The peak error, mean error, and mean square error between the ideal IDCT and the IDCT under test have to be less than certain small numbers given in the standard.

A few other items are required by the standard. One of them is the image-block updating rate. To prevent mismatched IDCT error and channel error propagation, every MB should be intra-coded at least once in every 132 transmitted picture frames. The contents of the transmitted bit stream must meet the requirements of a *hypothetical reference decoder* (HRD). For CIF pictures, every coded frame is limited to fewer than 256 kb/s; for QCIF, the limit is 64 kb/s. The HRD receiving buffer size is $B + 256$ kb/s, where $B = 4 \times R_{max}/29.97$ and R_{max} is the maximum connection (channel) rate. At every picture interval (1/29.97 sec), the HRD buffer is examined. If at least one complete coded picture is in the buffer, then the earliest picture data are removed from the buffer and decoded. The buffer occupancy, right after the above data have been removed, must be less than B.

Encoder Constraints and Options. Figure 12 shows a typical encoder structure. For the purpose of this discussion, the elements inside a standard compatible encoder can be classified, based on their functionalities, into two categories:

- The *basic coding operation* units, such as motion estimator, quantizer, transform, and variable-word-length encoder (VLE)
- The *coding parameter decision* units, such as the coding control in Figure 12. These units select the parameter values of the basic operation units, including motion vectors, quantization step size, and picture frame rate.

Although H.261 does not explicitly specify a standard encoder, most basic operation elements are strongly constrained by the standard. However, other crucial elements, such as the parameter decision unit, are still open to the design engineers. We briefly outline our observations below.

The VLE implements the VLC H.261 tables. The forward DCT is not specified, but it is expected that the DCT inside the encoder matches the decoder IDCT, and the forward DCT should be able to match its own IDCT.

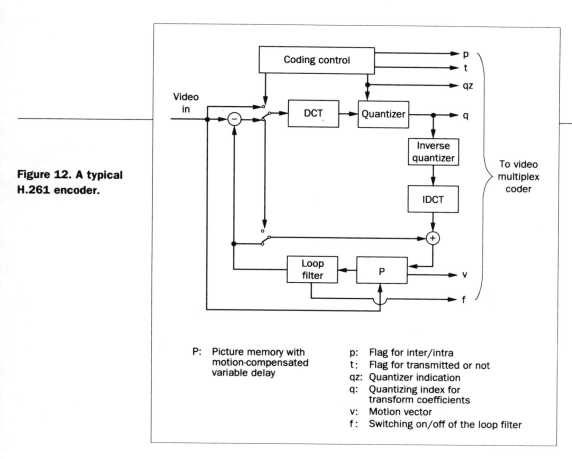

Figure 12. A typical H.261 encoder.

P: Picture memory with motion-compensated variable delay

p: Flag for inter/intra
t: Flag for transmitted or not
qz: Quantizer indication
q: Quantizing index for transform coefficients
v: Motion vector
f: Switching on/off of the loop filter

Because the inverse quantizer (IQ) is defined at the decoder, variations of the encoder quantizer are quite limited. From a theoretical viewpoint, however, it is not necessary for the decision levels of the encoder quantizer to be in the middle of two reconstruction levels. Also, encoder designers determine the criterion (a fixed or an adaptive threshold, for example) for selecting transform coefficients.

If motion compensation is selected, the motion estimator must be able to produce one motion vector for the entire MB. Block-matching motion estimation is used to produce such a motion vector; there can be several variations, such as hierarchical-motion estimation.[21] Because of the HRD model required by the standard, the encoded output bits of every frame must be regulated carefully. For example, successive frames producing small numbers of bits may violate the HRD requirement.

Although individual basic coding elements may affect the overall coding performance, the most critical and global influence on the encoder performance comes from the parameter decision units. The encoder must make several decisions, such as:
- How many frames should be transmitted, or conversely, how many should be skipped?
- What MTYPE should each macroblock use?
- What is the proper quantization step size?
- How do we control the buffer fullness so that it does not produce long delay and does not violate the HRD requirements?

Also, it is important to keep the hardware simple for practical applications. Many issues discussed have been investigated in the past; however, a complete solution has not been found.

MPEG First-Phase Standard

MPEG is an international standard[22-25] for the compression of digital audio and video transmission. The MPEG first-phase (MPEG-1) video compression standard, aimed primarily at coding video for digital storage media, at rates of 1 to 1.5 Mb/s, is well suited for a wide range of applications at a variety of bit rates. The standard mandates real-time decoding and supports features to facilitate interactivity with stored bit stream. It only specifies a syntax for the bit stream and the decoding process; sufficient flexibility is allowed for encoding complexity. Encoders can be designed for optimal tradeoff of performance versus complexity, depending on the specific application.

MPEG was chartered by the ISO to standardize a coded representation of video and audio suitable for digital storage media, such as compact disk – read-only memory (CD-ROM), digital audio tape (DAT), etc. The group's goal, however, has been to develop a *generic* standard, one that can be used in other digital video applications, such as telecommunication. The MPEG standard has three parts:
- Part 1 describes the synchronization and multiplexing of video and audio
- Part 2 describes video
- Part 3 describes audio.

459

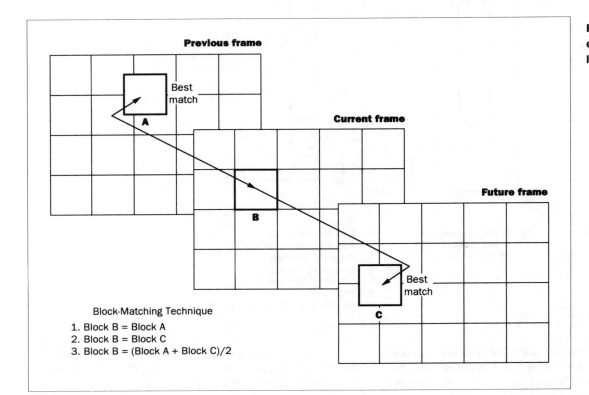

Figure 13. Motion-compensated interpolation.

Previous frame

Best match

A

Current frame

B

Future frame

Best match

C

Block-Matching Technique
1. Block B = Block A
2. Block B = Block C
3. Block B = (Block A + Block C)/2

An overview of the video portion of the MPEG standard follows.

Requirements of the Standard. Uncompressed digital video requires an extremely high transmission bandwidth. Digitized North American Television Standards Committee (NTSC) resolution video, for example, has a bit rate of approximately 100 Mb/s. With digital video, compression is necessary to reduce the bit rate to suit most applications. The required degree of compression is achieved by exploiting the spatial and temporal redundancy present in a video signal. However, the compression process is inherently lossy, and the signal reconstructed from the compressed bit stream is not identical to the input video signal. Compression typically introduces artifacts into the decoded signal.

The primary requirement of the MPEG video standard is that it should achieve the highest possible quality of the decoded video at a given bit rate. In addition to picture quality, different applications stipulate additional requirements. For instance, multimedia applications require the ability to access, i.e., decode, any video frame in a short time. The ability to perform fast search directly on the bit stream — forward and backward — is

extremely desirable if the storage medium has "seek" capabilities. Most applications require some degree of resilience to bit errors. It is also useful to be able to edit compressed bit streams directly while maintaining decodability. A variety of video formats should be supported.

Compression Algorithm Overview. References 23 and 25 describe the basic algorithms and syntax of the MPEG standard and Reference 25 details video coding using this standard. Here, we present the background and the basic information necessary for understanding this standard.

Exploiting spatial redundancy. The compression approach of MPEG video uses a combination of the ISO JPEG (still image) and CCITT H.261 (videoconferencing) standards. Because video is a sequence of still images, it is possible to compress or encode a video signal using techniques similar to JPEG. Such methods of compression are called intraframe coding techniques, where each frame of video is individually and independently compressed or encoded. Intraframe coding exploits the spatial redundancy that exists between adjacent pixels of a frame.

As in JPEG and H.261, the MPEG video-coding

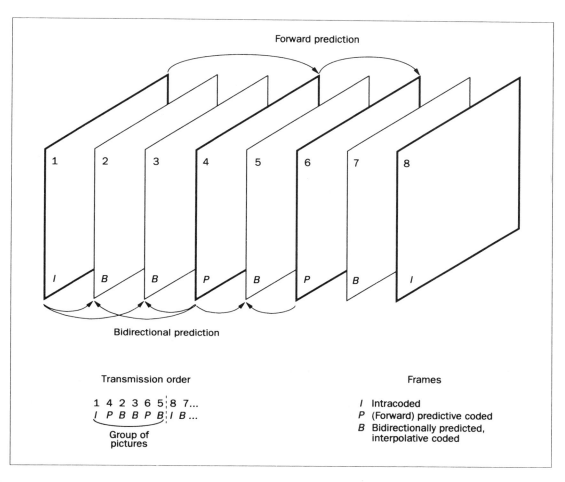

Figure 14. Group of pictures.

Forward prediction

Bidirectional prediction

Transmission order

1 4 2 3 6 5 8 7...
I P B B P B I B ...
Group of pictures

Frames

I Intracoded
P (Forward) predictive coded
B Bidirectionally predicted,
interpolative coded

algorithm employs a block-based two-dimensional DCT. A frame is first divided into 8×8 blocks of pixels, and the two-dimensional DCT is then applied independently on each block. This operation results in an 8×8 block of DCT coefficients in which most of the energy in the original (pixel) block is typically concentrated in a few low-frequency coefficients. A quantizer is applied to each DCT coefficient that sets many of them to zero. This quantization is responsible for the lossy nature of the compression algorithms in JPEG, H.261 and MPEG video. Compression is achieved by transmitting only the coefficients that survive the quantization operation and by entropy-coding their locations and amplitudes.

This standard allows the quantization operation to achieve a higher level of adaptation, a key factor in achieving good picture quality. Reference 26 details the relevant details of a quantizer adaptation scheme applicable within this context.

Exploiting temporal redundancy. Many of the interactive requirements discussed earlier can be satisfied by intraframe coding. However, as in H.261, the quality achieved by intraframe coding alone is not sufficient for typical video signals at bit rates around 1.5 Mb/s. Temporal redundancy results from a high degree of correlation between adjacent frames. The H.261 algorithm exploits this redundancy by computing a frame-to-frame difference signal called the *prediction error*. In computing the prediction error, the technique of motion compensation is employed to correct for motion. A block-based approach is adopted for motion compensation, where a block of pixels, called a *target block*, in the frame to be encoded is matched with a set of blocks of the same size in the previous frame, called a *reference frame*. The block in the reference frame that "best matches" the target block is used as the prediction for the latter, i.e., the prediction error is computed as the difference between

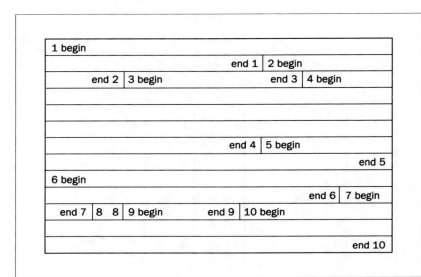

Figure 15. Possible arrangement of slices in a 256 X 192 picture.

The figure shows slices labeled: 1 begin; end 1, 2 begin; end 2, 3 begin, end 3, 4 begin; end 4, 5 begin; end 5; 6 begin; end 6, 7 begin; end 7, 8, 8, 9 begin, end 9, 10 begin; end 10.

the target block and the best-matching block. This best-matching block is associated with a motion vector that describes the displacement between it and the target block. The motion vector information is also encoded and transmitted along with the prediction error. The prediction error itself is transmitted using the DCT-based intraframe encoding technique summarized above. In MPEG video (as in H.261), the block size for motion compensation is chosen to be 16×16, representing a reasonable tradeoff between the compression provided by motion compensation and the cost associated with transmitting the motion vectors.

Bidirectional temporal prediction. Bidirectional temporal prediction, also called motion-compensated interpolation, is a key feature of MPEG video. In bidirectional prediction, some of the video frames are encoded using two reference frames, one in the past and one in the future. A block in those frames can be predicted by another block from the past reference frame (*forward prediction*), or from the future reference frame (*backward prediction*), or by the average of two blocks, one from each reference frame (*interpolation*). In every case, the block from the reference frame is associated with a motion vector, so that two motion vectors are used with interpolation. Motion-compensated interpolation for a block in a bidirectionally predicted frame is illustrated in Figure 13. Frames that are bidirectionally predicted are never themselves used as reference frames.

Bidirectional prediction provides a number of advantages. The primary one is that the compression obtained is typically higher than can be obtained from forward prediction. To obtain the same picture quality, bidirectionally predicted frames can be encoded with fewer bits than frames using only forward prediction. However, bidirectional prediction introduces extra delay in the encoding process, because frames must be encoded out of sequence. Further, it entails extra encoding complexity because block matching (the most computationally intensive encoding procedure) has to be performed twice for each target block, once with the past reference and once with the future reference.

Features of the Bit-Stream Syntax. The MPEG video standard specifies the *syntax* of the bit stream and, thus, the decoder. The standard also specifies how this bit stream is to be parsed and decoded to produce a decompressed video signal. However, a specific encoding method is not mandatory; different algorithms can be employed at the encoder so long as the resulting bit stream is consistent with the specified syntax. For example, the details of the block-matching procedure are not part of the standard. This is also true in H.261.

The bit-stream syntax should be flexible to support the variety of applications envisaged for the MPEG video standard. To this end, the overall syntax is constructed in several layers, each performing a different logical function. The outermost layer is called the *video sequence* layer, which contains basic parameters such as the size of the video frames, the frame rate, the bit rate, and certain other global parameters. A wide range of values is supported for all these parameters.

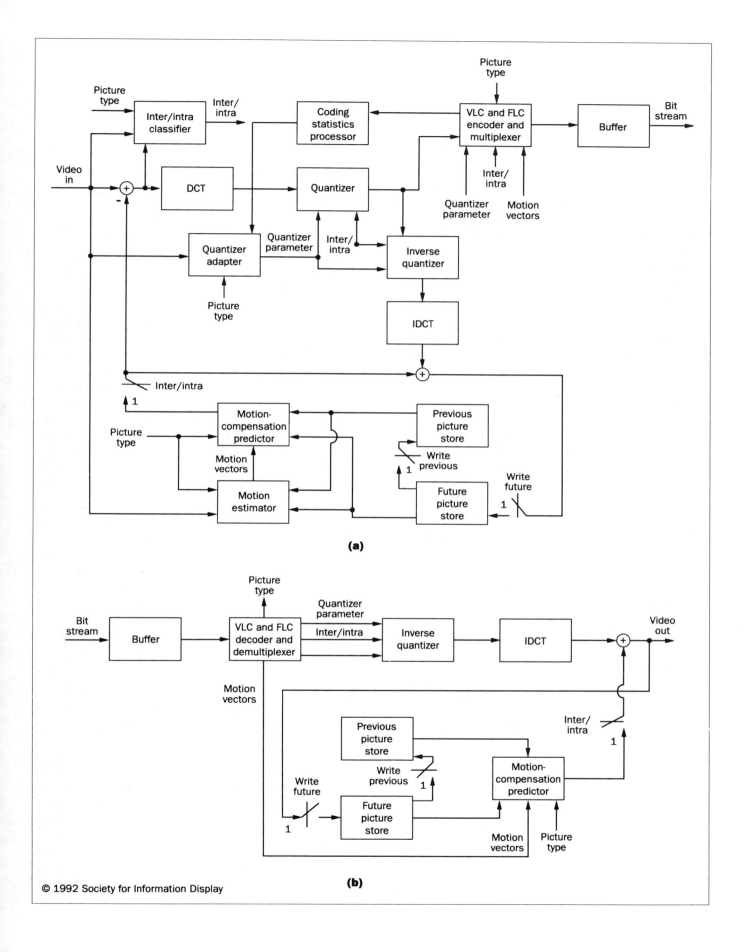

(a)

(b)

Inside the video sequence layer is the GOP layer, which provides support for random access, fast search, and editing. A sequence is divided into a series of GOPs, where each GOP contains an intracoded frame (I-frame) followed by an arrangement of (forward) predictive-coded frames (P-frames) and bidirectionally predicted, interpolative-coded frames (B-frames). Figure 14 shows a GOP example with six frames, 1 to 6. This GOP contains I-frame 1, P-frames 4 and 6, and B-frames 2, 3, and 5. The encoding and transmission order of the frames in this GOP is shown at the bottom of Figure 14. B-frames 2 and 3 are encoded after P-frame 4, using P-frame 4 and I-frame 1 as reference. We note that B-frame 7 in Figure 14 is part of the next GOP because it is encoded after I-frame 8. Random access and fast search are enabled by the availability of the I-frames, which can be decoded independently and serve as entry points for further decoding. The MPEG video standard allows GOPs to be of arbitrary structure and length. The GOP layer is the basic unit for editing an MPEG video bit stream.

The compressed bits produced by encoding a frame in a GOP constitute the *picture layer*. The picture layer first contains information on the type of frame that is present (I, P, or B), and the position of the frame in display order. The bits corresponding to the motion vectors and the DCT coefficients are packaged in the *slice* layer, the *macroblock* layer, and the *block* layer. Here, the block is the 8×8 DCT unit, the macroblock the 16×16 motion compensation unit, and the slice is a string of macroblocks of arbitrary length running from left to right and top to bottom across the frame. The slice layer is intended to be used for resynchronization during the decoding of a frame, in the event of bit errors. Prediction registers used in the differential encoding of motion vectors are reset at the start of a slice. It is again the responsibility of the encoder to choose the length of each slice. Figure 15 shows an example in which slice lengths vary throughout the frame. In the macroblock layer, the motion vector bits for a macroblock are followed by the block layer, which consists of the bits for the DCT coefficients of the 8×8 blocks in the macroblock. Figure 16 shows an MPEG video encoder and decoder. The different layers in the syntax and their use are illustrated in Table III.

Figure 16. A typical (a) MPEG-1 encoder and (b) MPEG-1 decoder.[25]

Table III. Layers of MPEG Video Bit-Stream Syntax

Syntax layer	Functionality
Sequence layer	Context unit
Group of pictures layer	Random access unit: video coding
Picture layer	Primary coding unit
Slice layer	Resynchronization unit
Macroblock layer	Motion compensation unit
Block layer	DCT unit

In demonstrations of MPEG video at a bit rate of 1.2 Mb/s, noninterlaced frames of size of 352 pixels by 240 lines at a frame rate of 29.97 per second have been used, with 2:1 color subsampling both horizontally and vertically. This resolution is roughly equivalent to one field of an interlaced NTSC frame. The quality achieved by the MPEG video encoder at this bit rate has often been compared to that of VHS. Although the MPEG video standard was originally intended for operation in the neighborhood of the above bit rate, a much wider range of resolution and bit rates is supported by the syntax. The MPEG video standard thus provides a generic bit-stream syntax that can be used for a variety of applications. The MPEG-video Committee Draft ISO CD 11172-2 provides all the details of the syntax, complete with informative sections on encoder procedures that are outside the scope of the standard.[22]

MPEG Second-Phase Standard. Currently, the second phase of MPEG (MPEG-2) is in progress. This phase is aimed at coding the video signals created by CCIR 601, e.g., 720 pixels, 480 lines, 30 frames per second, 2:1 interlace at bit rates of 2 Mb/s, or higher.

The first-phase standard, MPEG-1, focused on coding of single-layer (nonscalable) video of progressive format. The MPEG-2 standard is addressing issues of improved functionality by using scalable video coding. To initiate technical work for this phase of the MPEG standard, a worldwide video coding competition was held at Kurihama, Japan, in November 1991. Nearly 30 international organizations, including AT&T, submitted a video-coding scheme to this contest. AT&T's scheme was judged one of the best. Immediately after this competition, a collaborative phase of work began and, thus far, has resulted in a compromise scheme that retains many of the best features of the best performing schemes.

In the MPEG-2 standard, the main improvements in nonscalable coding result from emphasis on interlaced video. Various forms of frame/field motion-compensated predictions have been adapted to increase the coding efficiency. Frame/field DCT coding and quantization have also been adapted. All optimization experiments are being performed at bit rates between 4 and 9 Mb/s.

The MPEG-2 standard is also addressing scalable video coding for a range of applications where video needs to be decoded and displayed at a variety of resolution scales. Among the noteworthy applications of interest are multipoint video conferencing, window display on workstations, video communications on asynchronous transfer mode networks, and high-definition television (HDTV) with embedded standard TV.

In scalable video coding, which can be achieved in the *spatial* or the *frequency* domain, it is assumed that given an encoded video bit stream, decoders of various complexities can decode and display appropriate-size replicas of the original video. A scalable video encoder and corresponding highest resolution decoder are likely to have increased complexity compared to a single-layer encoder/decoder. However, this increase in complexity may be well justified in applications where increased functionality and error resilience are important.

Conclusion

Image coding standards are crucial to the robust growth of visual services in communication and computer systems. Without them, communication between terminals and systems becomes extremely inconvenient and costly. In the absence of standards, economies of scale in the manufacture of user devices, board systems, and VLSI chips may be lost.

The JBIG, JPEG, P×64, and MPEG standards provide compression algorithms for all types of images that might be carried on multimedia services. With the onset of inexpensive chips, high-speed communication, and large capacity disk storage, all elements needed for rapid growth are in place.

References

1. J. R. Allen et al., "VCTV: A Video-on-Demand Market Test," *AT&T Technical Journal*, Vol. 72, No. 1, January/February 1993, pp. 7–14.
2. ISO Committee Draft 11544, *Coded representation of picture and audio information — Progressive bi-level image compression*, ISO/IEC IS 11544, to be published in 1993.
3. Horst Hampel et al., "Technical features of the JBIG standard for progressive bi-level image compression," *Signal Processing: Image Communication*, Vol. 4, No. 2, April 1992, pp. 103–110.
4. R. Hunter and A. H. Robinson, "International digital facsimile coding standards," *Proceedings of the IEEE*, Vol. 68, No. 7, July 1980, pp. 854–867.
5. CCITT Recommendation T.4, *Standardization of Group 3 facsimile apparatus for document transmission*, Geneva, 1980.
6. CCITT Recommendation T.6, *Facsimile coding schemes and coding control functions for Group 4 facsimile apparatus*, Malaga–Torremolinos, 1984.
7. ISO Committee Draft 10918-1, *Digital compression and coding of continuous-tone still images — Part 1: Requirements and guidelines*, ISO/IEC DIS 10918-1, 1991.
8. R. W. Hamming, *Coding and Information Theory*, Prentice-Hall, Englewood Cliffs, New Jersey, 1980, pp. 96–98.
9. A. S. Tanenbaum, *Computer Networks*, Prentice-Hall, Inc., Englewood Cliffs, New Jersey, 1981.
10. N. Abramson, *Information Theory and Coding*, McGraw-Hill, New York, N. Y., 1963, pp. 61–62.
11. *Digital Compression and Coding of Continuous-Tone Still Images, Part 2: Compliance Testing*, ISO/IEC CD 10918-2, 1991.
12. A. N. Netravali and B. G. Haskell, *Digital Pictures: Representation and Compression*, Plenum Press, New York, 1988.
13. D. A. Huffman, "A Method for the Construction of Minimum-Redundancy Codes," *Proc. IRE*, No. 40, September 1952, pp. 1098–1101.
14. J. Amsterdam, "Data Compression with Huffman Coding," *BYTE*, Vol. 11, No. 5, May 1986, pp. 99–108.
15. G. G. Langdon, Jr., "An Introduction to Arithmetic Coding," *IBM J. Res. Develop.*, Vol. 28, No. 2, March 1984, pp. 135–149.
16. I. H. Witten, R. M. Neal, and J. G. Cleary, "Arithmetic Coding for Data Compression," *Communications of the ACM*, Vol. 30, No. 6, June 1987, pp. 520–540.
17. N. Ahmed, T. Natarajan, and K. R. Rao, "Discrete Cosine Transform," *IEEE Transactions on Computers*, Vol. C-23, No. 1, January 1974, pp. 90–93.
18. R. J. Clarke, *Transform Coding of Images*, Academic Press, Orlando, Florida, 1985.
19. H. Lohscheller, "A subjectively adapted image communication system," *IEEE Transactions on Communications*, Vol. COM-32, December 1984, pp. 1316–1322.
20. CCITT, *Recommendation H.261 — Video Codec for Audiovisual Services at px64 kbit/s*, Geneva, August 1990.
21. M. Bierling and R. Thoma, "Motion Compensating Field Interpolation Using a Hierarchically Structured Displacement Estimator," *Signal Processing*, Vol. 11, No. 4, Dec. 1986, pp. 387–404.
22. ISO Committee Draft 11172, *Information Technology-Coding of moving pictures and associated audio for digital storage media up to about 1.5 Mbit/s*, to be published in 1993.
23. D. J. LeGall, "MPEG: A Video Compression Standard for Multimedia Applications," *Communications of the ACM*, Vol. 34, No. 4, April 1991, pp. 47–58.
24. R. K. Jurgen, "Digital Video," *IEEE Spectrum*, Vol. 29, No. 3, March 1992, pp. 24–30.
25. A. Puri, "Video Coding Using the MPEG-1 Compression Standard," *Proc. International Symposium: Society for Information Display*, Boston, Massachusetts, May 1992, pp. 123–126.
26. A. Puri and R. Aravind, "Motion-Compensated Video Coding with Adaptive Perceptual Quantization," *IEEE Transactions on Circuits and Systems for Video Technology*, Vol. CSVT-1, December 1991, pp. 351–361.

The Digital Hierarchy — A Blueprint for Television in the 21st Century

By G. Reitmeier, C. Carlson, E. Geiger, and D. Westerkamp

The establishment of a new standard for HDTV is an opportunity to create a technologically advanced standard that will serve current and future applications of video well into the next century. This article describes a digital approach that provides efficiency and flexibility through a hierarchical approach to data compression. The digital hierarchy concept is a novel approach to transcoding digital video among several data rates. Also described are some of the industry requirements that the authors believe will be important in the era of HDTV, and the ability of a digital hierarchy to satisfy them is evaluated.

With his recent support of a simulcast approach for high-definition television (HDTV) broadcasting, Chairman Sikes of the FCC has provided the opportunity for the U.S. to set a technologically advanced video standard that will serve us well into the next century. The nature of television distribution and consumer electronics requires the establishment of standards that will last for many decades, in spite of rapid advances in technology. Such long-lived standards are essential to preserve the consumer's investment and allow a continually evolving system. This article will describe some desirable characteristics and an approach that the authors believe should be considered in the selection of a standard.

In retrospect, the NTSC television standard has served the U.S. very well for nearly 50 years.[1] (The first meeting of the NTSC was held July 31, 1940. The monochrome NTSC standard was established in 1942; color was added in the 1950s.) The longevity of this standard over a period containing such rapid technological progress is a tribute to the vision and leadership of those involved in the standardization process. Even more amazing is the plethora of new products and uses for video that have been developed around a standard that was established in 1941.[2] (The FCC approved the NTSC proposals and authorized full commercial telecasting in new rules issued April 30, 1941, which became effective July 1, 1941.) The broadcasting industry developed video recording and editing, migrated to compatible color, added special effects, and evolved to sophisticated post-production systems. Today's typical consumer has several TV receivers in the home, in addition to sophisticated camcorders and VCRs. There are many technical and economic lessons that can be learned from this history.

With the establishment of simulcast HDTV, the U.S. will undoubtedly be selecting its video standard for the next 50 years. We know that today's technology will be obsolete in 10 years, but we must be sure that the standards we set will have a much longer lifetime. We can be almost certain that over the next 50 years there will be new applications for HDTV, and that new technologies will make it possible to increase the level of HDTV resolution and picture quality beyond what we envision today. If, as an industry, we can plan for these advances within the framework of the simulcast standard that we are in the process of setting, we will create an HDTV standard with an extended lifetime. This will have great economic and social benefits compared to standards that might otherwise be doomed to early technical obsolescence.[3]

Some Industry Requirements for HDTV

In this section, the authors will present our view of some of the industry requirements for HDTV. Some of the factors in identifying these needs are driven by the belief that there are several structural needs that must be accommodated in order to support industry interrelationships among HDTV program producers, delivery systems, and consumer electronics manufacturers. These structural needs acknowledge that HDTV must be introduced in the context of today's complex industry environment. Other factors in identifying industry requirements are driven by the belief that providing good value to the consumer (i.e., the public) is in the best interest of all industry segments. For example, in the design of any video delivery system, there are tradeoffs that can be made between broadcasting and receiver costs. Biasing these tradeoffs in favor of the consumer was essential to the success of the NTSC standard, and we believe that similar decisions will provide market acceptance and growth for HDTV. With these thoughts in mind, we suggest several requirements that an HDTV standard should satisfy.

Bandwidth Efficiency

It is always desirable to make efficient use of bandwidth. Additional capacity in a delivery medium can invariably be used either to increase performance or to send additional channels of audio or video. In television, the primary limit in available bandwidth is imposed by the 6-MHz spectrum allocations for terrestrial broadcast channels. This channel was selected to be just wide enough to transmit 525-line 2:1 interlaced pictures at a 60-Hz field rate. In order to squeeze higher resolution and wider aspect ratio HDTV pictures into this channel, about five times more bandwidth reduction is required. This will require powerful compression techniques that result in excellent bandwidth efficiency.

Variable Quality

Analog technology provides us with an extensive continuum of cost/performance tradeoffs that we can apply to the design of video systems and components. Consider the case of VHS, S-VHS, and 8mm VCRs, which differ greatly in their signal processing and use of recording bandwidth. Even though they all use 525 lines, each tape standard makes different tradeoffs in technical parameters such as bandwidth, signal-to-noise ratio (SNR), track width, etc. The ability to vary quality is essential to consumer electronics manufacturers, who to a large extent compete on the basis of delivering the best performance at the appropriate cost for a particular product or market segment.

One example of variable quality is the choice of extended play modes on the VCR, which allow extra recording time at the sacrifice of some picture quality. By far the smoothest example of the analog continuum is the performance of terrestrial broadcasting systems, which enjoy graceful degradation characteristics as the receivers' distances from the transmitter are increased. HDTV must provide for quality variations so that manufacturers, service providers, and consumers have the ability to select levels of cost and performance appropriate for a variety of products and uses.

Reprinted with permission from *SMPTE J.*, vol. 101, no. 7, pp. 466–470, July, 1992.

Multiple Delivery Media

HDTV must have a cost-effective implementation for all of today's delivery media, including terrestrial broadcast, cable, and prerecorded cassettes. In addition, an HDTV standard should also anticipate the successful introduction of new delivery media and be able to make use of the new capabilities that they will provide. Some obvious candidates to contemplate are higher-density magnetic recording, direct broadcasting satellites, optical videodiscs, and optical fiber. Which, if any, of these new delivery media will succeed in the market will depend upon their cost, performance, features, and unique service characteristics, as well as the value they provide to the consumer relative to existing media. We can be certain that innovative new HDTV uses will emerge that we cannot envision today, but careful accommodation of the media that we can foresee will lead to a more robust, longer-lived standard.

Economical Transcoding and Interface

The needs of bandwidth efficiency, variable quality, and multiple delivery media lead to the conclusion that a variety of HDTV products will inevitably be developed that exhibit different levels of performance. In order to achieve this, they will record, transmit, or display different amounts of information. This, in turn, creates a need for efficient transcoding among these various forms of HDTV, so that signals can be exchanged among products without being subjected to extensive signal processing. This signal processing would not only be expensive, but it could potentially introduce artifacts in the HDTV picture.

In analog systems, we take for granted the ability to combine components with different levels of performance. Again considering the case of VCRs, we note that although the many products all have internally different formats, they share a common interface to the television receiver and one another. When we copy a tape from one format to another, we transcode from one level of the analog continuum to another, usually going through an intermediate representation (NTSC), which may be higher or lower in quality than the recorded signal. HDTV standards should provide for easy interconnection to one another by the consumer, with a single interface definition that accommodates a variety of different data rates and the resulting levels of picture quality.

Evolutionary Increases in Performance

The opportunity to successfully establish a new television standard can occur only once in a lifetime. The success and longevity of NTSC can be partly attributed to the fact that a long series of performance improvements were possible within the scope of the standard. A very important observation is that given the camera and display technology of the 1940s, a 525-line television system was excessive. Nevertheless, the limits of system performance were set well beyond the limits of available cameras and displays. This foresightedness allowed for many decades of performance improvements, which could be made without "bumping into" fundamental limitations imposed by the standard. With HDTV, we have the opportunity to repeat this foresightedness, and even to improve upon it.

Accommodating New Applications

Television was established as a mass medium for live entertainment broadcasting, and the technical parameters of the NTSC standard reflect this view. An example of this is interlace, which was invented as an economical solution to reduce flicker by providing a 60-Hz display rate. The inventors of interlace never envisioned today's sophisticated editing and special effects, and the difficulties and degradation that it creates in that environment. Likewise, the creators of NTSC could not have envisioned all of today's uses of the standard, including delivery of programming to consumers by terrestrial broadcasting, cable, and prerecorded cassette, not to mention the consumer producing his own programs with a small, lightweight camcorder.

HDTV standards must permit systems to be developed and implemented using current technology, but if the standards are to survive for the next 50 years (and they must), then HDTV standards must also provide room for new applications. Several recent U.S. Government reports cite many applications of HDTV, in areas as diverse as entertainment, medicine, defense, and others. While HDTV must accommodate all of today's uses of video, we can also be certain that innovative new uses for HDTV will emerge that we cannot envision today.

The Key Technology — Digital Data Compression

We are clearly in an era of digital technology. Computing technology and its underlying digital semiconductors have exhibited explosive growth during the last decade, and seem to be developing at an ever-increasing rate. Associated rapid developments in digital recording, optical media, and fiber communications have all been fueled by the computer revolution. Display technology is also being driven by computer workstation requirements, where 1000-line resolution is already common. With these rapid advances in mind, we must ask ourselves how long 1000-line television systems can be called "advanced." Why should HDTV be *limited* to 1000 lines? Should we not be setting a standard that anticipates even higher resolutions and provides the industry with an evolutionary growth path to achieve them? Today's digital technology environment raises such questions, which we believe should be addressed in the process of establishing an HDTV standard.

We believe that digital technology is the key to meeting the industry requirements that we have just discussed. Among these requirements, the need for bandwidth efficiency stands out as an extremely strong driver of technology. As we previously described, the difficult task of transmitting HDTV in a 6-MHz terrestrial broadcast channel will require at least four times more bandwidth efficiency than is achieved with the 525-line NTSC standard.

Proponents of analog HDTV systems (such as MUSE and EUREKA) advocate adaptive subsampling techniques to achieve the required bandwidth reduction. These techniques represent the state of the art in video bandwidth compression that can be achieved in conjunction with analog transmission. Essentially, adaptive subsampling techniques are more sophisticated versions of interlacing, which use digital processing to discard certain samples that can be accurately predicted by their neighbors in space and time. Unfortunately, since a large number of samples must be discarded in order to achieve the required bandwidth, visually important information can often be missing from the compressed video signal. The result is that, like interlace, it is inevitable that such techniques will introduce motion and flicker artifacts on certain critical picture material.

Digital data compression is a rapidly maturing technology, however, which is changing the limits of picture quality that can be achieved in a given bandwidth. For delivery media where it is feasible to use more than 6-MHz bandwidth, it is virtually certain that digital data compression approaches can economically provide outstanding picture quality. If terrestrial broadcast is served by an inferior analog or hybrid standard, higher-performance digital systems are likely to be utilized in other media, resulting in a very significant increment in picture quality. A proliferation of incompatible transmission standards is clearly not in the interest of either broadcasters or consumer electronics manufacturers. Thus, a critical technical goal for the entire industry to achieve is the development of a digital system that will deliver outstanding HDTV picture quality within a 6-MHz channel.

In order to achieve this goal, it will be necessary to extend the state of the art of data compression. One promising approach is to exploit the temporal redundancy in a video sequence. This can be done by using sophisticated motion analysis techniques to derive a set of motion vectors, which can be efficiently encoded and used as a very accurate predictor for

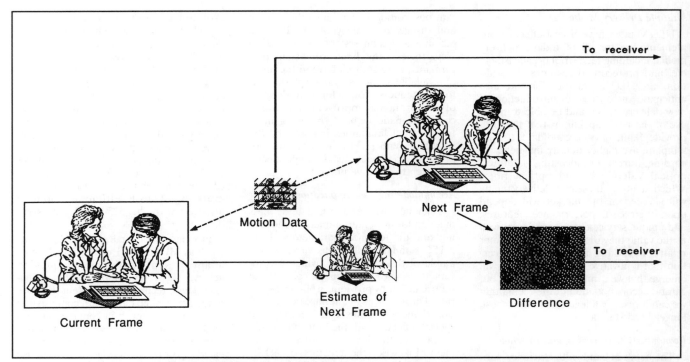

Figure 1. In motion-compensated data compression, consecutive frames are compared to derive motion vectors, which efficiently estimate the next frame. The difference between the estimate and the actual frame is spatially compressed and transmitted to the receiver along with encoded motion data.

the following frame. Thus, still portions of the scene, or those that exhibit predictable changes between successive frames, can be encoded entirely by a description of the predictor. The residual information can be spatially encoded, with any distortions optimized to minimize their perceptible impact. This concept is illustrated in Fig. 1. We believe that in the long term, the rapid growth of digital technology will result in the ability of digital HDTV systems to meet the need for bandwidth efficiency economically, with picture quality that is far superior to that of analog approaches.

Imitating Analog — The Digital Hierarchy Concept

Unfortunately, a normal characteristic of digital systems is to perform perfectly until exhibiting catastrophic failure. This "brick wall" performance of digital systems is precisely the opposite of the analog continuum, and it severely restricts the options of video system designers. A good example of this can be found in terrestrial broadcasting. The coverage area of a digital HDTV simulcast system will be limited primarily by co-channel interference restrictions on radiated power. A conventional digital system is likely to produce outstanding pictures within most of its coverage area, but would produce no picture at all just outside of its coverage contour. More importantly, the audience near the fringe area would likely experience complete loss of service during periods of exceptionally poor transmission conditions. What is more desirable is a system that

produces degraded pictures at the edge of its service contour under such conditions, but which still continues to provide service to its audience.

As previously cited, similar needs exist throughout consumer electronics, including the example of producing VCRs with Slow Play and Extended Play levels of performance. The need to develop digital techniques that mimic the performance characteristics of the analog continuum resulted in the digital hierarchy concept. These techniques will provide us with the ability to make the performance tradeoffs and provide the graceful degradation we rely upon to produce and deliver video products and services.

There have been many proposals for augmentation systems to improve the performance of analog systems. From a technical perspective, one of the shortcomings of these approaches is the fact that signal separation and recombination is subject to transmission noise. This is a particular problem when trying to improve picture quality by adding additional low-level high-frequency information, which can be completely obscured by a small amount of noise. And, in analog approaches, there is no way to improve the receiver SNR performance by adding augmentation signals. However, once a baseline digital standard is established, digital augmentation schemes will immediately become feasible. Since digital information is exactly reproducible, augmentation is a natural approach to extending the performance of digital systems. In fact, augmentation sig-

nals can be used either to improve resolution or to reduce artifacts (e.g., increase the SNR). With this understanding, we can now introduce the digital hierarchy concept as a nested set of video data structures, where each level of the hierarchy uses additional data rate to improve picture quality and resolution.

The digital hierarchy concept is illustrated in Fig. 2. We define Level 0 as the lowest level of the hierarchy, where we must choose a basic data compression scheme and a data rate. It is essential to perform very efficient high-quality compression at this data rate, employing sophisticated encoding techniques. The next level of the hierarchy is constructed by adding more information to improve the quality of the video picture. We move to this level by encapsulating the entire data stream from Level 0, and inserting additional Level 1 data packets into the bit stream. Assume, for example, that Level 1 of the hierarchy corresponded to a data rate suitable for terrestrial broadcast, say 20 Mbits/sec. Then Level 0 information might occupy a 5-Mbit/sec portion of the channel. If Level 0 information were coded more robustly than Level 1 information, then even under poor reception conditions a receiver could at least make a Level 0 picture. Although the Level 0 picture would exhibit more coding artifacts than the Level 1 picture, the alternative of a "noisy" picture should certainly be more acceptable than a blank screen.

Similarly, Level 2 is composed by encapsulating all of the entire Level 1 data and

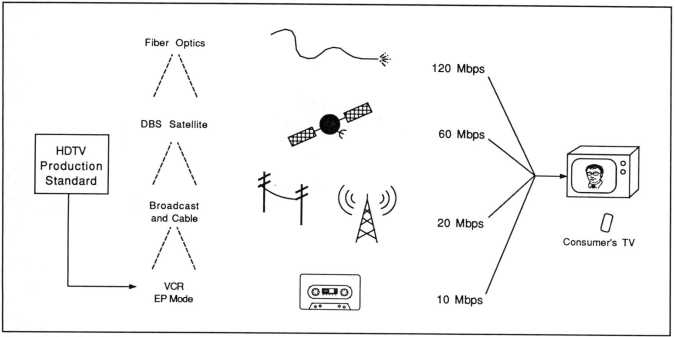

Figure 2. The digital hierarchy concept allows a single standard to accommodate multiple delivery media and different data rates, with commensurate levels of picture quality. Compressed video data structures at each higher rate are a superset of the data at lower rates. Higher data rate levels of the digital hierarchy can allow for higher resolution or fewer compression artifacts.

using the excess data rate of the Level 2 channel to send additional information. The additional information could be used to further reduce the noise level of the picture, or, alternatively, additional high-frequency detail could be added to the picture. At Level 2, Level 1 performance is the fallback for poor reception conditions. Additional levels can be defined as required. Essentially, once the basic compression technique and data protocols are established, each new layer of the hierarchy is a kind of augmentation signal. The important difference, compared to analog augmentation signals, is that digital techniques can more efficiently encode and decode the augmentation, based on processing in the "coded" domain rather than the image domain. This will lead to more cost-effective receivers and VCRs, and allow a single interface that can interconnect video components operating at different data rates within the digital hierarchy.

One of the most important aspects of the digital hierarchy is that it can be structured to optimize performance at the lowest level. Some other hierarchical proposals have optimized at the middle or highest levels of transmission capacity, which results in rapidly degrading video quality at the lower levels. Such an approach leaves the terrestrial broadcaster in an extremely uncompetitive position. We believe that the digital hierarchy approach is the digital approach that can best serve the broadcaster and consumer electronics manufacturer alike. As described in a previous section, we anticipate

that a crucial application of the hierarchy concepts will be to provide for graceful degradation to digital HDTV terrestrial broadcasting, thus providing a reliable service contour in digital systems.

Transcoding Concepts in the Digital Hierarchy

To date, most HDTV proposals have focused on a fixed, single set of video parameters and channel bandwidth, thus resulting in only one level of performance. The David Sarnoff Research Center and Thomson Consumer Electronics have recognized the need to produce and interconnect different consumer products with varying levels of performance. This, in turn, implies that these products will necessarily have to operate at different data rates. HDTV signals will thus have to be transcoded from one data rate to another when they are exchanged among consumer products with different performance levels. This is not a trivial task, however, since the signals will be comprised of heavily compressed data. The normal technique of transcoding is to decompress the data stream, reproducing the high-resolution video frames, and then recompress the signals, possibly using a completely different compression algorithm. This process is much the same as performing a standards conversion, and it will increase costs, introduce artifacts, and result in complex interface requirements. It is essential that recording media operating at different data rates have a simple way of transcoding from one rate to another, without having to perform complex de-

compression and recompression.

Thus, there is an opportunity to create less costly HDTV products if the signal standard is designed with this transcoding need in mind. Video data compression can be thought of as a kind of open systems interconnect (OSI)[4] model, composed of different layers of representation, as shown in Fig. 3. At the highest level is a motion picture, composed of its individual pixels. The next level down in the representation allows us to separate the video sequence into a set of component parts, (e.g., motion vectors and subband decomposition of the frame-by-frame residual information). Beneath this level, statistical code tables are computed to remove the redundancy from the components, subject to certain distortion rules. The resulting variable-rate data can be assembled into packets corresponding to the compressed data for each component part. At the next lower level, the packets are merged into a serial bit stream. Finally, this bit stream is mapped onto symbols that are transmitted over the physical channel.

The goal of the digital hierarchy is to permit digital HDTV signals to be transcoded between different data rates at the lowest possibly layer of representation. This will most likely occur at the packet level, where packets corresponding to particular component parts can be discarded to move from a higher data rate to a lower one. Moving from lower to higher data rates simply involves "padding" additional packets filled with dummy information, so that the data stream format of the higher rate can be preserved.

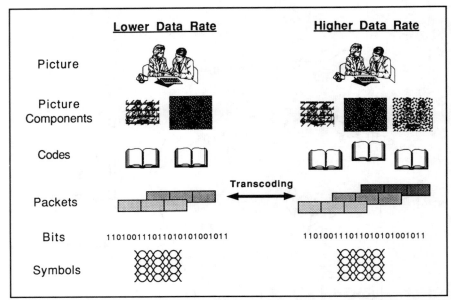

Figure 3. Transcoding in the digital hierarchy. Data-compressed video can be described by a layered representation analogous to the OSI data communications model. Transcoding between different data rates is more efficient at the lower layers of the model; providing for low-cost interoperability among a variety of products and services.

Benefits of the Digital Hierarchy Approach

If we understand the definition of a standard to mean a fixed, single set of video parameters, then meeting the requirements that we have outlined becomes impossible. On the other hand, we will see that it is quite possible to meet these industry requirements if we take advantage of the flexibility that the digital hierarchy concept provides.

First, efficient digital data compression will allow the efficient bandwidth use that is required for HDTV. Second, with a digital hierarchy, a single standard can be defined that provides variable quality commensurate with the data rate of the delivery channel. Thus the digital hierarchy is ideally suited to accommodate our third requirement for multiple delivery media, each having its own channel characteristics, data rate, and resulting level of picture quality. It is further interesting to note that in a digital system, additional channel capacity can be used to deliver more programming (at lower levels of picture quality) as well as to increase the level of picture quality. This flexibility, enabled by digital delivery and the digital hierarchy concept, should prove to be extremely important in helping service providers and consumer electronics manufacturers to meet an ever-increasing range of demands from the consumer.

Our fourth requirement for simple transcoding and interface is provided by the digital hierarchy's ability to achieve simple transcoding between its levels, which can be performed by dropping or adding packets of certain priority. This means that media operating at different data rates have a simple way of transcoding from one rate to another, without having to perform complex decompression and recompression, which will inevitably increase costs, introduce artifacts, and result in complex interface requirements.

The digital hierarchy anticipates our fifth requirement for evolutionary increases in performance in two ways. First, as computing and data compression technology advances, the basic performance of Level 0 can continue to improve with higher quality encoders at the studio. This will impact the performance of the entire hierarchy. Second, as more delivery bandwidth becomes available, and as display technology advances, the digital hierarchy can accommodate open-ended growth in system performance.

This leads directly to satisfying our sixth requirement for accommodating new applications, which include out-of-the-home uses, ranging from theaters to defense applications. These additional uses of a digital hierarchy standard will serve to accelerate technology development and will provide additional economies of scale to broadcasters and consumers alike.

Conclusion

The opportunity to successfully establish a new television standard can occur only once in a lifetime. The success and longevity of NTSC can be partly attributed to the fact that a long series of performance improvements were possible within the scope of the standard, which continue to this day. This foresightedness allowed for many decades of performance improvements, which could be made without bumping into fundamental performance limitations imposed by the standard.

With HDTV, we have the opportunity not only to repeat this foresightedness, but to improve upon it. The digital hierarchy is an approach that uses the flexibility of digital systems to avoid premature obsolescence and provide for the ongoing performance improvements that will be needed during the lifetime of an HDTV standard. It is a digital approach that mimics and improves upon the characteristics of the analog continuum. Just as in analog systems, additional bandwidth can produce either more resolution or improved SNR. The various levels of the digital hierarchy provide for cost/performance tradeoffs that will enable a wide variety of products to use the HDTV standard. It inherently provides for open-ended growth of system performance and display technology, without the penalty of obsoleting an entire standard and its related infrastructure.

HDTV standards will surely be developed for all of today's video applications and delivery media. Looking into the future, it is inevitable that new delivery media and display technology will emerge, along with the continued rapid advances in digital semiconductors. These technology advances will inevitably lead to the creation of new applications for HDTV. The opportunity to establish an HDTV standard should not be wasted on a system with fixed parameters that will satisfy the needs of only one application and rapidly grow obsolete. Rather, it is time for the video industry to establish a standard that is inherently digital, incorporating all of the flexibility that this technology is capable of delivering. In the long term, we believe that this will provide tremendous benefits in the form of new product opportunities and expanding markets. The digital hierarchy concept provides a flexible, expandable approach to HDTV that will ensure the longevity of the next television standard well into the next century.

Author's note: Many of the considerations and concepts discussed in this paper became significant contributions to the development of the Advanced Digital Television (ADTV) system that is being proposed to the FCC and its Advisory Committee by the Advanced Television Research Consortium (David Sarnoff Research Center, Thomson Consumer Electronics, North American Philips, NBC, and Compression Labs Inc.)

References

1. J. H. Udelson, *The Great Television Race,* The University of Alabama Press, 1982.
2. Ibid., p. 156
3. National Telecommunications and Information Administration, U.S. Dept. of Commerce. "Advanced Television, Related Technologies, and the National Interest," March 1989.
4. H. Zimmermann, "Standard Layer Model," *Computer Network Architects and Protocols,* Ed. P. E. Green, Jr., Plenum Press: New York, 1982.

Fiber Upgrade Strategies Using High-Bit-Rate Copper Technologies for Video Delivery

D. L. Waring, D. S. Wilson, and T. R. Hsing

Abstract—Continuing advances in digital subscriber line technology are now making it possible to transport 1.5 Mb/s over the nonloaded copper loop plant, 3 to 4 Mb/s over carrier serving area loops and above 10 Mb/s over drop wiring from fiber to the curb (FTTC) systems. These bit rates will allow the local exchange carriers to enter the "video dial tone" market using highly compressed digital video. Initially, all copper access techniques can be used. One channel of VCR quality video can be provided over the nonleaded loop plant, to about 75% of homes. NTSC quality video or two channels of VCR quality video can be delivered over CSA's, to about 55% of homes. With time, the penetration of fiber into the feeder network will increase the number of customers who can receive the latter service. The establishment of a successful video dial tone offering using copper technologies should fuel demand for enhanced quality and additional channels, further accelerating deployment of fiber in the feeder network and into the distribution network in support of FTTC systems. Copper drops served by FTTC can support multiple simultaneous channels of high-quality compressed digital video.

I. Introduction

OVER the past decade the telecommunications industry has accelerated deployment of fiber-based transmission systems. Fiber is well on its way to displacing copper as the transmission medium of choice in the long-haul network. In the local exchange network, fiber is now being used to provide access to many large business customers. Most downtown metropolitan areas have fiber rings in place or planned, providing gigibits-per-second capacities. In more suburban settings, fiber is beginning to penetrate the feeder network, providing high bandwidth to remote electronic hub sites. Several years of intensive research and development are now making Fiber to the Curb (FTTC) systems cost-effective for providing conventional copper-based voice telephone service in new-construction applications. Deployment of FTTC systems marks the beginning of displacement of copper in the distribution portion of the network serving smaller business and residential customers.

Scientists and engineers quickly recognized the tremendous potential of fiber. Not only is the bandwidth potential orders of magnitude greater than copper phone lines, but fiber is immune to most interference mechanisms that plague wire pair transmission, such as crosstalk between pairs within a cable and coupling of impulse noise and induction of ac power line currents into the conductors. Thus a single fiber to the residence holds the potential of providing all the bandwidth necessary for access to an advanced, information age network providing a broad range of voice, data and video services.

It has become increasingly recognized by policy makers that a fiber-based broad-band network infrastructure is necessary for a healthy, increasingly services-based business economy, and that ubiquitous extension of such a network to smaller businesses and residences is crucial. Access to broad-band service capabilities will play an important role in enabling smaller companies to remain competitive, will facilitate environmentally friendly work-at-home arrangements and will bring about "distance learning" and other educational capabilities. Administrations around the world are looking for ways to evolve their voice-based public networks toward flexible, high bandwidth Information Age networks.

The cornerstone of this strategy has been rightfully focused on fiber. But progress has been slowed by simple economics, in which relatively expensive optoelectronics equipment, although continuing to decline in price, is still more expensive than copper-based transmission equipment for most narrow-band services. Thus, operating companies continue to deploy copper cable to meet demand for voice services [1]. Although it would be strategically desirable to meet this service demand with fiber, there is strong business pressure to meet existing service demand in the most cost-effective way possible. This business reality is being exacerbated by the recent trend toward deregulation around the globe, with less government subsidization and a stronger correlation between the price a customer is charged for a particular service with the actual cost of that service.

The industry has pursued at least two strategies to accelerate deployment of fiber. Intensive research and development continues to drive down the cost of fiber-based transmission systems. The industry is very close to achieving first-cost parity with copper for providing voice or plain ordinary telephone service (POTS). This marks the beginning of the end for the copper distribution network, since new service demand and retrofit of deteriorating copper plant will together eventually drive copper out of the network. However, since the annual service growth and retrofit rates are a few percent of the total embedded base of lines, several decades will be required to convert the network on this basis.

A second strategy is to identify and expedite introduction of new broad-band services which require increased bandwidth and generate new revenues. The new revenues can then be used to drive fiber deployment. This scenario has led to rapid deployment of fiber access to business customers. For residential customers in suburban areas, there has been

Manuscript received June 10, 1992; revised July 17, 1992.
The authors are with Bellcore, Morristown, NJ 07962.
IEEE Log Number 9203610.

Reprinted from *IEEE J. Lightwave Technol.*, vol. 10, no. 11, pp. 1743–1750, Nov. 1992.

a "chicken and egg" problem, in which many experts believe higher bandwidth services will generate significant new revenues once ubiquitous broad-band access is economically available, but initial service demand isn't sufficient to justify fiber deployment.

A possible exception is entertainment video, which is a well-established market generating billions of dollars in sales annually. The market is very competitive and likely to become increasingly so with the well-established broadcast, cable television, theater and VCR tape markets, and new entries such as direct broadcast satellite. Entry of the Local Exchange Carriers (LEC's) into entertainment video seemed unlikely from a regulatory point of view until just recently. The FCC has been promoting LEC entry into "video dial tone," a switched video service in which a user chooses among a wide selection of video material and receives real-time response. Some members of Congress are also supportive of LEC video delivery, and it is possible that the LEC's will enter the market at some point in the future. FTTC architectures can be upgraded to deliver video over the same fiber that provides POTS to a residence, and there is much active research in this area, [2], [3].

A third strategy to upgrade the network is now emerging and will be the focus of this paper. Continuing advances in adaptive filtering, parallel processing, channel coding techniques and very large scale integration (VLSI) are making it possible to transmit much higher bit rates over the embedded copper plant than were previously thought possible. The digital subscriber line (DSL) developed for ISDN Basic Rate Access transmits 160 kb/s over the nonloaded copper plant. The high-bit-rate digital subscriber line (HDSL) has just become commercially available and will provide DS1-rate (1.544 Mb/s) access over two carrier serving area (CSA) loops [4]. The asymmetric digital subscriber line (ADSL) is being actively studied with the objective of providing one-way 1.5 Mb/s delivery from the network to the customer, a low-speed digital return channel and conventional analog POTS, all over a single nonloaded telephone line. These emerging high-bit-rate copper technologies are making it possible to utilize existing copper loops to introduce new wide-band service capabilities. Equally rapid advances in video compression are making it feasible to deliver a limited video capability, where one channel of "VCR" quality video can be received over an ordinary phone line.

In this paper we focus on how recent advances in high-bit-rate copper technology, coupled with advances in video compression, are making it possible to begin to offer limited video and other wide-band service capabilities to residential customers, and how these new copper-based technologies will coexist with and support the emergence of fiber in the access network. We begin in Section II with a brief overview of the access network, to better understand how we can gain maximum utility from the embedded copper base during the transition period. In Section III we briefly describe fundamentals of high-bit-rate copper technology. Section IV describes the ADSL and how it can be used to cost-effectively introduce new compressed video and other wide-band services. An important attribute of this approach is that investment in upgrading the network can be made incrementally, using

copper facilities already in place and adding access electronics as needed on a per-customer basis. However, the capabilities provided by ADSL will be limited, and as demand for service grows fiber will be required to support enhanced video quality and multiple simultaneous channels. Section V describes how hybrid architectures, consisting of fiber-based remote electronics feeding ADSL and very-high-bit-rate asymmetric digital subscriber lines (VADSL's) can provide increasing amounts of ubiquitous bandwidth as fiber penetrates the distribution network. Section VI concludes with the authors' thesis that high-bit-rate copper technologies will play an important role in supporting the evolution of fiber in the residential access network by increasing the speed and ubiquity with which the LEC's can offer new video and wide-band services, helping to build a base of service demand that will in turn accelerate additional fiber deployment.

II. PERSPECTIVE ON THE ACCESS NETWORK

A few years after inventing the telephone, Alexander Graham Bell patented twisted pair wiring (1881). Since then, the worldwide subscriber loop plant has grown to become one of the world's most valuable technological assets. For the U.S. public network, there are over 140 million subscriber access lines, representing an investment of over $80 billion. Thus there is significant motivation to find ways to utilize this asset fully. To do so requires a knowledge of copper plant topology.

Cables are designed to limit crosstalk. The tip and ring conductors are twisted into a pair, and pairs with different twist lengths are stranded together into a binder group, typically consisting of 25 to 50 pairs. Cables emanating from a central office are made up of many binder groups. These feeder cables run to a feeder-distribution interface (FDI) where smaller distribution cables begin to fan out to businesses and residences. A typical telephone line consists of many sections of cable of different gauges spliced together, including bridged taps which are open-ended pairs intentionally placed for service flexibility or resulting from service churn. The wide variation in loop make-ups results in considerable variability in transmission characteristics from loop to loop. To service rural customers, load coils are placed on long loops to add inductance to the pair which in turn flattens the voice channel response. This comes at the expense of severe attenuation above the voice channel, which ends around 4000 Hz. Load coils can be found on any length loop, but they are generally not used until loops exceed 18 kft in length. Fig. 1 depicts the nature of the loop plant today.

Telephone companies are beginning to mechanize their loop records, but the great bulk of loop make-ups are manually recorded on drawings called plats. Furthermore, service churn and maintenance activity result in multiple rearrangements in the field which aren't always accurately updated in the records. Loop transmission systems can only work over loops of certain maximum length, depending on wire gauge and bridged tap make-up. Determining whether a given loop "qualifies," either by direct measurement or by looking at cable records, is an expensive and time-consuming process. However, it is a simpler matter just to determine whether a loop is loaded or

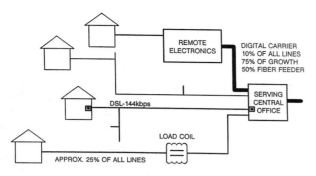

Fig. 1.   Existing U.S. loop plant.

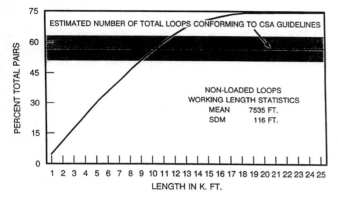

Fig. 2.   Make-up of nonloaded copper loop plant from 1983 loop survey.

By the early 1980's most companies were deploying DLC using the CSA guidelines. Today a little over 10% of all POTs lines are served from DLC remote terminals. And more than half of the new growth in voice service is now being provisioned by DLC. In some wire centers, loops emanating directly from the Central Office have been qualified for the CSA compliance, such that the area immediately surrounding the office can be thought of as a CSA. Thus, with time, telephone companies will have an increasing proportion of their nonloaded plant pre-qualified for CSA compliance. Loop transmission systems that can operate over the CSA can then be quickly provisioned. An estimated 55% of the loop plant will conform to CSA guidelines (Fig. 2), but only a portion of this population is currently qualified in records as CSA complaint.

III.   Emergence of Digital Subscriber Line Technology

High-performance transmission over copper loops requires precision equalization and echo cancellation in order to restore distorted signals. Historically this treatment was provided with electronic circuitry which could be adjusted for optimal performances on a given loop. This is necessary because, as we have seen, loop make-ups can vary significantly. In the 1970s provisioning of transmission equipment required considerable manual intervention by trained telephone company personnel. Detailed settings were calculated in design centers, based on loop make-ups, but often it was necessary to make additional measurements in the field in order to fine tune equalizers and echo cancellers. In the late 1970's this process was being automated by smart test sets which would excite the loop, make measurements, calculate settings and automatically download them into the equipment. But about that same time the application of adaptive filtering techniques began to emerge as an even more promising technology.

Adaptive filtering is a broad discipline with many commercial applications. Adaptive filtering was being utilized in the voice-band modem field, and scientists and engineers began to look at its application to transmission of digital signals over subscriber loops. An architecture called the digital subscriber line (DSL), shown in Fig. 3, emerged in the early 1980s, which uses self-adaptive digital equalizers and echo cancellers. As the fields of digital signal processing and VLSI continued to experience rapid advance, the equalizers and echo cancellers used in a DSL were able to achieve increasingly high levels of performance cost-effectively.

The DSL offers several significant benefits for the subscriber loop application. Since the DSL filters are self-adaptive, telephone company personnel simply install the units and turn on power. If there is not too much loss caused by excessively long loops, the electronics will automatically adjust themselves for optimal transmission on that given loop. As an example, the equalizer adaptation algorithms typically minimize an error signal at the digital detector and in so doing compensate for the particular make-up of the loop to which it is connected, including attenuation and rolloff due to length and multiple reflections due to gauge changes and bridged taps. Crosstalk noise is also simultaneously minimized. Furthermore, these

not, since cables tend to be loaded in bulk and the records can be accessed more quickly and are generally more accurate. Since most nonloaded loops do not exceed 18 kft (5.49 km) in length, there is great utility in a loop transmission system that can achieve 18 kft coverage. Then the loop provisioning process consists of simply selecting a spare nonloaded loop, of any makeup, serving the customer site. Fig. 2, derived from the 1983 Loop Survey [5], shows that about 75% of the loop plant is nonloaded, and practically all of it is less than 18 kft in length.

For ranges shorter than 18 kft, a complicated loop qualification process is necessary. However, the telephone companies have begun this process for carrier serving areas (CSA's). CSA guidelines were developed in the 1970s in conjunction with deployment of Digital Loop Carrier (DLC) [6]. A DLC system provides voice service from a remote terminal placed in the outside plant. The remote terminal time division multiplexes voice channels together and transports them back to the Central Office over T-carrier or, increasingly, over fiber in the feeder route. Remote terminals are strategically placed near clusters of customers, shortening the copper loops used to provide analog voice service. CSA guidelines disallow loaded loops and limit the length of nonloaded loops to up to 9 kft (2.74 km) of 26 gauge or 12 kft (3.65 km) of 24 gauge cable. The number and lengths of allowable bridged taps are also restricted [7]. These length restrictions limit transmission and signaling loss and allow for cost-reduced channel unit design. The architects of the CSA guidelines also recognized that the shorter, better controlled loops would be more amenable to supporting emerging digital services.

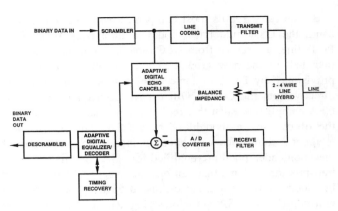

Fig. 3. Typical DSL transceiver.

adaptive systems continue to track the channel with time so that as a particular loop's characteristics change, due to temperature variations for example or as the crosstalk characteristics affecting that loop change, the DSL will continuously adjust itself, always seeking optimal performance.

By the early 1980s many research and exploratory development organizations were developing DSL's. At that time 56 kb/s data service was being deployed and the focus of the DSL effort was to provide voice service and digital data service. Digital switching was rapidly penetrating the network, and there was a strategy to digitize the last link to the customer, making possible an end-to-end all digital network. Common channel signaling was also emerging as a way to avoid problems arising from in-band signaling techniques and to increase network flexibility and features. The DSL work was focused by the new ANSI Committee, where a standard was initiated for ISDN Basic Rate Access [8]. This effort resulted in the definition of a 160 kb/s standard, broken into two 64 kb/s Bearer or "B" channels and a 16 kbt/s Delta or "D" channel for signaling purposes. The final 16 kb/s is used for framing and overhead functions by the network. An important part of the ISDN deliberations was detailed analysis to ensure that the DSL could achieve 18 kft coverage, thus covering virtually all of the nonloaded loop plant.

As the ISDN standard neared completion and semiconductor vendors began developing single chip DSLs, researchers began to look at even higher bit rate applications. One of the first to emerge was the high-bit-rate digital subscriber line or HDSL. HDSL is a transparent replacement for T-carrier, used in the access network for providing DS1 private line service. In many cases DS1 service is provided to large businesses directly with fiber, but a substantial fraction of the service is still being provisioned by T-carrier. T-carrier requires considerable engineering, to remove bridged taps and segregate binder groups. HDSL will provide repeaterless DS1 access over CSA loops, without bridged tap removal, without binder group separation and without repeaters. From a technology point of view, HDSL is a relatively straightfoward extension of the techniques used in the DSL for basic rate access. The DS1 signal rate requires about an order of magnitude increase in throughput over the DSL. It is currently not possible to achieve this capacity over 18 kft loops in the presence of crosstalk. Therefore attention became focused on the CSA as a range

of operation for the HDSL. Two pairs are used in an HDSL, where each pair carries half of the DS1 payload. The baud rate of the HDSL is thus about 5 times faster than the DSL, requiring faster signal processing hardware and larger numbers of filter taps. However, just in the few years since development of the DSL, VLSI advances are now making it possible to implement these more powerful HDSL transceivers on a single chip. Field trials of commercial HDSL systems are now being conducted [9].

The focus of the DSL was to digitize the local loop and to provide "narrow-band" voice and data services. The HDSL is one of several access technologies a telephone company can use to provide DS1 service, a service currently used almost exclusively by business customers. During the development of HDSL there was considerable interest in its applicability to residential customers, but the HDSL architecture is not optimally suited to a residential setting. The need for two pairs and the CSA range limit are not significant restrictions in a business setting, but many residential areas are beyond CSA range and have ratios of pairs per living unit as low as 1.3. The desire to deliver wide-band services to the residence led to a Bellcore proposal for the asymmetric digital subscriber line (ADSL).

IV. ADSL FOR VIDEO AND OTHER WIDE-BAND SERVICES OVER COPPER

The ADSL provides a new asymmetric digital transport capability to the residence. In one direction, from the network to the customer, 1.5 Mb/s of digital data is delivered. Digital communication in the reverse direction is much slower, somewhere in the range of 9.6 to 16 kb/s. This low-speed control channel is sufficient to pass keystrokes and mouse movements into the network, and the network can respond in real-time.

The ADSL will modulate the digitally encoded data channels and place them above the voice-band, enabling conventional analog voice service or POTS to operate at baseband. The objective is for ADSL to be transparent to POTS service, with the ringing and signaling voltages passing through the ADSL units to the station sets. If local power fails, the asymmetric digital service will go down, but POTS will still operate normally.

This architecture results in three separate signal components appearing simultaneously on one pair. The three channels are indicated in Fig. 4. Their spectra are separated in frequency by line coupling and filtering circuitry, with the POTS operating at baseband, the low-speed control channel operating above the voice-band, and the high-speed signal operating above that. Several modulation schemes and bandwidth allocations are being studied. The tradeoffs are complex, involving issues of severe loop loss at the extremes of the nonloaded plant, spectral compatibility with other services in the plant, impulse noise at the residence, coupling of POTS signaling transients into the digital receivers and radio frequency interference [10]. Fig. 5 shows the overlapping spectra of the DSL for ISDN Basic Rate Access, HDSL and conventional T-carrier. The industry is working to resolve this complex set of technical feasibility issues. Activity is now being focused by an ADSL Study Project in ANSI Working Group T1E1.4.

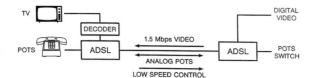

Fig. 4. ADSL architecture.

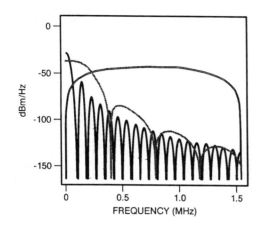

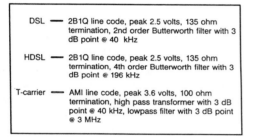

DSL	——	2B1Q line code, peak 2.5 volts, 135 ohm termination, 2nd order Butterworth filter with 3 dB point @ 40 kHz
HDSL	——	2B1Q line code, peak 2.5 volts, 135 ohm termination, 4th order Butterworth filter with 3 dB point @ 196 kHz
T-carrier	——	AMI line code, peak 3.6 volts, 100 ohm termination, high pass transformer with 3 dB point @ 40 kHz, lowpass filter with 3 dB point @ 3 MHz

Fig. 5. Spectral occupancy of loop transmission systems.

The asymmetric capability of the ADSL will be ideal for advanced videotex services [11]. Databases and high-resolution graphics can be rapidly manipulated by the user. The emergence of video disc-based multimedia applications, such as digital video interactive (DVI) and compact disc interactive (CD-I), will be synergistic with the ADSL. Since the raw data rate of a compact disc player is around 1.5 Mb/s, users can run applications across the public network with the same level of performance as a local copy. Fig. 6 shows a network architecture for such a gateway service. As software applications and application databases continue to proliferate, expand and change rapidly with time, leasing of services across the network may become attractive, somewhat of a throwback to the days of leased access to mainframe computers.

Remarkable advances in video compression have come about in just the last few years. Several standards bodies have been working on algorithms to compress digital video. CCITT's recommendation H.261 was developed for real-time video teleconferencing. This algorithm is capable of running over a range of transmission rates, from 64 kb/s up to 2.048 Mb/s. Although the algorithm was designed for a two-way videoconference, certain applications may emerge in which there is just one direction of video transmission.

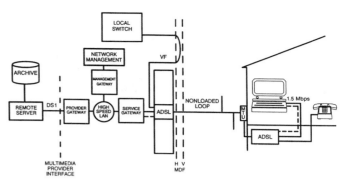

Fig. 6. ADSL in a multimedia application.

For example, educational applications are envisioned in which a lecture is encoded in real-time and transmitted to remote classrooms and students at home [12]. A rate of 1.5 Mb/s will provide sufficient quality of coverage of the lecturer and the blackboard or visuals such as used on an overhead projector.

The ISO Joint Photographic Experts Group or JPEG has developed a compression standard for still-image applications such as graphic rates, color facsimile, and desk-top publishing. Another video compression standard, the ISO Moving Picture Experts Group or MPEG recommendation, was developed for storage of full-motion video. Both JPEG and MPEG were developed for use with common mass storage devices such as Winchester disc drives, optical discs and compact disc ROM (CD-ROM) devices. These standards along with H.261 and resultant low cost coders and decoders will help stimulate and support sophisticated multimedia and education applications.

But the MPEG standard has grown beyond its computer-based origins. At higher bit rates, MPEG video is of sufficient quality for entertainment purposes such as viewing movies. Intensive research over the last several years has brought MPEG video, compressed to around 1.3 Mbit/s, to the threshold of "VCR" quality. To be of VCR quality, non-technical subjects have to rate MPEG video as having picture quality comparable to a VHS tape played in a conventional VCR. The 1.3 Mb/s rate allows for compressed high-quality audio and overhead to all be delivered within the bandwidth of a DS1 signal. Thus, using ADSL, a movie-on-demand service can be provided in which a customer receives a menu of available selections, pages through the menu or other aids such as movie reviews, makes a selection and receives the movie on command. The MPEG standard also accommodates pause and even fast-forward and fast-reverse features. A possible getting started network architecture for such a service is shown in Fig. 7. This scenario has only become possible within the last several years through advances in ADSL and MPEG, and is now drawing much attention as a way for LEC's to begin offering video services.

Video dial tone using ADSL will have its limitations. Only one channel can be offered and the quality will not be sufficient for enhanced television formats having expanded resolution. Customers on loaded loops cannot receive service. When encoding a movie off-line, the MPEG parameters can be

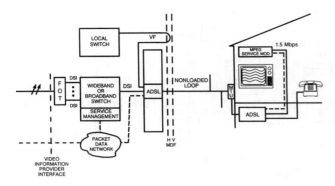

Fig. 7. ADSL in a video dial tone application.

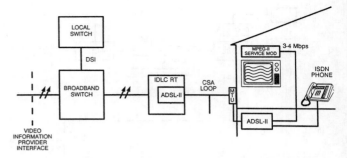

Fig. 8. Higher speed ADSL for fiber-fed CSA applications.

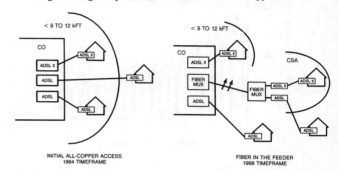

Fig. 9. One or two channels of digital video supported by ADSL and ADSL-II.

optimized manually on a scene-by-scene basis, much as is done for colorization. However, when using real-time hardware encoders such as at live events, this fine tuning will not be possible and picture quality may suffer.

Offsetting these disadvantages are several attractive aspects of an ADSL-based video dial tone offering. The nonloaded loop plant represents over 100 million potential U.S. customers and the facilities are already in place. The ADSL and MPEG electronics can be added on a per-customer basis, thus limiting up-front investment. The public switched network is well suited to video dial tone applications, and although only one channel can be provided over ADSL, if the inventory of available movies is large and if access is on demand this offering may be satisfactory to a significant percentage of customers.

An ADSL-based video on demand offering may provide the LEC's with the best way to enter the video entertainment market in the near future at a competitive price. To provide a full range of video services, however, will require higher bandwidth. This bandwidth will be provided by fiber. Fiber is beginning to penetrate the feeder plant, primarily in conjunction with the deployment of digital loop carrier (DLC) in the residential environment. Penetration of fiber-fed DLC is still relatively low, serving about 5% of residential customers today. But DLC has become the vehicle of choice for provisioning new voice service demand and over the next decade the provisioning of fiber-fed CSA's will grow. This leads to the feasilibity of higher speed ADSL's, operating over the shorter CSA loops.

Early feasibility studies indicate that bit rates of 3 to 4 Mb/s may be possible over CSA's. This higher rate will allow for simultaneous viewing of two different channels within a home, or one channel of higher quality video. An MPEG-II standards effort is now underway, examining compression algorithms for digital video at nominal bit rates of between 3 to 10 Mb/s. At 3 to 4 Mb/s, MPEG-II video approaches NTSC quality and could support improved or enhanced television receivers (Full HDTV, however, will require 16 Mb/s or more). Thus an ADSL-II architecture could be defined, supporting one-way delivery of between 3 to 4 Mb/s in addition to a narrow-band full-duplex channel for control, and conventional POTS operating at baseband. Alternatively, the high-speed channel could operate above ISDN Basic Rate Access, as depicted in Fig. 8. In this case the ISDN "D" channel would be used for control of the 3–4 Mb/s service.

V. A FIBER/COPPER EVOLUTION OF THE ACCESS NETWORK

ADSL can potentially provide one channel of VCR-quality video to customers on nonloaded loops to about 75% of homes. ADSL-II can potentially provide 2 channels of VCR-quality video or one channel of NTSC quality video to about 55% of homes. Initially most of these latter customers will be located within a short distance from wire centers, and loop qualification will be necessary in many cases to ensure customer loops meet CSA guidelines. This all-copper getting started scenario is shown in Fig. 9(a).

As provisioning based on CSA guidelines increases and as fiber penetrates the feeder network, more customers can potentially be served by ADSL-II, as depicted in Fig. 9(b). This evolution has the advantage that, while fiber enhances the service-providing capability of the LEC's, it is not necessary to deploy fiber to begin entering the video market. A significant base of customers can be reached by copper only, allowing the LEC's to establish a presence as a viable video distribution channel. Once a market base is established, it will help to drive the evolution toward increasing fiber penetration of the feeder network to support more service capability to more customers.

The market for video on demand could help stimulate the conversion of customers currently served by long loaded loops to be upgraded to fiber-fed remote electronics. Although it would be expensive to shorten these loops and remove load coils, this may be the least expensive method to provide higher bandwidth to many of these typically scattered, rural customers. Thus the number of homes served by loaded loops, currently 25%, would begin to shrink as customers receive wide-band digital service.

In the latter half of the 1980s, the telecommunications industry invested heavily in research and development of fiber

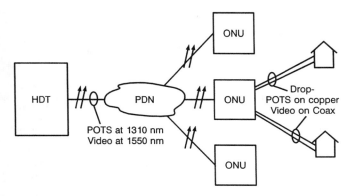

Fig. 10. Video upgrade to FTTC systems using wave division multiplexing.

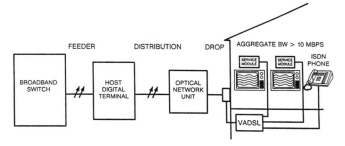

Fig. 11. VADSL technology supporting FTTC.

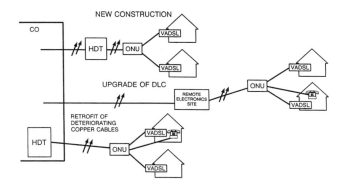

Fig. 12. VADSL and fiber in the distribution network supporting integrated broad-band access.

to the curb (FTTC) systems, searching for components and architectures that would reduce costs. Today, FTTC systems can provide POTS service as cost-effectively as traditional copper loops for certain situations. FTTC systems can achieve first-cost parity with copper where customer densities can support approximately 4 to 8 living units per optical network unit. FTTC costs will continue to drop with time and deployment will accelerate through this decade. LEC's will strategically position their access network by provisioning POTS service with FTTC as soon as it becomes financially viable. FTTC systems can be easily upgraded to provide wide-band and broad-band services. Fig. 10 shows one way to upgrade, using a different wavelength to transport digital video over the same fiber that provides POTS service. Similar techniques can be used to transport more conventional analog video. A separate coaxial drop can be installed from the optical network unit to deliver new video services to the residence. The fiber backbone and the coaxial drop have the potential to deliver multiple channels per household and there is sufficient bandwidth to support HDTV formats.

Another option for the final drop connection to the customer is to continue to use twisted pair. Drop lengths of typically 500 ft to up to 1000 ft could support bit rates in excess of 10 Mb/s using very high-bit-rate asymmetric digital subscriber line or VADSL technology. A VADSL could provide several channels of one-way high-quality video, along with narrowband ISDN services as depicted in Fig. 11. If the customer still wants to maintain conventional POTS service, a separate drop can be used to provide the new video capabilities. Or, the existing drop could be reused with the customer migrating to ISDN Basic Rate Service. Some experts believe there should and will be a trend toward integration of communications equipment within the customer premises; on the premises there will be local area communications with control functions centralized at a gateway to service providers, such as the local telephone company, the cable television provider, a cellular/microcellular transceiver and a broadcast receiver. A VADSL architecture, in which all LEC services are delivered to the customer across one interface, may have benefit in such an environment. Back in the network, the single VADSL termination in the optical network unit may have cost advantages compared to multiple drops, particularly as voice and video services become increasingly digitized.

Some lawmakers and regulators are encouraging an environment in which the LECs could transport many channels of broadcast video, similar to current multi-channel cable offerings. The most probable architecture for providing such a service is one with fiber in the feeder and fiber and coax in the distribution plant, with early offerings providing analog video, migrating with time to digital video. It may be that the experience and strength of the LEC's in the area of switching will drive them more toward switched video capabilities. Studies have shown that a maximum of 3 to 4 simultaneous channels are required per household. Thus 3 or 4 channels of video dial tone of sufficient quality, each offering access to a large array of programming, may serve the needs of many customers. Fig. 12 depicts how such a network could evolve. FTTC will begin to penetrate the network in new-construction and retrofit applications. Continued deployment of next-generation DLC systems will drive fiber into the feeder network, presenting additional opportunity to deploy FTTC systems. The LEC's can provide a robust video dial tone capability using VADSL technology over short drop wiring. In some cases this will be bundled with ISDN Basic Rate Access, but if the customer prefers, conventional POTS service will be maintained.

VI. CONCLUSIONS

The ADSL will allow the LEC's to use the existing embedded copper plant to begin offering video dial tone services to residential customers. Since existing telephone lines are used and ADSL electronics are added on a per-customer basis, the access costs are relatively low and can be deferred until time of service growth. This strategy will allow the LEC's to enter the video business and establish a base of customers. With time, demand for multiple simultaneous channels and higher quality video will grow. This expanded capability can again be provided with an all copper "ADSL-II" access technology, reaching more than half of all residences. Successful establishment of a video market, and subsequent growth, will accelerate penetration of fiber in the feeder network, over and above its current growth due to provisioning of voice services from digital loop carrier. Fiber in the feeder network will in turn support ADSL-II access to additional customers, potentially including those who previously received voice service over loaded loops. Continued growth in demand for higher quality video dial tone services could be supported by FTTC systems, where fiber now extends into the distribution network and VADSL technology is used to deliver multiple simultaneous channels of high-quality video over drop wiring.

This scenario is one of incremental increases in access bandwidth to the residence, in conjunction with increasing penetration of fiber in the loop plant. High-bit-rate copper technology can help LEC's grow the base of demand for wide-band services in a methodical fashion, a demand which ultimately will be supported by fiber.

REFERENCES

[1] "Domestic review and forecast," Telephony, December 16, 1991, p. 16.
[2] S. S. Wagner and R. C. Menendez, "Evolutionary architectures and techniques for video distribution on fiber," IEEE Commun. Mag., p. 17, Dec. 1989.
[3] R. Olshansky and G. Joyce, "Subscriber distribution networks using compressed digital video," this issue.
[4] "High-speed digital subscriber lines," IEEE Journal on Selected Areas in Commun., vol. 9, no. 6, Aug. 1991.
[5] "Characterization of Subscriber Loops for Voice and ISDN Services (1983 Subscriber Loop Survey Results)," ST-TSY-000041, Bellcore, 1987.
[6] T. P. Byrne et al., "Positioning the subscriber loop network for digital services," IEEE Trans. on Commun., vol. COM-30, no. 9, p. 2006, Sept. 1982.
[7] TR-TSY-000057, "Functional Criterial for Digital Loop Carrier Systems, Bellcore, Issue 1, April 1987.
[8] American National Standard for Telecommunications, "Integrated Services Digital Network (ISDN)-Basic Access Interface for Use on Metallic Loops for Application on the Network Side of the NT (Layer 1 Specification)," T1.601-1988.
[9] Perspectives, p. 76, Telephony, February 24, 1992.
[10] D. L. Waring, "The asymmetric digital subscriber line (ADSL): A new transport technology for delivering wide-band capabilities to the residence," IEEE Globecom '91 Proc., pp. 1979-1986, December 2-5, 1991.
[11] R. L. Knoll, "Videotex around the globe," Bellcore exchange magazine, pp. 17-21, Mar./Apr. 1991.
[12] L. M. Gomez, "Erasing barriers to learning through telecommunications," Bellcore exchange, Nov./Dec. 1991.

Visual Telephone

Susumu Ichinose, Hiroshi Sakai, Yoshiaki Nakamura and Kumi Takita

There are growing expectations that a broadband ISDN (B-ISDN) in corporating asynchronous transfer mode (ATM) transmission, intelligent terminal, human interface and video coding technologies will be the answer to our hope for having various visual telecommunication services. The visual telephone is based on the B-ISDN, and is considered to provide almost all conceivable visual telecommunications services. To bring this visual telephone to reality, the progress of various technologies is necessary. This paper provides an outline of the visual telephone service and related technologies and the following four papers each describes one of these technologies in detail.

Foreword

In the twenty-first century, digitalization of networks will be developed further and high-speed broadband, intelligent services are expected to be realized.

In the years to come, customers will be able to easily and freely select and utilize advanced services, but to realize such services, i.e., advanced communication services, it is very important to upgrade visual communication services, intelligent services and personal services. It is easy to imagine that a personal and intelligent advanced visual communication service using visual telephones will be the most important among the above mentioned advanced communication services.

Advanced visual communication services cannot be developed alone, as shown in Fig. 1, but inevitably will require the development of network and terminal services. These network services must be backed by B-ISDN, intelligent networks and visual communication technologies.

The terminal services must made use of human interface (HI) and video coding technologies. Various visual communication services, the most important of which is the visual

telephone, can be brought into actual operation with these technologies.

This paper shows the future of the visual telephone by describing these technologies and also shows the relationship of the sub-

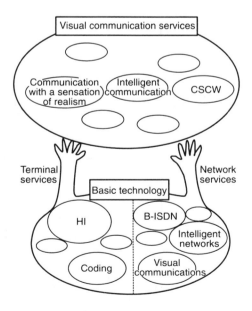

Figure 1. Services/Technologies Supporting Visual Communication Services

Reprinted with permission from *NTT Review,* vol. 5, no. 2, pp. 61–66, March 1993. © Japan Publications Trading Company.

jects covered in the four following papers.

Vision of Services in the Twenty-first Century

Advanced communication services to be realized in the twenty-first century will likely be built on three pillars: VI&P (Visual communication services , Intelligent services and Personal services).

In visual communication services, visual telephone/conferencing, video information and other services will be realized with high definition, large screen, stereoscopic displays.

In intelligent services, automatic interpretation, intelligent support and customized services will become available.

Finally in personal services, personal number service, flexible charging, privacy protection and portable telephone service will be implemented.

The realization of visual communication services in the twentieth century was pre-

dicted in the late nineteenth century. It is good for all of us that the long-waited video communication services are likely to be realized during the period from the late twentieth century to the early twenty-first century. But it is not easy to realize the services. It is expected that there will be various technological, social and cultural problems that will hinder their implementation.

Future of Network Services

3.1 Evolution Process of Networks

Telephone service networks widely used at present will be converted to ISDN (Integrated Services Digital Networks) with the further development of facsimiles, data communications and video telephones. Once the usefulness of networks is improved, there will be a greater requirement for the networks to send more information quicker and more economically. B-ISDN that allows the sending of

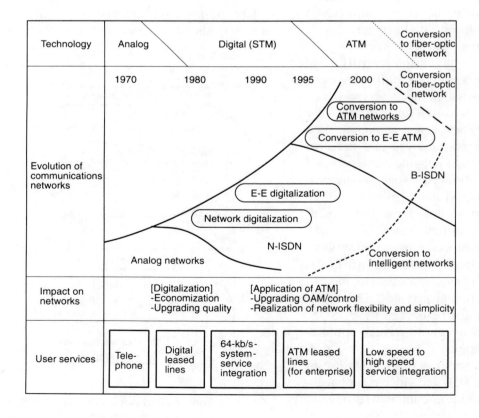

Figure 2. Evolution of Networks

broadband signals, video signals in particular, will be brought into service as the network of the twenty-first century.

Figure 2 shows evolution of networks[1].

Analog networks will be converted to ISDN from now to about the year 2000 and the age of B-ISDN is expected to come in the twenty-first century. B-ISDN, based on ATM (Asynchronous Transfer Mode) technology, allows a wide variety of communications to be made over a single network system. Once B-ISDN has become widely available, almost all information to be transported will be video, thus creating a new culture of visual communications.

3.2 Intelligent Networks

Effects are being made to make networks advanced and intelligent for providing a wide range of useful services economically, with high quality.

Intelligent networks are based on a new network architecture, and are composed of a high-level function layer including network service supervising points (NSSP) and network service points (NSP), a transmission layer where digital exchanges play central roles, and signaling subnetworks for the easy exchange of information within and between layers. Various services such as toll free service, are implemented with this configuration. Networks will start now to be quickly converted to intelligent ones, and as the sue of ATM in them increases, they will provide more visual information services.

3.3 Visual Communication Services

Visual communication services can be divided into two major forms: a two-way video communication service in which video signals are transmitted both ways, and a one-way video communication service in which video signals are transmitted one way.

(1) Two-Way Visual Communication Service

This service is needed to provide video telephone/video conferencing, and also is needed for video walls in satellite offices to visually show their environments to one another.

For this service, a network must provide a high-speed two-way digital circuit between two communicating parties, which requires upgrading of the network. This service will be first introduced for businesses and later for home use as the service areas of B-ISDN spread.

(2) One-Way Visual Communication Service

Video communication service includes not only a two-way service but also extends to a one-way service in which video signals are sent in one direction only, from the transmitting side to the receiving side. In certain areas, the demand for this service may sometimes be larger than that for two-way service. The one-way visual communication described here is not a large-scale communication medium such as broadcasting nor a one-to-one small-scale communication medium. It will be conveniently used as a medium-scale communication medium in between the large- and small-scale communication media. There is a network-casting service currently being offered that is this type of service[2]. In this network-casting service, information is replicated by the network's information copying function at the nearest point of the users and simultaneously delivered to a large number of users. In this case, the network is used in common by a large number of users to decrease charges sharply and allowing the users to enjoy the convenience of visual communications.

Perspective of Visual Telephone

4.1 Basic System

The visual telephone is different from the conventional video telephone/conferencing in that the latter is for visual communication between parties in separate locations in which the parties can only see each other's faces, while the former is for conveying as much visual information on and around the communicating parties as possible. With video telephone/conferencing, the communicating parties must keep eye contact with each other all the time but with the visual telephone they do not need to, because it utilizes as much video information on both ends as possible to convey the atmosphere to each other to the maximum extent. Its basic system is intended to build up a communication environment with a realistic sense of participation. It improves the human interface by utilizing large-screen, high-definition, stereoscopic display technology and audio processing technology, and makes high-speed, high-quality communication possible with high-efficiency video coding technology and terminal construction technology.

4.1.1 Human Interface Technology

(1) Eye-contact Display Technology

When a viewer watches a screen, it is desirable that an image displayed on the screen is always taken from an angle favorable to the viewer. Especially in face-to-face communications, it is important that the speaker's eyes meet the eyes of the listener. A method to use a half-mirror in front of the display screen has been proposed to obtain eye contact, but until now there has been a serious drawback in that the equipment required is too large. A new method has been proposed to electrically control the transparency and translucence of a liquid crystal screen, taking video pictures during the period when the screen is transparent and displaying during translucence[3], and is shown in Fig. 3. For face-to-face communication, the lines of sight of both sides should meet each other, and the study will be continued actively. This technology will be discussed in detail in one of following papers.

(2) Large Screen Display Technology

An HDTV (High definition TV) projector using liquid crystal panels has started to be seen on the market. In several years, it will be possible to project high definition television pictures. But to enjoy the pictures while working in a brightly illuminated room, the development of power saving, self-luminescence, large-screen, high-definition display technologies are necessary.

(3) Stereoscopic Display Technology

To make the sense of participation more realistic, stereoscopic display technology, together with large-screen and high-definition

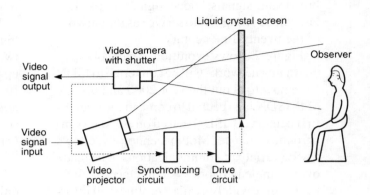

Figure 3. Eye Contact Display Technology

display technologies are also important. A stereoscopic display is a system to give a stereoscopic feeling to viewers with stereoscopic signals that are essential for the system. For this purpose, such special glasses as polarizing glasses has been used up to the present. But for face-to-face communications, putting on special glasses is not allowed because it spoils the natural appearance. A new stereoscopic display technology is proposed to overcome the drawbacks of wearing glasses[4]. This technology controls the system to always give stereoscopic images into the viewer's eyes by tracing the movement of the viewer's head. Figure 4 shows an experimental model of head-tracing-type stereoscopic display equipment.

The experimental model is the same in configuration as the input display equipment

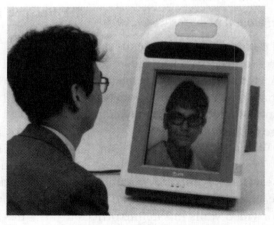

Figure 4. Stereoscopic Display Equipment

for a stereoscopic video telephone. The model contains a built-in 15-inch stereoscopic display, stereo camera, microphone/speaker, and head detection sensor. Experiments show that the observers are able to keep stereoscopic images in a wide range of positions with the experimental model.

The technologies connected with this area are expected to be further developed along with development of large-screen, flat-display technology.

There is also another high-fidelity three-dimensional display system: moving picture holography. Holography; however, has been mainly used in still pictures on dry photography plates up to now because it requires the formation of minute patterns the size of which is in the order of 1 μm. Several experiments are being carried out to make moving picture holography[5].

A three-dimensional display providing a stereoscopic image medium is expected with the development of high-density writing in the future, but considerable time will be required before actual development. The development of compression technology and finding ways to transmit enormous amounts of information are also important subjects.

4.1.2 Video Coding Methods

Direct coding, prediction, transform coding, and motion-compensation coding are the methods generally used for video coding. The methods are shown in Table 1.

These coding methods are used to encode waveforms to send and exactly reproduce into original images at the receiving end. On the other hand, intelligent coding methods are not for exactly encoding waveforms themselves but for encoding the sender's communication purpose contained in the waveforms as essential information. This will become the most important coding method of the future because it can convey more than the atmosphere at the sending end. The present level of coding is in between waveform coding and intelligent coding. The study of analysis and synthesis coding methods, which is an intermediate level, is being carried out by several research institutes in Japan and other

Table 1. Methods of Video Coding

Generation Division	Coding System	Applied Knowledge	Bit Rate
Zero Generation	Direct	Amplitude distribution	10^7–10^8
First Generation	Prediction, transform	Correlation between picture elements	10^6–10^7
Second Generation	Motion compensation	Motion information	10^4–10^6
Third Generation	Analysis/synthesis	2D-structure information	10^3–10^4
Forth Generation		3D-structure information	10^2–10^3
Fifth Generation	Intelligent	Concept model	10^1–10^2

countries. This method will be described in detail in a following paper.

4.1.3 Terminal Configuration Technology

The configuration of the visual telephone should provide a communication bus, control bus and video/audio signal lines as external interfaces as shown in Fig. 5 for connections with other systems such as an external camera, a large-screen display and a work station[7]. With this configuration, a work station can be connected to a basic module to provide various services through these interfaces.

The basic module is composed of a communication adaptor, media multiplexer, CODECs and terminal communication controller. The communication adaptor handles ATM transmission and call-processing procedures of B-ISDN. ATM transmission is carried out by sending packets called "cells" on an ATM 150 Mb/s transmission circuit. The media multiplexer multiplexes stereo audio signals of a bit rate between 64 kb/s and 1.5 Mb/s, and video signals between 6 and 32 Mb/s into a single channel. For ATM transmission, the function to establish and recover frame-synchronism which function detects loss of information and protects CODECs from malfunctioning is required because transmitted information is discarded when traffic is congested.

A CODEC carries out coding and decoding of video or audio signals at a speed corresponding to required services. The video signals are digital TV signals of studio quality that meet CCIR Rec. 601 (Encoding parameters of digital television for studios), and signals of HDTV quality are possible. The audio signals can be of high-fidelity sound

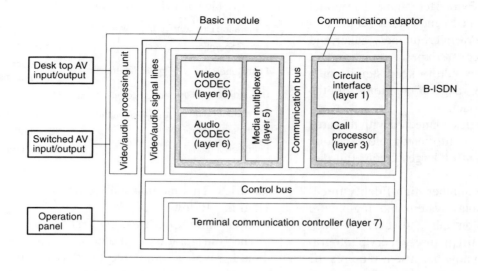

Figure 5. An Example of Terminal Configuration

equivalent to that of stereophonic record players or of a sound equivalent to that of telephone conversation. The terminal communication controller controls the functions of the basic module according to call origination/termination or terminal operation by users. This configuration for visual telephone terminals allows a visual communications service with highly advanced functions.

4.2 Applications

Many applications can be developed from the basic system of the visual telephone. Among the basic technologies for the applications, a technology for separated parties to work together through a communications network and a technology to check through long video recordings or quickly retrieve necessary information out of it are important. The fundamental technologies of collaboration and video handling on which the above mentioned technologies are based will be discussed in detail in the following papers.

In this section, some unique applications are explained.

(1) CSCW System

Generally speaking, activities of the staff in an organization are usually collaborations within small groups. The CSCW (Computer-Supported Cooperative Work) system is used to help carry out such collaboration for a party utilizing computers and networks. A system for a party to effectively utilize this CSCW by holding a teleconference with multiple parties in separate locations is called PMTC (Personal Multimedia Multipoint Teleconference) system[8].

This system allows multiple parties in separate locations to effectively work together by simultaneously displaying on a large screen at each location pictures from the sending party and ones from the receiving parties. This type of collaboration systems will quickly become popular in the near future.

(2) Intelligent Communication System

An intelligent communication system which utilizes intelligent coding technology is proposed[6]. Figure 6 shows configuration of the system.

In this system, individual databases for individual users and a common database for the whole system are distributed to different locations, and users exchange data between these databases as necessary. The users can receive data they need by converting data obtained from those databases into a form suitable for displays they use and combining them on such displays.

(3) Systems for Telecommunications with Realistic Sensation

Several systems have been proposed to realize virtual reality. In these systems, head mount displays and data gloves are employed to allow the operator to make the robots do the actual work instead of the operator[9][10]. For communications use, there is a system to provide an atmosphere as if users in separate locations were attending a meeting together, sitting around a conference table, by displaying the pictures of individual users on corresponding TV monitors[11].

Figure 7 shows a teleconferencing system with realistic sensation, which system consolidates all related technologies. This is a system that allows teleconferencing with realistic sensation by utilizing three-dimensional video information, audio, characters and all other means[12].

Figure 8 illustrates an example of a future communication system with realistic sensation. It shows a scene that an observer on the earth is talking with a crew of a space station about a base construction plan on the moon with the help from humanized computer graphics robot (CG)[13]. It is expected that these communication systems with realistic sensation become a reality in the twenty-first century.

Conclusion

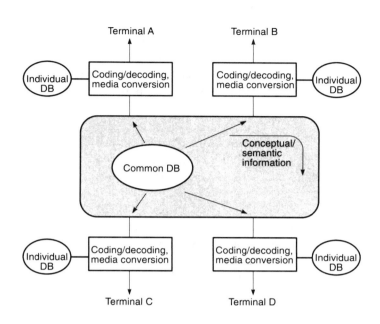

Figure 6. Intelligent Communication System

This paper has described perspectives for the future of visual communication services taking the visual telephone as the central topic. There are countless possibilities for the future of visual communication services; they cannot be foreseen from the direction of current telecommunications services.

Surely, visual communication services will

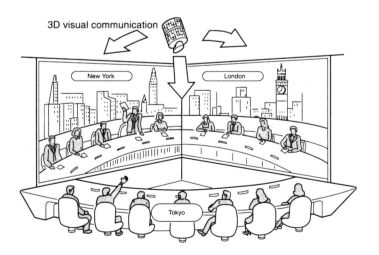

Figure 7. An Example of Teleconferencing System with Realistic Sensation

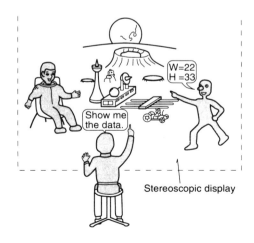

Figure 8. An Example of Communication System of a Realistic Sensaion

485

create a new type of culture. The authors also hope that visual communication services will lead to a more prosperous society.

In addition, the four important technologies described in this paper will be described in detail in the following four papers.

References

(1) H. Ishikawa, et al.: "Prospect of Advanced Telecommunication Network and Services," NTT Gijutsu Journal, Vol.1, No.9, pp.4-8, Dec, 1989 (in Japanese).

(2) T. Tanaka, et al.: "A Study of the NET-WORK CASTING in B-ISDN," 1992 Spring Nat. Conv. IEICE, D-703, 1992 (in Japanese).

(3) Shiwa, et al.: "A Large-Screen Visual Telecommunication Device Enabling Eye Contact," SID 91 Digest, pp.327-328 (1991).

(4) S. Ichinose, et al.: "Head Tracking Stereoscopic Display Technique," Trans. IEICE, Vol. J73-C-II, No. 3, pp.218-225, 1990 (in Japanese).

(5) K. Satou, et al.: "Basic Research of Holographic Television", 1991 Nat. Conv. JSAP, 28p-A-14, 1991 (in Japanese).

(6) H. Harashima: "Intelligent Image Coding and Communication," J.Inst. TV Eng., Vol. 42, No.6, pp.519-525, 1988 (in Japanese).

(7) Y. Nakamura, et al.: "A Study of Communication UIMS," 1992 Fall Nat. Conv. IEICE, A-169, 1992 (in Japanese).

(8) N. Kanemaki, et al.: "A Study of Multimedia Communication Space for Desktop Teleconferencing," 1991 Spring Nat. Conv. IEICE, GD-2, 1991 (in Japanese).

(9) S. Tachi: "Tele-Existence," J. Robotics Soc. Jpn., Vol.4, No.3, pp.295-300, 1986 (in Japanese).

(10) F. Scott: "Virtual Interface Environment", NASA Technical Report.

(11) S. Sabri, et al.: "Video Conferencing System," Proc. IEEE, Vol.73, No.4, pp.671-688 (1985).

(12) K. Akiyama, et al.: "Telecommunication System in the 21st Century," J. IEICE, Vol.73, No.12, pp.1355-1359, 1990 (in Japanese).

(13) H. Yasuda, et al.: "3-Dimensional Visual Telecommunication", J. Inst. TV Eng., Vol.43, No.8, pp.786-789, 1989 (in Japanese).

ISDN Personal Video

Paul E. Crouch
J. Al Hicks
John J. Jetzt

Desktop personal video telephony has become an area of increased interest among telecommunications professionals. This interest has been spurred by the combination of increased availability and lower cost for the bandwidth required for video transmission, and significant advances in video compression technology. Although analog technology current supports video telephony, the Integrated Services Digital Network (ISDN) will increase the growth and development of video telecommunications.

Introduction

ISDN's performance qualities make it an excellent and effectively noise-free transmission medium for voice, data, and video. Its error rate is on the order of 10^7 errors per transmitted bit. In addition, many ISDN interfacing arrangements have been designed to allow clear-channel communications without any processing in the network such as level changes and echo control.

Thus, ISDN provides a major advantage in terms of quality and bandwidth when compared to today's analog interface arrangements. Although it has been initially expensive, as ISDN is increasingly adopted, it will become more and more economical to operate through economies of scale. Conformity with international standards makes ISDN an even more logical choice for high quality telephone transmission.

Today the telecommunications community is thinking positively about desktop personal video telephony: real-time, two-way video and audio communication involving two or more people. Although video telephony has long been technically possible and even seriously proposed, until lately several major problems prevented its introduction, the primary one being that the bandwidth (i.e., data transmission rate) required for video transmission was prohibitively expensive and was not generally available.

Today, technology has met this challenge. Wideband transmission has become less expensive at the same time that video compression techniques have reduced the bandwidth required for video. As a result, the formerly "futuristic" video telephone is becoming a reality. As the technical and economic feasibility of videotelephony is proven, it will stop being "the wave of the future" and will move instead into the present. All signs suggest that the remainder of the Nineties will be a "video decade" where personal video will become commonplace.

We have already seen the introduction of a practical analog video telephone, the AT&T Videophone 2500, which uses the existing switched analog telephone network for its connectivity. However, significant advantages for personal video telephony can be gained by using ISDN.

Video Compression Technology and ISDN

Video compression technology has significantly reduced the bandwidth needed for video transmission. Moreover, as exemplified by the Videophone 2500, video compression technology is ready for practical, printed circuit board-sized applications that can be a part of a practical video telephone. Also, because of evolving compression standards, video compression technology also is becoming compatible with different vendors' video telephones.

High quality, economically priced cameras and displays for personal-sized video telephones are becoming available. Hence, video telephony is benefiting from the growth of demand in the consumer electronics market, i.e., from the cameras used in video camcorders, and the displays used in electronic games, and miniature TVs.

Reprinted with permission from *AT&T Technical Journal,* vol. 72, no. 1, pp. 33–40, Jan./Feb. 1993.

Transmission bandwidth is also more available and less expensive than in the past. ISDN is ideally suited to video telephony, and is being increasingly deployed. Full domestic and international ISDN connectivity is not far off.

Local video applications, even for the personal computer (PC), are now available. Thus, it is now technically possible to use the PC in the developing world of ISDN personal video. ISDN terminal products with standards-based digital transmission are already appearing on business desktops. Such terminals are ideal for integrating voice telephony services with personal video.

ISDN Personal Video in Society

In many ways we are already living in a video society. Certainly Cable News Network (CNN) and Music Television (MTV) have become influential in our culture. Video was once a medium where people passively watched professionally produced material. Today, however, daily use of personal video equipment such as camcorders and VCRs has become commonplace.

The proliferation of video technology has accustomed people to seeing themselves on a screen, and has overcome older habits of being "camera shy." No longer is it a novelty to see oneself on a video display. More and more, video is becoming accepted as "the next best thing to being there." In this new environment, it is natural for people to expect video telephones to become more widely available. Indeed, market studies show an emerging demand.

Also, increasing numbers of people are no longer "computer-shy." For many people, the personal computer is becoming almost as familiar as the telephone. High quality personal computer peripherals have encouraged people to expect integrated desktop solutions with entirely new dimensions of functionality, including personal video.

ISDN Personal Video in Business

Business is often quick to adopt new technologies to save money in existing operations, to seize new market opportunities, and to exploit the business potential inherent in the new technology. There is a growing demand for multimedia applications—including video—on the desktop. It is easy to see how video can increase business efficiency by adding a dimension to the ways people communicate and work today. Nor is it difficult to imagine new opportunities for video in the business world. For example, real estate brokers could share pictures on-line with prospective buyers. Banks could add "live" video tellers to remote automatic teller machines (ATMs). And travel agencies could enhance promotional descriptions with live pictures.

The Personal Uses of Video Technology

Even for those with business video experience, personal video will be a new medium. How will this new medium handle the user's needs?

Experience From Video Teleconferencing.
Many business people are accustomed to video teleconferencing. The business community has a large installed base of video teleconference rooms and equipment. Some units already "roll around," i.e., are portable or at least transportable. The next logical step is the desktop.

But personal video is more than just a smaller version of what business people are used to. In many ways, personal video has features in common with "room-to-room" video teleconferencing. A primary function of both business and personal video is communication by "talking heads," i.e., people talking face-to-face or even eye-to-eye over a video link. Teleconference users have learned that existing video teleconferencing equipment can function effectively to bring people together. In some ways, the equipment can make communication more spontaneous and more focused than face-to-face meetings. They can also make such meetings less costly in terms of time and travel.

A certain formality accompanies the room-to-room medium. The rooms are usually shared facilities with limited availability. Users must make appointments (at both ends) and leave their normal office or work space to use the rooms. This alone tends to reduce the sense of spontaneity. Seating and surroundings are often fixed; and equipment and controls often require training for effective use. When the medium and its uses are examined, personal video can be seen as more than miniaturized room teleconferencing. People expect more from desktop personal video service than they get in today's video teleconference room.

Furthermore, personal video is likely to have more diverse uses than in business-related video teleconferencing. The challenge for developers of personal video terminals is to make them adaptable to different situations while keeping them simple and user friendly.

The Personalities of Personal Video. "Face-to-face" mode comes immediately to mind when one thinks of personal video usage. This mode is the straightforward enhancement of a voice telephone call with a real time video picture of the person at the far end. There may be other modes, but this is the common denominator: personal video will always need to be person-to-person.

In the face-to-face mode, the personal video terminal will need to find a place in the user's ordinary workspace. To be accepted, personal video terminals must be designed to lend warmth, friendliness, spontaneity of use, and informality. In its own way, the video terminal must be as available and as easy to use as the voice telephone.

In the role of person-to-person communicator, personal video is an intimate medium. Personal video demands good eye contact. It should be adaptable to different lighting conditions and adjustable to different workspace "moods." Instead of the user going to the video (as in teleconferencing), the video must go to the user, who may wish to use video from different parts of the workspace.

The personal video feature controls should be friendly and obvious. The user needs to be readily aware of both the transmitted and received images. The quality of the video image should be easily adjustable. As an extension to the "mute" function in voice-only communications, the user may also need to invoke "video privacy," which allows temporary suspension of video transmission to the other end.

But personal video has modes beyond person-to-person. Sometimes it is important to see and communicate visually with the people at the other end, either individually or as a group in the teleconferencing room, to share other visual media such as pictures, applications, graphics, text, and documents. Video terminals can address this need by providing an optional graphics mode, as well as a mode for alternative video sources such as videotapes, CD players, and auxiliary cameras. These modes will be especially important for the "business personality" of personal video. They will have their own set of requirements to be successful. It should be easy to change from the face-to-face mode to the graphics or auxiliary video modes and to manipulate the features of each mode.

Residential users will have access to other "personalities" of personal video, and the various types of users in this category must be considered. Full-time work-at-home people or electronic commuters may have the same or similar needs as regular business users, but personal businesses operating from a home might have different needs. At the same time, ordinary personal callers in the residence should not be intimidated by the technology.

Technical Keys to Success

The technology is now in place to develop ISDN video terminals. Two keys to success are at hand:
- Standards being developed by the International Telegraph and Telephone Consultative Committee (CCITT) and International Standards Organization (ISO) have encouraged interoperability between and among products from different vendors.
- Low-cost custom silicon video codec chip sets, such as the AT&T Microelectronics AVP-4000 video-codec chip set, introduced in April 1992, are available.

CCITT Standards and Interoperability

Interoperability of personal video terminals will be achieved by complying with standards for ISDN and for video and audio compression.

In the 1980s, promulgating the CCITT Group 3 standard for facsimile transmission amounted to an open systems standard and was the linchpin for the phenomenal success of facsimile technology. It provided an international interoperability standard for fax communications. The fax industry went from the proprietary domain, where machines from one vendor could not operate with machines from other vendors, to the open systems domain, where all vendors' fax machines could

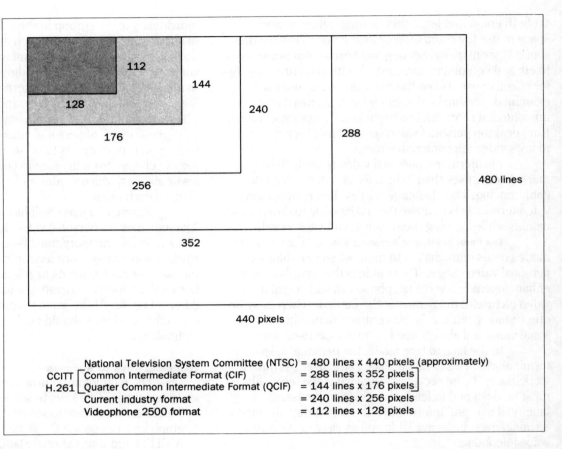

Figure 1. The relative relationship of some video processing formats. A video telephone or video conferencing system built to conform to CCITT standard H.261 must support the quarter common intermediate format (QCIF), 144 lines by 176 pixels, and, optionally, full common intermediate format (CIF), 288 lines by 352 pixels.

	National Television System Committee (NTSC)	= 480 lines x 440 pixels (approximately)
CCITT	Common Intermediate Format (CIF)	= 288 lines x 352 pixels
H.261	Quarter Common Intermediate Format (QCIF)	= 144 lines x 176 pixels
	Current industry format	= 240 lines x 256 pixels
	Videophone 2500 format	= 112 lines x 128 pixels

interoperate. By 1982, every new fax machine entering the market had Group 3 compatibility.

Similarly, in the video communications area, in December 1990 the CCITT promulgated the H-series family of standards. These included H.261, a digital video compression standard for video telephony and video conferencing. H.261 is expected to have the same effect on the video telephony and the video conferencing business during the 1990s that the Group 3 standard had on the fax business during the 1980s. Before the H.261 standard was adapted, the video telephony and video conferencing business was proprietary. All new video telephony products will probably be H.261-compatible.

The H.261 standard is often referred to as the P×64 standard, where P is an integer between 1 and 30. It covers video codecs operating from 40 kilobits per second (kb/s) to 1.92 megabits per second (Mb/s). Within the H.261 standard, the quarter common intermediate format (QCIF) is specified as the standard video

processing format for the video frame. The QCIF video frame consists of 144 lines and 176 pixels per line. The common intermediate format (CIF) is specified as an optional video processing format with 288 lines and 352 pixels per line.

CIF is different from the current domestic de facto standard video processing format in the video conferencing business, and is used by Compression Labs, Inc., PictureTel Corp., and others. That format is 240 lines and 256 pixels per line, about one quarter the resolution of the National Television System Committee (NTSC) 525-line standard. The 525-line broadcast standard produces about 480 lines of analog video output. With interlaced scanning, each of the two fields has about 240 lines. The resulting color resolution is equal to about 330 lines with 440 pixels per line.

Figure 1 illustrates the relative relationship of some video processing formats. Any video telephone or video conferencing system built to conform to H.261

Table I. CCITT H-series standards

Number	Definition
H.221	Frame structure for audiovisual services
H.230	Control and indication for audiovisual services
H.242	Establishing communication between audiovisual terminals
H.261	Video codec for audiovisual services at P×64 kb/s
H.320	Narrow-band visual telephone systems and terminal equipment

Table II. CCITT G-series audio standards

Number	Bit rate	Frequency
G.711	64 kb/s	3 kHz
G.722	64 kb/s	7 kHz (high fidelity)
G.728	16 kb/s	3 kHz

must support QCIF (144 lines by 176 pixels) and, optionally, full CIF (288 lines by 352 pixels).

H.261 processing for QCIF video frames operates as follows:

- Each input QCIF frame (up to 30 per second) is digitized and broken into one luminance subframe and two independent chrominance subframes. The luminance (Y) subframe consists of 144 lines, each containing 176 8-bit pixels.
- The chrominance sub-frames are subsampled further. Each contains 72 lines by 88 pixels of red and blue color-difference (R-Y and B-Y) signals.
- The digital compression algorithms—really the heart of the H.261 standard—now reduce the number of bits required to transmit the video. The compression scheme includes elements such as predictive coding, lossy compression by using the discrete cosine transform and quantization (i.e., not all coefficients are transmitted), motion compensation, further digital temporal and spatial filtering, and Huffman-like encoding.

CCITT H.261 is actually part of a suite of standards that includes H.221, H.230, H.242, and H.320. Table I briefly describes the content of each standard. To conform to H.261 and thus be able to interoperate with other vendors' products, a video telephone or video conferencing product must conform to all H-series standards.

An H.261-compliant video telephone or video conferencing system must also support one or more CCITT audio standards. Table II briefly outlines three G-series audio standards. These standards specify the encoding and decoding of audio signals and the compression into various bit rates. It is assumed that virtually every H.261-compliant product will support the G.711 standard for 3 kilohertz (kHz) voice at 64kb/s. While the G.722 standard for 7 kHz voice at 64 kb/s allows better audio quality, it is probable that some vendors will not choose to

implement the G.722 algorithm. In 112 to 128 kb/s applications, the G.728 standard for 3 kHz voice at 16 kb/s will probably be implemented by many vendors. It will allow more bandwidth to achieve better video quality.

H.261 also includes a mode for high resolution still frame video. In the context of 2-way video communication, this mode will allow alternative transmission of high resolution still frames. This high resolution still frame mode can be used to transmit text, graphics, drawings or photographs.

Custom Silicon Video Codec. The CCITT standards for video telephony have encouraged custom silicon development. The AT&T Microelectronics chip set (AVP-4000) consists of three chips: an encoder, decoder, and systems controller. When used with a digital signal processor, such as the DSP3210, the AVP-4000 chip set provides all the functionality required for video (H.261) and audio (G.711, G.722, and G.728). The chip set also supports the H.xxx suite of standards necessary for full H.261 compliance. The AVP-4000 supports both CIF (288 lines by 352 pixels) and QCIF (144 lines by 176 pixels). This chip set will serve as a strategic core technology within AT&T, and will provide the video codec engine for future video products across AT&T business units. The video codec engine will be the platform for a range of ISDN videotelephones, video PCs, and multimedia workstations.

Why ISDN?

As the name itself implies, ISDN was created as a communications interface to integrate and communicate many types of digital signals. The Basic Rate Interface (BRI), specified in the CCITT I.430 standard, provides the now familiar "2B+D" connectivity. The term *2B* means that two full-duplex 64 kb/s bearer channels are available to carry signals from a source to a destination. These channels allow transmission of digitized voice, circuit-switched or packet-switched data, as well as video signals.

The D-channel is a full-duplex 16 kb/s out-of-band signaling channel. It is always used for call set-up and control, and can also be used to transport user

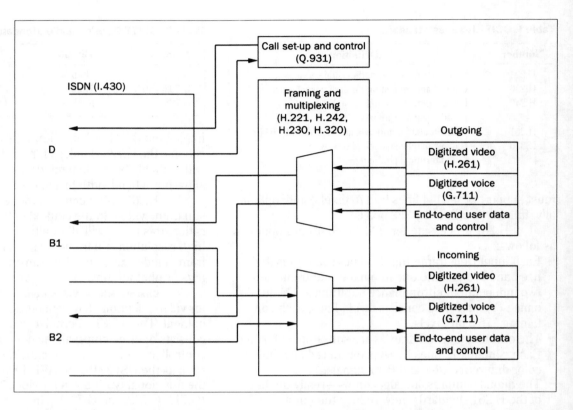

Figure 2. An overview of the video telephony terminal equipment interface to ISDN. The 2B+D capacity of ISDN is depicted as a conduit enclosing the separate parallel B- and D-channels.

packet-data. In video telephony, one or both B-channels are used to transmit the digitized voice and video signals, together with the end-to-end framing and user control signals. The D-channel is used for call setup, and optionally may be used for independent packet data calls.

Interfacing Video Telephony to ISDN. Figure 2 shows an overview of the video telephony terminal equipment interface to ISDN. The 2B+D capacity of ISDN is depicted as a conduit enclosing the separate parallel B- and D-channels. (The BRI, as defined in CCITT I.430, is a serial channel with the B- and D- channels multiplexed together in a 192 kb/s full-duplex channel.)

The terminal equipment uses the D-channel for the initial set-up and teardown of the call through the network. The terminal equipment also multiplexes, demultiplexes, and frames the digital inputs and outputs for the B-channels. The multiplexing and framing of these signals is specified in CCITT H.221. The inputs and outputs are the compressed digital video (H.261), the digital audio (G.711, G.722, or G.728), and the end-to-end user data and control signals.

It is interesting to note that much of the necessary end-to-end user control signaling could theoretically be provided over the D-channel via Q.931 signaling. Instead, the standards facilitate end-to-end control and signaling through in-band data on the B-channels via the H.221 protocol. In this way, ISDN video terminal equipment can interwork with video terminals that are not on ISDN, or are on separate "islands of ISDN," where digital trunking capabilities from end to end or the means to transmit the required ISDN information elements are lacking.

Providing End-to-End Digital Connectivity. ISDN is by definition a digital transmission interface for its terminal endpoints. Thus, each ISDN call is inherently digital, at least between the terminal equipment and the local switch, such as the AT&T Definity® and Legend® customer premises products, and the AT&T 5ESS® switch local central office. Standards-compliant video telephony requires end-to-end digital connectivity. As with data calls, digital switching and trunking must be provided for video calls throughout each leg of the total network connection. However, among the digital facilities provided

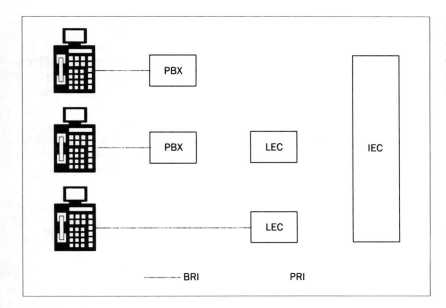

Figure 3. ISDN videotelephony networking alternatives, showing connections to the interexchange carrier (IEC) with and without a private branch exchange (PBX) or local exchange carrier (LEC).

today for data calls, some are not suitable for video calls, and some are more suitable than others.

The best facilities for video connectivity are those providing clear, unrestricted 64 kb/s channels for the ISDN B-channels. These facilities, as well as common channel signaling through Signaling System 7 (SS7), are increasingly provided by the Local Exchange Carriers (LECs). There are also 56 kb/s channels that provide clear, unrestricted connectivity. In the absence of available 64 kb/s channels, video telephony can operate over 56 kb/s facilities. But less bandwidth will necessarily reduce the quality of the video.

Some existing digital facilities cannot be identified as available for video. To establish the required end-to-end circuit-switched data connection, the network must be able to sense the circuit capabilities. The problem is that the network cannot identify some unrestricted data channels. Therefore, the call must be denied. As out-of-band control signaling (SS7) becomes universal, this problem will probably be reduced or completely eliminated.

Signaling and Control for the Transmission System.
When a call is made, the ISDN endpoint shows the type of call desired through the bearer capability information element. In the call setup process, one purpose of this element is to specify the transmission facilities needed for successful call completion. Some examples of bearer capabilities mentioned in CCITT I.451 include: speech,

G.711 audio, G.722 audio, video, restricted digital information, and unrestricted digital information.

Although a video bearer capability is mentioned in the CCITT standard, it has not yet been adopted as common usage by equipment providers and telephone companies. For the present, the speech bearer capability and the unrestricted digital information bearer capabilities for 64 kb/s and 56 kb/s are all that are generally available for video telephony to use.

For now, it is probable that the following scenario will be used to set up most personal video calls:
- An ordinary voice call is set up to the desired station.
- After the voice call is answered, one or two unrestricted circuit-switched data calls are set up.
- The original voice call is dropped.

There are several reasons for first setting up an ordinary voice call. Sometimes it is not known whether the called station has video capability. Even if it is known, it may not be desirable to add video until the the parties at both ends agree. Either way, voice calls are *always* possible between stations, whereas unrestricted data calls are not available everywhere. Furthermore, voice calls have desirable call handling features that currently are not available with data calls. These are the common features used in establishing contact with the right party: items such as call coverage, voice messaging (e.g., Audix), call forwarding, transfer, and hold.

However, the voice call cannot be used for video. Even if the network uses digital facilities for the voice call, it may insert loss or echo cancellation that would corrupt data transmission. Therefore, when video is to be added to the call, unrestricted circuit-switched data calls (if available) must be established to link the endpoints. Then, to allow as much bandwidth as possible for video, the voice portion of the call may be compressed using G.728 and then conveyed using H.221. Data call setup may involve several attempts to use different bearer capabilities to search out available transmission channels. This process will be improved wherever SS7 is adopted.

Incoming video calls may be distinguished from ordinary incoming data calls through low-layer capability message elements. These message elements are used for end-to-end signaling to show exactly what type of circuit switched data call is being established.

A Scenario to Eliminate Islands of ISDN. ISDN video calls require unrestricted circuit-switched data connectivity, but such connectivity is not yet universally available. At present we have "islands of ISDN" that lack digital trunking capabilities from end to end or the means to transmit the required ISDN information elements. These islands are being bridged and gradually eliminated as SS7 is adopted and as tariffs are established that permit circuit-switched data connectivity.

High quality, high bit-rate digital video service can be provided in several ways (Figure 3). The usual way of achieving circuit-switched data connectivity on IntraLATA calls is to obtain the service from the appro-priate LEC. ISDN video endpoints may interface directly to the local central office. Alternatively, ISDN video endpoints on a PBX system may interface to the central office indirectly through T1 lines or ISDN Primary Rate Interface (PRI) service. If equipment or tariff limitations prohibit the service provisioning through the LEC network, then connectivity may be possible through an interexchange carrier (IEC) such as AT&T. For InterLATA video calls, both LECs and IECs are likely to be involved in the needed service, unless the customer has direct connection to an IEC.

Summary

A combination of positive factors is paving the way for ISDN personal video:

- Reasonably priced endpoints are achievable.
- Standards are in place that can promote rapid video development.
- Although not fully in place today, a blueprint for ISDN deployment exists.

In short, no major technical issue stands in the way.

The precise form and features of the first generation of ISDN personal video products is being addressed. In addition, the same ISDN and audio/video compression technologies will be used to provide a wide range of video products and services beyond "talking heads." What happens now will truly be a function of customer-driven forces.

A Standards-Based Multimedia Conferencing Bridge

David N. Horn
Terry G. Lyons
John C. Mitchell
Dale L. Skran

Standardizing video, audio, and data exchange formats under the auspices of the International Telegraph and Telephone Consultative Committee (CCITT) will make possible a large new market in standard videoconferencing devices. This paper describes a possible solution for multipoint, multimedia conferencing in such an environment.

Introduction

Current trends in information systems technology include integrating computing and communications, multimedia multiparty conferencing, distance learning, computer supported collaborative work (CSCW), hypermedia systems, and other distributed multimedia services.

The impact of these advances may revolutionize society. Multimedia conferencing is not only a way to reduce travel so people can work together in a global marketplace; it also is a method to help people work together more effectively and more productively, regardless of their locations. By bringing computer tools and on-line information access to the meeting room, the decision-making process can be improved, and intellectual property such as designs or documents can be created during the meeting.

The volume of information bombarding us is overwhelming. Hypermedia systems (i.e., multidimensional, multimedia documents), may need to interactively access information located at many places over a network. Computer-based information processing tools will soon become essential to assimilate this information.

Video compression and the Integrated Services Digital Network (ISDN) are "enabling" technologies that help make this revolution possible. Another required enabling technology is a set of standards, protocols, and a signaling system to access these revolutionary new services.

These new services present two major communications requirements.

Multimedia Requirements. The network must transport multimedia rather than today's primarily audio-oriented unimedia. Multimedia includes audio, video, and other data, i.e., all digital equipment *excluding* audio and video, even though the audio and video may be digitized. To transport multimedia information, multiple network connections may need to be associated with each other and also synchronized. An ISDN Basic Rate Interface (BRI) provides two 64 kilobytes per second (kb/s) B channels plus a 16 kb/s D (signaling) channel, to offer 128 kb/s of usable bandwidth. Because multichannel call routing is not yet generally available, a user may have to request two separate B channel calls. These may be routed over the network through totally different routes and hence incur different delays.

Multiparty Operation Requirements. Group work implies multiparty operation. Thus, two new requirements must be considered:

- Signaling for managing multimedia, multiparty calls. The signaling aspect is complex. There is a need for flexible conference dynamics, e.g., adding or dropping parties, and changing media bandwidth allocation. Also, each user may have more than one line to the network, and each site may have more than one user. Access privileges (e.g., password control for entering a conference) and billing also must be considered.

- There must be provisions for media-specific bridging, i.e., audio bridging, video bridging, and data bridging. These media-specific bridging requirements are covered in detail in the next section.

Implementation Problems. The problems with implementing these multimedia, multiparty services on today's ISDN network include:

Reprinted with permission from *AT&T Technical Journal,* vol. 72, no. 1, pp. 41–49, Jan./Feb. 1993.

- Signaling on the D channel is only between the endpoint and the nearest network termination (i.e., the private branch exchange [PBX] or the local central office). User-to-user signaling is limited at best, and is not universally supported through existing networks.
- All basic unrestricted digital network services are point-to-point.

Multimedia Conference Bridge System Architecture

This section introduces a solution based on a multimedia conference bridge, or, using CCITT terminology, a multipoint control unit (MCU). The MCU is connected to the network via one or more digital trunk interfaces. It can be connected to a central office switch, a PBX, or any other convenient point that is accessible via dial-up point-to-point services from the user terminals. Figure 1 illustrates the configuration.

To conduct a multiparty, multimedia conference, point-to-point clear-channel circuit connections based on the conventional (Q.931) ISDN signaling procedures are established between the user terminals and the MCU. The MCU performs several basic functions.

Conference Management. Conference management involves making and receiving calls, negotiating and dynamically managing the bandwidth allocated to each media, adding and dropping conferees, and managing the media-specific bridges.

Audio Bridging. In addition to the basic audio bridging function of audio summation and gain control, a multimedia audio bridge should perform the following extra functions:
- Audio energy level monitoring, for optional video control and talker indication.
- Transcoding between different types of speech codings. Transcoding allows conferees with different quality speech encoding methods to talk together, without dropping to the lowest common denominator in terms of quality.
- Muting idle channels to reduce background noise.
- Delaying the audio to match any video delay introduced by video processing at the video bridge.

Video Bridging. Video compression hardware takes raw digitized video at approximately 45 megabits per second (Mb/s) and compresses it to a lower data rate (56 kb/s to 1.536 Mb/s) for transmission over the network. The hardware is still expensive, though very-large-scale integration (VLSI) technology is expected to

Panel 1. Terms and Acronyms in This Paper	
AGC	AudioGraphic Conference (application)
AVPS	audio visual protocol stack
BAS	bit rate allocation signal
BRI	Basic Rate Interface
CCITT	International Telegraph and Telephone Consultative Committee
CELP	code-excited linear prediction
CIF	common intermediate format
CSCW	computer supported collaborative work
GCC	generic conference control
HSD	high speed data
ISDN	Integrated Services Digital Network
JPEG	Joint Photographic Experts Group
LSD	low speed data
MCS	multipoint communications service
MCU	multipoint control unit
MLP	multilayer protocol
PBX	private branch exchange
PCM	pulse code modulation
VLSI	very-large-scale integration

bring the cost down rapidly. The compression and decompression causes a delay of several hundred milliseconds, and the picture quality is generally inferior to TV quality, especially for rapidly moving objects or images—such as normal printed text—with highly detailed content. Quality depends greatly on bandwidth: 128 kb/s video is much better than 56 kb/s video.

Given a conference where each party has only one source of compressed video and one display, one video bridging technique allows all users to view a particular user's video source. This means that the contents of the single compressed video source must be multicast (i.e., copied) to multiple destinations. The switching could be controlled either by a chairperson, who decides who sees what, or automatically by audio energy level, i.e. everyone sees the current loudest talker, except himself or herself, who sees the previous talker. Each viewer could also be allowed to make his or her choice of video source. Multi-window video, where the viewer can simultaneously can see multiple video sources in windows, is possible, but is currently expensive, adds delay, and causes loss of quality.

Data Bridging. The type of data bridging required depends on the application. Some applications may only

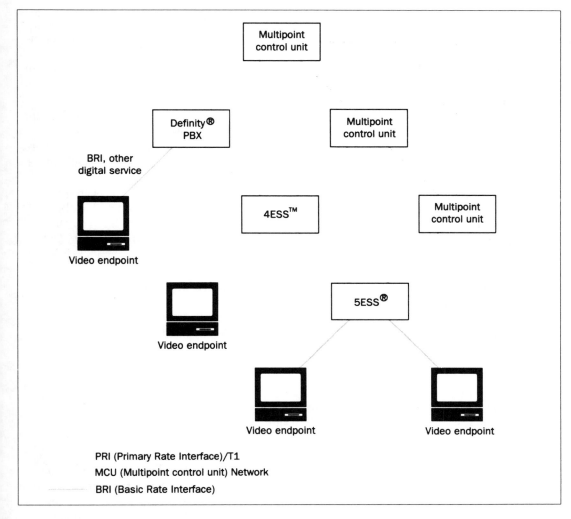

Figure 1. A diagram of a Multipoint Control Unit (MCU) layout, showing connections to the network through digital trunk interfaces.

require each party to receive data from a single source. Here, as with video bridging discussed earlier, the MCU must be able to multicast streams of data from one source to multiple destinations. Neither flow control nor contention resolution is needed. To receive data from a different source, the data bridge has to be reconfigured. More demanding applications, such as CSCW, may require any party to be able to send data to any set of destinations at any time. To satisfy this need, a true multipoint packet data protocol is presently being defined by the CCITT, and will be described more fully later in this paper.

Returning to the overall system architecture (see Figure 1), the MCU can be deployed anywhere in the network, including the customer's premises or the premises of a third party service provider. Multiple MCUs can be linked together in one conference, and one MCU can simultaneously support multiple conferences. All interactions with the network use only existing point-to-point services. Conference and application-related signaling between users and the MCU, and between users, is conducted "in-band" within the B channel circuits between the users and the MCU, and is transparent to the network. This implies a layered signaling scheme where protocols such as Q.931 are used for signaling between the network and the user/MCU for connections. In-band signaling is used for multimedia, multipoint call control and higher level service control.

Emerging Multi-Media Standards

Late in 1990, the CCITT approved the P×64 recommendations for point-to-point video conferencing, including H.221 (framing), H.230 (control and indication), H.242 (channel setup), H.261 (video compression), and H.320 (endpoint description). Collectively, the point-to-point P×64 recommendations were an initial plan for standardized videophone services. Until recently, all video codecs were based on proprietary algorithms and technology. With the arrival of the P×64 recommendations, interoperability between and among equipment from different manufacturers is now possible. The expectation is that this event will lead to lower video codec costs, just as Group 3 fax standards led to lower fax equipment costs and an explosion in market penetration.

In May 1991, 14 manufacturers (including one from the U. S.) passed interoperability tests in Japan. By March 1992, several American manufacturers (Compression Labs, Inc., PictureTel, and VideoTelecom) demonstrated P×64 interoperability. H.320 provides a good starting point for understanding the P×64 specifications because it contains an overview of the component elements of a videotelephony device.[1]

In May 1992, text was frozen on H.231, H.243 (multi-point control units), and H.233 (privacy). Also, G.728 [16 kilobits per second (kb/s) toll-quality audio] was accepted in its final form. These new recommendations provide for a wider range of standardized video services. Additional recommendations for encryption key exchange and Joint Photographic Experts Group (JPEG) still image transfer are being developed. Thus, P×64 continues to gather momentum.

Media Standards: Video. The core of the P×64 series of recommendations is H.261,[2] a specification for using a hybrid of discrete cosine transform (DCT) and differential pulse code modulation (PCM) to compress real-time video down to rates varying from 56 to 64 kb/s to 1.92 Mb/s. H.261 covers both P×56/64 kb/s (p = 1, 2, ... 6) and M×384 kb/s (m = 1, 2, .. 5). Two video quality modes are provided for: CIF (common intermediate format) and QCIF (quarter-CIF). CIF provides for a 288 lines by 352 pixel picture, and QCIF for a 144 line by 176 pixel picture.

Media Standards: Voice. Several audio standards are encompassed in the P×64 recommendations. However, all endpoints are required to support G.711 pulse code modulation (PCM). Other audio options likely to be widely used include G.722 sub-band adaptive differential pulse code modulation (ADPCM) of 7 kilohertz (kHz) speech for higher fidelity (at rates of 48, 56, and 64 kb/s) and G.728 low-delay (LD) codebook excited linear prediction (CELP).

G.728 is a new recommendation that provides for near-PCM quality audio at a data rate of 16 kb/s using a CELP algorithm. Using this algorithm is especially important for video telephony because it makes available more bandwidth for video and data.

Media Standards: Data. Two standards are provided for bridging data, simple broadcast and Multi-Layer Protocol, described in detail later. Simple data broadcast is provided at two rates, low speed data (LSD) and high speed data (HSD). LSD ranges from 300 b/s to 64 kb/s and HSD from 64 kb/s to 384 kb/s.

Bandwidth Management. Although H.261 is the most publicized part of P×64, H.221[3] is at the core of its effectiveness. This framing protocol allows the following elements to be combined flexibly into a single multi-media multiplex:

- Audio
- Video
- HSD and/or LSD
- Multilayer protocol (MLP)
- Control signals, including: frame alignment signal (FAS), bit rate allocation signal (BAS), and encryption control signal (ECS).

H.221 also supports bundling 56 to 64 kb/s pipes to form wider bandwidth connections, replacing a function now performed by a variety of proprietary devices that do not interoperate. Thus, H.221 is an internationally accepted open architecture for "inverse" multiplexing.

For example, in a 128 kb/s call we might observe 7 khz audio encoded at 56 kb/s, with the remaining bandwidth allocated to video and control. Dynamically, this might change to 16 kb/s CELP audio and 14.4 kb/s LSD with the remaining bandwidth allocated to video. HSD at 64 kb/s could be provided with the video turned off. Figure 2 shows a sample allocation of 384 kb/s of bandwidth on an H0 channel.

Point-to-Point Conference Control. Point-to-point conference control is covered by H.230[4] and H.242.[5] There are two kinds of BAS codes, commands and capabilities. Each capability, when sent, informs the far end

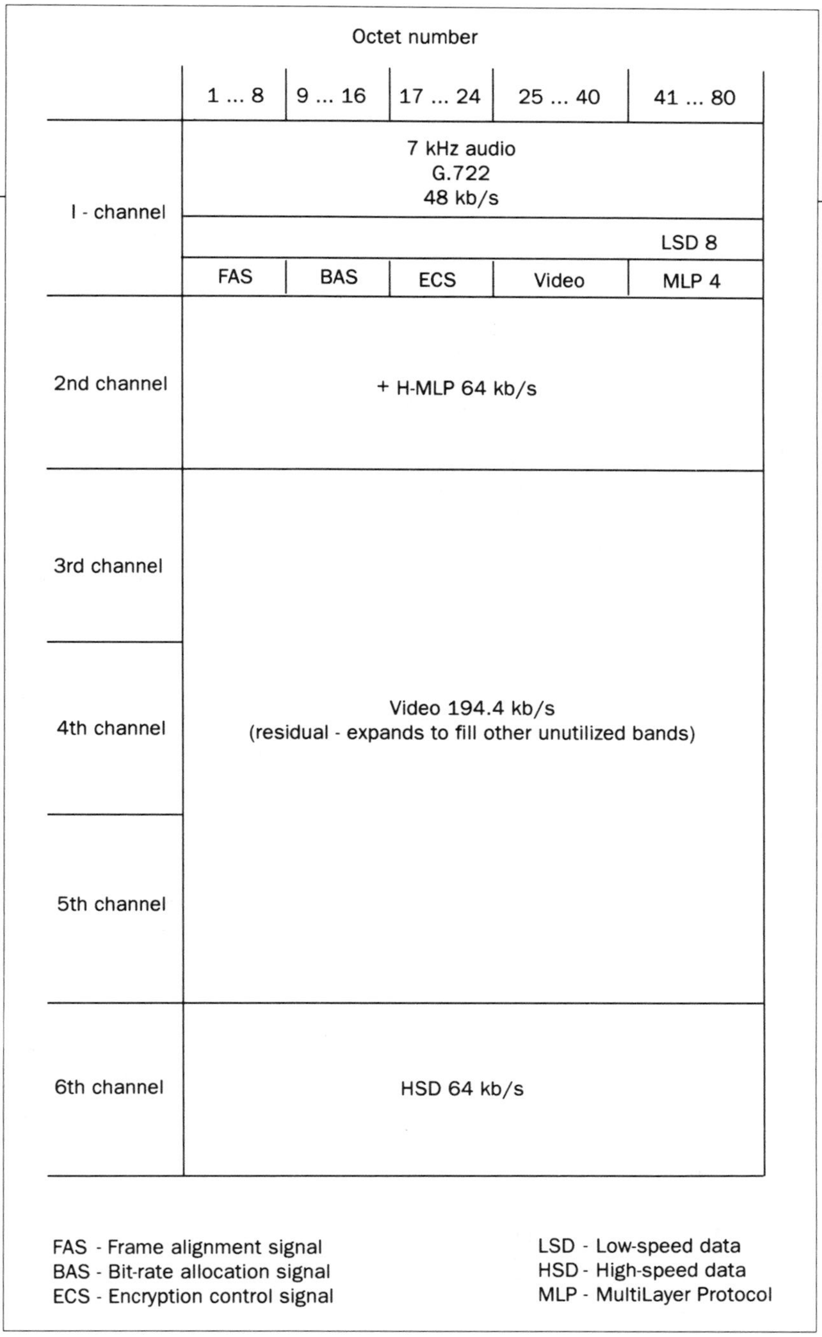

	1 … 8	9 … 16	17 … 24	25 … 40	41 … 80
I - channel	7 kHz audio G.722 48 kb/s				
					LSD 8
	FAS	BAS	ECS	Video	MLP 4
2nd channel	+ H-MLP 64 kb/s				
3rd channel	Video 194.4 kb/s (residual - expands to fill other unutilized bands)				
4th channel					
5th channel					
6th channel	HSD 64 kb/s				

FAS - Frame alignment signal
BAS - Bit-rate allocation signal
ECS - Encryption control signal

LSD - Low-speed data
HSD - High-speed data
MLP - MultiLayer Protocol

Figure 2. A specimen 384 kb/s bandwidth allocation.

that the sender can accept a given set of commands. For example, the audio capability "A-law" shows support for G.711 A-law PCM. Such a terminal could be expected to respond to the commands *A-law*, *OU*, and *A-law OF* (unframed and framed A-law PCM).

A session begins with a capability exchange. Each endpoint sends the other a set of capabilities that it wishes to disclose. The session is then presumably held at the highest common rates. The capability exchange may occur at any time during the call, and may be used to add or remove capabilities dynamically.

Multi-Point Conference Control. The MCU recommendation for P×64 has been frozen since May 1992. Final approval by the CCITT is expected early in 1993. Its major components are:

- H.231, multi-point control units for audiovisual systems using digital channels up to 2 Mb/s.
- H.243, basic MCU procedures for establishing communications between three or more audiovisual terminals using digital channels up to 2 Mb/s.

H.231 describes the overall architecture of an MCU, illustrated in Figure 3. H.243 addresses differences in

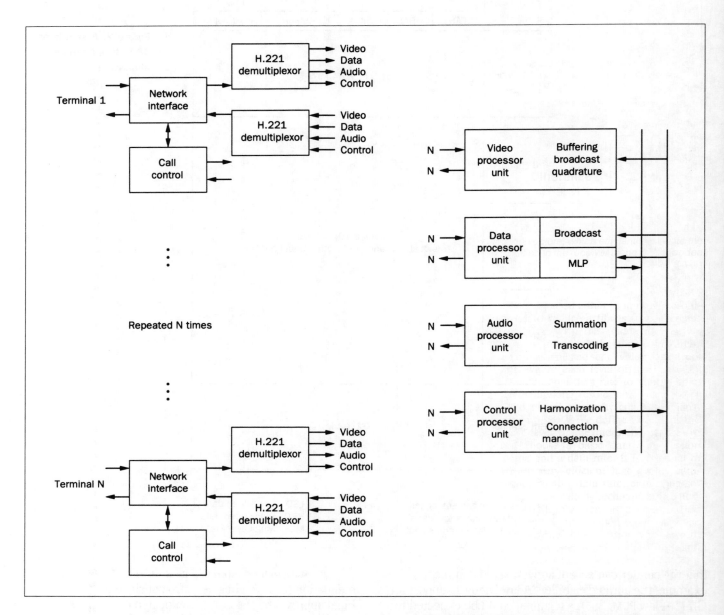

Figure 3. The generic architecture of an MCU following the H.231 standard, using H.221 multiplexers and demultiplexers.

operation between multi-point and point-to-point. It also describes management features that are significant only in a multi-point situation. Areas covered include:

- Terminal numbering
- Chair control of video broadcast
- In-band identification of endpoints for security purposes
- Multi-point control of LSD and HSD data broadcast, with the MCU controlling a token for each type of data

- Cascading of MCUs, a feature that allows customers to conference a larger group than a single MCU would normally support, or possibly to save on toll charges.

The overall philosophy is to provide a useful but simple set of commands, while leaving more complex features such as multi-level hierarchies of MCUs to the control of MLP.

Multilayer Protocol. The G- and H-series recommendations of Study Group XV described above focus on audio-video encodings and provide rudimentary support for data. They specify how the LSD and HSD channels of H.221 can be allocated to one transmitter at a time, allowing it to broadcast an arbitrary bit stream to other parties. Although H.221 permits opening another data channel labeled MLP (including a high-speed component, H-MLP), its use is not detailed. H.231 merely states that MLP data handling in an MCU consists of processing telematic information and conference control signals. The implied requirement, a distinguishing characteristic of MLP, is that it support interactive data exchange among multiple transmitters.

Study Group VIII has been developing a full MLP specification. The current study period culminated in a framework of five projected recommendations:
- T.121 AGC. AudioGraphic Conference, a core application that gives terminals a shared visual space of still images, annotations, and manipulations.
- T.122 MCS. Multipoint Communication Service, a new type of data communication offering on-demand point-to-point and multipoint virtual data channels, an option of uniformly sequenced delivery, and tokens to arbitrate resource contention.
- T.123 AVPS. Audio Visual Protocol Stack, a specified set of lower layer protocols to support MCS, for ISDN and for other important networks.
- T.124 GCC. Generic Conference Control, an application combining terminal-to-terminal, terminal-to-MCU, and MCU-to-MCU commands and indications.
- T.125 MCSP. Multipoint Communication Service Protocol, detailing how control information is exchanged over AVPS to implement the MCS service definition contained in T.122.

Figure 4 represents the relationship of these components. Agreement has been reached so far on the contents of T.122 and T.123. These are being sent to the CCITT plenary for approval in the first half of 1993.

MCS is implemented through a hierarchy of MCUs that cooperate to replicate and distribute the data of multiple transmitting terminals. Participants are assigned individual, addressable user identifiers. Destination channel numbers are indexes into distribution lists held by the MCUs. Receivers are allowed to join channels with data of interest to them (either known beforehand or advertised over other channels). Reliable connections between individual terminals and MCUs, as provided by AVPS, are combined into an overall flow that respects the rate of the slowest receiver. MCS is designed to bridge heterogeneous lower layers, allowing data conferences to include terminals on both ISDN and local area networks. MCS has the potential to become an open interface for multipoint interactions. It can support groupware applications other than AGC.

Services Architecture

The type of services offered by an MCU are not specified by the P×64 recommendations. MCU's services are expected to offer bridging features similar to those provided by audio-only bridges, including:
- Meet-me conferences, where conferees get a number in advance that will connect them to the conference. An optional password may be required to join it.
- Dial-out conferences, where the MCU calls each conferee to initiate the conference.
- Progressive conferences, in which a conferee calls successive parties and adds them to the conference one at a time.
- Reservation systems.
- Remote maintenance.
- Attendant screening of conferees for added security.

Limitations and Future Directions

The current standards have some limitations:
- Deployed ISDN networks do not fully support the multi-use information transfer capability for audiovisual services (previously designated 7 kHz audio) with interworking to ordinary telephone services.
- The bandwidth allocated to different media under H.221 is constant for long periods of time. It cannot expand to accommodate instantaneous demands for video or data during peaks in use, nor contract during intervals when a signal is idle.
- H.221 packages a single set of media streams into a P×64 digital connection. Transporting multiple video

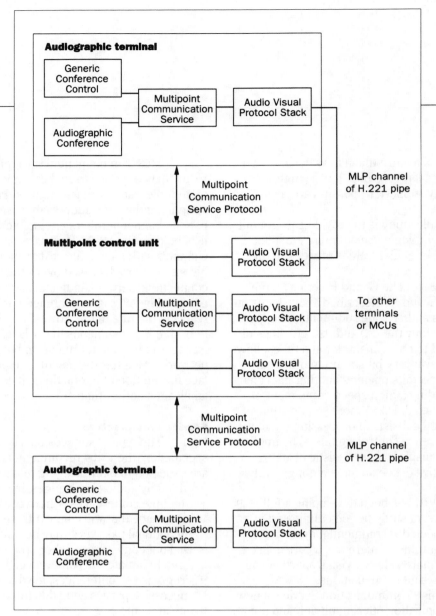

streams within a conference requires that multiple P×64 connections be set up. This affects the ability of cascaded MCUs to offer viewers a choice of video sources originating outside their respective parts of a conference.

- Encryption key management and authentication are not provided for in H.233 (privacy). A separate recommendation for these areas is currently being prepared.
- Standards for transfer of JPEG images in the context of video teleconferences have not yet been completed, but are currently being developed.

Future developments may redress these limitations and expand services in other ways:

- Audiovisual calls can be endowed with features that make ordinary telephony more convenient to use, including call forwarding, additional call offering,

hold, transfer, and conference.
- Packet switched framing, which is natural for data, can also be applied to the audio encoding. Audiographic streams may be transported in this way through a multi-service frame relay network or a local area network. Many logical streams could be accessed through a single network interface, with efficient use of bandwidth on demand.
- Broadband ISDN applies similar concepts of cell relay to higher transmission speeds. It supports the multiplexing of several virtual circuits over a virtual path between endpoints. With the completion of H.261, work on video coding in Study Group XV (where the P×64 recommendation originated) has shifted to this domain.
- The multipoint communication of MCS, currently built on a set of point-to-point connections between

terminals and MCUs, could evolve to using future switched multipoint network services. This would require work in advance on multipoint transport layer protocols.

- New service offerings can be built around repositories for storing multimedia information. These may include message recording for later retrieval, broadcast distribution to large numbers of subscribers, or interactive sequencing through audiovisual programs.

Summary

We have presented an open architecture for implementing a new generation of multimedia, multi-party applications and services on the current network, using existing signaling and services. The signaling model is layered, using the existing messages to signal for point-to-point connections to a MCU, then using in-band signaling for higher-layer services.

The key to success and interoperability is to define and adhere to the right set of standards. Each layer should be powerful enough to support the sophisticated applications of the future, yet general enough to support arbitrary applications including the multimedia equivalent to "plain old telephone service."

We expect the development of new and powerful multimedia applications will develop hand in hand with the deployment of MCUs.

References

1. "Narrow-Band Visual Telephone Systems and Terminal Equipment, CCITT Recommendation H.320, International Telegraph and Telephone Consultative Committee, Geneva, Switzerland, 1990.
2. "Video Codec for Audiovisual Services at P×64 kb/s," CCITT Recommendation H.261, International Telegraph and Telephone Consultative Committee, Geneva, Switzerland, 1990.
3. "Frame Structure for a 64 to 1920 kb/s Channel in Audiovisual Services," CCITT Recommendation H.221, International Telegraph and Telephone Consultative Committee, Geneva, Switzerland, 1990.
4. "Frame-Synchronous Control and Indication Signals for Audiovisual Systems," CCITT Recommendation H.230, International Telegraph and Telephone Consultative Committee, Geneva, Switzerland, 1990.
5. "System for establishing communications between audiovisual terminals using digital channels up to 2 Mbit/s," CCITT Recommendation H.242, International Telegraph and Telephone Consultative Committee, Geneva, Switzerland, 1990.

(Manuscript received June 18, 1992)

Packet Video and Its Integration into the Network Architecture

GUNNAR KARLSSON STUDENT MEMBER, IEEE, AND MARTIN VETTERLI, MEMBER, IEEE

Abstract—Packet video is investigated from a systems point of view. The most important issues to its transmission are identified and studied in the context of a layered network architecture model. This leads to a better understanding of the interactions between network and signal handling. The functions at a particular layer can thereby be made least dependent on network implementation and signal format. In the model, the higher layers provide format conversion, hierarchical source coding, error recovery, resynchronization, cost/quality arbitration, session setup and tear-down, packetization, and multiplexing. Provisions from the network layers pertain mainly to real-time transmission. Special consideration is given to hierarchical source coding, error recovery, statistical behavior, and timing aspects. Simulation results are presented for a subband coding system.

I. INTRODUCTION

TODAY'S fiber technology offers a transmission capacity that can easily handle high bit rates like those required for video transmission. This can lead to the development of networks which truly integrate all types of information services. By basing such a network on packet switching, the services (video, voice, and data) can be dealt with in a common format. Packet switching is more flexible than circuit switching in that it can emulate the latter (while the opposite is not possible), and vastly different bit rates can be multiplexed together. Also, the network's statistical multiplexing of variable rate sources may also yield a higher utilization of the channel capacity than what is obtainable with fixed capacity allocation. Most of these arguments have been brought forth and verified in a number of projects like MAGNET at Columbia University [1], [2], Prelude at CNET [3], [4], and PARIS at IBM [5]. Video coding for packet transmission has been considered by a number of authors [6]–[11]. Other issues of importance for packet video include error recovery [12], [7], [13], [9], [11], video resynchronization [14], [6], [11], and statistical analysis and modeling of the variable bit rate of coded video [15]–[19], [11]. The abstracts of the recent workshop on packet video give a good overview of new results in the field [20].

Manuscript received April 15, 1988; revised December 16, 1988. This work was supported by the National Science Foundation under Grant CDR-84-21402. This paper was presented in part at the Second International Workshop on Packet Video, Torino, Italy, September 7–9, 1988.

G. Karlsson was with the Department of Electrical Engineering, Columbia University, New York, NY. He is now with IBM Research Division, Zürich Research Laboratory, CH-8803 Rüschlikon, Switzerland.

M. Vetterli is with the Department of Electrical Engineering, Columbia University, New York, NY 10027.

IEEE Log Number 8927586.

The amount of information in a video signal depends on the activity in the captured scene. When compressed, the resulting bit rate may be highly varying, which is referred to as variable bit rate coding. Most compression methods produce a variable output rate. Only when a fixed output rate is enforced, as with circuit-switched transmission, is the compression varied in order to keep the transmitted rate within the prescribed limit of the channel. Since this is done regardless of the information content in the signal, the quality of the received signal may vary with the compression. (Generally, the effect is reduced by appropriate buffering.) In contrast, statistical multiplexing in packet networks allows the transmission rate to vary in order to reflect the information contents of the signal. It is consequently expected that the receiver will perceive a constant video quality. Throughout the paper, we will assume that variable rate coding is being used.

In the case of variable-rate transmission of real-time information, we can no longer assume the separation of source, channel, and receiver as a valid paradigm. The transmitter of a compressed video signal will require various amounts of capacity over time and the packet network provides a channel whose capacity changes depending on the total load of the network. The receiver, in turn, has to function together with the channel where packets are lost or delayed. Hence, there are strong dependencies between the entities involved, which require consideration of the global system. A structured way of considering the entire system of packet video is to place the required functions in their proper context, a network architecture model, so that the interactions between functions can be determined [21], [2]. This model may also help to design a system which minimizes a function's dependency on the format of the video signal. The model is illustrated in Fig. 1. By using the Open Systems Interconnection model [22] of the International Standards Organization as the starting point for discussion, we are provided with an adequate terminology that is not contingent upon any specific network implementation. Note that the OSI model was not designed to support real-time transmission. The network architecture model will be considered mainly from a video processing point of view. The control flows will not be covered.

The paper is organized as follows. First some signal processing issues of packet video coding and transmission are analyzed in more detail. These are hierarchical source

Reprinted from *IEEE J. Selected Areas Commun.*, vol. 7, no. 5, pp. 739–751, June 1989.

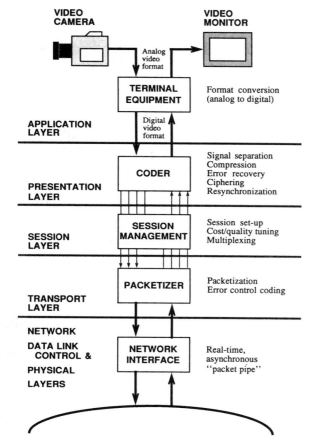

Fig. 1. The major functions of the higher layers of the packet video network architecture model. Note that the arrows indicate signal flows.

coding, error recovery, and the statistical behavior of variable-rate coded video signals. In Section III, video transmission considerations are covered pertaining to the lower layers of the model. Section IV presents the video-related functions fitted into the higher layers. Transmission delays and resynchronization of the video are discussed in Section V. Section VI presents simulation results of a packet video scheme based on subband coding with error recovery, indicating practical solutions to some of the issues raised throughout the paper.

II. SIGNAL PROCESSING ISSUES OF PACKET VIDEO

A number of issues in packet video call for signal processing solutions. These issues include source coding and error recovery. This section describes them in more detail. (They are related to the network architecture model in Section IV.) Also in this section, the statistical behavior of a compressed video signal is discussed. The properties of the varying capacity requirement matter for the network design, while semantics and syntax of the video signal are irrelevant.

A. Hierarchical Source Coding

Hierarchical coding, known also as layered coding or embedded coding, is a technique first developed for packet voice transmission [23], wherein a signal is separated into subsignals of various importance to be coded and transmitted separately. This general technique, illustrated in Fig. 2, may be advantageously extended to video coding and transmission as well [7], [11]. In this way, the coding of a subsignal can be tailored to the information it carries and the subsignal can be transmitted with a priority reflecting its importance. Network congestion, where buffer overflow leads to packet discard, will affect mainly the subsignals of low importance. Thus, hierarchical coding offers a way of achieving error control by preventing loss of perceptually important information. Yet another reason is the possibility of cost/quality tuning for a session [7], [9]. This refers to the fact that high video quality can be traded for reduced transmission cost. A potential problem with hierarchical coding appears if some of the compressed subsignals yield low output rates; the packetization delay may become intolerable for fixed-length packets. The solution would be to multiplex low bit-rate subsignals, or, alternatively, to stuff them with dummy information to artificially raise the rate.

In our definition of functionality, the process of separating (and recombining) the input signal does not include the compression of the resulting subsignals. The signal separation ought to be such that the total amount of data bits in the subsignals equals the amount of bits in the input. Moreover, it is desirable to require the signal separation and recombination to be lossless. This way the information loss is limited to the compression and transmission, which partly can be controlled through compression level and transmission priorities. Given these constraints, there exist several feasible ways of separating a signal into subsignals. The better methods are those which also lead to improved overall compression. Alternatives include bit-plane separation [23], subband analysis/synthesis [24], and unitary transforms [25].

Bit-plane separation means that the most important information consists of the most significant bits of the image, and, progressively down through the bit layers, the least important subsignal is composed of the least significant bits. This separation has the peculiarity that the most important subsignal would yield the highest compression, while the least important one, which contains virtually no correlation, may only be compressed to a slight degree. This is the reverse of the other methods. We have found subband analysis to be an attractive way of decomposing a signal for coding and transmission [7]–[9] since the subbands have a natural hierarchy. The use of subband coding as hierarchical coding will be presented in Section VI. For unitary block transforms, common block sizes lead to 64 and 256 channels, respectively, a prohibitively large number for independent transmission which would thus require some multiplexing. Since a transform is applied on subblocks of the image, all transform coefficients with the same index could be gathered from the subblocks to form a subsignal (commonly known as Mandala reordering). Zonal encoding may thereby eliminate entire subsignals by not allocating any bits to them.

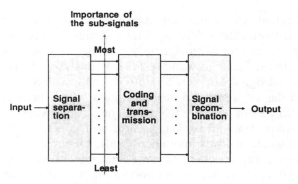

Fig. 2. A hierarchical coding system. The signal is separated into subsignals of various importance which may be coded and transmitted independently of one another. When received and decoded, the subsignals are recombined to form the output signal.

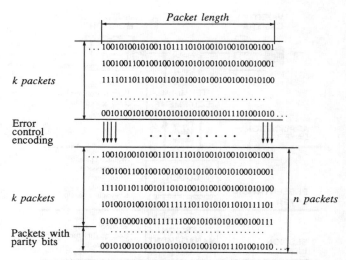

Fig. 3. Error correction encoding should be applied perpendicular to the segmented bit stream to achieve bit interleaving. The figure illustrates the case when a systematic block code is used.

B. Error Recovery

Along with the advantages of packet transmission, such as services integration and variable bit rate transmission, inevitably comes the problem of lost packets. Packet loss is caused by bit errors in the packet's address field, leading the packet astray in the network, and network congestion, leading to discard of packets due to filled buffers. Statistical properties differ for the two causes: bit-error can realistically be modeled as an uncorrelated process which results from noise in the transmission channel [22]. Packet loss due to network congestion is not so straightforward; it depends on the transmission rate in relation to the total network capacity, as well as the resource allocation and the sizes of the network buffers. A thorough analysis of the topic in the case of packet voice can be found in [26].

There are mainly two approaches to error recovery: first, the use of error control codes, and second, error concealment by use of visual redundancy. The former offers perfect recovery from error until the number of errors exceeds the limit of the used code. In contrast, the latter method never gives perfect recovery but it can be engineered to be nearly imperceptible. Its advantage, however, is that it works, although with decreasing effectiveness, regardless of the number of errors experienced during transmission. It is worth noting that while complete and correct delivery are the foremost constraints on data transmission, video as well as voice signals can tolerate some information loss (which of course is exploited already at the compression stage).

1) Error Control Coding: If error control coding is applied along the bit stream of a signal, a lost packet means that a burst of hundreds of bits has to be corrected; a formidable task which would require codes of unreasonable lengths. Fig. 3 depicts a better solution. Here the signal is put into packets after which the error control coding is performed across the information field of the packets (i.e., bit interleaving) [12]. The error control codes used can be block codes or convolutional codes [27]. In both cases, the codes should preferably be *systematic* since it speeds up the decoding: if no error is present, the information packets remain unaltered.

For an (n, k) block code, the number of packets that need to be stored is equal to the number of information bits of the code, k. Since all k packets must be created before the encoding can take place, the coding introduces a periodically varying delay. This can be avoided when the code is systematic by using copies of the information-bearing packets in the calculation of the parity symbols. Note that the same delays are incurred at the decoder, where they cannot be avoided. The minimum distance that the code should provide is governed by the network's probability of packet loss and the correlation of such loss. In most packet-switched networks, there is no absolute bound on the packet loss, whereby the number of lost packets can exceeded what the code can correct. Consequently, some other correction, such as the one presented next, needs to be invoked to avoid breakdown of the video session.

2) Error Concealment by Use of Visual Redundancy: Error concealment by use of visual redundancy takes place after the source decoding but before the signal recombination of the hierarchical source coding system (see Fig. 2). The general requirements for this method are that the error propagation is limited and that the locations of the lost values are known, i.e., they can be treated as erasures [7], [9]. The way these two properties can be obtained will depend on the source coding method used for the subsignals. Generally, recursive coding methods (e.g., DPCM) are less suitable for this type of error recovery than FIR-based methods, such as transform and subband coding. This is due to the strong linkage created between samples in the compressed signal. Section IV-B presents how the erasure property may be obtained.

An erased area of an image may be approximately concealed by spatial and temporal interpolation, or statistical image reconstruction methods. However, the latter are usually too computationally complex to be performed at video rate. Whether information in the surrounding areas, and previous and following video frames should be used in the interpolation depends on the signal separation method used in the hierarchical coding. Regardless of the success of the concealment, in a perceptual sense, the limited error propagation guarantees that the session never needs to be terminated for any amount of lost packets. An encouraging performance of error concealment by use of visual redundancy is indicated by simulation results in Section VI-B.

C. Statistical Behavior of Video Signals

The previously discussed issue shows how stochastic properties of the network, i.e., packet loss and variable delays, influence the development of the signal processing functions. Similarly, knowledge of the statistical behavior of variable rate coded video will be necessary for proper network design. This relationship is illustrated in Fig. 4, which also reinforces the argument about dependencies between source, channel, and receiver, as mentioned in the Introduction. However, variable rate coded video signals are problematic to describe since they are highly varying, with a bursty behavior. The bursts correspond to activity in the captured scene and they may therefore last several seconds. Consequently, the varying rate cannot be sufficiently smoothed out through buffering since it would introduce unacceptable delays. However, when the rates of all video sessions are summed in the channel, the total rate exhibits less burstiness as a result of the statistical multiplexing that takes place (assuming independent sources) [15]-[19], [11]. As the number of sources increases, the ratio of the standard deviation to the mean of the summed rate goes towards zero. Hence, statistical multiplexing may yield a higher channel utilization than what is possible in circuit switching.

Voice signals have been successfully modeled by a two-state (voice/silence) Markov chain. For video there is no direct analog such as motion/no motion. However, there has been a model derived from the voice model, in which the total output rate from N video sources is taken as the aggregate rate from several $(\gg N)$ independent on–off sources [18]. Thus, the rate variations are modeled as discrete steps, where each step corresponds to the output from an on–off source, and where only one such source may change state at a time (i.e., a birth–death process). While the model does not capture features of the video rate of a single source, such as its burstiness, the model may serve well for statistically multiplexed sources.

III. THE LOWER LAYERS OF THE NETWORK ARCHITECTURE MODEL

The previous section described some signal processing issues of packet video. Their corresponding functions will be part of the higher layers of the network model. First, however, the lower network layers need to be briefly discussed. These layers comprise the physical link layer, the data link control layer, and the network layer (see Fig. 1).

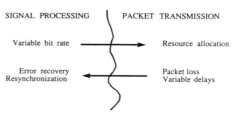

Fig. 4. The interactions between signal processing and transmission. The behavior of variable rate coded video will affect decisions on resource allocation. That, in turn, will influence the network's behavior in terms of packet loss and delay variations, which has to be remedied at the receiver by error recovery and resynchronization.

They form a network node, as opposed to the higher layers which typically reside in equipment on the customer's premises. If the division of functionalities between the layers is kept as suggested in this paper, then all of the lower layers may be designed without consideration of the signal type. The only requirement is that the layers have to support real-time services; it is irrelevant whether it is video or voice (except in need for capacity). Generally, this requires the lower layers to be as simple as possible without any processing of the information; any sophisticated signal handling is better performed at the higher layers where the signal's format and importance are known. Thus, the network may be described as a real-time, asynchronous "packet pipe," where packets inserted at one end come out orderly at the other end, although some will contain errors and others might have been lost.

The requirements for the physical link are adequate capacity and low bit-error rate. It is, however, difficult to quantify these parameters—in general, they are determined by the physical limits of the state-of-the-art technology. To give a sense of the needs involved in a general network carrying video, consider transmitting 30 channels with broadcast video quality at 45 Mbits/s. This would require a link with a capacity in excess of 1.35 Gbits/s. An average of no more than one bit error per video frame for each of these sessions (i.e., 900 errors per second) would correspond to a bit-error probability of less than 7×10^{-7} for the 1.35 Gbit/s link.

Most of the tasks commonly associated with data link control for data transmission are incompatible with real-time services. For example, automatic repeat request is unsuitable as an error handling technique for real-time transmission. Even though the propagation and processing delays may be short, retransmission will introduce delay variations which are to be avoided. In short, there will foreseeably be no processing of data-link frames that contain real-time information. Therefore, data-link control is reduced to deal only with link-management issues.

The network layer provides end-to-end communication and shields the transport layer above from any physical aspects of the transfer medium [22]. The functions associated with the network layer during a data transfer phase include: routing (switching), congestion control, and packet duplication for broad- and multicast sessions. The necessity to keep end-to-end delays and packet delay jitter under control requires video transmission to be conducted over a fixed route, a virtual circuit, which also guarantees that packets are delivered in order. The logical channel number should be protected in order to avoid packet loss, or worse, intrusion (delivery of unwanted packets) due to bit error in the address field. Since the delivery of video packets cannot be warranted by retransmission, the network layer should, through the use of congestion control, maximize the probability of successful and timely delivery. In order to perform such a control in a sensible manner, the layer should provide transmission priorities. Priorities may not be necessary if capacity reservations are available. Lowered transmission quality due to congestion can thereby be avoided by allocating generous amounts of capacity to important signals.

In summary, the network layers should act as a real-time "packet pipe" where order is maintained. However, some of the delivered packets may contain bit errors while others have been lost. To minimize the loss of important data, the network layer ought to provide priority classes. Finally, for multiparty sessions, addressing has to allow multiple destinations and the network nodes must provide packet duplication.

IV. The Higher Layers of the Network Architecture Model

The higher layers are the transport, session, presentation, and application layers (see Fig. 1). In these layers, we place functions for which specific video issues come into consideration. As seen in the previous section, the lower layers are not video specific, but rather they provide general real-time service which could serve voice as well as video. Each of these layers would shield the layer above from some of the physical structure of the link, so that at the network layer the notion of a virtual network is created whose physical implementation is irrelevant. There is a duality between this and the way we would like to see the video-specific, higher layers: an upper layer has to shield its service provider from some of the peculiarities of the format of the video signal. The higher layers will therefore be presented top-down to illustrate how the format dependence is incrementally reduced.

While the lower layers are resident in the network nodes, the upper four are at the customer's premises. In that sense, a packet video coder is seen as being the set of functions associated with the upper four layers. With a network that provides real-time transmission, the user's choice of video format, compression method, and encryption can be made independently of the network. Hence, the network does not restrict the introduction of new signal formats or more advanced compression methods.

A. The Application Layer

The application layer forms the boundary between the user and the network. For the signal, it provides analog inputs and outputs which adhere to the standard of the user's choice and the analog-to-digital and digital-to-analog conversions. This layer is thus dependent on both the

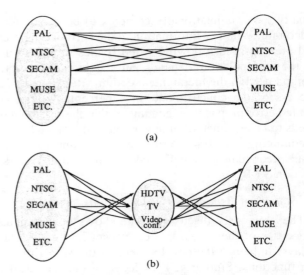

Fig. 5. Cross-compatibility between video formats: (a) direct format to format conversion, and (b) the use of a limited set of intermediate formats.

analog and digital video formats. To possibly obtain compatibility between different analog video formats, and to limit the variety of digital formats [see Fig. 5(a)], a highly reduced set of digital video formats could be used, as shown in Fig. 5(b). The allowed set of formats has to be such that any possible analog video format can be obtained from its members.

B. The Presentation Layer

The presentation layer holds functions which perform some type of signal conversion. Both the signal separation and the compression of hierarchical source coding would be performed within the context of the presentation layer. The other functions include ciphering, error concealment by use of visual redundancy, and video resynchronization. Resynchronization will be covered separately in Section V. Owing to the reduced number of digital video formats stemming from the application layer, presentation layer implementations can be restricted to one class (or standard) for each format.

Error concealment performed by utilizing visual redundancy, as explained in Section II-B2, relies entirely on the assumption that error propagation is limited and that the locations of lost data are known. However, one cannot expect lost data to be aligned to particular points in a video frame, such as the beginning of a scan line; nor can the number of erased values be deduced. The information about the ideal splitting points of the bit stream is local to the presentation layer where the video format is known, while the packet length is known only at the transport layer. Consequently, limited error propagation has to be achieved locally at the presentation layer by adding control information to the bit stream. A feasible way of doing this is to insert synchronization flags after every ith sample in a subsignal [13]. The distance between flags should be chosen so that the values may be concealed reasonably well if lost, while adding little overhead. The flags have

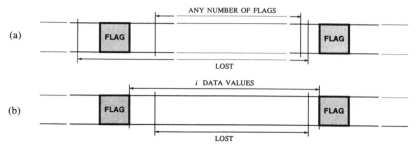

Fig. 6. Two cases of lost data: (a) one or more flags are missing, and (b) no flags are missing but intermediate data values have nevertheless been lost.

to consist of a unique identifier followed by a sequence number to indicate location and, in case of error, the number of erased segments. The flag's uniqueness has to be guaranteed by bit stuffing or reserved codewords. The latter appears advantageous if variable length codewords are being used: the flags are inserted before the variable length coding and they are transformed, as any other value, into their reserved codeword. One lost flag would imply that two data segments have been erased at least partly, as in Fig. 6(a), while the case shown in Fig. 6(b) would be detected since the segment would not yield i samples. All correctly received segments of a video frame would be decoded before the concealment is made, which in turn is done before the signal recombination.

C. The Session Layer

The session layer is mainly responsible for session setup and tear-down. Additionally, in our model, the session layer implements the functions which would be invoked only a limited number of times over an entire session. These functions are in contrast to continuously invoked functions, such as the compression. The session layer should provide not only different types of sessions, but also flexibility in the quality of the sessions. The functions of the session layer are completely freed from the format of the video signal. The layer receives a set of subsignals belonging to a single session and, owing to the format independence, some of these may carry sound information. Hence, it is here, at the session layer, that a complete session of integrated real-time services is created.

1) Session Types: One can foresee several types of video sessions, which can be end-to-end negotiated or locally negotiated. The former can be the common point-to-point session, but also multicast and multidrop sessions. We define a multicast session as a one-to-many communication where transmission to each receiver has been negotiated, and all destinations are explicitly addressed during the data transfer phase. Multidrop is analogous, except the communication is from many to one. A conference session would typically consist of multicast outgoing transmission and multidrop return. Both these sessions could be setup and torn-down together and all session management could apply to them equally. Only

one type of locally negotiated session is conceived, namely broadcast. It is considered to be based on permanent virtual circuits. The session setup is thus negotiated only with the local network node. To receive a broadcast channel, the associated virtual circuit is tapped at the node. (For more details see [28].) Multidrop is similar to broadcast in that the receiver chooses, at any point in time, which virtual circuit to tap by switching between the incoming circuits at the local node.

2) Session Quality: The session quality depends on two parts: source coding and transmission. In conjunction with hierarchical coding, a desirable quality and output bit rate may be achieved through transmission of an appropriate set of subsignals. The greater the number of subsignals, the higher the quality and the output rate. If the coding method can provide more than one compression mode, a greater flexibility in the cost/quality tradeoff may be obtained by changing compression of the subsignals. For transmission, at issue is the degree to which the session may be affected by network congestion. This is contingent upon the resource sharing policy used by the network management. A prodigal resource allocation may be likened to a circuit-switched system while a parsimonious one will yield a higher capacity utilization, but also more delay and packet loss. For a given resource allocation policy a more consistent quality is obtained if a higher number of the transmitted subsignals is given high transmission priority, rather than only the most important one. The transmission quality may be raised further by requesting the transport layer to perform error control encoding on a desired set of subsignals. So, the lossless session quality is set through the number of transmitted subsignals, and the allowed deterioration under network congestion is decided through the use of the transmission priorities and error control coding.

It is our opinion that packet video, compressed with hierarchical coding, would be advantageously transmitted as a hybrid of synchronous and asynchronous time division [28]. The hierarchy's most important subsignal would be transmitted with a fixed reservation of network resources, while the less significant subsignals would have to vie for their share of capacity. This hybrid of allocation policies reduces the stress on the error recovery mechanisms while it still yields higher channel utilization than does pure synchronous time division. The feasibility of such a scheme is discussed in conjunction with the simulation results given in Section VI-B1.

D. The Transport Layer

Functions associated with the transport layer are the segmentation of a data stream into packets, the reassembly of the stream at the receiver, and error control coding. Since the network service is restricted to virtual circuits, all packets are guaranteed an orderly delivery and reordering is therefore not of concern. The transport layer serves all subsignals emanating from the hierarchical coding at the presentation layer and other associated signals, such as sound, which have been added to the session at the session layer. Each such signal would be independently segmented, but the packetized signals would be multiplexed onto the same route at the network layer. Sound and video information will thereby follow a single path so that the delay difference between the two is minimized. Note that the segmentation process does not have information about the video format (such as beginning of frame or scan line); the bit stream may therefore be cut at any point.

For error recovery relying on error correcting codes, the amount of data received has to equal the amount transmitted, or it would place the error correcting encoder and decoder out of phase. Consequently, the transport layer at the destination node has to detect lost packets and replace them with dummy packets so that synchronization can be maintained. Since orderly delivery is guaranteed, end-to-end sequence numbers may suffice for this purpose; a detected gap in the sequence indicates the loss of one or more packets. The necessary range of the sequence numbers has to be determined in relation to the channel code used, so that all gap lengths can be detected which can be corrected by the code. Note that packet intrusion would cause a similar problem by increasing the number of packets received. However, we require the network layer to protect the address field of the packet so that intrusion cannot occur (see Section III). Delays introduced by the channel coding depend on the code length n and the packet size: long packets and codewords give longer delays but less overhead. However, this tradeoff can be resolved without affecting the functions in the layers above, which are independent of packet format. Consequently, the choice between the use of variable or fixed length packets can be made locally as well. While fixed length packets simplify segmentation and packet handling along the transmission path, variable lengths of the packets could be used to keep the packetization delay constant.

Note that end-to-end retransmission is not a possible error recovery method. First, multicast and broadcast sessions would not be feasible if a retransmission scheme was in effect. Consider that different packets may be lost on the various paths of transmission which can result in unreasonable requests for retransmission, proportional to

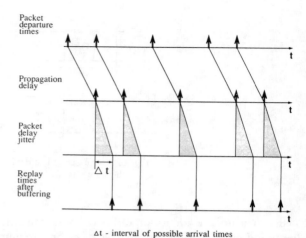

Fig. 7. The delays in a packet-switched network are composed of a fixed part due to the propagation delay, and a variable (jitter) part which is due to waiting time in buffers.

the number of recipients. Second, there is a risk of positive feedback: assume a congested network where all video providers experience packet loss. The strict delay constraint would bar random waiting times before retransmission. So if all providers rely on retransmission for error recovery, the congestion could be aggravated and might lead to more severe performance degradation [7], [9].

V. RESYNCHRONIZATION OF VIDEO

The timing problems of packet video are twofold. First, there are variations in transmission delays, referred to as packet delay jitter. Analogous to packet loss, these variations are an inherent problem with packet transmission. Packet delay jitter can be removed by buffering the packets at the receiver, whereby the delay becomes fixed and equal to the maximal value. This is illustrated in Fig. 7. Transmission delays are irrelevant for one-way sessions, such as broadcast TV. For video conversations (video and voice), in contrast, end-to-end delays are of foremost importance, since long delays impede information exchange. Increased packet loss is therefore accepted in order to achieve reduced delays. Video, as an information carrier, is subordinate to sound, and the video delay has to be bound only to provide lip-synchronization. Lip-synchronization error appears to be unobjectionable for video-to-voice lags in the range of -90 to $+120$ ms [29].

Second, the absence of a common time reference for the encoder and the decoder adds further complications to the reconstruction of a synchronous video signal. According to its clock, the decoder might thus expect data at a higher or lower rate than is being transmitted. Fig. 8 shows the various cases: (a) the clock frequencies are equal, (b) the receiver clock is fast compared to the transmitter clock, and (c) the receiver clock is slow relative to the one at the transmitter. Commonly, the transmission clock frequency is deduced from the arriving packets [14],

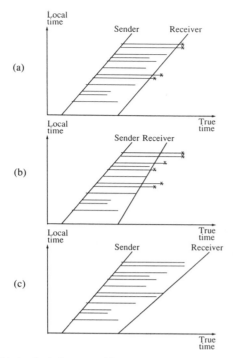

Fig. 8. In (a) the clocks have equal frequencies, and only the packets which are unduly delayed by the network are considered lost (marked by x). In (b) the receiver clock is fast compared to the sender, thus more packets are considered lost. If the receiver clock is slow, as in (c), too much time is allowed for arriving packets.

[6], [11]. This can be done by monitoring the level of the input buffer [14], or by synchronizing the receiver clock to time information in the packets (by use of a phase-locked loop) [6], [11]. Both methods are, however, complicated by packet delay jitter and, if used, variable rate coding. There are also cases when the receiver clock cannot adapt to the received data rate. For example, when video is received from more than one sender (as with multidrop in Section IV-C1), only one of the signals can be used for clock adjustment. So, the frame rates of the other received video signals have to be altered to match the playout rate. This could be performed by occasionally repeating or skipping frames, possible in combination with motion-compensated temporal filtering. (For more details see [28].)

VI. RESULTS FROM A PACKET VIDEO SIMULATION

In this section, results are presented pertaining to hierarchical source coding with error recovery, and the statistical behavior of its output rate. The simulation involved a subband coding scheme and error concealment by use of visual redundancy. The latter was simulated by random discard of packets; no actual network was used in the simulation. The full details of the coding scheme and associated results can be found in [7]–[9], [28]. The coding scheme is designed to provide quality sufficient for video conferences. The investigation was aimed at robust transmission and low complexity, rather than maximal compression.

A. Subband Coding of Video—The Implementation

We have investigated subband coding as hierarchical coding for packet networks. In this method, the signal separation of Fig. 2 is referred to as subband *analysis* and the recombination as *synthesis*. The analysis of a video signal is, in our scheme, achieved by splitting the frequency spectrum in all three dimensions (i.e., temporally, vertically, and horizontally) to obtain a total of 11 three-dimensional frequency regions. This is illustrated in Fig. 9. Following the filtering, the subbands are obtained by subsampling the signals in each dimension to the new Nyquist frequencies. As pointed out in Section II-A, signal separation and recombination should ideally be lossless, and should not increase the amount of data that need to be coded. The filters used enable a perfect reconstruction of the analyzed signal in the absence of coding and transmission loss [30], and the sum of data in the subbands equals that of the input. Also, the information in each subband is amenable to well-tailored quantization schemes which may be adjusted according to perceptual criteria. Thereby compression can be highest in subbands where distortion is least visible.

Subband 1, resulting from low-pass filterings in all three dimensions, retains a high variance of its intensity distribution, which is similar to that of the input. All of the other bands have greatly reduced variance and they can be sufficiently encoded by PCM. Subband 1, in contrast, needs more powerful encoding, which must be weighed against a possible reduction in robustness. As a compromise, the band is encoded with first-order one-dimensional DPCM. The prediction error and the PCM values are run-length encoded. The coding scheme has a low complexity, and can actually be implemented without multiplications [8]. It is worth noting that subband analysis may also be used for size reduction if up-sampling and synthesis filtering is bypassed [31].

B. Simulation Results

The subband coding scheme was simulated using a monochrome sequence consisting of 100 512 × 480 images, with 8 bits per pixel, which corresponds to a bit rate of 60 Mbits/s. According to our results, the argument that variable rate may give a constant quality appears to hold. The average rate of the total output is 2.7 Mbits/s with a standard deviation of 0.62 Mbits/s. In contrast, the mean signal-to-noise ratio (SNR) is 30.4 dB, with a standard deviation of only 0.3 dB!

The subband coding yields a separation of the image information, which results in vastly different behavior of the output rates. In Fig. 10, the mean rate and standard deviation have been plotted for all subbands. As shown, the temporal low-pass bands are generally less variant than the temporal high-pass bands, with the exception of band 5. This band is vertically high-pass filtered, which yields a large variance due to the interlaced format of the video. Fig. 11 shows the temporal behavior (i.e., burstiness and constancy) of four subbands. Owing to the temporal sub-

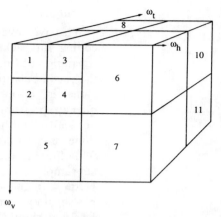

Fig. 9. The 11 frequency regions of the subband analysis. The total region is initially split along the midpoints of each frequency axis. The one which contains both low temporal and low spatial frequencies is split into four spatial-frequency regions.

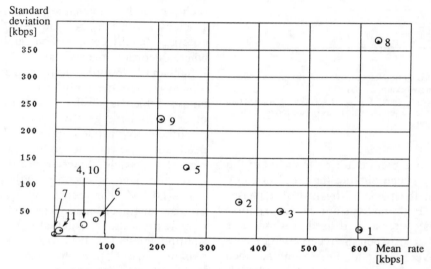

Fig. 10. Mean rate and standard deviation of all subbands (for the band's indexes see Fig. 9).

sampling, the frame rate is only 15 frames per second. Note that the bursts last for several frames. Hence, only limited smoothing can be obtained by buffering, if the end-to-end delay should meet the real-time constraint (Section V-A). In addition, the figure hints that rates from the sub-bands are correlated. The standard deviation of the summed rate is 0.62 Mbits/s. If the bands were independent, the sum-of-variances would give 0.45 Mbits/s as standard deviation.

1) Session Quality: In Fig. 12, the output rate is plotted against the SNR for selected subsets of all subbands. This can serve as an indication of how degradation can vary with available transmission capacity. The pictures in Fig. 13 represent the quality associated with the four cases in Fig. 12. Cost/quality tuning (see Section IV-B2) may be achieved by omitting less important subbands in order to yield a desired output rate. The possible range of quality and output rates corresponds to those of Fig. 12. Note

that packet loss is a temporary quality decrease along this curve, while cost/quality is a permanent one for the session.

The DPCM encoded subband 1 will require the highest possible transmission priority and, if possible, capacity reservation according to its maximum rate. Since its output rate is nearly constant, such a policy would not waste resources. In fact, its maximum rate in the simulation is 619 kbits/s as compared to a mean of 604 kbits/s. The other subbands can be transmitted with lower priority since they are not necessary for the continuity of the session; only its quality. A resource allocation could, in the case, guarantee capacity according to the mean rates of the bands. Thus, they will have to compete for unassigned portions of the network capacity when need be. An even lower allocation class would correspond to subbands which have no guaranteed capacity and therefore have to vie for their entire bandwidth. Priority assignment and ca-

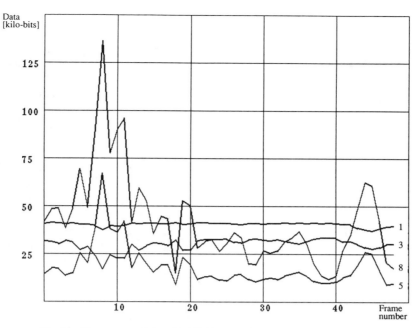

Fig. 11. The amount of data (in kilobits) per frame for four subbands (1, 3, 5, and 8). Note that the sequence length is halved due to the temporal subsampling.

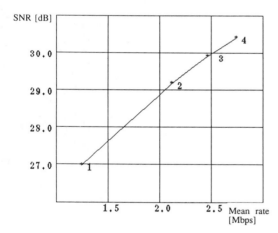

Fig. 12. The SNR as a function of bit rate. Case 1 consists of subbands 1 and 8; case 2: 1–4, and 8; case 3: 1–6, and 8; and case 4 includes all subbands.

pacity allocation for a subband could be made according to mean, variance, and visual importance, as given by Figs. 10 and 12.

2) Packetization Delays: The packetization delays, corresponding to the subbands' output rates, have been tabulated in Table I for 1024-bit packets (as used in [1] and [2]). The maximum delay is not an exact figure since it is not calculated by integration of the variable bit rate, but it is calculated from a constant rate, equal to the minimum of the variable rate. The table illustrates a potential problem with hierarchical coding: excessive packetization delay. When calculating the permissible end-to-end delay, the maximum packetization delay has to be used. Bands such as 7 and 11 may be either multiplexed, or omitted permanently. However, bursty subbands which at any point in time may yield a low bit rate are potential

problems, such as subbands 4, 6, 9, and 10 in the table. While multiplexing can eliminate the maximum delay, the added rates of these bursty bands may require unacceptable processing needs at rate peaks. One solution would be to avoid transmission of a packet that required more than the allowed time for its packetization.

3) Modeling of the Variable Output Rate: The output of each subband may be more easily modeled than the total rate (see Figs. 10 and 11). For example, subbands 1, 2, and 3 could be modeled as constant rate sources. The subbands 5, 8, and 9 could be modeled as simple, but cross-correlated, on–off sources, with the average time in the on-state equal to the average duration of the bursts. The remaining subbands could be excluded from the modeling because of their minor contribution to the total bit rate. An investigation of the statistical properties of the output rates of a subband coding scheme is reported in [19], where the simulation results include ten video sequences, each of 2 min duration.

C. Error Recovery

Our study covers error concealment by use of visual redundancy, as discussed in Section II-B2; it does not include the use of error correcting codes. We have found that subband coding offers a good framework for performing error recovery [7], [9]. First, synchronization flags are added according to the method of Section IV-B so that the location and number of lost packets are known. The encoding is memoryless, except for subband 1, which will need only one PCM value per synchronization flag in order to limit the error propagation (hence, the simple encoding). It is therefore possible to obtain restricted error propagation with limited overhead. Second, only subband 1 requires some form of computed concealment of the era-

513

(a)

(b)

(c)

(d)

(e)

Fig. 13. Pictures representing the cases in Fig. 12. (a) The original. (b)–
(e) show cases 1–4.

TABLE I

PACKETIZATION DELAYS FOR THE SUBBANDS. THE PACKET SIZE WAS 1024 BITS. (FOR BAND 7, THE MINIMUM BIT RATE IS 0, AS CALCULATED FROM THE MINIMUM NUMBER OF BITS PER FRAME. HENCE, THE CORRESPONDING MAXIMUM PACKETIZATION DELAY IS NOT VALID).

Sub-band	Mean [ms]	Max [ms]
1	1.7	1.8
2	2.8	4.0
3	2.3	4.0
4	16.1	93.9
5	3.9	7.5
6	12.3	280.1
7	4053.8	----
8	1.6	5.7
9	4.9	59.5
10	17.6	38.6
11	79.4	397.3

Fig. 14. The effect of packet loss. Five packets, of 1024 bits each, were lost, which corresponds to 2.9 percent of all the packets in the frame. The affected subbands (2, 5, 9, 10, and 11) were chosen at random, as were the particular packets.

sures. The other subbands recover to near invisibility of the errors by setting the erasures equal to zero (the mean). For subband 1, the erasures were patched over by using the corresponding area from the previous frame. The performance of this error recovery method was simulated by randomly erasing 1024-bit packets. For lack of a better model, the simulated loss was taken to be uncorrelated over time and between subbands. Representative images are shown in Figs. 14 and 15; in Fig. 14, five randomly chosen bands, not including subband 1, have suffered loss of one packet each, and Fig. 15 shows a case when subband 1 has been affected by a lost packet. Apparently, the method works well for areas without motion, but subband 1 leaves visible error in areas with motion. This inconsistency can be eliminated by using motion estimation to find the appropriate area to be used as concealment. Spatial filtering can then further reduce the visibility of error by smoothing along the border of the replaced area. This was demonstrated in a related study [28].

VII. CONCLUSIONS

Packet video has been studied from a system point of view and the functions necessary for video communications have been addressed. On signal processing issues, particular consideration was given to coding, error recovery, and the statistical properties of the transmission rate, for which simulation results were also presented. In terms of the network model, the lower layers would provide real-time transmission without regard to the signal's format. It is believed that network sessions should be conducted over virtual circuits, and that the network should provide for priorities if congestion control is exercised. The functionality should also include provisions for multiple destinations. Video-specific functions were discussed in the context of the higher layers. The functions could be ar-

Fig. 15. Packet loss in subband 1 cannot be satisfactorily substituted from the corresponding area in the previous frame when there are high amounts of motion.

ranged so that the dependence on the video signal's format is stepwisely reduced. The issues included format conversion, hierarchical coding, provisions to limit error propagation, session types, session quality and cost, and packetization. The timing problems inherent in an asynchronous network were also covered. Network delays are irrelevant for one-way sessions, but critical for two-way sessions, where the video delay has to be bound to give lip-synchronization. In addition to the network delays, there might be a disparity between the sender and the receiver clocks, which might be remedied by repeating or skipping video frames. Simulation results were presented for a hierarchical packet video coder based on the technique of subband coding. It appears that subband coding is a promising way of doing hierarchical source coding. The complexity is low and, in terms of quality and compression, the scheme promises a performance similar to transform coding. The simulation also verified various conjectures, like variable rate constant quality coding, cost/quality tradeoffs, and recovery from packet loss.

ACKNOWLEDGMENT

The authors thank Bell Communications Research for providing the image sequence; J-Y Cochennec of CNET, A. Lazar and S-Q Li of Columbia, J. Ma of IBM, and M. Garrett of Bellcore for helpful discussions; and the reviewers for their constructive comments.

REFERENCES

[1] A. A. Lazar et al., "MAGNET: Columbia's integrated network testbed," *IEEE J. Select. Areas Commun.*, vol. SAC-3, pp. 859–871, Nov. 1985.

[2] A. A. Lazar and J. S. White, "Packetized video on MAGNET," *Opt. Eng.*, vol. 26, pp. 596–602, July 1987.

[3] P. Gonet, "Fast packet approach to integrated broadband networks," *Networks*, vol. 9, pp. 292–298, Dec. 1986.

[4] M. Devault et al., "The prelude ATD experiment: Assessments and future prospects," *IEEE J. Select. Areas Commun.*, vol. 6, pp. 1528–1537, Dec. 1988.

[5] I. Cidron and I. S. Gopal, "PARIS: An approach to integrated high-speed private networks," *Int. J. Digital Analog Cabled Syst.*, vol. 1, pp. 77–85, 1988.

[6] W. Verbiest and M. Duponcheel, "Video coding in an ATD environment," in *Proc. Third Int. Conf. New Syst. Services Telecommun.*, Liège, Belgium, Nov. 1986, pp. 249–253.

[7] G. Karlsson and M. Vetterli, "Subband coding of video signals for packet-switched networks," in *Proc. SPIE Conf. Visual Commun. Image Processing II*, vol. 845, Cambridge, MA, Oct. 1987, pp. 446–456.

[8] ——, "Three dimensional sub-band coding of video," in *Proc. ICASSP '88*, New York, Apr. 1988, pp. 1100–1103.

[9] ——, "Sub-band coding of video for packet networks," *Opt. Eng.*, vol. 27, pp. 574–586, July 1988.

[10] N. Ohta et al., "Variable rate video coding using motion compensated DCT for asynchronous transfer mode network," in *Proc. IEEE 1988 Int. Commun. Conf.*, Philadelphia, PA, June 1988, pp. 1257–1261.

[11] W. Verbiest et al., "The impact of the ATD concept on video coding," *IEEE J. Select. Areas Commun.*, vol. 6, pp. 1623–1632, Dec. 1988.

[12] P. J. Lee "Forward error correction coding for packet loss protection," presented at First Int. Packet Video Workshop, Columbia Univ., New York, May 1987.

[13] G. Aartsen et al., "Error resilience of a video codec for low bit rates," in *Proc. ICASSP '88*, New York, Apr. 1988, pp. 1312–1315.

[14] J-Y Cochennec et al., "Asynchronous time-division networks: Terminal synchronization for video and sound signals," in *Proc. GLOBECOM '85*, New Orleans, LA, Dec. 1985, pp. 791–794.

[15] B. G. Haskell, "Buffer and channel sharing by several interframe picturephone coders," *Bell Syst. Tech. J.*, vol. 51, pp. 261–289, Jan. 1972.

[16] T. Koga et al., "Statistical performance analysis of an interframe encoder for broadcast television signals," *IEEE Trans. Commun.*, vol. COM-29, pp. 1888–1875, Dec. 1981.

[17] S-S Huang, "Source modelling for packet video," in *Proc. IEEE 1988 Int. Commun. Conf.*, Philadelphia, PA, June 1988, pp. 1262–1267.

[18] B. Maglaris et al., "Performance models of statistical multiplexing in packet video communications," *IEEE Trans. Commun.*, vol. COM-36, pp. 834–844, July 1988.

[19] P. Douglas et al., "Statistical analysis of the output rate of a sub-band video coder," in *Proc. SPIE Conf. Visual Commun. Image Processing III*, Cambridge, MA, Nov. 1988, pp. 1011–1025.

[20] Abstracts from the Second International Workshop on Packet Video, Torino, Italy, Sept. 7–9, 1988.

[21] L. Chiariglione and L. Corgnier, "System considerations for picture communication," in *Proc. IEEE 1984 Int. Commun. Conf.*, Amsterdam, May 1984, pp. 245–249.

[22] M. Schwartz, *Telecommunication Networks*, Reading, MA: Addison-Wesley, 1987.

[23] T. Bailly et al., "A technique for adaptive voice flow control in integrated packet networks," *IEEE Trans. Commun.*, vol. COM-28, pp. 325–333, Mar. 1980.

[24] M. Vetterli, "Multi-dimensional sub-band coding: Some theory and algorithms," *Signal Processing*, vol. 6, pp. 97–112, Feb. 1984.

[25] H. G. Musmann et al., "Advances in picture coding," *Proc. IEEE*, vol. 73, pp. 523–548, Apr. 1985.

[26] S-Q Li, "Study of packet loss in packet voice systems," *IEEE Trans. Commun.*, to be published.

[27] R. E. Blahut, *Theory and Practice of Error Control Codes*. Reading, MA: Addison-Wesley, 1983.

[28] G. Karlsson, "Sub-band coding for packet video," Ph.D. dissertation, Dep. Elec. Eng., Columbia University, May 1989.

[29] J-Y Cochennec, private communication.

[30] D. J. Le Gall and A. Tabatabai, "Sub-band coding of digital images using symmetric short kernel filters and arithmetic coding techniques," in *Proc. ICASSP 88*, New York, Apr. 1988, pp. 761–764.

[31] D. J. Le Gall and H. Gaggioni, "Transmission of HDTV signals under 140 Mbit/s using subband decomposition and discrete transform coding," in *Proc. Second Int. Workshop Signal Proc. HDTV*, L'Aquila, Italy, Feb. 1988, paper 64.

Constraints on Variable Bit-Rate Video for ATM Networks

Amy R. Reibman, *Member, IEEE* and Barry G. Haskell, *Fellow, IEEE*

Abstract—We consider constraints on the encoded bit rate of a video signal that are imposed by a channel and encoder and decoder buffers. We present conditions that ensure that the video encoder and decoder buffers do not overflow or underflow when the channel can transmit a variable bit rate. Using these conditions and a commonly proposed network-user contract, we examine the effect of a network policing function on the allowable variability in the encoded video bit rate. We describe how these ideas might be implemented in a system that controls both the encoded and transmitted bit rates. Finally, we present the performance of video that has been encoded using the derived constraints for the leaky bucket channel.

I. INTRODUCTION

TRADITIONALLY, video has been transmitted using channels that have constant rate. Because most video compression algorithms use variable length codes to improve compression, a buffer at the encoder is necessary to translate the variable rate output by the encoder into the constant-rate channel. A similar buffer is necessary at the decoder to translate the constant channel bit rate into a variable bit rate.

Recently, however, there has been much interest in sending video over broadband integrated services digital networks (B-ISDN). These networks are able to support variable bit rates by partitioning user data into a sequence of "cells" and inputting them to the network asynchronously. For this reason B-ISDN is referred to as an asynchronous transfer mode (ATM) network. ATM networks may allow video to be transmitted on a channel with variable rate.

In this paper, we examine the constraints imposed on the encoded video bit-rate as a result of encoder and decoder buffering. In particular, we show that for a constant-rate channel, it is possible to prevent the decoder buffer from overflowing or underflowing simply by ensuring that the encoder buffer never underflows or overflows, this is no longer the case for a variable-rate channel. Additional constraints must be imposed on the encoding rate, the channel rate, or both.

In addition, we also examine the effect of a proposed ATM network policing function on the encoded video bit rate. In general, network-imposed policing functions have the effect of limiting the bit rate that the network will

Manuscript received December 3, 1991; revised April 6, 1992. Paper was recommended by Associate Editor Yasuhiko Yasuda.

The authors are with AT&T Bell Laboratories, Holmdel, NJ 07733-3030.

IEEE Log Number 9202479.

guarantee to the user. Because video requires that certain information be received, it is therefore necessary for the video system to constrain its bit rate onto the network to ensure that it does not exceed that allowed by the policing function. Hence, we also examine the constraint on the encoded video bit rate imposed by these policing functions.

This paper is organized as follows. In Section II, we describe the ATM networks and the role of network policing functions. In Section III, we present constraints imposed by the encoder and decoder buffers on both the encoded and transmitted bit rates. In Section IV, we examine how channel constraints can further restrict the encoded and transmitted bit-rates. Sections V and VI present a system that jointly controls the encoded and transmitted bit-rates. Section VII presents some examples illustrating the improvements that can result by using a variable-rate channel. Section VIII concludes the paper with a discussion.

II. ATM NETWORKS

ATM networks are often proposed for transmitting video because they can accommodate the bit rate necessary for high-quality video, and because the quality of the video can benefit from the variable bit rate that the ATM network can theoretically provide. As a result, recent research has gone into developing video compression algorithms that have unconstrained bit rates but achieve constant quality [1]. By having the user select a desired quality, these algorithms can provide better compressed video than algorithms designed for a constant-rate channel, even when both algorithms produce the same average rate.

However, if the bit rate of all streams were to vary arbitrarily, the network would be unable to provide guaranteed delivery of all packets. Two solutions to this have been proposed. The first solution is to have the user assign a priority (high or low) to each packet submitted to the network. The high-priority packets are guaranteed by the network; the low-priority packets can be dropped by the network. The second solution (which is still necessary even given the first) is to assume that a contract exists between the network and the user. The network guarantees that the cell loss rate (CLR) for high-priority packets will not exceed an agreed-to value, provided that the user does not submit too many. A policing function monitors the user output and either drops packets in excess of the

Reprinted from *IEEE Trans. Circuits Syst.*, vol. 2, no. 4, pp. 361–372, Dec. 1992.

contract or marks these excess packets as low priority, possibly to be dropped later in the network.

The advantages of priority labeling, both for video [2]–[6] and for the network [7] have been well established. In addition, the effect of a policing function on the network behavior has also been studied [8]–[10]. A discussion of a unified approach to controlling congestion is given in [11]. In this paper we concentrate on examining the effect of the policing functions on the video quality.

For video, the existence of a policing function has a significant effect on the output bit rate because some information is essential to the decoder, e.g., timing data, start-of-picture codes, etc. If this information is not received, the video decoder will be unable to decode anything. Therefore, it is essential to the video user that all high-priority packets are received. This implies that the network should *never* drop high-priority packets or, equivalently, that the network should never change the marking of a high-priority packet to low priority. Therefore, it is essential that the video algorithm control its output bit rate to ensure that the network-imposed policing function does not detect any excess high-priority packets.

III. VIDEO BUFFER VERIFICATION FOR GENERAL VARIABLE-RATE CHANNELS

In this section, we present conditions necessary to guarantee that the buffers at the video encoder and decoder do not overflow or underflow. These conditions are presented both in terms of a constraint on the encoder rate and a constraint on the channel rate. The channel rate may be variable but is not otherwise constrained.

Clearly, if either buffer overflows, information is lost. Encoder buffer underflow is only a problem if the channel has constant bit rate and cannot be turned off; in this case, something must always be transmitted. Because encoder buffer underflow can always be avoided by sending stuffing bits, it is not considered a problem.

However, the concept of decoder buffer underflow is less intuitive since the decoder is generally capable of removing bits from its buffer faster than bits arrive. The decoder buffer is said to underflow when the decoder must display a new frame (which happens, e.g., every one-thirtieth of a second), but no new frame has been decoded. Therefore, three things must happen simultaneously: 1) the decoder buffer is empty, 2) the next-frame frame memory is not full, and 3) it is time to display a freshly decoded frame. For this reason, we discretize the problem using the uncoded frame period. A smaller period could be used if necessary in systems having relatively small buffer sizes.

For a constant bit-rate channel, it is possible to determine upper bounds on encoder and decoder buffer sizes such that if the encoder's output rate is controlled to ensure no encoder buffer overflow or underflow, then the decoder buffer will also never underflow or overflow. As we will see, the problem becomes more difficult when the channel may transmit a variable bit rate, for example, when transmitting video across packet (ATM) networks.

A. Buffer Dynamics

Examples of the encoder and decoder buffer dynamics are shown in Figs. 2 and 3, respectively. We define $E(t)$ to be the number of bits (or bytes or packets) output by the encoder at time t. The channel bit rate $R(t)$ is variable. $B^e(t)$ and $B^d(t)$ are the instantaneous fullnesses of the encoder and decoder buffers, respectively. Each buffer has a maximum size, $B^e_{\max}$ and $B^d_{\max}$, that cannot be exceeded. Given $B^e_{\max}$, the encoder is designed to ensure its buffer never overflows, i.e.,

$$0 \le B^e(t) \le B^e_{\max} \quad \forall t. \tag{1}$$

Here we examine conditions on the buffers and the channel to ensure the decoder buffer never overflows or underflows, i.e.,

$$0 \le B^d(t) \le B^d_{\max} \quad \forall t. \tag{2}$$

First, we discretize the problem by defining E_i ($i = 1, 2, \cdots$) to be the number of bits in the interval $[(i-1)T, iT)$, where T is the duration of one uncoded frame as output from the camera or fed to the display. Therefore,

$$E_i = \int_{(i-1)T}^{iT} E(t)\, dt. \tag{3}$$

Similarly, let R_i be the number of bits that are transmitted during the ith frame period:

$$R_i = \int_{(i-1)T}^{iT} R(t)\, dt. \tag{4}$$

The encoder buffer receives bits at rate $E(t)$ and outputs bits at rate $R(t)$. Therefore, assuming empty buffers prior to startup at time $t = 0$

$$B^e(t) = \int_0^t [E(s) - R(s)]\, ds \tag{5}$$

and the encoder buffer fullness after encoding frame i is

$$B^e_i = B^e(iT) = \int_0^{iT} [E(s) - R(s)]\, ds. \tag{6}$$

This can be written explicitly as

$$B^e_i = \sum_{j=1}^{i} E_j - \sum_{j=1}^{i} R_j \tag{7}$$

or recursively as

$$B^e_i = B^e_{i-1} + E_i - R_i. \tag{8}$$

After the decoder begins to receive data, it waits LT s before starting to decode. We assume for clarity that L is an integer, although this is not necessary. At the decoder, we define a new time index τ, which is zero when decoding starts.

$$t = \tau + LT + \text{channel.delay}. \tag{9}$$

The encoder can calculate the initial fullness of the decoder buffer $B^d(0)$ (when $\tau = 0$) if L is predetermined or sent explicitly as a decoder parameter. It is given by

$$B_0^d = \sum_{j=1}^{L} R_j. \tag{10}$$

The decoder buffer fullness at time $\tau = iT$ is then given by

$$B_i^d = B_{i-1}^d + R_{L+i} - E_i \tag{11}$$

$$B_i^d = B_0^d + \sum_{j=1}^{i} R_{L+j} - \sum_{j=1}^{i} E_j. \tag{12}$$

For $(i-1)T < \tau < iT$, the decoder buffer fullness varies, depending on the channel rate $R(t)$ and the rate at which the decoder extracts data from its buffer. In general in this interval, the decoder buffer fullness could rise up to the larger of $B_{i-1}^d + E_{i-1}$ or $B_i^d + E_i$, or fall to the smaller of $B_{i-1}^d - E_i$ of $B_i^d - E_{i+1}$.

There are two useful expressions for B_i^d when the channel has variable rate, each derived using (12) and (10).

$$B_i^d = \sum_{j=1}^{L} R_j + \sum_{j=L+1}^{L+i} R_j - \sum_{j=1}^{i} E_j$$

$$= \sum_{j=i+1}^{i+L} R_j - \left(\sum_{j=1}^{i} E_j - \sum_{j=1}^{i} R_j \right)$$

$$= \sum_{j=i+1}^{i+L} R_j - B_i^e \tag{13}$$

or

$$B_i^d = \sum_{j=i+1}^{i+L} E_j - \left(\sum_{j=1}^{i+L} E_j - \sum_{j=1}^{i+L} R_j \right)$$

$$= \sum_{j=i+1}^{i+L} E_j - B_{i+L}^e. \tag{14}$$

Equation (13) expresses B_i^d as a function of the cumulative channel rates over the last L frames and the encoder buffer fullness L frames ago, when frame i was encoded. Equation (14) expresses it as a function of the cumulative encoder rates over the last L frames and the encoder buffer fullness now, or when frame $i + L$ is encoded. This is an expression that the encoder can compute directly from its observations.

B. Buffer Verification

We now combine equations from Section III-A with (1) and (2), to obtain conditions necessary to prevent encoder and decoder buffer underflow and overflow using a general variable-rate channel. To prevent encoder buffer overflow and underflow, from (1) and (8) we have

$$0 \le B_{i-1}^e + E_i - R_i \le B_{max}^e \tag{15}$$

$$R_i - B_{i-1}^e \le E_i \le R_i + B_{max}^e - B_{i-1}^e \tag{16}$$

which is a constraint on the number of bits per coded frame for a given channel rate. For example, when the channel has a constant rate, the encoder prevents its buffer from overflowing or underflowing by varying the quality of coding [12]. If the encoder sees that its buffer is approaching fullness, it reduces the bit rate being input to the buffer by reducing the quality of coding, using a coarser quantizer on the data. Conversely, if encoder buffer underflow threatens, the encoder can generate more input data, either by increasing the quality of coding or by outputting stuffing data that are consistent with the coding syntax.

Alternatively, to achieve constant picture quality, we can instead let the number of bits per frame E_i be unconstrained, and force the channel rate R_i to accommodate. Rewriting (15), we get

$$0 \ge -B_{i-1}^e - E_i + R_i \ge -B_{max}^e$$

$$E_i - (B_{max}^e - B_{i-1}^e) \le R_i \le B_{i-1}^e + E_i \tag{17}$$

encoder overflow condition   encoder underflow condition

Therefore, encoder buffer overflow and underflow can be prevented by constraining either the encoded bit rate per frame period (16), or the transmitted bit rate per frame period (17).

To prevent decoder buffer overflow and underflow, we combine (2) and (11) to obtain

$$0 \le B_{i-1}^d + R_{i+L} - E_i \le B_{max}^d \tag{18}$$

$$R_{i+L} + B_{i-1}^d - B_{max}^d \le E_i \le R_{i+L} + B_{i-1}^d \tag{19}$$

which is a constraint on the encoder bit rate for a given channel rate.

Alternatively, we can again allow the number of bits per frame to be unconstrained and examine the constraint on the channel rate R_i.

$$E_i - B_{i-1}^d \le R_{i+L} \le E_i + (B_{max}^d - B_{i-1}^d)$$

or, for $i > L$,

$$E_{i-L} - B_{i-L-1}^d \le R_i \le E_{i-L} + (B_{max}^d - B_{i-L-1}^d).$$

decoder underflow   decoder overflow

condition   condition

$$\tag{20}$$

This provides a restriction on the channel rate R_i that depends on the encoder activity L frames ago.

Even if the channel rate is completely controllable, a restriction still exists on E_i, the number of bits used to encode frame i. This constraint is necessary to prevent simultaneous overflow of both buffers. (Note that simultaneous underflow of both buffers is not a problem. The upper bound of (17) is always greater than the lower bound of (20).)

It can be seen either by combining the lower bound of (17) with the upper bound of (20),

$$E_i - (B_{\max}^e - B_{i-1}^e) \le R_i \le E_{i-L} + (B_{\max}^d - B_{i-L-1}^d)$$

$$E_i \le E_{i-L} + (B_{\max}^e - B_{i-1}^e) + (B_{\max}^d - B_{i-L-1}^d) \quad (21)$$

or by noting that because the delay is L, the system must store L frames worth of data,

$$0 \le \sum_{j=i-L+1}^{i} E_j \le B_{\max}^d + B_{\max}^e. \quad (22)$$

These bounds arise because of the finite memory of the video system. The system can store no more than $B_{\max}^d + B_{\max}^e$ bits at any given time, but it must store L frames of data always. Therefore, these L frames cannot be coded with too many bits. In the case of equality for either (21) or (22), both buffers are completely full at the end of frame i.

In this section, we have considered the case where the channel delay is constant. To accommodate the variable channel delay expected in an ATM network, the largest expected channel delay should be used in (9). In addition, the decoder buffer should be large enough to contain the additional bits that may arrive with shorter delay. Thus if the minimum channel delay is Δ and the maximum channel delay is $\Delta + \delta$, (9) becomes

$$t = \tau + LT + \Delta + \delta \quad (23)$$

and the decoder buffer constraint of (18) becomes

$$0 \le B_{i-1}^d + R_{i+L} - E_i \le B_{\max}^d - \max_i \int_{iT}^{iT+\delta} R(s)\,ds. \quad (24)$$

IV. Buffer Verification for Channels with Rate Constraints

A. Fixed-Rate Channel

If the channel has a fixed bit rate, then the buffer verification problem simplifies. In particular, it is possible to guarantee that the decoder buffer never overflows or underflows, provided that the encoder buffer never overflows or underflows.

For the constant-rate channel let $R_i = RT$ be the number of bits transmitted during one uncoded frame period of duration T. The initial fullness of the decoder buffer when decoding starts is

$$B^d(0) = B_0^d = LRT. \quad (25)$$

The key to simplification is in (12), which reduces to

$$B_j^d = B_0^d - B_j^e \quad (26)$$

when the channel has constant rate. Note that this equation is not true for a variable-rate channel since, in that case,

$$B_j^d = B_0^d + \sum_{i=1}^{j} R_{L+i} - \sum_{i=1}^{j} E_i$$

$$\ne B_0^d + \sum_{i=1}^{j} R_i - \sum_{i=1}^{j} E_i$$

$$= B_0^d - B_j^e. \quad (27)$$

Because B_j^e is always positive, the decoder buffer is never as full at the end of a frame as it was before decoding started. Therefore, to prevent decoder buffer overflow, using (26), the decoder buffer size can be chosen solely to ensure that it can handle the initial buffer fullness, plus the number of bits for one frame. In most cases, the decoder is much faster than the channel rate, so we can choose $B_{\max}^d = LRT + \delta$ where δ is small.

In addition, we know that the decoder buffer will never underflow, provided that

$$0 \le B_j^d = LRT - B_j^e, \quad (28)$$

or, provided that $B_j^e \le LRT$. Therefore, if we choose $B_{\max}^e = LRT$, and ensure that the encoder buffer never overflows, the decoder buffer will never underflow. Herein lies the simplicity of the constant-rate channel: it is possible to ensure that the decoder buffer does not overflow or underflow simply by ensuring that the encoder buffer does not overflow or underflow.

We now discuss the choice of the decoder delay L and indicate how the delay enables a variable encoder bit rate, even though the channel has a fixed rate. The encoder buffer fullness can be written as

$$B_j^e = \sum_{k=1}^{j} E_k - jRT \le LRT. \quad (29)$$

Reorganizing,

$$\sum_{k=1}^{j} E_k \le (L+j)RT$$

so that

$$L \ge \sum_{k=1}^{j} E_k/RT - j, \quad \forall j \quad (30)$$

which indicates the trade-off between the necessary decoder delay and the variability in the number of encoded bits per frame. Because a variable number of bits per frame can provide better image quality, (30) also indicates the trade-off between the allowable decoder delay and the image quality.

Insight into how (30) involves the variability in the number of bits per coded frame can be seen by examining the two extremes of variability. First, suppose that all frames have the same number of bits $E_i = RT$. Then, $L \ge 0$, and no decoder delay is necessary. At the other extreme, suppose all the transmitted bits were for frame 1; then $L \geq E_1/RT - 1$. In this case, the decoder must wait until (most of) the data for the first frame have been received.

Therefore, the constant-rate channel provides the simplicity of ensuring no decoder buffer overflow or underflow by monitoring encoder buffer underflow or overflow. In addition, even though the channel has constant rate, with the use of a delay, it is possible to obtain some variability in the number of bits per encoded frame.

B. Leaky-Bucket Channel

We show that for the channel whose rate is controlled by a leaky-bucket policing function, the conditions on the encoder bit rate are somewhat weaker than those for a fixed-rate channel. Therefore, we can get some additional flexibility on the encoder bit rate.

When the network implements a leaky-bucket policing function, it keeps a counter indicating the fullness of an imaginary buffer inside the network. The input to the imaginary buffer (henceforth called the "bucket" here) is R_i bits for frame period i. The output rate of the bucket is $\overline{R}$ bits per frame period. The bucket size is $N_{\max}$. Hence, the instantaneous bucket fullness is

$$N_i = \max\left\{0, N_{i-1} + R_i - \overline{R}\right\}. \tag{31}$$

If the bucket never underflows, N_i can be written as

$$N_i = \sum_{j=1}^{i} R_j - i\overline{R}. \tag{32}$$

However, (32) actually provides only a lower bound on the bucket fullness since the actual bucket fullness may be larger if bucket underflow has occurred.

To ensure that the policing mechanism does not mark high-priority packets as droppable, rate R_i must be such that the bucket never overflows, i.e.,

$$N_i \leq N_{\max} \quad \forall i$$

or

$$R_i \leq N_{\max} - N_{i-1} + \overline{R} \tag{33}$$

Equation (33) defines the leaky-bucket constraint on the rate that is input to the network. Even if the bucket does underflow, the rate can also be upper bounded by

$$R_i \leq N_{\max} - \sum_{j=1}^{i-1} R_j + i\overline{R}. \tag{34}$$

Combining (34) with (17), which constrains the rate to prevent encoder buffer underflow and overflow, we have a

necessary condition on the encoded rate:

$$E_i \leq N_{\max} + B_{\max}^e - \sum_{j=1}^{i-1} R_j + i\overline{R} - B_{i-1}^e$$

$$\leq N_{\max} + B_{\max}^e + i\overline{R} - \sum_{j=1}^{i-1} R_j - \left(\sum_{j=1}^{i-1} E_j - \sum_{j=1}^{i-1} R_j\right)$$

$$\leq N_{\max} + B_{\max}^e + i\overline{R} - \sum_{j=1}^{i-1} E_j$$

$$E_i \leq B_{\max}^E + \overline{R} - B_{i-1}^E \tag{35}$$

where $B_{\max}^E = N_{\max} + B_{\max}^e$ is the size of a virtual encoder buffer and

$$B_i^E = \sum_{j=1}^{i} E_j - i\overline{R}$$

is the fullness of the virtual encoder buffer at time i.

Therefore, the encoder output bit rate E_i must be constrained (by the compression algorithm) to ensure that a virtual encoder buffer of size $B_{\max}^E$ does not overflow, assuming a constant output rate of $\overline{R}$ bits per frame. Because this constraint is less strict than preventing an actual encoder buffer with the same drain rate but smaller size $B_{\max}^e$ from overflowing or underflowing, we have a potential advantage over a channel with constant rate.

However, this is not the only constraint. In fact, preventing decoder buffer overflow can impose a stronger constraint. In particular, the right side of the decoder rate constraint (20) may actually be more strict than the leaky-bucket rate constraint (33). As a result, we may not actually be able to obtain the full flexibility in the encoder bit rate equivalent to using a virtual encoder buffer of a larger size.

It is possible, however, to reduce the actual delay at the decoder without sacrificing the flexibility in the encoded bit rate. Theoretically, we can obtain the same flexibility in the encoded bit rate that is available with a constant-rate channel and decoder delay L when we use a leaky-bucket channel with zero delay, provided that $L = N_{\max}/\overline{R}$ and $N_{\max} = B_{\max}^e = B_{\max}^d$. However, recall that we will certainly be paying for both $N_{\max}$ and $\overline{R}$.

V. Coding System with Joint Channel and Encoder Rate Control

In this section, we describe a method whereby the number of encoded bits for each video frame and the number of bits transmitted across the variable rate channel are selected jointly. The necessity arises as described previously: with a variable bit-rate channel, the decoder buffer imposes a constraint on the transmitted bit rate that is different than that imposed by the encoder buffer. This method also provides the flexibility of having channel bit rates that are less than the maximum allowed by the channel, which may be desirable when the channel is not constrained solely by its peak rate.

A. System Description

Fig. 1 describes a system incorporating these concepts. In Fig. 1, a video signal is applied to the video encoder. The video encoder produces an encoded video bit stream

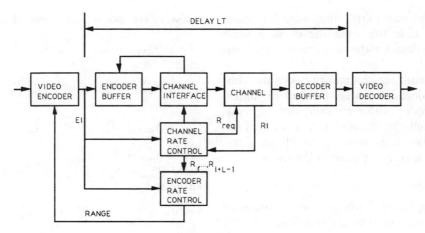

Fig. 1. System.

that is stored in the encoder buffer before being transmitted via the channel interface to the variable-rate channel. After being transmitted across the variable-rate channel, the video bit stream is stored in the decoder buffer. The bit stream from the decoder buffer is input to the video decoder, which outputs a video signal. The delay from encoder buffer input to decoder buffer output, exclusive of channel delay, is exactly LT s. The value of the delay L is known a priori, as are the encoder and decoder buffer sizes $B_{\max}^e$ and $B_{\max}^d$.

The video encoder can encode the video signal using any method that allows the number of bits that are produced to be controlled (see, e.g., [12]). A range indicating the number of bits that can be produced is provided by the encoder rate control device. The video encoder produces a bit stream that contains E_i number of bits in one frame period, which is within the range given by the encoder rate control device. These bits are input to the encoder buffer and stored until they are transmitted.

The channel rate control device takes as input the actual number of bits output in each frame period by the video encoder. It computes estimated channel rates R_i, $\cdots, R_{i+L-1}$, describing the number of bits that will be transmitted across the channel in the following L frame periods. These rates are chosen to prevent encoder and decoder buffer overflow and underflow and to conform to the channel constraint. The channel rate control device sends the estimated value of R_i to channel as R_{req}. We assume here that the channel grants the request, in which case $R_i = R_{\mathrm{req}}$. (If the request is not granted, the channel rate control device can selectively discard information from the bit stream. However, such information discarding is an emergency measure only since our express purpose is to avoid such discarding.) If the encoder buffer empties, the channel interface unit immediately terminates transmission. In most cases, this will cause a reduction of R_i.

The encoder rate control device computes a bound on the number of bits that the video encoder may produce without overflowing or underflowing either the encoder or decoder buffers. It takes as input the actual number of bits E_i output in each frame period by the encoder. It also takes as input the channel rate values that are selected by the channel rate control device. The bound output by the encoder rate control device is computed to guarantee that neither the encoder nor decoder buffers overflow or underflow.

B. Encoder and Channel Rate-Control Devices

We describe here the joint operation of the encoder and channel rate-control devices. To simplify the discussion, we assume that the channel allows transmission at the requested rate. This is not an unreasonable assumption because the channel rate-control device is selecting estimated channel rates to conform to the channel constraints negotiated between the channel and the video system.

Joint operation of the encoder and channel rate-control devices:

1) Initialize buffer fullness variables prior to encoding frame $i = 1$: $B_i^e = B_i^d = 0$. Initialize leaky bucket fullness N_i.
2) Estimate the future channel rates, future leaky-bucket fullnesses, and future decoder-buffer fullnesses for the next L frames. For the channel rates, we utilize inequalities (20) and (33), where for $k \le 0, E_k = 0$. Leaky-bucket and decoder-buffer fullnesses are given, respectively, by (31) and (12). Rewriting them, we get for $j = i, i + 1, \cdots, i + L - 1$

$$E_{j-L} - B_{j-L-1}^d \le R_j \le E_{j-L} + \left(B_{\max}^d - B_{j-L-1}^d \right)$$

decoder underflow   decoder overflow condition
    condition   (36)

$$R_j \le N_{\max} - N_{j-1} + \overline{R} \qquad (37)$$

$$N_j = \max \left\{ 0, N_{j-1} + R_j - \overrightarrow{R} \right\} \qquad (38)$$

$$B_{j-L}^d = B_{j-L-1}^d + R_j - E_{j-L}. \qquad (39)$$

Several selection methods for the estimated rates are discussed in Section VI. These methods may ideally consider the fact that a frame with a large number of bits has just occurred or is imminent. They may also consider the cost of transmitting at a given rate. When $i \leq L$, no frames are being decoded and the decoder buffer is only filling. In general, the sum of $R_1, \cdots, R_L$ should be chosen to exceed the expected encoded bit rate of the first few frames in order to avoid decoder buffer underflow.

3) Calculate an upper bound on R_{i+L} using the leaky-bucket constraint (37):

$$R_{i+L} \leq R_{i+L}^{ub} = N_{\max} - N_{i+L-1} + \overline{R}. \quad (40)$$

4) Calculate an upper bound on E_i using constraints on encoder buffer overflow from inequality (16) and decoder buffer underflow from inequality (19).

$$E_i \leq B_{\max}^e + R_i - B_{i-1}^e \quad (41)$$

$$E_i \leq R_{i+L}^{ub} + B_{i-1}^d. \quad (42)$$

The minimum of these two upper bounds on E_i is output by the encoder rate control device to the video encoder.

5) Encode frame i to get E_i bits.
6) Using the actual value of E_i, recompute R_i, the actual number of bits transmitted this frame period. (This may be necessary if the encoder buffer would underflow, thus making the actual R_i less than that estimated.)

$$R_i = B_{i-1}^e + E_i. \quad (43)$$

7) Use actual values of E_i and R_i to compute actual values of B_i^e, N_i, and B_{i-L}^d using (8), (38), and (39), respectively.
8) Increment i, and go to step 2).

VI. RATE-CONTROL STRATEGIES

In this section, we describe an encoder rate control algorithm, and two channel rate-control algorithms for the leaky bucket. Other channel constraints could have been used instead. In the encoder rate-control algorithm, the quantizer step size used by the encoder is chosen to ensure not only that the encoder buffer does not overflow but also that the decoder buffer does not underflow when the corresponding data is decoded. In the channel rate-control algorithms, we select the channel rate R_i based on the channel constraints as well as the decoder buffer fullness.

Voeten *et al.* [13] present an encoder rate-control algorithm that considers the gabarit channel constraint and the encoder buffer. Bits are submitted to the channel as fast as the channel constraint allows. The decoder buffer is not considered.

A. Encoder Rate Control

To control the encoder rate in order to ensure no encoder or decoder buffer overflow or underflow, we select the quantizer step size to be used by the encoder.

Our selection of quantizer step size is modified from the Reference Model 8 (RM8) simulation encoder [12].

In the RM8 simulation encoder, the quantizer step size is selected based solely on the fullness of the encoder buffer. With the encoder buffer size chosen to be $B_{\max}^e = P * 6400$, the RM8 buffer control selects

$$Q = 2 * \text{INT}(32 * B^e(t)/B_{\max}^e) + 2 \quad (44)$$

where INT( ) denotes truncation to a fraction without rounding.

We make two modifications to the RM8 encoder rate control algorithm. The first modification is introduced to prevent the decoder buffer from underflowing when the frame currently being encoded is finally decoded. We rewrite the constraint of (42) as

$$E_i \leq R_{i+L}^{ub} + \left[B_{\max}^d - (B_{\max}^d - B_{i-1}^d) \right] \quad (45)$$

and, comparing this to the encoder buffer overflow constraint (41), we set

$$Q = 2 * \text{INT}\Big(32 * \max \Big\{ B^e(t)/B_{\max}^e,$$

$$\left[B_{\max}^d - B^d(t + LT))/B_{\max}^d \right] \Big\} \Big) + 2. \quad (46)$$

Note that the value of the decoder buffer fullness is a prediction of what we expect the decoder buffer fullness to be when the current frame is decoded.

If the channel rate is constant, (46) does not select a different quantizer than RM8. However, if the channel rate is variable, the quantization control in (46) is necessary to prevent the current frame from being encoded with more bits than the system can transmit before this frame is to be decoded.

However, an additional modification must be made to the quantization strategy to enable the leaky bucket to empty when scene activity is low. If we start with a full leaky bucket and choose Q as in (46), the leaky bucket would never empty and we would always transmit at the average channel rate. As with RM8, the quantizer step size can decrease arbitrarily to increase the number of encoded bits per frame and keep the encoder buffer from underflowing. However, if we can enable the leaky bucket to empty, the channel rate can subsequently be larger than average, and the leaky-bucket channel can allow better performance than a peak-rate channel. Thus, a second modification to the RM8 quantizer step size is necessary to obtain some advantages from a variable bit-rate channel.

Rather than encoding fairly still parts of the sequence with progressively smaller quantizer step sizes, we assume the user has preselected a minimum quantizer step size together with the resultant maximum quality. Therefore, if a scene is still, it will be encoded with quantizer $Q = Q_{\min}$, and its average encoded bit rate will be less than $\overline{R}$.

Thus, we choose the quantizer step size to be

$$Q = \max \left\{ Q_{\min}, 2 * \text{INT}\left(32 * \max \left\{ B^e(t) / B^e_{\max}, \right.\right.\right.$$

$$\left.\left.\left. \left[B^d_{\max} - B^d(t + LT) \right] / B^d_{\max} \right\} \right) + 2 \right\}.$$

By selecting a minimum step size, the user sets an upper bound on the quality that can be received. (A given quantizer step size does not ensure a given image quality; however the two are closely related.) Although the user makes a small sacrifice in still image quality by choosing, say $Q_{\min} > 4$, such a choice may yield overall better quality.

B. Leaky-Bucket Channel Rate Control

We compare two rate control algorithms for the leaky bucket. Both use the basic procedure of Section V-B; however, they differ in the selection of R_i. The first algorithm is greedy, always choosing the maximum rate allowed by both the channel and the decoder-buffer fullness. The second algorithm is conservative, selecting a channel rate to gradually fill the decoder buffer if the leaky bucket is not full.

Greedy Leaky-Bucket Rate-Control Algorithm (GLB): For the greedy algorithm (GLB), we choose the maximum rate that both the channel and the decoder buffer will allow. Therefore,

$$R_i = \min \left\{ B^e_i, E_{i-L} + B^d_{\max} - B^d_{i-L-1}, N_{\max} - N_{i-1} + \overline{R} \right\}. \quad (47)$$

The first constraint prevents the encoder buffer from underflowing, the second constraint prevents the decoder buffer from overflowing, and the third constraint prevents the leaky bucket from overflowing. Equation (47) is also used to obtain the estimated rates.

Considering only the encoder buffer fullness, the greedy leaky-bucket algorithm appears optimal. Because we transmit at the maximum rate allowed by both the network and the decoder buffer, the encoder buffer is kept as empty as possible, providing the most room to store newly encoded data. If we were to transmit at less than the maximum rate, then the bits that would remain in the encoder buffer would still need to be transmitted later. However, this algorithm may actually suffer in performance because it fills the bucket as fast as possible. The gain in performance provided by the leaky bucket could be of longer duration if the leaky bucket filled more slowly.

Conservative Leaky-Bucket Rate-Control Algorithm (CLB): The second rate-control algorithm for the leaky bucket is more conservative. The rate is chosen to either fill the leaky bucket, to fill the decoder buffer (if this will take fewer than $\overline{R}$ b), or to take L frames to fill the decoder buffer. The estimated rate R_i is assigned as follows:

$$tmp = E_{i-L} + B^d_{\max} - B^d_{i-L-1};$$

$$if(tmp > \overline{R})\, tmp = \overline{R} + \left(E_{i-L} + B^d_{\max} - B^d_{i-L-1} - \overline{R} \right)/L;$$

$$R_i = \min \left(tmp, N_{\max} - N_i + \overline{R} \right).$$

Because the rate is smaller than the maximum, we will see that we can extend the duration of the improvement provided by the leaky bucket, although we may limit the magnitude of the improvement.

VII. SIMULATION EXAMPLES

In this section, we numerically compare the video quality of the rate-control strategies described in Section VI to the video quality produced using a channel with a peak rate constraint. We examine the results for the table tennis and ferris wheel CIF sequences. The table tennis sequence contains several scenes with varying average bit rates, whereas the Ferris wheel sequence contains one scene with two periods in which a wheel is rotating in front of the camera and an interim period in which the wheels are rotating perpendicular to the camera near the edges of the image.

A. Simulation Approach

We simulate using the basic compression algorithm of RM8. The only modification is in the quantizer step-size selection (described in Section VI) and the buffer regulation algorithm. For each frame period, we estimate the current rate R_i and an upper bound on the future rate R^{ub}_{i+L}. We assume that both the current and future rates are divided as evenly as possible across the frame. They may not be exactly evenly divided if the encoder buffer started empty and the encoded bit rate at the beginning of the frame is small. The interval between recomputing buffer variables is 11 macroblocks. In addition to recomputing the encoder-buffer fullness, we also recompute the estimated future decoder-buffer fullness and the current leaky-bucket fullness.

For our examples, intraframe coding was used periodically every 60 frames, as well as when a scene change occurs. We use $P = 58$ to select the nominal average rate of $P * 64$ kb/s second, or 3.712 Mb/s. As a result, the nominal average number of transmitted bits per frame period is $\overline{R} = 123733$ b.

Of the six variables (the delay, the encoder- and decoder-buffer sizes, the bucket size, the nominal average channel rate, and the minimum quantizer step size), we examine the effect of changing the minimum quantizer step-size $Q_{\min}$ and the leaky bucket size $N_{\max}$. Default parameters are those specified by RM8: $B^e_{\max} = B^d_{\max} = LT\overline{R}$, where $L = 3$. We assume the network bucket is full initially, i.e., $N_0 = N_{\max}$.

B. Simulation Results

Quantizer Step-Size: We begin by illustrating the effect of a judicious choice of $Q_{\min}$ using the Ferris wheel sequence. Fig. 4(a) shows the peak signal-to-noise ratio

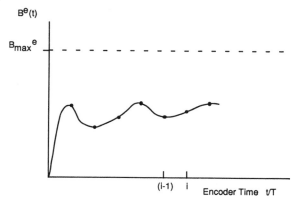

Fig. 2. Encoder buffer dynamics.

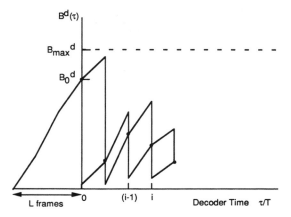

Fig. 3. Decoder buffer dynamics.

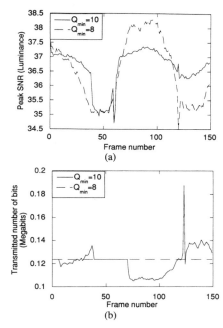

Fig. 4. Effect of $Q_{\min}$. (a) Peak SNR. (b) Transmitted number of bits per frame.

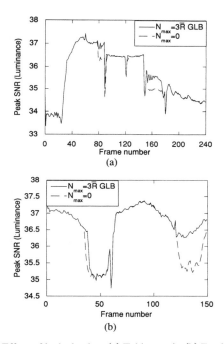

Fig. 5. Effect of leaky bucket. (a) Table tennis. (b) Ferris wheel.

(PSNR $= 10 \log_{10}$ [(mean squared error)$/255 * 255$] as a function of time when the minimum quantizer step sizes are $Q_{\min} = 8$ and 10, with a leaky-bucket size of $N_{\max} = 3\overline{R}$ using the GLB rate control algorithm. When $Q_{\min} = 8$, the quality varies greatly as a function of image content. However, when $Q_{\min} = 10$, the image quality is fairly constant from frame 60 onward. If the viewer cannot distinguish between images with a PSNR greater than 37, then the larger PSNR for frames 68–114 when $Q_{\min} = 8$ is effectively wasted.

The associated channel rates for each case are shown in Fig. 4(b). When $Q_{\min} = 8$, the number of bits transmitted by the channel during each frame period is constant, $R_i = \overline{R} \; \forall i$. When $Q_{\min} = 10$, we have a variable-channel bit rate, although it is constrained by the leaky bucket. The actual average channel rate when $Q_{\min} = 8$ is 3.712 Mb/s, whereas it is 3.651 Mb/s when $Q_{\min} = 10$. Alternatively, if we use $Q_{\min} = 12$ (not shown), the quantizer step size is always $Q_{\min}$. This produces an actual average rate of 3.083 Mb/s that is significantly below the nominal.

Leaky-Bucket Size: Next we examine the effect of changing the leaky bucket size $N_{\max}$. For simplicity, we first examine the two cases $N_{\max} = 0$ and $N_{\max} = 3\overline{R}$. When $N_{\max} = 0$, the channel rate can be no larger than $\overline{R}$; however, it can be less if the encoder buffer is empty.

The PSNR for the table tennis and ferris wheel sequences are shown in Fig. 5(a) and (b), respectively, for $N_{\max} = 0$ and for $N_{\max} = 3\overline{R}$ with the greedy leaky-bucket

(GLB) algorithm. For the table tennis sequence, $Q_{\min} = 8$, whereas for the ferris wheel sequence, $Q_{\min} = 10$. For each sequence, the PSNR when $N_{\max} = 3\overline{R}$ is always at least as good as when $N_{\max} = 0$. However, for the table tennis sequence, $N_{\max} = 3\overline{R}$ performs better than $N_{\max} = 0$ between frames 78 and 92 and between frames 151 and 176. For the ferris wheel sequence, $N_{\max} = 3\overline{R}$ performs slightly better than $N_{\max} = 0$ between frames 35 and 40 and performs significantly better from frame 120 onward. During the rest of each sequence, the presence of a nonzero leaky bucket has little effect.

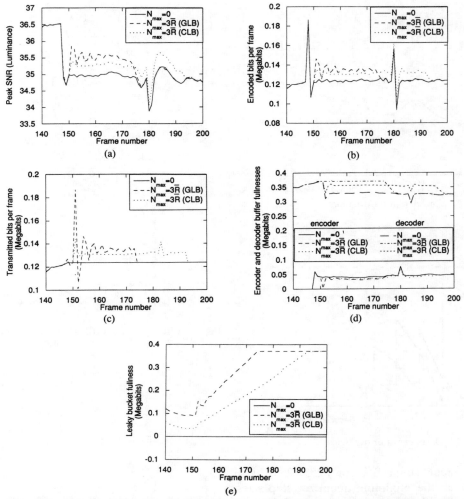

Fig. 6. Effect of leaky bucket, and table tennis. (a) PSNR. (b) Encoded bits per frame E_i. (c) Transmitted bits per frame R_i. (d) Encoder and decoder buffer fullnesses B_i^e and B_i^d. (e) Leaky bucket fullness N_i.

An explanation of the performance improvement of the leaky bucket is best found by simultaneously examining graphs of the PSNR, encoded bit rate E_i, the channel bit rate R_i, the encoder- and decoder-buffer fullnesses B_i^e and B_i^d, and the leaky-bucket fullness N_i. These are shown for the table tennis sequence in Fig. 6, and for the ferris wheel sequence in Fig. 7, expanded to show the regions of interest. The conservative leaky-bucket (CLB) algorithm with $N_{\max} = 3\bar{R}$ is also shown in the same figures.

For both sequences, at the start of the intervals shown, the leaky bucket is not full (Figs. 6(e) and 7(e)). Therefore, when the scene activity increases (whether because of a scene change (table tennis) or just increased activity (ferris wheel)), both algorithms (GLB and CLB) select the transmitted rate (Figs. 6(c) and 7(c)) to be larger than average. This keeps the encoder buffer (Figs 6(d) and 7(d)) emptier, which allows more encoded bits per frame (Figs. 6(b) and 7(b)), producing improved image quality (Figs. 6(a) and 7(a)). For the table tennis sequence, the improvement is approximately 0.5 dB over a range of 25–45 frames, whereas for the ferris wheel sequence, the improvement is over 1 dB for at least 30 frames.

The conservative algorithm (CLB) does not perform as well as the greedy algorithm (GLB) when both are performing better than no leaky bucket. However, the CLB performs better than no leaky bucket over a longer period since the leaky bucket does not fill as quickly.

Next, we examine the effect that increasing the bucket size has on the image quality. Fig. 8(a) and (b) show the PSNR and leaky-bucket fullnesses for $N_{\max} = 0, \bar{R}, 2\bar{R}, 3\bar{R}, 4\bar{R}, 5\bar{R}$ using the GLB for the table tennis sequence. In general, as the bucket size increases, performance does not decrease. That is, for a particular frame, $N_{\max} = 3\bar{R}$ may not perform better than $N_{\max} = 2\bar{R}$; however, as $N_{\max}$ increases, the duration of improvement lengthens. $N_{\max} = \bar{R}$ provides significant improvement over $N_{\max} = 0$ for only 7 frames, whereas $N_{\max} = 5\bar{R}$ outperforms $N_{\max} = 0$ for over 40 frames.

VIII. DISCUSSION AND CONCLUSIONS

We have presented constraints on the variable transmission rate and the encoded rate of compressed video that is imposed by encoder and decoder buffers. A system is presented that controls both the encoded and transmitted bit rates to satisfy these constraints. This solution is

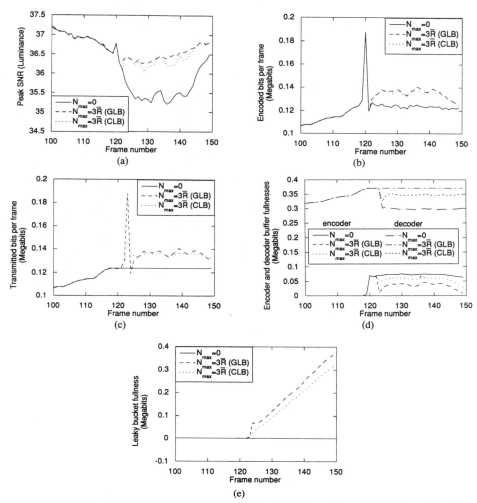

Fig. 7. Effect of leaky bucket, and Ferris wheel. (a) PSNR. (b) Encoded bits per frame E_i. (c) Transmitted bits per frame R_i. (d) Encoder and decoder buffer fullnesses B_i^e and B_i^d. (e) Leaky bucket fullness N_i.

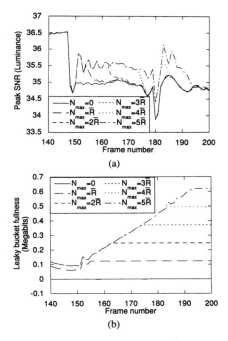

Fig. 8. Effect of leaky-bucket size, table tennis. (a) Peak SNR. (b) Leaky-bucket fullness.

essential if the decoder buffer size is fixed a priori. We presented an encoder rate control algorithm, and two channel rate control algorithms for the leaky bucket channel. The performance of each was illustrated on video sequences.

In general, the leaky bucket will improve image quality in two situations: at an intraframe when the leaky bucket is not full, and when the scene activity increases while the leaky bucket is not full. However, to obtain the improvement, the selection of $Q_{\min}$ is critical. If $Q_{\min}$ is too small, the leaky bucket will be full when the scene activity increases. Alternatively, if $Q_{\min}$ is too large, the quality will be limited by $Q_{\min}$ rather than the encoder buffer fullness.

Also, the magnitude of the quality improvement is often not significant. For the results shown, the magnitude of the improvement is limited by the decoder buffer fullness. More significant improvements may be available if the decoder buffer is not kept nearly as full.

More sophisticated encoder rate control algorithms are possible, including those that use adaptive quantization based on scene content. More sophisticated channel rate control algorithms are also possible. For example, the rate control algorithm could forecast when an intraframe will be encoded and attempt to empty the encoder buffer in advance. However, the results presented here do indicate the extent to which quality improvement is possible by using a leaky-bucket channel constraint.

Overall, if the user selects a maximum quality they are willing to receive, using a leaky-bucket channel instead of a constant-rate channel may allow them to achieve overall better image quality. However, because of the presence of the channel constraint, it will not be possible to obtain truly constant image quality.

REFERENCES

[1] J. C. Darragh and R. L. Baker, "Fixed distortion subband coding of images for packet-switched networks," *IEEE J. Selected Areas Commun.*, vol. 7, no. 5, pp. 789–800, June 1989.

[2] M. Ghanbari, "Two-layer coding of video signals for VBR networks," *IEEE J. Selected Areas Commun.*, vol. 7, no. 5, pp. 771–781, June 1989.

[3] A. R. Reibman, "DCT-based embedded coding for packet video," *Image Communication*, June 1991.

[4] G. Karlsson and M. Vetterli, "Packet video and its integration into the network architecture," *IEEE J. Selected Areas Commun.*, vol. 7, no. 5, pp. 739–751, June 1989.

[5] F. Kishino, K. Manabe, Y. Hayashi, and H. Yasuda, "Variable bit-rate coding of video signals for ATM networks," *IEEE J. Selected Areas Commun.*, vol. 7, no. 5, pp. 801–806, June 1989.

[6] M. Nomura, T. Fujii, and N. Ohta, "Layered packet-loss protection for variable rate video coding using DCT," in *Second Int. Workshop on Packet Video*, 1988.

[7] G. Ramamurthy and B. Sengupta, "Modeling and analysis of a variable bit rate video multiplexer," in *Proc. 7th ITC Seminar*, 1990.

[8] E. P. Rathgeb, "Modeling and performance comparison of policing mechanisms for ATM networks," *IEEE J. Selected Areas Commun.*, vol. 9, no. 3, pp. 325–334, April 1991.

[9] M. Butto, E. Cavallero, and A. Tonietti, "Effectiveness of the 'leaky bucket' policing mechanism in ATM networks," *IEEE J. Selected Areas Commun.*, vol. 9, no. 3, pp. 335–342, April 1991.

[10] L. Dittmann, S. B. Jacobsen, and K. Moth, "Flow enforcement algorithms for ATM networks," *IEEE J. Selected Areas Commun.*, vol. 9, no. 3, pp. 343–350, April 1991.

[11] A. E. Eckberg, Jr., D. T. Luan, and D. M. Lucantoni, "An approach to controlling congestion in ATM networks," *Int. J. Digital and Analog Communication Syst.*, vol. 3, pp. 199–209, 1990.

[12] "Description of reference model 8 (RM8)," Tech. Rep. 525, CCITT SGXV Working Party XV/4, 1989.

[13] B. Voeten, F. V. der Putten, and M. Lamote, "Preventive policing in video codecs for ATM networks," in *Fourth Int. Workshop on Packet Video*, pp. G1.1–G1.6, 1991.

Chapter 5
Digital Video in Multimedia: Technology for Mass Applications

C.A.A.J. GREEBE and R. McFARLANE

PHILIPS LABORATORIES
345 SCARBOROUGH ROAD
BRIARCLIFF MANOR, NY 10510

The most significant advance in information delivery in the past few years, which will bring multimedia to the masses, is the emergence of digital compressed video, which grew out of the original need to transmit and receive images over telephone lines for videoconferencing. The art of digital compression of moving images is now approaching maturity. Acceptable quality NTSC video can now be transmitted over a T1 telephone line (1.5 Mb/s) and high quality NTSC video needs only to occupy about one-fourth of a present cable or DBS channel. Equipment for this kind of delivery will become available in the U.S. in 1994. Concurrently, both the cable operators and the telephone companies have been deploying fiber-optic lines to replace twisted pair copper and coax, as technological advances make the transition cost-effective.

The combination of fiber-optic networks and digital compressed video will allow at least a ten-fold increase in the number of programs a cable network can provide (500 programs); it could offer, for example, all the "blockbuster" movies on demand (say at 15-minute intervals). The network will be able to devote some program channels for data at a 5-Mb/s rate each, orders of magnitude faster than conventional teletext. These channels, which can carry arbitrary mixes of data, still pictures, video, and audio, can be combined to provide 30 Mb/s for each 6-MHz band, and will be the vehicles for new consumer multimedia service via cable.

The advances in compressed digital video and audio will provide the ingredients for making mass delivery of multimedia programming at reasonable cost. As the multimedia services enter the consumer market, many observers foresee a merging of the television set and the personal computer to various extents, initially via the use of set-tops with the TV sets. This increased intelligence and computing power of the viewing device will bring customized interactive data services to the consumer, and will require novel consumer-friendly interfaces. Today, the best evidence of the coming multimedia revolution is in the acceptance of the CD-ROM and new multimedia embodiments such as CD-I as the storage elements of choice.

The digital compact disc, which evolved from the analog optical videodisc technology developed in the early 1970s, was created to give the consumer one hour of pure digital stereo sound. However, the digital stream can be regarded as 600 Mbytes of pure data, delivered at a rate of 1.4 Mbit/s and containing any combination of text, pictures, graphics, sound, or software. The compact disc in this application becomes the compact disc read-only memory (CD-ROM) requiring a computer to manage the data stream.

While the CD-ROM could store large volumes of text and graphics, its value as a storage device for multimedia was realized only after the development of video compression, which provided substantial reduction in the storage requirements for moving pictures. Applying the compression method of MPEG (Motion Picture Expert Group), an accepted world standard, the CD-ROM has evolved into a multimedia memory. The most popular implementation is the compact disc interactive (CD-I) which today can deliver full motion video of better than VHS quality at a rate of 1.2 Mbit/s, with 0.2 M/bit/s for stereo audio of CD quality. Five playback modes are supported by the current CD-I player: normal play, slow motion forward (variable), freeze frame, single picture forward, and scan. Prior to the recent realization of MPEG-1 full motion video, the CD-I representation of video was restricted to pictures of 1/9 the full screen size and at low picture-refresh rates—15 Hz. The quality of the video, which is compressed in non-real-time, using human intervention for optimum results, has been characterized as better than VHS quality, or good enough to be considered by telephone companies for video-on-demand service over existing copper pairs.

As the delivery of multimedia for the masses evolves rapidly towards real-time delivery, the consumer will be faced with the problem of navigating through the multitude of live and prerecorded video offerings, and new multimedia transactional, educational, and entertainment services. Today analog cable networks with 50 to 65 channels find it necessary to devote at least two channels for directory service, a "barker channel" providing video-based advertising for a dozen pay-per-view offerings, and a teletext-style channel for traditional program listing. In future cable and switched-network systems, using fiber and compressed digital video, the directory can be more extended, more descriptive, and easier to operate (user friendly) than present schemes.

A digital channel occupying the same bandwidth as the present analog channel (6 MHz) can support a data rate of 3.5 Mbytes/s, three orders of magnitude faster than teletext. At this speed, a database of several megabytes can be downloaded in a few seconds, providing a form of "super" teletext. Using a few buttons on an infrared remote control, the television viewer can exercise local interactivity. Navigation via an interactive television guide would employ text, graphics, still pictures, and video clips to make the search for the desired program more interesting.

The future addition of a low-speed data return path, via the remote control to the cable headend or telephone network, will enable full interactivity and, with the downloading of program software to more intelligent receivers, the techniques of the multimedia television guide will be open to new applications that are transactional in nature, such as teleshopping, distance learning, and games.

FURTHER READING

[1] D. Andrew, "MPEG encoding of full screen video for compact disc interactive," *Philips Research Labs-Redhill Review,* pp. 59–61, 1991.

[2] G. Davenport et al., "Cinematic primitives for multimedia," *IEEE Computer Graphics and Applications,* July, pp. 67–74, 1991.

[3] P. Ford, "Microsoft windows with multimedia extensions: standards, simplicity, and success in multimedia," *CD-ROM Professional,* pp. 53–55, 1992.

[4] C. Goldfarb, "A standard for structured hypermedia interchange," *Computer,* August, pp. 81–84, 1991.

[5] P. Hallenbeck and J. Hallenbeck, "Personal home TV programming," *Proc. ICCE,* pp. 310–311, 1990.

[6] E. Hoffert et al., "QuickTime: an extensible standard for digital multimedia," *37th Annual Int. Computer Conf. COMPCON,* pp. 15–20, Spring 1992.

[7] R. MacNeil, "Capturing multimedia design knowledge using TYRO, the constraint based designer apprentice," *Proc. SPIE V. 1460,* pp. 94–102, 1991.

[8] B. Mandalia et al., "Flexible hardware architecture for multimedia communications processing," *IEEE Int. Conf. Communications,* pp. 961–965, 1989.

[9] M. Mills, "Media composition for casual users," *37th Annual IEEE Int. Computer Conf.,* pp. 52–57, 1992.

[10] S. Mountford, "When TVs are computers are TVs (panel)," *ACM Conf. Human Factors in Computing Systems,* pp. 227–230, 1992.

[11] M.M. Mourad, "Some issues in the implementation of multimedia communication system," *2nd IEEE Workshop on Future Trends Distrib. Computing Systems,* pp. 4–13, 1990.

[12] N. Negroponte, "Media room," *Proc. SID,* vol. 22, no. 2, pp. 109–113, 1981.

[13] N. Negroponte, "Media technology, lunatic fringe," *Proc. 35th. Nat'l. Conf. Advancement of Research,* pp. 192–203, 1991.

[14] N. Negroponte, "Products and services for computer networks," *Scientific American,* Sept., pp. 76–83, 1991.

[15] D. Penna and S. Turner, "CD ROM—new applications for the compact disc," *Philips Research Labs-Redhill Review,* pp. 41–42, 1985.

[16] J. Piesing, "A design tool system for compact disc interactive," *Philips Research Labs-Redhill Review,* pp. 62–63, 1991.

[17] N. Richards, "Showing photo CD pictures on CD-I," *Philips Research Labs-Redhill Review,* pp. 11–14, 1990.

[18] T. Salamone, "Multimedia: state-of-the-art and future outlook," *Proc. NCGA 1990 Conf.,* pp. 234–239, 1990.

[19] M. Shiels, "A frame language for compact disc interactive," *Philips Research Labs-Redhill Review,* pp. 56–58, 1991.

[20] R. Steinmetz et al., "Generic support for distributed multimedia applications," *IEEE Int. Conf. Communications,* pp. 1451–1457, 1990.

[21] R. Steinmetz, "Synchronization properties in multimedia systems," *IEEE J. Selected Areas in Communications,* April, pp. 401–412, 1990.

[22] J. van der Meer, "The full motion system for CD-I," *IEEE Trans. Consumer Electronics,* vol. 38, no. 4, pp. 910–920 1992.

[23] J. Wendorf and H. Strubbe, "Fast digital data channels enable new cable services," *NCTA Technical Papers,* pp. 173–178, 1992.

FAST DIGITAL DATA CHANNELS ENABLE NEW CABLE SERVICES

J. Wendorf and H. Strubbe

Philips Laboratories, Briarcliff Manor, NY

Abstract

With the advent of digital delivery systems in CATV, fast data channels of multiple megabytes per second are feasible. Such channels open new possibilities for multimedia interactive applications. They can be used to provide an enhanced TV guide service that includes still pictures or even video clips. They can provide an electronic advertising magazine with pictures. Under appropriate conditions, they can lead to a variety of CD-I like applications. This paper outlines some of the new cable services made possible with fast, one way data channels, and explains the issues to be addressed in developing those services.

Keywords: television, cable, digital, teletext, multimedia, database, CD-I, TV guide.

INTRODUCTION

For many years broadcasters have included digital data in the video signals they send to TV receivers. Examples are teletext [1,2] and closed caption systems [3]. We consider such data channels "slow", as they carry less than 2 Kbytes/second. For closed captions, the rate is only 60 bytes per second. If in place of video an entire 6 MHz TV channel is used only for data, much higher rates are possible. For example, full channel teletext could carry roughly 0.5 Mbytes/second.

The advent of digital delivery systems in cable TV (CATV) provides the opportunity for even faster data channels of multiple megabytes per second. In the Philips Digital Video system [4], each 6 MHz TV channel can carry roughly 3.5 Mbytes/second. Such fast data channels open new possibilities for multimedia interactive applications.

In the following section we explain the concept of locally interactive applications, based on the repeated, one way transmission of complete databases. This is the primary technique for exploiting fast data channels. We then describe three applications that use this technique: an electronic TV guide, an electronic advertising magazine, and a system help and tutorial facility.

Following these examples we explain how a wide variety of applications, including currently unforeseen applications, can be supported through the transmission and loading of an application's code, along with its database. We then describe a further extension, the use of local storage such as a digital tape or optical disc, to capture all or selected portions of a database for later play back. Finally, we discuss some of the database design issues, including the overall structure of the database and the format of its constituent data items.

FAST DATA CHANNELS

In this paper we assume a one way transmission channel, as supported by most current CATV systems. With a two way interactive channel, many applications would be handled differently. We do not expect two way fast data channels to be widely available at low cost in the near future. However, the addition of a separate, slow back channel to a one way fast data channel is an extension that will be considered in our future work.

We also assume a single, 6 MHz TV channel is being used. In the future, multiple adjacent channels could be combined to provide even faster digital data channels.

With a one way data channel, it is not possible to send a query to a remote database to obtain a specified item of interest. Instead, the entire database can be transmitted from the remote location and scanned sequentially by a receiver to find and extract the required information. This is the basic technique used in teletext systems.

With a fast data channel of 3.5 Mbytes/second, a database of several megabytes can be transmitted within a few seconds. If the database is transmitted repeatedly, a query about the database can be answered within the time it takes to transmit the database again, in this example within a few seconds.

The underlying query handling system within the receiver is conceptually quite simple. It merely waits until the required data are transmitted again and picks them up at that time. In this way an application can interact with a user and provide responses to the user's input, based on the contents of the database. In practice, the high data rate of the transmission channel necessitates the inclusion of special hardware in the receiver, to scan the data stream for the items of interest and extract them for use in the application.

The scanning hardware can be simple, such as comparing a fixed bit field within each block or packet of the database against a given pattern. The scanning hardware could also be quite complex, such as matching each data item against a Boolean combination of several variable length and variable position fields, or against a complex relational database query [5].

The structure and format of the database, and the complexity of the query handling software within the receiver, are strongly affected by the type of scanning hardware

used. In this paper we assume simple hardware, like the fixed bit field matcher described above. Some of the associated database design issues are discussed later, in the section on Database Format.

For databases larger than a few megabytes, the query response time can become unacceptably long, because of how long it takes to transmit the database each time. Depending on the application, this problem can be alleviated to some extent by one of two techniques. First, copies of the most frequently accessed data items can be repeated at regular intervals throughout the database. Second, copies of the most likely items to be accessed next can be cached by the receiver, usually in RAM. Both of these techniques are discussed in more detail in the section on Database Format.

To give a more concrete impression of approximately how much data can be carried in a given time on a fast data channel of 3.5 Mbytes/second, the following list provides a number of examples. These examples assume that state of the art digital compression techniques are employed:

- 5000 full TV screen text pages in 1 second.

- 300 fax pages in 1 second.

- 1200 two page letters in 1 second.

- 15 novels in 1 second.

- 25 one minute voice messages in 1 second.

- 15 high quality video stills in 1 second.

- 300 small color still pictures in 1 second.

- A daily newspaper with black and white pictures in 1 second.

- A weekly newsmagazine with color pictures in 3 seconds.

- The contents of four 800K floppy disks in 1 second.

- One full CD-ROM or CD-I disk (600 Mbytes) in 3 minutes.

EXAMPLE APPLICATIONS

We now briefly describe three example applications that are based on the repeated, one way transmission of multiple megabyte databases. First we consider an enhanced electronic TV guide service that demonstrates some of the features made possible by fast data channels. There already exist some electronic TV guides. Two examples are SuperGuide [6], built into the UNIDEN UST4800 satellite decoder, and InSight [7], soon to be broadcast via the PBS network. However, because these systems work with relatively low data rates, they only present the user with screens and menus consisting of text.

By exploiting a fast data channel, an electronic TV guide can be augmented with still pictures, audio clips, and even video clips. These can be used to attract consumers to the shows, for instance to advertise pay-per-view offerings. A still picture can be used as an identifier for a show, both to make it more attractive and to make it more immediately recognizable. This is particularly valuable for children who cannot comprehend text. Some shows, such as movies, can have their identifying pictures replaced by video clips. This would be like the clips shown on current "preview" channels, or like the "trailers" shown in movie theaters, and hence be much more effective for attracting viewers.

The size of the text portion of a TV guide database, containing schedule information and brief summaries of all the shows over a one week period, is roughly 1 Mbyte. There are approximately 1000 different shows in one week, each of which could have a separate identifying still picture. Each of those pictures requires roughly 5 Kbytes of storage. Thus, the total size of the TV guide database, including still pictures, is roughly 6 Mbytes. It can be transferred on a fast data channel in under two seconds.

Video clips require much larger amounts of information to be transferred. A fast data channel can simultaneously carry over 15 VHS quality, full screen movies, or over 100 small, picture-in-picture (PIP) size movies. By reserving half the bandwidth of the data channel for video clips, over 50 continuously repeating, PIP size clips could be provided. The text and still pictures part of the TV guide database could then be transferred in about four seconds.

Four seconds is too long for a viewer to wait for information about a TV show, so parts of the TV guide database would have to be cached in the receiver. Only information about the shows that are currently playing or coming up in the near future need be cached, since that is what the viewer will most often be interested in. As the viewer looks further into the future, it will take him/her a few seconds to study each screen of information. During that time the data for successively later shows can be cached, so that the information will be immediately available when needed.

Because of the quantities of data involved, video clips are never cached. Instead, they are played in real time, beginning at whatever point they are currently showing. Since each clip is typically quite short (30 to 60 seconds) and repeated continuously, starting in the midst of a clip should be acceptable to most viewers.

Our second example is an advertising magazine that uses a database of classified ads and optional associated pictures. A mechanism to search through the magazine by category or by keyword would make this more powerful than its printed equivalent. Color pictures, audio, and video could be exploited by advertisers to attract and inform a highly targeted audience of viewers. The viewers of an ad are those who, through their interactions and selections, have already indicated an interest in the product or service.

The size of the advertising magazine database, excluding video clips, would be comparable to a weekly newsmagazine with color pictures. Thus, it would take about 3 seconds to transmit on a fast data channel. Data caching techniques similar to those discussed above for the TV guide can be used to ensure that the system response times are acceptable.

A third example application is a system help and tutorial facility that can explain to users how to operate their receivers, and introduce them to the various TV, audio and data services available. By pressing a HELP button on the remote at any time, users can obtain context sensitive help information. Procedures can be explained and demonstrated through tutorial sequences. Pictures, audio and video can significantly enhance the learning experience.

The text part of the help database, along with simple illustrations, would probably be less than 1 Mbyte. With more elaborate pictures for demonstration sequences, the size might grow to around 2 Mbytes. This can still be transmitted in under one second. Hence it may be possible to provide the help facility without any caching of the database.

LOADING APPLICATION CODE

The flexibility of the data receiving device to support a wide variety of applications, including currently unforeseen applications, can be supported through a mechanism for loading application code. One obvious approach is to transmit an application's code along with its database. The receiver would first load the application code and begin executing it. The application code would then interact with the user and access information from the database as required.

If the data processing computer inside the receiver conforms to an open standard, third party software developers and service providers will be encouraged to produce applications for use with the system. A wide variety of applications would then be available. For example, one could imagine a "Video Game of the Week" data service channel that transmitted the code and data of multimedia video games, with the selection of games changing on a weekly basis.

For the standard data processing computer, we advocate a Compact Disc Interactive (CD-I) compatible platform [8]. CD-I was designed especially with consumers and TVs in mind. It has been adopted by a number of consumer electronics manufacturers, and an increasing selection of products and applications based on the standard are now becoming available. Although CD-I was originally developed with compact disc technology in mind, much of the standard and many of the existing software development tools can be readily adapted to the fast data channel environment.

LOCAL STORAGE

A further extension of the data receiving device, to increase its range of capabilities, is the addition of local mass storage facilities. We discussed earlier the use of RAM for caching selected data items from the transmitted database. With local mass storage, such as an optical disc, large portions or the entire contents of a database could be captured. For example, the complete contents of a compact disc would normally take about three minutes to transmit, which is too long to wait for the retrieval of a selected data item. However, if the transmitted data is first stored onto a local disc, it could be "replayed" later with faster interaction.

Local mass storage opens additional application possibilities. For example, music libraries or video game libraries could be made available on data service channels. Subscribers could then create personal collections of their favorite music or games by capturing selected items from the transmitted libraries and storing them on digital tapes or optical discs. The various copyright issues to be addressed by such applications, while very important, will not be discussed in this paper.

Another way to exploit local mass storage is to combine a local database with a transmitted database. For example, the contents of an encyclopedia could be stored on a CD-I disc. The latest updates to the encyclopedia could be transmitted on a fast data channel. By combining the two databases, the user would have interactive access to the latest information in a very large database. Updates to the CD-I disc could then be made at relatively infrequent intervals.

DATABASE FORMAT

Having looked at some of the potential applications of fast digital data channels, we can now summarize some of the associated database design issues. First it should be noted that although the above multimedia databases are transmitted over a TV channel, the format of their pictures, video and sound need not be identical with the compressed video and audio formats of a digital cable TV system. Sometimes the TV formats are the most convenient to use, such as for the encoding of video clips. But in other cases different formats might be preferred.

The type of data processing computer used, in our case a CD-I compatible platform, has a strong influence on the format of data items. To maintain CD-I compatibility, most items, such as still pictures, graphical objects, and even application code, will follow CD-I conventions. However, some database providers may prefer to supply their information in other formats. This can be accommodated by converting the data into a CD-I compatible form, either before transmission or after it is captured in the receiver. The needs of the database scanning hardware and software could also force additional restructuring of the data items to facilitate retrieval.

One major concern when designing the overall structure of the database is to minimize the number of times the user might have to wait for long periods to receive requested information. Two main techniques are available for dealing with this problem: repetition and caching. Repetition involves copying the most frequently accessed data items and transmitting them more frequently, thereby reducing the expected latency. The down side is that the overall size of the database increases, and thus the time to receive the less frequently accessed data items increases.

The second technique is caching. This involves storing in the receiver the most likely information to be requested next. The main problem is determining what information should be cached. This also has to be traded off against the amount of memory, usually RAM, to be used for the cache. Caching can be especially effective for hypertext structured applications where the user is presented with screens of information that are linked together in a predetermined fashion. While the user is viewing one screen, all of the screens directly linked to it can be retrieved. One of those screens will be what the user wants to see next.

For accessing the database information in different ways, index files can be transmitted along with the database and cached in the receiver. For example, the TV guide database might have one index file containing pointers to all of the shows for each channel, and a second index file with pointers to all of the shows for each time slot. By carefully designing the index files according to the application's needs, it should be possible to answer most queries in a single scan of the database, looking for an item identified by a particular pointer. Simple scanning hardware that matches a fixed bit field in each block or packet of the database against a given pointer/identifier is all that is needed.

CONCLUSION

In this paper we have explained how the fast digital data channels, made possible by the advent of digital delivery systems in CATV, can enable new cable services. We described a variety of locally interactive, multimedia applications, based on the repeated, one way transmission of complete databases. We also discussed some of the issues involved in the design of those applications.

Work is currently proceeding on the development of an experimental system that can support the types of applications discussed above. For demonstration purposes, an experimental, enhanced, electronic TV guide is being developed as an initial application. Studies by ourselves and others indicate that users like the concept of an electronic TV guide, and are even willing to pay for it. We believe that the TV guide may be the driving application that finally leads to the broad acceptance of interactive services by American consumers.

Throughout the paper, a single 6 MHz TV channel was assumed as the basis for a fast digital data channel. However, nothing prevents multiple adjacent channels from being combined into a single, even faster data channel in the future. This will enable even more elaborate interactive, multimedia applications to be developed.

ACKNOWLEDGMENTS

The ideas and work presented in this paper are the result of comments and contributions from many people. We especially want to thank Paul Rutter, Jhumkee Iyengar, Bill Lord, Brian Johnson, and everyone associated with the Briarcliff TV Data Services project.

REFERENCES

[1] Electronic Industries Association, *Joint EIA/CVCC Recommended Practice for Teletext: North American Basic Teletext Specification (NABTS)*, EIA-516, May 1988.

[2] UK Department of Trade and Industry, *World System Teletext and Data Broadcasting System Technical Specification*, 1986.

[3] J. Lentz, *et al.*, *Television Captioning for the Deaf: Signal and Display Specifications*, Rep. No. E-7709-C, PBS, May 1980.

[4] M. Balakrishnan and W. Mao, "An MPEG Standard Based Video Compression System and Applications", May 1992, in these Proceedings.

[5] T. Bowen, *et al.*, "A Scale Database Architecture for Network Services", *IEEE Communications*, Jan. 1991, pp. 52-59.

[6] P. Hallenbeck and J. Hallenbeck, "Personal Home TV Programming Guide", in *Proc. of ICCE 1990*, pp. 310-311.

[7] Chicago Tribune, "One-Button Recording Latest VCR Technology", Sept. 12, 1990, p. 3.

[8] Philips and Sony, *Compact Disc Interactive Full Functional Specification*, Sept. 1990.

FAM-20.3

PERSONAL HOME TV PROGRAMMING GUIDE

Peter D. Hallenbeck
SuperGuide
3500 Jordan Oaks Drive
Efland, NC 27243

Jill J. Hallenbeck
Research Triangle Institute
P.O. Box 12194
Research Triangle Park, NC 27709

Abstract

The SuperGuide system is a low-cost, home-oriented, interactive, electronic, on-screen programming guide. When integrated with the TV tuner, remote control, and other devices, an exciting new component and capability emerges.

Introduction

The increase in the numbers and types of television programming available is a small part of today's information explosion. Television has grown from three networks and PBS to over 100 services. In addition to video overchoice, "tier-ing" and marketing have muddied the waters by allowing customers to subscribe to bits, pieces, and packages of programming. When deciding what to view, customary paper programming guides must show all possibilities. The viewer must wade through all of this information, selecting from descriptions of shows in packages to which he has subscribed. Then, by memory or little pieces of paper which are often lost in the dimly lit confines of the video viewing emporium, the viewer must translate the service (e.g., CBS network programming) to a channel and set the TV to that channel. For home satellite viewing, the act of tuning a service is complicated enough to keep many subscribers from fully realizing the potential of their system. The new SuperGuide system is an interactive programming guide which can receive a broadcast database of programming for only those services to which a viewer subscribes and present only that information on the TV screen. The presentation is controlled by the user's hand-held remote control unit. When the viewer selects the show, the Guide, connected to the TV, tunes in the show. In the case of direct to-home satellite information, the satellite and transponder (channel) for a service are used to make all tuning automatic. Additionally, shows are bundled together by *type* so the viewer may choose to have the Guide customized on-the-fly for only one *type* (e.g., movies or sports) of programming. Perhaps the best way to describe the system is to state that people do not watch *Channel 5* or *CBS* but, in fact, watch *I Love Lucy* or *Wall Street Week*. The goal of the Guide is to let the customer select the show. Matters concerning subscriptions, tuning, and networks are secondary to the content (or lack of it) of what is watched.

Background

The original SuperGuide system was developed in 1985. The hardware consisted of a simple discrete chip circuit board with a black and white bitmap display generator, 256 Kbytes of dynamic RAM, a radio frequency modem, some peripherals, and a power supply. The data for the Guide was transmitted on a satellite audio subcarrier using a narrow audio channel format. The signal was a Frequency Shift Key (FSK) modulated signal with a total bandwidth of 130 KHz. The signal was a simple asynchronous serial format, the same which has been used for years to communicate with computer terminals. The low cost of microprocessor serial port chips made this a good choice.

The transmission rate was a surprisingly low 4800 bits per second. If the quality of a home satellite system was as good as a commercial system, the system could have run four times faster. The quality of the systems, however, dictated the lower speed so the customers could load the listings into their unit with few or no errors. Even at this low rate, about two percent of the systems could not receive the information well enough to use it and about 20 percent of the systems load the information with some errors in the data.

All the uplink site equipment was custom-built due to our inability to locate equipment which could do FSK modulation at this low rate. This allowed us to design an inexpensive receiver for the data and adjust the manner in which the data was formated and transmitted to match and work with the receiver.

The bitmap display was chosen because it was the only way to print characters on the screen using proportional spacing, which not only reduces the "computery" look of the screen but also increases the printable number of characters per line. The graphic ability of the bitmap display also allows for the drawing of various lines and custom symbols (e.g., stereo headphones) borrowed from printed guides. This reinforces the programming guide concept in the TV viewer's mind. The bitmap size was 256 across by 190 down. This was enough for a 16-line display with a 5 x 7 font. It was later discovered that this font was too small for bleary-

Reprinted from *ICCE 1990 Digest*, pp. 310–311, 1992.

eyed end-of-the-day use. A test of a 7 x 9 font was so well accepted that it is the only font used in the new system.

The 256 Kbytes of memory has both the bitmap display (8 Kbytes), variables and stack space for the program (8 Kbytes), and the storage for the listings and service information (240 Kbytes). The original Guide loaded the listing for all the services available, much as the paper guides print the listings for all available services. The listings are stored in the local box to allow for immediate response to any actions taken by the viewer. This local storage makes the system very different from a teletext system and allows for many original features. A mechanism for selecting and showing only a viewer's favorite services allows the Guide to show only the programming to which the viewer subscribes. The same mechanism allows the listings to be searched for various subsets of programming, such as sports or movies, and presents one of those subsets on the TV screen. A small 100-word dictionary helped compress the listings about ten percent. The 256 Kbytes of memory could hold about four days of programming with 120 services.

The New SuperGuide System

Design of the new system began in 1988. Keeping in mind the perils of any "second system," we set out to correct the "undocumented features" in the first system and incorporate many of the little things we learned about people interactions with the original SuperGuide system. Many of the lessons learned apply to any interactive consumer device, such as VCR on-screen event programming and future IEEE Home Bus controllers. The hardware changes focus on the quality of the display, the data modem, and a secure encryption system. A gate array and a standard cell chip allow an increase in performance and a decrease in price.

The biggest change in the display is the addition of color and a 512 x 200 pixel display. The fonts are 7 x 9, stored on a 15 x 12 matrix. To keep the luminance bandwidth below 3 MHz, there is the restriction that three pixels in a row must be either *on* or *off*. This allows for extremely "smooth" characters due to the partial overlap of pixels. Color was added to attract customers. The new display format holds 14 lines of text on a screen, with 30 to 40 characters per line when in proportional space mode. Multiple fonts are supported. The data modem is a synchronous bitstream, with an on-board digital clock extractor. A 40-bit Error Correction Code was added so that burst errors of up to 17 bits could be corrected. This corrects for not only regular FM satellite transmission noise but also for the dreaded local "vacuum cleaner" noise. When a person in the house turns on a heavy appliance, sometimes even a light switch, a spike of noise couples through the receiver system and can cause an error.

The great DRAM crunch of '88 made us determined to significantly increase how much information we could store in a given amount of memory. We decided to switch to an active download system. The original system loaded all listings like an electronic mailbox with a paper guide placed inside of it. The new SuperGuide system examines each show and de-

termines if it should be kept. It dynamically builds the single database of listings. A 4000-word dictionary compresses the text in the listings by 50 percent. The combined result of these two changes is one half the memory can store twice as many days of programming for a typical viewer. The DRAM requirements reduced eight 256K x 1 chips to a single 256K x 4.

The technical challenges of the system are immense. The hardware, which costs less that $40, has about as much power as the first Macintosh system. The broadcast database, the equivalent of a weekly programming guide, must be electronically "laid up," formated, and transmitted at least twice a day. The subscription price has to be less than a paper guide. The system must be secure or subscription revenue will be lost. Five years from now the system should cost about $10 to add to a TV or cable converter box.

Finally, the biggest challenge of all was to make Super-Guide *easy* enough to use so people *could* use it, yet *functional* enough so people *will* use it. Hierarchical menus are used throughout the Guide. Operation of all the menus, as well as the Guide itself, requires six buttons on the handheld: cursor keys *up* and *down*, page *forward* and page *back* keys, a *select* key and a *return* key. The biggest problem we've seen in most human interfaces is inconsistency. By forcing a consistency of use of these buttons, the education time for a viewer is about one minute. People are educated by showing them how to use the programming Guide first. Motivation: owners want to watch TV. Other functions (e.g., setup and article viewing) operate in the exact same manner, so by the time the owners have learned to use the Guide, they have the knowledge to use all the other features of the unit. It is similar to the problem of someone who only sets up his VCR for recording once a week. The procedure is done so infrequently that is is a challenge each time. If the procedure were done daily, the viewer would remember how to do it. Along those same lines, SuperGuide takes a show you want to record and passes the information to a standard event timer in a VCR or satellite receiver. Due to a lack of devices which can accept this information (i.e., Start time, Stop time, and Channel) from an external source, this is a feature waiting for the right hardware. When the VCRs which have bus interfacing exist, SuperGuide will be ready to make recording on your VCR truly as simple as finding the show you want to record and pressing a single button.

Conclusion

The new SuperGuide system will fit in well with tomorrow's world and will help people manage some of the information they deal with each day. Who knows, it might even save a few trees!

CDROM—New Applications for the Compact Disc

D.E. Penna and S.R. Turner

Introduction

The Compact Disc was developed by Philips to give the consumer one hour of pure digital stereo sound. However that digital data no longer has to be just sound. When connected to a personal computer the compact disc can net as a vast data store of 600 Mbytes containing any combination of text, pictures, graphics, sound or software. In this form it is known as CDROM which stands for Compact Disc Read Only Memory.

Such a low cost mass store based on the consumer player opens the way to a whole series of new applications from the serious, like electronic reference books and interactive educational programs, to the fun such as adventure games and activity simulation.

CDROM Parameters

The CDROM is a very secure medium of 600 Mbytes. The three layer error correction code (ECC) gives an extremely low error rate of 1 in 10^9 bytes for soft errors and 1 in 10^{12} bytes for hard errors. The data rate is 1.41 Mbs[1] which reduces due to the ECC overhead to an effective 150 Kbyte/s of useable data. The disc spins at a constant linear velocity of 1.3m/s giving a relatively low rotational speed of 200-300 rpm. The access time is partly dependent on this rotational speed and partly the control electronics in the player. Professional players are able to traverse the disc in 3 s while domestic versions are somewhat slower. The fastest access time is 200 ms while typical access times within an application are 0.5 to 1 s.

Thus CDROM is approximately half way between a floppy and a hard disc in terms of data rate and access speed but has tremendous capacity and is very accurate.

An Electronic Picture and Sound Dictionary on Compact Disc

A reasonable existing technology paper dictionary contains around 80,000 entries and consists of 11 Mbytes of text. Thus 50 copies of such a dictionary could be placed on one disc. Even the full Oxford English Dictionary contains only 230 Mbytes of text which would occupy just over a third of a disc. The Encyclopedia Britannica is very similar at 280 Mbytes.

As an experiment we have created part of an English language dictionary (the letter 'O') and placed it on a CDROM. In order to offer improvements over the paper dictionary some 15% of the entries in the electronic version have an associated colour picture and nearly all entries have the pronunciation of the word as an audible output. In addition selected entries have links to their antonyms and synonyms and also semantically related words.

The basic system consists of an adapted consumer compact disc player linked via a parallel interface to a home computer which drives a colour display. Initial selection of an entry is either from a scrolled list of the words or by direct keying of the required entry (Fig. 1).

An entry in the dictionary consists of (Fig. 2):

1) 300 to 1000 characters of text
   (typically 500 bytes)

2) a small run length coded colour
   pictures where appropriate
   (usually about 5 Kbytes)

3) an audible pronunciation of the word
   (PCM coding about
   10 Kbytes at 4 kHz bandwidth)

Thus the sound occupies most of the space. As not all entries have pictures the average data per entry is 12 Kbytes, so with the present coding 50,000 entries could be fitted on to a single disc. To achieve the full 80,000 entries on one disc an improved sound coding scheme which compressed the data by a factor of two would be needed instead of the very simple PCM coding used.

Particular attention was paid while creating this experimental disc to ensuring that the text of an entry was easily readable. Thus two anti-aliased soft character fonts, one italic and one normal were created and proportionally spaced text used. The display resolution of the experimental home computer was 384×256 with 8 bits per pixel via a colour look up table allowing up to 256 different colours on the screen.

The creation of text, pictures, and sound was a major task. A drawing package was used to create the pictures and the artist was given a defined area within which to create the colour picture. A special editor was devised to enable the digitised sound sequences to be edited down to just the pronunciation of the word. Finally a compiler was necessary to assemble each entry together with its associated text, picture, sound and cross references and then link all the entries together to produce a file on a VAX 11/780 which was then sent for Compact Disc mastering.

Animated Pictures

The high data rate from the disc, 150 Kbyte/s continuously for one hour, means that with certain restrictions it is possible to produce real time animation sequences direct from the disc. For example an area on the screen 256×128 pixels with 4 bits per pixel can be updated at nearly 10 picture/s. The home computer has to be able to handle this high data rate transferring the pictures from the disc to the screen memory continuously at one byte every 6.7 µs. However it is possible to have up to half the screen containing a realistic moving image with fixed or slowly changing data on the rest of the screen.

Conclusions

These experiments have shown the tremendous potential of CDROM as an inexpensive mass storage medium. To be economical it is not necessary to use its vast capacity and initially in the semi-professional market many applications needing only 50 Mbytes on a secure exchangeable medium are already viable. Even only 10% full the CDROM is equivalent to 50 floppy discs.

However when the creative applications writers have learnt how to exploit its ability to store still video pictures, graphics, animation, sound, text, and software it will be realised that a new interactive medium has been born. To this end a consumer standard for the coding on the disc is being developed.

Figures 1 and 2 not available at the time of this printing.

THE FULL MOTION SYSTEM FOR CD-I

Jan van der Meer
Philips Consumer Electronics
Eindhoven, The Netherlands

ABSTRACT

Compact Disc Interactive (CD-I) is the new multimedia system for home entertainment, education, training, publishing and other applications that combines audio, video, text, graphics, animation and interactivity. To extend CD-I with the capability to play moving natural pictures on full screen with associated audio of Compact Disc quality, the Full Motion system is defined. To play Full Motion sequences from CD-I disc requires compression of the audiovisual information to the CD-I bitrate. The Full Motion system applies a compression method based on the MPEG standard. This paper describes the features of the CD-I Full Motion system, application of the MPEG standard for Full Motion and the architecture of a Full Motion CD-I player.

1. INTRODUCTION

After an initial introduction on the professional and institutional market, CD-I has been introduced on the consumer market in the USA in October 1991, followed by Japan and United Kingdom in April 1992; the rest of Europe followed in September and October 1992. CD-I combines audio, video, text, graphics, animation and interactivity. The capability to play moving natural pictures is limited to partial screen (e.g. 1/9 of the screen) and low picture rates (e.g. 15 Hz). To improve this performance the Full Motion system is defined.

The Full Motion system introduces in CD-I the capability to play from one CD-I disc up to 72 minutes of moving natural pictures on full screen with audio on Compact Disc quality. Each Full Motion CD-I disc can be played on 50 Hz and a 60 Hz players. The Full Motion system offers a world standard with full compatibility between the 50 Hz and 60 Hz world.

The Full Motion system is defined as an extension of the CD-I Specification [1], without requiring any modification of this specification. As a consequence, Full Motion is a full compatible extension of CD-I. Each CD-I disc without Full Motion plays on CD-I players with Full Motion. Furthermore, each Full Motion CD-I disc "plays" also on CD-I players without Full Motion, although the Full Motion functions will not be available on such players.

CD-I discs are produced at authoring. The Full Motion system provides a variety of features to design Full Motion CD-I discs. An important feature at authoring is flexibility to optimize the discs for an application. For example, a trade-off can be made between audio quality and the number of audio streams. At a bitrate of 192 kbit/sec e.g. one audio stream in stereo of CD quality can be recorded or six audio streams in mono of speech quality. At Full Motion CD-I players a number of features is available to play back Full Motion CD-I discs. Section 2 of this paper presents the features provided by the Full Motion system at authoring and at the Full Motion CD-I player.

A typical Full Motion CD-I disc is expected to allocate 1.2 Mbit/sec for video on full screen, and 0.2 Mbit/sec for audio in stereo of CD quality; the total bitrate from disc equals 1.4 Mbit/sec. To compress the audiovisual information to these bitrates and to store the coded audio and video data on CD-I discs, the MPEG standard [2] is applied. The MPEG standard is defined by ISO/IEC as a generic standard, i.e. as an application independent standard. The application of this generic standard for Full Motion is discussed in section 3 of this paper.

In section 4 of this paper the architecture of the Full Motion CD-I player is presented. The Full Motion system is defined such, that 'Base Case' players, i.e. players without any extension, can be upgraded easily with Full Motion. In the architecture of the Full Motion CD-I player, Full Motion is an easy add-on function. This approach made it possible to prepare Base Case CD-I players for Full Motion. A consumer can upgrade a prepared player with Full Motion simply by installing a Full Motion cartridge (see figure 1).

Reprinted from *IEEE Trans. Consumer Electron.*, vol. 38, no. 4, pp. 910–920, Nov. 1992.

Figure 1   Installing a Full Motion cartridge in a Base Case CD-I player prepared for Full Motion.

2. FULL MOTION FEATURES

The Full Motion System provides a variety of features both at authoring and at the Full Motion CD-I Player. At authoring features are available to support the design of Full Motion CD-I discs. Flexibility to optimize discs to the requirements of the application is an important feature at authoring. Features available at a Full Motion CD-I Player support the user to play Full Motion CD-I Discs. These features include play back modes, presentation of played audiovisual information and full compatibility of discs between the 60 Hz and 50 Hz world. Beyond the features directly related to Full Motion, two additional features are provided. These features address handling of still pictures and use by applications of the available memory in a Full Motion Decoder, when this memory is not needed for decoding Full Motion data.

2.1   Features at authoring

Full Motion CD-I discs are produced at authoring. The CD-I application is specified and developed. The Full Motion audiovisual material is compressed in compliance with the MPEG standard. The resulting coded data are merged with the other CD-I data to create the Full Motion CD-I disc image.

After compressing an audio or video input signal, the coded data is stored in an MPEG audio or MPEG video stream. On a CD-I disc multiple MPEG audio and MPEG video streams can be recorded in parallel, e.g. for applications requiring audio in several languages. At the Full Motion CD-I Player, only one MPEG audio stream and one MPEG video stream can be played simultaneously. At authoring trade-offs can be made between the number of streams, the bitrate for each stream, the audio or picture quality of each stream and, in case of video, the picture size.

Audio can be coded in stereo and in mono. All fixed bitrates allowed by the MPEG standard can be used. The lowest bitrate for mono of 32 kbit/sec can be used for speech and other audio not requiring a very high quality. At a bitrate of 192 kbit/sec in stereo an audio quality can be achieved which is subjectively equal to the Digital Audio quality from Compact Disc.

The Full Motion system codes non-interlaced moving video. To support source material in 60 Hz and 50 Hz, several temporal formats can be used. Picture rates of (approximately) 24 Hz and 30 Hz support film and video based source material in 60 Hz, while source material in 50 Hz is supported by a picture rate of 25 Hz. The spatial format is a rectangle with a horizontal size in pixels and a vertical size in lines. The maximum picture area is limited; in case of 30 Hz to 352 pixels by 240 lines, and in case of 25 Hz to 352 pixels by 288 lines. However, the picture area can be used in a flexible way. Full screen pictures can be coded, but also wide and low pictures as well as high and narrow pictures (for an example see figure 2).

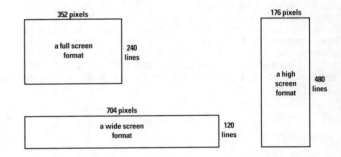

Figure 2   Example of spatial picture formats.

The bitrate to code video is a parameter. In case of a play back directly from a Full Motion CD-I Disc, the maximum bitrate is about 1.4 Mbit/sec. After storage of the sequence by the application, play back is also possible from memory. In that case a maximum bitrate of approximately 5 Mbit/sec is allowed e.g. for playing video with a very high picture quality.

Each Full Motion CD-I Disc can be played on each Full Motion CD-I Player, independently of the 60 Hz or 50 Hz display rate of the player. The Full Motion decoder reconstructs pictures at the picture rate they are coded, i.e. at about 24 Hz, 30 Hz or 25 Hz. The decoder is to produce a video output at a display rate of 60 Hz or 50 Hz. The Full Motion decoder therefore needs to apply a frame rate conversion from the coded picture rate to the required display rate of 60 Hz or 50 Hz. The conversion is applied in temporal direction without any impact on picture size in terms of number of pixels and lines. Due to this conversion, some aspect ratio distortion may occur. At authoring a pixel aspect ratio can be applied which is optimum for either a 60 Hz or a 50 Hz display, but which results in a noticeable distortion of the aspect ratio when the pictures are displayed at the other display rate. For compatibility reasons therefore an intermediate pixel aspect ratio is recommended which results in a minor distortion of the aspect ratio at both 60 Hz and 50 Hz displays; without reference to the original, this distortion is not noticeable in both cases.

For storage on a Full Motion CD-I disc, the audio and video material is compressed to the CD-I bitrate. A typical encoding environment is depicted in figure 3. The video signal from the source is filtered and sub-sampled to the SIF format [2] by a pre-processor. The SIF pictures are input to a video encoder. The audio signal from the source is provided to the audio encoder; in case of very low bitrates (speech quality) the audio may be pre-filtered first. In figure 3 some typical values are indicated for bitrates and bitrate reduction (BRR). To obtain highest picture quality, it is essential that the SIF pictures at the input of the video encoder are natural pictures of high quality, without spatial and temporal distortions. In general the pre-processor will apply therefore techniques to reduce e.g. noise and alias.

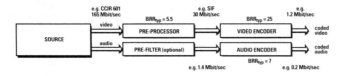

Figure 3   Typical audio and video encoding environment

The Full Motion system specifies the format of the coded bitstreams at the output of the encoders. The techniques to be applied for pre-processing and encoding techniques are not specified; they are at the discretion of the authoring tool. A major feature of the Full Motion system is therefore that each improvement of the encoding strategy can be applied at encoding. A continuous growth path to improve picture and audio quality is therefore expected, without any need to modify Full Motion CD-I players.

Applications can apply a variety of encoding tools. Audio encoding tools are available already for operation in real time. Currently video encoders are available for operation in non-real time. The speed of non-real time video encoders is increasing rapidly, due to speed optimization of the algorithms as well as due to faster computer based encoding platforms. Video encoders operating in real time are expected by the end of 1992.

Especially flexibility is available in coding video. To code a video sequence, the MPEG standard allows to use three types of pictures : Intra-pictures (I), Predicted pictures (P) and Interpolated pictures (bidirectional prediction : B). Intra-pictures provide entry points for random access, but only with moderate compression. Predicted pictures are coded with reference to a past picture (I or P picture). Bidirectional (B) pictures provide the highest amount of compression, but require both a past and a future reference picture (I or P picture) for prediction.

An example is given in figure 4; in this example the I and P picture are followed by two B pictures. The number of B pictures between two successive I or P pictures may vary. Coding of a B picture requires availability of the past and future reference picture. Each future reference picture is therefore coded prior to the B picture(s) using this reference picture. See figure 4. For each video sequence, the encoder decides which picture types are applied. Also the amount of bits to code each picture is at the discretion of the encoder.

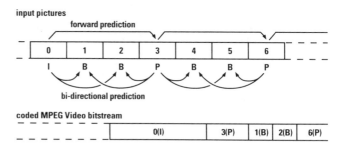

Figure 4   MPEG Video encoding

At the decoder, I pictures are reconstructed without using any information from other pictures. At these type of pictures play back can start. They are referred to as entry point pictures. The distance between entry point pictures is flexible. Applications can specify entry point pictures in a video sequence prior to encoding the sequence.

2.2 Features of Full Motion CD-I Player

Each Full Motion CD-I disc contains an application program. This application program controls play back of the disc on the Full Motion CD-I player, in interaction with the user. Part of such control is to decide which MPEG video stream and which MPEG audio stream are to be played, if any. The application can control separately decoding of MPEG audio data and decoding of MPEG video data. The Full Motion system allows for play back directly from disc, as well as from memory. In case of a play from memory, the data to be played is loaded in memory by the application. Play from disc and play from memory are mutually exclusive functions for audio as well as for video. The Full Motion system supports loops from memory, by means of which MPEG data stored in memory can be played continuously.

At the Full Motion CD-I player, MPEG audio can be played simultaneously with ADPCM audio. To play back MPEG audio, the play forward mode and the mute mode are available. In the play forward mode, MPEG audio is played back at normal speed forward. A play forward can be paused and continued. In the mute mode the audio output from the Full Motion decoder is muted. The audio signals at the output of the Full Motion decoder are provided to the external audio input of the Base Case audio section (see figure 5). The left and right MPEG audio signals are mixed with the left and right audio output signals from the ADPCM decoder.

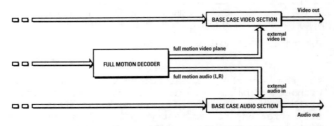

Figure 5   Mixing of audio and video from Full Motion decoder with Base Case audio and video

Coded MPEG Audio data is a concatenation of coded audio frames. An audio frame represents a number of audio samples. The decoder can reconstruct each audio frame without using information from other audio frames. Play back of MPEG Audio can therefore start at each audio frame.

On the play back modes of MPEG video there is some impact from the predictive video coding techniques applied in the MPEG standard. Play back can start at entry point pictures (I pictures). Entry point pictures are defined during encoding. The address of entry point pictures on a disc is known by the application. For reconstruction of P and B pictures, previously reconstructed reference pictures are required; therefore at these picture types play back cannot start.

At the decoder pictures are reconstructed in the same order as they are included in the bitstream. After reconstruction pictures need re-ordering. See figure 6. The re-ordered pictures are to be displayed at a frame rate of 50 Hz or 60 Hz, depending on the player type used for play back. The decoder applies a frame rate conversion to the required display rate. See figure 6.

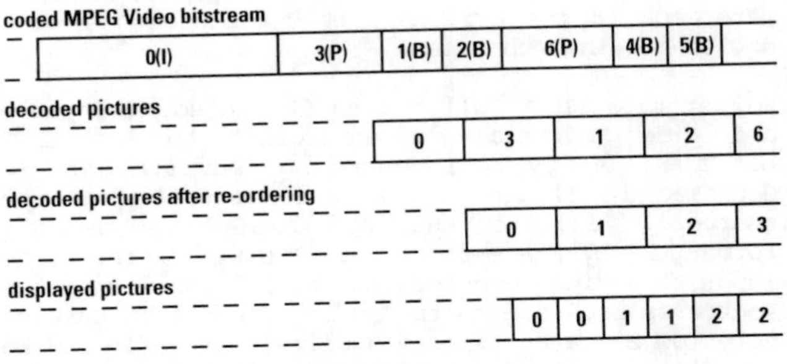

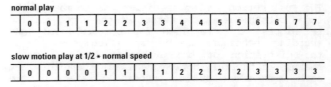

Figure 6   MPEG Video decoding

To play back MPEG video, five modes are available in the Full Motion system : play forward, slow motion forward, freeze, single picture forward and scan. In the play forward mode MPEG video is played back at normal speed forward.

In the slow motion forward mode MPEG video is played forward in slow motion. The application can select the slow motion speed from seven available speeds, defined by the formula :
slow motion speed = $(1/m)$ * normal speed,
where $m = 2, 3, 4, ..., 8$.
See example in figure 7. A play forward and a slow motion can be paused at each picture and can be continued at the paused picture.

normal play

0	0	1	1	2	2	3	3	4	4	5	5	6	6	7	7

slow motion play at 1/2 * normal speed

0	0	0	0	1	1	1	1	2	2	2	2	3	3	3	3

Figure 7   Displayed pictures at normal play and at slow motion

The freeze mode can be entered from the play mode at each picture. At entering the freeze mode, the currently displayed picture is frozen and the decoding stops, but the MPEG video stream continues. From the freeze mode, the play mode can be continued. In that case play back will continue at the first entry point picture (I picture) encountered in the MPEG video bitstream. For an example see figure 8.

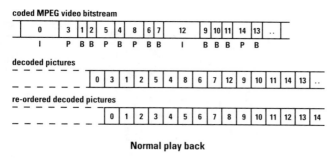

coded MPEG video bitstream

0	3	1	2	5	4	8	6	7	12	9	10	11	14	13	..
I	P	B	B	P	B	P	B	B	I	B	B	B	P	B

decoded pictures

| 0 | 3 | 1 | 2 | 5 | 4 | 8 | 6 | 7 | 12 | 9 | 10 | 11 | 14 | 13 | .. |

re-ordered decoded pictures

| 0 | 1 | 2 | 3 | 4 | 5 | 6 | 7 | 8 | 9 | 10 | 11 | 12 | 13 | 14 |

Normal play back

coded MPEG video bitstream

0	3	1	2	5	4	8	6	7	12	9	10	11	14	13	..
I	P	B	B	P	B	P	B	B	I	B	B	B	P	B

decoded pictures

| 0 | 3 | 1 | | | | | | 12 | | 14 | 13 | .. |

re-ordered decoded or frozen pictures

| 0 | 1 | 1 | 1 | 1 | 1 | 1 | 1 | 1 | 1 | 1 | 1 | 12 | 13 | 14 |

freeze command — continue command

Performance after freeze and continue commands

Figure 8 Normal play back and performance after freeze and continue commands; in this example the freeze command is issued during display of picture no 1, while the continue command is issued prior to encountering I picture no 12 in the MPEG video bitstream

In the single picture forward mode, pictures are played back one by one. By giving another single picture forward command, the next picture is displayed. The application can control the length of the display period of each picture by controlling the time interval between successive commands.

During the scan mode entry point pictures are seeked, reconstructed and displayed as a still picture for a nominal display period, during which the next entry point picture is seeked and decoded. The length of the nominal display period is controlled by the application. The application may scan entry point pictures in forward, reverse or random direction.

After decoding the MPEG video data, the Full Motion decoder displays reconstructed MPEG video pictures or a part thereof in the full motion video plane, available at the output of the decoder. The full motion video plane has a horizontal resolution of 384 or 360 pixels on a line, and is fully synchronized with the other planes, i.e. the base case video planes. The width of all planes is 384 or 360 pixels of normal resolution and the height of all planes is 240 or 280 lines. The field rate of the full motion video plane can be 60 Hz or 50 Hz, either interlaced or non-interlaced, exactly following the vertical timing of the base case video planes.

The application controls the part of the reconstructed picture to be displayed by means of a display window. The display window is a rectangle within the reconstructed picture; the reconstructed picture area within the display window is displayed in the full motion video plane. See figure 9. The reconstructed picture or the part thereof which is displayed may be smaller than the spatial size of the full motion video plane. In areas of the full motion video plane not covered by the displayed part of a reconstructed picture, a background color is displayed. The application can program one background color in RGB for the entire full motion video plane.

Figure 9 Display window from reconstructed picture displayed within full motion video plane

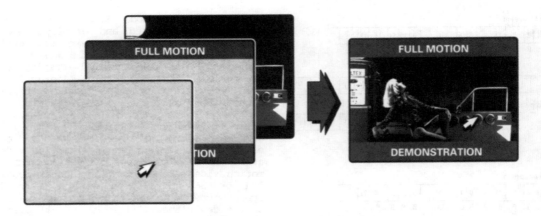

Figure 10 Overlay of the cursor plane, a base case
(e.g. RGB) plane and the full motion
video plane

The application can control the size and the position of the display window by means of the following parameters :
- height and width of window;
- position of window within reconstructed picture;
- position of window within full motion video plane.
By means of above parameters a variety of display functions can be realized. For example the window can be opened or closed slowly by modifying the size of the window each field period. Also scrolling within the reconstructed picture is possible, as well as scrolling within the full motion video plane. Another function available to applications is to blank the window; in that case the contents of the display window becomes 'black', i.e. R,G,B = 16,16,16.

At the output of the Full Motion decoder the full motion video plane is available. The full motion video plane is provided to the external video input of the Base Case video section (see also figure 5). By controlling this input, the application can replace the backdrop plane by the full motion video plane. When enabled, the full motion video plane will be visible in picture areas where transparency is defined for all enabled base case video planes, including the cursor (see figure 10). Note that an application can apply pixel accuracy in defining transparency.

2.3 Still Pictures

A still picture is a video sequence consisting of one picture. Non-interlaced still pictures with a picture area of up to 352 pixels by 288 lines can therefore be coded as a normal full motion sequence. For such still pictures the previous sections 2.1 and 2.2 are applicable.

The technique to compress still pictures, as provided by the MPEG standard, is more efficient than the methods available in a Base Case player. For a typical still picture, MPEG compression is approximately four times more efficient as DYUV compression (DPCM based) in the Base Case player. In a special mode, the Full Motion system therefore also supports MPEG based coding of interlaced still pictures.

For coding of interlaced still pictures the maximum picture area is 384 pixels by 576 lines. Flexibility is available to exploit this area for coding wide and low pictures as well as high and narrow pictures. After reconstruction, interlaced still pictures are displayed in the full motion video plane, with both the full motion video plane and the base case video planes in the interlace mode. The part of the still picture to be displayed is selected by means of a display window, as for non-interlaced pictures. The control of the full motion video plane, the control of the display window and the mixing with base case video planes is the same as for non-interlaced video; see section 2.2.

Default one reconstructed interlaced still picture can be stored. An extension mechanism is defined for Full Motion decoders with larger memories to store multiple reconstructed still pictures. The application can read the number of interlaced still picture which can be stored in the Full Motion decoder from a Device Status Descriptor (DSD). A DSD contains characteristics of a specific device in a player.

2.4 Memory extension

The Full Motion decoder in a CD-I player contains a memory bank of at least 4 Mbit, a.o. to handle MPEG video decoding and re-ordering as well as frame rate conversion. When the memory is not used for Full Motion video decoding, the memory can be used to extend the amount of system memory available to applications. In that case the Full Motion decoder serves as memory controller, such that the memory is transparently accessible by the application. The minimum size of the memory bank is 4Mbit. In the general case, the size of the memory bank applied in a Full Motion CD-I player is found from the formula :

Size memory bank = (B * 1) Mbit,

where B >= 4; B is an integer value. The application can find the size of the applied memory bank from a Device Status Descriptor (DSD), where the applied value of B is stored.

3. APPLICATION OF THE MPEG STANDARD FOR FULL MOTION

The MPEG standard is a generic standard for audiovisual coding, i.e. an application independent standard. The MPEG standard has been defined by working group WG11 of subcommittee SC29 of the joint technical committee JTC1 of the standardization bodies ISO and IEC. In this working group, the Moving Picture Experts Group (MPEG), experts from many countries, representing a.o. the computer industry, the VLSI industry, the telecommunication industry, and the consumer electronics industry, contributed to develop the MPEG standard.

The three companies collaborating in the Full Motion System for CD-I, Matsushita Electric Industry, Sony Corporation and Philips Consumer Electronics, decided to apply the MPEG standard for this system. The techniques developed by the MPEG Committee will enable many applications requiring digitally compressed video and audio. The storage media targeted by MPEG include, next to Compact Disc, also DAT and computer disks and it is expected that MPEG based technologies will eventually be used in a variety of communication channels, such as ISDN and local area networks and even in broadcasting applications.

The MPEG standard specifies an MPEG stream as a generic interchange format. To store an MPEG stream on a medium, a medium specific layer is required (see figure 11). In case of the Full Motion system, the medium is the CD-I disc or memory and the medium specific layer is the disc format.

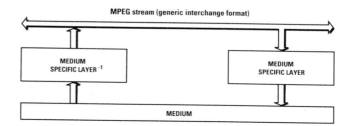

Figure 11   Storage of an MPEG stream on a medium.

The MPEG standard consists of three parts. In part 1 the system layer of the standard is specified, including the multiplex structure to combine MPEG audio and MPEG video data; furthermore timing information needed for synchronized play back is specified in part 1. [3] In part 2 of the MPEG standard the video coding layer is specified. [4][5] Part 3 specifies the audio coding layer.

A general MPEG encoding system is given in figure 12. Audio and video sources are providing inputs to audio and video encoders. The MPEG Audio and MPEG Video streams generated by the encoders are multiplexed into one MPEG stream. In one MPEG stream up to sixteen MPEG Video streams and up to thirty-two MPEG Audio streams can be multiplexed. Furthermore a System Time Clock is available with a nominal value of 90 kHz. The System Time clock is used for synchronization.

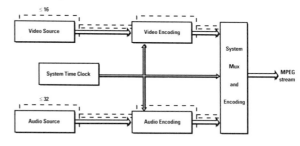

Figure 12   General MPEG encoding system

The MPEG multiplex structure consists of packs and packets. Each pack consists of a pack header and a number of packets. Each packet consists of a packet header and a data field; the data field contains data from one of the streams in the multiplex. For an example see figure 13.

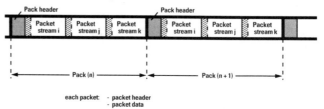

Figure 13   Example of MPEG multiplex structure with three streams (i, j and k).

For synchronization reasons, values of the System Time Clock are encoded in packet headers and pack headers. In packet headers Time Stamps (TS) are encoded. A Time Stamp indicates the value of the System Time Clock at the instant that a picture or audio frame enters the video or audio encoder. See figure 14. In the pack header the System Clock Reference (SCR) is encoded, indicating the value of the System Time Clock at the instant the SCR field exits the encoding system as part of the produced MPEG stream. At decoding, the inverse process is followed. From the SCR values in the pack headers, the System Time Clock is regenerated. Decoded pictures and audio frames are output of the decoders at the instants indicated by the Time Stamps. As a result, the mutual timing relations between audio and video at the output of the decoder are the same as at the input of the encoder.

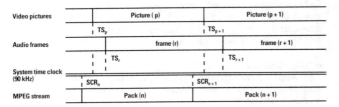

Figure 14   Synchronization between audio and video in MPEG, using the 90 kHz System Time Clock.

In the MPEG standard a number of parameters are defined; examples are the picture rate, the picture size, the audio sampling frequency and the bitrate. To make the MPEG standard suitable for many applications, these parameters usually have a large range. The picture size e.g. can be up to 4096 pixels by 4096 lines.

To define the parameter range covered, an application has to specify its 'MPEG profile'. The MPEG profile also defines the specific constraints from the application on the MPEG syntax and semantics. In the MPEG standard an MPEG profile has been defined already for target applications. The Full Motion system adopts the profile of CSPS (Constrained System Parameter Stream) as defined in the MPEG standard for the system layer, while the profile for the video coding layer of constrained parameters is supported. In the Full Motion system some video parameters are allowed to go beyond the constrained parameter range for video.

Next to its MPEG profile, an application has to specify the application specific characteristics. Examples are the medium specific layer (see figure 14) and how to use the MPEG stream in the application. For the Full Motion system the latter is summarized in section 2 of this paper. The medium specific layer for Full Motion CD-I discs is summarized in section 3.1. The MPEG profile applied by the Full Motion system is summarized in sections 3.2, 3.3 and 3.4 for the audio, video and systems parts of the MPEG standard. In section 3.5 synchronized playback of Full Motion sequences is described.

3.1   The medium specific layer for storage on CD-I disc

On a CD-I disc data is stored in sequentially recorded units called sectors. At a player CD-I discs are read at a constant rate of 75 sectors per second. Each CD-I sector consists of a header, a subheader and a datafield. The header and subheader provide a.o. information on the data type, the form, and coding information. The data type indicates the type of data stored in the sector; video sectors, audio sectors and data sectors are distinguished. The form (which may be 1 or 2) indicates whether error correction code is included in the datafield. Form 1 sectors contain 2048 Bytes of user data and 280 Bytes of error correction code. Form 2 sectors contain fully 2324 Bytes of user data without any error correction code. The coding information indicates the applied coding format of the sector. For example video sectors may contain DYUV, CLUT or RGB data and audio sectors may contain ADPCM data on compression level A, B or C.

To store Full Motion data on CD-I discs, the coding format options are extended. Two new coding formats are defined for video sectors : 'MPEG video' and 'MPEG still picture' for storage of MPEG coded non-interlaced moving picture data and interlaced still picture data. One new coding format is defined for audio sectors : 'MPEG audio' for storage of coded MPEG audio data. Each MPEG video sector, MPEG still picture sector and MPEG audio sector is a form 2 sector with a usable datafield of 2324 Bytes. Note that the Full Motion application program is stored in a normal data sector.

To store Full Motion data in sectors, the system part of the MPEG standard is applied. The multiplex structure provided by the system part is applied for a separate multiplex of MPEG video streams, MPEG still picture streams and MPEG audio streams. As a result three type of ISO11172 streams can be distinguished:
a) In this type of ISO 11172 stream MPEG video streams are multiplexed. In each ISO11172 stream of this type one or more (up to 16) MPEG video streams may be multiplexed. This type of ISO11172 streams is stored in MPEG video sectors.
b) In this type of ISO 11172 stream MPEG still picture streams are multiplexed. Each ISO11172 stream of this type may be a multiplex of one or more (up to 16) MPEG still picture streams. This type of ISO11172 streams is stored in MPEG still picture sectors.
c) In this type of ISO 11172 stream MPEG audio streams are multiplexed. In each ISO11172 stream of this type one or more (up to 32) MPEG audio streams may be multiplexed. This type of ISO11172 streams is stored in MPEG audio sectors.
Each ISO11172 stream is stored in an integer number of sectors.

3.2 MPEG audio profile

To code audio, the Full Motion system applies layer I and layer II of the audio part of the MPEG standard. Audio can be coded in stereo, in joint stereo (i.e. intensity stereo), in dual channel or in single channel. In case of intensity stereo, the redundancy between both stereo channels is exploited to improve the coding efficiency. All bitrates allowed by MPEG for layer I and layer II are supported; see figure 15. The applied audio sampling frequency is 44.1 kHz. For simple integration of the MPEG Audio decoding functions with Base Case decoding functions, other sampling frequencies are not allowed in the Full Motion system. The protection bit may be used to add redundancy to the MPEG audio data. Two options may be used for emphasis : no emphasis and 50/15 μsec emphasis. Other options, including CCITT J.17 emphasis are not allowed.

Layer I			Layer II		
bitrate	mono	stereo	bitrate	mono	stereo
32	yes	yes	32	yes	no
64	yes	yes	48	yes	no
96	yes	yes	56	yes	no
128	yes	yes	64	yes	yes
160	yes	yes	80	yes	no
192	yes	yes	96	yes	yes
224	yes	yes	112	yes	yes
256	yes	yes	128	yes	yes
288	yes	yes	160	yes	yes
320	yes	yes	192	yes	yes
352	yes	yes	224	no	yes
384	yes	yes	256	no	yes
416	yes	yes	320	no	yes
448	yes	yes	384	no	yes

Figure 15   Available audio bitrate options in kbit/sec
Note : stereo refers to dual channel mode, independent stereo mode or intensity stereo mode; mono refers to single channel mode.

3.3 MPEG video profile

The Full Motion system supports the constrained video parameters, defined in the video part of the MPEG standard, but some parameters have a larger range in the Full Motion system. The Full Motion system allows for a maximum bitrate for video of about 5 Mbit/sec. This bitrate exceeds the 1.856 Mbit/sec limit defined in the MPEG standard for the constrained video parameters. Furthermore, for coded interlaced still pictures the maximum picture size exceeds the picture size limit for the constrained video parameters. Finally, in the Full Motion system video coding with a variable bitrate is allowed.

The following summarizes the bounds specified in the video part of the MPEG standard for the constrained parameters. See the MPEG standard for the definition of parameters. The maximum picture width is 768 pixels, and the maximum height is 576 lines. The maximum picture area is 396 macroblocks. A macroblock is a rectangular block of 16*16 luminance pixels and corresponding chrominance pixels. The maximum number of macroblocks per second equals 396*25. The constrained parameters allow for picture rates of 23.976 Hz, 24 Hz, 25 Hz, 29.97 Hz and 30 Hz. The maximum size of the VBV buffer is 40 kByte, and the range of motion vectors on half pixel accuracy is bounded to approximately +/- 64 pixels. For further details see part 2 of the MPEG standard.

An MPEG video data stream may be a concatenation of sequences with different parameters. For example the picture rate or the picture size may change. The Full Motion system applies no constraints on the pixel aspect ratio. Applications should take into account however that Full Motion decoders do not compensate for aspect ratio distortion. Three aspect ratios options are recommended for practical use : one optimum ratio for 60 Hz displays, one optimum ratio for 50 Hz displays, and one intermediate ratio suitable for both 60 Hz and 50 Hz displays.

3.4 MPEG system profile

The system part of the MPEG standard applies a multiplex structure consisting of packs and packets. See also figure 13. In each MPEG video sector, MPEG still picture sector and MPEG audio sector one pack is stored. Each pack consists of a pack header and one or more packets. A packet consists of a packet header followed by data from one stream.

The System Clock Reference (SCR) parameter in the pack header indicates, in units of the System Time Clock, the nominal arrival time of the pack at the input of the Full Motion decoder (see also figure 14). At play back, the decoder uses the SCR parameter to control the System Time Clock. For example at the start of a play back, the decoder System Time Clock can be initialized to the value equal to the SCR value encoded in the header of the first pack entering the decoder.

In the Full Motion system the System Time Clock is locked to the rate of 75 Hz at which sectors are read from disc. As a consequence, in case of a play from disc, the difference between encoded SCR values in sectors from the same ISO11172 stream is a multiple of 1200 (1200*75 = 90000). Full motion data can be played from memory with sector rates of 1, 2, 3 or 4 times the nominal sector rate. In general therefore the SCR difference described above is a multiple of 1200, 600, 400 or 300.

In the Full Motion system the System Time Clock is locked furthermore to both the picture rate in MPEG video streams and MPEG still picture streams, and to the audio sampling frequency of 44.1 kHz. The locking to the picture rate and the audio sampling frequency is ensured at encoding.

Each ISO11172 stream within the Full Motion system is a CSPS stream (Constrained System Parameter Stream; see system part of MPEG standard).

3.5 Playback synchronization

Synchronization between MPEG audio and MPEG video is ensured implicitly by the MPEG standard. The decoder regenerates the System Time Clock and presents decoded pictures and audio frames based on Time Stamps. See also figure 14. In the Full Motion system, the MPEG audio decoder and the MPEG video decoder do not share the same System Time Clock. Both decoders have their own System Time Clock. Because both clocks are locked to the 75 Hz sector delivery rate, their mutual offset is constant during a play. The mutual offset to be applied is known by the application. At playback, synchronization between MPEG audio and MPEG video is achieved, when the required mutual offset is applied between both System Time Clocks.

The MPEG standard assumes instantaneous decoding without any processing delay. In practice processing delays occurs in MPEG audio and MPEG video decoders. Each processing delay consists of a variable and a fixed component. The variable component is to be within 40 msec for each MPEG audio or MPEG video decoder in a Full Motion CD-I player. Within a player, the fixed component is to be constant for each MPEG audio or MPEG video decoder. The maximum synchronization error in the presentation of MPEG video and MPEG audio is therefore +/- 40 msec. The value of the constant component of the MPEG processing delay is player dependent and stored in a DSD.

Synchronization between a Full Motion play and plays of ADPCM audio and Base Case video is the responsibility of the application. To compensate for the processing delay of MPEG audio and MPEG video data, applications should delay the ADPCM audio play and the Base Case video play. The required value for such compensating delay can be found from the constant component of the MPEG processing delay stored in a DSD. To make synchronization possible between application events and Full Motion events, the Full Motion decoder informs the application, upon request, about Full Motion events. Examples are 'start of display of next picture' and 'presentation starts of next audio frame'.

4. ARCHITECTURE OF FULL MOTION CD-I PLAYER

A CD-I Base Case player is extended with the capability to play Full Motion CD-I discs by implementing a Full Motion decoder in the player. The interface between the Full Motion decoder and the Base Case player is straight forward (see figure 16). The Full Motion decoder is connected to and controlled via the CPU bus. The transfer of Full Motion data from disc or memory to the decoder is also via the CPU bus. The audio and video outputs from the Full Motion decoder are provided to the external audio and video inputs of the Base Case audio and video sections. For video synchronization the pixel clock as well as horizontal and vertical synchronization signals from the Base Case video section are provided to the Full Motion decoder. To lock the decoders System Time Clocks to the sector rate, a CD data clock is provided to the Full Motion decoder; this clock can be e.g. the master clock to which data delivery by the CD drive is locked. The frequency of such clock is player dependent.

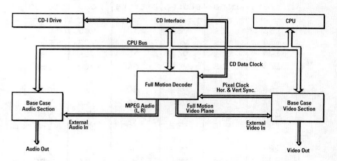

Figure 16   Full Motion decoder in a CD-I player

4.1   Structure of the Full Motion decoder

The Full Motion decoder basically consists of two functions, an MPEG video decoding function and an MPEG audio decoding function. Both MPEG decoding functions are in practice realized in a combination of hardware and software; which parts are realized in hardware and which in software is implementation dependent. The MPEG video processing hardware may consist of an MPEG video decoder IC with an external memory bank of at least 4Mbit. The memory bank can be used for multiple purposes during MPEG video decoding :
a) for buffering of coded input data,
b) for storage of reference pictures at decoding,
c) for re-ordering of decoded pictures, and
d) as display memory at frame rate conversion.
Next to the input buffer of 46 kByte, as defined by the MPEG standard, in total slightly more than three pictures of maximum size can be stored in 4 Mbit.

The MPEG audio decoder hardware may consist of an MPEG audio decoder IC. The MPEG video and audio decoding software are the MPEG video driver and the MPEG audio driver. Both drivers are hardware dependent. The application controls the Full Motion decoder by communicating with the MPEG video driver and the MPEG audio driver. The application communicates with both drivers via the Full Motion manager (see figure 17). The Full Motion manager is part of CD-RTOS, the compact disc real time operating system applied in CD-I. For the Full Motion system, the specification of CD-RTOS is therefore extended with the Full Motion manager, the calls between the application and the Full Motion manager, and the calls between the Full Motion manager and both the MPEG video driver and the MPEG audio driver.

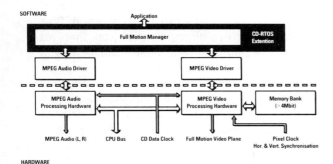

Figure 17 Structure of Full Motion decoder

5. CONCLUSION

In this paper the Full Motion system for CD-I is presented. The Full Motion System is a full compatible extension of the CD-I system. After compression, the audiovisual information is stored on CD-I disc at a data format which is fully MPEG compatible. In the architecture of a Full Motion CD-I player, Full Motion is an simple add-on function. The system provides a variety of features to produce and playback Full Motion CD-I discs. The major features are 50 Hz /60 Hz disc compatibility, a high futureproof flexibility, and the capability to play from one Full Motion CD-I disc up to 72 minutes of audiovisual material of high quality.

References

[1] Compact Disc Interactive Full Functional Specification
     September 1990
     Sony Corporation and NV Philips

[2] MPEG1 standard
     Coding of moving pictures and associated audio for digital storage media up to about 1.5 Mbit/sec.
     April 1992
     Draft international standard ISO/IEC DIS 11172
     ISO/IEC JTC1/SC29/WG11

[3] Le Gall, D.J. MPEG : A video compression standard for multimedia applications
     Communications of the ACM
     Volume 34, Number 4, April 1991

[4] Le Gall, D.J. The MPEG video compression algorithm
     Signal Processing : Image Communication
     Volume 4, Number 2, April 1992

[5] MacInnis, A.G. The MPEG systems coding specification
     Signal Processing : Image Communication
     Volume 4, Number 2, April 1992

QuickTime™: An Extensible Standard for Digital Multimedia

Eric Hoffert, Mark Krueger, Lee Mighdoll, Micheal Mills, Johnathan Cohen, Doug Camplejohn, Bruce Leak, Jim Batson, David Van Brink, Dean Blackketter, Michael Arent, Rich Williams, Chris Thorman, Mitch Yawitz, Ken Doyle, Sean Callahan

Apple Computer, Inc.

Abstract

QuickTime is an extensible standard for digital multimedia. It establishes a foundation for the representation of time-based objects and file formats, still image and video compression techniques, human interface conventions, and application programming interfaces. All of these representations can stay the same as we move towards an era of full-screen, full-motion digital video/high-resolution digital systems and as the underlying media technologies and compression schemes improve rapidly over time. QuickTime includes direct support in the operating system for audio/video synchronization and for still and moving image compression algorithms. Software-based video decompression is used as a means to permit dynamic media functionality in all color Macintosh computers. As a result, QuickTime brings dynamic media to a broad range of applications, including not only media authoring tools such as video editors and animation systems, but to mainstream tools such as word processors, databases, spreadsheets and electronic mail.

Introduction

QuickTime is a digital multimedia extension to the Macintosh operating system. It is a new architecture for dynamic data types, such as sound, video, MIDI and animation. Just as QuickDraw is a standard part of Macintosh system software that allows applications to integrate graphics in a consistent, mainstream fashion, QuickTime will become a standard part of Macintosh system sofware that will allow applications to integrate dynamic media in a consistent, mainstream fashion. In addition, much of the structure of QuickTime is general enough so that cross-platform usage and development is a potential application for the system.

The previous generation of work on personal computers has focused largely on the graphical representation and manipulation of two-dimensional screen objects. Most of the work concentrated on spatial metaphors—for rearranging objects on a screen or page, stretching or shrinking their size, editing and grouping them together into larger composite objects, changing their visual attributes, (such as color, opacity or texture), and ultimately printing the arrangement of objects onto a piece of paper. The concept of "cut and paste" for two-dimensional objects involves cutting a region from one image and pasting it elsewhere into a separate position on-screen or possibly into a separate image. This notion of "cut and paste" in the spatial domain has been very effective. It has facilitated the advent of desktop publishing, allowing personal computers to produce high quality output of text and graphics for paper reproduction and dissemination of information.

We have created a system that focuses on the manipulation of time-based objects. This work borrows a number of concepts from the manipulation of spatial objects—including stretching, shrinking, editing and changing of attributes, but all of these operations can now be applied to objects in the temporal domain. For example, stretching an object temporally makes it of longer duration, and editing an object in time, means removing some selection from its full duration. The concept of "cut and paste" for temporal objects involves cutting a selection from a temporal sequence and pasting it elsewhere at a seperate time offset and possibly into a separate temporal sequence. This notion of "cut and paste" in the temporal domain has proven to be very powerful and necessary for dealing with dynamic, real-time streams such as video, sound, animation, MIDI and other time-based information.

The fundamental notion of using the clipboard and scrapbook as pieces of temporary storage in the Macintosh operating system are maintained for dynamic media as well. It is now possible to cut and paste digital video and animation sequences through the clipboard and scrapbook, just as it has been possible to cut and paste text and graphics in the past.

Reprinted from *37th Annual Int. Computer Conference-COMPCON*, pp. 15–20, Spring 1992.

We have also developed a new means of expression for dynamic media—the dynamic document. Unlike desktop publishing, which produces traditional paper, and desktop video, which produces traditional analog video, the dynamic document facilitated by QuickTime exists only in electronic form. It forms the basis for a new medium of interactive communication, a hybrid of print, film, video and computers.

Overview

QuickTime is composed of a number of building blocks, as follows:

Movie file format

A new file format for the storage and manipulation of temporal media objects, called the Movie file format has been developed. The Movie file format was created to be used as a container for any type of dynamic data, or any object that changes over time. A Movie contains groups of homogeneous data, called tracks. Each of these tracks can have a distinct type, such as video, sound, MIDI or SMPTE. Tracks have their own time scales (such as 29.97 frames per second for NTSC video, or 44.1khz for digital audio) and each track can be offset in time from the begining of a Movie. The tracks are represented as pointers which refer to the actual data, called the media. This allows many different versions of a movie (also called edit lists) to be compactly stored, each of which refers back to the original data. It also makes cut and paste operations efficient, since only the data references are exchanged, rather than the actual data representation. This defers the need of moving large amounts of multimedia data through the various system components and I/O system, until a final edit or version of a sequence has been decided upon, or until a sequence needs to be sent to another computer for playback.

Like a real movie one might view in the cinema, a QuickTime movie has a number of different temporal representations. For example, embedded into the file format is a "poster", a single frame representative of the entire movie, as well as a "preview", a sequence of short duration (roughly 3–5 seconds) that is representative of the full-length movie. The movie, its poster and its preview are all stored seperately in the Movie file format, allowing access to the temporal data at a variety of different scales, each useful for a different context. The different temporal representation facilitates efficient multimedia browsing of large movie databases, allowing viewing of still images or short previews from

bandwidth starved networks and CDROM. It is also possible to view the poster frame of a movie directly from the Finder or a file dialogue when viewing files in a folder, without having to use any application.

The Movie format was intended as a cross-platform file format, allowing exchange of multimedia sequences with Windows, DOS, UNIX and other platforms. Apple is publishing the specification of the file format, and is encouraging third parties doing cross-platform development to use the file format as a container for exchanging dynamic data. The format is also extensible; it starts with track type definitions of video and sound, but it is feasible that there may be new types in the future, such as SMPTE, MIDI or other track types.

PICT file format extensions

The standard means for storing color images in the Macintosh environment has been extended considerably. The PICT format now allows images to be associated with different compression schemes, as well as with picture overlay information, such as masks, mattes and other data. Also, each PICT image can now contain a reduced size representation of an image, which is an 80 x 60 compressed "thumbnail" picture. The usage of a thumbnail image allows rapid browsing of high resolution still images remotely over networks, or locally from CDROM via the reduced resolution representation. The thumbnail image requires only 4 - 5Kbytes of additional data, making it a small fraction of the complete picture file for all but the smallest of pictures. In addition, the PICT extensions are backwards compatible, allowing any Macintosh application to immediately use compressed PICT images.

Macintosh Toolbox Extensions

QuickTime brings three new toolboxes to the existing Macintosh programmer's toolset in the areas of image compression, time management and modular software design.

Image Compression Manager

The image compression manager shields applications from the details of still and video compression and decompression by using device and algorithm independent services. It provides a seamless view of compression methods, independent of whether they are software or hardware based. New software compression schemes can be added to applications by adding a compressor component module, a small QuickTime code object, to the system folder. New hardware compression schemes can be added to the system by adding a compressor component, along with additional hardware VLSI or DSP compression technology. Applications can still use the same Movie file format and human interface standards with different software or hardware compression methods. The image compression manager takes care of display details such as clipping, scaling, crossing multiple screens and fast dithering. It also performs a number of tasks automatically, such as handling the display and processing for random access and reverse play functionality for temporally compressed sequences, as well as performing scene change detection and inserting automatic keyframes when necessary within a video data stream.

Movie Toolbox

The movie toolbox controls all temporal objects within QuickTime. It is used to associate time scales with Movie tracks, to perform editing and playback functions, and to deal with time based manipulations of selections of sequences. The toolbox allows manipulation of temporal data on a movie, track, or media basis. This toolbox controls the synchronization of multiple tracks with different time scales - for example, allowing 15 fps video to be synced with 22khz audio, or 10 fps animation to be synced with 8 khz audio. As long as each track is a recognized type, and has a specified time scale and duration, QuickTime can synchronize the tracks together. It also takes care of correctly joining together different video sequences, which may be of different compression types, frame rates and image resolutions when doing editing or playback functions.

The Movie Toolbox allows the usage of "alternate" tracks. Alternate tracks are typically tracks all of the same type (such as video), but each track can be used in a different context. For example, one can define alternate track types for a video sequence at a variety of different image resolutions; fast computers can use the hi-res tracks, and slow computers can use the lo-res tracks. Tracks for a video sequence can exist at different bit depths - a true-color track can be used for high-end color machines, and a one-bit per pixel track used for machines that have one-bit display, such as the recently introduced Apple notebook computers. For soundtracks, alternate tracks can be used to store the audio in different languages. Only the correct language is used for different international versions of a digital multimedia sequence. For the cases of video bit depth and soundtrack language, QuickTime ascertains what type of

system the user is working on, and selects the appropriate track from among the alternates automatically.

Like images, movies can have masks associated with their display windows. This allows an arbitrarily shaped movie to play on the screen; for example the silhouette of a person's head for a talking head sequence, or a circular movie showing the earth's rotation.

Timing Models

QuickTime also can function as the time manager of the system. It maintains global clocks of both video field rate and microsecond timing resolutions. All time based events are slaved to these global clocks. Time based events can be used with scheduling facilities available within QuickTime. For example, it is possible to queue up a variety of different events each of which can occur at a specific time. Scheduled events can be triggered not only based on time conditions at a specific time T (i.e., when $t < T$, $t > T$, $t = T$), but also on rate conditions as well for a specific rate R (i.e., when $r < R$, $r > R$, $r = R$).

Component Manager

Components are independent pieces of code which use a standardized interface and can be bound to programs or the operating system at run-time (without compilation). These components are in some ways like objects in an object oriented system, in that they can be flexibly re-used among different applications. Component software is a key building block of QuickTime, and the component manager manages all of the components in the system. The fundamental assumption in QuickTime is that media-based technologies will improve quickly over time. As a result, many of the building blocks of QuickTime are built as components that can easily be replaced or upgraded. Usage of the component manager allows adding or subtracing pieces of the operating system with ease. During the course of a user session, one or more media components may be installed or removed from the system for different functions. This allows flexible, user-customized functionality to be assembled by the user without writing any new software. A user can select their own compression schemes, video digitizer, audio digitizer, look and feel of the interface etc. to form the basis of their media capture, editing and playback environment.

In QuickTime, the following pieces of software are components:

- still image and video compressors
- video digitizer interface
- audio/video sequence grabber
- audio/video synchronization services
- timing facilities
- human interface elements

Allowing media technologies to become software components makes it easy to create flexible, general systems. For example, a developer can write an application to capture video, without knowing what video digitizer or compression scheme will be used by the end-user. All that is needed by the developer is to write software that adheres to the digitizer and compression component API, and the system will ensure that whatever video digitizer and compression scheme are available on the user's machine will be used correctly. This approach frees users from the previous difficulties in running multimedia software, which has required users to run software which is tied to particular pieces of hardware. Using the same software with different hardware, would involve an entire rewrite of the application.

Compression in QuickTime

QuickTime allows both software and hardware compression schemes to be used interchangebly in the system. Hardware compression schemes such as motion JPEG, MPEG, DVI and p*64 are all potential candidates for inclusion as QuickTime compressors. A variety of software based schemes can be expected as well. However, to keep QuickTime solely a piece of system software and to keep its cost low for the user, it was necessary to devise methods to achieve dynamic media functionality without requiring hardware compression, and to do so for a broad range of application areas. This was accomplished by development of a suite of software compression techniques for the areas of still images, animation and video. The next section details the software compression schemes at the heart of QuickTime.

"Free" Software Compression

QuickTime provides a basic set of software compression/decompression schemes that meet a wide range of compression needs for still images, animation and video. These compression schemes are intended to be a built-in feature of every Macintosh with a 68020 or better processor, including both color and black & white machines. Support for black & white machines, includes support for QuickTime movies to run on the Apple Computer Inc. portable PowerBook™ machines as well. Providing advanced functionality for "free" has

previous precedents at Apple such as Hypercard™ (an interactive media program that ships with every machine), and LocalTalk™, the built-in networking protocol and hardware that is a part of every Apple machine. Software compression and decompression is an egalitarian approach, since it allows everyone to be both author and recipient of a multimedia message. It is still useful, even as hardware based compression begins to proliferate, since users of hardware based compression systems can still send along software based versions of their movies as alternate QuickTime tracks, for those recipients who may not have hardware decompression capability. There are currently five compression schemes built into QuickTime:

- **Video**: the video compressor was designed to permit playback of digitized video sequences with synchronized sound at frame rates of 10 fps or better from magneto-optical, CDROM [6] or hard disk. The compressor can playback at resolutions between sixteenth and quarter screen or more, depending on CPU processing power, image complexity and video display processing speed. This compressor supports both spatial and temporal compression modes, and it is a lossy compression scheme, with compression ratios ranging from 5:1 to 50:1, depending on content and frame to frame coherency. The video compressor is somewhat tolerant of noise, but will show image blockiness as a picture quality artifact as the compression ratio is increased. The video compressor includes the functionality of being recompressible with minimal or no quality degradation, allowing sequences to be processed with special effects, or edited repeatedly in multiple passes without any appreciable image quality reduction.

- **Animation**: the animation compressor was designed to permit playback of digitally synthesized and rendered moving image sequences. It has comparable resolution and frame rate performance to the Video compressor, supports both spatial and temporal compression modes and can function in both a lossless and lossy compression mode, with compression ratios ranging from 3:1 to 500:1, depending on content. The animation compressor uses a run-length encoding format, is highly sensitive to noise, preferring large coherent areas in time and space, and will show image streaking as a picture quality artifact.

- **Photo**: the photo compressor is a fully compliant, fast software implementation of the baseline ISO

JPEG still image compression standard. The compression scheme is DCT based, and was designed to compress high-quality scanned or digitized true-color images to be visually lossless at a compression ratio of 10:1. The compressor implementation in QuickTime supports only a spatial, lossy compression mode with compression ratios ranging from 5:1 to 100:1, depending on content and tolerance for quality degradation. DCT image artifacts include ringing, chroma crawl and blurriness. Although the JPEG algorithm was designed primarily to handle still images, it is also capable of being used to represent motion sequences, and fast CISC or RISC processors can be used for software video decompression with JPEG.

• **Raw**: the raw compressor (also called "None") is a storage representation for images at all available bit depths, from one bit per pixel up to twenty four bits per pixel. This includes both direct color, as well as CLUT formats. The raw format can be thought of as uncompressed video, but since many bit depths are accomodated, one can think of the lower bit depth representations as a form of compression. For example, it is possible to take a twenty-four bit video clip and convert it to be one-bit per pixel (for playback on notebook computers with one bit displays), and achieve a compression ratio of 24:1. The raw compressor is a very convenient compression format on which to apply image and video processing techniques, as well as special effects, since these operations are generally defined in the spatial domain, not the transform or compressed bit formats of the available image compressors.

• **Graphics**: This compressor is optimized for high picture quality and fast playback of digital animation or video content on eight-bit displays. This compressor was included, since a large number of users still have eight-bit color as their standard frame buffer.

Human interface
Technology has always been important at Apple, but never more important than the issues of ease of use and consistency in the human interface. This tradition has been continued in the QuickTime project, and QuickTime sets new standards for the behavior of dynamic media across all applications. Included as new interface elements within QuickTime are a standardized controller for playing and editing moving image sequences, a consistent method for selecting image and video compression parameters, and elements for building a simple, real-time video capture system. In addition, there is now a detailed set of guidelines for digital multimedia application behavior, such as how

movies should behave in documents [3] (called dynamic documents), how movies are cut and pasted between applications and the scrapbook, and how applications should present the concept of movie references to a user, so that the separation between pointer and data is understood [4].

Applications
Whenever a new set of tools is developed, it is important to create examples that will fully exercise the tools. We have done this with QuickTime, and created a number of interactive digital multimedia showcases, to test, push and cajole our new tools:

• **The Digital News System at EDUCOM** [2] was a hypermedia news system that was digitally distributed over both local and wide-area networks at the educational conference EDUCOM in 1990. The hypermedia news consisted of compressed still images, digital audio, digital video, hypertext links, Postscript graphics and textual material. A digital news magazine was created by a multimedia design team every day for four days in a row at the conference, and the hypermedia news was available at seventy-five kiosk machines connected by Ethernet and T-1 links, which were scattered across the city of Atlanta at conference centers and hotels.

• **The Virtual Museum** [5] is an electronic museum that a user can "walk" through, using a 3D navigation metaphor. There are five rooms - atrium, medicine, botany, astronomy and environment. Users can walk from room to room at will and select paintings or scultpures in 3D perspective to get a close up look and explanation of an exhibit. 3D objects are "hot" in each frame with user selection of an object triggering different events of playing a sound or digital movie or jumping to a particular card in a Hypercard stack. The Virtual Museum was scripted in Hypertalk™. Exhibits could all be dynamic in nature, such as movies illustrating the evolution of the universe, the different stages of growth of a fetus with sonograms, the growth of a Rosebud Campion plant and other simulations. The widespread usage of both anmation and digital video in the museum was easily accomplished using QuickTime as a foundation technology.

References

[1] Liebhold, M. and Hoffert, E., "Towards an Open Environment for Digital Video", *Communications of the ACM: Special Issue on Digital Multimedia*, April 1991, Vol. 34, No. 4, pp. 104-112.

[2] Hoffert, E. and Gretsch, G., "The Digital News System at EDUCOM: A Convergence of Interactive Computing, Newspapers, Television and High-Speed Networks", *Communications of the ACM: Special Issue on Digital Multimedia*, April 1991, Vol. 34, No. 4, pp. 113-115.

[3] Yawitz, M., Mills, M. and Arent, M., "Movies in Text Processing Documents", *Human Interface Working Paper, Apple Computer Inc. QuickTime Developer CDROM Disk*, December 1991.

[4] Yawitz, M., Mills, M., Arent, M., Hoffert, E. and Small, I., "HI Guidelines for Movies With External Data", *Human Interface Working Paper, Apple Computer Inc. QuickTime Developer CDROM Disk*, December 1991.

[5] Miller, G. and Hoffert, E.,"The Virtual Museum", *submitted for publication*, January 1992.

[6] Hoffert, E., "CD-Playable QuickTime Movies", *Apple Computer Inc. QuickTime Developer CDROM Disk*, December 1991.

[7] Hoffert, E., "Capturing QuickTime Movies", *Apple Computer Inc. QuickTime Developer CDROM Disk*, December 1991.

[8] Apple Computer, Inc., QuickTime Documentation, *Apple Computer Inc. QuickTime Developer CDROM Disk*, December 1991.

Acknowledgements

The Quicktime team would like to thank Dave Nagel, Mike Liebhold, Andy Poupart, Dick Lyon, Gavin Miller, John Worthington and Ty Roberts for their encouragement, assistance and support.

Trademarks

UNIX is a trademark of AT&T Bell Laboratories.
DOS and Windows are trademarks of the Microsoft Corporation.
Macintosh, Hypercard, Powerbook, HyperTalk, LocalTalk and QuickTime are trademarks of Apple Computer, Inc.

MPEG Encoding of Full Screen Video for Compact Disc Interactive

Derek Andrew

Our objective is to allow high quality moving pictures to be stored and displayed on multimedia Compact Disc Interactive (CD-I) systems. This planned extension to provide full screen digital motion video requires a coding system that compresses the video data rate by a factor of 133 to 1.2Mbit/s. We have implemented the proposed Moving Picture Expert Group (MPEG) standard video compression system on a SUN-ANDROX workstation to provide a software facility which can encode a ten minute video sequence overnight. This solution brings MPEG encoding within practical reach of CD-I authoring establishments.

This article describes the various compression techniques used in the MPEG system, where the picture quality obtained depends on the picture content. For many picture sequences quality is already acceptable but some sequences give visible artefacts. The flexibility of the software encoder is being used to examine ways to enhance picture quality.

Introduction

Advances in digital video technology herald the era of digital video applied to video transmission, broadcast, teleconferencing, video telephony and multimedia information systems such as Compact Disc Interactive. The need for digital video compression is common to all these applications. The proposed MPEG[1,2] standard defines a system for digital video compression. Philips has been active in this standardisation process within the International Standards Organisation (ISO) and it now seems that a world standard has been achieved.

The original picture source signal may be obtained from film or video. It is first converted into a digital broadcast quality signal, probably in a format known as CCIR 601, at around 160 Mbit/s (CCIR is the International Consultative Radio Committee). The challenge is to compress that video signal to 1.2 Mbit/s, so that the pictures may be stored on the optical disc and displayed with acceptable quality using the standard CD-I disc reading system and an MPEG decoder. This CD-I application, requiring a compression factor of 133, is a severe test for the MPEG scheme.

Compression Techniques

The various techniques for compression which are combined within the MPEG system will now be discussed.

Pre-Processing

The CCIR 601 video is converted to a non-interlaced format with 352 pixels (picture elements) on 288 lines for a full screen image. Each picture has a luminance (Y) and two chrominance (U and V) elements. Both chrominance data sets are reduced to one quarter of the area of the luminance set for each picture. This pre-processing compresses the data from 160 to 30 Mbit/s.

Picture Typing

The picture sequence is classified into picture types (figure 1). Coded I pictures contain all the information

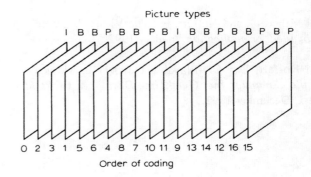

Figure 1. An MPEG sequence.

that the decoder needs to reconstruct them. Coded P pictures may contain difference information and are reconstructed by adding the differences to information copied from the latest previously decoded I or P picture. Coded B pictures also contain differences but the copied data added in the decoder may come from the P or I frames which occur just before or just after the B picture. For this reason the order of coding (shown in figure 1) is not the same as the left to right order of display. Coding efficiency decreases with picture type in the order B P and I. For CD-I applications, where the user interacts with the system, it is desirable for decoding to commence from entry points at many locations in the picture sequence. I frames provide these entry points.

Redundancy Between Consecutive Pictures (Temporal Redundancy)

In this coding scheme use is made of the characteristic of video sequences that there is often similarity between neighbouring pictures in a sequence. Each picture is divided into regions (blocks of 8 × 8 pixels). A previously coded picture is searched to find a block which matches that currently being coded. When a block is found which matches the data exactly, only the vector displacement information for the block is sent

Reprinted with permission from *Philips Research Labs-Redhill Review 1991*, pp. 59–61, 1992 © Philips Electronics.

to the decoder, thereby greatly reducing the data which must be transferred.

The search for a forward vector for a P type picture is illustrated in figure 2. In this example the P pictures are separated by three B pictures. The block to be coded in the P_1 picture is matched with a block of similar picture content from the previously coded P_0 picture. The vector arrow indicates the offset to this best matching

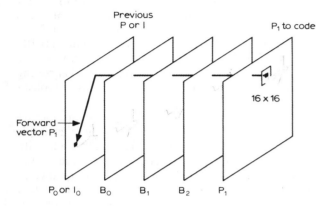

Figure 2. Forward vector for block in P_1.

block. The search for vectors is actually performed on blocks of 16×16 pixels. Each of the 8×8 blocks contained within the vector block may use the vector in the coding process. If the match is not perfect, the coder may specify the vector and an error block, i.e. the block containing the differences between the original and the copied block. For P-type frames there are three choices of coding 8×8 blocks, coding using the original 8×8 block, coding with optimum vector and error block, or coding with zero vector and error block.

For B-type pictures a search for two vectors is performed, a forward vector for a matching block in P_0 and a backward vector for a matching block in P_1. There are four options for coding B pictures: coding of the original block, coding with forward vector and error block, coding with backward vector and error block, or coding with forward and backward vector plus error block where the error is now the original block minus the mean of the blocks selected by the forward and backward vectors. The coder examines each possible mode of coding and attempts to select that mode which results in the minimum requirement for coded data. The efficiency of coding is variable and increases when similar objects are found in consecutive pictures.

Redundancy Within a Single Picture (Spatial Redundancy)
Either the 8×8 block representing the original data (INTRA coding) or the error block representing the

differences (INTER coding) is mathematically transformed, using a Discrete Cosine Transformation (DCT), into a frequency domain representation. This DCT provides no actual data compression. However, the advantage is, that after the DCT, the 8×8 coefficients can be approximated, with less disturbing influence on picture quality. The approximations are performed by the quantiser. The quantiser groups DCT coefficients into bands and assigns a single value to all coefficients within a band. The number of different possible quantised coefficients is less than the number of possible DCT coefficients in proportion to the number in each band. The table of code words needed to represent the quantised coefficients is similarly reduced. The compression can be varied by changing the size of the bands. Compression can also be increased by replacing all DCT coefficients below a threshold value by zero. Another variable to increase compression is to bias the quantiser, causing the coefficients representing the higher spatial frequencies to be grouped in wider bands. The variation of the characteristics of the quantiser influence picture quality, and must be dynamically adjusted as the content of the picture sequence changes in such a manner that quality remains as high as possible.

Zig-Zag Scan and Run Length Encoding
After quantisation and thresholding, several of the DCT coefficients of the coded block are generally zero. A coding scheme which transmits only non zero coefficients and the number (run length) of zero coefficients before the next non-zero one, results in data compression when many zeros exist. The efficiency of the run length coding is enhanced if the DCT coefficients are ordered in increasing spatial frequencies using the MPEG prescribed zig-zag scan of the 8×8 data block illustrated in figure 3.

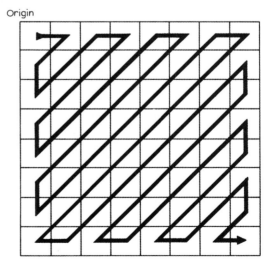

Figure 3. Quantiser zig-zag scan order for an 8×8 block.

Bit Stream Encoding

After quantisation and run length encoding the data is assembled as a coded bit stream. This bit stream has a structure and syntax conforming to the MPEG specification. A valid bit stream will allow reconstruction of the picture sequence using an MPEG defined decoder. The bit stream is provided with defined sets of headers which contain the data describing the characteristics of the video. The pictures are divided into sequences, groups of pictures, and single pictures. Each picture is further divided into slices, macro-blocks and blocks. Each subdivision is prefaced by a header code. The data describing the actual picture is inserted between the headers in the correct order. MPEG defines tables of code words which must be used to code all the header and picture data. The tables of code words all use a coding principle in which the most frequently occurring data entries in each table are coded using the shortest code words (Huffman coding).

Bit Rate Smoothing by Buffer Regulation

The bit stream assembled as described has a data rate which is variable and dependent on the picture content. The CD-I player has a fixed 1.2 Mbit/s video transfer rate. In order to match the two bit streams the coder must have a regulation system. The MPEG system also allows a buffer to be specified which can help to smooth the variations of the data rate. This buffer must never overflow or empty. The buffer regulator in the encoder simulates and monitors the state of this buffer. If there is any danger of overflow, the quantiser bands are made larger to increase data compression. In the case of the buffer being likely to empty the bands are made smaller and if necessary extra null code words are added to the bit stream. In general the buffer regulator must keep the quantiser bands at their smallest size compatible with the required average bit rate and allowable buffer state. If the buffer regulator is not optimum, picture quality will suffer considerably.

A Software Implementation of an MPEG Encoder

Encoding of video is an intensive computational task. To code 10 minutes of full screen video using the first Philips software encoding algorithm required three weeks of continuous processing using a main frame VAX. At PRL the more sophisticated MPEG encoding scheme has been programmed to operate on a single board ANDROX ICS-400 parallel processing system containing four Digital Signal Processors[3]. The ANDROX is controlled by a SUN sparc station. With this system, the time taken to code a video sequence is 100 times the sequence duration, so the ten minute video can now be coded overnight. This greatly improved efficiency and the ready availability of the SUN-ANDROX workstation brings MPEG encoding within practical reach of CD-I Authoring establishments.

The fact that picture quality depends on picture content means that some sequences, for example zooms and fades, are more difficult to encode with acceptable quality than others. The software implementation allows the influence on picture quality of each of the many coding parameters to be investigated. The improved speed of coding allows these investigations to proceed more rapidly. For many sequences quality is already acceptable, but work continues at PRL in order to provide further enhancements to the quality of full screen moving pictures on CD-I.

References

1 "Coding of moving pictures and associated audio", Committee Draft of Standard, ISO-IEC JTC/SC2/WG11 MPEG 90/176 Rev.2, 1990.
2 Le Gall, D., "MPEG: A Video Compression Standard for Multimedia Applications", Comm. of the ACM, No.4, vol.3, 1991.
3 Andrew, D., "An Experimental MPEG Software Encoder", Proc. Electronic Imaging International, pp.504–508, Miller-Freeman Expositions, 1991.

Showing Photo CD pictures on CD-I

N.D. Richards

Photo CD is a new Consumer product, which allows the amateur photographer to have standard 35mm negatives digitised by a commercial photoprocessor and recorded digitally on writable CD. It is then possible to display these pictures as very high quality images on a domestic television set. Both disc and player will be competitively priced. The system has been designed to be compatible with the CD-I audio visual system, which is about to be launched on the consumer market. The combination of Photo CD and CD-I provides an intelligent display system with an easy user interface and a wide range of attractive features.

Introduction

Photo CD (Compact Disc) is a new consumer product, jointly developed by Kodak and Philips. It provides a highly cost-effective means to transfer standard 35mm colour negatives in digital form to a CD-ROM (Read Only Memory) compact disc. These digital images may then be displayed on standard domestic television sets, computer displays or printed as extremely high quality colour prints.

Figure 1 Photo CD – a new consumer product.

A considerable advantage to the consumer is that no special camera is required. Any normal 35mm camera may be used to expose the negative, and existing negatives may also be converted to the digital disc format. Each disc is capable of recording over 100 images. Because the initial capture of the image is on film, with the digitisation being performed by the photoprocessor, then the resolution and quality of the digitised picture are far in excess of competing electronic capture systems. The disc may be updated, so that not all the pictures need to be written in a single operation.

The disc is a recordable CD disc, which is formatted as a CD-ROM XA bridge disc. The implications of using this format are that the same disc may be played back by either a general purpose computer system which is equipped with a CD-ROM XA drive, a dedicated Photo CD player, or a consumer CD-I (CD-Interactive) player.

Because the Photo CD system is offered to the market as an open system, it will be possible for Photo CD images to be used as cheap high quality input to computer desk top publishing systems, or the images displayed on suitably high resolution computer graphics terminals. However, our present interest is in the display of pictures in a domestic environment.

The Photo CD player will play back the digital images from disk and display them on either a 525 line or 625 line television receiver or monitor. As an alternative to displaying the Photo CD images on a dedicated player it is also possible to play back and display the pictures on a CD-I player. PRL has developed software techniques and prototype application programs to enable CD-I to be used for this purpose. In addition there has been close involvement in developing the coding standards.

Why Photo CD?

The object of Photo CD is to combine the high quality and convenience of photographic film with the advantages of digital storage, which for images mirror the well known advantages of digital audio. Once the analogue image has been digitised it can be arranged that the image is substantially immune from subsequent distortion and degradation. An unlimited number of perfect copies may be made of any image, and there need be no degradation resulting from prolonged storage or repeated showing. The random access feature of the compact disc, which has been very well received for selecting audio tracks, is even more valuable for accessing individual Photo CD pictures. The final major advantage is that digitisation makes

Reprinted with permission from *Philips Research Labs-Redhill Review 1990*, pp. 11–14, 1991. © Philips Electronics.

flexible manipulation of the images a possibility. Zoom with selective cropping, exposure and colour balance correction, titling and photomontage are all available in this new electronic darkroom.

The advantages of the Photo CD approach is that the digitisation equipment itself needs to be neither cheap nor portable, but can be shared by a very large number of users. Thus a cheap, high quality digitisation service is available to all users of existing 35 mm cameras. The possibility of making direct digital imaging cameras that are compatible with the Photo CD standard remains. But for the foreseeable future the combination of film and off-line scanning is likely to provide the best combination, and is identical with the approach used by the professional graphics industry.

Requirements of the Digital Coding Process

The design aim of the Photo CD coding system is to offer the advantages of a digital system, both for soft display on television systems and hard copy print output, without compromising the quality of the original photographic input.

The first, and most obvious, aspect of quality is the spatial resolution of the digitised pictures. A resolution of $3k \times 2k$ pixels has been adopted for 35 mm negatives, and this allows enlargements of poster size to be printed with good quality. Even higher resolutions are expected to be available in the future for larger format negatives.

The colorimetric aspects are also important. Here we have a problem arising from the fact that the Photo CD system is required to be suitable for generating both hard copy prints and television images on cathode ray tubes. So on the one hand we have a subtractive, non-linear colour system whose primaries are determined by cyan, yellow and magenta dyes or printing inks, and on the other an additive, differently non-linear system whose primaries are determined by the Cathode-Ray Tube (CRT) red, green and blue phosphors.

There are also problems of dynamic range. Compared with audio, the two potential display media have a comparatively low dynamic range. Prints have a range from white to black that is limited by both the density of the dyes or pigments and the surface reflections. Cathode ray tubes are limited by surface reflections and internal electron scattering. In both cases the effects amount to several percent so that achievable contrast ranges may only be in the range of 30 to 50. The source negative material has a much larger range, of at least 2.5 orders of magnitude. This is primarily to allow extended exposure latitude, and it is desirable to retain this extended range in the Photo CD system.

In addition to high picture quality, the system must have an adequate functional performance. It must be possible to pack a useful number of images on one disc,

the loading time from disc must be acceptable for the display application, and the complexity of the decoding should be well adapted to the capabilities of current dedicated hardware and general purpose computers.

As a measure of this last problem, we can consider the consequences of writing the raw digital colour image directly to disc. One image would consist of approximately 30 Mbytes, thus limiting the disc to 20 pictures. Even less acceptable would be the fact that each picture would take three minutes to load from disc. It is thus essential that the picture data should be compressed, and preferably organised in a way that facilitates rapid access to individual images.

Coding Photo CD Images

The 35 mm negatives are initially scanned by a solid state photosensitive array to give an image of $3k \times 2k$ pixels. Because the scanning device is connected to a powerful digital workstation it is possible to enhance the quality of the initial digital image in a number of ways. Self-calibration of the scanning device and correction of the known colour characteristics of the colour negative material (masking) are easily incorporated into the system. Relatively sophisticated algorithms for exposure compensation are also possible, and in the future it is to be expected that other means of providing digital image enhancement will be made available.

The coding process that is adopted (figure 2) is very similar to that used for producing digital television signals. This is no coincidence, because an important

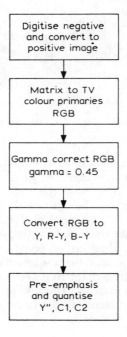

Figure 2 Coding Photo CD.

562

feature of Photo CD is the ability to show the pictures on a colour television display. However the coding has been adapted to the particular requirements of using the same data for making high resolution colour prints with an extended brightness and colour gamut.

The first modification to the coding process is the transformation of the three primary colour signals from the colour space of the image scanning system to that adopted for the colour television display system. The colours that can be reproduced by a colour CRT are defined by a colour triangle with vertices determined by the colours of the individual red, green and blue phosphors. The triangle lies inside the locus of pure spectral colours. It nearly, but not quite encompasses the locus of real surface colours available from pigments, but is deficient in both the magenta and cyan areas. This is shown in figure 3. The subtractive colour processes are themselves restricted in their available gamut (and in a much more complex and non-linear way). The cyan and magneta dyes or pigments used may well be capable of reproducing colours in the area where colour phosphors are most deficient. Even television systems of the future are likely to have a

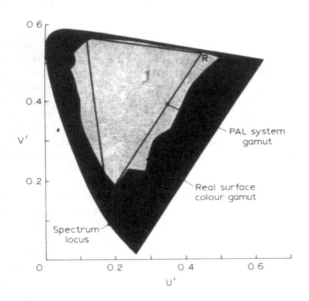

Figure 3 Range of colours reproducible by television system.

colour gamut that is not limited by the current phosphor set.

A possible solution would be to use neither colour television nor colour printing primaries for the encoding process, but to use hypothetical primaries that encompass the gamut of both display processes. However, an alternative solution is to make use of the fact that the whole of colour space may be defined by any practical set of primaries, e.g. the colour television set, provided that the red, green and blue values may take a range that exceeds the normal boundaries of

zero to unity. In particular, negative values may be allowed. These negative values must be ignored by the television system (negative light is not readily generated by the CRT), but are valid inputs to linear matrices that may be used to transform to a wider gamut colour space with alternative primaries. Adopting this approach ensures close compatibility with present video display systems, without losing the information that is required by systems with an extended colour gamut.

The first stage of coding is thus linear matrixing from the wide gamut colour space that is used by the digitising equipment to the colour space defined by the standard SMPTE (Society of Motion Picture and Television Engineers) phosphor set, retaining any negative values or values in excess of unity. The resulting red, green and blue values are then gamma corrected by the conventional 0.45 power law to give R, G and B, still preserving negative values. A luminance signal, Y, is generated from the gamma corrected R, G and B. Chrominance signals R-Y and B-Y define the colour. The Y signal thus formed will never take negative values, but may have a value that exceeds unity. The extended colour gamut coding also results in an increased range for the chrominance signals. This increased range of the signals, along with the desired dynamic range to give greater exposure latitude, is accommodated by a further process of scaling and offset prior to quantisation of the values to the final transmission code.

It will be seen that the coding is very similar to standard digital television coding. A simple look up table will convert to standard CCIR (International Radio Consultative Committee) YUV components with 0.45 law gamma correction (U and V are the transmitted colour signals). The only further requirement for video compatibility is that the display system should be able to deal with de-maxtrixed RGB signals that may take negative values.

Coding for Different Display Resolutions and Data Compression

It is not generally possible to convert a high resolution image to a lower resolution by a simple process of subsampling. It must be preceded by a low pass filtering process. Not only does this require computation time, but it requires that all of the data for the higher resolution image is accessed. This could result in very long access times for the video slideshow application. The Photo CD system overcomes this problem by storing a hierarchy of properly filtered and subsampled images on the disc. This is shown in table 1, and ranges from the highest resolution print file, through images suitable for differing television resolutions, including HDTV, and down to reduced area overview images.

Resolution	Application
3k × 2k	Print file
1k5 × 1k	HDTV
768 × 512	TV
384 × 256	TV/4
192 × 128	TV/16, (overview)

Table 1 Photo CD image resolutions.

The lower resolution images, i.e. from 768 × 512 downwards, consist of a Y image at the basic resolution and chrominance components subsampled by a factor of two both horizontally and vertically. This is a well established means of obtaining a factor of two data compression, with little visual loss in fidelity. Because very little of the total data resides in these lower resolution images and because it is desirable to have the least decoding overhead for these television based images, no further compression is used at these levels.

The two highest resolution images are encoded by a form of pyramid coding. Thus the 1.5k × 1k image is encoded by first subtracting the interpolated 768 × 512 image, to give a difference image. Because the higher resolution image only differs from the interpolated lower resolution image in the vicinity of sharp edges, the difference data has statistics that make it suitable for quantisation and variable length coding, which compresses the data from 8 bits per pixel to about 3 bits.

The 1.5k × 1k image is subsequently reconstructed from the 768 × 512 resolution image plus the compressed difference data.

A second stage of differencing enables the 3k × 2k image to be coded in a similar way, and at this level even higher data compressions are achieved.

A complete "image pack" of the different resolution images for one negative exposure compresses to about 5 Mbytes, thus allowing over 100 different pictures to be stored on one disc.

Combining Photo CD and CD-I

Because the coding of the images has been designed to be very similar to that adopted for digital television, it is possible to design cost-effective hardware for dedicated photo CD players. These players decode the images from the disc and display them on a standard domestic television receiver. Features like rotation of images, zoom magnification and favourite picture selection are all possible, as well as the playback of conventional CD audio.

Similarly, the encoding has been designed so as to present few decoding problems for the relatively powerful workstations used for image processing and quality desk-top publishing.

Our specific interest at PRL was in making it possible to use the CD-I interactive video system to display and manipulate the Photo CD images. The standard CD-I player is capable of displaying colour images in several different modes, depending on the particular application. Graphics and text are usually displayed in CLUT mode, using Colour Look-Up Tables to translate the 8 bit or 4 bit values into either one of 256 or 16 colours respectively. Natural photographic material is generally displayed using the DYUV mode. This is an eight bit display mode that uses delta PCM (Pulse Code Modulation) coding of YUV colour components to achieve compression of the colour data both on disc and in display memory. As a result of the differential PCM coding it is possible to display the complete gamut of colours used in colour television.

Because the Photo CD coding has been carefully designed to match the basic requirements of easy display on video systems, it has been possible to write software to run on standard CD-I players which converts Photo CD to a form that will display on the player.

In order to display Photo CD image data it is necessary first to translate the values to YUV by means of a look up table. This is followed by a delta PCM encoder which compresses the 8 bit YUV data to the 4 bit PCM codes that are used by the CD-I display. The CD-I player is programmed to recode the data as it is loaded from disc with only a few seconds delay. The player has sufficient memory to double buffer the pictures, and so this will generally disguise the loading and recoding time.

The normal resolution of the CD-I natural picture mode enables DYUV coded pictures to be displayed as either 384 × 256 non-interlaced or 384 × 512 interlaced images, which are comparable in quality with broadcast TV. However, it is possible to enhance the pictures further by means of a technique known as QHY coding[1]. This makes use of various unique features of the CD-I hardware to enhance the 384 × 512 images to 768 × 512, while still providing the full colour gamut that is a feature of DYUV coding. The increased resolution requires rather more time for loading and recoding, but results in displayed images which exceed the quality obtainable on most current broadcast receivers.

We have also written CD-I application programs which demonstrate the features which will be available from the combination of a CD-I player and Photo CD disc.

At the simplest level, it is possible to sequence through the pictures on disc under either automatic or manual control. The CD-I hardware enables the pictures to be sequenced either by an instantaneous cut from one image to the next, or by fades, dissolves and wipes of varying complexity. It is possible to pre-program all these effects, in addition to the order and duration of the pictures.

In order to make use of these features it is necessary to provide specific user interaction modes in which it is possible to review the contents of the disc and select the order and mode of viewing. In some respects these ergonomic aspects of the system present a greater challenge than the purely technical aspects, but we are assisted by the fact that we have a completely programmable system.

One of the more exciting features of the system is the possibility of selecting specific areas of the image and magnifying the image by ratios of 2, 4 or 8 times. Other ratios are available at the cost of a little more processing time. Here we see the advantage of having retained the high resolution of the film on disc.

Errors in exposure and colour balance may be corrected, and the pictures may be retouched by an electronic air brush. Many more features, such as the addition of titles and various photo-montage effects and digital enhancements to the picture, are available for the enthusiast.

All of these features may be made available on CD-I players, and a suitable CD-I application program will be incorporated in each Photo CD disc.

Acknowledgements

The work described in this article forms part of a collaboration between the Kodak and Philips Consumer Electronics development groups.

Reference

[1] Richards, N.D., "QHY – High Resolution Natural Picture Mode for CD-I", PRL Ann. Rev., pp.61–63, 1987

A Frame Language for Compact Disc Interactive

Martin Shiels

As the world of Compact Disc Interactive (CD-I) grows, there will be demand for more sophisticated software. PRL has been investigating how to provide more "intelligent" applications for CD-I, and part of that work has focused on the provision of knowledge representation languages. CD-I Frames is one such language. It implements the proven concept of "frames" in the demanding environment of CD-I. Consequently, much effort has been expended to ensure that the language provides useful features without sacrificing performance.

Introduction

Accomplishing the goal of introducing "intelligent" software into the world of CD-I means looking at knowledge representation languages. Once knowledge is represented, the system can reason with it to answer user queries and solve interesting problems. When working with knowledge, choosing the right representation language is critical and the choice is not always simple. There will invariably be a trade-off between the technical capabilities of the language and the constraints imposed by the hardware. For any representation language, the basic technical requirements are:

- Expressive Power – people need to communicate their knowledge effectively to the system; the representation language should lend itself well to how they naturally think about the subject.
- Understandability – people need to understand what the system knows; they should be able to inspect the knowledge and appreciate how it relates together.
- Accessibility – the system must be able to use the knowledge it has been given; it should be capable of finding related information simply and efficiently.

Frame languages, in general, are an attempt to meet these requirements. In our particular case, the following CD-I requirements must also be addressed:

- Performance – the time taken to respond to any user interaction should be less than one second.
- Minimum Memory Usage – the whole program (knowledge base plus user interface) must fit into the 1 Megabyte of random-access memory in a base-case CD-I player.
- Integration – any language must integrate with the tools and methods already in use by CD-I practitioners.

At PRL, the combination of these two sets of requirements led to a design philosophy that could be described as "Minimalist". To ensure compactness, we have provided only those features which are proven and worthwhile. To ensure efficiency, we have produced two versions: one optimised for run-time performance, the other designed to support the authoring process. The latter version contains knowledge integrity checkers and high-level tools such as a frame editor.

Features of a Frame

What is a frame? A frame is a chunk of knowledge or information that represents one concept or entity. For example, your car could be represented by a frame and its manufacturer by another. Each frame has a unique name and an arbitrary number of properties (or slots as they are called). Each slot can have a number of values. There is a special kind of slot called a relation that has values which are the names of other frames; in essence, a relation slot points to another frame or frames. Here is an example of a frame:

```
(citroen-ax

    (is-a car)
    (manufactured-by Citroen)
    (engine 1000 1100 1360)
    (trim E R TRS GT)
    (launched 1986)
)
```

Its name is "citroen-ax" and it has five slots. The "is-a" and "manufactured-by" slots are relation slots which point to the frames "car" and "Citroen". Figure 1 depicts these relations graphically. The other slots contain simple, data values.

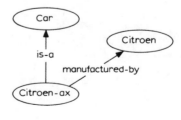

Figure 1. A simple frame network.

CD-I Frames

CD-I Frames is a frame language developed at PRL. A frame language is used to input, access and manipulate the frames in a knowledge base. CD-I Frames provides:

- An object-oriented representation. It is important to note the distinction here between object-oriented representations and object-oriented languages. In CD-I Frames it is the data that is object-oriented not the methods as in object-oriented languages.
- Inheritance over class hierarchies. CD-I frames provides two special relations for organising frames into class hierarchies. These are the "is-a" and "instance" relations. Figure 2 shows an example hierarchy. A frame can inherit slots and values via these relations. So, in the above example, "citroen-ax" can inherit all the properties associated with "car", such as the fact that all cars have at least three wheels. Inheritance permits the creation of compact knowledge bases.

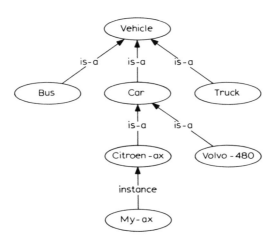

Figure 2. A class hierarchy.

- User-defined relations. To help the designer model real-world situations, CD-I Frames supports user-defined relations. In the above example, "manufactured-by" is a user-defined relation. Relations are the strength of a frame language; relations connect related information together and in doing so make it readily accessible to the system.
- Knowledge integrity checking. The usefulness of a knowledge base depends on its integrity. CD-I Frames provides error checking features which detect syntactic and semantic errors such as the creation of relational loops. The designer can also specify the kinds of values which are permitted in a given slot and the system will report any violations.
- Basic list processing. CD-I Frames is built using a package called Clisp, which provides the basics of LISP-like programming. Combined with CD-I Frames, this creates a powerful extension to the C programming language.

An Example Application: the Cook's Assistant

The question that needs to be answered is "Can CD-I Frames be used to produce applications that perform well on a base-case CD-I player?". One way to find out is by example. Here we take a program called the "Cook's Assistant" which was originally developed using the KnowledgeCraft tool kit[1]. The original CRL[1] and LISP code was rewritten in CD-I Frames and C. Its knowledge base consists of 96 dishes and over 200 food ingredients compiled from a well-known cook book. The program assists the user in the design and planning of a meal for a special occasion.

Analysing the program, we see that the actual program size is 216 Kilobytes. When the program is run it has to initialise the knowledge base, a process which consumes another 96 Kilobytes. On top of that, the program needs to allocate a further 50 Kilobytes to be used as a temporary work area. In total the Cook's Assistant (without its interface) needs 352 Kilobytes of memory which is well within base case player resources of 1 Megabyte.

Looking at the performance times we find that once the program is installed it takes a further four seconds of processing to initialise its knowledge base. Then during user interaction most response times are less than one second, exceptions are at most 2.5 seconds. These results, we would argue, meet the performance criteria for CD-I software.

Authoring Support

CD-I Frames is a programming extension to the C language. As such it is suitable for C programmers and database experts, but to be usable by a wider audience it needs higher-level authoring tools. One such tool is FRED, a frame editor, which has been developed at PRL. FRED lets the user create new frames and edit existing frames. Several navigation features are provided: you can go to a frame directly by entering its name, access it via an index, or jump to it by selecting its name in the currently viewed frame. The tool has a property sheet to let the user profile the tool's behaviour to their own requirements. Figure 3 shows the FRED user interface running under OpenWindows on a Sun workstation.

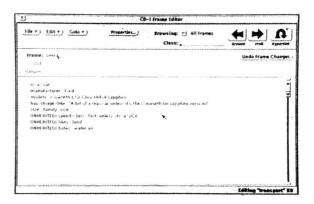

Figure 3. User interface to the frame editor FRED.

567

Future tools will include a graphical editor for creating and viewing knowledge structures such as class hierarchies. Another tool will be a user shell that lets the user try out CD-I Frames functions without having to write C code. With such a tool suite, CD-I Frames will become suitable for use by domain experts.

Conclusions

CD-I Frames is a solution to the problem of providing a useful knowledge representation language for CD-I. It combines a simple and natural style of representation with ease of understanding. The fact that information is related together means that it is readily accessible to the system and in turn that helps the system meet the demanding performance criteria for CD-I. As a language, CD-I Frames is suitable for C programmers, but with the frame editor and forthcoming tools, it will become suitable for domain experts and non CD-I practitioners.

Reference

1 Lloyd, P.R., "Bringing Intelligence to Interactive Multimedia Applications", PRL Annual Review, pp. 81 84, 1989.

A Design Tool System for Compact Disc Interactive

Jon Piesing

Compact Disc Interactive (CD-I) is a new consumer multimedia entertainment system on sale in the USA and Japan, and is being launched by Philips in Europe this year.

Many of the current generation of titles for CD-I were designed by designers who had very little knowledge of what the medium was capable of, and no way of finding out except by trying to communicate their ideas to a highly skilled C programmer for implementation. Production at this level is time consuming, expensive and frustrating for those involved. This article summarises the approach we have taken to try and reduce these problems.

Introduction

From a consideration of the main problems of current CD-I title production, we identified two main goals for our work on design tools :

- To enable non-programmers to have access to as much of the functionality of the CD-I medium as possible.
- To remove the programmer as far as possible from the routine aspects of CD-I title production.

What Makes CD-I Special?

The CD-I system was designed to be a consumer electronics product and not a computer. As example of this, the video hardware is optimised for the display of television style material, rather than attempting to provide the style of display used in PCs or workstations. Also the computer component of the CD-I system is optimised for cost, not for performance, and hence is not comparable in speed with PCs or workstations.

This design emphasis severely limits the applicability of design tools which were designed for PC or workstation based multimedia. Many of these have been tried as design tools for CD-I, with varying degrees of success. None of them allow a designer to design applications which remotely start exploiting what makes CD-I different from other multimedia platforms. Some of them have, however, proved very successful in niche areas such as animation, the best example of this being MacroMind Director.

Important Requirements

Within the goals described above, a number of requirements can be defined for design tools. The most important of these is that users of the tools should be as close to WYSIWYG (What You See Is What You Get) as possible, or perhaps even WYEIWYG (What You Experience Is What You Get). Not only does the designer need to be able to get accurate feedback on the effect of creative decisions, but this feedback needs to be available as soon as possible to the designer.

No single tool will able to address the needs and preferences of all designers and all titles. What is required is an architecture for tools to allow designers to chose from a range the one which is most appropriate to them, to the particular section of a particular title which they are working on at that time. This requires an environment to be created which allows multiple tools to work together, sharing the same data and application definition.

The second goal stated above is to remove the programmer from the routine aspects of title production as far as possible. However, particularly in consumer oriented titles, there will always be a need for programmers to add the extra features to enable a particular title to be distinctive and unique. This requires the tool environment and the application definition to be extensible, so that particular features of an application can be contracted to programmers where appropriate.

The Environment

Platforms

In order to give the designer a WYSIWYG interface with the best possible response time, the system which the tools run on must include a CD-I player in a way which is as tightly coupled as possible. A number of possible architectures were considered for this, in the end the one which was chosen for the first developments was an expanded CD-I player. This gives the tightest possible degree of coupling for the designer, and makes the validation that the tool will run on a base case player much more certain than some of the other options.

The User Interface

The user interface software which was developed for this package takes the form of a library which is highly compatible at the C programming language source code level with the XView libraries from Sun Microsystems. The degree of compatibility is sufficiently high that design tools for XView (such as DevGuide from Sun) may be used to generate C code which, when linked against the tool user interface library, produces a tool which runs on the expanded CD-I player itself.

Reprinted with permission from *Philips Research Labs-Redhill Review 1991,* pp. 62–63, 1992. © Philips Electronics.

As previously described, the performance of the CD-I system when used as a computer is not comparable with workstations or high end PCs. In order to achieve acceptable speed, below the XView level the library is very highly optimised for the CD-I player. In particular, there is no support for multitasking or for the X Windows layer.

The Language

The scripting/application definition language designed as part of this system is called CD-I Talk. The language is intended to be written by the same type of person who could write in HyperTalk. Unlike HyperTalk, the entire application in CD-I Talk is held in text files, there is no binary format.

Currently there is a fixed set of object classes with no inheritance of properties or methods. The list at time of writing is:

audio	context	cursor	font
hot spot	image	memory	palette
sequence	surface	text	timer

Of these, the two most important are the context and the surface. The context object is the basic unit of a CD-I Talk application. A single context represents one location within the CD-I application, and describes within it all the other objects local to that location and how they are used.

The surface object defines a displayable area of a screen. It is the only CD-I Talk object class which is directly displayable. All other objects such as images, hot spots and text must be linked to a surface in some way in order to be used. The actual display on the screen of the CD-I player is built up from a stack of surfaces, one on top of the other.

Design Tools

A number of design tools were identified as possibilities for early implementation. All of them should enable the user to edit a CD-I application defined in the CD-I Talk language. Together they provide a first attempt at covering a large range of user needs. Since the system is required to be extensible, better versions of the same or more specialised tools can be added into the environment later.

The initial set of intended tools comprises the following:

- Screen Layout Tool (i.e. visually oriented)
- Structure Editor (i.e. logically oriented)
- Script Editor/Debugger (i.e. script oriented)

A time oriented tool is also needed, but a bridge from an existing CD-I product could satisfy this need in the short term.

Another possible set of components are filters from other multimedia design tools into our system. As an experiment, a prototype filter was constructed from HyperCard to CD-I Talk.

"StructEd"

The tool currently called "StructEd" is a logically oriented design tool. Using it, the designer can build up the logical structure of a CD-I application in terms of a set of nodes and the links between them. The tool interfaces to other tools in order to add the appropriate detail needed to define the contents of the each node. The user interface of the tool is shown in figure 1.

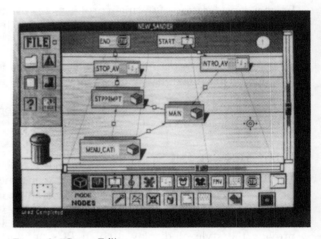

Figure 1. "StructEd".

Within the main working area, users can position nodes in whatever way means most to them. Detail not relevant at a particular point can be hidden by collecting it within a special type of node called a group. Groups can either be created empty and then filled or created by selecting a number of nodes and then grouping them.

Each node is assigned a type chosen from a range (currently fixed) and the when the user chooses to add detail to that node, another appropriate tool is invoked to do this.

"Media Showcase"

Media Showcase is the first part of this system to be released on the market. It comprises two of the tools listed in the Design Tools section above, the screen layout tool and the script editor/debugger.

The screen layout tool enables the user to design the visual appearance of a CD-I application, this includes the creation, specification and editing of surfaces, text, hot spots, cursors and images. It also enables the user to specify the order of the surfaces within the stack.

The script editor/debugger contains a context sensitive text editor for CD-I Talk and a CD-I Talk source debugger. The tool is closely connected to the CD-I Talk interpreter to enable the user to obtain the fastest and most accurate possible feedback when debugging. Common debugging features like single stepping and breakpoints are included (figure 2).

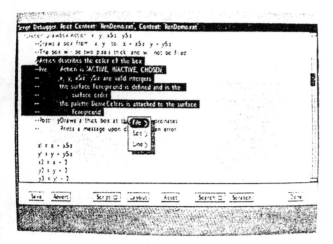

Figure 2. "Media Showcase" script editor.

Other Tools

As well as design tools, there need to be other tools in the system for creation of audio and video information where it is not being imported from outside. One of these under development is an audio digitising, encoding and editing tool (figure 3).

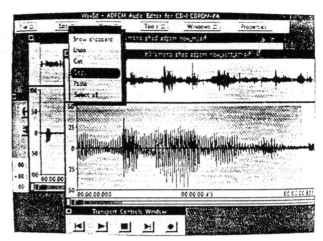

Figure 3. "WaveEd" audio tool.

Acknowledgements

The system described here has been the subject of a joint effort by engineers from three organisations: OptImage Interactive Services L.P. of Des Moines, Iowa, USA; Philips Advanced Projects Group, Mitcham, UK; and PRL, Redhill.

References

1 "Compact Disc-Interactive: A Designer's Overview", Kluwer, 1987.
2 "Balboa Run-Time Environment – Programmers Guide and Reference Guide", OptImage Interactive Services L.P, 1991.
3 "Media Showcase Users Guide", OptImage Interactive Services L.P, 1991.

Capturing Multimedia Design Knowledge Using TYRO, the Constraint Based Designer's Apprentice

Ron MacNeil
Visible Language Workshop
Massachusetts Institute of Technology
Cambridge, MA. USA

ABSTRACT

TYRO [MacNeil89,90] is a visual programming environment that uses a case based reasoning approach to capturing and reusing knowledge about the design of multimedia presentations. Case-based reasoning assumes that people solve problems by remembering relevant scenarios and modifying or adapting them to the the situation at hand, then storing this new approach away for future reuse. In TYRO, the designer constructs a case library by demonstrating solutions of prototypical multimedia problems and defining constraining relations between object sequences. Adaptation and augmentation of the case library takes place as trial presentations reveal failure conditions. The designer constructs rule objects which are combinations of condition objects and actions objects. Condition objects trigger when the failure condition is detected and action objects, or rules of thumb, fire and revise the constraint network, or revise the sequence of objects, etc. The resulting cases generated are stored and indexed for future use by the system.

INTRODUCTION

The Problem

One of the biggest challenges that will confront users of future globally networked computer systems, where multimedia transacting and browsing is the norm, is that without help from the system a typical user will drown in the wrong information before stumbling on the information he seeks. We assume that automatic presentation systems help people navigate, and act as power tools for more expert users, aiding in getting their points across to their colleagues more expeditiously.

The Approach

Since there currently isn't a formalized language of visual presentation, we have built an environment that allows expert users to "teach" the machine about multimedia presentations. We attempt to place multimedia design applications in a framework where knowledge-based reasoning can be applied, e.g. a powerful object-oriented inferencing environment interfaced to a multimedia graphics environment. We provide a visual programming interface that allows multimedia designers to build templates while designing. The reasoning approach chosen, case-based reasoning, is from work by Roger Schank [Riesbeck, Schank 89] and his colleagues done at Yale in the 1970's and 1980's.

Reprinted with permission from *Proc of SPIE*, R MacNeil, "Capturing Multimedia Design Knowledge Using TYRO, the Constraint Based Designer Apprentice," vol. 1460, pp. 94–102, 1991. © Proceedings of SPIE.

Why Case-based Reasoning

Case-based reasoning assumes that people solve problems by remembering cases that most closely resemble the situation at hand and then adapting them to fit current specifics.

Lets use the example of visiting a restaurant. As we enter the restaurant we retrieve from memory the case (or script) that we always use when entering a restaurant. This is a series of steps one of which is waiting for the maitre d' to seat you. But in this case no one is around. So now we have to try to repair the script by retrieving another case which deals with asking for assistance. Finally we find someone who can seat us. If we are to learn from this experience, we will store this particular (repaired) case away in memory and resuing this case might cause us not to come back to this restaurant again, especially if we are in a hurry.

The practice of graphic and multimedia design has striking similarities. There are canonical approaches to a wide range of communication tasks which the experienced practicioner develops over time. Innovative designs are generated by reusing old approaches with slight modifications to fit the current problem domain. Young designers learn the craft by studying the work of the "old masters", not, typically, by listening to the older designers lecture. The cases contain the real knowledge.

DESIGN EXAMPLE

TYRO's job is to provide an environment which supports building cases or templates which capture and transfer the intent of the conceptual groupings of the design without getting in the way of the process of exploring a design idea. To do this we will work through a design example.

The example chosen was developed by Steve Librande, a graduate student at the VLW, while working at a company that specializes in producing low-cost promotional slide-tapes. The client company operates ambulances equipped with teams of emergency medical technichians dispatched to accident sites. The goal of the presentation is to give viewers both facts about the company and a sense of the employees and the kind of jobs they do. It must be interesting to watch, yet the entertainment value must not detract from the factual communication portions. In this case the entertainment factor results from the beat and pacing of the sounds, as well as the relationship of sounds and images.

INTRODUCTION

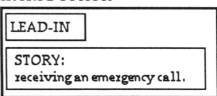

COMMUNICATION BODY

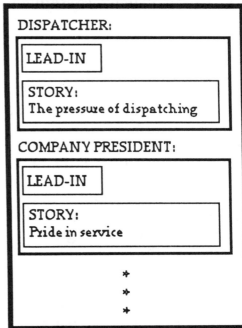

RECAP-RESOLUTION

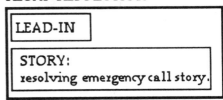

Fig. 1.

The form of the piece is quite simple. The basic element is a module which starts with a short lead-in, of not more than 10sec duration, followed by the "story" narrated either by a speaker or by the sound and sights of a situation. The broad outline follows the classic sequence: introduction, body of communication, recapitulation. In this sequence the introduction and recap are basic modules, and the body is a sequence of these modules, all of them variations on the theme of getting to know the jobs and people at the client company.

The production method was simple and economical as well. The design process started with storyboarding which shows with rather crude drawings the sequence of visual highlights accompanied by verbal descriptions of narration and sound effects. 35mm slides were then shot and live sound recordings made of the working environment, interviews, and recreations of accident scenes. This single image approach was chosen over video because of the lower production costs of assembling lap-dissolve slide sequences as compared to video editing. The style and approach used here can be useful for presenting many different types of material such as the work of a laboratory, activities in a museum, salient points of a data base.

For the purposes of this paper I will "reverse engineer" the example, trying to show how one creates a presentation, while building templates which capture the conceptual essense of the approach.

TYRO ENVIRONMENT
TYRO is built in Apple's Macintosh Common Lisp [Steele90] and CLOS [Keene89] and runs on a MacSE/30 with 8MB of RAM and SuperMac hi-res color card.

The top-level interface to TYRO is comprised of Browsers and Editors. Fig 2. shows the Still Image, Sound, Midi, Narration Browsers that have been loaded with all of the elements that might possibly be used in the presentation. The challenge for a browser is to make obvious the most significant and distinguishing aspects of the indexed objects. While TYRO Browsers only go part of the way to answering this challenge they at least provide both a name index and a visual view of the data. In the case of digitized sound one would see an energy or frequency plot, for midi data one would see a piano-roll plot, for narration one would see a color-coded script printout, for slides one would see a postage stamp version of the slide.

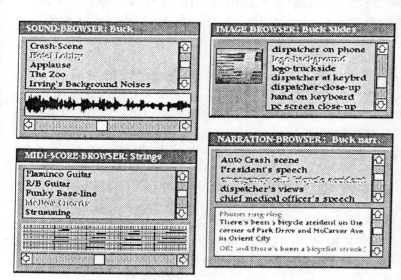

Fig. 2.

ARLOtje

After the elements have been logged into the appropriate browser, they must also begin to have a life in ARLOtje [Haase89], the representation language for building representation languages. ARLOtje has tools for natural language understanding, case-based reasoning and recently, analogy mapping. Its base ontology knows about humans, inanimate objects, time and space, and can be easily extended to include specialized knowledge on a particular domain.

Fig 3. shows a simple visual interface to ARLOtje with a beginning set of slots and relations appropriate to the example domain. In the figure we have just created relations speaking-over and speaking-to, and are currently asserting that the dispatcher shown in the Image Browser slide named "dispatcher on phone" is speaking over a telephone. We need to tell ARLOtje enough about each of the elements so that it can make inferences about the appropriateness of an element to be used in a candidate case.

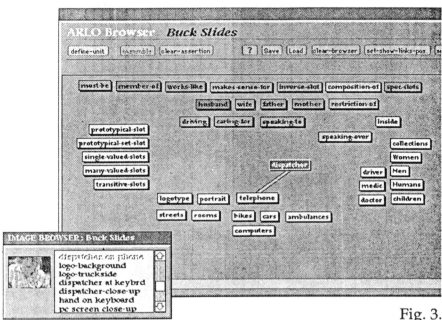

Fig. 3.

Likewise ARLOtje's story reader will be run over the narration, and generate scripts which will be useful later in case matching . Finally, the salient elements of the "sound effects" portion of the audio and midi-data tracks need to be entered into ARLOtje.

Automatic Logging

It is fair to say that the element logging and knowledge-base assimilation is a currently very tedious and time consuming process. Unfortunately there are some daunting problems and missing black boxes that keep us from automating this process. For example, one would like to generate the voice annotation automatically, rather than having to stop, rewind and type the narration by hand into a word processor. The work of Victor Zue [Zue90] and Dragon Systems shows promise. One would like to extract the relevant environmental and sound-effect sounds from audio and video recordings for synchronization and context generation. In this area the work of Michael Hawley [Hawley91] shows promise. Of course one would also like to have an object recognition algorithm to help automate the very tedious process of slide and video sequence logging. Work in scene recognition and part recognition for robotics applications shows that if one can work with a very limited set of object types one can make some small headway.

BUILDING "INTRO" TEMPLATE

The template building session begins by double-clicking the "Templates" button in the Template-Browser (Fig 4). This creates a new Template object, prompts for its name, and also creates a Template-Editor, Level 1 in Fig 5.

Fig 5. shows the multiple levels of detail accessible through the Template-Editor and the three view types on each level: logical, spatial and temporal. Double-clicking on the sub-template Lead-in opens it up (shown in Level 2) to reveal the elements in this part and their constraining relations. Double-clicking on any of these elements opens up another level to reveal Temporal and Spatial Editors for those objects. One of the goals of TYRO is to have visual programming editors for every object, so that for example, double-clicking on a constraint would open up a Constraint editor. At this time, alas, all the multimedia constraints are hard coded, and one cannot create new constraints by visual programming.

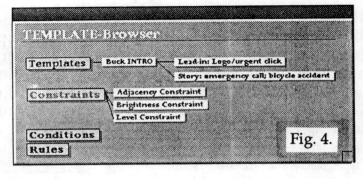

Fig. 4.

MULTIMEDIA CONSTRAINTS

At the very heart of TYRO's ability to generate presentations automatically is the notion of multimedia constraints [Leler88][Feiner89]. These can be either uni-directional or bi-directional .

Uni-directional constraints are found in every conducted or scripted medium. All the parameterized controls such as cross-fade between images, cross-fade between sounds, scaling, translation, and rotation of image parts should be modelled as constraining relations to allow an arithmetic solver to determine new values given a changed context. This kind of constraint can be created directly in the Temporal-Editor in one of the control tracks. For example when an image is sent to the Temporal-Editor from the Image-Browser in Fig. 6. it creates an associated fade-control constraint with its default set to full value for the duration of the image. The values for this constraint can be modified by dragging control points to cause a cross-fade, or slow-in fast-out etc. Likewise for constraints imposed on the midi and sound data.

When designing a presentation, one of the first things the designer must decide is what modality is in charge; whether the sound or the image will drive the pacing and type of elements chosen. If these relationships are modelled as bi-directional constraints then a symbolic constraint resolution system can be employed and allow the designer to change his mind about what modality is in charge while allowing a quick test to see what the effect of that change is.

For example, research in musical score reading [Rosenthal 91] now allows one to detect the beat in a stream of midi-data. One could build a constraint which aligned image change after a certain number of beats, or one could choose a musical score on whether it had a particular beat, if one knew the rate the images should change.

As one can see in Fig. 6. the structure of the Lead-In Template is very simple. It is built with two elements: the company logo and a midi-score of a muffled click that reminds one of a fast heartbeat. It cross-fades to the beginning of the Story comprised of shots of one side of a telephone call showing the dispatcher, what she sees, environmental sounds, and dialogue transcribed in a Narration Track.

The Lead-In Templates found in the body of the presentation are different from this one in that they should introduce a specific topic or person in the case of a mini biography.

We introduce two new objects, the Condition, and the Rule as one way of subclassing Templates.

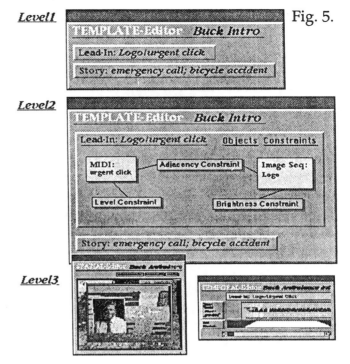

Fig. 5.

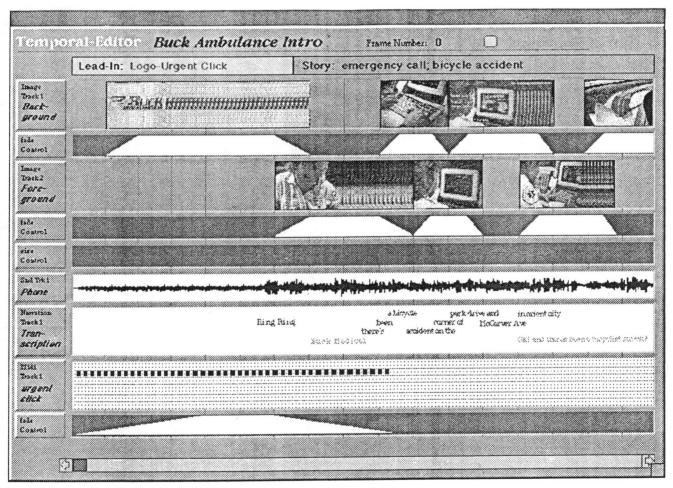

Fig. 6.

Building the Rule Object

Double-clicking on the Conditions button in Template Browser prompts for the name of a new condition to build, and opens up a Condition Editor window which allows the user to build a condition object using visual programming means. Currently Condition objects are coded by hand in ARLOtje Lisp code. In this case, the condition we wish to detect is the fact that there is just one speaker in the transcribed Narration Track. Detecting that condition will happen when ARLOtje's story reader parses the narration. ARLOtje will return the subject of the narration for use by the Rule object.

A Rule is created by double clicking on the Rules button. This opens a Rule Editor window into which is inserted the Condition object and Action object. The narration used in this case is the voice of a dispatcher, so the goal of the rule object is to find a picture of the dispatcher and return that. The Temporal Editor shows the example image chosen. It is inserted just after the dispatcher starts speaking. This Rule then gets added to the Lead-In Template.

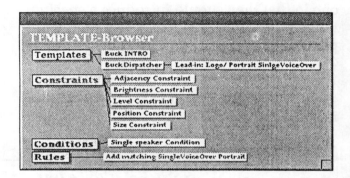

We decide to make the portrait smaller than full frame and place it on top of the logo background image. To do this, we demonstrate its position and size by direct manipu-

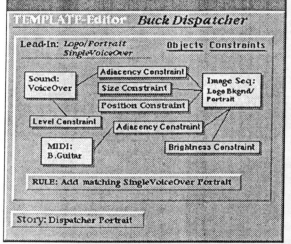

Fig. 7.

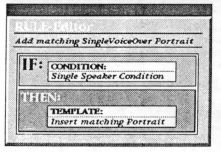

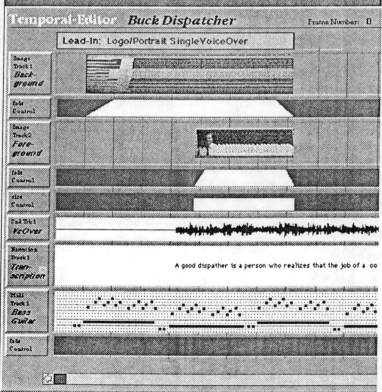

578

lation of the image in the Spatial Editor. The result is that uni-directional constraints appear in the Temporal and Template Editors. We plan to bring forward spatial relation constraints from earlier versions of TYRO that would allow the user to specify constraining relationships between image and graphic elements.

Related Work
Laura Robin's thesis at the VLW [Robin 89] was the inspiration for the element Browser and Temporal and Spatial editors found in this work. For a more detailed description see the paper in this proceedings.

MUSE [Hodges-et al89] is a toolkit for building multimedia learning environments developed at MIT's Project Athena. It integrates full motion video with graphics and sound and has the notion of constraints between multimedia objects. To date all the knowledge lives in the directed graph link structure imposed by the authors.

COMET [Feiner, McKeown90] is an environment for generating muli-media explanations developed at Columbia Univ. Its architecture includes a single content planner, media coordinator, bi-directional links between text and graphics generators and a media layout component. Each of these components has at least one knowledge base. To date all examples, both graphics and knowledge bases, have been hand coded.

Conclusions and Future Work
TYRO has been extended with the addition of multimedia element Browsers, Temporal Editor, ARLOtje Browser to allow multimedia designers to build case libraries of templates which represent high level chunks of design knowledge. Work needs to be done in several areas. Earlier versions of TYRO allowed the user to build most of the primitive constraints and extend object types in Editors using visual programming techniques, and this capability needs to be restored. We also plan to bring on-line recent work on ARLOtje that uses the notion of analogy mapping. This would allow designers to continue a typical practice of designing by drawing analogies to earlier works, specifying similarities or differences. Finally we need to find ways of visualizing the reasoning process so users can extend the reasoner's capabilities.

Acknowledgements
Major support for the work described in this paper was provided by NYNEX and DARPA. I would like to thank Nathan Felde and Sergio Canetti at NYNEX's Media Lab as well as Prof. Muriel Cooper, Prof. Nicholas Negroponte, Dr. Henry Lieberman of MIT's Media Lab for their continued support of this project. The Visible Language Workshop is also supported by grants and equipment from Paws Inc., Apple Computer, Digital Equipment Corp.

This effort was sponsored in part by the Rome Laboratories, by the Air Force System Command and the Defense Advanced Research Projects Agency (DARPA) under contract # F30602-89-C-0022. The views and conclusions of this document are those of the author and should not be interpreted as necessarily representing the official policies, expressed or implied, of the Rome Laboratories, of the AFSC , DARPA or the United States government.

References

[Feiner, McKeown 90] Steven Feiner, Kathleen McKeown, Coordinating Text and Graphics in Explanation Generation, Proceedings of AAAI-90.

[Haase 90], Ken Haase, ARLOtje Internals Manual, Internal Document, The Media Laboratory, MIT, 1990.

[Hawley 91], Mike Hawley, personal communication, The Media Laboratory, MIT, 1991.

[Hodges-etal89] Matthew Hodges, Russell Sasnett, Mark Ackerman A Construction Set for Multimedia Applications, IEEE Software January 1989.

[Keene89] Sonya E. Keene, Object-Oriented Programming in Common Lisp, A Programmers guide to CLOS, Addison Wesley, 1989.

[Leler 88], William Leler, Constraint Programming Languages, Addison Wesley, 1988.

[MACNEIL 89] Ron MacNeil, TYRO, a Constraint-based Graphic Designer's Assistant, Proceedings of the IEEE 1989 Workshop on Visual Languages.

[MACNEIL 90] Ron MacNeil, ADAPTIVE PERSPECTIVES: Case-Based Reasoning with TYRO, the Graphic Designer's Apprentice, Proceedings of the IEEE 1990 Workshop on Visual Languages.

[RIESBECK,SCHANK 89], Christopher Riesbeck, Roger Schank, Inside Case-Based Reasoning, Lawrence Erlbaum Associates, Publishers.1989

[Robin 89] Laura Robin Temporal Adaptation of Multimedia Scripts, MSVS Thesis, Media Laboratory, MIT 1989.

[Rosenthal91] David Rosenthal, Music and Cognition Group, Media Lab, MIT, Emulation of Human Rhythm Perception, submitted to Computer Music Journal, 1991

[Steele90] Guy L. Steele, Common Lisp the Language Second Edition, Digital Press 1990.

[Zue90] Victor Zue, J. Glass, D.Goodine, M. Phillips, S. Seneff The SUMMIT Speech Recognition System: Phonological Modelling and Lexical Access, Proceedings from ICASSP: 49-52, Albuquerque, NM, 1990.

Author Index

Subject Index

Editor's Biography

Theodore S. Rzeszewski was born in Chicago, IL. He received the BSEE and MSEE degrees from the University of Illinois, Urbana, and professional degree of Electrical Engineer as well as an honorary Doctorate Degree from Illinois Institute of Technology/Midwest College of Engineering (IIT/MCE), Wheaton, IL.

His professional experience combines corporate and academic service. He has worked at the Communications and the Consumer Products Divisions of Motorola, Hazeltine Research, AT&T Bell Labs, and Matsushita Electric. Ted joined Matsushita as Manager of Advanced Development in June 1990. Previously, he served as Manager of Technical Operations of Matsushita Applied Research Laboratory. He was at Bell Labs from 1982 to 1990. His interests include digital video, high definition television, cable television, multimedia, and fiber optic communications.

His compatible HDTV system was one system under consideration by the ATSC. Ted was project engineer on the first micro-computer controlled frequency synthesizer for TV. His other accomplishments include 31 U.S. Patents and approximately 20 papers published in technical journals, books, and conference records. He has edited two previous IEEE Press Books and been chairman for the 1991 and 1992 EIA/IEEE Digital Video Workshop.

Ted was an Associate Professor at MCE, and designated a Todd Professor at IIT where he taught a course on digital video. Also, he is a fellow of the IEEE, and a member of Phi Eta sigma, and Eta Kappa Nu.